Prof. Ric[...]
U Wisconsin Law School
975 Bascom Mall
Madison WI   53706
(608) 263 - 7409

☐ - π/Δ; appellant/appellee; petitioner/respondent

☐ Negligence = ~~focus on~~ focus on : RTL
Common Law, Natural law; non-statutory, Banana Peel/Falling Ladder law

☐ If. notes cite to previous or subsequent case, read it.
i.e. p. 171; n. 3.

☐ Sample question and sample "B" answer.

☐ duty/breach = prima facie (extent of harm left to jury) (1st day)
Some harm/any harm
i.e. can be "negligent" w/o harm, but no CoA as matter of law

☐ See p. 196 Get Wisconsin's medical malpractice statutes

☐ see p. 199 n 3 ⊗ = to "parse" a sentence for "elements" of CoA

☐ See p. 146 Learned Hand equation B<PL (B = burden of taking adequate precautions;
P = probability of occurrence
L = gravity of resulting injury)

☐ Issue - "the most important thing for this class re: exam (spotting the issue)"
R rule/reasoning of court - the most impt thing re exam - outline of fully stated rules
A analysis of your own/application of rule - most important - analysis/app
Conclusion - holding

☐ Briefing = Case History
Key Facts/Evidence
Issue
G/Rule - quote of c/r, set of Rules + Exceptions or variations,
S/Holding - like or spec exc or variation combined w/ ruling or order (application of rule = reasoning)
Rationale of Court
Commentary

☐ Cross Reference Res Ipsa Loq. with/ alternative causes/liability
(compare)

- Strict Liability - purpose of statute is to deter CoA or completely
☐ cf negligence per se - although intended π + harm, purpose may be other: i.e. Crime

☐ — Wisconsin cases. See pp. 249, n.4; p. 258, n. 9; p. 268, n. 5; p 280 o; p. 287, n. 23; p. 31, n.3; p 103, n.2; p.257, n.1;

☐ - Procedural distinction b/w prima facie v case in chief

    Pf = possibility | upon wh/ fair minds can differ

    CiC = probability |

☐ 1st day – explains DV, NOV, where facts come from
    — Briefing

☐ 2nd day – Socratic – on case and notes
    — How do you know what facts are?
    (why did authors put case here n for subsequent days)

☐ Kim to say 1st day = cases [in book] will be incongruent, inconsistent, incompatible, or The legal term of art = irreconcilable
  — — Case or notes may indicate maj r min positions wh/ you should include in your outline and Know for exam.
  — — if not indicated you should know and be prepared to present bothe arguments in an exam.

Law Review Articles: See p. 287, n. 5; p 289, n.4 (Posner);

University Casebook Series

March, 1991

ACCOUNTING AND THE LAW, Fourth Edition (1978), with Problems Pamphlet (Successor to Dohr, Phillips, Thompson & Warren)

George C. Thompson, Professor, Columbia University Graduate School of Business.
Robert Whitman, Professor of Law, University of Connecticut.
Ellis L. Phillips, Jr., Member of the New York Bar.
William C. Warren, Professor of Law Emeritus, Columbia University.

ACCOUNTING FOR LAWYERS, MATERIALS ON (1980)

David R. Herwitz, Professor of Law, Harvard University.

ADMINISTRATIVE LAW, Eighth Edition (1987), with 1989 Case Supplement and 1983 Problems Supplement (Supplement edited in association with Paul R. Verkuil, Dean and Professor of Law, Tulane University)

Walter Gellhorn, University Professor Emeritus, Columbia University.
Clark Byse, Professor of Law, Harvard University.
Peter L. Strauss, Professor of Law, Columbia University.
Todd D. Rakoff, Professor of Law, Harvard University.
Roy A. Schotland, Professor of Law, Georgetown University.

ADMIRALTY, Third Edition (1987), with Statute and Rule Supplement

Jo Desha Lucas, Professor of Law, University of Chicago.

ADVOCACY, see also Lawyering Process

AGENCY, see also Enterprise Organization

AGENCY—PARTNERSHIPS, Fourth Edition (1987)

Abridgement from Conard, Knauss & Siegel's Enterprise Organization, Fourth Edition.

AGENCY AND PARTNERSHIPS (1987)

Melvin A. Eisenberg, Professor of Law, University of California, Berkeley.

ANTITRUST: FREE ENTERPRISE AND ECONOMIC ORGANIZATION, Sixth Edition (1983), with 1983 Problems in Antitrust Supplement and 1990 Case Supplement

Louis B. Schwartz, Professor of Law, University of Pennsylvania.
John J. Flynn, Professor of Law, University of Utah.
Harry First, Professor of Law, New York University.

BANKRUPTCY, Second Edition (1989), with 1990 Case Supplement

Robert L. Jordan, Professor of Law, University of California, Los Angeles.
William D. Warren, Professor of Law, University of California, Los Angeles.

BANKRUPTCY AND DEBTOR–CREDITOR LAW, Second Edition (1988)

Theodore Eisenberg, Professor of Law, Cornell University.

BUSINESS CRIME (1990)

Harry First, Professor of Law, New York University.

BUSINESS ORGANIZATION, see also Enterprise Organization

BUSINESS PLANNING, Temporary Second Edition (1984)

David R. Herwitz, Professor of Law, Harvard University.

BUSINESS TORTS (1972)

Milton Handler, Professor of Law Emeritus, Columbia University.

CHILDREN IN THE LEGAL SYSTEM (1983) with 1990 Supplement (Supplement edited in association with Elizabeth S. Scott, Professor of Law, University of Virginia)

Walter Wadlington, Professor of Law, University of Virginia.
Charles H. Whitebread, Professor of Law, University of Southern California.
Samuel Davis, Professor of Law, University of Georgia.

CIVIL PROCEDURE, see Procedure

CIVIL RIGHTS ACTIONS (1988), with 1990 Supplement

Peter W. Low, Professor of Law, University of Virginia.
John C. Jeffries, Jr., Professor of Law, University of Virginia.

CLINIC, see also Lawyering Process

COMMERCIAL AND DEBTOR–CREDITOR LAW: SELECTED STATUTES, 1990 EDITION

COMMERCIAL LAW, Second Edition (1987)

Robert L. Jordan, Professor of Law, University of California, Los Angeles.
William D. Warren, Professor of Law, University of California, Los Angeles.

COMMERCIAL LAW, Fourth Edition (1985), with 1990 Case Supplement

E. Allan Farnsworth, Professor of Law, Columbia University.
John Honnold, Professor of Law, University of Pennsylvania.

COMMERCIAL PAPER, Third Edition (1984), with 1990 Case Supplement

E. Allan Farnsworth, Professor of Law, Columbia University.

COMMERCIAL PAPER, Second Edition (1987) (Reprinted from COMMERCIAL LAW, Second Edition (1987))

Robert L. Jordan, Professor of Law, University of California, Los Angeles.
William D. Warren, Professor of Law, University of California, Los Angeles.

COMMERCIAL PAPER AND BANK DEPOSITS AND COLLECTIONS (1967), with Statutory Supplement

William D. Hawkland, Professor of Law, University of Illinois.

COMMERCIAL TRANSACTIONS—Principles and Policies, Second Edition (1991)

Alan Schwartz, Professor of Law, Yale University.
Robert E. Scott, Professor of Law, University of Virginia.

COMPARATIVE LAW, Fifth Edition (1988)

Rudolf B. Schlesinger, Professor of Law, Hastings College of the Law.
Hans W. Baade, Professor of Law, University of Texas.
Mirjan P. Damaska, Professor of Law, Yale Law School.
Peter E. Herzog, Professor of Law, Syracuse University.

UNIVERSITY CASEBOOK SERIES—Continued

COMPETITIVE PROCESS, LEGAL REGULATION OF THE, Fourth Edition (1990), with 1989 Selected Statutes Supplement

Edmund W. Kitch, Professor of Law, University of Virginia.
Harvey S. Perlman, Dean of the Law School, University of Nebraska.

CONFLICT OF LAWS, Ninth Edition (1990)

Willis L. M. Reese, Professor of Law, Columbia University.
Maurice Rosenberg, Professor of Law, Columbia University.
Peter Hay, Professor of Law, University of Illinois.

CONSTITUTIONAL LAW, Eighth Edition (1989), with 1990 Case Supplement

Edward L. Barrett, Jr., Professor of Law, University of California, Davis.
William Cohen, Professor of Law, Stanford University.
Jonathan D. Varat, Professor of Law, University of California, Los Angeles.

CONSTITUTIONAL LAW, CIVIL LIBERTY AND INDIVIDUAL RIGHTS, Second Edition (1982), with 1989 Supplement

William Cohen, Professor of Law, Stanford University.
John Kaplan, Professor of Law, Stanford University.

CONSTITUTIONAL LAW, Eleventh Edition (1985), with 1990 Supplement (Supplement edited in association with Frederick F. Schauer, Professor, Harvard University)

Gerald Gunther, Professor of Law, Stanford University.

CONSTITUTIONAL LAW, INDIVIDUAL RIGHTS IN, Fourth Edition (1986), (Reprinted from CONSTITUTIONAL LAW, Eleventh Edition), with 1990 Supplement (Supplement edited in association with Frederick F. Schauer, Professor, Harvard University)

Gerald Gunther, Professor of Law, Stanford University.

CONSUMER TRANSACTIONS, Second Edition (1991), with Selected Statutes and Regulations Supplement

Michael M. Greenfield, Professor of Law, Washington University.

CONTRACT LAW AND ITS APPLICATION, Fourth Edition (1988)

Arthur Rosett, Professor of Law, University of California, Los Angeles.

CONTRACT LAW, STUDIES IN, Third Edition (1984)

Edward J. Murphy, Professor of Law, University of Notre Dame.
Richard E. Speidel, Professor of Law, Northwestern University.

CONTRACTS, Fifth Edition (1987)

John P. Dawson, late Professor of Law, Harvard University.
William Burnett Harvey, Professor of Law and Political Science, Boston University.
Stanley D. Henderson, Professor of Law, University of Virginia.

CONTRACTS, Fourth Edition (1988)

E. Allan Farnsworth, Professor of Law, Columbia University.
William F. Young, Professor of Law, Columbia University.

CONTRACTS, Selections on (statutory materials) (1988)

CONTRACTS, Second Edition (1978), with Statutory and Administrative Law Supplement (1978)

Ian R. Macneil, Professor of Law, Cornell University.

UNIVERSITY CASEBOOK SERIES—Continued

COPYRIGHT, PATENTS AND TRADEMARKS, see also Competitive Process; see also Selected Statutes and International Agreements

COPYRIGHT, PATENT, TRADEMARK AND RELATED STATE DOCTRINES, Third Edition (1990), with 1989 Selected Statutes Supplement and 1981 Problem Supplement

Paul Goldstein, Professor of Law, Stanford University.

COPYRIGHT, Unfair Competition, and Other Topics Bearing on the Protection of Literary, Musical, and Artistic Works, Fifth Edition (1990), with 1990 Statutory Supplement

Ralph S. Brown, Jr., Professor of Law, Yale University.
Robert C. Denicola, Professor of Law, University of Nebraska.

CORPORATE ACQUISITIONS, The Law and Finance of (1986), with 1990 Supplement

Ronald J. Gilson, Professor of Law, Stanford University.

CORPORATE FINANCE, Third Edition (1987)

Victor Brudney, Professor of Law, Harvard University.
Marvin A. Chirelstein, Professor of Law, Columbia University.

CORPORATION LAW, BASIC, Third Edition (1989), with Documentary Supplement

Detlev F. Vagts, Professor of Law, Harvard University.

CORPORATIONS, see also Enterprise Organization

CORPORATIONS, Sixth Edition—Concise (1988), with 1990 Case Supplement and 1990 Statutory Supplement

William L. Cary, late Professor of Law, Columbia University.
Melvin Aron Eisenberg, Professor of Law, University of California, Berkeley.

CORPORATIONS, Sixth Edition—Unabridged (1988), with 1990 Case Supplement and 1990 Statutory Supplement

William L. Cary, late Professor of Law, Columbia University.
Melvin Aron Eisenberg, Professor of Law, University of California, Berkeley.

CORPORATIONS AND BUSINESS ASSOCIATIONS—STATUTES, RULES, AND FORMS (1990)

CORRECTIONS, SEE SENTENCING

CREDITORS' RIGHTS, see also Debtor-Creditor Law

CRIMINAL JUSTICE ADMINISTRATION, Fourth Edition (1991)

Frank W. Miller, Professor of Law, Washington University.
Robert O. Dawson, Professor of Law, University of Texas.
George E. Dix, Professor of Law, University of Texas.
Raymond I. Parnas, Professor of Law, University of California, Davis.

CRIMINAL LAW, Fourth Edition (1987)

Fred E. Inbau, Professor of Law Emeritus, Northwestern University.
Andre A. Moenssens, Professor of Law, University of Richmond.
James R. Thompson, Professor of Law Emeritus, Northwestern University.

CRIMINAL LAW AND APPROACHES TO THE STUDY OF LAW, Second Edition (1991)

John M. Brumbaugh, Professor of Law, University of Maryland.

CRIMINAL LAW, Second Edition (1986)

Peter W. Low, Professor of Law, University of Virginia.
John C. Jeffries, Jr., Professor of Law, University of Virginia.
Richard C. Bonnie, Professor of Law, University of Virginia.

CRIMINAL LAW, Fourth Edition (1986)

Lloyd L. Weinreb, Professor of Law, Harvard University.

CRIMINAL LAW AND PROCEDURE, Seventh Edition (1989)

Ronald N. Boyce, Professor of Law, University of Utah.
Rollin M. Perkins, Professor of Law Emeritus, University of California, Hastings College of the Law.

CRIMINAL PROCEDURE, Third Edition (1987), with 1990 Supplement

James B. Haddad, Professor of Law, Northwestern University.
James B. Zagel, Chief, Criminal Justice Division, Office of Attorney General of Illinois.
Gary L. Starkman, Assistant U. S. Attorney, Northern District of Illinois.
William J. Bauer, Chief Judge of the U.S. Court of Appeals, Seventh Circuit.

CRIMINAL PROCESS, Fourth Edition (1987), with 1990 Supplement

Lloyd L. Weinreb, Professor of Law, Harvard University.

DAMAGES, Second Edition (1952)

Charles T. McCormick, late Professor of Law, University of Texas.
William F. Fritz, late Professor of Law, University of Texas.

DECEDENTS' ESTATES AND TRUSTS, Seventh Edition (1988)

John Ritchie, late Professor of Law, University of Virginia.
Neill H. Alford, Jr., Professor of Law, University of Virginia.
Richard W. Effland, late Professor of Law, Arizona State University.

DISPUTE RESOLUTION, Processes of (1989)

John S. Murray, President and Executive Director of The Conflict Clinic, Inc., George Mason University.
Alan Scott Rau, Professor of Law, University of Texas.
Edward F. Sherman, Professor of Law, University of Texas.

DOMESTIC RELATIONS, see also Family Law

DOMESTIC RELATIONS, Second Edition (1990)

Walter Wadlington, Professor of Law, University of Virginia.

EMPLOYMENT DISCRIMINATION, Second Edition (1987), with 1990 Supplement

Joel W. Friedman, Professor of Law, Tulane University.
George M. Strickler, Professor of Law, Tulane University.

EMPLOYMENT LAW, Second Edition (1991), with Statutory Supplement

Mark A. Rothstein, Professor of Law, University of Houston.
Andria S. Knapp, Visiting Professor of Law, Golden Gate University.
Lance Liebman, Professor of Law, Harvard University.

ENERGY LAW (1983) with 1986 Case Supplement

Donald N. Zillman, Professor of Law, University of Utah.
Laurence Lattman, Dean of Mines and Engineering, University of Utah.

UNIVERSITY CASEBOOK SERIES—Continued

ENTERPRISE ORGANIZATION, Fourth Edition (1987), with 1987 Corporation and Partnership Statutes, Rules and Forms Supplement

Alfred F. Conard, Professor of Law, University of Michigan.
Robert L. Knauss, Dean of the Law School, University of Houston.
Stanley Siegel, Professor of Law, University of California, Los Angeles.

ENVIRONMENTAL POLICY LAW 1985 Edition, with 1985 Problems Supplement (Supplement in association with Ronald H. Rosenberg, Professor of Law, College of William and Mary)

Thomas J. Schoenbaum, Professor of Law, University of Georgia.

EQUITY, see also Remedies

EQUITY, RESTITUTION AND DAMAGES, Second Edition (1974)

Robert Childres, late Professor of Law, Northwestern University.
William F. Johnson, Jr., Professor of Law, New York University.

ESTATE PLANNING, Second Edition (1982), with 1985 Case, Text and Documentary Supplement

David Westfall, Professor of Law, Harvard University.

ETHICS, see Legal Profession, Professional Responsibility, and Social Responsibilities

ETHICS OF LAWYERING, THE LAW AND (1990)

Geoffrey C. Hazard, Jr., Professor of Law, Yale University.
Susan P. Koniak, Professor of Law, University of Pittsburgh.

ETHICS AND PROFESSIONAL RESPONSIBILITY (1981) (Reprinted from THE LAWYERING PROCESS)

Gary Bellow, Professor of Law, Harvard University.
Bea Moulton, Legal Services Corporation.

EVIDENCE, Sixth Edition (1988 Reprint), with 1990 Case Supplement (Supplement edited in association with Roger C. Park, Professor of Law, University of Minnesota)

John Kaplan, Professor of Law, Stanford University.
Jon R. Waltz, Professor of Law, Northwestern University.

EVIDENCE, Eighth Edition (1988), with Rules, Statute and Case Supplement (1990)

Jack B. Weinstein, Chief Judge, United States District Court.
John H. Mansfield, Professor of Law, Harvard University.
Norman Abrams, Professor of Law, University of California, Los Angeles.
Margaret Berger, Professor of Law, Brooklyn Law School.

FAMILY LAW, see also Domestic Relations

FAMILY LAW Second Edition (1985), with 1991 Supplement

Judith C. Areen, Professor of Law, Georgetown University.

FAMILY LAW AND CHILDREN IN THE LEGAL SYSTEM, STATUTORY MATERIALS (1981)

Walter Wadlington, Professor of Law, University of Virginia.

FEDERAL COURTS, Eighth Edition (1988), with 1990 Supplement

Charles T. McCormick, late Professor of Law, University of Texas.
James H. Chadbourn, late Professor of Law, Harvard University.
Charles Alan Wright, Professor of Law, University of Texas, Austin.

UNIVERSITY CASEBOOK SERIES—Continued

FEDERAL COURTS AND THE FEDERAL SYSTEM, Hart and Wechsler's Third Edition (1988), with 1989 Case Supplement, and the Judicial Code and Rules of Procedure in the Federal Courts (1989)

Paul M. Bator, Professor of Law, University of Chicago.
Daniel J. Meltzer, Professor of Law, Harvard University.
Paul J. Mishkin, Professor of Law, University of California, Berkeley.
David L. Shapiro, Professor of Law, Harvard University.

FEDERAL COURTS AND THE LAW OF FEDERAL–STATE RELATIONS, Second Edition (1989), with 1990 Supplement

Peter W. Low, Professor of Law, University of Virginia.
John C. Jeffries, Jr., Professor of Law, University of Virginia.

FEDERAL PUBLIC LAND AND RESOURCES LAW, Second Edition (1987), with 1990 Case Supplement and 1990 Statutory Supplement

George C. Coggins, Professor of Law, University of Kansas.
Charles F. Wilkinson, Professor of Law, University of Oregon.

FEDERAL RULES OF CIVIL PROCEDURE and Selected Other Procedural Provisions, 1990 Edition

FEDERAL TAXATION, see Taxation

FOOD AND DRUG LAW (1980), with Statutory Supplement

Richard A. Merrill, Dean of the School of Law, University of Virginia.
Peter Barton Hutt, Esq.

FUTURE INTERESTS (1970)

Howard R. Williams, Professor of Law, Stanford University.

FUTURE INTERESTS AND ESTATE PLANNING (1961), with 1962 Supplement

W. Barton Leach, late Professor of Law, Harvard University.
James K. Logan, formerly Dean of the Law School, University of Kansas.

GOVERNMENT CONTRACTS, FEDERAL, Successor Edition (1985), with 1989 Supplement

John W. Whelan, Professor of Law, Hastings College of the Law.

GOVERNMENT REGULATION: FREE ENTERPRISE AND ECONOMIC ORGANIZATION, Sixth Edition (1985)

Louis B. Schwartz, Professor of Law, Hastings College of the Law.
John J. Flynn, Professor of Law, University of Utah.
Harry First, Professor of Law, New York University.

HEALTH CARE LAW AND POLICY (1988)

Clark C. Havighurst, Professor of Law, Duke University.

HINCKLEY, JOHN W., JR., TRIAL OF: A Case Study of the Insanity Defense (1986)

Peter W. Low, Professor of Law, University of Virginia.
John C. Jeffries, Jr., Professor of Law, University of Virginia.
Richard C. Bonnie, Professor of Law, University of Virginia.

INJUNCTIONS, Second Edition (1984)

Owen M. Fiss, Professor of Law, Yale University.
Doug Rendleman, Professor of Law, College of William and Mary.

INSTITUTIONAL INVESTORS, (1978)

David L. Ratner, Professor of Law, Cornell University.

UNIVERSITY CASEBOOK SERIES—Continued

INSURANCE, Second Edition (1985)

William F. Young, Professor of Law, Columbia University.
Eric M. Holmes, Professor of Law, University of Georgia.

INSURANCE LAW AND REGULATION (1990)

Kenneth S. Abraham, University of Virginia.

INTERNATIONAL LAW, see also Transnational Legal Problems, Transnational Business Problems, and United Nations Law

INTERNATIONAL LAW IN CONTEMPORARY PERSPECTIVE (1981), with Essay Supplement

Myres S. McDougal, Professor of Law, Yale University.
W. Michael Reisman, Professor of Law, Yale University.

INTERNATIONAL LEGAL SYSTEM, Third Edition (1988), with Documentary Supplement

Joseph Modeste Sweeney, Professor of Law, University of California, Hastings.
Covey T. Oliver, Professor of Law, University of Pennsylvania.
Noyes E. Leech, Professor of Law Emeritus, University of Pennsylvania.

INTRODUCTION TO LAW, see also Legal Method, On Law in Courts, and Dynamics of American Law

INTRODUCTION TO THE STUDY OF LAW (1970)

E. Wayne Thode, late Professor of Law, University of Utah.
Leon Lebowitz, Professor of Law, University of Texas.
Lester J. Mazor, Professor of Law, University of Utah.

JUDICIAL CODE and Rules of Procedure in the Federal Courts, Students' Edition, 1989 Revision

Daniel J. Meltzer, Professor of Law, Harvard University.
David L. Shapiro, Professor of Law, Harvard University.

JURISPRUDENCE (Temporary Edition Hardbound) (1949)

Lon L. Fuller, late Professor of Law, Harvard University.

JUVENILE, see also Children

JUVENILE JUSTICE PROCESS, Third Edition (1985)

Frank W. Miller, Professor of Law, Washington University.
Robert O. Dawson, Professor of Law, University of Texas.
George E. Dix, Professor of Law, University of Texas.
Raymond I. Parnas, Professor of Law, University of California, Davis.

LABOR LAW, Eleventh Edition (1991), with 1991 Statutory Supplement

Archibald Cox, Professor of Law, Harvard University.
Derek C. Bok, President, Harvard University.
Robert A. Gorman, Professor of Law, University of Pennsylvania.
Matthew W. Finkin, Professor of Law, University of Illinois.

LABOR LAW, Second Edition (1982), with Statutory Supplement

Clyde W. Summers, Professor of Law, University of Pennsylvania.
Harry H. Wellington, Dean of the Law School, Yale University.
Alan Hyde, Professor of Law, Rutgers University.

LAND FINANCING, Third Edition (1985)

The late Norman Penney, Professor of Law, Cornell University.
Richard F. Broude, Member of the California Bar.
Roger Cunningham, Professor of Law, University of Michigan.

LAW AND MEDICINE (1980)

Walter Wadlington, Professor of Law and Professor of Legal Medicine, University of Virginia.
Jon R. Waltz, Professor of Law, Northwestern University.
Roger B. Dworkin, Professor of Law, Indiana University, and Professor of Biomedical History, University of Washington.

LAW, LANGUAGE AND ETHICS (1972)

William R. Bishin, Professor of Law, University of Southern California.
Christopher D. Stone, Professor of Law, University of Southern California.

LAW, SCIENCE AND MEDICINE (1984), with 1989 Supplement

Judith C. Areen, Professor of Law, Georgetown University.
Patricia A. King, Professor of Law, Georgetown University.
Steven P. Goldberg, Professor of Law, Georgetown University.
Alexander M. Capron, Professor of Law, University of Southern California.

LAWYERING PROCESS (1978), with Civil Problem Supplement and Criminal Problem Supplement

Gary Bellow, Professor of Law, Harvard University.
Bea Moulton, Professor of Law, Arizona State University.

LEGAL METHOD (1980)

Harry W. Jones, Professor of Law Emeritus, Columbia University.
John M. Kernochan, Professor of Law, Columbia University.
Arthur W. Murphy, Professor of Law, Columbia University.

LEGAL METHODS (1969)

Robert N. Covington, Professor of Law, Vanderbilt University.
E. Blythe Stason, late Professor of Law, Vanderbilt University.
John W. Wade, Professor of Law, Vanderbilt University.
Elliott E. Cheatham, late Professor of Law, Vanderbilt University.
Theodore A. Smedley, Professor of Law, Vanderbilt University.

LEGAL PROFESSION, THE, Responsibility and Regulation, Second Edition (1988)

Geoffrey C. Hazard, Jr., Professor of Law, Yale University.
Deborah L. Rhode, Professor of Law, Stanford University.

LEGISLATION, Fourth Edition (1982) (by Fordham)

Horace E. Read, late Vice President, Dalhousie University.
John W. MacDonald, Professor of Law Emeritus, Cornell Law School.
Jefferson B. Fordham, Professor of Law, University of Utah.
William J. Pierce, Professor of Law, University of Michigan.

LEGISLATIVE AND ADMINISTRATIVE PROCESSES, Second Edition (1981)

Hans A. Linde, Judge, Supreme Court of Oregon.
George Bunn, Professor of Law, University of Wisconsin.
Fredericka Paff, Professor of Law, University of Wisconsin.
W. Lawrence Church, Professor of Law, University of Wisconsin.

LOCAL GOVERNMENT LAW, Second Revised Edition (1986)

Jefferson B. Fordham, Professor of Law, University of Utah.

UNIVERSITY CASEBOOK SERIES—Continued

MASS MEDIA LAW, Fourth Edition (1990)

Marc A. Franklin, Professor of Law, Stanford University.
David A. Anderson, Professor of Law, University of Texas.

MUNICIPAL CORPORATIONS, see Local Government Law

NEGOTIABLE INSTRUMENTS, see Commercial Paper

NEGOTIATION (1981) (Reprinted from THE LAWYERING PROCESS)

Gary Bellow, Professor of Law, Harvard Law School.
Bea Moulton, Legal Services Corporation.

NEW YORK PRACTICE, Fourth Edition (1978)

Herbert Peterfreund, Professor of Law, New York University.
Joseph M. McLaughlin, Dean of the Law School, Fordham University.

OIL AND GAS, Fifth Edition (1987)

Howard R. Williams, Professor of Law, Stanford University.
Richard C. Maxwell, Professor of Law, University of California, Los Angeles.
Charles J. Meyers, late Dean of the Law School, Stanford University.
Stephen F. Williams, Judge of the United States Court of Appeals.

ON LAW IN COURTS (1965)

Paul J. Mishkin, Professor of Law, University of California, Berkeley.
Clarence Morris, Professor of Law Emeritus, University of Pennsylvania.

PENSION AND EMPLOYEE BENEFIT LAW (1990)

John H. Langbein, Professor of Law, University of Chicago.
Bruce A. Wolk, Professor of Law, University of California, Davis.

PLEADING AND PROCEDURE, see Procedure, Civil

POLICE FUNCTION, Fifth Edition (1991)

Reprint of Chapters 1–10 of Miller, Dawson, Dix and Parnas's CRIMINAL JUSTICE ADMINISTRATION, Fourth Edition.

PREPARING AND PRESENTING THE CASE (1981) (Reprinted from THE LAWYERING PROCESS)

Gary Bellow, Professor of Law, Harvard Law School.
Bea Moulton, Legal Services Corporation.

PROCEDURE (1988), with Procedure Supplement (1989)

Robert M. Cover, late Professor of Law, Yale Law School.
Owen M. Fiss, Professor of Law, Yale Law School.
Judith Resnik, Professor of Law, University of Southern California Law Center.

PROCEDURE—CIVIL PROCEDURE, Second Edition (1974), with 1979 Supplement

The late James H. Chadbourn, Professor of Law, Harvard University.
A. Leo Levin, Professor of Law, University of Pennsylvania.
Philip Shuchman, Professor of Law, Cornell University.

PROCEDURE—CIVIL PROCEDURE, Sixth Edition (1990)

Richard H. Field, late Professor of Law, Harvard University.
Benjamin Kaplan, Professor of Law Emeritus, Harvard University.
Kevin M. Clermont, Professor of Law, Cornell University.

PROCEDURE—CIVIL PROCEDURE, Fifth Edition (1990)

Maurice Rosenberg, Professor of Law, Columbia University.
Hans Smit, Professor of Law, Columbia University.
Rochelle C. Dreyfuss, Professor of Law, New York University.

PROCEDURE—PLEADING AND PROCEDURE: State and Federal, Sixth Edition (1989), with 1990 Case Supplement

David W. Louisell, late Professor of Law, University of California, Berkeley.
Geoffrey C. Hazard, Jr., Professor of Law, Yale University.
Colin C. Tait, Professor of Law, University of Connecticut.

PROCEDURE—FEDERAL RULES OF CIVIL PROCEDURE, 1990 Edition

PRODUCTS LIABILITY AND SAFETY, Second Edition, (1989), with 1989 Statutory Supplement

W. Page Keeton, Professor of Law, University of Texas.
David G. Owen, Professor of Law, University of South Carolina.
John E. Montgomery, Professor of Law, University of South Carolina.
Michael D. Green, Professor of Law, University of Iowa

PROFESSIONAL RESPONSIBILITY, Fifth Edition (1991), with 1991 Selected Standards on Professional Responsibility Supplement

Thomas D. Morgan, Professor of Law, George Washington University.
Ronald D. Rotunda, Professor of Law, University of Illinois.

PROPERTY, Sixth Edition (1990)

John E. Cribbet, Professor of Law, University of Illinois.
Corwin W. Johnson, Professor of Law, University of Texas.
Roger W. Findley, Professor of Law, University of Illinois.
Ernest E. Smith, Professor of Law, University of Texas.

PROPERTY—PERSONAL (1953)

S. Kenneth Skolfield, late Professor of Law Emeritus, Boston University.

PROPERTY—PERSONAL, Third Edition (1954)

Everett Fraser, late Dean of the Law School Emeritus, University of Minnesota.
Third Edition by Charles W. Taintor, late Professor of Law, University of Pittsburgh.

PROPERTY—INTRODUCTION, TO REAL PROPERTY, Third Edition (1954)

Everett Fraser, late Dean of the Law School Emeritus, University of Minnesota.

PROPERTY—FUNDAMENTALS OF MODERN REAL PROPERTY, Second Edition (1982), with 1985 Supplement

Edward H. Rabin, Professor of Law, University of California, Davis.

PROPERTY, REAL (1984), with 1988 Supplement

Paul Goldstein, Professor of Law, Stanford University.

PROSECUTION AND ADJUDICATION, Fourth Edition (1991)

Reprint of Chapters 11–26 of Miller, Dawson, Dix and Parnas's CRIMINAL JUSTICE ADMINISTRATION, Fourth Edition.

PSYCHIATRY AND LAW, see Mental Health, see also Hinckley, Trial of

PUBLIC UTILITY LAW, see Free Enterprise, also Regulated Industries

REAL ESTATE PLANNING, Third Edition (1989), with Revised Problem and Statutory Supplement (1991)

Norton L. Steuben, Professor of Law, University of Colorado.

REAL ESTATE TRANSACTIONS, Revised Second Edition (1988), with Statute, Form and Problem Supplement (1988)

Paul Goldstein, Professor of Law, Stanford University.

RECEIVERSHIP AND CORPORATE REORGANIZATION, see Creditors' Rights

REGULATED INDUSTRIES, Second Edition, (1976)

William K. Jones, Professor of Law, Columbia University.

REMEDIES, Second Edition (1987)

Edward D. Re, Chief Judge, U. S. Court of International Trade.

REMEDIES, (1989)

Elaine W. Shoben, Professor of Law, University of Illinois.
Wm. Murray Tabb, Professor of Law, Baylor University.

SALES, Second Edition (1986)

Marion W. Benfield, Jr., Professor of Law, University of Illinois.
William D. Hawkland, Chancellor, Louisiana State Law Center.

SALES AND SALES FINANCING, Fifth Edition (1984)

John Honnold, Professor of Law, University of Pennsylvania.

SALES LAW AND THE CONTRACTING PROCESS, Second Edition (1991)

(Reprinted from Commercial Transactions, Second Edition (1991)
Alan Schwartz, Professor of Law, Yale University.
Robert E. Scott, Professor of Law, University of Virginia.

SECURED TRANSACTIONS IN PERSONAL PROPERTY, Second Edition (1987) (Reprinted from COMMERCIAL LAW, Second Edition (1987))

Robert L. Jordan, Professor of Law, University of California, Los Angeles.
William D. Warren, Professor of Law, University of California, Los Angeles.

SECURITIES REGULATION, Sixth Edition (1987), with 1990 Selected Statutes, Rules and Forms Supplement and 1990 Cases and Releases Supplement

Richard W. Jennings, Professor of Law, University of California, Berkeley.
Harold Marsh, Jr., Member of California Bar.

SECURITIES REGULATION, Second Edition (1988), with Statute, Rule and Form Supplement (1988)

Larry D. Soderquist, Professor of Law, Vanderbilt University.

SECURITY INTERESTS IN PERSONAL PROPERTY, Second Edition (1987)

Douglas G. Baird, Professor of Law, University of Chicago.
Thomas H. Jackson, Dean of the Law School, University of Virginia.

SECURITY INTERESTS IN PERSONAL PROPERTY (1985) (Reprinted from Sales and Sales Financing, Fifth Edition)

John Honnold, Professor of Law, University of Pennsylvania.

SELECTED STANDARDS ON PROFESSIONAL RESPONSIBILITY, 1991 Edition

UNIVERSITY CASEBOOK SERIES—Continued

SELECTED STATUTES AND INTERNATIONAL AGREEMENTS ON UNFAIR COMPETITION, TRADEMARK, COPYRIGHT AND PATENT, 1989 Edition

SELECTED STATUTES ON TRUSTS AND ESTATES, 1991 Edition

SOCIAL RESPONSIBILITIES OF LAWYERS, Case Studies (1988)

Philip B. Heymann, Professor of Law, Harvard University.
Lance Liebman, Professor of Law, Harvard University.

SOCIAL SCIENCE IN LAW, Second Edition (1990)

John Monahan, Professor of Law, University of Virginia.
Laurens Walker, Professor of Law, University of Virginia.

TAXATION, FEDERAL INCOME (1989)

Stephen B. Cohen, Professor of Law, Georgetown University

TAXATION, FEDERAL INCOME, Second Edition (1988), with 1990 Supplement (Supplement edited in association with Deborah H. Schenk, Professor of Law, New York University)

Michael J. Graetz, Professor of Law, Yale University.

TAXATION, FEDERAL INCOME, Sixth Edition (1987)

James J. Freeland, Professor of Law, University of Florida.
Stephen A. Lind, Professor of Law, University of Florida and University of California, Hastings.
Richard B. Stephens, late Professor of Law Emeritus, University of Florida.

TAXATION, FEDERAL INCOME, Successor Edition (1986), with 1990 Legislative Supplement

Stanley S. Surrey, late Professor of Law, Harvard University.
Paul R. McDaniel, Professor of Law, Boston College.
Hugh J. Ault, Professor of Law, Boston College.
Stanley A. Koppelman, Professor of Law, Boston University.

TAXATION, FEDERAL INCOME, OF BUSINESS ORGANIZATIONS (1991)

Paul R. McDaniel, Professor of Law, Boston College.
Hugh J. Ault, Professor of Law, Boston College.
Martin J. McMahon, Jr., Professor of Law, University of Kentucky.
Daniel L. Simmons, Professor of Law, University of California, Davis.

TAXATION, FEDERAL INCOME, OF PARTNERSHIPS AND S CORPORATIONS (1991)

Paul R. McDaniel, Professor of Law, Boston College.
Hugh J. Ault, Professor of Law, Boston College.
Martin J. McMahon, Jr., Professor of Law, University of Kentucky.
Daniel L. Simmons, Professor of Law, University of California, Davis.

TAXATION, FEDERAL INCOME, OIL AND GAS, NATURAL RESOURCES TRANSACTIONS (1990)

Peter C. Maxfield, Professor of Law, University of Wyoming.
James L. Houghton, CPA, Partner, Ernst and Young.
James R. Gaar, CPA, Partner, Ernst and Young.

TAXATION, FEDERAL WEALTH TRANSFER, Successor Edition (1987)

Stanley S. Surrey, late Professor of Law, Harvard University.
Paul R. McDaniel, Professor of Law, Boston College.
Harry L. Gutman, Professor of Law, University of Pennsylvania.

UNIVERSITY CASEBOOK SERIES—Continued

TAXATION, FUNDAMENTALS OF CORPORATE, Second Edition (1987), with 1989 Supplement

Stephen A. Lind, Professor of Law, University of Florida and University of California, Hastings.
Stephen Schwarz, Professor of Law, University of California, Hastings.
Daniel J. Lathrope, Professor of Law, University of California, Hastings.
Joshua Rosenberg, Professor of Law, University of San Francisco.

TAXATION, FUNDAMENTALS OF PARTNERSHIP, Second Edition (1988)

Stephen A. Lind, Professor of Law, University of Florida and University of California, Hastings.
Stephen Schwarz, Professor of Law, University of California, Hastings.
Daniel J. Lathrope, Professor of Law, University of California, Hastings.
Joshua Rosenberg, Professor of Law, University of San Francisco.

TAXATION, PROBLEMS IN THE FEDERAL INCOME TAXATION OF PARTNERSHIPS AND CORPORATIONS, Second Edition (1986)

Norton L. Steuben, Professor of Law, University of Colorado.
William J. Turnier, Professor of Law, University of North Carolina.

TAXATION, PROBLEMS IN THE FUNDAMENTALS OF FEDERAL INCOME, Second Edition (1985)

Norton L. Steuben, Professor of Law, University of Colorado.
William J. Turnier, Professor of Law, University of North Carolina.

TORT LAW AND ALTERNATIVES, Fourth Edition (1987)

Marc A. Franklin, Professor of Law, Stanford University.
Robert L. Rabin, Professor of Law, Stanford University.

TORTS, Eighth Edition (1988)

William L. Prosser, late Professor of Law, University of California, Hastings.
John W. Wade, Professor of Law, Vanderbilt University.
Victor E. Schwartz, Adjunct Professor of Law, Georgetown University.

TORTS, Third Edition (1976)

Harry Shulman, late Dean of the Law School, Yale University.
Fleming James, Jr., Professor of Law Emeritus, Yale University.
Oscar S. Gray, Professor of Law, University of Maryland.

TRADE REGULATION, Third Edition (1990)

Milton Handler, Professor of Law Emeritus, Columbia University.
Harlan M. Blake, Professor of Law, Columbia University.
Robert Pitofsky, Professor of Law, Georgetown University.
Harvey J. Goldschmid, Professor of Law, Columbia University.

TRADE REGULATION, see Antitrust

TRANSNATIONAL BUSINESS PROBLEMS (1986)

Detlev F. Vagts, Professor of Law, Harvard University.

TRANSNATIONAL LEGAL PROBLEMS, Third Edition (1986) with 1991 Revised Edition of Documentary Supplement

Henry J. Steiner, Professor of Law, Harvard University.
Detlev F. Vagts, Professor of Law, Harvard University.

TRIAL, see also Evidence, Making the Record, Lawyering Process and Preparing and Presenting the Case

CASES AND MATERIALS

ON

TORTS

By

WILLIAM L. PROSSER
Late Professor of Law, University of California,
Hastings College of the Law

JOHN W. WADE
Dean and Distinguished Professor of Law, Emeritus,
Vanderbilt University School of Law

VICTOR E. SCHWARTZ
Adjunct Professor of Law, Georgetown Law Center and
University of Cincinnati Law School
Partner, Crowell & Moring
Washington, D.C.

EIGHTH EDITION

Westbury, New York
THE FOUNDATION PRESS, INC.
1988

Library of Congress Cataloging-in-Publication Data

Prosser, William Lloyd, 1898–
    Cases and materials on torts / by William L. Prosser, John W.
Wade, Victor E. Schwartz.—8th ed.
        p.   cm.—(University casebook series)
    Includes index.
    ISBN 0–88277–641–X
    1. Torts—United States—Cases. I. Wade, John W. II. Schwartz,
Victor E. III. Title. IV. Series.
KF1249.P7 1988
346.7303—dc19
[347.3063]   88–7124
                                                                  CIP

    Prosser, et al. Torts 8th Ed. UCB
    4th Reprint—1991

TO
RICHARD DAVISON, M.D.
and
MARY MOODY WADE
*The first has kept one of the editors alive and well;
the second has kept the other editor very happy.*

*

xix

PREFACE

During the 37–year lifetime of this casebook, Tort law has continuously displayed much ferment and change. Both the courts and the legislatures are responding to demands for change, often at cross-purposes. A Torts casebook may need some updating the same year it is published. In four to six years a new edition is mandated. It has now been six years since we published the seventh edition. We have endeavored in this edition to demonstrate the significant developments of those six years, placing emphasis on the contemporary law of Torts and depicting incipient trends.

In this process we have esteemed the help given by many of our users, both Torts professors and students. They have suggested new cases and new avenues of thought to explore. We have also welcomed general suggestions for improvement of the book. These suggestions have helped to create and maintain a product that captures the new, while sustaining the tradition and stability needed in a work of this nature.

Principles established in the beginning continue to serve as guidelines for each new edition:

1. Select and carefully edit cases that are vivid, provocative and teachable.

2. Prepare full notes providing stimulating points for classroom discussion and giving the student an understanding of details that cannot be treated fully in class because of time limitations.

3. Include in the notes a generous supply of citations to significant cases and law review articles for further study. This means that the casebook can serve not only as a teaching tool, but also as a valuable reference or research book. Many people, both in law school and practice, have told us that they have found it very useful in quickly directing them to a more detailed discussion of a particular topic. In this connection we greatly appreciate receiving citations to cases suitable for setting out or citing in the next edition, and reprints or citations to useful articles.

4. Use an overall presentation that does not attempt to mold the course in accordance with any preconceived approaches or concepts of the editors but affords a full opportunity to present and explore various points of view and to utilize various teaching styles.

5. Provide appropriate treatment of all parts of Tort law, arranged so that the book can easily be adapted to a first-year course of variable length and to optional advanced courses or seminars.

6. Afford proper attenton to the growing significance of statutes in Tort law and the effects of new and controversial efforts to enact further statutory changes in the law.

This edition, in following these guidelines, is like the earlier ones in organization and size, although this edition has fewer pages than the previous one. There are some slight modifications in arrangement. A new chapter on Civil Rights Torts has been added by enlarging Section 2 of the Miscellaneous chapter (then Ch. 22) and adding some recent Supreme Court cases to give a more adequate portrayal of the present state of the law (making it now Ch. 20). The chapters after the one on Nuisance (Ch. 16) have been rearranged by moving the chapter on Misrepresentation (then Ch. 17), and making it Chapter 21, just before the chapter on Interference with Advantageous Relationships (now Ch. 22). The purpose of the change is to place together the two major chapters on Business Torts. The prediction in the seventh edition that the topic of business torts gives "promise of becoming the next burgeoning field of Tort law, following professional negligence and products liability" (p. ii) has been entirely fulfilled.

Each chapter in the book has been carefully reviewed and re-edited to keep it up to date. The most extensive changes have been made in the chapters on Negligence, Proximate Cause, Product Liability, Defamation and Interference With Advantageous Relationships.

While the size of this casebook may give pause to some teachers, we believe that all students should be given an opportunity to become acquainted with all of the topics that the book covers. Our suggestion is that a first-year course of five or six hours be supplemented by an optional two-hour course for upper-class students. Experience has shown that this plan works well.

In previous editions of this casebook, the deletion of a part of the text from a published opinion was indicated by the use of lacunae (***), but if the deletion was confined to citations of cases and other authorities, this was indicated by the word "citation" in brackets. In the present edition the first part of this practice is continued but the form of the reference when only citations are omitted has been modified. The letter "c" is used for "citation." To indicate that several citations have been deleted, "cc" is used. The letter is capitalized or not, depending on whether the citation was placed in the middle of a sentence or started a new sentence.

JOHN W. WADE
VICTOR E. SCHWARTZ

April 1988

ACKNOWLEDGMENTS

1. *Pictures*. Grateful acknowledgment is made to the following for their kind assistance in locating or their courtesy in supplying or granting permission to publish pictures, as follows:

Palsgraf pictures. William J. Pallas, Assistant General Counsel, Long Island Railroad.

Wagon Mound pictures. John Fairfax & Sons, Ltd., Sydney, N.S.W., Australia.

St. Francis Hotel picture. The hotel.

MacPherson Buick Model. Buick Motor Division of General Motors Corporation.

Pictures of New York Court of Appeals and of some individual Justices. Professor Robert J. Tyman, Albany Law School.

Pictures of California Supreme Court and of individual Justices. Professor T.A. Smedley, Hastings Law School.

Pictures of Supreme Court of Oregon. Retired Justice Ralph M. Holman.

Advisory Committee to the Reporter of Restatement (Second) of Torts. Paul A. Wolkin, Executive Vice President, American Law Institute.

Pictures of the parties and house in Katko v. Briney. Bruce A. Palmer, Esq., Oskaloosa, Iowa.

Pictures of the bridge in Dillon v. Twin State Gas and Electric Co. Peter H. Bornstein, Esq., Berlin, New Hampshire.

Pictures of Judge Andrews in *Palsgraf* case. Retired Judge Francis Bergan.

Picture of Justice Francis in *Henningsen* case. Rutgers Law Review.

Picture of the New Jersey Supreme Court. Stephen W. Townsend, Clerk of the Court.

Especial appreciation is due to Ms. Bernice Loss, in charge of the Art Collection at Harvard Law School, for her courtesy in making available the following pictures: Lords Abinger, Blackburn, Cairns, Ellenborough and Herschell, Lord Justice Bowen, Chief Baron Pollock, Chief Justices Holt, Shaw and Tindall, Justices Cardozo and Holmes, Judge Learned Hand, and Dean Bohlen.

2. *Reprints*. Appreciative acknowledgment is also made to the following for permission to include the indicated selections:

American Law Institute. Certain sections from the Restatement, Second, Torts.

ACKNOWLEDGMENTS

National Conference of Commissioners on Uniform State Laws. Certain Uniform and Model Acts.

Matthew Bender & Co. Three paragraphs from A. Larson, The Law of Workmen's Compensation.

3. *Editorial Assistance.*

Grateful appreciation is extended to the following for their valuable contribution to the editorial work on this edition:

Liberty Mahshigian, Esq., of Crowell and Moring in Washington, D.C., for her research, writing, and good counsel.

Professor Craig Joyce of the University of Houston School of Law, for professional proof-reading of the page proof.

Professor David R. Smith of the Vanderbilt Law School for preparing preliminary drafts of two Chapters.

SUMMARY OF CONTENTS

*

TABLE OF CONTENTS

TABLE OF CONTENTS

CHAPTER X. DAMAGES

CHAPTER XI. WRONGFUL DEATH AND SURVIVAL
(Page 539)

CHAPTER XII. DEFENSES

CHAPTER XIII. IMPUTED NEGLIGENCE

CHAPTER XIV. STRICT LIABILITY

CHAPTER XV. PRODUCTS LIABILITY

CHAPTER XXIII. SOME UNCLASSIFIED TORTS

CHAPTER XXIV. COMPENSATION SYSTEMS AS SUBSTITUTES FOR TORT LAW

*

TABLE OF CASES

Principal cases are in italic type. Cases cited or discussed are in roman type. References are to Pages.

lv

CASES AND MATERIALS

ON

TORTS

*

Chapter I

DEVELOPMENT OF LIABILITY BASED UPON FAULT

"Tort" comes from the Latin word "tortus," which means twisted, and the French word "tort," which means injury or wrong. A tort is a civil wrong, other than a breach of contract, for which the law provides a remedy. This area of law imposes duties on persons to act in a manner that will not injure other persons. A person who breaches a tort duty has committed a tort and may be liable in a lawsuit brought by a person injured because of that tort.

Over the years, tort law has normally been a part of the common law, developed by the courts through the opinions of the judges in the cases before them. In some areas, however, statutes have long been common—e.g., trespass to real property, limitation of actions; and statutes have been more frequently used in recent years.

Modern Tort Law—Beyond the Casebooks Into the Field of Public Debate. From the time this casebook began with its first edition in the early 1950's, tort law was of concern primarily to law students, law professors and attorneys who practiced in the field. The public, in general, knew very little, if anything, about the subject. In the past decade or so, however, this has changed quite dramatically. Prior to coming to law school, you probably had read about so-called "liability crises"; that doctors have been "struggling" to obtain insurance; that product manufacturers have gone out of business or declined to put on the market new and useful products, all because of problems in the area of "tort law."

Both the Federal Government and state governments have studied these "crises." More legislation affecting tort law has been enacted in recent years than in decades during the past. As you study the law of torts, you may find that you will be reading news stories about the subject from a new perspective. You may decide that many stories oversimplify the tort system and perhaps miss important points. It is important to pay attention to these stories, however, for the subject you are dealing with is very live, very real and at the center of major public policy debates.

In studying the subject, you should consider the major purposes of tort law. They include: (1) to provide a peaceful means for adjusting the rights of parties who might otherwise "take the law into their own hands"; (2) to deter wrongful conduct; (3) to encourage socially responsible behavior; and, (4) to restore injured parties to their original condition, insofar as the law can do this, by compensating them for their injury. Should people always be compensated when they have

National Health Care

1

to restore a sense of harmony to the community

been injured by the action of another? If your answer to this question is in the affirmative, think about whether it is necessary always to have a trial, with a plaintiff, a defendant and lawyers. On the other hand, if tort law should not compensate every person who is injured by another, what are appropriate rules and standards to determine whom to compensate and under what circumstances? This is the primary problem to which the law of torts addresses itself.

It is important to remember, also, that in back of the tort system is an insurance system. Even the layman knows that most people who are sued in tort law have some form of liability insurance. The "crises" that have occurred in tort law have often arisen when there has been an availability or affordability difficulty with regard to liability insurance. This, in turn, may lead to problems that more directly affect the public—a fireworks exhibit is not held, a physician refuses to deliver a baby, a useful product is not marketed.

The casebook will explore the system that has been accused of having caused these crises. Evaluate it carefully, and remember that you are not only learning a legal subject, but also becoming an educated person who can and should participate in the debate about the direction tort law should take now and into the next century.

Historical Origins. Historians have differed as to how the law of torts began. There is one theory that it originated with liability based upon "actual intent and actual personal culpability," with a strong moral tinge, and slowly formulated external standards which took less account of personal fault. O. Holmes, The Common Law, Lecture I (1881). It seems quite likely that the most flagrant wrongs were the first to receive redress.

Another, and more generally accepted theory, is that the law began by making a person act at his peril if he caused physical harm, and gradually developed toward the acceptance of moral standards as the basis of liability. Wigmore, Responsibility for Tortious Acts: Its History, 7 Harv.L.Rev. 315, 383 & 441 (1894). Ames, Law and Morals, 22 Harv.L.Rev. 97 (1908). It has been suggested that there has been no steady progression, and that there have been "unmoral" periods, and others in which stress has been laid upon moral fault. Isaacs, Fault and Liability, 31 Harv.L.Rev. 954, 965 (1918).

Certainly at one time the law was not very much concerned with the moral responsibility of the defendant. "The thought of man shall not be tried," said Chief Justice Brian, in Y.B. 7 Edw. IV, f. 2, pl. 2 (1468), "for the devil himself knoweth not the thought of man." The courts were interested primarily in keeping the peace between individuals by providing a substitute for private vengeance, and the party injured was just as likely to take the law into his own hands when the injury was an innocent one. The person who hurt another by pure accident or in self-defense was required to make good the damage inflicted. "In all civil acts," it was said, in Lambert v. Bessey, T.Raym.

421, 83 Eng.Rep. 220 (K.B.1681), "the law doth not so much regard the intent of the actor, as the loss and damage of the party suffering."

Forms of action. In the early English law, after the Norman conquest, remedies for wrongs were dependent upon the issuance of writs to bring the defendant into court. In the course of the thirteenth century the principle was established that no one could bring an action in the King's common law courts without the King's writ. As a result of the jealous insistence of the nobles and others upon the prerogatives of their local courts, the number of writs that the King could issue was limited, and their forms were strictly prescribed. There were, in other words, "forms of action," and unless the plaintiff's claim could be fitted into the form of some established and recognized writ, he was without a remedy in the King's courts. The result was a highly formalized system of procedure that governed and controlled the law as to the substance of the wrongs that might be remedied.

The writs available for remedies that were purely tortious in character were two—the writ of trespass and the writ of trespass on the case, often called action on the case.

The form of action in trespass had originally a criminal character. It would lie only in cases of forcible breaches of the King's peace, and it was only on this basis that the royal courts assumed jurisdiction over the wrong. The purpose of the remedy was at first primarily that of punishment of the crime; but to this there was added later the satisfaction of the injured party's claim for redress. If the defendant was found guilty, damages were awarded to the successful plaintiff, and the defendant was imprisoned, and allowed to purchase his release by payment of a fine. What similarity remains between tort and crime is to be traced to this common beginning. See Woodbine, The Origin of the Action of Trespass, 33 Yale L.J. 799 (1923), 34 Yale L.J. 343 (1934); F. Maitland, The Forms of Action at Common Law, 65 (1941).

Writs in trespass were confined to forcible acts in breach of the King's peace. The writ of trespass on the case developed out of a practice of applying to the Chancellor, in cases in which no writ could be found in the Register to cover the plaintiff's claim, for a special writ, in the nature of trespass, drawn to fit the particular case. Historians have differed as to the origin of this practice. Attempts to trace it are found in C. Fifoot, History and Sources of the Common Law: Tort and Contract, 66–74 (1949), and Kiralfy, The Action on the Case, Chapter I (1951).

Whatever may have been its origin, it was through this action on the case, rather than through trespass, that most of the modern law of both tort and contract developed. Thus, in the field of tort law, actions for nuisance, conversion, deceit, defamation, malicious prosecution, interference with economic relations and the modern action for negligence all developed out of the action on the case.

The distinction between trespass and case lay in the direct and immediate application of force to the person or property of the plaintiff.

Trespass would lie only for direct and forcible injuries; case, for other tangible injuries to person or property. The classic illustration is that of a log thrown into the highway. A person struck by the rolling log could maintain trespass against the thrower, since the injury was direct and immediate; but one who came along later and was hurt by stumbling over the stationary log in the road could maintain only an action on the case. Leame v. Bray, 3 East 593, 102 Eng.Rep. 724 (1802).

The distinction was not one between intentional and negligent conduct. The emphasis was upon the causal sequence, rather than the character of the defendant's wrong. Trespass would lie for all forcible, direct injuries, even though they were not intended, while the action on the case might be maintained for injuries intended but not forcible or not direct. There were, however, two significant points of difference between the two actions. Trespass, because of its quasi-criminal character, required no proof of any actual damage, since the invasion of the plaintiff's rights by the criminal conduct was regarded as a tort in itself; while in the action on the case, which developed purely as a civil remedy, there could ordinarily be no liability unless actual damage was proved. Also, in its earlier stages trespass was identified with the view that liability might be imposed without regard to the defendant's fault, while case from the beginning required proof of either a wrongful intent or negligence.

The criminal aspect of trespass disappeared in 1697, when the statute of 5–6 William & Mary, c. 12, abolished the fine, and left the action as an exclusively civil remedy. Out of adherence to precedent, however, the courts continued to allow the action even though no real injury was suffered. They were, however, disinclined to extend the scope of trespass beyond the existing precedents, perhaps because of the belief that punishment was primarily the function of the criminal law and the civil action should be used only to compensate for harm done. This explains the restrictions in modern law on actions for assault, offensive but harmless battery, and false imprisonment. If harm was done, the injured party could still sue in case and recover, even though the defendant's wrong did not amount to a trespass. If no harm was done, the recovery of punitive damages in a civil action was limited to the most flagrant types of cases, where the criminal law did not apply, or was not effective as a deterrent.

ANONYMOUS

King's Bench, 1466
Y.B. 5 Edw. IV, folio 7, placitum 18.

BRIAN. In my opinion if a man does a thing he is bound to do it in such a manner that by his deed no injury or damage is inflicted upon others. As in the case where I erect a building, and when the timber is being lifted a piece of it falls upon the house of my neighbor and bruises

[handwritten: 5 entirely without fault]

his house, he will have a good action, and that, although the erection of my house was lawful and the timber fell without my intent.

Similarly, if a man commits an assault upon me and I cannot avoid him if he wants to beat me, and I lift my stick in self-defense in order to prevent him, and there is a man in back of me and I injure him in lifting my stick, in that case he would have an action against me, although my lifting the stick was lawful to defend myself and I injured him without intent. *[handwritten: — without fault]*

[handwritten margin: movement is voluntary; but intended, negligence or by accident]

1. This passage, translated from the Norman French, is one of the few bits and fragments of the early English law of torts that have come down to us. Brian, who became Chief Justice of the Court of Common Pleas in 1471, was apparently only arguing as counsel in this case; but he appears to have been stating accepted law.

WEAVER v. WARD
King's Bench, 1616.
Hobart 134, 80 Eng. Rep. 284.

[handwritten: No Holding]

Weaver brought an action of trespass of assault and battery against Ward. The defendant pleaded, that he was amongst others by the commandment of the Lords of the Council a trained soldier in London, of the band of one Andrews captain; and so was the plaintiff, and that they were skirmishing with their muskets charged with powder for the exercise in re militari [in a military matter], against another captain and his band; and as they were so skirmishing the defendant casualiter & per infortunium & contra voluntatem suam [accidentally and by misfortune and against his will] in discharging his piece did hurt and wound the plaintiff, which is the same, &c. absque hoc [without this], that he was guilty aliter sive alio modo [otherwise or in another manner].

[handwritten margin: No Fault, Again]

And upon demurrer by the plaintiff, judgment was given for him; for though it were agreed, that if men tilt or turney in the presence of the King, or if two masters of defence playing their prizes kill one another, that this shall be no felony; or if a lunatick kill a man, or the like, because felony must be done animo felonico [with a felonious mind]; yet in trespass, which tends only to give damages according to hurt or loss, it is not so; and therefore if a lunatick hurt a man, he shall be answerable in trespass; and therefore no man shall be excused of a trespass (for this is in the nature of an excuse, and not of a justification, prout ei bene licuit [as is properly permitted to him]), except it may be judged utterly without his fault. *[handwritten: = No Fault?]*

[handwritten margin: Crime requires intent, thus no crime.]

[handwritten margin: H]

As if a man by force take my hand and strike you, or if here the defendant had said, that the plaintiff ran cross his piece when it was discharging, or had set forth the case with the circumstances, so as it had appeared to the Court that it had been inevitable and that the defendant had committed no negligence to give occasion to the hurt.

1. This is apparently the earliest known case in which it was clearly recognized that a defendant might not be liable, even in an action of trespass, for a purely accidental injury occurring entirely without his fault. Note that the burden rests upon the defendant to plead and prove his freedom from all fault.

2. The next two centuries see a gradual blurring of the distinction between trespass and case. The procedural distinction is now long antiquated, although some vestige of it still remains in jurisdictions retaining common law pleading in a modified form. Modern law has almost entirely abandoned the artificial classification of injuries as direct and indirect, and looks instead to the intent of the wrongdoer or his negligence.

3. The first step was taken when the action on the case was held to cover injuries which were merely negligent but were directly inflicted, as in Williams v. Holland, 10 Bing. 112, 131 Eng.Rep. 848 (1833). Although this left the plaintiff an election between trespass and case, the action of case came to be used quite generally in all cases of negligence, whether direct or indirect, while trespass remained as the remedy for intentional injuries inflicted by acts of violence. Terms such as battery, assault and false imprisonment, which were varieties of trespass, gradually came to be associated only with intent, and negligence emerged as a separate tort. The shift was a slow one, and the courts seem to have been quite unconscious of it at the time. When in the nineteenth century the old forms of action were replaced in most jurisdictions by the modern code procedure, the new classification remained. There was occasional confusion, and some talk, for example, of a negligent battery, as in Anderson v. Arnold's Ex'r, 79 Ky. 370 (1881), but, in general, these old trespass terms are now restricted to cases of intent.

4. Although we no longer have "forms of action," it usually is helpful from the vantage point of advocacy to place one's claim under a tort "label" that will be familiar to the court: e.g., "battery," "assault," "defamation," "nuisance."

5. With certain exceptions, actions for injuries to the person, or to tangible property, now require proof of an intent to inflict them, or of failure to exercise proper care to avoid them. As to the necessity of proving actual damage, the courts have continued the distinctions found in the older actions of trespass and case; and whether the damage is essential to the existence of a cause of action for a particular tort may depend very largely upon its ancestry in terms of the old procedure.

6. The story of the change in the law is narrated in Goodhart and Winfield, Trespass and Negligence, 49 L.Q.Rev. 358 (1933); Prichard, Trespass, Case and the Rule in Williams v. Holland, Cambridge L.J. 234 (1964); Gregory, Trespass to Negligence to Absolute Liability, 37 Va.L.Rev. 359 (1951); Roberts, Negligence: Blackstone to Shaw to? An Intellectual Escapade in a Tory Vein, 50 Cornell L.Q. 191 (1964). A thoughtful perspective on the problems of this chapter is Malone, Ruminations on the Role of Fault in the History of the Common Law of Torts, 31 La.L.Rev. 1 (1970).

BROWN v. KENDALL

Supreme Judicial Court of Massachusetts, 1850.
60 Mass. (6 Cush.) 292.

This was an action of trespass for assault and battery　*　*　*
[Two dogs, owned by plaintiff and defendant, were fighting. Defendant
tried to separate them by beating them with a stick. In doing so he
backed up toward the plaintiff, and in raising his stick over his
shoulder, hit plaintiff in the eye, and injured him.]

Whether it was necessary or proper for the defendant to interfere
in the fight between the dogs; whether the interference, if called for,
was in a proper manner, and what degree of care was exercised by each
party on the occasion; were the subject of controversy between the
parties, upon all the evidence in the case　*　*　*

[The trial judge, refusing to give requested instructions to the
contrary, instructed the jury that if beating the dogs was a necessary
act which defendant was under a duty to do, defendant was required to
use only ordinary care in doing it; but if it were only a proper and
permissible act, defendant was liable unless he exercised extraordinary
care; and that the burden of proving the extraordinary care was on the
defendant.]

The jury under these instructions returned a verdict for the plaintiff; whereupon the defendant alleged exceptions.

SHAW, C.J.　*　*　* The facts set forth in the bill of exceptions
preclude the supposition, that the blow, inflicted by the hand of the
defendant upon the person of the plaintiff, was intentional. The whole
case proceeds on the assumption, that the damage sustained by the
plaintiff, from the stick held by the defendant, was inadvertent and
unintentional; and the case involves the question how far, and under
what qualifications, the party by whose unconscious act the damage
was done is responsible for it. We use the term "unintentional" rather
than involuntary, because in some of the cases, it is stated, that the act
of holding and using a weapon or instrument, the movement of which is
the immediate cause of hurt to another, is a voluntary act, although its
particular effect in hitting and hurting another is not within the
purpose or intention of the party doing the act.

It appears to us, that some of the confusion in the cases on this
subject has grown out of the long-vexed question, under the rule of the
common law, whether a party's remedy, where he has one, should be
sought in an action of the case, or of trespass. This is very distinguishable from the question, whether in a given case, any action will lie.
The result of these cases is, that if the damage complained of is the
immediate effect of the act of the defendant, trespass *vi et armis* lies; if
consequential only, and not immediate, case is the proper remedy. [Cc]

In these discussions, it is frequently stated by judges, that when
one receives injury from the direct act of another, trespass will lie. But
we think this is said in reference to the question, whether trespass and

Chief Justice Shaw

not case will lie, assuming that the facts are such, that some action will lie. These *dicta* are no authority, we think, for holding, that damage received by a direct act of force from another will be sufficient to maintain an action of trespass, whether the act was lawful or unlawful, and neither wilful, intentional, or careless. * * *

We think, as the result of all the authorities, the rule is correctly stated by Mr. Greenleaf, that the plaintiff must come prepared with evidence to show either that the *intention* was unlawful, or that the defendant was *in fault;* for if the injury was unavoidable and the conduct of the defendant was free from blame, he will not be liable. 2 Greenl. Ev. §§ 85 to 92; [c]. If, in the prosecution of a lawful act, a casualty purely accidental arises, no action can be supported for an injury arising therefrom. [Cc] In applying these rules to the present case, we can perceive no reason why the instructions asked for by the defendant ought not to have been given; to this effect, that if both plaintiff and defendant at the time of the blow were using ordinary care, or if at that time the defendant was using ordinary care, and the plaintiff was not, or if at that time, both the plaintiff and defendant were not using ordinary care, then the plaintiff could not recover.

In using this term, ordinary care, it may be proper to state, that what constitutes ordinary care will vary with the circumstances of cases.   In general, it means that kind and degree of care, which prudent and cautious men would use, such as is required by the exigency of the case, and such as is necessary to guard against probable danger.   A man, who should have occasion to discharge a gun, on an open and extensive marsh, or in a forest, would be required to use less circumspection and care, than if he were to do the same thing in an inhabited town, village, or city.   To make an accident, or casualty, or as the law sometimes states it, inevitable accident, it must be such an accident as the defendant could not have avoided by the use of the kind and degree of care necessary to the exigency, and in the circumstances in which he was placed.

We are not aware of any circumstances in this case, requiring a distinction between acts which it was lawful and proper to do, and acts of legal duty.   There are cases, undoubtedly, in which officers are bound to act under process, for the legality of which they are not responsible, and perhaps some others in which this distinction would be important.   We can have no doubt that the act of the defendant in attempting to part the fighting dogs, one of which was his own, and for the injurious acts of which he might be responsible, was a lawful and proper act, which he might do by proper and safe means.   If, then, in doing this act, using due care and all proper precautions necessary to the exigency of the case, to avoid hurt to others, in raising his stick for that purpose, he accidentally hit the plaintiff in his eye, and wounded him, this was the result of pure accident, or was involuntary and unavoidable, and therefore the action would not lie.   *   *

The court instructed the jury, that if it was not a necessary act, and the defendant was not in duty bound to part the dogs, but might with propriety interfere or not as he chose, the defendant was responsible for the consequences of the blow, unless it appeared that he was in the exercise of extraordinary care, so that the accident was inevitable, using the word not in a strict but a popular sense.   This is to be taken in connection with the charge afterwards given, that if the jury believed, that the act of interference in the fight was unnecessary, (that is, as before explained, not a duty incumbent on the defendant,) then the burden of proving extraordinary care on the part of the defendant, or want of ordinary care on the part of the plaintiff, was on the defendant.

The court are of opinion that these directions were not conformable to law.   If the act of hitting the plaintiff was unintentional, on the part of the defendant, and done in the doing of a lawful act, then the defendant was not liable, unless it was done in the want of exercise of due care, adapted to the exigency of the case, and therefore such want of due care became part of the plaintiff's case, and the burden of proof was on the plaintiff to establish it. [Cc]

Perhaps the learned judge, by the use of the term extraordinary care, in the above charge, explained as it is by the context, may have intended nothing more than that increased degree of care and diligence, which the exigency of particular circumstances might require, and which men of ordinary care and prudence would use under like circumstances, to guard against danger. If such was the meaning of this part of the charge, then it does not differ from our views, as above explained. But we are of opinion, that the other part of the charge, that the burden of proof was on the defendant, was incorrect. Those facts which are essential to enable the plaintiff to recover, he takes the burden of proving. The evidence may be offered by the plaintiff or by the defendant; the question of due care, or want of care, may be essentially connected with the main facts, and arise from the same proof; but the effect of the rule, as to the burden of proof, is this, that when the proof is all in, and before the jury, from whatever side it comes, and whether directly proved, or inferred from circumstances, if it appears that the defendant was doing a lawful act, and unintentionally hit and hurt the plaintiff, then unless it also appears to the satisfaction of the jury, that the defendant is chargeable with some fault, negligence, carelessness, or want of prudence, the plaintiff fails to sustain the burden of proof, and is not entitled to recover.

New trial ordered.

---

1. Why a new trial? Why not simply a judgment for the defendant?

2. What has gone on in the law since the Anonymous Case in 1466? How would Justice Shaw have decided Weaver v. Ward?

3. This decision is the earliest clear statement of the rule commonly applied, that liability must be based on legal fault.

4. While Brown v. Kendall dealt with a defendant who was separating dogs, most tort defendants in Massachusetts at the time were industrial employers. Does this fact, plus the social policy of the time, have a bearing on the legal change reflected in the opinion?

5. In some jurisdictions, the old distinction between trespass and case survived until comparatively recent dates, in the form of decisions holding that if the injury is one for which trespass would lie the defendant must sustain the burden of proving that he was not at fault, while if only case would lie the burden of proving fault is on the plaintiff. The distinction was not finally abandoned in England until Fowler v. Lanning, [1959] 1 Q.B. 426.

COHEN v. PETTY

Court of Appeals of the District of Columbia, 1933.
62 App.D.C. 187, 65 F.2d 820.

GRONER, ASSOCIATE JUSTICE.　Plaintiff's declaration alleged that on December 14, 1930, she was riding as a guest in defendant's automobile; that defendant failed to exercise reasonable care in its operation, and drove it at a reckless and excessive rate of speed so that he lost control of the car and propelled it off the road against an embankment on the side of the road, as the result of which plaintiff received permanent injuries.　The trial judge gave binding instructions, and the plaintiff appeals.　　　~ *bought Δ's facts*

There were four eyewitnesses to the accident, namely, plaintiff and her sister on the one side, and defendant and his wife on the other.　All four were occupants of the car.　Defendant was driving the car, and his wife was sitting beside him.　Plaintiff and her sister were in the rear seat.　＊　＊　＊　After passing the Country Club, and when somewhere near Four Corners and five or six miles from Silver Spring, the automobile suddenly swerved out of the road, hit the abutment of a culvert, and ran into the bank, throwing plaintiff and her sister through the roof of the car onto the ground.

Plaintiff's sister estimated the speed of the car just before the accident somewhere between thirty-five and forty miles an hour, and plaintiff herself, who had never driven a car, testified she thought it was nearer forty-five.　The place of the accident was just beyond a long and gradual curve in the road.　Plaintiff testified that just before the accident, perhaps a minute, she heard the defendant, who, as we have said, was driving the car, exclaim to his wife, "I feel sick," and a moment later heard his wife exclaim in a frightened voice to her husband, "Oh, John, what is the matter?"　Immediately thereafter the car left the road and the crash occurred.　Her sister, who testified, could not remember anything that occurred on the ride except that, at the time they passed the Country Club, the car was being driven about thirty-five or forty miles an hour and that the occupants of the car were engaged in a general conversation.　The road was of concrete and was wide.　Plaintiff, when she heard defendant's wife exclaim, "What is the matter?" instead of looking at the driver of the car, says she continued to look down the road, and as a result she did not see and does not know what subsequently occurred, except that there was a collision with the embankment.

Defendant's evidence as to what occurred just before the car left the road is positive and wholly uncontradicted.　His wife, who was sitting beside him, states that they were driving along the road at the moderate rate of speed when all of a sudden defendant said, "Oh, Tree, I feel sick"—defendant's wife's name is Theresa, and he calls her Tree. His wife looked over, and defendant had fainted.　"His head had fallen back and his hand had left the wheel and I immediately took hold of the wheel with both hands, and then I do not remember anything else until I waked up on the road in a strange automobile." The witness further testified that her husband's eyes were closed when she looked, and that his fainting and the collision occurred in quick sequence to his previous statement, "Oh, Tree, I feel so sick." The defendant himself testified that he had fainted just before the crash, that he had never fainted before, and that so far as he knew he was in good health, that on the day in question he had had breakfast late, and had had no luncheon, but that he was not feeling badly until the moment before the illness and the fainting occurred. * * *

(I)   The sole question is whether, under the circumstances we have narrated, the trial court was justified in taking the case from the jury. We think its action was in all respects correct.

 It is undoubtedly the law that one who is suddenly stricken by an illness, which he had no reason to anticipate, while driving an automobile, which renders it impossible for him to control the car, is not chargeable with negligence. [Cc]

(H)   In the present case the positive evidence is all to the effect that defendant did not know and had no reason to think he would be subject to an attack such as overcame him. Hence negligence cannot be predicated in this case upon defendant's recklessness in driving an automobile when he knew or should have known of the possibility of an accident from such an event as occurred.

As the plaintiff wholly failed to show any actionable negligence prior to the time the car left the road, or causing or contributing to that occurrence, and as the defendant's positive and uncontradicted evidence shows that the loss of control was due to defendant's sudden illness, it follows the action of the lower court was right. Even if plaintiff's own evidence tended more strongly than it does to imply some act of negligence, it would be insufficient to sustain a verdict and judgment upon proof such as the defendant offered here of undisputed facts, for in such a case the inference must yield to uncontradicted evidence of actual events.

Affirmed.

----

1. Defendant, asleep on the rear seat of an automobile, unconsciously pushed with his foot against the front seat in which plaintiff, the driver, was sitting. Plaintiff's arms were forced off of the wheel, the car crashed into a culvert and overturned, and plaintiff was injured. Is defendant liable? Lobert v. Pack, 337 Pa. 103, 9 A.2d 365 (1939).

2. Defendant, driving an automobile, went to sleep at the wheel. The car went into the ditch and injured the plaintiff. Is defendant liable for his conduct while he is asleep? What if he knew that he was getting sleepy and continued to drive? Bushnell v. Bushnell, 103 Conn. 583, 131 A. 432 (1925). Is this not always the case?

3. Defendant, knowing that he was subject to epileptic fits, drove an automobile. He was seized with a fit while driving and lost control of the car,

which ran into the plaintiff and injured him. Is defendant liable? Eleason v. Western Casualty & Surety Co., 254 Wis. 134, 35 N.W.2d 301 (1948). What if he had never had a fit before? Moore v. Capital Transit Co., 226 F.2d 57 (D.C. Cir.1955), cert. denied, 350 U.S. 966 (1956).

4. A patient was given prescription drugs (Prolixin, Decanoate and Thorazine) and discharged from the hospital, without being warned that they would impair his mental and physical abilities. The patient drove his automobile, lost control and struck a tree, injuring his passenger. Are the patient, the manufacturers of the drugs, the physicians and the hospital liable to the passenger? Cf. Kirk v. Michael Reese Hospital and Medical Center, 136 Ill. App.3d 945, 91 Ill.Dec. 420, 483 N.E.2d 906 (1985), rev'd, 117 Ill.2d 507, 111 Ill. Dec. 944, 513 N.E.2d 387 (1987).

5. Do you agree with the result of the principal case? What about the argument that anyone who drives an automobile should bear the risk that others will be injured if he suffers a heart attack while he is driving, and make good their loss? In a case where an epileptic had an unanticipated attack, plaintiff's counsel argued most strongly that since defendant had liability insurance, he should bear the risk. Was the argument a good one? See Hammontree v. Jenner, 20 Cal.App.3d 528, 97 Cal.Rptr. 739 (1971). The court rejected this contention.

6. See Kaufman and Kantrowitz, The Case of the Sleeping Motorist, 25 N.Y.U.L.Q.Rev. 362 (1950).

SPANO v. PERINI CORP.

Court of Appeals of New York, 1969.
25 N.Y.2d 11, 250 N.E.2d 31, 302 N.Y.S.2d 527, on remand,
33 A.D.2d 516, 304 N.Y.S.2d 15 (1969).

FULD, CHIEF JUDGE. The principal question posed on this appeal is whether a person who has sustained property damage caused by blasting on nearby property can maintain an action for damages without a showing that the blaster was negligent. Since 1893, when this court decided the case of Booth v. Rome, W. & O.T.R.R. Co., 140 N.Y. 267, 35 N.E. 592, 24 L.R.A. 105, it has been the law of this State that proof of negligence was required unless the blast was accompanied by an actual physical invasion of the damaged property—for example, by rocks or other material being cast upon the premises. We are now asked to reconsider that rule.

The plaintiff Spano is the owner of a garage in Brooklyn which was wrecked by a blast occurring on November 27, 1962. There was then in that garage, for repairs, an automobile owned by the plaintiff Davis which he also claims was damaged by the blasting. Each of the plaintiffs brought suit against the two defendants who, as joint venturers, were engaged in constructing a tunnel in the vicinity pursuant to a contract with the City of New York. The two cases were tried together, without a jury, in the Civil Court of the City of New York, New York County, and judgments were rendered in favor of the plaintiffs. The judgments were reversed by the Appellate Term and the Appellate Division affirmed that order, granting leave to appeal to this court.

It is undisputed that, on the day in question (November 27, 1962), the defendants had set off a total of 194 sticks of dynamite at a construction site which was only 125 feet away from the damaged premises. Although both plaintiffs alleged negligence in their complaints, no attempt was made to show that the defendants had failed to exercise reasonable care or to take necessary precautions when they were blasting. Instead, they chose to rely, upon the trial, solely on the principle of absolute liability * * *

The concept of absolute liability in blasting cases is hardly a novel one. The overwhelming majority of American jurisdictions have adopted such a rule. [Cc] Indeed, this court itself, several years ago, noted that a change in our law would "conform to the more widely (indeed almost universally) approved doctrine that a blaster is absolutely liable for any damages he causes, with or without trespass". [C]

We need not rely solely however upon out-of-state decisions in order to attain our result. Not only has the rationale of the *Booth* case [c] been overwhelmingly rejected elsewhere but it appears to be fundamentally inconsistent with earlier cases in our own court which had held, long before *Booth* was decided, that a party was absolutely liable for damages to neighboring property caused by explosions. (See, e.g., Hay v. Cohoes Co., 2 N.Y. 159; Heeg v. Licht, 80 N.Y. 579.) In the *Hay* case (2 N.Y. 159, supra), for example, the defendant was engaged in blasting an excavation for a canal and the force of the blasts caused large quantities of earth and stones to be thrown against the plaintiff's house, knocking down his stoop and part of his chimney. The court held the defendant *absolutely* liable for the damage caused * * *

Although the court in *Booth* drew a distinction between a situation—such as was presented in the *Hay* case—where there was "a physical invasion" of, or trespass on, the plaintiff's property and one in which the damage was caused by "setting the air in motion, or in some other unexplained way," [c], it is clear that the court, in the earlier cases, was not concerned with the particular manner by which the damage was caused but by the simple fact that any explosion in a built-up area was likely to cause damage. Thus, in Heeg v. Licht, 80 N.Y. 579, the court held that there should be absolute liability where the damage was caused by the accidental explosion of stored gunpowder, even in the absence of a physical trespass (p. 581):

"The defendant had erected a building and stored materials therein, which from their character were liable to and actually did explode, causing injury to the plaintiff. The fact that the explosion took place tends to establish that the magazine was dangerous and liable to cause damage to the property of persons residing in the vicinity. * * * The fact that the magazine was liable to such a contingency, which could not be guarded against or averted by the greatest degree of care and vigilance, evinces its dangerous character, * * * In such a case, the rule which exonerates a party engaged in a lawful business, when free from negligence, has no application."

Such reasoning should, we venture, have led to the conclusion that the *intentional* setting off of explosives—that is, blasting—in an area in which it was likely to cause harm to neighboring property similarly results in absolute liability. However, the court in the *Booth* case rejected such an extension of the rule for the reason that "[t]o exclude the defendant from blasting to adapt its lot to the contemplated uses, at the instance of the plaintiff, would not be a compromise between conflicting rights, but an extinguishment of the right of the one for the benefit of the other" [c]. The court expanded on this by stating, "This sacrifice, we think, the law does not exact. Public policy is sustained by the building up of towns and cities and the improvement of property. Any unnecessary restraint on freedom of action of a property owner hinders this."

This rationale cannot withstand analysis. The plaintiff in *Booth* was not seeking, as the court implied, to "exclude the defendant from blasting" and thus prevent desirable improvements to the latter's property. Rather, he was merely seeking compensation for the damage which was inflicted upon his own property as a result of that blasting. The question, in other words, was not *whether* it was lawful or proper to engage in blasting but *who* should bear the cost of any resulting damage—the person who engaged in the dangerous activity or the innocent neighbor injured thereby. Viewed in such a light, it clearly appears that *Booth* was wrongly decided and should be forthrightly overruled * * *

[The court here considered the evidence of causation of the plaintiffs' damage, and concluded that it was sufficient.]

Even though the proof was not insufficient as a matter of law, however, the Appellate Division affirmed on the sole ground that no negligence had been proven against the defendants and thus had no occasion to consider the question whether, in fact, the blasting caused the damage. That being so, we must remit the case to the Appellate Division so that it may pass upon the weight of the evidence. [Cc]

The order appealed from should be reversed, with costs, and the matter remitted to the Appellate Division for further proceedings in accordance with this opinion.

---

1. The early common law strict liability of the type of Weaver v. Ward has persisted most stubbornly in connection with trespass to real property and has been exorcised only in contemporary times. Thus, in Randall v. Shelton, 293 S.W.2d 559 (Ky.1956), defendant's truck ran over a small stone in the gravel highway and the tire cast it out so that it hit plaintiff, who was standing in her yard, and injured her. The appellate court found no negligence and held that the defendant's motion for judgment notwithstanding the verdict should have been granted. To do this, it had to overrule an earlier Kentucky case in which a runaway street car invaded plaintiff's property and did damage. The special rule for trespass explains some of the early New York cases discussed in the opinion of the principal case.

2. The procedural distinction long made in New York, between an action of trespass for blasting causing physical invasion by casting rocks on the plaintiff's land, for which there was strict liability, and the action of nuisance for vibration or concussion which shook plaintiff's house to pieces, which would require proof of negligence, has long been denounced as a marriage of procedural technicality with scientific ignorance. It has lingered on in a small number of states, where older decisions have not yet been overruled. See, for example, Coalite, Inc. v. Aldridge, 285 Ala. 137, 229 So.2d 539 (1969). The principal case has no doubt given it its death blow.

3. The question of strict liability for damage to land by blasting and other activities that have been deemed extrahazardous is considered at greater length in Chapter 14, on strict liability.

4. For the present, it is sufficient to note that this case represents one type of situation in which strict liability may be applied, without any showing of intent or negligence, by the considerable majority of the courts that have considered the question. This has sometimes been called absolute liability, or liability without fault. The Restatement of Torts § 519, conferred the name of "ultrahazardous activity" upon these cases. The Restatement (Second) of Torts has concluded that a better name is "abnormally dangerous activities," since today the emphasis is more upon the abnormal character of what the defendant does in relation to its surroundings rather than upon the high degree of danger alone.

5. Strict liability has also been imposed upon manufacturers of products when defects in their wares have caused injury. This position is now generally followed when the defect causing the injury was caused by an error in the manufacturing process. There is less agreement as to the application of strict liability for failure to use a safer design or to warn of dangers.

In Beshada v. Johns–Manville Products Corp., 90 N.J. 191, 447 A.2d 539 (1982), strict liability was applied against manufacturers of asbestos for failure to warn about dangers, regardless of whether the dangers were known or knowable at the time of manufacture.

6. Several recent decisions show a judicial "trend" away from fault as the basis of tort liability. See, for example, Hayes v. Ariens Co., 391 Mass. 407, 462 N.E.2d 273 (1984); Elmore v. Owens–Illinois, Inc., 673 S.W.2d 434 (Mo.1984); Dart v. Wiebe Mfg., Inc., 147 Ariz. 242, 709 P.2d 876 (1985). This trend in the law of torts has been alleged to contribute to the high cost and unavailability of liability insurance.

7. One justification for imposing liability without regard to fault is the argument that the defendant is better able than the plaintiff to absorb the cost of an accident. See Halphen v. Johns–Manville Sales Corp., 484 So.2d 110, 117 (La.1986).

8. Strict liability involves a good many problems that are to be considered later in Chapters 15 and 16. For present purposes, note merely that there are three possible bases of tort liability:

A. Conduct intended to cause harm.

B. Negligent conduct creating an unreasonable risk of causing harm not intended.

C. Conduct subject to strict liability, without intent or negligence, to the extent that it has survived from the early law or has been re-established by modern ideas of policy.

9.   These will be considered in turn, which will carry us through Chapter 15.   The remainder of this book covers particular fields of case law in which special problems arise, and in most of which intent, negligence and strict liability are all involved and intermingled as possible bases for recovery.

Little Neil Armstrong, or Setter yet, Columbus
–seeing beyond the horizon of his experience
–foreseeing laws of physics
what do we do – she him

Chapter II

INTENTIONAL INTERFERENCE WITH PERSON OR PROPERTY

¿ Haven't we all seen it before? (pulling chair out –pke)
¿ Should Δ have known she would sit where her chair was? – w/substantial certainty

¿ what are the facts?
π's v. Δ's =
¿ which did Trct buy? } Why?
¿ which is before SCt?

1. INTENT

(Gen. Denning) UW graduate took CA. bar exam
in swivel seats, she stood, seat swiveled,
plop, flat on pants? should
building or seat makers be liable? Don't
they know people sit back down
from whence they got up?

Ruth GARRATT v. DAILEY

Supreme Court of Washington, 1955
46 Wash.2d 197, 279 P.2d 1091.

(Case of "intent" turning on facts)

HILL, JUSTICE. The liability of an infant for an alleged battery is presented to this court for the first time. Brian Dailey (age five years, nine months) was visiting with Naomi Garratt, an adult and a sister of the plaintiff, Ruth Garratt, likewise an adult, in the back yard of the plaintiff's home, on July 16, 1951. It is plaintiff's contention that she came out into the back yard to talk with Naomi and that, as she started to sit down in a wood and canvas lawn chair, Brian deliberately pulled it out from under her. The only one of the three present so testifying was Naomi Garratt. (Ruth Garratt, the plaintiff did not testify as to how or why she fell.) The trial court, unwilling to accept this testimony, adopted instead Brian Dailey's version of what happened, and made the following findings:

"III. * * * that while Naomi Garratt and Brian Dailey were in the back yard the plaintiff, Ruth Garratt, came out of her house into the back yard. Some time subsequent thereto defendant, Brian Dailey, picked up a lightly built wood and canvas lawn chair which was then and there located in the back yard of the above described premises, moved it sideways a few feet and seated himself therein, at which time he discovered the plaintiff, Ruth Garratt, about to sit down at the place where the lawn chair had formerly been, at which time he hurriedly got up from the chair and attempted to move it toward Ruth Garratt to aid her in sitting down in the chair; that due to the defendant's small size and lack of dexterity he was unable to get the lawn chair under the plaintiff in time to prevent her from falling to the ground. That plaintiff fell to the ground and sustained a fracture of her hip, and other injuries and damages as hereinafter set forth.

"IV. That the preponderance of the evidence in this case establishes that when the defendant, Brian Dailey moved the chair in question *he did not have any wilful or unlawful purpose* in doing so; that *he did not have any intent to injure* the plaintiff, or any intent to bring about any *unauthorized* or *offensive* contact with her person or any objects appurtenant thereto; that the circumstances which immedi-

¿ any contact? = harmful

18

ately preceded the fall of the plaintiff established that the defendant, *Brian Dailey, did not have purpose, intent or design to perform a prank or to effect an assault and battery upon the person of the plaintiff.*" (Italics ours, for a purpose hereinafter indicated.)

It is conceded that Ruth Garratt's fall resulted in a fractured hip and other painful and serious injuries. To obviate the necessity of a retrial in the event this court determines that she was entitled to a judgment against Brian Dailey, the amount of her damage was found to be $11,000. Plaintiff appeals from a judgment dismissing the action and asks for the entry of a judgment in that amount or a new trial.

The authorities generally, but with certain notable exceptions, [c] state that when a minor has committed a tort with force he is liable to be proceeded against as any other person would be. * * *

In our analysis of the applicable law, we start with the basic premise that Brian, whether five or fifty-five, must have committed some wrongful act before he could be liable for appellant's injuries. * * *

It is urged that Brian's action in moving the chair constituted a battery. A definition (not all-inclusive but sufficient for our purpose) of a battery is the intentional infliction of a harmful bodily contact upon another. * * *

We have in this case no question of consent or privilege. We therefore proceed to an immediate consideration of intent and its place in the law of battery. In the comment on clause (a) of § 13, the Restatement says:

"*Character of Actor's Intention.* In order that an act may be done with the intention of bringing about a harmful or offensive contact or an apprehension thereof to a particular person, either the other or a third person, the act must be done for the purpose of causing the contact or apprehension or with knowledge on the part of the actor that such contact or apprehension is substantially certain to be produced." [C]

We have here the conceded volitional act of Brian, i.e., the moving of a chair. Had the plaintiff proved to the satisfaction of the trial court that Brian moved the chair while she was in the act of sitting down, Brian's action would patently have been for the purpose or with the intent of causing the plaintiff's bodily contact with the ground, and she would be entitled to a judgment against him for the resulting damages. [Cc]

The plaintiff based her case on that theory, and the trial court held that she failed in her proof and accepted Brian's version of the facts rather than that given by the eyewitness who testified for the plaintiff. After the trial court determined that the plaintiff had not established her theory of a battery (i.e., that Brian had pulled the chair out from under the plaintiff while she was in the act of sitting down), it then

[handwritten top margin: intent (definition) – to voluntarily commit act with the purpose of bringing about harmful of offensive contact with the knowledge that ~~really~~ harm is substantial certain to result.]

[handwritten left margin: one element of battery]

became concerned with whether a battery was established under the facts as it found them to be.

In this connection, we quote another portion of the comment on the "Character of actor's intention," relating to clause (a) of the rule from [Restatement, (First) Torts, 29, § 13]:

[handwritten left margin: What is Restatement]

"It is not enough that the act itself is intentionally done and this, even though the actor realizes or should realize that it contains a very grave risk of bringing about the contact or apprehension. Such realization may make the actor's conduct negligent or even reckless but unless he realizes that to a substantial certainty, the contact or apprehension will result, the actor has not that intention which is necessary to make him liable under the rule stated in this section." *[handwritten: say, "grave risk" or "substantial certainty"]*

[handwritten right margin: "does" grave risk sound like it me subst. cert. Test practically = when you argue your side, why do you say...]

A battery would be established if, in addition to plaintiff's fall, it was proved that, when Brian moved the chair, he knew with substantial certainty that the plaintiff would attempt to sit down where the chair had been. If Brian had any of the intents which the trial court found, in the italicized portions of the findings of fact quoted above, that he did not have, he would of course have had the knowledge to which we have referred. The mere absence of any intent to injure the plaintiff or to play a prank on her or to embarrass her, or to commit an assault and battery on her would not absolve him from liability if in fact he had such knowledge. [C] Without such knowledge, there would be nothing wrongful about Brian's act in moving the chair and, there being no wrongful act, there would be no liability.

[handwritten right margin: whether in the pos of sitting or not qres = as whether he knew]

[handwritten left margin: ? is intent to injure necessary? No]

[handwritten left margin circle: I]

While a finding that Brian had no such knowledge can be inferred from the findings made, we believe that before the plaintiff's action in such a case should be dismissed there should be no question but that the trial court had passed upon that issue; hence, the case should be remanded for clarification of the findings to specifically cover the question of Brian's knowledge, because intent could be inferred therefrom. If the court finds that he had such knowledge the necessary intent will be established and the plaintiff will be entitled to recover, even though there was no purpose to injure or embarrass the plaintiff. [C] If Brian did not have such knowledge, there was no wrongful act by him and the basic premise of liability on the theory of a battery was not established.

[handwritten left margin circle: H]

It will be noted that the law of battery as we have discussed it is the law applicable to adults, and no significance has been attached to the fact that Brian was a child less than six years of age when the alleged battery occurred. The only circumstance where Brian's age is of any consequence is in determining what he knew, and there his experience, capacity, and understanding are of course material.

[handwritten left margin: Age]

From what has been said, it is clear that we find no merit in plaintiff's contention that we can direct the entry of a judgment for $11,000 in her favor on the record now before us.

Nor do we find any error in the record that warrants a new trial.

     *   *   *

The cause is remanded for clarification, with instructions to make definite findings on the issue of whether Brian Dailey knew with substantial certainty that the plaintiff would attempt to sit down where the chair which he moved had been, and to change the judgment if the findings warrant it. * * *

Remanded for clarification.

[On remand, the trial judge concluded that it was necessary for him to consider carefully the time sequence, as he had not done before; and this resulted in his finding "that the arthritic woman had begun the slow process of being seated when the defendant quickly removed the chair and seated himself upon it, and that he knew, with substantial certainty, at that time that she would attempt to sit in the place where the chair had been." He entered judgment for the plaintiff in the amount of $11,000, which was affirmed on a second appeal in Garratt v. Dailey, 49 Wash.2d 499, 304 P.2d 681 (1956).]

_____

1. Can a child five years and nine months old have an intent to do harm to another? And if so, how can that intent be "fault"? Suppose that a boy of seven, playing with a bow and arrow, aims at a girl of five and hits her, and she is injured. Is he liable? Weisbart v. Flohr, 260 Cal.App.2d 281, 67 Cal.Rptr. 114 (1968). See Weisiger, Tort Liability of Minors and Incompetents, 1951 U.Ill.L.F. 227. See generally Restatement (Second) of Torts § 8A.

2. Can a two-year-old child who bites an infant be liable for an intentional tort? See Fromenthal v. Clark, 442 So.2d 608 (La.App.1983), cert. denied, 444 So.2d 1242 (1984).

3. Can a young child commit a tort requiring a "malicious" state of mind? Ortega v. Montoya, 97 N.M. 159, 637 P.2d 841 (1981). Some states have parental responsibility statutes, making parents liable for their child's malicious torts.

SPIVEY v. BATTAGLIA
Supreme Court of Florida, 1972.
258 So.2d 815.

DEKLE, JUSTICE. * * * Petitioner (plaintiff in the trial court) and respondent (defendant) were employees of Battaglia Fruit Co. on January 21, 1965. During the lunch hour several employees of Battaglia Fruit Co., including petitioner and respondent, were seated on a work table in the plant of the company. Respondent, in an effort to tease petitioner, whom he knew to be shy, intentionally put his arm around petitioner and pulled her head toward him. Immediately after this "friendly unsolicited hug," petitioner suffered a sharp pain in the back of her neck and ear, and sharp pains into the base of her skull. As a result, petitioner was paralyzed on the left side of her face and mouth.

An action was commenced in the Circuit Court of Orange County, Florida, wherein the petitioners, Mr. and Mrs. Spivey, brought suit against respondent for, (1) negligence, and (2) assault and battery. Respondent, Mr. Battaglia, filed his answer raising as a defense the claim that his "friendly unsolicited hug" was an assault and battery as a matter of law and was barred by the running of the two-year statute of limitations on assault and battery. Respondent's motion for summary judgment was granted by the trial court on this basis. The district court affirmed on the authority of McDonald v. Ford, [223 So.2d 553 (Fla.App.1969)].

Tr Ct = Δ -summary
RR = SoL
Ct App = aff'd
S.

(I) The question presented for our determination is whether petitioner's action could be maintained on the negligence count, or whether respondent's conduct amounted to an assault and battery as a matter of law, which would bar the suit under the two-year statute (which had run).

In *McDonald* the incident complained of occurred in the early morning hours in a home owned by the defendant. While the plaintiff was looking through some records, the defendant came up behind her, laughingly embraced her and, though she resisted, kissed her hard. As the defendant was hurting the plaintiff physically by his embrace, the plaintiff continued to struggle violently and the defendant continued to laugh and pursue his love-making attempts. In the process, plaintiff struck her face hard upon an object that she was unable to identify specifically. With those facts before it, the district court held that what actually occurred was an assault and battery, and not negligence. The court quoted with approval from the Court of Appeals of Ohio in Williams v. Pressman, 113 N.E.2d 395, at 396 (Ohio App.1953):

" * * * an assault and battery is not negligence, for such action is intentional, while negligence connotes an unintentional act." ? or unintentional re -should be result.

(R) The intent with which such a tort liability as assault is concerned is not necessarily a hostile intent, or a desire to do harm. Where a reasonable man would believe that a particular result was *substantially certain* to follow, he will be held in the eyes of the law as though he had intended it. It would thus be an assault (intentional). However, the knowledge and appreciation of a risk, short of substantial certainty, is not the equivalent of intent. Thus, the distinction between intent and negligence boils down to a matter of degree. "Apparently the line has been drawn by the courts at the point where the known danger ceases to be only a foreseeable risk which a reasonable man would avoid (negligence), and becomes a substantial certainty." In the latter case, the intent is legally implied and becomes an assault rather than unintentional negligence.

R = re: intent

Would Brian, given facts on remand, be better held for Negligence?

The distinction between the unsolicited kisses in *McDonald,* supra, and the unsolicited hug in the present case turns upon this question of intent. In *McDonald,* the court, finding an assault and battery, necessarily had to find initially that the results of the defendant's acts were "intentional." This is a rational conclusion in view of the struggling involved there. In the instant case, the DCA must have found the same intent. But we cannot agree with that finding in these circumstances. It cannot be said that a reasonable man in this defendant's position would believe that the bizarre results herein were "substantially cer-

(R) intend results

(H)

tain" to follow. This is an unreasonable conclusion and is a misapplication of the rule in *McDonald*. This does not mean that he does not become liable for such unanticipated results, however. The settled law is that a defendant becomes liable for reasonably foreseeable consequences, though the exact results and damages were not contemplated.

but liable in Negl., not Battery

Acts that might be considered prudent in one case might be negligent in another. Negligence is a relative term and its existence must depend in each case upon the particular circumstances which surrounded the parties at the time and place of the events upon which the controversy is based.

The trial judge committed error when he granted summary final judgment in favor of the defendant. The cause should have been submitted to the jury with appropriate instructions regarding the elements of negligence. Accordingly, certiorari is granted; the decision of the district court is hereby quashed and the cause is remanded with directions to reverse the summary final judgment.

(H) not Battery as a matter of law

It is so ordered.   *Was there battery? No RTL = no substantial certainty of result*
What effect of SCts ruling? remanded, ▲ possibly liable for Negligence

1. Distinguish:

A. The intent to do an act. The defendant fires a rifle, or drives an automobile in excess of the speed limit.

B. The intent to bring about the consequences—the bullet, or the car, hits a man. It is this that is always important in determining whether there is an intentional tort. See Etcher v. Blitch, 381 So.2d 1119 (Fla.App.1979), cert. denied, 386 So.2d 636 (1980).

battery must have both

2. Distinguish:

A. The defendant does not act. He is carried onto plaintiff's land against his will. Smith v. Stone, Style 65, 82 Eng.Rep. 533 (1647).

B. He acts intentionally, but under fear or threats. Twelve armed men compel him to enter plaintiff's land and steal a horse. Gilbert v. Stone, Style 72, 82 Eng.Rep. 539 (1648).

C. He acts intentionally, but without any desire to affect the plaintiff, or any certainty that he will do so. He rides a horse, which runs away with him and runs the plaintiff down. Gibbons v. Pepper, 1 Ld.Raym. 38, 91 Eng.Rep. 922 (1695).

D. He acts with the desire to affect the plaintiff, but for an entirely permissible or laudable purpose. He shoots the plaintiff in self-defense, or as a soldier defending his country.

In which of these is there an intent to do harm? *B, D*

3. In some cases it may not seem important to distinguish between negligent and intentionally wrongful conduct: the defendant will be held liable in either situation. Nevertheless, the distinction may be legally significant. Thus:

A. Will defendant be liable for punitive damages? See infra, Chapter 10, Section 3.

B. Will the defense of contributory negligence be available to defendant? See infra page 569, note 10.

C. Will defendant's employer be liable under the doctrine of *respondeat superior*? See infra page 649.

D. How far will the law trace the consequences of defendants' wrongful act? See Tate v. Canonica, 180 Cal.App.2d 898, 5 Cal.Rptr. 28 (1960) (liability for causing suicide).

E. Will the defendant be protected under a liability insurance policy? See Allstate Ins. Co. v. Hiseley, 465 F.2d 1243 (10th Cir.1972). Cloud v. Shelby Mut. Ins. Co., 248 So.2d 217 (Fla.App.1971).

F. Has the state statute of limitations run? See the principal case.

G. Will an employer be subject to liability to an employee in spite of a general worker compensation immunity shield?

An exception is sometimes permitted for intentional wrongdoing. Does an employer's intentional failure to train an employee to perform a dangerous task supply the requisite intent to injure under the workers' compensation intentional injury exception? See Reed Tool Co. v. Copelin, 689 S.W.2d 404 (Tex. 1985). What about an employer's deliberate exposure of employees to dangerous products? See Millison v. E.I. du Pont de Nemours & Co., 101 N.J. 161, 501 A.2d 505 (1985). In Blankenship v. Cincinnati Milacron Chemicals, Inc., 69 Ohio St.2d 608, 433 N.E.2d 572 (1982), cert. denied, 459 U.S. 857 (1982), the court held that the relevant workers' compensation statute did not expressly prohibit lawsuits based on intentional torts and harm caused by an employer's intentional conduct was not an injury arising out of the "normal course" of employment. Note, however, that not all jurisdictions hearing suits for intentional torts have gone as far as Ohio in broadening their concept of "intentional." But compare Bardere v. Zafir, 102 A.D.2d 422, 477 N.Y.S.2d 131 (1984), aff'd, 63 N.Y.2d 850, 472 N.E.2d 37, 482 N.Y.S.2d 261 (1984), holding that in the absence of a showing of "specific acts [by the employer] directed at causing harm to particular employees" the doctrine will not apply.

4. Does this mean that a court's characterization of a defendant's conduct as "negligent" or "intentional" is influenced by the legal effect of its finding? Cf. Lambertson v. United States, 528 F.2d 441 (2d Cir.1976), cert. denied, 426 U.S. 921 (1976).

RANSON v. KITNER

Appellate Court of Illinois, 1888.
31 Ill.App. 241.

CONGER, J. This was an action brought by appellee against appellants to recover the value of a dog killed by appellants, and a judgment rendered for $50.

The defense was that appellants were hunting for wolves, that appellee's dog had a striking resemblance to a wolf, that they in good faith believed it to be one, and killed it as such.

Many points are made, and a lengthy argument failed to show that error in the trial below was committed, but we are inclined to think that no material error occurred to the prejudice of appellants.

The jury held them liable for the value of the dog, and we do not see how they could have done otherwise under the evidence. Appellants are clearly liable for the damages caused by their mistake, notwithstanding they were acting in good faith.

We see no reason for interfering with the conclusion reached by the jury, and the judgment will be affirmed.

1. Did the defendant intend to kill the dog? The court calls it "mistake." Why not accident?

2. Distinguish:

A. Whether the mistake prevents the existence of an intent to affect the person or property in question. Defendant shoots at an animal, not knowing whose or what it is. Does he intend to kill it? Defendant, seeking to arrest A, gets the wrong man and arrests B. Does he intend to arrest B? Seigel v. Long, 169 Ala. 79, 53 So. 753 (1910). What if a surgeon operates on the wrong patient? Gill v. Selling, 125 Or. 587, 267 P. 812 (1928).

B. Whether the mistake will protect the defendant against liability for the result he intended to cause. There is general agreement that it does not where the defendant by mistake appropriates property of the plaintiff. If he is not to be liable for his mistake, he is unjustly enriched. Perry v. Jefferies, 61 S.C. 292, 39 S.E. 515 (1901) (cutting and removing timber from plaintiff's land under a reasonable belief that defendant owned it); Dexter v. Cole, 6 Wis. 319, 70 Am. Dec. 465 (1858) (driving off plaintiff's sheep, believed to be defendant's).

3. On the other hand, some of the defendant's privileges depend, not upon the existence of a fact, but upon the reasonable belief that the fact exists. Defendant, seeing the plaintiff reach for a handkerchief in his pocket, reasonably believes that he is reaching for a gun, and attacks plaintiff to defend himself. See infra, page 107. Mistakes as to the existence of a privilege are dealt with below in connection with the privilege itself.

4. See generally Whittier, Mistake in the Law of Torts, 15 Harv.L.Rev. 335 (1902).

McGUIRE v. ALMY

Supreme Judicial Court of Massachusetts, 1937.
297 Mass. 323, 8 N.E.2d 760.

QUA, JUSTICE. This is an action of tort for assault and battery. The only question of law reported is whether the judge should have directed a verdict for the defendant.

The following facts are established by the plaintiff's own evidence: In August, 1930, the plaintiff was employed to take care of the defendant. The plaintiff was a registered nurse and was a graduate of a training school for nurses. The defendant was an insane person. Before the plaintiff was hired she learned that the defendant was a "mental case and was in good physical condition," and that for some time two nurses had been taking care of her. The plaintiff was on "24 hour duty." The plaintiff slept in the room next to the defendant's room. Except when the plaintiff was with the defendant, the plaintiff kept the defendant locked in the defendant's room. * * *

On April 19, 1932, the defendant, while locked in her room, had a violent attack. The plaintiff heard a crashing of furniture and then knew that the defendant was ugly, violent and dangerous. The defendant told the plaintiff and a Miss Maroney, "the maid," who was with the plaintiff in the adjoining room, that if they came into the defendant's room, she would kill them. The plaintiff and Miss Maroney looked into the defendant's room, "saw what the defendant had done," and "thought it best to take the broken stuff away before she did any harm to herself with it." They sent for a Mr. Emerton, the defendant's brother-in-law. When he arrived the defendant was in the middle of her room about ten feet from the door, holding upraised the leg of a low-boy as if she were going to strike. The plaintiff stepped into the room and walked toward the defendant, while Mr. Emerton and Miss Maroney remained in the doorway. As the plaintiff approached the defendant and tried to take hold of the defendant's hand which held the leg, the defendant struck the plaintiff's head with it, causing the injuries for which the action was brought.

The extent to which an insane person is liable for torts has not been fully defined in this Commonwealth. * * *

Turning to authorities elsewhere, we find that courts in this country almost invariably say in the broadest terms that an insane person is liable for his torts. As a rule no distinction is made between those torts which would ordinarily be classed as intentional and those which would ordinarily be classed as negligent, nor do the courts discuss the effect of different kinds of insanity or of varying degrees of capacity as bearing upon the ability of the defendant to understand the particular act in question or to make a reasoned decision with respect to it, although it is sometimes said that an insane person is not liable for torts requiring malice of which he is incapable. Defamation and malicious prosecution are the torts more commonly mentioned in this connection. * * * These decisions are rested more upon grounds of public policy and upon what might be called a popular view of the requirements of essential justice than upon any attempt to apply logically the underlying principles of civil liability to the special instance of the mentally deranged. Thus it is said that a rule imposing liability tends to make more watchful those persons who have charge of the defendant and who may be supposed to have some interest in preserving his property; that as an insane person must pay for his support, if he is financially able, so he ought also to pay for the damage which he does; that an insane person with abundant wealth ought not to continue in unimpaired enjoyment of the comfort which it brings while his victim bears the burden unaided; and there is also a suggestion that courts are loath to introduce into the great body of civil litigation the difficulties in determining mental capacity which it has been found impossible to avoid in the criminal field.

The rule established in these cases has been criticized severely by certain eminent text writers both in this country and in England, principally on the ground that it is an archaic survival of the rigid and formal mediaeval conception of liability for acts done, without regard to fault, as opposed to what is said to be the general modern theory that liability in tort should rest upon fault. Notwithstanding these criticisms, we think, that as a practical matter, there is strong force in the reasons underlying these decisions. They are consistent with the general statements found in the cases dealing with the liability of infants for torts, [cc] including a few cases in which the child was so young as to render his capacity for fault comparable to that of many insane persons, [cc]. Fault is by no means at the present day a universal prerequisite to liability, and the theory that it should be such has been obliged very recently to yield at several points to what have been thought to be paramount considerations of public good. Finally, it would be difficult not to recognize the persuasive weight of so much authority so widely extended.

But the present occasion does not require us either to accept or to reject the prevailing doctrine in its entirety. For this case it is enough to say that where an insane person by his act does intentional damage to the person or property of another he is liable for that damage in the same circumstances in which a normal person would be liable. This means that in so far as a particular intent would be necessary in order to render a normal person liable, the insane person, in order to be liable, must have been capable of entertaining that same intent and must have entertained it in fact. But the law will not inquire further into his peculiar mental condition with a view to excusing him if it should appear that delusion or other consequence of his affliction has caused him to entertain that intent or that a normal person would not have entertained it. * * *

Coming now to the application of the rule to the facts of this case, it is apparent that the jury could find that the defendant was capable of entertaining and that she did entertain an intent to strike and to injure the plaintiff and that she acted upon that intent. See American Law Institute Restatement, Torts, §§ 13, 14. We think this was enough. * * *

[The rest of the opinion holds that whether the plaintiff consented to the attack or assumed the risk of it is an issue to be left to the jury. There was no evidence that the defendant had previously attacked any one or made any serious threat to do so. The plaintiff had taken care of the defendant for fourteen months without being attacked. When the plaintiff entered the room the defendant was breaking up the furniture, and it could be found that the plaintiff reasonably feared that the defendant would do harm to herself. Under such circumstances it cannot be ruled as a matter of law that the plaintiff assumed the risk.]

Judgment for the plaintiff on the verdict.

1. Can an insane person have an intent to do harm to another? And if so, how can such an intent be "fault"? How does the lunatic differ from the automobile driver who suffers a heart attack, in Cohen v. Petty, supra, page 11?

2. The American decisions are unanimous in their agreement with the principal case. The result has, however, been much criticized. See, e.g., Bohlen, Liability in Tort of Infants and Insane Persons, 23 Mich.L.Rev. 9 (1924); Curran, Tort Liability of the Mentally Ill and Mentally Deficient, 21 Ohio St. L.J. 52 (1960). Good, recent discussions of the whole problem include Fridman, Mental Incompetency, 79 Law Q.Rev. 502 (1963), 80 Law Q.Rev. 84 (1964); and Note, Insanity as a Defense, 54 Marq.L.Rev. 245 (1971).

3. It has been held, however, that the insanity may prevent the specific kind of intent necessary for certain torts, such as deceit, when the defendant is to be held liable only if he knows that he is not speaking the truth. See Irvine v. Gibson, 117 Ky. 306, 77 S.W. 1106 (1904); Chaddock v. Chaddock, 130 Misc. 900, 226 N.Y.S. 152 (1927); Beaubeauf v. Reed, 4 La.App. 344 (1926).

4. Even if an insane person lacks the ability to form the intent to commit a tort, an action may lie against persons responsible for controlling the insane person, based on negligent supervision. See Rausch v. McVeigh, 105 Misc.2d 163, 431 N.Y.S.2d 887 (1980).

TALMAGE v. SMITH

Supreme Court of Michigan, 1894.
101 Mich. 370, 59 N.W. 656.

MONTGOMERY, J. The plaintiff recovered in an action of trespass. The case made by plaintiff's proofs was substantially as follows: * * * Defendant had on his premises certain sheds. He came up to the vicinity of the sheds, and saw six or eight boys on the roof of one of them. He claims that he ordered the boys to get down, and they at once did so. He then passed around to where he had a view of the roof of another shed, and saw two boys on the roof. The defendant claims that he did not see the plaintiff, and the proof is not very clear that he did, although there was some testimony from which it might have been found that he was within his view. Defendant ordered the boys in sight to get down, and there was testimony tending to show that the two boys in defendant's view started to get down at once. Before they succeeded in doing so, however, defendant took a stick, which is described as being two inches in width, and of about the same thickness, and about 16 inches long, and threw it in the direction of the boys; and there was testimony tending to show that it was thrown at one of the boys in view of the defendant. The stick missed him, and hit the plaintiff just above the eye with such force as to inflict an injury which resulted in the total loss of the sight of the eye. * * * George Talmage, the plaintiff's father, testifies that defendant said to him that he threw the stick, intending it for Byron Smith,—one of the boys on the roof,—and this is fully supported by the circumstances of the case. * * *

The circuit judge charged the jury as follows: "If you conclude that Smith did not know the Talmage boy was on the shed, and that he did not intend to hit Smith, or the young man that was with him, but

(handwritten top margin)
① Had to be intended to hit, not just frighten.
② Force had to be excessive, beyond reasonable.
(RTL = defending property – we'll see later)

simply, by throwing the stick, intended to frighten Smith, or the other *(handwritten: assault)* *(handwritten right margin: see p. 31 "imminent apprehension")*
young man that was there, and the club hit Talmage, and injured him,
as claimed, then the plaintiff could not recover. If you conclude that
Smith threw the stick or club at Smith, or the young man that was with
Smith,—intended to hit one or the other of them,—and you also
conclude that the throwing of the stick or club was, under the circum-
stances, reasonable, and not excessive, force to use towards Smith and *(handwritten right margin: ① SE of property; although ② intent may still transfer)*
the other young man, then there would be no recovery by this plaintiff.
But if you conclude from the evidence in this case that he threw the
stick, intending to hit Smith, or the young man with him,—to hit one of
them,—and that that force was unreasonable force, under all the
circumstances, then [the defendant] would be doing an unlawful act, if
the force was unreasonable, because he had no right to use it. He
would be liable then for the injury done to this boy with the stick.
* * *" [The jury rendered a verdict for the plaintiff.]

We think the charge is a very fair statement of the law of the case. *(handwritten: Sct agrees w/ Rules of Trct)*
* * * The right of the plaintiff to recover was made to depend upon
an intention on the part of the defendant to hit somebody, and to inflict
an unwarranted injury upon some one. Under these circumstances,
the fact that the injury resulted to another than was intended does not *(handwritten: R/H)*
relieve the defendant from responsibility. * * *

The judgment will be affirmed, with costs.

(handwritten: yes — what about Brown p. 7? Intended B)
(handwritten: see Brown 1968 thing (def (battery? yes = Ransen p. 24), instead hit W. State?)

1. This doctrine of "transferred intent" was derived originally from the
criminal law, and goes back to the time when tort damages were awarded as a
side issue in criminal prosecutions. It is familiar enough in the criminal law,
and has been applied in several tort cases where the defendant has shot at A, or
thrown a rock at him, and has unintentionally hit B instead. See, for example,
Lopez v. Surchia, 112 Cal.App.2d 314, 246 P.2d 111 (1952) (shooting); Carnes v.
Thompson, 48 S.W.2d 903 (Mo.1932) (striking); Singer v. Marx, 144 Cal.App.2d
637, 301 P.2d 440 (1956) (throwing a missile).

2. The doctrine is discussed in Prosser, Transferred Intent, 45 Tex.L.Rev.
650 (1967). The conclusion there is that it applies whenever both the tort
intended and the resulting harm fall within the scope of the old action of
trespass—that is, where both involve direct and immediate application of force
to the person or to tangible property. There are five torts that fell within the
trespass writ: battery, assault, false imprisonment, trespass to land, and
trespass to chattels. When the defendant intends any one of the five, and
accidentally accomplishes any one of the five, he is liable.

3. Thus he is liable when he shoots to frighten A (assault) and the bullet
unforeseeably hits a stranger (battery). Brown v. Martinez, 68 N.M. 271, 361
P.2d 152 (1961). Or when he shoots at a dog (trespass to chattels) and hits a
man (battery). Corn v. Sheppard, 179 Minn. 490, 229 N.W. 869 (1930).

4. On the other hand, when either the tort intended or the one accomplished does not fall within the trespass action, the doctrine does not apply.
Thus when defendant commits a murder in a house, and causes loss of value to
the owner. Clark v. Gay, 112 Ga. 777, 38 S.E. 81 (1901). Or when he inflicts a

(handwritten bottom: Use this re: sample exam)

beating upon A, and causes mental distress to a bystander. McGee v. Vanover, 148 Ky. 737, 147 S.W. 742 (1912).

Volitional Act
Intent
  purposely to cause Tort (Battery) ← *harmful + offensive contact*
knowingly w/ substantial certainty That tort will result ← *particular result*
Cause
  Harm (physical)
  or
∴ Indignity

2. BATTERY

COLE v. TURNER
Nisi Prius, 1704.
6 Modern Rep. 149, 90 Eng.Rep. 958.

At Nisi Prius, upon evidence in trespass for assault and battery, Holt, C.J., declared:

1. That the least touching of another in anger is a battery.

harm must be intended

2. If two or more meet in a narrow passage, and without any violence or design of harm, the one touches the other gently it will be no battery.

3. If any of them use violence against the other, to force his way in a rude inordinate manner, it is a battery; or any struggle about the passage, to that degree as may do hurt, is a battery.

---

1. In United States v. Ortega, 4 Wash.C.C. 531, Fed.Cas.No. 15,971 (E.D. Pa.1825), defendant, in an offensive manner, approached the plaintiff, took hold of the breast of his coat, and said that he demanded satisfaction. Is this a battery?

2. What about spitting in the plaintiff's face? Alcorn v. Mitchell, 63 Ill. 553 (1872). Or forcibly removing his hat? Seigel v. Long, 169 Ala. 79, 53 So. 753 (1910). Or an attempted search of his pockets? Piggly–Wiggly Alabama Co. v. Rickles, 212 Ala. 585, 103 So. 860 (1925).

3. What if a ~~man~~ *woman* touches a ~~woman~~ *man* in an indecent manner? Skousen v. *in Criminal = 4th degree sexual assault* Nidy, 90 Ariz. 215, 367 P.2d 248 (1961). Cf. Gates v. State, 110 Ga.App. 303, 138 S.E.2d 473 (1964) (stranger touching ~~woman~~ *men* on the buttocks).

4. What about tapping plaintiff on the shoulder to attract his attention? "Pardon me, sir, could you direct me, etc."? Coward v. Baddeley, 4 H. & N. 478, 157 Eng.Rep. 927 (1859).

5. With the modern shift of emphasis to intent and negligence, as distinguished from trespass and case, "battery" has become exclusively an intentional tort. Thus there is no battery when defendant negligently, or even recklessly, drives his car into plaintiff and injures him, without intending to hit him. Cook v. Kinzua Pine Mills Co., 207 Or. 34, 293 P.2d 717 (1956). The same shift of emphasis accounts for the modern cases allowing recovery when the contact inflicted is not direct and immediate, but indirect.

RESTATEMENT (SECOND) OF TORTS (1965)

"§ 13. Battery: Harmful Contact   *Garratt v. Daily rule*

"An actor is subject to liability to another for battery if

"(a) he acts intending to cause a harmful or offensive contact with the person of the other or a third person, or an imminent apprehension of such a contact, and
need only intend this, (F)

"(b) a harmful contact with the person of the other directly or indirectly results." *this results*

Cf: p. 28, 9 ; Δ intended only to scare

"§ 18. Battery: Offensive Contact

"(1) An actor is subject to liability to another for battery if

"(a) he acts intending to cause a harmful or offensive contact with the person of the other or a third person, or an imminent apprehension of such a contact, and

"(b) an offensive contact with the person of the other directly or indirectly results.

"(2) An act which is not done with the intention stated in Subsection (1, a) does not make the actor liable to the other for a mere offensive contact with the other's person although the act involves an unreasonable risk of inflicting it and, therefore, would be negligent or reckless if the risk threatened bodily harm."

Suppose in Putney p 28, A had only meant to scare, see

1. Has the "black letter" law of battery undergone any substantial changes since Cole v. Turner in 1704? *is this substantially certain, or reasonably foreseeable*

2. When defendant intentionally causes plaintiff to undergo an offensive contact and the resulting injuries are more extensive than a reasonable person might have anticipated, the defendant will still be liable for those injuries. See Baldinger v. Banks, 26 Misc.2d 1086, 201 N.Y.S.2d 629 (1960) (six-year-old boy shoves four-year-old girl). A similar case is Harrigan v. Rosich, 173 So.2d 880 (La.App.1965), where defendant, wishing to get rid of the plaintiff, pushed him with his finger, and said, "Go home, old man." *extent of harm is given/irrelevant — Read This b/c may not get to damages -- so use + pieces*

non standard — take "it" you find it

3. In Vosburg v. Putney, 80 Wis. 523, 50 N.W. 403 (1891), one schoolboy, during a class hour, playfully kicked another on the shin. He intended no harm, and the touch was so slight that the plaintiff actually did not feel it. It had, however, the effect of "lighting up" an infection in the leg from a previous injury, and as a result the plaintiff suffered damages found by the jury to be $2,500. Is there liability for battery? See Reynolds, Tortious Battery: Is "I Didn't Mean Any Harm" Relevant?, 37 Okla.L.Rev. 715 (1984).

4. Does it make any difference that the defendant is trying to help the plaintiff? In Clayton v. New Dreamland Roller Skating Rink, Inc., 14 N.J. Super. 390, 82 A.2d 458 (1951), cert. denied, 13 N.J. 527, 100 A.2d 567 (1953), plaintiff fell at a skating rink and broke her arm. Over the protests of plaintiff and her husband, defendant's employees proceeded to manipulate the arm in an attempt to set it. Is this battery? *Harmful or offensive? re: purpose = Surgeon?*

5. Can the plaintiff by prohibiting a contact that would not be offensive to a reasonable person, such as a tap on the shoulder to attract attention, make

the defendant liable when he inflicts it? The Restatement (Second) of Torts § 19, leaves the question open. See Richmond v. Fiske, 160 Mass. 34, 35 N.E. 103 (1893), where defendant, against orders, entered plaintiff's bedroom and woke him up to present a milk bill. This was held to be battery; but no doubt it would be offensive to a reasonable person.

6. Can there be liability for battery for a contact of which plaintiff is unaware at the time? What if a woman is kissed while she is asleep, and upon waking and being informed of it is annoyed? Cf. McCraney v. Flanagan, 47 N.C.App. 498, 267 S.E.2d 404 (1980) (intercourse). Or an unauthorized surgical operation is performed while plaintiff is under an anaesthetic? Does it make any difference whether the operation is harmful or beneficial? See Mohr v. Williams, infra, page 97.

7. Is the transmission of a disease, such as herpes, through sexual activity a battery? Does consent to the sexual activity operate as a defense? See Liability in Tort for the Sexual Transmission of Disease: Genital Herpes and the Law, 70 Cornell L.Rev. 101 (1984); Baruch, AIDS In the Courts: Tort Liability for the Sexual Transmission of Acquired Immune Deficiency Syndrome, 22 Tort & Ins. L.J. 165 (1987).

FISHER v. CARROUSEL MOTOR HOTEL, INC.

Supreme Court of Texas, 1967.
424 S.W.2d 627.

[Action for assault and battery. Plaintiff, a black, was invited to attend a meeting concerning telemetry equipment at defendant's motor hotel. The meeting included a buffet luncheon. As plaintiff was standing in line with others, he was approached by one of defendant's employees, who snatched the plate from his hand, and shouted that no Negro could be served in the club. Plaintiff was not actually touched, and was in no apprehension of physical injury; but he was highly embarrassed and hurt by the conduct in the presence of his associates. The jury returned a verdict for $400 actual damages for his humiliation and indignity, and $500 exemplary damages in addition. The trial court set aside the verdict and gave judgment for the defendants notwithstanding the verdict. This was affirmed by the Court of Civil Appeals. Plaintiff appealed to the Supreme Court.]

GREENHILL, JUSTICE * * * Under the facts of this case, we have no difficulty in holding that the intentional grabbing of plaintiff's plate constituted a battery. The intentional snatching of an object from one's hand is as clearly an offensive invasion of his person as would be an actual contact with the body. "To constitute an assault and battery, it is not necessary to touch the plaintiff's body or even his clothing; knocking or snatching anything from plaintiff's hand or touching anything connected with his person, when done in an offensive manner, is sufficient." Morgan v. Loyacomo, 190 Miss. 656, 1 So.2d 510 (1941).

Such holding is not unique to the jurisprudence of this State. In S.H. Kress & Co. v. Brashier, 50 S.W.2d 922 (Tex.Civ.App.1932, no writ), the defendant was held to have committed "an assault or trespass upon the person" by snatching a book from the plaintiff's hand. The jury findings in that case were that the defendant "dispossessed plaintiff of the book" and caused her to suffer "humiliation and indignity."

The rationale for holding an offensive contact with such an object to be a battery is explained in 1 Restatement (Second) of Torts § 18 (Comment p. 31) as follows:

"Since the essence of the plaintiff's grievance consists in the offense to _RTL_ the dignity involved in the unpermitted and intentional invasion of the inviolability of his person and not in any physical harm done to his body, it is not necessary that the plaintiff's actual body be disturbed. Unpermitted and intentional contacts with anything so connected with the body as to be customarily regarded as part of the other's person and therefore as partaking of its inviolability is actionable as an offensive contact with his person. There are some things such as clothing or a cane or, indeed, anything directly grasped by the hand which are so intimately connected with one's body as to be universally regarded as part of the person."

We hold, therefore, that the forceful dispossession of plaintiff Fisher's plate in an offensive manner was sufficient to constitute a battery, and the trial court erred in granting judgment notwithstanding the verdict on the issue of actual damages. * * *

Damages for mental suffering are recoverable without the necessity for showing actual physical injury in a case of willful battery because _C'sA = not dependent on actual harm_ the basis of that action is the unpermitted and intentional invasion of _damages = dependent on actual harm_ the plaintiff's person and not the actual harm done to the plaintiff's body. Restatement (Second) of Torts § 18. Personal indignity is the _± punitive_ essence of an action for battery; and consequently the defendant is liable not only for contacts which do actual physical harm, but also for those which are offensive and insulting. [Cc]. We hold, therefore, that plaintiff was entitled to actual damages for mental suffering due to the willful battery, even in the absence of any physical injury. [The court then held that the defendant corporation was liable for the tort of its employee.]

The judgments of the courts below are reversed, and judgment is here rendered for the plaintiff for $900 with interest from the date of the trial court's judgment, and for costs of this suit.

Did color have anything to do with it? should it have?

1. What would have been the result if plaintiff had not been black, but merely was subject to having his plate removed abruptly? Suppose the waiter had not touched plaintiff's plate, but said in a loud voice, "Get out, we don't serve Negroes here!"? What if the doorman at the hotel shouted a racial epithet and kicked plaintiff's car when he was about to leave. Battery?

2. Does the utilization of the tort of battery confuse things? Why not characterize what happened as "intentional infliction of emotional harm"? See Browning v. Slenderella Systems, 54 Wash.2d 440, 341 P.2d 859 (1959). On the other hand, might the case be regarded as one of imaginative lawyering, assuming the state was not ready to recognize intentional infliction of emotional harm as a tort? What other remedies might have been available to plaintiff?

See Colley, Civil Actions for Damages Arising Out of Violations of Civil Rights, 17 Hastings L.J. 189 (1965).

3. Defendant, unreasonably suspecting the plaintiff of shoplifting, forcibly seized a package from under her arm and opened it. Morgan v. Loyacomo, 190 Miss. 656, 1 So.2d 510 (1941). *Intent harmful or offensive? No. Suppose white store owner did this consistently to black customers? different inten*

4. A is standing with his arm around B's shoulder, and leaning on him. C, passing by, violently jerks B's arm, as a result of which A falls down. To whom is C liable for battery? Reynolds v. Pierson, 29 Ind.App. 273, 64 N.E. 484 (1902).

5. For general treatments of battery, see Carpenter, Intentional Invasion of Interest of Personality, 13 Or.L.Rev. 227, 275 (1934); Vold, The Legal Allocation of Risk in Assault, Battery and Imprisonment, 17 Neb.L.Rev. 149 (1938); Restatement (Second) of Torts §§ 13–20 (1966); 1 Harper and James, Torts §§ 3.1–3.3 (2d ed. 1986); Prosser and Keeton on Torts (5th ed. 1984) § 11. (Hereafter no general references to treatises will be given.)

3. ASSAULT

Ques #1 = what's the name of this case?

I DE S ET UX. v. W DE S

At the Assizes, 1348.
Y.B.Lib.Ass. folio 99, placitum 60.

I de S and M, his wife, complain of W de S concerning this, that the said W, in the year, etc., with force and arms did make an assault upon the said M de S and beat her. And W pleaded not guilty. And it was found by the verdict of the inquest that the said W came at night to the house of the said I and sought to buy of his wine, but the door of the tavern was shut and he beat upon the door with a hatchet which he had in his hand, and the wife of the plaintiff put her head out of the window and commanded him to stop, and he saw and he struck with the hatchet but did not hit the woman. Whereupon the inquest said that it seemed to them that there was no trespass since no harm was done. *Trot = Δ*

THORPE, C.J. There is harm done and a trespass for which he shall recover damages since he made an assault upon the woman, as has been found, although he did no other harm. Wherefore tax the damages, etc. And they taxed the damages at half a mark. Thorpe awarded that they should recover their damages, etc., and that the other should be taken. And so note that for an assault a man shall recover damages, etc.

And "I" said, "hey M, stick your head out the window and run interference with W's hatchet,

1. This is the great-grandparent of all assault cases. Why allow the action if "no harm was done"? *So that I can recover in assault."*

Sapp v. Hill's Wife [handwritten]

WESTERN UNION TELEGRAPH CO. v. HILL

Court of Appeals of Alabama, 1933.
25 Ala.App. 540, 150 So. 709.

Action for damages for assault by J.B. Hill against the Western Union Telegraph Company. From a judgment for plaintiff, defendant appeals.

SAMFORD, JUDGE. The action in this case is based upon an alleged assault on the person of plaintiff's wife by one Sapp, an agent of defendant in charge of its office in Huntsville, Ala. The assault complained of consisted of an attempt on the part of Sapp to put his hand on the person of plaintiff's wife coupled with a request that she come behind the counter in defendant's office, and that, if she would come and allow Sapp to love and pet her, he "would fix her clock."

The first question that addresses itself to us is, Was there such an assault as will justify an action for damages?

While every battery includes an assault, an assault does not necessarily require a battery to complete it. What it does take to constitute an assault is an unlawful attempt to commit a battery, incomplete by reason of some intervening cause; or, to state it differently, to constitute an actionable assault there must be an intentional, unlawful, offer to touch the person of another in a rude or angry manner under such circumstances as to create in the mind of the party alleging the assault a well-founded fear of an imminent battery, coupled with the apparent present ability to effectuate the attempt, if not prevented. * * *

What are the facts here? Sapp was the agent of defendant and the manager of its telegraph office in Huntsville. Defendant was under contract with plaintiff to keep in repair and regulated an electric clock in plaintiff's place of business. When the clock needed attention, that fact was to be reported to Sapp, and he in turn would report to a special man, whose duty it was to do the fixing. At 8:13 o'clock p.m. plaintiff's wife reported to Sapp over the phone that the clock needed attention, and, no one coming to attend the clock, plaintiff's wife went to the office of defendant about 8:30 p.m. There she found Sapp in charge and behind a desk or counter, separating the public from the part of the room in which defendant's operator worked. The counter is four feet and two inches high, and so wide that, Sapp standing on the floor, leaning against the counter and stretching his arm and hand to the full length, the end of his fingers reaches just to the outer edge of the counter. The photographs in evidence show that the counter was as high as Sapp's armpits. Sapp had had two or three drinks and was "still slightly feeling the effects of whisky I felt all right; I felt good and amiable." When plaintiff's wife came into the office, Sapp came from towards the rear of the room and asked what he could do for her. She replied: "I asked him if he understood over the phone that my clock was out of order and when he was going to fix it. He stood there and looked at me a few minutes and said: 'If you will come back here

*Suppose Ranson dog?
or the wolf?*

*physical
evidence
v.
testimony
v
for jury*

and let me love and (pet you,) I will fix your clock.' This he repeated and reached for me with his hand, he extended his hand toward me, he did not put it on me; I jumped back. I was in his reach as I stood there. He reached for me right along here (indicating her left shoulder and arm)." The foregoing is the evidence offered by plaintiff tending to prove assault. Per contra, aside from the positive denial by Sapp of any effort to touch Mrs. Hill, the physical surroundings as evidenced by the photographs of the locus tend to rebut any evidence going to prove that Sapp could have touched plaintiff's wife across that counter even if he had reached his hand in her direction <u>unless she was leaning</u> against <u>the counter or</u> Sapp should have stood upon something so as to elevate him and allow him to reach beyond the counter. However, there is testimony tending to prove that, notwithstanding the width of the counter and the height of Sapp, Sapp could have reached from six to eighteen inches beyond the desk in an effort to place his hand on Mrs. Hill. The evidence as a whole <u>presents a question for the jury.</u> This was the view taken by the trial judge, and in the several rulings bearing on this question there is no error. * * *

*Court bound by
factfinders finding*

[Reversed on the ground that Sapp had not acted within the scope of his employment.] *what does This have to do with it? (suing Engel)*
Why not sue Sapp? (Old Sapp probably has no money) "deep pocket"
Explain quickly "respondeat superior"/ This is basically it

1. Defendant, standing three or four feet from plaintiff, made a "kissing sign" at her by puckering his lips and smacking them. He did not touch her, and made no effort to kiss her, or to use any force. Is this an assault? Fuller v. State, 44 Tex.Crim. 463, 72 S.W. 184 (1903).

2. Defendant, a hundred yards from plaintiff, starts running toward him, throwing rocks as he runs. At what point does this become an assault? Cf. State v. Davis, 23 N.C. (1 Ired.) 125, 35 Am.Dec. 735 (1840); Grimes v. State, 99 Miss. 232, 54 So. 839 (1911). *"apparent present ability to effectuate"*

3. What about mere preparation, such as bringing a gun along for an interview? Penny v. State, 114 Ga. 77, 39 S.E. 871 (1901). *No, must have act ("words constitute act)*

4. Must the plaintiff be put in fear, as distinguished from mere apprehension of contact? Suppose this case arose today and a modern Mrs. Hill was President of the Woman's Self–Defense League whose motto was "We Fear No Men!" Assault? Cf. Brady v. Schatzel, [1911] Q.St.R. 206, 208; Coleman v. Employment Security Dept., 25 Wash.App. 405, 607 P.2d 1231 (1980). Is there an important distinction between apprehension and fear? *-- Wimp can cause apprehension in a bully, if not fear*

"apprehension"—"apparent"

5. Is there an assault if defendant threatens the plaintiff with an unloaded gun? See Allen v. Hannaford, 138 Wash. 423, 244 P. 700 (1926). Suppose the gun remains on defendant's lap? See Castiglione v. Galpin, 325 So.2d 725 (La.App.1976).

6. In State v. Barry, 45 Mont. 598, 124 P. 775 (1912), it was held that there was no assault where the plaintiff did not know that a gun was aimed at him with intent to shoot him until it was all over. The Restatement (Second) of Torts § 22, has agreed. On the other hand, in People v. Pape, 66 Cal. 366, 5 P. 621 (1885), defendant put gunpowder in plaintiff's stove, intending to blow him up. Plaintiff did not know about it until after the gunpowder was discovered and removed. Defendant was convicted of an assault. *should have been
Trespass to land, chattel*

[handwritten top margin: Person throw jackhammer at you from behind, intending to hit, but misses. Criminal? yes. Tort? No — Interest of state against such behavior — If you were not hit, nor apprehended the possibility of being hit, are you harmed?]

7. A major distinction between a criminal assault and an assault in tort is that for a criminal assault, a victim need not have an apprehension or fear of contact. A criminal assault occurs if the defendant intends to injure the victim and has the ability to do so. For the tort of assault, the victim must have an apprehension of contact, and it is not necessary that the defendant have the actual ability to carry out the threatened contact. Commonwealth v. Slaney, 345 Mass. 135, 185 N.E.2d 919 (1962). Depending upon which classification is chosen, a defendant could be subject to either criminal prosecution or civil damages. *[margin: only apparent]*

8. Does a complaint state a cause of action for assault if one paragraph of the complaint asserts that the defendants threatened to strike the plaintiffs with blackjacks and that the threats placed the plaintiffs in fear that a battery will be committed against them and a subsequent paragraph asserts that the defendants showed the plaintiffs that the defendants were carrying blackjacks? Cucinotti v. Ortmann, 399 Pa. 26, 159 A.2d 216 (1960). *[handwritten: How imminent is imminent?]*

9. Is there an assault in the following cases, where the words were accompanied by a threatening gesture? *[handwritten: evidence of factual apprehension]* *[margin: what is point of these questions?]*

A. "Were you not an old man, I would knock you down." State v. Crow, 23 N.C. (1 Ired.) 375 (1840).

B. "If it were not for your gray hairs, I would tear your heart out." Commonwealth v. Eyre, 1 Serg. & Rawle 347 (Pa.1815).

C. "I have a great mind to hit you." State v. Hampton, 63 N.C. 13 (1868).

10. What about: "If you do not pay me my money, I will have your life"? Keefe v. State, 19 Ark. 190 (1857).

11. Can words make an assault out of conduct that would otherwise not be sufficient for the tort? Suppose that while defendant and plaintiff are engaged in a violent quarrel, defendant reaches for his hip pocket. Does it make any difference whether he says, "I'll blow your brains out," or "Pardon me, I need a handkerchief"? *[handwritten: Factual evidence of intent]* *[margin: what is point of this ques?]*

12. What about words which threaten harm from an independent source? "Look out! There is a rattlesnake behind you!"

13. Can an assault occur if a man has sexual intercourse with a woman while she is either asleep or unconscious, and she has no recollection of the event, but she is angry when she later discovers that it occurred? McCraney v. Flanagan, 47 N.C.App. 498, 267 S.E.2d 404 (1980). Suppose she was falsely told that it occurred?

4. FALSE IMPRISONMENT

[margin: Act (includes words) / Intent – purposely knowingly / subjective re: plaintiff / Cause = reasonable apprehension of imminent contact (battery) H+0 / Present + Apprehend / Ability to commit]

[margin right: elements — ① intent ② direct restraint (acts or words) ③ person or property ④ against will ⑤ no reasonable means of exit ⑥ to an area (not necessarily restraint to person)]

BIG TOWN NURSING HOME, INC. v. NEWMAN
Court of Civil Appeals of Texas, 1970.
461 S.W.2d 195.

McDONALD, CHIEF JUSTICE. This is an appeal by defendant Nursing Home from a judgment for plaintiff Newman for actual and exemplary damages in a false imprisonment case. *[margin: Πct = Π]*

Plaintiff Newman sued defendant Nursing Home for actual and exemplary damages for falsely and wrongfully imprisoning him against his will from September 22, 1968 to November 11, 1968. * * *

Plaintiff is a retired printer 67 years of age, and lives on his social security and a retirement pension from his brother's printing company. He has not worked since 1959, is single, has Parkinson's disease, arthritis, heart trouble, a voice impediment, and a hiatal hernia. He has served in the army attaining the rank of Sergeant. He has never been in a mental hospital or treated by a psychiatrist. Plaintiff was taken to defendant nursing home on September 19, 1968, by his nephew who signed the admission papers and paid one month's care in advance. Plaintiff had been arrested for drunkenness and drunken driving in times past (the last time in 1966) and had been treated twice for alcoholism. Plaintiff testified he was not intoxicated and had nothing to drink during the week prior to admission to the nursing home. The admission papers provided that patient "will not be forced to remain in the nursing home against his will for any length of time." Plaintiff was not advised he would be kept at the nursing home against his will. On September 22, 1968, plaintiff decided he wanted to leave and tried to telephone for a taxi. Defendant's employees advised plaintiff he could not use the phone, or have any visitors unless the manager knew them, and locked plaintiff's grip and clothes up. Plaintiff walked out of the home, but was caught by employees of defendant and brought back forceably, and thereafter, placed in Wing 3 and locked up. Defendant's Administrator testified Wing 3 contained senile patients, drug addicts, alcoholics, mentally disturbed, incorrigibles and uncontrollables, and that "they were all in the same kettle of fish." Plaintiff tried to escape from the nursing home five or six times but was caught and brought back each time against his will. He was carried back to Wing 3 and locked and taped in a "restraint chair", for more than five hours. He was put back in the chair on subsequent occasions. He was not seen by the home doctor for some 10 days after he was admitted, and for 7 days after being placed in Wing 3. The doctor wrote the social security office to change payment of plaintiff's social security checks without plaintiff's authorization. Plaintiff made every effort to leave and repeatedly asked the manager and assistant manager to be permitted to leave. The home doctor is actually a resident studying pathology and has no patients other than those in two nursing homes. Finally, on November 11, 1968, plaintiff escaped and caught a ride into Dallas, where he called a taxi and was taken to the home of a friend. During plaintiff's ordeal he lost 30 pounds. There was never any court proceeding to confine plaintiff. * * *

False imprisonment is the direct restraint by of one person of the physical liberty of another without adequate legal justification. There is ample evidence to sustain [the jury's finding that plaintiff was falsely imprisoned]. * * *

Defendant placed plaintiff in Wing 3 with insane persons, alcoholics and drug addicts knowing he was not in such category; punished plaintiff by locking and taping him in the restraint chair; prevented him from using the telephone for 51 days; locked up his clothes;

told him he could not be released from Wing 3 until he began to obey the rules of the home; and detained him for 51 days during which period he was demanding to be released and attempting to escape.

* * *

Defendant may be compelled to respond in exemplary damages if the act causing actual damages is a wrongful act done intentionally in violation of the rights of plaintiff. [Cc]

Defendant acted in the utter disregard of plaintiff's legal rights, knowing there was no court order for commitment, and that the admission agreement provided he was not to be kept <u>against his will</u>.

* * *

However, from this record, we are of the opinion that the * * * judgment of the trial court is excessive. * * *

[Plaintiff subsequently agreed to a remittitur suggested by the court, and the judgment below, so reformed, was affirmed.]

---

1. Plaintiff has a ticket to enter defendant's race track. Defendant refuses to admit him. Is this false imprisonment? Marrone v. Washington Jockey Club, 35 U.S.App.D.C. 82 (1910). Suppose the exclusion is on the basis of race. See 42 U.S.C.A. § 2000a, treated infra page 77, at note 6.

2. In Cullen v. Dickenson, 33 S.D. 27, 144 N.W. 656 (1913), the defendant prevented plaintiff from entering a dance hall, under the mistaken belief that she was under eighteen years of age. It was held that under modern code procedure this was a tort for which plaintiff could recover damages, although not false imprisonment.

3. Can there be false imprisonment in a moving automobile? Cieplinski v. Severn, 269 Mass. 261, 168 N.E. 722 (1929). In an entire city? Allen v. Fromme, 141 App.Div. 362, 126 N.Y.S. 520 (1910). In the state of Rhode Island? Or Texas? When plaintiff is not permitted to leave the United States? There are no decisions.

4. If one exit of a room or a building is locked with plaintiff inside, but another reasonable means of exit is left open, there is no imprisonment. Davis & Allcott Co. v. Boozer, 215 Ala. 116, 110 So. 28 (1926); Furlong v. German-American Press Ass'n, 189 S.W. 385, 389 (Mo.1916) ("If a way of escape is left open which is available without peril of life or limb, no imprisonment"). See also the classic case of Bird v. Jones, 7 A. & E., N.S., 742, 115 Eng.Rep. 668 (1845).

5. The Restatement (Second) of Torts § 36, comment a, treats the means of escape as unreasonable if it involves exposure of the person as when the plaintiff is in the water and defendant steals his clothes, or material harm to the clothing, or danger of substantial harm to another. Plaintiff is obviously not required to make his escape by crawling through a sewer.

6. A means of escape is clearly not a reasonable one if the plaintiff does not know of its existence, and it is not apparent. Talcott v. National Exhibition Co., 144 App.Div. 337, 128 N.Y.S. 1059 (1911).

7. If the only means of escape could cause physical danger to plaintiff, and he could remain "imprisoned" without any risk of harm, he may not recover for

In other words, must he make / escapee? No

injuries he suffers in making his escape. See Sindle v. New York City Transit Authority, 33 N.Y.2d 293, 307 N.E.2d 245, 352 N.Y.S.2d 183 (1973).

8. Along with battery and assault, false imprisonment has now become exclusively an intentional tort. The Restatement (Second) of Torts § 35, Comment h, points out, however, that for negligence resulting in the confinement of another a negligence action will lie, but only if some actual damage results. Cf. Mouse v. Central Sav. & Trust Co., 120 Ohio St. 599, 7 Ohio L.Abs. 334, 167 N.E. 868 (1929). What would be the result if defendant double-parks his automobile and thus prevents plaintiff from driving to an important business meeting?

1st

(#) Must know of constraint while it is happening

(2)(4) = but for π to establish CoA; if doesn't, reluctantly in effect, 1st RQ is meaningless

PARVI v. CITY OF KINGSTON
Court of Appeals of New York, 1977.
41 N.Y.2d 553, 362 N.E.2d 960, 394 N.Y.S.2d 161.

[Plaintiff was in a drunken condition in downtown Kingston one night. He was picked up by the police and told them he had no place to go. Rather than arrest him, they drove him out of town and left him on a discontinued golf course to "sleep it off." There was conflicting testimony as to whether he went willingly or asked to be dropped off. On cross examination he admitted that he had no recollection of what had happened that night.

Trct = Δ/dismissed ¼ to trial
App Div = aff'd/Δ

Action for false imprisonment. The trial court dismissed the case and the Appellate Division affirmed.]

FUCHSBERG, JUSTICE. * * * [The element of] consciousness of confinement is a more subtle and more interesting subissue in this case. On that subject, we note that, while respected authorities have divided on whether awareness of confinement by one who has been falsely imprisoned should be a *sine qua non* for making out a case, [cc] *Broughton* [v. State of New York], 37 N.Y.2d p. 456, 373 N.Y.S.2d p. 92, 335 N.E.2d p. 313 has laid that question to rest in this State. Its holding gives recognition to the fact that false imprisonment, as a dignitary tort, is not suffered unless its victim knows of the dignitary invasion. Interestingly, the Restatement (Second) of Torts § 42 too has taken the position that there is no liability for intentionally confining another unless the person physically restrained knows of the confinement or is harmed by it. *you do not analyze harm unless issue of lack of knowledge arises, int'n all other clam are not*

Real Issue
sub (I)
present consciousness later recollection?

However, though correctly proceeding on that premise, the Appellate Division, in affirming the dismissal of the cause of action for false imprisonment, erroneously relied on the fact that Parvi, after having provided additional testimony in his own behalf on direct examination, had agreed on cross that he no longer had any recollection of his confinement. In so doing, that court failed to distinguish between a later recollection of consciousness and the existence of that consciousness at the time when the imprisonment itself took place. The latter, of course, is capable of being proved though one who suffers the consciousness can no longer personally describe it, whether by reason of lapse of memory, incompetency, death or other cause. Specifically, in this case, while it may well be that the alcohol Parvi had imbibed or

Sub (H) = awareness at time of constraint

the injuries he sustained, or both, had had the effect of wiping out his recollection of being in the police car against his will, that is a far cry from saying that he was not conscious of his confinement at the time when it was actually taking place. And, <u>even if plaintiff's sentient</u> *RTR* <u>state at the time of his imprisonment was something less than total sobriety, that does not mean that he had no conscious sense of what was then happening to him.</u> To the contrary, there is much in the *= record = in Δ's answer* record to support a finding that the plaintiff indeed was aware of his arrest at the time it took place. By way of illustration, <u>the officers described Parvi's responsiveness to their command that he get into the car, his colloquy while being driven to Coleman Hill and his request to be let off elsewhere.</u> At the very least, then, it was for the jury, in the (H) first instance, to weigh credibility, evaluate inconsistencies and determine whether the burden of proof had been met. * * *

          Reversed.

— would bar recovery =

BREITEL, Chief Judge (dissenting). * * * [P]laintiff has failed even to make out a prima facie case that he was conscious of his purported confinement, and that he failed to consent to it. His memory of the entire incident had disappeared; at trial, Parvi admitted that he no longer had any independent recollection of what happened on the day of his accident, and that as to the circumstances surrounding his entrance into the police car, he only knew what had been suggested to him by subsequent conversations. In light of this testimony, Parvi's conclusory statement that he was ordered into the car against his will is insufficient, as a matter of law, to establish a prima facie case. * * *

Breitel's point? procedural. Fuchsberg may be correct if Δ...'s evidence gets before jury; But Breitel says it is for (H) to get it there, not officers. (of course, in pleadings, the proper allegation, whether or not ... can prove, is ...)

1. The mother of a 16–year–old boy who is disoriented and ill instructed a police officer to take her son to a particular hospital. Is there false imprisonment if the officer takes the boy to the wrong hospital? What if the boy dies? See Haisenleder v. Reeder, 114 Mich.App. 258, 318 N.W.2d 634 (1982). Or what if the plaintiff, a sufferer from diabetes who is unconscious from insulin shock, is wrongfully arrested and confined in jail overnight in the belief that he is drunk, but is released before he regains consciousness. Is there a tort? See Prosser, False Imprisonment: Consciousness of Confinement, 55 Colum.L.Rev. 847 (1955); Restatement (Second) of Torts § 42.

Done at trial then officers testimony may prove this case

2. Called upon to make an emergency evaluation, a doctor diagnoses a person as mentally ill and has her detained in a mental institution. Is this false imprisonment? See Carter v. Landy, 163 Ga.App. 509, 295 S.E.2d 177 (1982). The doctor's exercise of reasonable care and use of proper medical procedures are relevant as to whether the detention was lawful.

HARDY v. LaBELLE'S DISTRIBUTING CO.
Supreme Court of Montana, 1983.
203 Mont. 263, 661 P.2d 35.

The fine art of preparing your witness.

GULBRANDSON, JUSTICE. * * * Defendant, LaBelle's Distributing Company (LaBelle's) hired Hardy as a temporary employee on December 1, 1978. She was assigned duty as a sales clerk in the jewelry department.

On December 9, 1978, another employee for LaBelle's, Jackie Renner, thought she saw Hardy steal one of the watches that LaBelle's had in stock. Jackie Renner reported her belief to LaBelle's showroom manager that evening.

On the morning of December 10, Hardy was approached by the assistant manager of LaBelle's jewelry department and told that all new employees were given a tour of the store. He showed her into the showroom manager's office and then left, closing the door behind him.

There is conflicting testimony concerning who was present in the showroom manager's office when Hardy arrived. Hardy testified that David Kotke, the showroom manager, Steve Newsom, the store's loss prevention manager, and a uniformed policeman were present. Newsom and one of the policemen in the room testified that another policeman, instead of Kotke, was present.

Hardy was told that she had been accused of stealing a watch. Hardy denied taking the watch and agreed to take a lie detector test. According to conflicting testimony, the meeting lasted approximately from twenty to forty-five minutes.

Hardy took the lie detector test, which supported her statement that she had not taken the watch. The showroom manager apologized to Hardy the next morning and told her that she was still welcome to work at LaBelle's. The employee who reported seeing Hardy take the watch also apologized. The two employees then argued briefly, and Hardy left the store.

Hardy brought this action claiming that defendants had wrongfully detained her against her will when she was questioned about the watch.

On appeal Hardy raises basically two issues: (1) Whether the evidence is sufficient to support the verdict and judgment and (2) Whether the District Court erred in the issuance of its instructions. The two key elements of false imprisonment are the restraint of an individual against his will and the unlawfulness of such restraint. [Cc] The individual may be restrained by acts or merely by words which he fears to disregard. [Cc]

Here, there is ample evidence to support the jury's finding that Hardy was not unlawfully restrained against her will. While Hardy stated that she felt compelled to remain in the showroom manager's office, she also admitted that she wanted to stay and clarify the situation. She did not ask to leave. She was not told she could not leave. No threat of force or otherwise was made to compel her to stay. Although she followed the assistant manager into the office under pretense of a tour, she testified at trial that she would have followed him voluntarily if she had known the true purpose of the meeting and that two policemen were in the room. Under these circumstances, the jury could easily find that Hardy was not detained against her will.

[Cc] See also, Meinecke v. Skaggs (1949), 123 Mont. 308, 213 P.2d 237, and Roberts v. Coleman (1961), 228 Or. 286, 365 P.2d 79. * * *

[The court also found that the District Court did not err in issuance of jury instructions on the law of false imprisonment, and affirmed the District Court's judgment in favor of defendants.]

---

1. An employee is suspected of stealing property from her employer and is told a trip to her home is necessary to recover the property. If the employee feels mentally compelled for fear of losing her job to go in an automobile with her supervisor to her home, has she been confined involuntarily? What if she agrees to go along, but during the automobile trip she asks to stop and call her husband and is denied permission to do so? See Faniel v. Chesapeake & Potomac Tel. Co., 404 A.2d 147 (D.C.App.1979).

2. Retention of plaintiff's property may provide the "restraint" necessary to constitute false imprisonment. See Fischer v. Famous Barr Co., 646 S.W.2d 819 (Mo.App.1982), where plaintiff set off the security alarm when exiting a store because the salesperson forgot to remove the sensor tag from an article of clothing she had purchased. Because an employee of the store took possession of the bag containing her purchases, plaintiff felt she had to follow the employee back to the fourth floor where she made her purchase. Compare Marcano v. Northwestern Chrysler–Plymouth Sales, Inc., 550 F.Supp. 595 (N.D. Ill.1982), where plaintiff went to a car dealership to discuss a dispute over payments on her loan and voluntarily gave her keys to the dealer so he could inspect the car. The dealer locked the car and kept the keys. Plaintiff stayed at the dealership for five hours because she had no other way to get home. The court held that there was no false imprisonment because she could have left and because the defendant did not intend to confine her personally, but only to keep her car.

3. False imprisonment has not been extended beyond such direct duress to person or to property. If the plaintiff submits merely to persuasion, and accompanies the defendant to clear himself of suspicion, without any implied threat of force, the action does not lie. Hunter v. Laurent, 158 La. 874, 104 So. 747 (1925); James v. MacDougall & Southwick Co., 134 Wash. 314, 235 P. 812 (1925). Suppose the defendant says to the plaintiff, "You must remain in this room, or I will never speak to you again"? Compare Fitscher v. Rollman & Sons Co., 31 Ohio App. 340, 167 N.E. 469 (1929), where defendant threatened to make a scene on the street unless plaintiff remained.

4. It is generally agreed that false imprisonment resembles assault, in that threats of future action are not enough. Thus the action does not lie where the defendant merely threatens to call the police and have the plaintiff arrested unless he remains. Sweeney v. F.W. Woolworth Co., 247 Mass. 277, 142 N.E. 50 (1924); Priddy v. Bunton, 177 S.W.2d 805 (Tex.Civ.App.1943).

5. On the shopkeeper's privilege to detain a suspected thief, which might have been involved in the last case, see Bonkowski v. Arlan's Department Store, infra page 119.

[handwritten margin: narrow issue.]

[handwritten margin top: Threat of losing unsecured, unterenured, job is not enough force for F.I.]

[handwritten margin right: △   π   Moral pressure is not enough.]

COLUMBIA SUSSEX CORP., INC. v. HAY

Court of Appeals of Kentucky, 1981.
627 S.W.2d 270.

[handwritten margin left: Tr Ct = π / Ct App = rev'd /s (retained in failing to D.V.) / Whose facts should be adhered to? π / Did Ct? Not really]

WHITE, J. This appeal is taken from slander and false imprisonment awards rendered by a jury in the Boone Circuit Court.

On February 26, 1979, the Best Western Hotel of Richwood, Kentucky, was robbed. At that time appellee, Mrs. Hay, was manager of the hotel, which was owned and operated by appellant, Columbia Sussex Corporation. Appellant William J. Yung was president and appellant David Diehl was General Manager of Columbia Sussex.

During the holdup the robber revealed knowledge of a special warning alarm attached to the cash register. If certain bills were lifted therefrom the alarm was activated. Mr. Yung felt that such knowledge revealed that the robber had inside information. Consequently, he called Mrs. Hay into his office to inform her that lie detector tests would be given to her employees and her.

Evidently upset over being asked to participate in the testing, Mrs. Hay inquired whether Mr. Yung was insinuating that one of them had done it. To this he responded, "that is just exactly what I am saying, *[handwritten: —goes to slander]* you will be surprised to find out which one did it." Further testimony implies that there were others present (Mr. Beagle, a Columbia Sussex vice-president, and/or some of the employees); however, none were called to establish that such words had, indeed, been heard and understood.

Subsequently, Mr. Diehl told Mrs. Hay to gather her workers for the polygraph. He is then [supposed] to have said that Mr. Yung definitely felt that one of them (Mrs. Hay or her subordinates) was *[handwritten: —goes to slander]* involved in the crime and that he tended to agree with him. Mrs. Hay testified by name that several others were present when this was said; however, none was called to corroborate this assertion.

[handwritten margin: →] Regarding the false imprisonment issue, testimony establishes that Mrs. Hay inquired of Mr. Diehl what would happen if they did not take the test. His answer was that they could leave, indicating that their jobs would be lost. Ultimately, each employee who was called took the polygraph examination. At the time that the tests were administered, each, including Mrs. Hay, signed a paper, which acknowledged that the subject was taking the test under neither coercion nor duress. Mrs. Hay's testimony is that she did, indeed, submit under duress inasmuch as her job rested on such and that she informed the polygraph operator that her only lie was that she was taking it without coercion. The operator was not called.

Although the results of the tests were never formally given to the employees, testimony revealed that they established no connection between a worker and the robbery. No arrest had been made prior to trial. * * *

Turning now to that aspect of the action dealing with false impris- onment, appellants urge that the trial court erred in failing to direct a verdict on this issue. We agree. (H)

The key element of false imprisonment is that one is involuntarily restrained. Mrs. Hay testified that she had signed, and there was introduced into evidence the copy of, a statement which asserted that she was not taking the test under either coercion or duress. At trial Mrs. Hay recanted, alleging that she, indeed, had been coerced under threat of losing her job. She further testified that she had informed the polygraph operator of this at the time the test was conducted.

Prosser speaks to involuntary submission based upon threats of force. He continues by emphasizing that:

> "It is essential * * * that the restraint be against the plain- tiff's will; and if he agrees of his own free choice to surrender his freedom of motion, as by remaining in a room * * * to clear himself of suspicion * * * rather than yielding to the constraint of a threat, then there is no imprisonment.

> * * * Moral pressure, as where the plaintiff remains with the defendant to clear himself of suspicion of theft * * * is not enough." Prosser at pp. 44–45.

Herein, Mrs. Hay did not submit an order to cleanse her reputation but rather to retain her job. A job is not a vested property right or interest absent additional considerations such as tenure, contract, etc., none of which was present here. [Cc] Her situation at Best Western was terminable at will and as such was a mere benefit.

What threat against person or property, therefore, was leveled to restrict her freedom of movement? If restraint resulting from the protection of one's reputation against suspicion of criminal activity is deemed merely to have emanated from an exhibition of moral pressure rather than from a threat against person or property, certainly the restraint evidenced by one's interest in retaining an untenured position must also fall short of the standard necessary to prove false imprison- ment.

Furthermore, on the question of voluntariness, other than Mrs. Hay's denials in pleadings and upon the stand, there was nothing to establish that the submission was anything other than voluntary. From the record the only indication of displeasure was her inquiry as to what would happen if they did not submit. The response, as noted, was that their jobs would be lost. Appellee then signed the release.

The release itself is in two parts. The first is the voluntary consent to the polygraph examination. It reveals that without duress or coercion and having been advised of her legal rights Mrs. Hay, in signing, agreed to the testing. The second part, signed at the conclu- sion of the testing, indicates that although knowledgeable of being able to leave at any time during the examination, appellee chose to remain of her own free will.

Mrs. Hay offered no more than herself as witness to indicate her state of mind at that time. The polygraph operator was not called to confirm her story. The results of the polygraph were not introduced to show that a lie had been told in the matter of voluntary consent. None of the motel employees testified that Mrs. Hay had revealed feelings of coercion or duress. (One worker acknowledged that she, under identical circumstances, had voluntarily taken the examination).

If a release and consent form is to have any validity at all upon which those associated with the giving of polygraph examinations may rely, clearly it is not to be subject to defeat by unsubstantiated later assertions that although the document was signed, the examinee had not in truth intended at that time to subscribe to its contents.

To prosecute successfully a claim for false imprisonment, there must have been established: (1) Defendant's act by force or threats of force against person or property (2) Which with intent caused plaintiff to be confined to an area certain.

In this instance the burden was upon Mrs. Hay not only to establish the requisites of the cause but also in doing so to overcome the presumptive effect of voluntariness which the release form carried. Appellee clearly failed to establish her prima facie case; thus, the lower court was in error in denying appellants' motion for a directed verdict upon this issue. * * *

[The court rejected appellants' additional argument that the acts complained of, slander and false imprisonment, were compensable only under the state's workers' compensation act because they arose within the employment relationship.]

The judgment of the Boone Circuit Court is reversed and remanded with instructions to retry the issue of slander in accordance with the law cited herein and to enter a final judgment in the issue of false imprisonment in favor of appellants Columbia Sussex, Yung and Diehl.

ENRIGHT v. GROVES

Colorado Court of Appeals, 1977.
39 Colo.App. 39, 560 P.2d 851.

SMITH, JUDGE. Defendants Groves and City of Ft. Collins appeal from judgments entered against them upon jury verdicts awarding plaintiff $500 actual damages and $1,000 exemplary damages on her claim of false imprisonment.

The evidence at trial disclosed that on August 25, 1974, Officer Groves, while on duty as a uniformed police officer of the City of Fort Collins, observed a dog running loose in violation of the city's "dog leash" ordinance. He observed the animal approaching what was later identified as the residence of Mrs. Enright, the plaintiff. As Groves approached the house, he encountered Mrs. Enright's eleven-year-old son, and asked him if the dog belonged to him. The boy replied that it was his dog, and told Groves that his mother was sitting in the car

parked at the curb by the house. Groves then ordered the boy to put
the dog inside the house, and turned and started walking toward the
Enright vehicle.

Groves testified that he was met by Mrs. Enright with whom he
was not acquainted. She asked if she could help him. Groves responded by demanding her driver's license. She replied by giving him her
name and address. He again demanded her driver's license, which she
declined to produce. Groves thereupon advised her that she could *radical !*
either produce her driver's license or go to jail. Mrs. Enright responded by asking, "Isn't this ridiculous?" Groves thereupon grabbed one of
her arms, stating, "Let's go!" * * *

She was taken to the police station where a complaint was signed
charging her with violation of the "dog leash" ordinance and bail was
set. Mrs. Enright was released only after a friend posted bail. She was
later convicted of the ordinance violation. * * *

Appellants contend that Groves had probable cause to arrest Mrs.
Enright, and that she was in fact arrested for and convicted of violation
of the dog-at-large ordinance. They assert, therefore, that her claim for
false imprisonment or false arrest cannot lie, and that Groves' use of
force in arresting Mrs. Enright was permissible. We disagree. *H*

False arrest arises when one is taken into custody by a person who *False Arrest*
claims but does not have proper legal authority. W. Prosser, Torts § 11
(4th ed.). Accordingly, a claim for false arrest will not lie if an officer
has a valid warrant or probable cause to believe that an offense has
been committed and that the person who was arrested committed it.
Conviction of the crime for which one is specifically arrested is a
complete defense to a subsequent claim of false arrest. [Cc]

Here, however, the evidence is clear that Groves arrested Mrs. *Tr. ct = finding*
Enright, not for violation of the dog leash ordinance, but rather for *RTL*
refusing to produce her driver's license. This basis for the arrest is
exemplified by the fact that he specifically advised her that she would
either produce the license or go to jail. We find no statute or case law *RTL*
in this jurisdiction which requires a citizen to show her driver's license
upon demand, unless, for example, she is a driver of an automobile and
such demand is made in that connection. * * *

Here, there was no testimony that Groves ever even attempted to
explain why he was demanding plaintiff's driver's license, and it is
clear that she had already volunteered her name and address. Groves
admitted that he did not ask Mrs. Enright if she had any means of
identification on her person, instead he simply demanded that she give
him her driver's license.

We conclude that Groves' demand for Mrs. Enright's driver's license was not a lawful order and that refusal to comply therewith was
not therefore an offense in and of itself. Groves was not therefore
entitled to use force in arresting Mrs. Enright. Thus Groves' defense

Why is this significant

*Suppose that after verifying that the woman was indeed
Mrs. Enright, that he then planned to arrest her? If this were
his rationale, should he not have arrested when she gave name, w/ or w/o
license? yes*

based upon an arrest for and conviction of a specific offense must, as a matter of law, fail.   *   *   *

Judgment affirmed.

[Handwritten: Could officer have lawfully arrested ∏ after she identified herself w/ probable cause of crime (dog leash violation)? Should he validate by asking for ID to eliminate mistakes? Is there better ID th. Driver's license]

1. Is it necessary that the defendant be an officer? Suppose a filling station attendant asserts legal authority to detain the plaintiff, and plaintiff submits? Daniel v. Phillips Petroleum Co., 229 Mo.App. 150, 73 S.W.2d 355 (1934). Plaintiff, attempting to leave defendant's train, fell and broke his leg. A cab was called to take him to the hospital. Defendant's conductor told plaintiff that the law required him to remain and fill out a statement about the accident. Plaintiff did so, and the cab was held for fifteen or twenty minutes, during which plaintiff was in considerable pain, while the statement was filled out and signed. This was held to be false imprisonment. Whitman v. Atchison, T. & S.F.R. Co., 85 Kan. 150, 116 P. 234 (1911).

2. A private citizen who aids a policeman in making a false arrest can be held liable to plaintiff for false imprisonment. See Annot., 98 A.L.R.3d 542 (1980).

3. Regardless of the unreasonableness of the arrest, no action for false imprisonment will lie if the plaintiff actually committed the crime. See Taco Bell, Inc. v. Saleme, 701 S.W.2d 78 (Tex.App.1985). *[Handwritten: 3 is correct]*

WHITTAKER v. SANDFORD

Supreme Judicial Court of Maine, 1912.
110 Me. 77, 85 A. 399.

[Handwritten margin: (H) Need not be bodily constrained, but confined to area]

[Handwritten margin: (A) Failure to release constitutes "restraint"]

[Plaintiff was a member of a religious sect, of which defendant was the leader. The sect had a colony in Maine and at Jaffa, in Syria, the latter of which plaintiff had joined. Plaintiff decided to abandon the movement and to return to America. Defendant asked her to come back to America on his yacht rather than by steamer; and when plaintiff suggested that she might not be let off of the yacht until she was "won to the movement again," defendant assured her repeatedly that under no circumstances would she be detained on board. Plaintiff accepted the assurance and sailed for America on the yacht. On arrival in port defendant refused to furnish her with a boat so that she could leave the yacht. She remained on board for nearly a month and finally obtained her release by a writ of habeas corpus. She brought an action for false imprisonment. The jury returned a verdict in her favor for $1100. Defendant excepted to the court's instructions, and appeals from an order denying his motion for a new trial.]

[Handwritten margin: presumably filed by family]

[Handwritten margin: Trct = π (verdict)]

SAVAGE, J.   *   *   * The court instructed the jury that the plaintiff to recover must show that the restraint was physical, and not merely a moral influence; that it must have been actual physical restraint, in the sense that one intentionally locked into a room would be physically restrained but not necessarily involving physical force upon the person; that it was not necessary that the defendant, or any person by his direction, should lay his hand upon the plaintiff; that if the plaintiff was restrained so that she could not leave the yacht Kingdom by the

[Handwritten margin: Rule]

intentional refusal to furnish transportation as agreed, she not having it in her power to escape otherwise, it would be a physical restraint and unlawful imprisonment. We think the instructions were apt and sufficient. If one should, without right, turn the key in a door, and thereby prevent a person in the room from leaving, it would be the simplest form of unlawful imprisonment. The restraint is physical. The four walls and the locked door are physical impediments to escape. Now is it different when one who is in control of a vessel at anchor, within practical rowing distance from the shore, who has agreed that a guest on board shall be free to leave, there being no means to leave except by rowboats, wrongfully refuses the guest the use of a boat? The boat is the key. By refusing the boat he turns the key. The guest is as effectually locked up as if there were walls along the sides of the vessel. The restraint is physical. The impassable sea is the physical barrier. * * *

A careful study of the evidence leads us to conclude that the jury were warranted in finding that the defendant was guilty of unlawful imprisonment. This, to be sure, is not an action based upon the defendant's failure to keep his agreement to permit the plaintiff to leave the yacht as soon as it should reach shore. But his duty under the circumstances is an important consideration. It cannot be believed that either party to the agreement understood that it was his duty merely to bring her to an American harbor. The agreement implied that she was to go ashore. There was no practical way for her to go ashore except in the yacht's boats. The agreement must be understood to mean that he would bring her to land, or to allow her to get to land, by the only available means. The evidence is that he refused her a boat. His refusal was wrongful. The case leaves not the slightest doubt that he had the power to control the boats, if he chose to exercise it. It was not enough for him to leave it to the husband to say whether she might go ashore or not. She had a personal right to go on shore. If the defendant personally denied her the privilege, as the jury might find he did, it was a wrongful denial.

---

1. A woman tells her boyfriend she does not want to date him anymore, but agrees to ride with him to the store and back. When they return to her parents' house and she opens the car door, the boyfriend suddenly starts the car off, making it dangerous for her to exit the moving vehicle. False imprisonment? See Noguchi v. Nakamura, 2 Hawaii App. 655, 638 P.2d 1383 (1982).

2. In Talcott v. National Exhibition Co., 144 App.Div. 337, 128 N.Y.S. 1059 (1911), plaintiff was one of a crowd seeking admission to the baseball game between the Chicago Cubs and the New York Giants that played off the tie for the 1908 National League pennant. This game had been caused by a one-to-one tie in an earlier game between the same teams, produced when Fred Merkle of the Giants pulled his famous "bonehead play" in failing to touch second base. For two fascinating accounts of that game told by other players in it, see L. Ritter, The Glory of Their Times 98–100 and 124–218 (1966); the book has a picture of the after-game crowd in the Polo Grounds at p. 126. The Giants, who

would have won the pennant except for the Merkle error, lost the playoff game. Plaintiff succeeded in entering an enclosure where tickets were sold, but found that he could not get in. Defendant closed the entrance gates behind him to prevent injuries from the crush. There was another exit, of which defendant failed to inform plaintiff, and he remained within the enclosure for more than an hour. In his action for false imprisonment, a verdict and judgment in his favor were affirmed. It was held that while the defendant might have been justified in closing the gates, it was then under a duty to inform plaintiff of the other exit.

3. Members of a religious cult are abducted by their relatives and subjected to deprogramming. Is this false imprisonment? Eilers v. Coy, 582 F.Supp. 1093 (D.Minn.1984).

4. False imprisonment may occur without being readily apparent on the surface. Thus, in Griffin v. Clark, 55 Idaho 364, 42 P.2d 297 (1935), plaintiff had intended to go home by train. Defendant intercepted her voyage at an intermediate stop, entered the train, seized her handbag and took it to an automobile. Plaintiff followed, demanding her bag. While she did so the train left the station. Plaintiff then went along with defendant and her handbag in defendant's automobile and an accident ensued. The court found sufficient evidence of false imprisonment. While the court also found evidence of defendant's negligent driving, he may have been held liable to plaintiff although no negligence was proved. Why? Cf. Note 2, page 43.

5. See Restatement (Second) of Torts § 45; Note, 7 S.Cal.L.Rev. 102 (1934).

5. INTENTIONAL INFLICTION OF MENTAL DISTRESS

STATE RUBBISH COLLECTORS ASS'N v. SILIZNOFF

Supreme Court of California, 1952.
38 Cal.2d 330, 240 P.2d 282.

[The State Rubbish Collectors Association sued Siliznoff to collect on certain notes. Siliznoff counterclaimed, asking that the notes be cancelled because of duress and want of consideration. In addition he sought general and punitive damages because of alleged "assaults" made on him. The evidence was that Siliznoff had collected an account from the Acme Brewing Company which the Association regarded as within the territory of another member of the Association named Abramoff. The defendant was called before the Association and ordered to pay over the collected money to Abramoff, as a result of which he signed the notes in question. Further facts appear in the opinion.

The jury returned a verdict for Siliznoff on the original complaint, and also for Siliznoff on the counterclaim. Siliznoff obtained a judgment against the Association for $1,250 general and special damages and $4,000 punitive damages. The Association appealed the judgment.]

TRAYNOR, J. * * * Plaintiff's primary contention is that the evidence is insufficient to support the judgment. Defendant testified that: * * *

Andikian [an inspector of the Association] told defendant that " 'We will give you up till tonight to get down to the board meeting and make some kind of arrangements or agreements about the Acme Brewery, or otherwise we are going to beat you up.' * * * He says he either would hire somebody or do it himself. And I says, 'Well, what would they do to me?' He says, well, they would physically beat me up first, cut up the truck tires or burn the truck, or otherwise put me out of business completely. He said if I didn't appear at that meeting and make some kind of an agreement that they would do that, but he says up to then they would let me alone, but if I walked out of that meeting that night they would beat me up for sure." Defendant attended the meeting and protested that he owed nothing for the Acme account and in any event could not pay the amount demanded. He was again told by the president of the association that "that table right there [the board of directors] ran all the rubbish collecting in Los Angeles and if there was any routes to be gotten that they would get them and distribute them among their members * * *." After two hours of further discussion defendant agreed to join the association and pay for the Acme account. He promised to return the next day and sign the necessary papers. He testified that the only reason "they let me go home, is that I promised that I would sign the notes the very next morning." The president "made me promise on my honor and every- thing else, and I was scared, and I knew I had to come back, so I believe he knew I was scared and that I would come back. That's the only reason they let me go home." Defendant also testified that because of the fright he suffered during his dispute with the association he became ill and vomited several times and had to remain away from work for a period of several days.

Plaintiff contends that the evidence does not establish an assault against defendant because the threats made all related to action that might take place in the future; that neither Andikian nor members of the board of directors threatened immediate physical harm to defen- dant. [C] We have concluded, however, that a cause of action is established when it is shown that one, in the absence of any privilege, intentionally subjects another to the mental suffering incident to seri- ous threats to his physical well-being, whether or not the threats are made under such circumstances as to constitute a technical assault.

In the past it has been frequently stated that the interest in emotional and mental tranquillity is not one that the law will protect from invasion in its own right. [Cc] As late as 1934 the Restatement of Torts took the position that "The interest in mental and emotional tranquillity and, therefore, in freedom from mental and emotional disturbance is not, as a thing in itself, regarded as of sufficient impor- tance to require others to refrain from conduct intended or recognizably likely to cause such a disturbance." Restatement, Torts, § 46, com- ment c. The Restatement explained the rule allowing recovery for the mere apprehension of bodily harm in traditional assault cases as an historical anomaly (§ 24, comment c), and the rule allowing recovery for insulting conduct by an employee of a common carrier as justified by the necessity of securing for the public comfortable as well as safe service (§ 48, comment c).

The Restatement recognized, however, that in many cases mental distress could be so intense that it could reasonably be foreseen that illness or other bodily harm might result. If the defendant intentionally subjected the plaintiff to such distress and bodily harm resulted, the defendant would be liable for negligently causing the plaintiff bodily harm. Restatement, Torts, §§ 306, 312. Under this theory the cause of action was not founded on a right to be free from intentional interference with mental tranquillity, but on the right to be free from negligent interference with physical well-being. A defendant who intentionally subjected another to mental distress without intending to cause bodily harm would nevertheless be liable for resulting bodily harm if he should have foreseen that the mental distress might cause such harm.

The California cases have been in accord with the Restatement in allowing recovery where physical injury resulted from intentionally subjecting the plaintiff to serious mental distress. [Cc]

The view has been forcefully advocated that the law should protect emotional and mental tranquillity as such against serious and intentional invasions, [cc] and there is a growing body of case law supporting this position. [Cc] In recognition of this development the American Law Institute amended section 46 of the Restatement of Torts in 1947 to provide:

"One who, without a privilege to do so, intentionally causes severe emotional distress to another is liable (a) for such emotional distress, and (b) for bodily harm resulting from it."

In explanation it is stated that "The interest in freedom from severe emotional distress is regarded as of sufficient importance to require others to refrain from conduct intended to invade it. Such conduct is tortious. The injury suffered by the one whose interest is invaded is frequently far more serious to him than certain tortious invasions of the interest in bodily integrity and other legally protected interests. In the absence of a privilege, the actor's conduct has no social utility; indeed it is anti-social. No reason or policy requires such an actor to be protected from the liability which usually attaches to the wilful wrongdoer whose efforts are successful." (Restatement of the Law, 1948 Supplement, Torts, § 46, comment d.)

There are persuasive arguments and analogies that support the recognition of a right to be free from serious, intentional and unprivileged invasions of mental and emotional tranquillity. If a cause of action is otherwise established, it is settled that damages may be given for mental suffering naturally ensuing from the acts complained of [cc], and in the case of many torts, such as assault, battery, false imprisonment and defamation, mental suffering will frequently constitute the principal element of damages. [C] In cases where mental suffering constitutes a major element of damages it is anomalous to deny recovery because the defendant's intentional misconduct fell short of producing some physical injury.

It may be contended that to allow recovery in the absence of physical injury will open the door to unfounded claims and a flood of litigation, and that the requirement that there be physical injury is necessary to insure that serious mental suffering actually occurred. The jury is ordinarily in a better position, however, to determine whether outrageous conduct results in mental distress than whether that distress in turn results in physical injury. From their own experience jurors are aware of the extent and character of the disagreeable emotions that may result from the defendant's conduct, but a difficult medical question is presented when it must be determined if emotional distress resulted in physical injury. [C] Greater proof that mental suffering occurred is found in the defendant's conduct designed to bring it about than in physical injury that may or may not have resulted therefrom. * * *

In the present case plaintiff caused defendant to suffer extreme fright. By intentionally producing such fright it endeavored to compel him either to give up the Acme account or pay for it, and it had no right or privilege to adopt such coercive methods in competing for business. In these circumstances liability is clear. * * *

The judgment is affirmed.

1. Why not assault? Why not false imprisonment? Assuming neither tort occurred, how many attorneys in 1952 would have thought of bringing a cross-complaint in this case for "intentional infliction of emotional harm"? How many judges would have adopted it?

2. But what form of tort has been unleashed? Is it as definite in character as those that arose out of the writ of trespass? What result in the main case if the Association had only threatened to close down Siliznoff's business, but had not made threats to his physical well-being? Do you agree that the jury can more easily determine whether conduct is outrageous than whether physical injury resulted from emotional harm? If so, does this fact suggest that a claim should be allowed?

3. The seminal case to allow recovery for the intentional infliction of mental distress as a distinct tort was Wilkinson v. Downton, [1897] 2 Q.B. 57, in which a practical joker amused himself by telling the plaintiff that her husband had been smashed up in an accident, and was lying at The Elms in Leytonstone with both legs broken; and that she was to go to him at once in a cab with two pillows to fetch him home. The shock to her nervous system caused serious physical illness with permanent consequences, and at one time threatened her reason. Why the defendant was held liable is unclear to the reader of the opinion and apparently to the court as well.

4. Some states recognize the tort, but restrict its application to situations in which plaintiff has suffered "physical consequences." See Duty v. General Fin. Co., 154 Tex. 16, 273 S.W.2d 64 (1954); Clark v. Associated Retail Credit Men, 105 F.2d 62 (D.C.Cir.1939).

5. On the other hand, there are now numerous decisions in which, upon the basis of extreme outrage, the recovery has been allowed. Recovery for mental distress without physical injury is allowed only if the defendant's conduct exceeds the "limits of social toleration." Consider the following: Wilson v. Wilkins, 181 Ark. 137, 25 S.W.2d 428 (1930) (mob threat to harm plaintiff if he were not out of town by nightfall); Savage v. Boies, 77 Ariz. 355, 272 P.2d 349 (1954) (police decoyed plaintiff into confinement by telling her that her husband and child were injured and in the hospital); Christofferson v. Church of Scientology, 57 Or.App. 203, 644 P.2d 577 (1982), cert. denied, 459 U.S. 1206 (1983) and cert. denied, 459 U.S. 1227 (1983) (plaintiff sued a religious organization for scheming to gain control of her mind and to force her into a life of service to the organization and for a course of retaliatory conduct after she disassociated herself from the organization); Young v. Stensrude, 664 S.W.2d 263 (Mo.App.1984) (woman attended business meeting in defendant's office, where male employee of defendant showed a pornographic movie in a room with four other men while making obscene remarks to the woman); Nelson v. Ford Motor Credit Co., 621 S.W.2d 573 (Tenn.App.1981) (credit company mistakenly sent debt-collection notices and letters to plaintiffs, threatening to repossess plaintiffs' automobiles).

6. The Racketeer Influenced and Corrupt Organization Act ("RICO"), 18 U.S.C.A. § 164, provides certain plaintiffs with additional civil remedies when defendants are found to be involved in a "pattern of racketeering activity." Vietnamese Fishermen's Ass'n v. Knights of the K.K.K., 518 F.Supp. 993 (S.D. Tex.1981).

7. As the principal case indicates, § 46 of the Restatement of Torts was changed in the 1948 Supplement to recognize the cause of action for the intentional infliction of severe emotional distress, and to allow recovery "(a) for such emotional distress, and (b) for bodily harm resulting from it." This has been retained by the Restatement (Second) of Torts, § 46, where it is said that liability exists when the defendant's conduct is "extreme and outrageous," and a caveat leaves open the possibility of further expansion.

8. Is it necessary that the defendant intended to cause the mental disturbance, or that it be substantially certain to follow, within the rule stated in Garratt v. Dailey, supra page 18? What if there is merely a high degree of probability, and the defendant acts in conscious disregard of it, so that his conduct is "wilful," "wanton," or "reckless"? See Restatement (Second) of Torts § 46.

SLOCUM v. FOOD FAIR STORES OF FLORIDA

Supreme Court of Florida, 1958.
100 So.2d 396.

DREW, JUSTICE. This appeal is from an order dismissing a complaint for failure to state a cause of action. Simply stated, the plaintiff sought money damages for mental suffering or emotional distress, and an ensuing heart attack and aggravation of pre-existing heart disease, allegedly caused by insulting language of the defendant's employee directed toward her while she was a customer in its store. Specifically, in reply to her inquiry as to the price of an item he was marking, he replied: "If you want to know the price, you'll have to find out the best way you can * * * you stink to me." She asserts, in the alternative, that the language was used in a malicious or grossly reckless manner, "or with intent to inflict great mental and emotional disturbance to said plaintiff."

No great difficulty is involved in the preliminary point raised as to the sufficiency of damages alleged, the only direct injury being mental or emotional with physical symptoms merely derivative therefrom. [C] While that decision would apparently allow recovery for mental suffering, even absent physical consequences, inflicted in the course of other intentional or malicious torts, it does not resolve the central problem in this case, i.e. whether the conduct here claimed to have caused the injury, the use of insulting language under the circumstances described, constituted an actionable invasion of a legally protected right. Query: does such an assertion of a deliberate disturbance of emotional equanimity state an independent cause of action in tort?

Appellant's fundamental argument is addressed to that proposition. The case is one of first impression in this jurisdiction, and she contends that this Court should recognize the existence of a new tort, an independent cause of action for intentional infliction of emotional distress.

A study of the numerous references on the subject indicates a strong current of opinion in support of such recognition, in lieu of the strained reasoning so often apparent when liability for such injury is predicated upon one or another of several traditional tort theories.

* · * · *

A most cogent statement of the doctrine covering tort liability for insult has been incorporated in the Restatement of the Law of Torts, 1948 supplement, sec. 46, entitled "Conduct intended to cause emotional distress only." It makes a blanket provision for liability on the part of "one, who, without a privilege to do so, intentionally causes severe emotional distress to another," indicating that the requisite intention exists "when the act is done for the purpose of causing the distress or with knowledge * * * that severe emotional distress is substantially certain to be produced by [such] conduct." Comment (a), Sec. 46, supra. Abusive language is, of course, only one of the many means by which the tort could be committed.

However, even if we assume, without deciding, the legal propriety of that doctrine, a study of its factual applications shows that a line of demarcation should be drawn between conduct likely to cause mere "emotional distress" and that causing "severe emotional distress," so as to exclude the situation at bar. [C] "So far as it is possible to generalize from the cases, the rule which seems to be emerging is that there is liability only for conduct exceeding all bounds which could be tolerated by society, of a nature especially calculated to cause mental damage of a very serious kind." [C] And the most practicable view is that the functions of court and jury are no different than in other tort actions where there is at the outset a question as to whether the conduct alleged is so legally innocuous as to present no issue for a jury. [C]

This tendency to hinge the cause of action upon the degree of the insult has led some courts to reject the doctrine in toto. [C] Whether or not this is desirable, it is uniformly agreed that the determination of whether words or conduct are actionable in character is to be made on an objective rather than subjective standard, from common acceptation. The unwarranted intrusion must be calculated to cause "severe emotional distress" to a person of ordinary sensibilities in the absence of special knowledge or notice. There is no inclination to include all instances of mere vulgarities, obviously intended as meaningless abusive expressions. While the manner in which language is used may no doubt determine its actionable character, appellant's assertion that the statement involved in this case was made to her with gross recklessness, etc., cannot take the place of allegations showing that the words were intended to have real meaning or serious effect.

A broader rule has been developed in a particular class of cases, usually treated as a distinct and separate area of liability originally applied to common carriers. Rest.Torts, per. ed., sec. 48. The courts have from an early date granted relief for offense reasonably suffered by a patron from insult by a servant or employee of a carrier, hotel, theater, and most recently, a telegraph office. The existence of a special relationship, arising either from contract or from the inherent nature of a non-competitive public utility, supports a right and correlative duty of courtesy beyond that legally required in general mercantile or personal relationships. [Cc]

In view of the concurrent development of the cause of action first above described, there is no impelling reason to extend the rule of the latter cases. Their rationale does not of necessity cover the area of business invitees generally, where the theory of respondeat superior underlying most liabilities of the employer would dictate some degree of conformity to standards of individual liability. This factor, together with the stringent standards of care imposed in a number of the carrier cases [c], may have influenced the treatment of the subject by editors of the Restatement, where the statement of the carrier doctrine is quite limited in scope and classified separately from the section covering the more general area of liability under consideration. But whether or not these rules are ultimately adopted in this jurisdiction, the facts of the present case cannot be brought within their reasonable intendment.

Affirmed.

1. Why is the intentional infliction of mental disturbance by the insult not a tort in itself?

2. "Against a large part of the frictions and irritations and clashing of temperaments incident to participation in community life, a certain toughening of the mental hide is a better protection than the law could ever be. * * * Of course there is danger of getting into the realm of the trivial in this matter of

insulting language. No pressing social need requires that every abusive outburst be converted into a tort; upon the contrary, it would be unfortunate if the law closed all the safety valves through which irascible tempers might legally blow off steam." Magruder, Mental and Emotional Disturbance in the Law of Torts, 49 Harv.L.Rev. 1033, 1035, 1053 (1936).

3. A South Carolina gentleman, incensed at his inability to get a telephone number, so far forgets his chivalry as to call the operator a God damned woman, and to say that if he were there he would break her God damned neck. The unprecedented experience, according to her allegations, causes her extreme mental disturbance, and leaves her a nervous wreck. Does this state a cause of action? Brooker v. Silverthorne, 111 S.C. 553, 99 S.E. 350 (1919).

4. Compare Halliday v. Cienkowski, 333 Pa. 123, 3 A.2d 372 (1939) ("Scotch bitch," "bastard," and "bum"); Atkinson v. Bibb Mfg. Co., 50 Ga.App. 434, 178 S.E. 537 (1935) (foreman cursing discharged woman, with open knife in his hand); Kramer v. Ricksmeier, 159 Iowa 48, 139 N.W. 1091 (1913) (profanity and abuse over the telephone, with threats of future violence); Barry v. Baugh, 111 Ga.App. 813, 143 S.E.2d 489 (1965) ("crazy").

5. Insult statutes in Mississippi, Virginia and West Virginia, which had their origin as part of anti-dueling codes, provide an action for "all words which, from their usual construction and acceptation are considered as insults, and lead to violence and breach of the peace." They are treated in Wade, Tort Liability for Abusive and Insulting Language, 4 Vand.L.Rev. 63 (1950), which discusses liability in general.

The constitutionality of these statutes may be in question today as possibly being in conflict with the free-speech provisions of the First Amendment. In criminal cases, they are deemed valid only when the words used are likely to incite an immediate breach of the peace. See Gooding v. Wilson, 405 U.S. 518, 523 (1972). Virginia has merged its insult statute into the state's law of libel with the result that truth is an absolute defense and defendant's comments may be privileged. See Old Dominion Branch v. Austin, 213 Va. 377, 192 S.E.2d 737 (1972), rev'd on other grounds, 418 U.S. 264 (1974).

6. Common carriers and innkeepers have been held to a higher standard of conduct and may be liable for using insulting language to their passengers and patrons. See, e.g., Lipman v. Atlantic Coast Line R.R. Co., 108 S.C. 151, 93 S.E. 714 (1917) (carrier); Emmke v. DeSilva, 293 F. 17 (8th Cir.1923) (hotel). But cf. Wallace v. Shoreham Hotel Corp., 49 A.2d 81 (D.C.Mun.App.1946) (restaurant).

HARRIS v. JONES
Court of Appeals of Maryland, 1977.
281 Md. 560, 380 A.2d 611.

MURPHY, CHIEF JUDGE. * * * The plaintiff, William R. Harris, a 26–year–old, 8–year employee of General Motors Corporation (GM), sued GM and one of its supervisory employees, H. Robert Jones, in the Superior Court of Baltimore City. The declaration alleged that Jones, aware that Harris suffered from a speech impediment which caused him to stutter, and also aware of Harris' sensitivity to his disability, and his insecurity because of it, nevertheless "maliciously and cruelly ridiculed * * * [him] thus causing tremendous nervousness, increasing the physical defect itself and further injuring the mental attitude fostered by the Plaintiff toward his problem and otherwise intentionally inflicting emotional distress." (It was also alleged in the declaration that Jones' actions occurred within the course of his employment with GM and that GM ratified Jones' conduct.)

The evidence at trial showed that Harris stuttered throughout his entire life. While he had little trouble with one syllable words, he had great difficulty with longer words or sentences, causing him at times to shake his head up and down when attempting to speak.

During part of 1975, Harris worked under Jones' supervision at a GM automobile assembly plant. Over a five-month period, between March and August of 1975, Jones approached Harris over 30 times at work and verbally and physically mimicked his stuttering disability. In addition, two or three times a week during this period, Jones approached Harris and told him, in a "smart manner," not to get nervous. As a result of Jones' conduct, Harris was "shaken up" and felt "like going into a hole and hide."

On June 2, 1975, Harris asked Jones for a transfer to another department; Jones refused, called Harris a "troublemaker" and chastised him for repeatedly seeking the assistance of his committeeman, a representative who handles employee grievances. On this occasion, Jones, "shaking his head up and down" to imitate Harris, mimicked his pronunciation of the word "committeeman," which Harris pronounced "mmitteeman." * * *

Harris had been under the care of a physician for a nervous condition for six years prior to the commencement of Jones' harassment. He admitted that many things made him nervous, including "bosses." Harris testified that Jones' conduct heightened his nervousness and his speech impediment worsened. He saw his physician on one occasion during the five-month period that Jones was mistreating him; the physician prescribed pills for his nerves.

Harris admitted that other employees at work mimicked his stuttering. Approximately 3,000 persons were employed on each of two shifts, and Harris acknowledged the presence at the plant of a lot of "tough guys," as well as profanity, name-calling and roughhousing among the employees. He said that a bad day at work caused him to become more nervous than usual. He admitted that he had problems with supervisors other than Jones, that he had been suspended or relieved from work 10 or 12 times, and that after one such dispute, he followed a supervisor home on his motorcycle, for which he was later disciplined.

On this evidence, * * * the jury awarded Harris $3,500 compensatory damages and $15,000 punitive damages against both Jones and GM. [This was reversed by the Court of Special Appeals.]

In concluding that the intentional infliction of emotional distress, standing alone, may constitute a valid tort action, the Court of Special

Appeals relied upon Restatement (Second) of Torts, ch. 2, Emotional Distress, § 46 (1965), which provides, in pertinent part:

"§ 46. Outrageous Conduct Causing Severe Emotional Distress

"(1) One who by extreme and outrageous conduct intentionally or recklessly causes severe emotional distress to another is subject to liability for such emotional distress, and if bodily harm to the other results from it, for such bodily harm."

The court noted that the tort was recognized, and its boundaries defined, in W. Prosser, Law of Torts § 12, at 56 (4th ed. 1971), as follows:

"So far as it is possible to generalize from the cases, the rule which seems to have emerged is that there is liability for conduct exceeding all bounds usually tolerated by decent society, of a nature which is especially calculated to cause, and does cause, mental distress of a very serious kind."

The trend in other jurisdictions toward recognition of a right to recover for severe emotional distress brought on by the intentional act of another is manifest. Indeed, 37 jurisdictions appear now to recognize the tort as a valid cause of action. * * *

[F]our elements * * * must coalesce to impose liability for intentional infliction of emotional distress:

   ① The conduct must be intentional or reckless;

   ② The conduct must be extreme and outrageous;

   ③ There must be a causal connection between the wrongful conduct and the emotional distress;

   ④ The emotional distress must be severe. * * *

[The intermediate Court of Special Appeals had found that the first two elements were established but reversed on the ground that the last two elements were not.]

Whether the conduct of a defendant has been "extreme and outrageous," so as to satisfy that element of the tort, has been a particularly troublesome question. Section 46 of the Restatement, comment d, states that "Liability has been found only where the conduct has been so outrageous in character, and so extreme in degree, as to go beyond all possible bounds of decency, and to be regarded as atrocious, and utterly intolerable in a civilized community." The comment goes on to state that liability does not extend, however: "to mere insults, indignities, threats, annoyances, petty oppressions, or other trivialities. The rough edges of our society are still in need of a good deal of filing down, and in the meantime plaintiffs must necessarily be expected and required to be hardened to a certain amount of rough language, and to occasional acts that are definitely inconsiderate and unkind. * * *"

In determining whether conduct is extreme and outrageous, it should not be considered in a sterile setting, detached from the surroundings in which it occurred. [C] The personality of the individual to whom the misconduct is directed is also a factor. "There is a difference between violent and vile profanity addressed to a lady, and the same language to a Butte miner and a United States marine." Prosser, Intentional Infliction of Mental Suffering: A New Tort, 37 Mich.L.Rev. 874, 887 (1939). * * *

It is for the court to determine, in the first instance, whether the defendant's conduct may reasonably be regarded as extreme and outrageous; where reasonable men may differ, it is for the jury to determine whether, in the particular case, the conduct has been sufficiently extreme and outrageous to result in liability. * * *

While it is crystal clear that Jones' conduct was intentional, we need not decide whether it was extreme or outrageous, or causally related to the emotional distress which Harris allegedly suffered.[2] The fourth element of the tort—that the emotional distress must be severe—was not established by legally sufficient evidence justifying submission of the case to the jury. That element of the tort requires the plaintiff to show that he suffered a severely disabling emotional response to the defendant's conduct. The severity of the emotional distress is not only relevant to the amount of recovery, but is a necessary element to any recovery. * * *

Assuming that a causal relationship was shown between Jones' wrongful conduct and Harris' emotional distress, we find no evidence, legally sufficient for submission to the jury, that the distress was "severe" within the contemplation of the rule requiring establishment of that element of the tort. The evidence that Jones' reprehensible conduct humiliated Harris and caused him emotional distress, which was manifested by an aggravation of Harris' pre-existing nervous condition and a worsening of his speech impediment, was vague and weak at best. * * * While Harris' nervous condition may have been exacerbated somewhat by Jones' conduct, his family problems antedated his encounter with Jones and were not shown to be attributable to Jones' actions. Just how, or to what degree, Harris' speech impediment worsened is not revealed by the evidence. Granting the cruel and insensitive nature of Jones' conduct toward Harris, and considering the position of authority which Jones held over Harris, we conclude that the humiliation suffered was not, as a matter of law, so intense as to constitute the "severe" emotional distress required to recover for the tort of intentional infliction of emotional distress.

Judgment affirmed; costs to be paid by appellant.

_____

1. How culpable must defendant's conduct be before it reaches the level of being extreme enough to be deemed tortious? Some guidelines can be found in decided cases. Thus, it is generally held that the mere solicitation of a woman

2. The fact that Harris may have had some pre-existing susceptibility to emotional distress does not necessarily preclude al distress does not necessarily preclude liability if it can be shown that the conduct intensified the pre-existing condition of psychological stress. [Cc]

to illicit intercourse is not only not an assault but does not give rise to any other cause of action. Reed v. Maley, 115 Ky. 816, 74 S.W. 1079 (1903). "The view being, apparently, that there is no harm in asking." Magruder, Mental and Emotional Disturbance in the Law of Torts, 49 Harv.L.Rev. 1033, 1035 (1936). What about homosexual solicitations?

In Samms v. Eccles, 11 Utah 2d 289, 358 P.2d 344 (1961), a respectable married woman was hounded by continued telephone calls from May to December, some of them late at night; and on one occasion defendant even resorted to a form of advertising by coming to her home and making an indecent exposure of his person. The court said that under any usual circumstances such solicitation would not be actionable ("It seems to be a custom of long standing and one which in all likelihood will continue"), but found such "aggravated circumstances" in this case as to make the defendant liable. In accord, Mitran v. Williamson, 21 Misc.2d 106, 197 N.Y.S.2d 689 (1960).

2. Courts are reluctant to subject either internal family disputes or petty but strongly felt antagonisms to the sanctions of tort law. However, when conduct exceeds all reasonable bounds of behavior tolerated by society, courts are likely to find that a claim has been stated. Cf. Halio v. Lurie, 15 A.D.2d 62, 222 N.Y.S.2d 759 (1961) (man who had jilted a woman wrote her jeering verses and taunting letters); Flamm v. Van Nierop, 56 Misc.2d 1059, 291 N.Y.S.2d 189 (1968) (defendant constantly drove behind plaintiff at a "dangerously close distance," phoned him unnecessarily at his home and business and either hung up or remained on the line in silence, and "dashed" at him in public places).

3. Is there any common theme or set of similar factors running through the following cases? *I am at a total loss here. Anybody, what do you think.*

A. State Rubbish Collectors Association v. Siliznoff, supra page 50.

B. Defendant, a private detective, representing that he was a police officer, threatened to charge the plaintiff, a resident alien, with espionage unless she turned over to him certain private letters in her possession. She suffered severe mental disturbance, and was made seriously ill. The defendant was held liable. Janvier v. Sweeney, [1919] 2 K.B. 316.

C. Defendants, school authorities, called a high school girl to the school office, and bullied and badgered her for a considerable length of time, threatening her with prison and with public disgrace for herself and her family, unless she confessed to immoral conduct with various men. They succeeded in extorting from her a confession of misconduct, of which she was innocent. She suffered severe mental disturbance, and resulting illness. Defendants were held liable. Johnson v. Sampson, 167 Minn. 203, 208 N.W. 814 (1926).

D. *Collecting Agencies.* While reasonable attempts to collect a debt lead to no liability, even though they may be expected to, and do, cause serious mental distress—Berrier v. Beneficial Finance, Inc., 234 F.Supp. 204 (D.C.Ind. 1964); Passman v. Commercial Credit Plan of Hammond, Inc., 220 So.2d 758 (La.App.1969)—more excessive conduct may produce a different result. Thus:

Defendant, a creditor, had plaintiff called to the telephone of her neighbor, with the message that it was an emergency call. Defendant began the conversation by telling plaintiff that "this is going to be a shock; it is as much of a shock to me to have to tell you as it will be to you." When plaintiff said that she was prepared for the message, the defendant let her have it: "This is the Federal Outfitting Company—why don't you pay your bill?" Plaintiff suffered severe nervous shock and resulting serious illness. A complaint alleging these facts was held to state a cause of action. Bowden v. Spiegel, Inc., 96 Cal.App.2d

793, 216 P.2d 571 (1950). A veterinarian and an animal hospital threaten to "do away with" plaintiffs' little dog unless plaintiffs paid in cash and in full a bill for treating the dog for injuries suffered when struck by an automobile. See Lawrence v. Stanford and Ashland Terrace Animal Hospital, 655 S.W.2d 927 (Tenn.1983).

By mistake a credit was listed as a debt and a promise to correct it was not carried out, so that harassment automatically continued. Moorhead v. J.C. Penney Co., 555 S.W.2d 713 (Tenn.1977). See Berger, The Bill Collector and the Law, 17 DePaul L.Rev. 327 (1968); Fair Debt Collection Practices Act, 15 U.S. C.A. §§ 801–818.

E. There are similar cases involving the outrageous tactics of insurance adjusters seeking to force a settlement. Frishett v. State Farm Mut. Auto. Ins. Co., 3 Mich.App. 688, 143 N.W.2d 612 (1966); Continental Cas. Co. v. Garrett, 173 Miss. 676, 161 So. 753 (1935). See also, as to refusal of a liability insurer to settle a claim, Fletcher v. Western Nat. Life Ins. Co., 10 Cal.App.3d 376, 89 Cal. Rptr. 78 (1970). When the insurance company is reasonable in its refusal to settle a claim, it will not be held liable simply because its client happened to be an excessive worrier about fiscal problems. See Rossignol v. Noel, 289 A.2d 691 (Me.1972).

F. Other cases have involved evicting landlords, Kaufman v. Abramson, 363 F.2d 865 (4th Cir.1966), and even high pressure salesmen. See Turner v. ABC Jalousie Co., 251 S.C. 92, 160 S.E.2d 528 (1968).

4. The plaintiff's sensitivities may be a factor in defendant's conduct being deemed extreme and outrageous. Cf. Korbin v. Berlin, 177 So.2d 551 (Fla.App. 1965), where defendant approached a six-year-old girl and said to her: "Do you know that your mother took a man away from his wife? Do you know that God is going to punish them? Do you know that a man is sleeping in your mother's room? God will punish them." It was alleged that the child suffered serious mental distress and resulting physical injury. Should a demurrer to a complaint pleading these facts be overruled? Cf. Delta Fin. Co. v. Ganakas, 93 Ga. App. 297, 91 S.E.2d 383 (1956).

5. Should abuse of plaintiff's sensitivity for race or religion be similarly regarded? In Alcorn v. Anbro Eng'g Inc., 2 Cal.3d 493, 468 P.2d 216, 86 Cal. Rptr. 88 (1970), plaintiff, a black man, was employed by defendant as a truck driver and was also shop steward for the local union. Defendant's foreman discharged him for attempting to countermand orders, and in the course of the altercation repeatedly called him a "goddam nigger." A claim was allowed. In Browning v. Slenderella Systems, 54 Wash.2d 440, 341 P.2d 859 (1959), plaintiff was refused service on the basis of her race. The court allowed a claim but reduced damages from $750 to a "nominal amount," finding that she had suffered only brief momentary personal embarrassment.

6. Should special protection be accorded to pregnant women? When a creditor came to the house of a woman seven months pregnant and screamed profanity, abuse and accusations of dishonesty in the presence of others and she suffered severe emotional disturbance which resulted in a miscarriage, she was allowed to recover in Kirby v. Jules Chain Stores Corp., 210 N.C. 808, 188 S.E. 625 (1936). See Bartow v. Smith, 149 Ohio St. 301, 78 N.E.2d 735 (1948), a holding that otherwise was overruled by Yeager v. Local Union 20, 6 Ohio St.3d 369, 453 N.E.2d 666 (1983).

7. Other physical conditions that affect plaintiff may be taken into account when defendant is aware of them. Plaintiff was suffering from arterial

hypertension, as a result of which he had lost his sight, but was slowly recovering. Knowing his condition, the defendants, representing a creditor to whom plaintiff owed $61.80, wrote him three letters in which they threatened suit, attachment and garnishment and permanent ruination of his credit unless he paid the bill, which he was unable to do. Worry over these letters aggravated plaintiff's condition, and caused him to suffer a relapse and severe attacks of hypertension. Defendants were held liable. Clark v. Associated Retail Credit Men, 105 F.2d 62 (D.C.Cir.1939) (excellent opinion of Edgerton, J., too long to set out in full).

8. Should protection also be given to the hypersensitive or idiosyncratic plaintiff? In one early landmark case protection was allowed. Plaintiff, an eccentric old woman, believed that a pot of gold had been buried in her back yard, and was constantly digging for it. Defendant buried a pot with other contents where she would dig it up. When she did so, he caused her to be escorted by a procession in triumph to the city hall, where she opened the pot under circumstances of extreme public humiliation. She suffered acute mental distress, with resulting serious illness, which apparently further unsettled her reason and contributed to her early death. The "pot of gold" came in the form of a judgment, but only to her heirs. Nickerson v. Hodges, 146 La. 735, 84 So. 37 (1920). Certain emotional human weaknesses for potentially harmful goods may be exploited by sellers of alcohol and tobacco. Should they be liable under an emotional harm theory? See White, Intentional Exploitation of Man's Known Weaknesses, 9 Hous.L.Rev. 889 (1972).

TAYLOR v. VALLELUNGA

District Court of Appeal of California, 1959.
171 Cal.App.2d 107, 339 P.2d 910.

O'DONNELL, JUSTICE pro tem. * * * In the first count, plaintiff Clifford Gerlach alleges that on December 25, 1956, defendants struck and beat him causing him bodily injury for which he seeks damages. In the second count, plaintiff and appellant Gail E. Taylor incorporates by reference the charging allegations of the first count and proceeds to allege that she is the daughter of plaintiff Clifford Gerlach, that she was present at and witnessed the beating inflicted upon her father by defendants, and that as a result thereof, she suffered severe fright and emotional distress. She seeks damages for the distress so suffered. It is not alleged that any physical disability or injury resulted from the mental distress. A general demurrer to the second count of the complaint was interposed by defendants. The demurrer was sustained and appellant was granted ten days leave to amend. Appellant failed to amend and judgment of dismissal of the second count was entered. The appeal is from the judgment of dismissal.

The California cases have for some time past allowed recovery of damages where physical injury resulted from intentionally subjecting the plaintiff to serious mental distress. [C] In the Siliznoff case [supra page 50] the Supreme Court extended the right of recovery to situations where no physical injury follows the suffering of mental distress, saying that "a cause of action is established when it is shown that one, in the absence of any privilege, intentionally subjects another to the mental suffering incident to serious threats to his physical well-being, whether or not the threats are made under such circumstances as to constitute a technical assault." [C] In arriving at this result the court relied in substantial part upon the development of the law in this field of torts as traced by the American Law Institute, and it quotes with approval [c] section 46, as amended, of the Restatement of Torts, (Restatement of the Law, 1948 Supplement, Torts, § 46) which reads: "One who, without a privilege to do so, intentionally causes severe emotional distress to another is liable (a) for such emotional distress, and (b) for bodily harm resulting from it." In explanation of the meaning of the term "intentionally" as it is employed in said section 46, the Reporter says in subdivision (a) of that section: "An intention to cause severe emotional distress exists when the act is done for the purpose of causing the distress or with knowledge on the part of the actor that severe emotional distress is substantially certain to be produced by his conduct. See Illustration 3." Illustration 3 referred to reads as follows: "A is sitting on her front porch watching her husband B, who is standing on the sidewalk, C, who hates B and is friendly to A, *whose presence is known to him,* stabs B, killing him. C is liable to A for the mental anguish, grief and horror he causes." [Emphasis added.]

The failure of the second count of the complaint in the case at bar to meet the requirements of section 46 of the Restatement of Torts is at once apparent. There is no allegation that defendants knew that appellant was present and witnessed the beating that was administered to her father; nor is there any allegation that the beating was administered for the purpose of causing her to suffer emotional distress, or, in the alternative, that defendants knew that severe emotional distress was substantially certain to be produced by their conduct. * * *

—Judgment affirmed.

1. Why not "transferred intent," as in Talmage v. Smith, supra page 28? There is one case, Lambert v. Brewster, 97 W.Va. 124, 125 S.E. 244 (1924), in which it was mentioned by way of analogy when plaintiff recovered for mental disturbance at the peril of another. Is it desirable to extend the liability to every one who may be shocked or frightened at conduct directed at a third person? What if three million people witness an assassination of a President on television? Defendant plays a practical joke on a neighbor that humiliates him and produces physical illness. This result produces severe emotional disturbance on members of his family. How far does liability go?

2. A case allowing recovery when plaintiff was present is Hill v. Kimball, 76 Tex. 210, 13 S.W. 59 (1890), where defendant inflicted a violent, bloody battery upon two persons in the presence of a pregnant woman and she suffered a miscarriage as the result of her mental disturbance. See also Rogers v. Williard, 144 Ark. 587, 223 S.W. 15 (1920).

3. In Knierim v. Izzo, 22 Ill.2d 73, 174 N.E.2d 157 (1961), defendant threatened a woman that he would murder her husband and then, out of her presence, carried out the threat. Her claim was upheld. How did it differ from the main case?

4. When a five-year-old girl was molested by a teenage baby sitter, the child's mother who learned about it later was allowed a claim against the sitter but not against his parents for the emotional distress she suffered from learning about what had happened. See Schurk v. Christensen, 80 Wash.2d 652, 497 P.2d 937 (1972). How might this case be distinguished from the main case?

5. A number of courts have required that plaintiff be present at the time. Thus, recovery was denied in Koontz v. Keller, 52 Ohio App. 265, 3 N.E.2d 694 (1936), where defendant murdered plaintiff's sister, and she later discovered the body, and in Ellsworth v. Massacar, 215 Mich. 511, 184 N.W. 408 (1921), where plaintiff made a later discovery of an attack on her husband. Should this be a "black letter" requirement? What if she were to learn of it ten years later? The Restatement has included it as a restriction, but has supplied a "caveat." See Restatement (Second) of Torts § 46(2).

6. *Dead Bodies.* A good many cases have allowed recovery for mental distress at the intentional mutilation or disinterment of a dead body, or for interference with proper burial. See, for example, Alderman v. Ford, 146 Kan. 698, 72 P.2d 981 (1937); Gostkowski v. Roman Catholic Church, 262 N.Y. 320, 186 N.E. 798 (1933); Papieves v. Lawrence, 437 Pa. 373, 263 A.2d 118 (1970) (deliberate misburial to conceal accident). In most of these cases, the courts have talked of a property right in the body, said to be in the next of kin or a group of close relatives, which serves as a foundation for the action for mental disturbance. Apart from the difficulty of deciding who owns it, this is at best an unsatisfactory kind of property, which cannot be sold or conveyed unless it should happen to be willed to a hospital, can be used only for the one purpose of burial, and not only has no pecuniary value but is a source of liability for funeral expenses. But suppose an eye from the body had been willed to X, a blind person who might be able to see again. Y, who hated X, mutilated the eye. What should be the basis, if any, of X's claim against Y?

In Gadbury v. Bleitz, 133 Wash. 134, 233 P. 299 (1925), where the body was held without burial with demand for payment of another debt, the court avoided difficulties surrounding right of ownership by recognizing that the tort was in reality the intentional infliction of mental distress upon the survivors by extreme outrage. In accord is Stephens v. Waits, 53 Ga.App. 44, 184 S.E. 781 (1936).

7. The classic article on the infliction of mental distress is Magruder, Mental and Emotional Distress in the Law of Torts, 49 Harv.L.Rev. 1033 (1936). For general review of this Section, see Prosser, Insult and Outrage, 44 Calif.L. Rev. 40 (1956); Wade, Tort Liability for Abusive and Insulting Language, 4 Vand.L.Rev. 63 (1950); Leibson, Recovery of Damages for Emotional Distress Caused by Physical Injury to Another, 15 J.Fam.L. 163 (1976); Gilvelber, The Right to Minimum Social Decency and the Limits of Evenhandedness: Intentional Infliction of Emotional Distress by Outrageous Conduct, 82 Colum.L.Rev. 42 (1982).

Intentional

6. TRESPASS TO LAND

DOUGHERTY v. STEPP

difference b/w intentional & negligent trespass

Supreme Court of North Carolina, 1835.
18 N.C. 371.

? "broke the close"

This was an action of trespass quare clausum fregit, tried at Buncombe on the last Circuit, before his Honor Judge Martin. The only proof introduced by the plaintiff to establish an act of trespass, was, that the defendant had entered on the unenclosed land of the plaintiff, with a surveyor and chain carriers, and actually surveyed a part of it, claiming it as his own, but without marking trees or cutting bushes. This, his Honor held not to be a trespass, and the jury under his instructions, found a verdict for the defendant, and the plaintiff appealed. * * *

Trct = Δ
Sct = rev'd

implied RTL at Trct = no damage, no harm done

RUFFIN, CHIEF JUSTICE. In the opinion of the Court, there is error in the instructions given to the jury. The amount of damages may depend on the acts done on the land, and the extent of injury to it therefrom. But it is an elementary principle, that every unauthorized, and therefore unlawful entry, into the close of another, is a trespass. From every such entry against the will of the possessor, the law infers some damage; if nothing more, the treading down the grass or herbage, or as here, the shrubbery.

as in "enclosure"?

extent of damage is a factual question?

Judgment reversed, and new trial ordered.

Know differences —will not come up above

1. We are here concerned only with intentional trespass to land. There may be negligent trespass, but it is governed by the ordinary rules applicable to negligence actions. One of these is that when the entry upon the land is merely negligent, proof of some actual damage is essential to the cause of action. Thus, the word trespass may be used to describe the kind of interest that defendant has invaded. Traditionally, that interest has been described as the right to exclusive possession of land. Restatement (Second) of Torts § 165.

2. Is the trespass intentional when the defendant enters the land in the honest and reasonable belief that it is his own? See Glade v. Dietert, 156 Tex. 382, 387, 295 S.W.2d 642, 645 (1956) (dictum). Cf. Ranson v. Kitner, supra page 24. *no el of another" element*

if AP who if trespass of trespass of trespass sol runs

3. Why nominal damages when the trespass does no harm? Why bother? The explanation sometimes given is that the action of trespass is normally either a suit really intended to try title, or is directed at the vindication of the legal right, without which the defendant's conduct, if repeated, might ripen into a prescriptive right. Hence there is no room for the application of the maxim, *de minimis non curat lex.* See 1 T. Street, Foundations of Legal Liability, 25 (1906). On the other hand, if the law declared that there was no cause of action for invasions that caused only nominal damages, it would not be possible to acquire a "prescriptive" right. At common law, one reason underlying the rule was to keep the peace. See F. Harper and James, Torts § 1.8 at 31 (2d ed. 1986). Is the rule justified today? See Keeton, Trespass, Nuisance and Strict Liability, 59 Colum.L.Rev. 457, 468 (1959).

4. When a trespassory invasion is found, the fact that defendant's conduct was socially useful or even beneficial to plaintiff was usually deemed not controlling. See Harmony Ditch Co. v. Sweeney, 31 Wyo. 1, 222 P. 577 (1924); Longenecker v. Zimmerman, 175 Kan. 719, 267 P.2d 543 (1954).

BRADLEY v. AMERICAN SMELTING AND REFINING CO.

Supreme Court of Washington, 1985.
104 Wash.2d 677, 709 P.2d 782.

CALLOW, JUSTICE. * * * Plaintiff's property is located some 4 miles north of defendant's smelter. Defendant's primary copper smelter (also referred to as the Tacoma smelter), has operated in its present location since 1890. * * * As a part of the industrial process of smelting copper at the Tacoma smelter, various gases such as sulfer dioxide and particulate matter, including arsenic, cadmium and other metals, are emitted. Particulate matter is composed of distinct particles of matter other than water, which cannot be detected by the human senses.

The insistence that a trespass involve an invasion by a "thing" or "object" was repudiated in the well known (but not particularly influential) case of Martin v. Reynolds Metals Co., [221 Or. 86, 342 P.2d 790 (1959)], which held that gaseous and particulate fluorides from an aluminum smelter constituted a trespass for purposes of the statute of limitations: "[L]iability on the theory of trespass has been recognized where the harm was produced by the vibration of the soil or by the concussion of the air which, of course, is nothing more than the movement of molecules one against the other." The view recognizing a trespassory invasion where there is no "thing" which can be seen with the naked eye undoubtedly runs counter to the definition of trespass expressed in some quarters. [Citing the Restatement of Torts and Prosser]. It is quite possible that in an earlier day when science had not yet peered into the molecular and atomic world of small particles, the courts could not fit an invasion through unseen physical instrumentalities into the requirement that a trespass can result only for a direct invasion. But in this atomic age even the uneducated know the great and awful force contained in the atom and what it can do to a man's property if it is released. In fact, the now famous equation $E = MC^2$ has taught us that mass and energy are equivalents and that our concept of "things" must be reframed. If these observations on science in relation to the law of trespass should appear theoretical and unreal in the abstract, they become very practical and real to the possessor of land when the unseen force cracks the foundation of his house. The force is just as real if it is chemical in nature and must be awakened by the intervention of another agency before it does harm. * * *

[*Martin*] was an action in trespass brought against the defendant corporation for causing gases and fluoride particulates to settle on the plaintiffs' land making it unfit for livestock. * * * The court stated: "Trespass and private nuisance are separate fields of tort liability relating to actionable interference with the possession of land. They may be distinguished by comparing the interest invaded; and actionable invasion of a possessor's interest in the exclusive possession of land is a trespass; an actionable invasion of a possessor's interest in the use and enjoyment of his land is a nuisance."

We hold that theories of trespass and nuisance are not inconsistent, that the theories may apply concurrently, and that the injured party may proceed under both theories when the elements of both actions are present. * * *

Having held that there was an intentional trespass, we adopt, in part, the rationale of Borland v. Sanders Lead Co., 369 So.2d 523, 529 (Ala.1979), which stated in part: "Although we view this decision as an application, and not an extension, of our present law of trespass, we feel that a brief restatement and summary of the principles involved in this area would be appropriate. Whether an invasion of property interest is a trespass or a nuisance does not depend upon whether the intruding interest is 'tangible' or 'intangible.' Instead, an analysis must be made to determine the interest interferred with. If the intrusion interferes with the right to exclusive possession of property, the law of trespass applies. If the intrusion is to the use and enjoyment of property, the law of nuisance applies. As previously observed, however, the remedies of trespass and nuisance are not necessarily mutually exclusive. * * *

"Under the modern theory of trespass, the law presently allows an action to be maintained in trespass for invasions that, at one time, were considered indirect and, hence, only a nuisance. In order to recover in trespass for this type of invasion [i.e., the asphalt piled in such a way as to run onto plaintiff's property, or the pollution emitting from a defendant's smoke stack, such as in the present case], a plaintiff must show (1) an invasion affecting an interest in the exclusive possession of his property; (2) an intentional doing of the act which results in the invasion; (3) reasonable foreseeability that the act done could result in an invasion of plaintiff's possessory interest; and (4) substantial damages to the res."

We accept and approve the elements of trespass by airborne pollutants as set forth in the Borland case. * * *

When airborne particles are transitory or quickly dissipate, they do not interfere with a property owner's possessory rights and, therefore, are properly denominated as nuisances. [Cc] When, however, the particles or substance accumulates on the land and does not pass away, then a trespass has occurred. [Cc] While at common law any trespass entitled a landowner to recover nominal or punitive damages for the invasion of his property, such a rule is not appropriate under the circumstances before us. No useful purpose would be served by sanctioning actions in trespass by every landowner within a hundred miles of a manufacturing plant. Manufacturers would be harassed and the litigious few would cause the escalation of costs to the detriment of many. The elements that we have adopted for an action in trespass from Borland require that a plaintiff has suffered actual and substan-tial damages. Since this is an element of the action, the plaintiff who cannot show that actual and substantial damages have been suffered should be subject to dismissal of his cause upon a motion for summary judgment. *   *   *

The United States District Court for the Western District of Washington shall be notified for such further action as it deems appropriate.

[handwritten: What about gas = Can it violate exclusive possession? Can it "accumulate"?]

1. Since the tort protects plaintiff's alleged right to exclusive possession of his land, traditionally there has been a requirement that the invasion be a physical one which usually must be accomplished by a tangible mass. See Ryan v. Emmetsburg, 232 Iowa 600, 4 N.W.2d 435 (1942). Thus, in Amphitheaters, Inc. v. Portland Meadows, 184 Or. 336, 198 P.2d 847 (1948), it was held to be no trespass where race track lights were reflected onto plaintiff's outdoor movie theater. Would any action lie? *Nuisance = use and enjoyment*

2. Trespass has often been contrasted with the tort of nuisance which protects plaintiff's use and enjoyment of his land. In an action for nuisance, courts usually require some actual damage, do not require a physical invasion of land, and take account of the social utility of defendant's activity. On classification between trespass and nuisance, see Note, 60 Colum.L.Rev. 877 (1960).

HERRIN v. SUTHERLAND
Supreme Court of Montana, 1925.
74 Mont. 587, 241 P. 328.

[handwritten: (I) = whether airspace is land? c/L = upwards to infinity (H) = Yes, within limits RTR = modernity; e.g. airplanes etc.]

*   *   * [T]he defendant, while engaged in hunting ducks and other migratory game birds, and while standing on the lands of another, repeatedly discharged a Winchester shotgun at water fowl in flight over plaintiff's said premises *   *   * "to plaintiff's damage in the sum of $10." *   *   *

After defendant's general demurrer *   *   * was overruled, he declined to answer, and his default was entered. Upon the suggestion of counsel for plaintiff that only nominal damages would be demanded, the court rendered judgment in favor of the plaintiff for damages in the sum of $1. From this judgment the defendant has appealed.

CALLAWAY, C.J. *   *   * It must be held that when the defendant, although standing upon the land of another, fired a shotgun over plaintiff's premises, dwelling and cattle, he interfered with the "quiet, undisturbed, peaceful enjoyment of the plaintiff," and thus committed a technical trespass at least. The plaintiff was the owner of the land. "Land," says Blackstone, "in its legal significance has an indefinite extent, upwards as well as downwards; whoever owns the land possesses all the space upwards to an indefinite extent; such is the maxim of the law." *   *   *

Sir Frederick Pollock, in the tenth edition of his valuable work on Torts, page 363, observes that it has been doubted whether it is a trespass to pass over land without touching the soil, as one may in a balloon, or to cause a material object as a shot fired from a gun, to pass over it. * * * Continuing, he observes:

"As regards shooting, it would be strange if we could object to shots being fired point blank across our land only in the event of actual injury being caused, and the passage of the foreign object in the air above our soil being thus a mere incident and a distinct trespass to person or property."

But he concludes that when taking into account the extreme flight of projectiles fired from modern artillery which may pass thousands of feet above the land, the subject is not without difficulty. That shortly it will become one of considerable importance is indicated by the rapid approach of the airplane as an instrumentality of commerce, as is suggested in a valuable note found in 32 Harvard Law Review, 569. However, it seems to be the consensus of the holdings of the courts in this country that the air space, at least near the ground, is almost as inviolable as the soil itself. * * * It is a matter of common knowledge that the shotgun is a firearm of short range. To be subjected to the danger incident to and reasonably to be anticipated from the firing of this weapon at water fowl in flight over one's dwelling house and cattle would seem to be far from inconsequential, and while plaintiff's allegations are very general in character, it cannot be said that a cause of action is not stated, for nominal damages at least. * * *

The judgment is affirmed.

---

1. A, disturbed at night by the howling of a cat on the roof of B's adjoining house, shoots the cat. The bullet remains in the cat, and neither bullet nor cat touches the ground. Is this a trespass to B's land? Davies v. Bennison, 22 Tasmanian L.Rep. 52 (1922).

2. During a dispute between neighbors over a backyard fence, one of them extends her arm over the fence, without touching it. Is this a trespass? Hannabalson v. Sessions, 116 Iowa 457, 90 N.W. 93 (1902).

What about a scaffold that hangs over plaintiff's property? See Geller v. Brownstone Condominium Ass'n, 82 Ill.App.3d 334, 37 Ill.Dec. 805, 402 N.E.2d 807 (1980).

3. *"Cujus est solum, ejus est usque ad coelum et ad inferos."* [Whose is the soil, his it is also unto the sky and the depths.] Coke, Littleton, 4a. How practical a rule today?

CITY OF NEWARK v. EASTERN AIRLINES
United States District Court, District of New Jersey, 1958.
159 F.Supp. 750.

[Three cities, two townships and six individuals joined as plaintiffs in an action seeking to enjoin several defendants from flying over their land at such altitude as to constitute a nuisance or a trespass to the land, and to recover damages for the flights. The opinion is that of the trial court.]

WILLIAM F. SMITH, DISTRICT JUDGE. * * * The enactment of the Civil Aeronautics Act, 49 U.S.C.A. § 401 et seq., was a proper exercise by Congress of the power granted by the Commerce Clause of the Constitution, Article I, Section 8, Clause 3. This legislation clearly evidenced the intent of Congress to preempt the exclusive power of regulation and control in the field of interstate air commerce. There was created thereunder a Civil Aeronautics Board, 49 U.S.C.A. § 421, charged with the responsibility of, and vested with the authority to: first, encourage and develop in the public interest "an air-transportation system properly adapted to the [present and future] needs of the foreign and domestic commerce of the United States, of the Postal Service, and of the national defense"; and second, regulate "air commerce in such manner as to best promote its development and safety." [Cc] The Board was empowered to supervise and control by rule, regulation and order the entire field of interstate air commerce. [C] It was also made the final arbiter of the public interest.

Section 3 of the Act, 49 U.S.C.A. § 403, provides: "There is recognized and declared to exist in behalf of any citizen of the United States a public right of freedom of transit in air commerce through the navigable airspace of the United States." The term "navigable airspace" is defined in general terms in Section 10 of the Air Commerce Act of 1926, 49 U.S.C.A. § 180, as follows: "* * * the term 'navigable airspace' means airspace above the minimum safe altitudes of flight prescribed by the Civil Aeronautics Authority * * *." The term is not otherwise defined by statute, but is defined by regulation.

The Civil Aeronautics Board, pursuant to the authority vested in it to prescribe and revise from time to time "air traffic rules governing the flight of * * * aircraft, including rules as to safe altitudes of flight," Section 601(a)(7) of the Act, 49 U.S.C.A. § 551(a)(7), promulgated § 60.17, 14 C.F.R., which prescribed minimum safe altitudes. This rule defined the "navigable airspace" in the manner contemplated by the statutes hereinabove cited. [The court here reviewed the applicable regulations of the Civil Aeronautics Board.]

We are of the opinion that the term "navigable airspace," as thus defined, includes not only the space above the minimum altitude of 1,000 feet prescribed by the regulation but also that space below the fixed altitude and apart from the immediate reaches above the land. The latter limits are not defined with mathematical certainty but by a formula which, as the Civil Aeronautics Board explains, "applies the standard of necessity to accomplish specified ends and in so doing produces the maximum flight paths for climb and descent that are consistent with the safest operating techniques and practices." [Cc] It has been held that this airspace is in the public domain. United States v. Causby, 1946, 328 U.S. 256, 266. [Cc] * * *

There are contained in the second count the individual claims of the plaintiffs for damages and for injunctive relief predicated upon an alleged trespass to realty. These claims are jointly pleaded but for the purposes of adjudication must be regarded as separate and distinct claims. The claims present common questions of law and fact of which identical principles are determinative. It might be well, therefore, to first consider these principles.

There no longer can be any doubt that the public enjoys a "right of freedom of transit in air commerce through the navigable airspace of the United States." [C] The right was recognized by the Supreme Court in the case of United States v. Causby, supra, [c] wherein it is stated: "It is ancient doctrine that at common law ownership of the land extended to the periphery of the universe—*Cujus est solum ejus est usque ad coelum.* But that doctrine has no place in the modern world. The air is a public highway, as Congress has declared. Were that not true, every transcontinental flight would subject the operator to countless trespass suits. Common sense revolts at the idea. To recognize such private claims to the airspace would clog these highways, seriously interfere with their control and development in the public interest, and transfer into private ownership that to which only the public has a just claim." It was therein held [c]: "The airspace, *apart from the immediate reaches above the land,* is part of the public domain." (Emphasis by the Court.)

It was further held in the Causby case, [c] "The landowner owns at least as much of the space above the ground as he can occupy or use in connection with the land." The Supreme Court cited with approval Hinman v. Pacific Air Transport, in which it was held, at page 758 of 84 F.2d: the landowner owns "so much of the space above the ground as [he] can occupy or make use of, in connection with the enjoyment of [the] land. This right is not fixed. It varies with [the] varying needs and is coextensive with them." The rule, as we interpret it, is that the landowner owns not only as much of the space above the ground as he occupies but also as much thereof as he may use in connection with the land. The airspace which lies above the immediate reaches of his land as thus defined is in the public domain and may be used by the public as navigable airspace. It follows "that the flight of aircraft across the land of another cannot be said to be a trespass without taking into consideration the question of altitude." [C] * * *

The principles do not foreclose the right of the landowner to maintain an action for trespass to realty in a proper case but the action may not rest on evidence that the aircraft in flight passed across his land in the navigable airspace above the immediate reaches thereof. There must be evidence not only that the aircraft passed over his lands from time to time but also that there was an unlawful invasion of the immediate reaches of his land; in other words, there must be evidence that the aircraft flights were at such altitudes as to interfere substantially with the landowner's possession and use of the airspace above the surface.

The evidence offered by the plaintiffs in support of their individual claims must be examined in the light of these recognized principles.

When thus examined, the insufficiency of the evidence to support the claims becomes apparent.   *   *   *

Claim of Irving S. Jay (One of a number of claims)

This plaintiff lives at 333 Itaska Street, Hillside, N.J., in a house which is more than three and a half miles from the start of the takeoff run. He testified generally that he and the members of his family were, and are, disturbed by the noise and vibration caused by planes which pass over his house.

He was asked, "Will you tell us just what happened and what you saw?" He answered: "Yes. During the period that I am home I noticed that there are anywhere from thirty to fifty planes until one o'clock in the morning, that is, the period from six o'clock at night to one o'clock in the morning. Some near, some far, some very, very close. These planes come over, both coming from the Airport and going to the Airport. They come over with a terrible roar; they come over, they shake the house; they have caused cracks in the ceiling, they have caused the dishes to jingle in the cupboard, they have caused us to wake up at night. They disturb my sleep and my family's sleep." [C] When asked as to the identity of the planes, he answered: "American, Eastern, TWA and several others like that." When pressed further, he added: "United," and "Mohawk." [C] It appears from his testimony that these identifications were made during the summer months. When asked "how many of the planes that come over from 6 P.M., to 8 A.M., did you identify?", apparently referring to observations made by the plaintiff during the winter months, he answered, "I couldn't identify any." The testimony was otherwise so indefinite that it would be impossible for the Court to determine with any reasonable degree of certainty the frequency with which any one or more of the aircraft of any one or more of the defendant airlines passed over the property of the plaintiff. *did it matter?*

A deficiency of evidence, common to the claims of the other plaintiffs, is present here. A careful examination of the plaintiff's testimony discloses that he did not venture an approximation of the altitudes at which planes crossed his property. There is clearly no evidence which will support a determination that aircraft passed below the navigable airspace and within the immediate reaches of the land, a determination of fact which is necessary if the Court is to adjudge any one or more of the defendants guilty of a trespass to realty. *failed to allege proper facts*

We do not mean to suggest that the plaintiff must prove with mathematical exactitude the altitudes at which aircraft ordinarily passed over his property; this might very well be an impossible task. There must be some evidence, however, which will enable the Court to make a determination that the aircraft flights were at altitudes below the navigable airspace, which is in the public domain, and within the superadjacent airspace immediately above the land. The ultimate determination must be predicated upon a consideration of aircraft altitudes, and therefore some evidence as to altitudes, for example, well-grounded approximations, is necessary. A determination that there has been a continuing trespass may not rest on mere speculation and conjecture.

The claim for injunctive relief asserted by this plaintiff under the second count must, therefore, be dismissed because of the insufficiency of the evidence.

[The claim of plaintiff Jay for damages on the ground of nuisance was dismissed because the damages proved were less than the federal jurisdictional amount of $3,000.]

What about cities now allowing building taller Than their capitol

1. Congress has now expressly placed "air space needed to insure safety in take-off and landing aircraft" in the public domain. See 49 U.S.C.A. § 1301(24). The Federal Aviation Administration has minimum safe altitudes for aircraft. 14 C.F.R. § 91.79 (1981). Flights above these altitudes are no longer trespasses.

2. The Restatement of Torts, §§ 159, 194, provided that air travel was a trespass but may be privileged. For historical treatment, see R. Wright, The Law of Air Space (1968); Sweeny, Adjusting the Conflicting Interests of Landowner and Aviator in Anglo–American Law, 3 J.Air L. & Com. 329 and 531 (1932); Thurston, Trespass to Air Space, in Harvard Legal Essays, 501 (1934). The Restatement (Second) of Torts § 159, now provides that air travel is a trespass only if it "enters into immediate reaches of the air space next to the land, and * * * interferes substantially with the others' use and enjoyment of *Nuisance* the land." This is essentially the position in Hinman v. Pacific Air Transport, 84 F.2d 755 (9th Cir.1936); Freeman v. United States, 167 F.Supp. 541 (D.Okl. 1958) ("immediate reaches").

3. In effect, the Restatement approach changes a fundamental aspect of the tort of trespass (see Dougherty v. Stepp, supra, page 66). Some courts have been more explicit in doing so and have held that flight by aircraft is never trespassory and plaintiff's remedy lies in negligence or nuisance. See Atkinson v. Bernard, Inc., 223 Or. 624, 355 P.2d 229 (1960); Nestle v. Santa Monica, 6 Cal.3d 920, 496 P.2d 480, 101 Cal.Rptr. 568 (1972). What is the advantage to plaintiff in these approaches?

4. When government overflights have substantially affected habitability of the land below, a court may find a "taking" within the meaning of the Fifth Amendment to the United States Constitution and the government will be required to compensate the owner. This was the true "holding" of United States v. Causby, 328 U.S. 256 (1946). Local government is subject to the same constitutional responsibility. See Griggs v. Allegheny County, 369 U.S. 84 (1962) (county operated airport). *Does local govt have authority of eminent domain?*

5. For treatment of noise and vibration as a nuisance and of the application of inverse condemnation, see Alevizos v. Metropolitan Airports Comm'n, infra page 831 and notes. Remedies for ground damage as the result of airline crashes are considered in the chapters on negligence and strict liability.

6. The interest in the possession of land also extends below the surface, and may present similar problems there. The question frequently arises in connection with mining law. It is held by most jurisdictions that it is a trespass to mine under another's land. North Jellico Coal Co. v. Helton, 187 Ky. 394, 219 S.W. 185 (1920); Chartiers Block Coal Co. v. Mellon, 152 Pa. 286,

25 A. 597 (1893). In many of the western states, however, the miner is permitted to follow the vein wherever it may lead, so long as it is unbroken. On "slant drilling" of oil wells, see Note, 27 Calif.L.Rev. 192 (1939).

7. In Edwards v. Sims, 232 Ky. 791, 24 S.W.2d 619 (1929), the plaintiff owned a tract of land on a hill. Defendant discovered on his adjoining land the entrance to a cave, which extended a considerable distance under plaintiff's land. Defendant developed the cave, advertised it, and conducted tourists through it. Plaintiff brought suit to compel a survey of the cave and an accounting, claiming that the repeated entries by defendant and his tourists were trespasses upon plaintiff's land and that defendant was accountable to plaintiff for a portion of the profits he had made. Plaintiff also asked an injunction preventing further trespasses on that part of the cave under his land. The trial court ordered the survey. The Court of Appeals refused to prohibit it, relying on the maxim "cujus est solum," and saying: "the owner of realty * * * is entitled to the free and unfettered control of his own land above, upon, and beneath the surface. So whatever is in a direct line between the surface of the land and the center of the earth belongs to the owner of the surface." Both an injunction and damages were awarded. The dissenting opinion of Logan, J., is well worth reading as a piece of literature. But cf. Boehringer v. Montalto, 142 Misc. 560, 254 N.Y.S. 276 (1931) (sewer line at depth of 150 feet).

ROGERS v. BOARD OF ROAD COM'RS FOR KENT COUNTY

Supreme Court of Michigan, 1948.
319 Mich. 661, 30 N.W.2d 358.

REID, JUSTICE. Plaintiff instituted this suit to recover damages because of the death of her husband, Theodore Rogers, which plaintiff claims was caused by the trespass and negligence of the defendant board of county road commissioners. Defendant filed a motion to dismiss, based on the pleadings and on the ground of governmental immunity. The lower court granted defendant's motion and dismissed the cause. Plaintiff appeals from the judgment of dismissal of her cause.

Plaintiff claims that for two winter seasons previous to the date of the fatal injury to her husband the defendant board of road commissioners had obtained a license to place a snow fence in decedent's field parallel to the roadway past decedent's farm. Plaintiff claims in her declaration that the placing of the snow fence there was with the distinct understanding and agreement between the defendant and decedent that all of the fence together with the anchor posts should be removed by defendant at the end of each winter season when the necessity for snow fences for that season no longer existed. [The defendant failed to remove an anchor post, and plaintiff's husband, driving his mowing machine, was thrown to the ground when the bar of the machine struck the post, and received injuries that caused his death.] * * *

The court dismissed plaintiff's cause of action, ruling that the action was plainly an action based upon negligence, that there was no basis for any finding of trespass and that the defense of governmental immunity applied to the facts set forth in plaintiff's declaration.

Failure to remove the anchor stake upon expiration of the license to have it on defendant's land was a continuing trespass and is alleged by plaintiff to have been a proximate cause of the damage for which she seeks to recover.

"§ 160. Failure to remove a thing placed on the land pursuant to a license or other privilege

"A trespass, actionable under the rule stated in § 158, may be committed by the continued presence on the land of a structure, chattel or other thing which the actor or his predecessor in legal interest therein has placed thereon

"(a) with the consent of the person then in possession of the land, if the actor fails to remove it after the consent has been effectively terminated, or

"(b) pursuant to a privilege conferred on the actor irrespective of the possessor's consent, if the actor fails to remove it after the privilege has been terminated, by the accomplishment of its purpose or otherwise." Restatement of the Law, Torts, p. 368. * * *

The judgment of the court dismissing the cause of action is reversed and the cause remanded for such further proceedings as shall be found necessary.

———

1. A privileged entry onto the land of another may be limited not only by time and space, but also by purpose. In Brown v. Dellinger, 355 S.W.2d 742 (Tex.Civ.App.1962), two children who were permitted to play on their neighbor's property on one occasion improperly ignited a charcoal burner in the garage and caused $28,000 worth of damages. They were treated as trespassers. In Rossi v. Ventresca Bros. Constr. Co., 94 Misc.2d 756, 405 N.Y.S.2d 375 (1978), the owner of an automobile parked overnight in a shopping center parking lot was held liable as a trespasser for damages incurred by the parking-lot owner in having the automobile towed away.

2. At common law trespass would not lie unless defendant entered the land illegally (breaking of the close). As the principal case reflects, the distinction between trespass and case is no longer controlling, and a trespass can arise today when a visitor who entered land with the consent of the possessor "overstays" his welcome. Of course, the visitor must be informed that he no longer has the possessor's consent to remain.

3. Should the possessor have the right to revoke the welcome mat for any reason? Suppose he simply does not like the visitor's looks? See Mitchell v. Mitchell, 54 Minn. 301, 55 N.W. 1134 (1893); Davis v. Stone, 120 Mass. 228 (1876). See generally Gibson, Visitor's Refusal to Leave Premises, 21 Clev.St.L. Rev. 154 (1972).

4. *Consequences of Trespass.* Note that in the principal case the defendant is held liable to the wife for the death of her husband resulting from the trespass, without any question of negligence in failing to remove the anchor post. Compare the following:

A. Defendant, a trespasser, entered plaintiff's blacksmith shop, and built a fire in the forge. After he left, and without any showing of negligence on the part of defendant, the shop caught fire and was destroyed. Defendant was held liable for the loss of the shop on the basis of the trespass. Wyant v. Crouse, 127 Mich. 158, 86 N.W. 527 (1901).

B. Defendant's employee, delivering a package at plaintiff's residence, entered a side door into a sun porch, left the door open, and crossed the porch to knock at an inner door. Plaintiff's feeble-minded child, whom defendant did not see, fell through the open door and was injured. There was evidence that the employee had been told not to make deliveries by way of that porch. On this basis, the jury were permitted to find that he was a trespasser, and to return a verdict against defendant. Keesecker v. G.M. McKelvey Co., 64 Ohio App. 29, 27 N.E.2d 787 (1940), on appeal, 141 Ohio St. 162, 47 N.E.2d 211 (1940).

5. So far as appears from the decided cases, the rule is limited to physical harm to person or property, occurring on the premises, and to the possessor of the land and the members of his family. The rule is discussed in Prosser, Transferred Intent, 45 Tex.L.Rev. 650, 658–671 (1967).

6. *Restrictions on Right to Exclude Persons from Premises.* Some of the federal civil rights acts require certain landowners and possessors of land to make their premises open to the public without discrimination, and the Constitution is held to impose other restrictions.

A. *Anti-discrimination Statutes.* The Federal Civil Rights Act of 1964, 42 U.S.C.A. § 2000a, requires all places of public accommodation whose business affects interstate commerce to serve customers "without discrimination or segregation on the ground of race, color, religion, or national origin." In Hamm v. Rock Hill, 379 U.S. 306 (1964), rehearing denied, 379 U.S. 995, it was held by a 5–4 vote that this statute entitles blacks not only to enter a restaurant and demand service, but to remain and insist upon it after they are ordered to leave, and that they cannot be prosecuted for criminal trespass when they do so. In accord is Dilworth v. Riner, 343 F.2d 226 (5th Cir.1965), as to a civil suit for trespass. Cf. Restatement (Second) of Torts § 886.

The Civil Rights Act of 1871, 42 U.S.C.A. § 1983, provides a possible civil remedy for persons who are deprived of Constitutional rights by individuals acting under color of any state law or custom. See Adickes v. S.H. Kress & Co., 398 U.S. 144 (1970) (white person who accompanied blacks denied service at lunch counter).

The Civil Rights Act of 1870, 42 U.S.C.A. § 1981, provides that persons of all races have the right to make contracts that can be made by members of the white race. This may prohibit a commercial landholder from restricting entry solely on the basis of race. See Gonzales v. Fairfax–Brewster School, Inc., 363 F.Supp. 1200 (D.Va.1973), modified, 515 F.2d 1082 (4th Cir.1975), aff'd, 427 U.S. 160 (1976). Recently, the Civil Rights Act of 1870 has been construed by the Supreme Court of the United States to cover persons of distinct ethnic backgrounds as well as persons of the non-Caucasion "race." St. Francis College v. Al–Khazraji, ___ U.S. ___, 107 S.Ct. 2022, 95 L.Ed.2d 582 (1987) (professor of Arab ancestry who was denied tenure could bring § 1981 discrimination claim against his employer.) On the same day, the Supreme Court held that Jewish persons could bring a claim under 42 U.S.C.A. § 1982, since at the time of enactment of § 1982 "Jews and Arabs were among the peoples then considered to be distinct races and hence within the protection of statute." Shaare Tefila Congregation v. Cobb, ___ U.S. ___, 107 S.Ct. 2019, 95 L.Ed.2d 594 (1987).

B. *Freedom of Speech.* A private individual may control territory so extensive that it may become "public" for the purposes of First Amendment freedom of speech. See Marsh v. Alabama, 326 U.S. 501 (1946) (company town). This limits the owner's power to restrict entry and expression upon his land; he would have the same responsibility as the government to allow peaceful picketing. The case of Amalgamated Food Employees Union v. Logan Valley Plaza, Inc., 391 U.S. 308 (1968), was read by some to impose this obligation upon owners of large shopping centers, but in Lloyd Corp. v. Tanner, 407 U.S. 551 (1972), the Supreme Court held that only employees of the center engaged in a labor dispute had the right to picket. Then in Hudgens v. N.L.R.B., 424 U.S. 507 (1976), the Court overruled the *Logan Valley* case and returned the state of the law to *Marsh:* Private property would be deemed public for First Amendment purposes only when the landowner had virtually supplanted a municipal government. In Pruneyard Shopping Center v. Robins, 447 U.S. 74 (1980), the Supreme Court found that a provision in the California constitution that allows individuals to exercise their free speech rights on the property of a privately-owned shopping center does not violate the owner's property rights. Nuances of this topic are usually treated in Constitutional Law. See generally Schwartz, A Landholder's Right to Possession of Property Versus A Citizen's Right of Free Speech: Tort Law As A Resource For Conflict Resolution, 45 U.Cin.L.Rev. 1 (1976); Henely, Property Rights and First Amendment Rights: Balance and Conflict, 62 A.B.A.J. 77 (1976).

7. TRESPASS TO CHATTELS

GLIDDEN v. SZYBIAK

Supreme Court of New Hampshire, 1949.
95 N.H. 318, 63 A.2d 233.

Actions at law under the provisions of R.L. c. 180, §§ 23, 24, to recover for a dog bite sustained by the plaintiff Elaine Glidden upon September 29, 1946, and for medical expenses incurred by her father, Harold Glidden. Trial by the Court, with verdicts for the plaintiffs. The plaintiff Elaine Glidden, who was four years old at the time of the occurrence here involved, left her home about noon on the day of her injury, to go to a neighborhood store for candy. On the porch of the store Elaine encountered a dog named Toby and engaged in play with him. She eventually climbed on his back and pulled his ears. The dog snapped at her and bit her nose, inflicting wounds for which a recovery is sought. She was treated by two physicians and a successful result obtained. Such scars as were left are "in no way disfiguring but discernible on close view." The dog Toby was owned by the defendant Jane Szybiak, an unmarried daughter of the other two defendants, 26 years of age at the time of the trial, living with her parents. * * * The defendants also excepted to the denial of their motions for judgment at the close of the evidence. The Court also made the following finding: "Elaine is found to have been of such tender years as to be incapable of being guilty of contributory negligence in her conduct toward the dog Toby. If she was too young to be guilty of negligence, she cannot be found to have been guilty of a trespass or a tort at the

time she received her injury." To this finding the defendants duly
excepted.

BRANCH, CHIEF JUSTICE. The statute under which these actions
were brought reads as follows: "23. Liability of owner. Any person to
whom or to whose property damage may be occasioned by a dog not
owned or kept by him shall be entitled to recover such damage of the
person who owns or keeps the dog, or has it in possession, unless the
damage was occasioned to him while he was engaged in the commission
of a trespass or other tort."

It is the contention of the defendants that the plaintiff Elaine was
engaged in the commission of a trespass at the time of her injury and
is, therefore, barred from recovery under the statute. The law in
regard to a trespass to chattels is thus summarized in the Restatement
of the Law of Torts, s. 218: "One who without consensual or other
privilege to do so, uses or otherwise intentionally intermeddles with a
chattel which is in possession of another is liable for a trespass to such
person if, (a) the chattel is impaired as to its condition, quality or value,
or (b) the possessor is deprived of the use of the chattel for a substantial
time, or (c) bodily harm is thereby caused to the possessor or harm is
caused to some person or thing in which the possessor has a legally
protected interest." In comment (f) to clauses (a) and (b), it is pointed
out that "the interest of a possessor of a chattel in its inviolability,
unlike the similar interest of a possessor of land, is not given legal
protection by an action for nominal damages for harmless intermed-
dlings with the chattel. * * * Sufficient legal protection of the
possessor's interest in the mere inviolability of his chattel is afforded by
his privilege to use reasonable force to protect his possession against
even harmless interference." —

No claim was advanced at the trial that the dog Toby was in any
way injured by the conduct of the plaintiff Elaine. Consequently she
could not be held liable for a trespass to the dog. Consequently her
conduct did not constitute a trespass which will prevent her recovery
under the statute here invoked. * * *

Judgment on the verdict against the defendant Jane. * * *

---

1. Might plaintiff have avoided defendant's argument on this issue altogether? What did the New Hampshire legislature mean by "trespass"?

2. The earliest cases in which trespass was applied to chattels involved
asportation, or carrying off, and a special form of the writ, known as trespass de
bonis asportatis ("d.b.a.") was developed for such situations. Later the action
was extended to cases where the chattels were damaged but not taken, as
where animals were killed or beaten. It at last became applicable to any
physical interference with a chattel in the possession of the plaintiff. Thus
Parker v. Mise, 27 Ala. 480, 62 Am.Dec. 776 (1855) (shooting dog); Bruch v.
Carter, 32 N.J.L. 554 (1867) (moving horse from one place to another); Cole v.
Schweer, 159 Ill.App. 278 (1910) (releasing fish).

3. Trespass to chattels is now quite universally limited to intentional interferences with them. Thus in Mountain States Tel. & Tel. Co. v. Horn Tower Const. Co., 147 Colo. 166, 363 P.2d 175 (1961), it was held that there was no trespass when defendant unintentionally severed plaintiff's telephone conduit. An action will of course lie for negligent interference which causes damage, but it has been absorbed into the general field of negligence actions, and no longer is called trespass.

4. But as in the case of trespass to land, the tort is treated as intentional even though the defendant acts under an innocent mistake, as where he drives off the plaintiff's sheep, believing that they are his own. Dexter v. Cole, 6 Wis. 319, 70 Am.Dec. 465 (1858).

5. The only doubtful question as to trespass to chattels is whether the action will lie without proof of any actual damage to the chattel. If there is actual dispossession, as in Wintringham v. Lafoy, 7 Cow. 735 (N.Y.1827), where an officer by mistake levied execution upon goods belonging to the plaintiff, the deprivation of possession is regarded as damage in itself, and no other is required. But where there is merely interference with the chattel, as by laying hands on a horse or an automobile, the few American decisions have held that the action cannot be maintained without proof of damage. Marentille v. Oliver, 2 N.J.L. 358 (1808); Paul v. Slason, 22 Vt. 231, 54 Am.Dec. 75 (1850); Graves v. Severens, 40 Vt. 636 (1868). In accord is the Restatement (Second) of Torts, § 218. What should be the result if defendant places a bumper sticker for a Democratic candidate on a Republican's car?

6. English writers have contended that the analogy of trespass to land should apply to trespass to chattels, and that there is a real necessity for an action for nominal damages to protect property from intermeddlers. See Salmond and Henston, Torts 89–90 (18th ed. 1981), citing several British cases apparently holding this, including Thurston v. Charles, 21 T.L.R. 659 (K.B.1905), holding liability for showing a private letter to an unauthorized person (£400 damages).

7. The development of the action of trover, and the tort of conversion, provided a convenient substitute for trespass to chattels, and has made that action more or less obsolete. It survives as a possible remedy for interferences of a minor character, when the plaintiff wants to keep the chattel and sue for the harm.

8. CONVERSION

(A) NATURE OF THE TORT

PEARSON v. DODD

United States Court of Appeals, District of Columbia Circuit, 1969.
410 F.2d 701, cert. denied, 395 U.S. 947, 89 S.Ct. 2021, 23 L.Ed.2d 465 (1969).

J. SKELLY WRIGHT, CIRCUIT JUDGE: This case arises out of the exposure of the alleged misdeeds of Senator Thomas Dodd of Connecticut by newspaper columnists Drew Pearson and Jack Anderson. The District Court has granted partial summary judgment to Senator Dodd, appellee here, finding liability on a theory of conversion. At the same time, the court denied partial summary judgment on the theory of invasion of privacy. Both branches of the court's judgment are before us on interlocutory appeal. We affirm the District Court's denial of summary judgment for invasion of privacy and reverse its grant of summary judgment for conversion.

The undisputed facts in the case were stated by the District Court as follows: " * * * [O]n several occasions in June and July, 1965, two former employees of the plaintiff, at times with the assistance of two members of the plaintiff's staff, entered the plaintiff's office without authority and unbeknownst to him, removed numerous documents from his files, made copies of them, replaced the originals, and turned over the copies to the defendant Anderson, who was aware of the manner in which the copies had been obtained. The defendants Pearson and Anderson thereafter published articles containing information gleaned from these documents."

[For another part of this case involving the tort of invasion of privacy, see, infra page 957].

The District Court ruled that appellants' receipt and subsequent use of photocopies of documents which appellants knew had been removed from appellee's files without authorization established appellants' liability for conversion. We conclude that appellants are not guilty of conversion on the facts shown.

Dean Prosser has remarked that "[c]onversion is the forgotten tort." That it is not entirely forgotten is attested by the case before us. History has largely defined its contours, contours which we should now follow except where they derive from clearly obsolete practices or abandoned theories.

Conversion is the substantive tort theory which underlay the ancient common law form of action for trover. A plaintiff in trover alleged that he had lost a chattel which he rightfully possessed, and that the defendant had found it and converted it to his own use. With time, the allegations of losing and finding became fictional, leaving the question of whether the defendant had "converted" the property the only operative one.

The most distinctive feature of conversion is its measure of damages, which is the value of the goods converted. The theory is that the "converting" defendant has in some way treated the goods as if they were his own, so that the plaintiff can properly ask the court to decree a forced sale of the property from the rightful possessor to the converter.

Because of this stringent measure of damages, it has long been recognized that not every wrongful interference with the personal property of another is a conversion. Where the intermeddling falls short of the complete or very substantial deprivation of possessory rights in the property, the tort committed is not conversion, but the lesser wrong of trespass to chattels.

The Restatement (Second) of Torts has marked the distinction by defining conversion as: " * * * [A]n intentional exercise of dominion or control over a chattel which so seriously interferes with the right of another to control it that the actor may justly be required to pay the other the full value of the chattel." Less serious interferences fall under the Restatement's definition of trespass.

The difference is more than a semantic one. The measure of damages in trespass is not the whole value of the property interfered with, but rather the actual diminution in its value caused by the interference. More important for this case, a judgment for conversion can be obtained with only nominal damages, whereas liability for trespass to chattels exists only on a showing of actual damage to the property interfered with. Here the District Court granted partial summary judgment on the issue of liability alone, while conceding that possibly no more than nominal damages might be awarded on subsequent trial. Partial summary judgment for liability could not have been granted on a theory of trespass to chattels without an undisputed showing of actual damages to the property in question.

It is clear that on the agreed facts appellants committed no conversion of the physical documents taken from appellee's files. Those documents were removed from the files at night, photocopied, and returned to the files undamaged before office operations resumed in the morning. Insofar as the documents' value to appellee resided in their usefulness as records of the business of his office, appellee was clearly not substantially deprived of his use of them.

This of course is not an end of the matter. It has long been recognized that documents often have value above and beyond that springing from their physical possession. They may embody information or ideas whose economic value depends in part or in whole upon being kept secret. The question then arises whether the information taken by means of copying appellee's office files is of the type which the law of conversion protects. The general rule has been that ideas or information are not subject to legal protection, but the law has developed exceptions to this rule. Where information is gathered and arranged at some cost and sold as a commodity on the market, it is properly protected as property. Where ideas are formulated with labor and inventive genius, as in the case of literary works or scientific researches, they are protected. Where they constitute instruments of fair and effective commercial competition, those who develop them may gather their fruits under the protection of the law.

The question here is not whether appellee had a right to keep his files from prying eyes, but whether the information taken from those files falls under the protection of the law of property, enforceable by a suit for conversion. In our view, it does not. The information included the contents of letters to appellee from supplicants, and office records of other kinds, the nature of which is not fully revealed by the record. Insofar as we can tell, none of it amounts to literary property, to scientific invention, or to secret plans formulated by appellee for the conduct of commerce. Nor does it appear to be information held in any way for sale by appellee, analogous to the fresh news copy produced by a wire service. * * *

Because no conversion of the physical contents of appellee's files took place, and because the information copied from the documents in those files has not been shown to be property subject to protection by suit for conversion, the District Court's ruling that appellants are guilty of conversion must be reversed.

So ordered.

1. Conversion is a tort whose detailed complications exceed the time that can conveniently be allotted to it in any Torts course. There are thousands of conversion cases, but most of them have been concerned only with settling the title to disputed goods, and there are relatively few in which the tort itself has been in issue. The topic of conversion has tended to be shunted back and forth between the courses in Torts and Property and so to be covered in neither. Many of the practical problems relating to title and conversion are covered in Article 2 of the Uniform Commercial Code and law school courses in sales or commercial law.

Few legal writers have displayed much interest in the topic of conversion. There is a good little book, Warren, Trover and Conversion (1936), and the following articles: Ames, History of Trover 11 Harv.L.Rev. 277, 374 (1898); Salmond, Observations on Trover and Conversion, 21 Law Q.Rev. 43 (1905); Clark, The Test of Conversion, 21 Harv.L.Rev. 1084 (1908); Warren, Qualifying as Plaintiff in an Action for Conversion, 49 Harv.L.Rev. 1084 (1936); Prosser, The Nature of Conversion, 42 Cornell L.Q. 168 (1957); Faust, Distinction Between Conversion and Trespass to Chattel, 37 Or.L.Rev. 256 (1958); Note, 21 Cornell L.Q. 112 (1935).

2. Plaintiff and defendant owned a house as tenants in common. A dispute over ownership arose, and defendant and her agent entered the house, took possession of it, and changed the locks on the door. She then removed plaintiff's furniture from the house and put it in storage, after informing plaintiff that she would do so if he did not remove it and then notifying him where it was available. The trial court held that plaintiff could recover the full value of the furniture on the basis of conversion, but the appellate court reversed and held that "[w]here the conduct complained of does not amount to a substantial interference with possession or the right [to the property], but consists of intermeddling with or use and damage to the personal property, the owner has a cause of action for trespass or case, and may recover only the actual damages suffered by reason of the impairment of the property or the loss of its use." See Zaslow v. Kroenert, 29 Cal.2d 541, 176 P.2d 1 (1946).

3. Vary the *Zaslow* facts as follows:

A. The same facts, except that defendant removes the furniture to a warehouse at a distance, so that plaintiff is subject to substantial inconvenience and expense in recovering it. This is a conversion. Forsdick v. Collins, 1

Starkie 173, 171 Eng.Rep. 437 (1816); and cf. Electric Power Co. v. Mayor of New York, 36 App.Div. 383, 55 N.Y.S. 460 (1899).

B. The same facts, except that defendant does not notify plaintiff. This is a conversion. McGonigle v. Victor H. Belleisle Co., 186 Mass. 310, 71 N.E. 569 (1904); Borg & Powers Furniture Co. v. Reiling, 213 Minn. 539, 7 N.W.2d 310 (1943).

C. The same facts, except that defendant stores the furniture in his own name, with the intent to keep it for himself. This is a conversion. Hicks Rubber Co. Distributors v. Stacy, 133 S.W.2d 249 (Tex.Civ.App.1939).

D. The same facts, except that while the furniture is in the warehouse, and before plaintiff can remove it, it is destroyed by fire. This is a conversion. McCurdy v. Wallblom Furniture & Carpet Co., 94 Minn. 326, 102 N.W. 873 (1905).

4. What would be the elements of damage in an action of trespass d.b.a.?

5. A conversion may occur when one who is authorized to use a chattel uses it in a manner exceeding the authorization. See Swish Mfg. Southeast v. Manhattan Fire & Marine Ins., 675 F.2d 1218 (11th Cir.1982) (lease permitted use of aircraft for transporting passengers and lessee used aircraft for transportation of contraband).

RUSSELL–VAUGHN FORD, INC. v. ROUSE
Supreme Court of Alabama, 1968.
281 Ala. 567, 206 So.2d 371.

[Plaintiff went to defendant's place of business to discuss trading his Falcon for a new Ford. Continuing discussions, he visited again, with his wife and children, and a third time, with a friend.

On this last occasion, a salesman asked him for the keys to his Falcon and he turned them over while inspecting new cars. The difference between the two cars had been raised by defendant, and plaintiff declined to trade on this basis. He asked for his keys and all of the employees denied knowing where they were. Despite his frequent demands the employees laughed at him as if the entire matter was a "big joke." Plaintiff called the police department, and after a policeman arrived, one of the salesmen threw the keys to plaintiff "with the statement that he was a cry baby and that 'they just wanted to see him cry a while.'"

Suit against defendant company and two salesmen for conversion of the Falcon. The jury returned a general verdict for $5,000, and defendants appealed.]

SIMPSON, JUSTICE.   *   *   * The appellants have made several assignments of error. Initially it is argued that the facts of this case do not make out a case of conversion. It is argued that the conversion if at all, is a conversion of the keys to the automobile, not of the automobile itself. It is further contended that there was not under the case here presented a conversion at all. We are not persuaded that the law of Alabama supports this proposition. As noted in Long–Lewis Hardware Co. v. Abston, 235 Ala. 599, 180 So. 261:

"It has been held by this court that 'the fact of conversion does not necessarily import an acquisition of property in the defendant.' Howton v. Mathias, 197 Ala. 457, 73 So. 92, 95. The conversion may consist, not only in an appropriation of the property to one's own use, but in its destruction or in exercising dominion over it in exclusion or defiance of *plaintiff's right.*" [Cc] (Emphasis added).

It is not contended that the plaintiff here had no right to demand the return of the keys to his automobile. Rather, the appellants seem to be arguing that there was no conversion which the law will recognize under the facts of this case because the defendants did not commit sufficient acts to amount to a conversion. We cannot agree. A remarkable admission in this regard was elicited by the plaintiff in examining one of the witnesses for the defense. It seems that according to salesmen for Russell–Vaughn Ford, Inc. it is a rather usual practice in the automobile business to "lose keys" to cars belonging to potential customers. We see nothing in our cases which requires in a conversion case that the plaintiff prove that the defendant appropriated the property to his own use; rather, as noted in the cases referred to above, it is enough that he show that the defendant exercised dominion over it in exclusion or defiance of the right of the plaintiff. We think that has been done here. The jury so found and we cannot concur that a case for conversion has not been made on these facts.

Further, appellants argue that there was no conversion since the plaintiff could have called his wife at home, who had another set of keys and thereby gained the ability to move his automobile. We find nothing in our cases which would require the plaintiff to exhaust all possible means of gaining possession of a chattel which is withheld from him by the defendant, after demanding its return. On the contrary, it is the refusal, without legal excuse, to deliver a chattel, which constitutes a conversion. Compton v. Sims, 209 Ala. 287, 96 So. 185.

We find unconvincing the appellants contention that if there were a conversion at all, it was the conversion of the automobile keys, and not of the automobile. In Compton v. Sims, supra, this court sustained a finding that there had been a conversion of cotton where the defendant refused to deliver to the plaintiff "warehouse tickets" which would have enabled him to gain possession of the cotton. The court spoke of the warehouse tickets as a symbol of the cotton and found that the retention of them amounted to a conversion of the cotton. So here, we think that the withholding from the plaintiff after demand of the keys to his automobile, without which he could not move it, amounted to a conversion of the automobile. * * *

Affirmed.

_____

1. Vary this case as follows:

A. A salesman by mistake drives plaintiff's automobile a short distance to another lot owned by defendant. As soon as he realizes the mistake, he returns the automobile undamaged to plaintiff. This is not a conversion. Cf. Blackinton v. Pillsbury, 260 Mass. 123, 156 N.E. 895 (1927); Hushaw v. Dunn, 62 Colo. 109, 160 P. 1037 (1916).

B. The automobile is sold to a third party before the discovery was made and cannot be located or is destroyed. This is a conversion. Cf. Donahue v. Shippee, 15 R.I. 453, 8 A. 541 (1887).

C. The salesman attempted to steal the auto, but returned it only when he saw a policeman near the showroom. This is a conversion. Cf. Lawyers' Mortgage Inv. Co. v. Paramount Laundries, 287 Mass. 357, 191 N.E. 398 (1934); Hutchinson v. Merchants' & Mechanics' Bank, 41 Pa. 42 (1861).

D. The salesman "gives" the car to X, who gets in it to drive off. Who is liable?

2. In Gulf, C. & S.F.R. Co. v. Wortham, 154 S.W. 1071 (Tex.Civ.App.1913), defendant railroad, having in its possession goods shipped by A to himself, by mistake delivered them to B. The mistake was discovered immediately and the goods were promptly taken back from B and delivered to A. It was held that there was no conversion.

3. There must be a major interference with the plaintiff's right of control over the chattel sufficiently significant to justify requiring him to pay the full value of the chattel. In Donovan v. Barkhausen Oil Co., 200 Wis. 194, 227 N.W. 940 (1929), plaintiff's car was damaged in a collision, to the extent of a crumpled fender, a loosened bumper, and a shallow dent in the body. Plaintiff left the car with defendant, with instructions not to allow anyone to touch it. Defendant went ahead and repaired the damage. It was held that this was not a conversion.

If a dealer entrusted with a car for sale drives it, on one occasion, for ten miles on his own business, it is not a conversion. Cf. Jeffries v. Pankow, 112 Or. 439, 223 P. 745 (1924).

4. A type of case that once was common is Doolittle v. Shaw, 92 Iowa 348, 60 N.W. 621 (1894). Defendant rented a horse from plaintiff, to be driven to Manchester and back. Defendant drove the horse six or seven miles into the country beyond Manchester, without damaging it. It was held that this was not a conversion. But if the horse had been seriously injured in an accident while it was beyond Manchester, with or without the defendant's fault, there would have been a conversion. Palmer v. Mayo, 80 Conn. 353, 68 A. 369 (1907); Baxter v. Woodward, 191 Mich. 379, 158 N.W. 137 (1916).

One of the minor mysteries of the law is why there have been no similar cases involving automobiles. In Grossman Chevrolet Co. v. Enockson, 86 N.W.2d 644 (N.D.1957), a car rental dealer sued a sublessee of an automobile when the vehicle had been kept beyond the rental period and badly damaged in an accident. Plaintiff was permitted to recover for damage to the car, but the theory was based on negligence. Could there have been recovery on any basis if the bailee had not been negligent in having the accident?

The Restatement (Second) of Torts has undertaken to identify the factors that influence courts in determining if a conversion has taken place when there has been interference with a chattel. It provides:

"§ 222A.   What Constitutes Conversion

"(1) Conversion is an intentional exercise of dominion or control over a chattel which so seriously interferes with the right of another to control it that the actor may justly be required to pay the other the full value of the chattel.

"(2) In determining the seriousness of the interference and the justice of requiring the actor to pay the full value the following factors are important:

"(a) the extent and duration of the actor's exercise of dominion or control;

"(b) the actor's intent to assert a right in fact inconsistent with the other's right of control;

"(c) the actor's good faith;

"(d) the extent and duration of the resulting interference with the other's right of control;

"(e) the harm done to the chattel;

"(f) the inconvenience and expense caused to the other."

The ways in which an actor may convert a chattel—i.e., intentionally exercise dominion and control over it that so seriously interferes with the owner's right to control it that it is just to require the actor to pay its full value—include the following:

(1) acquiring possession of it—e.g., stealing the chattel;

(2) damaging or altering it—e.g., intentionally running over an animal and killing it;

(3) using it—e.g., a bailee seriously violates the terms of the bailment;

(4) receiving it—e.g., obtaining possession after a purchase from a thief;

(5) disposing of it—e.g., a bailee wrongfully sells the chattel;

(6) misdelivering it—e.g., delivery to wrong person by mistake so that the chattel is lost; and

(7) refusing to surrender it—e.g., bailee refuses to return the chattel.

See Restatement (Second) of Torts § 223 and following sections.

(B) Effect of Good Faith

An individual may be subject to liability for conversion although he was not subjectively at fault. This can occur in at least two ways:

1. When the defendant intends to affect the chattel in a manner inconsistent with the plaintiff's right of control, the fact that he acted in good faith, and under a mistake, does not prevent liability for conversion. Thus, if a bailee delivers goods to an imposter or on the

basis of a forged document, he is liable to the bailor or owner. See Baer v. Slater, 261 Mass. 153, 158 N.E. 328 (1927) (defendant delivers goods to imposter); Potomac Ins. Co. v. Nickson, 64 Utah 395, 231 P. 445 (1924) (garage delivers car to person who presented a stolen duplicate parking ticket); Suzuki v. Small, 214 App.Div. 541, 212 N.Y.S. 589 (1925) (steel sent to wrong company). Compare Ranson v. Kitner, supra page 24.

Some special rules have developed at common law for the protection of bailees and servants who deal with the chattels of third persons under directions from their bailors or employers. These are rules of commercial convenience and the reason underlying them is clearly the practical necessity of permitting someone to receive goods for storage or safekeeping or transportation, without inquiry as to the title of the person from whom they are received. If, for example, a garage accepting an automobile for overnight parking were to be held liable for conversion when it turned out to be a stolen car, there would be few people willing to operate a parking garage.

A owns goods. B steals them from him, and turns them over to C, a carrier, for shipment to a distant point. Neither the receipt of the stolen goods nor the transportation nor the redelivery to B, the thief, will make C liable to A for conversion of the goods, so long as C acts in good faith, without notice of A's claim to the goods. This is also true if C delivers the goods at destination to D in accordance with B's directions. The rules are also applied to a servant who receives the goods from his employer.

This privilege does not extend to the case in which the bailee or servant himself negotiates the transaction by which A's goods are converted. Thus, if A's goods are stolen by B, and C, who is D's servant, himself buys them from B on behalf of D, and takes delivery, he is liable to A for conversion. This is also true when C is the servant of B, and negotiates the sale and delivery to D. Good faith is no defense in this case. Thus an auctioneer who sells and delivers stolen goods becomes a converter. See Note, 45 Calif.L.Rev. 776 (1957).

Nor does the privilege extend to a case in which the goods are in the hands of the bailee or servant, and they are claimed from him by both the bailor or employer and the true owner. In this case, the bailee or servant is required, at his peril, to see that he delivers to the right person, and he becomes liable for conversion if he delivers to the wrong one. His remedy is to interplead the claimants, or under modern statutes to deposit the goods in court.

2. The other major area in which an innocent conversion may take place concerns good faith purchasers. An innocent purchaser cannot obtain a title from a thief. The purchaser acts at his peril and may be sued in conversion by the true owner.

Complications arise when A induces B to sell him goods by fraud. In this case, title passes to A, but the equity courts permitted B to rescind the transaction because of the fraud and recover back his goods.

At a later stage, the law courts took over the equitable principle and permitted B to rescind the transaction of his own motion, and recover from A as if consent never had been given. This meant that B could maintain trover against A. The remedy remained essentially the equitable one of rescission even after it was taken over by the law courts. The plaintiff must act promptly, must himself do equity and must in all other respects conform to equitable principles. See, for example, Thurston v. Blanchard, 39 Mass. (22 Pick.) 18 (1839).

Since it is fundamental that a bona fide purchase cuts off equitable rights, this right to rescind for fraud is terminated when a bona fide purchaser acquires both title and possession from the defrauding party. There is thus a distinction between stolen goods, as to which the legal title does not pass and a bona fide purchaser is therefore not protected, and goods obtained by fraud, as to which the title does pass, subject to an equity of rescission, which is cut off by a bona fide purchase.

(C) NECESSITY OF DEMAND; RETURN OF CHATTEL

Demand. Some states have followed the rule that possession by a bona fide purchaser or other innocent converter is not in itself a sufficiently serious defiance of the owner's rights, and hold that he is liable only when he refuses to return the goods on demand. See Gillet v. Roberts, 57 N.Y. 28 (1874); Parker v. Middlebrook, 24 Conn. 207 (1855).

In most states, however, a conversion occurs as soon as the defendant takes dominion and control over the goods in a manner inconsistent with plaintiff's ownership. See Hovland v. Farmers Union Elevator Co., 67 N.D. 71, 269 N.W. 842 (1936). In these states, there may be a separate act of conversion for an initial taking of possession and for a later refusal to return on demand, and the owner can elect between them. Restatement (Second) of Torts § 229.

Return. When a converter offers to return the converted goods and the owner accepts, the return does not bar the action for conversion, but it must be taken into account to mitigate the damages recovered. If the chattel is in the same condition as when it was taken, has not changed in value and the plaintiff has suffered no special damage through being deprived of possession, the effect may be to reduce his recovery to nominal damages.

When the plaintiff refuses to accept the offered return, the older rule was that the defendant could not force the goods back upon him in reduction of the damages. The plaintiff could insist upon the full value of the goods as his measure of damages, and the defendant had to keep them. He had, in Professor Warren's phrase, "bought something."

The English courts and some American jurisdictions have held that when the conversion is an innocent one committed under an honest mistake, the court may require the plaintiff to take back the goods and credit the defendant with their value, in any case in which the goods are undamaged and there has been no change in the plaintiff's position. The matter is within the sound discretion of the trial court, and even in these jurisdictions there is no absolute right to the return as a matter of law. See Rutland & W.R. Co. v. Bank of Middlebury, 32 Vt. 639 (1850). The Restatement (Second) of Torts has followed this approach in § 922.

Payment of the chattel's value by a converter to the original owner effectuates a common law forced sale of the chattel and precludes the original owner's further recovery of damages for subsequent conversions. Baram v. Farugia, 606 F.2d 42 (3d Cir.1979). Is a judgment for plaintiff sufficient for this purpose too?

(D) DAMAGES

The measure of damages for conversion is the value of the property converted. Normally this is the market value—what the property could have been sold for in the open market by a willing seller to a willing buyer. For elaboration on this and indication of other recoverable damages, see Restatement (Second) of Torts § 927.

The value is normally determined as of the time of the conversion, so that it becomes important to decide whether a demand is necessary. The theory is that if the chattel is available on the market, the owner should mitigate his damages by purchasing another chattel. But he is not expected to do this at the very moment of the conversion. While some courts would give him the highest intermediate value between the time of conversion and the time of the suit or the judgment, the rule approved by most commentators would give him the highest intermediate value between the time of conversion and a reasonable time for making a replacement. If there is no market value, other methods may be used, such as manufacturing cost, less depreciation. See Restatement (Second) of Torts § 911.

In determining market value, the focus is on the market in which the goods would have to be replaced. Goodpasture, Inc. v. M/V Pollux, 688 F.2d 1003 (5th Cir.1982), reh'g denied, 693 F.2d 133 (1982), cert. denied, 460 U.S. 1084 (1983).

Sometimes the property destroyed or damaged has little market worth, but has a peculiar value to the owner. Usually damages cannot be recovered for sentiment, but if defendant's conduct is outrageous, plaintiff may be able to recover damages for emotional harm suffered from the loss. See La Porte v. Associated Independents, Inc., 163 So.2d 267 (Fla.1964) (pet dachshund). See also Windeler v. Scheers Jewelers, 8 Cal.App.3d 844, 88 Cal.Rptr. 39 (1970) (plaintiff told jeweler of great sentimental value of ring; recovery allowed in claim for negligence).

Punitive damages may be allowed when the conversion was malicious but not when it was done innocently.

(E) WHAT MAY BE CONVERTED

Because of its origin as an action against the finder of lost goods, trover was limited to the conversion of things that were capable of being lost and found. It would lie for any chattel, but not for land, which in the eyes of the law could not be lost. Hence the dispossession or withholding of real property could not be a conversion. Nor could the severance of timber, minerals, crops or fixtures attached to the land. Once there was severance, however, the goods became chattels and the plaintiff could bring trover for their removal from the land. These rules are still applied.

Since intangible rights, such as those of a stockholder in a corporation, could not be lost and found, the original common law rule was that they could not be the subject of a conversion. This has been considerably modified. See Rubin, Conversion of Choses in Action, 10 Fordham L.Rev. 415 (1941). It was first held that damages could be recovered for the conversion of intangible rights when they were merged and identified with a special instrument, such as a promissory note, a check, a bill of lading or a stock certificate, and that instrument itself was converted. This has now been generally extended to permit recovery for the conversion of rights of a kind customarily merged with such an instrument, such as those of a stockholder, without any conversion of the stock certificate. Herrick v. Humphrey Hardware Co., 73 Neb. 809, 103 N.W. 685 (1905) (refusal to register a transfer on the books of the corporation, depriving the new owner of his rights as a stockholder).

Look again at Pearson v. Dodd, 410 F.2d 701 (D.C.Cir.1969), supra page 80, for a ruling on the conversion of private papers.

The decisions are still in agreement that there can be no conversion of intangible rights which are not customarily merged in an instrument, such as the goodwill of a business. Powers v. Fisher, 279 Mich. 442, 272 N.W. 737 (1937); Illinois Minerals Co. v. McCarty, 318 Ill.App. 423, 48 N.E.2d 424 (1943). In Meier v. Wilkins, 15 App.Div. 97, 44 N.Y.S. 274 (1897), it was held that the right to occupy a market stall under a license could not be converted; and in Mackay v. Benjamin Franklin Realty & Holding Co., 288 Pa. 207, 135 A. 613 (1927), it was held that an architect's ideas for a building could not be converted. Most of the decisions agree that there can be no conversion of an ordinary debt or account, apart from any other chattel.

There is perhaps no very good reason why conversion should not lie for the misappropriation of any intangible right, except that thus far there has been no particular need for the action, since other remedies have been sufficient.

(F) WHO MAY MAINTAIN THE ACTION

Trover, like trespass, was founded upon the plaintiff's possession. From this has come the rule that anyone in possession of a chattel at the time of a conversion can maintain an action for it. Thus a finder can recover for conversion. See Aigler, Rights of Finders, 21 Mich.L. Rev. 664, 57 Am.L.Rev. 511 (1928); Moreland, Rights of Finders, 16 Ky. L.J. 1 (1927). The same is true of a bailee to whom the chattel is loaned, although he has no other interest in it, or a sheriff who has seized it on execution.

Modern law has discovered new reasons for permitting the possessor to recover. It is said that possession is sufficient title against the wrongdoer who has no rights at all; and that the party in possession is the proper party to account to the true owner for the amount recovered, and to adjust with him any question as to their respective rights. See Warren, Qualifying as Plaintiff in an Action for Conversion, 49 Harv.L. Rev. 1084, 1095 (1936).

Recovery has been permitted even when the plaintiff's possession is wrongful, and in defiance of the true owner. Thus one converter may recover from another. Jeffries v. Great Western R. Co., 5 El. & Bl. 802, 119 Eng.Rep. 680 (1856). In this case, however, the plaintiff usually has had some colorable claim of right to the chattel; and it has been held that in the absence of such a claim he cannot recover. Turley v. Tucker, 6 Mo. 583, 35 Am.Dec. 449 (1840); Rexroth v. Coon, 15 R.I. 35, 23 A. 37 (1885). In Anderson v. Gouldberg, 51 Minn. 294, 53 N.W. 636 (1892), a thief was permitted to maintain an action of replevin, but an action for conversion may be more doubtful. Compare the cases refusing to allow recovery for conversion of property possessed for an illegal purpose. Miller v. Chicago & N.W.R. Co., 153 Wis. 431, 141 N.W. 263 (1913) (slot machine); Suttori v. Peckham, 48 Cal.App. 88, 191 P. 960 (1920) (fish taken in violation of law).

Trover was also extended to permit recovery by one who did not have possession, but had the immediate right to it, as in the case of a bailor at will who was entitled to possession on demand. Manders v. Williams, 4 Exch. 339, 154 Eng.Rep. 1242 (1849). Or a mortgagee after default. Nichols & Shepard Co. v. Minnesota Thresher Mfg. Co., 70 Minn. 528, 73 N.W. 415 (1897). This, too, has carried over into the modern law of conversion.

The common law rule was that trover would not lie in favor of one who was entitled only to future possession of the chattel, as in the case of a lessor for a term not yet expired or the conditional seller of goods when there has been no default in payment. Gordon v. Harper, 7 Term Rep. 9, 101 Eng.Rep. 828 (1796); Newhall v. Kinsburg, 131 Mass. 445 (1881). There was, however, a remedy in the form of an action on the case for the damages sustained by the one entitled to future possession. Since the abolition of the forms of action under modern procedure, many courts have called this action one for the conversion of the plaintiff's interest in the chattel, as in Morin v. Hood, 96 N.H. 485, 79 A.2d 4 (1951) (mortgagee); Redd Chemical & Nitrate Co. v. W.T. Clay Merc. Co., 219 Ala. 478, 122 So. 652 (1929) (equitable lien). It probably makes very little difference whether it is called conversion or not, so long as it is understood that the plaintiff recovers only the value of his own interest.

Chapter III

PRIVILEGES

1. CONSENT

O'BRIEN v. CUNARD S.S. CO.

Supreme Judicial Court of Massachusetts, 1891.
154 Mass. 272, 28 N.E. 266.

Tort, for an assault, and for negligently vaccinating the plaintiff, who was a steerage passenger on the defendant's steamship. The trial court directed a verdict for the defendant, and the plaintiff brings exceptions.

KNOWLTON, J. * * * To sustain the first count, which was for an alleged assault, the plaintiff relied on the fact that the surgeon who was employed by the defendant vaccinated her on ship-board, while she was on her passage from Queenstown to Boston. On this branch of the case the question is whether there was any evidence that the surgeon used force upon the plaintiff against her will. In determining whether the act was lawful or unlawful, the surgeon's conduct must be considered in connection with the surrounding circumstances. If the plaintiff's behavior was such as to indicate consent on her part, he was justified in his act, whatever her unexpressed feelings may have been. In determining whether she consented, he could be guided only by her overt acts and the manifestations of her feelings. [Cc] It is undisputed that at Boston there are strict quarantine regulations in regard to the examination of emigrants, to see that they are protected from small-pox by vaccination, and that only those persons who hold a certificate from the medical officer of the steam-ship, stating that they are so protected, are permitted to land without detention in quarantine, or vaccination by the port physician. It appears that the defendant is accustomed to have its surgeons vaccinate all emigrants who desire it, and who are not protected by previous vaccination, and give them a certificate which is accepted at quarantine as evidence of their protection. Notices of the regulations at quarantine, and of the willingness of the ship's medical officer to vaccinate such as needed vaccination, were posted about the ship in various languages, and on the day when the operation was performed the surgeon had a right to presume that she and the other women who were vaccinated understood the importance and purpose of vaccination for those who bore no marks to show that they were protected. By the plaintiff's testimony, which, in this particular, is undisputed, it appears that about 200 women passengers were assembled below, and she understood from conversation with them that they

94

were to be vaccinated; that she stood about 15 feet from the surgeon, and saw them form in a line, and pass in turn before him; that he "examined their arms, and, passing some of them by, proceeded to vaccinate those that had no mark;" that she did not hear him say anything to any of them; that upon being passed by they each received a card, and went on deck; that when her turn came she showed him her arm; he looked at it, and said there was no mark, and that she should be vaccinated; that she told him she had been vaccinated before, and it left no mark; "that he then said nothing; that he should vaccinate her again;" that she held up her arm to be vaccinated; that no one touched her; that she did not tell him she did not want to be vaccinated; and that she took the ticket which he gave her, certifying that he had vaccinated her, and used it at quarantine. She was one of a large number of women who were vaccinated on that occasion, without, so far as appears, a word of objection from any of them. They all indicated by their conduct that they desired to avail themselves of the provisions made for their benefit. There was nothing in the conduct of the plaintiff to indicate to the surgeon that she did not wish to obtain a card which would save her from detention at quarantine, and to be vaccinated, if necessary, for that purpose. Viewing his conduct in the light of the surrounding circumstances, it was lawful; and there was no evidence tending to show that it was not. The ruling of the court on this part of the case was correct. * * *

Exceptions overruled.

---

1. Suppose that in the course of an argument defendant announces that he is going to punch plaintiff in the nose. Plaintiff stands his ground but says and does nothing, and defendant punches him. Is there consent?

2. On a park bench in the moonlight, a young man informs a girl that he is going to kiss her. She says and does nothing, and he kisses her. Is he liable for battery?

HACKBART v. CINCINNATI BENGALS, INC.
United States Court of Appeals, Tenth Circuit, 1979.
601 F.2d 516, cert. denied, 444 U.S. 931, 100 S.Ct. 275, 62 L.Ed.2d 188 (1979).

WILLIAM E. DOYLE, CIRCUIT JUDGE. The question in this case is whether in a regular season professional football game an injury which is inflicted by one professional football player on an opposing player can give rise to liability in tort where the injury was inflicted by the intentional striking of a blow during the game.

The injury occurred in the course of a game between the Denver Broncos and the Cincinnati Bengals, which game was being played in Denver in 1973. The Broncos' defensive back, Dale Hackbart, was the recipient of the injury and the Bengals' offensive back, Charles "Booby" Clark, inflicted the blow which produced it. * * *

The trial court's finding was that Charles Clark, "acting out of anger and frustration, but without a specific intent to injure * * * stepped forward and struck a blow with his right forearm to the back of the kneeling plaintiff's head and neck with sufficient force to cause both players to fall forward to the ground." Both players, without complaining to the officials or to one another, returned to their respective sidelines since the ball had changed hands and the offensive and defensive teams of each had been substituted. Clark testified at trial that his frustration was brought about by the fact that his team was losing the game. * * *

Despite the fact that the defendant Charles Clark admitted that the blow which had been struck was not accidental, that it was intentionally administered, the trial court ruled as a matter of law that the game of professional football is basically a business which is violent in nature, and that the available sanctions are imposition of penalties and expulsion from the game. Notice was taken of the fact that many fouls are overlooked; that the game is played in an emotional and noisy environment; and that incidents such as that here complained of are not unusual. * * *

Indeed, the evidence shows that there are rules of the game which prohibit the intentional striking of blows. Thus, Article 1, Item 1, Subsection C, provides that: "All players are prohibited from striking on the head, face or neck with the heel, back or side of the hand, wrist, forearm, elbow or clasped hands." Thus the very conduct which was present here is expressly prohibited by the rule which is quoted above.

The general customs of football do not approve the intentional punching or striking of others. That this is prohibited was supported by the testimony of all of the witnesses. They testified that the intentional striking of a player in the face or from the rear is prohibited by the playing rules as well as the general customs of the game. Punching or hitting with the arms is prohibited. Undoubtedly these restraints are intended to establish reasonable boundaries so that one football player cannot intentionally inflict a serious injury on another. Therefore, the notion is not correct that all reason has been abandoned, whereby the only possible remedy for the person who has been the victim of an unlawful blow is retaliation. * * *

In sum, having concluded that the trial court did not limit the case to a trial of the evidence bearing on defendant's liability but rather determined that as a matter of social policy the game was so violent and unlawful that valid lines could not be drawn, we take the view that this was not a proper issue for determination and that plaintiff was entitled to have the case tried on an assessment of his rights and whether they had been violated. * * *

Reversed and remanded for a new trial.

Ⓝ 1. Defendant taps plaintiff on the shoulder to attract his attention for a reasonable purpose. May consent be assumed? Wiffin v. Kincard, 2 Bos. & P.N.R. 471, 127 Eng.Rep. 713 (1807); Coward v. Baddeley, 4 Hurl. & N. 478, 157 Eng.Rep. 927 (1859). Is this a battery, to begin with?

Consent? Battery?

(?) 2. What about a course of rough-house practical joking between the parties in the past? Wartman v. Swindell, 54 N.J.L. 589, 25 A. 356 (1892).

(?) 3. Plaintiff and defendant were opposing players in a baseball game. Defendant, not trying to break up a double play, slid into second base and upset plaintiff, who was injured. Is there liability? Tavernier v. Maes, 242 Cal.App. 2d 532, 51 Cal.Rptr. 575 (1966). What about one player clipping another in a football game?

(N) 4. Does a hockey player consent to violent bodily contact if he remains seated on his team's bench when, during a brawl on the ice, an opposing player strikes him? See Overall v. Kadella, 138 Mich.App. 351, 361 N.W.2d 352 (1984).

(N) 5. Local custom permits the public to take fish in small lakes and ponds. Defendant passes over plaintiff's property to reach such a lake. Consent? See Marsh v. Colby, 39 Mich. 626 (1878).

(I)= whether consent to medical attention/surgery is req'd? or at physician's discretion?)

MOHR v. WILLIAMS
Supreme Court of Minnesota, 1905.
95 Minn. 261, 104 N.W. 12.

(H)= req'd; exc= ① in emergency ② in course of present operation

[Plaintiff consulted defendant, an ear specialist, concerning trouble with her right ear. On examining her, he found a diseased condition of the right ear, and she consented to an operation upon it. When she was unconscious under the anaesthetic, defendant concluded that the condition of the right ear was not serious enough to require an operation; but he found a more serious condition of the left ear, which he decided required an operation. Without reviving the plaintiff to ask her permission, he operated on the left ear. The operation was skillfully performed, and was successful. Plaintiff nevertheless brought an action for battery. In the court below the jury returned a verdict in *Tr Ct= π* favor of the plaintiff for $14,322.50. The trial judge denied defendant's motion for judgment notwithstanding the verdict, but granted a new trial on the ground that the damages were excessive. Both parties appeal.]

BROWN, J. * * * The evidence tends to show that, upon the first examination of plaintiff, defendant pronounced the left ear in good condition, and that, at the time plaintiff repaired to the hospital to submit to the operation on her right ear, she was under the impression that no difficulty existed as to the left. In fact, she testified that she had not previously experienced any trouble with that organ. It cannot be doubted that ordinarily the patient must be consulted, and his *G/R* consent given, before a physician may operate upon him. * * *

The physician impliedly contracts that he possesses, and will exercise in the treatment of patients, skill and learning, and that he will exercise reasonable care and exert his best judgment to bring about favorable results. The methods of treatment are committed almost exclusively to his judgment, but we are aware of no rule or principle of law which would extend to him free license respecting surgical operations. Reasonable latitude must, however, be allowed the physician in a particular case; and we would not lay down any rule which would unreasonably interfere with the exercise of his discretion, or prevent him from taking such measures as his judgment dictated for the welfare of the patient in a case of emergency. If a person should be injured to the extent of rendering him unconscious, and his injuries were of such a nature as to require prompt surgical attention, a physician called to attend him would be justified in applying such medical or surgical treatment as might reasonably be necessary for the preservation of his life or limb, and consent on the part of the injured person would be implied. And again, if, in the course of an operation to which the patient consented, the physician should discover conditions not anticipated before the operation was commenced, and which, if not removed, would endanger the life or health of the patient, he would, though no express consent was obtained or given, be justified in extending the operation to remove and overcome them. But such is not the case at bar. The diseased condition of plaintiff's left ear was not discovered in the course of an operation on the right, which was authorized, but upon an independent examination of that organ, made after the authorized operation was found unnecessary. Nor is the evidence such as to justify the court in holding, as a matter of law, that it was such an affection as would result immediately in the serious injury of plaintiff, or such an emergency as to justify proceeding without her consent. She had experienced no particular difficulty with that ear, and the questions as to when its diseased condition would become alarming or fatal, and whether there was an immediate necessity for an operation, were, under the evidence, question of fact for the jury.

The contention of defendant that the operation was consented to by plaintiff is not sustained by the evidence. At least, the evidence was such as to take the question to the jury. This contention is based upon the fact that she was represented on the occasion in question by her family physician; that the condition of her left ear was made known to him, and the propriety of an operation thereon suggested, to which he made no objection. It is urged that by his conduct he assented to it, and that plaintiff was bound thereby. It is not claimed that he gave his express consent. It is not disputed but that the family physician of plaintiff was present on the occasion of the operation, and at her request. But the purpose of his presence was not that he might participate in the operation, nor does it appear that he was authorized to consent to any change in the one originally proposed to be made. Plaintiff was naturally nervous and fearful of the consequences of being placed under the influence of anaesthetics, and the presence of her family physician was requested under the impression that it would allay and calm her fears. The evidence made the question one of fact for the jury to determine.

The last contention of defendant is that the act complained of did not amount to an assault and battery. This is based upon the theory that, as plaintiff's left ear was in fact diseased, in a condition dangerous and threatening to her health, the operation was necessary, and having been skillfully performed at a time when plaintiff had requested a like operation on the other ear, the charge of assault and battery cannot be sustained; that, in view of these conditions, and the claim that there was no negligence on the part of defendant, and an entire absence of any evidence tending to show an evil intent, the court should say, as a matter of law, that no assault and battery was committed, even though she did not consent to the operation. In other words, that the absence of a showing that defendant was actuated by a wrongful intent, or guilty of negligence, relieves the act of defendant from the charge of an unlawful assault and battery. We are unable to reach that conclusion, though the contention is not without merit. It would seem to follow from what has been said on the other features of the case that the act of defendant amounted at least to a technical assault and battery. If the operation was performed without plaintiff's consent, and the circumstances were not such as to justify its performance without, it was wrongful; and, if it was wrongful, it was unlawful. As remarked in 1 Jaggard on Torts, 437, every person has a right to complete immunity of his person from physical interference of others, except in so far as contact may be necessary under the general doctrine of privilege; and any unlawful or unauthorized touching of the person of another, except it be in the spirit of pleasantry, constitutes an assault and battery. In the case at bar, as we have already seen, the question whether defendant's act in performing the operation upon plaintiff was authorized was a question for the jury to determine. If it was unauthorized, then it was, within what we have said, unlawful. It was a violent assault, not a mere pleasantry; and, even though no negligence is shown, it was wrongful and unlawful. The case is unlike a criminal prosecution for assault and battery, for there an unlawful intent must be shown. But that rule does not apply to a civil action, to maintain which it is sufficient to show that the assault complained of was wrongful and unlawful or the result of negligence. [C]

The amount of plaintiff's recovery, if she is entitled to recover at all, must depend upon the character and extent of the injury inflicted upon her, in determining which the nature of the malady intended to be healed and the beneficial nature of the operation should be taken into consideration, as well as the good faith of the defendant.

Order affirmed.

[Reference to the records of the District Court of Ramsey County, Minnesota, discloses that on the second trial the plaintiff received a verdict and judgment for $39. There was no appeal.]

1. Why did plaintiff's attorney sue under a theory of battery instead of ordinary negligent medical malpractice? Should there be recovery if defendant used all reasonable care in the operation? What result if plaintiff had lost her hearing in her left ear even though defendant used all reasonable care in the operation? Cf. Rogers v. Board of Road Commissioners, supra page 75.

2. Plaintiff, a boy 15 years of age, was run over by a train and his foot was crushed. When he arrived at the hospital he was unconscious and slowly

bleeding to death. Defendant, the house surgeon, concluded that immediate amputation of the foot was necessary to save the boy's life. Finding no relatives present, he performed the operation. Is he liable? Why? Luka v. Lowrie, 171 Mich. 122, 136 N.W. 1106 (1912).

What if the plaintiff had remained conscious, and had insisted on prohibiting the operation, saying that he would rather die than lose his foot? See Mulloy v. Hop Sang, 1 W.W.R. 714 (Alberta C.A.) (1935).

3. The principal case has for years been regarded as the leading case on unauthorized operations. It is still sound law. There has, however, been a rather marked change in the attitude of the courts, brought about primarily by the fact that all surgery of any consequence is today performed in hospitals, which have their own rules and standardized practices. To these the plaintiff may well be taken, in the absence of any evidence to the contrary, to consent. See Barnett v. Bachrach, 34 A.2d 626 (Mun.App.D.C.1943) (surgeon discovered inflamed appendix during course of another operation); Kennedy v. Parrott, 243 N.C. 355, 90 S.E.2d 754 (1956) (in operation for appendicitis surgeon discovered enlarged cysts on plaintiff's ovaries, and proceeded to puncture them).

4. Thus in a good many cases it has been found that the consent is sufficiently general in its terms to justify the physician in doing whatever he thinks necessary in the course of the operation. See for example Rothe v. Hull, 352 Mo. 926, 180 S.W.2d 7 (1944); Baxter v. Snow, 78 Utah 217, 2 P.2d 257 (1931). Further, many hospitals today use specialized consent forms drafted with legal assistance. <u>What should they say?</u> *ask*

5. What if the plaintiff specifically insists that the operation shall go thus far, and no further? For example, she consents to an incision and an examination of her stomach under ether, but expressly and emphatically forbids anything more. If the surgeon goes ahead and removes part of her stomach, is he liable? Schloendorff v. Society of New York Hospital, 211 N.Y. 125, 105 N.E. 92 (1914). See Powell, Consent to Operative Procedures, 21 Md.L.Rev. 189 (1961).

6. Brother Joseph Fox, an 86–year–old member of a Catholic Order, had previously expressed a desire not to have his life artificially prolonged by use of a respirator if he became permanently unconscious. That condition came to pass following a cardiac arrest in a hernia operation. Should his expression constitute sufficient authority to "pull the plug"? Matter of Storar, 52 N.Y.2d 363, 438 N.Y.S.2d 266, 420 N.E.2d 64, cert. denied, 454 U.S. 858 (1981); see generally Annot., 93 A.L.R.3d 671 (1964). For a more recent decision in this area, see Bartling v. Glendale Adventist Medical Center, 184 Cal.App.3d 961, 229 Cal.Rptr. 360 (1986).

7. When plaintiff refused to consent to a transfusion on religious grounds, the court in Application of the President and Directors of Georgetown College, 331 F.2d 1000 (D.C.Cir.1964), granted a declaratory judgment to proceed. A similar request was denied in In re Osborne, 294 A.2d 372 (D.C.App.1972), where a bedside record disclosed that the patient would regard a transfusion under any circumstances as violative of his religious beliefs. A concurring judge believed the patient's right to deny consent should be upheld even if it were not placed on religious grounds. See generally Vodiga, Euthanasia and the Right to Die, 51 Chi.–Kent L.Rev. 7 (1974); Note, Informed Consent and the Dying Patient, 83 Yale L.J. 1632 (1974); Note, The Right of a Patient to Refuse Blood Transfusions: A Dilemma of Conscience and Law for Patient, Physician

and Hospital, 3 U.San Fernando V.L.Rev. 91 (1974); Annot., 9 A.L.R.3d 1391 (1966).

8. In the case of a minor child, consent of the parent is necessary to any major surgical operation, except in an emergency. Zoski v. Gaines, 271 Mich. 1, 260 N.W. 99 (1935) (9½ years); Bonner v. Moran, 126 F.2d 121 (D.C.Cir.1941) (15 years).

But a minor 17 or 18 years of age has been held capable of legally consenting, at least to minor operations. Gulf & S.I.R. Co. v. Sullivan, 155 Miss. 1, 119 So. 501 (1928); Lacey v. Laird, 166 Ohio St. 12, 139 N.E.2d 25 (1956). Is consent from a parent necessary to prescribe a contraceptive pill? Must a minor female have parental consent for an abortion? Ballard v. Anderson, 4 Cal.3d 873, 484 P.2d 1345, 95 Cal.Rptr. 1 (1971). *Is abortion a battery? if w/o consent?*

Generally, a competent adult can consent for himself, but should a patient's husband's consent be necessary for a physician to perform a hysterectomy or other sterilizing operation on his wife? See Murray v. Vandevander, 522 P.2d 302 (Okl.App.1974). Is the husband's consent necessary for an abortion? *what is purpose of consent in context of tort.*

9. When a parent refuses on religious or other grounds to allow a hospital to provide emergency medical treatment for the child, courts are likely to grant a hospital's application to overrule the parent. See Annot., 52 A.L.R.3d 1118 (1973). The battleground here focuses on operations that will improve the child's comfort, but are not immediately necessary to save the child's life. Compare In re Sampson, 29 N.Y.2d 900, 328 N.Y.S.2d 686, 278 N.E.2d 918 (1972) (approving) with In re Green, 448 Pa. 338, 292 A.2d 387 (1972) (disallowing). See also Simpson, Misrepresentation of Medical Students in Teaching Hospitals, 23 Med.Trial Tech.Q. 233 (1977).

The latest problem in this area involves parents who "consent" on behalf of *would you* their child to be a donor in a transplant operation for the benefit of a brother or sister. See Hart v. Brown, 29 Conn.Supp. 368, 289 A.2d 386 (1972). Should a parent or anyone have this power?

10. A useful discussion of many of these problems can be found in McCoid, A Reappraisal of Liability for Unauthorized Medical Treatment, 41 Minn.L. Rev. 381 (1957).

DE MAY v. ROBERTS

Supreme Court of Michigan, 1881.
46 Mich. 160, 9 N.W. 146.
Tr Ct = π
S Ct = aff'd

MARTSON, C.J. The declaration in this case in the first count sets forth that the plaintiff was at a time and place named a poor married woman, and being confined in child-bed and a stranger, employed in a professional capacity defendant De May who was a physician; that *Doc allowed guest to be in room.* defendant visited the plaintiff as such, and against her desire and intending to deceive her wrongfully, etc., introduced and caused to be present at the house and lying-in room of the plaintiff and while she was in the pains of parturition the defendant Scattergood, who intruded upon the privacy of the plaintiff, indecently, wrongfully and unlawfully *plaintiff alleges* laid hands upon her and assaulted her, the said Scattergood, which was well known to defendant De May, being a young unmarried man, a stranger to the plaintiff and utterly ignorant of the practice of medicine, while the plaintiff believed that he was an assistant physician, a competent and proper person to be present and to aid her in her extremity. * * *

The evidence on the part of the plaintiff tended to prove the allegations of the declaration. On the part of the defendants evidence was given tending to prove that Scattergood very reluctantly accompanied Dr. De May at the urgent request of the latter; that the night was a dark and stormy one, the roads over which they had to travel in getting to the house of the plaintiff were so bad that a horse could not be rode or driven over them; that the doctor was sick and very much fatigued from overwork, and therefore asked the defendant Scattergood to accompany and assist him in carrying a lantern, umbrella and certain articles deemed necessary upon such occasions; that upon arriving at the house of the plaintiff the doctor knocked, and when the door was opened by the husband of the plaintiff, De May said to him "that I had fetched a friend along to help carry my things;" he, plaintiff's husband, said all right, and seemed to be perfectly satisfied. They were bid to enter, treated kindly and no objection whatever made to the presence of defendant Scattergood. That while there Scattergood, at Dr. De May's request, took hold of plaintiff's hand and held her during a paroxysm of pain, and that both of the defendants in all respects throughout acted in a proper and becoming manner actuated by a sense of duty and kindness. * * *

Dr. De May therefore took an unprofessional young unmarried man with him, introduced and permitted him to remain in the house of the plaintiff, when it was apparent that he could hear at least, if not see all that was said and done, and as the jury must have found, under the instructions given, without either the plaintiff or her husband having any knowledge or reason to believe the true character of such third party. It would be shocking to our sense of right, justice and propriety to doubt even but that for such an act the law would afford an ample remedy. To the plaintiff the occasion was a most sacred one and no one had a right to intrude unless invited or because of some real and pressing necessity which it is not pretended existed in this case. The plaintiff had a legal right to the privacy of her apartment at such a time, and the law secures to her this right by requiring others to observe it, and to abstain from its violation. The fact that at the time, she consented to the presence of Scattergood supposing him to be a physician, does not preclude her from maintaining an action and recovering substantial damages upon afterwards ascertaining his true character. In obtaining admission at such a time and under such circumstances without fully disclosing his true character, both parties were guilty of deceit, and the wrong thus done entitles the injured party to recover the damages afterwards sustained, from shame and mortification upon discovering the true character of the defendants. * * *

Judgment for plaintiff affirmed.

1. Defendant gives plaintiff some chocolate candy, which contains an irritant poison. In ignorance of this fact, plaintiff eats the candy, and is made ill. Is there liability for a battery? Cf. Commonwealth v. Stratton, 114 Mass. 303, 19 Am.Rep. 350 (1873). On the effect, in general, of fraud and mistake on consent, see Restatement (Second) of Torts § 892B; Fischer, Fraudulently Induced Consent to Intentional Torts, 46 U.Cin.L.Rev. 71 (1977).

2. Defendant, a "magnetic healer," undertakes to treat plaintiff, a girl of 18, for a nervous illness. At his direction, she removes all her clothing, and he massages her body and takes indecent liberties with her person. She submits in the belief that this is necessary for the treatment of her illness. Is defendant liable? Cf. Bartell v. State, 106 Wis. 342, 82 N.W. 142 (1900).

3. Defendant, a salesman of artificial limbs, calls on plaintiff, a woman with an artificial leg. Representing himself to be a doctor, he induces her to expose her person, and to permit him to lay hands on her. He is in fact a doctor, but of theology. Battery? Commonwealth v. Gregory, 132 Pa.Super. 507, 1 A.2d 501 (1938).

4. Suppose that A consents to sexual intercourse with B, in ignorance of the fact that B has a sexually communicable illness. A contracts the disease. Has she an action against B? Kathleen K. v. Robert B., 150 Cal.App.3d 992, 198 Cal.Rptr. 273 (1984). Crowell v. Crowell, 180 N.C. 516, 105 S.E. 206 (1920); cf. De Vall v. Strunk, 96 S.W.2d 245 (Tex.Civ.App.1936).

5. What if a woman consents to sexual intercourse with a man only after he assured her that "I can't possibly get anyone pregnant," knowing that the statement was false? Barbara A. v. John G., 145 Cal.App.3d 369, 193 Cal.Rptr. 422 (1983).

6. What if A consents to sexual intercourse with B in return for money and is paid with a counterfeit bill?

7. Plaintiff is in a saloon, so drunk that he does not know what he is doing. Defendant induces him to drink a large quantity of whiskey, as a result of which he dies almost immediately. A battery? Cf. Hollerud v. Malamis, 20 Mich.App. 748, 174 N.W.2d 626 (1969) (drunk consenting to Indian wrestling match).

8. Plaintiff consents to an operation under a general anesthetic only on condition that her own physician is present during the operation. He was not present. Is the consent vitiated? Pugsley v. Privette, 220 Va. 892, 263 S.E.2d 69 (1980). What is the effect of allowing a resident to perform the operation under the supervision of the designated surgeon? Suppose the designated surgeon was not present at all.

9. *"Informed Consent."* A recent development in the law of medical malpractice is the doctrine of "informed consent," requiring a physician or surgeon to disclose to his patient the risks of proposed medical or surgical treatment. If he does not do so and goes ahead knowing that the patient is unaware of the risk, he may be liable when injury results from the treatment.

In early cases, this liability was placed on the ground of battery, by analogy to De May v. Roberts, and the cases in the preceding notes. Among the cases so holding have been Bang v. Charles T. Miller Hospital, 251 Minn. 427, 88 N.W.2d 186 (1958); Gray v. Grunnagle, 423 Pa. 144, 223 A.2d 663 (1966).

Around 1960, the failure to disclose the risk began to be treated as a breach of the doctor's professional duty, and hence as a matter of negligence. The cases now generally proceed on that basis. The matter is therefore treated infra. When the physician exceeds the boundaries of consent, the matter is still treated as battery as set forth in Mohr v. Williams. Some courts have recently attempted to broaden the battery theory in these types of situations. See Shultz, Informed Choice to Patient Choice: A New Protected Interest, 95 Yale L.J. 219 (1985).

10. If the main case arose today, a modern Scattergood might be a licensed physician's assistant. A state statute or regulation of a health board would define what he was permitted to do. These statutes and regulations differ in their preciseness and are a source of potential liability. See Note, The Expanding Role of the Physician's Assistant, 76 W.Va.L.Rev. 162 (1973); Schwartz, The Allied Health Professions and Malpractice Liability, New Developments in Medicine (ICLE 1974).

If they consent to means, can consent to possible consequences be implied.

HART v. GEYSEL

Supreme Court of Washington, 1930.
159 Wash. 632, 294 P. 570.

MAIN, J. This action was brought by the administrator of the estate of Hamilton I. Cartwright, deceased, who died as the result of a blow received in a prize fight. To the amended complaint, which will be referred to as the complaint, each of the defendants interposed a demurrer which was sustained. The plaintiff refused to plead further and elected to stand upon the complaint. A judgment was entered dismissing the action, from which the plaintiff appeals.

February 5, 1929, Hamilton I. Cartwright and Cecil Geysel engaged in a prize fight in the city of Seattle, during which Cartwright received a blow which caused his death. In the complaint there are no facts showing that the mutual combat was engaged in in anger, that there was malicious intent to seriously injure, or that there was excessive force.

The controlling question is whether the action can be maintained for wrongful death when the encounter, though unlawful, was entered into with the consent of both parties.

Section 2556, Rem.Comp.Stat., makes prize fighting unlawful and provides that one engaging therein shall be guilty of a gross misdemeanor, with a proviso which is not here material. * * *

Upon the question stated, the adjudicated cases, as well as the textwriters, are in conflict. One line supports what is known as the majority rule, and the other, the minority. The majority rule has been stated as follows:

Majority "Where the parties engage in mutual combat in anger, each is civilly liable to the other for any physical injury inflicted by him during the fight. The fact that the parties voluntarily engaged in the combat is no defense to an action by either of them to recover damages for personal injuries inflicted upon him by the other." [Cc]

— — does not go to lawfulness

The minority rule has been stated as follows: *minority* Ⓡ

"Where parties engage in a mutual combat in anger, the act of each is unlawful and relief will be denied them in a civil action; at *—goes to lawfulness* least, in the absence of a showing of excessive force or malicious intent to do serious injury upon the part of the defendant." * * *

In each of the cases which support the majority rule, the combat was entered into in anger, with a malicious intent to seriously injure, and in some of them the question of excessive force was present as bearing upon the question of damages. In the cases which support the minority rule, the encounter, or fist fight, as it may be called, was entered into in anger, from which it would be necessarily inferred that there was an intent to do injury.

The majority rule carries into a civil action, where one party sues the other for damages for something which has been done in violation of positive law, the principle applied in criminal prosecutions by the state to the effect that the consent of one or both of the parties does not ℝ prevent such a prosecution. The minority rule does not apply this principle when a civil action is brought by one of the parties against the other for damages which have been sustained in a combat consented to by both parties, but which was in violation of positive law. The authorities supporting the majority rule recognize that if the thing done is (not) one prohibited by positive law, for which a penalty is imposed, then consent is a complete defense in a civil action for damages. The majority rule is an exception to two generally well-recognized and accepted principles of law: (a) That one who has consented to suffer a particular invasion of his private right has no right to complain; and (b) that no one shall profit by his own wrongdoing. The minority rule recognizes and applies these principles.

The facts in the case now before us do not bring it within the authorities supporting the majority rule, because here there are no *ℝℝ against maj.* facts which show anger, malicious intent to injure, or excessive force. Ⓐ *min. rule* It may be stated that the facts of this case do not contain one element of the minority rule, that of anger. It is unnecessary, as we view it, in Ⓗ the present case to adopt either rule. It is sufficient to say that in our opinion one who engages in prize fighting, even though prohibited by positive law, and sustains an injury, should not have a right to recover any damages that he may sustain as the result of the combat, which he expressly consented to and engaged in as a matter of business or sport. To enforce the criminal statute against prize fighting, it is not necessary to reward the one that got the worst of the encounter at the expense of his more fortunate opponent. This view is supported by the rule tentatively adopted by the American Law Institute [and now § 60 of the First and Second Restatements of Torts.]

The appellant cites a number of cases which hold that consent to an abortion by a patient is no defense to a subsequent action for damages against the doctor for performing the operation in a negligent manner, but if that be the rule in such cases it is not necessarily applicable to the facts now before us. We here distinctly do not express any opinion upon whether consent to an abortion precludes a right of recovery for the negligent act of the doctor in performing the operation.

The judgment will be affirmed.

----

(4) do not discuss

1. The question of when plaintiff's consent should be invalidated because defendant violated a criminal statute is not free from difficulty. Some of the considerations include: (a) the policy of denying compensation to an intentional wrongdoer who himself may have committed a crime and been injured as a result of it; (b) the effect of deterring him, and others like him, by denying him recovery if he gets hurt; (c) the effect of potential liability in deterring defendant, and others like him; (d) the fact that plaintiff has after all been intentionally battered by defendant; (e) the policy expressed by the maxim, *In pari delicto potior est conditio defendentis* [In equal guilt, the position of the defendant is the stronger].

2. A growing number of courts and the Restatement (Second) of Torts § 892C have followed the position espoused in Hudson v. Craft, 33 Cal.2d 654, 204 P.2d 1 (1949). Plaintiff's consent will be nullified if the defendant's conduct violated a criminal statute designed to protect a class of persons to which plaintiff belongs. Under that theory, how would the following cases be decided?

A. Plaintiff, a female 15 years of age, consents to intercourse with a 50–year–old man in a state that would regard his conduct as unlawful carnal knowledge. Most courts have held plaintiff's consent to be ineffective. See Bishop v. Liston, 112 Neb. 559, 199 N.W. 825 (1924); Gaither v. Meacham, 214 Ala. 343, 108 So. 2 (1926).

But a competent adult woman cannot maintain an action for her own seduction when she has consented, even if intercourse between unmarried adults is illegal in the state. Defendant's overpowering personality or extraordinary powers of persuasion are not tantamount to "duress" that would nullify consent. See Rouse v. Creech, 203 N.C. 378, 166 S.E. 174 (1932).

B. Defendant provides plaintiff's decedent with sleeping pills, knowing he intends to use them to commit suicide. The state's criminal law prohibits both aiding and abetting suicide and attempted suicide. Schwartz, Civil Liability for Causing Suicide: A Synthesis of Law and Psychiatry, 24 Vand.L.Rev. 217, 220–222 (1971), evaluating the factors set forth in supra note 1, suggests that a claim should be allowed. See also 12 Loy.L.A.L.Rev. 967 (1979).

C. Defendant physician provides plaintiff with an abortion at a period in her pregnancy when the action could still be deemed illegal. Prior to Roe v. Wade, 410 U.S. 113 (1973), which limited the power of states to declare abortions illegal, courts were about evenly divided on the question of whether the consent of the woman upon whom the operation was performed barred her recovery. One line of cases, as in Miller v. Bennett, 190 Va. 162, 56 S.E.2d 217 (1949); and Sayadoff v. Warda, 125 Cal.App.2d 626, 271 P.2d 140 (1954), held that the consent is a bar. Milliken v. Heddesheimer, 110 Ohio St. 381, 144 N.E. 264 (1924), held that it is not.

Should the answer to this question depend on whether plaintiff's conduct was also illegal and the parties were in pari delicto? Suppose the defendant negligently performed the operation. Has plaintiff "consented" to that conduct? See Wolcott v. Gaines, 225 Ga. 373, 169 S.E.2d 165 (1969); Henrie v. Griffith, 395 P.2d 809 (Okl.1964) (negligent post-operative care). Some courts have held, however, as in Nash v. Meyer, 54 Idaho 283, 31 P.2d 273 (1934), that the plaintiff will not be aided by allowing recovery for her own criminal conduct, even where there is negligence.

3. The classic article on the general subject is Bohlen, Consent as Affecting Civil Liability for Breaches of the Peace, 24 Colum.L.Rev. 849 (1924).

2. SELF–DEFENSE *Read*

The privilege of self-defense is normally covered in Criminal Law, and detailed discussion must be left to that course. Cases involving tort liability are rather infrequent. When they arise, the criminal law rules are carried over and applied without much variation. The following brief summary will indicate how self-defense fits into the tort picture:

(1) *Existence of Privilege.* Anyone is privileged to use reasonable force to defend himself against a threatened battery on the part of another. The recognition of this privilege came as late as about 1400, and it always has been a matter to be pleaded and proved by the defendant.

(2) *Retaliation.* ~not privileged~ The privilege is one of defense against threatened battery, and not one of retaliation. When the battery is no longer threatened, the privilege terminates; and thereafter the defendant himself becomes liable for battery. Germolus v. Sausser, 83 Minn. 141, 85 N.W. 946 (1901); cf. Drabek v. Sabley, 31 Wis.2d 184, 142 N.W.2d 798 (1966) (battery and false imprisonment of boy who had thrown a snowball).

Even if a person initially was an aggressor, once he has retreated he has a right to self-defense against the person he initially threatened. Edgar v. Emily, 637 S.W.2d 412 (Mo.App.1982) (after coming to his sister's house with a stick, defendant walked back to his jeep intending to leave, and his sister came at him with a hatchet or hammer and hit him in the face with her fist; he then hit his sister with the stick in self-defense).

(3) *Reasonable Belief.* The privilege exists when the defendant reasonably believes that the force is necessary to protect himself against battery, even though there is in fact no necessity. This is an instance in which a reasonable mistake on the part of the actor will protect him. The reason that the rule in Ranson v. Kitner, supra page 24, is not applied is apparently the importance attached by the courts to "self-preservation as the first law of nature."

A. Plaintiff and defendant were on bad terms. They met in the highway, and defendant accosted plaintiff, asking why plaintiff had been slandering him. Plaintiff, who had a bad reputation for shooting people, suddenly put his hand into his pocket. Defendant, believing that he was about to draw a revolver, struck him on the head with a cane and knocked him down. It was held that the jury should have been instructed that defendant was liable only if he had no reasonable grounds to fear an immediate attack by plaintiff. Keep v. Quallman, 68 Wis. 451, 32 N.W. 233 (1887).

B. Defendant ejected from a dance an intoxicated individual named Noble, who had not paid his admission fee. Defendant was then informed that Noble was outside, "getting some bricks." Defendant stepped into the doorway, looking out into the darkness for Noble. At this moment, plaintiff, arriving late for the dance, came running rapidly up the steps, which were dimly lighted. Defendant, believing that he was being attacked by Noble, struck plaintiff and knocked him down the steps. Defendant was held not liable. Crabtree v. Dawson, 119 Ky. 148, 83 S.W. 557 (1904).

4. *Provocation.* Should insults, verbal threats, or opprobrious language justify the exercise of self-defense? Almost every court that has passed upon the question has held that they do not. See Crotteau v. Karlgaard, 48 Wis.2d 245, 179 N.W.2d 797 (1970) ("Get out of the way, you dumb son of a bitch"); Prell Hotel Corp. v. Antonacci, 86 Nev. 390, 469 P.2d 399 (1970). For a long time, some Louisiana courts permitted this line of defense, but recently that state joined the others. See Morneau v. American Oil Co., 272 So.2d 313 (La.1973), noted in 34 La.L.Rev. 137 (1973). In many states, the offending words can be introduced on the issue of punitive damages, and in some states they may mitigate compensatory damages.

Although the general rule of law is relatively clear, its application in the context of disputes is not. Thus, if the abusive words are accompanied by an actual threat of physical violence reasonably warranting an apprehension of imminent bodily harm, one may be privileged to defend, see Silas v. Bowen, 277 F.Supp. 314 (D.S.C.1967); and one does not have to wait for the blow to fall before acting. See Martin v. Estrella, 107 R.I. 247, 266 A.2d 41 (1970). Further, when accompanied by an overt hostile act, oral abuse may amount to a challenge to fight and constitute consent. Restatement (Second) of Torts § 69.

5. *Amount of Force.* The privilege is limited to the use of force that is or reasonably appears to be necessary for protection against a threatened battery. Differences in age, size and relative strength are proper considerations. Thus, a 5′ 6″, 135–pound middle-aged man was permitted to ward off a 6′ 6″, 230–pound young athlete with a shot aimed near his feet. Silas v. Bowen, 277 F.Supp. 314 (D.S.C.1967) (it missed and hit plaintiff). Similarly a small ten-year-old was permitted to throw a broom at a larger ten-year-old in McDonald v. Terrebonne Parish School Bd., 253 So.2d 558 (La.App.1971), cert. denied, 260 La. 128, 255 So.2d 353 (1971) (it missed and took out plaintiff's eye). But a teenage boy engaged in a fistfight with another was not justified in using a baseball bat to protect himself from the threatened injury in Andrepont v. Naquin, 345 So.2d 1216 (La.App.1977). To justify resistance with a deadly weapon, defendant must have a reasonable appre-

hension of loss of life or great bodily injury. See Greenberg v. Mobil Oil Corp., 318 F.Supp. 1025 (N.D.Tex.1970).

6. *Retreat.* One basic disagreement in approach to the privilege of self-defense focuses on whether the defendant must retreat if he can do so without increasing his danger, rather than stand his ground and use force. It is settled that he may stand his ground and use any force short of that likely to cause serious injury. The common law rule was that, rather than kill his assailant or seriously wound him, defendant must "retreat to the wall." A minority of the American courts still apply this rule, and it is adopted by the Restatement (Second) of Torts § 65. The majority, chiefly in the south and west, have insisted upon a higher importance of the dignity and honor of the individual and have held that the defendant may stand his ground and use deadly force, and even kill his assailant. Since it is usually difficult or impossible to retreat effectively from a man with a gun, the question no longer has the importance that it once had.

7. *Injury to Third Party.* A small number of cases have dealt with the situation in which the defendant, defending himself against A, unintentionally shoots B instead. So far as "transferred intent" is concerned, the privilege of self-defense is carried over, and the defendant is held not to be liable to B in the absence of some negligence toward him. And in determining whether there is negligence, the emergency, and the necessity of defense against A, are still to be considered. Morris v. Platt, 32 Conn. 75 (1864); Shaw v. Lord, 41 Okl. 347, 137 P. 885 (1914). Cf. Thompson v. Beliauskas, 341 Mass. 95, 167 N.E.2d 163 (1960) (defense of property).

8. A good review of the whole subject of self-defense is in Perkins, Self–Defense Re-examined, 1 U.C.L.A.L.Rev. 133 (1954). See also Annot., 44 A.L.R.3d 1078 (1973).

3. DEFENSE OF OTHERS

1. *Nature of Privilege.* A privilege similar to that of self-defense is recognized for the defense of third persons. The early common law recognized a feudal privilege in the master of the household to defend members of his family and his servants against attack. Most of the cases have involved members of the same family defending one another, or the relation of master and servant, as in Frew v. Teagarden, 111 Kan. 107, 205 P. 1023 (1922).

As in the case of self-defense, the closest questions concern whether defendant used reasonable force in the circumstances. See, upholding the privilege, e.g., Boyer v. Waples, 206 Cal.App.2d 725, 24 Cal.Rptr. 192 (1962) (plaintiff, who had previously made serious threats to members of defendant's family and was seen outside the defendant's home at night with an object in hand that looked like dynamite, but was, in fact, a flashlight, was shot and wounded); McCullough v. McAnelly, 248 So.2d 7 (La.App.1971), cert. denied, 259 La. 748, 252 So.2d 451 (1971) (three teenaged boys attacked defendant's son and would not desist when warned; father shot and wounded one). Compare Lopez v. Surchia, 112 Cal.App.2d 314, 246 P.2d 111 (1952) (defendant shot boy who was fighting with defendant's son—privilege denied.)

2. *Mistake.* The Restatement (Second) of Torts § 76, has taken the position that the privilege extends to the defense of any third person, including a stranger, if the actor reasonably believes that the circumstances are such as to give the third person the privilege of self-defense and that the intervention is necessary. Although there are not many cases, it appears that "Every man has the right of defending any man by reasonable force against unlawful force." Salmond, Law of Torts 44 (8th ed. 1934); Brouster v. Fox, 117 Mo.App. 711, 93 S.W. 318 (1906); Beavers v. Calloway, 270 App.Div. 873, 61 N.Y.S.2d 804 (1946), aff'd, 271 App.Div. 820, 66 N.Y.S.2d 613.

3. *Reasonable Mistake.* One question over which the courts have differed is that of the effect of a reasonable mistake as to the necessity for taking action. A slight majority of the courts holds that the intervenor steps into the shoes of the person he is defending, and is privileged only when that person would be privileged to defend himself. If it turns out that he has intervened to help the aggressor, he is liable. Robinson v. Decatur, 32 Ala.App. 654, 29 So.2d 429 (1947); State v. Cook, 78 S.Ct. 253, 59 S.E. 862 (1907); People v. Young, 11 N.Y.2d 274, 229 N.Y.S.2d 1, 183 N.E.2d 319 (1962).

Other courts hold that the defendant is privileged to use reasonable force to defend another even when he is mistaken in his belief that intervention is necessary, so long as his mistake was reasonable. The Restatement (Second) of Torts § 76, has adopted this position.

4. DEFENSE OF PROPERTY

KATKO v. BRINEY
Supreme Court of Iowa, 1971.
183 N.W.2d 657.

MOORE, CHIEF JUSTICE. The primary issue presented here is whether an owner may protect personal property in an unoccupied boarded-up farm house against trespassers and thieves by a spring gun capable of inflicting death or serious injury.

We are not here concerned with a man's right to protect his home and members of his family. Defendants' home was several miles from the scene of the incident to which we refer infra.

Plaintiff's action is for damages resulting from serious injury caused by a shot from a 20–gauge spring shotgun set by defendants in a bedroom of an old farm house which has been uninhabited for several years. Plaintiff and his companion * * * had broken and entered the house to find and steal old bottles and dated fruit jars which they considered antiques. * * *

The jury returned a verdict for plaintiff and against defendants for $TG = \widehat{\pi}$ $20,000 actual and $10,000 punitive damages.

After careful consideration of defendants' motions for judgment notwithstanding the verdict and for new trial, the experienced and capable trial judge overruled them and entered judgment on the verdict. Thus we have this appeal by defendants. * * *

[The house was inherited from Mrs. Briney's grandparents and had been unoccupied for some time. There had been a series of intrusions.] Defendants through the years boarded up the windows and doors in an attempt to stop the intrusions. They had posted "no trespass" signs on the land several years before 1967. The nearest one was 35 feet from the house. On June 11, 1967 defendants set "a shotgun trap" in the north bedroom. After Mr. Briney cleaned and oiled his 20–gauge shotgun, the power of which he was well aware, defendants took it to the old house where they secured it to an iron bed with the barrel pointed at the bedroom door. It was rigged with wire from the doorknob to the gun's trigger so it would fire when the door was opened. Briney first pointed the gun so an intruder would be hit in the stomach but at Mrs. Briney's suggestion it was lowered to hit the legs. He admitted he did so "because I was mad and tired of being tormented" but "he <u>did not intend to injure anyone</u>." He gave no explanation of why he used a loaded shell and set it to hit a person already in the house. Tin was nailed over the bedroom window. The spring gun could not be seen from the outside. No ⟨warning⟩ of its presence was posted. * * *

[Plaintiff] entered the old house by removing a board from a porch window which was without glass. * * * As he started to open the north bedroom door the shotgun went off striking him in the right leg above the ankle bone. Much of his leg, including part of the tibia, was

Mr. and Mrs. Edward Briney in front of their vacant farmhouse near Oskaloosa, Iowa

Everything is in book because of some great significance. Plaintiff Marvin E. Katko *Warren Beatty?*

blown away. Only by * * * assistance was plaintiff able to get out of *his companion?* the house and after crawling some distance was put in his vehicle and rushed to a doctor and then to a hospital. He remained in the hospital 40 days. * * *

There was undenied medical testimony plaintiff had a permanent deformity, a loss of tissue, and a shortening of the leg. * * *

The main thrust of defendants' defense in the trial court and on *"does not preclude"* this appeal is that "the law permits use of a spring gun in a dwelling or warehouse for the purpose of preventing the unlawful entry of a burglar or thief." * * *

Instruction 6 stated: "An owner of premises is prohibited from willfully or intentionally injuring a trespasser by means of force that either takes life or inflicts great bodily injury; and therefore a person owning a premise is prohibited from setting out 'spring guns' and like dangerous devices which will likely take life or inflict great bodily injury, for the purpose of harming trespassers. The fact that the trespasser may be acting in violation of the law does not change the rule. The only time when such conduct of setting a 'spring gun' or a like dangerous device is justified would be when the trespasser was committing a felony of violence or a felony punishable by death, or where the trespasser was endangering human life by his act."

* * * *¿ So ok if Δ is in the house, sleeping, sets gun? Sounds like it.*

The overwhelming weight of authority, both textbook and case law, (H) supports the trial court's statement of the applicable principles of law.

* * *

Restatement of Torts § 85, page 180, states: "The value of human life and limb, not only to the individual concerned but also to society, so outweighs the interest of a possessor of land in excluding from it those whom he is not willing to admit thereto that a possessor of land has, as is stated in § 79, no privilege to use force intended or likely to cause death or serious harm against another whom the possessor sees about to enter his premises or meddle with his chattel, unless the intrusion threatens death or serious bodily harm to the occupiers or users of the premises. * * * A possessor of land cannot do indirectly and by a mechanical device that which, were he present, he could not do immediately and in person. Therefore, he cannot gain a privilege to install, for the purpose of protecting his land from intrusions harmless to the lives and limbs of the occupiers or users of it, a mechanical device whose only purpose is to inflict death or serious harm upon such as may intrude, by giving notice of his intention to inflict, by mechanical means and indirectly, harm which he could not, even after request, inflict directly were he present." * * *

The facts in Allison v. Fiscus, 156 Ohio St. 120, 100 N.E.2d 237, decided in 1951, are very similar to the case at bar. There plaintiff's right to damages was recognized for injuries received when he feloniously broke a door latch and started to enter defendant's warehouse with intent to steal. As he entered a trap of two sticks of dynamite buried under the doorway by defendant owner was set off and plaintiff seriously injured. The court held the question whether a particular trap was justified as a use of reasonable and necessary force against a trespasser engaged in the commission of a felony should have been submitted to the jury. The Ohio Supreme Court recognized plaintiff's right to recover punitive or exemplary damages in addition to compensatory damages. * * *

In addition to civil liability many jurisdictions hold a landowner criminally liable for serious injuries or homicide caused by spring guns or other set devices. [Cc] * * *

[The court declined to rule on whether punitive damages were allowable in this type of case because defendant's attorney had not raised that issue in the trial court.]

Study and careful consideration of defendants' contentions on appeal reveal no reversible error.

Affirmed.

LARSON, JUSTICE [dissented, noting that the trial judge's instructions "failed to tell the jury it could find the installation was not made with the intent or purpose of striking or injuring the plaintiff," and that the

principle espoused by the court had never been applied to a burglar, but
only "in the case of a mere trespasser in a vineyard."]

should there be a difference here

---

1. The Brineys had to sell 80 acres of their 120–acre farm in order to pay
the judgment in this case. Their appeal to equity to block enforcement of the
judgment failed. See Briney v. Katko, 197 N.W.2d 351 (1971). Further
background about the case can be found in Palmer, Katko v. Briney: A Study
in American Gothic, 56 Iowa L.Rev. 1219 (1971).

2. A strange development later arose between the parties. When the 80
acres were put up for judgment sale and there were no bids above the minimum
price of $10,000, three neighbors purchased the land for a dollar more, expect-
ing to hold it for Briney until he won his appeal. When he did not win, they
leased the land back to him for enough to pay taxes and their interest costs on
the money they had borrowed. || Some years later, the neighbors decided to sell.
One of them bought the property for $16,000 and sold it to his son for $16,500.
Briney and Katko then got together and jointly sued the neighbors to establish
a constructive trust on their profit. Just before the case came to trial, it was
settled for a sum large enough to pay the remainder of Briney's judgment to
Katko.

Briney then continued farming it paying judgment in indebtness profit

3. The United Press International reported the results of the trial court
decision in this case, stating in part that Katko was "shot and seriously injured
in the *home* of Mr. and Mrs. Edward Briney." (Emphasis added.) A public
outcry about the decision resulted in the introduction of "Briney Bills" in
several state legislatures. The Nebraska Legislature enacted a self-defense act
that provided in part that "no person * * * shall be placed in * * *
jeopardy * * * for protecting, by any means necessary, himself, his family, or
his real or personal property * * *." The statute was held to be unconstitutional by the Supreme Court of Nebraska on the unusual ground of improper
delegation of sentencing authority. See State v. Goodseal, 186 Neb. 359, 183
N.W.2d 258 (1971), cert. denied, 404 U.S. 845 (1971).

4. As in the case of self-defense, the privilege to defend property is limited
to the use of force reasonably necessary to the situation as it appears to the
defendant. Here again a reasonable mistake as to the necessity will protect
him. Smith v. Delery, 238 La. 180, 114 So.2d 857 (1959); Bunten v. Davis, 82
N.H. 304, 133 A. 16 (1926). But a reasonable mistake as to the existence of the
privilege will not, as when the invader is on the land as a matter of right.

5. What constitutes reasonable force is normally a question for the jury,
but there are several recognized limitations. When the invasion is peaceful
and occurs in the presence of the possessor, the use of any force at all will be
unreasonable unless a request has been made to depart. Chapell v. Schmidt,
104 Cal. 511, 38 P. 892 (1894) (defendant caned elderly person who was picking
flowers); Emmons v. Quade, 176 Mo. 22, 75 S.W. 103 (1903). A request does not
have to be made, however, when the conduct of the intruder would indicate to a
reasonable person that it would be useless or that it could not safely be made in
time. See Higgins v. Minaghan, 78 Wis. 602, 47 N.W. 941 (1891); State v.
Cessna, 170 Iowa 726, 153 N.W. 194 (1915).

6. When the invasion occurs in the presence of the possessor, he may
repel him by use of physical force short of infliction of serious bodily injury.
See Palmer v. Smith, 147 Wis. 70, 132 N.W. 614 (1911); Ulmer v. Seelman, 159

Mich. 253, 123 N.W. 1124 (1909); McIlvoy v. Cockran, 9 Ky. (2 A.K. Marsh.) 271 (1820).

7. *Use of Force Calculated to Cause Death or Serious Injury.* The principal case caused a good deal of re-thinking about when, if ever, force calculated to cause death or serious injury may be utilized to defend possession. It is one of the few cases in which a burglar or a thief was able to recover civil damages from his intended victim.

A. When the privilege of self-defense enters the picture in that the invader threatens the personal safety of the defendant or his family, the defendant may use deadly force if it is necessary in the circumstances. This is likely to occur when the invader attempts to enter the homestead at night. See Tipsword v. Potter, 31 Idaho 509, 174 P. 133 (1918); Coleman v. New York & N.H.R. Co., 106 Mass. 160 (1870).

B. Still another privilege may also apply. There is a privilege to use reasonable force to prevent the commission of a crime. With a serious felony like burglary the amount of permissible force is greater, and some courts permit a deadly force. See Scheuermann v. Scharfenberg, 163 Ala. 337, 50 So. 335 (1909); Gray v. Combs, 30 Ky. 478 (1832).

C. In Ilott v. Wilkes, 3 B. & Ald. 304, 106 Eng.Rep. 674 (1820), it was held that a landowner who placed spring guns on his land to keep off poachers was not liable to a trespasser who was shot. The result of this decision was a storm of public disapproval, which led to an act of Parliament making the setting of such devices a crime. In Bird v. Holbrook, 4 Bing. 628, 130 Eng.Rep. 911 (1824), a case which arose before the statute was passed, but was decided afterward, the court overruled the Ilott case and a defendant who set a spring gun was held liable to a trespasser.

D. Most American courts such as the main case and the Restatement (Second) of Torts § 85 have followed Bird v. Holbrook, supra. Many jurisdictions have placed the restrictions on the use of deadly force in their state statutory codes. See statutes collected in Posner, Killing or Wounding to Protect a Property Interest, 14 J.L. & Econ. 201, 228–232 (1971). Some statutes and some cases appear to allow the use of deadly force against serious invasions of property, such as burglary, that may be costly to the possessor. There is also some authority that the right of peaceful habitation may be protected by the use of deadly force. See Model Penal Code § 3.06(d)(i) (1962). Compare Bramble v. Thompson, 264 Md. 518, 287 A.2d 265 (1972) (German Shepherd).

E. The general rule prohibiting deadly force is modified in some states by permitting it if defendant gives the plaintiff clear notice of the danger. See Starkey v. Dameron, 92 Colo. 420, 21 P.2d 1112 (1933) (dictum); State v. Marfaudille, 48 Wash. 117, 92 P. 939 (1907). This is especially likely to occur when defendant's use of force involved a vicious dog. See Hood v. Waldrum, 58 Tenn.App. 512, 434 S.W.2d 94 (1968); Sappington v. Sutton, 501 P.2d 814 (Okl. 1972). Compare Loomis v. Terry, 17 Wend. 496, 31 Am.Dec. 306 (N.Y.1837) (no warning, defendant liable). Barbed wire may give notice in and of itself. See Quigley v. Clough, 173 Mass. 429, 53 N.E. 884 (1899). What privilege is operating in these cases?

In some jurisdictions, even posted warnings will not protect the landholder if he would not be privileged to use this amount of force were he there in person. See State v. Plumlee, 177 La. 687, 149 So. 425 (1933); State v. Childers, 133 Ohio St. 508, 14 N.E.2d 767 (1938).

F. Another line of defense that may work for the landholder is the argument that he intended only to frighten and not to injure the intruder. See Allison v. Fiscus, 156 Ohio St. 120, 100 N.E.2d 237 (1951), discussed in the principal case.

8. The limitations on the possessor's privilege may also restrict his power to eject the plaintiff from his property into a position of unreasonable physical danger. Thus a tramp stealing a ride on a railroad train cannot be thrown off at forty miles an hour. Chesapeake & O. Ry. Co. v. Ryan Adm'r, 183 Ky. 428, 209 S.W. 538 (1919).

In Depue v. Flateau, 100 Minn. 299, 111 N.W. 1 (1907), this was extended even further. Plaintiff, a travelling cattle buyer, called at defendant's farmhouse on a cold winter evening, and was asked to stay for dinner. During dinner plaintiff was overcome by a "fainting spell," and became very weak and seriously ill. He asked permission to stay over night, which was refused. Defendant led him out to his sleigh, put him into it, adjusted the robes around him, and threw the reins, which he was too weak to hold, over his shoulders. Defendant then started the horses on the road to town. Plaintiff was found the following morning by the side of the road about three-quarters of a mile away, badly frost-bitten, and nearly frozen to death. Defendant was held liable. Suppose the landowner places a drunken guest in his car to go home?

9. On the other hand, if the plaintiff's presence endangers the personal safety of those on the premises, the privilege of self-defense, or that of defense of third persons, may justify the ejection. In Tucker v. Burt, 152 Mich. 68, 115 N.W. 722 (1908), plaintiff, a member of the family of the janitor of an apartment house, fell ill with a highly contagious and infectious disease. Defendant, the owner of the building, ejected her. She was able to get to a hospital in a taxi. It was held that defendant was not liable.

10. See Bohlen and Burns, The Privilege to Protect Property by Dangerous Barriers and Mechanical Devices, 35 Yale L.J. 535 (1926); Hart, Injuries to Trespassers, 47 Law Q.Rev. 92, 101–105 (1931).

5. RECOVERY OF PROPERTY *Disregard*

HODGEDEN v. HUBBARD
Supreme Court of Vermont, 1846.
18 Vt. 504, 46 Am.Dec. 167.

[Trespass for assault and battery, and for taking and carrying away a stove. Plaintiff buyer had purchased the stove on credit at the warehouse of defendants, and carried it away. Defendants discovered almost at once that plaintiff had misrepresented his assets and credit and that he was financially irresponsible. They immediately started out in pursuit, and overtook the plaintiff about two miles away, where they took the stove away from him by force. His resistance was such that the defendants used violence and applied force to his person with "great rudeness and outrage." Plaintiff drew a knife, and he was then forcibly held by one of the defendants while the other took possession of the stove.

The court charged the jury that, although plaintiff was guilty of misrepresentation and fraud in obtaining the stove, the defendants were still not justified in forcibly taking it from him, or using force against his person, but must resort to redress by legal process; and that if they found that the force was used, the defendants would be liable. Verdict for plaintiff for $1.00 damages. Exceptions by defendants.]

WILLIAMS, CH. J. It is admitted, in this case, that the property in the stove did not pass to the plaintiff, that, though the plaintiff obtained possession of the stove, yet it was by such means of falsehood and fraud, criminal in the eye of the law, as made the possession unlawful, and that, although the consent of the owner was apparently obtained to the delivery of the possession to the plaintiff, yet, as it respects the plaintiff, and so far as the right of property was concerned, no such consent was given. * * *

In the present case the defendants had clearly a right to retake the property, thus fraudulently obtained from them, if it could be done without unnecessary violence to the person, or without breach of the peace. * * *

In this case before us it is stated, that it did not appear "how much force was used, or its character," before the defendants were assaulted by the plaintiff. To obtain possession of the property in question no violence to the person of the plaintiff was necessary, or required, unless from his resistance. * * * The plaintiff had no lawful possession, nor any right to resist the attempt of the defendants to regain the property, of which he had unlawfully and fraudulently obtained the possession. By drawing his knife he became the aggressor, inasmuch as he had no right thus to protect his fraudulent attempt to acquire the stove, and the possession of the same, and it was the right of the defendants to hold him by force, and, if they made use of no unnecessary violence, they were justified; if they were guilty of more, they were liable. * * *

The judgment of the county court is reversed.

––––––––

1. The privilege of an owner dispossessed of a chattel to use force to recapture it appears to have been first recognized in cases in which there was only a momentary interruption of his possession, so that it was easy to regard him as in effect defending his original possession rather than interfering with that of another. This was extended later to situations in which the wrongdoer had obtained the chattel by force or fraud, and had made his escape with it, but the pursuit was "fresh." These limitations have continued to be applied to the privilege. As to the requirement of force or fraud, see Watson v. Rheinderknecht, 82 Minn. 235, 84 N.W. 798 (1901).

2. Fresh pursuit is limited to prompt discovery of the dispossession, and prompt and persistent efforts to recover the chattel. Any undue lapse of time during which the pursuit has not been commenced, or has come to a halt, will mean that the owner is no longer privileged to fight himself back into possession, but must resort to the law. Bobb v. Bosworth, 16 Ky. 81, 12 Am.Dec. 273

(1808); Barr v. Post, 56 Neb. 698, 77 N.W. 123 (1898), rev'd, 59 Neb. 361, 80 N.W. 1041 (1899); Restatement (Second) of Torts § 103.

3. The privilege is limited to force reasonable under the circumstances. As in the case of the defense of possession, it is not reasonable to use any force calculated to inflict serious bodily harm to protect the property interest. Gortarez v. Smitty's Super Value, Inc., 140 Ariz. 97, 680 P.2d 807 (1984) (shopowner's use of a choke hold on teenage boy after chasing him in parking lot because of suspected shoplifting was not reasonable). Restatement (Second) of Torts § 106. But if the wrongdoer resists, the owner may use any force reasonably required to defend his own person. Gyre v. Culver, 47 Barb. (N.Y.) 592 (1867); Hamilton v. Barker, 116 Mich. 684, 75 N.W. 133 (1898). Ordinarily a resort to any force at all will not be justified until a demand has been made for the return of the property; but this is not required when it reasonably appears that demand would be useless or dangerous. Restatement (Second) of Torts § 104.

4. The few cases dealing with the point indicate that this privilege differs from the privilege of defending the original possession, in that the loss due to a reasonable mistake must fall on the one who makes it. S.H. Kress & Co. v. Musgrove, 153 Va. 348, 149 S.E. 453 (1929); see Estes v. Brewster Cigar Co., 156 Wash. 465, 287 P. 36 (1930); Restatement (Second) of Torts § 100, comment d, adding "unless the mistake was induced by the other."

5. The question frequently arises in cases of conditional sales of such things as automobiles, pianos, refrigerators and television sets, where the buyer has purchased on the installment plan, has been given possession, and has defaulted in his payments. Title has remained in the seller, and upon such default he is entitled to possession; and if he can retake the chattel peaceably he may do so without liability. On the other hand, since he has voluntarily surrendered possession in the first place, he has no privilege to recapture it by force; and if the buyer will not give up the chattel, he must resort to his legal remedy. Roberts v. Speck, 169 Wash. 613, 14 P.2d 33 (1932). There have been quite a few cases—not all in agreement—dealing with what constitutes the use of force (for example, the use of a skeleton key).

6. The courts are not agreed as to whether a clause in the contract giving the seller the privilege to use force is effective. A few of the older decisions have held that it is. Lambert v. Robinson, 162 Mass. 34, 37 N.E. 753 (1894); W.T. Walker Furniture Co. v. Dyson, 32 U.S.App.D.C. 90 (1908). The prevailing view of the later decisions is that the clause is void as inviting a breach of the peace. Girard v. Anderson, 219 Iowa 142, 257 N.W. 400 (1934), is one of the best decisions. Is the problem one of the scope of the privilege of recapture or whether consent should be invalidated?

7. The retaking of possession by a seller under a conditional sale, on default by the buyer, is now controlled by § 9–503 of the Uniform Commercial Code, which provides that "unless otherwise agreed a secured party has on default the right to take possession of the collateral. In taking possession a secured party may proceed without judicial process if this can be done without breach of the peace." The constitutionality of this provision was thrown somewhat in doubt by the holding in Fuentes v. Shevin, 407 U.S. 67 (1972), that a statutory replevin procedure allowing the taking of repossession without notice or hearing and without judicial order or supervision is unconstitutional. The principle in *Fuentes* seemed to be restricted in Mitchell v. W.T. Grant Co., 416 U.S. 600 (1974) (sequestration), but was substantially restored by North

Georgia Finishing, Inc. v. Di–Chem, Inc., 419 U.S. 601 (1975) (garnishment). While there is some disagreement, it seems likely that the UCC provision will be upheld. See Shirley v. State Nat'l Bank of Connecticut, 493 F.2d 739 (2d Cir. 1974), cert. denied, 419 U.S. 1009 (1974); and see the extensive symposium in 47 So.Cal.L.Rev. 1–164 (1973).

BONKOWSKI v. ARLAN'S DEPARTMENT STORE

See p. 43 n. 5

Court of Appeals of Michigan, 1968.
12 Mich.App. 88, 162 N.W.2d 347.

NEAL E. FITZGERALD, JUDGE. This appeal from a jury verdict for false arrest and slander, rendered against the defendant store whose agent stopped and questioned the plaintiff whom he suspected of larceny, surprisingly presents questions that are novel to the appellate courts of this jurisdiction.

The plaintiff, Mrs. Marion Bonkowski, accompanied by her husband, had left the defendant's Saginaw, Michigan store about 10:00 p.m. on the night of December 18, 1962 after making several purchases, when Earl Reinhardt, a private policeman on duty that night in the defendant's store, called to her to stop as she was walking to her car about 30 feet away in the adjacent parking lot. Reinhardt motioned to the plaintiff to return toward the store and when she had done so, Reinhardt said that someone in the store had told him the plaintiff had put three pieces of costume jewelry into her purse without having paid for them. Mrs. Bonkowski denied she had taken anything unlawfully, but Reinhardt told her he wanted to see the contents of her purse. On a cement step in front of the store, plaintiff emptied the contents of her purse into her husband's hands. The plaintiff produced sales slips for the items she had purchased, and Reinhardt, satisfied that she had not committed larceny, returned to the store.

Plaintiff brought this action against Earl Reinhardt and Arlan's Department Store, seeking damages on several counts. She complains that as a result of defendant's tortious acts she has suffered numerous psychosomatic symptoms, including headaches, nervousness, and depression. Arlan's Department Store filed a third-party complaint against Earl Reinhardt's employer, Gerald Kaweck, doing business as Michigan Security Police Service, who defaulted. On the counts of false arrest and slander the case went to the jury, who returned a verdict of $43,750. The defendant's motions for judgment notwithstanding the verdict, remittitur, and new trial were denied by the trial court. * * *

We conclude the plaintiff established a case entitling her to go to the jury on a charge of false arrest. [The court first concluded that the private policeman Reinhardt was the agent of defendant department store, which was responsible for his acts.]

To the common-law tort of false arrest, privilege is a common-law defense, and we recognize as applicable here a privilege similar to that recognized by the American Law Institute in the Restatement (Second) of Torts. In section 120A, the Institute recognizes a privilege in favor of a merchant to detain for reasonable investigation a person whom he reasonably believes to have taken a chattel unlawfully. We adopt the concept embodied in section 120A, and we state the rule for this action as follows: if defendant Arlan's agent, Earl Reinhardt, reasonably believed the plaintiff had unlawfully taken goods held for sale in the defendant's store, then he enjoyed a privilege to detain her for a reasonable investigation of the facts.

The Commissioners' [sic; Institute's] comment states the strong reason behind recognizing such a privilege:

"The privilege stated in this section is necessary for the protection of a shopkeeper against the dilemma in which he would otherwise find himself when he reasonably believes that a shoplifter has taken goods from his counter. If there were no such privilege, he must either permit the suspected person to walk out of the premises and disappear, or must arrest him, at the risk of liability for false arrest if the theft could not be proved." 1 Restatement (Second) of Torts, page 202.

That the problem of shoplifting, faced by merchants, has reached serious dimensions is common knowledge, and we find compelling reason to recognize such a privilege, similar to that recognized in other jurisdictions. [Cc]

In Montgomery Ward & Co., Inc., v. Freeman, the United States Court of Appeals for the Fourth Circuit, in a case arising in Virginia and involving a detention considerably longer than the detention here of [Mrs.] Bonkowski, reversed a verdict for the plaintiff because of the trial court's too narrow instruction on the point of justifiable detention and sent the case back, stating that "the instruction should submit the reasonableness of the detention to the jury and should set out the facts which, if found, would constitute reasonable grounds for the defendant's conduct." 199 F.2d 720, 724.

The privilege we recognize here goes beyond that set forth in the Restatement, for the Commissioners [sic] there stated a caveat that "the Institute expresses no opinion as to whether there may be circumstances under which this privilege may extend to the detention of one who has left the premises but is in their immediate vicinity." 1 Restatement (Second) of Torts page 202.

In their comment, the Commissioners [sic] state that, by their caveat, in the absence of express authority, they intended to leave the question open. 1 Restatement (Second) of Torts page 204. We think the privilege should be so extended here because we think it entirely reasonable to apply it to the circumstances of the case at bar, for the reason that a merchant may not be able to form the reasonable belief justifying a detention for a reasonable investigation before a suspected person has left the premises. In *Montgomery Ward*, supra, the court recognized the privilege as applicable even though the plaintiff was stopped by a manager after she had left the store.

On remand, on the cause for false arrest, therefore, it will be the duty of the jury to determine in accordance with the rule we have set down, whether or not the defendant's agent, Earl Reinhardt, reasonably believed the plaintiff had unlawfully taken any goods held for sale at the defendant's store. If the jury finds the defendant's agent did so reasonably believe, then it must further determine whether the investigation that followed was reasonable under all the circumstances. If the jury finds the defendant does not come within this privilege, then from the facts as discussed above, it could find a false arrest. * * *

Reversed and remanded for new trial in accordance with this opinion. The award of costs to await final determination of the cause.

[In Bonkowski v. Arlan's Department Store, 383 Mich. 90, 174 N.W. 2d 765 (1970), the Supreme Court of Michigan dismissed the false imprisonment claim on the ground that there was insufficient evidence that defendant intended to take plaintiff into custody. In dictum, the court affirmed the existence of the privilege.]

---

1. Shoplifting is a major problem for merchants. It costs them, in the aggregate, millions of dollars every year, which the public of course pays. It puts the merchant in the dilemma that, if he has the suspected person arrested he may be liable for false imprisonment if it turns out that there was no theft or if a jury fails to convict, while if he does nothing, and permits the suspect to walk out, the merchandise and all hope of proof will disappear forever.

2. Although some states have adopted this privilege by case law (see Collyer v. S.H. Kress Co., 5 Cal.2d 175, 54 P.2d 20 (1936)), it is statutory in many jurisdictions. The scope of the privilege differs in the various states and it is hazardous for an attorney to advise a client about the privilege without researching the current state law. Among the more important variables are:

A. Whether force can be utilized and, if so, how much. The Restatement would allow reasonable force short of bodily harm. A "request" to stay must be made if it is practicable to do so. See Restatement (Second) of Torts § 120A, Comment k. If the merchant is not allowed to use force, is the privilege of any real benefit?

B. What constitutes "reasonable grounds" or "probable cause" to detain a shopper and whether that issue is to be decided by the court or a jury. See Moore v. Pay'N Save Corp., 20 Wash.App. 482, 581 P.2d 159 (1978), and Annot., 47 A.L.R.3d 989 (1973).

C. What constitutes a reasonable time or manner of detention? Most courts would agree that defendant is liable when he demands a signed confession, and says that he will detain the plaintiff until it is signed. Moffatt v. Buffums', Inc., 21 Cal.App.2d 371, 69 P.2d 424 (1937); W.T. Grant Co. v. Owens, 149 Va. 906, 141 S.E. 860 (1928). Defendant also is liable when he threatens to detain the plaintiff until he pays. Cox v. Rhodes Avenue Hospital, 198 Ill.App. 82 (1916).

D. Whether the privilege should extend beyond the premises. Should the answer to this problem vary with the type of business in which the defendant is engaged?

E. Who is entitled to the privilege? Some states have extended the privilege beyond merchants to suppliers of services when defendant has failed to pay. See Standish v. Narragansett S.S. Co., 111 Mass. 512, 15 Am.Rep. 66 (1873).

3. The privilege is one of investigation only. If the defendant purports to arrest the plaintiff, he is liable if he does not have the legal authority to do so. Lindquist v. Friedman's, Inc., 366 Ill. 232, 8 N.E.2d 625 (1937). And also if the plaintiff is assaulted or bullied.

4. The merchant's privilege usually does not protect him against an action for slander, and if he accuses the suspect in front of others he may be subject to liability for defamation.

Re-entry Upon Real Property

5. May one use force to retake possession of real property? A minority of states permit an individual who has the legal right to immediate possession of land to attempt to retake possession by use of reasonable force short of causing death or serious injury. See Shorter v. Shelton, 183 Va. 819, 33 S.E.2d 643 (1945).

6. Most states provide the lawful owner with a quick and inexpensive remedy usually called "Forcible Entry and Detainer." This fact has led a growing number of courts to hold that the rightful owner can retake possession of his land only if he does not use force. Further, the party in peaceful possession may have a claim for assault and battery or trespass to his goods occurring in the course of a forcible entry. See Lobdell v. Keene, 85 Minn. 90, 88 N.W. 426 (1901). A claim for intentional infliction of emotional harm has been allowed when the invading owner's conduct was extreme and outrageous. See Daluiso v. Boone, 71 Cal.2d 484, 455 P.2d 811, 78 Cal.Rptr. 707 (1969).

7. The basic policy decision inherent in these cases can be traced to a 1381 statute, 5 Richard II, c. 2, which made it a criminal offense for one entitled to possession of land to enter and recover it by force. Aside from a temporary aberration in Newton v. Harland, 1 Man. & G. 644, 133 Eng.Rep. 490 (1840), however, the English courts did not utilize the statute to allow the party in peaceful possession a civil claim against the invader. See Turner v. Meymott, 1 Bing. 158, 130 Eng.Rep. 64 (1823), and Hemmings v. Stoke Poges Golf Club, [1920] 1 K.B. 720. The English law is thus contrary to the majority American rule.

8. If a tenant consents in the lease to a forcible entry by the landlord in the case of non-payment of rent, should that agreement shield the landlord from liability based on an invasion? See Princess Amusement Co. v. Smith, 174 Ala. 342, 56 So. 979 (1911); Goshen v. People, 22 Colo. 270, 44 P. 503 (1896); Backus v. West, 104 Or. 129, 205 P. 533 (1922).

6. NECESSITY *Read*

Read Reporter
— Was case ok trespass damages or gov'H
"takings" compensation.
Apparently, both are denied. See n.3.

Public necessity = not liable

SUROCCO v. GEARY

Supreme Court of California, 1853.
3 Cal. 69, 58 Am.Dec. 385.

MURRAY, CHIEF JUSTICE. This was an action, commenced in the court below, to recover damages for blowing up and destroying the plaintiffs' house and property, during the fire of the 24th of December, 1849.

Geary, at that time Alcalde of San Francisco, justified, on the ground that he had authority, by virtue of his office, to destroy said building, and also that it had been blown up by him to stop the progress *of fire* of the conflagration then raging.

It was in proof, that the fire passed over and burned beyond the building of the plaintiffs', and that at the time said building was destroyed, they were engaged in removing their property, and could, had they not been prevented, have succeeded in removing more, if not all of their goods.

The cause was tried by the court sitting as a jury, and a verdict *Trct = Π* rendered for the plaintiffs, from which the defendant prosecutes this *Sct = revd/a* appeal under the Practice Act of 1850.

The only question for our consideration is, whether the person who Ⓘ tears down or destroys the house of another, in good faith, and under apparent necessity, during the time of a conflagration, for the purpose of saving the buildings adjacent, and stopping its progress, can be held personally liable in an action by the owner of the property destroyed.

*   *   *

The right to destroy property, to prevent the spread of a conflagra- *G/R* tion, has been traced to the highest law of necessity, and the natural rights of man, independent of society or civil government. "It is referred by moralists and jurists to the same great principle which justifies the exclusive appropriation of a plank in a shipwreck, though the life of another be sacrificed; with the throwing overboard goods in a tempest, for the safety of a vessel; with the trespassing upon the lands of another, to escape death by an enemy. It rests upon the maxim, *Necessitas inducit privilegium quod jura privata* " [Necessity provides a privilege for private rights].

The common law adopts the principles of the natural law, and places the justification of an act otherwise tortious precisely on the same ground of necessity. [C] *(what necessity was at play?)*

This principle has been familiarly recognized by the books from the time of the saltpetre case, and the instances of tearing down houses to prevent a conflagration, or to raise bulwarks for the defense of a city, are made use of as illustrations, rather than as abstract cases, in which its exercise is permitted. At such times, the individual rights of property give way to the higher laws of impending necessity.

A house on fire, or those in its immediate vicinity, which serve to communicate the flames, becomes a nuisance, which it is lawful to abate, and the private rights of the individual yield to the considerations of general convenience, and the interests of society. Were it otherwise, one stubborn person might involve a whole city in ruin, by *RTL* refusing to allow the destruction of a building which would cut off the flames and check the progress of the fire, and that, too, when it was perfectly evident that his building must be consumed. * * *

The counsel for the respondent has asked, who is to judge of the necessity of the destruction of property?

This must, in some instances, be a difficult matter to determine. The necessity of blowing up a house may not exist, or be as apparent to the owner, whose judgment is clouded by interest, and the hope of saving his property, as to others. In all such cases the conduct of the individual must be regulated by his own judgment as to the exigencies of the case. If a building should be torn down without apparent or actual necessity, the parties concerned would undoubtedly be liable in an action of trespass. But in every case the necessity must be clearly shown. It is true, many cases of hardship may grow out of this rule, and property may often in such cases be destroyed, without necessity, by irresponsible persons, but this difficulty would not be obviated by making the parties responsible in every case, whether the necessity existed or not.

The legislature of the State possess the power to regulate this subject by providing the manner in which buildings may be destroyed, and the mode in which compensation shall be made; and it is to be hoped that something will be done to obviate the difficulty, and prevent the happening of such events as those supposed by the respondent's counsel.

In the absence of any legislation on the subject, we are compelled to fall back upon the rules of the common law.

The evidence in this case clearly establishes the fact, that the blowing up of the house was necessary, as it would have been consumed had it been left standing. The plaintiffs cannot recover for the value of the goods which they might have saved; they were as much subject to the necessities of the occasion as the house in which they were situate; and if in such cases a party was held liable, it would too frequently happen, that the delay caused by the removal of the goods would render the destruction of the house useless.

The court below clearly erred as to the law applicable to the facts of this case. The testimony will not warrant a verdict against the defendant.

Judgment reversed.

---

1. Defendant is fighting a forest fire that threatens an entire county. From an airplane he sprays fire-retardant chemicals onto plaintiff's land, which damage plaintiff's timber. Is defendant liable? Stocking v. Johnson Flying Service, 143 Mont. 61, 387 P.2d 312 (1963).

2. Defendant, a public officer, burns the clothing worn by a person who has died of smallpox. Is he liable to the new owner of the clothing? Cf. Seavey v. Preble, 64 Me. 120 (1874); State v. Mayor of Knoxville, 80 Tenn. 146, 47 Am.

Rep. 331 (1883). Putnam v. Payne, 13 Johns. (N.Y.) 312 (1816) (shooting mad dog in the street).

3. In December, 1941, the United States Army destroyed stored petroleum, terminal facilities, and vital parts of the plant of an oil company in Manila, in order to prevent them from falling into the hands of the advancing Japanese army. It was held that this was privileged, and not a compensable taking for public use, the theory of the majority being that it was not the Army's conduct but an act of war that was the cause of the destruction. See United States v. Caltex, Inc., 344 U.S. 149 (1952). Contra, that the Crown has no such privilege, Burmah Oil Co., Ltd. v. Lord Advocate, [1964] 2 All E.R. 348. *— Saddam/Iraq, was not ↓ precedent* *— after revolution, U.S. sovereign, attained more sovereignty than Crown?*

4. To be privileged, must the defendant be a public officer? In Harrison v. Wisdom, 54 Tenn. 99 (1872), private citizens of the town of Clarksville, Tenn., destroyed all the liquor in the town just before the entry of the Union army. It *God save the liquor?* was held that the court properly charged the jury that if they found that there was imminent impending danger, and a real public necessity, this was privileged. To the same effect is Restatement (Second) of Torts §§ 196 and 262. Suppose it only appeared to be necessary.

5. If the "champion of the public" is not to be held liable, should not the city or other community whose interests he protects be required to make compensation to the plaintiff? See Hall and Wigmore, Compensation for Property Destroyed to Stop the Spread of a Conflagration, 1 Ill.L.Rev. 501 (1907), written just after the San Francisco earthquake of 1906.

In the past, governmental immunity has prevented liability, but as indicated in Chapter 12, that doctrine is rapidly disappearing from the law. When governmental immunity is abrogated, however, the state is usually deemed liable "in the same manner and to the same extent as a private individual under like circumstances." See 28 U.S.C.A. § 2674 (Federal Tort Claims Act). Is this approach sensible in regard to the privilege of public necessity?

Some jurisdictions have provided for compensation by statute.

6. Do the constitutional provisions against taking private property for public use without due compensation have any application here?

7. Should the principle of necessity apply to destruction of personal property? See South Dakota Dept. of Health v. Heim, 357 N.W.2d 522 (S.D.1984) (state destroyed plaintiff's herd of elk which were suffering from a contagious disease). *If 'it burns, then insurance; if destroyed to prevent more fire, no ins. (?)*

8. What about fire insurance? For years the policies excepted destruction of property to prevent spread of fire. The Standard Fire Insurance Policy now provides that the policy does not apply to destruction by order of public authorities, except to prevent spread of fire caused by a reason not excluded. Does this take care of the problem?

Private necessity = liable

VINCENT v. LAKE ERIE TRANSP. CO.
Supreme Court of Minnesota, 1910.
109 Minn. 456, 124 N.W. 221.

(1) whether π can recover when Δ deliberately acted out of necessity, deliberately mooring ship to π's dock, damaging π.
Subj - Must Δ stay w/ ship even in a tempestuous storm?
Tract = π

Action by R.C. Vincent and others against the Lake Erie Transportation Company. Verdict for plaintiffs. From an order denying a new trial, defendant appeals.

O'BRIEN, J. The steamship Reynolds, owned by the defendant, was for the purpose of discharging her cargo on November 27, 1905, moored to plaintiff's dock in Duluth. While the unloading of the boat was taking place a (storm) from the northeast developed, which at about 10 o'clock p.m., when the unloading was completed, had so grown in violence that the wind was then moving at 50 miles per hour and continued to increase during the night. There is some evidence that one, and perhaps two, boats were able to enter the harbor that night, but it is plain that navigation was practically suspended from the hour mentioned until the morning of the 29th, when the storm abated, and during that time no master would have been justified in attempting to navigate his vessel, if he could avoid doing so. After the discharge of the cargo the Reynolds signaled for a tug to tow her from the dock, but none could be obtained because of the severity of the storm. If the lines holding the ship to the dock had been cast off, she would doubtless have drifted away; but, instead, the lines were kept fast, and as soon as one parted or chafed it was replaced, sometimes with a larger one. The vessel lay upon the outside of the dock, her bow to the east, the wind and waves striking her starboard quarter with such force that she was constantly being lifted and thrown against the dock, resulting in its damage, as found by the jury, to the amount of $500.

We are satisfied that the character of the storm was such that it would have been highly imprudent for the master of the Reynolds to have attempted to leave the dock or to have permitted his vessel to drift away from it. * * * Nothing more was demanded of them than ordinary prudence and care, and the record in this case fully sustains the contention of the appellant that, in holding the vessel fast to the dock, those in charge of her exercised good judgment and prudent seamanship. * * *

The appellant contends by ample assignments of error that, because its conduct during the storm was rendered necessary by prudence and good seamanship under conditions over which it had no control, it cannot be held liable for any injury resulting to the property of others, and claims that the jury should have been so instructed. An analysis of the charge given by the trial court is not necessary, as in our opinion the only question for the jury was the amount of damages which the plaintiffs were entitled to recover, and no complaint is made upon that score.

The situation was one in which the ordinary rules regulating property rights were suspended by forces beyond human control, and if, without the direct intervention of some act by the one sought to be held liable, the property of another was injured, such injury must be attributed to the (act of God) and not to the wrongful act of the person sought to be charged. If during the storm the Reynolds had entered the harbor, and while there had become disabled and been thrown against the plaintiffs' dock, the plaintiffs could not have recovered. Again, if while attempting to hold fast to the dock the lines had parted, without any negligence, and the vessel carried against some other boat or dock in the harbor, there would be no liability upon her owner. But here those in charge of the vessel deliberately and by their direct efforts held her in such a position that the damage to the dock resulted, and, having thus preserved the ship at the expense of the dock, it seems to us that her owners are responsible to the dock owners to the extent of the injury inflicted.   *   *   *

In Ploof v. Putnam, 81 Vt. 471, 71 A. 188 (1908), the Supreme Court of Vermont held that where, under stress of weather, a vessel was without permission moored to a private dock at an island in Lake Champlain owned by the defendant, the plaintiff was not guilty of trespass, and that the defendant was responsible in damages because his representative upon the island unmoored the vessel, permitting it to drift upon the shore, with resultant injuries to it. If, in that case, the vessel had been permitted to remain, and the dock had suffered an injury, we believe the shipowner would have been held liable for the injury done.

Theologians hold that a starving man may, without moral guilt, take what is necessary to sustain life; but it could hardly be said that the obligation would not be upon such person to pay the value of the property so taken when he became able to do so. And so public necessity, in times of war or peace, may require the taking of private property for public purposes; but under our system of jurisprudence compensation must be made.

Let us imagine in this case that for the better mooring of the vessel those in charge of her had appropriated a valuable cable lying upon the dock. No matter how justifiable such appropriation might have been, it would not be claimed that, because of the overwhelming necessity of the situation, the owner of the cable could not recover its value.

This is not a case where life or property was menaced by any object or thing belonging to the plaintiff, the destruction of which became necessary to prevent the threatened disaster. Nor is it a case where, because of the act of God, or unavoidable accident, the infliction of the injury was beyond the control of the defendant, but is one where the defendant prudently and advisedly availed itself of the plaintiff's property for the purpose of preserving its own more valuable property, and the plaintiffs are entitled to compensation for the injury done.

Order affirmed.

[The dissenting opinion of LEWIS, J. is omitted.]

---

1. The cases all appear to be in agreement with the principal case. See Newcomb v. Tisdale, 62 Cal. 575 (1881); Bohlen, Incomplete Privilege to Inflict Intentional Invasions of Interests of Property and Personality, 39 Harv.L.Rev. 307 (1926). See also Restatement (Second) of Torts, §§ 197 and 263. If defendant has not been at fault, why should he pay? For one view, see Fletcher, Fairness and Utility in Tort Doctrine, 85 Harv.L.Rev. 537, 546 (1972). Might the same approach be followed in regard to other privileges, such as self defense?

Public or Private necessity? — Who decides?

Ⓝ 2. What result in the principal case if it was necessary to moor the vessel to allow crewmen to escape onto land? See Mouse's Case, 12 Co.Rep. 63, 77 Eng.Rep. 1341 (1609).

Ⓝ 3. A traveler upon the public highway is normally held to be privileged to turn out to avoid an obstruction, and to pass over the abutting land. Morey v. Fitzgerald, 56 Vt. 487, 48 Am.Rep. 511 (1884); Irwin v. Yeagar, 74 Iowa 174, 37 N.W. 136 (1888). Also Dodwell v. Missouri Pac. R. Co., 384 S.W.2d 643 (Mo. 1964) (boy crawling through train that blocked crossing).

Extortioner sued?

Ⓝ 4. An extortioner threatens to drop a package of explosives if not paid $1 million. Defendant's negotiations fail and the extortioner drops the package. (1) Defendant leaps behind the plaintiff and is protected. (2) He pulls the plaintiff in front of him. Cf. Laidlaw v. Sage, 158 N.Y. 73, 52 N.E. 679 (1899).

Ⓝ 5. Should the necessity privilege ever extend to the taking of life? In criminal law the answer has generally been "No." Thus, in Arp v. State, 97 Ala. 5, 12 So. 301 (1893), the court affirmed the trial court's refusal to allow the defendant to be excused on the basis that two other men armed with shotguns had been present and threatened to kill him unless he murdered the deceased. On the other hand, § 2.09 of the Model Penal Code permits coercion as a defense if the force or threat of force was such that a person "of reasonable firmness in his situation would be unable to resist." Which is the better approach in tort law? With the Arp case, compare Crabtree v. Dawson, supra page 108. Are the two distinguishable?

6. In Regina v. Dudley, 15 Cox C.C. 624, 14 Q.B.D. 273 (1884), four survivors of a shipwreck were adrift in an open boat, a thousand miles from land, and dying of hunger. Three of them killed the fourth, a boy, and ate him. They were held criminally liable for his death. In United States v. Holmes, 1 Wall.Jr. 1, Fed.Cas. No. 15,383 (E.D.Pa.1842), after a passenger ship had hit an iceberg and sunk, nine members of her crew and thirty-two passengers were adrift in a badly overloaded lifeboat. The wind freshened, the sea began to rise, and the boat was in imminent danger of being swamped. The crew then threw overboard six of the passengers to lighten the boat. The following morning the survivors were rescued by a passing ship. Holmes, who had taken a leading part in throwing the passengers over, was tried for manslaughter, convicted and sentenced to hard labor for a long term, which the court subsequently reduced to six months. The president later remitted the sentence. The story is told in full in Hicks, Human Jettison (1927). What should be the position of tort law in these situations?

7. For an exhaustive and most stimulating discussion about the theoretical jurisprudence of many of these problems, see Fuller, The Case of the Speluncean Explorers, 62 Harv.L.Rev. 616 (1949).

7. AUTHORITY OF LAW *disregard*

The defense of legal authority is a subject for a course, a casebook or a text in itself. It can only be touched on here.

If the defendant is duly commanded or authorized by law to do what he does, he is of course not liable for doing it. The problem is to discover how far the legal sanction extends. A case illustrating how easily a physician can fall into error and be subject to liability when he attempts to justify his conduct under a state commitment statute is

Stowers v. Wolodzko, 386 Mich. 119, 191 N.W.2d 355 (1971). A good study of the matter is Jennings, Tort Liability of Administrative Officers, 21 Minn.L.Rev. 263 (1937); see also Restatement (Second) of Torts § 895D.

A distinction is commonly made between acts (1) that call for administrative judgment, such as those of a prosecuting attorney in deciding whether to seek an indictment, or a school board dismissing a pupil, which are called "discretionary" or "quasi-judicial," and (2) those requiring less personal judgment, such as remitting a prisoner to jail or dipping sheep, which are called "ministerial" only.

This subject is treated further in Chapter 12, Section 3(E).

Arrest

One common form of action under authority of law is arrest of the person, which consists of taking him into the custody of the law. An arrest may be made under a warrant, which is a signed order issued by a court directing that the person in question be arrested; or it may be made without a warrant.

Arrest under a warrant, or the seizure of goods under civil process, to which the same rules apply, is an act generally considered to be "ministerial," so that the officer is liable if he acts improperly. If the court issuing the warrant is entirely without jurisdiction to do it, it is commonly held that the invalid order affords the officer no protection. Warren v. Kelly, 80 Me. 512, 15 A. 49 (1888); Smith v. Hilton, 147 Ala. 642, 41 So. 747 (1906). But if the court has general jurisdiction to issue similar process, it is generally held that the officer is privileged if the warrant is "fair on its face," even though there may be errors and irregularities in its issue that affect the jurisdiction of the court in the particular case. Vittorio v. St. Regis Paper Co., 239 N.Y. 148, 145 N.E. 913 (1924); David v. Larochelle, 296 Mass. 302, 5 N.E.2d 571 (1936).

Even if the warrant is entirely valid, however, it does not protect the officer unless he carries out the order given him, even though he makes a perfectly reasonable mistake in good faith. Thus an officer who has a warrant for the arrest of A, and who reasonably believes B to be A and arrests him, is liable to B for false arrest.

Arrest without a warrant normally is covered in the course in criminal law. It may be made by a police officer, or by a private citizen. The common law imposed limitations upon the authority of each, with that of the private citizen, as might be expected, more narrowly restricted. The original common law rules concerning arrest without a warrant were as follows:

1. Either an officer or a citizen may arrest without a warrant to prevent a felony, or a breach of the peace that is being committed or reasonably appears about to be committed, in his presence.

2. An officer may make an arrest if he has information that affords reasonable grounds for thinking that a felony has been committed and that he has the right criminal.

3. The citizen may arrest without a warrant if a felony has in fact been committed, and he has reasonable grounds to suspect the man he arrests; but his authority depends upon the fact of the crime, and he must take the full risk if none has been committed.

4. For a past breach of the peace that is not a felony, an officer or a citizen may arrest without a warrant only if the offense was committed in his presence and he is in fresh pursuit.

5. For mere misdemeanors the old common law rule was that neither the officer nor the citizen could arrest without a warrant. This has now been modified in some jurisdictions to extend the power to an officer when the misdemeanor is committed in his presence.

These common law rules have been extensively changed by the modern penal codes, and, for any particular jurisdiction, reference must be made to the statutes.

There is a good Note on all this in 65 Colum.L.Rev. 502 (1965).

Assuming that an arrest would be lawful, an officer may also be subject to liability if he uses excessive force in the process of apprehending the suspect.

8. DISCIPLINE *disregard*

Parent and Child. There are a number of relations in which the necessity of some orderly discipline gives persons who have the control of others the privilege of exercising reasonable force and restraint upon them. One of the most important examples of this privilege is that given to a parent or one who is deemed to stand in place of a parent. See Clasen v. Pruhs, 69 Neb. 278, 95 N.W. 640 (1903); Fortinberry v. Holmes, 89 Miss. 373, 42 So. 799 (1907) (one caring for a child). See also cases collected in Annot., 19 A.L.R.2d 423, 451 (1951). The scope of the privilege was rarely tested for many years because parents were held to be immune from suits by their children. Interestingly enough, this very immunity arose in a case where a court may have been unwilling to delineate the scope of the privilege. See Hewlett v. George, 68 Miss. 703, 9 So. 885 (1891) (claim of false imprisonment).

Recently, a growing number of courts have abandoned the concept of tort immunity between parent and child, especially in the area of intentional torts. (For details, see Chapter 12, Section 3(A).) More cases dealing with the scope of this privilege may therefore arise in the future. In Gillett v. Gillett, 168 Cal.App.2d 102, 335 P.2d 736 (1959), an aunt who stood *in loco parentis* to a young child was held liable when she inflicted serious bodily injuries on the child in the course of disciplining her for an act of minor misbehavior. Are there practical reasons why there may not be too many cases of a child suing a parent even when immunity has been abolished? See Paulsen, Child Abuse

Reporting Laws—The Scope of the Legislation, 67 Colum.L.Rev. 1 (1967).

While some decisions have stated that a parent delegates his authority to discipline his child to a teacher when the youngster is in school, the teacher's privilege to discipline is more properly predicated on the need to maintain reasonable order in the classroom. See LaFrentz v. Gallagher, 105 Ariz. 255, 462 P.2d 804 (1969); Suits v. Glover, 260 Ala. 449, 71 So.2d 49 (1954). Thus it may be exercised even though the parent objects.

Most litigation has concerned the scope of the privilege. See Note, Right of a Teacher to Administer Corporal Punishment to a Student, 5 Washburn L.Rev. 75 (1965); Annot., 43 A.L.R.2d 469 (1955). It is not defined with precision.

First, there is some uncertainty as to whether it extends to activities conducted away from school that have only a slight connection with the educational program. See Annot., 53 A.L.R.3d 112 (1968).

Second, an instructor will be subject to liability for using "excessive" force. See Johnson v. Horace Mann Mut. Ins. Co., 241 So.2d 588 (La.App.1970). Significant variables gleaned from the cases include: (1) the nature of the punishment, (2) the conduct of the student, (3) the age and physical condition of the student, and (4) the motive of the instructor, e.g., did he act in anger or out of dislike, rather than in an attempt to discipline. See Story v. Martin, 217 So.2d 758 (La.App.1969); Tinkham v. Kole, 252 Iowa 1303, 110 N.W.2d 258 (1961).

Local school regulations may limit the teacher's privilege. See Simms v. School Dist. No. 1, 13 Or.App. 119, 508 P.2d 236 (1973).

The question of the constitutionality of school discipline was formally raised in Baker v. Owen, 395 F.Supp. 294 (M.D.N.C.), aff'd, 423 U.S. 907 (1975). The three-judge court held that it is not unconstitutional for teachers to administer reasonable corporal punishment for disciplinary purposes. Due process requires minimal procedural measures, including: (1) "except for those acts of misconduct which are so anti-social or disruptive in nature as to shock the conscience, corporal punishment may never be used unless the student was informed beforehand that specific misbehavior could occasion its use, and, subject to this exception, it should never be employed as a first line of punishment for misbehavior," (2) "a teacher or principal must punish corporally in the presence of a second school official (teacher or principal), who must be informed beforehand and in the student's presence of the reason for the punishment," and (3) "an official who has administered such punishment must provide the child's parent, upon request, a written explanation of his reasons and the name of the second official who was present." The punishment in question was held not to violate the Eighth Amendment prohibition of cruel and inhuman punishment. On corporal punishment in the public schools, see Ingraham v. Wright, 430 U.S. 651 (1977). Cf. Thomas v. Bedford, 389 So.2d 405 (La.App.1980).

Spouses. There was at one time a privilege in the husband to discipline his wife, by "moderate correction," "restraining" her by "domestic chastisement"—although there is probably no truth in the persistent legend that he was privileged to beat her with a stick "no thicker than his thumb." See Bradley v. State, 1 Miss. 156 (1824). This "gentle" rule for the preservation of family peace and harmony has long since been discarded, in the light of the altered status of married women in modern law; and in jurisdictions where husband and wife can sue one another for personal torts, the wife may recover without the defense of any such privilege.

Others. Other examples of the privilege of discipline are those of military and naval officers over their subordinates, which are largely governed by military law and dealt with by courts martial; and the authority of the master of a ship over both the crew and the passengers. Again the privilege, in the latter case, is limited to force reasonable under the circumstances; and the captain will be liable if he puts a passenger in irons for calling him the landlord of a floating hotel. King v. Franklin, 1 F. & F. 360, 175 Eng.Rep. 764 (1858).

9. JUSTIFICATION IN GENERAL *Read*

SINDLE v. NEW YORK CITY TRANSIT AUTHORITY

New York Court of Appeals, 1973.
33 N.Y.2d 293, 307 N.E.2d 245, 352 N.Y.S.2d 183.

JASEN, JUDGE. At about noon on June 20, 1967, the plaintiff, then 14 years of age, boarded a school bus owned by the defendant, New York City Transit Authority, and driven by its employee, the defendant Mooney. It was the last day of the term at the Elias Bernstein Junior High School in Staten Island and the 65 to 70 students on board the bus were in a boisterous and exuberant mood. Some of this spirit expressed itself in vandalism, a number of students breaking dome lights, windows, ceiling panels and advertising poster frames. There is no evidence that the plaintiff partook in this destruction.

The bus made several stops at appointed stations. On at least one occasion, the driver admonished the students about excessive noise and damage to the bus. When he reached the Annadale station, the driver discharged several more passengers, went to the rear of the bus, inspected the damage and advised the students that he was taking them to the St. George police station.

The driver closed the doors of the bus and proceeded, bypassing several normal stops. * * *

The plaintiff, joined with his father, then commenced an action to recover damages for * * * false imprisonment. * * * At the close of the plaintiffs' case, the court denied defendants' motion to amend their answers to plead the defense of justification. The court also excluded all evidence bearing on the justification issue.

TrCt = π
Ct App = rev'd

Procedural Holding

We believe that it was an abuse of discretion for the trial court to deny the motion to amend and to exclude the evidence of justification. It was the defendants' burden to prove justification—a defense that a plaintiff in an action for false imprisonment should be prepared to meet—and the plaintiffs could not have been prejudiced by the granting of the motion to amend. The trial court's rulings precluded the defendants from introducing any evidence in this regard and were manifestly unfair. Accordingly, the order of the Appellate Division must be reversed and a new trial granted.

In view of our determination, it would be well to outline some of the considerations relevant to the issue of justification. In this regard, we note that, generally, restraint or detention, reasonable under the circumstances and in time and manner, imposed for the purpose of preventing another from inflicting personal injuries or interfering with or damaging real or personal property in one's lawful possession or custody is not unlawful. (Cf. Penal Law, §§ 35.20, 35.25; see, also, General Business Law, § 218, which affords a retail merchant a defense to an action for false arrest and false imprisonment where a suspected shoplifter is reasonably detained for investigation or questioning.) Also, a parent, guardian or teacher entrusted with the care or supervision of a child may use physical force reasonably necessary to maintain discipline or promote the welfare of the child. (Penal Law, § 35.10.) — *New York, 1973*

Similarly, a school bus driver, entrusted with the care of his student-passengers and the custody of public property, has the duty to take reasonable measures for the safety and protection of both—the passengers and the property. In this regard, the reasonableness of his actions—as bearing on the defense of justification—is to be determined from a consideration of all the circumstances. At a minimum, this would seem to import, a consideration of the need to protect the persons and property in his charge, the duty to aid the investigation and apprehension of those inflicting damage, the manner and place of the occurrence, and the feasibility and practicality of other alternative courses of action. * * *

For the reasons stated, the order of the Appellate Division should be reversed and the case remitted for a new trial.

---

1. What privileges did the court rely on "by analogy"? Are there others—not mentioned by the court—that might be relevant? For a recent case that cited *Sindle*, see Matter of Malone, 105 A.D.2d 455, 480 N.Y.S.2d 603 (1984) (attorney raised defense of justification in that he had been acting in his "official" capacity as Inspector General when he advised client to testify falsely).

2. Can you think of other examples of conduct that might "justify" an apparent intentional tort although they do not fit within the traditional common law privileges discussed in this chapter?

3. In Peterson v. Sorlien, 299 N.W.2d 123 (Minn.1980), cert. denied, 450 U.S. 1031 (1981), the Supreme Court of Minnesota held that the parent-child

relationship justified limitations the defendant parents placed upon their adult child's mobility during "deprogramming" that would otherwise support a judgment of false imprisonment. See LeMoult, Deprogramming Members Of Religious Sects, 46 Fordham L.Rev. 599, 635 (1978). On the other hand, good intentions would not justify the unlawful restraint of a young girl even though the defendant sincerely believed that the girl's best interests would be served by the discipline imposed in a cloister. Gallon v. House of Good Shepherd, 158 Mich. 361, 122 N.W. 631 (1909). Cf. Smith v. Sisters of Good Shepherd, 87 S.W. 1083 (Ky.1905).

Chapter IV
NEGLIGENCE

1. HISTORY

Negligence was scarcely recognized as a separate tort before the earlier part of the nineteenth century. Prior to that time, the word had been used in a very general sense to describe the breach of any legal obligation, or to designate a mental element, usually one of inadvertence or inattention or indifference, entering into the commission of other torts. As a result, some writers once maintained that negligence was merely one way of committing any tort, just as some courts, for example, spoke occasionally of a negligent "battery."

One of the earliest appearances of what we now know as the tort of negligence was in the liability of those who professed to be competent in certain "public" callings. A carrier, an innkeeper, a blacksmith, or a surgeon was regarded as holding himself out to the public as one in whom confidence might be reposed, and hence as assuming an obligation to give proper service, for the breach of which, by any negligent conduct, he might be liable. But in other fields such as trespass and nuisance the idea developed, thinly disguised, that there might be liability for negligence; and in later years the action on the case produced a large, undigested group of situations in which negligence was the essence of the tort.

Somewhere around the year 1825, negligence began to emerge out of the action on the case, and to be recognized as a separate basis of tort liability, independent of other causes of action. Its rise coincided to a marked degree with the Industrial Revolution in England. "It was probably stimulated a good deal by the enormous increase of industrial machinery in general and by the invention of railways in particular. At that time railway trains were notable neither for speed nor for safety. They killed any object from a Minister of State to a wandering cow, and this naturally reacted upon the law." P. Winfield, Law of Tort 404 (5th ed. 1950).

The separate recognition of negligence was undoubtedly greatly encouraged by the disintegration of the old forms of action, and the disappearance of the distinction between direct and indirect injuries, found in trespass and case. Intentional injuries, whether direct or indirect, began to be grouped as a distinct field of liability, and negligence took separate form as the basis for unintended torts. Today, it is no longer disputed that distinct problems and principles, as well as distinct questions of policy, arise in negligence cases.

135

For the history of negligence in early law, and its development as an independent tort, see Winfield, The History of Negligence in the Law of Torts, 42 L.Q.Rev. 184 (1926); Wigmore, Responsibility for Tortious Acts: Its History, 7 Harv.L.Rev. 315, 441, 453 (1894).

2. ELEMENTS OF CAUSE OF ACTION

"Negligence" is the word used to describe the conduct of the defendant. But a cause of action for negligence requires more than negligent conduct. There must be a duty and there must be consequences. The traditional formula for the elements necessary to the cause of action includes the following:

1. A duty to use reasonable care. This is an obligation recognized by the law, requiring the actor to conform to a certain standard of conduct, for the protection of others against unreasonable risks.

2. A failure to conform to the required standard. This is commonly called breach of the duty. These two elements go to make up what the courts usually have called negligence; but the term frequently is applied to the second alone. Thus it may be said that the defendant was negligent, but is not liable because he was under no duty to the plaintiff not to be.

3. A reasonably close causal connection between the conduct and the resulting injury. This is commonly called "proximate cause," or sometimes "legal cause." It involves a combination of two elements—causation in fact, and legal limitation. They receive separate treatment in Chapters 5 and 6, infra.

4. Actual loss or damage resulting to the interests of another. The action for negligence developed chiefly out of the old form of action on the case; and it retained the rule of that action that pleading and proof of damage was an essential part of the plaintiff's case. While the modern law of torts has retained the requirement that proof of damage is an essential part of the law of negligence, the question of what is damage is less certain than it once was, e.g., is fear of getting a disease in the future damage? This will be explained in Chapters 5 and 6, infra.

It is clear that nominal damages to vindicate a technical right cannot be recovered in a negligence action if no actual damage has occurred. If defendant's risk-creating negligent conduct threatens but does not harm plaintiff, however, he may be able to obtain an injunction and stop the activity as a "nuisance."

3. A NEGLIGENCE FORMULA

LUBITZ v. WELLS
Superior Court of Connecticut, 1955.
19 Conn.Sup. 322, 113 A.2d 147.

Did father breach duty?

TROLAND, Judge.   The complaint alleges that James Wells was the owner of a golf club and that he left it for some time lying on the ground in the backyard of his home.   That thereafter his son, the defendant James Wells, Jr., aged eleven years, while playing in the yard with the plaintiff, Judith Lubitz, aged nine years, picked up the golf club and proceeded to swing at a stone lying on the ground.   In swinging the golf club, James Wells, Jr., caused the club to strike the plaintiff about the jaw and chin.

Negligence alleged against the young Wells boy is that he failed to warn his little playmate of his intention to swing the club and that he did swing the club when he knew she was in a position of danger.

In an attempt to hold the boy's father, James Wells, liable for his son's action, it is alleged that James Wells was negligent because although he knew the golf club was on the ground in his backyard and that his children would play with it, and that although he knew or "should have known" that the negligent use of the golf club by children would cause injury to a child, he neglected to remove the golf club from the backyard or to caution James Wells, Jr., against the use of the same.

The demurrer challenges the sufficiency of the allegations of the complaint to state a cause of action or to support a judgment against the father, James Wells.

what is ...?

It would hardly be good sense to hold that this golf club is so obviously and intrinsically dangerous that it is negligence to leave it lying on the ground in the yard.   The father cannot be held liable on the allegations of this complaint.   [Cc]

The demurrer is sustained.

---

1. Is a householder negligent for leaving in his backyard an object such as a baseball bat, or a hose with a nozzle, which one boy might pick up and swing at another?

2. Why might the boy be found negligent if the father was not?   What result if plaintiff had tripped over the club?   What if the article had been a hoe?   A loaded shotgun?   Cf. Johnson v. Krueger, 36 Colo.App. 242, 539 P.2d 1296 (1975).

3. A twelve-year-old boy lost his eye from a pellet fired from a slingshot manned by his eleven-year-old playmate.   Was it negligence to sell the slingshot?   See Moning v. Alfonso, 400 Mich. 425, 254 N.W.2d 759 (1977).

4. Defendant, facing a clear fairway, drove a golf ball from the tee without crying "Fore!"   The ball hooked badly, curved, and struck the plaintiff, who

was playing on another fairway 125 yards away. Is this negligence? Rose v. Morris, 97 Ga.App. 764, 104 S.E.2d 485 (1958). Is it negligence not to cry "Fore!" when the defendant sees the ball begin to hook?

5. Defendant parks his car on the edge of a city street without a curb, in front of a house where a mother and small child are sitting. He goes across the street to visit a friend there. He comes back in 20 minutes, gets in the car and drives off. There is a crunch and he stops to find that he had run over the toddler, who had crawled under the car. Was he negligent? Williams v. Jordan, 208 Tenn. 456, 346 S.W.2d 583 (1961).

BLYTH v. BIRMINGHAM WATERWORKS CO.

Court of Exchequer, 1856.
11 Exch. 781, 156 Eng.Rep. 1047.

[Defendant had installed water mains in the street, with fire plugs at various points. The plug opposite the plaintiff's house sprung a leak during a severe frost, because the connection between the plug and the water main was forced out by the expansion of freezing water. As a result, a large quantity of water escaped through the earth and into plaintiff's house, causing damage. The apparatus had been laid down 25 years ago, and had worked well during that time. The trial court left the question of defendant's negligence to the jury, which returned a verdict for plaintiff. Judgment was entered on the verdict, and defendant appealed.]

ALDERSON, B. I am of opinion that there was no evidence to be left to the jury. The case turns upon the question, whether the facts proved show that the defendants were guilty of negligence. Negligence is the omission to do something which a reasonable man, guided upon those considerations which ordinarily regulate the conduct of human affairs, would do or doing something which a prudent and reasonable man would not do. The defendants might have been liable for negligence, if unintentionally, they omitted to do that which a reasonable person would have done, or did that which a person taking reasonable precautions would not have done. A reasonable man would act with reference to the average circumstances of the temperature in ordinary years. The defendants had provided against such frosts as experience would have led men, acting prudently, to provide against; and they are not guilty of negligence, because their precautions proved insufficient against the effects of the extreme severity of the frost of 1855, which penetrated to a greater depth than any which ordinarily occurs south of the polar regions. Such a state of circumstances constitutes a contingency against which no reasonable man can provide. The result was an accident for which the defendants cannot be held liable.

Verdict to be entered for the defendants.

[The concurring opinions of MARTIN, B., and BRAMWELL, B., are omitted.]

1. In 1951, plaintiff's goods, in freight cars in the yards of defendant railroad company at Topeka, were destroyed by a flood that swept over the yards. There never had been any prior flood which had come anywhere near the yards; and when defendant first learned that the water was likely to reach them, it was too late to move the cars. Is defendant negligent in not moving them sooner? Ismert–Hincke Milling Co. v. Union Pacific R. Co., 238 F.2d 14 (10th Cir.1956).

2. Is a contractor constructing a building in Chicago required to take precautions against an earthquake? In San Francisco?

3. If the reasonable person will take into consideration foreseeable danger, does this involve anticipation, not only of an unusual natural force but also of a negligent act of a third person or a negligent act of the plaintiff?

4. May it be negligence to fail to take precautions against a stroke of lightning? Tex–Jersey Oil Corp. v. Beck, 292 S.W.2d 803 (Tex.Civ.App.1956).

GULF REFINING CO. v. WILLIAMS

Supreme Court of Mississippi, 1938.
183 Miss. 723, 185 So. 234.

Action by Willie Williams against the Gulf Refining Company and others for injuries allegedly resulting from defect in gasoline container which caused a fire. From a judgment for plaintiff, defendants appeal.

GRIFFITH, JUSTICE. Appellants are the distributors of petroleum products, including gasoline. Shortly before the injury here complained of, appellants, from their station at Canton, sold and delivered to a planter in that vicinity a drum of gasoline for use in farm tractors. Appellee was the planter's employee and was engaged in operating a tractor. The drum of gasoline had been taken to the field, but no attempt had been made to use it, until for the first time since its delivery, appellee undertook to remove the bunghole cap from the drum in order to replenish the fuel in the tractor, whereupon there was a sudden outburst of fire, caused, as the jury was justified in concluding upon the evidence, by a spark which was produced by the condition of unrepair in the threads of the bung cap, as will be later mentioned.

Appellee was severely burned by the sudden fire, and recovered judgment in an action therefor, from which judgment this appeal is prosecuted.

The chief argument of appellants is that the proof shows that an explosion or fire in drawing gasoline from a drum, when, or on account of, taking off the bung cap is an unusual, extraordinary and improbable occurrence, so much so that some of the witnesses say that no such happening had ever before been heard of by them; and that, therefore, appellant cannot be held liable as for a failure to anticipate the danger of any such improbable occurrence. And appellants call attention to language used by the courts wherein the declaration is made that there is no liability when the occurrence is unusual, extraordinary, and improbable. * * *

This general language has led to the occasional misunderstanding as to what may be termed the degree of probability which is meant by these expressions, as used in the law of negligence; and it is sometimes supposed and argued that unless such a foreseeable consequence is one which is more likely to happen than not to happen there can be no liability. * * *

When the inquiry is upon an issue whether a certain alleged fact existed or happened in the past, it is not sufficient to prove only or no more than a possibility, however substantial the possibility may be, so long as it is only a possibility. There the proof must establish the fact as a probability, using that word in its ordinary and common acceptation. * * * But when the inquiry is one of foreseeability, is as regards a thing that may happen in the future and to which the law of negligence holds a party to anticipation as a measure of duty, that inquiry is not whether the thing is to be foreseen or anticipated as one which will probably happen, according to the ordinary acceptation of that term, but whether it is likely to happen, even though the likelihood may not be sufficient to amount to a comparative probability. * * *

The test as respects foreseeability is not the balance of probabilities, but the existence, in the situation in hand, of some real likelihood of some damage and the likelihood is of such appreciable weight and moment as to induce, or which reasonably should induce, action to avoid it on the part of a person of a reasonably prudent mind.

The drum, or gasoline container, involved herein was of standard material, construction and manufacture, and of the kind in general use; and had it been in reasonably good repair there would, of course, be no liability. But the proof is that the drum had been in use nine years; that the threads in the bung plug or bung cap were broken, bent and jagged; that this condition had been brought about by repeated hammering on the bung cap during the course of its use,—a condition which had attracted the attention of one of appellants' employees before the container was sent out on this occasion. There is no adequate proof to show that appellee had equal knowledge or appreciation of the significance of this fact, or any knowledge which was sufficient to put the use at his risk as by the so-called assumption thereof, as contended for by appellants,—leaving aside whether, if the facts were otherwise, there would be assumption of risk, rather than contributory negligence.) [C] The proof is sufficient to show that a person of ordinary prudence, and mindful of the duty of cautious care with which appellants were charged, should have known of the condition aforesaid and should reasonably have anticipated, as a likelihood of weight and moment, that a sudden fire or explosion would be caused by the stated condition of unrepair; and hence appellants are liable for the injury to appellee which resulted.

Affirmed.

1. In Tullgren v. Amoskeag Mfg. Co., 82 N.H. 268, 133 A. 4 (1926), defendant escorted an employee with a "sick headache" home and left her to walk about 700 feet over a difficult road. On reaching her home she died. On motion for rehearing after reversing a directed verdict for defendant, the court said in part: "For a person to be careless it is not necessary that damage as a more rather than a less probable result should be anticipated. * * * Danger consists in the risk of harm, as well as the likelihood of it, and a danger calling for anticipation need not be of more probable occurrence than less. If there is some probability of harm sufficiently serious that ordinary men would take precautions to avoid it, then failure to do so is negligence. That the danger will more probably than otherwise not be encountered on a particular occasion does not dispense with the exercise of care. One who crosses a railroad track may not reasonably anticipate that a train will in fact be met but, by reason of the risk that one may be, he is called upon to do what is reasonably required to find out. In going around a sharp turn on a highway, where the view is obstructed, a driver may be careless toward opposite travel in speed or other ways, though the probabilities may be against meeting any one. If the chance is so great that ordinary men would drive differently, then it is careless not to do so. * * * The test is not of the balance of probabilities, but of the existence of some probability of sufficient moment to induce action to avoid it on the part of a reasonable mind."

2. An electric power company strung a copper wire along irregularly spaced poles. The wire blended into the autumn countryside. Should the company be liable when the wire is struck by a helicopter? See Arizona Public Service Co. v. Brittain, 107 Ariz. 278, 486 P.2d 176 (1971).

3. In Pease v. Sinclair Refining Co., 104 F.2d 183 (2d Cir.1939), plaintiff, a science teacher in a high school, wrote to defendant requesting an advertised free "science exhibit," consisting of bottles of petroleum products. Defendant sent him the exhibit, but one bottle, which was labeled "kerosene," was filled with water. Is this negligence?

4. In Paris v. Stepney Borough Council, [1951] A.C. 367, plaintiff, a man with one eye, was employed by defendant at garage work that required him on occasion to hammer on metal. Defendant did not supply him with goggles for the work. While he was hammering to drive out a rusty bolt, a chip flew off the bolt, struck him in the eye, and blinded him. Was this negligence? Suppose he had both eyes and one was blinded. Johnson v. Wichita Valley R. Co., 104 S.W.2d 128 (Tex.Civ.App.1950).

5. The toilet to a railway coach car was heated by steam passing through an uninsulated iron pipe that went around the corner under the lavatory. Plaintiff, a passenger, fainted and fell with her face against the pipe, seriously burning it. Is the railroad negligent? Hauser v. Chicago, Rhode Island & Pacific Ry., 205 Iowa 940, 219 N.W. 60 (1928).

CHICAGO, B. & Q.R. CO. v. KRAYENBUHL

Supreme Court of Nebraska, 1902.
65 Neb. 889, 91 N.W. 880.

[Action to recover for personal injuries sustained by plaintiff, a child four years old, in playing on a railroad turntable maintained by defendant. The trial resulted in a verdict and judgment for plaintiff, and defendant brings error.

The turntable was located between two branches of defendant's line. A path or footway, in common use by the general public and by plaintiff's family, passed within about 70 feet of the turntable. The turntable had a movable bolt by which it could be held in position and was provided with a padlock. The defendant's rules required its employees to keep the turntable locked when not in use, but there was evidence that this rule was frequently disregarded and that one of the staples was so loose that the turntable could be unfastened without difficulty. Plaintiff, in company with other young children, found the turntable unlocked and unguarded. Plaintiff got on the turntable, and when the other children set it in motion, plaintiff's foot was caught between the rails and severed at the ankle joint.

The court first held that the fact that the children were trespassers on the defendant's property did not deprive them of the right to enforce defendant's duty to use reasonable care to make its premises safe. As to this, see infra pages 478–82.]

ALBERT, C. * * * It is true, as said in Loomis v. Terry, 17 Wend. 497, 31 Am.Dec. 306, "the business of life must go forward"; the means by which it is carried forward cannot be rendered absolutely safe. * * * The business of life is better carried forward by the use of dangerous machinery; hence the public good demands its use, although occasionally such use results in the loss of life or limb. It does so because the danger is insignificant, when weighed against the benefits resulting from the use of such machinery and for the same reason demands its reasonable, most effective, and unrestricted use, up to the point where the benefits resulting from such use no longer outweigh the danger to be anticipated from it. At that point the public goods demands restrictions. For example, a turntable is a dangerous contrivance, which facilitates railroading; the general benefits resulting from its use outweigh the occasional injuries inflicted by it; hence the public good demands its use. We may conceive of means by which it might be rendered absolutely safe, but such means would so interfere with its beneficial use that the danger to be anticipated would not justify their adoption; therefore the public good demands its use without them. But the danger incident to its use may be lessened by the use of a lock which would prevent children, attracted to it, from moving it; the interference with the proper use of the turntable occasioned by the use of such lock is so slight that it is outweighed by the danger to be anticipated from an omission to use it; therefore the public good, we think demands the use of the lock. The public good would not require the owner of a vacant lot on which there is a pond to fill up the pond or inclose the lot with an impassable wall to insure the safety of children resorting to it, because the burden of doing so is out of proportion to the danger to be anticipated from leaving it undone. [C] But where there is an open well on a vacant lot, which is frequented by children, of which the owner of the lot has knowledge, he is liable for injuries sustained by children falling into the well, because the danger to be anticipated from the open well, under the circumstances, outweighs the

slight expense or inconvenience that would be entailed in making it
safe. * * *

Hence, in all cases of this kind in the determination of the question
of negligence, regard must be had to the character and location of the
premises, the purpose for which they are used, the probability of injury
therefrom, the precautions necessary to prevent such injury, and the
relations such precautions bear to the beneficial use of the premises.
The nature of the precautions would depend on the particular facts in
each case. In some cases a warning to the children or the parents
might be sufficient; in others, more active measures might be required.
But in every case they should be such as a man of ordinary care and
prudence would observe under like circumstances. If, under all the
circumstances, the owner omits such precautions as a man of ordinary
care and prudence, under like circumstances, would observe, he is
guilty of negligence. * * *

[The judgment was reversed for error in instructions to the jury
amounting to improper comment on the evidence.]

---

1. Is it dangerous to operate a train? An automobile? An airplane? A
lawn mower? Should the act of operating one always be negligence? Should it
ever be negligence? Would it be negligence today for a railroad to have a
turntable at all?

2. Defendant, excavating in the highway, set out an open flare pot at
night to give warning of the excavation. It left the flare pot until 10 A.M. in a
street in which it knew that children were accustomed to play. A child
meddled with the flare pot and was seriously burned. Should defendant be
liable? Why? Ott v. Washington Gas Light Co., 205 F.Supp. 815 (D.D.C.1962),
aff'd, 317 F.2d 138 (4th Cir.1963).

DAVISON v. SNOHOMISH COUNTY

Supreme Court of Washington, 1928.
149 Wash. 109, 270 P. 422.

BEALS, J. Plaintiffs instituted this action against Snohomish county as defendant, seeking to recover damages alleged to have been
suffered by them as the result of negligence of defendant in the
construction and maintenance of the elevated approach to a bridge
known as the Bascule bridge across Ebey slough. In the southwesterly
approach to this bridge there is a right angle turn towards the south
just easterly of the slough, and at this point the causeway or approach
to the bridge is at quite an elevation above the ground level. The
bridge itself is approximately 18 feet wide; the approach leading to the
bridge proper at the curve just to the east of the bridge increases in
width to a maximum of 30.9 feet, narrowing again to 18 feet at the end
of the turn.

At about 8 o'clock in the evening of November 11, 1926, plaintiffs
were driving their Ford automobile toward the city of Snohomish, and
proceeded to cross the bridge from the west to east at a low rate of

speed. Plaintiff Edwin F. Davison was driving, and, as the car rounded the curve to the east of the slough, he lost control, the car skidded, struck the railing on the east or outer edge of the approach just around the curve, broke through the railing, and, with plaintiffs, fell to the ground. Both plaintiffs suffered severe and painful injuries, and the automobile was wrecked; for all of which damage plaintiffs prayed for judgment in a large amount.

Defendant answered plaintiffs' complaint, denying all the allegations of negligence on its part and affirmatively pleading contributory negligence on the part of plaintiffs. The action came on regularly for trial, and resulted in a verdict in plaintiffs' favor in the sum of $2,500. Defendant seasonably moved for judgment in its favor notwithstanding the verdict, or, in the alternative, for a new trial. Both of these motions were denied by the trial court, which thereupon entered judgment upon the verdict, from which judgment defendant appeals.

* * *

[Respondents contended that the bridge was unsafe because of] the insufficiency of the railing or guard to prevent respondents' automobile from skidding off the approach * * *.

The use of the automobile as a means of transportation of passengers and freight has, during recent years, caused certain changes in the law governing the liability of municipalities in respect to the protection of their roads by railings or guards. A few years ago, when people traveled either on foot or by horse-drawn vehicles, a guardrail could to a considerable extent, actually prevent pedestrians or animals drawing vehicles from accidentally leaving the roadbed; but as a practical proposition, municipalities cannot be required to protect long stretches of roadway with railings or guards capable of preventing an automobile, moving at a rapid rate, from leaving the road if the car be in any way deflected from the roadway proper and propelled against the railing. As was said by this court in the case of Leber v. King County, 69 Wash. 134, 124 P. 397:

"Roads must be built and traveled, and to hold that the public cannot open their highways until they are prepared to fence their roads with barriers strong enough to hold a team and wagon when coming in violent contact with them, the condition being the ordinary condition of the country, would be to put a burden upon the public that it could not bear. It would prohibit the building of new roads and tend to the financial ruin of the counties undertaking to maintain the old ones."

This principle applies with special force to elevated causeways constructed of wood, such as the approach from which respondents' automobile fell, as upon such a structure the railing can be anchored or secured only to the deck of the causeway. Upon the ground, in situations of special danger, strength can be given to a guard or railing by driving posts into the earth, and a guard of any desired strength can be constructed in that manner. A concrete viaduct can be constructed with side walls of considerable resisting power; but the same degree of protection cannot be expected from a guard or railing along the side of an elevated frame causeway or viaduct. Respondents introduced some testimony to the effect that the posts which supported the railing were, to some extent, rotted. We have carefully considered this testimony, and, for the purposes of this opinion, assume that it was true; but we still do not think that it was sufficient to take the case to the jury upon the question of appellant's negligence in connection with the condition of the railing at the time of the accident. * * *

The judgment is reversed, with directions to dismiss the action.

——————

1. Compare the later decision of the same court in Bartlett v. Northern Pacific R. Co., 74 Wash.2d 881, 447 P.2d 735 (1968). With almost identical facts the trial court had granted summary judgment to the defendant on the basis of the Davison case. The Supreme Court reversed and remanded, saying: "The reasoning in Davison * * * was based on the impracticality as a matter of engineering and on prohibitive costs. We do not consider the ideas of the court, expressed 40 years ago, as necessarily authoritative on the engineering and financial phases of the same problem today. We are satisfied that the parties should have the opportunity of presenting their evidence as to the practicality (cost wise or otherwise) of guardrails or barriers on dangerous or misleading roadways to stop slow-moving vehicles." Who ultimately pays the cost if plaintiff prevails?

2. Defendant constructed its railway track so that it approached and crossed a public highway at a narrow acute angle, with the track close beside the highway for a considerable distance before the crossing. While plaintiff was riding his horse on the highway, the horse took fright at the approach of a train, as a result of which plaintiff was injured. The train was operated with due care. Is defendant liable for negligence in the construction of the track? Beatty v. Central Iowa R. Co., 58 Iowa 242, 12 N.W. 332 (1882).

3. In determining whether a choice of alternatives is reasonable, must the risk of harm to third persons be taken into account? Defendant's engineer, operating a train, unexpectedly finds a truck load of furniture on a crossing ahead of him. He can stop the train abruptly and avoid the collision, but if he does he will almost certainly throw his passengers about and injure them. What is he to do? Lucchese v. San Francisco–Sacramento R. Co., 106 Cal.App. 242, 289 P. 188 (1930).

4. Defendant, driving a truck heavily loaded with pipe, is suddenly confronted with a situation requiring him to stop suddenly or injure the plaintiff's intestate. If he stops the pipe may be expected to shift forward and crush him to death. What is he to do? Thurmond v. Pepper, 119 S.W.2d 900 (Tex.Civ. App.1938). Who decides?

UNITED STATES v. CARROLL TOWING CO.

United States Circuit Court of Appeals, Second Circuit, 1947.
159 F.2d 169.

[Libel in admiralty for the sinking of libellant's barge, which broke adrift from a pier through the negligence of defendant's servants in shifting its mooring lines. The trial court divided the damages, according to the admiralty rule, because it found contributory negligence of the libellant in not having a custodian on board the barge at the time.]

LEARNED HAND, CIRCUIT JUDGE. * * * It appears from the foregoing review that there is no general rule to determine when the absence of a bargee or other attendant will make the owner of the barge liable for injuries to other vessels if she breaks away from her moorings. However, in any cases where he would be so liable for injuries to others, obviously he must reduce his damages proportionately, if the injury is to his own barge. It becomes apparent why there can be no such general rule, when we consider the grounds for such a liability. Since there are occasions when every vessel will break from her moorings, and, since, if she does, she becomes a menace to those about her, the owner's duty, as in other similar situations, to provide against resulting injuries is a function of three variables: (1) The probability that she will break away; (2) the gravity of the resulting injury, if she does; (3) the burden of adequate precautions. Possibly it serves to bring this notion into relief to state it in algebraic terms: if the probability be called P; the injury L; and the burden B; liability

Judge Learned Hand

B < L x P² or B < PL
= if the burden is less, then : liability or not? liability
duty or not?

depends upon whether B is less than L multiplied by P; i.e., whether B is less than PL.

Applied to the situation at bar, the likelihood that a barge will break from her fasts, and the damage she will do, vary with the place and time; for example, if a storm threatens, the danger is greater; so it is, if she is in a crowded harbor where moored barges are constantly being shifted about. On the other hand, the barge must not be the bargee's prison, even though he lives aboard; he must go ashore at times. * * * We hold that it is not in all cases a sufficient answer to a bargee's absence without excuse, during working hours, that he has properly made fast his barge to a pier, when he leaves her. In the case at bar the bargee left at five o'clock on the afternoon of January 3rd, and the flotilla broke away at about two o'clock in the afternoon of the following day, twenty-one hours afterwards. The bargee had been away all the time, and we hold that his fabricated story was affirmative evidence that he had no excuse for his absence. At the locus in quo—especially during the short January days and in the full tide of war activity—barges were being constantly drilled in and out. Certainly it was not beyond reasonable expectation that, with the inevitable haste and bustle, the work might not be done with adequate care. In such circumstances we hold—and that is all that we do hold—that it was a fair requirement that the Conners Company should have a bargee aboard (unless he had some excuse for his absence), during the working hours of daylight.

some cases = yes
80 yrs. had
duty = meaning
not enough

duty to foresee

really

duty =

— and that his absence was tantamount to breach

[The decree was affirmed as to the division of damages.]

then what was all the shit about?

1. In Conway v. O'Brien, 111 F.2d 611, 612 (2d Cir.1940), Judge Learned Hand stated in part: "The degree of care demanded of a person by an occasion is the resultant of three factors: the likelihood that his conduct will injure others, taken with the seriousness of the injury if it happens, and balanced against the interest which he must sacrifice to avoid the risk. All these are practically not susceptible of any quantitative estimate, and the second two are generally not so, even theoretically. For this reason a solution always involves some preference, or choice between incommensurables, and it is consigned to a jury because their decision is thought most likely to accord with commonly accepted standards, real or fancied." Is this statement consistent with the approach taken in the principal case? Is a court well equipped to weigh these considerations? A jury? *Yes. Aff'd*

2. An urban electric utility fails to insulate its high tension wires and the decedent is electrocuted when his ladder comes in contact with a wire. Negligence? Amici curiae "complain of the increased costs of more adequate insulation. When the likelihood of danger to human life is to be balanced against the costs of insulation, we do not think the latter is a good argument." Kingsport Util. v. Brown, 201 Tenn. 393, 299 S.W.2d 656 (1950).

human life, even one, always wins — what about 65 mph speed limit

3. Is it negligence to fail to design an automobile hood so that if it flies up while the car is going it will not block all vision and produce a wreck? Evidence showed that there were 6 or 7 such happenings in 7 or 8 years and

that it would cost up to $10 to make a change. Cf. Roach v. Kononen, 269 Or. 457, 525 P.2d 125 (1974).

4. See Terry, Negligence, 29 Harv.L.Rev. 40 (1915); Seavey, Negligence— Subjective or Objective, 41 Harv.L.Rev. 1 (1927); Edgerton, Negligence, Inadvertence and Indifference, 39 Harv.L.Rev. 849 (1926).

RESTATEMENT (SECOND) OF TORTS (1965)

§ 291. Unreasonableness; How Determined; Magnitude of Risk and Utility of Conduct

Where an act is one which a reasonable man would recognize as involving a risk of harm to another, the risk is unreasonable and the act is negligent if the risk is of such magnitude as to outweigh what the law regards as the utility of the act or of the particular manner in which it is done.

Magnitude of risk > utility of act × manner which is done

§ 292. Factors Considered in Determining Utility of Actor's Conduct

In determining what the law regards as the utility of the actor's conduct for the purpose of determining whether the actor is negligent, the following factors are important:

(a) the social value which the law attaches to the interest which is to be advanced or protected by the conduct;

(b) the extent of the chance that this interest will be advanced or protected by the particular course of conduct;

(c) the extent of the chance that such interest can be adequately advanced or protected by another and less dangerous course of conduct.

§ 293. Factors Considered in Determining Magnitude of Risk

In determining the magnitude of the risk for the purpose of determining whether the actor is negligent, the following factors are important:

(a) the social value which the law attaches to the interests which are imperiled;

(b) the extent of the chance that the actor's conduct will cause an invasion of any interest of the other or of one of a class of which the other is a member;

(c) the extent of the harm likely to be caused to the interests imperiled;

(d) the number of persons whose interests are likely to be invaded if the risk takes effect in harm.

gross negligence v. negligence?

4. THE STANDARD OF CARE

2 Issues:
① duty re: fire – duty to know risk   *What is a "rick"?*
② subjective or objective test   *What will happen if hay is not properly stacked?*

(A) THE REASONABLE PRUDENT PERSON

"what he knew," goes to
both; obj. test answers
both

VAUGHAN v. MENLOVE

Q = Real or Hypothetical person?
A = Hypothetical
(next case = whose hyp?)

Court of Common Pleas, 1837.
3 Bing. (N.C.) 467, 132 Eng.Rep. 490.

[Defendant built a hay rick near the boundary of his land not far
from the plaintiff's cottages. It was alleged that the rick was likely to *risk*
ignite, thereby endangering the plaintiff's cottages, of which the defendant had notice; that the defendant was negligent in maintaining the
rick in this dangerous condition; and that the rick did ignite and the
fire spread to plaintiff's land, burning his cottages. Defendant denied
that he was negligent.]

At the trial it appeared that the rick in question had been made by
the defendant near the boundary of his own premises; that the hay was
in such a state when put together, as to give rise to discussions on the
probability of fire; that though there [were] conflicting opinions on the
subject, yet during a period of five weeks, the defendant was repeatedly
warned of his peril; that his stock was insured; and that upon one
occasion, being advised to take the rick down to avoid all danger, he
said, "he would chance it." He made an aperture or chimney through
the rick; but in spite, or perhaps in consequence of his precaution, the
rick at length burst into flames from the spontaneous heating of its
materials; the flames communicated to the defendant's barn and sta-
bles, and thence to the plaintiff's cottages, which were entirely destroyed.

Patterson, J., before whom the cause was tried, told the jury that
the question for them to consider, was, whether the fire had been
occasioned by gross negligence on the part of the defendant; adding,
that he was bound to proceed with such reasonable caution as a
prudent man would have exercised under such circumstances.

A verdict having been found for the plaintiff, a rule nisi for a new *fact = π*
trial was obtained, on the ground that the jury should have been *①*
directed to consider, not, whether the defendant had been guilty of *objective*
gross negligence with reference to the standard of ordinary prudence, a *or*
standard too uncertain to afford any criterion; but whether he had *subjective*
acted bona fide to the best of his judgment; if he had, he ought not to
be responsible for the misfortune of not possessing the highest order of
intelligence. The action under such circumstances, was of the first
impression. *held to a duty of average intelligence* *of first impression*

TINDAL, C.J. I agree that this is a case primae impressionis; but I
feel no difficulty in applying to it the principles of law as laid down in
other cases of a similar kind. * * * [T]hough the defendant did not

Chief Justice Tindal

= even objective test for what Δ must know in order to perform duty.

himself light the fire, yet mediately, he is as much the cause of it as if he had himself put a candle to the rick; for it is (well known) that hay will ferment and take fire if it be not carefully stacked. It has been decided that if an occupier burns weeds so near the boundary of his own land that damage ensues to the property of his neighbor, he is liable to an action for the amount of injury done, (unless) the accident were occasioned by a sudden blast which he could not foresee. * * *

re: duty G/R

It is contended, however, that the learned Judge was wrong in leaving this to the jury as a case of gross negligence, and that the question of negligence was so mixed up with reference to what would be the conduct of a man of ordinary prudence that the jury might have thought the latter the rule by which they were to decide; that such a rule would be too uncertain to act upon; and that the question ought to have been whether the defendant had acted honestly and bona fide to the best of his own judgment. * * * The care taken by a prudent man has always been the rule laid down; and as to the supposed difficulty of applying it, a jury has always been able to say whether, taking that rule as their guide, there has been negligence on the occasion in question.

Instead, therefore, of saying that the liability for negligence should be co-extensive with the judgment of each individual, which would be as variable as the length of the foot of each individual, we ought rather to adhere to the rule which requires in all cases a regard to caution such as a man of ordinary prudence would observe. That was in substance the criterion presented to the jury in this case, and therefore the present rule must be discharged.

[The concurring opinions of PARK and VAUGHAN, JJ., are omitted. GASLEE, J., concurred in discharging the rule.]

1. How can an honest mistake in judgment be "fault"? Did Chief Justice Tindal present defendant's best argument? What was it?

2. The standard formula for instructing the jury has been that of "a reasonable man of ordinary prudence." Variations on this have, however, been upheld, if they obviously mean the same thing. Thus the "ordinarily prudent man," Osborne v. Montgomery, 203 Wis. 223, 234 N.W. 372 (1931); the "typical prudent man," Warrington v. New York Power & Light Corp., 252 App.Div. 364, 300 N.Y.S. 154 (1937); the "average person of ordinary prudence," Charbonneau v. MacRury, 84 N.H. 501, 153 A. 457 (1931).

"The 'reasonable man' has been described by Greer, L.J. as 'the man in the street' or 'the man in the Clapham omnibus', or, as I recently read in an American author, 'the man who takes the magazines at home, and in the evening pushes the lawn mower in his shirt sleeves.'" Hall v. Brooklands Club, [1933] 1 K.B. 205, 224. For whimsical treatments, see A. Herbert, Uncommon Law 1–6 (7th ed. 1952); R. Megarry, The Clapham Omnibus, in Miscellany-at-Law 260 (1955).

3. The courts have quite jealously guarded the integrity of the instruction to the jury, and in particular the entirely hypothetical character of the "reasonable man." Thus in Freeman v. Adams, 63 Cal.App. 225, 218 P. 600 (1923), it was held reversible error to charge the jury that:

"In determining what a reasonable and prudent man would do under the circumstances, you will remember that presumably a jury is composed of such reasonable and prudent persons, and you may each ask yourself, Did the defendants do, or fail to do, anything which, under the circumstances, I would not have done or would have done?"

Courts have traditionally referred to this mythical person in the masculine gender. Obviously, this form of description is now outdated. The form used here is the reasonable, prudent person.

4. "* * * In applying the universally accepted standard of care: that of the ordinary, reasonable and prudent man under the circumstances, the term 'ordinary' should be given its true meaning by not requiring the conduct of an extraordinarily careful person. Such an 'ordinary' man is not necessarily a supercautious individual devoid of human frailties and constantly preoccupied with the idea that danger may be lurking in every direction about him at any

time. We appreciate that to require such constant apprehension of danger from every possible source would indeed be beyond normal conduct and would be too exacting a standard." Whitman v. W.T. Grant Co., 16 Utah 2d 81, 395 P.2d 918, 920 (1964).

5. See Seavey, Negligence—Subjective or Objective, 41 Harv.L.Rev. 1 (1927); Green, The Negligence Issue, 37 Yale L.J. 1029 (1928), reprinted in Green, Judge and Jury 153 (1930); James, The Qualities of the Reasonable Man in Negligence Cases, 16 Mo.L.Rev. 1 (1951); Reynolds, The Reasonable Man of Negligence Law: A Health Report on the "Odious Creature," 23 Okla.L.Rev. 410 (1970).

DELAIR v. McADOO
Supreme Court of Pennsylvania, 1936.
324 Pa. 392, 188 A. 181.

KEPHART, CHIEF JUSTICE. Plaintiff brought an action in trespass to recover for damages to his person and property sustained as a result of a collision between his automobile and that owned by the defendant. The accident occurred when defendant, proceeding in the same direction as plaintiff, sought to pass him. As defendant drew alongside of plaintiff, the left rear tire of his car blew out, causing it to swerve and come into contact with the plaintiff's car. The latter's theory at trial was that defendant was negligent in driving with defective tires. The jury found for plaintiff in the sum of $7,500. The court below granted defendant a new trial on the ground that the verdict was excessive, but refused his motion for a judgment n.o.v. Its ruling on the latter motion is here for review. * * *

It has been held in other states that the question whether a particular person is negligent in failing to know that his tires are in too poor a condition for ordinary operation on the highways is a question of fact for the jury. [Cc] In the instant case the testimony relative to the defect was as follows: A witness for the plaintiff stated that the tire "was worn pretty well through. You could see the tread in the tire— the inside lining." The witness later described this inside lining as the "fabric." The fact that the tire was worn through to and into the fabric over its entire area was corroborated by another witness. The repairman who replaced the tire which had blown out stated that he could see "the breaker strip" which is just under the fabric of a tire. This testimony was contradicted by the defendant.

A jury is just as well qualified to pass judgment as to the risk of danger in the condition of an article in universal use under a given state of facts as experts. We have in this state more than a million automobiles and trucks, approximately two for every three families. Their daily use over the highways is common, and requires a certain amount of knowledge of the movable parts, particularly the tires; it is imperative that a duty or standard of care be set up that will be productive of safety for other users of the highways. Any ordinary individual, whether a car owner or not, knows that when a tire is worn through to the fabric, its further use is dangerous and it should be removed. When worn through several plies, it is very dangerous for further use. All drivers must be held to a knowledge of these facts. An owner or operator cannot escape simply because he says he does not know. He must know. The hazard is too great to permit cars in this condition to be on the highway. It does not require opinion evidence to demonstrate that a trigger pulled on a loaded gun makes the gun a dangerous instrument when pointed at an individual, nor could one escape liability by saying he did not know it was dangerous. The use of a tire worn through to the fabric presents a similar situation. The rule must be rigid if millions are to drive these instrumentalities which in a fraction of a second may become instruments of destruction to life and property. There is no series of accidents more destructive or more terrifying in the use of automobiles than those which come from "blow-outs." The law requires drivers and owners of motor vehicles to know the condition of those parts which are likely to become dangerous where the flaws or faults would be disclosed by a reasonable inspection. It will assume they do know of the dangers ascertainable by such examination.

Order affirmed.

1. This case is sent back for a new trial. In the light of the opinion, how should the trial judge handle it? What does he say to the jury?

2. Compare Michigan City v. Rudolph, 104 Ind.App. 643, 12 N.E.2d 970 (1938), holding that the driver is held to the knowledge that an automobile will go out of control if it is driven fast through loose sand.

3. Are there any facts which every mentally competent adult knows? The law of gravity—something dropped will fall? Seaboard Air Line R. Co. v. Hackney, 217 Ala. 382, 115 So. 869 (1928). The principle of leverage—one end of a balanced board will fly up if the other is trod on? Cf. City of Huntingburg v. First, 15 Ind.App. 552, 43 N.E. 17 (1896). The fact that wood and paper will burn? Lillibridge v. McCann, 117 Mich. 84, 75 N.W. 288 (1898).

4. Suppose the individual has led a life that has not brought him into contact with information common in the particular community. A city dweller who never has seen a bull or a mule, or heard anything about their characteristics, visits a friend in the country, and makes a misguided attempt to fraternize with the animals. Tolin v. Terrell, 133 Ky. 210, 117 S.W. 290 (1909). What about an Eskimo flown to New York and suddenly deposited in the city streets, where he sees his first traffic signal and is fascinated by the pretty colored lights? See Seavey, Negligence—Subjective or Objective? 41 Harv.L.Rev. 1, 19 (1927).

5. Distinguish ignorance from the breach of a duty to find out. A stranger in a town is suddenly confronted with a purple traffic light. In Gobrecht v. Beckwith, 82 N.H. 415, 135 A. 20 (1926), defendant, a landlord, installed a gas heater in a closed and almost unventilated bathroom, in ignorance of the fact that it would fill the room with carbon monoxide. Plaintiff, a tenant, used the bathroom, lighted the heater, and was poisoned. It was held that defendant could be found negligent in not making inquiry or investigation as to the safety of the heater, but that plaintiff could reasonably rely on the landlord.

6. Suppose persons who do not hold themselves out as having superior knowledge or training do actually have them. Should they be required to exercise those superior qualities to avoid harm to others? For example, in the principal case, suppose the defect was a latent one, but defendant could have easily discovered it because his hobby was auto mechanics. Should he be held liable? The Restatement (Second) of Torts suggests an affirmative answer in § 289, Comment *m*.

7. There is an exhaustive collection of cases on what the reasonable person will know in a Note in 23 Minn.L.Rev. 628 (1939).

8. It is commonly held that the reasonable person will not forget what is actually known, and that forgetfulness does not excuse negligence. But when distracted attention, lapse of time or other similar factors make it reasonable to forget, it can be found that there is no negligence. See Ferrie v. D'Arc, 31 N.J. 92, 155 A.2d 257 (1959), rev'g 55 N.J.Super. 65, 150 A.2d 83 (1959).

TRIMARCO v. KLEIN
Court of Appeals of New York, 1982.
56 N.Y.2d 98, 436 N.E.2d 502, 451 N.Y.S.2d 52.

FUCHSBERG, JUDGE. After trial by jury in a negligence suit for personal injuries, the plaintiff, Vincent N. Trimarco, recovered a judgment of $240,000. A sharply divided Appellate Division, 82 A.D.2d 20, 441 N.Y.S.2d 62, having reversed on the law and dismissed the complaint, our primary concern on this appeal is with the role of the proof plaintiff produced on custom and usage. The ultimate issue is whether he made out a case.

The controversy has its genesis in the shattering of a bathtub's glass enclosure door in a multiple dwelling in July, 1976. Taking the testimony most favorably to the plaintiff, as we must in passing on the presence of a prima facie case, we note that, according to the trial testimony, at the time of the incident plaintiff, the tenant of the apartment in which it happened, was in the process of sliding the door open so that he could exit the tub. It is undisputed that the occurrence was sudden and unexpected and the injuries he received from the lacerating glass most severe.

The door, which turned out to have been made of ordinary glass variously estimated as one sixteenth to one quarter of an inch in thickness, concededly would have presented no different appearance to the plaintiff and his wife than did tempered safety glass, which their uncontradicted testimony shows they assumed it to be. Nor was there any suggestion that defendants ever brought its true nature to their attention. * * *

As part of his case, plaintiff, with the aid of expert testimony, developed that, since at least the early 1950's, a practice of using shatterproof glazing materials for bathroom enclosures had come into common use, so that by 1976 the glass door here no longer conformed to accepted safety standards. This proof was reinforced by a showing that over this period bulletins of nationally recognized safety and consumer organizations along with official Federal publications had joined in warning of the dangers that lurked when plain glass was utilized in "hazardous locations", including "bathtub enclosures". Over objection, the trial court also allowed in sections 389–m and 389–o of New York's General Business Law, which, enacted in 1972 though effective only as of July 1, 1973, required, on pain of criminal sanctions, that only "safety glazing material" be used in all bathroom enclosures after the effective date; however, the court carefully cautioned the jury that, because the statute did not apply to existing installations, of which the glass in question was one, it only was to be considered "along with all the other proof in this case, as a standard by which you may measure the conduct of the defendants". And, on examination of the defendants' managing agent, who long had enjoyed extensive familiarity with the management of multiple dwelling units in the New York City area, plaintiff's counsel elicited agreement that, since at least 1965, it was customary for landlords who had occasion to install glass for shower enclosures, whether to replace broken glass or to comply with the request of a tenant or otherwise, to do so with "some material such as plastic or safety glass".

   In face of this record, in essence, the rationale of the majority at the Appellate Division was that, "assuming that there existed a custom and usage at the time to substitute shatterproof glass" and that this was a "better way or a safer method of enclosing showers" [c] unless prior notice of the danger came to the defendants either from the plaintiff or by reason of a similar accident in the building, no duty devolved on the defendants to replace the glass either under the common law or under section 78 of the Multiple Dwelling Law. To this the court added that, were it not dismissing, it would have ordered a new trial because, in its view, the admission of the afore-mentioned sections of the General Business Law, even with the reservations attached by the Trial Judge, constituted reversible error. * * *

   Our analysis may well begin by rejecting defendants' contention that the shower door was not within the compass of section 78 of the Multiple Dwelling Law. From early on, it was understood that this statute was enacted in recognition of the reality that occupants of tenements in apartment houses, notwithstanding their control of the rented premises, as a practical matter looked to their landlords for the safe maintenance of the tenanted quarters as well. The result was that, if responsibility for keeping "every part thereof * * * in good repair" was not placed on the landlords, defects would remain un-remedied [cc]. * * *

   Which brings us to the well-recognized and pragmatic proposition that when "certain dangers have been removed by a customary way of doing things safely, this custom may be proved to show that [the one charged with the dereliction] has fallen below the required standard" [c]. Such proof, of course, is not admitted in the abstract. It must bear on what is reasonable conduct under all the circumstances, the quintes-sential test of negligence.

It follows that, when proof of an accepted practice is accompanied by evidence that the defendant conformed to it, this may establish due care [c] and, contrariwise, when proof of a customary practice is coupled with a showing that it was ignored and that this departure was a proximate cause of the accident, it may serve to establish liability. [c]. Put more conceptually, proof of a common practice aids in "formulat[ing] the general expectation of society as to how individuals will act in the course of their undertakings, and thus to guide the common sense or expert intuition of a jury or commission when called on to judge of particular conduct under particular circumstances" (Pound, Administrative Application of Legal Standards, 44 ABA Rep, 445, 456–457).

The source of the probative power of proof of custom and usage is described differently by various authorities, but all agree on its potency. Chief among the rationales offered is, of course, the fact that it reflects the judgment and experience and conduct of many (2 Wigmore, Evidence [3d ed], § 461; Prosser, Torts [4th ed], § 33). Support for its relevancy and reliability comes too from the direct bearing it has on feasibility, for its focusing is on the practicality of a precaution in actual operation and the readiness with which it can be employed (Morris, Custom and Negligence, 42 Col.L.Rev. 1147, 1148). Following in the train of both of these boons is the custom's exemplification of the opportunities it provides to others to learn of the safe way, if that the customary one be. (See Restatement (Second) Torts § 295A, Comments *a, b*.)

From all this it is not to be assumed customary practice and usage need be universal. It suffices that it be fairly well defined and in the same calling or business so that "the actor may be charged with knowledge of it or negligent ignorance" (Prosser, Torts [4th ed], § 33, p. 168; Restatement (Second) Torts § 295A, p. 62, Comment *a*).

However, once its existence is credited, a common practice or usage is still not necessarily a conclusive or even a compelling test of negligence (1 Shearman & Redfield, Negligence [rev ed], § 10). Before it can be, the jury must be satisfied with its reasonableness, just as the jury must be satisfied with the reasonableness of the behavior which adhered to the custom or the unreasonableness of that which did not [c]. After all, customs and usages run the gamut of merit like everything else. That is why the question in each instance is whether it meets the test of reasonableness. As Holmes' now classic statement on this subject expresses it, "[w]hat usually is done may be evidence of what ought to be done, but what ought to be done is fixed by a standard of reasonable prudence, whether it usually is complied with or not" (*Texas & Pacific Ry. Co. v. Behymer*, 189 U.S. 468, 470, 23 S.Ct. 622, 622–23, 47 L.Ed. 905).

So measured, the case the plaintiff presented, even without the insertion of sections 389–*m* and 389–*o* of the General Business Law, was enough to send it to the jury and to sustain the verdict reached. The expert testimony, the admissions of the defendant's manager, the data on which the professional and governmental bulletins were based, the evidence of how replacements were handled by at least the local building industry for the better part of two decades, these in the aggregate easily filled that bill. Moreover, it was also for the jury to decide whether, at the point in time when the accident occurred, the modest cost and ready availability of safety glass and the dynamics of the growing custom to use it for shower enclosures had transformed what once may have been considered a reasonably safe part of the apartment into one which, in the light of later developments, no longer could be so regarded.

Furthermore, the charge on this subject was correct. The Trial Judge placed the evidence of custom and usage "by others engaged in the same business" in proper perspective, when, among other things, he told the jury that the issue on which it was received was "the reasonableness of the defendant's conduct under all the circumstances". He also emphasized that the testimony on this score was not conclusive, not only by saying so but by explaining that "the mere fact that another person or landlord may have used a better or safer practice does not establish a standard" and that it was for the jurors "to determine whether or not the evidence in this case does establish a general custom or practice". *Jury decides if custom exist, if custom is reasonable, if act conformed to custom, if act was reasonable*

Ergo = custom is to be considered as w/in "circumstances"

Nevertheless, we reverse and order a new trial because the General Business Law sections should have been excluded. * * *

Order reversed, with costs, and case remitted to Supreme Court, Bronx County, for a new trial in accordance with the opinion herein.

————————

1. Who is interested in introducing evidence of the custom, plaintiff or defendant? Why? *p. 156*

2. On the use of expert evidence to prove that an industry custom is not the most effective way to test a steam boiler to make certain that it is safe from the danger of exploding, see Marsh Wood Products Co. v. Babcock and Wilcox, 207 Wis. 209, 240 N.W. 392 (1932).

3. Defendant, driving an automobile on a private road, where no statute is applicable, drives on the left side of the road. In the absence of special circumstances, can he be found negligent in doing so? Not to be negligent? Cf. Eamiello v. Piscitelli, 133 Conn. 360, 51 A.2d 912 (1947) (walking on wrong side of road). What about special circumstances? Suppose the right side of the road is full of dangerous potholes? Compare Texas & Pacific R. Co. v. Behymer, 189 U.S. 468 (1903), quoted in the principal case, where it was railway custom to make up a train by bumping cars together with brakemen standing on top of them; and this was done on one occasion when the cars were covered with sheet ice.

4. What if a custom violates a statute? Suppose everyone in town habitually jaywalks, crossing the street in the middle of the block? Cf. Fowler v. Key System Transit Lines, 37 Cal.2d 65, 230 P.2d 339 (1951). Suppose a custom is arguably careless behavior. Should a jury be permitted to consider it? Cf. Easterly v. Advance Stores Co., 432 F.Supp. 7 (E.D.Tenn.1976).

5. Are there customs that are so clearly unreasonable that they are not even to be admitted in evidence to prove due care? In Mayhew v. Sullivan Mining Co., 76 Me. 100 (1884), defendant mining company did not guard or even light ladder-holes in the platforms in its mine. A workman fell through such a hole and was injured. Barrow, J.: "If the defendants had proved that in every mining establishment that has existed since the days of Tubal Cain, it has been the practice to cut ladder-holes in their platforms, situated as this was while in daily use for mining operations, without guarding or lighting them, and without notice to contractors or workmen, it would have no tendency to show that the act was consistent with ordinary prudence or a due regard for the safety of those who were using their premises by their invitation."

6. The classic article on this topic is Morris, Custom and Negligence, 42 Colum.L.Rev. 1147 (1942), reprinted in Morris, Studies in the Law of Torts 214 (1952). See also James, Particularizing Standards of Conduct in Negligence Trials, 5 Vand.L.Rev. 697, 709–714 (1952).

CORDAS v. PEERLESS TRANSPORTATION CO.

City Court of New York, New York County, 1941.

27 N.Y.S.2d 198.

CARLIN, JUSTICE. This case presents the ordinary man—that problem child of the law—in a most bizarre setting. As a lonely chauffeur in defendant's employ he became in a trice the protagonist in a breath-bating drama with a denouement almost tragic. It appears that a man, whose identity it would be indelicate to divulge, was feloniously relieved of his portable goods by two nondescript highwaymen in an alley near 26th Street and Third Avenue, Manhattan; they induced him to relinquish his possessions by a strong argument ad hominem couched in the convincing cant of the criminal and pressed at the point of a most persuasive pistol. Laden with their loot, but not thereby impeded, they took an abrupt departure, and he, shuffling off the coil of that discretion which enmeshed him in the alley, quickly gave chase through 26th Street toward 2d Avenue, whither they were resorting "with expedition swift as thought" for most obvious reasons. Somewhere on that thoroughfare of escape they indulged the stratagem of separation ostensibly to disconcert their pursuer and allay the ardor of his pursuit. He then centered on for capture the man with the pistol, whom he saw board the defendant's taxicab which quickly veered south toward 25th Street on 2d Avenue, where he saw the chauffeur jump out while the cab still in motion, continued toward 24th Street; after the chauffeur relieved himself of the cumbersome burden of his fare the latter also is said to have similarly departed from the cab before it reached 24th Street.

The chauffeur's story is substantially the same except that he states that his uninvited guest boarded the cab at 25th Street while it was at a standstill waiting for a less colorful fare; that his "passenger" immediately advised him "to stand not upon the order of his going but go at once," and added finality to his command by an appropriate gesture with a pistol addressed to his sacroiliac. The chauffeur in reluctant acquiescence proceeded about fifteen feet, when his hair, like unto the quills of the fretful porcupine, was made to stand on end by the hue and cry of the man despoiled, accompanied by a clamorous concourse of the law-abiding who paced him as he ran; the concatenation of "stop thief," to which the patter of persistent feet did maddingly beat time, rang in his ears as the pursuing posse all the while gained on the receding cab with its quarry therein contained. The hold-up man sensing his insecurity suggested to the chauffeur that in the event there was the slightest lapse in obedience to his curt command that he, the chauffeur, would suffer the loss of his brains, a prospect as horrible to an humble chauffeur as it undoubtedly would be to one of the intelligentsia.

The chauffeur, apprehensive of certain dissolution from either Scylla, the pursuers, or Charybdis, the pursued, quickly threw his car out of first speed in which he was proceeding, pulled on the emergency, jammed on his brakes and, although he thinks the motor was still running, swung open the door to his left and jumped out of his car. He confesses that the only act that smacked of intelligence was that by which he jammed the brakes in order to throw off balance the hold-up man, who was half-standing and half-sitting with his pistol menacingly poised. Thus abandoning his car and passenger the chauffeur sped toward 26th Street and then turned to look; he saw the cab proceeding south toward 24th Street, where it mounted the sidewalk. The plaintiff-mother and her two infant children were there injured by the cab, which, at the time, appeared to be also minus its passenger, who, it appears, was apprehended in the cellar of a local hospital where he was pointed out to a police officer by a remnant of the posse, hereinbefore mentioned. He did not appear at the trial. The three aforesaid plaintiffs and the husband-father sue the defendant for damages, predicating their respective causes of action upon the contention that the chauffeur was negligent in abandoning the cab under the aforesaid circumstances. Fortunately the injuries sustained were comparatively slight. * * *

Negligence has been variously defined but the common legal acceptation is the failure to exercise that care and caution which a reasonable and prudent person ordinarily would exercise under like conditions or circumstances. * * * Negligence is "not absolute or intrinsic," but "is always relevant to some circumstances of time, place or person." In slight paraphrase of the world's first bard it may be truly observed that the expedition of the chauffeur's violent love of his own security outran the pauser, reason, when he was suddenly confronted with unusual emergency which "took his reason prisoner." The learned attorney for the plaintiffs concedes that the chauffeur acted in an emergency but claims a right to recovery upon the following proposition taken verbatim from his brief: "It is respectfully submitted that the value of the interest of the public at large to be immune from being injured by a dangerous instrumentality such as a car unattended while in motion is very superior to the right of a driver to abandon same while it is in motion, even when acting under the belief that his life is in danger and by abandoning same he will save his life."

To hold thus under the facts adduced herein would be tantamount to a repeal by implication of the primal law of nature written in indelible characters upon the fleshy tablets of sentient creation by the Almighty Law-giver, "the supernal Judge who sits on high." There are those who stem the turbulent current for bubble fame, or who bridge the yawning chasm with a leap for the leap's sake, or who "outstare the sternest eyes that look, outbrave the heart most daring on the earth, pluck the young sucking cubs from the she-bear, yea, mock the lion when he roars for prey" to win a fair lady, and these are the admiration of the generality of men; but they are made of sterner stuff than the ordinary man upon whom the law places no duty of emulation. The law would indeed be fond if it imposed upon the ordinary man the obligation to so demean himself when suddenly confronted with a danger, not of his creation, disregarding the likelihood that such a contingency may darken the intellect and palsy the will of the common legion of the earth, the fraternity of the ordinary man—whose acts or omissions under certain conditions make the yardstick by which the law measures culpability or innocence, negligence or care. * * *

Returning to our chauffeur. If the philosophic Horatio and the martial companions of his watch were "distilled almost to jelly with the act of fear" when they beheld "in the dead vast and middle of the night" the disembodied spirit of Hamlet's father stalk majestically by "with a countenance more in sorrow than in anger," was not the chauffeur, though unacquainted with the example of these eminent men-at-arms more amply justified in his fearsome reactions when he was more palpably confronted by a thing of flesh and blood bearing in its hand an engine of destruction which depended for its lethal purpose upon the quiver of a hair? When Macbeth was cross-examined by Macduff as to any reason he could advance for his sudden dispatch of Duncan's grooms he said in plausible answer, "Who can be wise, amazed, temperate and furious, loyal and neutral in a moment? No man." * * *

Kolanka v. Erie Railroad Co., 215 App.Div. 82, 86, 212 N.Y.S. 714, 717, says: "The law in this state does not hold one in an emergency to the exercise of that mature judgment required of him under circumstances where he has an opportunity for deliberate action. He is not required to exercise unerring judgment, which would be expected of him, were he not confronted with an emergency requiring prompt action." The circumstances provide the foil by which the act is brought into relief to determine whether it is or is not negligent. If under normal circumstances an act is done which might be considered negligent, it does not follow as a corollary that a similar act is negligent if performed by a person acting under an emergency, not of his own making, in which he suddenly is faced with a patent danger with a moment left to adopt a means of extrication.

[handwritten top margin: Did Shakespeare use the word "pluck" twice? p. 160]

The chauffeur—the ordinary man in this case—acted in a split second in a most harrowing experience. To call him negligent would be to brand him coward; the court does not do so in spite of what those swaggering heroes, "whose valor plucks dead lions by the beard", may bluster to the contrary. The court is loathe to see the plaintiffs go without recovery even though their damages were slight, but cannot hold the defendant liable upon the facts adduced at the trial. Motions, upon which decision was reserved, to dismiss the complaint are granted, with exceptions to plaintiffs. Judgment for defendant against plaintiffs dismissing their complaint upon the merits.

[handwritten right margin: Cardin would do well to extricate the "the's" from his quintessence]

[handwritten: Was the real RTL That T's had only slightly suffered [and] That Δ had had enough.]

1. Compare Vincent v. Lake Erie Transp. Co., supra page 125. Why a different result? Would it make any difference if plaintiff in the principal case had been killed or seriously injured? Should it? Some legal scholars have observed that society tends to prevent direct taking of life while permitting indirect, but statistically certain, deaths. See Calabresi, Reflections on Medical Experiments in Humans, 98 Daedalus 387 (1969); Ely, The Wages of Crying Wolf: A Comment on Roe v. Wade, 82 Yale L.J. 920, 927 (1973).

[handwritten right margin: Why a certain standard of ship in tempestuous storm?]

2. In the principal case, the judge acted as a trier of fact. However, most legal disputes surrounding the emergency doctrine arise in regard to whether a judge should have instructed a jury about "the reasonable person in an emergency." See Miller v. Reilly, 21 Md.App. 465, 319 A.2d 553 (1974) (failure to apply emergency brake). Since the jury is usually instructed to view the reasonable person "in the circumstances," of what importance is the instruction?

3. Does the emergency excuse the actor from the standard of the reasonable man? What if his conduct is found to be unreasonable even in the light of the emergency? Lederer v. Connecticut Co., 95 Conn. 520, 111 A. 785 (1920); Lunzer v. Pittsburgh & L.E.R. Co., 296 Pa. 393, 145 A. 907 (1929).

4. There is general agreement that if the emergency is created by the negligence of the actor himself, the emergency doctrine does not apply. See for example Casey v. Siciliano, 310 Pa. 238, 165 A. 1 (1933). It has been said, however, that it is not the conduct after the emergency has arisen which the law does not excuse, but the negligent conduct which brought it about. Windsor v. McKee, 22 S.W.2d 65 (Mo.App.1929). *— What if emergency is created not by N.*

5. Are there situations in which one may be required to anticipate an emergency, and be prepared to meet it? What if defendant is driving past a school, and a boy suddenly comes darting out of a driveway on a bicycle? Cf. Bybee Bros. v. Imes, 288 Ky. 1, 155 S.W.2d 492 (1941); Conery v. Tackmaier, 34 Wis.2d 511, 149 N.W.2d 575 (1967). *— Definitely shouldn't jump out of car.*

6. See Reynolds, Put Yourself in an Emergency—How Will You Be Judged? 62 Ky.L.J. 366 (1973); Evans, the Standard of Care in Emergencies, 31 Ky.L.J. 207 (1943).

*[handwritten bottom:
(H) - one need not place (or keep) her life in danger (unless Δ creates the danger)
— Δ did what the reasonable man of ordinary prudence would do under the circumstances (emergency)]*

Duty of handicapped (handwritten)

Issue is State's [handwritten marginalia] not blind persons, not Respondeat sup. necessarily tort on blind man

ROBERTS v. STATE OF LOUISIANA

Court of Appeal of Louisiana, 1981.
396 So.2d 566.

LABORDE, JUDGE. In this tort suit, William C. Roberts sued to recover damages for injuries he sustained in an accident in the lobby of the U.S. Post Office Building in Alexandria, Louisiana. Roberts fell after being bumped into by Mike Burson, the blind operator of the concession stand located in the building.

Plaintiff sued the State of Louisiana, through the Louisiana Health and Human Resources Administration, advancing two theories of liability: respondeat superior and negligent failure by the State to properly supervise and oversee the safe operation of the concession stand. The stand's blind operator, Mike Burson, is not a party to this suit although he is charged with negligence.

Tr Ct = Δ [The trial court ordered plaintiff's suit dismissed.]

Ct App = Aff'd We affirm the trial court's decision for the reasons which follow.

On September 1, 1977, at about 12:45 in the afternoon, operator Mike Burson left his concession stand to go to the men's bathroom located in the building. As he was walking down the hall, he bumped into plaintiff who fell to the floor and injured his hip. Plaintiff was 75 years old, stood 5'6" and weighed approximately 100 pounds. Burson, on the other hand, was 25 to 26 years old, stood approximately 6' and weighed 165 pounds. * * *

Respondeat Superior Even though Burson was not joined as a defendant, his negligence or lack thereof is crucial to a determination of the State's liability. Because of its importance, we begin with it.

Plaintiff contends that operator Mike Burson traversed the area from his concession stand to the men's bathroom in a negligent manner. To be more specific, he focuses on the operator's failure to use his cane even though he had it with him in his concession stand. *fact*

duty of blind In determining an actor's negligence, various courts have imposed differing standards of care to which handicapped persons are expected to perform. Professor William L. Prosser expresses one generally recognized modern standard of care as follows:

= just another circumstance "As to his physical characteristics, the reasonable man may be said to be identical with the actor. The man who is blind . . . is entitled to live in the world and to have allowance made by others for his disability, and he cannot be required to do the impossible by conforming to physical standards which he cannot meet . . . . At the same time, the conduct of the handicapped individual must be reasonable in the light of his knowledge of his infirmity, which is treated merely as one of the circumstances under which he acts . . . . It is sometimes said that a blind man must use a greater degree of care than one who can see; but it is now generally agreed that as a fixed rule this is inaccurate,

but still reasonableness

taking account of blindness. (handwritten)

[handwritten top margin: reasonable blind person of ordinary prudence under similar circumstances]

[handwritten: the same or]

[handwritten circled: R]

and that the correct statement is merely that <u>he must take the precautions, be they more or less, which the ordinary reasonable man would take if he were blind.</u>" W. Prosser, *The Law of Torts*, Section 32, at Page 151–52 (4th ed. 1971).

[handwritten right margin: R Why did Prosser put this here.]

A careful review of the record in this instance reveals that Burson *[handwritten circled: H]* was acting as a reasonably prudent blind person would under these particular circumstances.

Mike Burson is totally blind. Since 1974, he has operated the concession stand located in the lobby of the post office building. It is one of twenty-three vending stands operated by blind persons under a (program) funded by the federal government and implemented by the State through the Blind Services Division of the Department of Health and Human Resources. Burson hired no employees, choosing instead to operate his stand on his own. * * *

[handwritten left margin: e tries to o; gets sued. ir?]

On the date of the incident in question, Mike Burson testified that he left his concession stand and was on his way to the men's bathroom when he bumped into plaintiff. He, without hesitancy, <u>admitted that at the time he was not using his cane,</u> explaining that he relies on his <u>facial sense which he feels is an adequate technique for short trips inside the (familiar) building.</u> Burson testified that he does use a cane to get to and from work.

[handwritten right margin: Circumstances]

Plaintiff makes much of Burson's failure to use a cane when traversing the halls of the post office building. Yet, our review of the testimony received at trial indicates that <u>it is not uncommon for blind people to rely on other techniques when moving around in a (familiar) setting.</u> For example George Marzloff, the director of the Division of Blind Services, testified that he can recommend to the blind operators that they should use a cane but he knows that when they are in a setting in which they are comfortable, he would say that nine out of ten will not use a cane and in his personal opinion, if the operator is in a relatively busy area, the cane can be more of a hazard than an asset.

[handwritten right margin: Finding]

*[handwritten: *]*

* * *

The only testimony in the record that suggests that Burson traversed the halls in a negligent manner was that elicited from <u>plaintiff's</u> expert witness, William Henry Jacobson. Jacobson is an instructor in peripathology, which he explained as the science of movement within the surroundings by visually impaired individuals. Jacobson, (admitting that he conducted no study or examination of Mike Burson's mobility skills and that he was unfamiliar with the State's vending program,) nonetheless testified that he would require a blind person to use a cane in traversing the areas outside the concession stand.

[handwritten right margin: Experts for sale. How does one choose expert? What relevance. Is this subjective rather than objective reas. person?]

* * *

Upon our review of the record, we feel that plaintiff has failed to show that Burson was negligent. Burson testified that he was very familiar with his surroundings, having worked there for three and a half years. He had special mobility training and his reports introduced into evidence indicate good mobility skills. He explained his decision to rely on his facial sense instead of his cane for these short trips in a manner which convinces us that it was a reasoned decision. Not only was Burson's explanation adequate, there was additional testimony from other persons indicating that such a decision is not an unreasonable one. Also important is the total lack of any evidence in the record showing that at the time of the incident, Burson engaged in any acts which may be characterized as negligence on his part. For example, there is nothing showing that Burson was walking too fast, not paying attention, et cetera. Under all of these circumstances, we conclude that Mike Burson was not negligent.

Our determination that Mike Burson was not negligent disposes of our need to discuss liability on the part of the State.

For the above and foregoing reasons, the judgment of the trial court dismissing plaintiff's claims against defendant is affirmed and all costs of this appeal are assessed against the plaintiff-appellant.

Affirmed.

---

1. Accord, as to the other physical disabilities: Otterbeck v. Lamb, 85 Nev. 456, 456 P.2d 855 (1972) (deaf); Stephens v. Dulaney, 78 N.M. 53, 428 P.2d 27 (1967) (no sense of smell); Mahan v. State of New York to Use of Carr, 172 Md. 373, 191 A. 575 (1937) (short stature, unable to see over hood of automobile). Duvall v. Goldin, 139 Mich.App. 342, 362 N.W.2d 275 (1984) (epileptic); Burgess v. Shreveport, 471 So.2d 690 (La.1985), reh'g denied (elderly person); Hodges v. Jewel Cos., 72 Ill.App.3d 263, 28 Ill.Dec. 571, 390 N.E.2d 930 (1979) (polio victim on crutches).

2. Is a blind man negligent in going out on the street unaccompanied? See Hill v. Glenwood, 124 Iowa 479, 100 N.W. 522 (1904), where the blind man was the injured party. Suppose he had gone out without a cane. Smith v. Sneller, 147 Pa.Super. 231, 24 A.2d 61, aff'd, 345 Pa. 68, 26 A.2d 452 (1942). Should contributory negligence of the plaintiff be treated differently?

3. Will the reasonable person with a physical handicap always exercise more care than one without it? Should it make any difference if the party with a physical handicap is a plaintiff or a defendant?

4. Suppose that instead of being physically handicapped, the actor has superior endowments—he is stronger, can see farther or is wiser. Is it sufficient for him to exercise ordinary abilities or must he exercise his superior ones? See Restatement (Second) of Torts § 289(b).

5. What about the obligation of the defendant to take the possibility of such a disability as blindness into account? See Fletcher v. Aberdeen, 54 Wash. 2d 174, 338 P.2d 743 (1959).

6. See ten Broek, The Right to Live in the World: The Disabled in the Law of Torts, 54 Cal.L.Rev. 841 (1966); Weisiger, Negligence of the Physically Infirm, 24 N.C.L.Rev. 187 (1945).

7. *Intoxication.* This is probably to be classed as a physical infirmity. Nevertheless the courts have consistently refused to make any allowance for it where it is "voluntary," or even negligent. Why? Is voluntary intoxication negligence in itself? What if the defendant has been intentionally smoking

marijuana? For treatment of the numerous problems see McCoid, Intoxication and its Effect Upon Civil Responsibility, 42 Iowa L.Rev. 38 (1956).

8. What is defendant's obligation toward one who is intoxicated? One of the most famous judicial utterances is in Robinson v. Pioche, Bayerque & Co., 5 Cal. 460 (1885): "A drunken man is as much entitled to a safe street as a sober one, and much more in need of it."

ROBINSON v. LINDSAY

Supreme Court of Washington, 1979.
92 Wash.2d 410, 598 P.2d 392.

UTTER, CHIEF JUSTICE. An action seeking damages for personal injuries was brought on behalf of Kelly Robinson who lost full use of a thumb in a snowmobile accident when she was 11 years of age. The petitioner, Billy Anderson, 13 years of age at the time of the accident, was the driver of the snowmobile. After a jury verdict in favor of Anderson, the trial court ordered a new trial.

The single issue on appeal is whether a minor operating a snowmobile is to be held to an adult standard of care. The trial court failed to instruct the jury as to that standard and ordered a new trial because it believed the jury should have been so instructed. We agree and affirm the order granting a new trial.

The trial court instructed the jury under WPI 10.05 that: "In considering the claimed negligence of a child, you are instructed that it is the duty of a child to exercise the same care that a reasonably careful child of the same age, intelligence, maturity, training and experience would exercise under the same or similar circumstances." Respondent properly excepted to the giving of this instruction and to the court's failure to give an adult standard of care.

The question of what standard of care should apply to acts of children has a long historical background. Traditionally, a flexible standard of care has been used to determine if children's actions were negligent. Under some circumstances, however, courts have developed a rationale for applying an adult standard.

In the courts' search for a uniform standard of behavior to use in determining whether or not a person's conduct has fallen below minimal acceptable standards, the law has developed a fictitious person, the "reasonable man of ordinary prudence." That term was first used in Vaughan v. Menlove, 132 Eng.Rep. 490 (1837).

Exceptions to the reasonable person standard developed when the individual whose conduct was alleged to have been negligent suffered from some physical impairment, such as blindness, deafness, or lameness. Courts also found it necessary, as a practical matter, to depart considerably from the objective standard when dealing with children's behavior. Children are traditionally encouraged to pursue childhood activities without the same burdens and responsibilities with which adults must contend. [C] As a result, courts evolved a special standard of care to measure a child's negligence in a particular situation.

Prosser, et al. Torts 8th Ed. UCB—6

In Roth v. Union Depot Co., 13 Wash. 525, 43 P. 641 (1896), Washington joined "the overwhelming weight of authority" in distinguishing between the capacity of a child and that of an adult. As the court then stated, at page 544, 43 P. at page 647: "[I]t would be a monstrous doctrine to hold that a child of inexperience—and experience can come only with years—should be held to the same degree of care in avoiding danger as a person of mature years and accumulated experience."

The court went on to hold, at page 545, 43 P. at page 647: "The care or caution required is according to the capacity of the child, and this is to be determined, ordinarily, by the age of the child. * * * [A] child is held * * * only to the exercise of such degree of care and discretion as is reasonably to be expected from children of his age."

* * * In the past we have always compared a child's conduct to that expected of a reasonably careful child of the same age, intelligence, maturity, training and experience. This case is the first to consider the question of a child's liability for injuries sustained as a result of his or her operation of a motorized vehicle or participation in an inherently dangerous activity.

Courts in other jurisdictions have created an exception to the special child standard because of the apparent injustice that would occur if a child who caused injury while engaged in certain dangerous activities were permitted to defend himself by saying that other children similarly situated would not have exercised a degree of care higher than his, and he is, therefore, not liable for his tort. Some courts have couched the exception in terms of children engaging in an activity which is normally one for adults only. See, e.g., Dellwo v. Pearson, 259 Minn. 452, 107 N.W.2d 859 (1961) (operation of a motorboat). We believe a better rationale is that when the activity a child engages in is inherently dangerous, as is the operation of powerful mechanized vehicles, the child should be held to an adult standard of care.

Such a rule protects the need of children to be children but at the same time discourages immature individuals from engaging in inherently dangerous activities. Children will still be free to enjoy traditional childhood activities without being held to an adult standard of care. Although accidents sometimes occur as the result of such activities, they are not activities generally considered capable of resulting in "grave danger to others and to the minor himself if the care used in the course of the activity drops below that care which the reasonable and prudent adult would use * * *." Daniels v. Evans, 107 N.H. 407, 408, 224 A.2d 63, 64 (1966).

Other courts adopting the adult standard of care for children engaged in adult activities have emphasized the hazards to the public if the rule is otherwise. We agree with the Minnesota Supreme Court's language in its decision in Dellwo v. Pearson, *supra,* 259 Minn. at 457–58, 107 N.W.2d at 863:

"Certainly in the circumstances of modern life, where vehicles moved by powerful motors are readily available and frequently operated by immature individuals, we should be skeptical of a rule that would allow motor vehicles to be operated to the hazard of the public with less than the normal minimum degree of care and competence."

[handwritten: = factor of duty is less; on capacity/character of Δ, but rather on risk to π]

Dellwo applied the adult standard to a twelve-year-old defendant operating a motor boat. Other jurisdictions have applied the adult standard to minors engaged in analogous activities. Goodfellow v. Coggburn, 98 Idaho 202, 203–04, 560 P.2d 873 (1977) (minor operating tractor); Williams v. Esaw, 214 Kan. 658, 668, 522 P.2d 950 (1974) (minor operating motorcycle); Perricone v. DiBartolo, 14 Ill.App.3d 514, 520, 302 N.E.2d 637 (1973) (minor operating gasoline-powered minibike); Krahn v. LaMeres, 483 P.2d 522, 525–26 (Wyo.1971) (minor operating automobile). The holding of minors to an adult standard of care when they operate motorized vehicles is gaining approval from an increasing number of courts and commentators. [C]

The operation of a snowmobile likewise requires adult care and competence. Currently 2.2 million snowmobiles are in operation in the United States. 9 Envir.Rptr. (BNA) 876 [1978 Current Developments]. Studies show that collisions and other snowmobile accidents claim hundreds of casualties each year and that the incidence of accidents is particularly high among inexperienced operators. [C]

At the time of the accident, the 13–year–old petitioner had operated snowmobiles for about 2 years. When the injury occurred, petitioner was operating a 30–horsepower snowmobile at speeds of 10–20 miles per hour. The record indicates that the machine itself was capable of 65 miles per hour. Because petitioner was operating a powerful motorized vehicle, he should be held to the standard of care and conduct expected of an adult. *[handwritten: (H)]*

The order granting a new trial is affirmed.

---

1. The standard usually is stated to be "what it is reasonable to expect of children of like age, intelligence and experience." See Restatement (Second) of Torts § 283A; Cleveland Rolling Mill Co. v. Corrigan, 46 Ohio St. 283, 20 N.E. 466 (1889). What significance should be attached to a child's testimony that he understood the danger associated with his conduct? See Norfolk & Portsmouth Belt Line R. v. Barker, 275 S.E.2d 613 (Va.1981). *[handwritten: G/R]*

2. This means that more may be required of a child of superior intelligence for his age than of one who is mentally backward. Compare Jones v. Firemen's Ins. Co. of Newark New Jersey, 240 So.2d 780 (La.App.1970), with Robertson v. Travis, 393 So.2d 304 (La.App.1980). *[handwritten: = same minimal intelligence & knowledge req'd of all adults, at least until "old age"]*

3. The question is normally one for the jury; but if the conclusion is that the child has behaved unreasonably in view of his estimated capacity, he may still be found negligent as a matter of law.

4. There are two or three decisions in which a similar allowance has been made for the physical and mental deficiencies of old age, but all have involved plaintiffs. LaCava v. New Orleans, 159 So.2d 362 (La.App.1964); Johnson v. St.

Paul City R. Co., 67 Minn. 260, 69 N.W. 900 (1897); Kitsap County Transp. Co. v. Harvey, 15 F.2d 166 (9 Cir.1927). See Note, Negligence and the Elderly: A Proposal for a Relaxed Standard of Care, 17 J.Mar.L.Rev. 874 (1984).

5. A minority of the courts have adopted arbitrary age limits. See Kuhns v. Brugger, 390 Pa. 331, 135 A.2d 395 (1957). Thus a child under the age of seven is, as a matter of law, incapable of any negligence; one between seven and 14 is presumed incapable, but may be proved capable; one over 14 is presumed capable, but may be proved incapable. These arbitrary rules have been taken over from the common law rules as to the capacity of children to commit crime. They were originally derived from the civil law which goes back to the Bible, with its emphasis upon multiples of the mystic number seven.

6. Most courts now reject these arbitrary limits. There is an excellent review of both sides of the question in the majority and dissenting opinions in Tyler v. Wood, 285 Mich. 460, 280 N.W. 827 (1938). But even the courts which refuse to hold that a child under seven is not capable of negligence will still hold that extremely young children are without the capacity. See, for example, Verni v. Johnson, 295 N.Y. 436, 68 N.E.2d 431 (1946).

7. The maximum age to which the special rule as to children has been applied appears to be seventeen, in Charbonneau v. MacRury, 84 N.H. 501, 153 A. 457 (1931). But cf. Dorais v. Paquin, 113 N.H. 187, 304 A.2d 369 (1972) (17-year-old held to adult standard in walking on wrong side of road). In Atlanta Gas Light Co. v. Brown, 94 Ga.App. 351, 94 S.E.2d 612 (1956), it was "presumed" that a 20–year–old was as capable as an adult.

8. As reflected in the decision in the principal case, the Restatement (Second) of Torts has taken the position that the special rule should not be applied when the actor engages "in an activity which is normally undertaken only by adults, and for which adult qualifications are required." What activities fit within this rule? Thus far it has been deemed applicable when a child was driving an automobile, Nielson v. Brown, 232 Or. 426, 374 P.2d 896 (1962); a motorboat, Dellwo v. Pearson, 259 Minn. 452, 107 N.W.2d 859 (1961), and when a teen-ager was playing golf, Neumann v. Shlansky, 58 Misc.2d 128, 294 N.Y.S.2d 628 (1968), aff'd, 63 Misc.2d 587, 312 N.Y.S.2d 951 (1971) (Gullota, J., dissenting), aff'd, 36 A.D.2d 540, 318 N.Y.S.2d 925 (1971). The rule was applied to a plaintiff riding a motorcycle in Harrelson v. Whitehead, 236 Ark. 325, 365 S.W.2d 868 (1963), and Daniels v. Evans, 107 N.H. 407, 224 A.2d 63 (1966). In accord, as to motor scooters is Adams v. Lopez, 75 N.M. 503, 407 P.2d 50 (1965). The rule was not applied to plaintiffs who were bicycle riding in Williams v. Gilbert, 239 Ark. 935, 395 S.W.2d 333 (1965); and Bixenman v. Hall, 251 Ind. 527, 242 N.E.2d 837 (1969). Or the use of guns, in Purtle v. Shelton, 251 Ark. 519, 474 S.W.2d 123 (1972).

9. The court in Dellwo v. Pearson, supra note 8, said in dictum that: "There may be a difference between the standard of care that is required of a child in protecting himself against hazards and the standard that may be applicable when his activities expose others to hazards." This distinction was rejected in Dunn v. Teti, 280 Pa.Super. 399, 421 A.2d 782 (1980), where the court held that a child's conduct should be judged by the same standard whether he is plaintiff or a defendant.

10. Most of the decisions on children have involved plaintiffs, and the question has been one of their contributory negligence in looking out for their own safety. It is contended in James, Accident Liability Reconsidered: The Impact of Liability Insurance, 57 Yale L.J. 549, 554–556 (1948), that child

[Handwritten top margin: General Issue: Reasonable ——— person under circ's. or / Reasonable person under circ's, including ——— or / Neither. (not taken into account).]

defendants should be held to the standard of adults, for the reason that in practice they do not pay for the injuries they inflict, and such payment comes, if at all, from another person, or from insurance which the child has not furnished. See also James, The Qualities of the Reasonable Man in Negligence Cases, 16 Mo.L.Rev. (1951).

There has been little support in case law for James' view. See Faith v. Massengill, 104 Ga.App. 348, 121 S.E.2d 657 (1961) (explicitly rejecting the dual standard); 38 Ore.L.Rev. 268 (1959). Does it solve more problems than it creates?

11. See Shulman, The Standard of Care Required of Children, 33 Yale L.J. 617 (1927); Bohlen, Liability in Tort of Infants and Insane Persons, 23 Mich.L. Rev. 9 (1924); Gray, The Standard of Care for Children Revisited, 45 Mo.L.Rev. 597 (1980).

[Handwritten: 1) Insanity as complete defense Insanity (negates intent; but negligence?) 2) As category for duty 3) As factor in circumstances "Sudden" insanity vs. anticipated or known]

[Handwritten left margin: Tr Ct = π (jury) SCt = Aff'd]

BREUNIG v. AMERICAN FAMILY INS. CO. *[handwritten: — when does duty attach]*

Supreme Court of Wisconsin, 1970.
45 Wis.2d 536, 173 N.W.2d 619. *[handwritten: Note: Madison epilepsy case]*

[Action for personal injuries received by plaintiff when his truck was struck by an automobile driven on the left side of the highway by Mrs. Erma Veith. The action was brought against defendant insurance company under Wisconsin procedure which permits direct action against a liability insurer. The jury returned a verdict for plaintiff, and defendant appealed.]

[Handwritten right margin: Good RZL if req'd no-fault ins., but WI does not so require.]

[Handwritten: otherwise π sues Δ; Δ sues Ins. ¿ effect on jury swing Δ vis-a-vis Ins.?]

HALLOWS, CHIEF JUSTICE. There is no question that Erma Veith was subject at the time of the accident to an insane delusion which directly affected her ability to operate her car in an ordinarily prudent manner and caused the accident. * * *

The evidence established that Mrs. Veith, while returning home after taking her husband to work, saw a white light on the back of the car ahead of her. She followed this light for three or four blocks. Mrs. Veith could not remember anything else except landing in a field, lying on the side of the road, and people talking. She recalled awaking in the hospital.

[Handwritten right margin: ping ping ping]

The psychiatrist testified Mrs. Veith told him she was driving on a road when she believed that God was taking ahold of the steering wheel and was directing her car. She saw the truck coming and stepped on the gas in order to become air-borne because she knew she could fly because Batman does it. To her surprise she was not air-borne before striking the truck, but after the impact she was flying. * * * The psychiatrist testified Erma Veith was suffering from "schizophrenic reaction, paranoid type, acute." He stated that from the time Mrs. Veith commenced following the car with the white light and ending with the stopping of her vehicle in the cornfield, she was not able to operate the vehicle with her conscious mind, and that she had no knowledge or forewarning that such illness or disability would likely occur. * * *

[Handwritten right margin: a major character missing from the recent film series (but can't get much closer than Madonna)?]

[Handwritten: Key Fact]

[Handwritten bottom: How politically incorrect can you get?]

[Handwritten bottom right: (G/R) — likely to get any compensatory, not punitive damages.]

G/R = If no notice, knowledge, forewarning of insanity effect, may vitiate responsibility.

170   NEGLIGENCE   Ch. 4 G/R

The case was tried on the theory that some forms of insanity are a defense to and preclude liability for negligence. [C] Not all types of insanity vitiate responsibility for a negligent tort. The question of liability in every case must depend upon the kind and nature of the insanity. The effect of the mental illness or mental hallucination must be such as to affect the person's ability to understand and appreciate the duty which rests upon him to drive his car with ordinary care, or if the insanity does not affect such understanding and appreciation, it must affect his ability to control his car in an ordinarily prudent manner. And in addition, there must be an absence of notice or forewarning to the person that he may be suddenly subject to such a type of insanity or mental illness. * * * *

The policy basis of holding a permanently insane person liable for his tort is: (1) Where one of two innocent persons must suffer a loss it should be borne by the one who occasioned it; (2) to induce those interested in the estate of the insane person (if he has one) to restrain and control him; and (3) the fear an insanity defense would lead to false claims of insanity to avoid liability. Same re: criminal law — not punishment, compensatory.

The cases holding an insane person liable for his torts have generally dealt with pre-existing insanity of a permanent nature and the question here presented was neither discussed nor decided. The plaintiff cites Sforza v. Green Bus Lines (1934) 150 Misc. 180, 268 N.Y.S. 446; Shapiro v. Tchernowitz (1956) 3 Misc.2d 617, 155 N.Y.S.2d 1011; Johnson v. Lambotte (1961) 147 Colo. 203, 363 P.2d 165, for holding insanity is not a defense in negligence cases. *Sforza* and *Shapiro* are New York trial court decisions which do not discuss the question here presented and are unconvincing. In *Johnson,* the defendant was under observation by order of the county court and was being treated in a hospital for "chronic schizophrenic state of paranoid type." On the day in question, she wanted to leave the hospital and escaped therefrom and found an automobile standing on a street with its motor running a few blocks from the hospital. She got into the car and drove off, having little or no control of the car. She soon collided with the plaintiff. Later she was adjudged mentally incompetent and committed to a state hospital. *Johnson* is not a case of sudden mental seizure with no forewarning. The defendant knew she was being treated for mental disorder and hence would not come under the nonliability rule herein stated. distinguishing on facts = sudden mental seizure = duty = Circ act / reas = forewarning = duty = not to do act

We think the statement that insanity is no defense is too broad when it is applied to a negligence case where the driver is suddenly overcome without forewarning by a mental disability or disorder which incapacitates him from conforming his conduct to the standards of a reasonable man under like circumstances. These are rare cases indeed, but their rarity is no reason for overlooking their existence and the justification which is the basis of the whole doctrine of liability for negligence, i.e., that it is unjust to hold a man responsible for his

G/R

Insanity is not a defense; rather, a question of duty

does not belong here. In effect, isn't this what judge is saying a Circs / reas would be conduct which he is incapable of avoiding and which incapability was unknown to him prior to the accident.

We need not reach the question of contributory negligence of an insane person or the question of comparative negligence as those problems are not now presented. All we hold is that a sudden mental incapacity equivalent in its effect to such physical causes as a sudden heart attack, epileptic seizure, stroke, or fainting should be treated alike and not under the general rule of insanity.

next case

"w/o forewarning" (epilepsy)?

An interesting case holding this view in Canada is Buckley & Toronto Transp. Comm'n v. Smith Transport, Ltd. [1946] Ont.Rep. 798, 4 Dom.L.Rep. 721, which is almost identical on the facts with the case at bar. There, the court found no negligence when a truck driver was overcome by a sudden insane delusion that his truck was being operated by remote control of his employer and as a result he was in fact helpless to avert a collision. *Professor gets same delusion.*

[The court then considered whether Mrs. Veith had any warning or knowledge that would reasonably lead her to believe that hallucinations would occur and be such as to affect her driving an automobile. It concluded that, notwithstanding the testimony of the psychiatrist that in his opinion she did not, there was sufficient evidence of her past conduct to permit the jury to conclude that she believed she had a special relationship to God and was the chosen one to survive at the end of the world, and that she could believe that God would take over the direction of her life to the extent of driving her car. The question was held therefore to be properly left to the jury. Various other questions were also considered.]

Judgment affirmed. *Min = Reasonable insane person under the circ's.*
Reasonable person under the circ's, including insanity.
"under the circumstances"
Reasonable person under circ's (disregarding insanity) Maj (R)

1. Most courts have not deemed insanity to be material in defense of negligence actions; the defendant is judged by the standard of the reasonable person. See, for example, Johnson v. Lambotte, 147 Colo. 203, 363 P.2d 165 (1961); Cross v. Kent, 32 Md. 581 (1870); Williams v. Hays, 143 N.Y. 442, 38 N.E. 449 (1894); Ellis v. Fixico, 174 Okl. 116, 50 P.2d 162 (1935).

2. This has been true even in the case of "sudden insanity." See Kuhn v. Zabotsky, 9 Ohio St.2d 129, 224 N.E.2d 137 (1967).

3. The foundation for the rule can be traced to the ancient case of Weaver v. Ward, supra page 5. Does the principal case represent an improvement? Is it in accord with current understanding of psychiatric illness? Does an "insane" defendant actually "know" about his condition and have the ability to make a rational decision not to drive? Can you articulate the distinction between negligent and intentional conduct where the defendant is insane?

4. Who was the actual "defendant" in the principal case? What bearing does that have on the problem? *Directly sue insurance Co. in W.I.*

5. The Restatement of Torts, § 283, originally took no position as to the standard to be applied to an insane person in negligence cases. In the Restatement (Second) of Torts § 283B, this has been changed to state that he is to be held in all respects to the standard of the reasonable person who is sane.

not under the circumstances or even similar circumstances (like w/ children) see next page

See also § 895J. Is this totally consistent with the rule on children? Should it be?

6. There are a few cases on the contributory negligence of insane plaintiffs. They appear to agree that the recovery is barred <u>only when the insanity did not prevent the plaintiff from understanding the danger and taking action.</u> Emory Univ. v. Lee, 97 Ga.App. 680, 104 S.E.2d 234 (1958); De Martini v. Alexander Sanitarium, 192 Cal.App.2d 442, 13 Cal.Rptr. 564 (1961); Johnson v. Texas & Pac. R. Co., 16 La.App. 464, 133 So. 517, 135 So. 114 (1931).

7. See Alexander and Szasz, Mental Illness as an Excuse for Civil Wrongs, 43 Notre Dame Law. 24 (1967); Bohlen, Liability in Tort of Infants and Insane Persons, 23 Mich.L.Rev. 9 (1924); Green, Public Policy Underlying the Law of Mental Incompetency, 38 Mich.L.Rev. 1189 (1940); Ague, The Liability of Insane Persons in Tort Actions, 60 Dickinson L.Rev. 211 (1956); Wilkinson, Mental Incompetency as a Defense to Tort Liability, 17 Rocky Mt.L.Rev. 38 (1944); Curran, Tort Liability of the Mentally Ill and Mentally Deficient, 21 Ohio St.L.J. 52 (1960); Note, Tort Liability of the Mentally Ill in Negligence Actions, 93 Yale L.J. 153 (1983).

LYNCH v. ROSENTHAL

Court of Appeals of Kansas City, Missouri, 1965.
396 S.W.2d 272.

SPERRY, COMMISSIONER. Ronald G. Lynch sued Fred Rosenthal for damages because of personal injuries received when he got his right arm caught in a corn picker operated by defendant. Plaintiff had a verdict and judgment for $10,000.00, and defendant appeals.

Plaintiff was twenty-two years of age when the accident occurred, and twenty-four when the case was tried. He was a single man and lived at the farm home of defendant and his wife and family consisting originally, of six children. Defendant's wife took plaintiff and his sister out of the State Home for subnormal, or retarded children, at Marshall, Missouri, when plaintiff was twelve years of age. Plaintiff had, at that time, been in the home for about seven years. He could not talk. He had never gone to school and, when defendant's wife attempted to enter plaintiff in school, he was rejected as unsuitable because of his size, age and mental condition. He was never adopted by defendant but lived in the home with the family. He was given room, board, clothing and some spending money and he helped with the farm and household work. He ate at the family table and was treated like defendant's children. Sometimes, he worked for neighbors and for others, but he was never an <u>employee</u> of defendant in a legal sense. * * *

Plaintiff stated that defendant told him to pick up corn behind the picker; that he told him to walk behind the picker; that he walked about three feet behind and to the right of the picker. (He also said that he walked twenty feet to the right of the picker). He stated that, as he walked near the rear of the picker, a corn stalk was pulled up and cast against his shins; that he stumbled and fell into the picker; that he caught at a metal shield near the open husking rollers, and his right arm went into the rollers; that he then got up on the drawbar with his left foot; that defendant did not warn him about walking in close proximity to the picker; that he knew that it was dangerous to get too close to moving parts of machinery. * * *

Dr. Lytton, a qualified child psychiatrist, was a witness for plaintiff. He testified to the effect that he examined plaintiff and administered certain tests commonly used in such cases. He gave it as his opinion that plaintiff had the mental capacity of a child of from nine and one half to ten and one half years of age; that he had an I.Q. of 65 as compared to a national average of 100; that he is not mentally ill, just has a low mental capacity; that he is unlike a normal ten year old child in that he cannot use his actual mental ability in a meaningful way; that most ten year olds can ride a bicycle; that, since plaintiff can not do so, he has a mental level of less than ten years; that he does not have the ability to appreciate the danger of moving machinery, but he can comprehend a warning to stay away from it; that he can not do a simple syllogism; that he is incapable of abstract reasoning; that most ten year olds can tell time but plaintiff cannot; that there are three classifications of subnormal mentality, to-wit: moron, low moron, and idiot; that plaintiff is a low moron; that the extent of his mental incapacity would be apparent to any normal person who might live around him. * * *

Defendant pleaded and submitted the issue of plaintiff's contributory negligence. He now urges that he was contributorily negligent as a matter of law.

In support of this contention he points out that plaintiff stated in evidence that he knew that it was dangerous to get too close to the husking machinery of a corn picker, that he might be hurt if he did. However, there was medical evidence to the effect that plaintiff's mental condition was such that he would understand a direct warning to stay away from such machinery, which defendant did not give, but that he might not be able to understand the reason therefor. The extent of his mental deficiency was fully explored in the evidence, and the testimony of Dr. Lytton and Mrs. Rosenthal made his mental condition clear. Plaintiff also testified, and the jury had an opportunity to judge that issue from his testimony for they saw the witness and heard his testimony. There was evidence from which the jury could have found that his full usable mentality was below that of a ten year old child. In Cathey v. DeWeese, Mo., 289 S.W.2d 51, the court considered the question of whether a seventeen year old ninth grade boy, of average intelligence and ability, was guilty of contributory negligence as a matter of law, when his foot got caught in a hay baler. The court said (55–56) that, although he had seen the printed sign of danger appearing on the machine and knew, independently, that it was dangerous to come in contact with the rollers of the machine, that such was not sufficient for the trial court to declare contributory negligence as a matter of law. The court said " * * * the question is whether, by reason of his youthfulness and inexperience, reasonable minds could differ as to his *realization* and *appreciation* of the danger". The verdict in plaintiff's favor was ordered re-instated. The facts in that case were far stronger in support of a ruling of contributory negligence than they are in the case at bar. * * *

The judgment is affirmed.

———

1. "If, for instance, a man is born hasty and awkward, is always hurting himself or his neighbors, no doubt his congenital defects will be allowed for in the courts of Heaven, but his slips are no less troublesome to his neighbors than if they sprang from guilty neglect. His neighbors accordingly require him, at his peril, to come up to their standard, and the courts which they establish decline to take his personal equation into account." Holmes, The Common Law 108 (1881). See also Seavey, Negligence—Subjective or Objective? 41 Harv.L. Rev. 1 (1927).

2. There appear to be no cases on the negligence of mentally deficient adult defendants, when it does not amount to insanity. There are, however, several cases as to the contributory negligence of plaintiffs. These divide as follows:

A. Wright v. Tate, 208 Va. 291, 156 S.E.2d 562 (1967), appears to stand alone in refusing to make any allowance for the plaintiff's mental deficiency, and holding him to the standard of the ordinary intelligent reasonable person. Snead, J.: "If the rule were otherwise, there would be a different standard for each level of intelligence, resulting in confusion and uncertainty in the law."

B. Allowance is made for the mental deficiency if it has prevented the plaintiff from comprehending his danger and taking action to avoid it, but not otherwise.

C. There are a few cases making allowance even for the plaintiff's inability to exercise the judgment of a reasonable person. Seattle Elec. Co. v. Hovden, 190 Fed. 7 (9th Cir.1911); Dassinger v. Kuhn, 87 N.W.2d 720 (N.D. 1958).

3. One line of theory adopted today by some psychologists is that certain individuals are "accident prone." That is to say, that because of psychological drives explained as based on a Freudian suppressed desire for self-punishment or self-destruction, they have an unusual propensity for getting into accidents, which they cannot control. Whether the explanation is true or not, there are certainly a great many individuals who are frequently involved in accidents. Many of them, perhaps, merely have slow reactions to danger. Are the "accident prone" individuals to be excused from liability?

4. See James and Dickinson, Accident Proneness and Accident Law, 63 Harv.L.Rev. 769 (1950); McNiece and Thornton, Automobile Accident Prevention and Compensation, 27 N.Y.U.L.Rev. 585, 591–597 (1952).

5. Can voluntary intoxication be used as a defense against negligent conduct? See Schwartz v. Johnson, 152 Tenn. 586, 280 S.W. 32 (1926).

(B) The Professional

HEATH v. SWIFT WINGS, INC.
Court of Appeals of North Carolina, 1979.
40 N.C.App. 158, 252 S.E.2d 526.

On 3 August 1975 a Piper 180 Arrow airplane crashed immediately after takeoff from the Boone–Blowing Rock Airport. * * *

Plaintiff's evidence, except to the extent it is quoted from the record, is briefly summarized as follows: Mary Payne Smathers Curry, widow of Vance Smathers, observed the takeoff of the Piper aircraft shortly after 5:00 o'clock on 3 August 1975. She observed Fred Heath load and reload the passengers and luggage, apparently in an effort to improve the balance of the aircraft. He also "walked around [the airplane] and looked at everything * * *. She remembers seeing him and thinking that he's doublechecking it to be sure no one has slashed the tires." The airplane engine started promptly and the plane was taxied to the end of the runway where it paused for approximately five minutes before takeoff. The airplane came very close to the end of the runway before takeoff. However "[t]he engine sounded good the entire time, and she did not recall hearing the engine miss or pop or backfire." After takeoff, the airplane "gained altitude but it didn't go up very high" and then "leveled off pretty low". * * *

William B. Gough, Jr., a free-lance mechanical engineering consultant and pilot, testified concerning the operation and flight performance of the Piper 180 Arrow. He testified concerning the many factors affecting the takeoff capabilities of the Piper and the calculations to be made by the pilot before takeoff, utilizing flight performance charts. He testified that in his opinion, according to his calculations, the pilot should have used flaps to aid in the takeoff. Furthermore, he stated that in his opinion the reasonably prudent pilot should have made a controlled landing in the cornfield shortly after takeoff if he were experiencing difficulty attaining flight speed, and that if he had done so [he, his wife and son, and Smathers] would have survived. * * *

After the customary motions at the conclusion of all the evidence, the case was submitted to the jury upon voluminous instructions by the trial court. The jury returned a verdict answering the following issue as indicated: "1. Was Fred Heath, Jr., negligent in the operation of PA–28R 'Arrow' airplane on August 3, 1975 as alleged in the complaint?" Answer: "No". Plaintiff appeals assigning error to the exclusion of certain evidence and to the charge to the jury. * * *

MORRIS, CHIEF JUDGE. * * * Assignment of error No. 4 is directed to the trial court's charge concerning the definition of negligence and the applicable standard of care:

Trct jury instruction "Negligence, ladies and gentlemen of the jury, is the failure of someone to act as a reasonably and careful and prudent person would under the same or similar circumstances. Obviously, this could be the doing of something or the failure to do something, depending on the circumstances. (With respect to aviation negligence could be more **at** specifically defined as the failure to exercise that degree of ordinary **issue** care and caution, which an ordinary prudent pilot having the same training and experience as Fred Heath, would have used in the same or similar circumstances.")

It is a familiar rule of law that the standard of care required of an individual, <u>unless altered by statute</u>, is the conduct of the <u>reasonably</u> *makes it sou* <u>prudent man under the same or similar circumstances.</u> [Cc] While the */as tho' par* standard of care of the reasonably prudent man remains constant, the *the circ's* quantity or degree of care required varies significantly with the attendant circumstances. [Cc]

Subjective: i.e., in order to determine jury needed to know Heath's training and experience; and judge against himself

The trial court improperly introduced a <u>subjective standard of care</u> *See p. 174, n.2* into the definition of negligence by referring to the "ordinary care and caution, which an ordinary prudent pilot *having the same training and experience as Fred Heath,* would have used in the same or similar circumstances." (Emphasis added.) We are aware of the authorities which support the application of a greater standard of care than that of the ordinary prudent man for persons shown to possess <u>special skill in a</u> particular endeavor. See generally Prosser, Law of Torts (4th ed.) § 32. Indeed, our courts have long recognized (that) <u>one who engages in a business, occupation, or profession must exercise the requisite degree of learning, skill, and ability of that calling with reasonable and ordinary care.</u> See e.g., <u>Insurance Co. v. Sprinkler Co.</u>, 266 N.C. 134, 146 S.E.2d 53 (1966) (fire sprinkler contractor); <u>Service Co. v. Sales Co.</u>, 261 N.C. 660, 136 S.E.2d 56 (1964) (industrial designer); <u>Hunt v. Bradshaw</u>, 242 N.C. 517, 88 S.E.2d 762 (1955) (physician); <u>Hodges v. Carter</u>, 239 N.C. 517, 80 S.E.2d 144 (1954) (attorney). <u>Furthermore</u> the <u>specialist within a profession may be held to a standard of care greater than that required of the general practitioner.</u> [C] Nevertheless, the professional standard remains an (objective) standard. For example, the recognized standard for a physician is established as "the standard of professional competence and care customary in similar communities among physicians engaged in his field of practice." <u>Dickens v. Everhart</u>, 284 N.C. at 101, 199 S.E.2d at 443.

Such objective standards avoid the evil of imposing a different standard of care upon each individual. The instructions in this case concerning the pilot's standard of care are (misleading) at best, and a misapplication of the law. <u>They permit the jury to consider Fred Heath's own particular experience and training, whether outstanding or inferior, in determining the requisite standard of conduct, rather than applying a minimum standard generally applicable to all pilots.</u> The plaintiff is entitled to an instruction holding Fred Heath to the objective minimum standard of care applicable to all pilots.   *   *   *

Subjective: a std of care for Fred
objective: a std of care for pilots

This matter was well tried by both counsel for plaintiff and counsel for defendants, and several days were consumed in its trial. Nevertheless, for prejudicial errors in the charge, there must be a

New trial.

HARRY C. MARTIN and CARLTON, JJ., concur.

1. A growing proportion of negligence litigation involves persons rendering services. The basic principles involved are relatively uncomplicated: the reasonable prudent person takes on the profession of the actor and an objective standard is applied. See The Germanic, 196 U.S. 589 (1904) (shipmaster—"external standard" applied by Justice Holmes); Mertz v. Connecticut Co., 217 N.Y. 475, 112 N.E. 166 (1916) ("the prudent and competent motorman").

2. When the person rendering the service holds himself out as having superior knowledge, training and skill, he is held to a standard that expresses this. This has been consistently true of the traditional professions; it has more recently applied to the groups newly aspiring to the title of professional, and is coming to apply to artisans and craftsmen. The standard, however, is still expressed in objective form—the knowledge, training and skill (or ability and competence) of an ordinary member of the profession in good standing. Not the "average" member; this would literally mean that half of the members could meet the standard. The expression "in good standing," is held to be too vague in Gridley v. Johnson, 476 S.W.2d 475 (Mo.1978).

3. The "professional" normally contracts to render services, and the cause of action grows out of this contract. But the suit is usually in tort for damage caused by negligence. There is no need to contract specifically to exercise the normal skill of the professional—the law imposes the duty. Ordinarily, the professional is liable only for negligence, and he does not guarantee his work to be safe. But he may guarantee it. See Tierney, The Contractual Aspects of Malpractice, 19 Wayne L.Rev. 1457 (1973).

4. *Expert Testimony.* When the professional is engaged in work that is technical in nature—not a matter of "common knowledge"—a lay jury is not in a position to understand without explanation the nature of the work or the application of the standard of care to this work. For practical reasons, a plaintiff must offer expert evidence on these matters or the judge may well decide that the jury does not have sufficient evidence on which to make a determination as to negligence and will direct a verdict for the defendant. As a general rule this is the extent of the requirement of expert testimony. See Aetna Ins. Co. v. Hellmuth, Obata & Kassabaum, Inc., 392 F.2d 472 (8th Cir. 1968). But for one profession—medicine—the courts have usually laid down a "rule of law" that expert testimony is required.

5. Professional negligence is now commonly called malpractice. On the subject in general, see Eddy, Professional Negligence (1955); T. Roady and Andersen (eds.), Professional Negligence (1960) (reprint of symposium in 12 Vand.L.Rev. 535–850); D. Partlett, Professional Negligence (1985); Restatement (Second) of Torts § 299A; Comment, Professional Negligence, 121 U.Pa.L.Rev. 627 (1973).

6. Representative treatments of negligence for the major professions include the following:

Attorneys. Gillen, Legal Malpractice, 12 Washburn L.J. 281 (1973); Haughy, Lawyers' Malpractice; A Comparative Appraisal, 48 Notre Dame Law. 888 (1973); Gaudineer, Ethics and Malpractice, 26 Drake L.Rev. 88 (1976); Houser, Legal Malpractice: An Overview, 55 N.D.L.Rev. 185 (1979); Mallen, Malpractice at a Glance, 5 Cal.Law 34 (1985); Wade, The Attorney's Liability for Negligence, 12 Vand.L.Rev. 735 (1959).

Doctors. D. Louisell and Williams, Medical Malpractice, chs. 8, 9 (1973); B. Shartel and Plant, The Law of Medical Practice, ch. 3 (1959); J. Walz and Inbau, Medical Jurisprudence, chs. 4–6 (1971); King, In Search of a Standard of Care for the Medical Profession: The "Accepted Practice" Formula, 28 Vand.L. Rev. 1213 (1975); Linden, The Negligent Doctor, 11 Osgoode Hall L.J. 31 (1973); McCoid, The Care Required of Medical Practitioners, 12 Vand.L.Rev. 549 (1959); Beresford, Professional Liability of Psychiatrists, 21 Defense L.J. 123 (1972); Garner, Landmark Decisions in Dental Malpractice, 16 Defense L.J. 11 (1967); Note, 23 Vand.L.Rev. 729 (1970).

Architects and Engineers. Bell, Professional Negligence of Architects and Engineers, 12 Vand.L.Rev. 711 (1959); Seybold, Liability of Architects or Engineers to Their Clients, in Defense Research Institute, Liability of Architects and Engineers 3 (1969); Peck & Hock, Liability of Engineers for Structural Design Errors: State of the Art Considerations in Defining the Standard of Care, 30 Villanova L.Rev. 403 (1985).

Teachers. Proehl, Tort Liability of Teachers, 12 Vand.L.Rev. 723 (1959); Seitz, Tort Liability of Teachers and Administrators for Negligent Conduct Toward Pupils, 20 Cleve.St.L.Rev. 551 (1971); Vacca, Teacher Malpractice, 8 U.Rich.L.Rev. 447 (1974).

A new form of potential malpractice has arisen called "educational malpractice." See Donohue v. Copiague Union Free School Dist., 47 N.Y.2d 440, 391 N.E.2d 1352, 418 N.Y.S.2d 375 (1979). These cases have generally been unsuccessful partly because of difficulties in determining why the student failed to learn and partly because of problems in financing an award. See Wade, An Overview of Professional Negligence, 17 Mem.St.L.Rev. 465 (1987). How does failure to educate a child to read and write differ from failure to teach him how to use a golf club? See Brahatoek v. Millard Sch. Dist., District # 17, 202 Neb. 86, 273 N.W.2d 680 (1979). See also Elson, Common Law Remedies for the Educational Harms Caused by Incomplete or Careless Teaching, 33 Notre Dame Law. 306 (1977); Foster, Educational Malpractice: A Tort for The Untaught?, 19 U.B.C.L.Rev. 161 (1985).

Accountants. Defense Research Institute, Professional Liability; Liability of Accountants (1972); Brodsky and Swanson, The Expanded Liability of Accountants for Negligence, 12 Sec.Reg.L.J. 252 (1984). See also infra pages 1048–62.

Clergy. Nally v. Grace Community Church, 157 Cal.App.3d 912, 204 Cal. Rptr. 303, noted 1985 Ariz.St.L.J. 213 (1984); Hester v. Barnett, 723 S.W.2d 544 (Mo.App.1987). In the past, few lawsuits were brought against members of the clergy. This appears to have changed. Why? Can you articulate ways in which members of the clergy might commit *negligent* malpractice? See Klee, Clergy Malpractice: Bad News for the Good Samaritan or a Blessing in Disguise? 17 Toledo L.Rev. 209 (1985); Note, Clergy Malpractice: Making Clergy Accountable to a Lower Power, 14 Pepperdine L.Rev. 137 (1986).

7. The standard is appropriately modified for specialists in a particular profession holding themselves out to have higher skills. See Rosenbaum, The

Degree of Skill and Care Legally Required of a Medical or Surgical Specialist 49 Medico–Legal J. 85 (1932); Notes, 30 Albany L.Rev. 282 (1966) (attorneys), 16 St. Louis U.L.J. 497 (1972) (doctors). Also for paraprofessionals, Wade, Tort Liability of Paralegals and Lawyers Who Utilize Their Services, 24 Vand.L.Rev. 1133 (1971); Left, Medical Devices and Paramedical Personnel: A Preliminary Context for Emerging Problems, 1967 Wash.U.L.Q. 332.

Cf below for

Legal Malpractice

HODGES v. CARTER — *read case in reporters = confusing*

Supreme Court of North Carolina, 1954.
239 N.C. 517, 80 S.E.2d 144.

Civil action to recover compensation for losses resulting from the alleged negligence of defendant D.D. Topping and H.C. Carter, now deceased, in prosecuting, on behalf of plaintiff, certain actions on fire insurance policies.

On 4 June 1948 plaintiff's drug store building located in Bellhaven, N.C., together with his lunch counter, fixtures, stock of drugs and sundries therein contained, was destroyed by fire. At the time plaintiff was insured under four policies of fire insurance against loss of, or damage to, said mercantile building and its contents. He filed proof of loss with each of the four insurance companies which issued said policies. The insurance companies severally rejected the proofs of loss, denied liability, and declined to pay any part of the plaintiff's losses resulting from said fire.

H.C. Carter and D.D. Topping were at the time attorneys practicing in Beaufort and adjoining counties. As they were the ones from whom plaintiff seeks to recover, they will hereafter be referred to as the defendants. — * — * — *why impt to point out?*

On 3 May 1949 defendants, in behalf of plaintiff, instituted in the Superior Court of Beaufort County four separate actions—one against each of the four insurers. Complaints were filed and summonses were issued, directed to the sheriff of Beaufort County. In each case the summons and complaint, together with copies thereof, were mailed to the Commissioner of Insurance of the State of North Carolina. The *Note —* Commissioner accepted service of summons and complaint in each case and forwarded a copy thereof by registered mail to the insurance company named defendant therein.

Thereafter each defendant made a special appearance and moved to dismiss the action against it for want of proper service of process for that the Insurance Commissioner was without authority, statutory or otherwise, to accept service of process issued against a foreign insurance company doing business in this State. When the special appearance and motion to dismiss came on for hearing at the February Term 1950, the judge presiding concluded that the acceptance of service of process by the Insurance Commissioner was valid and served to subject the movants to the jurisdiction of the court. Judgment was entered in each case denying the motion therein made. Each defendant excepted and appealed. This Court reversed. Hodges v. New Hampshire Fire

Insurance Co., 232 N.C. 475, 61 S.E.2d 372. See also Hodges v. Home
Insurance Co., 233 N.C. 289, 63 S.E.2d 819.

On 4 March 1952 plaintiff instituted this action in which he alleges
that the defendants were negligent in prosecuting his said actions in
that they failed to (1) have process properly served, and (2) sue out alias
summonses at the time the insurers filed their motions to dismiss the
actions for want of proper service of summons, although they then had
approximately sixty days within which to procure the issuance thereof.

Defendants, answering, deny negligence and plead good faith and
the exercise of their best judgment.

At the hearing in the court below the judge, at the conclusion of
plaintiff's evidence in chief, entered judgment of involuntary nonsuit.
Plaintiff excepted and appealed.

BARNHILL, CHIEF JUSTICE. * * * Ordinarily when an attorney
engages in the practice of the law and contracts to prosecute an action
in behalf of his client, he impliedly represents that (1) he possesses the
requisite degree of learning, skill, and ability necessary to the practice
of his profession and which others similarly situated ordinarily possess;
(2) he will exert his best judgment in the prosecution of the litigation
entrusted to him; and (3) he will exercise reasonable and ordinary care
and diligence in the use of his skill and in the application of his
knowledge to his client's cause. [Cc]

An attorney who acts in good faith and in an honest belief that his
advice and acts are well founded and in the best interest of his client is
not answerable for a mere error of judgment or for a mistake in a point
of law which has not been settled by the court of last resort in his State
and on which reasonable doubt may be entertained by well-informed
lawyers. [Cc]

Conversely, he is answerable in damages for any loss to his client
which proximately results from a want of that degree of knowledge and
skill ordinarily possessed by others of his profession similarly situated,
or from the omission to use reasonable care and diligence, or from the
failure to exercise in good faith his best judgment in attending to the
litigation committed to his care. [Cc]

When the facts appearing in this record are considered in the light
of these controlling principles of law, it immediately becomes manifest
that plaintiff has failed to produce a scintilla of evidence tending to
show that defendants breached any duty the law imposed upon them
when they accepted employment to prosecute plaintiff's actions against
his insurers or that they did not possess the requisite learning and skill
required of an attorney or that they acted otherwise than in the utmost
good faith.

The Commissioner of Insurance is the statutory process agent of
foreign insurance companies doing business in this State, G.S. § 58–153,
Hodges v. New Hampshire Insurance Co., 232 N.C. 475, 61 S.E.2d 372,
and when defendants mailed the process to the Commissioner of Insur-

ance for his acceptance of service thereof, they were following a custom which had prevailed in this State for two decades or more. Foreign insurance companies had theretofore uniformly ratified such service, appeared in response thereto, filed their answers, and made their defense. The right of the Commissioner to accept service of process in behalf of foreign insurance companies doing business in this State had not been tested in the courts. Attorneys generally, throughout the State, took it for granted that under the terms of G.S. § 58–153 such acceptance of service was adequate. And, in addition, the defendants had obtained the judicial declaration of a judge of our Superior Courts that the acceptance of service by the Commissioner subjected the defendants to the jurisdiction of the court. Why then stop in the midst of the stream and pursue some other course?

Doubtless this litigation was inspired by a comment which appears[1] in our opinion on the second appeal, Hodges v. Home Insurance Co., 233 N.C. 289, 63 S.E.2d 819. However, what was there said was pure dictum, injected—perhaps ill advisedly—in explanation of the reason we could afford plaintiff no relief on that appeal. We did not hold, or intend to intimate, that defendants had been in any wise neglectful of their duties as counsel for plaintiff.

The judgment entered in the court below is

Affirmed.

---

1. The dictum in the Hodges case, referred to in the last major paragraph of the principal case, reads as follows: "At the time defendant entered its motion to dismiss the original action, the plaintiff still had more than sixty days in which to sue out an alias summons and thus keep his action alive. He elected instead to rest his case upon the validity of the service had. The unfortunate result is unavoidable." The statute of limitations had thus run and no new suit could be brought. As a result the loss fell on the insured. Is this where it should fall?

2. *Error of Judgment.* While most treatments of the standard of care for professionals have been confined to the element of knowledge and skill, there are, as the opinion in this case indicates, two other significant elements. The first is the exercise of a discerning judgment in the exercise of a reasonable discretion. It is usually expressed by saying that a doctor or lawyer is not liable for a "mere error of judgment." He is, however, required to exercise his own best judgment.

3. The leading case is Lucas v. Hamm, 56 Cal.2d 583, 364 P.2d 685, 15 Cal. Rptr. 821 (1961), where a will had trust provisions that violated the rules of perpetuities and restraint on alienation. Of these topics, it was said that "few, if any, areas of the law have been more fraught with more confusion or concealed traps for the unwary draftsman," and the court held the attorney not liable. The same attitude is taken regarding doctors, particularly in the use of discretion in making a diagnosis. See Blankenship v. Baptist Memorial Hosp., 26 Tenn.App. 131, 168 S.W.2d 491 (1942).

4. *Use of Due Care.* The other element involves the professional's use of due care in the use of his skill and knowledge. The "antidote" to Lucas v.

Hamm is Smith v. Lewis, 13 Cal.3d 349, 530 P.2d 589, 118 Cal.Rptr. 621 (1975). Defendant attorney, representing a wife in a divorce proceeding, failed to claim for his client her interests under the California community property law in her husband's retirement benefits. He mistakenly believed that they were not subject to the claim. The trouble was that he failed to research the topic and could have found the law relatively clear that the retirement rights were community property. The court upheld a judgment for $100,000. See generally Annot., 78 A.L.R.3d 255 (1977).

A prime illustration of this type of negligence for lawyers is failure to file a suit before the running of the statute of limitations. This involves no exercise of judgment. Lally v. Kuster, 177 Cal. 783, 171 P. 961 (1918); Watkins v. Sheppard, 278 So.2d 890 (La.App.1973). While a doctor may not be liable for a mistake of diagnosis, he is liable if he negligently fails to obtain the requisite data on which to exercise his trained discretion. Butts v. Watts, 290 S.W.2d 777 (Ky.1958); Merchants Nat'l Bank & Trust Co. v. United States, 272 F.Supp. 409 (D.N.D.1967).

5. While engaged in litigation an attorney may run into problems involving all three aspects of negligence. See the treatment in the important case of Woodruff v. Tomlin, 616 F.2d 924 (6th Cir.1980), involving negligence in the conduct of litigation.

6. In attorney negligence cases the plaintiff-client must show that but for the attorney's negligence the client would have been successful in prosecuting or defending the claim. See Togstad v. Vesely, Otto, Miller & Keefe, 291 N.W.2d 686 (Minn.1980). Would it be more difficult for a plaintiff-client to bring a successful attorney-negligence case where the claim is that the attorney inadequately prepared for trial or where the claim is that the attorney missed the statute of limitations?

7. "A careful lawyer might readily advise a client that he was entitled to a piece of real property, and that it was proper to bring an action for its recovery, while at the same time he would unhesitantly reject a title which involved the same question as to which he advised a suit." Byrnes v. Palmer, 18 App.Div. 1, 45 N.Y.S. 479, 482 (1897).

8. An attorney appointed to represent an indigent defendant in a criminal trial is not entitled to any degree of immunity from suit for malpractice brought by that defendant. Ferri v. Ackerman, 440 U.S. 907 (1979).

[handwritten: ⌊ acting on behalf of ~~the~~ State]

BOYCE v. BROWN

[handwritten: Trct - Δ (DV.)]

Supreme Court of Arizona, 1938.
51 Ariz. 416, 77 P.2d 455.

[handwritten margin: Medical Malpractice ② Expert Testimony req'd unless Gross Negligence]

LOCKWOOD, JUDGE. Berlie B. Boyce and Nannie E. Boyce, his wife, hereinafter called plaintiffs, brought suit against Edgar H. Brown, hereinafter called defendant, to recover damages for alleged malpractice by the defendant upon the person of Nannie E. Boyce. The case was tried to a jury and, at the close of the evidence for plaintiffs, the [handwritten: lwr ct=dv. for ⌐] court granted a motion for an instructed verdict in favor of the defendant, on the ground that there was no competent testimony that he was guilty of any acts of commission or omission sufficient, as a matter of law to charge him with malpractice. Judgment was rendered on the verdict, and, after the usual motion for new trial was overruled, this appeal was taken. * * *

The sole question for our consideration, therefore, is whether, taking the evidence as strongly as is reasonably possible in support of plaintiffs' theory of the case, as we must do when the court instructs a verdict in favor of defendant, there was sufficient evidence to sustain a judgment in favor of plaintiffs. *   * *

About September 1, 1927, plaintiffs engaged the services of defendant, who for many years had been a practicing physician and surgeon in Phoenix, to reduce a fracture of Mrs. Boyce's ankle. This was done by means of an operation which consisted, in substance, of making an incision at the point of fracture, bringing the broken fragments of bone into apposition, and permanently fixing them in place by means of a metal screw placed in the bone. Defendant continued to attend Mrs. Boyce for three or four weeks following such operation until a complete union of the bone had been established, when his services terminated. There is no serious contention in the record that defendant did not follow the approved medical standard in the treatment of the fractured bone up to this time. No further professional relations existed between the parties until seven years later, in November, 1934, when Mrs. Boyce again consulted him, complaining that her ankle was giving her considerable pain. He examined the ankle, wrapped it with adhesive tape, and then filed the edge of an arch support, which he had made for her seven years before, and which, from use, had grown so thin that the edge was sharp. About a week later he removed the bandage. Her ankle, however, did not improve after this treatment, but continued to grow more painful until January, 1936, some two years later. At this last-mentioned time she returned to defendant, who again examined the ankle. A few days later she went to visit Dr. Kent of Mesa, who, on hearing the history of the case, and noticing some discoloration and swelling, caused an X-ray of the ankle to be made. This X-ray showed that there had been some necrosis of the bone around the screw. Dr. Kent operated upon Mrs. Boyce, removing the screw, and she made an uneventful recovery, the ankle becoming practically normal.

There are certain general rules of law governing actions of malpractice, which are almost universally accepted by the courts, and which are applicable to the present situation. We state them as follows: (1) One licensed to practice medicine is presumed to possess the degree of skill and learning which is possessed by the average member of the medical profession in good standing in the community in which he practices, and to apply that skill and learning, with ordinary and reasonable care, to cases which come to him for treatment. If he does not possess the requisite skill and learning, or if he does not apply it, he is guilty of malpractice. [C] (2) Before a physician or surgeon can be held liable as for malpractice, he must have done something in his treatment of his patient which the recognized standard of good medical practice in the community in which he is practicing forbids in such cases, or he must have neglected to do something which such standard requires. [C] (3) In order to sustain a verdict for the plaintiffs in an action for malpractice, the standard of medical practice in the commu-

expert testimony to establish standard + deviation therefrom.

expert testimony

expert testimony a requirement.

nity must be shown by affirmative evidence, and, unless there is evidence of such a standard, a jury may not be permitted to speculate as to what the required standard is, or whether the defendant has departed therefrom. [Cc] (4) Negligence on the part of a physician or surgeon in the treatment of a case is never presumed, but must be affirmatively proven, and no presumption of negligence nor want of skill arises from the mere fact that a treatment was unsuccessful, failed to bring the best results, or that the patient died. [C] (5) The accepted rule is that negligence on the part of a physician or surgeon, by reason of his departure from the proper standard of practice, must be established by expert medical testimony, unless the negligence is so grossly apparent that a layman would have no difficulty in recognizing it. [Cc] (6) The testimony of other physicians that they would have followed a different course of treatment than that followed by the defendant is not sufficient to establish malpractice unless it also appears that the course of treatment followed deviated from one of the methods of treatment approved by the standard in that community. [C] *or unless course of treatment followed was not an accepted course (unless fully informed)*

also expert testimony

This is what is argued re: X-Ray

With these principles of the law governing the relation of physician and patient, and malpractice actions arising out of that relation as a guide, let us consider the record to see whether plaintiffs presented sufficient evidence to sustain a judgment in their favor. Two questions present themselves to us: (a) What was the treatment which defendant gave Mrs. Boyce in November, 1934? and (b) What was the medical standard which he was required to conform to, under all the circumstances, in giving her treatment at that time? The treatment given, according to her own testimony, consisted in an ordinary examination of the ankle, the smoothing of an arch support which she was then wearing, and the wrapping of the ankle with adhesive tape, with the suggestion that the tape be left on for a few days. About a week later Mrs. Boyce returned and the tape was taken off. The evidence does not show that she ever came back to defendant for further treatment in November, 1934, or, indeed, until January, 1936. The next question is whether the examination and treatment given by defendant departed from the established standard for cases like that of Mrs. Boyce. The only testimony we have which, in any manner, bears upon medical standards or the proper treatment of Mrs. Boyce in November, 1934, is that of Dr. Kent, who performed the operation on the ankle in January, 1936, and of defendant. The latter testified that he did what was required by Mrs. Boyce's condition as it existed then. Dr. Kent's testimony as to the condition he found in 1936, and what he did, is clear and distinct. He was asked as to how long prior to that time the screw should have been removed, and stated that he could not answer; that, if the ankle was in the same condition as it was when he operated, he would say that the screw should have been removed, but that it was impossible for him to testify as to when the condition justifying removal arose. He was questioned more fully and answered substantially that his first conclusion, if he had been in the position of defendant, when Mrs. Boyce called on the latter in November, 1934, would have been

key fact FACT

that arthritis in the ankle joint was causing the pain, but that he would not have been fully satisfied without having an X-ray made of the ankle. On cross-examination he testified that the method of uniting bone used by defendant was a standard one, and that the screw was not removed, as a rule, unless it made trouble. Nowhere, however, did Dr. Kent testify as to what was the proper standard of medical care required at the time defendant treated Mrs. Boyce in 1934, or as to whether, in his opinion, the treatment given deviated from that standard. The nearest he came to such testimony was the statement that he personally would have had an X-ray taken, but he did not say the failure to do so was a deviation from the proper standard of treatment.

Counsel for plaintiffs, in their oral argument, apparently realized the weakness of their evidence on the vital point of what the proper medical standard required in 1934, and based their claim of negligence almost entirely upon the failure of defendant to take an X-ray of Mrs. Boyce's ankle at that time. They urge that this comes within the exception to the general rule, in that a failure to do so is such obvious negligence that even a layman knows it to be a departure from the proper standard. We think this contention cannot be sustained. It is true that most laymen know that the X-ray usually offers the best method of diagnosing physical changes of the interior organs of the body, and particularly of the skeleton, short of an actual opening of the body for ocular examination, but laymen cannot say that in all cases where there is some trouble with the internal organs that it is a departure from standard medical practice to fail to take an X-ray. Such things are costly and do not always give a satisfactory diagnosis, or even as good a one as other types of examination may give. In many cases the taking of an X-ray might be of no value and put the patient to unnecessary expense, and, in view of the testimony in the present case as to the arthritis which Mrs. Boyce had, and which Dr. Kent testified would have been his first thought as to the cause of Mrs. Boyce's pain in 1934, we think it is going too far to say that the failure to take an X-ray of Mrs. Boyce's ankle at that time was so far a departure from ordinary medical standards that even laymen would know it to be gross negligence. Since, therefore, there was insufficient evidence in the record to show that defendant was guilty of malpractice, under the rules of law above set forth, the court properly instructed a verdict in favor of the defendant.

The judgment of the superior court is affirmed.

1. The summary in this case was an accurate statement of the law when made and has been modified since in only minor respects.

2. *Customary Practice.* For the professions in general, evidence as to customary practice is admissible and may prove very influential. For the medical profession, it is usually found to be controlling and the jury are usually told that the plaintiff cannot recover unless he proves that the defendant's conduct was not in accord with recognized medical practice. It is not enough

[handwritten top margin: The reasonable physician of ordinary prudence under same or similar circ's. (locality rule) would get "informed consent"]

that a doctor testify that he would not follow the defendant's practice; he must also testify that the practice was not recognized as valid. There are some occasions, however, where a customary practice is held to be negligence. See, e.g., Ault v. Hall, 119 Ohio St. 422, 164 N.E. 518 (1928); Incollingo v. Ewing, 444 Pa. 263, 299, 282 A.2d 206 (1971). The locality rule as discussed in the principal case is also held to apply to the rule that compliance with a recognized custom will not be negligence. Gresham v. Ford, 192 Tenn. 310, 241 S.W.2d 408 (1951); see Morrison v. McNamara, infra page 192.

3. *Testimony.* The greatest significance of the locality rule and the customary-practice rule comes when they are joined with the rule that expert evidence is required. To show what is the standard of learning or the customary practice in a small town, the only expert is a doctor who knows about this (or a similar) small town. What are the chances of getting that doctor to testify? *[handwritten: exp. in D's favor?]*

4. In the principal case, do you suppose that the defendant was probably not negligent or just not proved to be negligent? Did plaintiff lose because her attorney negligently failed to ask the right questions of Dr. Kent or because Dr. Kent was not ready to testify frankly on this issue? Why not get some other witness? *[handwritten margin: legal malpractice]*

5. The courts have evolved several doctrines to alleviate this problem— the "common-knowledge rule," the doctrine of informed consent (Scott v. Bradford, infra this page) and an expanded application of "res ipsa loquitur." As to the latter, see Holmes v. Gamble, infra page 245.

6. In cases where a plaintiff brings an action based in contract, some courts have held that an express warranty of result between doctor and plaintiff is not necessary. Sciacca v. Polizzi, 403 So.2d 728 (La.1981).

[handwritten: Duty = circ = breach of must cause harm / reas]

[handwritten: Duty = informed consent = breach of must cause patient to proceed — one test (undisclosed risk) must cause harm]

SCOTT v. BRADFORD

[handwritten: (surgeon) Self-determination?]

Supreme Court of Oklahoma, 1979.
606 P.2d 554.

[handwritten: Medical Malpractice]

DOOLIN, JUSTICE. This appeal is taken by plaintiffs in trial below, from a judgment in favor of defendant rendered on a jury verdict in a medical malpractice action. *[handwritten: Trct = ∆]*

Mrs. Scott's physician advised her she had several fibroid tumors on her uterus. He referred her to defendant surgeon. Defendant admitted her to the hospital where she signed a routine consent form prior to defendant's performing a hysterectomy. After surgery, Mrs. Scott experienced problems with incontinence. She visited another physician who discovered she had a vesico-vaginal fistula which permitted urine to leak from her bladder into the vagina. This physician referred her to an urologist who, after three surgeries, succeeded in correcting her problems.

Mrs. Scott, joined by her husband, filed the present action alleging medical malpractice, claiming defendant failed to advise her of the risks involved or of available alternatives to surgery. She further maintained had she been properly informed she would have refused the surgery. *[handwritten: Why? Will she have to prove this?]* *[handwritten: top of p. 189]* *[handwritten: re: cause]*

[handwritten bottom: duty to get consent / duty to inform / duty to ensure consent is based on information]

The case was submitted to the jury with instructions to which plaintiffs objected. The jury found for defendant and plaintiffs appeal.

* * *

The issue involved is whether Oklahoma adheres to the doctrine of informed consent as the basis of an action for medical malpractice, and if so did the present instructions adequately advise the jury of defendant's duty.

Anglo–American law starts with the premise of thoroughgoing self-determination, each man considered to be his own master. This law does not permit a physician to substitute his judgment for that of the patient by any form of artifice. The doctrine of informed consent arises out of this premise.

Consent to medical treatment, to be effective, should stem from an understanding decision based on adequate information about the treatment, the available alternatives, and the collateral risks. This requirement, labeled "informed consent," is, legally speaking, as essential as a physician's care and skill in the *performance* of the therapy. The doctrine imposes a duty on a physician or surgeon to inform a patient of his options and their attendant risks. If a physician breaches this duty, patient's consent is defective, and physician is responsible for the consequences.

If treatment is completely unauthorized and performed without any consent at all, there has been a battery. However, if the physician obtains a patient's consent but has breached his duty to inform, the patient has a cause of action sounding in negligence for failure to inform the patient of his options, regardless of the due care exercised at treatment, assuming there is injury.

The first buds of court decisions heralding this new medical duty are found in Salgo v. Leland Stanford, Jr., University Board of Trustees, 154 Cal.App.2d 560, 317 P.2d 170 (1957). That court grounded the disclosure requirement in negligence law, holding a physician violates a duty to his patient and subjects himself to liability if he withholds any facts which are necessary to form the basis of an intelligent consent by the patient to the proposed treatment. The court strongly suggested a physician is obligated not only to disclose *what* he intends to do, but to supply information which addresses the question of *whether* he should do it. This view was a marked divergence from the general rule of "professional standard of care" in determining what must be disclosed. Under that standard, earlier decisions seemed to perpetuate medical paternalism by giving the profession sweeping authority to decide unilaterally what is in the patient's best interests. Under the "professional standard of care" a physician needed only to inform a patient in conformance with the prevailing medical practice in the community.

More recently, in perhaps one of the most influential informed consent decisions, Canterbury v. Spence, 150 U.S.App.D.C. 263, 464 F.2d 772 (D.C.Cir.1972), cert. den. 409 U.S. 1064, the doctrine received perdurable impetus. Judge Robinson observed that suits charging

failure by a physician adequately to disclose risks and alternatives of
proposed treatment were not innovative in American law. He emphasized the fundamental concept in American jurisprudence that every
human being of adult years and sound mind has a right to determine
what shall be done with his own body. True consent to what happens
to one's self is the informed exercise of a choice. This entails an
opportunity to evaluate knowledgeably the options available and the
risks attendant upon each. It is the prerogative of every patient to
chart his own course and determine which direction he will take.

The decision in *Canterbury* recognized the tendency of some jurisdictions to turn this duty on whether it is the custom of physicians
practicing in the community to make the particular disclosure to the
patient. That court rejected this standard and held the standard
measuring performance of the duty of disclosure is conduct which is
reasonable under the circumstances: "[We can not] ignore the fact that
to bind disclosure obligations to medical usage is to arrogate the
decision on revelation to the physician alone." We agree. A patient's
right to make up his mind whether to undergo treatment should not be
delegated to the local medical group. What is reasonable disclosure in
one instance may not be reasonable in another. We decline to adopt a
standard based on the professional standard. We, therefore, hold the
scope of a physician's communications must be measured by his patient's need to know enough to enable him to make an intelligent
choice. In other words, full disclosure of all material risks incident to
treatment must be made. There is no bright line separating the
material from the immaterial; it is a question of fact. A risk is
material if it would be likely to affect patient's decision. When nondisclosure of a particular risk is open to debate, the issue is for the
finder of facts.

This duty to disclose is the first element of the cause of action in
negligence based on lack of informed consent. However, there are
exceptions creating a privilege of a physician not to disclose. There is
no need to disclose risks that either ought to be known by everyone or
are already known to the patient. Further, the primary duty of a
physician is to do what is best for his patient and where full disclosure
would be detrimental to a patient's total care and best interests a
physician may withhold such disclosure, for example, where disclosure
would alarm an emotionally upset or apprehensive patient. Certainly
too where there is an emergency and the patient is in no condition to
determine for himself whether treatment should be administered, the
privilege may be invoked. The patient has the burden of going forward with evidence tending
to establish prima facie the essential elements of the cause of action.
The burden of proving an exception to his duty and thus a privilege not
to disclose, rests upon the physician as an affirmative defense.

The cause of action, based on lack of informed consent, is divided
into three elements, the duty to inform being the first, the second is

[handwritten top margin: Causation = not whether lack of [informed] consent caused harm (given ultimate[treat] caused harm) re: informed consent but whether lack of [informed] consent caused decision to proceed or not to proceed, harm resulting? Therefore, subissue arises]

causation, and the third is injury. The second element, that of causation, requires that plaintiff patient would have chosen no treatment or a different course of treatment had the alternatives and material risks of each been made known to him. If the patient would have elected to proceed with treatment had he been duly informed of its risks, then the element of causation is missing. In other words, a causal connection exists between physician's breach of the duty to disclose and patient's injury when and only when disclosure of material risks incidental to treatment would have resulted in a decision against it. A patient obviously has no complaint if he would have submitted to the treatment if the physician had complied with his duty and informed him of the risks. This fact decision raises the difficult question of the correct standard on which to instruct the jury.

The court in Canterbury v. Spence, supra, although emphasizing principles of self-determination permits liability only if non-disclosure would have affected the decision of a fictitious "reasonable patient," even though actual patient testifies he would have elected to forego therapy had he been fully informed.

Decisions discussing informed consent have emphasized the *disclosure* element but paid scant attention to the consent element of the concept, although this is the root of causation. Language in some decisions suggest the standard to be applied is a subjective one, i.e., whether that particular patient would still have consented to the treatment, reasonable choice or otherwise. [Cc]

Although the *Canterbury* rule is probably that of the majority, its "reasonable man" approach has been criticized by some commentators as backtracking on its own theory of self-determination. The *Canterbury* view certainly severely limits the protection granted an injured patient. To the extent the plaintiff, given an adequate disclosure, would have declined the proposed treatment, and a reasonable person in similar circumstances would have consented, a patient's right of self-determination is *irrevocably lost.* This basic right to know and decide is the reason for the full-disclosure rule. Accordingly, we decline to jeopardize this right by the imposition of the "reasonable man" standard.

If a plaintiff testifies he would have continued with the proposed treatment had he been adequately informed, the trial is over under either the subjective or objective approach. If he testifies he would not, then the causation problem must be resolved by examining the credibility of plaintiff's testimony. The jury must be instructed that it must find plaintiff would have refused the treatment if he is to prevail.

Although it might be said this approach places a physician at the mercy of a patient's hindsight, a careful practitioner can always protect himself by insuring that he has adequately informed each patient he treats. If he does not breach this duty, a causation problem will not arise.

The final element of this cause of action is that of injury. The risk must actually materialize and plaintiff must have been injured as a result of submitting to the treatment. Absent occurrence of the undisclosed risk, a physician's failure to reveal its possibility is not actionable.

In summary, in a medical malpractice action a patient suing under the theory of informed consent must allege and prove:

(1) defendant physician failed to inform him adequately of a material risk before securing his consent to the proposed treatment;

(2) if he had been informed of the risks he would not have consented to the treatment;

(3) the adverse consequences that were not made known did in fact occur and he was injured as a result of submitting to the treatment.

As a defense, a physician may plead and prove plaintiff knew of the risks, full disclosure would be detrimental to patient's best interests or that an emergency existed requiring prompt treatment and patient was in no condition to decide for himself.

Because we are imposing a new duty on physicians, we hereby make this opinion prospective only, affecting those causes of action arising after the date this opinion is promulgated.

The trial court in the case at bar gave rather broad instructions upon the duty of a physician to disclose. The instructions objected to did instruct that defendant should have disclosed material risks of the hysterectomy and feasibility of alternatives. Instructions are sufficient when considered as a whole they present the law applicable to the issues. Jury found for defendant. We find no basis for reversal.

Affirmed. * * *

BARNES, JUSTICE, concurring in part, dissenting in part: I concur with the majority opinion in all respects except I would adopt the reasonable man test set out in Canterbury v. Spence, 150 U.S.App.D.C. 263, 464 F.2d 772 (D.C.Cir.1972), cert. den. 409 U.S. 1064.

1. The doctrine of informed consent has had a very checkered career. Developed first as a basis for vitiating the consent and holding that an action of battery would lie, it proved to be too strong a remedy for the evil it purported to cure. The battery theory is now generally abandoned, except, of course, where the operation goes beyond the consent. Some courts still retain it, however. See Congrove v. Holmes, 37 Ohio Misc. 95, 66 Ohio Op. 295, 308 N.E.2d 765 (1973).

2. With the abandonment of the battery theory, the courts held that the question was whether the doctor was negligent in failing to disclose the particular risks. This brought into play the doctrine of customary practice and the need of having expert medical testimony that it was not good medical practice to fail to inform of the risk. That proved even more difficult than obtaining testimony that other conduct was negligent.

3. As a result, a good number of courts have been holding, on one theory or another, that the question of whether the patient should be informed of the risk should not depend upon established medical practice but upon a suitable standard that the jury could apply without expert testimony.

4. The principal case gives a good up-to-date treatment. See also Adams v. Richland Clinic, Inc., P.S., 37 Wash.App. 650, 681 P.2d 1305 (1984); Pratt v. Univ. of Minn. Affiliated Hosp. and Clinics, 38 Ed.Law Rep. 1287, 403 N.W.2d 865 (Minn.1987) (nondisclosure in genetic counseling); Shenefield v. Greenwich Hosp. Ass'n, 10 Conn.App. 239, 522 A.2d 829 (1987) (vasectomy operation).

5. Two California cases broaden considerably the scope of the duty of a doctor to inform of risks. In Truman v. Thomas, 27 Cal.3d 285, 611 P.2d 902, 165 Cal.Rptr. 308 (1980), a patient declined to take a pap test and the physician was held liable for failing to warn her of the risks involved in declining to take it. In Tresemer v. Barke, 86 Cal.App.3d 656, 150 Cal.Rptr. 384 (1978), defendant had installed a Dalkon Shield contraceptive intrauterine device in plaintiff at a time when they were commonly used and there was no knowledge of any dangers. Two years later, information of serious dangers from its use became available. The defendant's failure to notify plaintiff and give her the opportunity to have it removed was held to be a breach of duty arising from "a confidential relationship between doctor and patient," since there is an "imposed continuing status of physician-patient where the danger arose from that relationship." At least one court, however, has preferred to impose liability in work involving only the administration of drugs. Boyer v. Smith, 345 Pa. Super. 66, 497 A.2d 646 (1985).

6. For a similar broadening of the duty of an attorney, see Togstad v. Vesely, Otto, Miller & Keefe, 291 N.W.2d 686 (Minn.1980). Can you identify any rule in the law of attorney-negligence similar to informed consent in doctor negligence?

7. The topic has fascinated law review writers. See Plant, An Analysis of "Informed Consent," 36 Fordham L.Rev. 639 (1968); McCoid, A Reappraisal of Liability for Unauthorized Medical Treatment, 41 Minn.L.Rev. 381 (1957); Meisel, The Expansion of Liability for Medical Accidents from Negligence to Strict Liability by Way of Informed Consent, 56 Neb.L.Rev. 51 (1977).

8. *Causation.* Informed consent raises one problem that can be only mentioned at this early point in the course. Liability is being imposed even though there was no other negligence in performing the operation or administering the treatment. If so, it must be on the basis that if the risk had been disclosed the patient would not have agreed to be subjected to the risk by undergoing the operation or the treatment. How do we know? Can we rely on the patient's interested judgment after the event, whether it is honest or not? Can we resort to the reasonable prudent person again? Is that true causation? Observe the differing viewpoints in the two opinions in the principal case.

9. Other causation problems can arise with professional services. If an attorney negligently lets the statute run without filing suit, what is he liable for? The value of the suit? How can we tell what, if anything, it was worth without trying it? Does the client then have to win two separate suits in one?

10. Some of the professional-services cases involve another problem to be taken up later. Is the defendant liable to people who were not in privity of contract with him? A lawyer draws up a will which is invalid. Can the intended beneficiary of a legacy recover now that the testator is dead?

[handwritten: Locality rule applies to small, rural communities]

MORRISON v. MacNAMARA *[handwritten: Medical Malpractice]*

District of Columbia Court of Appeals, 1979.
407 A.2d 555.

[handwritten: Is this also a question of causation?]

[Appellant Morrison reported to appellee medical laboratory in Washington, D.C., for a urethral smear test for trichomonas, a urinary tract infection. The test was administered while Morrison was standing. Morrison had an adverse reaction to the test—he fainted and struck his head on a metal blood pressure stand and on the floor, causing permanent loss of his senses of smell and taste, among other injuries.

At trial, Morrison presented an expert witness from Michigan who testified that the test often causes the patient to feel faint and that the "national standard of care" requires that the patient sit or lie down during the test. The trial court refused to allow the testimony, holding that expert witnesses in medical malpractice cases must come from the same community as the defendant. Morrison appeals that ruling. Appellees presented expert witnesses from Washington area laboratories who testified that they always administered the test with the patient standing.]

[handwritten left margin: national = sit/lie down; Wash DC = standing up; (I) locality rule]

[handwritten: Trct = Δ]

[handwritten: geographical community]

NEWMAN, CHIEF JUDGE: * * * At the close of all the evidence, appellant submitted several jury instructions which were based on the national standard of care. Appellant maintained that in view of the national certification of the laboratory, the laboratory was under a duty to adhere to nationally accepted standards for administering the urethral smear test, and that the jury should be so instructed. Appellees argued that the laboratory owed only the duty to adhere to that standard of medical care recognized in the Washington, D.C. metropolitan area. The trial court agreed with appellees.

* * * In medical malpractice, a term referring to ordinary negligence concepts in the area of medical diagnosis, treatment, and the like, the duty of care is generally formulated as that degree of reasonable care and skill expected of members of the medical profession under the same or similar circumstances. * * *

[handwritten: R] The locality rule states that the conduct of members of the medical profession is to be measured solely by the standard of conduct expected of other members of the medical profession in the same locality or the same community. [Cc]

This doctrine is indigenous to American jurisprudence and appears to have developed in the late nineteenth century. [Cc] The rule was designed to protect doctors in rural areas who, because of inadequate training and experience, and the lack of effective means of transportation and communication, could not be expected to exhibit the skill and care of urban doctors. * * *

[handwritten right margin: RTR for locality rule; still plausible?]

In addition, it was argued that in view of the ability of urban areas to attract the most talented doctors, a rule which would hold rural doctors to urban standards of care would precipitate the departure of

[handwritten at top: — whether to sit or stand; a question — of access? education?]

doctors from rural areas and thereby leave rural communities without sufficient medical care. [Cc] In sum, the locality rule was premised on the notion that the disparity in education and access to advances in medical science between rural and urban doctors required that they be held to different standards of care. *[handwritten margin: access to technology?]*

The cases in this jurisdiction exhibit a lack of uniformity on the issue of the geographic area in which the conduct of members of the medical profession is to be measured. For example, a number of cases state that members of the medical profession are held to the skill and learning exercised by members of their profession in the District of *[handwritten: same community]* Columbia. [Cc] In other cases, the standard is referred to as that degree of care exercised by other members of the medical profession in the District or a similar locality. [Cc] Finally, a number of cases have *[handwritten: similar community]* articulated the medical standard of care without referring to any geographic limitation whatsoever. [Cc] Since courts in this jurisdiction were never directly presented with this issue, the empirical validity of the assumptions behind the locality rule has not previously been examined.

Even a cursory analysis of the policy behind the locality doctrine *[handwritten: locality rule does not apply in urban area.]* reveals that whatever relevance it has to the practice of medicine in remote rural communities, it has no relevance to medical practice in the District of Columbia. Clearly the nation's capital is not a community isolated from recent advances in the quality of care and treatment of patients. Rather, it is one of the leading medical centers in quality health care. * * * *[handwritten: #1; RTL; locality]*

Moreover, any purported disparity between the skills of practitioners in various urban centers has for the most part been eliminated. Unlike the diversified and often limited training that was available a hundred years ago, medical education has been standardized throughout the nation through a system of national accreditation. [Cc] Moreover, the significant improvements in transportation and communication over the past hundred years cast further doubt on continued vitality of the doctrine. * * * In sum, the major underpinnings of the locality doctrine no longer obtain. The locality rule has been quite properly criticized as a relic of the nineteenth century which has no relevance to the realities of modern medical practice. [Cc] *[handwritten margin: RTL for discarding locality rule altogether — even in rural areas? or still need Wash DC?]*

Quite apart from the locality rule's irrelevance to contemporary medical practice, the doctrine is also objectionable because it tends to immunize doctors from communities where medical practice is generally below that which exists in other communities from malpractice liability. [Cc] Rather than encouraging medical practitioners to elevate the quality of care and treatment of patients to that existing in other communities, the doctrine may serve to foster substandard care, by testing the conduct of medical professionals by the conduct of other medical professionals in the same community.

The locality rule is peculiar to medical malpractice. Architects are not held to a standard of conduct exercised by other architects in the

District or a similar locality. [C] Moreover, the conduct of lawyers is not measured solely by the conduct of other lawyers in the District or a similar community. [Cc]

Despite these criticisms, the locality rule is still followed in several jurisdictions. * * *

Courts which have abandoned the locality rule have taken different approaches in defining the geographical boundary within which the conduct of a medical practitioner is to be measured. For example, a number of courts have modified the locality rule by extending the geographical reference group of the standard of care to include that of "the same or similar localities." [Cc]

This approach has been criticized because of the difficulty in determining whether two communities are similar. [Cc] In addition, the similar locality formulation has been criticized for containing the same deficiencies as the traditional locality rule, *i.e.,* if the standard of conduct in a similar community is substandard, the similar locality rule would immunize those medical professionals whose conduct conforms to the substandard medical practice in a similar community. [Cc]

Other courts, noting that medical standards have been nationalized largely through a system of national board certification, have adopted a national standard of care, and accordingly have eliminated any reference to a geographically defined area in their formulation of the standard of care applicable to medical professionals. [Cc] The import of these decisions is that health care professionals who are trained according to national standards and who hold themselves out to the public as such, should be held to a national standard of care.

We are in general agreement with those courts which have adopted a national standard of care. Varying geographical standards of care are no longer valid in view of the uniform standards of proficiency established by national board certification. * * *

Although we have found no cases which address the issue of the standard of care applicable to a clinical laboratory, the same reasons which justify the application of a national standard of care to physicians and hospitals appear to apply with equal validity to medical laboratories. Medical laboratories are often staffed and operated by doctors who undergo the same rigorous training as other physicians. The opportunities for keeping abreast of medical advances that are available to doctors are equally available to clinical laboratories. Indeed medical laboratories are often an integral part of a hospital. [C] Moreover, clinical laboratories generally conduct many of the routine tests that would normally be performed by physicians and hospitals. Accordingly, they owe similar duties in their care and treatment of patients. [C]

Thus we hold that at least as to board certified physicians, hospitals, medical laboratories, and other health care providers, the standard of care is to be measured by the national standard. It follows that an instruction which compares a nationally certified medical professional's conduct exclusively with the standard of care in the District or a similar community is erroneous.

In the present case, appellees concede that they are a nationally certified medical laboratory and that they hold themselves out to the public as such. Appellant's expert witness testified at trial that the proper procedure to be employed in conducting a urethral smear test, according to national standards, is with the patient in a sitting or prone position. Appellees' expert witnesses who were all from the Washington metropolitan area testified that they were not aware of any national standards for conducting the test and that they always conducted the test with the patient in a standing position. However, the trial court instructed the jury that the appellees' conduct is to be compared solely with the standard of care prevailing in Washington, D.C. Thus, in effect the jury was instructed to ignore the testimony of appellant's expert witness on the standard of care. This instruction was error. The conflict in expert testimony was for the jury to resolve. Accordingly, we vacate the judgment in favor of appellees and order a new trial. * * * Reversed.

---

1. It has been traditional with the medical profession to state the standard of knowledge and skill in terms of a practitioner in good standing in the community in which the defendant practices or in a similar one. This apparently arose in the days in which medical education was not standardized and there was wide variance in the knowledge and skill of doctors in different parts and areas of the country. To a large extent, this factual situation has disappeared and the law is changing, too. Thus, some courts have held that there is a minimum national standard especially for specialists. Murphy v. Little, 112 Ga.App. 517, 145 S.E.2d 760 (1965) (setting broken arm); Wentling v. Jenny, 206 Neb. 335, 293 N.W.2d 76 (1980) (treatment of breast cancer); Roberts v. Tardif, 417 A.2d 444 (Me.1980) (national standard of care). Other courts have extended the scope of the locality. Flock v. J.C. Palumbo Fruit Co., 63 Idaho 220, 118 P.2d 707 (1941). And a number of courts have abolished the rule entirely. E.g., Brune v. Belinkoff, 354 Mass. 102, 235 N.E.2d 793 (1968); Shilkret v. Annapolis Emergency Hosp. Ass'n, 276 Md. 187, 349 A.2d 245 (1975); Hall v. Hilbun, 466 So.2d 856 (Miss.1985). But cf. Gambill v. Stroud, 258 Ark. 766, 531 S.W.2d 945 (1976). See generally Note, An Evaluation of Changes in the Medical Standard of Care, 23 Vand.L.Rev. 729 (1970).

As the principal case suggests, the locality rule has not been generally followed in regard to the other professions.

2. The locality rule can create serious injustice in some situations. Suppose there are only a few doctors in the community where the events occurred and none of them will testify against a colleague. But does the rule in the principal case create injustice for the medical profession? Suppose it spawns "professional experts" who travel from city to city, testifying in medical malpractice cases against doctors. *Still must be telling the truth, presumably*

3. There was no "medical malpractice" crisis when the locality rule was the majority law in the United States. Is this an appropriate reason to reject its demise? Can a reasonable "middle ground" between the rule of the principal case and the traditional locality rule be formed?

The "Medical Malpractice Crisis" and Statutory Change in the Common Law.

In the latter part of the 1970's and again in the mid–1980's, an increase in the number of medical malpractice suits produced sudden sharp rises in the premiums for malpractice liability insurance. This in turn produced alarm sometimes amounting to dismay within the profession and insistent demands that the state legislatures find ways of alleviating the harm. Almost every state passed legislation of some sort. Much of the blame was placed by the lobbyists on the law of negligence, and various modification of the substantive law of torts were rushed through the legislatures. The statutes have varied considerably and there is no uniformity in them. Changes were made in the standard of care, the doctrine of informed consent (see infra page 190), the doctrine of res ipsa loquitur (see infra page 248), the collateral source rule (see infra page 515), the statute of limitations (see infra page 606), imposing limits on the amount that could be received for pain and suffering or on the total amount recovered in a malpractice action, and prohibiting the setting forth in a complaint of the amount sued for. Changes of other types were also made. Many states required submission of the case to a screening board before bringing action, others required submission to arbitration and others sought to impose restrictions on the contingent-fee system. The statutes were supplemented by some individual doctors by bringing a tort action against the patient (and his attorney) for bringing an unwarranted civil action (see infra page 1009).

This latter device did not prove to be very successful, and state supreme courts held a number of the statutory provisions to be unconstitutional for various reasons; but most of the states still have some of the statutory modifications in effect. An attorney must therefore carefully investigate the code of his state when any malpractice claim arises. Unfortunately, it is not feasible to do much more here than issue this alert. The crisis atmosphere has now spread to all areas of professional malpractice. See Report of the Tort Policy Working Group on the Causes, Extent and Policy Implications of the Current Crisis in Insurance Availability and Affordability, 7–8 (February, 1986).

Legislative provisions in 22 states are collected and summarized in 5 The INCL Brief 12–18 (Oct. 1975). See also Redish, Legislative Response to the Medical Malpractice Insurance Crisis: Constitutional Implications, 55 Tex.L.Rev. 759 (1977); Smith, Battling a Tort Frontier: Constitutional Attacks on Medical Malpractice Laws, 38 Okla.L.Rev. 195 (1985); B. Levin & Coye (eds.), Tort Reforms and Related Proposals: Annotated Bibliography on Products Liability and Medical Malpractice, 135–233 (A.B.A.1979); Bell, Legislative Intrusions into the Common Law of Medical Malpractice: Thoughts About the Deterrent Effect of Tort Liability, 35 Syracuse L.Rev. 939 (1984).

[handwritten: factor in circumstances] *[handwritten: Authors agree w/ Care by degrees rather than lumping all as factors as of "circumstances"]*

(C) AGGRAVATED NEGLIGENCE

1. *"Degrees" of Care.* It is obvious, and elementary, that the care required by the standard of the reasonable person will vary according to the risk. As the danger increases, the actor is required to exercise caution commensurate with it, and so to be more careful. Those who deal with things that are known to be dangerous, such as explosives or electricity, must exercise more care than one who is merely walking down the street. Likewise, those who have accepted a special responsibility toward others, as in the case of a common carrier which becomes responsible for the safety of passengers, must exercise more care in accordance with the duty undertaken. On many occasions, this has been expressed in instructions to the jury, approved on appeal, that the carrier, or the person dealing with special danger, must exercise "the highest degree of care," or "the utmost caution characteristic of very careful prudent persons." See, for example, Peck v. Fanion, 124 Conn. 549, 1 A.2d 143 (1938); Pennsylvania Co. v. Roy, 102 U.S. 451 (1880). On "reasonable care" vs. "extraordinary care" regarding the use of firearms, see the opinions in Everette v. New Kensington, 262 Pa. Super. 28, 396 A.2d 467 (1978).

[handwritten margin: difference?]

There are a good many other decisions in which this has been held to be error, on the ground that there are no "degrees" of care recognized by the law, but merely amounts of care, greater or less; that the care required of the actor is always the same under the traditional formula, that of a reasonable person under like circumstances; and that the greater danger, or the greater responsibility, are merely circumstances that require a greater amount of care. See Union Traction Co. v. Berry, 188 Ind. 514, 124 N.E. 737 (1919); Rea v. Simowitz, 225 N.C. 575, 35 S.E.2d 871 (1945); Frederick v. Detroit, 370 Mich. 425, 121 N.W.2d 918 (1963). While this is undoubtedly correct as a matter of principle, in a number of cases the instruction, although erroneous, has been held not to be prejudicial.

2. *"Degrees" of Negligence.* A different attempt, carried to considerable lengths in the last century, has been to distinguish "degrees" of negligence, breaking it down into different kinds of conduct, with different legal consequences. This idea was lifted from the Roman law by Chief Justice Holt in a bailment case, Coggs v. Bernard, 2 Ld.Raym. 909, 92 Eng.Rep. 107 (1704). As it developed, the distinction was made between "slight" negligence, defined as a failure to use great care; ordinary negligence, or failure to use reasonable care; and "gross" negligence, which is failure to exercise even slight care. See Green, High Care and Gross Negligence, 23 Ill.L.Rev. 4 (1928); Elliott, Degrees of Negligence, 6 So.Cal.L.Rev. 91 (1932).

These distinctions were subjected to a good deal of criticism almost from the start. In Wilson v. Brett, 11 M. & W. 113, 152 Eng.Rep. 737 (1843), Baron Rolfe made a much quoted statement that gross negligence is merely the same thing as ordinary negligence, "with the addition of a vituperative epithet." In some of the very early cases, this was true. "Gross negligence" was an expression used to mean nothing more than negligence. See, for example, Vaughan v. Menlove, supra, page 149. But when it is intended to mean more, "gross" negligence is readily understood by the ordinary person as involving an extreme departure from ordinary standards of conduct, and it is very probable that Judge Magruder's students at the Harvard Law School knew what he meant when he explained "Chief Justice Rugg's famous distinctions among negligence, gross negligence and recklessness as being the distinctions among a fool, a damned fool, and a God-damned fool." Harvard Law Record, April 16, 1959.

In practice, however, it proved extraordinarily difficult to set any lines of demarcation; and these distinctions filled the courts with vexatious appeals in which they were asked to rule upon particular conduct as a matter of law. During the latter half of the nineteenth century, the courts of Illinois and Kansas were deluged with appeals, as a result of their adoption of a rule that contributory negligence was not a defense when the negligence of the defendant was found to be "gross," and that of the plaintiff "slight" in comparison. Both courts finally threw up their hands and threw out the distinctions, declaring that henceforth only one kind of negligence, measured by the standard of the reasonable person, was to be recognized. The story is told in Malone, The Formative Era of Contributory Negligence, 41 Ill.L.Rev. 151 (1946).

Since then, "gross" and "slight" negligence have been under a cloud, and discredited with the courts. They have largely lost their significance in the common law, both in England and in most States. Some vestiges still remain in the law of bailments, where some courts still hold that a gratuitous bailee owes his bailor only the duty of slight care, and so is liable only for gross negligence in looking after the goods. See, for example, Altman v. Aronson, 231 Mass. 588, 121 N.E. 505 (1919). The words "gross negligence" occasionally appear as words of art in automobile guest statutes. In that context, they have been construed to mean "the absence of slight care." See, for example, Hennon v. Hardin, 78 Ga.App. 81, 50 S.E.2d 236 (1948). On occasion they have been treated as synonyms for "recklessness." See Jackson v. Edwards, 144 Fla. 187, 197 So. 833 (1940).

3. *Recklessness.* A standard of conduct theoretically more culpable than gross negligence is "recklessness." Often called "wanton or willful misconduct," it purports to indicate a classification between negligence and intentional torts. While some courts have indicated that it differs from ordinary negligence in that the actor must have exercised a deliberate and conscious disregard for a known probability of harm to another, the Restatement (Second) of Torts and many courts have deemed the "recklessness" standard to be an objective one.

There is less consensus among the courts as to the nature of the standard or as to the instruction to be given to the jury. The Restatement (Second) defines it as follows in § 500:

"The actor's conduct is in reckless disregard of the safety of another if he does an act or intentionally fails to do an act which it is his duty to the other to do, knowing or having reason to know of facts which would lead a reasonable man to realize, not only that his conduct creates an unreasonable risk of physical harm to another, but also that such risk is substantially greater than that which is necessary to make his conduct negligent."

It will be helpful to "parse" this sentence by dividing it into its primary elements. For an opinion analyzing it in careful detail, see Williamson v. McKenna, 223 Or. 366, 354 P.2d 56 (1960).

In Universal Concrete Pipe Co. v. Bassett, 130 Ohio St. 567, 200 N.E. 843 (1936), Stephenson, J., after expressing in forcible language his distaste for the concept, quoted from § 282 of the Restatement, as to the respects in which the effect of recklessness differs from that of ordinary negligence, as follows:

"1. the rule that contributory negligence is no defense to an act intended to invade the plaintiff's interest is applied where the conduct is in reckless disregard of the plaintiff's interest;

"2. greater culpability is recognized by the imposition of punitive damages in many jurisdictions;

"3. there is a pronounced tendency to regard reckless conduct as the legal cause of a particular harm, although the actor's conduct if merely negligent would not have been so considered;

"4. in some jurisdictions the liability of a landowner to a trespasser or a gratuitous licensee is imposed only when the presence of the trespasser or licensee is known and the risk created by the actor's conduct is out of all proportion to its social utility;

"5. in the construction of statutes which specifically refer to gross negligence, that phrase is sometimes construed as equivalent to reckless disregard;

"6. in those jurisdictions where the distinction between trespass and trespass on the case is still of importance, reckless disregard is assimilated to intend harm to the extent that an action for trespass will lie."

Automobile Guest Statutes

The use of the expressions "recklessness," "gross negligence" and "willful and wanton conduct" evolved for the most part in connection with statutes providing that the driver of an automobile is liable only for some form of aggravated misconduct to one who is riding as a guest in his car.

The principle of limiting the duty that a driver owes to his automobile guest originated in the Massachusetts case of Massaletti v. Fitzroy, 228 Mass. 487, 118 N.E. 168 (1917). The court derived the principle from what it regarded as an analogous situation—the relationship between a gratuitous bailee and his bailor. While the Massaletti decision had only a minor impact on the case law of other states, it had an enormous impact on state legislatures. As late as 1970, over half the states had adopted guest statutes.

The many legislatures that followed *Massaletti* were persuaded by a persistent lobby on the part of some liability insurance companies. Rationales included the possibility of collusion between host and injured guest in manufacturing a claim against the host's insurer, a fair allocation of a limited insurance fund to pedestrians and persons in other cars in preference to "guests," and savings in fuel by encouraging car pools. Until the mid–1970's, no guest statute was repealed.

The statutes filled the courts with cases, in which a good many knotty little problems of interpretation arose; and the efforts of many courts to get around the statute in cases of manifest hardship led to some rather peculiar law. First of all, who was a "guest"? What was the effect of sharing expenses, of the host's business interest in offering the ride, of an employer's order prohibiting the driver from taking free riders, of stowaways, of a passenger's demand to be let out of the car? Once each state had settled those questions, there was the further problem of whether the driver's conduct in the particular case fit into the state's definition of "gross negligence," "recklessness," or "willful and wanton." A major subissue was whether or not plaintiff needed to prove that the defendant had actual knowledge of the risk involved. Compare Bailey v. Brown, 34 Ohio St.2d 62, 63 Ohio Op.2d 92, 295 N.E.2d 672 (1973), with Williamson v. McKenna, 223 Or. 366, 354 P.2d 56 (1960). See also Note, 17 Hast.L.J. 337 (1966); 2 F. Harper & James, Law of Torts, 950–958 (1950).

In Brown v. Merlo, 8 Cal.3d 855, 506 P.2d 212, 106 Cal.Rptr. 388 (1973), the Supreme Court of California held that the California guest statute denied "equal protection of the laws" to nonpaying automobile guests. See also Ramey v. Ramey, 273 S.C. 680, 258 S.E.2d 883 (1979). Eleven other state supreme courts found the guest statutes unconstitutional under state or federal constitutional provisions, and many state legislatures have repealed their guest statutes, recognizing their incompatibility with modern notions of risk distribution. In 1986 only six states required aggravated negligence for liability to guests; of these six, Illinois limits the application of the statute to hitchhikers, Ill.Rev. Stat., ch. 95½, §§ 10–210, and Texas limits it to close relatives. Tex. Civ.Prac. & Rem. § 72.001 (1986).

The legacy of the guest statutes is each state's definition of aggravated negligence, which today most often arises when juries decide whether to award punitive damages. See Chapter 10, section 3. Is it proper to apply a guest statute definition of "recklessness" to determine whether punitive damages—a quasi-criminal penalty—should be imposed?

5.　RULES OF LAW

Section 285 of the Restatement (Second) of Torts provides as follows:

§ 285.　How Standard of Conduct Is Determined

The standard of conduct of a reasonable man may be

(a) established by a legislative enactment or administrative regulation which so provides, or

(b) adopted by the court from a legislative enactment or an administrative regulation which does not so provide, or

(c) established by judicial decision, or *meant to be broken – Rule of Law*

(d) applied to the facts of the case by the trial judge or the jury, if there is no such enactment, regulation, or decision. *– first impression*

Clause (a) is illustrated by the so-called Dram–Shop Acts. See, e.g., Conn.Gen.Stat.Ann. § 30–102; Ill.Rev.Stat. Ch. 43, § 135; McGough, Dram Shop Acts, 1967 ABA Section of Insurance, Negligence and Compensation Law 448.

Clause (b) is treated in detail in Section 6, Violation of Statute, infra page 209.

Clause (c) is covered in the current Section (Rules of Law).

Clause (d) is illustrated by most of the cases in the preceding Section (The Standard of Care). — —

For an indication of the distinction between clauses (c) and (d), consider the case of Qualcast (Wolverhampton) Ltd. v. Haynes, [1959] A.C. 743, [1959] 2 All E.R. 38 (H.L.): Plaintiff was an experienced moulder. Steel spats were made available by defendant employer for its moulders as they carried ladles of molten metal, but plaintiff had not been directed to wear them. He operated without spats and was badly burned when he spilled a ladle. Action against the defendant for failing to warn him. The trial judge (without a jury) held for the plaintiff, stating, "Now, if I were not bound by authority I should decide that the plaintiff was so experienced that he needed no warning and that what he did was with the full knowledge of the risks involved and that there was no negligence on the part of the defendants. But I feel in view of the [unreported] authorities cited to me that such a decision would be wrong and I feel compelled to come to a different conclusion." *① What does judge mean?*

The case came to the House of Lords. Lord Somervell of Harrow: "When negligence cases were tried with juries the judge would direct them as to the law above. The question whether on the facts in that particular case there was or was not a failure to take reasonable care was a question for the jury. There was not, and could not be, complete uniformity of standard. One jury would attribute to the reasonable man a greater degree of prescience than would another. The jury's decision did not become part of our law citable as a precedent. In those days it would only be in very exceptional circumstances that a judge's direction would be reported or be citable. So far as the law is concerned they would all be the same. Now that negligence cases are mostly tried without juries, the distinction between the functions of the judge and jury is blurred. A judge naturally gives reasons for the conclusion formerly arrived at by a jury without reasons. It may sometimes be difficult to draw the line, but if the reasons given by a judge for arriving at the conclusion previously reached by a jury are to be treated as 'law' and citable, the precedent system will die from a surfeit of authorities. * * *

"In the present case, * * * the learned county court judge felt himself bound by certain observations in different cases which were not, I think, probably intended by the learned judges to enunciate any new principles or gloss on the familiar standard of reasonable care. It must be a question on the evidence in each case whether, assuming a duty to provide some safety equipment, there is a duty to advise everyone, whether experienced or inexperienced, as to its use. * * *

"I have come to the conclusion that the learned judge's first impulse was the right conclusion on the facts as he found them, and for the reasons he gives. I will not elaborate these reasons or someone might cite my observations as part of the law of negligence."

POKORA v. WABASH RY. CO.

Supreme Court of the United States, 1934.
292 U.S. 98, 54 S.Ct. 580, 78 L.Ed. 1149.

[Plaintiff, driving a truck, approached a level railroad crossing at which defendant had four tracks. Because of boxcars standing on the first track, five or ten feet to the north of the crossing, he could not see the tracks to the north. He stopped, looked as well as he could, and listened, but heard no bell or whistle. He then drove slowly ahead, and when he reached the main track was struck by a passenger train from the north, coming at a speed of about thirty miles an hour. The trial court directed a verdict for defendant, on the ground that plaintiff's conduct was contributory negligence as a matter of law, and this was affirmed by the Circuit Court of Appeals. Certiorari was granted by the Supreme Court.]

MR. JUSTICE CARDOZO delivered the opinion of the Court. * * * The Circuit Court of Appeals (one judge dissenting) affirmed, resting its judgment on the opinion of this court in B. & O.R. Co. v. Goodman, 275 U.S. 66, 48 S.Ct. 24, 72 L.Ed. 167. * * *

The argument is made, however, that our decision in B. & O.R. Co. v. Goodman, supra, is a barrier in the plaintiff's path, irrespective of the conclusion that might commend itself if the question were at large. There is no doubt that the opinion in that case is correct in its result. Goodman, the driver, traveling only five or six miles an hour, had, before reaching the track, a clear space of eighteen feet within which the train was plainly visible. With that opportunity, he fell short of the legal standard of duty established for a traveler when he failed to look and see. This was decisive of the case. But the court did not stop there. It added a remark, unnecessary upon the facts before it, which has been a fertile source of controversy. "In such circumstances it seems to us that if a driver cannot be sure otherwise whether a train is dangerously near he must stop and get out of his vehicle, although obviously he will not often be required to do more than to stop and look."

There is need at this stage to clear the ground of brushwood that may obscure the point at issue. We do not now inquire into the existence of a duty to stop, disconnected from a duty to get out and reconnoitre. The inquiry, if pursued, would lead us into the thickets of conflicting judgments. Some courts apply what is often spoken of as the Pennsylvania rule, and impose an unyielding duty to stop, as well as to look and listen, no matter how clear the crossing or the tracks on either side. * * *

Other courts, the majority, adopt the rule that the traveler must look and listen, but that the existence of a duty to stop depends upon the circumstances, and hence generally, even if not invariably, upon the judgment of the jury. * * * The subject has been less considered in this court, but in none of its opinions is there a suggestion that at any and every crossing the duty to stop is absolute, irrespective of the danger. Not even in B. & O.R. Co. v. Goodman, supra, which goes farther than the earlier cases, is there support for such a rule. To the contrary, the opinion makes it clear that the duty is conditioned upon the presence of impediments whereby sight and hearing become inadequate for the traveler's protection.

Choice between these diversities of doctrine is unnecessary for the decision of the case at hand. Here the fact is not disputed that the plaintiff did stop before he started to cross the tracks. If we assume that by reason of the box cars, there was a duty to stop again when the obstructions had been cleared, that duty did not arise unless a stop could be made safely after the point of clearance had been reached. * * * For reasons already stated, the testimony permits the inference that the truck was in the zone of danger by the time the field of vision was enlarged. No stop would then have helped the plaintiff if he remained seated on his truck, or so the triers of fact might find. His case was for the jury, unless as a matter of law he was subject to a duty to get out of the vehicle before it crossed the switch, walk forward to the front, and then, afoot, survey the scene. We must say whether his failure to do this was negligence so obvious and certain that one conclusion and one only is permissible for rational and candid minds.

Standards of prudent conduct are declared at times by courts, but they are taken over from the facts of life. To get out of a vehicle and reconnoitre is an uncommon precaution, as everyday experience informs us. Besides being uncommon, it is very likely to be futile, and sometimes even dangerous. If the driver leaves his vehicle when he nears a cut or curve, he will learn nothing by getting out about the perils that lurk beyond. By the time he regains his seat and sets his car in motion, the hidden train may be upon him. * * * Often the added safeguard will be dubious though the track happens to be straight, as it seems that this one was, at all events as far as the station, about five blocks to the north. (A train traveling at a speed of thirty miles an hour will cover a quarter of a mile in the space of thirty seconds.) It may thus emerge out of obscurity as the driver turns his back to regain the waiting car, and may then descend upon him suddenly when his car is on the track. Instead of helping himself by getting out, he might do better to press forward with all his faculties alert. So a train at a neighboring station, apparently at rest and harmless, may be transformed in a few seconds into an instrument of destruction. At times the course of safety may be different. One can figure to oneself a roadbed so level and unbroken that getting out will be a gain. Even then the balance of advantage depends on many circumstances and can be easily disturbed. Where was Pokora to leave his truck after getting out to reconnoitre? If he was to leave it on the switch, there was the possibility that the box cars would be shunted down upon him before he could regain his seat. The defendant did not show whether there was a locomotive at the forward end, or whether the cars were so few that a locomotive could be seen. If he was to leave his vehicle near the curb, there was even stronger reason to believe that the space to be covered in going back and forth would make his observations worthless. One must remember that while the traveler turns his eyes in one direction, a train or a loose engine may be approaching from the other.

Illustrations such as these bear witness to the need for caution in framing standards of behavior that amount to rules of law. The need is the more urgent when there is no background of experience out of which the standards have emerged. They are then, not the natural flowerings of behavior in its customary forms, but rules artificially developed, and imposed from without. Extraordinary situations may not wisely or fairly be subjected to tests or regulations that are fitting for the commonplace or normal. In default of the guide of customary conduct, what is suitable for the traveler caught in a mesh where the ordinary safeguards fail him is for the judgment of a jury. * * * The opinion in Goodman's Case has been a source of confusion in the federal courts to the extent that it imposes a standard for application by the judge, and has had only wavering support in the courts of the states. We limit it accordingly.

The judgment should be reversed, and the cause remanded for further proceedings in accordance with this opinion.

It is so ordered.

———

1. In Baltimore & Ohio R. Co. v. Goodman, 275 U.S. 66 (1927), Justice Holmes concluded his opinion with: "It is true * * * that the question of due

Justice Holmes

care very generally is left to the jury. But we are dealing with a standard of conduct, and when the standard is clear it should be laid down once and for all by the courts." *Holmes = Do 'justice, Sir, do justice!' Hand = "That is not my Job. My job is to apply to law."*

Do you think that Justice Holmes really intended to declare a rule to which there could be no possible exceptions? How would he handle exceptional circumstances?

2. The decision created something of a furor. See Note, Aftermath of the Supreme Court's Stop, Look and Listen Rule, 43 Harv.L.Rev. 926 (1930). The rule stated has had something of a checkered history. In Green, The Duty

Problem in Negligence Cases, 29 Colum.L.Rev. 255, 275 (1929), there is a short account of the economic background. When the railroads were new and poverty-stricken, it was considered more reasonable to put the burden of protecting himself upon the vehicle driver by an ironclad rule. Is there still the same justification?

3. Notwithstanding all the criticism, the general rule still has held up. In nearly all jurisdictions, it is still usually negligence as a matter of law not to look and listen when approaching a known railroad crossing, and not to slow down or even stop when obstructed vision or something else in the situation calls for it. See, for example, Chicago, R.I. & P.R. Co. v. McFarlin, 336 F.2d 1 (10th Cir.1964).

4. But over the years too many cases arose in which special circumstances made the rule an unreasonable one. Thus crossing gates were left open, as in Wabash R. Co. v. Glass, 32 F.2d 697 (6th Cir.1929). Or the driver relied on the absence of a customary flagman or flasher signal, as in Wabash R. Co. v. Walczak, 49 F.2d 763 (6th Cir.1931). Or it was clear that the conduct specified would have added nothing to the driver's safety, as in Torgeson v. Missouri–Kansas–Texas R. Co., 124 Kan. 798, 262 P. 564 (1928).

5. A similar fate has overtaken similar "rules of law," formerly stated by a good many courts as absolute, such as the rule that it is always negligence to drive an automobile at such a speed that it is impossible to stop within the range of vision. Usually this is true. But the "rule" has had to give way when the driver is suddenly blinded by the lights of an approaching car, as in Emerson v. Bailey, 102 N.H. 360, 156 A.2d 762 (1959). Or a car ahead with a visible tail-light turns out to be backing up. Cerny v. Domer, 13 Ohio St.2d 117, 235 N.E.2d 132 (1968). Or there is a dense fog, and a sudden obstacle of an entirely unusual and unexpected kind turns up, such as the house being moved in the middle of the street in Morehouse v. Everett, 141 Wash. 399, 252 P. 157 (1926).

6. Compare the "rule" that a pedestrian crossing the street must continue to look all the way across. McKinney v. Yelavich, 352 Mich. 687, 90 N.W.2d 883 (1958) contains an excellent discussion of reducing negligence to fixed rules in this situation. See also Notes, 25 Fordham L.Rev. 371 (1956); 12 Wyo.L.J. 116 (1958).

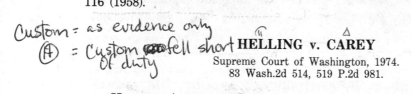

HELLING v. CAREY

Supreme Court of Washington, 1974.
83 Wash.2d 514, 519 P.2d 981.

HUNTER, ASSOCIATE JUSTICE. This case arises from a malpractice action instituted by the plaintiff (petitioner), Barbara Helling.

The plaintiff suffers from primary open angle glaucoma. Primary open angle glaucoma is essentially a condition of the eye in which there is an interference in the ease with which the nourishing fluids can flow out of the eye. Such a condition results in pressure gradually rising above the normal level to such an extent that damage is produced to the optic nerve and its fibers with resultant loss in vision. The first loss usually occurs in the periphery of the field of vision. The disease usually has few symptoms and, in the absence of a pressure test, is often undetected until the damage has become extensive and irreversible.

The defendants (respondents), Dr. Thomas F. Carey and Dr. Robert C. Laughlin, are partners who practice the medical specialty of ophthalmology. Ophthalmology involves the diagnosis and treatment of defects and diseases of the eye.

The plaintiff first consulted the defendants for myopia, nearsightedness, in 1959. At that time she was fitted with contact lenses. She next consulted the defendants in September, 1963, concerning irritation caused by the contact lenses. Additional consultations occurred in October, 1963; February, 1967; September, 1967; October, 1967; May, 1968; July, 1968; August, 1968; September, 1968; and October, 1968. Until the October 1968 consultation, the defendants considered the plaintiff's visual problems to be related solely to complications associated with her contact lenses. On that occasion, the defendant, Dr. Carey, tested the plaintiff's eye pressure and field of vision for the first time. This test indicated that the plaintiff had glaucoma. The plaintiff, who was then 32 years of age, had essentially lost her peripheral vision and her central vision was reduced to approximately 5 degrees vertical by 10 degrees horizontal.

Thereafter, in August of 1969, after consulting other physicians, the plaintiff filed a complaint against the defendants alleging, among other things, that she sustained severe and permanent damage to her eyes as a proximate result of the defendants' negligence. During trial, the testimony of the medical experts for both the plaintiff and the defendants established that the standards of the profession for that specialty in the same or similar circumstances do not require routine pressure tests for glaucoma upon patients under 40 years of age. The reason the pressure test for glaucoma is not given as a regular practice to patients under the age of 40 is that the disease rarely occurs in this age group. Testimony indicated, however, that the standards of the profession do require pressure tests if the patient's complaints and symptoms reveal to the physician that glaucoma should be suspected.

The trial court entered judgment for the defendants following a defense verdict. The plaintiff thereupon appealed to the Court of Appeals, which affirmed the judgment of the trial court. Helling v. Carey, No. 1185–41918–1 (Wn.App., filed Feb. 5, 1973). The plaintiff then petitioned this Court for review, which we granted.

We find this to be a unique case. The testimony of the medical experts is undisputed concerning the standards of the profession for the specialty of ophthalmology. * * * The issue is whether the defendants' compliance with the standard of the profession of ophthalmology, which does not require the giving of a routine pressure test to persons under 40 years of age, should insulate them from liability under the facts in this case where the plaintiff has lost a substantial amount of her vision due to the failure of the defendants to timely give the pressure test to the plaintiff.

[handwritten top margin: Rule = no distinction/ degrees of duty based on ⊓; all deserve the same (at least re adult)]

[handwritten left margin: RTL = akin to equal prot.]

The incidence of glaucoma in one out of 25,000 persons under the age of 40 may appear quite minimal. However, that one person, the plaintiff in this instance, is entitled to the same protection, as afforded persons over 40, essential for timely detection of the evidence of glaucoma where it can be arrested to avoid the grave and devastating result of this disease. The test is a simple pressure test, relatively *[handwritten: RTL]* inexpensive. There is no judgment factor involved, and there is no doubt that by giving the test the evidence of glaucoma can be detected. The giving of the test is harmless if the physical condition of the eye permits. The testimony indicates that although the condition of the plaintiff's eyes might have at times prevented the defendants from administering the pressure test, there is an absence of evidence in the record that the test could not have been timely given.

Justice Holmes stated in Texas & Pac. Ry. v. Behymer, 189 U.S. 468, 470, 23 S.Ct. 622, 623, 47 L.Ed. 905 (1903): "What usually is done may be evidence of what ought to be done, but what ought to be done is fixed by a standard of reasonable prudence, whether it usually is complied with or not." *[handwritten: We've heard this before, tending to negate "custom" as std.]*

In The T.J. Hooper, 60 F.2d 737, on page 740 (2d Cir.1932), [Judge] Hand stated: "[I]n most cases reasonable prudence is in fact common prudence; but strictly it is never its measure; a whole calling may have *[handwritten: discarding "custom]* unduly lagged in the adoption of new and available devices. It never may set its own tests, however persuasive be its usages. *Courts must in the end say what is required; there are precautions so imperative that even their universal disregard will not excuse their omission.*" (Italics ours.)

Under the facts of this case reasonable prudence required the timely giving of the pressure test to this plaintiff. The precaution of giving this test to detect the incidence of glaucoma to patients under 40 years of age is so imperative that irrespective of its disregard by the standards of the ophthalmology profession, it is the duty of the courts to say what is required to protect patients under 40 from the damaging results of glaucoma.

[handwritten left margin: "Rule of Law"] (H) We therefore hold, as a matter of law, that the reasonable standard that should have been followed under the undisputed facts of this case was the timely giving of this simple, harmless pressure test to this plaintiff and that, in failing to do so, the defendants were negligent, *[handwritten left margin: Cause = but/for, Legal =]* which proximately resulted in the blindness sustained by the plaintiff for which the defendants are liable.

There are no disputed facts to submit to the jury on the issue of the defendants' liability. Hence, a discussion of the plaintiff's proposed instructions would be inconsequential in view of our disposition of the case.

The judgment of the trial court and the decision of the Court of Appeals is reversed, and the case is remanded for a new trial on the issue of damages only.

UTTER, Associate Justice [concurs with opinion].

1. The year after this case was decided, the state legislature passed an act providing that in an action for "professional negligence" the plaintiff must "prove by a preponderance of the evidence that the defendant * * * failed to exercise that degree of skill, care and learning <u>possessed</u> by other persons in the same profession and that as a proximate result of such failure the plaintiff suffered damages. * * *" Wash.Rev.Code Ann. § 4.24.290. The court of appeals held that this statute overruled the *Helling* case in Gates v. Jensen, 20 Wash.App. 81, 579 P.2d 374 (1978). But the case was reversed by the supreme court and *Helling* held still effective, in Gates v. Jensen, 92 Wash.2d 246, 595 P.2d 919 (1979), on the ground that the statute spoke of the defendant's failure to exercise that degree of skill, care and learning *possessed* by other persons in the same profession, not that exercised by them.

2. Should this "rule of law" prove of aid to the doctors? After this they will know what to do and will not have to worry about whether the test for glaucoma should be given in the particular case. Was it fair to the defendants in this case? Is the rule clear enough?

3. Could similar rules be adopted for attorneys? Would it be desirable?

6. VIOLATION OF STATUTE

OSBORNE v. McMASTERS

Supreme Court of Minnesota, 1889.
40 Minn. 103, 41 N.W. 543.

Action for damages by M. Osborne, administrator, against S.R. McMasters, for the death of plaintiff's intestate, resulting from the use of poison sold without a label by defendant's clerk in the course of his employment. Judgment for plaintiff, and defendant appeals.

MITCHELL, J. Upon the record in this case it must be taken as the facts that defendant's clerk in his drug-store, in the course of his employment as such, sold to plaintiff's intestate a deadly poison without labeling it "Poison," as required by statute; that she, in ignorance of its deadly qualities, partook of the poison which caused her death. * * * It is now well settled, certainly in this state, that where a statute or municipal ordinance imposes upon any person a specific duty for the protection or benefit of others, if he neglects to perform that duty he is liable to those for whose protection or benefit it was imposed for any injuries of the character which the statute or ordinance was designed to prevent, and which were proximately produced by such neglect. * * * It is immaterial whether the duty is one imposed by the rule of common law requiring the exercise of ordinary care not to injure another, or is imposed by a statute designed for the protection of others. In either case the failure to perform the duty constitutes negligence, and renders the party liable for injuries resulting from it. The only difference is that in the one case the measure of legal duty is to be determined upon common-law principles, while in the other the statute fixes it, so that the violation of the statute constitutes conclusive evidence of negligence, or, in other words, negligence *per se*. The action in the latter case is not a statutory one, nor does the statute give the right of action in any other sense, except that it makes an act negligent which otherwise might not be such or at least only evidence of negligence. All that the statute does is to establish a fixed standard by which the fact of negligence may be determined. The gist of the action is still negligence, or the non-performance of a legal duty to the person injured. * * *

Judgment affirmed.

1. Compare the remarks of Traynor, J. in Clinkscales v. Carver, 22 Cal.2d 72, 136 P.2d 777 (1943): "A statute that provides for a criminal proceeding only does not create a civil liability; if there is no provision for a remedy by civil action to persons injured by a breach of the statute it is because the Legislature did not contemplate one. A suit for damages is based on the theory that the conduct inflicting the injuries is a common-law tort, in this case the failure to exercise the care of a reasonable man at a boulevard stop. The significance of the statute in a civil suit for negligence lies in its formulation of a standard of conduct that the court adopts in the determination of such liability. (See Holmes, The Common Law, 120–129 (1881); Morris, The Relation of Criminal Statutes to Tort Liability, 46 Harv.L.Rev. 453 (1932).) The decision as to what the civil standard should be still rests with the court, and the standard formulated by a legislative body in a police regulation or criminal statute becomes the standard to determine civil liability only because the court accepts it. In the absence of such a standard the case goes to the jury, which must determine whether the defendant has acted as a reasonably prudent man would act in similar circumstances. The jury then has the burden of deciding not only what the facts are but what the unformulated standard is of reasonable conduct. When a legislative body has generalized a standard from the experience of the community and prohibits conduct that is likely to cause harm, the court accepts the formulated standards and applies them." See also Rudes v. Gottschalk, 159 Tex. 552, 324 S.W.2d 201, 205 (1959).

2. Why give any effect at all in a civil action for negligence to a statute which merely specifies a crime, and provides only for a criminal penalty? What about the following arguments?

A. The reasonable person will always obey the criminal law. Is this true? Should it be a question for the jury? What about a statute such as the legendary one providing that when two railroad trains approach a crossing each shall stop and neither shall move forward until the other has passed by?

B. The legislature intended, or is "presumed" to have intended, a civil remedy for the violation. What is the probability as to the state of mind of the legislature: (1) it did intend to provide a civil remedy, but did not say so; (2) it intended not to provide one and therefore omitted it; (3) it never thought about the matter at all?

C. The statute gives rise to a right. A right without a remedy is useless and the court supplies an appropriate remedy. *Ubi ius ibi remedium.*

D. The court adopts the standard of conduct from the criminal statute and lays it down as a rule of law in the civil action. See the preceding section. See Chapter 23, Section 1, infra, on the effect of statutes on torts other than negligence.

3. Must the court accept the statute as controlling? See the next case. See also Stevens v. Luther, 105 Neb. 184, 180 N.W. 87 (1920) (six mile an hour speed limit); Stafford v. Chippewa Valley Electric R. Co., 110 Wis. 331, 85 N.W. 1036 (1901) (requirement that a street bell be rung continuously).

4. What if a criminal statute is invalid, and totally ineffective for criminal prosecutions? For example, an ordinance establishing an arterial stop sign, and requiring drivers to stop under criminal penalty, was never properly published, as required for the adoption of such ordinances. Does this prevent the court, in a negligence action, from adopting the stop as a required standard of conduct? A number of cases say, no. See Lewis v. Miami, 127 Fla. 426, 173 So. 150 (1937); Ponca City v. Reed, 115 Okl. 166, 242 P. 164 (1925); Clinkscales v. Carver, 22 Cal.2d 72, 136 P.2d 777 (1943).

STACHNIEWICZ v. MAR–CAM CORP.

Supreme Court of Oregon, 1971.
259 Or. 583, 488 P.2d 436.

HOLMAN, JUSTICE. The patron of a drinking establishment seeks to recover against the operator for personal injuries allegedly inflicted by other customers during a barroom brawl. The jury returned a verdict for defendant. Plaintiff appealed.

From the evidence introduced, the jury could find as follows:

A fight erupted in a bar between a group of persons of American Indian ancestry, who were sitting in a booth, and other customers who were at an adjacent table with plaintiff. One of plaintiff's friends had refused to allow a patron from the booth to dance with the friend's wife because the stranger was intoxicated. Thereafter, such threats as "Hey, Whitey, how big are you?" were shouted from the booth at plaintiff and his companions. One of the persons at the table, after complaining to the bartender, was warned by him, "Don't start trouble with those guys." Soon thereafter, those individuals who had been sitting in the booth approached the table and one of them knocked down a person who was talking to a member of plaintiff's party. With that, the brawl commenced.

After a short melee, someone shouted "Fuzz!" and those persons who had been sitting in the booth ran out a door and into the parking lot, with one of plaintiff's friends in hot pursuit. Upon reaching the door, the friend discovered plaintiff lying just outside with his feet wedging the door open.

Plaintiff suffered retrograde amnesia and could remember nothing of the events of the evening. No one could testify to plaintiff's whereabouts at the time the [disturbance occurred] or to the cause of the vicious head injuries which plaintiff displayed when the brawl was ended.

The customers in the booth had been drinking in defendant's place of business for approximately two and one-half hours before the affray commenced.

The principal issue is whether, as plaintiff contends, violations of ORS 471.410(3) and of Oregon Liquor Control Regulation No. 10–065(2) constitute negligence as a matter of law. The portion of the statute relied on by plaintiff reads as follows:

"(3) No person shall give or otherwise make available any alcoholic liquor to a person visibly intoxicated * * *."

The portion of the regulation to which plaintiff points provides:

"(2) No licensee shall permit or suffer any loud, noisy, disorderly or boisterous conduct, or any profane or abusive language, in or upon his licensed premises, or permit any visibly intoxicated person to enter or remain upon his licensed premises."

The trial court held that a violation of either the statute or the regulation did not constitute negligence per se. It refused requested instructions and withdrew allegations of negligence which were based on their violation.

A violation of a statute or regulation constitutes negligence as a matter of law when the violation results in injury to a member of the class of persons intended to be protected by the legislation and when the harm is of the kind which the statute or regulation was enacted to prevent. [Cc] The reason behind the rule is that when a legislative body has generalized a standard from the experience of the community and prohibits conduct that is likely to cause harm the court accepts the formulation. Justice Traynor in Clinkscales v. Carver, 22 Cal.2d 72, 136 P.2d 777 (1943).

However, in addition, it is proper for the court to examine preliminarily the appropriateness of the standard as a measure of care for civil litigation under the circumstances presented. F. James, Jr., "Statutory Standards and Negligence in Accident Cases," 11 La.L.Rev. 95, 111–12 (1950–51); Restatement (Second) of Torts § 286, comment d (1965). The statute in question prevents making available alcohol to a person who is *already visibly intoxicated*. This makes the standard particularly inappropriate for the awarding of civil damages because of the extreme difficulty, if not impossibility, of determining whether a third party's injuries would have been caused, in any event, by the already inebriated person. Unless we are prepared to say that an alcoholic drink given after visible intoxication is the cause of a third party's injuries as a matter of law, a concept not advanced by anyone, the standard would be one almost impossible of application by a factfinder in most circumstances. * * * * *

The regulation promulgated by the commission is an altogether different matter. * * *

ORS 471.030, entitled "Purpose of Liquor Control Act," provides, in part, as follows:

"(1) The Liquor Control Act shall be liberally construed so as:

"(a) To prevent the recurrence of abuses associated with saloons or resorts for the consumption of alcoholic beverages." * * *

An examination of the regulation discloses that it concerns matters having a direct relation to the creation of physical disturbances in bars which would, in turn, create a likelihood of injury to customers. A common feature of our western past, now preserved in story and reproduced on the screen hundreds of times, was the carnage of the barroom brawl. No citation of authority is needed to establish that the "abuses associated with saloons," which the Liquor Control Act seeks to prevent, included permitting on the premises profane, abusive conduct and drunken clientele (now prohibited by the regulation) which results in serious personal injuries to customers in breach of the bar owner's duty to protect his patrons from harm. We find it reasonable to assume that the commission, in promulgating the regulation, intended to prevent these abuses, and that they had in mind the safety of patrons of bars as well as the general peace and quietude of the community. In view of the quoted purpose of the Act and of the history of injury to innocent patrons of saloons, we cannot assume otherwise.

In addition, we see no reason why the standard is not an appropriate one for use in the awarding of civil damages. Because plaintiff was within the class of persons intended to be protected by the regulation and the harm caused to him was the kind the statute was intended to prevent, we hold that the trial court erred in not treating the alleged violations of the regulation as negligence as a matter of law. * * *

We believe it would be fair for the jury to infer, in the circumstances set forth in the statement of the facts, that plaintiff was injured by one of the persons in the booth who had created the disturbance and that the injuries would not have occurred except for defendant's violation of the commission's regulation, as alleged.

The judgment of the trial court is reversed and the case is remanded for a new trial.

1. What is the basis upon which a court seeks to select or reject a criminal statute as a standard of care in a particular tort suit? This is not a readily solvable problem. The court must determine that:

A. The party seeking to charge the other with violation of the statute is a member of the class the legislature intended to protect. See Thomas v. Baltimore & O.R. Co., 19 Md.App. 217, 310 A.2d 186 (1973) (plaintiff who knew of location of railway crossing not in class to be protected by regulation requiring warning); Erickson v. Kongsli, 40 Wash.2d 79, 240 P.2d 1209 (1952) (abutting landowner's property damaged when defendant made an illegal left turn—not in class to be protected); Distad v. Cubin, 633 P.2d 167 (Wyo.1981) (violation of regulations on emergency treatment not negligence per se when plaintiff did not appear to need emergency care—not in class to be protected).

What result in the principal case if an employee of the drinking establishment had been injured in the melee?

B. The hazard that occurred was one the legislature intended to prevent. The leading case on the "different hazard" is Gorris v. Scott, L.R. 9 Ex. 125 (1874), where a contagious diseases act required that animals shipped by boat be kept in pens, to avoid the spread of disease. Plaintiff's sheep were washed overboard from defendant's boat during a storm, because they were not in pens. It was held that the violation of the statute did not make the defendant liable for the loss of the sheep.

What result in the principal case if plaintiff had been injured when an intoxicated person had stumbled and fallen upon him? *element of intent? = No: same result*

2. The Restatement (Second) of Torts spells out in greater detail these requirements in § 287, and it states in § 288:

"The court will not adopt as the standard of conduct of a reasonable man the requirements of a legislative enactment or an administrative regulation whose purpose is found to be exclusively

"(a) to protect the interests of the state or any subdivision of it as such, or

"(b) to secure to individuals the enjoyment of rights or privileges to which they are entitled only as members of the public, or

"(c) to impose upon the actor the performance of a service which the state or any subdivision of it undertakes to give the public, or

"(d) to protect a class of persons other than the one whose interests are invaded, or

"(e) to protect another interest than the one invaded, or

"(f) to protect against other harm than that which has resulted, or

"(g) to protect against any other hazards than that from which the harm has resulted."

3. Because state legislative history is usually scanty and also difficult to obtain, there may be wide latitude for a court to decide who is in the "class" or what was the "hazard" that the legislature had in mind. On occasion the court may rely on the title or the preamble of the statute. Compare Kelly v. Henry Muhs Co., 71 N.J.Law 358, 59 A. 23 (1904), with Drake v. Fenton, 237 Pa. 8, 85 A. 14 (1912).

federalism   4. *Federal Legislation.* There is no "doctrine" of negligence per se in federal laws. If there is no general federal common law of negligence as a √ result of Erie R. Co. v. Tompkins, 304 U.S. 64 (1938), the federal courts are in no position to adopt a criminal statutory rule of conduct as a civil rule of conduct replacing the general standard of care. The result is that they find it necessary to "imply" a civil action from the criminal statute, thus placing the responsibility for the action on the Congress. See infra Chapter 23, section 1.

5. The states do have a "doctrine" of negligence per se. Should violation *Tort Work/* √ of a federal statute be a basis for finding negligence per se in a state court? *Study/Paper/Art* Surprisingly, there is very little consideration of this problem. See Steagall v. Dot Mfg. Corp., 223 Tenn. 428, 446 S.W.2d 515 (1969), where the court assumed that violation of the Federal Hazardous Substances Act might be negligence per se but found no proximate cause. In a case of first impression in Idaho, a state court found that violation of Occupational Safety and Health Administration regulations constituted negligence per se as a matter of state law. Sanchez v. Galey, 112 Idaho 609, 733 P.2d 1234 (1986). In diversity cases where they are applying state law, federal courts have sometimes assumed, without careful consideration, that the state court would apply negligence per se to a federal statute. See Orthopedic Equip. Co. v. Eutsler, 276 F.2d 455 (4th Cir.1960) (Federal Food, Drug & Cosmetic Act—Virginia law); Gober v. Revlon, Inc., 317 F.2d 47 (4th Cir.1963) (same—California law). On the Occupational Safety and

Health Act of 1970, see Annots., 79 A.L.R.3d 962 (1977); 35 A.L.R.Fed. 461 (1977).

NEY v. YELLOW CAB CO.

Illinois Supreme Court, 1954.
2 Ill.2d 74, 117 N.E.2d 74.

MAXWELL, JUSTICE. * * * The Appellate Court here affirmed the trial court's judgment fixing liability on the defendant for violation of a section of the Uniform Traffic Act. The plaintiff charged that defendant, by its servant, negligently permitted its taxicab to remain unattended on a Chicago street without first stopping the engine or locking the ignition or removing the key, contrary to a section of said act. The undisputed facts reveal that a thief stole the taxicab and while in flight ran into plaintiff's vehicle causing property damage. Defendant's motion to dismiss the complaint was based on the theory that the acts or omissions of the defendant did not constitute actionable negligence, nor the proximate cause of the damage. Briefly stated, plaintiff contended that the defendant's violation of the statute was negligence and the proximate cause of the damage.

The statute in question, section 92 of article XIV of the Uniform Traffic Act, provides: "(a) No person driving or in charge of a motor vehicle shall permit it to stand unattended without first stopping the engine, locking the ignition and removing the key, or when standing upon any perceptible grade without effectively setting the brake thereon and turning the front wheels to the curb or side of the highway. (b) No person shall operate or drive a motor vehicle who is under fifteen years of age." Ill.Rev.Stat.1953, chap. 95½, par. 189; Jones Ann.Stat. 85.221.

The defendant takes the position that this particular statute is not an antitheft measure but is a traffic regulation, the violation of which could impose no liability on the owner or operator of the vehicle for the misconduct of a thief, for the reason that, under such circumstances, the violation of the statute is not actionable negligence in that the misconduct is neither negligence with relation to the resulting injury, nor its proximate cause. The plaintiff, on the other hand, contends that the statute is a safety measure for the benefit of the public; that its violation is prima facie evidence of negligence; and that reasonable persons might reasonably foresee that its violation could result in the consequences which occurred here. The plaintiff further contends that irrespective of the statute there would be a common-law liability under the same circumstances, and that in either event the questions of negligence and proximate cause are, under the facts alleged and admitted here, questions of fact and not questions of law. * * *

We have carefully studied the reasoning of our Appellate Courts and the courts of the other jurisdictions, in the light of these distinctions, and conclude that the issue presented requires our determination of the following questions: (a) What was the legislative intention? (b)

Is the violation of the statute the <u>proximate cause</u> of the injury? (c) Is the act of the thief an intervening, independent, efficient force which breaks the causal connection between the original wrong and the injury?

Labeling of the statute does not solve the problem. Defendant urges that the statute is a traffic regulation and not an antitheft measure, and from this premise reasons to a conclusion of nonliability. It seems to argue that if it were an antitheft measure liability would attach in this case. * * * We think the key to the construction of the statute with regard to the legislative intention appears in the statute itself. The requirement that the brakes be set and the wheels turned to the curb on a grade is no material theft deterrent. The second subparagraph of the section prohibiting persons under fifteen years of age from operating a motor vehicle indicates to us that the legislature was thinking about the danger to the public in permitting persons lacking in experience, judgment, knowledge and maturity to operate such vehicles. <u>We cannot but conclude that this entire section is a public safety measure.</u> This being so, what harm did the legislature foresee and attempt to prevent by prohibiting the leaving of an unat- tended motor vehicle with the key in the ignition? <u>The motor vehicle with the key in its ignition in itself could obviously do no harm.</u>

Consequently, there enters into our consideration the question of foreseeability as to intervention of outside agencies not under the control of the person in charge of the motor vehicle. The drawing of lines of demarcation in problems of cause and effect is often difficult in the study of formal logic and these difficulties are not minimized in the field of jurisprudence. We cannot say that the legislature intended to distinguish between certain types of outside agencies without express- ing such distinction. Such a distinction would be too tenuous a ground to serve as a basis for decision in view of the broad general sweep of the statutory language employed. The legislature has here used clear and express terms making it the duty of persons in charge of motor vehicles to do certain acts upon leaving their vehicles unattended. The motiva- tion of such legislation is not the State's desire to punish but rather its interest in public welfare for protection of life, limb and property by prevention of recognized hazards.

<u>The violation of the statute is prima facie evidence of negligence under the prevailing rule of this State.</u> [Cc] This in itself creates no liability. <u>The injury must have a direct and proximate connection with the violation of the statute</u> before liability will be held to exist. It is the existence of this cause and effect relationship which makes the negligence of the defendant actionable.

Where an independent agency intervenes, the solution of the prob- lem becomes aggravated. * * *

A further problem is presented when the independent agency is an illegal or criminal act. <u>Wrongful acts of independent third persons, not actually intended by the defendant, are not regarded by the law as</u>

natural consequences of his wrong, and he is not bound to anticipate the general probability of such acts, any more than a particular act by this or that individual. The rule applies a fortiori to criminal acts. The intervention of a criminal act, however, does not necessarily interrupt the relation of cause and effect between negligence and an injury. If at the time of the negligence, the criminal act might reasonably have been foreseen, the causal chain is not broken by the intervention of such act. * * *

The speed and power of automobiles have increased to the extent that safety experts are now showing keen awareness of their potentials even in the hands of rightful owners and careful operators. Incidents of serious havoc caused by runaway thieves or irresponsible juveniles in stolen or "borrowed" motor vehicles frequently shock the readers of the daily press. With this background must come a recognition of the probable danger of resulting injury consequent to permitting a motor vehicle to become easily available to an unauthorized person through violation of the statute in question. The percentage of cases of this nature or the incidence of injury done where an independent force has intervened after such violation, however, is not the standard or measure of liability. We are here concerned only with the question as to whether or not this intervening force is without or within the range of reasonable anticipation and probability. * * *

* * * [W]e recall the reasoning of Justice Cardozo, that the range of reasonable apprehension is at times for the court, and at times, if varying inferences are possible, a question for the jury. The possibility of varying inferences in a case such as the one before us has been amply demonstrated. * * *

We are in agreement with the court below in our belief that reasonable men might differ on the question where there were special circumstances surrounding the defendant's violation of the statute which may be the proximate cause of the damage that followed. We * * * believe that under the circumstances as presented in the case before us we find no persuasive authority and no impelling reasoning for this court to hold, *as a matter of law,* that no actionable negligence can exist.

Questions of negligence, due care and proximate cause are ordinarily questions of fact for a jury to decide. The right of trial by jury is recognized in the Magna Charta, our Declaration of Independence and both our State and Federal constitutions. It is a fundamental right in our democratic judicial system. Questions which are composed of such qualities sufficient to cause reasonable men to arrive at different results should never be determined as matters of law. The debatable quality of issues such as negligence and proximate cause, the fact that fair-minded men might reach different conclusions, emphasize the appropriateness and necessity of leaving such questions to a fact-finding body. The jury is the tribunal under our legal system to decide that type of issue. To withdraw such questions from the jury is to usurp its function. [C]

For the foregoing reasons, it is our opinion that the Appellate Court was correct in affirming the judgment of the municipal court of Chicago.

Judgment affirmed.

HERSHEY, J., dissenting. The majority opinion is contradictory within itself. It first concludes that section 92 of article XIV of the Uniform Traffic Act [C] is not an antitheft statute, but is, in fact, a public safety measure. Although the opinion fails to answer in specific fashion its question as to what harm the legislature foresaw and attempted to prevent by the passage of this act, it does ultimately determine that the statute was to prevent accidents caused by a thief in stealing the vehicle. This determination is manifest by the majority's adoption of the Appellate Court determination. The majority thus finds the statute, or at least that part of the statute rendering it unlawful to fail to remove the keys from a parked vehicle, to be an antitheft measure. * * *

The majority concludes that all parts of this statute, except that portion referring to the keys, indicate an intention on the part of the legislature to prevent harm to the public by an inadvertent or negligent movement of a parked vehicle, or through its being driven by a young person devoid of experience, judgment, knowledge, or maturity. It finds that the legislature's purpose in relation to those portions of the statute was not to deter theft. However, the majority then concludes that the portion directing the removal of the keys from the vehicle was to prevent the operation of the vehicle and possible public harm by a thief in flight. The slightest experience renders everyone cognizant of the fact that the removal of automobile ignition keys is only a minor deterrent, if any, to the theft of an automobile and a subsequent flight from detection and pursuit. Consequently, it is only reasonable and logical to construe the legislature's intention in the passage of this portion of the statute in the same light as is attributed to the remainder of the section. One can only conclude, therefore, that the legislature required the removal of the key to prevent a mere negligent or inadvertent starting of the automobile and an ensuing uncontrolled movement thereof. Obviously the legislature could not presume by such legislation to prevent a wilful movement of the vehicle by an unauthorized person. It is generally recognized that one may leave a motor vehicle standing unattended in a public street temporarily, without being guilty of negligence, provided he takes the ordinary precautions of securing it by the appliances with which it is equipped for that purpose, and that if it is thereafter set in motion by the wilful or negligent act of a third person, such wilful or negligent act will be deemed the proximate cause of the accident or injury resulting therefrom and the owner will not be liable. * * *

[handwritten: Ergo, not neg. per se (dissent)]
[handwritten: ≠ Neg. Per se?]

This section, not being an antitheft measure, and not making the failure to remove the key an absolute act of negligence, cannot constitute the proximate cause of this injury. *[handwritten: Does this follow?]* But for the intervention of the theft the failure to remove the key could not have caused this injury. Moreover, unless the thief was in immediate flight from the scene of his theft, the act of thievery could not even be a factor contributing to the injury. * * * *[handwritten: Is dissent's outcome any different? (finds for Δ)]*

[handwritten: Dissent implies that ① Causation is a question of law, not fact.]

1. The principal case illustrates how much discretion a court may have in determining the purpose of a statute. Was the purpose of this key-in-the-car statute to prevent theft of the car, with resulting loss to the owner and his insurance company and an increased burden on the police? Cf. Anderson v. Theisen, 231 Minn. 369, 43 N.W.2d 272 (1950). To prevent the car from being started up by children or other irresponsible people? Cf. Bouldin v. Sategna, 71 N.M. 329, 378 P.2d 370 (1963). To prevent joy-riding teenagers from "taking it out for a spree"? To prevent it from being stolen by a tense thief, endangering people in the vicinity while trying to make his getaway?

2. Observe how the two opinions in this case argue for a single purpose. May there not be more than one purpose? Cf. Hines v. Foreman, 243 S.W. 479 (Tex.Comm.App.1923). The statute prohibited use of a "cut-out" in the exhaust pipe leading to the muffler, in order to make a zooming or roaring noise. Plaintiff had his cut-out open driving down the streets of a Texas city. He approached a railroad track, and unknown to him because of the noise of the cutout, there was a train coming and he was engaged in a race that ended in a tie. The issue was whether he was contributorily negligent, and he claimed that the statute was irrelevant because its purpose was to prevent harassing noises. Held, it had a double purpose, and one of them was to eliminate noises preventing him from hearing traffic hazards.

3. This statute is part of the Uniform Vehicle Code prepared and revised by the National Committee on Uniform Traffic Laws and Ordinances and continuously monitored and revised. It is in a chapter on safety provisions and committee members have stated that it was intended as a safety measure. Is this relevant? For a strong case holding that the purpose includes a thief making a getaway, with the opinion written by Judge Edgerton, a former torts teacher, see Ross v. Hartman, 139 F.2d 14 (D.C.Cir.1943).

4. Who makes the decision as to the purpose of the statute—judge or jury? *[handwritten: more appropriately, is a ques. of law or fact?]*

5. How long and how far away should the owner be liable for dangerous driving by the thief? Cf. Liberto v. Holfeldt, 221 Md. 62, 155 A.2d 698 (1959) (five days later, considerable distance across city); Wannebo v. Gates, 227 Minn. 194, 34 N.W.2d 695 (1948) (getaway only). *[handwritten: √=see re:]* Suppose the thief intentionally runs into a policeman he thinks is trying to arrest him? Berko v. Freda, 172 N.J. Super. 436, 412 A.2d 821 (1980). See Peck, An Exercise Based on Empirical Data: Liability for Harm Caused by Stolen Automobiles, 1969 Wis.L.Rev. 909; Wade, Torts—1961 Tennessee Survey, 15 Vand.L.Rev. 952, 955 (1962).

6. Both opinions in the principal case became heavily involved in the problem of proximate cause. There should be no problem of proximate cause if *[handwritten: = Cause: yes]* the event is within the hazard that the statute is intended to avert. By *[handwritten: proximate: no]* deciding the purpose of the statute, the court eliminates the proximate cause problem. See Ross v. Hartman, supra n. 3. Is there an element of begging the question by following this procedure? But it may simplify some of the difficul-

ties of proximate cause. Look for it later when the subject of proximate cause is taken up.

7. See Morris, The Role of Criminal Statutes in Negligence Actions, 49 Col.L.Rev. 21 (1949), reprinted in Morris, Studies in the Law of Torts, 141 (1952) (especially valuable); Morris, The Relation of Criminal Statutes to Tort Liability, 49 Harv.L.Rev. 453 (1933); Thayer, Public Wrong and Private Action, 27 Harv.L.Rev. 317 (1914). See also James, Statutory Standards and Negligence in Accident Cases, 11 La.L.Rev. 95 (1950).

Professors Thayer and Morris have postulated that courts may be reluctant to utilize a statute when it would create a new duty entirely unknown at common law. There is some support for this in the cases. See Brown v. Kelly, 42 N.J. 362, 200 A.2d 781 (1964); and Fitzwater v. Sunset Empire, Inc., 263 Or. 276, 502 P.2d 214 (1972), both declining to find that ordinances requiring abutting landowners to keep sidewalks in repair and remove snow and ice were enacted for the benefit of pedestrians. Decisions on this issue may have been influenced, at least initially, by the fact that the statute creates an affirmative duty.

8. A statute requires that a seller of a "deadly weapon receive positive identification" of the purchaser from two residents of the state, and keep a record of name, age, address and other details. Defendant sells a gun without complying, and the purchaser uses it on the plaintiff in the course of an armed robbery. Should the defendant be liable? Cf. Hetherton v. Sears, Roebuck & Co., 593 F.2d 526 (3d Cir.1979), second appeal, 652 F.2d 1152 (3d Cir.1981).

9. Once the statute is declared "out of the case," what issues remain?

10. The effect of the violation of criminal (and other) statutes and regulations on the law of torts is not confined by any means to the tort of negligence and the doctrine of negligence per se. It has been generally recognized that in furtherance of the purpose of particular legislation and to insure its effectiveness, a court may, despite the absence of a provision to this effect, supply a civil action for damages according relief to a person for whose benefit conduct of another was either proscribed or required by the legislation. Restatement (Second) of Torts § 874A. The usual explanation is that the right is "implied" from the legislation. See infra Chapter 23, Section 1.

BROWN v. SHYNE

Court of Appeals of New York, 1926.
242 N.Y. 176, 151 N.E. 197.

LEHMAN, J. The plaintiff employed the defendant to give chiropractic treatment to her for a disease or physical condition. The defendant had no license to practice medicine, yet, he held himself out as being able to diagnose and treat disease, and, under the provisions of the Public Health Law (Const.Laws, c. 45), he was guilty of a misdemeanor. The plaintiff became paralyzed after she had received nine treatments by the defendant. She claims, and upon this appeal we must assume, that the paralysis was caused by the treatment she received. She has recovered judgment in the sum of $10,000 for the damages caused by said injury. * * *

At the close of the plaintiff's case the plaintiff was permitted to amend the complaint to allege "that in so treating the plaintiff the defendant was engaged in the practice of medicine contrary to and in violation of the provisions of the Public Health Law of the state of New York in such case made and provided, he at the time of so treating plaintiff not being a duly licensed physician or surgeon of the state of New York." Thereafter the trial judge charged the jury that ["from the violation of the statute the jury might infer negligence which produced injury to the plaintiff."] * * * Whole CoA is given

In so charging the jury * * * the trial justice in my opinion erred.

The provisions of the Public Health Law prohibit the practice of medicine without a license granted upon proof of preliminary training, and after examination intended to show adequate knowledge, are of course intended for the protection of the general public against injury which unskilled and unlearned practitioners might cause. If violation of the statute by the defendant was the proximate cause of the plaintiff's injury, then the plaintiff may recover upon proof of violation. If violation of the statute has no direct bearing on the injury, proof of the violation becomes irrelevant. For injury caused by neglect of duty imposed by the penal law there is civil remedy; but, of course, the injury must follow from the neglect. — see Assumption p. 220

Proper formulation of general standards of preliminary education and proper examination of the particular applicant should serve to raise the standards of skill and care generally possessed by members of the profession in this state; but the license to practice medicine confers no additional skill upon the practitioner, nor does it confer immunity from physical injury upon a patient if the practitioner fails to exercise care. Here, injury may have been caused by lack of skill or care; it would not have been obviated if the defendant had possessed a license yet failed to exercise the skill and care required of one practicing medicine. True, if the defendant had not practiced medicine in this state, he could not have injured the plaintiff, but the protection which the statute was intended to provide was against risk of injury by the unskilled or careless practitioner, and, unless the plaintiff's injury was caused by carelessness or lack of skill, the defendant's failure to obtain a license was not connected with the injury. The plaintiff's cause of action is for negligence or malpractice. The defendant undertook to treat the plaintiff for a physical condition which seemed to require remedy. Under our law such treatment may be given only by a duly qualified practitioner who has obtained a license.

The defendant in offering to treat the plaintiff held himself out as qualified to give treatment. He must meet the professional standards of skill and care prevailing among those who do offer treatment lawfully. If injury follows through failure to meet those standards, the plaintiff may recover. The provisions of the Public Health Law may result in the exclusion from practice of some who are unqualified. Even a skilled and learned practitioner who is not licensed commits an offense against the state; but against such practitioners the statute was not intended to protect, for no protection was needed, and neglect to obtain a license results in no injury to the patient and, therefore, no private wrong. The purpose of the statute is to protect the public against unfounded assumption of skill by one who undertakes to prescribe or treat for disease. In order to show that the plaintiff has been injured by defendant's breach of the statutory duty, proof must be given that defendant in such treatment did not exercise the care and skill which would have been exercised by qualified practitioners within the state, and that lack of skill and care caused the injury. Failure to obtain a license as required by law gives rise to no remedy if it has caused no injury.

For these reasons the judgments should be reversed, and a new trial granted, with costs to abide the event.

[The dissenting opinion of CRANE, J., is omitted.]

1. Who is more likely to use reasonable care in practicing medicine, the class of persons who are licensed or unlicensed? Should this make any difference in the principal case?

2. In Whipple v. Grandchamp, 261 Mass. 40, 158 N.E. 270 (1927), a medical licensing statute was held to establish standards of skill and competence, and a chiropractor practicing medicine with no license was held negligent as a matter of law. Can the two cases be reconciled?

3. Statutes requiring drivers' licenses for the operation of an automobile have received, in general, the same treatment. New Hampshire used to be an exception. In Johnson v. Boston & Maine R. Co., 83 N.H. 350, 143 A. 516 (1928), it was held that the legislature has made a "positive limitation of right," and for the protection of those on the highway had ruled out even competent drivers. "There is no other practical way to accomplish the desired result. The fit can protect themselves by procuring a license. If they do not, they cannot complain of being classed with the unfit."

Following this, the legislature amended the statute in 1937 to provide that driving without a license "in any civil action shall be prima facie evidence of unfitness to drive." The Johnson case was overruled "in its entirety," and the question is now merely one of whether the driver was in fact competent to drive. Fuller v. Sirois, 97 N.H. 100, 82 A.2d 82 (1951).

4. Statutes requiring the registration of automobiles and license plates are commonly held to be merely for purposes of taxation, and to aid the police, and not to give rise to any civil action based upon the violation.

Massachusetts formerly had a unique rule that anyone driving an unregistered car was a "trespasser on the highway," and therefore liable for all injuries he caused, and could not recover himself except for injuries caused intentionally or recklessly. After the Massachusetts court, in Comeau v. Harrington, 333 Mass. 768, 130 N.E.2d 554 (1955), had expressed disapproval of the doctrine, but said that any change must be for the legislature, the legislature changed the rule in 1959 by an amendment to the licensing section. It is now provided that the violation shall not be a defense in an action by the violator, but shall be deemed evidence of negligence in an action against him. Mass.Laws 1959, c. 250.

5. See generally Gregory, Breach of Criminal Licensing Statutes in Civil Litigation, 36 Cornell L.Q. 622 (1951).

[handwritten: Purpose of lights = to be and be seen]

MARTIN v. HERZOG
Court of Appeals of New York, 1920.
228 N.Y. 164, 126 N.E. 814.

[handwritten: re: Contributory negligence → same case as negligence, except by π rather than Δ]

Action by Elizabeth Martin, as administratrix of William J. Martin, deceased, against Samuel A. Herzog and another. Judgment for the plaintiff against the named defendant was reversed by the Appellate Division (176 App.Div. 614, 163 N.Y.Supp. 189), and plaintiff appeals.

[handwritten margin: Trct = π; App.Div. = rev'd/Δ; Ct App = Aff'd/Δ]

[Plaintiff's decedent was killed in a collision between the buggy he was driving, and defendant's automobile. It was after dark, and decedent was driving the buggy without lights, in violation of a criminal statute requiring lights. The trial judge refused defendant's request for an instruction that the absence of a light on the plaintiff's vehicle was "prima facie evidence of contributory negligence," and instructed instead that the jury might consider the absence of lights as some evidence of negligence, but that it was not conclusive evidence. He also granted plaintiff's request for an instruction that "the fact that the plaintiff's intestate was driving without a light is not negligence in itself." The jury returned a verdict for the plaintiff, on which judgment was entered. The Appellate Division reversed for error in the instructions. Plaintiff now appeals to the Court of Appeals.]

CARDOZO, J. * * * We think the unexcused omission of the statutory signals is more than some evidence of negligence. It is negligence in itself. Lights are intended for the guidance and protection of other travelers on the highway. Highway Law, § 329a. By the very terms of the hypothesis, to omit, willfully or heedlessly, the safeguards prescribed by law for the benefit of another that he may be preserved in life or limb, is to fall short of the standard of diligence to which those who live in organized society are under a duty to conform. That, we think, is now the established rule in this state. [Cc]

[handwritten margin: R — Negl. per se; intended class of π; type of harm]

In the case at hand, we have an instance of the admitted violation of a statute intended for the protection of travelers on the highway, of whom the defendant at the time was one. Yet the jurors were instructed in effect that they were at liberty in their discretion to treat the omission of lights either as innocent or as culpable. They were allowed to "consider the default as lightly or gravely" as they would (Thomas, J., in the court below). They might as well have been told that they could use a like discretion in holding a master at fault for the omission of a safety appliance prescribed by positive law for the protection of a workman. [Cc] Jurors have no dispensing power, by which they may relax the duty that one traveler on the highways owes under the statute to another. It is error to tell them that they have. The omission of these lights was a wrong, and, being wholly unexcused, was also a negligent wrong. No license should have been conceded to the triers of the facts to find it anything else.

Neg per se + cause =

We must be on our guard, however, against confusing the question of negligence with that of the causal connection between the negligence and the injury. A defendant who travels without lights is not to pay damages for his fault, unless the absence of lights is the cause of the disaster. A plaintiff who travels without them is not to forfeit the right to damages, unless the absence of lights is at least a contributing cause of the disaster. To say that conduct is negligence is not to say that it is always contributory negligence. "Proof of negligence in the air, so to speak, will not do." Pollock Torts (10th Ed.) p. 472.

Now for jury to decide!

We think, however, that evidence of a collision occurring more than an hour after sundown between a car and an unseen buggy, proceeding without lights, is evidence from which a causal connection may be inferred between the collision and the lack of signals. [Cc] If nothing else is shown to break the connection, we have a case, prima facie sufficient, of negligence contributing to the result.

Are there degrees of gravity of harm which affects the scope of intent?

We are persuaded that the tendency of the charge, and of all the rulings, following it, was to minimize unduly, in the minds of the triers of the facts, the gravity of the decedent's fault. Errors may not be ignored as unsubstantial, when they tend to such an outcome. A statute designed for the protection of human life is not to be brushed aside as a form of words, its commands reduced to the level of cautions, and the duty to obey attenuated into an option to conform.

The order of the Appellate Division should be affirmed, and judgment absolute directed on the stipulation in favor of the defendant, with costs in all courts.

[The dissenting opinion of HOGAN, J., is omitted.]

1. The great majority of the courts take the position stated by Cardozo in this case, that when a statute applies to the facts, an unexcused violation is "negligence per se," which must be declared by the court and not left to the jury.

2. California treats such a violation as giving rise to a "presumption" of negligence, which becomes negligence as a matter of law unless the presumption is rebutted. Since it can be rebutted only by showing an excuse for the violation, this appears to come out at much the same place as the "negligence per se" rule. Vermont formerly held the same way, but has apparently swung over to "negligence per se." See Shulins v. New England Ins. Co., 360 F.2d 781 (2d Cir.1966).

3. A minority of about half a dozen states, such as Massachusetts and New Jersey, hold that the violation is only evidence of negligence, which the jury may accept or reject as it sees fit.

4. The California court had quite a workout on all this in Satterlee v. Orange Glenn School District, 29 Cal.2d 581, 177 P.2d 279 (1947), with Traynor, Edmonds and Carter, JJ., each writing an opinion, and taking a different one of

(handwritten margin notes: ① per se / ② presumption / ③ evidence)

the foregoing three positions. Edmonds carried the majority of the court with his "presumption" theory. The case has a good exposition of the arguments.

5. Ordinances, in general, have been treated in the same manner as statutes. A few states, such as New York and Michigan, which hold the violation of a statute to be negligence per se, have treated the violation of an ordinance as only evidence of negligence. Kentucky once made this distinction, in the case of a foolish ordinance providing a speed limit of six miles an hour for railway trains. Louisville & N.R. Co. v. Dalton, 102 Ky. 290, 43 S.W. 431 (1897). The case was overruled, and the violation of any ordinance held negligence per se, in Greyhound Terminal v. Thomas, 307 Ky. 44, 209 S.W.2d 478 (1947). *(margin: exam – use ordinance)*

6. There is a similar conflict as to the effect of the regulations of administrative bodies, acting under statutory authority. These are sometimes given the effect of negligence per se, sometimes held to be only evidence of negligence. There is more of a tendency toward the latter position than in the case of statutes. See Hassan v. Stafford, 472 F.2d 88 (3d Cir.1973), noted in 77 Temp.L.Rev. 739 (1974); Morris, The Role of Administrative Safety Measures in Negligence Actions, 28 Tex.L.Rev. 143 (1949).

7. Advisory safety codes promulgated by governmental authority, industry or voluntary associations may be admissible on the issue of negligence if properly identified and shown through expert testimony to have general acceptance in the industrial community. See Lemery v. O'Shea Dennis, Inc., 112 N.H. 199, 291 A.2d 616 (1972); Philo, Use of Safety Standards, Codes and Practices in Tort Litigation, 41 Notre Dame Law. 1 (1965). Many jurisdictions reject them, however, on the ground that they are hearsay. See Annot., 75 A.L.R.2d 778 (1961). *(margin: disregard)*

8. The fact that a statute is inapplicable, either because it is not intended for the protection of the class of persons in which the plaintiff is included, or because it was not intended for protection against the particular risk, does not necessarily rule it out entirely as evidence bearing on the issue of negligence. Thus in Hansen v. Kemmish, 201 Iowa 1008, 208 N.W. 277 (1926), a statute, intended only to prevent the misbreeding of animals, provided that hogs should be confined by fences of specified strength. Defendant fenced his hogs with a fence of less strength; one of them broke through the fence, escaped into the highway, and wrecked plaintiff's car. It was held that, while the statute did not define a standard of conduct to be adopted as a matter of law, the jury could consider it as bearing on the kind of fence necessary for the proper confinement of hogs. *(margin: re exam: "alternatively…)*

ZENI v. ANDERSON

Supreme Court of Michigan, 1976.
397 Mich. 117, 243 N.W.2d 270.

(handwritten: Excuse for violating statute. / Rebuttable Presumption)

WILLIAMS, JUSTICE.   *   *   * The accident which precipitated this action occurred one snowy morning, March 7, 1969, when the temperature was 11° F, the sky was clear and the average snow depth was 21 inches. Plaintiff Eleanor Zeni, then a 56–year–old registered nurse, was walking to her work at the Northern Michigan University Health Center in Marquette. Instead of using the snow-covered sidewalk, which in any event would have required her to walk across the street

significance?

twice to get to her job, she traveled along a well-used pedestrian snowpath, with her back to oncoming traffic.

sure she was

Defendant Karen Anderson, a college student, was driving within the speed limit in a steady stream of traffic on the same street. Ms. Anderson testified that she had turned on the defroster in the car and her passenger said she had scraped the windshield. An eyewitness whose deposition was read at trial, however, testified that defendant's windshield was clouded and he doubted that the occupants could see out. He also testified that the car was traveling too close to the curb and that he could tell plaintiff was going to be hit.

Defendant's car struck the plaintiff on the driver's right side. Ms. Anderson testified she first saw the plaintiff between a car parked on the right-hand side of the road and defendant's car, and that she did not hear nor feel her car strike Ms. Zeni. The eyewitness reported seeing plaintiff flip over the fender and hood. He said when he went over to help her his knees were on or inside the white line delineating a parking space. A security officer observed blood stains on the pavement approximately 13 feet from the curb.

Ms. Zeni's injuries were serious and included an intra-cerebral subdural hematoma which required neurosurgery. She has retrograde amnesia and therefore, because she does not remember anything from the time she began walking that morning until sometime after the impact, there is no way to determine whether she knew defendant was behind her. Following an extended period of convalescence, plaintiff, still suffering permanent disability, could return to work on only a part-time basis.

Testimony at trial indicated that it was common for nurses to use the roadway to reach the Health Center, and a security officer testified that in the wintertime it was safer to walk there than on the one sidewalk. Apparently, several days before the accident, Ms. Zeni had indeed fallen on the sidewalk. Although she was not hurt when she fell, the Director of University Security was hospitalized when he fell on the walk.

Statute

Defendant, however, maintained that plaintiff's failure to use that sidewalk constituted contributory negligence because, she said, it violated M.C.L.A. § 257.655; M.S.A. § 9.2355, which requires:

"Where sidewalks are provided, it shall be unlawful for pedestrians to walk upon the main traveled portion of the highway. Where sidewalks are not provided, pedestrians shall, when practicable, walk on the left side of the highway facing traffic which passes nearest."
* * *

tr ct = π
ct App = revd/Δ
s ct = revd/π

[There was a jury verdict for plaintiff in the trial court. The court of appeals reversed because of instructions on the subject of last clear chance. Discussion of last clear chance is omitted.]

A. *Violation of Statute as Rebuttable Presumption.* In a growing number of states, the rule concerning the proper role of a penal statute in a civil action for damages is that violation of the statute which has been found to apply to a particular set of facts establishes only a prima facie case of negligence, a presumption which may be rebutted by a showing on the part of the party violating the statute of an adequate excuse under the facts and circumstances of the case. The excuses may not necessarily be applicable in a criminal action, since, in the absence of legislatively-mandated civil penalties, acceptance of the criminal statute itself as a standard of care in a civil action is purely discretionary. See Comment and Illustrations, 2 Restatement (Second) of Torts § 288A, pp. 33–37.

Michigan cases have in effect followed this rule. For example, over a 65 year period, cases concerning the effect in a negligence action of violation of the statute requiring vehicles to keep to the right side of the road have almost consistently adopted a rebuttable presumption approach, even though the language of the statute is not written in terms of a presumption. * * *

We think the test of the applicable law was well stated by our brother Justice Fitzgerald when he was a judge on the Court of Appeals. In Lucas v. Carson, 38 Mich.App. 552, 196 N.W.2d 819 (1972), he analyzed a case where, in spite of defendant's precautions, her vehicle "inexplicably slid into the rear of plaintiff's stopped car" where plaintiff was waiting at a traffic signal. * * *

First, in analyzing whether the presumption of negligence attributed to a rear-end collision had been rebutted in the case before them, the Court of Appeals acknowledged that the usual grounds for rebuttal, sudden emergency, did not appear in this case. In effect accepting defendant's contention that the doctrine of sudden emergency was not the sole basis for rebutting a presumption of negligence, the Court held:

"The general rule appears to be that evidence required to rebut this presumption *as a matter of law* should be positive, unequivocal, strong, and credible. In the case at bar, defendant driver contended that she was at all times driving in a reasonable and prudent manner. * * * [T]here was sufficient evidence at least to generate a jury question regarding rebutting of the presumption." * * *

This is the approach we follow today. * * *

[An] attraction of this approach is that it is fair. "If there is sufficient excuse or justification, there is ordinarily no violation of a statute and the statutory standard is inapplicable." Satterlee v. Orange Glenn School Dist. of San Diego County, 29 Cal.2d 581, 594, 177 P.2d 279, 286 (1947) (dissenting in part). It would be unreasonable to adhere to an automatic rule of negligence "where observance would subject a person to danger which might be avoided by disregard of the general rule." Tedla v. Ellman, 280 N.Y. 124, 131–132, 19 N.E.2d 987, 991 (1939).

The approach is logical. Liability without fault is not truly negligence, and in the absence of a clear legislative mandate to so extend liability, the courts should be hesitant to do so on their own. Because these are, after all, criminal statutes, a court is limited in how far it may go in plucking a statute from its criminal milieu and inserting it into the civil arena. The rule of rebuttable presumption has arisen in part in response to this concern, and in part because of the reluctance to go to the other extreme and in effect, discard or disregard the legislative standard. * * *

B. Violation of Statute as Negligence Per Se. While some Michigan cases seem to speak of negligence per se as a kind of strict liability, Holbert v. Staniak, 359 Mich. 283, 290, 102 N.W.2d 186 (1960), an examination indicates that there are a number of conditions that attempt to create a more reasonable approach than would result from an automatic application of a per se rule.

[Reference is made here to the court's construing the statute, determining its purpose and applying principles of proximate cause.]

Despite such limitations, the judge-made rule of negligence per se has still proved to be too inflexible and mechanical to satisfy thoughtful commentators and judges. It is forcefully argued that no matter how a court may attempt to confine the negligence per se doctrine, if defendant is liable despite the exercise of due care and the availability of a reasonable excuse, this is really strict liability, and not negligence. Prosser, The Law of Torts (4th ed.), § 36, p. 197. Since it is always possible that the Legislature's failure to deal specifically with the question of private rights was not accidental, and that there might have been no legislative intent to change the law of torts, such treatment of the statute may well be a gross perversion of the legislative will. It is troublesome, too, that "potentially ruinous civil liability" may follow from a "minor infraction of petty criminal regulations", [c] or may, in a jurisdiction burdened by contributory negligence, serve to deprive an otherwise deserving plaintiff of a much-needed recovery. * * *

C. Violation of Statute as Evidence of Negligence. Just as the rebuttable presumption approach to statutory violations in a negligence context apparently arose, at least in part, from dissatisfaction with the result of a mechanical application of the per se rule, a parallel development in our state with respect to infractions of ordinances and of administrative regulations, has been that violations of these amount to only evidence of negligence. [Cc]

We have not, however, chosen to join that small minority which has decreed that violation of a statute is only evidence of negligence. In view of the fairness and ease with which the rebuttable presumption standard has been and can be administered, we believe the litigants are thereby well served and the Legislature is given appropriate respect.

D. Application of Statutory Standard to This Case. We have seen, therefore, that while some of our Michigan cases seem to present negligence per se as an unqualified rule, the fact of the matter is that there are a number of qualifications which make application of this rule not really a per se approach at all. Not only must the statutory purpose doctrine and the requirement of proximate cause be satisfied, but the alleged wrongdoer has an opportunity to come forward with evidence rebutting the presumption of negligence.

An accurate statement of our law is that when a court adopts a penal statute as the standard of care in an action for negligence, violation of that statute establishes a prima facie case of negligence, with the determination to be made by the finder of fact whether the party accused of violating the statute has established a legally sufficient excuse. If the finder of fact determines such an excuse exists, the appropriate standard of care then becomes that established by the common law. Such excuses shall include, but shall not be limited to, those suggested by the Restatement (Second) of Torts § 288A, and shall be determined by the circumstances of each case.

In the case at bar, moreover, the statute itself provides a guideline for the jury, for a violation will not occur when it is impracticable to use the sidewalk or to walk on the left side of a highway. This is ordinarily a question for the finder of fact, [c] and thus the statute itself provides not only a legislative standard of care which may be accepted by the court, but a legislatively mandated excuse as well. * * *

* * * [W]e find the jury was adequately instructed as to the effect of the violation of this particular statute on plaintiff's case. * * *

The Court of Appeals is reversed and the trial court is affirmed. Costs to plaintiff.

---

1. Section 288A of the Second Restatement, referred to in the principal case, reads as follows:

"(1) An excused violation of a legislative enactment or an administrative regulation is not negligence.

"(2) Unless the enactment or regulation is construed not to permit such excuse, its violation is excused when

"(a) the violation is reasonable because of the actor's incapacity;

"(b) he neither knows nor should know of the occasion for compliance;

"(c) he is unable after reasonable diligence or care to comply;

"(d) he is confronted by an emergency not due to his own misconduct;

"(e) compliance would involve a greater risk of harm to the actor or to others."

This list is "not intended to be exclusive."

2. When a prosecution under a criminal statute is involved, the "soft spot" is normally the discretionary authority of the district attorney in deciding whether to prosecute. Within that discretion, he can determine that the accused's conduct was sufficiently excusable that a prosecution would not be fair. There is no such "soft spot" in a civil action for negligence. The plaintiff has been injured and he wants compensation regardless of any excuse that the defendant might present. To prevent unjust results, the common law has come to recognize that excuses should be recognized in some instances.

3.   The principal case classifies the approaches to this problem into three groups: (1) negligence per se, (2) prima facie negligence and (3) some evidence of negligence.   Most commentators would agree with this classification.   But there may be disagreement on the content of the first two groups.   The Restatement espouses the negligence per se approach, but it also permits excuses as indicated in § 288A.   The two concepts are regarded as fitting together in an accurate delineation of the per se approach.   The second classification (prima facie negligence) would then apply to jurisdictions in which the issue goes to the jury even when there is no credible evidence of a recognized excuse, but merely testimony that the defendant acted with due care.   It is in this situation alone that a distinction exists between the two classes.   These differing classifications, of course, are merely a matter of semantics.   What significance do they have on the content of an instruction to the jury?

4.   In light of the Restatement (Second) of Torts and the principal case, how might the following situations be decided?

A.   A statute provides that no vehicle shall be driven on the highway at night without a tail light.   Without any fault or knowledge of defendant, his tail light goes out while he is driving at night, and as a result plaintiff is injured in a collision with him.   Brotherton v. Day & Night Fuel Co., 192 Wash. 362, 73 P.2d 788 (1937).   What if defendant discovered that the light was out, but continued to drive carefully to a near-by filling station?   Taber v. Smith, 26 S.W.2d 722 (Tex.Civ.App.1930).

B.   A statute prohibits automobile drivers from passing at an intersection. Defendant approaches an intersection concealed from view and not marked by any warning sign, of whose existence he is ignorant, and as he reaches it attempts to pass.   Hullander v. McIntyre, 78 S.D. 453, 104 N.W.2d 40 (1960).

C.   A child, too young to know or appreciate the statute, crosses a street in the middle of the block?   Morby v. Rogers, 122 Utah 540, 252 P.2d 231 (1953); Maker v. Wellin, 214 Or. 332, 327 P.2d 793, 329 P.2d 1114 (1958).   Suppose an adult does not know of the jay-walking statute?

D.   Defendant drives on the left side of the road to avoid hitting a child who has darted out from the right.   Burlie v. Stephens, 113 Wash. 182, 193 P. 684 (1920); Sims v. Eleazer, 116 S.C. 41, 106 S.E. 854 (1921).   Would it be negligence *not* to violate the statute?

FREUND v. DeBUSE
Supreme Court of Oregon, 1972.
264 Or. 447, 506 P.2d 491.

Denecke, Justice.   The plaintiff alleged he was injured when the car he was driving was struck in the rear by defendant's pickup.   The defendant testified the collision occurred because his brakes unexpectedly failed.   The jury returned a verdict for the defendant and plaintiff appeals.

The plaintiff contends the trial court erred in failing to instruct the jury that the defendant was liable.   The basis of plaintiff's motion was that the defendant was negligent per se because his brakes were not "adequate to control the movement of and to stop and hold such [his]

Oregon Supreme Court (1972)
Seated: McAllister, O'Connell, C.J., Denecke
Standing: Howell, Holman, Tongue, Bryson

vehicle" and his brakes were not "maintained in good working order," all in violation of ORS 483.444. The defendant's testimony was that after the collision he "tore apart" his wheel and found a broken brake drum which was the cause of the brake failure.

Just weeks ago in Barnum v. Williams, 264 Or. 71, 504 P.2d 122 (1972), we expressed the difficulty this court has had in the application of the negligence per se doctrine. The *Barnum* case involved an "operational" motor vehicle statute, driving on the "wrong side" of the road. We held "that if a party is in violation of a motor vehicle statute, such a party is negligent as a matter of law unless such party introduces evidence from which the trier of fact could find that the party was acting as a reasonably prudent person under the circumstances." [C] The issue here is whether this rule also should be applied to violations of motor vehicle equipment statutes. We hold it should.

Initially, the law of Oregon was that violation of a statute setting the standard required for motor vehicle equipment was negligence per se. We stated that it was negligence per se although the violator might have acted as a reasonably prudent person. Nettleton v. James, 212 Or. 375, 386, 319 P.2d 879 (1958). In the same case, however, we stated that if the violation of the equipment statute was because of a "latent defect" the operator might not be liable.

In McConnell v. Herron, 240 Or. 486, 493, 402 P.2d 726 (1965), in which the defendant had defective brakes, we departed from the strict negligence per se doctrine. We stated: " * * * We are now of the opinion that the motor vehicle code was not intended to eliminate the element of fault from the law of torts. * * *. Accordingly, we apply to equipment defects the same rule we have applied in the past to operational errors. Liability in both situations is based upon fault rather than upon a theory of absolute liability." 240 Or. at 491, 402 P.2d at 729.

We did not, however, "apply to equipment defects the same rule we have applied in the past to operational errors." Instead, we adopted a rule somewhere between the rule applicable to operational errors and our former rule for equipment statute violations. We stated a party would be excused from a violation of an equipment statute if he could prove "that his noncompliance was caused by circumstances beyond his control and that it was impossible, regardless of his degree of care, for him to comply with the statute." [C]

We were quickly called upon to apply the standard applied in McConnell v. Herron, supra, to violations of both equipment and operational statutes. In Pozsgai v. Porter, 249 Or. 84, 86–88, 435 P.2d 818 (1968) we acknowledge that we were applying a different negligence per se rule for violations of equipment statutes than for violations of operational statutes. We admitted that "theoretically" there may be "no justification for the rule of McConnell which treats the violation of safety equipment statutes differently than the violation of operational statutes." [C]

In Ainsworth v. Deutschman, 251 Or. 596, 446 P.2d 187 (1968), we held that the statement of the rule in McConnell v. Herron, supra, for violations of the equipment statutes was incorrect. We adopted the suggested language in Pozsgai v. Porter, supra, and stated that violations of equipment statutes would not be negligence per se if such violations could not be avoided by the exercise of the highest degree of care, although it was not "impossible, regardless of the degree of care he might have exercised, for him to comply with the statute." [C]

There is no logical or empirical basis for treating violations of vehicle equipment statutes differently than vehicle operational statutes and our experience has taught us that attempts to preserve any distinction have resulted in confusion.

McConnell v. Herron, supra, and Ainsworth v. Deutschman, supra, are overruled insofar as they hold that violations of vehicle equipment statutes are negligence per se unless the violator can establish that the violation occurred despite his exercise of a standard of care higher than that of a reasonably prudent person. We hold, as we did in Barnum v. Williams, supra, "that if a party is in violation of a motor vehicle [equipment] statute, such a party is negligent as a matter of law unless such party introduces evidence from which the trier of fact could find that the party was acting as a reasonably prudent person under the circumstances." [C]

The next question is whether *fair minds could differ as to* the evidence introduced by the defendant is sufficient for a jury to find that the defendant acted as a reasonably prudent person despite his violation of the statute. We find that it is.

The vehicle was a 1955 pickup which defendant had purchased in 1968, about eight months prior to the collision. The jury could find that the defendant had no prior trouble with the brakes except that about three weeks before the collision he adjusted them. He testified that because of normal wear of the brake lining he had to push the brake pedal down too far to get braking. He corrected this by adjusting the pedal.

The defendant testified the broken brake drum caused the brake failure in this manner:

"A. * * * [Y]our brake drum is round with brake lining. They push out against the brake drum. And this brake drum cracked and spread out under the pressure of the application of the brakes, allowing the—excessive amount of fluid to enter the wheel cylinder. The piston that pushes the brake lining out, causing the brake pedal to go to the floor. * * *

"Q. Where does all that fluid go when you push on your pedal?

"A. You have a wheel cylinder drum. It is a small cylinder on a wheel with a piston in it. During normal braking, the brake lining will only push so far and you will only travel a short distance, but due to the broken drum, you travel the whole distance; the cylinder absorbs all the fluid that was in the master cylinder."

We find this to be sufficient evidence to enable the jury to find that the defendant acted as a reasonably prudent person. When there is no prior warning of any possible defect in the brakes a reasonable vehicle operator is not required to "tear apart" the wheel to inspect for a defect.

ha ha

Affirmed.

McALLISTER, JUSTICE (dissenting). In my dissenting opinion in *Barnum v. Williams*, Or., 504 P.2d 122, 127 (1972) I pointed out that the majority had incorrectly interpreted our prior cases involving motor vehicle operational statutes. In the present case the majority overrules our prior decisions involving safety equipment statutes. In my opinion the two lines of cases, although applying different standards, were, prior to *Barnum*, entirely consistent. For the reasons stated in my dissent in that case, I cannot join the majority in abandoning the rule of negligence per se. *Is the court abandoning it?*

Moreover, in my opinion, the defendant failed to meet his burden of proof that he could not even, by the exercise of the highest degree of care, discover the defect in the brake drum.

I dissent.

---

1. This case illustrates the difficulties one court has had in attempting to find the most suitable adjustment for applying a bad-brakes statute. Other states have experienced similar difficulties with the construction of this type of statute, and the interpretations range all the way from strict liability, making the defendant liable if his brakes fail to execute properly without regard to whether the condition was discoverable or not, Spalding v. Waxler, 2 Ohio St.2d 1, 31 Ohio Op.2d 1, 205 N.E.2d 890 (1965), to ordinary negligence, essentially making the statute ineffective in any respect, Phillips v. Britannia Hygienic Laundry Co., [1923] 1 K.B. 539. Cf. Maloney v. Rath, 69 Cal.2d 442, 445 P.2d 513, 71 Cal.Rptr. 897 (1968), allowing an excuse but holding that the duty to use care to maintain the brakes in compliance with the statute cannot be delegated even to a repairman.

2. Certain types of statutes are commonly interpreted to make the defendant liable without regard to his negligence or excuse for the violation. They include:

A. Child labor acts, providing under criminal penalty that no minor under a minimum age shall be employed in certain occupations, as in Krutlies v. Bulls Head Coal Co., 249 Pa. 162, 94 A. 459 (1915); Blanton v. Kellioka Coal Co., 192 Ky. 220, 232 S.W. 614 (1921).

B. Pure Food Acts that prohibit the commercial sale of adulterated food. Doherty v. S.S. Kresge Co., 227 Wis. 661, 278 N.W. 437 (1938); Bolitho v. Safeway Stores, 109 Mont. 213, 95 P.2d 443 (1937).

C. The Federal Safety Appliance Act, requiring that railway cars used in interstate commerce be equipped with automatic couplers and other safety devices, in good operating condition. O'Donnell v. Elgin, J. & E.R. Co., 338 U.S. 384 (1949). Accord, St. Louis S.W.R. Co. v. Williams, 397 F.2d 147 (5th Cir. 1968) (Boiler Inspection Act).

D. Various factory acts making specific requirements for the safety of employees. Koenig v. Patrick Const. Corp., 298 N.Y. 313, 83 N.E.2d 133 (1948); Continental Can Co. v. Horton, 250 F.2d 637 (8th Cir.1957).

E. One court has held that strict or absolute liability will apply to all violations of OSHA regulations of hazardous substances that are related to Federal Employers' Liability Act claims. Hebel v. Conrail, Inc., 444 N.E.2d 870 (Ind.App.1983).

F. "Safe place" statutes, requiring lights and other protection in tenement houses, or premises open to the public. Monsour v. Excelsior Tobacco Co., 115 S.W.2d 219 (Mo.App.1938); Smulczeski v. City Center of Music and Drama, 3 N.Y.2d 498, 146 N.E.2d 769 (1957).

G. Statutes prohibiting the sale of firearms and other dangerous objects to minors. See Note, 20 La.L.Rev. 796 (1960).

3. When strict liability is imposed because no excuse is permitted, it often is held that the legislative purpose cannot be given full effect unless the

defenses of contributory negligence and assumption of risk are made unavailable to the defendant.

4. *Reasonable Care Per Se.* Suppose defendant shows that he complied with all regulatory statutes and administrative regulations. Should his conduct be deemed "reasonable care per se"? See Raymond v. Riegel Textile Corp., 484 F.2d 1025 (1st Cir.1973) (Flammable Fabrics Act); Black v. Pub. Serv. Elec. & Gas Co., 56 N.J. 63, 265 A.2d 129, 136 (1970) (evidence of care); Wilson v. Piper Aircraft Corp., 282 Or. 61, 577 P.2d 1322 (1978). Should the answer depend on how completely the product or activity is regulated by government?

---

7. PROOF OF NEGLIGENCE

(A) COURT AND JURY: CIRCUMSTANTIAL EVIDENCE

GODDARD v. BOSTON & MAINE R.R. CO.

Supreme Judicial Court of Massachusetts, 1901.
179 Mass. 52, 60 N.E. 486.

Action by Wilfred H. Goddard against the Boston & Maine Railroad Company for personal injuries received by falling upon a banana skin lying upon the platform at defendant's station at Boston. The evidence showed that [plaintiff] was a passenger who had just arrived, and was about the length of the car from where he alighted when he slipped and fell. There was evidence that there were many passengers on the platform. Verdict directed for defendant, and plaintiff excepts.

HOLMES, C.J. The banana skin upon which the plaintiff stepped and which caused him to slip may have been dropped within a minute by one of the persons who was leaving the train. It is unnecessary to go further to decide the case.

Exceptions overruled.

ANJOU v. BOSTON ELEVATED RAILWAY CO.

Supreme Judicial Court of Massachusetts, 1911.
208 Mass. 273, 94 N.E. 386.

Action by Helen G. Anjou against the Boston Elevated Railway Company. Verdict was directed for defendant, and the case reported.

RUGG, J. The plaintiff arrived on one of defendant's cars on the upper level of the Dudley Street terminal; other passengers arrived on the same car, but it does not appear how many. She waited until the crowd had left the platform, when she inquired of one of defendant's uniformed employés the direction to another car. He walked along a narrow platform, and she, following a few feet behind him toward the stairway he had indicated, was injured by slipping upon a banana peel. It was described by several who examined it in these terms: It "felt dry, gritty, as if there were dirt upon it," as if "trampled over a good deal," as "flattened down, and black in color," "every bit of it was black, there wasn't a particle of yellow," and as "black, flattened out and gritty." It was one of the duties of employés of the defendant, of whom there was one at this station all the time, to observe and remove whatever was upon the platform to interfere with the safety of travelers. These might have been found to be the facts.

The inference might have been drawn from the appearance and condition of the banana peel that it had been upon the platform a considerable period of time, in such position that it would have been seen and removed by the employés of the defendant if they had been reasonably careful in performing their duty. Therefore there is something on which to base a conclusion that it was not dropped a moment before by a passenger, and Goddard v. Boston & Maine R.R., 179 Mass. 52, 60 N.E. 486 is plainly distinguishable. The obligation rested upon the defendant to keep its station reasonably safe for its passengers It might have been found that the platform was suffered to remain in such condition as to be a menace to those rightfully walking upon it. Hence there was evidence of negligence on the part of the defendant, which should have been submitted to the jury. [Cc]

In accordance with the terms of the report, let the entry be:

Judgment for the plaintiff for $1,250 with costs.

[Normally, this case would have been reversed for a new trial. For some reason (perhaps to avoid expense of a new trial), defense counsel apparently agreed to an entry of judgment against his client if he lost on appeal.]

JOYE v. GREAT ATLANTIC AND PACIFIC TEA CO.

United States Court of Appeals, Fourth Circuit, 1968.
405 F.2d 464.

CRAVEN, CIRCUIT JUDGE: Willard Joye slipped and fell on a banana in defendant's A & P supermarket. In his diversity suit in the district court the jury returned a verdict for him in the amount of $10,000 and defendant appeals. We reverse because we are unable to find in the record sufficient evidence to present a jury issue as to constructive notice to defendant of a dangerous condition. Without such notice, in the context of the case, and under South Carolina law which we must apply, the district court should have granted defendant's Rule 50(b) motion for judgment n.o.v. * * *

There was no evidence that the A & P (1) put the banana on the floor or (2) had actual notice of its presence. Thus plaintiff's case turns on the sufficiency of the evidence to establish constructive notice. [C]

Plaintiff offered no direct evidence below as to how long the banana had been on the floor before the accident. The circumstantial evidence taken most favorably to the plaintiff shows that the floor may not have been swept for as long as 35 minutes. No one saw the banana until *after* Joye fell on it. It was then described as dark brown in color, having dirt and sand on it. There was dirt on the floor near the banana, and the banana was sticky around the edges. From this evidence we think the jury could not tell whether the banana had been on defendant's floor for 30 seconds or 3 days. * * *

Because it cannot be determined from the evidence how long (even the broadest range of approximation) the banana may have been on the floor, we reverse the judgment of the district court and remand to that court with instructions to enter judgment in favor of the defendant, The Great Atlantic & Pacific Tea Company.

Reversed.

JASKO v. F.W. WOOLWORTH CO.

Supreme Court of Colorado, 1972.
177 Colo. 418, 494 P.2d 839.

[Plaintiff was injured when she slipped on a piece of pizza that was on the terrazzo floor near the "pizza-hoagie counter" in defendant's store.]

GROVES, JUSTICE. * * * We address ourselves solely to the necessity of notice of the specific condition, which under the facts of this case is of first impression in this court. * * *

In her attempt to meet the requirement of notice, plaintiff did not claim or show that the alleged pizza was placed or dropped on the floor directly by the defendant or its employees, or that defendant knew of its presence. [C] Rather, it was her contention that defendant's method of selling pizza was one which leads inescapably to such mishaps as her own, and that in such a situation conventional notice requirements need not be met. We agree.

The dangerous condition was created by the store's method of sale. The steps taken to constantly clean the floor show that the store owner recognized the danger.

The practice of extensive selling of slices of pizza on waxed paper to customers who consume it while standing creates the reasonable probability that food will drop to the floor. Food on a terrazzo floor will create a dangerous condition. In such a situation, notice to the proprietor of the specific item on the floor need not be shown.

The basic notice requirement springs from the thought that a dangerous condition, when it occurs, is somewhat out of the ordinary. * * * In such a situation the storekeeper is allowed a reasonable time, under the circumstances, to discover and correct the condition, unless it is the direct result of his (or his employees') acts. However, when the operating methods of a proprietor are such that dangerous conditions are continuous or easily foreseeable, the logical basis for the notice requirement dissolves. Then, actual or constructive notice of the specific condition need not be proved. * * *

The ruling of the Court of Appeals is reversed and the cause remanded to it for further remand to the trial court and new trial.

1. Can these cases be reconciled?

2. Why not require the defendant to prove that it was not negligent—that is, that it was not responsible for the substance plaintiff slipped on? Plaintiff has no information, and can get none, as to what defendant's employees have or have not done; defendant knows, or can perhaps find out.

3. To what extent is plaintiff's disadvantage remedied by statutes permitting him to call defendant, or his servants or agents, to the stand and cross-examine them as to the facts without being bound by their testimony? By "discovery" or "interrogatory" procedure under which, in advance of trial, either party may require the other to answer questions under oath?

4. Plaintiff has two separate burdens of proof on the issue of negligence—the burden of coming forward with enough evidence to avoid a directed verdict against him and if he hurdles that, the burden of persuading the trier of fact to find in his favor. In most situations plaintiff discharges the first burden by convincing the judge that reasonable jurors could find on a more-probable-than-not basis that plaintiff's contention is correct. Plaintiff must then persuade the jury that the preponderance of the evidence is in his favor.

5. What kind of evidence has plaintiff introduced in these cases? How reliable is it? There are footprints in the mud, and a hundred eyewitnesses testify on oath that they sat there the whole time and no one passed by. Can the jury find that some one did? Would you expect them to? Cf. Phoenix Refining Co. v. Powell, 251 S.W.2d 892 (Tex.Civ.App.1952) (tire skid marks); Macfie v. Kaminski, 219 Neb. 524, 364 N.W.2d 31 (1985) (proof of skid).

6. In what circumstances can one infer that defendant has been negligent with regard to a foreign substance on the floor of his premises? What if plaintiff only proves a pattern of recurring conditions, such as litter on the floor of a cafeteria, where customers either eat at the counter or carry their food without trays? See Bozza v. Vornado, Inc., 42 N.J. 355, 200 A.2d 777 (1964). Suppose there had been evidence of notable customers?

7. Problems involved in proving facts in tort cases, as any competent trial lawyer will affirm, are often more difficult than developing the relevant rules of law. See, for example, S. Schreiber, Trial Evidence in Civil Cases (1969); L. Schwartz, Trial of Automobile Accident Cases v. 1–6 (1968); G. Lacy, Scientific Automobile Accident Reconstruction (1968).

8. Although a Torts course can only introduce the students to problems of proof, it is important for them to have a continuing sensitivity to the problems throughout the law school career. This awareness will be developed in courses in evidence, trial practice and legal clinic, as well as in continuing legal education programs after graduation from law school.

[handwritten at top: = a presumption of negligence]

(B) RES IPSA LOQUITUR

[handwritten: "Well then, don't argue w/ this; this is just something I need to know; it's in Latin, after all.]

BYRNE v. BOADLE

Court of Exchequer, 1863.
2 H. & C. 722, 159 Eng.Rep. 299.

[handwritten: Gets Duty/Breach/CoA / (cause) to jury (only) / Shifts BoP to ∆ for case in chief / That ∆ was not N, ∆ did not cause]

[Action for negligence. The plaintiff's evidence was that he was walking in a public street past the defendant's shop, and that a barrel of flour fell upon him from a window above the shop, knocked him down, and seriously injured him. There was no other evidence. The Assessor was of the opinion that there was no evidence of negligence for the jury, and nonsuited the plaintiff, reserving leave to him to move the Court of Exchequer to enter the verdict for him for £50 damages. Plaintiff obtained a rule nisi.] *[handwritten left margin: (Civil Grand Jury?)]* *[handwritten right margin: TrCt = ∆ (dismiss)]*

[handwritten: as in PF case?]

Charles Russell now shewed cause. First, there was no evidence to connect the defendant or his servants with the occurrence. * * * It is consistent with the evidence that the purchaser of the flour was superintending the lowering of it by his servant, or it may be that a stranger was engaged to do it without the knowledge or authority of the defendant. [Pollock, C.B. The presumption is that the defendant's servants were engaged in removing the defendant's flour; if they were not it was competent to the defendant to prove it.] *[handwritten: BoP on ∆ (why the presumption?)]*

Secondly, assuming the facts to be brought home to the defendant or his servants, these facts do not disclose any evidence for the jury of negligence. The plaintiff was bound to give affirmative proof of negli-*[handwritten: 6/12]* gence. But there was not a scintilla of evidence, unless the occurrence is of itself evidence of negligence. There was not even evidence that the barrel was being lowered by a jigger-hoist as alleged in the declaration. [Pollock, C.B. There are certain cases of which it may be said res ipsa loquitur, and this seems one of them. In some cases the Courts have held that the mere fact of the accident having occurred is evidence of negligence, as, for instance, in the case of railway collisions.]

POLLOCK, C.B. We are all of opinion that the rule must be absolute to enter the verdict for the plaintiff. The learned counsel was quite right in saying that there are many accidents from which no presumption of negligence can arise, but I think it would be wrong to lay down as a rule that in no case can a presumption of negligence arise from the *[handwritten: = RIL]* fact of an accident. Suppose in this case the barrel had rolled out of the warehouse and fallen on the plaintiff, how could he possibly ascertain from what cause it occurred? It is the duty of persons who keep barrels in a warehouse to take care that they do not roll out, and I think that such a case would, beyond all doubt, afford prima facie evidence of negligence. A barrel could not roll out of a warehouse *[handwritten: 6/12 of RIL]* without some negligence, and to say that a plaintiff who is injured by it must call witnesses from the warehouse to prove negligence seems to me preposterous. * * * The present case upon the evidence comes to this, a man is passing in front of the premises of a dealer in flour, and

[handwritten at bottom: why? Would they not tell the truth, under oath?]

Chief Baron Pollock

there falls down upon him a barrel of flour. I think it apparent that the barrel was in the custody of the defendant who occupied the premises, and who is responsible for the acts of his servants who had the control of it; and in my opinion the fact of its falling is prima facie evidence of negligence, and the plaintiff who was injured by it is not bound to show that it could not fall without negligence, but if there are any facts inconsistent with negligence it is for the defendant to prove them.

[The concurring opinions of BRAMWELL, B., CHANNELL, B., and PIG-OTT, B., are omitted.]

---

1. What kind of evidence of defendant's negligence has plaintiff offered? How persuasive is it? What about the possibility that some trespassing tramp entered the premises and rolled the barrel out of the window? Suppose the defendant in the principal case was merely a deliverer of flour and not the

*then π would have been remiss for not suing the owner
if π had not.*

owner of the shop? Cf. Hake v. George Wiedemann Brewing Co., 23 Ohio St.2d 65, 52 Ohio Op.2d 366, 262 N.E.2d 703 (1970).

2. *Res Ipsa Loquitur.* "The thing speaks for itself." This is an old phrase, found in Cicero and other ancient writers; and it has been used from time to time in other connections in the law. Chief Baron Pollock was an English gentleman, with a classical education, as was counsel to whom he spoke. Just what did he mean by it? This question has been put in Latin: Res ipsa loquitur, sed quid in infernos dicet? *but what in the hell does it mean?* ✓

3. There has been considerable denunciation of the use of the phrase in negligence cases. See, for example, Bond, C.J., dissenting in Potomac Edison Co. v. Johnson, 160 Md. 33, 152 A. 633 (1930): "It adds nothing to the law, has no meaning which is not more clearly expressed for us in English, and brings confusion to our legal discussions. It does not represent a doctrine, is not a legal maxim, and is not a rule." Also Lord Shaw, in Ballard v. North British R. Co., [1923] Sess.Cas.H.L. 43, 56: "If that phrase had not been in Latin, nobody would have called it a principle."

4. The first attempt to state the rule of Byrne v. Boadle was that of Chief Justice Erle in Scott v. London & St. Katherine Docks Co., 3 H. & C. 596, 159 Eng.Rep. 665 (1865): "There must be reasonable evidence of negligence; but where the thing is shown to be under the management of the defendant or his servants, and the accident is such as in the ordinary course of things does not happen if those who have the management use proper care, it affords reasonable evidence, in the absence of explanation by the defendants, that the accident arose from want of care."

*duty to inspect
strict liability
for common
carriers*

5. Shortly after 1870, this principle became entangled and confused with an older and quite different rule. In Christie v. Griggs, 2 Camp. 79, 170 Eng. Rep. 1088 (1809), the axle of a stagecoach broke and a passenger was injured. Sir James Mansfield declared that the burden lay upon the common carrier to prove that the injury was not caused by its negligence. Later decisions explained this on the basis of the special responsibility which the carrier had undertaken under its contract to transport the passenger safely.

6. The two principles became intermingled and ultimately merged in cases of injuries to passengers under the name of "res ipsa loquitur"; and much of the confusion that has surrounded the doctrine is due to this merger.

7. On "res ipsa loquitur" generally, see Atiyah, Res Ipsa Loquitur in England and Australia, 35 Mod.L.Rev. 337 (1972); Carpenter, The Doctrine of Res Ipsa Loquitur, 1 U.Chi.L.Rev. 519 (1934); Malone, Res Ipsa Loquitur and Proof by Inference, 4 La.L.Rev. 70 (1941); Morris, Res Ipsa Loquitur in Texas, 26 Tex.L.Rev. 257, 761 (1948); Prosser, Res Ipsa Loquitur in California, 37 Cal. L.Rev. 183 (1949), reprinted in Prosser, Selected Topics on the Law of Torts 302 (1954); James, Proof of the Breach in Negligence Cases, 37 Val.U.L.Rev. 179 (1951).

COX v. NORTHWEST AIRLINES, INC.

United States Court of Appeals, Seventh Circuit, 1967.
379 F.2d 893, cert. denied, 389 U.S. 1044, 88 S.Ct. 788, 19 L.Ed.2d 836.

CASTLE, CIRCUIT JUDGE. The appellant, Northwest Airlines, Inc., *Tr ct = ∆ π* prosecutes this appeal from a judgment entered against it in an admiralty action instituted in the District Court by the libellant-appellee, Irene Cox, administratrix. Libellant sought recovery of damages under the Death on the High Seas Act (46 U.S.C.A. § 761 et seq.) for the death of her husband. The action was tried to the court without a jury. The court made and entered findings of fact and conclusions of law, and awarded judgment against the appellant for $329,956.59.

The record discloses that the libellant's decedent, her husband, Randall S. Cox, a Captain in the United States Army, 29 years of age, was a passenger on appellant's Douglas DC–7C airplane N290, flight 293, which crashed in the Pacific Ocean on June 3, 1963 during a flight from McChord Air Force Base, near Seattle, Washington, to Elmendorf, Alaska, at approximately 11:12 A.M. at a point about one hundred sixteen miles west-southwest of Annette Island off the west coast of Canada. The flight had taken off from McChord at about 8:32 A.M. after having been briefed on the weather by both its dispatch office at the Seattle Airport and by a U.S. Air Force weather specialist at McChord, and having followed the usual procedures in preparation for flight. The crew reported by radio at 11:07 A.M. that it had been over Domestic Annette at 11:06 at an altitude of 14,000 feet and requested clearance to climb to 18,000 feet. No reason for the requested change in altitude was given. Domestic Annette is a fix-point at which directional radio bearings are obtained along the air route from McChord to Elmendorf. This was the last known transmission made by the crew of the aircraft. On the following day, June 4, 1963, floating debris was sighted in the Pacific Ocean about 35 nautical miles west of Domestic Annette. Approximately 1,500 pounds of wreckage identified as being from the aircraft, including life vests still encased in their plastic containers and extremely deformed seat frames, was recovered. The bodies of none of the crew or passengers were ever recovered.

* * *

The court's conclusion that the negligence of appellant was the proximate cause of decedent's death is predicated upon the court's finding that:

"[A]s a result of the occurrence Randall S. Cox met his death. The instrumentality which produced the death of Randall S. Cox was under the exclusive control and management of the [appellant] and that the occurrence in question was such as does not ordinarily occur in the absence of negligence, and, further, that there is no possibility of contributing conduct which would make Randall S. Cox responsible; that the facts herein justify a finding of negligence."

The appellant recognizes that the doctrine of res ipsa loquitur may properly have application in actions involving airline accidents. But the appellant contends that in the instant case it was error to apply that doctrine in resolving the issue of liability because there is substantial proof of the exercise of due care by the appellant and no countervailing evidence of specific negligence or even of unusual circumstances. Appellant urges that evidence of due care on its part precludes any inference of negligence arising from the occurrence in the absence of at least minimal supporting evidence and, therefore, libellant has not sustained the burden of proof requisite to an ultimate finding of negligence and has failed to prove her case by a preponderance of the evidence.

The evidence of due care to which appellant alludes concerns its maintenance records and procedures with respect to the aircraft involved; the qualified and certified status, and the competence, of the operating personnel of the aircraft and of the dispatcher; the safety training received by the crew; and the evidence that the flight was properly dispatched and the weather normal.

There is no evidence as to the cause of the aircraft's crash into the ocean or concerning what happened to affect the operation of the aircraft during the period following 11:07 A.M. and prior to the crash. In the absence of such evidence, the probative value of appellant's general evidence of due care is not of substantial import. Whether due care was exercised by the operating personnel of the aircraft in the face of whatever occurred to affect the operation of the aircraft can be appraised only in the light of knowledge of what that occurrence was, whether human or mechanical failure or some other incident, and of what if anything was or could have been done about it.

We perceive nothing in appellant's due care evidence which precludes an application of the res ipsa loquitur doctrine or conditions such application upon the libellant's responding with evidence to support some specific negligent act or omission on the part of appellant. Here, the cause of the crash which resulted in the death of Randall S. Cox is wholly unexplained. And, as was cogently observed in Johnson v. United States, 333 U.S. 46, 49, 68 S.Ct. 391, 393, 92 L.Ed. 468:

"No act need be explicable only in terms of negligence in order for the rule of *res ipsa loquitur* to be invoked. The rule deals only with permissible inferences from unexplained events."

We are of the opinion that the court properly applied the doctrine of res ipsa loquitur and that its finding of negligence was a permissible one—warranted though not compelled [c]—and that the court's conclusion on the issue of appellant's liability is thus supported by the evidence and the application of correct legal criteria. * * *

The judgment of the District Court is affirmed insofar as it adjudicates the issue of the liability of the appellant, Northwest Airlines, Inc., to the libellant, and the cause is remanded to the District Court with directions that the court modify the judgment by reducing the amount of damages awarded therein to conform with the views herein expressed. * * *

1. How does the court know that this accident would be unlikely to occur in absence of negligence on the part of defendant? How could an attorney persuade the court that this was true? What about the possibility that the plaintiff himself had caused the crash or that another passenger brought a bomb aboard?

2. What would you expect the rule to be forty or fifty years ago, when an airplane crashed without explanation? See Wilson v. Colonial Air Transport, 278 Mass. 420, 180 N.E. 212 (1932); Herndon v. Gregory, 190 Ark. 702, 81 S.W.2d 849 (1935).

3. In United States v. Kesinger, 190 F.2d 529 (10th Cir.1951), the court reached a similar conclusion when, without explanation, defendant's plane crashed into plaintiff's barn. The court said:

"In the past decade tremendous improvements have been effected in the design and construction of airplanes, and in the operation and maintenance thereof. Today, an airplane operated under normal weather conditions is a reasonably safe means of transportation. On the basis of passenger miles flown it is relatively as safe as other methods of public transportation. The rates charged by insurance carriers for insurance of passengers are the same whether the passenger travels by train, bus or airplane. An airline which has operated in the states of Colorado, Kansas, Oklahoma, New Mexico and Texas during the past 15 years recently received a special award from the National Safety Council. During the period of its operation the airline had flown 437,262,000 passenger miles without a passenger fatality and without a serious accident. An international airline was also given an award by the National Safety Council for having completed 1,637,300,000 passenger miles without a passenger or crew fatality. An airplane of a proven safe type of design taking off for an ordinary routine flight under normal weather conditions does not crash in the ordinary course of things, unless there has been a failure to properly inspect, service and maintain it, or unless it is not operated with due care."

How did the court acquire this information? Did it have to pass muster under the exclusionary rules of evidence? See Davis, Judicial Notice, 55 Colum.L.Rev. 945 (1955).

4. What result in the instant case if Northwest had acquired the plane in question from Douglas the day before the accident happened? Cf. Campbell v. First Nat'l Bank, 370 F.Supp. 1096 (D.N.M.1973). What if a plane, flying through smooth air, suddenly and without any warning strikes a "bump," and a passenger is thrown from his seat? Cudney v. Midcontinent Airlines, 363 Mo. 922, 254 S.W.2d 662 (1953); Ness v. West Coast Airlines, Inc., 90 Idaho 111, 410 P.2d 965 (1965). Or hot tea is spilled into his lap from a tray? Lazarus v. Eastern Air Lines, 292 F.2d 748 (D.C.Cir.1961). See generally McLarty, Res Ipsa Loquitur in Airline Passenger Litigation, 37 Va.L.Rev. 55 (1951).

5. How persuasive is the inference of negligence in the following cases?

(a) When truck brakes fail, the owner is at fault. See Harris v. Irish Truck Lines, Inc., 11 Cal.3d 373, 521 P.2d 481, 113 Cal.Rptr. 489 (1974).

(b) When a television set catches fire and burns, the manufacturer was negligent. See Gast v. Sears Roebuck & Co., 39 Ohio St.2d 29, 68 Ohio Op.2d 17, 313 N.E.2d 831 (1974).

(c) When the doors of a self-service elevator close on a person, the owner of the building is at fault. Isaacs v. Warren Terrace, Inc., 31 Ohio Misc. 65, 59 Ohio Op.2d 405, 60 Ohio Op.2d 214, 277 N.E.2d 88 (1971).

(d) When a human body falls upon a work of art, the person who fell was negligent. See Krebs v. Corrigan, 321 A.2d 558 (D.C.App.1974).

(e) When an automobile leaves the travelled portion of a highway and overturns or crashes into a stationary object, the driver was at fault. See Badela v. Karpowich, 152 Conn. 360, 206 A.2d 838 (1965).

(f) When a single automobile crashes, the driver is at fault. Mets v. Granrud, 606 P.2d 1384 (Mont.1980).

(g) When a fertilizer plant explodes, the person in control of the plant was negligent. Collins v. N–Ren Corp., 604 F.2d 659 (10th Cir.1979).

6. Can the inference of negligence ever be so strong as to suggest "gross negligence," "recklessness" or "wilful or wanton" conduct? See Annot., 23 A.L.R.3d 1083 (1969).

HOLMES v. GAMBLE

Supreme Court of Colorado, En Banc 1982.
655 P.2d 405.

DUBOFSKY, JUSTICE. We granted certiorari to review the judgment of the Colorado Court of Appeals in Holmes v. Gamble, 624 P.2d 905 (Colo.App.1980), affirming a Denver District Court order directing verdicts for both defendants in a medical malpractice action. We affirm the judgment, but determine that the Court of Appeals applied the wrong standard in upholding the district court's ruling that the plaintiff failed to establish a prima facie case of res ipsa loquitur.

Holmes was a Vail building contractor who suffered severe injury to his knee when a ditch in which he was working collapsed. Rescuers dug Holmes out of the ditch where he was buried waist-deep. A doctor in Vail referred Holmes to the defendant William E. Gamble, a Denver orthopedic surgeon, for immediate knee surgery. After a sedative was administered to Holmes, his brother transported him from Vail to Denver in the back of a station wagon. Dr. Gamble, assisted by the defendant anesthesiologist, Dr. Carl F. Heaton, operated on Holmes' knee the following day. Holmes was anesthetized and unconscious during the entire operation.

Awakening from anesthesia the morning after the operation, Holmes experienced numbness and tingling in the last three fingers of both hands. Holmes testified that he noticed these sensations immediately after regaining consciousness. His mother and brother, who were present in his hospital room when he awakened, corroborated his testimony. Holmes also testified that he described the numbness and tingling to Dr. Gamble later that day and that Gamble told him that the sensations could have been caused by pressure on his elbows during the operation. Dr. Gamble testified that he was not sure whether Holmes told him of this condition the day after the operation but believed that Holmes first mentioned it almost two weeks later. A medical history taken by a neurologist whom Holmes consulted three weeks after the operation recited that Holmes had not become aware of the sensations until several days after the operation. The neurologist diagnosed the sensations as symptoms of bilateral ulnar neuropathy—a condition which can be caused by traumatic injury to nerves in the elbows. Holmes' use of his hands became increasingly impaired by a loss of strength and by curling of the fingers. Neurosurgery was performed on one elbow, and by the time of the trial, Holmes had recovered some but not full use of both hands.

Holmes sued Doctors Gamble and Heaton for malpractice, alleging that the ulnar neuropathy affecting his hands was triggered by traumatic injuries to the nerves in his elbows caused by the doctors' negligent failure to properly position him on the operating table during his knee operation. Because he possessed no direct evidence of the events which had transpired during the operation, Holmes attempted to invoke the doctrine of *res ipsa loquitur* to create a presumption that his neural disorder was a proximate result of the defendants' negligence. His *prima facie* case consisted of the following circumstantial evidence: never before had he exhibited any symptoms of ulnar neuropathy; the cave-in injured only his lower body; undue force was not exerted on his upper body or extremities during the rescue; medical examinations conducted preoperatively in Vail and at the Denver hospital disclosed no evidence of trauma to the elbow nerves; he was transported from Vail to Denver in a careful manner; he experienced no numbness or tingling in his fingers between the time he was injured in the cave-in and the time he was anesthetized by Dr. Heaton; and he experienced those sensations for the first time immediately upon regaining full consciousness following the operation. Holmes also presented medical testimony that: trauma to the elbow nerve often causes ulnar neuropathy; improper positioning on an operating table can cause trauma to a patient's elbow nerves; a doctor who improperly positions a patient on an operating table fails to use the reasonable degree of knowledge, skill and training possessed by other physicians practicing the same specialty; and, if a surgical patient has never experienced symptoms of ulnar neuropathy before being anesthetized, the onset of those symptoms immediately after the patient regains consciousness justifies an inference, to a reasonable degree of medical certainty, that the neuropathy was triggered between the time anesthesia was administered and the time the patient awoke.

The district court directed a verdict for the defendant Heaton at the close of the plaintiff's evidence but did not rule on whether the plaintiff had established the elements of *res ipsa loquitur*. * * *

At the close of the evidence, the district court granted Dr. Gamble's motion for a directed verdict and ruled that the doctrine of *res ipsa loquitur* did not apply to the case. The Court of Appeals upheld the ruling * * *

Holmes argues that both courts below misconceived the scope of the inquiry a trial court must make to resolve the preliminary question of whether a plaintiff has adduced sufficient circumstantial evidence of negligence for the doctrine of *res ipsa loquitur* to apply. The Court of Appeals' holding is erroneous, Holmes contends, in declaring that a plaintiff must establish the elements of *res ipsa loquitur* "by a preponderance of the evidence" to withstand a defense motion for a directed verdict.

Under the doctrine of *res ipsa loquitur,* a rebuttable presumption of a defendant's negligence arises if the plaintiff's circumstantial evidence shows that: (1) the event is the kind which ordinarily does not occur in the absence of negligence; (2) responsible causes other than the defendant's negligence are sufficiently eliminated by the evidence; and (3) the negligence is within the scope of the defendant's duty to the plaintiff. [C] For the case to be submitted to the jury on a theory of *res ipsa loquitur,* the circumstantial evidence of these three elements must be such that it is more likely that the event was caused by negligence than that it was not. Where the probabilities are at best evenly balanced between negligence and its absence, it becomes the duty of the court to direct a verdict for the defendant. [Cc]

The scope of the inquiry permitted by this standard of review is narrower than and inconsistent with the inquiry undertaken by the district court and approved by the Court of Appeals in this case. A verdict may not be directed against a plaintiff who relies on *res ipsa loquitur* to establish a *prima facie* case of presumed negligence because he fails to establish by a preponderance of the evidence that the injury was of the kind which ordinarily does not occur in the absence of negligence. The expression "preponderance of the evidence" connotes the evidence which is "most convincing and satisfying in the controversy between the parties," [c] and involves the determination of disputed factual questions, the credibility of witnesses, and the probative value of the evidence adduced by the parties. Instead, the proper inquiry by the trial court is directed to the legal sufficiency of the plaintiff's evidence. It involves no weighing of the evidence; rather, the evidence and all legitimate inferences therefrom are to be construed in a light most favorable to the plaintiff. [Cc]

Therefore, we hold that the courts below erred in applying the preponderance of the evidence standard to an evaluation of the sufficiency of the plaintiff's *prima facie* case of *res ipsa loquitur.* To withstand a defense motion for a directed verdict on a cause of action premised on *res ipsa loquitur,* a plaintiff must adduce evidence, which, when viewed in a light most favorable to the plaintiff, establishes that the existence of each element of that doctrine is more probable than not.

Applying the correct standard to the facts of this case, we conclude that the district court and the Court of Appeals correctly ruled that the plaintiff had not established a *prima facie* case of *res ipsa loquitur* against either defendant. Taking all of the evidence and inferences therefrom in the light most favorable to Holmes, we find that it is at least equally likely that a cause other than the defendants' negligence was the basis of Holmes' injury. * * * All of the evidence of pressure to the armpits was linked to causes other than actions of the defendants—*i.e.,* lifting Holmes from the ditch, supporting him while walking, loading him into his brother's station wagon, and his use of crutches after the operation.

Finally, even if damage to the ulnar nerve alone could cause symptoms of numbness and tingling in three fingers—a result which the evidence showed to be extremely unlikely—Holmes has similarly failed to show that it is more probable that the damage to the nerves was caused by positioning on the operating table than by the cave-in or by pressure on his elbows during the ride from Vail to Denver. The evidence produced at trial demonstrated that Holmes' arms were placed in different positions throughout the operation, so that it was unlikely for the nerves in both elbows to have been damaged by pressure during the operation.

The judgment of the Court of Appeals is affirmed.

---

1. Should res ipsa loquitur apply in the following cases?

A. Plaintiff awakes with his leg partially paralyzed after defendant anesthetist administered spinal anesthesia. Ayers v. Parry, 192 F.2d 181 (3d Cir. 1951).

B. Plaintiff, insane, is given electric shock treatment by defendant physician. In the course of the treatment one of her bones is broken. This is all the evidence. Farber v. Olkon, 40 Cal.2d 503, 254 P.2d 520 (1953).

C. Plaintiff undergoes a surgical operation. Afterward she is returned to her hospital room, and left in an unconscious condition for an hour. When she recovers consciousness, she has a second-degree burn on her stomach in the exact shape of a hot water bottle. Cf. Timbrell v. Suburban Hosp., 4 Cal.2d 68, 47 P.2d 737 (1935).

D. After surgery for a tumor of the spinal cord, plaintiff begins to hemorrhage. Defendant surgeon, having failed in other efforts to stop the bleeding, reopens the incision and packs the wound with a cellulosic material and sews it up. Plaintiff wakes up paralyzed below the incision. Brannon v. Wood, 251 Or. 349, 444 P.2d 558 (1968).

2. Plaintiff suffers a broken jaw as the result of an oral surgeon's efforts to extract a wisdom tooth. If an expert testifies that such an event does not usually occur in the absence of negligence, should this provide a basis for the application of res ipsa loquitur? See Morgan v. Children's Hosp., 18 Ohio St. 3d 185, 480 N.E.2d 464 (1985); Mayor v. Dowsett, 240 Or. 196, 400 P.2d 234 (1965). Is this peculiar to malpractice cases? See Fricke, The Use of Expert Evidence in Res Ipsa Loquitur Cases, 5 Vill.L.Rev. 59 (1959); Note, 106 U.Pa. L.Rev. 731 (1958). Would an expert make a difference in any of the cases above?

3. *Availability of Expert Testimony.* Physicians and surgeons sometime decline to testify against one another in medical malpractice cases. See Markus, Conspiracy of Silence, 14 Clev.–Mar.L.Rev. 520 (1965). A survey made by the Boston University Law–Medicine Research Institute, and reported in Medical Economics, Aug. 28, 1961, found that out of 214 doctors, only 31% of the specialists and 27% of the general practitioners said that they would be willing to appear for the plaintiff where a surgeon, operating on a diseased kidney, removed the wrong one. This has been termed, by plaintiffs' attorneys, a "conspiracy of silence." In Agnew v. Parks, 172 Cal.App.2d 756, 343 P.2d 118 (1959), a suit was actually brought against a group of doctors for "conspiracy to obstruct the ends of justice" by refusal to testify; and in L'Orange v. Medical

Protective Co., 394 F.2d 57 (6th Cir. 1968), an insurance company was held liable for cancelling a dentist's liability insurance because he testified.

4. There are two types of cases in which sending a case to the jury on the basis of res ipsa loquitur may produce a result unfair to the defendant. The first is that of the "calculated risk." The defendant is aware of the serious risks involved, but determines, in the exercise of his medical judgment, that the patient's condition warrants the taking of that risk in order to cure him. The other involves the case of a "bad result" that is very rare but one that may come about despite the exercise of all due care. The problem is whether the happening of the event gives rise to a reasonable inference of negligence, not whether the injury would normally occur or not. For further discussion, see Siverson v. Weber, 57 Cal.2d 834, 372 P.2d 97, 22 Cal.Rptr. 337 (1962); Fehrman v. Smirl, 20 Wis.2d 1, 121 N.W.2d 255, 122 N.W.2d 439 (1963).

5. *Effect of specific pleading of negligence.* No less than four positions have been taken by the courts, as to whether the plaintiff, by his specific pleading of negligence, has lost his right to rely upon *res ipsa loquitur:* (a) that he has lost it entirely; (b) that he may take advantage of *res ipsa loquitur* to the extent that the inference of negligence to be drawn supports his specific allegations; (c) that he may rely on *res ipsa* only if the specific pleading is accompanied by a general allegation of negligence; and (d) that it is available without regard to the form of the pleading. Which is the best rule? Is any of the four unfair to plaintiff, or to defendant? See discussion in Vogreg v. Shepard Ambulance Co., 47 Wash.2d 659, 289 P.2d 350 (1955).

6. Similar positions have been taken as to the effect of the introduction of specific evidence of negligent conduct. What if the plaintiff's specific evidence tells the complete story of how the accident happened and just what the defendant did? Is there any room for the application of *res ipsa loquitur*? Augspurger v. Western Auto Supply Co., 257 Iowa 777, 134 N.W.2d 913 (1963).

Compare the following: "When the plaintiff shows that the railway car in which he was a passenger was derailed, there is an inference that the defendant railroad has somehow been negligent. When the plaintiff goes further and shows that the derailment was caused by an open switch, the plaintiff destroys any inference of other causes; but the inference that the defendant has not used proper care in looking after its switches is not destroyed, but considerably strengthened. If the plaintiff goes further still and shows that the switch was left open by a drunken switchman on duty, there is nothing left to infer; and if the plaintiff shows that the switch was thrown by an escaped convict with a grudge against the railroad, the plaintiff has proven himself out of court." W. Prosser and W. Keeton, Torts, 260 (5th ed. 1984).

7. As part of medical malpractice reform legislation (see page 196 supra), a number of states have codified the res ipsa loquitur doctrine, limiting its application to specific medical mishaps. One statute allows a "rebuttable inference of negligence" only for foreign bodies unintentionally left in the body following surgery, an explosion or fire originating in a substance used for treatment, or a surgical procedure on the wrong part of the body. 18 Del.Code Ann. tit. 18, § 6853 (Supp.1986). Are there other acts that would not require expert testimony to prove negligence? See Lacy v. G.D. Searle & Co., 484 A.2d 527 (Del.Super.1984).

Case of the UFC (unidentified Flying Chair)

— LARSON v. ST. FRANCIS HOTEL

read w/ Ybarra

District Court of Appeal of California, 1948.
83 Cal.App.2d 210, 188 P.2d 513.

Larson = multiple Δ's/causes = no RIL

Ybarra = multiple Δ's/causes = RIL

BRAY, JUSTICE. The accident out of which this action arose was *among them* apparently the result of the <u>effervescence and ebullition of San Franciscans in their exuberance of joy</u> on V–J day, August <u>14, 1945.</u> Plaintiff (who is not included in the above description), while walking on the

→ *finally, peace -- so what happened?*

The St. Francis Hotel, viewed from Union Square.
Post Street runs to the right of the Hotel

sidewalk on Post Street adjoining the St. Francis Hotel, just after
stepping out from under the marquee, was struck on the head by a
heavy, over-stuffed arm chair, knocked unconscious, and received injuries for which she is asking damages from the owners of the hotel.
Although there were a number of persons in the immediate vicinity, no
one appears to have seen from whence the chair came nor to have seen
it before it was within a few feet of plaintiff's head, nor was there any
identification of the chair as belonging to the hotel. However, it is a
reasonable inference that the chair came from some portion of the
hotel. For the purposes of this opinion, we will so assume, in view of
the rule on nonsuit cases that every favorable inference fairly deducible
from the evidence must be drawn in favor of plaintiff, and that all the
evidence must be construed most strongly against the defendants. [C]

At the trial, plaintiff, after proving the foregoing facts and the
extent of her injuries, rested, relying upon the doctrine of res ipsa
loquitur. On motion of defendant the court granted a nonsuit. The
main question to be determined is whether under the circumstances
shown, the doctrine applies. The trial court correctly held that it did
not.

In Gerhart v. Southern California Gas Co., 56 Cal.App.2d 425, 132
P.2d 874, 877, cited by plaintiff, the court sets forth the test for the
applicability of the doctrine. " * * * for a plaintiff to make out a
case entitling him to the benefit of the doctrine, *he must prove* (1) that
there was an accident; (2) that the thing or instrumentality which
caused the accident was at the time of and prior thereto under the
exclusive control and management of the defendant; (3) *that the accident was such that in the ordinary course of events, the defendant using
ordinary care, the accident would not have happened.* * * * The
doctrine of res ipsa loquitur applies only where the cause of the injury
is shown to be under the exclusive control and management of the
defendant and can have no application * * * to a case having a
divided responsibility where an unexplained accident may have been
attributable to one of several causes, for some of which the defendant is
not responsible, and when it appears that the injury was caused by one
of two causes for one of which defendant is responsible but not for the
other, plaintiff must fail, if the evidence does not show that the injury
was the result of the former cause, or leaves it as probable that it was
caused by one or the other." [Emphasis added.]

Applying the rule to the facts of this case, it is obvious that the
doctrine does not apply. While, as pointed out by plaintiff, the rule of
exclusive control "is not limited to the actual physical control but
applies to the right of control of the instrumentality which causes the
injury" it is not clear to us how this helps plaintiff's case. A hotel does
not have exclusive control, either actual or potential, of its furniture.
Guests have, at least, partial control. Moreover, it cannot be said that
with the hotel using ordinary care "the accident was such that in the
ordinary course of events * * * it would not have happened." On the
contrary, the mishap would quite as likely be due to the fault of a guest

or other person as to that of defendants. The most logical inference from the circumstances shown is that the chair was thrown by some such person from a window. It thus appears that this occurrence is not such as ordinarily does not happen without the negligence of the party charged, but, rather, one in which the accident ordinarily might happen despite the fact that the defendants used reasonable care and were totally free from negligence. To keep guests and visitors from throwing furniture out windows would require a guard to be placed in every room in the hotel, and no one would contend that there is any rule of law requiring a hotel to do that. * * * *thus, no RIL or shifting Prof BoP to Δ.

The judgment appealed from is affirmed.

No = No proof that π had control at all;

1. Must the possibility that the event has been caused by the conduct of a third person, for which defendant is not responsible, be entirely eliminated? Defendant parks his automobile on the side of a hill. Shortly afterward, without explanation, the automobile runs away down the hill and injures plaintiff. What are the possibilities? Can plaintiff get to the jury? Glaser v. Schroeder, 269 Mass. 337, 168 N.E. 809 (1929); Borg & Powers Furniture Co. v. Clark, 194 Minn. 305, 260 N.W. 316 (1935). A court allowed plaintiff's case to be heard by the jury although there was a four-hour lapse of time after defendant parked her car. See Hill v. Thompson, 484 P.2d 513 (Okl.1971). Compare Hughes v. Jolliffe, 50 Wash.2d 554, 313 P.2d 678 (1957).

2. A television catches fire in plaintiff's home. How does he persuade a court to invoke res ipsa loquitur against the manufacturer when the set left the factory several months before the incident in question? See Gast v. Sears Roebuck & Co., 39 Ohio St.2d 29, 68 Ohio Op.2d 17, 313 N.E.2d 831 (1974). Generally, what should the plaintiff do to eliminate his own conduct as a cause of the accident? Is it enough that he testifies that he did nothing unusual, and only made use of the thing furnished him by defendant for the purpose for which it was furnished?

3. Hot water escapes through a ruptured fitting on a radiator in a tenant's apartment, causing personal injury and damaging property. Should defendant landlord's "right to control" the instrumentality be sufficient to invoke res ipsa loquitur? See Niman v. Plaza House, Inc., 471 S.W.2d 207 (Mo. 1971), noted 38 U.Mo.L.Rev. 371 (1973). Some of the older cases required that defendant have "exclusive control". Thus, in Kilgore v. Shepard Co., 52 R.I. 151, 158 A. 720 (1932), plaintiff sat down on a chair in defendant's store, and it collapsed and injured him. Recovery was denied because plaintiff, and not defendant, was in "control" of the chair at the time. Contra: Gow v. Multnomah Hotel, 191 Or. 45, 224 P.2d 552 (1950); Rose v. Melody Lane of Wilshire, 39 Cal.2d 481, 247 P.2d 335 (1952).

4. *Defendant's Superior Knowledge.* It has sometimes been said that the basis of res ipsa loquitur is the defendant's superior knowledge, or ability to obtain evidence, as to just what has occurred; or in other words, that the purpose of the rule is to "smoke out" evidence that the defendant has or can get, and the plaintiff cannot. This has often been stated as an additional reason for applying res ipsa loquitur when it was otherwise applicable, or for refusing to apply it when it was otherwise inapplicable, as in Hughes v. Jolliffe, 50 Wash.2d 554, 313 P.2d 678 (1957).

5. If superior knowledge on the part of defendant is essential to res ipsa loquitur, what effect should modern discovery procedures have on the principle? Or the modern evidence rule that one may cross examine defendant as an adverse witness? The court in Krebs v. Corrigan, 321 A.2d 558, 561 (D.C.App. 1974), stated that: "The doctrine exists because of the realization that examination of a defendant as an adverse witness is not a viable way to discover the cause of an accident." There are holdings that a plaintiff is not precluded from invoking res ipsa loquitur because he has not attempted to obtain evidence through discovery procedures. Menth v. Breeze Corp., 4 N.J. 428, 73 A.2d 183 (1950); Bone v. General Motors Corp., 322 S.W.2d 916 (Mo.1959).

6. Several writers have contended that defendant's superior knowledge is the primary, if not the sole, purpose of the rule. This is the thesis of the book by Shain, Res Ipsa Loquitur (1945). The late Professor Carpenter was a vigorous advocate of this position. Carpenter, The Doctrine of Res Ipsa Loquitur in California, 10 So.Cal.L.Rev. 166 (1937); Carpenter, Res Ipsa Loquitur, 10 So.Cal.L.Rev. 467 (1937). A more recent article developing the same arguments at length is Jaffe, Res Ipsa Loquitur Vindicated, 1 Buffalo L.Rev. 1 (1951).

7. In a few cases, the court has refused to let the plaintiff get to the jury on the inference of negligence because the defendant did not know what had occurred and could not find out. See, for example, Appalachian Ins. Co. v. Knutson, 358 F.2d 679 (8th Cir.1966); Wilson v. East St. Louis & Interurban Water Co., 295 Ill.App. 603, 15 N.E.2d 599 (1938).

8. Most of the cases, however, hold that res ipsa loquitur applies, even though the defendant's knowledge is not superior to that of the plaintiff. See, for example, Johnson v. Foster, 202 So.2d 520 (Miss.1967) (car unaccountably leaves highway and overturns; both parties dead); Nicol v. Geitler, 188 Minn. 69, 247 N.W. 8 (1933) (similar; guest dead, driver disappeared); Burkett v. Johnston, 39 Tenn.App. 276, 282 S.W.2d 647 (1955) (similar; both dead); Haasman v. Pacific Alaska Air Express, 100 F.Supp. 1 (D.Alaska 1951), aff'd, 198 F.2d 550 (9th Cir.1952) (lost plane); Judson v. Giant Powder Co., 107 Cal. 549, 40 P. 1020 (1885) (nitroglycerin factory blew up; the "witnesses who saw and knew, like all things else around, save the earth itself, were scattered to the four winds").

9. Might defendant's superior knowledge be regarded as a requirement when the inference of defendant's negligence is relatively weak, but be dispensed with when it is relatively strong? Is it helpful to go further and look at the three basic ingredients of res ipsa loquitur in the context of an interdependent calculus with the strength of one factor supporting the weakness of the other?

10. *Car leaving highway.* There is general agreement that the fact that an automobile leaves the traveled portion of the highway and overturns, or crashes into a stationary object, is enough, in the absence of explanation, to make out a res ipsa loquitur case against the driver. Badela v. Karpowich, 152 Conn. 360, 206 A.2d 838 (1965); Bavis v. Fonte, 241 Md. 123, 215 A.2d 739 (1966); Tanski v. Jackson, 269 Minn. 304, 130 N.W.2d 492 (1964); Bagby v. Commonwealth, 424 S.W.2d 119 (Ky.1968).

YBARRA v. SPANGARD
Supreme Court of California, 1944.
25 Cal.2d 486, 154 P.2d 687.

Action by Joseph Roman Ybarra against Lawrence C. Spangard
and others for injuries resulting from allegedly improper treatment by
physicians and nurses. From a judgment of nonsuit, plaintiff appeals.
Reversed.

GIBSON, CHIEF JUSTICE. This is an action for damages for personal
injuries alleged to have been inflicted on plaintiff by defendants during
the course of a surgical operation. The trial court entered judgments of
nonsuit as to all defendants and plaintiff appealed.

On October 28, 1939, plaintiff consulted defendant Dr. Tilley, who
diagnosed his ailment as appendicitis, and made arrangements for an
appendectomy to be performed by defendant Dr. Spangard at a hospital
owned and managed by defendant Dr. Swift. Plaintiff entered the
hospital, was given a hypodermic injection, slept, and later was awakened by Drs. Tilley and Spangard and wheeled into the operating room
by a nurse whom he believed to be defendant Gisler, an employee of Dr.
Swift. Defendant Dr. Reser, the anesthetist, also an employee of Dr.
Swift, adjusted plaintiff for the operation, pulling his body to the head
of the operating table and, according to plaintiff's testimony, laying him
back against two hard objects at the top of his shoulders, about an inch
below his neck. Dr. Reser then administered the anesthetic and
plaintiff lost consciousness. When he awoke early the following morning he was in his hospital room attended by defendant Thompson, the
special nurse, and another nurse who was not made a defendant.

Plaintiff testified that prior to the operation he had never had any
pain in, or injury to, his right arm or shoulder, but that when he
awakened he felt a sharp pain about half way between the neck and the
point of the right shoulder. He complained to the nurse, and then to
Dr. Tilley, who gave him diathermy treatments while he remained in
the hospital. The pain did not cease but spread down to the lower part
of his arm, and after his release from the hospital the condition grew
worse. He was unable to rotate or lift his arm, and developed paralysis
and atrophy of the muscles around the shoulder. He received further
treatments from Dr. Tilley until March, 1940, and then returned to
work, wearing his arm in a splint on the advice of Dr. Spangard.
* * *

Plaintiff's theory is that the foregoing evidence presents a proper
case for the application of the doctrine of res ipsa loquitur, and that the
inference of negligence arising therefrom makes the granting of a
nonsuit improper. Defendants take the position that, assuming that
plaintiff's condition was in fact the result of an injury, there is no
showing that the act of any particular defendant, nor any particular
instrumentality, was the cause thereof. They attack plaintiff's action
as an attempt to fix liability "en masse" on various defendants, some of

whom were not responsible for the acts of others; and they further point to the failure to show which defendants had control of the instrumentalities that may have been involved. Their main defense may be briefly stated in two propositions: (1) that where there are several defendants, and there is a division of responsibility in the use of an instrumentality causing the injury, and the injury might have resulted from the separate act of either one of two or more persons, the rule of res ipsa loquitur cannot be invoked against any one of them; and (2) that where there are several instrumentalities, and no showing is made as to which caused the injury or as to the particular defendant in control of it, the doctrine cannot apply. We are satisfied, however, that these objections are not well taken in the circumstances of this case. * * *

The present case is of a type which comes within the reason and spirit of the doctrine more fully perhaps than any other. The passenger sitting awake in a railroad car at the time of a collision, the pedestrian walking along the street and struck by a falling object or the debris of an explosion, are surely not more entitled to an explanation than the unconscious patient on the operating table. Viewed from this aspect, it is difficult to see how the doctrine can, with any justification, be so restricted in its statement as to become inapplicable to a patient who submits himself to the care and custody of doctors and nurses, is rendered unconscious, and receives some injury from instrumentalities used in his treatment. Without the aid of the doctrine a patient who received permanent injuries of a serious character, obviously the result of someone's negligence, would be entirely unable to recover unless the doctors and nurses in attendance voluntarily chose to disclose the identity of the negligent person and the facts establishing liability. [Cc] If this were the state of the law of negligence, the courts, to avoid gross injustice, would be forced to invoke the principles of absolute liability, irrespective of negligence, in actions by persons suffering injuries during the course of treatment under anesthesia. But we think this juncture has not yet been reached, and that the doctrine of res ipsa loquitur is properly applicable to the case before us.

The condition that the injury must not have been due to the plaintiff's voluntary action is of course fully satisfied under the evidence produced herein; and the same is true of the condition that the accident must be one which ordinarily does not occur unless some one was negligent. We have here no problem of negligence in treatment, but of distinct injury to a healthy part of the body not the subject of treatment, nor within the area covered by the operation. The decisions in this state make it clear that such circumstances raise the inference of negligence and call upon the defendant to explain the unusual result.

The argument of defendants is simply that plaintiff has not shown an injury caused by an instrumentality under a defendant's control, because he has not shown which of the several instrumentalities that he came in contact with while in the hospital caused the injury; and he has not shown that any one defendant or his servants had exclusive control over any particular instrumentality. Defendants assert that some of them were not the employees of other defendants, that some did not stand in any permanent relationship from which liability in tort would follow, and that in view of the nature of the injury, the number of defendants and the different functions performed by each, they could not all be liable for the wrong, if any.

We have no doubt that in a modern hospital a patient is quite likely to come under the care of a number of persons in different types of contractual and other relationships with each other. For example, in the present case it appears that Drs. Smith, Spangard and Tilley were physicians or surgeons commonly placed in the legal category of independent contractors; and Dr. Reser, the anesthetist, and defendant Thompson, the special nurse, were employees of Dr. Swift and not of the other doctors. But we do not believe that either the number nor relationship of the defendants alone determines whether the doctrine of res ipsa loquitur applies. Every defendant in whose custody the plaintiff was placed for any period was bound to exercise ordinary care to see that no unnecessary harm came to him and each would be liable for failure in this regard. Any defendant who negligently injured him, and any defendant charged with his care who so neglected him as to allow injury to occur, would be liable. The defendant employers would be liable for the neglect of their employees; and the doctor in charge of the operation would be liable for the negligence of those who became his temporary servants for the purpose of assisting in the operation.

* * *

It may appear at the trial, that, consistent with the principles outlined above, one or more defendants will be found liable and others absolved, but this should not preclude the application of the rule of res ipsa loquitur. The control at one time or another, of one or more of the various agencies or instrumentalities which might have harmed the plaintiff was in the hands of every defendant or of his employees or temporary servants. This, we think, places upon them the burden of initial explanation. Plaintiff was rendered unconscious for the purpose of undergoing surgical treatment by the defendants; it is manifestly unreasonable for them to insist that he identify any one of them as the person who did the alleged negligent act. * * *

[I]f we accept the contention of defendants herein, there will rarely be any compensation for patients injured while unconscious. A hospital today conducts a highly integrated system of activities, with many persons contributing their efforts. There may be, e.g., preparation for surgery by nurses and interns who are employees of the hospital; administering of an anesthetic by a doctor who may be an employee of the hospital, an employee of the operating surgeon, or an independent contractor; performance of an operation by a surgeon and assistants who may be his employees, employees of the hospital, or independent contractors; and post surgical care by the surgeon, a hospital physician, and nurses. The number of those in whose care the patient is placed is not a good reason for denying him all reasonable opportunity to recover for negligent harm. It is rather a good reason for re-examination of the statement of legal theories which supposedly compel such a shocking result.

We do not at this time undertake to state the extent to which the reasoning of this case may be applied to other situations in which the doctrine of res ipsa loquitur is invoked. We merely hold that where a plaintiff receives unusual injuries while unconscious and in the course of medical treatment, all those defendants who had any control over his body or the instrumentalities which might have caused the injuries may properly be called upon to meet the inference of negligence by giving an explanation of their conduct.

The judgment is reversed.

[On the second trial, each of the defendants except the owner of the hospital gave evidence, and each testified that while he was present he saw nothing occur that could have produced the injury to plaintiff's arm and shoulder. The trial court, without a jury, found that this did not overcome the inference of negligence, and found against all of them. This was affirmed, on the basis of the above opinion, in Ybarra v. Spangard, 93 Cal.App.2d 43, 208 P.2d 445 (1949).]

---

1. This decision was approved and followed, upon similar facts, in Oldis v. La Societe Francaise de Bienfaisance Mutuelle, 130 Cal.App.2d 461, 279 P.2d 184 (1955); Frost v. Des Moines Still College of Osteopathy, 248 Iowa 294, 79 N.W.2d 306 (1956); and Beaudoin v. Watertown Memorial Hosp., 32 Wis.2d 132, 145 N.W.2d 166 (1966). On the other hand it was rejected in Rhodes v. De Haan, 184 Kan. 473, 337 P.2d 1043 (1959); and Talbot v. Dr. W.H. Groves' Latter–Day Saints Hosp., Inc., 21 Utah 2d 73, 440 P.2d 872 (1968). The case is criticized in Seavey, Res Ipsa Loquitur: Tabula in Naufragio, 63 Harv.L.Rev. 643 (1950). A good article is Thode, The Unconscious Patient; Who Should Bear the Risk of Unexplained Injuries to a Healthy Part of His Body?, 1969 Utah L.Rev. 1. Compare a situation where plaintiff brought a claim against one physician but did not eliminate another physician who participated in the operation as a cause of her harm. Jones v. Harrisburg Polyclinic Hosp., 437 A.2d 1134 (Pa.1981).

2. How far is the decision to be explained on the basis of the special responsibility undertaken by the defendants toward the plaintiff? By the refusal of the medical profession to testify? In Gobin v. Avenue Food Mart, 178 Cal.App.2d 345, 2 Cal.Rptr. 822 (1960), the court explained the *Ybarra* case as based upon the special obligation of the medical people to their patient, and refused to extend it by applying res ipsa loquitur against the manufacturer, wholesaler and retailer of a defective dart gun that injured the purchaser.

3. Does the principal case mean that plaintiff can always make out a res ipsa loquitur case against two or more defendants by showing that his injury must necessarily have been caused by the negligence of one of them? Suppose the injury could have occurred on one of several occasions. See Loizzo v. St. Francis Hosp., 121 Ill.App.3d 172, 76 Ill.Dec. 677, 459 N.E.2d 314 (1984). What if plaintiff proves that his goods were in the hands of either A or B as bailee, and have been damaged in a negligent manner? Turner v. North American Van Lines, 287 S.W.2d 384 (Mo.App.1956).

4. Courts have applied res ipsa loquitur against multiple defendants in a few special situations. In Loch v. Confair, 372 Pa. 212, 93 A.2d 451 (1953), and Nichols v. Nold, 174 Kan. 613, 258 P.2d 317 (1953), it was applied against the bottler and the retailer of bottled beverages which exploded. Both states impose strict liability, in the form of a "warranty" to the consumer, upon sellers of food products.

In Gilbert v. Korvette, Inc., 457 Pa. 602, 327 A.2d 94 (1974), plaintiff was injured by an escalator in a Korvette's store. The court found that the rule of res ipsa loquitur supported the conclusion that both the store operator and escalator operator were responsible causes of the injury and that each may be subjected to liability.

In Dement v. Olin–Mathieson Chem. Corp., 282 F.2d 76 (5th Cir.1960), defendant A manufactured dynamite and sold it to defendant B, which resold it together with a cap of its own manufacture. The dynamite and cap exploded prematurely, and injured a workman. The court applied res ipsa loquitur against both A and B, stressing the fact that each had cooperated to contribute to the final unified product.

5. In several states all this may be affected by statutes that permit the plaintiff to join defendants in one action and plead that they are liable in the alternative. It has been held that in order to carry out the purpose of these statutes, they must be interpreted to mean that the plaintiff, by showing that one or the other is liable, can get by a motion for nonsuit or dismissal and can get to the jury if defendants offer no evidence. Hummerstone v. Leary, [1921] 2 K.B. 664; S. & C. Clothing Co. v. United States Trucking Corp., 216 App.Div. 482, 215 N.Y.S. 349 (1926); Thermoid Rubber Co. v. Baird Rubber & Trading Co., 124 Misc. 774, 249 N.Y.S. 277 (1925). But if, at the close of the whole case, there is not sufficient evidence against any defendant, a verdict must still be directed against the plaintiff. Julius Klugman's Sons v. Oceanic Steam Nav. Co., 42 F.2d 461 (S.D.N.Y.1930).

6. Nine Wauwatosa High School Band mothers individually cooked turkeys from which turkey salad was made. Plaintiff ate the turkey salad and suffered food poisoning. Should res ipsa loquitur be invoked against all of them? Does the situation differ from the principal case? See Samson v. Riesing, 62 Wis.2d 698, 215 N.W.2d 662 (1974).

7. The case of Anderson v. Somberg, 67 N.J. 291, 338 A.2d 1 (1975), presents a different type of solution. While plaintiff was undergoing an operation to remove an intravertebral disc, the tip of a rongeur (a surgical instrument) broke off and fell into the spinal column where it could not be located. He brought action for the resulting injury, joining the surgeon, the hospital (which kept the instruments), the supplier and the manufacturer of the rongeur. The court held that the jury should be instructed that one of the defendants must be found liable and that it should decide which defendant was responsible. On the retrial the jury found against the manufacturer (and the supplier); and the decision was affirmed in 158 N.J.Super. 384, 386 A.2d 413 (1978), cert. denied, 423 U.S. 923 (1978). Are there any constitutional problems involved?

8. Can res ipsa loquitur be applied against two defendants, neither of whom was in exclusive control, if both were under a duty of reasonable care to prevent the occurrence? For example, a sign falls into the street from the front of a building; both the landlord and his tenant were under a duty to inspect it for defects. Smith v. Claude Neon Lights, 110 N.J.L. 326, 164 A. 423 (1933).

Cf. Bond v. Otis Elevator, 388 S.W.2d 681 (Tex.1965), on remand, 391 S.W.2d 519 (1965) (fall of elevator; building owner and elevator company both responsible for maintenance).

9. *Common Carriers and Collisions Between Vehicles.* There is general agreement that when plaintiff's car collides with defendant's, neither driver has a res ipsa loquitur case against the other. Why? Does not each driver have superior knowledge as to what he has done himself?

10. When the collision injures a third person, such as a bystander on the sidewalk, most of the decisions have held that he does not have a *res ipsa* case against either driver. Busch v. Los Angeles Ry. Corp., 178 Cal. 536, 174 P. 665 (1918); Union Traction Co. v. Alstadt, 195 Ind. 389, 143 N.E. 879 (1924).

11. When one of the vehicles is operated by a common carrier, and the injury is to its passenger, many courts apply res ipsa loquitur against the carrier alone. See Capital Transit Co. v. Jackson, 80 U.S.App.D.C. 162, 149 F.2d 839 (1945). But see Reardon v. Boston Elevated R. Co., 247 Mass. 124, 141 N.E. 857 (1923).

12. Why res ipsa loquitur against the carrier, but not against the other driver, when the evidence against each is the same? The reason sometimes given is that, since the carrier is held to the highest degree of care, it is more probable that the collision was due to some negligence on the part of the carrier than of the other driver. See James, Proof of the Breach in Negligence Cases, 37 Va.L.Rev. 179 (1951); and cf. Simpson v. Gray Line Co., 226 Or. 71, 358 P.2d 516 (1961), holding that a tire blowout on a bus creates a res ipsa case against the carrier. A better explanation may be simply that this is a survival of the older rule which once placed the burden of proof upon the carrier; and that its basis is the special responsibility undertaken toward the passenger.

13. There is a good discussion of the whole problem of multiple defendants in McCoid, Negligence Actions Against Multiple Defendants, 7 Stan.L.Rev. 480 (1955).

SULLIVAN v. CRABTREE

Court of Appeals of Tennessee, 1953.
36 Tenn.App. 469, 258 S.W.2d 782.

FELTS, JUDGE. Plaintiffs sued for damages for the death of their adult son, Robert Sullivan, who was killed while a guest in a motor truck which swerved off the highway and overturned down a steep embankment. Suit was brought against both the owner and the driver of the truck, but a nonsuit was taken as to the owner, and the case went to trial against the driver alone. There was a verdict and judgment in his favor, and plaintiffs appealed in error.

The truck was a large trailer-tractor truck * * *. Its driver Crabtree * * * permitted Sullivan to ride with him as a guest in the cab of the truck.

The road on which he was driving was a paved first-class Federal-state highway (U.S. 41, Tenn. 2), but coming down the mountain from Monteagle to Pelham it had a number of moderate grades and pretty sharp curves. It was midafternoon, and the weather was dry and clear. As Crabtree was approaching a curve another truck overtook and passed him, and just after it did so, Crabtree's truck suddenly swerved from his right side over to his left, ran off the left shoulder, overturned down a steep embankment, and crushed Sullivan to death.

D's evid = rebutting presumption

Defendant testified that there was some loose gravel on the road, which had perhaps been spilled there by trucks hauling gravel, and the pavement was broken a little on the right-hand side; and that when he "hit the edge of the curve on the right-hand side" he "lost control of the truck," and it turned from his right side across to the left, and ran off the shoulder of the highway. On cross-examination he further said:

"Q. Can you tell the Jury now what caused you to lose control of the truck and permit it to run off the road down the embankment? A. No. The brakes could have gave way, or the brakes could have grabbed or it could have been a particular wheel grabbed, because on a tractor, if the brakes happen to grab on it, the load is so much heavier than the tractor, it whips either way and takes control of the tractor and you have nothing to do with it.

"Q. Did that happen in this case? A. It is possible. * * *

"Q. You can't tell us just what did cause the accident or cause you to lose control of the truck? A. Probably hitting the edge of the pavement or it could have been several different things. Like one going off the mountain, if it is pulled out with the wrecker, you don't know whether a hose got connected up in there and when you turned the curve break a hose, cut it or break it loose. The brakes are cut on and off with a catch there like that, and it is easy for a hose to get loose."

Such being the undisputed facts, plaintiffs contend that defendant was guilty, as a matter of law, of negligence causing the death sued for, and that there was no evidence to support a verdict for defendant. They show a duty of care owing by defendant to the deceased under our rule that a driver must use ordinary care for the safety of his guest [c] and to make out a breach of that duty, or proximate negligence, they invoke the rule of res ipsa loquitur.

They insist that the facts of this case brought it within the rule of res ipsa loquitur requiring a finding of negligence, in the absence of an explanation disproving negligence; that since there was no such explanation, since defendant did not know why he lost control of the truck or what caused the accident, the jury were bound to find that it was caused by his negligence and could not reasonably render a verdict in his favor. * * *

The maxim res ipsa loquitur means that the facts of the occurrence evidence negligence; the circumstances unexplained justify an inference of negligence. In the principle of proof employed, a case of res ipsa loquitur does not differ from an ordinary case of circumstantial evidence. Res ipsa loquitur is not an arbitrary rule but rather "a common sense appraisal of the probative value of circumstantial evidence." Boykin v. Chase Bottling Works, 32 Tenn.App. 508, 520–523, 222 S.W.2d 889, 896.

This maxim does not generally apply to motor vehicle accidents but it may apply to such an accident where the circumstances causing it were within the driver's control and the accident was such as does not usually occur without negligence. So where a motor vehicle, without apparent cause, runs off the road and causes harm, the normal inference is that the driver was negligent, and res ipsa loquitur is usually held to apply. * * *

So we agree with learned counsel for plaintiffs that the facts of this case brought it within the maxim res ipsa loquitur. The accident was such as does not usually occur without negligence, and the cause of it was in control of the driver, or rather it resulted from his loss of control of the truck, which he could not explain. —

While we agree that these facts made a case of res ipsa loquitur, we do not agree that they, though unexplained, required an inference or finding of negligence, or that the jury could not reasonably refuse to find negligence and return a verdict for defendant, or that there was no evidence to support their verdict for him.

It is true there has been confusion in the cases as to the procedural effect of res ipsa loquitur, some cases giving it one and some another of these three different effects:

(1) It warrants an inference of negligence which the jury may draw or not, as their judgment dictates. [Cc]

(2) It raises a presumption of negligence which requires the jury to find negligence if defendant does not produce evidence sufficient to rebut the presumption. [Cc]

(3) It not only raises such a presumption but also *shifts the ultimate burden of proof* to defendant and requires him to prove by a preponderance of all the evidence that the injury was not caused by his negligence. [Cc]

The effect of a case of res ipsa loquitur, like that of any other case of circumstantial evidence varies from case to case, depending on the particular facts of each case; and therefore such effect can no more be fitted into a fixed formula or reduced to a rigid rule than can the effect of other cases of circumstantial evidence. The only generalization that can be safely made is that, in the words of the definition of res ipsa loquitur, it affords "reasonable evidence," in the absence of an explanation by defendant, that the accident arose from this negligence.

The weight or strength of such "reasonable evidence" will necessarily depend on the particular facts of each case, and the cogency of the inference of negligence from such facts may of course vary in degree all the way from practical certainty in one case to reasonable probability in another.

In exceptional cases the inference may be so strong as to require a directed verdict for plaintiff, as in cases of objects falling from defendant's premises on persons in the highway, such as Byrne v. Boadle (1863), 2 H. & C. 720, 159 Eng.Reprint 299 (a barrel of flour fell from a window of defendant's warehouse); McHarge v. M.M. Newcomer & Co., 117 Tenn. 595, 100 S.W. 700, 9 L.R.A., N.S., 298 (an awning roller fell from defendant's building); and Turnpike Co. v. Yates, supra (a toll gate or pole fell on a traveler); cf. Annotation, 153 A.L.R. 1134.

In the ordinary case, however, res ipsa loquitur merely makes a case for the jury—merely permits the jury to choose the inference of defendant's negligence in preference to other permissible or reasonable inferences. [Cc]

We think this is true in the case before us. The cause of the death sued for was defendant's loss of control of the truck. This may have been due to his own negligence, or it may have been due to no fault of his—an unavoidable accident resulting from the brakes giving way or the breaking of some part of the control mechanism of the truck. Since such conflicting inferences might be reasonably drawn from the evidence, it was for the jury to choose the inference they thought most probable; and we cannot say that there was no evidence to support their verdict for defendant. * * *

All the assignments of error are overruled and the judgment of the Circuit Court is affirmed.

1. Most cases are in accord with the principal case as to the procedural effect of res ipsa loquitur: it warrants the inference of negligence that the jury may draw or not, as its judgment dictates. See George Foltis, Inc. v. New York, 287 N.Y. 108, 38 N.E.2d 455 (1941).

Most of the courts have recognized, however, that there may be exceptional cases where the inference of negligence will be so compelling that the jury cannot be permitted to reject it, and a verdict must be directed for the plaintiff in the absence of evidence to explain it away. One such case is the head-on collision of two trains on the same track in Moore v. Atchison, T. & S.F.R. Co., 28 Ill.App.2d 340, 171 N.E.2d 393 (1961). "The time will probably never come when a collision resulting from an attempt to have two trains going at full speed, in opposite directions, pass each other, on the same track, will not be held to be negligence in law." Rouse v. Hornsby, 67 F. 219, 221 (8th Cir.1895).

2. Some of these courts have given res ipsa loquitur a greater procedural effect when the action is brought by an injured passenger against his carrier. See, for example, Greyhound Corp. v. Brown, 269 Ala. 520, 113 So.2d 916 (1959), and Transcontinental Bus System v. Simons, 367 P.2d 160 (Okl.1961), shifting the burden of proof to the defendant. This is obviously a carry-over from the original rule that, because of the special responsibility undertaken by the carrier, it had the burden of proof.

3. The "presumption" position is taken by about half a dozen courts, as in Schechter v. Hann, 305 Ky. 794, 205 S.W.2d 690 (1947). The number was formerly much larger, but it has been cut down by overruling decisions in several states.

4. The burden of proof is shifted to the defendant in a few states. Cf. Weiss v. Axler, 137 Colo. 544, 328 P.2d 88 (1958). Some other states shift the burden of proof in passenger cases only.

5. California adopted a unique rule in Burr v. Sherwin Williams Co., 42 Cal.2d 682, 268 P.2d 1041 (1954). Recognizing that the procedural effect of res ipsa loquitur will vary with the strength of the inference, whether defendant is a carrier and the like, the court declared that for the convenience of judges a uniform instruction to the jury was desirable, and therefore ruled that in every res ipsa case the jurors are to be instructed that the inference arises, and they must draw it. But in Exploration Drilling Co. v. Heavy Transp., Inc., 220 Cal. App.2d 397, 33 Cal.Rptr. 747 (1963), this was limited to cases in which all of the elements of res ipsa loquitur are established beyond dispute.

6. See Heckel and Harper, Effect of the Doctrine of Res Ipsa Loquitur, 22 Ill.L.Rev. 724 (1928); Prosser, The Procedural Effect of Res Ipsa Loquitur, 20 Minn.L.Rev. 241 (1936); Carpenter, The Doctrine of Res Ipsa Loquitur in California, 10 So.Calif.L.Rev. 166 (1937); Rosenthal, The Procedural Effect of Res Ipsa Loquitur in New York, 22 Cornell L.Q. 39 (1936); Prosser, Res Ipsa Loquitur in California, 37 Calif.L.Rev. 183 (1949), reprinted in Prosser, Selected Topics on the Law of Torts, 302 (1954); Shain, Res Ipsa Loquitur (1945).

GOLDSTEIN v. LEVY

Supreme Court of New York, Appellate Term, 1911.
74 Misc. 463, 132 N.Y.S. 373.

Action by Dora Goldstein against Etta Levy. From an order setting aside a verdict for plaintiff, plaintiff appeals.

SEABURY, J. This action was brought to recover damages for personal injuries alleged to have been caused by the defendant's negligence. The plaintiff purchased a ticket and went into a music hall owned and controlled by the defendant. Above the place where plaintiff was seated there was suspended from the dome of the hall a chandelier containing about 21 electric lights, used for lighting the hall in order that the patrons might witness the performance. A shade surrounding one of these lights broke, and a piece of it fell upon the plaintiff, causing the injuries complained of. The accident occurred on a Thursday, and the defendant proved that on the previous Monday she had the chandelier and shades examined by the electrician employed for that purpose; also that the chandelier and shade had been in like manner inspected every week prior to the accident, and for the period of six years prior to the accident no similar accident occurred, and the globes had never been discovered to be defective or in a dangerous condition. The defendant, however, offered no evidence to explain the cause of the accident.

In our opinion the facts above recited called for the application of the rule res ipsa loquitur, and the burden was upon the defendant to explain the accident in such a manner as to overcome the presumption of negligence raised by the plaintiff's proof. This the defendant did not do. Evidence tending to show that inspections were carefully and regularly made is insufficient to establish that the accident itself was not caused by the defendant's negligence. The circumstances and character of the occurrence were such as to call for the application of the doctrine of res ipsa loquitur. The accident was unusual. The plaintiff could not be expected to define its exact cause. If the inspections which the defendant claimed were made had been carefully made, it is not inconceivable that the defect which caused the shade to fall might have been discovered. If one may be held liable for the fall of a wall upon a pedestrian * * * or an innkeeper for the fall of plaster from a ceiling upon a guest * * *, we can see no good reason why the same principle which was applied in those cases should not be held applicable here.

The facts proved by the plaintiff established a prima facie case, which was put in issue by the proof of care which the defendant claims she exercised. The issue was properly submitted to the jury for their determination, and in our opinion the verdict of the jury in favor of the plaintiff cannot properly be held to be contrary to the evidence or the law. In our judgment, the learned trial court erred in setting aside the verdict.

Order reversed, with costs, and verdict reinstated, with costs to the appellant.

———

1. Defendant's bus suddenly went into the ditch, and injured a passenger. Defendant's driver testifies that the bus was properly inspected and maintained and that he drove with all proper care, and that he does not understand how the bus got into the ditch. Can a verdict be directed for defendant? Francisco v. Circle Tours Sightseeing Co., 125 Or. 80, 265 P. 801 (1928). Cf. Cox v. Northwest Airlines, Inc., supra page [241].

2. A dead mouse is found baked inside a loaf of bread from defendant's bakery, and plaintiff is injured by eating the bread. Defendant introduces evidence of many witnesses who testify that all possible care was used in the bakery and that such precautions were taken that it was impossible for mice to get into the product. A directed verdict? Cf. Doyle v. Continental Baking Co., 262 Mass. 516, 160 N.E. 325 (1928); Gustafson v. Gate City Co-op. Creamery, 80 S.D. 430, 126 N.W.2d 121 (1964) (glass in butter).

3. Suppose defendant produces substantial evidence of a nonnegligent explanation as to how and why the accident happened? For example, in the principal case, what if defendant showed that a 10–year–old boy had shot the chandelier with a BB gun through an open window? Should this rebut res ipsa loquitur and entitle defendant to a directed verdict? See Siegler v. Kuhlman, 3 Wash.App. 231, 473 P.2d 445, 450 (1970), rev'd, 81 Wash.2d 448, 502 P.2d 1181 (1972) (accident caused by mechanical failure that defendants could not have guarded against by exercise of reasonable care).

4. Think of all of the ways negligence law has changed over the past 50 years to make it easier for an injured person to bring a claim against an ordinary lay person and a professional. Has the law made it "too easy," as some so-called "tort reformers" have alleged? Or has the law rid itself of unfair barriers that blocked the rights of injured parties? Or do we have a situation in which each change is fair on its individual merits, but taken together with other changes has created unfairness for defendants?

Chapter V

CAUSATION IN FACT

---

1. SINE QUA NON

PERKINS v. TEXAS AND NEW ORLEANS RY. CO.

Supreme Court of Louisiana, 1962.
243 La. 829, 147 So.2d 646.

SANDERS, JUSTICE. This is a tort action. Plaintiff, the 67–year-old widow of Tanner Perkins, seeks damages for the death of her husband in the collision of an automobile, in which he was riding, with a train of the defendant railroad. The district court awarded damages. The Court of Appeal affirmed. We granted certiorari to review the judgment of the Court of Appeal.

The tragic accident which gave rise to this litigation occurred at the intersection of Eddy Street and The Texas and New Orleans Railroad Company track in the town of Vinton, Louisiana, at approximately 6:02 a.m., after daylight, on September 28, 1959. At this crossing Eddy Street runs north and south, and the railroad track, east and west. Involved was a 113–car freight train pulled by four diesel engines traveling east and a Dodge automobile driven by Joe Foreman in a southerly direction on Eddy Street. Tanner Perkins, a guest passenger, was riding in the front seat of the automobile with the driver.

Located in the northwest quadrant of the intersection of the railroad track and Eddy Street was a warehouse five hundred feet long. A "house track" paralleled the main track on the north to serve the warehouse. This warehouse obstructed the view to the west of an automobile driver approaching the railroad crossing from the north on Eddy Street. It likewise obstructed the view to the north of trainmen approaching the crossing from the west. Having previously served on this route, the engineer and brakeman were aware of this obstruction.

To warn the public of the approach of trains, the defendant railroad had installed at the crossing an automatic signal device consisting of a swinging red light and a bell. At the time of the accident, this signal was operating. A standard Louisiana railroad stop sign and an intersection stop sign were also located at the crossing.

Proceeding east, the train approached the intersection with its headlight burning, its bell ringing, and its whistle blowing.

The engineer, brakeman, and fireman were stationed in the forward engine of the train. The engineer was seated on the right or

265

south side, where he was unable to observe an automobile approaching from the left of the engine. The brakeman and fireman, who were seated on the left or north side of the engine, were looking forward as the train approached the intersection. These two crewmen saw the automobile emerge from behind the warehouse. At that time the front wheels of the automobile were on or across the north rail of the house track. The fireman estimated that the train was approximately 60 feet from the crossing when the automobile emerged from behind the warehouse. The brakeman, however, estimated that the train was 30 to 40 feet from the crossing at the time the automobile came into view. Both crewmen immediately shouted a warning to the engineer, who applied the emergency brakes. The train struck the right side of the automobile and carried it approximately 1250 feet. The two occupants were inside the automobile when it came to rest. Both were killed.

The speed of the automobile in which Tanner Perkins was riding was variously estimated from 3-4 miles per hour to 20-25 miles per hour.

The plaintiff and defendant railroad concede in their pleadings that Joe Foreman, the driver of the automobile, was negligent in driving upon the track in front of the train and that his negligence was a proximate cause of the death of Tanner Perkins.

It is conceded that the railroad's safety regulations imposed a speed limit of 25 miles per hour on trains in the town of Vinton. The plaintiff has conceded in this Court that this self-imposed speed limit was a safe speed at the crossing. The train was in fact traveling at a speed of 37 miles per hour.

Applicable here is the rule that the violation by trainmen of the railroad's own speed regulations adopted in the interest of safety is evidence of negligence. * * *

We find, as did the Court of Appeal, that the trainmen were negligent in operating the train 12 miles per hour in excess of the speed limit.

* * * [T]he prime issue in this case is whether the excessive speed of the train was a cause in fact of the fatal collision.

It is fundamental that negligence is not actionable unless it is a cause in fact of the harm for which recovery is sought. It need not, of course, be the sole cause. Negligence is a cause in fact of the harm to another if it was a substantial factor in bringing about that harm. Under the circumstances of the instant case, the excessive speed was undoubtedly a substantial factor in bringing about the collision if the collision would not have occurred without it. On the other hand, if the collision would have occurred irrespective of such negligence, then it was not a substantial factor. [Cc]

In the instant case the train engineer testified that at a speed of 25 miles per hour he would have been unable to stop the train in time to avoid the accident. Other facts of record support his testimony in this regard. With efficient brakes, the mile-long train required 1250 feet to stop at a speed of 37 miles per hour. It is clear, then, that even at the concededly safe speed of 25 miles per hour, the momentum of the train would have, under the circumstances, carried it well beyond the crossing. This finding, of course, does not fully determine whether the collision would have been averted at the slower speed. The automobile was also in motion during the crucial period. This necessitates the further inquiry of whether the automobile would have cleared the track and evaded the impact had the train been moving at a proper speed at the time the trainmen observed the automobile emerge from behind the warehouse. Basic to this inquiry are the speed of the automobile and the driving distance between it and a position of safety. [C]

The testimony of the witnesses is in hopeless conflict as to the speed of the automobile at the time of the collision.

* * * Despite these deficiencies in the evidence, the plaintiff argues that had the train been traveling at a proper speed the driver of the automobile would "conceivably" have had some additional time to take measures to avert disaster and the deceased would have had some additional time to extricate himself from danger. Hence, the plaintiff reasons, the collision and loss of life "might not" have occurred.

On the facts of this case, we must reject the escape theory advanced in this argument. Because of the deficiencies in the evidence which we have already noted, it is devoid of evidentiary support. The record contains no probative facts from which the Court can draw a reasonable inference of causation under this theory. In essence, the argument is pure conjecture.

Based upon the evidence of record, it appears almost certain that the fatal accident would have occurred irrespective of the excessive speed of the train. It follows that this speed was not a substantial factor in bringing about the accident.

We conclude that the plaintiff has failed to discharge the burden of proving that the negligence of the defendant was a cause in fact of the tragic death. The judgment in favor of plaintiff is manifestly erroneous.

For the reasons assigned, the judgment of the Court of Appeal is reversed, and the plaintiff's suit is dismissed at her cost.

---

1. In the principal case, if the collision was a cause of the plaintiffs' deaths, why should the defendant have avoided liability?

2. Defendant truck driver negligently failed to signal for a left turn. Plaintiff crashed into the truck. Can defendant win the case by establishing that plaintiff was not looking and would not have seen the signal if it had been given? Rouleau v. Blotner, 84 N.H. 539, 152 A. 916 (1931) ("if he were a deaf man, the failure to sound whistle, bell or horn would be immaterial"); cf. Gustad v. Allen, 520 P.2d 594 (Colo.App.1974).

3. Defendant excavates a hole in the sidewalk, and leaves it unguarded and unlighted. Plaintiff, a traveler on the sidewalk, accidentally falls into it in the dark. Is defendant's negligence a cause of his injury? What if a third person negligently bumps into plaintiff, and knocks him into the hole? Village of Carterville v. Cook, 129 Ill. 152, 22 N.E. 14 (1889). Suppose the third person intentionally shoves him into it? Milostan v. Chicago, 148 Ill.App. 540 (1904).

4. The mate of defendant's steam trawler falls overboard, and disappears immediately. Defendant's lifeboat is lashed to the deck instead of being suspended from davits, and is equipped with only one oar. Is this negligence a cause of his death? Ford v. Trident Fisheries Co., 232 Mass. 400, 122 N.E. 389 (1919).

5. Defendant, cutting ice on a lake, was negligent in failing to fence the opening as required by statute, in failing to give warning of its location, and in not having ropes or other appliances at hand to rescue anyone who fell in. Plaintiff's horses ran away, plunged into the opening, and were drowned. The evidence was that the horses were uncontrollable and could not have been stopped or directed, and that they went under the ice and could not have been rescued. Is defendant's negligence a cause of their loss? Stacy v. Knickerbocker Ice Co., 84 Wis. 614, 54 N.W. 1091 (1893). See also Haft v. Lone Palm Hotel, 3 Cal.3d 756, 478 P.2d 465, 91 Cal.Rptr. 745 (1970), where a motel operator failed to fulfill a statutory obligation to provide either a lifeguard for a motel pool or post a suitable warning that no lifeguard was present. A father and son, last seen playing in the pool, were found at the bottom. Was the motel operator's negligence a cause of the death? Would the presence of a lifeguard have prevented the drowning? See Rovegno v. San Jose Knights of Columbus Hall Ass'n, 108 Cal.App. 591, 291 P. 848 (1930).

6. In Technical Chemical Co. v. Jacobs, 480 S.W.2d 602 (Tex.1972), defendant failed to put a warning on a can of refrigerant. Plaintiff started using it without reading the instructions. Was defendant's failure to warn a cause of plaintiff's injury?

7. Defendant railroad violated a statute in failing to display a warning sign at a railroad crossing. Plaintiff, who was injured at the crossing, knew from prior experience of the danger. Was defendant's negligence a cause in fact of plaintiff's injuries? See Thomas v. Baltimore & Ohio R. Co., 19 Md.App. 217, 310 A.2d 186 (1973).

8. Can this be reduced to a rule? For an attempt, see Strachan, Scope and Application of the "But For" Causal Test, 33 Mod.L.Rev. 386 (1970). Two excellent articles on causation in fact are Malone, Ruminations on Cause–In–Fact, 9 Stan.L.Rev. 60 (1958); and Zwier, "Cause in Fact" in Tort Law—A Philosophical and Historical Examination, 31 DePaul L.Rev. 769 (1982). Two elaborate books are Becht and Miller, The Test of Causation in Fact (1961); and Hart and Honoré, Causation (1960). The latter deals with both the philosophical and legal aspects of both cause in fact and "proximate cause."

2. PROOF OF CAUSATION

REYNOLDS v. TEXAS & PAC. RY. CO.
Court of Appeals of Louisiana, 1885.
37 La.Ann. 694.

[Plaintiff and his wife sought damages against defendant company for injuries she suffered when she fell down a stairway.]

FENNER, J. * * * The train was behind time. Several witnesses testify that passengers were warned to "hurry up." Mrs. Reynolds, a corpulent woman, weighing two hundred and fifty pounds, emerging from the bright light of the sitting-room, which naturally exaggerated the outside darkness, and hastening down these unlighted steps, made a misstep in some way and was precipitated beyond the narrow platform in front and down the slope beyond, incurring the serious injuries complained of. [The trial court, without a jury, gave judgment to the plaintiffs for $2,000 damages. Defendant appealed.]

[Defendant] contends that, even conceding the negligence of the company in [failing to light the stairway or provide a handrail], it does not follow that the accident to plaintiff was necessarily caused thereby, but that she might well have made the misstep and fallen even had it been broad daylight. We concede that this is possible, and recognize the distinction between post hoc and propter hoc. But where the negligence of the defendant greatly multiplies the chances of accident to the plaintiff, and is of a character naturally leading to its occurrence, the mere possibility that it might have happened without the negligence is not sufficient to break the chain of cause and effect between the negligence and the injury. Courts, in such matters, consider the natural and ordinary course of events, and do not indulge in fanciful suppositions. The whole tendency of the evidence connects the accident with the negligence. * * *

Judgment affirmed.

1. Suppose the stairway had been well lighted and had only lacked a handrail? Should it make any difference that defendant violated an ordinance? See Blue Grass Restaurant Co. v. Franklin, 424 S.W.2d 594 (Ky.1968).

2. If a life preserver had been thrown to a drowning man, would he have caught it and been saved? Kirincich v. Standard Dredging Co., 112 F.2d 163 (3d Cir.1940). Would an adequate number of campus police have prevented trespassing boys from shooting a student in the eye with an air rifle? Stockwell v. Board of Trustees of Stanford University, 64 Cal.App.2d 197, 148 P.2d 405 (1944). How are these questions to be decided?

KRAMER SERVICE, INC. v. WILKINS

Supreme Court of Mississippi, 1939.
184 Miss. 483, 186 So. 625.

[The plaintiff, a guest in the defendant's hotel, received a cut on his forehead from a piece of glass that fell from a broken transom when the plaintiff opened the door. There was evidence that the condition of disrepair had existed long enough to charge defendant with notice of it. The wound did not heal, and two years after the injury plaintiff went to a specialist in skin diseases, who found that at the point of the injury a skin cancer had developed, which was not fully cured at the time of the trial, some three years after the original injury. The defendant appeals a jury verdict for the plaintiff.]

GRIFFITH, JUSTICE. * * * Appellant requested an instruction to the effect that the cancer or any prolongation of the trouble on account thereof should not be taken into consideration by the jury, but this instruction was refused.

Two physicians or medical experts, and only two, were introduced as witnesses, and both were specialists in skin diseases and dermal traumatisms. One testified that it was possible that a trauma such as appellee suffered upon his temple, could or would cause a skin cancer at the point of injury, but that the chances that such a result would ensue from such a cause would be only one out of one hundred cases. The other testified that there is no causal connection whatever between trauma and cancer, and went on to illustrate that if there were such a connection nearly every person of mature age would be suffering from cancer. * * *

There is one heresy in the judicial forum which appears to be Hydraheaded, and although cut off again and again, has the characteristic of an endless renewal. That heresy is that proof that a past event possibly happened, or that a certain result was possibly caused by a past event, is sufficient, in probative force to take the question to a jury. Such was never the law in this state, and we are in accord with almost all of the other common-law states. * * * It is not enough that negligence of one person and injury to another coexisted, but the injury must have been caused by the negligence. Post hoc ergo propter hoc is not sound as evidence or argument. Nor is it sufficient for a plaintiff, seeking recovery for alleged negligence by another toward the plaintiff, to show a possibility that the injury complained of was caused by negligence. Possibilities will not sustain a verdict. It must have a better foundation. * * *

Taking the medical testimony in this case in the strongest light in which it could be reasonably interpreted in behalf of the plaintiff, this testimony is that as a possibility a skin cancer could be caused by an injury such as here happened, but as a probability the physicians were in agreement that there was or is no such a probability.

And the medical testimony is conclusive on both judge and jury in this case. That testimony is undisputed that after long and anxious years of research the exact cause of cancer remains unknown—there is no dependably known origin to which it can be definitely traced or ascribed. If, then, the cause be unknown to all those who have devoted their lives to a study of the subject, it is wholly beyond the range of the common experience and observation of judges and jurors, and in such a case medical testimony when undisputed, as here, must be accepted and acted upon, in the same manner as is other undisputed evidence; otherwise the jury would be allowed to resort to and act upon nothing else than the proposition post hoc ergo propter hoc, which, as already mentioned, this Court has long ago rejected as unsound, whether as evidence or as argument.

In all other than the exceptional cases now to be mentioned, the testimony of medical experts, or other experts, is advisory only; but we repeat that where the issue is one which lies wholly beyond the range of the experience or observation of laymen and of which they can have no appreciable knowledge, courts and juries must of necessity depend upon and accept the undisputed testimony of reputable specialists, else there would be no substantial foundation upon which to rest a conclusion. * * *

Affirmed as to liability; reversed and remanded on the issue of the amount of the damages [in allowing recovery for the skin cancer in addition to the original cut on the forehead].

_____

1. Why not decide this case on the basis of Reynolds v. Texas & Pacific Ry. Co.? How much is proved by the fact that, out of a good many square inches of skin on the human body, the cancer developed at the exact point of the unhealed cut? Compare Emery v. Tilo Roofing Co., 89 N.H. 165, 195 A. 409 (1937), where a fire started at a place on a roof where workmen had been smoking cigarettes, shortly after they had left it. What if plaintiff eats peanuts, and then develops cancer of the stomach? What if a woman develops breast cancer after breaking her leg in a fall precipitated by defendant's negligence? Cf. Daly v. Bergstedt, 267 Minn. 244, 126 N.W.2d 242 (1964). Or if a child becomes "actively schizophrenic" after a comparatively minor automobile accident? See Steinhauser v. Hertz Corp., 421 F.2d 1169 (2d Cir.1970).

2. What effect upon this decision if there was expert medical testimony that, more probably than not, the cut played a substantial part in producing the cancer? See Hanna v. Aetna Ins. Co., 23 Ohio Misc. 27, 52 Ohio Op.2d 316, 259 N.E.2d 177 (1970); Lee v. Blessing, 131 Conn. 569, 41 A.2d 337 (1945). What result if medical experts testify that plaintiff's smoking of cigarettes caused his lung cancer—should the jury hear the case? See Pritchard v. Liggett & Myers Tobacco Co., 295 F.2d 292, 296 (3d Cir.1961). For a discussion of some of the medical and legal aspects of these problems, see Small, Gaffing at a Thing Called Cause, 31 Tex.L.Rev. 630 (1953).

3. Should a broadcasting company be held negligently liable for airing scenes of violent acts on television, when those scenes may incite others to perform similar acts? See Olivia N. v. National Broadcasting Co., Inc., 74 Cal. App.3d 383, 141 Cal.Rptr. 511 (1977), cert. denied, 435 U.S. 1000 (1978) (nine-

year-old girl "artificially raped" with a bottle by her attackers, also minors, who had watched a similar incident depicted in a television drama). Do the First and Fourteenth Amendments preclude the media's tort liability in these types of claims? What problems in proving causation would a plaintiff encounter?

[handwritten: Duty to act is breached (omission), Thus by necessity, cause is something else.]

HERSKOVITS v. GROUP HEALTH COOPERATIVE OF PUGET SOUND

[handwritten: See Reynolds p. 269] *[handwritten: Δ does not cause harm; but has duty to prevent. = omission]*

Supreme Court of Washington, 1983.
99 Wash.2d 609, 664 P.2d 474.

[handwritten left margin: TrCt = Δ SCt = rev'd, remand reinstate CoA]

DORE, JUSTICE. This appeal [from the trial court's action in granting defendant's motion for summary judgment] raises the issue of whether an estate can maintain an action for professional negligence as a result of failure to timely diagnose lung cancer, where the estate can show probable reduction in statistical chance for survival but cannot show and/or prove that with timely diagnosis and treatment, decedent probably would have lived to normal life expectancy.

Both counsel advised that for the purpose of this appeal we are to *assume* that the respondent Group Health Cooperative of Puget Sound and Dr. William Spencer negligently failed to diagnose Herskovits' cancer on his first visit to the hospital and proximately caused a 14 percent reduction in his chances of survival. It is undisputed that Herskovits had less than a 50 percent chance of survival at all times herein.

The main issue we will address in this opinion is whether a patient, with less than a 50 percent chance of survival, has a cause of action against the hospital and its employees if they are negligent in diagnosing a lung cancer which reduces his chances of survival by 14 percent.

* * *

We are persuaded by the reasoning of the Pennsylvania Supreme Court in Hamil v. Bashline, 481 Pa. 256, 392 A.2d 1280 (1978). While *Hamil* involved an original survival chance of greater than 50 percent, we find the rationale used by the *Hamil* court to apply equally to cases such as the present one, where the original survival chance is less than 50 percent. The plaintiff's decedent was suffering from severe chest pains. His wife transported him to the hospital where he was negligently treated in the emergency unit. The wife, because of the lack of help, took her husband to a private physician's office, where he died. In an action brought under the wrongful death and survivorship statutes, the main medical witness testified that if the hospital had employed proper treatment, the decedent would have had a substantial chance of surviving the attack. The medical expert expressed his opinion in terms of a 75 percent chance of survival. It was also the doctor's opinion that the substantial loss of a chance of recovery was the result of the defendant hospital's failure to provide prompt treatment. The defendant's expert witness testified that the patient would have died regardless of any treatment provided by the defendant hospital.

[Handwritten margin notes top of page: "another 'cause' all its own." / "If duty had been performed, harm would not have resulted." / "Doesn't 'but for' in fact address the question?"]

The *Hamil* court distinguished the facts of that case from the general tort case in which a plaintiff alleges that a defendant's act or omission set in motion a force which resulted in harm. In the typical tort case, the "but for" test, requiring proof that damages or death probably would not have occurred "but for" the negligent conduct of the defendant, is appropriate. In *Hamil* and the instant case, however, the defendant's act or omission failed in a *duty* to protect against harm from *another source.* Thus, as the *Hamil* court noted, the fact finder is put in the position of having to consider not only what *did* occur, but also what *might have* occurred. *Hamil* states at p. 271: "Such cases by their very nature elude the degree of certainty one would prefer and upon which the law normally insists before a person may be held liable. Nevertheless, in order that an actor is not completely insulated because of uncertainties as to the consequences of his negligent conduct, Section 323(a) [of the Torts Restatement] tacitly acknowledges this difficulty and permits the issue to go to the jury upon a less than normal threshold of proof." (Footnote omitted.) The *Hamil* court held that once a plaintiff has demonstrated that the defendant's acts or omissions have increased the risk of harm to another, such evidence furnishes a basis for the jury to make a determination as to whether such increased risk was in turn a substantial factor in bringing about the resultant harm. * * *

Where percentage probabilities and decreased probabilities are submitted into evidence, there is simply no danger of speculation on the part of the jury. More speculation is involved in requiring the medical expert to testify as to what would have happened had the defendant not been negligent.

Both counsel have agreed for the purpose of arguing this summary judgment, that the defendants were negligent in failing to make a diagnosis of cancer on Herskovits' initial visit in December 1974, and that such negligence was the proximate cause of reducing his chances of survival by 14 percent. It is undisputed that Herskovits had less than a 50 percent chance of survival at that time. Based on this agreement and Dr. Ostrow's deposition and affidavit, a prima facie case is shown. We reject Group Health's argument that plaintiffs *must show* that Herskovits "probably" would have had a 51 percent chance of survival if the hospital had not been negligent. We hold that medical testimony of a reduction of chance of survival from 39 percent to 25 percent is sufficient evidence to allow the proximate cause issue to go to the jury.

Causing reduction of the opportunity to recover (loss of chance) by one's negligence, however, does not necessitate a total recovery against the negligent party for all damages caused by the victim's death. Damages should be awarded to the injured party or his family based only on damages caused directly by premature death, such as lost earnings and additional medical expenses, etc.

We reverse the trial court and reinstate the cause of action.

[Handwritten notes in margins: "G/R" "u = but for" "=distinction?" "Prima Facie" "R/H" "What about " " in bringing about risk?" "Are we not asking whether there is harm." "all damages" "damages = 14% of ___?" "What will ∆ argue now? No 'cause' at all?" "¿death saved medical expenses? Well, no."]

[ROSELLINI, J., concurs. The concurring opinion of PEARSON, J., differed from the majority in urging that medical testimony showing a substantial reduction in plaintiff's chance of survival should establish a prima facie issue of proximate cause. WILLIAMS, C.J., STAFFORD and UTTER, JJ., concur with PEARSON, J. BRACHTENBACHY and DIMMICK, JJ., dissent.]

------

1. For a general discussion of this area of law, see King, Causation, Valuation, and Chance in Personal Injury Torts Involving Preexisting Conditions and Future Consequences, 90 Yale L.J. 1353 (1981) (cited in concurring opinion of principal case).

2. A difficult and recurring problem in medical malpractice cases occurs when a physician has made a negligent diagnosis, yet it is questioned whether a correct diagnosis would have saved the patient. Who should have the burden of proof on this issue? What should that burden be? See Cooper v. Sisters of Charity, 27 Ohio St.2d 242, 56 Ohio Op.2d 146, 272 N.E.2d 97 (1971). Another problem occurs when a physician or hospital staff negligently delays treatment, which substantially reduces a patient's chance of survival. See Waffen v. United States Dept. of Health & Human Services, 799 F.2d 911 (4th Cir.1986).

3. Cases dealing with informed consent, supra pages 186–91 can present a special problem in the area of cause in fact. Should plaintiff patient be able to hurdle the issue if he testifies that he would not have undergone the medical procedure if defendant physician had informed him of the risk? Some courts have said that an objective test is preferable, i.e., what would a prudent person in the patient's position have decided if adequately informed of the peril? Is that sufficient proof of what this plaintiff would have done? Should not plaintiff's testimony on the issue be enough? See Cobbs v. Grant, 8 Cal.3d 229, 502 P.2d 1, 11, 104 Cal.Rptr. 505 (1972); Canterbury v. Spence, 150 U.S.App. D.C. 263, 464 F.2d 772, 791 (1972).

4. Establishing causation in fact can be a substantial burden in a suit against an attorney for professional negligence. An attorney fails to file a suit for his client before the statute of limitations runs. What must the client prove besides negligence? Suppose the attorney was negligent in failing to cite to a court relevant cases that might have avoided jail for his client. What must the client prove in an action against the attorney? See Martin v. Hall, 20 Cal.App. 3d 414, 97 Cal.Rptr. 730 (1970).

IN RE "AGENT ORANGE" PRODUCT LIABILITY LITIGATION MDL NO. 381

United States District Court, Eastern District, New York, 1984.
597 F.Supp. 740.

WEINSTEIN, C.J. In 1979 a class action was commenced charging the United States government and a major portion of the chemical industry with deaths and dreadful injuries to tens of thousands of Vietnam veterans who came in contact with herbicides used in the war in Southeast Asia. The suit also claimed that as a result of the veterans' exposure, their children suffer severe birth defects. After five years of numerous motions and extensive discovery a tentative settlement was reached on the eve of trial.

The sole question before this court is whether the case against the chemical companies should now be settled * * *

[The court approved a preliminary settlement agreement, advising both parties to accept the proposal. The court then explored the legal complexities that both parties would face in the event the plan was rejected and a full trial was necessary.]

There are serious factual problems with plaintiffs' case, the chief one being doubt that present scientific knowledge would support a finding of causality * * *

Many plaintiffs suffer from diseases that can be caused by dioxin. Dioxin caused the diseases. The logical and practical difficulty with their argument is that the diseases referred to may result from causes other than dioxin poisoning * * *

The effect of exposure to dioxin has been and is being studied at least as intensively as that of any other toxic substance * * *

As with most statistical studies of this kind, it cannot be proven conclusively that [for example] a particular child's birth defect was or was not "caused" (in a tort law sense) by the father's exposure to Agent Orange. Nonetheless, the data to date does not support any claim of birth defect sufficient to allow a jury finding in favor of a member of the class. Since plaintiffs would have the burden of proof at a trial, the "weakness" of any statistical data would tend to favor defendants' position. * * *

[T]he result of an enormous scientific effort to be helpful on causation has, from the plaintiffs' point of view, left the case at best open. This is not sufficient to support a recovery in tort law even though it may suffice to permit regulation of products that might contain dioxin or support a public policy decision to use public funds to compensate exposed Vietnam veterans or their children with medical problems. * * *

In conclusion, all that can be said is that persuasive evidence of causality has not been produced. * * *

Defendants contend that even if anyone was injured by Agent Orange, plaintiffs cannot establish that the harm to any one of them was caused by any individual defendant. * * *

The seven chemical company defendants, Dow Chemical Co., Hercules, Inc., The Monsanto Company, Diamond Shamrock Chemicals Corporation, Thompson Chemical Corporation, T.H. Agriculture & Nutrition, and Uniroyal, Inc., manufactured over 99% of a herbicide called Agent Orange used by the military in Vietnam between 1965 and 1970. * * *

In Vietnam, in preparation for spraying, the drums were drained into large tanks and their contents mixed with those of other drums, making identification of the individual manufacturer's Agent Orange impossible. Even if the Agent Orange had not been mixed, connecting an individual defendant's product with a person in contact with it would be virtually impossible because of lack of records.

Plaintiffs have several difficult legal hurdles to overcome. The first results from the conceded inability of any veteran to identify the manufacturer of the herbicide to which he was exposed. Second, all of the ailments and conditions class members allegedly suffer from, with the possible exception of chloracne, are not unique to Agent Orange or dioxin exposure and occur in the population at large. Thus, even if it is possible to establish by a preponderance of the evidence that some members of the class were injured because it is shown that those diseases occur in a higher percentage of the class members than would be statistically expected, it may be impossible to prove who those members are. * * *

Traditional tort principles would dictate that causation be determined on a case-by-case basis using the preponderance-of-the-evidence rule. [Cc] The rule provides an "'all or nothing' approach, whereby [assuming all other elements of the cause of action are proven], the plaintiff becomes entitled to full compensation for those . . . damages that are proved to be 'probable' (a greater than 50 percent chance), but is not entitled to any compensation if the proof does not establish a greater than 50 percent chance." Jackson v. Johns–Manville Sales Corp., 727 F.2d 506, 516 (5th Cir.1984).

Under the "strong" version of the preponderance rule, statistical correlations alone indicating that the probability of causation exceeds fifty percent are insufficient; some "particularistic" or anecdotal evidence, that is, "proof that can provide direct and actual knowledge of the causal relationship between the defendant's tortious conduct and the plaintiff's injury," is required. [Cc] * * *

The "weak" version of the preponderance rule would allow a verdict solely on statistical evidence; the "all-or-nothing" approach converts the statistical probability into a legally absolute finding that the causal connection did or did not exist in the case. C. McCormick, Handbook on the Law of Damages, 118 (1935). * * *

There would appear to be little harm in retaining the requirement for "particularistic" evidence of causation in sporadic accident cases since such evidence is almost always available in such litigation. In mass exposure cases, however, where the chance that there would be particularistic evidence is in most cases quite small, the consequence of retaining the requirement might be to allow defendants who, it is virtually certain, have injured thousands of people and caused billions of dollars in damages, to escape liability. Because of this fact and the fact that "particularistic evidence * * * is * * * no less probabilistic than * * * statistical evidence," the "weak" version of the preponderance rule appears to be the preferable standard to apply in mass exposure cases—particularly where, as here, all claimants and defendants are joined in one suit. * * *

There is a strong likelihood that even if some causal link could be established between Agent Orange and the diseases and conditions from which plaintiffs claim they are suffering, it would be impossible in most cases to identify the individual class members who were injured by Agent Orange. Given the desirability of resolving the indeterminate plaintiff problem using a form of proportional liability or some other acceptable method, a dismissal of the class action would be unwarranted. The statistical theory, available data, and public policy are far from settled. Particularly during this period of rapidly changing scientific approaches and increased threats to the environment, we should not unduly restrict development of legal theory and practice—both substantive and procedural—by dismissing a class action such as the one now before us although the hazards of an ultimate dismissal must be considered in assessing the fairness of the settlement.

[The settlement was tentatively approved.]

———————

1. Traditionally, strict proof of causation has not always been required; courts may turn to circumstantial evidence as contrasted with direct proof. See Beyer v. White, 22 N.J.Super. 137, 144, 91 A.2d 606, 609 (1952) (workers' compensation case) ("But plaintiff was not obliged to establish proximate cause by direct indisputable evidence. The matter may rest upon legitimate inference, so long as the proof will justify a reasonable and logical inference as distinguished from mere speculation.").

2. Generally, a plaintiff must establish causation by a preponderance of the evidence. In workers' compensation cases, the burden is sometimes eased and "reasonable probability" may be enough. See McAllister v. Workmen's Compensation Appeals Bd., 69 Cal.2d 408, 445 P.2d 313, 71 Cal.Rptr. 697 (1968) (whether fireman's continued inhalation of smoke during his career caused lung cancer). Why do courts take this approach?

3. Application of the preponderance rule to mass exposure cases may, however, result in unfairness to both plaintiffs and defendants. Why?

4. Causation standards may differ if the issue is product regulation, i.e., should a sugar substitute be banned because it may cause cancer? Contrast a tort suit: did the sugar substitute cause plaintiff's stomach cancer? Why and how is this true? Who bears the cost in each instance?

5. See Rosenberg, The Causal Connection in Mass Exposure Cases: A "Public Law" Vision of the Tort System, 97 Harv.L.Rev. 851 (1984), urging the courts to move away from traditional tort doctrine in mass exposure cases.

6. Recently, a number of lawsuits were brought against the manufacturer of a prescription drug to treat morning sickness, alleging that the drug Bendectin caused birth defects. In the 17 cases that had gone to trial at the time this casebook went to press, the drug was found not to be the cause of birth defects in 12 of the cases. The other five cases are being appealed by the manufacturer. There is strong controversy about whether specific studies support the claims that Bendectin causes birth defects, yet there are still thousands of lawsuits involving Bendectin pending around the country.

7. Legislation (the High Risk Occupational Disease Notification and Prevention Act) was pending before Congress in 1987 that would create a new bureaucracy in the Department of Health and Human Services to study and

identify "hazardous" substances in the workplace. If the Federal government determines that something in the workplace "may be associated with" an illness or disease, it would send notifications to all employees currently exposed to the substance and all employees who had been exposed for the past 30 years. Current employees who are notified would be entitled to receive medical monitoring and, upon a doctor's order, a transfer to a "less hazardous" job at the previous wage—all at the employer's expense. See High Risk Occupational Disease Notification and Prevention Act, S. 79 and H.R. 162, 100th Cong., 1st Sess. (1987). Note that the trigger for notification and these benefits is a finding that a substance "may be associated with" an illness or disease. Would this be a reasonable standard for proof of causation in tort cases? Why or why not?

3. CONCURRENT CAUSES

HILL v. EDMONDS

Supreme Court of New York, Appellate Division, 1966.
26 A.D.2d 554, 270 N.Y.S.2d 1020.

MEMORANDUM BY THE COURT. In a negligence action to recover damages for personal injury, plaintiff appeals from a judgment of the Supreme Court, Queens County, entered June 21, 1965, which dismissed the complaint as against defendant Bragoli upon the court's decision at the close of plaintiff's case upon a jury trial. * * *

At the close of plaintiff's case the court dismissed the complaint against the owner of a tractor truck who on a stormy night left it parked without lights in the middle of a road where the car in which plaintiff was a passenger collided with it from the rear. From the testimony of the driver of the car the court concluded that she was guilty of negligence and was solely responsible for the collision. That testimony was that she saw the truck when it was four car lengths ahead of her and that she saw it in enough time to turn. At other points, however, she indicated that she did not know just what happened, that she swerved to avoid the truck, "and the next thing I knew I woke up. I was unconscious." Assuming, *arguendo*, that she was negligent, the accident could not have happened had not the truck owner allowed his unlighted vehicle to stand in the middle of the highway. Where separate acts of negligence combine to produce directly a single injury each tortfeasor is responsible for the entire result, even though his act alone might not have caused it. [Cc] Accordingly, the complaint against the truck owner must be reinstated and a new trial had.

---

1. As a horse-drawn street car stopped for a railroad crossing, the railroad's employee negligently raised the crossing gates, although a train was approaching. The street car driver negligently proceeded onto the crossing without looking, whereupon the railroad lowered the gates, shutting in the street car on the railroad track. Passengers on the street car, seeing the train coming, stampeded in panic, and plaintiff, one of the passengers, was pushed off

of the car and injured. Who is liable? Washington & Georgetown R. Co. v. Hickey, 166 U.S. 521 (1897).

2. Plaintiff's horse fell into an excavation made by a traction company and left unguarded at night. It scrambled out, and promptly fell into a second and adjoining excavation, left in the street by the town authorities. After it climbed out again, and in consequence of both falls, the horse took fright and ran away. The horse was injured and the wagon was broken. The traction company and the town were acting entirely independently. Are they each liable for the entire damage? Carstesen v. Stratford, 67 Conn. 428, 35 A. 276 (1896).

ANDERSON v. MINNEAPOLIS, ST.P. & S.ST. M. R.R. CO.

Supreme Court of Minnesota, 1920.
146 Minn. 430, 179 N.W. 45.

LEES, C. This is a fire case brought against the defendant railway company. * * * Plaintiff had a verdict. The appeal is from an order denying a motion in the alternative for judgment notwithstanding the verdict or for a new trial. * * *

[A forest fire, which originated in a bog and was found by the jury to have been caused by the negligence of the defendant, swept over a large area. It merged with another fire of independent and uncertain origin, and the combined fires burned over plaintiff's property. The defendant contends that the following instruction to the jury was in error:]

"If the plaintiff was burned out by some fire other than the bog fire, which other fire was not set by one of the defendant's engines, then, of course, defendant is not liable. * * * If plaintiff was burned out by fire set by one of the defendant's engines in combination with some other fire not set by any of its engines, then it is liable.

"If you find that other fire or fires not set by one of defendant's engines mingled with one that was set by one of the defendant's engines, there may be difficulty in determining whether you should find that the fire set by the engine was a material or substantial element in causing plaintiff's damage. If it was, the defendant is liable, otherwise it is not. * * *

"If you find that the bog fire was set by the defendant's engine and that some greater fire swept over it before it reached the plaintiff's land, then it will be for you to determine whether that bog fire * * * was a material or substantial factor in causing plaintiff's damage. If it was * * * the defendant is liable. If it was not, the defendant is not liable."

The following proposition is stated in defendant's brief and relied on for reversal:

"If plaintiff's property was damaged by a number of fires combining, one * * * being the fire pleaded * * * the others being of no responsible origin, but of such sufficient or superior force that they would have produced the damage to plaintiff's property regardless of the fire pleaded, then defendant was not liable."

This proposition is based on Cook v. Minneapolis, St. P. & S.S.M. Ry. Co., 98 Wis. 624, 74 N.W. 561. * * * If the Cook case merely declares that one who negligently sets a fire is not liable if another's property is damaged, unless it is made to appear that the fire was a material element in the destruction of the property, there can be no question about the soundness of the decision. But if it decides that if such fire combines with another of no responsible origin, and after the union of the two fires they destroy the property, and either fire independently of the other would have destroyed it, then irrespective of whether the first fire was or was not a material factor in the destruction of the property, there is no liability, we are not prepared to adopt the doctrine as the law of this state. If a fire set by the engine of one railroad company unites with a fire set by the engine of another company, there is joint and several liability, even though either fire would have destroyed plaintiff's property. But if the doctrine of the Cook case is applied and one of the fires is of unknown origin, there is no liability. * * * [T]here [should] be liability in such a case. We, therefore hold that the trial court did not err in refusing to instruct the jury in accordance with the rule laid down in the Cook case. * * *

We find no error requiring a reversal, and hence the order appealed from is affirmed.

1. As plaintiff was driving his horse and wagon down a narrow road, two motorcycles, independently operated by two defendants, roared past him, one on each side. The horse took fright and ran away, and plaintiff was injured. Either motorcycle alone would have been sufficient to frighten the horse. Who is liable? Corey v. Havener, 182 Mass. 250, 65 N.E. 69 (1902).

2. A stabs B with a knife. C then fractures B's skull with a rock. Either injury would be fatal. B dies from the effect of both. Who is liable for his death? Wilson v. State, 24 S.W. 409 (Tex.Cr.App.1893); People v. Lewis, 124 Cal. 551, 57 P. 470 (1899). Should the answer be the same in criminal and tort law?

3. A car rental company rents a car with defective brakes. The driver negligently fails to see the plaintiff and hits him. Who, if anyone, is liable? See Prosser and Keeton, Torts 267, n. 27 (5th ed. 1984).

4. While defendant is suffering from terminal cancer, he is negligently hit by defendant's automobile and killed. How does this case differ from the principal case and those cited in note 2, supra? See Follett v. Jones, 252 Ark. 950, 481 S.W.2d 713 (1972).

5. In Cook v. Minneapolis, St. P. & S.S.M.R. Co., 98 Wis. 624, 74 N.W. 561 (1898), where two fires merged as in the principal case, the court refused to hold a defendant liable where the other fire was of innocent origin. Is this sound? In Kingston v. Chicago & N.W.R. Co., 191 Wis. 610, 211 N.W. 913 (1927), the court modified the effect of the Cook case by holding that the burden was upon the defendant to prove the innocent origin of the other fire.

G/c = But/for

Exc = Substantial factor – if multiple causes / concurrent

6. The "substantial factor" test would retain "but for" causation as an essential precondition except in situations, such as the principal case, in which two or more actively operating forces, for only one of which the defendant was responsible, combine to bring about the harm, while each alone would have been sufficient to bring about the harm. See Restatement (Second) of Torts §§ 431–433 (1965).

"Substantial factor" was taken by the trial judge in the *Anderson* case from an article by Jeremiah Smith, Legal Cause in Actions of Tort, 25 Harv.L.Rev. 103, 223, 229 (1911). It obviously has the advantage of eliminating cases in which the defendant has made a proved, but insignificant, contribution to the result—as where he throws a lighted match into a forest fire.

"Alternative Liability"

4. PROBLEMS IN DETERMINING WHICH PARTY CAUSED THE HARM

= what about Cf. K
Agent Orange ? represented 99% of them
Not GTSL, but independent Tortfeasors each of which must prove the other caused harm; or, both being negligent, both will share damages

SUMMERS v. TICE + Simonson

Supreme Court of California, 1948.
33 Cal.2d 80, 199 P.2d 1.

– Only one caused harm, did not combine, but which?
– Shifts BoP to ∆.

TrCt = π
SCt = affl'd

Actions by Charles A. Summers against Harold W. Tice and against Ernest Simonson for negligently shooting plaintiff while hunting. From judgments for plaintiff, defendants appeal, and the appeals were consolidated pursuant to stipulation.

[Plaintiff and the two defendants were members of a hunting party. Both defendants negligently fired, at the same time, at a quail and in the plaintiff's direction. Plaintiff was struck in the eye by a shot from one gun. There was no other satisfactory evidence.]

facts/evidence

CARTER, J. * * * The problem presented in this case is whether the judgment against both defendants may stand. It is argued by defendants that they are not joint tort feasors, and thus jointly and severally liable, as they were not acting in concert and that there is not sufficient evidence to show which defendant was guilty of the negligence which caused the injuries—the shooting by Tice or that by Simonson. * * * The one shot that entered plaintiff's eye was the major factor in assessing damages and that shot could not have come from the gun of both defendants. It was from one or the other only.

I

"in concert"

Independent / TFs
not "in concert"
Cf = p. 280 ∆'

It has been held that where a group of persons are on a hunting party, or otherwise engaged in the use of firearms, and two of them are negligent in firing in the direction of a third person who is injured thereby, both of those so firing are liable for the injury suffered by the third person, although the negligence of only one of them could have caused the injury. * * *

These cases speak of the action of defendants as being in concert as the ground of decision, yet it would seem they are straining that concept and the more reasonable basis appears in Oliver v. Miles, 144 Miss. 852, 110 So. 666. There two persons were hunting together. Both shot at some partridges and in so doing shot across the highway injuring plaintiff who was traveling on it. The court stated they were acting in concert and thus both were liable. The court then stated: "We think that * * * each is liable for the resulting injury to the boy, although no one can say definitely who actually shot him. *To hold otherwise would be to exonerate both from liability, although each was negligent, and the injury resulted from such negligence.*" [Emphasis added.] * * *

— again Knowledge of A

When we consider the relative position of the parties and the results that would flow if plaintiff was required to pin the injury on one of the defendants only, a requirement that the burden of proof on that subject be shifted to defendants becomes manifest. They are both wrongdoers—both negligent toward plaintiff. They brought about a situation where the negligence of one of them injured the plaintiff, hence it should rest with them each to absolve himself if he can. The injured party has been placed by defendants in the unfair position of pointing to which defendant caused the harm. If one can escape the other may also and plaintiff is remediless. Ordinarily defendants are in a far better position to offer evidence to determine which one caused the injury. This reasoning has recently found favor in this Court. [The court refers here to its earlier holding in Ybarra v. Spangard, supra page 254].

Shifts BoP

RTL =

RTL =

[T]he same reasons of policy and justice shift the burden to each of defendants to absolve himself if he can—relieving the wronged person of the duty of apportioning the injury to a particular defendant, apply here where we are concerned with whether plaintiff is required to supply evidence for the apportionment of damages. If defendants are independent tort feasors and thus each liable for the damage caused by him alone, and, at least, where the matter of apportionment is incapable of proof, the innocent wronged party should not be deprived of his right to redress. The wrongdoers should be left to work out between themselves any apportionment. * * *

Whether Joint TFs or Independent TFs, each liable;
Joint TFs = JSL
Independent TFs = amongst each other
— actually the same result?

The judgment is affirmed.

Not really, one party may be the deep pocket, or answered, etc.; one judgment proved

1. In accord, on similar facts, are Bowman v. Redding & Co., 449 F.2d 956 (D.C.Cir.1971); and Cook v. Lewis, [1952] 1 Dom.L.Rep. 1, [1951] B.C.Rep. 830. The Restatement (Second) of Torts, § 433B, has approved the rule. What is the relation of this case to Ybarra v. Spangard, supra page 254?

2. In two motels, the pool was operated in violation of statute, without attendants or warning. The burden of proof for causation was put on the defendant in Haft v. Lone Palm Hotel, 3 Cal.3d 756, 91 Cal.Rptr. 745, 478 P.2d 465 (1970) (father and son drowned); but was put on the plaintiffs in Smith v. Americania Motor Lodge, 39 Cal.App.3d 1, 113 Cal.Rptr. 771 (1974) (two small children). How should they compare with the principal case and each other?

3. Two automobiles, negligently driven by A and B, collide. Immediately, a car negligently driven by C piles into the wreck. Somewhere in the process plaintiff, a passenger in A's car, is killed. There is no other evidence. What result? Cummings v. Kendall, 41 Cal.App.2d 549, 107 P.2d 282 (1940); Murphy v. Taxicabs of Louisville, Inc., 330 S.W.2d 395 (Ky.1959); cf. Petersen v. Parry, 92 Idaho 647, 448 P.2d 653 (1968) (two cars collide; all occupants killed).

4. A number of defendants spew pollution into the air and damage *real* plaintiff's property, but he cannot show which one caused what damage. Is this *case* enough to apply the principal case? See Katz, The Function of Tort Liability in Technology Assessment, 38 U.Cin.L.Rev. 587, 617–620 (1969).

5. Should it make any difference in the principal case if plaintiff sues only one defendant, without joining the other? What if there were ten hunters in the principal case?

Trct — Δ (dis'd)
SCt — π (rev'd)

SINDELL v. ABBOTT LABORATORIES

Supreme Court of California, 1980.
26 Cal.3d 588, 607 P.2d 924, 163 Cal.Rptr. 132, cert. denied, 449 U.S. 912, 101
S.Ct. 285, 66 L.Ed.2d 140 (1980).

MOSK, JUSTICE. This case involves a complex problem both timely Ⓘ and significant: may a plaintiff, injured as the result of a drug administered to her mother during pregnancy, who knows the type of drug involved but cannot identify the manufacturer of the precise product, hold liable for her injuries a maker of a drug produced from an identical formula?

[Plaintiff alleged that her mother ingested a drug, diethylstilbestrol (DES), which was marketed by the defendants, five drug companies. The drug was also marketed by approximately 195 other companies. The drug, a synthetic estrogen, was used for the purpose of preventing a miscarriage. Plaintiff, now an adult, alleged that she developed a cancer as a result of her mother's ingesting the drug. She also indicated that she could not identify the manufacturer of the drug. The trial court dismissed the action.

This court held that (1) the case was not the same as Summers v. Tice because not all the defendants were before the court, and (2) there was no "concert of action" among the defendants. See infra page 354].

A third theory upon which plaintiff relies is the concept of industry-wide liability, or according to the terminology of the parties, "enterprise liability." This theory was suggested in Hall v. E.I. Du Pont de Nemours & Co., Inc. (E.D.N.Y.1972) 345 F.Supp. 353. In that case, plaintiffs were 13 children injured by the explosion of blasting caps in 12 separate incidents which occurred in 10 different states between 1955 and 1959. The defendants were six blasting cap manufacturers, comprising virtually the entire blasting cap industry in the United States, and their trade association. There were, however, a number of Canadian blasting cap manufacturers which could have supplied the caps. The gravamen of the complaint was that the practice of the industry of omitting a warning on individual blasting caps and of failing to take other safety measures created an unreasonable risk of harm, resulting in the plaintiffs' injuries. The complaint did not identify a particular manufacturer of a cap which caused a particular injury.

The court reasoned as follows: there was evidence that defendants, acting independently, had adhered to an industry-wide standard with regard to the safety features of blasting caps, that they had in effect delegated some functions of safety investigation and design, such as labelling, to their trade association, and that there was industry-wide cooperation in the manufacture and design of blasting caps. In these circumstances, the evidence supported a conclusion that all the defendants jointly controlled the risk. Thus, if plaintiffs could establish by a preponderance of the evidence that the caps were manufactured by one of the defendants, the burden of proof as to causation would shift to all the defendants. The court noted that this theory of liability applied to industries composed of a small number of units, and that what would be fair and reasonable with regard to an industry of five or ten producers might be manifestly unreasonable if applied to a decentralized industry composed of countless small producers. * * *

We decline to apply this theory in the present case. At least 200 manufacturers produced DES; *Hall*, which involved 6 manufacturers representing the entire blasting cap industry in the United States, cautioned against application of the doctrine espoused therein to a large number of producers. (345 F.Supp at p. 378.)

Moreover in *Hall*, the conclusion that the defendants jointly controlled the risk was based upon allegations that they had delegated some functions relating to safety to a trade association. There are no such allegations here, and we have concluded above that plaintiff has failed to allege liability on a concert of action theory. * * *

If we were confined to the theories of *Summers* and *Hall*, we would be constrained to hold that the judgment must be sustained. Should we require that plaintiff identify the manufacturer which supplied the DES used by her mother or that all DES manufacturers be joined in the action, she would effectively be precluded from any recovery. As defendants candidly admit, there is little likelihood that all the manufacturers who made DES at the time in question are still in business or that they are subject to the jurisdiction of the California courts. There are, however, forceful arguments in favor of holding that plaintiff has a cause of action.

In our contemporary complex industrialized society, advances in science and technology create fungible goods which may harm consumers and which cannot be traced to any specific producer. The response of the courts can be either to adhere rigidly to prior doctrine, denying recovery to those injured by such products, or to fashion remedies to meet these changing needs. * * *

The most persuasive reason for finding plaintiff states a cause of action is that advanced in *Summers*: as between an innocent plaintiff and negligent defendants, the latter should bear the cost of the injury. Here, as in *Summers*, plaintiff is not at fault in failing to provide evidence of causation, and although the absence of such evidence is not attributable to the defendants either, their conduct in marketing a drug the effects of which are delayed for many years played a significant role in creating the unavailability of proof.

From a broader policy standpoint, defendants are better able to bear the cost of injury resulting from the manufacture of a defective product. As was said by Justice Traynor in *Escola* [v. Coca Cola Bottling Co.], "[t]he cost of an injury and the loss of time or health may be an overwhelming misfortune to the person injured, and a needless one, for the risk of injury can be insured by the manufacturer and distributed among the public as a cost of doing business." (24 Cal.2d p. 462, 150 P.2d p. 441; see also Rest.2d Torts, § 402A, com. c, pp. 349–350.) The manufacturer is in the best position to discover and guard against defects in its products and to warn of harmful effects; thus, holding it liable for defects and failure to warn of harmful effects will provide an incentive to product safety. [Cc] These considerations are particularly significant where medication is involved, for the consumer is virtually helpless to protect himself from serious, sometimes permanent, sometimes fatal, injuries caused by deleterious drugs.

Where, as here, all defendants produced a drug from an identical formula and the manufacturer of the DES which caused plaintiff's injuries cannot be identified through no fault of plaintiff, a modification of the rule of *Summers* is warranted. As we have seen, an undiluted *Summers* rationale is inappropriate to shift the burden of proof of causation to defendants because if we measure the chance that any particular manufacturer supplied the injury-causing product by the number of producers of DES, there is a possibility that none of the five defendants in this case produced the offending substance and that the responsible manufacturer, not named in the action, will escape liability.

But we approach the issue of causation from a different perspective: we hold it to be reasonable in the present context to measure the likelihood that any of the defendants supplied the product which allegedly injured plaintiff by the percentage which the DES sold by each of them for the purpose of preventing miscarriage bears to the entire production of the drug sold by all for that purpose. Plaintiff asserts in her briefs that Eli Lilly and Company and 5 or 6 other companies produced 90 percent of the DES marketed. If at trial this is established to be the fact, then there is a corresponding likelihood that this comparative handful of producers manufactured the DES which caused plaintiff's injuries, and only a 10 percent likelihood that the offending producer would escape liability.

If plaintiff joins in the action the manufacturers of a substantial share of the DES which her mother might have taken, the injustice of shifting the burden of proof to defendants to demonstrate that they could not have made the substance which injured plaintiff is significantly diminished. * * *

The presence in the action of a substantial share of the appropriate market also provides a ready means to apportion damages among the defendants. Each defendant will be held liable for the proportion of the judgment represented by its share of that market unless it demonstrates that it could not have made the product which caused plaintiff's injuries. * * *

Under this approach, each manufacturer's liability would approximate its responsibility for the injuries caused by its own products. Some minor discrepancy in the correlation between market share and liability is inevitable; therefore, a defendant may be held liable for a somewhat different percentage of the damage than its share of the appropriate market would justify. It is probably impossible, with the passage of time, to determine market share with mathematical exactitude. * * * As we said in *Summers* with regard to the liability of independent tortfeasors, where a correct division of liability cannot be made "the trier of fact may make it the best it can." (33 Cal.2d at p. 88, 199 P.2d at p. 5.)

We are not unmindful of the practical problems involved in defining the market and determining market share, but these are largely matters of proof which properly cannot be determined at the pleading stage of these proceedings. Defendants urge that it would be both unfair and contrary to public policy to hold them liable for plaintiff's injuries in the absence of proof that one of them supplied the drug responsible for the damage. Most of their arguments, however, are based upon the assumption that one manufacturer would be held responsible for the products of another or for those of all other manufacturers if plaintiff ultimately prevails. But under the rule we adopt, each manufacturer's liability for an injury would be approximately equivalent to the damages caused by the DES it manufactured.

The judgments are reversed.

BIRD, C.J., and NEWMAN and WHITE, JJ., concur.

RICHARDSON, CLARK and MANUAL, JJ., dissent.

1. State supreme courts are sharply divided as to whether a claim should be allowed in this context. See Zafft v. Eli Lilly & Co., 676 S.W.2d 241, 247 (Mo.1984), where the court refused to abandon traditional tort law principles and denied plaintiff's claim. (Gunn, J., dissenting).

2. Among courts allowing a claim, there exists a division of opinion about how to handle the case.

A. Two states have adopted a modified version of the *Sindell* theory of alternative liability. See Abel v. Eli Lilly & Co., 418 Mich. 311, 343 N.W.2d 164, 174 (1984), cert. denied, 469 U.S. 833 (1984), adding that once all tortfeasors are joined, each may be found jointly and severally liable. See also Martin v. Abbott Laboratories, 102 Wash.2d 581, 689 P.2d 368, 380 (1984), where the court specifically rejected the requirement that the plaintiff join defendants representing a substantial share of the market; Shackil v. Lederle Laboratories, 219 N.J.Super. 601, 530 A.2d 1287 (App.Div.1987), where the court adopted an approach that shifts the burden to defendants, once plaintiff has joined the manufacturers of a substantial share of the market, to exculpate themselves by proving non-participation, possession of reduced market share, or that their product engendered a lower risk.

　B.　A "risk contribution" theory was adopted by the Wisconsin Supreme Court in Collins v. Eli Lilly & Co., 116 Wis.2d 166, 342 N.W.2d 37, 49–51, 53 (1984), cert. denied, 469 U.S. 826 (1984). The theory is in essence the *Sindell* "market share" theory with two differences: plaintiff need only sue one manufacturer, thereby eliminating the substantial share of the market requirement, and percentage of liability is based on comparative negligence, with market share only one of the factors used to make that finding.

　C.　A New York court found a "concert of action" in a DES case. See Bichler v. Eli Lilly & Co., 79 A.D.2d 317, 436 N.Y.S.2d 625 (1981), aff'd, 55 N.Y.2d 571, 436 N.E.2d 182, 450 N.Y.S.2d 776 (1982). The court found that the defendants acted in concert because they had engaged in "conscious parallel activity." Should that be enough to eliminate plaintiff's burden to prove causation?

　3.　When a claim has been allowed, courts have differed about the proper "theory" even within the same state. Compare Burke v. Johns–Manville Sales Corp., No. C–1–81–289 (S.D.Ohio Oct. 27, 1981), with Gorniak v. Combustion Eng'g, Inc., No. C78–465 (N.D.Ohio July 6, 1981).

　4.　The *Sindell* decision itself was based on a student law review contribution. See Comment, DES and a Proposed Theory of Enterprise Liability, 46 Fordham L.Rev. 963 (1978). In addition, check Fisher, Products Liability—An Analysis of Market Share Liability, 34 Vand.L.Rev. 1623 (1981); Delgado, Beyond Sindell: Relaxation of Cause–In–Fact Rules for Indeterminate Plaintiffs, 70 Calif.L.Rev. 881 (1982); Robinson, Multiple Causation in Tort Law: Reflections on the DES Cases, 68 Va.L.Rev. 713 (1982); Roberts and Royster, DES and the Identification Problem, 16 Akron L.Rev. 447 (1983); Biebel, DES Litigation and the Problem of Causation, 51 Ins.Couns.J. 223 (1984).

　5.　Would the legislature be a more effective forum to work out causational proof problems in mass tort cases? For an in-depth discussion of this alternative, see Schwartz and Mahshigian, Failure to Identify the Defendant in Tort Law: Towards a Legislative Solution, 73 Calif.L.Rev. 941 (1985). See also Elliot, Comment on Robinson, 14 J.Legal Stud. 79 (1985); Downey and Gulley, Theories of Recovery for DES Damage: Is Tort Liability the Answer? 4 J.Legal Med. 167 (1983).

　6.　Suppose plaintiff is exposed to toxic chemicals and receives minor injuries. Initially, plaintiff sues company for damages. Years later, plaintiff discovers that he may have developed cancer as a result of his earlier exposure. Should the doctrine of res judicata bar his recovery in a later action? Can the company assert that the statute of limitations has run? See Hagerty v. L. & L. Marine Serv. Inc., 788 F.2d 315 (5th Cir.1986); Herber v. Johns–Manville Corp., 785 F.2d 79 (3d Cir.1986). See also Nicolet, Inc. v. Nutt, 525 A.2d 146 (Del.1987) (cancer from asbestos).

Chapter VI

PROXIMATE OR LEGAL CAUSE

ATLANTIC COAST LINE R. CO. v. DANIELS

Court of Appeals of Georgia, 1911.
8 Ga.App. 775, 70 S.E. 203.

Ask student to paraphrase.

POWELL, J. * * * Cause and effect find their beginning and end in the limitless and unknowable. Therefore courts, in their finitude, do not attempt to deal with cause and effect in any absolute degree, but only in such a limited way as is practical and as is within the scope of ordinary human understanding. Hence arbitrary limits have been set, and such qualifying words as "proximate" and "natural" have come into use as setting the limits beyond which the courts will not look in the attempt to trace the connection between a given cause and a given effect. A plaintiff comes into court alleging, as an effect, some injury that has been done to his person or to his property. He shows that antecedent to the injury a wrongful act of another person occurred, and that, if this wrongful act had not occurred, the injury complained of would not (as human probabilities go) have occurred. We then say, in common speech, that the wrong was a cause of the injury. But to make such a standard (that, if the cause had not existed, the effect would not have occurred) the basis of legal responsibility would soon prove very unsatisfactory; for a *reductio ad absurdum* may be promptly established by calling to mind that, if the injured person had never been born, the injury would not have happened. So the courts ask another question: Was the wrongful act the proximate cause? * * *

---

1. For "proximate," we are indebted to Francis Bacon, Lord Chancellor, who in his time committed other sins. His maxim was: *In jure non remota causa, sed proxima, spectatur.* [In law, not the remote cause but the nearest one, is looked to.] According to the Random House Dictionary of the English Language (unabridged edition), proximate means "1. next; nearest; immediately before or after in order * * * 2. close, very near * * *" How important is the matter of physical distance between defendant's conduct and plaintiff's injury? See the discussion of the *Kinsman* cases, infra page 314, note 10.

forewarning of issues re: proximate: physical time

2. What about nearness or remoteness as to time? In City of Brady, Texas v. Finklea, 400 F.2d 352, 357 (5th Cir.1968), an electrician was electrocuted by wires suspended from a transformer cross arm that had been negligently installed by the city over 28 years before. The court stated that "lapse of time is but one element to be considered along with all relevant facts in the case." Cf. Bradler v. Craig, 274 Cal.App.2d 466, 79 Cal.Rptr. 401 (1969) (house built 18 years earlier).

3. The Restatement (Second) of Torts § 431 has substituted the term "legal cause" for proximate cause. Is this a more accurate term? Is it more

288

helpful in understanding the nature of proximate cause? Thus far, most courts have been inclined to retain the terminology of "proximate cause." Both terms are often used to include cause in fact.

4. Articles, notes and comments on "proximate cause" are legion. The topic has had a peculiar fascination for legal writers, and most of them have used it as a springboard to launch their own theories as to the proper basis of legal liability. At one extreme, there have been attempts to reduce it all to definite mechanical rules, as in Beale, The Proximate Consequences of an Act, 33 Harv.L.Rev. 633 (1920), and Carpenter, Proximate Cause, 14 S.Cal.L.Rev. 1, 115, 416 (1940), 15 S.Cal.L.Rev. 187, 304, 427 (1941), 16 S.Cal.L.Rev. 1, 61, 275 (1942). At the other extreme, there has been a rejection of all rules, and the position that the court must decide each case according to its ideas of "justice," as in Edgerton, Legal Cause, 72 U.Pa.L.Rev. 211, 343 (1924).

Among the principal landmarks of discussion have been the book by Leon Green, The Rationale of Proximate Cause (1927); Bohlen, The Probable or the Natural Consequences as a Test of Liability in Negligence, 40 U.Pa.L.Rev. 79, 148 (1901); Smith, Legal Cause in Actions of Tort, 25 Harv.L.Rev. 103, 223, 303 (1911); Green, Are There Dependable Rules of Causation? 77 U.Pa.L.Rev. 601 (1929); Goodhart, The Unforeseeable Consequences of a Negligent Act, 39 Yale L.J. 532 (1930); Campbell, Duty, Fault and Legal Cause, 1938 Wis.L.Rev. 402; Gregory, Proximate Cause in Negligence—A Retreat from "Rationalization," 6 U.Chi.L.Rev. 36 (1938); Morris, Proximate Cause in Minnesota, 34 Minn.L.Rev. 185 (1950); James and Perry, Legal Cause, 60 Yale L.J. 761 (1951); Eldredge, The Role of Foreseeable Consequences in Negligence Law, 23 Pa.B.A.Q. 158 (1952). See also the books by Robert Keeton, Legal Cause in the Law of Torts (1963), and Hart and Honoré, Causation in the Law of Torts (1959).

Some recent efforts by law review writers include Seidelson, Some Reflections on Proximate Cause, 19 Duq.L.Rev. 1 (1980); Shavell, Analysis of Causation and the Scope of Liability in the Law of Torts, 9 J.Legal Stud. 463 (1980); King, Causation, Valuation, and Chance in Personal Injury Torts Involving Preexisting Conditions and Future Consequences, 90 Yale L.J. 1353 (1981). For economic applications and ramifications of proximate cause, see Landes & Posner, Causation in Tort Law: An Economic Approach, 12 J.Legal Stud. 109 (1983); and Grady, Proximate Cause and the Law of Negligence, 69 Iowa L.Rev. 363 (1984).

1. UNFORESEEABLE CONSEQUENCES

RYAN v. NEW YORK CENTRAL R.R. CO.

Court of Appeals of New York, 1866.
35 N.Y. 210, 91 Am.Dec. 49.

HUNT, J. On the 15th day of July, 1854, in the city of Syracuse, the defendant, by the careless management, or through the insufficient condition of one of its engines, set fire to its woodshed, and a large quantity of wood therein. The plaintiff's house, situated at a distance of one hundred and thirty feet from the shed, soon took fire from the heat and sparks, and was entirely consumed, notwithstanding diligent efforts were made to save it. A number of other houses were also burned by the spreading of the fire. The plaintiff brings this action to recover from the railroad company the value of his building thus destroyed. The judge at the Circuit nonsuited the plaintiff, and the General Term of the fifth district affirmed the judgment.

The question may be thus stated: A house in a populous city takes fire, through the negligence of the owner or his servant; the flames extend to and destroy an adjacent building: Is the owner of the first building liable to the second owner for the damage sustained by such burning?

It is a general principle that every person is liable for the consequences of his own acts. He is thus liable in damages for the proximate results of his own acts, but not for remote damages. It is not easy at all times to determine what are proximate and what are remote damages.

* * *

If an engineer upon a steamboat or locomotive in passing the house of A., so carelessly manages its machinery that the coals and sparks from its fires fall upon and consume the house of A., the railroad company or the steamboat proprietors are liable to pay the value of the property thus destroyed. [C] Thus far the law is settled and the principle is apparent. If, however, the fire communicates from the house of A. to that of B., and that is destroyed, is the negligent party liable for his loss? And if it spreads thence to the house of C., and thence to the house of D., and thence consecutively through the other houses until it reaches and consumes the house of Z., is the party liable to pay the damages sustained by these twenty-four sufferers? The counsel for the plaintiff does not distinctly claim this, and I think it would not be seriously insisted that the sufferers could recover in such case. Where then is the principle upon which A. recovers and Z. fails?

* * *

I prefer to place my opinion upon the ground that in the one case, to-wit, the destruction of the building upon which the sparks were thrown by the negligent act of the party sought to be charged, the result was to have been anticipated the moment the fire was communicated to the building; that its destruction was the ordinary and natural result of its being fired. In the second, third or twenty-fourth case, as supposed, the destruction of the building was not a natural and expected result of the first firing. That a building upon which sparks and cinders fall should be destroyed or seriously injured must be expected, but that the fire should spread and other buildings be consumed is not a necessary or an usual result. That it is possible, and that it is not infrequent, cannot be denied. The result however depends, not upon any necessity of a further communication of the fire, but upon a concurrence of accidental circumstances, such as the degree of the heat, the state of the atmosphere, the condition and materials of the adjoining structures and the direction of the wind. These are accidental and varying circumstances. The party has no control over them, and is not responsible for their effects.

My opinion therefore is, that this action cannot be sustained, for the reason that the damages incurred are not the immediate but the remote result of the negligence of the defendants. The immediate result was the destruction of their own wood and sheds; beyond that, it was remote. * * *

To sustain such a claim as the present, and to follow the same to its legitimate consequences, would subject to a liability against which no prudence could guard, and to meet which no private fortune would be adequate. * * * A man may insure his own house or his own furniture, but he cannot insure his neighbor's building or furniture, for the reason that he has no interest in them. To hold that the owner must not only meet his own loss by fire, but that he must guarantee the security of his neighbors on both sides, and to an unlimited extent, would be to create a liability which would be the destruction of all civilized society. No community could long exist under the operation of such a principle. In a commercial country each man, to some extent, runs the hazard of his neighbor's conduct, and each, by insurance against such hazards, is enabled to obtain a reasonable security against loss. To neglect such precaution, and to call upon his neighbor on whose premises a fire originated, to indemnify him instead, would be to award a punishment quite beyond the offense committed. It is to be considered also that if the negligent party is liable to the owner of a remote building thus consumed, he would also be liable to the insurance companies who should pay losses to such remote owners. The principle of subrogation would entitle the companies to the benefit of every claim held by the party to whom a loss should be paid. * * *

The remoteness of the damage, in my judgment, forms the true rule on which the question should be decided, and which prohibits a recovery by the plaintiff in this case.

Judgment should be affirmed.

———

1. Compare the instant case with Ford v. Jeffries, 474 Pa. 588, 379 A.2d 111 (1977), where defendant was held liable when fire from his burning house spread next door to plaintiff's home, destroying it. Could the fact that defendant's house had caught fire just a few months before the accident have been a distinguishing factor? If the defendant could not anticipate that the fire would burn anything but its own building, how was it negligent at all? If the result is "not infrequent," why may it not be foreseen?

2. Assuming that it was negligent, was plaintiff's damage foreseeable? See City of Bishop v. South Texas Elec. Coop., 577 S.W.2d 331 (Tex.Civ.App. 1979) (plaintiff's firetruck destroyed in grassfire caused by defendant). The limitation to foreseeable consequences was first stated by Baron Pollock in Greenland v. Chaplin, 5 Ex. 243, 155 Eng.Rep. 104 (1850). A leading American case then adopted this position in Milwaukee & St. Paul R. Co. v. Kellogg, 94 U.S. 469 (1876).

3. At the opposite extreme from the principal case is Atchison, T. & S.F.R. Co. v. Stanford, 12 Kan. 354, 15 Am.Rep. 362 (1874), where a railroad that negligently set a fire next to its tracks was held liable to the owner of a farm nearly four miles away, to whose property the fire spread.

Kansas had, at the time of the decision, and still has, many miles of uninsured grain, and its community attitude toward railroads is not necessarily the same as that of New York. Do these factors account for the difference in opinion? Completely? Is there any essential reason why the two states should have the same rule?

4. Most of the decisions on fires spreading for a substantial distance have held the defendant liable. See, for example, Smith v. London & S.W.R. Co. [1870] L.R. 6 C.P. 14; Hoyt v. Jeffers, 30 Mich. 181 (1874); E.T. & H.K. Ide v. Boston & Maine R. Co., 83 Vt. 66, 74 A. 401 (1909).

Is case still good law in New York?

5. New York has since modified the rule to allow recovery by the first adjoining landowner, as distinct from the first building. Webb v. Rome, W. & O.R. Co., 49 N.Y. 420, 10 Am.Rep. 389 (1872). Or the first property to which the fire jumps, although it is not adjoining. Homac Corp. v. Sun Oil Co., 258 N.Y. 462, 180 N.E. 172 (1932). The New York Court of Appeals has said that the *Ryan* case "should not be extended beyond the precise facts which appear therein." See Frace v. N.Y.L.E. & W.R. Co., 143 N.Y. 182, 189, 38 N.E. 102 (1894). But on occasion the shadow of the old rule has barred a nonadjacent landowner's claim. See Rose v. Pennsylvania R. Co., 236 N.Y. 568, 142 N.E. 287 (1923). Pennsylvania at one time accepted the New York rule, but later rejected it in favor of a limitation of foreseeable distance. Pennsylvania R. Co. v. Hope, 80 Pa. 373, 21 Am.Rep. 100 (1876). Other courts have rejected the "first building" test.

6. Policy considerations weighed heavily in the principal case. How important was insurance? Could the defendant railroad have purchased liability insurance to cover this situation? Should the fact that the plaintiff could easily have purchased accident or fire insurance be utilized to restrict the liability of a negligent defendant to consequences that are less than reasonably foreseeable? Why?

7. The mention of "insurance" as a decisional factor, in the opinion of the principal case, has sustained academic interest for over 100 years. For examples, see Green & Smith, No–Fault and Jury Trial II, 50 Tex.L.Rev. 1297, 1303 (1972); Smith, The Miscegenetic Union of Liability Insurance and the Tort Process in the Personal Injury Claims System, 54 Cornell L.Rev. 645, 666 (1969); Ehrenzweig, Negligence Without Fault, 54 Calif.L.Rev. 1422, 1448, 1452 (1966); Franklin, When Worlds Collide: Liability Theories and Disclaimers Defective Products Cases, 18 Stan.L.Rev. 974, 984 and n. 64 (1966); Vinson, Proximate Cause Should Be Barred from Wandering Outside Negligence Law, 13 Fla.St. U.L.Rev. 215 (1985).

(I) whether Δ liable for aggravating pre-existing conditions? (thin skulled or egg shell skulled π?)

BARTOLONE v. JECKOVICH

Supreme Court of New York, 1984.
103 A.D.2d 632, 481 N.Y.S.2d 545.

(II) extent of damage is immaterial; if foreseeable, Δ is liable

note #3

DENMAN, JUSTICE.—On October 4, 1976 plaintiff was involved in a four-car chain reaction collision in Niagara Falls for which defendants were found liable. Plaintiff sustained relatively minor injuries consisting of whiplash and cervical and lower back strain for which he was treated with muscle relaxants and physical therapy but was not hospitalized. Subsequently, however, he suffered an acute psychotic breakdown from which he has not recovered. The theory on which plaintiff's case was tried was that the accident aggravated a pre-existing paranoid schizophrenic condition which has totally and permanently disabled him. * * *

At the time of the accident, plaintiff was a 48 year old man who lived alone in one room and worked out of a union hall as a carpenter. He was very proud of his physique and his strength, spending on the average of four hours daily at the local YMCA engaged in body building. On weekends, in order to conserve his strength, he pursued nonphysical interests such as painting and sculpture, singing and playing the guitar and trombone. Since the accident, plaintiff has been in a degenerative psychotic condition in which he is withdrawn, hostile, delusional, hears voices and sees shadows, refuses to cut his hair, shave or bathe and no longer participates in any of his former interests. In the words of his treating psychiatrist, he is "a life lost." — *at least until he gets his hands on those damages.*

Three psychiatrists and one neurosurgeon testified on behalf of plaintiff. From their testimony a strange and sad profile emerged: Plaintiff's mother had died of cancer when he was a very young boy. His sister had also died of cancer. Probably as a consequence, plaintiff had developed a fear and dislike of doctors and engaged in body building in order to avoid doctors and ward off illness. His bodily fitness was extremely important to him because it provided him with a sense of control over his life so that he was able to function in a relatively normal way. * * * Because he had such an intense emotional investment in his body, his perception of this impairment made him incapable of his former physical feats and he was thus deprived of the mechanism by which he coped with his emotional problems. As a consequence, he deteriorated psychologically and socially as well.
* * *

Defendants' expert, who had never seen the plaintiff, even at trial, agreed that plaintiff suffered from schizophrenia but stated that, in his opinion, it had not been exacerbated by the accident and that defendant was merely attempting to make money. The jury, who had an opportunity to see the plaintiff and hear his testimony, returned a verdict of $500,000. The court set that verdict aside stating that there was no basis on which the jury could conclude that plaintiff's total mental breakdown could be attributed to a minor accident.

P. ct = Jury - π
Judge = Nov = Δ

We find, to the contrary, that there was ample proof in the record to support the jury's verdict. There is precedent for such determination. In *Bonner v. U.S.*, 339 F.Supp. 640, plaintiff was a passenger in a car which was rear-ended. She received a whiplash injury resulting in cervical spasms and lumbar-sacral strain for which she was treated with muscle relaxants and physiotherapy. She later developed numbness, headaches, hearing difficulties, inability to keep her eyes open, deteriorated personal hygiene, degeneration in appearance, facial tics and jerking and twitching of her head, all of which were determined to be of a psychological rather than neurological origin. The psychiatric testimony established that she had a pre-existing underlying psychotic illness with which she was able to cope until the accident but that the

SCt = rev'd = π
pretty close facts! skeptical?

accident had precipitated a chronic psychosis which was totally disabling.

In *Steinhauser v. Hertz Corp.*, 421 F.2d 1169 (2d Cir.), plaintiff, a 14 year old girl, was riding as a passenger in a car with her parents when it was struck by another vehicle. The occupants did not suffer any bodily injuries. Within minutes after the accident, plaintiff began to behave in a bizarre manner. After a series of hospitalizations, she was diagnosed as suffering from a "schizophrenic reaction—acute—undifferentiated." The other evidence at trial was similar to the evidence in the case before us. Prior to the accident she had a " 'prepsychotic' personality" and displayed a predisposition to abnormal behavior. * * * Nevertheless, there was testimony that, had it not been for the accident, she might have been able to lead a normal life and that the accident was the precipitating cause of her psychosis. The trial court did not allow plaintiff's counsel to elicit testimony as to whether the accident could have been an aggravating cause of her condition. In reversing a verdict of no cause for action, the United States Court of Appeals for the Second Circuit stated that the evidence made clear that plaintiff had some degree of pathology which was activated into schizophrenia by the emotional trauma connected with the accident and that she was entitled to have that issue fairly weighed by a jury.

The circumstances of those cases as well as those of the case before us illustrate the truth of the old axiom that a defendant must take a plaintiff as he finds him and hence may be held liable in damages for aggravation of a pre-existing illness (see McCahill v. New York Transp. Co., 201 N.Y. 221, 94 N.E. 616). Nor may defendants avail themselves of the argument that plaintiff should be denied recovery because his condition might have occurred even without the accident. [Cc]

The record presents ample evidence that plaintiff, although apparently suffering from a quiescent psychotic illness, was able to function in a relatively normal manner but that this minor accident aggravated his schizophrenic condition leaving him totally and permanently disabled.

Accordingly, the order should be reversed and the jury's verdict reinstated.

Order unanimously reversed with costs, motion denied and verdict reinstated.

1. The seminal opinion on the rule that a defendant must take a plaintiff as he finds him is McCahill v. New York Transp. Co., 201 N.Y. 221, 94 N.E. 616 (1911). The same court that decided *McCahill* also decided Ryan v. New York Central R. Co., supra page 289. The *McCahill* opinion did not mention insurance. Who could best insure in the instant situation?

2. The courts are agreed upon the rule stated in this case, when unforeseeable consequences follow from a physical injury to the person of the plaintiff. Compare Keegan v. Minneapolis & St. L. R. Co., 76 Minn. 90, 78 N.W. 965 (1899), where death from inflammation of the heart resulted from a sprained ankle.

Also Baltimore City Passenger R. Co. v. Kemp, 61 Md. 74 (1883) (cancer); Ominsky v. Charles Weinhagen & Co., 113 Minn. 422, 129 N.W. 845 (1911) (loss of hair from fright); Thompson v. Lupone, 135 Conn. 236, 62 A.2d 861 (1948) (obesity of 261-pound woman delayed recovery from normal period of two weeks to eight months: "The defendants took her as they found her"). See also Lockwood v. McKaskill, 262 N.C. 663, 138 S.E.2d 541 (1964), noted in 43 N.C.L. Rev. 1001 (1965) (amnesia due to plaintiff's predisposition).

3. One of the illustrations running through the English cases, originating in Dulieu v. White, [1901] 2 K.B. 669, 679, is that of the man with the thin skull, who suffers death when a normal man would have had only a bump on the head.

4. Should the principle of this case be applied when a negligently inflicted physical injury aggravates a prior mental illness? Suppose plaintiff's expert witness, a psychiatrist, testifies that an automobile accident was "the precipitating cause of plaintiff's schizophrenia"? See Steinhauser v. Hertz Corp., 421 F.2d 1169, 1172–1173 (2d Cir.1970).

IN RE ARBITRATION BETWEEN POLEMIS AND FURNESS, WITHY & CO., LTD.

Court of Appeal, [1921] 3 K.B. 560.

BANKES, L.J. By a time charter party dated February 21, 1917, the respondents chartered their vessel to the appellants. * * * The vessel was employed by the charterers to carry a cargo to Casablanca in Morocco. The cargo included a quantity of benzine or petrol in cases. While discharging at Casablanca a heavy plank fell into the hold in which the petrol was stowed, and caused an explosion, which set fire to the vessel and completely destroyed her. The owners claimed the value of the vessel from the charterers, alleging that the loss of the vessel was due to the negligence of the charterers' servants. The charterers contended * * * that the damages claimed were too remote. The claim was referred to arbitration and the arbitrators stated a special case for the opinion of the Court. Their findings of fact are as follows: The arbitrators found that the ship was lost by fire; that the fire arose from a spark igniting the petrol vapor in the hold; that the spark was caused by the falling board coming into contact with some substance in the hold; and that the causing of the spark could not reasonably have been anticipated from the falling of the board, though some damage to the ship might reasonably have been anticipated, and stated the damages at £196, 165 1s. 11d. * * *

In the present case the arbitrators have found as a fact that the falling of the plank was due to the negligence of the defendants' servants. The fire appears to me to have been directly caused by the falling of the plank. Under these circumstances I consider that it is immaterial that the causing of the spark by the falling of the plank could not have been reasonably anticipated. The appellants' junior counsel sought to draw a distinction between the anticipation of the extent of damage resulting from a negligent act and the anticipation of the type of damage resulting from such an act. He admitted that it

What was unforeseeable to Δ? extent of harm (burned a little vs. a lot)
type of harm (harmed by falling plank vs. harm by fire)
result (fire? whole ship burning)
manner (fire? could plank have destroyed whole ship?)

296   PROXIMATE OR LEGAL CAUSE   Ch. 6

extent v. type

could not lie in the mouth of a person whose negligent act had caused damage to say that he could not reasonably have foreseen the extent of the damage, but he contended that the negligent person was entitled to rely upon the fact that he could not reasonably have anticipated the type of damage which resulted from his negligent act. I do not think that the distinction can be admitted. Given the breach of duty which constitutes the negligence, and given the damage as a direct result of that negligence, the anticipations of the person whose negligent act has produced the damage appear to me to be irrelevant. I consider that the damages claimed are not too remote. *what about fire case -- direct.*

SCRUTTON, L.J. * * * The second defense is that the damage is too remote from the negligence, as it could not be reasonably foreseen as a consequence. * * * [I]f the act would or might probably cause damage, the fact that the damage it in fact causes is not the exact kind of damage one would expect is immaterial, so long as the damage is in fact directly traceable to the negligent act, and not due to the operation of independent causes having no connection with the negligent act, except that they could not avoid its results. Once the act is negligent, the fact that its exact operation was not foreseen is immaterial. * * * In the present case it was negligent in discharging cargo to knock down the planks of the temporary staging, for they might easily cause some damage either to workmen, or cargo, or the ship. The fact that they did directly produce an unexpected result, a spark in an atmosphere of petrol vapor which caused a fire, does not relieve the person who was negligent from the damage which his negligent act directly caused. *(Do wooden planks normally cause sparks? Are planks on ships usually wet?)*

minor? after caveat? fire case? (wind, temp, etc)

For these reasons the experienced arbitrators and the judge appealed from came, in my opinion, to a correct decision, and the appeal must be dismissed with costs.

Appeal dismissed.

[The concurring opinion of WARRINGTON, L.J., is omitted.]

Do you agree that this case stands for the proposition that proximate = direct? What does direct mean?

1. The "rule" of this case has had considerable support in the United States. See, e.g., Christianson v. Chicago, St. P., M. & O.R. Co., 67 Minn. 94, 69 N.W. 640 (1896) ("consequences which follow in unbroken sequence, without an intervening efficient cause, from the original negligent act are natural and proximate"); Ramsey v. Carolina–Tennessee Power Co., 195 N.C. 788, 143 S.E. 861 (1928); Lynch v. Fisher, 34 So.2d 513 (La.App.1948). What is the reason underlying the rule? Is the rule similar in nature to the early common law distinction between trespass and case? See page 3, supra. What supported that rule?

Is this the same? Is "direct" = "result" the same as "unbroken sequence"? Seems not. Principal case is direct = fire case is unbroken sequence

2. Was the petrol vapor in the hold an independent cause? Was the entire chain of events foreseeable? What happens if you rub two dry sticks together? Was it negligence to start to unload with petrol vapor permeating the hold?

3. Distinguish between unforeseeability of the result that has occurred and unforeseeability of the manner in which it is brought about. It is quite

generally agreed that the latter will not relieve the defendant of responsibility. A remarkable illustration is Bunting v. Hogsett, 139 Pa. 363, 21 A. 31 (1890), where negligent operation of defendant's industrial "dinky" engine caused a collision with a train on a crossing. Just before the collision the engineer of the "dinky" reversed the engine, shut off the steam, and jumped. The collision jarred loose the throttle, and the "dinky" engine backed up, gathering momentum, and traveled around a loop to a second crossing, where there was a second collision with the train. Plaintiff, a passenger on the train, was injured in the second collision. Defendant was held liable. See also Hill v. Winsor, 118 Mass. 251 (1875).

4. *Intentional Torts.* In Derosier v. New England Tel. & Tel. Co., 81 N.H. 451, 130 A. 145 (1925), the court made the following statement of policy, which has been much quoted: "In determining how far the law will trace causation and afford a remedy, the facts as to the defendant's intent, his imputable knowledge, or his justifiable ignorance are often taken into account. The moral element is here the factor that has turned close cases one way or the other. For an intended injury the law is astute to discover even very remote causation. For one which the defendant merely ought to have anticipated it has often stopped at an earlier stage of the investigation of causal connection. And as to those where there was neither knowledge nor duty to foresee, it has usually limited accountability to direct and immediate results."

This is undoubtedly true, although, it has represented a general and often unexpressed tendency, rather than any clear and definite lines of demarcation. There have, however, been a few decisions in which liability for intended injury has clearly been carried farther than for the same injury negligently inflicted. See, for example, as to suicide resulting from intentional misconduct, the cases cited, infra page 333.

OVERSEAS TANKSHIP (U.K.) LTD. v. MORTS DOCK & ENGINEERING CO., LTD.

"WAGON MOUND NO. 1"

Privy Council, 1961
[1961] A.C. 388.

[Plaintiff Morts Dock operated a wharf for shipbuilding and ship repairing in the Port of Sydney, Australia. The freighter Wagon Mound, owned by the defendants, was moored about 600 feet away. She carelessly discharged into the bay a large quantity of furnace oil, which spread across the surface. The oil came in contact with the slipways of plaintiffs' wharf, and interfered with their use, thus causing minor damage, which was so slight that plaintiffs made no claim for it. The oil was ignited when cotton waste floating on its surface was set fire by molten metal dropped from the wharf by plaintiff's workmen. The fire seriously damaged the wharf, as well as two ships docked alongside of it. The trial court specifically found that defendants "did not know and could not reasonably be expected to have known" that the oil (which was stated by counsel to have a flash point of about 170° F.) was capable of being set afire when spread on water. Judgment was given for the plaintiff, which was affirmed by the Supreme Court of New South Wales. Defendants appealed to the Privy Council, where the decision was reversed. After reviewing In re Polemis, supra page 295, and a number of subsequent British decisions, the court continued:]

VISCOUNT SIMONDS: * * * Enough has been said to show that the authority of *Polemis* has been severely shaken though lipservice has from time to time been paid to it. In their Lordships' opinion it should no longer be regarded as good law. It is not probable that many cases will for that reason have a different result, though it is hoped that the law will be thereby simplified, and that in some cases at least palpable injustice will be avoided. For it does not seem consonant with current ideas of justice or morality that for an act of negligence, however slight or venial, which results in some trivial foreseeable damage the actor should be liable for all consequences however unforeseeable and however grave, so long as they can be said to be "direct." It is a principle of civil liability, subject only to qualifications which have no present relevance, that a man must be considered to be responsible for the probable consequences of his act. To demand more of him is too harsh a rule, to demand less is to ignore that civilized order requires the observance of a minimum standard of behaviour.

This concept applied to the slowly developing law of negligence has led to a great variety of expressions which can, as it appears to their Lordships, be harmonized with little difficulty with the single exception of the so-called rule in *Polemis*. For, if it is asked why a man should be

Morts Dock after the fire

Morts Dock was never rebuilt

responsible for the natural or <u>necessary</u> or probable consequences of his
act (or any other similar description of them) the answer is that it is not
because they are natural or necessary or probable, but because, since
they have this quality, it is judged by the standard of the reasonable
man, that he ought to have foreseen them.   Thus it is that over and
over again it has happened that in different judgments in the same case
and sometimes in a single judgment liability for a consequence has been
imposed on the ground that it was reasonably foreseeable or alternatively on the ground that it was natural or necessary or probable.   The
two grounds have been treated as coterminous, and so they largely are.
But, where they are not, the question arises to which the wrong answer
was given in *Polemis*.   For, if some limitation must be imposed upon
the consequences for which the negligent actor is to be held responsible—and all are agreed that some limitation there must be—why
should that test (reasonable foreseeability) be rejected which, since he is
judged by what the reasonable man ought to foresee, corresponds with
the common conscience of mankind, and a test (the "direct" consequence) be substituted which leads to nowhere but the never ending
and insoluble problems of causation.

   It is, no doubt, proper when considering tortious liability for
negligence to analyze its elements and to say that the plaintiff must
prove a duty owed to him by the defendant, a breach of that duty by the
defendant, and consequent damage.   But there can be no liability until

[Handwritten marginal annotations:]
1
In reality, test is foreseeability.
2
Would ordinary reasonable prudent person during ops near working wharf not foreseeing that it might catch fire?
Is he saying that result need not be direct? Not necessarily. Rather, that even some direct results may be entirely unforeseeable, too remote. But, may an indirect result be entirely foreseeable and probable? See p. 297, n. 4.

the damage has been done. It is not the act but the consequences on which tortious liability is founded. Just as (as it has been said) there is no such thing as negligence in the air, so there is no such thing as liability in the air. Suppose an action brought by A for damage caused by the carelessness (a neutral word) of B, for example a fire caused by the careless spillage of oil. It may of course become relevant to know what duty B owed to A, but the only liability that is in question is the liability for damage by fire. It is vain to isolate the liability from its content and to say that B is or is not liable and then to ask for what damage he is liable. For his liability is in respect of that damage and no other. If, as admittedly it is, B's liability (culpability) depends on the reasonable foreseeability of the consequent damage, how is that to be determined except by the foreseeability of the damage which in fact happened—the damage in suit? And, if that damage is unforeseeable so as to displace liability at large, how can the liability be restored so as to make compensation payable?

But, it is said, a different position arises if B's careless act has been shown to be negligent and has caused some foreseeable damage to A. Their Lordships have already observed that to hold B liable for consequences however unforeseeable of a careless act, if, but only if, he is at the same time liable for some other damage however trivial, appears to be neither logical nor just. This becomes more clear if it is supposed that similar unforeseeable damage is suffered by A and C but other foreseeable damage, for which B is liable, by A only. A system of law which would hold B liable to A but not to C for the similar damage suffered by each of them could not easily be defended. Fortunately, the attempt is not necessary. For the same fallacy is at the root of the proposition. It is irrelevant to the question whether B is liable for unforeseeable damage that he is liable for foreseeable damage, as irrelevant as would the fact that he had trespassed on Whiteacre be to the question whether he had trespassed on Blackacre. Again suppose a claim by A for damage by fire by the careless act of B. Of what relevance is it to that claim that he has another claim arising out of the same careless act? It would surely not prejudice his claim if that other claim failed; it cannot assist it if it succeeds. Each of them rests on its own bottom and will fail if it can be established that the damage could not reasonably be foreseen. * * * As Lord Denning said in King v. Phillips, [1953] 1 Q.B. 429 at p. 441, there can be no doubt since Bourhill v. Young that the test of *liability for shock* is foreseeability of *injury by shock*. Their Lordships substitute the word "fire" for "shock" and endorse this statement of the law. * * *

[The appeal was allowed, and the action for damages caused by negligence dismissed. The case was remanded to the Full Court of New South Wales for disposition of an alternative claim for liability on the basis of nuisance, since their Lordships thought that it would not be proper for them to come to any conclusion upon the material before them. The plaintiffs decided not to proceed further with the nuisance liability, and their litigation ended with this decision of the Privy Council.]

---

1. The rule of this case has been the underlying premise of many decisions in the United States. See, e.g., Mauney v. Gulf Refining Co., 193 Miss. 421, 9 So.2d 780 (1942) ("The area within which liability is imposed is that which is within the circle of reasonable foreseeability"). Thus:

A. When defendant served "foul smelling" shrimp, he risked causing patron to become ill, but not causing someone else to trip on her vomit. Crankshaw v. Piedmont Driving Club, 115 Ga.App. 820, 156 S.E.2d 208 (1967).

B. When defendant bus driver drove at an unreasonable speed in a snowstorm, he risked a collision with another vehicle, but not creating a snow-swirl that would blind another driver who followed in his wake. Metts v. Griglak, 438 Pa. 392, 264 A.2d 684 (1970).

C. When defendant manufacturer supplied a defective metal ring on a dog collar, it risked causing the owner to lose his dog, but not causing the dog to bite plaintiff. Oehler v. Davis, 223 Pa.Super. 333, 298 A.2d 895 (1972) (products liability case applying proximate-cause principles of negligence law).

D. When defendant allowed a rug to remain on the floor after the wind had blown its edge up, he risked that a customer would trip over it, but not that the wind would wrap it around the legs of a customer using another door. Lyvere v. Ingles Markets, Inc., 36 N.C.App. 560, 244 S.E.2d 437 (1978).

2. Professor (now Judge) Robert E. Keeton has suggested a general rule that helps to explain Wagon Mound I and other cases that espouse its approach to proximate cause. One of his three formulations of the rule is: "A negligent actor is legally responsible for that harm, and only that harm, of which the negligent aspect of his conduct is a cause in fact." R. Keeton, Legal Cause in the Law of Torts, 9 (1963). How helpful is this formulation? Is it similar to the rationale of the *Palsgraf* case, infra page 304? Compare it to the rule as to violation of statutes intended to protect plaintiffs against a particular risk. See supra, page 213, note 1, B. Should the same rule apply when there is no statute, and the defendant's conduct creates only a particular risk? Or do the written law and the policy of strict statutory construction afford a reason to make a distinction?

3. The decision in the principal case apparently put an end to forty years of dispute, in various legal articles and a number of more or less conflicting cases, over the soundness of the rule of In re Polemis. Two excellent articles in which the whole matter is reviewed, and the case itself discussed, are Fleming, The Passing of Polemis, 39 Can.Bar Rev. 489 (1961); and Williams, The Risk Principle, 77 L.Q.Rev. 179 (1961). See also Green, Foreseeability in Negligence Law, 61 Colum.L.Rev. 1401 (1961).

4. Since the Privy Council was the highest appellate court for the Commonwealth and its decisions not binding in England, there was initially some doubt whether the case would be accepted by the English courts. This was finally set to rest in Doughty v. Turner Mfg. Co., [1964] 1 Q.B. 518, where an asbestos cement cover was knocked into a vat filled with an extremely hot solution of sodium cyanide, which might have been expected to splash some of the molten substance upon anyone standing nearby. Although no injuries were sustained when the cover was initially knocked into the vat, the molten liquid, following the laws of chemistry, erupted a short time later and caused injury to

the plaintiff. His recovery in the trial court was reversed, because there was no reason for anyone to expect the eruption.

5. Other English decisions have made it clear that there are some limits on the requirement of foreseeability laid down in Wagon Mound No. 1. Thus the way in which the event occurs need not be foreseeable, so long as the event itself is to be anticipated. Hughes v. Lord Advocate, [1963] A.C. 837. And the rule as to the thin skull, where the consequences of an actual personal injury are unforeseeable, continues to be applied. Smith v. Leech Brain & Co., [1962] 2 Q.B. 405.

6. Plaintiff is shot and wounded by two gunmen. He later learns that the gunmen were paid to kill him by defendant, who had read "gun for hire" advertisements in a national magazine for mercenaries. Plaintiff claims, in an action against the magazine publisher, that the injuries he suffered were foreseeable by the magazine when it decided to place the ad. What result? See Norwood v. Soldier of Fortune Magazine, Inc., 651 F.Supp. 1397 (W.D. Ark.1987). *No cause in fact*

OVERSEAS TANKSHIP (U.K.) LTD. v. MILLER STEAMSHIP CO.

"WAGON MOUND NO. 2"

Privy Council, 1966.
[1967] 1 A.C. 617.

[The facts are the same as in the preceding case, but this action was brought, on the grounds of nuisance and negligence, by the owners of the two ships docked at the wharf. The trial court, Walsh, J., made more elaborate findings on the issue of foreseeability, as follows:

"(1) Reasonable people in the position of the officers of the *Wagon Mound* would regard the furnace oil as very difficult to ignite upon water. (2) Their personal experience would probably have been that this had very rarely happened. (3) If they had given attention to the risk of fire from the spillage, they would have regarded it as a possibility, but one which could become an actuality only in very exceptional circumstances. (4) They would have considered the chances of the required exceptional circumstances happening whilst the oil remained spread on the harbour waters as being remote. (5) I find that the occurrence of damage to the plaintiff's property as a result of the spillage not reasonably foreseeable by those for whose acts the defendant would be responsible. * * * (8) Having regard to those findings, and because of finding (5), I hold that the claim of each of the plaintiffs, framed in negligence, fails."

Judgment for the defendants was affirmed by the Supreme Court of New South Wales, and plaintiffs appealed to the Privy Council.]

LORD REID [after holding that the count in nuisance added nothing, since it must be a nuisance founded upon negligence]. It is now necessary to turn to the respondents' submission that the trial judge was wrong in holding that damage from fire was not reasonably foreseeable. * * *

In *The Wagon Mound (No. 1)* the Board were not concerned with degrees of foreseeability because the finding was that the fire was not foreseeable at all. So Lord Simonds had no cause to amplify the statement that the "essential factor in determining liability is whether the damage is of such a kind as the reasonable man should have foreseen." But here the findings show that some risk of fire would have been present to the mind of a reasonable man in the shoes of the ship's chief engineer. So the first question must be what is the precise meaning to be attached in this context to the words "foreseeable" and "reasonably foreseeable."

[The court here referred to Bolton v. Stone, [1951] A.C. 850, where the risk that a cricket ball would be driven out of the grounds and strike a plaintiff on an unfrequented public road was held to be "so small that in the circumstances a reasonable man would have been justified in disregarding it and taking no steps to eliminate it."]

But it does not follow that, no matter what the circumstances may be, it is justifiable to neglect a risk of such a small magnitude. A reasonable man would only neglect such a risk if he had some valid reason for doing so, e.g., that it would involve considerable expense to eliminate the risk. He would weigh the risk against the difficulty of eliminating it. * * *

In the present case there was no justification whatever for discharging the oil into Sydney Harbour. Not only was it an offence to do so, but it involved considerable loss financially. If the ship's engineer had thought about the matter, there could have been no question of balancing the advantages and disadvantages. From every point of view it was both his duty and his interest to stop the discharge immediately.

It follows that in their Lordships' view the only question is whether a reasonable man having the knowledge and experience to be expected of the chief engineer of the *Wagon Mound* would have known that there was a real risk of the oil on the water catching fire in some way; if it did, serious damage to ships or other property was not only foreseeable but very likely. * * *

The findings show that he ought to have known that it is possible to ignite this kind of oil on water, and that the ship's engineer probably ought to have known that this had in fact happened before. The most that can be said to justify inaction is that he would have known that this could only happen in very exceptional circumstances. But this does not mean that a reasonable man would dismiss such a risk from his mind and do nothing when it was so easy to prevent it. If it is clear that the reasonable man would have realized or foreseen and prevented the risk, then it must follow that the appellant is liable in damages.

* * *

Appeal (of the ship owners) allowed.

1. Has *Polemis* come in again by the back door, in the guise of foreseeability of the remotely possible? Are there many events which the reasonable person would not recognize as possible, with a slight degree of risk?

2. Compare the formula of Learned Hand in United States v. Carroll Towing Co., supra page 146. How does it relate to this case?

3. There are good discussions of Wagon Mound No. 2 in Goodhart, The Brief Life Story of the Direct Consequence Law in English Tort Law, 53 Va.L. Rev. 857 (1967); Smith, The Limits of Tort Liability in Canada: Remoteness, Foreseeability and Proximate Cause, included in Linden, Studies in Canadian Tort Law (1968); Green, The Wagon Mound No. 2—Foreseeability Revisited, 1967 Utah L.Rev. 197. Dean Green, in the article above, suggests that "foreseeability" is being "overloaded." Is he right?

4. What about applying the rule of *Wagon Mound No. 2* in cases of injury to the person? See Rowe, Demise of the Thin Skull Rule, 40 Mod.L.Rev. 377 (1977).

PALSGRAF v. LONG ISLAND R.R. CO.

Court of Appeals of New York, 1928.
248 N.Y. 339, 162 N.E. 99.

CARDOZO, C.J. Plaintiff was standing on a platform of defendant's railroad after buying a ticket to go to Rockaway Beach. A train stopped at the station, bound for another place. Two men ran forward to catch it. One of the men reached the platform of the car without mishap, though the train was already moving. The other man, carrying a package, jumped aboard the car, but seemed unsteady as if about to fall. A guard on the car, who had held the door open, reached forward to help him in, and another guard on the platform pushed him from behind. In this act the package was dislodged, and fell upon the rails. It was a package of small size, about fifteen inches long, and was covered by a newspaper. In fact it contained fireworks, but there was nothing in its appearance to give notice of its contents. The fireworks when they fell exploded. The shock of the explosion threw down some scales at the other end of the platform many feet away. The scales struck the plaintiff, causing injuries for which she sues.

The conduct of the defendant's guard, if a wrong in its relation to the holder of the package, was not a wrong in its relation to the plaintiff, standing far away. Relatively to her it was not negligence at all. Nothing in the situation gave notice that the falling package had in it the potency of peril to persons thus removed. Negligence is not actionable unless it involves the invasion of a legally protected interest, the violation of a right. "Proof of negligence in the air, so to speak, will not do." Pollock, Torts (11th Ed.) p. 455 * * *

The plaintiff, as she stood upon the platform of the station, might claim to be protected against intentional invasion of her bodily security. Such invasion is not charged. She might claim to be protected against unintentional invasion by conduct involving in the thought of reasonable men an unreasonable hazard that such invasion would ensue. These, from the point of view of the law, were the bounds of her

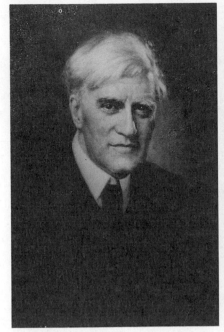 

Chief Judge Cardozo   Judge Andrews

immunity, with perhaps some rare exceptions, survival for the most part of ancient forms of liability, where conduct is held to be at the peril of the actor. [C] If no hazard was apparent to the eye of ordinary vigilance, an act innocent and harmless, at least to outward seeming, with reference to her, did not take to itself the quality of a tort because it happened to be a wrong, though apparently not one involving the risk of bodily insecurity, with reference to some one else. "In every instance, before negligence can be predicated of a given act, back of the act must be sought and found a duty to the individual complaining, the observance of which would have averted or avoided the injury." McSherry, C.J., in West Virginia Central & P.R. Co. v. State, 96 Md. 652, 666, 54 A. 669, 671. [Cc]

"The ideas of negligence and duty are strictly correlative." Bowen, L.J., in Thomas v. Quartermaine, 18 Q.B.D. 685, 694. The plaintiff sues in her own right for a wrong personal to her, and not as the vicarious beneficiary of a breach of duty to another.

A different conclusion will involve us, and swiftly too, in a maze of contradictions. A guard stumbles over a package which has been left upon a platform. It seems to be a bundle of newspapers. It turns out to be a can of dynamite. To the eye of ordinary vigilance, the bundle is abandoned waste, which may be kicked or trod on with impunity. Is a passenger at the other end of the platform protected by the law against the unsuspected hazard concealed beneath the waste? If not, is the

Scales of the type involved in *Palsgraf*

Scene of *Palsgraf* accident, taken a few years later
but with no change in features

result to be any different, so far as the distant passenger is concerned, when the guard stumbles over a valise which a truckman or a porter has left upon the walk? The passenger far away, if the victim of a wrong at all, has a cause of action, not derivative, but original and primary. His claim to be protected against invasion of his bodily security is neither greater nor less because the act resulting in the invasion is a wrong to another far removed. In this case, the rights that are said to have been violated, the interests said to have been invaded, are not even of the same order. The man was not injured in his person or even put in danger. The purpose of the act, as well as its effect, was to make his person safe. If there was a wrong to him at all, which may very well be doubted, it was a wrong to a property interest only, the safety of his package. Out of this wrong to property, which threatened injury to nothing else, there has passed, we are told, to the plaintiff by derivation or succession a right of action for the invasion of an interest of another order, the right to bodily security. The diversity of interests emphasizes the futility of the effort to build the plaintiff's right upon the basis of a wrong to some one else. Even then, the orbit of the danger as disclosed to the eye of reasonable vigilance would be the orbit of the duty. * * * *

The argument for the plaintiff is built upon the shifting meanings of such words as "wrong" and "wrongful," and shares their instability. What the plaintiff must show is "a wrong" to herself; i.e., a violation of her own right, and not merely a wrong to some one else, nor conduct, "wrongful" because unsocial, but not "a wrong" to any one. * * * The risk reasonably to be perceived defines the duty to be obeyed and risk imports relation; it is risk to another or to others within the range of apprehension. [C] This does not mean, of course, that one who launches a destructive force is always relieved of liability, if the force, though known to be destructive, pursues an unexpected path. "It was not necessary that the defendant should have had notice of the particular method in which an accident would occur, if the possibility of an accident was clear to the ordinarily prudent eye." Munsey v. Webb, 231 U.S. 150, 156. [Cc] Some acts, such as shooting are so imminently dangerous to any one who may come within reach of the missile however unexpectedly, as to impose a duty of prevision not far from that of an insurer. Even today, and much oftener in earlier stages of the law, one acts some times at one's peril. [Cc] Under this head, it may be, fall certain cases of what is known as transferred intent, an act willfully dangerous to A resulting by misadventure in injury to B. [Cc] These cases aside, wrong is defined in terms of the natural or probable, at least when unintentional. [Cc] The range of reasonable apprehension is at times a question for the court, and at times, if varying inferences are possible, a question for the jury. Here, by concession, there was nothing in the situation to suggest to the most cautious mind that the parcel wrapped in newspaper would spread wreckage through the station. If the guard had thrown it down knowingly and willfully, he would not have threatened the plaintiff's safety, so far as appearances could warn him. His conduct would not have involved, even then, an unreasonable probability of invasion of her bodily security. Liability can be no greater where the act is inadvertent.

Negligence, like risk, is thus a term of relation. Negligence in the abstract, apart from things related, is surely not a tort, if indeed it is understandable at all. * * *

The law of causation, remote or proximate, is thus foreign to the case before us. The question of liability is always anterior to the question of the measure of the consequences that go with liability. If there is no tort to be redressed, there is no occasion to consider what damage might be recovered if there were a finding of a tort. We may assume, without deciding, that negligence, not at large or in the abstract, but in relation to the plaintiff, would entail liability for any and all consequences, however novel or extraordinary. [Cc]

There is room for argument that a distinction is to be drawn according to the diversity of interests invaded by the act, as where conduct negligent in that it threatens an insignificant invasion of an interest in property results in an unforeseeable invasion of an interest of another order, as, e.g., one of bodily security. Perhaps other distinctions may be necessary. We do not go into the question now. The consequences to be followed must first be rooted in a wrong.

The judgment of the Appellate Division and that of the Trial Term should be reversed, and the complaint dismissed, with costs in all courts.

ANDREWS, J. (dissenting). Assisting a passenger to board a train, the defendant's servant negligently knocked a package from his arms. It fell between the platform and the cars. Of its contents the servant knew and could know nothing. A violent explosion followed. The concussion broke some scales standing a considerable distance away. In falling, they injured the plaintiff, an intending passenger.

Upon these facts, may she recover the damages she has suffered in an action brought against the master? The result we shall reach depends upon our theory as to the nature of negligence. Is it a relative concept—the breach of some duty owing to a particular person or to particular persons? Or, where there is an act which unreasonably threatens the safety of others, is the doer liable for all its proximate consequences, even where they result in injury to one who would generally be thought to be outside the radius of danger? This is not a mere dispute as to words. We might not believe that to the average mind the dropping of the bundle would seem to involve the probability of harm to the plaintiff standing many feet away whatever might be the case as to the owner or to one so near as to be likely to be struck by its fall. If, however, we adopt the second hypothesis, we have to inquire only as to the relation between cause and effect. We deal in terms of proximate cause, not of negligence. * * *

But we are told that "there is no negligence unless there is in the particular case a legal duty to take care, and this duty must be one

which is owed to the plaintiff himself and not merely to others."
Salmond Torts (6th Ed.) 24. This I think too narrow a conception.
Where there is the unreasonable act, and some right that may be
affected there is negligence whether damage does or does not result.
That is immaterial. Should we drive down Broadway at a reckless
speed, we are negligent whether we strike an approaching car or miss it
by an inch. The act itself is wrongful. It is a wrong not only to those
who happen to be within the radius of danger, but to all who might
have been there—a wrong to the public at large. Such is the language
of the street. Such the language of the courts when speaking of
contributory negligence.   *   *   *

Due care is a duty imposed on each one of us to protect society from
unnecessary danger, not to protect A, B, or C alone.

It may well be that there is no such thing as negligence in the
abstract. "Proof of negligence in the air, so to speak, will not do." In
an empty world negligence would not exist. It does involve a relationship between man and his fellows, but not merely a relationship
between man and those whom he might reasonably expect his act
would injure; rather, a relationship between him and those whom he
does in fact injure. If his act has a tendency to harm some one, it
harms him a mile away as surely as it does those on the scene.   *   *   *

The proposition is this: Every one owes to the world at large the
duty of refraining from those acts that may unreasonably threaten the
safety of others. Such an act occurs. Not only is he wronged to whom
harm might reasonably be expected to result, but he also who is in fact
injured, even if he be outside what would generally be thought the
danger zone. There needs be duty due the one complaining, but this is
not a duty to a particular individual because as to him harm might be
expected. Harm to some one being the natural result of the act, not
only that one alone, but all those in fact injured may complain. We
have never, I think, held otherwise.   *   *   * Unreasonable risk being
taken, its consequences are not confined to those who might probably
be hurt.   *   *   * An overturned lantern may burn all Chicago. We
may follow the fire from the shed to the last building. We rightly say
the fire started by the lantern caused its destruction.

A cause, but not the proximate cause. What we do mean by the
word "proximate" is that, because of convenience, of public policy, of a
rough sense of justice, the law arbitrarily declines to trace a series of
events beyond a certain point. This is not logic. It is practical politics.
Take our rule as to fires. Sparks from my burning haystack set on fire
my house and my neighbor's. I may recover from a negligent railroad.
He may not. Yet the wrongful act as directly harmed the one as the
other. We may regret that the line was drawn just where it was, but
drawn somewhere it had to be. We said the act of the railroad was not
the proximate cause of our neighbor's fire. "Cause" it surely was. The
words we used were simply indicative of our notions of public policy.
Other courts think differently.   *   *   *

Take the illustration given in an unpublished manuscript by a distinguished and helpful writer on the law of torts. A chauffeur negligently collides with another car which is filled with dynamite, although he could not know it. An explosion follows. A, walking on the sidewalk nearby, is killed. B, sitting in a window of a building opposite, is cut by flying glass. C, likewise sitting in a window a block away, is similarly injured. And a further illustration: A nursemaid, ten blocks away, startled by the noise, involuntarily drops a baby from her arms to the walk. We are told that C may not recover while A may. As to B it is a question for court or jury. We will agree that the baby might not. Because, we are again told, the chauffeur had no reason to believe his conduct involved any risk of injuring either C or the baby. As to them he was not negligent.

But the chauffeur being negligent in risking the collision, his belief that the scope of the harm he might do would be limited is immaterial. His act unreasonably jeopardized the safety of any one who might be affected by it. C's injury and that of the baby were directly traceable to the collision. Without that, the injury would not have happened. C had the right to sit in his office, secure from such dangers. The baby was entitled to use the sidewalk with reasonable safety.

The true theory is, it seems to me, that the injury to C, if in truth he is to be denied recovery, and the injury to the baby, is that their several injuries were not the proximate result of the negligence. And here not what the chauffeur had reason to believe would be the result of his conduct, but what the prudent would foresee, may have a bearing—may have some bearing, for the problem of proximate cause is not to be solved by any one consideration. It is all a question of expediency. There are no fixed rules to govern our judgment. There are simply matters of which we may take account. * * * There is in truth little to guide us other than common sense.

There are some hints that may help us. The proximate cause, involved as it may be with many other causes, must be, at the least, something without which the event would not happen. The court must ask itself whether there was a natural and continuous sequence between cause and effect. Was the one a substantial factor in producing the other? Was there a direct connection between them, without too many intervening causes? Is the effect of cause on result not too attenuated? Is the cause likely, in the usual judgment of mankind, to produce the result? Or, by the exercise of prudent foresight, could the result be foreseen? Is the result too remote from the cause, and here we consider remoteness in time and space. [C] Clearly we must so consider, for the greater the distance either in time or space, the more surely do other causes intervene to affect the result. When a lantern is overturned, the firing of a shed is a fairly direct consequence. Many things contribute to the spread of the conflagration—the force of the wind, the direction and width of streets, the character of intervening structures, other factors. We draw an uncertain and wavering line, but draw it we must as best we can.

* * * Once again, it is all a question of fair judgment, always keeping in mind the fact that we endeavor to make a rule in each case that will be practical and in keeping with the general understanding of mankind.

Here another question must be answered. In the case supposed, it is said, and said correctly, that the chauffeur is liable for the direct effect of the explosion, although he had no reason to suppose it would follow a collision. "The fact that the injury occurred in a different manner than that which might have been expected does not prevent the chauffeur's negligence from being in law the cause of the injury." But the natural results of a negligent act—the results which a prudent man would or should foresee—do have a bearing upon the decision as to proximate cause. We have said so repeatedly. What should be foreseen? No human foresight would suggest that a collision itself might injure one a block away. On the contrary, given an explosion, such a possibility might be reasonably expected. I think the direct connection, the foresight of which the courts speak, assumes prevision of the explosion, for the immediate results of which, at least, the chauffeur is responsible.

It may be said this is unjust. Why? In fairness he should make good every injury flowing from his negligence. Not because of tenderness toward him we say he need not answer for all that follows his wrong. We look back to the catastrophe, the fire kindled by the spark, or the explosion. We trace the consequences, not indefinitely, but to a certain point. And to aid us in fixing that point we ask what might ordinarily be expected to follow the fire or the explosion.

This last suggestion is the factor which must determine the case before us. The act upon which defendant's liability rests is knocking an apparently harmless package onto the platform. The act was negligent. For its proximate consequences the defendant is liable. If its contents were broken, to the owner; if it fell upon and crushed a passenger's foot, then to him; if it exploded and injured one in the immediate vicinity, to him also as to A in the illustration. Mrs. Palsgraf was standing some distance away. How far cannot be told from the record—apparently 25 or 30 feet, perhaps less. Except for the explosion, she would not have been injured. We are told by the appellant in his brief, "It cannot be denied that the explosion was the direct cause of the plaintiff's injuries." So it was a substantial factor in producing the result—there was here a natural and continuous sequence—direct connection. The only intervening cause was that, instead of blowing her to the ground, the concussion smashed the weighing machine which in turn fell upon her. There was no remoteness in time, little in space. And surely, given such an explosion as here, it needed no great foresight to predict that the natural result would be to injure one on the platform at no greater distance from its scene than was the plaintiff. Just how no one might be able to predict. Whether by flying fragments, by broken glass, by wreckage of machines or structures no one could say. But injury in some form was most probable.

Under these circumstances I cannot say as a matter of law that the plaintiff's injuries were not the proximate result of the negligence. That is all we have before us. The court refused to so charge. No request was made to submit the matter to the jury as a question of fact, even would that have been proper upon the record before us.

The judgment appealed from should be affirmed, with costs.

POUND, LEHMAN and KELLOGG, JJ., concur with CARDOZO, C.J.

ANDREWS, J., dissents in opinion in which CRANE and O'BRIEN, JJ., concur.

Judgment reversed, etc.

Who is P suing? (seemingly man w/ fireworks) but no, the RR.

1. Plaintiff on a motion for reargument pointed out that Mrs. Palsgraf stood much closer to the scene of the explosion than the majority opinion would suggest. Would this fact be likely to alter Judge Cardozo's decision in the case? See Palsgraf v. Long Island R. Co., 249 N.Y. 511, 164 N.E. 564 (1928).

2. The Record in this case is set out in Scott and Simpson, Cases on Civil Procedure, pp. 891–940 (1950). A study of it indicates that as described in the opinions, the event could not possibly have happened. These were apparently ordinary fireworks, and not bombs. Firecrackers were heard exploding; there was a "ball of fire" (from a Roman candle?), and a "mass of black smoke." All this happened in the pit below the edge of the platform, which would have protected the scale. No one testified to seeing it fall over. An appreciable interval elapsed after the first noise and smoke, during which Mrs. Palsgraf said to her daughter, "Elizabeth, turn your back." Then "the scale blew and hit me in the side." The platform was crowded, and there was no evidence of any other damage to anybody or anything. Plaintiff's original complaint, before amendment, alleged that the scale was knocked over by a stampede of frightened passengers. Would it make any difference in the decision?

what is author insinuating here?

The news story in the New York Times for August 25, 1924, p. 1, col. 4, differs in numerous details. It lists 13 persons injured, including Helen Polsgraf [sic], whose injury was "shock." It describes the events as happening at 11:25 a.m. at the East New York station, under the Atlantic Avenue stations, and a transfer point. There was a large crowd of excursionists, "jostling and pushing" to board a Jamaica express train. Three men, each carrying a large package, sought to board the train and a package fell to the tracks below. A large explosion rocked the car and tore away part of the platform and "overthrew a penny weighing machine more than ten feet away," smashing the glass and wrecking its mechanism. The police surmised that the three men, who disappeared, were Italians "bound for an Italian celebration somewhere on Long Island, where fireworks and bombs were to play an important role." The police decided that the event was an accident, with the man dropping the exploding package being jostled by the crowd. One of the other men dropped his parcel in the station as he fled, and it was found to contain fireworks of various kinds.

Further discussion of the facts is to be found in Prosser, Palsgraf Revisited, 52 Mich.L.Rev. 1 (1953); J. Noonan, Persons and Masks of the Law, c. 4 (1976); and Palsgraf Kin Tell Human Side of Famed Case, 66 Harv.L.Record [No. 8] 1

(Apr. 14, 1978). On the relationship of the case to the Restatement of Torts, see Prosser and Noonan, supra, and R. Keeton, A Palsgraf Anecdote, 56 Tex.L.Rev. 513 (1978).

3. Accepting the facts as stated, Mrs. Palsgraf was a passenger. She had bought her ticket, and started her trip by going upon the platform. Did the defendant owe her no duty? Was there no relation between them? This is ignored by both opinions. Would it make any difference?

4. If the "scale" in question could be toppled over by the explosion of fireworks some distance away, it may not have been steadily anchored to the railroad platform. Does this suggest an argument that might have allowed plaintiff to prevail under the language and rationale of Judge Cardozo's opinion?

5. How does the decision square with In re Polemis, supra page 295? The Restatement of Torts approved both cases, in § 281, and in § 433, Comment e. Are they consistent? How much sense does a reconciliation make?

6. Both opinions in *Palsgraf* have been cited scores of times; almost every practicing lawyer knows the case by name and it has served as a stimulus for legal writers to work out their own ideas, and endeavor to line up "duty" and "proximate cause." See, among many others, Green, The Palsgraf Case, 30 Colum.L.Rev. 789 (1930), reprinted in L. Green, Judge and Jury, ch. 8 (1930); Goodhart, The Unforeseeable Consequences of a Negligent Act, 39 Yale L.J. 449 (1930); Campbell, Duty, Fault and Legal Cause, 1938 Wis.L.Rev. 402; Cowan, The Riddle of the Palsgraf Case, 23 Minn.L.Rev. 46 (1938); Gregory, Proximate Cause in Negligence—A Retreat from Rationalization, 6 U.Chi.L.Rev. 36 (1938); Seavey, Mr. Justice Cardozo and the Law of Torts, 52 Harv.L.Rev. 372 (1939), 48 Yale L.J. 390 (1939), 39 Colum.L.Rev. 20 (1939); Ehrenzweig, Loss–Shifting and Quasi–Negligence: A New Interpretation of the Palsgraf Case, 8 U.Chi.L.Rev. 729 (1941); Prosser, Palsgraf Revisited, 52 Mich.L.Rev. 1 (1953), reprinted in Prosser, Selected Topics on the Law of Torts, 191 (1953); James, Scope of Duty in Negligence Cases, 47 Nw.U.L.Rev. 778 (1953); Thode, Tort Analysis: Duty–Risk v. Proximate Cause and the Rational Allocation of Functions Between Judge and Jury, 1977 Utah L.Rev. 1; Reynolds, Limits on Negligence Liability: Palsgraf at 50, 32 Okla.L.Rev. 63 (1979).

7. How important is all this as a practical matter? How often will a case involve direct causation and a clearly unforeseeable plaintiff? In a recurring situation, a vehicle negligently strikes a person, knocks his body off at an angle, hitting plaintiff who had been in a position of apparent safety. Is plaintiff "unforeseeable"? A number of courts have allowed recovery. See Kommerstad v. Great N.R. Co., 120 Minn. 376, 139 N.W. 713 (1913); Alabama Great S.R. Co. v. Chapman, 80 Ala. 615, 2 So. 738 (1886); Wolfe v. Checker Taxi Co., 299 Mass. 225, 12 N.E.2d 849 (1938). On the other hand, the Supreme Court of Pennsylvania has twice declared that this fact pattern presents an "unforeseeable" plaintiff. See Wood v. Pennsylvania R. Co., 177 Pa. 306, 35 A. 699 (1896) (train); Dahlstrom v. Shrum, 368 Pa. 423, 84 A.2d 289 (1951) (bus).

For some cases following *Palsgraf,* see Tucker v. Collar, 79 Ariz. 141, 285 P.2d 178 (1955) (defective machinery supplied by defendant to a tenant started a fire which burned the landlord's building); Diamond State Tel. Co. v. Atlantic Refining Co., 205 F.2d 402 (3d Cir.1953) (defendant negligently collided with a boat, and damaged plaintiff's cable, which defendant had no reason to expect to be attached to the boat); Radigan v. W.J. Halloran Co., 97 R.I. 122, 196 A.2d 160 (1963) (defendant negligently brought a crane into contact with an uninsulated high tension power line, and electricity passed through the crane, through an electrical conduit in the ground, and burned a hole in a gas main, which ultimately resulted in explosion of gas on the third floor of a fire station).

Palsgraf has been rejected by other cases. See Jackson v. B. Lowenstein & Bros., 175 Tenn. 535, 136 S.W.2d 495 (1940); Pfeifer v. Standard Gateway Theater, 262 Wis. 229, 55 N.W.2d 29 (1952). In the Jackson case, a customer in a department store fell on a defective mat at the top of the stairway. Her potential rescuer jostled another customer who fell and injured plaintiff who was around the corner of the stairs. Would this be decided in favor of plaintiff or defendant under the majority opinion in *Palsgraf?*

8. The *Palsgraf* Case also has been relied on in a few other types of cases which would appear to be better explained on other grounds. Thus:

A. Violation of statutes intended for the protection of a class of persons in which plaintiff is not included. Flynn v. Gordon, 86 N.H. 198, 165 A. 715 (1933); Chicago, B. & Q.R. Co. v. Murray, 40 Wyo. 324, 277 P. 703 (1929).

B. Mental distress suffered by the plaintiff at harm or peril to another, as where a mother sees her child run down before her eyes. Cote v. Litawa, 96 N.H. 174, 71 A.2d 792 (1950); Resavage v. Davies, 199 Md. 479, 86 A.2d 879 (1952).

C. Pecuniary loss to one resulting from injury to another, as in the case of an insurance company which has covered the risk. Sinram v. Pennsylvania R. Co., 61 F.2d 767 (2d Cir.1932). See State of Louisiana ex rel. Guste v. M/V Testbank, infra page 1108.

9. The suggestion in the next to the last paragraph of Cardozo's opinion, that defendant's negligence must not only create a risk of harm to the plaintiff, but to the particular interest of the plaintiff which is in fact invaded, was taken up by the Restatement of Torts § 281, Comment g. Illustration 3, there given, is to the effect that if the fireworks had put out the eye of the passenger with the package, he could not have recovered, since he was not threatened with harm to his interest in his eye. This is supported by one case, Texas & Pac. R. Co. v. Bigham, 90 Tex. 223, 38 S.W. 162 (1896), where harm was threatened to plaintiff's cattle, and they stampeded and inflicted personal injury on him. Most courts have rejected the distinction. Mitchell v. Friedman, 11 N.J.Super. 344, 78 A.2d 417 (1951) (harm to toilet, and personal injury); Brackett v. Bellows Falls Hydro–Elec. Corp., 87 N.H. 173, 175 A. 822 (1934) (harm to land, personal injury); Atherton v. Goodwin, 163 Kan. 22, 180 P.2d 296 (1947) (harm to scales, pecuniary loss). The Restatement (Second) of Torts § 281, Comment j, has rejected the limitation. An interesting discussion of the question by a writer who first supported the distinction, and then changed his mind, is Payne, Negligence and Interest: A Comment, 18 Mod.L.Rev. 43 (1955).

10. With the pair of *Wagon Mound* cases, compare the pair of *Kinsman* cases. Petition of Kinsman Transit Co., 338 F.2d 708 (2d Cir. 1964) ("Kinsman No. 1"), arose out of a "series of misadventures" that happened during the night of January 21, 1959. Employees of Kinsman Transit Company improperly moored a ship, the Shivas, at a dock operated by the Continental Grain Company, in the Buffalo River, at a point nearly three miles above a lift bridge maintained by the City of Buffalo. The river, winding and about 200 feet wide, was full of floating ice, which was moving with a rapid current. Ice and debris accumulated, building a wedge between the ship and the dock. Pressure from the wedge snapped the mooring lines and pulled out an improperly anchored "deadman," or mooring block.

The Shivas broke loose and drifted downstream. She collided with another ship, the Tewksbury, which had been properly moored at its dock. The collision broke the Tewksbury loose, and the two ships went on down the river together. Frantic telephone calls to city workers at the bridge to have them raise it in time went unanswered because one bridge crew had gone off duty, and another was late in coming on. By the time the second crew began to raise the drawbridge, it was too late. The ships crashed into the center of the bridge and caused it to collapse. Ice jammed in behind the wreckage; the river backed up, and property on the banks of the Buffalo River flooded as far upstream as the Continental dock.

On some twenty claims for such property damage, the trial court found negligence and liability on the part of Kinsman, Continental, and the City of Buffalo, and entered its decree accordingly. Affirming the trial court's decision, the Court of Appeals (Friendly, J.) stated:

"The weight of authority in this country rejects the limitation of damages to consequences foreseeable at the time of the negligent conduct when the consequences are 'direct,' and the damage, although other and greater than expectable, is of the same general sort that was risked. [Cc] Other American courts, purporting to apply a test of foreseeability to damages, extend that concept to such unforeseen lengths as to raise serious doubt whether the concept is meaningful; indeed, we wonder whether the British courts are not finding it necessary to limit the language of the Wagon Mound as we have indicated." Id. at 724–25.

The court also noted that as long as the actor's risk, no matter how small, was "of the same general sort, from the same forces, and to the same class of persons," id. at 725, then the actor would be liable if he failed to exercise due care.

The court realized, however, that there must be some limitation to this. "Somewhere a point will be reached when courts will agree that the link has become too tenuous—that what is claimed to be consequence is only fortuity." Id. Finally, the court echoed the words of Judge Andrews dissenting in *Palsgraf*, supra at pages 310, 311: "It is all a question of expediency, * * * of fair judgment, always keeping in mind the fact that we endeavor to make a rule in each case that will be practical and in keeping with the general understanding of mankind."

Suppose flooding had reached property up-river from the place where the Shivas had been docked? Cf. Note, 49 Minn.L.Rev. 1052 (1965).

Four years after the first *Kinsman* decision, the same court heard another complaint based upon the same facts. Petition of Kinsman Transmit Co. ("Kinsman No. 2"), 388 F.2d 821 (2d Cir.1968). This claim, however, was brought by owners of wheat stored aboard a ship berthed in the Buffalo harbor below the bridge. Because of the accident, the ship could not be moved and unloaded at the shipper's grain elevators located above the collapsed bridge; and the shipper was put to considerable additional expense for extra transportation and storage costs and for the purchase of replacement wheat.

Affirming the lower court's ruling, the court (Kaufman, J.) held that "the injuries to [the shippers] were too 'remote' or 'indirect' a consequence of defendant's negligence." Id. at 824. In effect, the Court was stating that the facts in the *Kinsman* No. 2 case had reached a point at which the consequences were too "tenuous" for liability.

The court noted, however, that the trial judge had reached the same result by differentiating between "negligent interference with contractual relations," and negligent of physical integrity of property, involved in *Kinsman No. 1.* The latter was entitled to protection; the former was not. The appellate court in *Kinsman No. 2* stated that it would "hesitate" to embrace the suggested distinction, although it reached the same result as the trial judge did on "remoteness" grounds alone. Do you find the distinction valid? Useful? Cf. State of Louisiana ex rel. Guste v. M/V Testbank, infra page 1108 and notes.

2. INTERVENING CAUSES

DERDIARIAN v. FELIX CONTRACTING CORP.

New York Court of Appeals, 1981.
51 N.Y.2d 308, 414 N.E.2d 666, 434 N.Y.S.2d 166.

[Defendant Felix Contracting Corporation, in performing a contract to install an underground gas main in Mount Vernon, N.Y., had excavated a worksite in the street. Plaintiff Derdiarian, employee of a subcontractor, was engaged in sealing a gas main.]

COOKE, CHIEF JUDGE. * * * On the afternoon of November 21, 1973, defendant James Dickens suffered an epileptic seizure and lost consciousness, allowing his vehicle to careen into the work site and strike plaintiff with such force as to throw him into the air. When plaintiff landed, he was splattered over his face, head and body with 400 degree boiling hot liquid enamel from a kettle struck by the automobile. The enamel was used in connection with sealing the gas main. Although plaintiff's body ignited into a fire ball, he miraculously survived the incident.

At trial, plaintiff's theory was that defendant Felix had negligently failed to take adequate measures to insure the safety of workers on the excavation site. * * *

To support his claim of an unsafe work site, plaintiff called as a witness Lawrence Lawton, an expert in traffic safety. According to Lawton, the usual and accepted method of safeguarding the workers is to erect a barrier around the excavation. Such a barrier, consisting of a truck, a piece of heavy equipment or a pile of dirt, would keep a car out of the excavation and protect workers from oncoming traffic. The expert testified that the barrier should cover the entire width of the excavation. He also stated that there should have been two flagmen present, rather than one, and that warning signs should have been posted advising motorists that there was only one lane of traffic and that there was a flagman ahead.

* * * Defendant Felix now argues that plaintiff was injured in a freakish accident, brought about solely by defendant Dickens' negligence, and therefore there was no causal link, as a matter of law, between Felix' breach of duty and plaintiff's injuries.

The concept of proximate cause, or more appropriately legal cause, has proven to be an elusive one, incapable of being precisely defined to cover all situations * * *.

Where the acts of a third person intervene between the defendant's conduct and the plaintiff's injury, the causal connection is not automatically severed. In such a case, liability turns upon whether the intervening act is a normal or foreseeable consequence of the situation created by the defendant's negligence. [Cc] If the intervening act is extraordinary under the circumstances, not foreseeable in the normal course of events, or independent of or far removed from the defendant's conduct, it may well be a superseding act which breaks the causal nexus. [Cc] Because questions concerning what is foreseeable and what is normal may be the subject of varying inferences, as is the question of negligence itself, these issues generally are for the fact finder to resolve.

There are certain instances, to be sure, where only one conclusion may be drawn from the established facts and where the question of legal cause may be decided as a matter of law. Those cases generally involve independent intervening acts which operate upon but do not flow from the original negligence. Thus, for instance, we have held that where an automobile lessor negligently supplies a car with a defective trunk lid, it is not liable to the lessee who, while stopped to repair the trunk, was injured by the negligent driving of a third party. [C] Although the renter's negligence undoubtedly served to place the injured party at the site of the accident, the intervening act was divorced from and not the foreseeable risk associated with the original negligence. And the injuries were different in kind than those which would have normally been expected from a defective trunk. In short, the negligence of the renter merely furnished the occasion for an unrelated act to cause injuries not ordinarily anticipated. [C]

By contrast, in the present case, we cannot say as a matter of law that defendant Dickens' negligence was a superseding cause which interrupted the link between Felix' negligence and plaintiff's injuries. From the evidence in the record, the jury could have found that Felix negligently failed to safeguard the excavation site. A prime hazard associated with such dereliction is the possibility that a driver will negligently enter the work site and cause injury to a worker. That the driver was negligent, or even reckless, does not insulate Felix from liability. [Cc] Nor is it decisive that the driver lost control of the vehicle through a negligent failure to take medication, rather than a driving mistake. [C] The precise manner of the event need not be anticipated. The finder of fact could have concluded that the foreseeable, normal and natural result of the risk created by Felix was the injury of a worker by a car entering the improperly protected work area. An intervening act may not serve as a superseding cause, and relieve an actor of responsibility, where the risk of the intervening act occurring is the very same risk which renders the actor negligent.

In a similar vein, plaintiff's act of placing the kettle on the west side of the excavation does not, as a matter of law, absolve defendant Felix of responsibility. Serious injury, or even death, was a foreseeable consequence of a vehicle crashing through the work area. The injury could have occurred in numerous ways, ranging from a worker being directly struck by the car to the car hitting an object that injures the worker. Placement of the kettle, or any object in the work area, could affect how the accident occurs and the extent of injuries. That defendant could not anticipate the precise manner of the accident or the exact extent of injuries, however, does not preclude liability as a matter of law where the general risk and character of injuries are foreseeable.

* * *

For the foregoing reasons, the order of the Appellate Division should be affirmed, with costs.

---

1. Why did plaintiff's attorney not seek to impose liability onto the automobile driver, Mr. Dickens? Does your answer have a bearing on whether this decision was correct?

2. *Intervening Negligence.* Distinguish:

A. Defendant is negligent only because he creates the risk that plaintiff will be injured through the negligence of a third party. Defendant sets off an auto alarm at 4:00 a.m. while attempting to repossess a car. In the resulting confusion, a neighbor is shot. Griffith v. Valley of Sun Recovery & Adjustment Bureau, Inc., 126 Ariz. 227, 613 P.2d 1283 (1980).

B. Defendant creates a risk of a particular result and the negligence of a third person, whether foreseeable or not, brings about that result. A wrecking company failed to secure a condemned house prior to demolition. Vagrants living in the house accidently burned the house down. Aetna Ins. Co. v. 3 Oaks Wrecking and Lumber Co., 65 Ill.App.3d 618, 21 Ill.Dec. 919, 382 N.E.2d 283 (1978).

C. Defendant creates a particular risk, and the unforeseeable negligence of a third person brings about an entirely different result. He parks his car blocking a fireplug, and a negligently driven automobile collides with it, so that a passenger in the second car is injured. Cf. Falk v. Finkelman, 268 Mass. 524, 168 N.E. 89 (1929).

Does liability stand upon the same footing in all three cases?

3. A rock radio station with an extensive teenage audience conducted a contest that rewarded the first contestant to locate a peripatetic disc jockey. Two minors driving in separate automobiles attempted to follow the disc jockey's automobile to its next stop. In the course of their pursuit, at speeds up to 80 m.p.h., one of the minors negligently forced a car off the highway, killing the driver. Wrongful death action against the radio station. What result? Weirum v. RKO Gen., Inc., 15 Cal.3d 40, 539 P.2d 36, 123 Cal.Rptr. 468 (1975).

4. Note that a plaintiff's own conduct can constitute an intervening cause that breaks the causal connection between defendant's negligence and the injury. However, in order to be a superseding cause, plaintiff's conduct must be more than contributory negligence that would be relevant in apportioning negligent conduct, and must, in addition to being unforeseeable, rise to such a

level of culpability as to replace defendant's negligence as the legal cause of the injury. For example, in Mesick v. State of New York, 118 A.D.2d 214, 504 N.Y.S.2d 279 (1986), plaintiff's conduct was not a superseding cause of his injuries when he swung himself from a rope tied to a tree branch out into a water hole and fell onto jagged rocks. There was evidence that the defendant, State of New York, was aware that the rope had been tied to the tree and was used by people who swam at the water hole.

5. Dealer negligently failed to tighten lug bolts on the wheels of Hairston's newly purchased automobile. A wheel fell off and Hairston brought the car safely to a stop on a bridge. A van stopped behind Hairston's auto, and the driver offered to assist Hairston. Hairston got out and was standing behind his car when Alexander's flatbed truck rammed into the van stopped behind Hairston, propelling the van into Hairston, who was killed. The court held the dealer liable even though the conduct of the driver of the flatbed truck was "inexcusable." His conduct, however, was not "so highly improbable and extraordinary an occurrence in this series of events as to bear no reasonable connection to the harm threatened" by the dealer's original negligence. The superseding act of Alexander's negligent driving was therefore in the "area of risk created by the negligence" of dealer not tightening the lug bolts. Hairston v. Alexander Tank and Equipment Co., 310 N.C. 227, 311 S.E.2d 559, 567 (1984).

6. Defendant, under an obligation to furnish a safe place to work, set plaintiff, its employee, at cleaning a coin-operated machine with gasoline in a small room in which there was a lighted gas heater with an open flame. While he was working, a rat escaped from the machine and ran to take refuge under a heater, where its fur, impregnated with gasoline fumes, caught fire from the flame. The rat "returned in haste and flames to its original hideout," and exploded the gasoline vapor inside the machine, injuring the plaintiff. Is defendant liable? United Novelty Co. v. Daniels, 42 So.2d 395 (Miss. 1949).

7. Should a drunk operator of a boat who causes an accident be fully liable? Suppose he claims that a superseding cause of the accident was the defective condition of the boat? See generally Annot., 35 A.L.R. 4th 104 (1985).

8. The cases in the prior section of this Chapter did not turn primarily on the effect of intervening causes. According to the Restatement (Second) of Torts § 441: "An intervening force is one which actively operates in producing harm to another after the actor's negligent act or omission has been committed."

According to McLaughlin, Proximate Cause, 39 Harv.L.Rev. 149, 159 (1925): "An intervening force is a force which is neither operating in the defendant's presence, nor at the place where the defendant's act takes effect at the time of the defendant's act, but comes into effective operation at or before the time of the damage."

9. The test for determining whether an intervening force constitutes a superseding cause is often couched in terms of foreseeability. See Restatement (Second) of Torts § 477 (1965). A person must foresee the normal consequences of his conduct, but is not responsible for extraordinarily negligent intervening acts of third persons. On considerations important in determining whether an intervening force is a superseding cause, see Restatement of Torts § 442.

10. *Act of God.* One standard type of "intervening force" is called an "act of God," "vis major" or "force of nature." In Kimble v. Mackintosh Hemphill Co., 359 Pa. 461, 59 A.2d 68, 71–72 (1948), defendant was not relieved of liability when a section of a negligently maintained roof crashed, falling onto and

killing plaintiff. The defendant claimed that the roof collapsed as a result of extremely high winds. The court stated, "We cannot say that the intervening cause [of the high winds] was vis major. One who fails in his duty to remedy a defective or dangerous condition is liable for injuries resulting therefrom, although the immediate cause of the injury is the wind. [Cc] The causal connection is not broken, and the original wrongdoer is liable for the injury sustained." Note how the issue in Kimble differs from Blyth v. Birmingham Waterworks Co., supra page 138. Is it consistent in principle with the *Anderson* "twin fires" case, supra page 279? The Restatement § 450 defines force of nature, and § 451 outlines the consideration that will make the force of nature a superseding cause.

11. In which of these situations should the defendant be exonerated?:

A. Defendant did not inspect a telephone pole for 14 years or replace it when it rotted. It is felled during a 12–inch snowfall and injures plaintiff. Bowman v. Columbia Tel. Co., 406 Pa. 455, 179 A.2d 197 (1962).

B. Defendant stops on the side of a highway during a fog in order to give plaintiff a ride. Plaintiff attempts to cross the highway and is hit by a third party. Augustine v. Hitzman, 287 Minn. 311, 178 N.W.2d 227 (1970).

C. A charter plane company negligently fails to supply one of its vehicles with sufficient fuel. The pilot is forced to make an emergency landing on a small island in the Pacific. A volcano erupts and kills a passenger. Cf. Doss v. Big Stone Gap, 145 Va. 520, 134 S.E. 563 (1926).

12. Can an employer's failure to follow manufacturer's instructions shield the otherwise negligent manufacturer from liability when an employee is injured while using the product? See Noel v. Esgard, Inc., 411 So.2d 1108 (La. App.1982). Does an action exist against the negligent employer? If the employee's claim is covered by workers' compensation insurance, will the employer's negligence be considered? See Varela v. American Petrofina Co., 658 S.W.2d 561 (Tex.1983), holding that the injured party had no claim against the negligent employer.

13. Remember that there may be more than one proximate cause of an injury and, therefore, more than one defendant may be held jointly and severally liable. Is it then correct to instruct the jury that the defendant's negligence must be "the" proximate cause of the injury? Is such an instruction necessarily prejudicial? Barringer v. Arnold, 358 Mich. 594, 101 N.W.2d 365 (1960); Gantt v. Sissell, 222 Ark. 902, 263 S.W.2d 916 (1954).

WATSON v. KENTUCKY & INDIANA BRIDGE & R.R. CO.

Court of Appeals of Kentucky, 1910.
137 Ky. 619, 126 S.W. 146.

[Through the negligence of the defendant railroad, a tank car full of gasoline was derailed and its valve broken, so that the gasoline ran into the street. One Duerr struck a match, igniting the gasoline vapor, and an explosion followed, injuring plaintiff, a bystander. Duerr testified that he struck the match to light a cigar, and that when he dropped the match the explosion occurred before it reached the ground. Other witnesses testified that Duerr had said to a companion, "Let's go set the damn thing on fire," that he struck the match against a fence

A rather imperative name for a judge.

and deliberately threw it into the gasoline vapor. The trial court directed a verdict for the defendant, and plaintiff appealed.]

SETTLE, J. * * * The lighting of the match by Duerr having resulted in the explosion, the question is, was that act merely a contributing cause, or the efficient and, therefore, proximate cause of appellant's injuries? The question of proximate cause is a question for the jury. In holding that Duerr in lighting or throwing the match acted maliciously or with intent to cause the explosion, the trial court invaded the province of the jury. There was, it is true, evidence tending to prove that the act was wanton or malicious, but also evidence conducing to prove that it was inadvertently or negligently done by Duerr. It was therefore for the jury and not the court to determine from all the evidence whether the lighting of the match was done by Duerr inadvertently or negligently, or whether it was a wanton and malicious act. * * *

If the presence on Madison street in the city of Louisville of the great volume of loose gas that arose from the escaping gasoline was caused by the negligence of the appellee Bridge & Railroad Company it seems to us that the probable consequence of its coming in contact with fire and causing an explosion was too plain a proposition to admit of doubt. Indeed, it was most probable that some one would strike a match to light a cigar or for other purposes in the midst of the gas. In our opinion, therefore, the act of one lighting and throwing a match under such circumstances cannot be said to be the efficient cause of the explosion. It did not of itself produce the explosion, nor could it have done so without the assistance and contribution resulting from the primary negligence, if there was such negligence, on the part of the appellee Bridge & Railroad Company in furnishing the presence of the gas in the street. This conclusion, however, rests upon the theory that Duerr inadvertently or negligently lighted and threw the match in the gas.

If, however, the act of Duerr in lighting the match and throwing it into the vapor or gas arising from the gasoline was malicious, and done for the purpose of causing the explosion, we do not think appellees would be responsible, for while the appellee Bridge & Railroad Company's negligence may have been the efficient cause of the presence of the gas in the street, and it should have understood enough of the consequences thereof to have foreseen that an explosion was likely to result from the inadvertent or negligent lighting of a match by some person who was ignorant of the presence of the gas or of the effect of lighting or throwing a match in it, it could not have foreseen or deemed it probable that one would maliciously or wantonly do such an act for the evil purpose of producing the explosion. Therefore, if the act of Duerr was malicious, we quite agree with the trial court that it was one which the appellees could not reasonably have anticipated or guarded against, and in such case the act of Duerr, and not the primary negligence of the appellee Bridge & Railroad Company, in any of the particulars charged, was the efficient or proximate cause of appellant's injuries. The mere

See n. 13 previous case

fact that the concurrent cause or intervening act was unforeseen will not relieve the defendant guilty of the primary negligence from liability, but if the intervening agency is something so unexpected or extraordinary as that he could not or ought not to have anticipated it, he will not be liable, and certainly he is not bound to anticipate the criminal acts of others by which damage is inflicted and hence is not liable therefor.

For the reasons indicated, the judgment is * * * reversed as to the Bridge & Railroad Company, and the cause remanded for a new trial consistent with the opinion.

1. *Intervening Intentional Misconduct.* Defendant service station attendant sold a small amount of gasoline to six-year-old Penny Jones. Penny falsely told the attendant that her mother had requested it. Later that day, Penny's four-year-old half-sister Candy threw a lighted match into the gasoline and the ensuing flames ignited her legs and dress. Is defendant liable? Can the principal case be distinguished? See Jones v. Robbins, 289 So.2d 104 (La.1974).

2. In Village of Carterville v. Cook, 129 Ill. 152, 22 N.E. 14 (1889), defendant excavated a hole in the sidewalk and a third person negligently jostled the plaintiff into it. Defendant was held liable. What if the third person had deliberately pushed plaintiff into the hole? Alexander v. New Castle, 115 Ind. 51, 17 N.E. 200 (1888); Milostan v. Chicago, 148 Ill.App. 540 (1909).

3. Defendant left the door of its elevator shaft unlocked and unguarded. A stranger, impersonating an elevator boy, politely ushered plaintiff through the door. She fell down the shaft and was injured. Is defendant liable? Cole v. German Savings & Loan Society, 124 F. 113 (8th Cir.1903).

4. In Parness v. Tempe, 123 Ariz. 460, 600 P.2d 764 (1979), a young boy was pushed to the ground by two others at a neighborhood recreation center. The center did not provide adequate supervision. Should it be liable for the intentional conduct of others?

5. *Intervening Criminal Acts.* Under ordinary circumstances, is it reasonably to be expected that any one will criminally tamper with a railroad track? Deyo v. New York Central R. Co., 34 N.Y. 9, 88 Am.Dec. 418 (1865). What if there is a strike in progress, with a record of continued violence on the part of the strikers? Int'l & G.N.R. Co. v. Johnson, 23 Tex.Civ.App. 160, 203, 55 S.W. 772 (1900). In the absence of any special circumstances, should the defendant anticipate forgery of a check? Benenson v. National Surety Co., 260 N.Y. 299, 183 N.E. 505 (1932). Assault upon a railway passenger? Hoff v. Public Service R. Co., 91 N.J.L. 641, 103 A. 209 (1918). A baseball umpire? Toone v. Adams, 262 N.C. 403, 137 S.E.2d 132 (1964).

6. It is probably impossible to state any comprehensive rule as to when a defendant will be liable for the intervening criminal act of a third person. See Restatement (Second) of Torts §§ 448–449 (1965); and see also Eldredge, Culpable Intervention as Superseding Cause, 86 U.Pa.L.Rev. 121 (1937), reprinted in Eldredge, Modern Tort Problems, 205 (1941); Feezer, Intervening Crime and Liability for Negligence, 24 Minn.L.Rev. 635 (1940). Some of the more common situations in which liability has been found are the following:

A. Defendant, by contract or otherwise, is under a duty to protect plaintiff against criminal misconduct, and fails to do so. See, e.g., Silva v. Showcase Cinemas Concessions of Dedham, Inc., 736 F.2d 810, 813 (1st Cir.1984), cert. denied, 469 U.S. 883 (1984), where the court held that a jury could reasonably find that a proximate cause of plaintiff's being stabbed to death was the theatre's failure adequately to patrol its premises. See also Cherry, Liability of Business Property Owners for Injury to Customers in Parking Lots by Criminal Attacks From Third Parties, 13 Real Est.L.J. 141 (1984). Similar liability may be imposed upon lessors and their duty to protect lessees, and a government's obligation to its citizens.

B. Defendant's affirmative act destroys or defeats a protection which plaintiff has placed around his person or property to guard them against crime. Defendant, who has leased floor space in plaintiff's jewelry store, goes to the store on a holiday, and leaves the key in the front door. Garceau v. Engel, 169 Minn. 62, 210 N.W. 608 (1926). Cf. Southwestern Bell Tel. Co. v. Adams, 199 Ark. 254, 133 S.W.2d 867 (1939) (defendant left windows of plaintiff's warehouse open). Contra, Andrews v. Kinsel, 114 Ga. 390, 40 S.E. 300 (1901).

C. Defendant brings into association with plaintiff a person whom he knows or should know to be peculiarly likely to commit crime, under circumstances creating a recognizable unreasonable risk that he will do so. The security agency for an apartment building hired a security guard with a violent record. The guard used his passkey to gain access to plaintiff's apartment, where he assaulted her. Who should be liable? Easley v. Apollo Detective Agency, 69 Ill.App.3d 920, 26 Ill.Dec. 313, 387 N.E.2d 1241 (1979).

Compare Hines v. Garrett, 131 Va. 125, 108 S.E. 690 (1921), where a railroad carried a young girl past her station, and put her off the train near a "hobo jungle," notoriously the haunt of criminal characters. On her way back to town, she was raped by two different persons unidentified. Is the railroad company liable?

D. Defendant has taken custody of a person of dangerous criminal tendencies, and fails to restrain him. Matron held liable for policeman's death when he was shot by juveniles who escaped from a youth center. Christensen v. Epley, 36 Or.App. 535, 585 P.2d 416 (1978). Contra, and much criticized, was Henderson v. Dade Coal Co., 100 Ga. 568, 28 S.E. 251 (1897), where a company using convict labor negligently guarded a brutal and vicious convict with a record of sexual offenses, and he escaped and raped the plaintiff. What if the convict were only a forger, with no record of violence, and he held up plaintiff with a gun in the course of his escape? Williams v. State, 308 N.Y. 548, 127 N.E.2d 545 (1955).

7. The following cases will help to test one's understanding of the rules and policy implications involved with regard to intervening criminal acts:

A. The State of New York was negligent in having only one attendant in a maximum-security closed ward. This led to the escape of a known dangerous psychotic. Some four hours after this occurred the escapee chanced upon an automobile with the keys in it, drove away and collided with plaintiff's automobile. Should the State be liable for this consequence? Dunn v. State, 29 N.Y.2d 313, 277 N.E.2d 647, 327 N.Y.S.2d 622 (1971).

B. Defendant insurance company issued a policy on the life of a small child, payable to her aunt as beneficiary. Under state law the policy was prohibited because the aunt did not have an insurable interest in the life of the child. The aunt murdered the child in the hope of collecting the life insurance.

Should the company be liable to the child's parents in a wrongful death action? See Liberty Nat'l Life Ins. Co. v. Weldon, 267 Ala. 171, 100 So.2d 696 (1958); cf. Galanis v. Mercury International Ins. Underwriters, 247 Cal.App.2d 690, 55 Cal.Rptr. 890 (1967) (suicide-bent person buys insurance at airport vending machine and causes plane to crash). See also Tarasoff v. Regents of The University of California, infra page 424.

8. *Keys Left in Car.* One fairly common proximate-cause puzzle involves an intervening criminal act and subsequent negligence by the intervenor. This occurs when defendant leaves keys in the ignition of his unlocked automobile. A thief drives off with the vehicle and negligently injures plaintiff in a subsequent collision. For treatment when a statute or ordinance is involved, see Ney v. Yellow Cab Co., supra page 215 and notes. When there is no statute or ordinance involved, most courts have declined to impose liability unless the vehicle has been left in an area where the crime is especially likely to happen. See Hergenrether v. East, 61 Cal.2d 440, 393 P.2d 164, 39 Cal.Rptr. 4 (1964); Annot., 45 A.L.R.3d 787 (1972). The fact that the vehicle is an extraordinarily dangerous one may also be a circumstance that suggests liability. See Richardson v. Ham, 44 Cal.2d 772, 285 P.2d 269 (1955). What is the likelihood that a motor vehicle thief will be involved in an accident? See Peck, An Exercise Based Upon Empirical Data—Liability for Harm Caused by Stolen Vehicles, 1969 Wis.L.Rev. 909. If an owner of a vehicle is liable in this context, should an automobile manufacturer also be liable if a thief is able to "jump the wires" on a vehicle? See Dean v. General Motors Corp., 301 F.Supp. 187 (E.D.La.1969).

KELLY v. GWINNELL

Supreme Court of New Jersey, 1984.
96 N.J. 538, 476 A.2d 1219.

[Defendant Gwinnell, after having driven co-defendant Zak home, spent an hour or two at Zak's home before leaving to return to his own home. During that time, Gwinnell consumed a number of drinks of scotch on the rocks with Zak and his wife. Later, Zak accompanied Gwinnell outside to his car, chatted with him, and watched as Gwinnell drove off to go home. On the way home, Gwinnell was involved in a head-on collision with an automobile operated by plaintiff Marie Kelly, who was seriously injured. Kelly sued Gwinnell and Gwinnell's employer, and those defendants in turn sued the Zaks in a third party action. Thereafter, plaintiff amended her complaint to include the Zaks as direct defendants. The trial court granted the Zaks' motion for summary judgment because as a matter of law a host is not liable for the negligence of an adult social guest who has become intoxicated at the host's home. The appellate court affirmed, noting that New Jersey has no Dram Shop Act imposing liability on the provider of alcoholic beverages and that New Jersey common law liability had been extended to a social host only when the guest was a minor.]

WILENTZ, C.J. This case raises the issue of whether a social host who enables an adult guest at his home to become drunk is liable to the victim of an automobile accident caused by the drunken driving of the guest. Here the host served liquor to the guest beyond the point at which the guest was visibly intoxicated. We hold the host may be liable under [certain] circumstances. * * *

"Negligence is tested by whether the reasonably prudent person at the time and place should recognize and foresee an unreasonable risk or likelihood of harm or danger to others." [Cc] When negligent conduct creates such a risk, setting off foreseeable consequences that lead to plaintiff's injury, the conduct is deemed the proximate cause of the injury. "[A] tortfeasor is generally held answerable for the injuries which result in the ordinary course of events from his negligence and it is generally sufficient if his negligent conduct was a substantial factor in bringing about the injuries." [Cc]

Under the facts here defendant provided his guest with liquor, knowing that thereafter the guest would have to drive in order to get home. Viewing the facts most favorably to plaintiff (as we must, since the complaint was dismissed on a motion for summary judgment), one could reasonably conclude that the Zaks must have known that their provision of liquor was causing Gwinnell to become drunk, yet they continued to serve him even after he was visibly intoxicated. By the time he left, Gwinnell was in fact severely intoxicated. A reasonable person in Zak's position could foresee quite clearly that this continued provision of alcohol to Gwinnell was making it more and more likely that Gwinnell would not be able to operate his car carefully. Zak could foresee that unless he stopped providing drinks to Gwinnell, Gwinnell was likely to injure someone as a result of the negligent operation of his car. * * *

[T]he only question remaining is whether a duty exists to prevent such risk or, realistically, whether this Court should impose such a duty. * * *

When [a] court determines that a duty exists and liability will be extended, it draws judicial lines based on fairness and policy. In a society where thousands of deaths are caused each year by drunken drivers, where the damage caused by such deaths is regarded increasingly as intolerable, where liquor licensees are prohibited from serving intoxicated adults, and where long-standing criminal sanctions against drunken driving have recently been significantly strengthened to the point where the Governor notes that they are regarded as the toughest in the nation, see Governor's Annual Message to the N.J. State Legislature, Jan. 10, 1984, the imposition of such a duty by the judiciary seems both fair and fully in accord with the State's policy.

We therefore [expand our prior decisions that limited liability to licensees who served liquor for profit or social hosts who served liquor to a minor and] hold that a host who serves liquor to an adult social guest, knowing both that the guest is intoxicated and [that he] will thereafter be operating a motor vehicle, is liable for injuries inflicted on a third party as a result of the negligent operation of a motor vehicle by the adult guest when such negligence is caused by the intoxication. We impose this duty on the host to the third party because we believe that the policy considerations served by its imposition far outweigh those asserted in opposition. While we recognize the concern that our ruling will interfere with accepted standards of social behavior; will intrude on and somewhat diminish the enjoyment, relaxation, and camaraderie that accompany social gatherings at which alcohol is served; and that such gatherings and social relationships are not simply tangential benefits of a civilized society but are regarded by many as important, we believe that the added assurance of just compensation to the victims of drunken driving as well as the added deterrent effect of the rule on such driving outweigh the importance of those other values. * * * We therefore reverse the [summary] judgment in favor of the defendants Zak and remand the case. * * *

GARIBALDI (dissenting). * * * The majority need not parade the horrors that have been caused by drunk drivers to convince me that there is always room for stricter measurers against intoxicated drivers. I too am concerned for the injured victim of a drunken driver. However, the almost limitless implications of the majority's decision lead me to conclude that the Legislature is better equipped to effectuate the goals of reducing injuries from drunken driving and protecting the interests of the injured party, without placing such a grave burden on the average citizen of this state. * * *

My reluctance to join the majority is not based on any exaggerated notion of judicial deference to the Legislature. Rather, it is based on my belief that before this Court plunges into this broad area of liability and imposes high duties of care on social hosts, it should carefully consider the ramifications of its actions. * * *

[T]his Court has, in the past, imposed civil liability on commercial licensees who serve alcoholic beverages to intoxicated patrons. Commercial licensees are subject to regulation by both the Alcoholic Beverage Commission (ABC) and the Legislature. It is reasonable to impose tort liability on licensees based on their violation of explicit statutes and regulations.

I have no quarrel with the imposition of such liability because of the peculiar position occupied by the licensee. A social host, however, is in a different position. * * *

A significant difference between an average citizen and a commercial licensee is the average citizen's lack of knowledge and expertise in determining levels and degrees of intoxication. Licensed commercial providers, unlike the average citizen, deal with the alcohol-consuming public every day. This experience gives them some expertise with respect to intoxication that social hosts lack. A social host will find it more difficult to determine levels and degrees of intoxication. * * *

The nature of home entertaining compounds the social host's difficulty in determining whether a guest is obviously intoxicated before serving the next drink. In a commercial establishment, there is greater control over the liquor; a bartender or waitress must serve the patron a drink. Not so in a home when entertaining a guest. At a social gathering, for example, guests frequently serve themselves or guests may serve other guests. Normally, the host is so busy entertaining he does not have time to analyze the state of intoxication of the guests. * * * Furthermore, the commercial bartender usually does not drink on the job. The social host often drinks with the guest, as the Zaks did here.) * * *

Further, it is not clear from the Court's opinion to what lengths a social host must go to avoid liability. Is the host obligated to use physical force to restrain an intoxicated guest from drinking and then from driving? Or is the host limited to delay and subterfuge tactics short of physical force? What is the result when the host tries to restrain the guest but fails? Is the host still liable? The majority opinion is silent on the extent to which we must police our guests.

The most significant difference between a social host and a commercial licensee, however, is the social host's inability to spread the cost of liability. The commercial establishment spreads the cost of insurance against liability among its customers. The social host must bear the entire cost alone. * * *

[The social host] may not have sufficient insurance to cover the limitless liability that the Court seeks to impose. These people may lose everything they own if they are found liable as negligent social hosts under the Court's scheme. The individual economic cost to every New Jersey citizen should be weighed before today's result is reached. * * *

---

1. In Coulter v. Superior Court, 21 Cal.3d 144, 577 P.2d 669, 145 Cal.Rptr. 534 (1978), the California court imposed liability on the host in a situation similar to that in the principal case. Before the year was out, however, the California legislature expressly "abrogated" the holding in the case "in favor of prior judicial interpretation finding the consumption of alcoholic beverages rather than the serving of alcoholic beverages as the proximate cause of injuries inflicted on another by an intoxicated person." Cal.Bus. & Prof.Code § 25602. Liability was continued, however, for a defendant furnishing a drink to "any obviously intoxicated minor." § 25602.1. The constitutionality of the 1978 amendments was upheld four years later by the California Supreme Court. Cory v. Shierloh, 29 Cal.3d 430, 433, 629 P.2d 8, 174 Cal.Rptr. 500 (1981).

Several courts have held social hosts liable for furnishing intoxicating liquors to minors. See Wiener v. Gamma Phi Chapter of Alpha Tau Omega Fraternity, 258 Or. 632, 485 P.2d 18 (1971) (fraternity found negligent for serving beer to minor who subsequently injured third party in automobile accident); cf. Sutter v. Hutchings, 254 Ga. 194, 327 S.E.2d 716 (1985). Why are courts more willing to impose liability when a minor is involved? But see Holmquist v. Miller, 367 N.W.2d 468, 471 (Minn.1985): "Thus it is clear from legislative and case history that the Civil Damages Act preempts a cause of action against a social host for negligently serving alcohol, whether it be to an adult or to a minor who subsequently injures a third party."

Maj

2. Almost all state supreme courts ruling on this issue have declined to impose liability on a social host when the recipient of the alcohol is an adult. See, e.g., Klein v. Raysinger, 504 Pa. 141, 470 A.2d 507, 510 (1983) ("Thus, the great weight of authority supports the view that in the case of an ordinary able-bodied man it is the consumption of the alcohol, rather than the furnishing of the alcohol, which is the proximate cause of any subsequent occurrence").

This issue is the subject of many recent law review articles. See, e.g., Notes, 11 Am.J.L. & Med. 229 (1985), 52 Tenn.L.Rev. 145 (1984), 23 Duq.L.Rev. 1307 (1985).

3. *Commercial Dispensers of Liquor.* A legislative response to early common law liability insulation of commercially licensed vendors was the Dram Shop Act. These acts generally provided a civil cause of action (as well as criminal sanctions) against furnishers of alcohol for damages resulting from a consumer's intoxicated state. Fourteen states currently enforce Dram Shop Acts. In addition, states that have repealed or are otherwise without a Dram Shop Act have enacted alcohol-beverage control laws, the violation of which will usually constitute negligence per se. As of 1986, approximately 12 states that have clearly ruled on the subject continue to adhere to the common law rule insulating commercial vendors from liability. See Ling v. Jan's Liquors, 237 Kan. 629, 703 P.2d 731, 739 (1985) for an appendix that briefly summarizes the present status of the civil liability of liquor vendors in all jurisdictions. It is clear that licensed vendors' supplying of liquor to patrons has become widely recognized as a proximate cause of injuries attributable to intoxicated persons. See Ontiveros v. Borak, 136 Ariz. 500, 667 P.2d 200 (1983). Courts have consistently been unwilling, however, to extend liability on these grounds to a social host. See Klein v. Raysinger, supra note 2. What are the policy considerations and tort law principles differentiating a licensee and a social host? See McGough, Dram Shop Acts, ABA Section of Insurance, Negligence and Compensation Law 448 (1967); Annot., 8 A.L.R.3d 1412 (1966). See also, Notes, 133 U.Pa.L.Rev. 867 (1985); 61 Ind.L.J. 85 (1985).

Yes

4. *Entrustment.* A car owner lends his vehicle to a person who is obviously intoxicated. The driver negligently runs into plaintiff. Should the owner be liable? See Deck v. Sherlock, 162 Neb. 86, 75 N.W.2d 99 (1956). Suppose the bailee is not intoxicated at the time but is a known alcoholic. See Powell v. Langford, 58 Ariz. 281, 119 P.2d 230 (1941). Should it make any difference that the automobile is given outright rather than loaned? Estes v. Gibson, 257 S.W.2d 604 (Ky.1953). Many courts have recognized the analogy between negligent sale of alcohol and the tort of negligent entrustment. See Buchanan v. Merger Enterprises, Inc., 463 So.2d 121, 126 (Ala.1984).

Sine qua non = Neg re: train? = yes — of conductor
but/for = Neg re: train? = no, No

Facts: Herbert fell off train
: π (cousin) went to look, rescue
: π fell

WAGNER v. INTERNATIONAL RY. CO.

Court of Appeals of New York, 1921.

232 N.Y. 176, 133 N.E. 437.

"Rescue Doctrine"

duty to prevent rescue.

Palsgraf guy

CARDOZO, J. The action is for personal injuries. The defendant operates an electric railway between Buffalo and Niagara Falls. There is a point on its line where an overhead crossing carries its tracks above those of the New York Central and the Erie. A gradual incline upwards over a trestle raises the tracks to a height of 25 feet. A turn is then made to the left at an angle of from 64 to 84 degrees. After making this turn, the line passes over a bridge, which is about 158 feet

Rule: G/R A rescuer of a victim of negligence is always forseeable to original negligent party (unless wanton, foolish, etc), need not have been invited (i.e. duty to prevent)

long from one abutment to the other. Then comes a turn to the right at about the same angle down the same kind of an incline to grade. Above the trestle, the tracks are laid on ties unguarded at the ends. There is thus an overhang of the cars, which is accentuated at curves. On the bridge, a narrow footpath runs between the tracks, and beyond the line of overhang there are tie rods and a protecting rail.

Plaintiff and his cousin Herbert boarded a car at a station near the bottom of one of the trestles. Other passengers, entering at the same time, filled the platform, and blocked admission to the aisle. The platform was provided with doors, but the conductor did not close them. Moving at from 6 to 8 miles an hour, the car without slackening, turned the curve. There was a violent lurch, and Herbert Wagner was thrown out, near the point where the trestle changes to a bridge. The cry was raised, "Man overboard." The car went on across the bridge, and stopped near the foot of the incline. Night and darkness had come on. Plaintiff walked along the trestle, a distance of 445 feet, until he arrived at the bridge, where he thought to find his cousin's body. He says that he was asked to go there by the conductor. He says, too, that the conductor followed with a lantern. Both these statements the conductor denies. Several other persons, instead of ascending the trestle, went beneath it, and discovered under the bridge the body they were seeking. As they stood there, the plaintiff's body struck the ground beside them. Reaching the bridge, he had found upon a beam his cousin's hat, but nothing else. About him there was darkness. He missed his footing, and fell.

The trial judge held that negligence toward Herbert Wagner would not charge the defendant with liability for injuries suffered by the plaintiff unless two other facts were found: First, that the plaintiff had been invited by the conductor to go upon the bridge; and, second, that the conductor had followed with a light. Thus limited, the jury found in favor of the defendant. Whether the limitation may be upheld is the question to be answered.

Danger invites rescue. The cry of distress is the summons to relief. The law does not ignore these reactions of the mind in tracing conduct to its consequences. It recognizes them as normal. It places their effects within the range of the natural and probable. The wrong that imperils life is a wrong to the imperiled victim; it is a wrong also to his rescuer. The state that leaves an opening in a bridge is liable to the child that falls into the stream, but liable also to the parent who plunges to its aid. [Cc] The railroad company whose train approaches without signal is a wrongdoer toward the traveler surprised between the rails, but a wrongdoer also to the bystander who drags him from the path. [Cc] The rule is the same in other jurisdictions. [Cc] The risk of rescue, if only it be not wanton, is born of the occasion. The emergency begets the man. The wrongdoer may not have foreseen the coming of a deliverer. He is accountable as if he had. [Cc]

Δ's argument:

The defendant says that we must stop, in following the chain of causes, when action ceases to be "instinctive." By this is meant, it seems, that rescue is at the peril of the rescuer, unless spontaneous and immediate. If there has been time to deliberate, if impulse has given way to judgment, one cause, it is said, has spent its force, and another has intervened. In this case the plaintiff walked more than 400 feet in going to Herbert's aid. He had time to reflect and weigh; impulse had been followed by choice; and choice, in the defendant's view, intercepts and breaks the sequence. We find no warrant for thus shortening the chain of jural causes. We may assume, though we are not required to decide, that peril and rescue must be in substance one transaction; that the sight of the one must have aroused the impulse to the other; in short, that there must be unbroken continuity between the commission of the wrong and the effort to avert its consequences. If all this be assumed, the defendant is not aided. Continuity in such circumstances is not broken by the exercise of volition. [Cc] So sweeping an exception, if recognized, would leave little of the rule. "The human mind," as we have said (People v. Majone, 91 N.Y. 211, 212), "acts with celerity which it is sometimes impossible to measure." The law does not discriminate between the rescuer oblivious of peril and the one who counts the cost. It is enough that the act, whether impulsive or deliberate, is the child of the occasion.

O/L = Caveat in its holding:

Δ's 2nd argument:

The defendant finds another obstacle, however, in the futility of the plaintiff's sacrifice. He should have gone, it is said, below the trestle with the others; he should have known, in view of the overhang of the cars, that the body would not be found above; his conduct was not responsive to the call of the emergency; it was a wanton exposure to a danger that was useless. [Cc] We think the quality of his acts in the situation that confronted him was to be determined by the jury. Certainly he believed that good would come of his search upon the bridge. He was not going there to view the landscape. The law cannot say of his belief that a reasonable man would have been unable to share it. He could not know the precise point at which his cousin had fallen from the car. If the fall was from the bridge, there was no reason why the body, caught by some projection, might not be hanging on high, athwart the tie rods or the beams. Certainly no such reason was then apparent to the plaintiff, or so a jury might have found. Indeed, his judgment was confirmed by the finding of the hat. There was little time for delay, if the facts were as he states them. Another car was due, and the body, if not removed, might be ground beneath the wheels. The plaintiff had to choose at once, in agitation and with imperfect knowledge. He had seen his kinsman and companion thrown out into the darkness. Rescue could not charge the company with liability if rescue was condemned by reason. "Errors of judgment," however, would not count against him if they resulted "from the excitement and confusion of the moment." [Cc] The reason that was exacted of him was not the reason of the morrow. It was reason fitted and proportioned to the time and the event.

Whether Herbert Wagner's fall was due to the defendant's negligence, and whether plaintiff, in going to the rescue, as he did, was foolhardy or reasonable in the light of the emergency confronting him, were questions for the jury.

The judgment of the Appellate Division and that of the Trial Term should be reversed, and a new trial granted, with costs to abide the event.

---

1. *Second Accident.* In the principal case, suppose that Herbert Wagner had been thrown out of the train onto a road and before he could be moved a car struck him and injured him further. Regardless of whether the driver of the car was negligent, the cases generally agree that the railway company would be liable for both injuries. See, e.g., Morrison v. Medaglia, 287 Mass. 46, 191 N.E. 133 (1934); Bunda v. Hardwick, 376 Mich. 640, 138 N.W.2d 305 (1965); cf. Sworden v. Gross, 243 Or. 83, 409 P.2d 897 (1966) (plaintiff himself negligent in producing first collision). The automobile driver, of course, would not liable for the first injuries.

2. *Attempt to Escape from Danger Created by Defendant.* In the principal case, suppose that Herbert Wagner, in attempting to hold onto something as the train was lurching, pulled plaintiff out of the train with him, injuring the plaintiff? The cases generally agree that the railway company would be liable for this injury. The classic decision is Tuttle v. Atlantic City R. Co., 66 N.J.L. 327, 49 A. 450 (1901), where a freight car jumped a track and lunged across the street. Plaintiff, on the sidewalk, ran from the car, fell and injured her knee. She was allowed to recover. See also Kroeger v. Safranek, 161 Neb. 182, 72 N.W.2d 831 (1955); Thornton v. Weaber, 380 Pa. 590, 112 A.2d 344 (1955).

3. *Attempt to Avert Danger Created by Defendant (Rescue).* In the principal case, suppose that plaintiff was a volunteer who offered to go up the trestle and look for Herbert Wagner. Unless he acts recklessly, a rescuer is usually allowed to recover for an injury he sustains.

4. A few of the numerous legal problems raised by the "rescue doctrine" are listed here. By his efforts the rescuer may injure himself, as in *Wagner*; or the rescued person, as in the physician cases, infra note 5; or a third person, as in Thomas v. Casey, 49 Wash.2d 14, 297 P.2d 614 (1956). Are the issues the same? Should they be answered the same way?

5. Suppose the injured rescuer is a professional—a policeman, a fireman or a life guard. See Nastasio v. Cinnamon, 295 S.W.2d 117 (Mo.1956). Compare Carter v. Taylor Diving & Salvage Co., 341 F.Supp. 628 (E.D.La.1972), aff'd mem., 470 F.2d 995 (5th Cir.1973) (doctor suffered heart attack as result of lengthy emergency treatment under strain), with Solgaard v. Guy F. Atkinson Co., 6 Cal.3d 361, 491 P.2d 821, 99 Cal.Rptr. 29 (1971) (doctor caught by landslide in seeking to reach injured person). And see the thorough treatment of the subject in Maltman v. Sauer, 84 Wash.2d 975, 530 P.2d 254 (1975).

6. Suppose the person rescued negligently put himself into a position of danger. Should he be liable to the person who was injured coming to his aid? See Dodson v. Maddox, 359 Mo. 742, 223 S.W.2d 434 (1949); Ruth v. Ruth, 213 Tenn. 82, 372 S.W.2d 285 (1963). Suppose the rescuee was in the act of taking his own life and clearly did not want to be rescued? See Talbert v. Talbert, 22 Misc.2d 782, 199 N.Y.S.2d 212 (1960).

7. What if the attempt at rescue is utterly foolish? A passenger about to alight from defendant's train hands her baby to a man on the platform. The train unexpectedly starts up and carries her away. A bystander heroically snatches up the child and runs after the train. He runs the length of the platform, losing ground steadily, and stumbles over a baggage truck at the far end. The child is injured. Liability? Atchison, T. & S.F.R. Co. v. Calhoun, 213 U.S. 1 (1909). Cf. Robinson v. Butler, 226 Minn. 491, 33 N.W.2d 821 (1948) (excited passenger seizing steering wheel of automobile). Suppose the rescuer was mistaken and the rescuee was not actually in danger? Cf. Ellmaker v. Goodyear Tire & Rubber Co., 372 S.W.2d 650 (Mo.App.1963).

8. What if plaintiff is injured while rescuing his own property? Defendant starts a fire that burns toward plaintiff's house, and plaintiff is burned while trying to put it out. Illinois Central R. Co. v. Siler, 229 Ill. 390, 82 N.E. 362 (1907). Suppose he tries to rescue the property of a third person? Stewart v. Jefferson Plywood Co., 255 Or. 603, 469 P.2d 783 (1970); Burnett v. Conner, 299 Mass. 604, 13 N.E.2d 417 (1938). The property of the defendant? Rushton v. Howle, 79 Ga.App. 360, 53 S.E.2d 768 (1949); Green v. Britton, 22 Conn. Super. 71, 160 A.2d 497 (1960).

9. What about the rescuer of a rescuer? Richards v. Kansas Electric Power Co., 126 Kan. 521, 268 P. 847 (1928); Brown v. Ross, 345 Mich. 54, 75 N.W.2d 68 (1956); Richardson v. United States, 248 F.Supp. 99 (E.D.Okl.1965).

10. *Attempt to Alleviate Harm Caused by Defendant.* The primary example of this is the case in which a physician treats the plaintiff's injuries and negligently aggravates them. Is the original defendant liable for the aggravation? The usual answer is in the affirmative. Jess Edwards, Inc. v. Goergen, 256 F.2d 542 (10th Cir.1958); Thompson v. Fox, 326 Pa. 209, 192 A. 107 (1937). But the intervening negligence may be so unusual that the court holds it to be superseding, as in Purchase v. Seelye, 231 Mass. 434, 121 N.E. 413 (1918), where the hospital made a mistake and operated on the wrong patient.

Suppose the injured party is being taken by an ambulance to the hospital for treatment. An accident en route causes additional injuries. Should it make any difference whether the second collision was caused by (1) the speed of the ambulance because of the emergency, (2) the causal negligence of the driver though no emergency was involved, or (3) the negligence of a third party in running into the ambulance? Atherton v. Devine, 602 P.2d 634 (Okl.1979).

11. *Second Injury Caused by Weakened Condition Resulting from First Injury.* There are some recurrent patterns falling into this classification, in which the cases have indicated a more or less crystallized response. The first involves the onset of a disease likely to attack one in a weakened condition—for example, the pneumonia in Beauchamp v. Saginaw Mining Co., 50 Mich. 163, 15 N.W. 65 (1883), or the hemolytic streptococcus infection in Wallace v. Ludwig, 292 Mass. 251, 198 N.E. 159 (1935). An earlier distinction depending on the time when the germs invaded the body has been abandoned, but it may still make a difference whether the disease was of a type which would attack a healthy person and produce the same result. See, e.g., Case of Upham, 245 Mass. 31, 139 N.E. 433 (1923) (appendicitis).

Another type of case involves a second breaking of a limb which had not fully recovered its original strength. The plaintiff usually recovers for the second injury. Squires v. Reynolds, 125 Conn. 366, 5 A.2d 877 (1939); Mitchell v. Legarsky, 95 N.H. 214, 60 A.2d 136 (1948). Factors that may affect the holding, however, include the length of time between the accidents, the location and nature of the second injury, the reasonableness of the plaintiff's conduct and the character of the second accident. See Linder v. Payette, 64 Idaho 656, 135 P.2d 440 (1943); Vance, Liability for Subsequent Injuries, 42 Tex.L.Rev. 86 (1963).

12. *Legal Concepts Affecting These Cases.* In the notes above, fact patterns for classifying the cases have been suggested. Running through some of these fact patterns with varying significance are several legal concepts which may affect the determination of legal cause. Consider how the following sets of contrasting concepts apply to the patterns above:

(A) Dependent vs. independent intervening cause. "A dependent intervening cause is one which operates in response to or is a reaction to the stimulus of a situation for which the actor has made himself responsible by his negligent conduct." Restatement (Second) of Torts § 441, Comment *c.* It is less likely to be held to be superseding than an independent intervening cause. *[This one is apropo]*

(B) Extent of liability vs. existence of liability. If tort liability already exists between the parties, the court may be more ready to extend it to additional or augmented harm than if there had been no liability.

(C) Normal intervening force vs. extraordinary intervening force. A normal intervening force is defined in the Restatement (Second) as "a normal consequence of a situation created by the actor's negligent conduct." § 443. "It means that the court or jury, looking at the matter after the event, and therefore knowing the situation which existed when the new force intervened does not regard its intervention as so extraordinary as to fall outside of the class of normal events." Id., Comment *b.* This is obviously based on a hindsight approach, but the concept can also be used with the foresight approach. Thus, one would assume knowledge of the initial incident and then ask himself what subsequent intervening forces would be readily foreseeable. In his dissenting opinion in the *Palsgraf* case, Judge Andrews expressed a similar idea in a different context. "I think the direct connection, the foresight of which the courts speak, assumes prevision of the explosion * * * And surely, given such an explosion as here, it needed no great foresight to predict that the natural result would be to injure one on the platform at no greater distance than the plaintiff." Supra, page 311. Is he talking about the same thing?

["Irresistible Impulse" = doctrine]

FULLER v. PREIS

New York Court of Appeals, 1974.
35 N.Y.2d 425, 322 N.E.2d 263, 363 N.Y.S.2d 568.

BREITEL, CHIEF JUDGE. Plaintiff executor, in a wrongful death action, recovered a jury verdict for $200,000. The Appellate Division set aside the verdict and judgment in favor of plaintiff executor and dismissed the complaint. In doing so, that court noted that even if it were not to dismiss the complaint, it would set the verdict aside as contrary to the weight of the credible evidence. Plaintiff executor appeals. *[Tct = π / App Div = revld/∆ / Ct App = revld/— new trial]*

Decedent, Dr. Lewis, committed suicide some seven months after an automobile accident from which he had walked away believing he was uninjured. In fact he had suffered head injuries with consequences to be detailed later. The theory of the case was that defendants, owner

Chief Judge Breitel

and operator of the vehicle which struck decedent's automobile, were responsible in tort for the suicide as a matter of proximate cause and effect. The issue is whether plaintiff's evidence of cause of the suicide was sufficient to withstand dismissal of the complaint.

There should be a reversal of the order of the Appellate Division and a new trial ordered. * * *

[An] act of suicide, as a matter of law, is not a superseding cause in negligence law precluding liability. An initial tort-feasor may be liable for the wrongful acts of a third party if foreseeable (see Restatement (Second) of Torts § 442A). * * *

Thus, there is neither public policy nor precedent barring recovery for suicide of a tortiously injured person driven "insane" by the consequence of the tortious act. [Cc] * * *

[T]his case was tried for all purposes in accordance with the prevailing law. Indeed, the jury was instructed, primarily, upon the theory of liability for a suicide by an accident victim suffering from ensuing mental disease, who was unable to control the "irresistible impulse" to destroy himself. The theory of the trial, therefore, determines the rule to be applied on the appeal.

Dr. Lewis was physically and mentally healthy immediately prior to the automobile accident in which he struck his head against the interior of his own vehicle. After the accident he suffered several epileptic seizures, often with unconsciousness. Before the accident he had never suffered a seizure. For seven months between the accident and his death, Dr. Lewis experienced no fewer than 38 separate seizures. * * *

The only authentic issue is whether the suicide was an "irresistible impulse" caused by traumatic organic brain damage. * * *

On the day of the suicide, only seven months after the accident, when Dr. Lewis had had three seizures, his daughter tried to speak with him but he did not respond. After the third seizure he seemed unable to recognize his wife, had a strange look, and locked himself in the bathroom. Twenty minutes later, his wife heard him mutter, "I must do it, I must do it", and then a gunshot rang out. Dr. Lewis had shot himself in the head and died the following day. * * *

In tort law, as contrasted with criminal law, there is recognition that one may retain the power to intend, to know, and yet to have an irresistible impulse to act and therefore be incapable of voluntary conduct. * * *

The issue in this case was, precisely, whether Dr. Lewis, who obviously knew what he was doing and intended to do what he did, nevertheless, was, because of mental derangement, incapable of resisting the impulse to destroy himself. Precedents and modern knowledge say that that could have been. The jury found that it was so. * * *

Of course, there may be and undoubtedly have been cases where the causal nexus becomes too tenuous to permit a jury to "speculate" as to the proximate cause of the suicide.

A suicide is a strange act and no rationalistic approach can fit the act into neat categories of rationality or irrationality. When the suicide is preceded by a history of trauma, brain damage, epileptic seizures, aberrational conduct, depression and despair, it is at the very least a fair issue of fact whether the suicide was the rational act of a sound mind or the irrational act or irresistible impulse of a deranged mind evidenced by a physically damaged brain. It would be illogical to conclude otherwise. Consequently, although the Appellate Division in exercise of its supervisory power to review the facts could set the jury verdict aside, it was impermissible for it to dismiss the complaint.

Since the Appellate Division, in reversing, stated that in any event it would have set the verdict aside as contrary to the weight of the evidence, the verdict in favor of plaintiff may not be reinstated and a new trial is required.

Accordingly, the order of the Appellate Division should be reversed, with costs, and a new trial directed.

————

1. If a suicide is a deliberate, intentional act by an individual, how can one individual be liable for the suicide of another? How is the problem affected by the concepts described in note 12, page 333? Are the decisions affected by policy reasons underlying the rhetoric of proximate cause?

2. Early decisions steadfastly denied claims based on causing suicide as long as the decedent had even the slightest awareness of what he was doing. See Scheffer v. Railroad Co., 105 U.S. 249 (1882); Brown v. American Steel and Wire Co., 43 Ind.App. 560, 88 N.E. 80 (1909); Daniels v. New York, N.H. & H.R. Co., 183 Mass. 393, 67 N.E. 424 (1903). Courts followed the view from ecclesiastical and early common law that a person who knowingly committed suicide was a culpable wrongdoer.

3. Even when defendant had engaged in extreme and outrageous conduct highly likely to cause severe emotional distress, decedent's cognitive recognition of his act would be deemed a superseding cause and bar any claim. See Salsedo v. Palmer, 278 Fed. 92 (2d Cir.1921); Stevens v. Steadman, 140 Ga. 680, 79 S.E. 564 (1913); Lancaster v. Montesi, 216 Tenn. 50, 390 S.W.2d 217 (1965) (sadistic physical and emotional torture). Recently some courts have allowed a claim in this type of situation although decedent was aware of his own conduct. See State for Use and Benefit of Richardson v. Edgeworth, 214 So.2d 579 (Miss. 1968); Tate v. Canonica, 180 Cal.App.2d 898, 5 Cal.Rptr. 28 (1960); Cauverien v. De Metz, 20 Misc.2d 144, 188 N.Y.S.2d 627 (Sup.Ct.1959).

4. Liability for negligently caused suicide was broadened when some courts stated that a wrongful death claim would be allowed not only when the decedent was unaware of what he was doing, but also when the decedent's injury caused an irresistible impulse to commit suicide. Padula v. State, 48 N.Y.2d 366, 398 N.E.2d 548, 422 N.Y.S.2d 943 (1979); Wallace v. Bounds, 369 S.W.2d 138 (Mo.1963); Long v. Omaha & C.B. St. R. Co., 108 Neb. 342, 187 N.W. 930 (1922). But most courts found an irresistible impulse only when decedent acted in a sudden frenzy; when he left a note or purchased poison the courts found control. In one decision the court relied on the efficient manner in which the decedent cut his throat to deny recovery. Brown v. American Steel and Wire Co., 43 Ind.App. 560, 88 N.E. 80 (1909).

The principal case is one of the few giving a broader interpretation of the irresistible impulse test. For a good review of the cases on this issue, see Grant v. F.P. Lathrop Constr. Co., 81 Cal.App.3d 796, 146 Cal.Rptr. 45 (1978).

5. Some workers' compensation cases have allowed a claim when a work-related accident was a substantial factor in the decedent's becoming incapable of normal judgment and committing suicide. See Delaware Tire Center v. Fox, 411 A.2d 606 (Del.Super.1980); Graver Tank & Mfg. Co. v. Industrial Commission, 97 Ariz. 256, 399 P.2d 664 (1965); Burnight v. Industrial Accident Commission, 181 Cal.App.2d 816, 5 Cal.Rptr. 786 (1960). Studies suggest that this test comports better with the psychiatric understanding of the cause of suicide than the irresistible impulse formula. See Schwartz, Civil Liability for Causing Suicide: A Synthesis of Law and Psychiatry, 24 Vand.L.Rev. 217, 232–236 (1971). Is it an appropriate one for tort law?

6. An affirmative duty to use care to prevent suicide is sometimes imposed by tort law upon certain classes of defendants. Problems of proximate

cause may still arise. As to hospitals, see Meier v. Ross General Hospital, 69 Cal.2d 420, 445 P.2d 519, 71 Cal.Rptr. 903 (1968); Annot., 60 A.L.R.3d 880 (1974). As to psychiatrists, see Fernandez v. Baruch, 52 N.J. 127, 244 A.2d 109 (1968); Furness v. Fitchett [1958] N.Z.U.L.Rev. 396; Morse, The Tort Liability of a Psychiatrist, 18 Syracuse L.Rev. 691 (1967). The cases involving pharmacists usually involve the illegal sale of a drug (e.g., barbiturate) to a person who uses it to commit suicide. The traditional answer has been no liability. See Scott v. Greenville Pharmacy, 212 S.C. 485, 48 S.E.2d 324 (1948); Eckerd's Inc. v. McGhee, 19 Tenn.App. 277, 86 S.W.2d 570 (1935). This position may be changing. See Runyon v. Reid, 510 P.2d 943 (Okl.1973); Annot. 58 A.L.R.3d 814. Compare the cases on liability of a seller of liquor, supra page 328.

BY WAY OF SYNTHESIS

The problem involved in the cases in this chapter is whether defendant's liability to plaintiff should be cut off even though the defendant's conduct was both negligent and a factual cause of the plaintiff's injury. Is there a system by which this problem can be handled and a test by which to make the determination?

1. It may first be suggested that the problem can be raised and treated by the court in connection with any one of the four elements of a negligence case—duty, breach of duty, causation or damage. The duty approach, for example, is espoused in the majority opinion in *Palsgraf* and is rather frequently used in cases of the unforeseeable plaintiff. Certain types of damage may be held not to be the basis of recovery. Negligence may be held not to be directed to the plaintiff. But most courts have treated the question in the causation element.

The problem is a difficult one, but the length of the treatment in this casebook and the amount of time allotted it in most courses may perhaps give an exaggerated impression of its importance. In the great majority of negligence cases, the problem does not arise at all; it comes up only in the fraction of negligence actions that involve unusual fact situations. How is it to be handled when it does arise?

There are many legal tests that have been devised by the courts and legal scholars—some rather precise and almost mechanical and some very broad and general. The more precise ones give an illusion of certainty. As a matter of fact, almost every jurisdiction has two distinct and apparently unrelated lines of authority—one with a broad scope of liability and the other with a narrow scope. They do not help the court especially to reach a decision on a case before it, but they do help substantially in explaining the decision after it has been reached.

This is not a situation, however, in which precision and certainty are essential. Neither party to the action engaged in his conduct in reliance upon a "rule" of proximate cause. The principal task of the court is to do justice as between these parties in their present situation. For this purpose, a weighing, evaluative process is required, rather than a clear-cut rule of law. This suggests the use of a standard similar to the one for determining whether a person was negligent (what a reasonable, prudent person would do under the same or similar circumstances). A standard allows the taking into consideration of competing factors or policy elements. Often these policy elements are not articulated or brought out into the open. For an analysis of some of them, see L. Green, Judge and Jury, Ch. 4, 5 (1930).

2. There are two general approaches to the problem of proximate cause—the hindsight, or direct-causation, approach and the foreseeability approach. Practically every jurisdiction has used both, at one time or another. In many instances they would be likely to produce the same result, but not always. In theory the foresight approach would produce a smaller ambit of liability.

But foreseeability is an accordion concept, depending upon the detail and precision with which foresight is required. Many torts teachers have found it helpful to express foreseeability in terms of the risk idea. "This position has been justified as more rational, since the factors which define negligence should also limit liability for negligence; as easier to administer, since it fixes the nearest thing to a definite boundary of liability which is possible; and more just, since negligence may consist of only a slight deviation from the community standard of conduct, and even be free from all moral blame, while its consequences may be catastrophic, and out of all proportion to the fault." Prosser and Keeton, Torts 282 (5th ed. 1984), citing Pollock, Liability for Consequences, 38 Law Q.Rev. 165 (1922); Goodhart, The Unforeseeable Consequences of a Negligent Act, 38 Yale L.J. 449 (1930); Seavey, Mr. Justice Cardozo and the Law of Torts, 52 Harv.L.Rev. 372 (1939), 48 Yale L.J. 390 (1939), 39 Colum.L.Rev. 20 (1939); Foster, Grant and Green, The Risk Theory and Proximate Cause, 32 Neb.L.Rev. 72 (1952); Wilson, Some Thoughts About Negligence, 2 Okla.L.Rev. 275 (1949); R. Keeton, Legal Cause in the Law of Torts (1963).

There is much force in these arguments, but they suggest far more in the way of certainty and precision than the test warrants. Consider a single illustration, adapted from Judge Magruder's opinion in Marshall v. Nugent, 222 F.2d 604 (1st Cir.1955).

Suppose that a truck is driven at excessive speed. It is relatively easy to say that the total risk, made up of the aggregate of all of the possibilities of harm, whether they are very probable or fantastic, is so great that the reasonable man of ordinary prudence would not do this, and therefore the driver is negligent. How easy is it, by a process of fragmentation of the risk, to separate out particular consequences and intervening factors, and to say that they are, or are not, significant parts of the original total foreseeable risk? Is it "foreseeable," in any sense that the reasonable driver could have the possibility in mind, and so take precautions against it, that:

(a) The driver will hit another car and kill a man?

(b) The car with which he collides will be thrown out of control, and hit a third car, or even a fourth? Springer v. Pacific Fruit Exchange, 92 Cal.App. 732, 268 P. 951 (1928).

(c) He will endanger a child in the street, and a person who tries to rescue it will sustain a broken arm? Wagner v. International R. Co., supra page 328.

(d) The truck will narrowly miss a pregnant woman, who will be frightened into a miscarriage? Cf. Mitnick v. Whalen Bros., 115 Conn. 650, 163 A. 414 (1932).

(e) He will hit a pedestrian, who will be left helpless in the street, and be run over by another car? Bunda v. Hardwick, 376 Mich. 640, 138 N.W.2d 305 (1965).

(f) He will cause a collision, which will leave wrecked cars blocking the highway, and another driver will run into the wreckage? Holmberg v. Villaume, 158 Minn. 442, 197 N.W. 849 (1924).

(g) He will hit a pedestrian, and while the man is unconscious, his watch will be stolen? Cf. Brauer v. New York Central R. Co., 91 N.J.L. 190, 103 A. 166 (1918).

(h) The person he injures will contract pneumonia because of his weakened condition, and die of it? Wallace v. Ludwig, supra page 332, note 11.

(i) The injured person may suffer a second accident six months later while he is walking on crutches? Squires v. Reynolds, supra page 332, note 11.

(j) The person he injures will receive negligent medical treatment, and die or be further injured because of it? Jess Edwards, Inc. v. Goergeen, supra page 332, note 10.

(k) The truck will knock a car up against a stone wall. The wall is weakened and, as a result, a stone falls off the top a day later and injures a pedestrian. Cf. In re Guardian Casualty Co., 253 App.Div. 360, 2 N.Y.S.2d 232 (1938).

All of these things have happened and there have been holdings that each was "proximate." Is it perhaps overloading the risk concept to make it the basis for determining each of these situations? Like the purpose-of-the-statute test (see supra note 1, page 213), from which it is derived, the risk test often approaches a begging of the question. One decides how broadly or narrowly to express the purpose of the criminal statute or the scope of the risk of an act of common law negligence with an awareness of what the result of that decision will be and with the decision perhaps influenced by it.

And yet, despite all of these difficulties, the risk approach, viewed entirely as an approach rather than as a definitive test, can be very helpful. It poses the problem in a way that can help to direct the line of thought of the decision-maker. If the idea is expressed in terms of a reasonably close relation between the harm threatened (or the risk created) and the injury incurred, then it is put in the form of a standard instead of a rule, and the need to exercise discretion in its application is made apparent. See Prosser, Selected Topics on the Law of Torts, 191, 233, 242 (1954); Wade, Book Review, 8 Vand.L.Rev. 657, 660–663 (1955).

3. For an interesting case in which the court expressly used the risk approach, see Hill v. Lundin & Associates, Inc., 260 La. 542, 256 So. 2d 620 (1972), where defendant contractor left an aluminum ladder standing against the side of a house after making emergency repairs following a hurricane, an unidentified third person moved it to the ground in the back yard, and plaintiff tripped over it in rushing to protect a small child from the ladder. Said the court, in part:

* * * "The same policy considerations which would motivate a legislative body to impose duties to protect from certain risks are applied by the court in making its determination. 'All rules of conduct, irrespective of whether they are the product of a legislature or are a part of the fabric of the court-made law of negligence, exist for purposes. They are designed to protect *some* persons under *some* circumstances against *some* risks. Seldom does a rule protect every victim against every risk that may befall him, merely because it is shown that the violation of the rule played a part in producing the injury. The task of defining the proper reach or thrust of a rule in its policy aspects is one that must be undertaken by the court in each case as it arises. How appropriate is the rule to the facts of this controversy? This is a question that the court cannot escape.' Malone, Ruminations on Cause–In–Fact, 9 Stanford L.Rev. 60, 73 (1956).

"This defendant's alleged misconduct, its alleged breach of duty was in leaving the ladder leaning against the house unattended. The risk encountered by the plaintiff which caused her harm was the ladder lying on the ground where it was placed by another, over which she tripped as she moved to protect the child. The record is devoid of any evidence tending to establish that the defendant could have reasonably anticipated that a third person would move the ladder and put it in the position which created this risk, or that such a 'naked possibility' was an unreasonable risk of harm. [C]

"A rule of law which would impose a duty upon one not to leave a ladder standing against a house does not encompass the risk here encountered. We are of the opinion that the defendant was under no duty to protect this plaintiff from the risk which gave rise to her injuries. The plaintiff has failed to establish legal and actionable negligence on the part of the defendant." 256 So.2d at 623.

What was the risk created by the defendant's conduct? Is the court responding to this by defining "the risk encountered by the plaintiff"? Might the risk have been defined broadly enough to cover the plaintiff's injury? How would the case be decided under the hindsight approach? By talking in terms of a superseding cause? Was the defendant negligent here? Is that the major issue?

Yes

4. From the consideration of the cases in this chapter, you should have obtained a "feel" for the problem, so that it is possible to tell promptly whether the answer is clear or so difficult that litigation may be warranted. You are not expected to be sure of the answer for all cases, but you should identify fact patterns in which application of the principles of proximate cause have become fairly well crystallized—for example, the thin-skull and rescue situations.

You should have become acquainted with the various legal tests and their ramifications and be able (1) to use or respond to them in argument, (2) able to present a lucid and logical legal argument for a particular result, and (3) liable to utilize or respond to such modifying adjectives for the word "cause" as active, efficient, natural and probable, foreseeable or unforeseeable, proximate, nearest and superseding and such terms as risk, unbroken sequence, just or expedient result, or dependent or independent intervening cause.

You ought to know how to argue the facts as well as the law. A few illustrations may be helpful in this regard. In Hines v. Morrow, 236 S.W. 183 (Tex.Civ.App.1921), defendant negligently left a mudhole in a highway. A's car drove into it and got stuck. B, a man with a wooden leg, attempted to pull A's car out of the mud with a tow rope. His wooden leg got stuck in the mud, and in order to extricate himself B took hold of the tail gate of the tow truck. As the truck moved, a loop in the tow rope lassoed his good leg and broke it. Clarence Morris in Proximate Cause in Minnesota, 34 Minn.L.Rev. 185 (1950), attributes the "peg leg" decision in the *Hines* case to the summary of the facts in plaintiff's brief, as follows: "The case stated in briefest form, is simply this: Appellee was on the highway, using it in a lawful manner, and slipped into this hole, created by appellant's negligence, and was injured in attempting to extricate himself."

If the plaintiff had used the same approach in stating the issue in Koehler v. Waukesha Milk Co., 190 Wis. 52, 208 N.W. 901 (1926), he would have said that the defendant left a glass milk bottle on the plaintiff's doorstep with a slight chip near the top, and the decedent perished as a result—with the consequence that he would probably have lost the case. Instead, he explained that the decedent had picked the bottle up and scratched a finger. The scratch had become infected, the infection had gone into blood poisoning (before the advent of penicillin) and the decedent died.

Compare Ramsey v. Carolina–Tennessee Power Co., 195 N.C. 788, 143 S.E. 861 (1928), where defendant railroad might have stated the facts as being that it had negligently "shunted" a freight car onto a spur track with too much force, with the result that the decedent quite a distance away inside a steam laundry plant was killed. How might the plaintiff state them instead?

5. If a trial court decides "as a matter of law" that the defendant's conduct was not a proximate cause of the plaintiff's injury, it directs a verdict for the defendant. This has happened in some of the cases in

this chapter. If there is an issue of proximate cause in the case and the trial court decides to let it go to the jury, it must instruct the jury as to the nature of the problem that it is to decide. What does the court say? There is no consensus. Model instructions from two different states can demonstrate the variety.

Arkansas. Model Jury Instructions (1974). AMI 501. "When I use the expression 'proximate cause,' I mean a cause which, in a natural and continuous sequence, produces damage and without which the damage would not have occurred.

"[This does not mean that the law recognizes only one proximate cause of damage. To the contrary, if two or more causes work together to produce damage, then you may find that each of them was a proximate cause.]"

AMI 503. "If, following any act or omission of a party, an event intervened which in itself caused any damage, completely independent of the conduct of that party, then his act or omission was not a proximate cause of the damage."

Texas. Pattern Jury Charges. Section 203. "Proximate cause means that cause which, in a natural and continuous sequence, unbroken by any new and independent cause, produces an event, and without which cause such event would not have occurred; and in order to be a proximate cause the act or omission complained of must be such that a person using ordinary care would have foreseen the event, or some similar event, which might reasonably result therefrom. There may be more than one proximate cause of an event.

"New and independent cause means the act or omission of a separate and independent agency, not reasonably foreseeable, which destroys the causal connection, if any, between the act or omission inquired about and the occurrence in question, and thereby becomes the immediate cause of such occurrence."

The charge is discussed in Green & Smith, Negligence Law, No-Fault and Jury Trial, 50 Tex.L.Rev. 1297, 1305–08 (1972).

Are these instructions meaningful to the average jury? Is that necessary? Would they do as the test for the court to apply? Would they produce the same result in such cases as *Palsgraf*, Derdiarian v. Felix Contracting Co. and Fuller v. Preis? Is it better for them to be complex and accurate, or simple and understandable? Do they suggest that the court should be more ready to decide the case itself or turn it over to the jury?

3. SHIFTING RESPONSIBILITY

Normally, when the defendant has negligently created a risk of harm to the plaintiff, the failure of a third person to intervene and take some action to prevent the risk from being realized, that is, to prevent the harm, will not affect the liability of the defendant when the harm in fact occurs. If, for example, the defendant negligently sets a grass fire that is burning toward the plaintiff's building, the failure of someone else to put out the fire does not relieve the defendant. Wiley v. West Jersey R. Co., 44 N.J.L. 247 (1882). The fact that the third person was under a duty to the plaintiff to extinguish the fire, and would be liable to the plaintiff for his failure to do so, makes no difference to the defendant's liability.

Thus in Diehl v. Fidelity Philadelphia Trust Co., 159 Pa.Super. 513, 49 A.2d 190 (1946), the defendant Metropolitan negligently discharged steam onto the sidewalk in front of a building owned by Fidelity. The steam condensed and froze, forming a coating of invisible ice on the pavement. With notice of the situation, Fidelity failed to clean off the ice although it was under a duty to do so. Plaintiff, a pedestrian, slipped on the ice, fell, and was injured. It was held that the failure of Fidelity to perform its duty did not relieve Metropolitan of liability, and that the two were liable as joint tortfeasors. *[Concurrent causes, two acts of N, combining substantial certainty, shifts BOP]*

This is unquestionably the usual conclusion in situations of this nature. There are, however, a few cases in which the conduct of the third person, whether action or inaction, has been held to relieve the defendant because the responsibility has been shifted from his shoulders. One fact pattern in which this has occurred involves defendant construction companies that have left dynamite caps lying about. They are found by a boy. He takes them home; his mother discovers that he has them, knows what they are, and takes them away from him. She *[superseding cause? place or less.]* subsequently leaves them lying where he finds them, plays with them and is injured. The responsibility is held to have shifted to the parent, relieving the defendant. See Peterson v. Martin, 138 Minn. 195, 164 N.W. 813 (1917); Pittsburg Reduction Co. v. Horton, 87 Ark. 576, 113 S.W. 647 (1908); Calkins v. Albi, 163 Colo. 370, 431 P.2d 17 (1967).

Although it may be said in these cases that the risk created by the defendant has terminated, the risk is still there, and very much alive. What has happened is that another person has taken control of it. When should that fact shield the original wrongdoer? It is probably not possible to find any general principle that will determine when the risk will be found to have shifted. The following two cases afford some basis for discussion of what factors will influence the conclusion of the court.

GOAR v. VILLAGE OF STEPHEN
[" independent intervening cause" "superseding cause"]

Supreme Court of Minnesota, 1923.
157 Minn. 228, 196 N.W. 171.

STONE, J. Action for personal injuries caused by electrical burns, wherein plaintiff had a verdict against both defendants, the Village of Stephen, a municipal corporation, and Minnesota Electric Distributing Company. The business of the latter corporation is the installation of electric distributing plants, and the generation and distribution of electricity in the territory served by it, which includes the Village of Stephen.

[Still court say "but for" village N, harm would not have occurred. N was a factor. But — b/c cos N was it a substantial factor?]

[TrCt = π re: both A's 1) Village 2) Elec. Co.]

Each defendant moved separately in the alternative for judgment notwithstanding the verdict or a new trial. The motions were denied upon condition that plaintiff consent to a reduction of the $12,500 verdict to $8,500. She so consented but both defendants have appealed.

While in her own home in Stephen, plaintiff was injured on August 10, 1922, by a high voltage current, or the escape of which, from its proper conductors into the Goar dwelling, one or both of the defendants is responsible. For convenience, we refer to the parties as plaintiff, the Village and the Company.

[The Company had installed a transformer pole for the Village. Under the terms of the contract the Company guaranteed the apparatus for one year from date of acceptance, but the Village assumed the responsibility of inspection during that time and of all maintenance thereafter. Two wires on the pole were set too close together, and "in the more or less constant but sometimes none too gentle breezes that play over the Red River Valley," they rubbed together until the insulation was worn through. The contact sent into plaintiff's residence a 2300 volt current. The accident occurred 17½ months after acceptance by the Village, and during that time the Village had made no inspections and done no maintenance work. It was held that the jury could find both the Village and the Company negligent.]

It does not follow, however, that the Company is liable, even though it was negligent in the manner indicated. The initial negligence was followed by the serious and wrongful inaction of the Village. Before the verdict against the Company can be sustained, we must resolve against it the question as to whether the negligence of the Village was a new agency severing causal connection between the Company's negligence and plaintiff's hurt; or whether, on the other hand, such negligence simply concurred with that of the Company so as to charge both defendants.

In such a case, the contractor has a right to rely upon the owner's assuming, immediately upon his acceptance of the work, the duty of inspection and maintenance, which confessedly was not performed here. If it had been, the plaintiff would not have been injured for the fact that the original clearance was lessening and growing dangerous would have been discovered before the insulation was worn through. It took a year and a half of neglect, and the consequent freedom of the elements to work their will, before any injury resulted.

Not only was the Village in exclusive control, and, in consequence, the only agency upon which rested the burden of inspection and maintenance, but the Company was deprived, upon its delivery of the plant to the Village, of the opportunity and means of protecting the property from deterioration, and itself from resulting liability.

While the law of contract does not help us, the presence in the case of the contract is a fact to which proper reference may be made, and which may be given its appropriate place with the other facts. One of the facts established by the contract is that the Village, by the guaran-

[handwritten marginalia: specific duty ≅ statute ⓝ per se → class of π / type of harm]

[handwritten marginalia: Village's to ensure that the co's duty was performed]

ty clause, assumed the duty, as between the two, of notifying the Company of any defect in the plant which it could be required to make good. As between the defendants, then, the Company has a much better standing than the Village. They could, by contract, adjust their reciprocal duties to suit themselves. The duty so allocated to the Village was not performed. As against the Company, it has no complaint, because, it must be assumed, had the decreasing clearance between the two wires been called to the Company's attention, the condition would have been rectified.

How serious and long continued must such obvious neglect be in order to become an independent cause of injury? Is there no limit of time beyond which a contractor will cease to be liable, with the owner, for an injury which could not have happened but for the negligence of the latter?

If the Company is liable in this case, there is no rule of law which would prevent the same result were the accident to occur ten years later. If, in the one case the Company's negligence be a proximate cause, it must be so in the other. If in the one situation the negligence of the Village be not an independent producing agency of injury, it cannot be in the other. We are dealing with a question of negligence, and cannot hold a defendant liable as an insurer. [C]

[handwritten marginalia: presumably here there is a rule of law? is this it?]

Our examination of the problem and the authorities, in the light of which it must be solved, leads us to the conclusion, and we so hold, as a matter of law, that, under the circumstances of this case, the negligence of the Village was an independent producing agency of such character, that it broke the causal connection between the negligence of the Company and plaintiff's injury, and thereby became the proximate cause of the latter. * * *

[handwritten marginalia: Ⓗ]

On the appeal of the Village there must be an affirmance, and on that of the Company, a reversal, with instructions to set aside the verdict against it, and for judgment in its favor.

So ordered.

[handwritten marginalia: What was Stephen's duty? = to inspect; to tell company;]

1. What if the accident had happened a week after the transformer pole was turned over by the Electric Company to the village? Suppose the Village had been immune from liability. Would this have made a difference in the liability of the Company?

2. A case of much the same type is Greenwood v. Lyles & Buckner, Inc., 329 P.2d 1063 (Okl.1958). Defendant contractor, constructing a new highway, excavated a drainage ditch across the end of the old one, and set up no barriers or warning signs. The State Highway Department, for which the work was done, neglected either to close the old highway to travel or to provide barriers or signs. Seven months after the work was completed plaintiff, driving on the old highway, ran into the ditch. It was held that the contractor was not liable. Why?

GORDON v. NIAGARA MACHINE AND TOOL WORKS

United States Court of Appeals, Fifth Circuit, 1978.
574 F.2d 1182.

[The opinion in this case was written by Judge Keady of the Northern District of Mississippi. The Court of Appeals for the Fifth Circuit reversed and remanded the decision because of inadequate proof for the conclusion. In the second trial, the judge found that additional proof was introduced that justified his decision and he wrote this opinion. The Fifth Circuit adopted the opinion as its own.]

PER CURIAM. We affirm the judgment below on the basis of Judge Keady's * * * opinion set out below: * * *

In this diversity action, plaintiff, Mrs. Ivy L. Gordon, on June 9, 1969, lost four fingers of her left hand when operating a punch power press in the course of her employment by Poloron Corporation (Poloron). The press, which was manufactured by defendant Niagara Machine and Tool Works (Niagara), cycled unexpectedly while being manually operated by plaintiff and while her hand was within the jaws, or shearing area, of the press.

The facts surrounding this injury, as determined at the original trial, are as follows. The press was manufactured by Niagara and in 1954 sold directly to its customer, Poloron, at New Rochelle, New York. Five years later, Poloron moved the machine to its Batesville, Mississippi plant, the site of the accident. * * *

The press was a multipurpose type, with an open back inclinable configuration, and adaptable to an almost infinite number of industrial uses calling for cutting, stamping, forming, etc. * * * The press could be set, by means of a selection button, to cycle continuously with an automatic feed of material at 90 strokes per minute or to "single-stroke" in a manually-fed operation.

The press being a multipurpose type, Niagara sold it "naked", that is, without dies, and without guards or safety apparatus, although Niagara did manufacture and market a line of safety attachments. In accordance with the custom in the power press industry, the selection of dies and appropriate guarding or safety devices was left to the purchaser. In this instance Poloron, after acquiring the machine, removed the foot treadle which Niagara had installed for manual operation, and replaced it with a two-palm button system made by Schreder Corporation. * * *

The only warning which Niagara furnished at the time of sale was contained within the course of a 31-page service manual supplied to Poloron with the press; it stated "Never place your hands under the slides or between the die unless the power is off and the slides blocked up." Niagara did not place a label, decal or other sign on the machine warning of danger, nor did it advise its customer of any need to affix such a warning on the machine where it could be seen by press operators. Instead, Niagara left it up to Poloron to instruct its employees as to what was in the service manual.

Mrs. Gordon was never notified or warned by Poloron of danger in placing her hands within the die area when the press was set for manual operation. On the day of her injury, she was operating the press, as instructed, in a single-stroke manually-fed shearing procedure. She was removing a piece of cut material from the pinch point of the press when the machine unexpectedly cycled, amputating her fingers. The unexpected cycling was, in our view, attributable to failure of the press clutch to hold after completion of the normal stroke. In any event, either this condition or some other mechanical failure of the press, and not the act of Mrs. Gordon, caused the press to "double trip" or repeat its stroke.

On the basis of the foregoing facts, this court concluded at the first trial that Niagara was negligent in failing effectively to warn press operators of the dangers of coming in contact with the die areas, and therefore was liable to an operator, ignorant of the hazard, who was injured by an unexpected cycling of the press, whatever the cause of such cycling, absent warning that the press, even when set for manual operation, had such proclivity. * * *

The Fifth Circuit reversed for lack of evidence to support our finding that *because* * * * Niagara had no reason to believe that Poloron's employees, including plaintiff, would not be informed by Poloron of the danger of bodily contact with the pinch point of the press because of the possibility of double tripping at any time. * * *

Upon retrial additional evidence was submitted to the court on the questions remanded for our decision. For the following reasons, after mature consideration, we determine on the basis of the whole record and the additional evidence submitted that our prior conclusion of liability was correct, and we adhere thereto.

[The court first addressed the issue of Niagara's duty to warn, particularly whether it fulfilled that duty by providing warnings to the purchaser, Polodron, or whether it was required to provide warnings directly on the press that could be read by Polodron's employees who would operate the press. This issue is dealt with in Chapter 15, Section 2(c), infra. The court held that Niagara did not fulfill its duty to warn by providing warnings to Polodron.]

We address the second concern expressed by the Fifth Circuit in its remand of the case for our further consideration—can Niagara's negligent failure to warn be regarded as a proximate cause of plaintiff's injuries, or was Poloron's failure to warn an intervening cause which absolved Niagara of its own breach of duty? * * *

Should Poloron's negligence, then, be said to be a superseding cause of plaintiff's injuries, thereby relieving Niagara from liability? In *Solomon v. Continental Baking Co.*, 172 Miss. 388, 160 So. 732 (1935), the general principles of superseding cause were succinctly stated:

Where an act of negligence is a substantial factor in bringing about an injury, it does not cease to be a legal and proximate cause thereof because of the intervention of a subsequent act of negligence of another which contributed to the injury, *if the prior act of negligence is still operating and the injury inflicted is not different in kind from that which would have resulted from the prior act.* (Emphasis added). [C]

§ 447 of the Restatement of Torts, which was carried forward as originally worded into the Second Restatement, sheds further light on the superseding cause question:

"§ 447. Negligence of Intervening Acts

The fact that an intervening act of a third person is negligent in itself or is done in a negligent manner does not make it a superseding cause of harm to another which the actor's negligent conduct is a substantial factor in bringing about, if

(a) the actor at the time of his negligent conduct should have realized that a third person might so act, or

(b) a reasonable man knowing the situation existing when the act of the third person was done would not regard it as highly extraordinary that the third person had so acted, or

(c) the intervening act is a normal consequence of a situation created by the actor's conduct and the manner in which it is done is not extraordinarily negligent."

Determination of the issue of superseding cause ordinarily presents factual questions to be answered by the trier of fact, and not disposed of as a matter of law. Under the test summarized in the *Solomon* case, the questions presented are (1) was Niagara's failure to warn a substantial cause of plaintiff's injury; (2) was Niagara's negligent conduct of a continuing nature; and (3) was plaintiff's injury resulting from Poloron's negligence the same type of injury expected to result from Niagara's negligence? Under the more detailed Restatement § 447 test, clauses (a), (b), and (c), though stated in the disjunctive, present a common question—was Poloron's negligent failure to warn reasonably foreseeable to Niagara?

Question (1), whether Niagara's failure to warn was a substantial cause of Mrs. Gordon's injuries, must be answered in the affirmative since she did not realize the danger of placing her hand within the die area of the press, in part because of Niagara's failure to make effective warning. Both Question (2), as to the continuing nature of Niagara's failure to warn, and Question (3), as to the similarity of Mrs. Gordon's injuries resulting from Poloron's intervening negligence to those resulting from Niagara's initial negligence, clearly call for affirmative answers. As the trier of the facts in this case, we find ample evidence exists to hold Niagara's negligence, though compounded by Poloron's dereliction, was not superseded as a proximate cause. * * *

Because the high degree of grave harm apt to befall operators ignorant of the double tripping proclivity of Niagara's press, the sub-

≈ burden of warning operators by placing sign directly on machine

stantial number of serious industrial accidents occurring to press operators and known to the power press industry in 1954 and long prior
thereto, and since it was not reasonable for Niagara to expect the
limited warning discernible only in a technical service manual furnished with the press would be communicated to press operators, we
find as a fact that Poloron's failure to issue proper warnings to its press
operators was reasonably foreseeable to Niagara.

Also to be considered on the issue of superseding cause is what
effect the passage of 15 years from the manufacture and sale of the
press had upon Niagara's negligence since Poloron also had a duty to
warn its employees, especially after it discovered the danger through
actual experience in operating Niagara presses. * * *

Although some factors might support a finding that Poloron's
negligence had superseded that of Niagara at the time of Mrs. Gordon's
injuries, viz., lapse of time, Poloron's relation to plaintiff, and Poloron's
knowledge of the danger, consideration of cogent factors compels us to
reach a different result. Highly significant are the grave dangers of
injury from operating a press absent positive, direct warnings for the
operator not to come in contact with the danger zone, and the appalling
nature of injuries likely to result. Additionally Niagara, by selling the
press without guarding of any kind and knowing that it was subject to
many uses through manual operation, knew or should have known that
industrial users of its presses, like Poloron, might well fail to observe its
safety warnings, making such neglect well within the range of foresee- *= re: summary*
ability by Niagara. * * * Because of these considerations, we do not *issue; summary*
feel it would be just to regard Poloron's negligence in failing to take *held.*
safety precautions as the sole proximate cause of plaintiff's injury.
* * * [E]ven if Poloron had advised its press operators of physical
danger, the failure of Niagara to affix explicit warnings on the machine
itself is an omission of such substantial and continuing effect as to have
a definite causal connection with plaintiff's injuries.

Moreover, Poloron's duty as an employer to warn of danger, and
Niagara's duty as the supplier of a dangerous chattel to warn should be
measured against the same standard of reasonable care. * * * *? Rest.?*

Poloron, of course, did not in any manner warn its press operators
of the dangerous characteristics of the press, much less attach a
warning plate to the machine. Unless Poloron's duty to warn *per se*
supersedes the chattel supplier's § 388 duty [to attach a warning plate
or sign], automatically absolving Niagara of liability for the plaintiff's
injuries suffered, at least in substantial part, because of Niagara's
negligent omission—a proposition which we cannot accept—established
principles of concurring negligence compel us to find that Niagara's
negligence proximately contributed to Mrs. Gordon's injuries. * * *

For the foregoing reasons, we issue an order reinstating our prior
judgment in this cause.

1. *Intervening Negligence.* When the defendant negligently sells a defective product, it is undisputed that the negligent failure of an intermediate party, such as a dealer or the plaintiff's employer, to discover the defect or to take precautions against its possible existence, does not relieve the defendant of responsibility. Ford Motor Co. v. Matthews, 291 So.2d 169 (Miss.1974) (even though a portion of a defective tractor had been rebuilt by the seller who did not discover the defect in that process).

The same is true of other foreseeable negligence. Ford Motor Co. v. Zahn, 265 F.2d 729 (8th Cir.1959) (sudden swerve of driver to avoid collision); Parkinson v. California Co., 233 F.2d 432 (10th Cir.1956) (workman lighting match in presence of gas); Herman v. Markham Air Rifle Co., 258 Fed. 475 (D.Mich.1918) (store customer negligently discharged air rifle at plaintiff); Steele v. Rapp, 183 Kan. 371, 327 P.2d 1053 (1958) (fellow employee dropped jug of inflammable nail polish remover); Comstock v. General Motors Corp., 358 Mich. 163, 99 N.W.2d 627 (1959) (garage service manager, moving car, forgot that its brakes were defective).

2. *Intervening Discovery.* How should these cases be decided?

A. A gas company agreed to give its empty propane gas tanks to a manufacturer. An agent of the manufacturer picked up a tank and discovered some seepage leaking from a valve. Nevertheless, he placed the tank some 10–15 feet from plaintiff's building. The "seepage" was petroleum that flowed into the building where it was ignited by a boiler. Should the gas company be held liable for this harm? See Aetna Insurance Co. v. Loveland Gas & Elec. Co., 369 F.2d 648 (6th Cir.1966).

B. Defendant made and installed in a department store an escalator, which was dangerously defective. A series of accidents occurred, in which customers suffered minor injuries. These were reported to the owner of the store, but he did not inform defendant, and the escalator continued in operation. Thereafter, plaintiff was seriously injured by reason of the defect. Is defendant liable? Drazen v. Otis Elevator Co., 96 R.I. 114, 189 A.2d 693 (1963).

3. What if the product sold is so highly dangerous to the user as to make it entirely unfit for its intended use? In Farley v. Edward E. Tower & Co., 271 Mass. 230, 171 N.E. 639 (1930), defendant manufactured and sold to dealers combs for use in "water wave" treatment in beauty shops. These combs were made of pyroxylin, a nitrocellulose or gun-cotton, resembling celluloid. They were highly inflammable and explosive, and unsafe for any hair treatment involving heat. Defendant knew that heat treatment was common in beauty shops, but sold the packages for resale, without any warning by labels or otherwise. Tower, a dealer, was well aware of the character of the combs, but resold some of them to a beauty shop without any warning. The combs were used in treating plaintiff's hair with heat; they caught fire, and plaintiff's head was burned. Is defendant liable?

Cf. Kentucky Independent Oil Co. v. Schnitzler, 208 Ky. 507, 271 S.W. 570 (1925) (gasoline mixed with kerosene); Clement v. Crosby & Co., 148 Mich. 293, 111 N.W. 745 (1907) (explosive stove polish); Warner v. Santa Catalina Island Co., 44 Cal.2d 310, 282 P.2d 12 (1955) (high-powered ammunition for shooting gallery).

4. In Ferraro v. Taylor, 197 Minn. 5, 265 N.W. 829 (1936), the defendant, operating a "drive yourself" automobile service, rented a car to one Taylor. The car had defective brakes, the steering wheel was out of order, the wind-

Sounds like The cars I rented in Albany. last week.

shield wiper would not work, and it was raining. In other words, Taylor could not see, could not steer and could not stop. He drove the car for a considerable distance through city traffic before colliding with the plaintiff. He testified that the car was "a pineapple," an "old melon," an "old wreck," and "this car was just like all the rest of them I ever rented over there. There is none of them in shape." Is defendant relieved of liability?

Look back at Gordon
— — was Niagara ssly liable? both

Chapter VII

JOINT TORTFEASORS

1. LIABILITY AND JOINDER OF DEFENDANTS

Δ (17 yrs old)   π
BIERCZYNSKI v. ROGERS

Supreme Court of Delaware, 1968.
239 A.2d 218.

G/R = if you collide while passing always join the car you were passing to argue that you both were racing

HERRMANN, JUSTICE. This appeal involves an automobile accident in which the plaintiffs claim that the defendant motorists were racing on the public highway, as the result of which the accident occurred.

TrCt = π
both B+R liable jointly

The plaintiffs Cecil B. Rogers and Susan D. Rogers brought this action against Robert C. Race and Ronald Bierczynski, ages 18 and 17 respectively, alleging concurrent negligences in that they violated various speed statutes and various other statutory rules of the road, and in that they failed to keep a proper lookout and failed to keep their vehicles under proper control. The jury, by answer to interrogatories in its special verdict, expressly found that Race and Bierczynski were each negligent and that the negligence of each was a proximate cause of the accident. Substantial verdicts were entered in favor of the plaintiffs against both defendants jointly. The defendant Bierczynski appeals therefrom. The defendant Race does not appeal; rather, he joins with the plaintiffs in upholding the judgment below.

FACTS:

[The evidence justified a finding that the automobiles driven by Bierczynski and Race engaged in a speed contest, as they came down a hill side-by-side at twice the legal speed. Ahead of them was the car of the plaintiffs, in the westbound lane. As they approached it, Race tried to get his car back into the eastbound lane. He lost control of it, and careened sideways, at about 70 miles per hour, into the front of plaintiffs' car. Bierczynski remained in the proper lane at all times, and brought his car to a stop in it, about 35 feet from the area of collision. It did not come in contact with the plaintiffs' vehicle.]

as a matter of law?

In many States, automobile racing on a public highway is prohibited by statute, the violation of which is negligence per se. [Cc] Delaware has no such statute. Nevertheless, speed competition in automobiles on the public highway is negligence in this State, for the reason that a reasonably prudent person would not engage in such conduct. This conclusion is in accord with the general rule, prevailing in other jurisdictions which lack statutes on the subject, that racing motor vehicles on a public highway is negligence. [Cc]

352

It is also generally held that all who engage in a race on the highway do so at their peril, and are liable for injury or damage sustained by a third person as a result thereof, regardless of which of the racing cars directly inflicted the injury or damage. The authorities reflect generally accepted rules of causation that all parties engaged in a motor vehicle race on the highway are wrongdoers acting in concert, *~as opposed to Tice v. Summers* and that each participant is liable for harm to a third person arising from the tortious conduct of the other, because he has induced and encouraged the tort. [Cc]

We subscribe to those rules; and hold that, as a general rule, participation in a motor vehicle race on a public highway is an act of concurrent negligence imposing liability on each participant for any injury to a non-participant resulting from the race. If, therefore, Race and Bierczynski were engaged in a speed competition, each was liable for the damages and injuries to the plaintiffs herein, even though Bierczynski was not directly involved in the collision itself. Bierczynski apparently concedes liability if a race had, in fact, been in progress. Clearly there was ample evidence to carry to the jury the issue of a race—and with it, implicit therein, the issue of proximate cause as to Bierczynski. * * * *B apparently argued there was no race. (Stopper w/in 35 ft) 11 yards)*

We find no error as asserted by the appellant. The judgments below are affirmed.

---

1. Observe that there were two decisions in this case: 1) that the two defendants could be joined in the same action and 2) that each was liable for the full amount of the judgment. The law of joinder has evolved over the years but it usually raises no serious problems. The problems for joinder are not as difficult as those for liability of joint tortfeasors.

2. *Joinder.* Originally, English law did not permit joinder in the absence of a concert of action as in the principal case. See Sadler v. Western Ry. Co., [1896] A.C. 450 (two trucks, acting independently, blocked both ends of a street, preventing access to plaintiff's land—separate actions required). With the advent of the Field Code in the middle of last century, a plaintiff was able to join in one action "any person who . . . . is a necessary party to the complete determination or settlement of the questions involved therein." Modern procedural codes or rules of court are based on the principle of the trial convenience and provide that joinder is permitted when the plaintiff's claims arise from "the same transaction, occurrence, or series of transactions or occurrences and if any question of law or fact common to all defendants will arise in the action." Fed.R.Civ.Proc. 20(a). Joinder, therefore, does not necessarily require that defendants be liable for the exact same injury.

3. It is held in most jurisdictions, however, that the plaintiff has the right to sue one tortfeasor alone, without joining others who may also be liable; and if he does, the defendant cannot, over the plaintiff's objection, compel the joinder of the others. See Sox v. Hertz Corp., 262 F.Supp. 531 (D.S.C.1967). However, most states now provide for third-party practice, and if a defendant has a right of contribution against a joint tortfeasor in the jurisdiction, he may implead him as a third-party defendant and attempt to establish his joint responsibility. See Knell v. Feltman, infra page 367.

Plaintiffs do joining; Defendants do impleading.

4. *Liability.* "Joint and several liability" means that each of several tortfeasors is liable jointly with the others for the amount of the judgment against them, and that each is also individually liable for the full amount. The plaintiff can collect from any one of them or any group. There are three types of factual situations in which joint and several liability is normally imposed. The instant case illustrates the first—that in which the tortfeasors acted in concert. The classic discussion is Prosser, Joint Torts and Several Liability, 25 Calif.L.Rev. 413 (1937); and see Jackson, Joint Torts and Several Liability, 17 Tex.L.Rev. 399 (1939).

5. Three defendants, acting in concert, set upon the plaintiff. One held him, which was false imprisonment; another battered him; the third stole his silver buttons. All three were held liable for the entire damages. Smithson v. Garth, 3 Lev. 324, 83 Eng.Rep. 711 (1691). Cf. Garrett v. Garrett, 228 N.C. 530, 46 S.E.2d 302 (1948); and the amusing version of Romeo and Juliet up to date in Tricoli v. Centalanza, 100 N.J.L. 231, 126 A. 214 (1924).

6. Suppose that X attacks and beats the plaintiff. Defendant takes no part in the attack, but encourages X to go ahead and prevents others from interfering. Is defendant liable? Hilmes v. Stroebel, 59 Wis. 74, 17 N.W. 539 (1883); Thompson v. Johnson, 180 F.2d 431 (5th Cir.1950). What if he merely stands by and approves, but does nothing active? People v. Luna, 140 Cal.App. 2d 662, 295 P.2d 457 (1956).

7. Did the principal case involve an express or implied agreement to injure plaintiff? If not, why are defendants deemed joint tortfeasors? Did they participate in the joint creation of a negligent risk? See also Lemons v. Kelly, 239 Or. 354, 360–61, 397 P.2d 784, 787 (1964); Annot., 13 A.L.R.3d 431 (1967).

8. Suppose, in the principal case, that Race and Bierczynski had not been drag racing, but had entered a contest to see which one could get first from one point in the city to another, with each selecting his own route. Race was speeding and hit the plaintiffs. Should Bierczynski, who went by a different route, be liable? Would it make any difference whether Bierczynski was also speeding? Whether the point of the contest was to see who could drive the fastest or who picked the shortest route?

9. Compare Sindell v. Abbott Laboratories, Inc., supra p. 283. Was there a concert of action in that case? The *Sindell* court thought not, but contrast Bichler v. Eli Lilly & Co., 79 A.D.2d 317, 436 N.Y.S.2d 625 (1981), aff'd, 55 N.Y.2d 572, 436 N.E.2d 182, 450 N.Y.S.2d 776 (1982), where the court found that product sellers acted in "conscious parallelism" by marketing the same product at the same time in the same way. Is this a "concert of action" under the principles of the *Bierczynski* case? See also Abel v. Eli Lilly & Co., 418 Mich. 311, 343 N.W.2d 164 (1984).

10. The second situation in which joint and several liability applies is that in which defendants fail to perform a common duty to the plaintiff. For example, an elevator falls and both the building owner and the elevator company failed to comply with the duty to maintain it. See Bond v. Otis Elevator Co., 388 S.W.2d 681 (Tex.1965). Included in this situation is that in which there is a vicarious-liability relationship between two parties (i.e., master and servant); each is independently liable to the plaintiff. See infra Chapter 13, Section 1(A). For the third situation, see the next two cases.

Generally = Comp N → presumes factfinder can
assign percentage of liability
= Court N → complete bar to P's recovery
yw ti → Δs
= if so, then why not between Δ's ? (this case)

Ch. 7   LIABILITY & JOINDER OF DEFENDANTS   355

CONEY v. J.L.G. INDUSTRIES, INC.

Supreme Court of Illinois, 1983.
97 Ill.2d 104, 454 N.E.2d 197, 73 Ill.Dec. 337.

[This is a wrongful death action brought by Coney as administrator of the estate of Clifford M. Jasper. Jasper died while operating a hydraulic aerial work platform, manufactured by defendant, and the action is based on strict products liability. There were two defenses: (1) that Jasper was guilty of contributory negligence, and (2) that his employer, V. Jobst & Sons, was also guilty of contributory negligence in failing to provide a "groundman," and in failing to "instruct and train Jasper on the operation of the platform." The trial court struck the defenses, but three questions were certified to the Supreme Court.

The three questions were:

"Whether the doctrine of comparative negligence or fault is applicable to actions or claims seeking recovery under products liability or strict liability in tort theories?

Whether the doctrine of comparative negligence or fault eliminates joint and several liability?

Whether the retention of joint and several liability in a system of comparative negligence or fault denies defendants equal protection of the laws in violation "of the Federal and state constitutions."

The court's answer to the first question was in the affirmative. This will be considered in more detail in the chapters on Defenses and Product Liability.]

THOMAS J. MORAN, JUSTICE: * * * The common law doctrine of joint and several liability holds joint tortfeasors responsible for the plaintiff's entire injury, allowing plaintiff to pursue all, some, or one of the tortfeasors responsible for his injury for the full amount of the damages. [Cc]

Defendant asserts joint and several liability is a corollary of the contributory negligence doctrine. Prior to Alvis [v. Ribar, 85 Ill.2d 1, 421 N.E.2d 886, 52 Ill.Dec. 23 (1981), judicially adopting pure comparative negligence,] a plaintiff who was guilty of even slight contributory negligence was barred from recovery. Defendant maintains that joint and several liability balanced this inequity by permitting a faultless plaintiff to collect his entire judgment from any defendant who was guilty of even slight negligence. With the adoption of comparative negligence where damages are apportioned according to each party's fault, defendant argues it is no longer rational to hold a defendant liable beyond his share of the total damages. Defendant relies primarily on a line of cases where joint and several liability was abolished or limited in the course of construing a statutory scheme of liability. [Cc]

The vast majority of jurisdictions, however, which have adopted comparative negligence have retained joint and several liability as a part of their comparative negligence doctrine [citing authorities from 16 states].

Generally, four reasons have been advanced for retaining joint and several liability:

RTL =

(1) The feasibility of apportioning fault on a comparative basis does not render an indivisible injury "divisible" for purposes of the joint and several liability rule. A concurrent tortfeasor is liable for the whole of an indivisible injury when his negligence is a proximate cause of that damage. In many instances, the negligence of a concurrent tortfeasor may be sufficient by itself to cause the entire loss. The mere fact that it may be possible to assign some percentage figure to the relative culpability of one negligent defendant as compared to another does not in any way suggest that each defendant's negligence is not a proximate cause of the entire indivisible injury.

= then π is not at fault; Thus, no Comp N.

(2) In those instances where the plaintiff is not guilty of negligence, he would be forced to bear a portion of the loss should one of the tortfeasors prove financially unable to satisfy his share of the damages. *But this begs ques. =; in Comp N, π is not w/o fault; so π's may be greater than one Δs, who may be liable for all. Is that fair?*

RTL = to make The π whole =

(3) Even in cases where a plaintiff is partially at fault, his culpability is not equivalent to that of a defendant. The plaintiff's negligence relates only to a lack of due care for his own safety while the defendant's negligence relates to a lack of due care for the safety of others; the latter is tortious, but the former is not.

(4) Elimination of joint and several liability would work a serious and unwarranted deleterious effect on the ability of an injured plaintiff to obtain adequate compensation for his injuries. [Cc]

In adopting comparative negligence, this court eliminated the total bar to recovery which a plaintiff had faced under contributory negligence. In return for allowing a negligent plaintiff to recover, this court said fairness requires that a plaintiff's damages be "reduced by the percentage of fault *attributable to him*." (Emphasis added.) (*Alvis v. Ribar* (1981), 85 Ill.2d 1, 25, 52 Ill.Dec. 23, 421 N.E.2d 886.) Were we to eliminate joint and several liability as the defendant advocates, the burden of the insolvent or immune defendant would fall on the plaintiff; in that circumstance, plaintiff's damages would be reduced beyond the percentage of fault *attributable to him*. We do not believe the doctrine of comparative negligence requires this further reduction. Nor do we believe this burden is the price plaintiffs must pay for being relieved of the contributory negligence bar. The *quid pro quo* is the reduction of plaintiff's damages. What was said in *American Motorcycle Association v. Superior Court* (1978), 20 Cal.3d 578, 590, 578 P.2d 899, 906, 146 Cal.Rptr. 182, 189, is applicable here: "[F]airness dictates that the 'wronged party should not be deprived of his right to redress,' * * * '[t]he wrongdoers should be left to work out between themselves any apportionment.'" * * *

Comp N =

Defendant concedes that where the plaintiff is free from fault each defendant should still be held jointly and severally liable. It also admits in its reply brief that the Act leaves unaffected the common law doctrine of joint and several liability. * * *

Now, under *Alvis*, damages are allocated according to fault. As such, defendant argues, *Alvis* mandates that a tortfeasor should be liable only to the extent that his negligent acts or omissions produced the damages.

We find nothing in *Alvis* which mandates either a shift in who shall bear the risk of the insolvent defendant or the elimination of joint and several liability. Defendant has not cited nor have we found persuasive judicial authority for the proposition that comparative negligence compels the abolition of joint and several liability. On the contrary, most jurisdictions which have adopted comparative negligence have retained the doctrine. Therefore, we hold that our adoption of comparative negligence in *Alvis* does not change the longstanding doctrine of joint and several liability. * * *

Prospective application of a new doctrine or rule of law does not violate the equal protection of laws under either the Federal or Illinois constitution. [Cc]

Therefore, in response to the questions posed, we conclude that (1) comparative fault is applicable to strict products liability actions; (2) comparative fault does not eliminate joint and several liability; and (3) retention of joint and several liability does not deny defendants equal protection of the laws. * * *

Affirmed and remanded, with directions.

BARTLETT v. NEW MEXICO WELDING SUPPLY, INC.
Court of Appeals of New Mexico, 1982.
98 N.M. 152, 646 P.2d 579, cert. denied, 98 N.M. 336, 648 P.2d 794 (1982).

WOOD, JUDGE * * * The automobile accident involved three vehicles. The car in front of plaintiffs' car signaled a right hand turn. This lead car turned into and then pulled out of a service station in a very fast motion. Plaintiff Jane Bartlett slammed on her brakes to avoid hitting the lead car. Defendant's truck was behind plaintiffs' car. Defendant's driver applied his brakes; however, the truck skidded into the rear of plaintiffs' car.

The driver of the lead car is unknown. Plaintiffs sued defendant on a theory of negligence. Defendant contended that the negligence of the unknown driver "caused or contributed to cause" the accident and resulting damages. * * *

The jury answered "special questions." It determined that plaintiffs' damages were $100,000.00, that plaintiffs were not negligent, that defendant was negligent, that defendant's negligence contributed to the accident and plaintiffs' damages to the extent of 30%, that the unknown driver was negligent and this negligence contributed to the accident and plaintiffs' damages to the extent of 70%.

Plaintiffs moved that judgment be entered in their favor in the amount of $100,000.00. This motion was not granted. Instead, the trial court ordered a new trial. * * *

We granted defendant's application for an interlocutory appeal.

In this case, in using the term "joint and several liability," we mean that either of two persons whose concurrent negligence contributed to cause plaintiffs' injury and damage may be held liable for the entire amount of the damage caused by them.

It is not disputed that this is a common law rule which existed in New Mexico prior to *Scott v. Rizzo*, 96 N.M. 682, 634 P.2d 1234 (1981), which adopted the opinion of the Court of Appeals in *Claymore v. City of Albuquerque*. In *Claymore,* this Court adopted pure comparative negligence. * * *

The question is whether, in a comparative negligence case, a concurrent tortfeasor is liable for the entire damage caused by concurrent tortfeasors. * * * The premise for the question to be answered is that, under the common law rule, either the defendant or the unknown driver could be held liable for the damage caused by their combined negligence.

The question has been answered in several states; most of these decisions are not helpful because the answer depended upon the contents of a comparative negligence. [The court discusses rulings in a number of states.]

The foregoing discussion shows that joint and several liability, for concurrent tortfeasors, has been retained by judicial decision in pure comparative negligence states. We recognize that this retention accords with 2 Restatement (Second) of Torts § 433A (1965). *See,* Comment h to § 433A. Retention also accords with the Uniform Comparative Fault Act, § 2. [For text of this Act, see infra pages 579–81.]

The retention of joint and several liability ultimately rests on two grounds; neither ground is defensible.

The first ground is the concept that a plaintiff's injury is "indivisible." The California Supreme Court, in *American Motorcycle Ass'n* [v. Superior Court, 20 Cal.3d 578, 146 Cal.Rptr. 182, 579 P.2d 899 (1978)] supra, followed this ground when it stated: "[T]he simple feasibility of apportioning fault on a comparative negligence basis does not render an indivisible injury 'divisible' for purposes of the joint and several liability. * * * In other words, the mere fact that it may be possible to assign some percentage figure to the relative culpability of one negligent defendant as compared to another does not in any way suggest that each defendant's negligence is not a proximate cause of the entire indivisible injury."

Thus, under the California Supreme Court decision, a concurrent tortfeasor, 1% at fault, is liable for 100% of the damage caused by concurrent tortfeasors, on the basis that the tortfeasor, 1% at fault, caused the entire damage. A practical answer, in this case, is that the jury found that defendant was 30% at fault and caused 50% of the damage.

Prosser, *Law of Torts*, 4th Edition, § 41, p. 241, states: "The law of joint tortfeasors rests very largely upon recognition of the fact that each of two or more causes may be charged with a single result."

Prosser, "Joint Torts and Several Liability," 25 Cal.L.Rev. 413 (1936–37), states that the rule holding a concurrent tortfeasor for the entire loss "grew out of the common law concept of the unity of the cause of action; the jury could not be permitted to apportion the damages, since there was but one wrong." The "unity" concept, in turn was based on common law rules of pleading and joinder. * * *

Joint and several liability is not to be retained in our pure comparative negligence system on a theory of one indivisible wrong. The concept of one indivisible wrong, based on common law technicalities, is obsolete, and is not to be applied in comparative negligence cases in New Mexico. [C]

The second ground is that joint and several liability must be retained in order to favor plaintiffs; a plaintiff should not bear the risk of being unable to collect his judgment. We fail to understand the argument. Between one plaintiff and one defendant, the plaintiff bears the risk of the defendant being insolvent; on what basis does the risk shift if there are two defendants, and one is insolvent? In our case, the risk factor arises because the concurrent tortfeasor, 70% at fault, is unknown. * * *

Joint and several liability is not to be retained in our pure comparative negligence system on the basis that a plaintiff must be favored.

We hold that defendant is not liable for the entire damage caused by defendant and the unknown driver. Defendant, as a concurrent tortfeasor, is not liable on a theory of joint and several liability. * * *

The trial court properly instructed the jury to consider the negligence and damage resulting from the negligence of the unknown driver.

The order granting a new trial is reversed. The cause is remanded with instructions to enter judgment in favor of plaintiffs, against defendant, for the 30% of plaintiffs' damages caused by defendant.

---

1. In these two cases, the negligent conduct of several tortfeasors combines to produce a particular injury to the plaintiff. The negligence of each of them is found to be a proximate cause of that injury. The injury has therefore been treated as indivisible and this has commonly been regarded as the third situation in which the principle of joint and several liability should be applied. But this position has been based upon two other major tort principles that have

been changing. The question is whether they should produce a change in this principle. Some of them have not yet been covered in this course and need a preliminary explanation. One principle involves contributory negligence, which at common law barred plaintiff's recovery but has been changed in all but a few states so that it now has the effect of diminishing the amount of plaintiff's recovery (details in Chapter 12, Section 1). A second principle involves contribution, which was not allowed at common law but is now generally followed, permitting a tortfeasor paying more than his share to recover, on either a pro-rata basis or a comparative-negligence basis (this Chapter, Section 3). ▸ from other ∆

2. It is now being urged that the concept of comparative negligence should be applied to the "indivisible" injury, so that each defendant is responsible for only that part of the injury that the percentage of fault apportioned to him bears to the total negligence of all tortfeasors. Otherwise, it is claimed, he will not be treated fairly. If each tortfeasor is able to pay his apportioned part, it is obvious that this form of several liability will produce exactly the same result as the traditional system of joint and several liability.

3. The difference arises when the shares of one or more tortfeasors are not collectible from them. Under joint and several liability, the plaintiff can collect from one (or more) of the tortfeasors (sometimes called "Mr. Deep Pocket") and leave it up to him either to obtain contribution from the others or to bear the loss himself. Under several liability, each tortfeasor pays no more than his allocated share, and, instead of Mr. Deep Pocket, the injured party necessarily bears the loss of any uncollected share. Which is the fairer method?

4. Should it make any difference whether the plaintiff is negligent or not? The Uniform Comparative Fault Act (infra page 579) continues joint and several liability but provides for the determination of each party's "equitable share of the obligation" in accordance with his percentage of fault. Then, in case one party's share is uncollectible, it provides for a reallocation of that share among the other parties, including the plaintiff, if he is at fault, according to their respective percentages of fault. Does this seem fair? Suppose the plaintiff is not at fault?

How should an immune party be treated? Note that in the *Bartlett* case, the 70% tortfeasor was a "hit and run" driver, and therefore not a party to the action. Is it appropriate to determine the percentage of a nonparty? If he should later be found, would that determination be binding on him?

5. All of this is being very hotly debated at the present time. A fully organized campaign has been vigorously pushing for statutory abolition of joint and several liability by the state legislatures, and it has attained considerable success.

Many of the statutes have categorically abolished joint and several liability, and substituted several liability. Some legislatures, however, have adopted compromise provisions. Thus, joint and several liability may be eliminated (1) only for noneconomic damages (e.g., pain and suffering, emotional distress, etc.); or (2) for defendants whose percentage of fault is below a certain threshold, or (3) for certain types of defendants, such as municipal corporations. There are other variables.

6. Would it be desirable to have the judge explain to the jury the consequences of their decision in setting the percentage of fault? See Kaeo v. Davis, 719 P.2d 387 (Hawaii 1986).

7. Does the principle of joint and several liability contribute to augmenting the cost and reducing the availability of liability insurance? What significance should the answer to this question have in a decision of whether to retain or abolish the principle?

8. See generally Miller, Extending the Fairness Principle of *Li* and American Motorcycle: Adoption of the Uniform Comparative Fault Act, 14 Pac. L.J. 835 (1983); Zavos, Comparative Fault and the Insolvent Defendant, 14 Loyola L.A.L.Rev., 770 (1981); Adler, Allocation of Responsibility After American Motorcycle v. Superior Court, 6 Pepperdine L.Rev. 1 (1978); Wade, Should Joint and Several Liability of Multiple Tortfeasors Be Abolished?, 10 Am.J. Trial Advoc. 193 (1987); Notes, 10 U.Cin.L.Rev. 342 (1982), 37 U.Fla.L.Rev. 288 (1984), 50 Mo.L.Rev. 501 (1985).

2. SATISFACTION AND RELEASE

BUNDT v. EMBRO
Supreme Court of New York, Queens County, 1965.
48 Misc.2d 802, 265 N.Y.S.2d 872.

[Action by five plaintiffs, who were passengers in one or the other of two automobiles which collided. The actions were against the owners and drivers, as well as a contractor who was repairing the highway, and who had negligently obstructed the view of a stop sign. Some of the defendants moved to amend their answer to interpose the defense of discharge and satisfaction, in that plaintiffs had recovered a judgment for the same injuries against the State of New York in the Court of Claims; and that this judgment had been satisfied.]

WILLIAM B. GROAT, JUSTICE. * * * "[I]t is elementary law that one who has been injured by the joint wrong of several parties may recover his damages against either or all; but, although there may be several suits and recoveries, there can be but one satisfaction. [Cc] The reason of the rule is that while there may be many perpetrators of a wrongful act, each of whom is separately liable, yet the act and its consequences are indivisible, and the injured person is, therefore, limited to a single satisfaction." [C] * * *

Nor does this court agree with plaintiffs' argument that the rule that the satisfaction of the judgment against one joint tort feasor discharges the others has no application to a Court of Claims judgment. Section 8 of the Court of Claims Act states:

"The state hereby waives its immunity from liability and action and hereby assumes liability and consents to have the same determined in accordance with the same rules of law as applied to actions in the supreme court against individuals or corporations, provided the claimant complies with the limitations of this article."

"By the adoption of such section the State places itself as to those making claims against the State, in the same position as a private individual or a corporation would be for his or its negligence." [C]

The Court of Claims determined that the state was negligent and the plaintiffs were awarded judgments for the injuries sustained. If defendants are joint tort feasors with the state, the fact that the judgment satisfied is a Court of Claims judgment should not prevent application of a rule which prevents double recovery for a single injury.

The state may also be a joint tortfeasor [c]. While the sovereign has always been immune from suit at common law, " '[w]hen, however, the state confers upon a court jurisdiction to hear and determine all claims against it, or all claims of a particular class, the situation in that court is the same as if the claim were against a private individual or corporation.' " [Cc]

Therefore, if the trial court shall determine that the defendants were in fact joint tort feasors with the state, the satisfaction of a judgment against the state would operate as a ⟨discharge⟩ of the defendants.

Can State seek contribution from other d's? Would it?

Accordingly, leave to amend is granted to the defendants.

Should other d's have to pay to state? What about punitives/exemplary? Why does π get for their negl also, aside from contribution? It already made whole?

1. The original English rule, now altered by statute, was that the plaintiff could obtain but one judgment against one or more "joint tortfeasors," meaning those who acted in concert. Since the act of each was the act of all, it was considered that there was only one cause of action against all of them, which was "merged" in the judgment, so that the judgment against one alone, even though unsatisfied, barred any later action against another. This rule is now repudiated everywhere in the United States, and ⟨it is held⟩ that the plaintiff may bring a series of separate actions against defendants liable for the same damage, and reduce each to judgment.

2. A quite distinct principle developed in England, and carried over to the United States, that the plaintiff was entitled to only one compensation, and that satisfaction of his claim, by full payment, would prevent its further enforcement. It is obvious that this rule is equitable in its nature, and that its purpose is to prevent unjust enrichment. It is now generally held to apply even when satisfaction is made by one who believes himself to be liable but actually is not. See Latham v. Des Moines Elec. Light Co., 232 Iowa 1038, 6 N.W.2d 853 (1942); Harris v. Roanoke, 179 Va. 1, 18 S.E.2d 303 (1942); King, Accord and Satisfaction by a Third Person, 15 Mo.L.Rev. 115 (1950); Note, 8 Vand.L.Rev. 509 (1955). Payments made by the tortfeasor's liability insurance company are of course made on his behalf.

3. A necessary corollary of the second rule was that any partial satisfaction of the claim must be credited to the other parties who are also liable.

4. Payments made to the injured party in his own behalf rather than by or in behalf of a tortfeasor are not credited to the benefit of the tortfeasors, even though they may afford duplicate compensation for some losses. If, for example, a plaintiff's medical fees are paid for by some source collateral to the defendant, such as a relative, employer or insurance company, the defendant should not "be permitted to profit by any gratuity extended to his victim, and consequently, the reasonable value of said services should be recoverable." Burke v. Byrd, 188 F.Supp. 384 (N.D.Fla.1960); see also Royer v. Eskovitz, 358 Mich. 279, 100 N.W.2d 306 (1960) (where employer paid employee's medical bills and later sued tortfeasor for recovery of payments, no assignment by

employee to employer shown). This the so-called collateral-source rule applies to insurance policies maintained by the injured party, to gratuities to him, to employment benefits and to benefits from social legislation.

For discussion, see Restatement (Second) of Torts § 920A; Fleming, The Collateral Source Rule and Loss Allocation in Tort Law, 54 Calif.L.Rev. 1478 (1966); Lambert, The Case for the Collateral–Source Rule, 3 Trial Law.Q. 52 (1965). See infra pages 515–18.

COX v. PEARL INVESTMENT CO.

Supreme Court of Colorado, 1969.
168 Colo. 67, 450 P.2d 60.

HODGES, JUSTICE. This is a negligence case which terminated in the trial court with a summary judgment in favor of the defendant on a showing that a purported release had been executed by the plaintiffs in favor of a joint tort-feasor. The common law rule of law that the release of one tort-feasor releases all others who may have liability was applied by the trial court.

As plaintiffs in the trial court, Mr. and Mrs. Cox sought recovery of damages for injuries which Mrs. Cox sustained when she fell on property owned by the defendant Pearl Investment Company. * * * When the summary judgment motion was considered by the trial court, it was shown that the tenant, Goodwill Industries, had previously paid the plaintiffs $2500 in consideration of the plaintiffs' execution of a document entitled "Covenant Not to Proceed with Suit." * * *

The plaintiffs' second assignment of error, however, does bring into focus another important issue concerning the legal effect to be given to the "Covenant Not to Proceed with Suit" involved here. The trial court denominated it a release and, without ascribing any dignity to the expressed words that the plaintiffs reserved "the right to sue any other person or persons against whom they may have or assert any claim on account of damages arising out of the above described accident," ruled that it therefore barred any action against the defendant as a joint tort-feasor.

Although Price v. Baker, 143 Colo. 264, 352 P.2d 90 supports the trial court, we no longer deem it advisable to further impose on our body of law the harshness and rigidity of the rule and rationale of *Price.* * * * In our present analysis of this issue, we are drawn toward only one conclusion. We can no longer countenance the continuation of a rule of law which is not only harsh and illogical, but which gives refuge and absolution to wrongdoers by depriving a litigant under these circumstances of probable just and full compensation for his injuries caused by wrongdoers. It is not possible to visualize any reasonable or compelling justification for persisting in the application of this harsh and unrealistic rule except on the basis of ancient formalisms, the reasons for which no longer prevail. * * *

In *Price,* we declared "this state has long followed the universal rule that the release of one joint tort-feasor is a release of all." We hereby confirm this to be still the rule in Colorado. Also, we agree with the proposition that a joint tort-feasor is not ipso facto released by a covenant not to sue. We do, however, now state that the instrument involved in Price v. Baker, which is substantially identical to the writing involved in the case at bar, was improvidently interpreted to be an absolute and full release of all joint tort-feasors.

The manifest intent of the parties to a contract should always be given effect unless it be in violation of law or public policy. This is fundamental in contract law. Where a contract has the effect of releasing one joint tort-feasor but expressly reserves the right to sue others who may be liable, it should not in law be treated otherwise. The expressed reservation in this instrument of the right to sue other joint tort-feasors evinces a clear-cut manifestation that the plaintiffs were not receiving full compensation; and if this is borne out, their right to bring an action against others who were the cause of their damages should not be foreclosed. The danger of over compensation or double compensation is no excuse for barring a claim against joint tort-feasors. Obviously, no court would permit the accomplishment of this possible contingency. And certainly, the non-settling joint tort-feasor is not prejudiced, but rather, he is benefited for he would be entitled to have the amount of the judgment reduced by the amount paid by his co-tortfeasor. * * *

To be particularly noted is the early case of Matheson v. O'Kane, 211 Mass. 91, 97 N.E. 638. The facts therein are quite similar to the facts of the instant case in that the released parties were authorized to plead the instrument in bar to any action filed by the plaintiffs. It was held that this did not constitute a release of other defendants and further stated:

" * * * But where it is evident that the consideration paid to the plaintiff was not intended to be full compensation for his injuries, and the agreement signed by him although in form a release was clearly intended to preserve the liability of those who were not parties to it, many of the courts have sought to give effect to that intention by construing the agreement as in legal effect a covenant not to sue and not a technical release."

4 Restatement of Torts § 885 which is modeled after numerous cases like *Matheson,* supra, provides that a release will be construed as a covenant not to sue where the right to proceed against the remaining tort-feasors is expressly reserved. This section emphasizes the importance of the expressed intent of the contracting parties.

In the supplemental brief of the defendant, it is urged that *Price,* supra, establishes the rule in Colorado that the document involved there which is essentially identical to the instrument here is an absolute release of all joint tort-feasors and therefore, should not now be repudiated under the doctrine of stare decisis. This doctrine is assiduously followed by this court. However, when, as here, a prior decision is adverse to the rules of fundamental law and initiates a

[handwritten: what about of second or Third opportunity?]

harsh and unrealistic rule, we believe it becomes incumbent upon us at the first opportunity presented to make a necessary change.

Accordingly, the judgment is reversed and the cause remanded to the trial court for further proceedings not inconsistent with the views expressed herein.

[handwritten: ∆ harms π, says "what can I do for you"; π gives laundry list, & ∆ does them all. Then π sues. Has ∆ been released? Has π been satisfied? receiving]

1. Distinguish between release and satisfaction. Satisfaction is acceptance of full compensation for the injury. A release is a surrender of the plaintiff's claim, which may be for only partial compensation, and may even be gratuitous. Releases in the early common law were under seal, which disposed of the question of consideration.

2. Distinguish between a release and a covenant not to sue. The theory of the covenant is that plaintiff does not surrender his cause of action, but contracts that he will not sue on it. The right is retained, but there is agreement not to enforce it. The protection to the defendant is that if the plaintiff sues, he will have a counterclaim or cross-action for breach of the covenant, in which the damages will equal any recovery by the plaintiff plus the expenses of defending the suit. This is well set out in Pellett v. Sonotone Corp., 26 Cal.2d 705, 160 P.2d 783 (1945). It is generally recognized by the courts that the covenant is a mere procedural device, invented by the ingenuity of counsel to get around the effect of a release.

3. In early common law the only negligent "joint tortfeasors" were those who acted in concert. Since the act of one was the act of all, a release to one of them was held to release the others, since there was but one cause of action, which was surrendered. Confusion as to the meaning of "joint tortfeasors" carried this rule over in the early American decisions to those who acted independently but could be joined because they were liable for the same damages. In addition, perhaps because of abolition of the seal, release was confused with satisfaction. See Abb v. Northern Pacific R. Co., 28 Wash. 428, 68 P. 954 (1902) (a release, even with express reservation of rights against other tortfeasors, is "conclusive evidence of satisfaction"). The result was, almost everywhere, an original American rule that a release to one tortfeasor releases all who are liable for the same damages, regardless of compensation paid or reservation of rights.

4. The original rule to the effect that the release of one joint tortfeasor releases all has been extensively changed, by decision or by statute. The present state of the law may be summarized as follows:

(a) A very small number of states refuse to recognize the covenant not to sue, and hold that either a release or a covenant releases the other tortfeasors, regardless of compensation or reservation of rights.

(b) A good many states distinguish between a release and a covenant not to sue, and hold that the release necessarily releases other tortfeasors, but the covenant does not unless full compensation has been paid.

(c) Some states hold that a release with express reservation of rights against other tortfeasors is to be treated as a covenant not to sue, regardless of words of release.

(d) An increasing number of states hold that even a release without such a reservation does not release other tortfeasors unless it shows an intention to do so or full compensation has been paid.

(e) Statutes in a good many states have provided that a release with an express reservation of rights against other tortfeasors does not release them. For example, the Uniform Joint Obligations Act, § 4. Or that they are released only when the terms so provide. Uniform Contribution Among Tortfeasors Act, § 4(a). See, however, Hester v. Gatlin, 332 So.2d 660 (Fla.App. 1976), where overbroad language in the release released a defendant who did not participate in the settlement.

5. When other tortfeasors are not released from all liability, it is generally agreed that payments made under either the release or the covenant not to sue must be credited in partial satisfaction of their liability. See DeMaris v. Brown, 27 Wash.App. 932, 621 P.2d 201 (1980), for "crediting" and the effect of comparative negligence in claims against the nonsettling tortfeasor.

6. What if the plaintiff, prior to any accident, signs an agreement releasing A from any liability? In a collision, plaintiff is injured by the concurrent negligence of A and B. Is B released? Western Express Co. v. Smeltzer, 88 F.2d 94 (6th Cir. 1937). Cf. Dakin v. Allis, 25 Wis.2d 49, 130 N.W.2d 191 (1964) (alienation of affections).

7. The whole problem is discussed at length in McKenna v. Austin, 77 App.D.C. 228, 134 F.2d 659 (1943). A good decision is Gronquist v. Olson, 242 Minn. 119, 64 N.W.2d 159 (1954). See Restatement (Second) of Torts § 885.

8. A negligently runs into the plaintiff and breaks his leg. B, a physician, negligently treats the break, with the result that the leg is permanently shorter. Suppose that plaintiff accepts a payment from A for the original injury and releases him, expecting to hold B liable for the aggravation. When he sues B, B relies on the common law rule as to the effect of the release of one join tortfeasor. Assuming that A's liability extends to the total injury (supra page 354), some cases have held that B was released by the release to A. Thompson v. Fox, 326 Pa. 209, 192 A. 107 (1937). The booby-trap aspect of this application has led a number of courts to decline to apply the rule to successive tortfeasors in a situation like this. Derby v. Prewitt, 12 N.Y.2d 100, 187 N.E.2d 556, 236 N.Y.S.2d 953 (1962); Fieser v. St. Francis Hosp. & School of Nursing, 212 Kan. 35, 510 P.2d 145 (1973). Other courts resort to construction of the "release" as a means of avoiding the trap.

9. Suppose there is only one tortfeasor. A release is signed on the basis of assumed injuries. It turns out that the injuries are actually much more extensive than assumed. What can the injured party do? Ordinarily he must seek to set the release aside on the ground of fraud or mistake. But a release may cover unknown as well as known injuries if the parties so intend. This problem is treated in other courses, such as Restitution or Remedies. For treatment, see D. Dobbs, Remedies, § 11.10 (1973); Havighurst, The Effect upon Settlement of Mutual Mistake as to Injuries, 12 Defense L.J. 1 (1963).

10. There may be issues as to the scope of a release. Suppose there is an automobile accident in which both drivers and two passengers in one car are injured. The driver of the car without passengers executes a general release of liability in favor of the other driver. Later the releasee and the two passengers file a lawsuit against the releasor for personal injuries they sustained. The releasor files a counterclaim against the releasee, seeking contribution for any damages awarded to the passengers. Will the release operate to waive the releasor's right of contribution from the releasee? See Rakowski v. Lucente, 104 Ill.2d 317, 472 N.E.2d 791, 84 Ill.Dec. 654 (1984).

11. What problems should an attorney contemplate before advising his client whether to sign a release? For example, is an attorney liable to his client when the client, upon the attorney's advice, signs a release and is later barred from bringing a legal action against the tortfeasor?

12. For a practical perspective, see Kemp, Strategy of Remaining Codefendant(s); When the Plaintiff Settles With One Codefendant, 36 Fed.Ins. & Corp.Couns.Q. 41 (1985).

3. CONTRIBUTION AND INDEMNITY

KNELL v. FELTMAN

United States Court of Appeals, District of Columbia, 1949.
85 U.S.App.D.C. 22, 174 F.2d 662.

WILBUR K. MILLER, CIRCUIT JUDGE. On May 19, 1945 Evelyn Langland and her husband were guest passengers in an automobile owned and operated by Kenneth E. Knell. At 12th Street and Pennsylvania Avenue, in the District of Columbia, the car in which they were riding collided with a taxicab owned by Ralph L. Feltman and operated by his employee, as a result of which Mrs. Langland was seriously injured. She and her husband sued Feltman to recover damages. After answering, Feltman filed a third-party complaint against Knell, asserting the collision was caused by the contributing or sole negligence of Knell.

[The jury found, in answer to special interrogatories, that both Feltman's servant and Knell were negligent, that the negligence of each contributed to the collision, and that plaintiffs' damages were $11,500. The court then awarded judgment in favor of plaintiffs against Feltman for $11,500, and upon payment of this by Feltman, judgment in favor of Feltman against Knell for $5,750.]

Is Feltman to be denied contribution because the Langlands neither asked nor obtained judgment against Knell? The gist of Knell's argument on this question is that the right to contribution exists only between tortfeasors liable in common to the plaintiff; that his liability to the plaintiff was not established by a judgment against him in favor of the plaintiffs; that, therefore, his and Feltman's common liability to the Langlands was not established, and that consequently Feltman cannot have contribution from him.

In addition to being balked by Rule 14(a) [of the Federal Rules of Civil Procedure, which provides that a defendant may bring into the action another person who may be liable to him for all or any part of the damages, even though the plaintiff does not seek a judgment against him], the appellant's theory that there can be no contribution unless the plaintiff has first obtained a judgment against both wrongdoers is untenable for still another reason. The right to seek contribution belongs to the tortfeasor who has been forced to pay, and the existence of the right cannot logically depend upon a selection of defendants made by the plaintiff. If it did so depend, the caprice or whim of the plaintiff, or his deliberate intention to fasten liability on one defendant alone, could preclude that defendant from having contribution to which he might otherwise be entitled. Moreover, such an application of the contribution doctrine would open the way to collusion between a plaintiff, and one against whom he has a cause of action to impose liability solely upon another against whom he has a cause of action for the same wrong.

For these reasons, we see no substance in the suggestion that contribution between concurrent tortfeasors can be enforced only if both are judgment debtors of the plaintiff.

We come now to consider whether the fact that Knell personally participated in the commission of the tort takes this case out of the ruling in George's Radio, [Inc. v. Capital Transit Co., 75 U.S.App.D.C. 187, 126 F.2d 219 (1944),] where both wrongdoers were "vicariously" negligent.

This consideration logically leads to an examination of the interesting history of the no-contribution doctrine, which is conventionally said to begin with Merryweather v. Nixan, 8 Term Rep. 186, 101 Eng.Rep. 1337 (K.B.1799). The plaintiff and defendant in that case had injured a mill by taking or damaging its machinery and the plaintiff, having satisfied the judgment of the mill owner, sued for contribution. The trial judge non-suited on the ground that "no contribution could by law be claimed as between joint wrongdoers." On appeal, affirming the trial court, Kenyon, C.J., stated "that he had never before heard of such an action having been brought, where the former recovery was for a tort." In 1799, the word "tort" was used only to describe wrongs of a wilful or intentional character.

Due to the brevity of the report and a misleading headnote, the Merryweather case has often been cited in support of the sweeping proposition that no contribution can be had between joint tortfeasors. It is plain, however, that the ruling of the case was limited to the denial of contribution between wilful or intentional wrongdoers.

Nevertheless, after a period of adherence to the true Merryweather holding, the majority of American courts have long flatly said there can be no contribution between joint or concurrent tortfeasors, without distinguishing between those who are intentional wrongdoers and those whose unpurposed negligence results in a tort.

Widespread revulsion against that rule, which Chief Justice Groner said "is not sustainable upon any fair basis of reasoning, is wrong, and should be overruled", was demonstrated when the legislatures of some fifteen states enacted alleviating statutes in one form or another. Dissatisfaction with the rule is further shown by the fact that many courts have "riddled it with exceptions."

Among the exceptions created by the consciences of courts is that contribution may be enforced among concurrent tortfeasors who are only vicariously negligent. Obviously the creation of this exception was a differentiation from the Merryweather situation where the wrongdoers were deliberately such; and so was a recognition, perhaps unconscious, of the true Merryweather rule. Thus went the reasoning: if the tort-feasors were not personally present and had not directed their agents to commit the tort, they could not have intentionally done wrong and, therefore, the harsh rule of no contribution should be relaxed in their favor. No reason appears for denying the same favorable treatment to the unintentionally negligent, even though he personally committed the tortious act.

We conclude that when a tort is committed by the concurrent negligence of two or more persons who are not intentional wrongdoers, contribution should be enforced; that a joint judgment against such tort-feasors is not a prerequisite to contribution between them, and it is immaterial whether they were, or any of them was, personally negligent. In other words, we adopt for the District of Columbia, without exception or reservation, the rule stated by Chief Justice Groner in the George's Radio case "that when the parties are not intentional and wilful wrongdoers, but are made so by legal inference or intendment, contribution may be enforced." * * *

Affirmed.

---

1. The rule that there can be no contribution among joint tortfeasors had its origin in 1799 in the case of Merryweather v. Nixan, 8 T.R. 186, 101 Eng. Rep. 1337 [K.B.1799]. There is a very meager report of the case, but it seems clear that there had been a joint judgment against two defendants in an action for conversion and that they had acted in concert, since they were joined at a time when joinder was possible only on this basis. One defendant was denied contribution from the other, apparently on the ground that he had acted intentionally and his claim rested upon what was, in the eyes of the law, entirely his own wrong.

2. The early American cases denied contribution in cases of wilful misconduct, but allowed it when the tort committed by the claimant was a matter of negligence or mistake. But once the door was thrown open to joinder in one action of those who had merely caused the same damage, the origin of the rule and the reason for it were lost to sight, and contribution was denied among all "joint tortfeasors." This became the majority common law rule.

3. Most of the writers have advocated contribution, at least when the claimant is not an intentional wrongdoer, on the ground that it is unfair to saddle the entire burden of a loss, for which two are responsible, upon one alone, while the other goes scot free. See Bohlen, Contribution and Indemnity Between Tortfeasors, 21 Cornell L.Q. 522 (1936), 22 id. 569 (1937); Leflar, Contribution and Indemnity Between Tortfeasors, 81 U.Pa.L.Rev. 130 (1932); Hodges, Contribution and Indemnity Among Tortfeasors, 26 Tex.L.Rev. 150 (1947); Gregory, Contribution Among Joint Tortfeasors: A Uniform Practice, 1938 Wis.L.Rev. 365; Kissel, Developments in Third Party Practice—Contribution and Indemnity, 71 Ill.B.J. 654 (1983); and for a concise up-to-date summary, see H. Woods, Some Observations on Contribution and Indemnity, 38 Ark.L. Rev. 44 (1984). An elaborate book discussing both contribution and comparative negligence is C. Gregory, Legislative Loss Distribution in Negligence Actions (1932).

4. See Gregory, Contribution Among Joint Tortfeasors: A Pragmatic Criticism, 54 Harv.L.Rev. 1156 (1954), which discusses the desirability of contribution as a matter of social policy. What issues are raised? What is the effect on insurance? Cf. Comment, Contribution and Distribution of Loss Among Tortfeasors, 25 Am.U.L.Rev. 203 (1975).

5. The common law rule has been extensively changed. Many states have changed it by statute to allow contribution; others by case law. The picture alters rapidly, and no list can long remain accurate. The basic alternatives are as follows:

(a) The traditional common law rule of no contribution—long the majority rule but now in a minority and diminishing. (b) Contribution allowed between joint tortfeasors but only if a joint judgment has been obtained against them—a statutory rule adopted in a few states. (c) Contribution generally allowed among negligent tortfeasors.

A substantial majority of the states now permit contribution, either by statute or judicial decision. See, e.g., Safeway Stores, Inc. v. Raytown, 633 S.W.2d 727 (Mo.1982); cf. H. Woods, Comparative Fault, §§ 1:11, 13:5 (1978). The Restatement (Second) of Torts has adopted this position. See § 886A. Three successive uniform acts have provided for it. See Uniform Contribution Among Tortfeasors Act (1939), Uniform Contribution Among Tortfeasors Act (1955), and Uniform Comparative Fault Act (1979).

6. The common law rule that contribution is not permitted among intentional wrongdoers has persisted, and there seems little inclination to change it. It is specifically enacted in several statutes. But see Southern Pacific Transp. Co. v. State of California, 115 Cal.App.3d 116, 171 Cal.Rptr. 187 (1981), where the court concluded that willful misconduct does not bar contribution among joint tortfeasors. A limitation to the general rule of not permitting contribution among joint tortfeasors occurs in admiralty cases and fraud in securities actions. See, e.g., Huddleston v. Herman & MacLeon, 640 F.2d 534, 556–559 (5th Cir.1981), rev'd in part on another issue, 459 U.S. 375 (1983) (contribution among co-defendants allowed in cases where defendants violated Rule 10b–5 of the Securities Act).

7. There is sharp disagreement on the basis for making division of damages among the tortfeasors. The majority rule, by analogy to contribution among sureties, has adopted an equal-division basis—half and half if there are two tortfeasors, by thirds if there are three, and so on. A growing number of jurisdictions, however, are deciding to make the division according to the relative fault of the parties. With the widespread adoption of a comparative-negligence principle in substitution for the common law rule of contributory negligence, this position is becoming much more significant. It seems necessary in a state which administers pure comparative negligence, and the Uniform Comparative Fault Act now provides specifically for it.

8. Most states permitting contribution do not require that a judgment be obtained against a tortfeasor before he pays and seeks contribution. He may settle out of court with the injured party and then obtain contribution. Of course, he has the burden of proving that the settlement was reasonable. See Nations & Cabello, Contribution and Indemnity: The Intricate Web in Tort Litigation, 24 S.Tex.L.J. 1 (1983), recognizing that a judgment is necessary in Texas between defendants before contribution can be sought, and examining inadequacies in the current status of contribution law.

[Handwritten margin notes:] Maj = equally divided — Min trend = acc'g to relative fault

9. Depending upon local procedure, a person being sued for negligence may join another person as a third-party defendant against whom he is seeking contribution, or may bring a separate action for contribution. How should contribution be figured when there are four tortfeasors, only three of whom are before the court? Should it make any difference whether the missing tortfeasor was out of state and unavailable for process? Should it make any difference whether the division of damages was on a pro rata basis or on a comparative fault basis?

10. A was injured by the collision of two cars. A brought an action against B, the owner and driver of one car; C, the owner of the second car; and D, the driver of the second car. A recovered a judgment against all three for $15,000. B paid half the judgment and C and D paid the other half. B now asserts that his pro rata share of the judgment is only $5,000 and that he is entitled to contribution of $1,250 each from C and D. What result? Martindale v. Griffin, 233 App.Div. 510, 253 N.Y.S. 578 (1931), aff'd, 259 N.Y. 530, 182 N.E. 167 (1932). Cf. Wold v. Grozalsky, 277 N.Y. 364, 14 N.E.2d 437 (1938).

11. Suppose separate judgments are obtained against two joint tortfeasors, one for $10,000 and the other for $15,000. How can a proper adjustment be made in calculating what each should pay? Cf. D.C. Transit Co. v. Slingland, 266 F.2d 465 (D.C.Cir.1959) (formula: each pays that percentage of the judgment against it that the larger of the judgments bears to the sum of both judgments).

YELLOW CAB CO. OF D.C., INC. v. DRESLIN

United States Court of Appeals, District of Columbia Circuit, 1950.
86 U.S.App.D.C. 327, 181 F.2d 626.

PROCTOR, CIRCUIT JUDGE. The question here concerns contribution between tortfeasors where the judgment creditor is the wife of the tortfeasor against whom contribution is sought.

A taxicab of appellant (hereafter called "Cab Co."), driven by its agent, and an automobile, driven by appellee (hereafter called "Dreslin"), collided. Dreslin's wife and others in his car were injured. They sued the Cab Co. for damages. Dreslin joined with them, claiming for loss of consortium, medical expenses for Mrs. Dreslin and damages to his automobile. Among its defenses, the Cab Co. pleaded contributory negligence of Dreslin. It also cross-claimed against him for damages to the taxicab and for contribution for any sums recovered by the other plaintiffs against it. The jury's verdict established the collision to have been caused by concurrent negligent operation of the two cars. Accordingly judgments for varying amounts were entered in favor of all plaintiffs except Dreslin. In addition a declaratory judgment was entered allowing the Cab Co. contribution against Dreslin upon the several judgments except that of Mrs. Dreslin. This was disallowed because, as the Court held, "the right to contribution arises from a joint liability," and as Dreslin was not liable in tort to his wife, there was no joint liability between him and the Cab Co. as to her. This appeal is confined to that single question.

We agree with the conclusion of the trial court. Neither husband nor wife is liable for tortious acts by one against the other. That is the

common law rule.   It prevails today in the District of Columbia.
* * *

The rights of contribution arise out of a common liability.   The rule "hinges on the doctrine that general principles of justice require that in the case of a common obligation, the discharge of it by one of the obligors without proportionate payment from the other, gives the latter an advantage to which he is not equitably entitled."   [C] Contribution, then, depends upon joint liability.   An injured party plaintiff in the suit from which a right of contribution develops must have had a cause of action against the party from whom contribution is sought.   Here there was no liability by Dreslin to his wife,—no right to action against him and the Cab Co., hence nothing to which a right of contribution could attach.

The argument that it would be inequitable to allow Mrs. Dreslin to be "enriched" at the sole expense of the Cab Co., permitting her husband, equally at fault, to escape any of the burden, overlooks the fact that preservation of domestic peace and felicity is the policy upon which the rule of immunity between husband and wife is based.
* * *

The judgment is affirmed.

-----

1.   This is the majority rule.   It also applies to parent-child immunity. Norfolk Southern R. Co. v. Gretakis, 162 Va. 597, 174 S.E. 841 (1934).   In the family-immunity cases, however, several recent cases have allowed contribution, on the ground that the immunity goes not to the existence of tort liability, but to plaintiff's lack of capacity to bring suit against the defendant.   Bedell v. Reagan, 159 Me. 292, 192 A.2d 24 (1963);   Bishop v. Nielsen, 632 P.2d 864 (Utah 1981).   This position would not be sustainable if the defendant's immunity is not just against a particular plaintiff but against tort liability in general.   See Bond v. Pittsburgh, 368 Pa. 404, 84 A.2d 328 (1951) (charitable immunity).   See Hertz, The Tort Triangle: Contribution from Defendants When Plaintiff Cannot Sue, 32 Me.L.Rev. 83 (1980).

2.   A similar problem arises in connection with worker's compensation statutes preventing the employee from suing the employer in tort.   A majority of the courts have construed the statute as being intended to cut off all possible liability, but some courts have disagreed.   Compare Hunsucker v. High Point Bending & Chair Co., 237 N.C. 559, 75 S.E.2d 768 (1953), with American Dist. Tel. Co. v. Kittleson, 179 F.2d 946 (8th Cir.1950) (indemnity).   For discussion, see 2 A. Larson, Workmen's Compensation, § 76 (1975);   Davis, Third Party Tortfeasor's Rights When Compensation Employers Are Negligent, 4 Hofstra L.Rev. 571 (1976);   Ramsden & Bowen, Workmen's Compensation: The Continuing Dilemma of Third–Party Actions, 21 Idaho L.Rev. 57 (1985).

3.   What should be the effect of an automobile-guest statute?   The courts have generally held that it bars contribution if the host is not liable to the guest.   Troutman v. Modlin, 353 F.2d 382 (8th Cir.1965);   Shonka v. Campbell, 260 Iowa 1178, 152 N.W.2d 242 (1967);   Annot., 26 A.L.R.3d 1274 (1969).   In the *Shonka* case, however, a dissenting judge forcefully argued that the principal purpose of the statute is to prevent collusive suits, and that an action by a third person for contribution does not come within this reason.

4. What if the statute of limitations has run against the liability to the injured person? Can the other tortfeasor who has paid a judgment still enforce contribution? Keleket X–Ray Corp. v. United States, 275 F.2d 167 (D.D.C.1960); Cooper v. Philadelphia Dairy Products Co., 34 N.J.Super. 301, 112 A.2d 308 (1955). See Kutner, Contribution Among Tortfeasors: The Effects of Statutes of Limitations and Other Time Limitations, 33 Okla.L.Rev. 203 (1980); Annots., 57 A.L.R.3d 927 (1974) (what statute of limitations applies), and 57 A.L.R.3d 867 (1974) (when statute begins to run).

5. What is the effect on the right to contribution of a release given by plaintiff to one tortfeasor? A is injured by the combined negligence of B and C. A accepts $1000 from B and gives him a covenant not to sue (or release retaining rights). He then sues C and obtains a judgment for $15,000 and C pays $14,000. Can C obtain contribution (for $6,500, in a pro-rata state? There have been three solutions, none of which is satisfactory. The first rule, followed in the 1939 Uniform Act, § 4, has permitted contribution. Buckley v. Basford, 184 F.Supp. 870 (D.Me.1960); State Farm Mut. Auto. Ins. Co. v. Continental Cas Co., 264 Wis. 493, 59 N.W.2d 425 (1953). The difficulty with this solution is that it discourages settlements; B is not ready to make a settlement unless he is relieved of all liability. The second rule, followed in the 1955 Uniform Act, § 4, provides that B is discharged from liability for contribution, so long as he acts "in good faith." This solution is conducive to collusion and productive of litigation on the issue of good faith; it may also be unfair to the other tortfeasors. See Roberts, The Good Faith Settlement: An Accommodation of Competing Goals, 17 Loy.L.A.L.Rev. 841 (1984); Note, 23 San Diego L.Rev. 227 (1986). The third solution, followed in the 1979 Uniform Comparative Negligence Act, provides that the settlement with B means the selling of half of the cause of action to him, with a resulting pro-rata reduction in the claim against C (who would be liable for $7,500). Theobald v. Angelos, 44 N.J. 228, 208 A.2d 129 (1965); Palestine Contractors, Inc. v. Perkins, 386 S.W.2d 764 (Tex.1964). This also discourages settlements; A will be reluctant to sell half of his claim for less than half of what he thinks it is worth. For discussion, see Notes, 21 Rutgers L.Rev. 130 (1966); 19 Sw.L.J. 650 (1965). Section 886 of the Restatement (Second) of Torts has a caveat on the issue.

6. *Mary Carter Agreements.* Named after an agreement approved in the case of Booth v. Mary Carter Paint Co., 202 So.2d 8 (Fla.App.1967), and sometimes called Gallagher covenants or Loan Receipt Agreements, these are secret agreements between a plaintiff and one (or more, but not all) defendants in a personal injury case. Under a typical agreement, the defendant contracts to "guarantee" to plaintiff a designated amount of money in case the plaintiff loses the case or recovers less than the stated amount. The plaintiff, in turn, contracts to refund the payment to the defendant in case the verdict against all the defendants exceeds the stated amount. Thus the contracting defendant, who remains a party in the case, has a concealed interest in the outcome and is benefited by the size of the judgment against the defendants. Numerous variations of the form exist. Some courts have approved the agreements. Others have held them to be against public policy and void. Lum v. Stinnett, 87 Nev. 402, 488 P.2d 347 (1971). Still others insist that the existence of the agreement be made known; there may be a requirement that the judge be informed or discovery may be sought and existence of the agreement be brought out to the jury by cross examination. Cf. General Motors Corp. v. Simmons, 558 S.W.2d 855 (Tex.1977); Cal.Code Civ.Proc., § 877.5 (1980). The most complete treatment is Entman, Mary Carter Agreements: An Assessment of

Attempted Solutions, 38 U.Fla.L.Rev. 521 (1986). See also Guiding Principles for Cooperation in the Defense of Multi–Party Litigation, 32 Fed.Ins.Coun.Q. [No. 1] 3 (1981).

TOLBERT v. GERBER INDUS., INC.

Supreme Court of Minnesota, 1977,
255 N.W.2d 362. *Made defective equipment – installed it*

OTIS, JUSTICE. This is an action brought by ~~Norman~~ Tolbert against Gerber Industries, Inc. (Gerber), the manufacturer, and Voldco, Inc. (Voldco), the installer of defective equipment which caused plaintiff's injury. Schuler Grain Company (Schuler), Tolbert's employer, was made a third-party defendant. The jury found that Gerber and Voldco were negligent and that the negligence of each was a direct cause of Tolbert's injury and awarded Tolbert $60,572. Pursuant to our comparative negligence statute, Minn.St. 604.01, the jury was instructed to attribute a percentage of negligence to each tortfeasor. They *Jury found G+SL anyway* attributed 100 percent of the negligence to Gerber and Voldco jointly and did not apportion percentages between them. The trial court * * * awarded Voldco 100–percent indemnity from Gerber. We reverse and remand for further proceedings.

The issue presented is one which prompts us to re-evaluate well-established common-law rules in light of recently adopted principles of comparative negligence. Specifically, the question is whether a negligent installer of defective equipment is entitled to 100–percent indemnity from the negligent manufacturer because the negligence of the former was "passive" or "secondary," or whether the joint tortfeasors should be responsible for the loss in accordance with their respective degrees of culpability. * *Why not jurys finding of G+SL* *(b/c compn. encourages assumption/percentage of fault)*

In Hendrickson v. Minnesota Power & Light Co., 258 Minn. 368, 372, 104 N.W.2d 843, 848 (1960), we reviewed our decisions concerning indemnity between joint tortfeasors [1] and adopted the following rules:

"* * * A joint tortfeasor may generally recover indemnity only in the following situations:

"(1) Where the one seeking indemnity has only a derivative or vicarious liability for damage caused by the one sought to be charged. *EmpR seeks indem from EmpE*

"(2) Where the one seeking indemnity has incurred liability by action at the direction, in the interest of, and in reliance upon the one sought to be charged. *EmpE seeks from EmpR*

"(3) Where the one seeking indemnity has incurred liability because of a breach of duty owed to him by the one sought to be charged.

This case "(4) *Where the one seeking indemnity has incurred liability merely because of failure, even though negligent, to discover or prevent the misconduct of the one sought to be charged.* *Couldn't be the case under Rule 2?*

---

1. As we use the term "joint tortfeasors" it includes "all cases where there is joint liability for a tort, whether the acts of those jointly liable were concerted, merely concurrent, or even successive in point of time." Leflar, Contribution and Indemnity Between Tortfeasors, 81 U. of Pa.L.Rev. 130, 131 note 9.

"(5) Where there is an express contract between the parties containing an explicit undertaking to reimburse for liability of the character involved." (Italics supplied.) - *insurance*

The instant case falls within Rule 4 of *Hendrickson.* In situations covered by Rules 1, 2, and 3, the party who seeks indemnity has been held liable even though not personally at fault. In cases under Rule 1, the liability of the party seeking indemnity is imposed upon him for the conduct of another. Indemnity in such a case is supported by the fundamental principle that one who is guilty of injurious misconduct is himself liable therefor. In cases under Rule 2, indemnity is granted to a party who justifiably relied upon representations made by another and thus is without personal fault, but whose actions are nevertheless tortious. In cases under Rule 3, the party seeking indemnity is again without personal fault, but is exposed to liability because of the failure of another to perform a duty which he was legally or contractually obligated to perform. Rule 5 deals with contractual indemnity and is thus distinguishable from Rules 1, 2, and 3 and from Rule 4.

Cases which fall under Rule 4 are of a very different type from the others. Aside from cases of contractual indemnity, the other rules concern parties seeking indemnity who are without personal fault, but who nevertheless are liable in tort. Rule 4, however, concerns parties who are themselves culpably negligent but who nevertheless seek to avoid responsibility for the injury they have caused. The typical example of this is where the party seeking indemnity has failed to discover or prevent the negligence or misconduct of another when an ordinarily prudent person would have done so. Previously, the rule has been interpreted to apply where the negligence of the party seeking indemnity was merely "passive" or "secondary" as contrasted with the "active" or "primary" negligence of the other tortfeasor.

Our current rule on indemnity in Rule 4 situations presents a trial court with a bewildering array of issues. First, the Court must determine if the negligence of the party was "passive" or "secondary" as opposed to the "active" or "primary" negligence of the other tortfeasor. Next the Court is expected to decide whether the negligence was "concurrent," in which case contribution and not indemnity is awarded. [Cc] It also must examine "the relative culpability of the conduct of the wrongdoers," but still it must award indemnity on an all-or-nothing basis. [C] Finally, it is admonished that such indemnity cannot be determined by "hard-and-fast rules and must turn on the facts of each case." [C] -

Indemnity provides a just result in cases under Rules 1, 2, and 3. Its application insures that liability for damages is borne by the negligent party. It prevents those only vicariously liable from bearing an unfair burden thrust upon them by others (i.e., tortious acts by servants or employees, people driving cars with the owner's consent, or anyone for whose negligence another is held to be liable under the law). In Rule 4 cases, however, indemnity is a blunt instrument for reallocating responsibility for damages.   It shifts the entire loss from one culpable wrongdoer to another.

[handwritten marginalia: Presumably it couldn't be collect from the other; but not the other;]

In the related area of contributory negligence, our legislature has abandoned the all-or-nothing approach of the common law by adopting a comparative negligence statute, Minn.St. 604.01. Tortfeasors must now accept responsibility for damages commensurate with their own relative culpability. Because indemnity in Rule 4 situations is an equitable doctrine,[10] we are at liberty to ameliorate the rigid common-law rules in keeping with legislative philosophy without an express statutory mandate.

By limiting the reallocation of loss between joint tortfeasors to contribution based upon relative fault, the more culpable tortfeasor will continue to bear a greater share of the loss, but at the same time his joint tortfeasor will not continue to escape all liability as in the past.

*   *   *

The jury found that both Gerber and Voldco were negligent and that the negligence of each was a direct cause of plaintiff's injury. Consequently, as between them, each will bear the cost of compensating plaintiff in proportion to its relative culpability.

The judgment of the district court is affirmed in so far as it awards plaintiff judgment against defendants Gerber and Voldco and dismisses the third-party claims against Schuler. With respect to the award to Voldco of indemnity against Gerber, the judgment is reversed and the matter is remanded for a new trial on the limited issue of apportionment of liability between Gerber and Voldco in accordance with the rule we here adopt.

Reversed and remanded.

KELLY, JUSTICE [dissented, with concurrence of three other justices].

---

1. Efforts similar to that in the *Hendrickson* case (quoted in the principal case) to list the situations under which one tortfeasor may have indemnity against another, were made in Panasuk v. Seaton, 277 F.Supp. 979 (D.Mont. 1968); and Jacobs v. General Accident Fire & Life Assurance Corp., 14 Wis.2d 1, 109 N.W.2d 462 (1961). See also Restatement (Second) of Torts § 886B, which sets forth as a general principle: "If two persons are liable in tort to a third person for the same harm, and one of them discharges the liability of both, he is entitled to indemnity from the other if the other would be unjustly enriched at his expense by the discharge of the liability." It lists six instances in the blackletter and discusses other applications in the comments.

2. Indemnity has sometimes been granted in situations outside the *Hendrickson* list. Consider the following:

A. A manufacturer puts out a dangerous product. The user discovers the defect but continues to use the product, injuring a third party. If the manufac-

---

10. The principles governing indemnity between joint tortfeasors grew out of the doctrines of quasi-contract and unjust enrichment. Restatement, Restitution, Part I, Introductory Note; Hendrickson v. Minnesota Power & Light Co., 258 Minn. 368, 370, 104 N.W.2d 843, 846 (1960).

turer pays, is he entitled to indemnity from the user? Cf. Campbell v. Joslyn
Mfg. & Supply Co., 65 Ill.App.2d 344, 212 N.E.2d 512 (1965) (yes); and Guarnieri
v. Kewanee–Ross Corp., 263 F.2d 413 (2d Cir.1959), modified, 270 F.2d 575
(1959) (no).   *— —this is not indemnity, but contribution*

   B.   A runs over the injured party. His injuries are exacerbated by the
negligent treatment of B, a physician. If A pays for the total damage, can he
obtain indemnity from B for the additional damage for the negligent treat- *= physician pays*
ment? The usual answer is yes. Gertz v. Campbell, 55 Ill.2d 84, 302 N.E.2d 40 *for all?*
(1973); Travelers Indem. Co. v. Trowbridge, 41 Ohio St.2d 11, 70 Ohio Op.2d 6,
321 N.E.2d 787 (1975). Should the same result be reached when A strikes
plaintiff and leaves him unconscious in the street and B runs over him, causing
additional injuries? *Contribution=yes   indemnity=no*
But here intervening act was foreseeable, not relieving δ'
   C.   The general rule has been that one joint tortfeasor who was merely
negligent is not entitled to indemnity from another who was guilty of gross or
deliberate misconduct. See Panasuk v. Seaton, 277 F.Supp. 979 (D.Mont.1968);
Jacobs v. General Acc. Fire & Life Assur. Corp., 14 Wis.2d 1, 109 N.W.2d 462
(1961). But cf. Heit v. Bixby, 276 F.Supp. 217 (E.D.Mo.1967) (corporate directors liable for ordinary negligence granted indemnity against directors engaged
in intentional misconduct); United Air Lines, Inc. v. Wiener, 335 F.2d 379 (9th
Cir.1964), cert. denied, 379 U.S. 951 (1964) (carrier subject to highest degree of
care vs. ordinary negligence).

   How would the *Tolbert* court treat these cases?

   3.   For general treatments of indemnity, see Davis, Indemnity Between
Negligent Tortfeasors: A Proposed Rationale, 37 Iowa L.Rev. 517 (1952); Merri-
am and Thornton, Indemnity Between Tortfeasors, 25 N.Y.U.L.Rev. 845 (1950);
Leflar, Contribution and Indemnity Between Tortfeasors, 81 U.Pa.L.Rev. 130
(1932); Bohlen, Contribution and Indemnity Between Tortfeasors, 21 Cornell
L.Q. 552 (1936), 22 id. 469 (1937); Sherk, Common Law Indemnity Among Joint
Tortfeasors, 7 Ariz.L.Rev. 59 (1965); Hodges, Contribution and Indemnity
Among Tortfeasors, 26 Tex.L.Rev. 150 (1947); Note, 28 Fordham L.Rev. 782
(1960); Woods, Some Observations on Contribution and Indemnity, 38 Ark.L.
Rev. 44 (1984).

   4.   Indemnity has traditionally called for the recovery of the total amount
paid by the first tortfeasor, or for nothing. In a number of states the rules have
become quite technical, especially if contribution is not allowed. In a comparative contribution state such as Minnesota, where the choice is not between all
or nothing, many of the traditional indemnity situations no longer seem
justified. For similar holdings in comparative negligence states, see American
Motorcycle Ass'n v. Superior Court, 20 Cal.3d 578, 578 P.2d 899, 146 Cal.Rptr.
182 (1978). The Federal courts concur. See, e.g., Loose v. Offshore Navigation,
Inc., 670 F.2d 493 (5th Cir.1982); B & B Auto Supply v. Central Freight Lines,
Inc., 603 S.W.2d 814 (Tex.1980); cf. Missouri Pac. Ry. v. Whitehead & Kales Co.,
566 S.W.2d 466 (Mo.1978). See also Sales, Contribution and Indemnity Between
Negligent and Strictly Liable Tortfeasors, 12 St. Mary's L.J. 323 (1980); Old-
ham & Maynard, Indemnity and Contribution Between Strictly Liable and
Negligent Defendants, 28 Fed.Ins.Coun.Q. 139 (1978).

   5.   Several states have espoused a doctrine of "equitable indemnity" in
which recovery is not for the total amount but in proportion to the relative
fault of the parties—thus approaching a merger of contribution and indemnity
from the opposite side. See Dole v. Dow Chemical Co., 30 N.Y.2d 143, 282
N.E.2d 288, 331 N.Y.S.2d 382 (1972); American Motorcycle Ass'n v. Superior

Court, 20 Cal.3d 578, 578 P.2d 899, 146 Cal.Rptr. 182 (1978); Safeway Stores, Inc. v. Nest–Kart, 21 Cal.3d 326, 579 P.2d 441, 146 Cal.Rptr. 550 (1978); cf. Skinner v. Reed–Prentice Div. Package Machinery Co., 70 Ill.2d 1, 15 Ill.Dec. 829, 374 N.E.2d 437 (1978). This has been caused largely by restrictive contribution statutes that the court could not change, so that it made a change in the common law of indemnity. It has sometimes led to judicial adoption of comparative negligence. See Note, If They're Partly to Blame, Why Should I Get Stuck With the Bill? 3 Cooley L.Rev. 343 (1985).

6. In Kohr v. Allegheny Airlines, Inc., 504 F.2d 400, 405 (7th Cir.1974), the court adopted a new "federal rule of contribution and indemnity for aviation collisions," which would be "on a comparative negligence basis. Under such an approach the trier of fact will determine on a percentage basis the degree of negligent involvement of each party in the collision. The loss will then be distributed in proportion to the allocable concurring fault." On relative fault in general as the basis for contribution and indemnity, see Annot., 53 A.L.R.2d 184 (1974).

4. APPORTIONMENT OF DAMAGES

BRUCKMAN v. PENA

Colorado Court of Appeals, 1971.
29 Colo.App. 357, 487 P.2d 566.

DWYER, JUDGE. * * * Plaintiff was injured on July 21, 1964, when the car in which he was riding collided with a truck driven by the defendant Bruckman and owned by the defendant Armored Motors Service. On June 11, 1965, plaintiff was injured in a second collision and certain injuries he had sustained in the first collision were aggravated. This action was commenced on June 25, 1965, and the only defendants named in the action are the owner and driver of the truck involved in the first collision.

[The jury returned a verdict in favor of plaintiff William Pena in the sum of $50,000.]

In seeking reversal, defendants assert that the court was in error in one of its instructions to the jury. * * *

The instruction complained of concerns the amount of damages recoverable from the defendants. The first part of the instruction, which is a proper statement of the law applicable to the case, is as follows:

"If you find that after the collision complained of Plaintiff, William Pena, had an injury which aggravated the ailment or disability received in the collision complained of, the Plaintiff is entitled to recover for the injury or pain received in the collision complained of; but he is not entitled to recover for any physical ailment or disability which he may have incurred subsequent to the collision.

"Where a subsequent injury occurs which aggravated the condition caused by the collision, it is your duty, if possible, to apportion the amount of disability and pain between that caused by the subsequent injury and that caused by the collision."

In addition to this correct statement of the law, the court further instructed the jury: "But if you find that the evidence does not permit such an apportionment, then the Defendants are liable for the entire disability." Defendants argue that this last statement in the instruction is in error. * * *

It is the general rule that one injured by the negligence of another is entitled to recover the damages proximately caused by the act of the tort-feasor, and the burden of proof is upon the plaintiff to establish that the damages he seeks were proximately caused by the negligence of the defendant. In accordance with this general rule, we hold that the instruction is in error because it permits the plaintiffs to recover damages against the defendants for injuries which the plaintiff received subsequent to any act of negligence on the part of the defendants and from causes for which the defendants were in no way responsible. The instruction erroneously places upon the defendants the burden of proving that plaintiff's disability can be apportioned between that caused by the collision here involved and that caused by the subsequent injury in order to limit their liability to the damages proximately caused by their negligence. Counsel for plaintiffs argues that the rules concerning apportionment of disability announced by our Supreme Court in Newbury v. Vogel, 151 Colo. 520, 379 P.2d 811, should also apply here. In *Newbury*, the Court stated:

"We find the law to be that where a pre-existing diseased condition exists, and where after trauma aggravating the condition disability and pain result, and no apportionment of the disability between that caused by the pre-existing condition and that caused by the trauma can be made, in such case, even though a portion of the present and future disability is directly attributable to the pre-existing condition, the defendant, whose act of negligence was the cause of the trauma, is responsible for the entire damage."

The pre-existing condition in the *Newbury* case was of non-traumatic origin, but the rules there announced also apply where the pre-existing condition was caused by trauma. [C] The reasons for the adoption of the *Newbury* rules are not present here. It is one thing to hold a tort-feasor who injures one suffering from a pre-existing condition liable for the entire damage when no apportionment between the pre-existing condition and the damage caused by the defendant can be made, but it is quite another thing to say that a tort-feasor is liable, not only for the damage which he caused, but also for injuries subsequently suffered by the injured person. We hold that the defendants here cannot be held liable for the plaintiff's subsequent injury and this is so whether or not such damage can be apportioned between the two injuries.

The plaintiffs also rely on the case of Maddux v. Donaldson, 362 Mich. 425, 108 N.W.2d 33, 100 A.L.R.2d 1. This case involved a chain-type collision, and plaintiff's injuries resulted from successive impacts which to all intents and purposes were concurrent. The court there held that where independent concurring negligent acts have proximately caused injury and damage which cannot be apportioned between the tort-feasors, each tort-feasor is jointly and severally liable for all of the injury and damage. This rule is not applicable where, as here, the second injury or aggravation of the first injury is attributable to a distinct intervening cause without which the second injury or aggravation would not have occurred. * * *

Judgments reversed and cause remanded for a new trial on the issues of damages alone.

———

1. A and B, driving separate cars, negligently collide. One car bounces over on the sidewalk, hits C and injures him. C's injury is indivisible and therefore not apportionable. A and B are each liable for the full injury. Seattle First Nat'l Bank v. Shoreline Concrete Co., 91 Wash.2d 230, 588 P.2d 1308 (1978).

2. If A and B separately hit the plaintiff and the combined effect of the two accidents is that C dies, the death is treated as an indivisible result. Glick v. Ballentine Produce Inc., 396 S.W.2d 609 (Mo.1965); Bolick v. Gallagher, 268 Wis. 421, 67 N.W.2d 860 (1955). So, also, if insanity results from the combined effect of the two accidents. Rooney v. New York, N.H. & H.R. Co., 173 Mass. 222, 53 N.E. 435 (1899). Suppose the first accident had caused him to lose the sight of one eye, and the second had put out his other eye? What happens if there is a merger of the pain and suffering from two separate injuries?

3. In the principal case, should it make any difference whether the second accident was caused by the negligence of a third party, or the plaintiff's negligence or was an unavoidable occurrence? Would there be any difference if the second accident had occurred the day after the first one? Is the distinction drawn in the opinion in the principal case between it and the *Newbury* case a valid one?

4. A comment on the principal case in 49 Den.L.J. 115 (1972), indicates that there was testimony in the trial below that plaintiff had suffered permanent brain damage in each of the accidents and that it was impossible to apportion the damage between them. How can the jury apportion? Compare McAllister v. Pennsylvania R. Co., 324 Pa. 65, 187 A. 415 (1936), where plaintiff suffered, six months apart, an injury to each leg, with some combined effect on the back. The doctor treating the first injury had died. The court held that there is a "reasonable basis of apportionment" when there is "some evidence to sustain the apportionment made, even though, due to circumstances of the particular case, the proofs do not attain the degree of precision which would make possible an exact dividing line between the injuries." In Loui v. Oakley, 50 Hawaii 260, 438 P.2d 393 (1968), involving four accidents, the court held that the jury should be told to make a "rough estimate" and if that were impossible, "to apportion the damages equally among the various accidents."

[handwritten top margin: G/R = π cannot aggregate multiple claims in order to establish minimum amount in controversy for diversity jurisdiction]

MICHIE v. GREAT LAKES STEEL DIVISION, NAT'L STEEL CORP.

[handwritten: — significance = J+SL means π claiming all damages against each, so as long as complete diversity, then amt in controversy met for each]

[handwritten: Diversity ques = 2 reqts 1) defendant state 2) amt in court = more than $10,000]

United States Court of Appeals, Sixth Circuit, 1974.
495 F.2d 213.

EDWARDS, CIRCUIT JUDGE. This is an interlocutory appeal from a District Judge's denial of a motion to dismiss filed by three corporations which are defendants-appellants herein. * * *

Appellants' motion to dismiss was based upon the contention that each plaintiff individually had failed to meet the requirement of a $10,000 amount in controversy for diversity jurisdiction set forth in 28 U.S.C.A. § 1332 (1970).

The facts in this matter, as alleged in the pleadings, are somewhat unique. Thirty-seven persons, members of thirteen families residing near LaSalle, Ontario, Canada, have filed a complaint against three corporations which operate seven plants in the United States immediately across the Detroit River from Canada. Plaintiffs claim that pollutants emitted by plants of defendants are noxious in character and that their discharge in the ambient air violates various municipal and state ordinances and laws. They assert that the discharges represent a nuisance and that the pollutants are carried by air currents onto their premises in Canada, thereby damaging their persons and property. Each plaintiff individually claims damages ranging from $11,000 to $35,000 from all three corporate defendants jointly and severally. There is, however, no assertion of joint action or conspiracy on the part of defendants. * * * *[handwritten: If divisible, then what? Some perhaps less than $10,000.]*

We believe the principal question presented by this appeal may be phrased thus: Under the law of the State of Michigan, may multiple defendants, whose independent actions of allegedly discharging pollutants into the ambient air thereby allegedly create a nuisance, be jointly and severally liable to multiple plaintiffs for numerous individual injuries which plaintiffs claim to have sustained as a result of said actions, where said pollutants mix in the air so that their separate effects in creating the individual injuries are impossible to analyze? *[handwritten circled: 1]*

* * *

In Maddux v. Donaldson, 362 Mich. 425, 108 N.W.2d 33 the Michigan Supreme Court cites Landers v. East Texas Salt Water Disposal Company, 151 Tex. 251, 248 S.W.2d 731, a pollution case, in support of the above stated proposition. The court indicated that

" * * * * [i]t is clear that there is a manifest unfairness in 'putting on the injured party the impossible burden of proving the specific shares of harm done by each. * * * Such results are simply the law's callous dullness to innocent sufferers. One would think that the obvious meanness [sic] of letting wrongdoers go scot free in such cases would cause the courts to think twice and to suspect some fallacy in their rule of law'. " * * *

It is the opinion of this court that the rule of *Maddux,* supra, and *Landers,* supra, cited therein is the better, and applicable rule in this air pollution case.

On this point we affirm the decision of the District Judge. This complaint appears to have been filed under the diversity jurisdiction of the federal courts. All parties have agreed that Michigan law alone controls.

Like most jurisdictions, Michigan has had great difficulty with the problems posed in tort cases by multiple causes for single or indivisible injuries. * * *

We believe that the issue was decided in the lengthy consideration given by the Michigan court in the *Maddux* case. There Justice Talbot Smith (now Senior Judge, United States District Court for the Eastern District of Michigan, Southern Division) in an opinion for the court majority (joined by the writer of this opinion) held:

"It is our conclusion that if there is competent testimony, adduced either by plaintiff or defendant, that the injuries are factually and medically separable, and that the liability for all such injuries and damages, or parts thereof, may be allocated with reasonable certainty to the impacts in turn, the jury will be instructed accordingly and mere difficulty in so doing will not relieve the triers of the facts of this responsibility. This merely follows the general rule that 'where the independent concurring acts have caused distinct and separate injuries to the plaintiff, or where some reasonable means of apportioning the damages is evident, the courts generally will not hold the tort-feasors jointly and severally liable.'

"But if, on the other hand, the triers of the facts conclude that they cannot reasonably make the division of liability between the tort-feasors, this is the point where the road of authority divides. Much ancient authority, not in truth precedent, would say that the case is now over, and that plaintiff shall take nothing. Some modern courts, as well, hold that his is merely the case of the marauding dogs and the helpless sheep relitigated in the setting of a modern highway. The conclusion is erroneous. Such precedents are not apt. When the triers of the facts decide that they cannot make a division of injuries we have, by their own finding, nothing more or less than an indivisible injury, and the precedents as to indivisible injuries will control. They were well summarized in Cooley on Torts in these words: 'Where the negligence of two or more persons concur in producing a single, indivisible injury, then such persons are jointly and severally liable, although there was no common duty, common design, or concert action.'" *Maddux v. Donaldson,* 362 Mich. 425, 432–433, 108 N.W.2d 33, 36 (1961). * * *

We recognize, of course, that the *Maddux* [case] involves multiple collisions causing allegedly indivisible injuries. Hence, appellants are free to argue that the rule stated does not necessarily apply to the nuisance category of torts with which we deal here. Indeed, appellants

[handwritten top margin: J+SL = attributed to indivisible harm? = or indivisible fault? = or both? (either)]

call our attention to what appears to be a contrary rule applicable to nuisance cases referred to in the *Maddux* opinion. Restatement of Torts § 881.

In the latest Restatement, however, both the old and the newer rule are recognized and as the Michigan court held in *Maddux,* the question of whether liability of alleged polluters is joint or several is left to the trier of the facts. Where the injury itself is indivisible, the judge or jury must determine whether or not it is practicable to apportion the harm among the tortfeasors. If not, the entire liability may be imposed upon one (or several) tortfeasors subject, of course, to subsequent right of contribution among the joint offenders.

Perhaps the best summary of the rationale for such a rule is found in Harper and James:

"In the earlier discussion of the substantive liability of joint tort-feasors and independent concurring wrongdoers who have produced indivisible harm it was indicated that there were four categories into which these parties may be placed: situations in which (1) the actors knowingly join in the performance of the tortious act or acts; (2) the actors failed to perform a common duty owed to the plaintiff; (3) there is a special relationship between the parties (e.g., master and servant or joint entrepreneurs); (4) although there is no concerted action nevertheless the independent acts of several actors concur to produce indivisible harmful consequences. * * * *

[handwritten right margin: 1-3 = harm need not be indivisible]

"While the Restatement of Torts contains a short and apparently simple statement of the rule in category four, this type of situation has caused a great deal of disagreement in the courts. Here joint and several liability is sometimes imposed for the harm caused by the independent concurring acts of a number of persons. In all the situations in which such recovery is permitted the court must find first that the harm for which the plaintiff seeks damages is "indivisible." This can mean that the harm is not even theoretically divisible (as death or total destruction of a building) or that the harm, while theoretically divisible, is single in a practical sense so far as the plaintiff's ability to apportion it among the wrongdoers is concerned (as where a stream is polluted as a result of refuse from several factories). In the first type of case almost uniformly courts will permit entire recovery from any or all defendants. There is conflict, however, in the second situation, with some well-reasoned recent cases recognizing that the plaintiff's right to recover for his harm should not depend on his ability to apportion the damage but that this is a problem which is properly left with the defendants themselves." 1 F. Harper & F. James, The Law of Torts § 10.1 at 697–98, 701–02 (1956). * * * *

Assuming plaintiffs in this case prove injury and liability as to several tort-feasors, the net effect of Michigan's new rule is to shift the burden of proof as to which one was responsible and to what degree from the injured party to the wrongdoers. The injustice of the old rule is vividly illustrated in an early Michigan case, Frye v. City of Detroit,

256 Mich. 466, 239 N.W. 886 (1932). There a pedestrian was struck by an automobile, thrown in the path of a street car and struck again. Since his widow could not establish which impact killed him, a verdict was directed against her case. * * *

In this diversity case Michigan law is not finally and conclusively declared. The District Judge, under Erie R. Co. v. Tompkins, 304 U.S. 64, 58 S.Ct. 817, 82 L.Ed. 1188 (1938), had to seek to establish what the Supreme Court of Michigan would do with this case on the basis of what it has already decided. Like the District Judge, we believe that the Michigan courts would apply the *Maddux* principles to the case at bar. Under *Maddux,* each plaintiff's complaint should be read as alleging $11,000 or more in damages against each defendant. Therefore, the principle of Zahn v. International Paper Co., 414 U.S. 291, 94 S.Ct. 505, 38 L.Ed.2d 511 (1973), which would disallow aggregation of plaintiffs' claims for the purpose of establishing diversity jurisdiction, does not apply to this case. * * *

As modified [in regard to punitive damages], the judgment of the District Court is affirmed.

-----

1. How does the problem in the principal case differ from the *Agent Orange, Sindell,* and *Bierczynski* cases supra? Recognize the difference between identifying a possible tortfeasor and apportioning responsibility.

2. For a case that compares what effect contribution and implied indemnity have in a jury's decision for assigning liability by allocating damages, see Jethroe v. Koehring Co., 603 F.Supp. 1200 (S.D.Ill.1985).

3. Three vicious dogs, having separate owners, invade a field and kill sheep belonging to plaintiff. Consider the following means of handling the legal problems: (a) plaintiff can recover only for sheep whose death he can prove was caused by a particular dog, see Nohre v. Wright, 98 Minn. 477, 108 N.W. 865, 8 Ann.Cas. 1071 (1906); King v. Ruth, 136 Miss. 377, 101 So. 500 (1924) (nominal damages only); (b) each owner may be held liable for a proportionate share of the sheep, cf. Anderson v. Halverson, 126 Iowa 125, 101 N.W. 781 (1904); Wilbur v. Hubbard, 35 Barb. 303 (N.Y.1861); (c) each owner is liable for all the sheep except those which he can prove his dog did not kill, cf. Nelson v. Nugent, 106 Wis. 477, 82 N.W. 287 (1900) ("circumstance that another dog was engaged in the same act does not lessen the liability unless we are able to apportion the damage done by each dog"); (d) the dogs acted in concert and each owner is liable for all sheep, cf. Stephens v. Schadler, 182 Ky. 833, 207 S.W. 704 (1919); (e) this was an indivisible result since the dogs may have combined on individual sheep, cf. Inhabitants of Worcester County v. Ashworth, 160 Mass. 186, 35 N.E. 773 (1893) ("practically impossible to tell what part of the damage was done by one dog"—statute). Suppose the dogs had chased the sheep off a cliff?

4. The principal case involved pollution by several defendants. It relied heavily on the *Maddux* case, involving successive collisions. Are the two situations logically the same or different? The Restatement (Second) of Torts § 433A provides that damages are to be "apportioned among two or more causes when (a) there are separate harms, or (b) there is a reasonable basis for

determining the contribution of each cause to single harm." Is this section relevant to the question?

5.   In both types of situations, earlier cases were inclined to be slow to find an indivisible result and to require the plaintiff to prove the source of his injury so that the jury might make a finding. See, e.g., Johnson v. Fairmont, 188 Minn. 451, 247 N.W. 572 (1933) (stream pollution); Chipman v. Palmer, 77 N.Y. 51 (1879) (same); Grzybowski v. Connecticut Co., 116 Conn. 292, 164 A. 632 (1933) (successive injuries); Frye v. Detroit, 256 Mich. 466, 239 N.W. 886 (1932) (same—see discussion in opinion of principal case).

6.   The principal case indicates the attitude of many of the more recent decisions in finding the defendants each liable for the total damage. Two different legal means are used to accomplish this result: (a) to find that the injury is indivisible and therefore not apportionable as a matter of substantive law, and (b) to hold that the burden of proof is upon the defendants to show factual basis for apportionment, with the result that apportionment is unavailable as a practical matter. Illustrations of the first approach are Holtz v. Holder, 101 Ariz. 247, 418 P.2d 584 (1966) (chain collision); Ruud v. Grimm, 252 Iowa 1266, 110 N.W.2d 321 (1961) (same); Landers v. East Texas Salt Water Disposal Co., 151 Tex. 251, 248 S.W.2d 731 (1952) (pollution). Illustrations of the second approach are Murphy v. Taxicabs of Louisville, 330 S.W.2d 395 (Ky. 1959) (chain collision); Maddux v. Donaldson, 362 Mich. 425, 108 N.W.2d 33 (1961) (same); Phillips Petroleum Co. v. Hardee, 189 F.2d 205 (5th Cir.1951) (pollution); Finnegan v. Royal Realty Co., 35 Cal.2d 409, 218 P.2d 17 (1950) (aggravation of injuries caused by failure to supply exit doors); see Restatement (Second) of Torts § 433B(2). Is there any significant difference between these two ideas?

7.   To what extent may the trend described in the previous note have been influenced by the corresponding trend toward allowing contribution between joint tortfeasors and modern code procedure authorizing third-party practice? The availability of contribution might produce a result that is regarded as adequately fair in a rough, general sense.

8.   Twenty-six defendants discharge waste into a stream. No one of them discharges enough to pollute the stream, but the combined discharge does pollute it. Is the plaintiff entitled to damages, and if so how much, from each defendant? Does it make any difference that the defendants, although not acting in concert, each knows what the others are doing? Woodland v. Portneuf Marsh Valley Irr. Co., 26 Idaho 789, 146 P. 1106 (1915); Sloggy v. Dilworth, 38 Minn. 179, 36 N.W. 451 (1888); Woodyear v. Schaefer, 57 Md. 1, 40 Am.Rep. 419 (1881); Warren v. Parkhurst, 45 Misc. 466, 92 N.Y.S. 725 (1904).

9. Two defendants independently pollute a stream by discharging oil into it. The oil on the surface catches fire, and the fire burns the plaintiff's barn. Can the damages be apportioned? Northrup v. Eakes, 72 Okl. 66, 178 P. 266 (1918); Phillips Petroleum Co. v. Vandergriff, 190 Okl. 280, 122 P.2d 1020 (1942). What if it poisons livestock? Tidal Oil Co. v. Pease, 153 Okl. 137, 5 P.2d 389 (1931). What about damage to crops? Phillips Petroleum Co. v. Hardee, 189 F.2d 205 (5th Cir.1951); Robillard v. Selah–Moxee Irrigation District, 54 Wash.2d 582, 343 P.2d 565 (1959); but cf. Griffith v. Kerrigan, 109 Cal.App.2d 637, 241 P.2d 296 (1952).

DILLON v. TWIN STATE GAS & ELECTRIC CO.

Supreme Court of New Hampshire, 1932.
85 N.H. 449, 163 A. 111.

Action by Henry Dillon, administrator, against the Twin State Gas & Electric Company, transferred to the Supreme Court on defendant's exception to the denial of its motion for directed verdict.

Action for negligently causing the death of the plaintiff's intestate, a boy of 14. A jury trial resulted in a disagreement.

The defendant maintained wires to carry electric current over a public bridge in Berlin. In the construction of the bridge there were two spans of girders on each side between the roadway and footway. In each span the girders at each end sloped upwards towards each other from the floor of the bridge until connected by horizontal girders about nineteen feet above the floor.

The wires were carried above the framework of the bridge between the two rows of girders. To light the footway of the bridge at its center a lamp was hung from a bracket just outside of one of the horizontal girders and crossing over the end of the girder near its connection with a sloping girder. Wires ran from a post obliquely downward to the lamp and crossed the horizontal girder a foot or more above it. The construction of the wire lines over and upon the bridge is termed aerial. The wires were insulated for weather protection but not against contact.

The decedent and other boys had been accustomed for a number of years to play on the bridge in the daytime, habitually climbing the sloping girders to the horizontal ones, on which they walked and sat and from which they sometimes dived into the river. No current passed through the wires in the daytime except by chance.

The decedent, while sitting on a horizontal girder at a point where the wires from the post to the lamp were in front of him or at his side, and while facing outwards from the side of the bridge, leaned over, lost his balance, instinctively threw out his arm, and took hold of one of the wires with his right hand to save himself from falling. The wires happened to be charged with a high voltage current at the time and he was electrocuted.

ALLEN, J. [after holding that the defendant was under a duty to the decedent to exercise reasonable care, and that the question of its negligence was for the jury]:

The circumstances of the decedent's death give rise to an unusual issue of its cause. In leaning over from the girder and losing his balance he was entitled to no protection from the defendant to keep from falling. Its only liability was in exposing him to the danger of charged wires. If but for the current in the wires he would have fallen down on the floor of the bridge or into the river, he would without doubt have been either killed or seriously injured. Although he died from electrocution, yet, if by

Two views of the bridge over the Androscoggin River in Berlin, N.H.

reason of his preceding loss of balance he was bound to fall except for the intervention of the current, he either did not have long to live or was to be maimed. In such an outcome of his loss of balance, the defendant deprived him, not of a life of normal expectancy, but of one too short to be given pecuniary allowance, in one alternative, and not of normal, but of limited, earning capacity, in the other.

If it were found that he would have thus fallen with death probably resulting, the defendant would not be liable, unless for conscious suffering found to have been sustained from the shock. In that situation his life or earning capacity had no value. To constitute actionable negligence there must be damage, and damage is limited to those elements the statute prescribes.

If it should be found that but for the current he would have fallen with serious injury, then the loss of life or earning capacity resulting from the electrocution would be measured by its value in such injured condition. Evidence that he would be crippled would be taken into account in the same manner as though he had already been crippled.

His probable future but for the current thus bears on liability as well as damages. Whether the shock from the current threw him back on the girder or whether he would have recovered his balance, with or without the aid of the wire he took hold of, if it had not been charged, are issues of fact, as to which the evidence as it stands may lead to different conclusions.

Exception overruled.

––––––––––

1. Plaintiff is suffering from a fatal illness, such as cancer, which will inevitably shorten his life. Defendant negligently kills him. The value of his life is to be measured by his anticipated future earnings, along with other factors. Is his illness to be taken into account? See Follett v. Jones, 252 Ark. 950, 481 S.W.2d 713 (1972); Fortner v. Koch, 272 Mich. 273, 261 N.W. 762 (1935); Denman v. Johnston, 85 Mich. 387, 48 N.W. 565 (1891). Cf. Pieczonka v. Pullman Co., 89 F.2d 353 (2d Cir.1937). Is the fact that the disease was certain to get worse to be taken into account? Henderson v. United States, 328 F.2d 502 (5th Cir.1964).

2. Plaintiff's house is on fire, and the firemen are delayed in reaching it because the defendant has wrongfully blocked the highway. The house is completely destroyed. For what damages is defendant liable? Felter v. Delaware & Hudson R. Corp., 19 F.Supp. 852 (D.Pa.1937), aff'd, 98 F.2d 868 (3d Cir. 1938).

3. Defendant blocks the passage of plaintiff's barge into a canal. Further on, the canal is already blocked by a landslide. What is the value of the right to enter the canal of which plaintiff has been deprived? Douglas, Burt & Buchanan Co. v. Texas & Pacific R. Co., 150 La. 1038, 91 So. 503 (1922).

4. Plaintiff is standing in the path of an avalanche when defendant negligently shoots him. Or plaintiff is about to embark for Europe on a ship, when defendant negligently shoots him; a week later the ship runs into an iceberg and sinks with everyone on board. Is the result the same?

5. Compare Morris v. St. Paul City R. Co., 105 Minn. 276, 117 N.W. 500 (1908), with Hawkins v. Front St. Cable R. Co., 3 Wash. 592, 28 P. 1021 (1892). In each case defendant negligently injured a pregnant woman, and caused a miscarriage; and defendant sought to balance against the pain she had suffered the pain normally to be expected from the birth of the child. In the one case (as shown by the record in the case) she was pregnant two months; in the other it was eight and one-half.

6. A gives plaintiff a slow poison, for which there is no known antidote, and which is certain to kill him in a week. Ten minutes later B negligently hits plaintiff with a car and kills him. For what damages should B be liable? Or in other words, of what has he deprived the plaintiff?

7. Can the principal case be harmonized with the "twin fires" decision, supra page 279?

8. See Peaslee, Multiple Causation and Damage, 47 Harv.L.Rev. 1127 (1934); King, Causation, Valuation and Chance in Personal Injury Torts Involving Preexisting Conditions and Future Consequences, 90 Yale L.J. 1353 (1981).

9. The first article in note 8 was written by the Chief Justice of New Hampshire, shortly after the *Dillon* case was decided. He raises this variation of the case: "The builder of a temporary bridge fails in his duty to set up a net for the protection of people who may fall from the stringers. An electric company wrongfully maintains charged wires immediately below the stringers. X falls from a stringer, is caught by the wires and electrocuted. Had he escaped the wires he would have been killed on the rocks below, but had there been a net he would not have reached the rocks." Consider the liability of the parties.

Chapter VIII

LIMITED DUTY

In Heaven v. Pender, 11 Q.B.D. 503 (C.A.1883), Brett, M.R., declared, "The proposition * * * is that whenever one person is by circumstances placed in such a position with regard to another that every one of ordinary sense who did think would at once recognize that if he did not use ordinary care and skill in his own conduct with regard to those circumstances, he would cause danger of injury to the person or property of the other, a duty arises to use ordinary care and skill to avoid such danger."

This is a noted passage much quoted by courts and writers, notwithstanding the fact that ten years later, in Le Lievre v. Gould, [1893] 1 Q.B. 491 (C.A.), Brett, who had become Lord Esher, was forced to retreat from his own words.

As a general proposition, applicable in the ordinary negligence case, where the defendant has taken some affirmative action such as driving an automobile, it holds good. That is to say, that whenever the automobile driver should reasonably foresee that his conduct will involve an unreasonable risk of harm to other drivers or to pedestrians, he is then under a duty to them to exercise the care of a reasonable person as to what he does or does not do.

There are, however, some defendants and some situations for which a duty does not arise. In other words, the defendant is under no legal obligation toward the plaintiff to act with the care of a reasonable person and is not liable even though his conduct falls short of that standard and the other is injured as a result. And this is true although the danger is obvious and the risk entirely unreasonable, considered merely as a risk. We have already met two such situations. One is that of the common law rule that a gratuitous bailee is liable only for gross negligence in looking after the goods, supra page 197. The other is that of the statutes making the driver liable to a gratuitous guest in his car only for aggravated misconduct, supra page 199. You will recall that some state courts have held the guest statutes to be violative of the equal protection clauses of the state or federal constitutions. Have these decisions any implication for limited duty rules in areas covered by this chapter?

This chapter deals with a miscellaneous group of situations in which a defendant may not be under the full obligation of reasonable conduct toward the plaintiff, even in the light of a foreseeable and unreasonable risk. Usually this is expressed by a holding that the defendant is under no duty to use care to protect the plaintiff, or that the duty is limited to doing only certain things. It should be understood at the outset that there is no magic in "duty." It is merely a word with which the court states its conclusion that there is no liability; and it means what the court wants it to mean in the particular case. No general formula ever has been devised to state when there is and when there is not a duty in negligence cases; and it is very likely that none ever will be.

Consider the words of Friedman, J., in Raymond v. Paradise Unified Sch. Dist., 218 Cal.App.2d 1, 31 Cal.Rptr. 847 (1963): "Generally speaking, each * * * proximate cause decision turns on its own facts and has little value as precedent. [C] A judicial declaration of duty, in contrast, may amount to a statement of law and thus create precedent, more or less influential according to its factual proximity to the case at hand.

"An affirmative declaration of duty simply amounts to a statement that two parties stand in such relationship that the law will impose on one a responsibility for the exercise of care toward the other. Inherent in this simple description are various and sometimes delicate policy judgments. The social utility of the activity out of which the injury arises, compared with the risks involved in its conduct; the kind of person with whom the actor is dealing; the workability of a rule of care, especially in terms of the parties' relative ability to adopt practical means of preventing injury; the relative ability of the parties to bear the financial burden of injury and the availability of means by which the loss may be shifted or spread; the body of statutes and judicial precedents which color the parties' relationship; the prophylactic effect of a rule of liability; in the case of a public agency defendant, the extent of its powers, the role imposed upon it by law and the limitations imposed upon it by budget; and finally, the moral imperatives which judges share with their fellow citizens—such are the factors which play a role in the determination of duty. [Cc] Occasions for judicial determination of a duty of care are infrequent, because in 'run of the mill' accident cases the existence of a duty may be—and usually is—safely assumed."

What the cases in this chapter have in common is that all of them represent compromises made by the law between the conflicting claims of plaintiffs demanding protection, and defendants insisting that they shall be free to go about their own affairs without bothering about the person who gets in their way.

The chapter does not represent a complete exposition of all situations in which the "duty" issue may be raised; that broad a perspective is impossible to obtain because the boundaries are set, in part, by the imagination and skill of plaintiff's lawyers, as well as the willingness of clients to press novel claims. Some of these issues, such as a manufacturer's duty to warn of newly discovered dangers in a product or parents' duty toward their children, are discussed in other parts of this casebook. As an introduction to this volatile topic, four key areas are presented in which the law relating to duty has been subject to important changes in recent years.

1. MENTAL DISTURBANCE AND RESULTING INJURY

DALEY v. LaCROIX

Supreme Court of Michigan, 1970.
384 Mich. 4, 179 N.W.2d 390.

T.M. KAVANAGH, JUDGE. * * * On July 16, 1963, about 10:00 p.m., defendant was traveling west on 15 Mile Road near plaintiffs' farm in Macomb county. Defendant's vehicle left the highway, traveled 63 feet in the air and 209 feet beyond the edge of the road and, in the process, sheared off a utility pole. A number of high voltage lines snapped, striking the electrical lines leading into plaintiffs' house and caused a great electrical explosion resulting in considerable property damage.

Plaintiffs claimed, in addition to property damage, that Estelle Daley suffered traumatic neurosis, emotional disturbance and nervous upset, and that Timothy Daley suffered emotional disturbance and nervousness as a result of the explosion and the attendant circumstances. * * *

The Court of Appeals (13 Mich.App. 26, 163 N.W.2d 666) affirmed the trial court's grant of a directed verdict upon the ground that Michigan law denies recovery for negligently caused emotional disturbance absent a showing of physical impact. * * *

Recovery for mental disturbance caused by defendant's negligence, but without accompanying physical injury or physical consequences or any independent basis for tort liability, has been generally denied with the notable exception of the *sui generis* cases involving telegraphic companies and negligent mishandling of corpses. * * *

[However], compensation for a purely mental component of damages where defendant negligently inflicts an *immediate physical injury* has always been awarded as "parasitic damages." * * *

The final bastion against allowing recovery [for negligent infliction of emotional harm] is the requirement of some impact upon the person of the plaintiff. It is this doctrine and its continued vitality in our State which we must now consider. * * *

In the landmark decision of Victorian Railways Commissioners v. Coultas, 13 A.C. 222 (1888), recovery for a much disputed damage to plaintiff's nervous system caused by defendant's oncoming train was denied upon the ground that:

"Damages arising from mere sudden terror unaccompanied by any actual physical injury, but occasioning a nervous or mental shock, cannot under such circumstances, their Lordships think, be considered a consequence which, in the ordinary course of things, would flow from the negligence of the gate-keeper. If it were held that they can, it appears to their Lordships that it would be extending the liability for negligence much beyond what that liability has hitherto been held to be. Not only in such a case as the present, but in every case where an accident caused by negligence had given a person a serious nervous shock, there might be a claim for damages on account of mental injury. The difficulty which now often exists in case of alleged physical injuries of determining whether they were caused by the negligent act would be greatly increased, and a wide field opened for imaginary claims."

As a further hedge against fraudulent or fancied claims and the feared flood of litigation, a large number of American courts in adopting the Victorian Railways Commissioners rule superimposed the additional requirement of a contemporaneous physical impact. * * *

The leading American authority of Mitchell v. Rochester Ry. Co. (1896), 151 N.Y. 107, 45 N.E. 354, with "remorseless logic" stated the position as follows (pp. 109, 110, 45 N.E. p. 354):

"Assuming that fright cannot form the basis of an action, it is obvious that no recovery can be had for injuries resulting therefrom. That the result may be nervous disease, blindness, insanity, or even a miscarriage, in no way changes the principle. These results merely show the degree of fright, or the extent of the damages. * * * Therefore the logical result of the respondent's concession would seem to be, not only that no recovery can be had for mere fright, but also that none can be had for injuries which are the direct consequences of it. * * * These considerations lead to the conclusion that no recovery can be had for injuries sustained by fright occasioned by the negligence of another, where there is no immediate personal injury."
* * *

The life of the law, however, has not been logic but experience. Bowing to the onslaught of exceptions [9] and the growing irreconcilability between legal fact and decretal fiction, a rapidly increasing majority of courts have repudiated the "requirement of impact" and have regarded the physical consequences themselves or the circumstances of the accident as sufficient guarantee.

Pertinently, the New York Court of Appeals in Battalla v. State (1961), 10 N.Y.2d 237, 219 N.Y.S.2d 34, 176 N.E.2d 729, expressly overruled its Mitchell v. Rochester Ry. Co., decision, supra, observing at p. 239, 219 N.Y.S.2d at p. 36, 176 N.E.2d at p. 730:

9. The divergent approaches of the courts to find an exception to the Rochester Ry. Co. rule is excellently summarized by Prosser, Torts (3d Ed.), pp. 350, 351:

"Apart from some quite untenable notions of causal connection, the theory seems to be that the 'impact' affords the desired guarantee that the mental disturbance is genuine. But the same courts have found 'impact' in minor contacts with the person which play no part in causing the real harm, and in themselves can have no importance whatever. 'Impact' has meant a slight blow, a trifling burn or electric shock, a trivial jolt or jar, a forcible seating on the floor, dust in the eye, or the inhalation of smoke. The requirement has even been satisfied by a fall brought about by a faint after a collision, or the plaintiff's own wrenching of her shoulder in reaction to the fright. 'The magic formula "impact" is pronounced; the door opens to a full joy of a complete recovery.' A Georgia circus case has reduced the whole matter to a complete absurdity by finding 'impact' where the defendant's horse 'evacuated his bowels' into the plaintiff's lap."

"Before passing to a resume of the evolution of the doctrine in this State, it is well to note that it has been thoroughly repudiated by the English courts which initiated it, rejected by a majority of American jurisdictions, abandoned by many which originally adopted it, and diluted, through numerous exceptions, in the minority which retained it. Moreover, it is the opinion of the scholars that *the right* to bring an action should be enforced."

Based upon close scrutiny of our precedential cases and the authority upon which they rested and cognizant of the changed circumstances relating to the factual and scientific information available, we conclude that the "impact" requirement of the common law should not have a continuing effect in Michigan and we therefore overrule the principle to the contrary contained in our previous cases.

We hold that where a definite and objective physical injury is produced as a result of emotional distress proximately caused by defendant's negligent conduct, the plaintiff in a properly pleaded and proved action may recover in damages for such physical consequences to himself notwithstanding the absence of any physical impact upon plaintiff at the time of the mental shock.

The rule we adopt today is, of course, subject to familiar limitations.

Generally, defendant's standard of conduct is measured by reactions to be expected of normal persons. Absent specific knowledge of plaintiff's unusual sensitivity, there should be no recovery for hypersensitive mental disturbance where a normal individual would not be affected under the circumstances. * * *

Further, plaintiff has the burden of proof that the physical harm or illness is the *natural result* of the fright proximately caused by defendant's conduct. In other words, men of ordinary experience and judgment must be able to conclude, after sufficient testimony has been given to enable them to form an intelligent opinion, that the physical harm complained of is a natural consequence of the alleged emotional disturbance which in turn is proximately caused by defendant's conduct. * * *

In view of the above holding it becomes necessary to discuss another issue raised by plaintiffs—whether, considering the evidence in the light most favorable to plaintiffs, sufficient evidence was presented to create a jury question. Denying plaintiffs' motion for a new trial which sought to set aside the directed verdict against plaintiffs Timothy and Estelle Daley, the trial court reasoned:

"There was no expert or medical testimony offered on behalf of the minor, Timothy. Extremely vague lay testimony was offered to the effect he was nervous. It was so vague and uncertain it did not, in the court's opinion, reach the dignity of possessing any evidentiary value whatever. It afforded the jury nothing into which the jury could put its 'damage-assessment teeth'. Vachon v. Todorovich, 356 Mich. 182 [, 97 N.W.2d 122].

"On behalf of Estelle Daley, Dr. Goldin, a psychiatrist, testified. Direct and cross examination were extensive. He testified clearly that she had been neurotic since childhood and the incident complained of did not cause her neurosis. Dr. Goldin indicated the incident could have broken down her 'balances' somewhat although she did not consult him until a year after the accident.

"The lay testimony was of the same type as was given in Timothy's claim. It was vague and uncertain and indefinite."

From an examination of the evidence presented on behalf of Timothy Daley, we believe that, even though the question is a close one, on favorable view, he presented facts from which under our new rule as announced in this case, a jury could reasonably find or infer a causal relation between defendant's alleged negligence and the injuries alleged. We conclude that Timothy Daley should be given an opportunity to prove his alleged cause of action, if he can do so, at a new trial.

Plaintiff Estelle Daley's claim that she suffered physical consequences naturally arising from the fright proximately caused by defendant's conduct is amply supported by the record. Her sudden loss of weight, her inability to perform ordinary household duties, her extreme nervousness and irritability, repeatedly testified to by plaintiffs, are facts from which a jury could find or infer a compensable physical injury.

The plaintiffs' testimony is also supported by the medical expert witness, who diagnosed plaintiff Estelle Daley as "a chronic psychoneurotic * * * in partial remission," and who attributed this state or condition to the explosion directly caused by defendant's acts:

"Q. I want to ask one more question, from everything that you know about this case, Doctor, do you feel there is a causal relationship between the explosion of July, 1963 and the symptoms that she has shown that you have reported?

"A. Yes, the trauma is the triggering point for her breaking the balance in her.

"Q. By trauma?

"A. Any trauma, may be emotional trauma or physical trauma, in this case having this explosive sound that she heard and the fears that were attendant with the explosive sounds."

We hold * * * that this record presents sufficient facts from which a jury could reasonably find, or infer therefrom, a causal relationship between the fright occasioned by defendant's negligence and the injuries alleged. in plaintiffs' complaint. The trial court erred in taking plaintiff Estelle Daley's case from the jury. [Cc] It follows that the trial court also erred in striking plaintiff Leonard H. Daley's claim for medical expenses.

The order of the trial court granting directed verdicts against plaintiffs Estelle Daley and Timothy Daley and the Court of Appeals' affirmance thereof are reversed and the causes remanded for new trials. * * *

Costs shall abide the final result.

DETHMERS, T.G. KAVANAGH, ADAMS and BLACK, JJ., concurred with T.M. KAVANAGH.

BRENNAN, CHIEF JUSTICE (dissenting). If this were a case where a definite and objective physical injury was produced without impact by the negligent act of the defendant, it might be appropriate to adopt the rule set forth in the Restatement (Second) of Torts § 436(2).

This is not such a case. Plaintiffs did not suffer definite and objective physical injury. Plaintiffs suffered, if anything, indefinite and subjective injury. Traumatic neurosis, emotional disturbance and nervous upset are the very type of complaints which ought to be eliminated by restricting "no impact" cases to those in which a definite and objective physical injury occurs.

I would affirm the trial court's grant of directed verdict.

KELLY, J., concurred with BRENNAN, C.J.

---

1. The requirement of an "impact" before there can be recovery even for physical consequences caused by mental disturbance was once the position of most of the American courts. At one time it was the rule of every state with a very large city. The explanation has been suggested, and borne out by the objections voiced before legislatures when changes have been proposed, that this was because of the extensive development of the racket of injury faking in such cities. Many of the decisions are collected in Annot., 64 A.L.R.2d 100 (1959) (superseded by the Modern Status of Intentional Infliction of Mental Distress As Independent Tort: "Outrage," 38 A.L.R. 4th 998 (1985)).

2. Is the "impact" rule completely devoid of sense? Are you quite sure that within the past two years you have not almost hit someone with an automobile? Can you swear that you have not frightened anyone? What if you were sued on a claim that you had caused a miscarriage? A few courts still retain the impact rule. E.g., Champion v. Gray, 478 So.2d 17 (Fla.1985), and Brown v. Cadillac Motor Car Div., 468 So.2d 903 (Fla.1985).

3. The policy reasons for and against allowing recovery despite the absence of an impact are vigorously and colorfully expounded in the dissenting opinions in two Pennsylvania cases. In Bosley v. Andrews, 393 Pa. 161, 169, 142 A.2d 263, 267 (1958), Musmanno, J., dissented against the continued application of the impact rule. In Niederman v. Brodsky, 436 Pa. 401, 413, 261 A.2d 84, 90 (1970), Bell, C.J., dissented against the overruling of the impact rule. The uninhibited language more readily used in a dissenting opinion makes entertaining reading.

4. As the principal case indicates, most courts that have abandoned the rule have said that there can be no recovery unless the mental disturbance is normal, and reasonably to be expected under the circumstances. Most of the leading cases allowing recovery have not presented a problem with regard to this issue: plaintiff has narrowly escaped imminent and serious harm to his own physical well being. See Strazza v. McKittrick, 146 Conn. 714, 156 A.2d 149 (1959) (truck struck back of plaintiff's house while she was in a nearby

room); Falzone v. Busch, 45 N.J. 559, 214 A.2d 12 (1965) (pedestrian almost struck by automobile).

5.　When plaintiff's alleged emotional suffering stems from other causes, the cases are more difficult to decide.　Thus:

A.　An intern negligently inserted into plaintiff's shoulder a catheter that broke into four small pieces.　Two pieces were located and surgically removed, but two others could not be found.　Plaintiff developed a "phobia" that the remaining bits of catheter might cause her to develop cancer in the future.　Is the intern liable for that consequence?　See Howard v. Mount Sinai Hosp., Inc., 63 Wis.2d 515, 217 N.W.2d 383 (1974).　Suppose a physician negligently misdiagnosed a patient's ailment as cancer when none existed in fact and the patient developed "cancerphobia"?　Ferrara v. Galluchio, 5 N.Y.2d 16, 152 N.E.2d 249, 176 N.Y.S.2d 996 (1958).

B.　Defendant sold plaintiff a water softener that caused a rusty discoloration of the water in plaintiff's home.　Plaintiff noticed the discoloration after she drank a cup of coffee made from this water, and claimed she suffered a heart attack as a result of her shock.　The court denied her claim.　See Caputzal v. Lindsay Co., 48 N.J. 69, 222 A.2d 513 (1966).　Is the denial of a claim best placed on the ground of proximate cause or duty?

C.　Defendant hospital performed an emergency operation that necessitated the amputation of plaintiff's leg.　After making a medical inspection of the dismembered leg, the hospital destroyed it by cremation.　Plaintiff alleged that he suffered severe mental anguish when he was informed about this disposition. Should he be allowed a claim?　See Browning v. Norton–Children's Hosp., 504 S.W.2d 713 (Ky.1974).

D.　A woman becomes upset and then physically ill after noticing a small object, which she thought was a worm, in a bottle of Coca–Cola she was drinking.　The object, which never touched her lips, was a piece of Good–N–Plenty candy.　Should she be allowed to recover for her emotional distress? See Ellington v. Coca–Cola Bottling Co., 717 P.2d 109 (Okl.1986).

E.　A person has been exposed to asbestos and incurs asbestosis (scarring of the lung).　In addition to damages for this injury, can he also recover damages for his fear of contracting lung cancer?　See Jackson v. Johns–Manville Sales Corp., 781 F.2d 394 (5th Cir.1986), cert. denied, ___ U.S. ___, 106 S.Ct. 3339, 92 L.Ed.2d 743 (1986).　Suppose there has been exposure to asbestos but no illness has yet occurred?

6.　Should fear of becoming ill or dying at a later date be compensable? The question arises today in litigation over toxic torts and latent diseases.　See, e.g., Gideon v. Johns–Manville Sales Corp., 761 F.2d 1129 (5th Cir.1985) (asbestos-related cancer); Techalloy Co. v. Reliance Ins. Co., 338 Pa.Super. 1, 487 A.2d 820 (1984) (toxic chemicals); Payton v. Abbott Laboratories, 386 Mass. 540, 437 N.E.2d 171 (1982) (diethylstilbestrol).　Need the fear be well-founded?　Is the impact rule really a problem here?

7.　A majority of the courts also hold, in accordance with the principal case, that even in the absence of an impact, if the mental disturbance produces as a natural result, physical harm to the plaintiff, recovery can be granted.　Is this proof of physical harm adequate in the principal case, or does it really amount to a recovery for mental disturbance alone?

8.　How should a court determine what is or is not a "physical injury" for the purposes of this rule?　Should it be left to the jury to decide the question on the basis of conflicting expert testimony? Is there any viable alternative to the "physical injury threshold"? Consider the statement of Judge McEntee in Petition of the United States, 418 F.2d 264 (1st Cir.1969): "The term 'physical' is not used in its ordinary sense for purposes of applying the 'physical consequences' rule. Rather, the word is used to indicate that the condition or illness for which recovery is sought must be one susceptible of objective determination. Hence, a definite nervous disorder is a 'physical injury' sufficient to support an action for damages for negligence." See also Wallace v. Coca Cola Bottling Plants, Inc., 269 A.2d 117 (Me.1970): "The mental and emotional suffering to be compensable must be substantial and manifested by objective symptomatology."

9. Shock is commonly regarded as a physical injury to the body rather than to the mind. Vanoni v. Western Airlines, 247 Cal.App.2d 793, 56 Cal. Rptr. 115 (1967). If plaintiff complains of loss of sleep, does he have a case for the jury? Suppose plaintiff is unable to conduct a normal social life because of his emotional harm? See Toms v. McConnell, 45 Mich.App. 647, 207 N.W.2d 140 (1973).

10. The uncertainty involved in tracing causation in fact from defendant's conduct to plaintiff's injuries was another reason why some courts clung to the impact rule. A very interesting opinion by a qualified medical writer, doubting the extent to which recovery really has been justified in negligent infliction of emotional harm cases decided from 1850 to 1944, is Smith, Relation of Emotions to Injury and Disease: Legal Liability for Psychic Stimuli, 30 Va.L.Rev. 193, 284–85 (1944). A helpful discussion of the causation issues from a medical perspective can be found in Selzer, Psychological and Legal Concepts of Disease Causation, 56 Cornell L.Rev. 951 (1971). The Supreme Court of Virginia has sponsored a procedural safeguard on this issue: plaintiff must prove causation in fact by "clear and convincing" evidence. Womack v. Eldridge, 215 Va. 338, 210 S.E.2d 145 (1974).

ST. ELIZABETH HOSPITAL v. GARRARD
Supreme Court of Texas, 1987.
730 S.W.2d 649.

RAY, JUSTICE. The question presented in this personal injury case is whether the physical manifestation requirement remains an element of claims for negligent infliction of mental anguish. The trial court dismissed the plaintiffs' case because their petition sought recovery for mental anguish damages, negligently inflicted, which were not alleged to have resulted in physical injury. The court of appeals held that this court had previously eliminated the physical manifestation requirement and reversed the judgment of the trial court and remanded the cause for trial. 708 S.W.2d 571. We hold that proof of physical injury is no longer required in order to recover for negligent infliction of mental anguish and therefore affirm the judgment of the court of appeals.

James and Sharon Garrard sued St. Elizabeth Hospital and Dr. H.R. Wilcox to recover mental anguish damages which resulted from the defendants' negligence. The Garrards' second amended petition alleges that Mrs. Garrard was admitted to St. Elizabeth Hospital for the anticipated delivery of her second child. At the time of delivery it was first discovered Sharon Garrard was carrying twins. A male infant was born alive and healthy, and a female infant was stillborn. The attending physician and Mr. Garrard agreed to have an autopsy performed on the stillborn infant. However, no autopsy was ever performed. Instead, the body of the infant was delivered to a mortuary and disposed of in an unmarked, common grave without the knowledge or consent of either parent. The Garrards allege specific acts of negligence committed by St. Elizabeth Hospital and Dr. Wilcox, the pathologist. Finally, the petition states:

"Each of the alleged acts and omissions of negligence were a proximate cause of the injuries and damages suffered by the plaintiffs. The plaintiffs have each suffered past mental anguish and will continue to suffer future mental anguish, including but not limited to:

"1) Never knowing the cause of death of their baby with resulting worry concerning future pregnancies.

"2) Never knowing where their baby was buried and therefore unable to do traditional memorializations such as placing flowers on a grave or visiting a grave site.

"3) Loss of the opportunity to conduct a funeral and experience that normal and usual time of grief necessary to the continuation of life as usual following a death."

Thus, the Garrards seek damages only for their mental anguish; they have not pleaded any facts suggesting the mental anguish manifested itself physically.

The defendants filed special exceptions contending that because the Garrards had not pleaded any intentional or willful act, gross negligence, breach of contract, *physical injury* or a cause of action under the wrongful death or survival statutes, they had failed to state a claim for which relief could be granted. The trial court sustained the exceptions and, following the Garrards' refusal to further amend their petition, dismissed the cause.

In reversing the ruling of the trial court, the court of appeals held that this court's decision in *Sanchez v. Schindler*, 651 S.W.2d 249 (Tex. 1983), authorized recovery for mental anguish damages without proof of physical injury or conduct worse than negligence. * * *

Texas first recognized the tort of negligent infliction of mental anguish in *Hill v. Kimball*, 76 Tex. 210, 13 S.W. 59 (1890). Therein, Justice Gaines, "[i]n a bold, closely reasoned opinion * * * presaged the ultimate trend of American law" by acknowledging the validity of a cause of action for negligently inflicted mental anguish. [C] The plaintiff in *Hill* had suffered a miscarriage after witnessing an incident involving profane language and bloodshed. Importantly, the *Hill* opinion analyzed the cause of action in light of traditional tort concepts. The court reasoned that recovery could not be denied if proof could be made that the injury proximately resulted from the actions of the defendant. Additionally, the jury would have to answer the question of whether the defendant acted negligently in light of the reasonably prudent man standard. Thus, negligent infliction of mental anguish became a tort cognizable under Texas law, to be administered using traditional tort concepts. The single deviation from traditional tort principles involved the element of damages. The court deemed improper a recovery for mental anguish, negligently inflicted, when the plaintiff's suffering failed to manifest itself physically.

However, in the almost 100 years following *Hill v. Kimball* both courts and legal scholars have condemned the physical manifestation requirement as an artificial device, the sole purpose of which is to guarantee the genuineness of claims for mental injury.[3] The specific arguments cited most frequently in support of abandoning the physical manifestation requirement are convincing. The requirement is overinclusive because it permits recovery for mental anguish when the suffering accompanies or results in any physical impairment, regardless of how trivial the injury. More importantly, the requirement is underinclusive because it arbitrarily denies court access to persons with valid claims they could prove if permitted to do so. [C]

Additionally, the requirement is defective because it "encourages extravagant pleading and distorted testimony." *Id.* To continue requiring proof of physical injury when mental suffering may be equally recognizable standing alone would force "victim[s] to exaggerate symptoms of sick headaches, nausea, insomnia, etc., to make out a technical basis of bodily injury upon which to predicate a parasitic recovery for the more grievous disturbance, the mental and emotional distress she endured." * * *

Moreover, medical research has provided modern mankind with a much more detailed and useful understanding of the interaction between mind and body. It is well recognized that certain psychological injuries can be just as severe and debilitating as physical injuries.

Clearly, freedom from severe emotional distress is an interest which the law should serve to protect. Indeed, we have not hesitated to

---

3. The following jurisdictions have rejected the physical manifestation requirement as a limitation on recovery for mental anguish damages: *Taylor v. Baptist Medical Center, Inc.,* 400 So.2d 369, 374 (Ala.1981); *Molien v. Kaiser Foundation Hospitals,* 27 Cal.3d 916, 923, 616 P.2d 813, 817, 167 Cal.Rptr. 831, 835 (1980); *Montinieri v. Southern New England Telephone Co.,* 175 Conn. 337, 398 A.2d 1180, 1184 (1978); *Rodrigues v. State,* 52 Hawaii 156, 472 P.2d 509, 519 (1970); *Barnhill v. Davis,* 300 N.W.2d 104, 108 (Iowa 1981); *Culbert v. Sampson's Supermarkets Inc.,* 444 A.2d 433, 438 (Me.1982); *Bass v. Nooney Co.,* 646 S.W.2d 765, 772 (Mo.1983); *Johnson v. Supersave Markets, Inc.,* 686 P.2d 209, 213 (Mont.1984); *James v. Lieb,* 221 Neb. 47, 375 N.W.2d 109, 116 (1985); *Portee v. Jaf-*fee, 84 N.J. 88, 417 A.2d 521, 526 (1980); *Schultz v. Baberton Glass Co.,* 4 Ohio St.3d 131, 447 N.E.2d 109, 113 (1983); *Sinn v. Burd,* 486 Pa. 146, 404 A.2d 672, 679 (1979); *Chappetta v. Bowman Transportation, Inc.,* 415 So.2d 1019, 1022–23 (La.Ct. App.1982).

Writers on the subject generally agree that the physical manifestation requirement is destined for extinction. *See generally* McCarthy, *Illinois Law in Distress: The "Zone of Danger" and "Physical Injury" Rules in Emotional Distress Litigation,* 19 J.Mar.L.Rev. 17 (1985); Comment, *Negligent Infliction of Emotional Distress: A Proposal for a Recognized Tort Action,* 67 Marq.L.Rev. 557 (1984).

defend peace of mind when we deemed the facts sufficient to guarantee the genuineness of the claim in the absence of physical manifestations of the mental injury. Having recognized that an interest merits protection, it is the duty of this court to continually monitor the legal doctrines of this state to insure the public is free from unwarranted restrictions on the right to seek redress for wrongs committed against them. The physical manifestation requirement is one such restriction. In *Moore v. Lillebo* we eliminated the requirement in wrongful death actions. The time has come to advance the common law to coincide with the modern trend. Thus, we hold that proof of physical injury resulting from mental anguish is no longer an element of the common law action for negligent infliction of mental anguish.

By eliminating the physical manifestation requirement Texas joins an established trend in American jurisprudence which recognizes the tort of negligent infliction of mental anguish without imposing arbitrary restrictions on recovery in such actions.[6] The distinction between physical injury and emotional distress is no longer defensible. The problem is one of proof, and to deny a remedy in all cases because some claims may be false leads to arbitrary results which do not serve the best interests of the public. Jurors are best suited to determine whether and to what extent the defendant's conduct caused compensable mental anguish by referring to their own experience.

Thus, we hold that the Garrards' petition states a cause of action despite the absence of allegations that the mental anguish suffered resulted in physical injury. The judgment of the court of appeals is affirmed.

Spears, Justice, concurring and dissenting. I concur in the court's judgment. This state has long recognized that establishing the mishandling of a corpse and establishing a feeling of closeness or love between the deceased and the one asking for damages is sufficient for a jury to consider mental anguish. [Cc]

However, instead of confining this decision within these well established parameters, the court takes the unnecessary step of abolishing the physical manifestation requirement of negligently inflicted severe mental anguish. Decisions reaffirming the physical manifestation requirement are summarily overruled. [Cc] In so doing, the court approves compensating mere sorrow, grief, anger or worry, and promoting spurious litigation. From that holding, I dissent. * * *

The court proposes that it is joining the "established trend" by dispensing with the requirement. Seven states, comprising a distinct

---

6. The supreme courts of seven American jurisdictions have adopted the tort of negligent infliction of mental anguish in a more or less pure form. *See Taylor v. Baptist Medical Center, Inc.; Molien v. Kaiser Foundation Hospitals; Montinieri v. Southern New England Telephone Co.; Rodrigues v. State; Bass v. Nooney Co.; Johnson v. Supersave Markets, Inc.; Sch-* *ultz v. Barberton Glass Co.* [all cited in footnote 3, supra.]

Comparable approaches are reflected in decisions by the House of Lords and the high court of Australia. *See McLoughlin v. O'Brian* [1982] 2 W.L.R. 982 *and Jaensch v. Coffey* (Austl.1984) 54 Argus L.R. 417.

minority, does not a trend make. In fact, over forty jurisdictions retain the physical manifestation requirement for the tort of negligent infliction of mental anguish. *See* Restatement (Second) of Torts § 436A (1965) (appendix). The wisdom of Restatement § 436A is persuasive: "If the actor's conduct is negligent as creating an unreasonable risk of causing either bodily harm or emotional disturbance to another, and it results in such emotional disturbance alone, without bodily harm or other compensable damage, the actor is not liable for such emotional disturbance."

---

1. As explained in the principal case, most states retain the physical manifestation requirement, but two exceptions are well recognized. The death-telegram rule (recovery for emotional harm resulting from negligent transmission by a telegraph company of a message announcing death) is a minority rule but followed by a number of the states. See Johnson v. State, 37 N.Y.2d 378, 372 N.Y.S.2d 638, 334 N.E.2d 590 (1975); Mentzer v. Western Union Tel. Co., 93 Iowa 752, 62 N.W. 1 (1895); Western Union Tel. Co. v. Redding, 100 Fla. 495, 129 So. 743 (1930). The Federal rule allows recovery if physical harm results. Kaufman v. Western Union Tel. Co., 224 F.2d 723 (5th Cir.1955), cert. denied, 350 U.S. 947 (1956); O'Brien v. Western Union Tel. Co., 113 F.2d 539 (1st Cir. 1940).

The second exception involves negligent interference with dead bodies. See Lott v. State, 32 Misc.2d 296, 225 N.Y.S.2d 434 (1962); cf. Corso v. Crawford Dog and Cat Hosp., 97 Misc.2d 530, 415 N.Y.S.2d 182 (1979) (substitution in casket of cat for beloved pet dog).

2. These two exceptions have generally been treated as discrete and independent. The principal case suggests that they may evolve into a broader principle of real significance. Can you speculate on its probable ramifications? Consider the earlier case of Espinosa v. Beverly Hosp., 114 Cal.App.2d 232, 249 P.2d 843 (1953), where a hospital attendant delivered to a new mother the wrong baby. She suffered severe emotional harm on learning that the child she brought home and cared for was not, in fact, her own. No recovery was allowed. How should the case be decided today? Consider also the facts in Whetham v. Bismarck Hosp., infra page 403.

3. The majority of states have abandoned the traditional rule that a plaintiff could not recover for mental injuries that were not connected with actual or threatened impact. See, e.g., Gates v. Richardson, 719 P.2d 193, 195, n. 1 (Wyo.1986) (cases from 37 jurisdictions rejecting the rule).

4. A different type of case is Molien v. Kaiser Foundation Hosp., 27 Cal.3d 916, 616 P.2d 813, 167 Cal.Rptr. 831 (1980). Defendant erroneously and negligently diagnosed a wife's condition as syphilis, instructed her to advise her husband of the diagnosis and submit to a blood test. Though his test proved negative, she blamed him as the source and the marriage broke up. Suit by the husband for infliction of mental distress and for loss of consortium. In holding that there might be recovery, the court declared that "the attempted distinction between physical and psychological injury merely clouds the issue. The essential question is one of proof." It held "that a cause of action may be stated for the negligent infliction of severe emotional distress," and also allowed recovery for loss of consortium. The decision has found some followers. Would the ruling permit a recovery by the children of the couple? By the husband's

mother? Might the factual situation have come within the incipient principle suggested in the principal case? For the possibility of a different basis for recovery, see infra pages 549 and 877.

5. Should it make any difference if the defendant is a doctor or a psychologist? Suppose a therapist decides to "date" a patient's sexual companion, having learned of the companion through the course of psychotherapy with his patient—now a plaintiff. See Rowe v. Bennett, 514 A.2d 802 (Me.1986). Should other special relationships deserve special treatment?

6. At the time this casebook was going to print, there was legislation pending in Congress called the "High Risk Occupational Disease Notification and Prevention Act" under which the federal government would conduct studies and notify workers if they have been exposed to something in the workplace that may put them at risk of incurring an illness or disease. See S. 79 and H.R. 162, 100th Cong., 1st Sess. (1987). What tort claims, if any, might arise out of this process? The legislation precluded the actual notifications from being used as evidence in lawsuits against employers and producers of workplace substances. Do you think that this alone would prevent lawsuits from being brought once an employee receives notification of being at risk of catching a disease?

WHETHAM v. BISMARCK HOSPITAL
Supreme Court of North Dakota, 1972.
197 N.W.2d 678.

ERICKSTAD, JUDGE. Martin and Dixie Whetham, the parents of Tami Lynn, a child born to them in the Bismarck Hospital on the 28th day of July 1970, commenced an action to recover from the Bismarck Hospital a judgment of $100,000. They assert that shortly after Dixie's admission to the Bismarck Hospital, Tami Lynn was born, and that in the process of bringing Tami Lynn to Dixie's hospital bed an employee of the Hospital, in Dixie's presence, dropped her onto the tiled floor of the hospital room. They assert further that Tami Lynn struck her head upon the floor with great force and violence, fracturing her skull, and that this resulted from the careless and negligent handling of the child by the employee; that as a direct and proximate result of that negligence, Dixie was forced helplessly to watch her daughter fall to the floor and to hear the sound of the impact; that as a direct and proximate result of such negligence, Dixie suffered a severe emotional and mental shock, for which she now seeks recovery in money damages.

The Whethams also ask for damages resulting from the additional medical expenses thereafter required to be expended for Tami's care and for the prolonged hospitalization of the mother while the child received this care.

The trial court, on a motion for summary judgment, dismissed that part of the complaint which asked for damages arising out of the suffering caused Dixie from the emotional and mental shock of observing her daughter fall to the floor.

Dixie has now appealed to this court from the judgment entered on the 16th day of August 1971 dismissing that part of the complaint. The complaint asserts that no claim is made on behalf of Tami Lynn for her injuries, for the reason that the full residual effects of her injuries are not yet known. * * *

There are two leading cases in the State of California on whether liability may be predicated on fright or nervous shock (with consequent bodily injury) induced solely by the plaintiff's apprehension of negligently caused danger or injury to a third person.

The first case is that of Amaya v. Home Ice, Fuel & Supply Co., 59 Cal.2d 295, 29 Cal.Rptr. 33, 379 P.2d 513 (1963). In *Amaya,* Justice Schauer, speaking for the majority of the California Supreme Court, after reviewing the law of California and the other States of the United States, noting the development of the law as contained in the Restatement of Torts, the administrative difficulties and the socio-economic and moral factors, concluded that under the circumstances recovery was not permitted.

Justice Schauer pointed out that there must be a stopping point to the liability of a negligent defendant and, quoting Professor Prosser, said:

" 'It is still unthinkable that any one shall be liable to the end of time for all of the results that follow in endless sequence from his single act. Causation cannot be the answer; in a very real sense the consequences of an act go forward to eternity, and back to the beginning of the world.' [Cc]

He then explained why he thought it unthinkable that anyone should be liable to the end of time.

"First, to the extent that the law intervenes in any area of human activity and declares that for certain consequences of that activity the actor shall be held civilly liable in damages, both the individual actor and society as a whole feel the effects of the restraint—a psychological effect in the form of a lessening of incentive, and an economic effect in the form of the cost of insurance necessary to enable the activity to continue. Yet it is recognized that no activity could survive an unlimited progression of such effects. Accordingly, when the general social utility of an activity is deemed to outweigh the particular interest with which it may clash, important policy reasons dictate that some limits be set to liability for its consequences. How do these considerations affect our problem? The law, both in California and in the many other jurisdictions which have passed on the question, now provides, as has been shown, that an actor who is merely negligent is not liable to one who claims injury through fright or shock induced by conduct directed not to the latter but to a third person. Thus, in cases where the defendant's conduct involved negligent driving of a motor vehicle the courts conclude that to extend liability to spectators who were not themselves in danger 'would, in our opinion, place an unreasonable burden upon users of highways.' [C] As the industrial society in which we live becomes still more complex and the use of the streets and highways and airways increases, a certain percentage of accidents therefrom appears to become statistically inevitable. There will be losses, and our present system of insurance attempts to compensate for them, and, of course, to spread the cost of compensation over those who do not, as well as those who do, cause such losses. But could that system—imperfect at best—adequately and fairly absorb the far-reaching extension of liability that would follow from judicial abrogation of the rule now before us? And what of the many other activities of everyday life that are either uninsurable or customarily uninsured, yet may well give rise to the type of 'spectator injury' here alleged? We conclude, rather, that the social utility of such activities outweighs the somewhat speculative interest of individuals to be free from the risk of the type of injury here alleged.

"The second reason for seeking a stopping point to the negligent defendant's liability is a related one. As long as our system of compensation is based on the concept of fault, we must also weigh 'the moral blame attached to the defendant's conduct.' [C] Here is felt the difference between the social importance of conduct that negligently causes harm and conduct that is intended to do so. It is often said that in the latter case the defendant will be held liable for a broader range of consequences because, as the consequences are intended, they are the more 'foreseeable.' But in many intentional tort cases the defendant has been held liable under this reasoning for consequences far beyond those which he actually intended. [C] It follows that, once more, 'foreseeability' is not the real answer. Rather, the increased liability imposed on an intentional wrongdoer appears to reflect the psychological fact that solicitude for the interests of the actor weighs less in the balance as his moral guilt increases and the social utility of his conduct diminishes." Amaya Home Ice, Fuel & Supply Co., supra, 29 Cal.Rptr. 33, 44, 45, 379 P.2d 513, 524, 525. * * *

In 1968, only five years after *Amaya*, and after changes in the membership of the court, the California Supreme Court overruled *Amaya* in Dillon v. Legg, 68 Cal.2d 728, 69 Cal.Rptr. 72, 441 P.2d 912.

Justice Tobriner, speaking for the majority in *Dillon*, believing that the difficulties of adjudication should not frustrate the principle that there be a remedy for every substantial wrong and yet realizing that potential infinite liability should be limited, concluded that the law of torts holds a defendant amenable only for injuries to others which to the defendant at the time were reasonably foreseeable. In noting that the court was dealing with a case in which the plaintiff suffered a shock which resulted in physical injury, and confining its opinion to that case, the court said:

"In determining, in such a case, whether defendant should reasonably foresee the injury to plaintiff, or, in other terminology, whether defendant owes plaintiff a duty of due care, the courts will take into account such factors as the following: (1) Whether plaintiff was located near the scene of the accident as contrasted with one who was a distance away from it. (2) Whether the shock resulted from a direct emotional impact upon plaintiff from the sensory and contemporaneous observance of the accident, as contrasted with learning of the accident from others after its occurrence. (3) Whether plaintiff and the victim were closely related, as contrasted with an absence of any relationship or the presence of only a distant relationship." Dillon v. Legg, supra, 69 Cal.Rptr. 72, 80, 441 P.2d 912, 920.

After laying down these guidelines, the court said that it would determine whether the accident and harm were reasonably foreseeable in light of the cited factors.

Applying the aforementioned factors, Justice Tobriner concluded that the presence of all the factors indicated that the plaintiff had alleged a sufficient prima facie case. He quoted Dean Prosser as follows:

" '[W]hen a child is endangered, it is not beyond contemplation that its mother will be somewhere in the vicinity, and will suffer serious shock.' (Prosser, The Law of Torts, supra, at p. 353. See also 2 Harper & James, The Law of Torts, supra, at p. 1039.)" Dillon v. Legg, supra, 69 Cal.Rptr. 72, 81, 441 P.2d 912, 921.

Justice Burke, dissenting in *Dillon,* had this to say:

"The majority, obviously recognizing that they are now embarking upon a first excursion into the 'fantastic realm of infinite liability' (*Amaya,* at p. 315 of 59 Cal.2d, 29 Cal.Rptr. 33, 379 P.2d 513), undertake to provide so-called 'guidelines' for the future. But notwithstanding the limitations which these 'guidelines' purport to impose, it is only reasonable to expect pressure upon our trial courts to make their future rulings conform to the spirit of the new elasticity proclaimed by the majority.

"Moreover, the majority's 'guidelines' (ante, 69 Cal.Rptr. pp. 80, 81, 441 P.2d pp. 920, 921) are simply a restatement of those suggested earlier by Professor Prosser (Prosser, Torts, 2d ed., 1955, p. 182); they have already been discussed and expressly rejected by this court in *Amaya* (59 Cal.2d pp. 312–313, 29 Cal.Rptr. 33, 379 P.2d 513). Upon analysis, their seeming certainty evaporates into arbitrariness, and inexplicable distinctions appear. As we asked in *Amaya:* What if the plaintiff was honestly *mistaken* in believing the third person to be in danger or to be seriously injured? What if the third person had assumed the risk involved? How 'close' must the relationship be between the plaintiff and the third person? I.e., what if the third person was the plaintiff's beloved niece or nephew, grandparent, fiancé, or lifelong friend, more dear to the plaintiff than her immediate family? Next, how 'near' must the plaintiff have been to the scene of the accident, and how 'soon' must shock have been felt? Indeed, what is the magic in the plaintiff's being actually present? Is the shock any less real if the mother does not know of the accident until her injured child is brought into her home? On the other hand, is it any less real if the mother is physically present at the scene but is nevertheless unaware of the danger or injury to her child until after the accident has occurred? No answers to these questions are to be found in today's majority opinion. Our trial courts, however, will not so easily escape the burden of distinguishing between litigants on the basis of such artificial and unpredictable distinctions." Dillon v. Legg, supra, 69 Cal. Rptr. 72, 86, 441 P.2d 912, 926. * * *

[W]e conclude that the trial court was correct in the instant case in dismissing that part of the complaint which sought to recover damages for the plaintiff's mental anguish at witnessing her daughter's injury negligently caused by an employee of the Hospital. It is our view that the plaintiff herein could recover only if the defendant's negligent act had threatened the plaintiff herself with harm or placed her within what is termed the zone of danger. The complaint contains no facts upon which such a contention could be supported. * * *

For the reasons stated in this opinion, the judgment of the trial court is affirmed.

---

1. Prior to 1968, case law authority was virtually unanimous in rejecting recovery by bystanders who suffered emotional harm on the basis of observing an injury that had been negligently inflicted upon another. Cases are collected in Annot., 29 A.L.R.3d 1337 (1970). The Restatement (Second) of Torts § 313, respected this authority, and declared that there could be no recovery unless the plaintiff was in the zone of physical danger. The explanation was sometimes expressed in terms of proximate cause but more frequently in terms of lack of duty as being outside the scope of the risk, in reliance upon the majority opinion in Palsgraf v. Long Island R. Co., supra page 304. A leading case to this effect was Waube v. Warrington, 216 Wis. 603, 258 N.W. 497, 98 A.L.R. 394 (1935). What should be the result if plaintiff was in the zone of physical danger, but suffered physical results from emotional distress based solely on fear for the safety of another? Cf. Williamson v. Bennett, 251 N.C. 498, 112 S.E.2d 48 (1960). Did the *Molien* case, supra page 402, present a "bystander" problem?

2. A change came about with the decision of Dillon v. Legg, 68 Cal.2d 728, 441 P.2d 912, 69 Cal.Rptr. 72, 29 A.L.R.3d 1316 (1968), described at length in the opinion of the principal case. The majority and dissenting opinions in *Dillon*, and particularly in the earlier case of Amaya v. Home Ice, Fuel & Supply Co., 59 Cal.2d 295, 379 P.2d 513, 29 Cal.Rptr. 33 (1963), constitute the best and most thorough treatment of the issues involved. Judge Tobriner, who wrote the majority opinion in *Dillon*, had also written the opinion of the intermediate court which was reversed in *Amaya;* his elevation to the Supreme Court had made the difference in vote.

3. Some courts have decided to keep their zone-of-danger limitation. Dillon v. Legg has been rejected by courts in Louisiana, Newman v. Baton Rouge, 260 So.2d 52 (La.App.1972), Welsh v. Davis, 307 F.Supp. 416 (D.Mont. 1969) (anticipating state law); Massachusetts, Dziokonski v. Babineau, 375 Mass. 555, 380 N.E.2d 1295 (1978); New Hampshire, Corso v. Merrill, 119 N.H. 647, 406 A.2d 300 (1979); New Jersey, Portee v. Jaffee, 84 N.J. 88, 417 A.2d 521 (1980); Wisconsin, Garfield v. United States, 297 F.Supp. 891 (W.D.Wis.1969) (anticipating Wisconsin law); and Vermont, Guilmette v. Alexander, 128 Vt.

116, 259 A.2d 12 (1969). And see the thorough treatment in the English Court of Appeals, McLaughlin v. O'Brien, [1981] Q.B. 99, [1981] 1 All E.R. 809.

On the other hand some courts have accepted it. See D'Amicol v. Alvarez Shipping Co., 31 Conn.Sup. 164, 326 A.2d 129 (1973) (mother and father witnessed death of son); Leong v. Takasaki, 55 Hawaii 398, 520 P.2d 758, 94 A.L.R.3d 471 (1974) (ten-year-old boy witnessed his step-grandmother being killed); Sinn v. Burd, 486 Pa. 146, 404 A.2d 672 (1979); D'Ambra v. United States, 354 F.Supp. 810 (D.R.I.), aff'd, 518 F.2d 275, cert. denied, 414 U.S. 1075 (1973) (anticipation as to Rhode Island law); cf. Barnhill v. Davis, 300 N.W.2d 104 (Iowa 1981); Culbert v. Sampson's Supermarkets, Inc., 444 A.2d 433 (Me. 1982); Keck v. Jackson, 122 Ariz. 114, 593 P.2d 668 (1979); Haught v. Maceluch, 681 F.2d 291 (5th Cir.1984), reh'g denied, 685 F.2d 1385 (5th Cir. 1982).

4. What happens now in a state that follows *Dillon?* Even though Pennsylvania followed *Dillon,* a claim by parents and the identical twin of the decedent for mental distress suffered upon learning of the death was rejected because plaintiffs did not witness the surgery that caused the death. Hoffner v. Hodge, 47 Pa.Cmwlth. 277, 407 A.2d 940 (1979). Suppose a mother is not at the scene, but learns about a tragedy to her son somewhat later? A California court in Archibald v. Braverman, 275 Cal.App.2d 253, 79 Cal.Rptr. 723 (1969), permitted the claim when defendant had made an illegal sale of explosives to a 13-year-old old who subsequently blew himself up. When a wife was called to an emergency room shortly after her husband received a serious auto injury, she was allowed to recover. See Deboe v. Horn, 16 Cal.App.3d 221, 94 Cal.Rptr. 77 (1971). See Annot., 5 A.L.R.4th 833 (1981). The *Dillon* guidelines were liberally construed in Tommy's Elbow Room, Inc. v. Kavorkian, 727 P.2d 1038 (Alaska 1986), where a plaintiff recovered damages for negligent infliction of emotional distress caused by injury to another, despite the fact that he had not actually witnessed a tortious event. Plaintiff was the father of a woman killed in an accident by a drunken driver; he had passed the accident scene, not realizing his daughter was involved, but later returned and saw his daughter being removed from a car.

On the other hand, in Jansen v. Children's Hosp. Medical Center, 31 Cal. App.3d 22, 106 Cal.Rptr. 883 (1973), a mother's claim was rejected although she suffered severe emotional injury as a result of witnessing the progressive decline and ultimate death of her daughter—allegedly a victim of a negligent diagnosis by the hospital. The court said that the *Dillon* decision contemplated "a sudden and brief event causing the child's injury."

5. In Kelley v. Kokua Sales & Supply, Inc., 56 Hawaii 204, 532 P.2d 673 (1975), plaintiff, located in California, suffered a heart attack after being informed about the death of his daughter and granddaughter in an automobile accident that occurred in Hawaii. Although the court accepted *Dillon,* it denied plaintiff's claim because he was not located "a reasonable distance from the scene."

6. What result if the injured plaintiff was not a relative? Suppose a woman loses the man with whom she is living? Cf. Drew v. Drake, 100 Cal. App.3d 555, 168 Cal.Rptr. 65 (1980).

7. See generally Goodhart, Emotional Shock and the Unimaginative Taxi-cab Driver, 69 Law Q.Rev. 347 (1953); Nolan and Ursin, Negligent Infliction of Emotional Distress: Coherence Emerging from Chaos, 33 Hastings L.J. 583 (1982); Stevens, Negligent Infliction of Emotional Distress by Physicians and

Hospitals, 28 Med.Tr.T.Q. 233 (1982); Miller, The Scope of Liability for Negligent Infliction of Emotional Distress: Making "The Punishment Fit the Crime," 1 U.Haw.L.Rev. 1 (1979); Maragos, Negligent Infliction of Mental Distress—Mixed Signals?, 8 W.St.U.L.Rev. 139 (1981); Note, Negligent Infliction of Mental Distress: Reaction to Dillon v. Legg in California and Other States, 25 Hastings L.J. 1248 (1974); Note, Administering the Tort of Negligent Infliction of Mental Distress: A Synthesis, 4 Cardozo L.Rev. 487 (1983); Annots., 77 A.L.R.3d 447 (1977); 94 A.L.R.3d 486 (1979).

8. The rule of Dillon v. Legg may eventually be consumed by the recently emerging "independent" cause of action for emotional distress. See Pearson, Liability to Bystanders for Negligently Inflicted Emotional Harm, 34 U.Fla.L. Rev. 477 (1982).

9. Should the physical manifestation rule apply in bystander cases? If not, where does one draw the line? Who pays for all of this? Look at your automobile liability insurance policy. Are you "covered" if you injure A and the event is witnessed by B and you are sued by B? What if you almost injure A but B witnessed the event and is even more frightened than A? Should either party be able to recover?

2. FAILURE TO ACT

HEGEL v. LANGSAM

Court of Common Pleas of Ohio, 1971.
29 Ohio Misc. 147, 55 Ohio Ops.2d 476, 273 N.E.2d 351.

BETTMAN, JUDGE. This matter is before the Court on defendant's motion for judgment on the pleadings. The gravamen of plaintiff's position is that the defendants permitted the minor plaintiff, a seventeen year old female student from Chicago, Illinois, enrolled at the University, to become associated with criminals, to be seduced, to become a drug user and further allowed her to be absent from her dormitory and failed to return her to her parents' custody on demand.

In our opinion plaintiffs completely misconstrue the duties and functions of a university. A university is an institution for the advancement of knowledge and learning. It is neither a nursery school, a boarding school nor a prison. No one is required to attend. Persons who meet the required qualifications and who abide by the university's rules and regulations are permitted to attend and must be presumed to have sufficient maturity to conduct their own personal affairs.

We know of no requirement of the law and none has been cited to us placing on a university or its employees any duty to regulate the private lives of their students, to control their comings and goings and to supervise their associations.

We do not believe that O.R.C. 3345.21 requiring a university to maintain "law and order" on campus, nor O.R.C. 2151.41, making it a crime to contribute to the delinquency of a child, have any bearing on the fact situation before us.

For these reasons we hold that plaintiffs have failed to state a cause of action and defendants' motion for judgment on the pleadings should be granted. * * *

———

1. Compare with the instant case, Duarte v. State, 84 Cal.App.3d 729, 148 Cal.Rptr. 804 (1978), holding a university liable for rape and murder in a student dormitory. Reconcilable?

Although a governmental unit was technically the defendant in this case, the court applied the same fundamental tort principles that have been applied to private parties. Thus:

A. Bigan enticed his friend Yania, a competent adult, to jump into a large open trench in a strip mining area. The trench contained water 8 to 10 feet in depth and Yania drowned. Bigan made no rescue effort. Should he be liable to Yania's widow? Yania v. Bigan, 397 Pa. 316, 155 A.2d 343 (1959).

B. Siegrist and Farwell drove around town stopping at various restaurants and drive-ins. At one stop a gang beat up Farwell; Siegrist escaped injury. Should he have a duty to obtain medical aid for his friend? Farwell v. Keaton, 396 Mich. 281, 240 N.W.2d 217 (1976).

2. Assuming that "governmental tort immunity" is not applicable (see pages 622–34), should the state's tort duty to rescue or protect be greater than a private individual's? Why? To date, most courts have applied the same duty obligation to the government as to private individuals. See e.g., Simpson's Food Fair, Inc. v. Evansville, 149 Ind.App. 387, 272 N.E.2d 871 (1971) (failure to provide police protection to grocer); Riss v. City of New York, infra page 627 (individual who was threatened did not obtain requested police protection); Lacey v. United States, 98 F.Supp. 219 (D.Mass.1951) (Coast Guard failed to undertake rescue effort); Annot., 46 A.L.R.3d 1084 (1972). For a thoughtful discussion of this question, see Shapo, Changing Frontiers in Torts: Vistas for the 70's, 22 Stan.L.Rev. 330 (1970).

3. Should professionals be under an obligation to assist an individual in need of their services? Although the American Medical Association's Principles of Medical Ethics, Number 5 provides that, in an emergency, a physician should render service to the best of his ability, tort law places no such obligation on the profession. See Hurley v. Eddingfield, 156 Ind. 416, 59 N.E. 1058 (1901). Should an attorney be under a duty to take a case?

Originally, before the idea of contract obligations had developed, those engaged in "public callings" were held to have undertaken an obligation to serve the public, which made them liable for failure to do so. This survives today in the rule that common carriers, innkeepers, and public utilities generally, are liable for failure to render service. See, for example, Nevin v. Pullman Palace Car Co., 106 Ill. 222, 46 Am.Rep. 688 (1883), where the defendant was held liable for failure to provide a sleeping car berth.

4. Several European countries have provisions in their penal codes imposing a duty to rescue. Typical is the Dutch Penal Code, Art. 450: "One who, witnessing the danger of death with which another is suddenly threatened, neglects to give or furnish him such assistance as he can give or procure without reasonable fear of danger to himself or to others, is to be punished, if the death of the person in distress follows, by a detention of three months at most, and an amende of three hundred florins at most." Cf. Vt.Stat.Ann. tit. 12, § 579 (1973); see Franklin, Vermont Requires Rescue: A Comment, 25

Stan.L.Rev. 51 (1972).　For others, see Rudzinski, The Duty to Rescue: A Comparative Analysis, in Ratcliffe, The Good Samaritan and the Law, 91 (1966).

5.　Plaintiff is dying of starvation in the midst of a large city, and no one will give him food.　Or he falls overboard from a boat in front of a crowd gathered to watch a crew race, and no one will save him.　Against whom is an action to lie?　Should the situation be different when the defendant is singled out, either by a request from the plaintiff or by the fact that he is the only one on the spot?　Should he be expected to endanger his own life in an attempt at rescue, if he has no boat and is a poor swimmer?　What if he could easily throw a life-preserver or a rope?　Or if he needed only to cry out a warning?

6.　This topic has engaged a good many writers, all of whom have agreed in denouncing the state of the law.　See Ames, Law and Morals, 22 Harv.L.Rev. 97 (1908); Bohlen, The Moral Duty to Aid Others as a Basis of Tort Liability, 56 U.Pa.L.Rev. 217 (1908); Bruce, Humanity and the Law, 73 Cent.L.J. 335 (1911); Snyder, Liability for Negative Conduct, 35 Va.L.Rev. 446 (1949); McNiece and Thornton, Affirmative Duties in Torts, 58 Yale L.J. 1272 (1949); Seavey, I Am Not My Guest's Keeper, 13 Vand.L.Rev. 699 (1960); Rudolph, The Duty to Act: A Proposed Rule, 44 Neb.L.Rev. 499 (1965); Landes & Posner, Salvors, Finders, Good Samaritans and Other Rescuers: An Economic Study of Law and Altruism, 7 J. Legal Stud. 83 (1978); Levmore, Waiting for Rescue: An Essay On the Evolution and Incentive Structure of the Law of Affirmative Obligations, 72 Va. L.Rev. 879 (1986); and see two books: Ratcliffe (ed.), The Good Samaritan and the Law (1966); M. Shapo, The Duty to Act: Tort Law, Power and Public Policy (1977).

L.S. AYRES & CO. v. HICKS
Supreme Court of Indiana, 1942.
220 Ind. 86, 40 N.E.2d 334, 41 N.E.2d 195, 356.

[Plaintiff, a boy six years old, accompanied his mother to defendant's department store while she was shopping.　Plaintiff fell, and got his fingers caught in defendant's escalator.　Defendant unreasonably delayed stopping the escalator, as a result of which plaintiff's injuries were aggravated.　Judgment for plaintiff, and a new trial denied. Defendant appeals.]

SHAKE, C.J.　[after holding that there was no negligence in the construction of the escalator].　It may be observed, on the outset, that there is no general duty to go to the rescue of a person who is in peril. So, in Hurley, Adm'r, v. Eddingfield, 1901, 156 Ind. 416, 59 N.E. 1058, it was held that a physician was not liable for failing without any reason to go to the aid of one who was violently ill and who died from want of medical attention which was otherwise unavailable.　The effect of this rule was aptly illustrated by Carpenter, C.J., in Buch v. Amory Mfg. Co., 1897, 69 N.H. 257, 260, 44 A. 809, 810, as follows:

"With purely moral obligations the law does not deal.　For example, the priest and Levite who passed by on the other side were not, it is supposed, liable at law for the continued suffering of the man who fell among thieves, which they might, and morally ought to have prevented or relieved."

There may be principles of social conduct so universally recognized as to be demanded that they be observed as a legal duty, and the relationship of the parties may impose obligations that would not otherwise exist. Thus, it has been said that, under some circumstances, moral and humanitarian considerations may require one to render assistance to another who has been injured, even though the injury was not due to negligence on his part and may have been caused by the negligence of the injured person. Failure to render assistance in such a situation may constitute actionable negligence if the injury is aggravated through lack of due care. [C] The case of Depue v. Flatau, 1907, 100 Minn. 299, 111 N.W. 1, lends support to this rule. It was there held that one who invited into his house a cattle buyer who called to inspect cattle which were for sale owed him the duty, upon discovering that he had been taken severely ill, not to expose him to danger on a cold winter night by sending him away unattended while he was in a fainting and helpless condition.

After holding that a railroad company was liable for failing to provide medical and surgical assistance to an employee who was injured without its fault but who was rendered helpless, by reason of which the employee's injuries were aggravated, it was said with the subsequent approval of this court, in Tippecanoe Loan, etc., Co. v. Cleveland, etc., R. Co., 1915, 57 Ind.App. 644, 649, 650, 104 N.E. 866, 868, 106 N.E. 739:

"In some jurisdictions the doctrine has been extended much further than we are required to do in deciding this case. It has been held to apply to cases where one party has been so injured as to render him helpless by an instrumentality under the control of another, even though no relation of master and servant, or carrier and passenger, existed at the time. It has been said that the mere happening of an accident of this kind creates a relation which gives rise to a legal duty to render such aid to the injured party as may be reasonably necessary to save his life, or to prevent a serious aggravation of his injuries, and that this subsequent duty does not depend on the negligence of the one party, or the freedom of the other party from contributory negligence, but that it exists irrespective of any legal responsibility for the original injury."

From the above cases it may be deduced that there may be a legal obligation to take positive or affirmative steps to effect the rescue of a person who is helpless or in a situation of peril, when the one proceeded against is a master or invitor, or when the injury resulted from use of an instrumentality under the control of the defendant. Such an obligation may exist although the accident or original injury was caused by the negligence of the plaintiff or through that of a third person and without any fault on the part of the defendant. Other relationships may impose a like obligation, but it is not necessary to pursue that inquiry further at this time.

In the case at bar the appellee was an invitee and he received his initial injury in using an instrumentality provided by the appellant and under its control. Under the rule stated above and on the authority of the cases cited this was a sufficient relationship to impose a duty upon the appellant. Since the duty with which we are presently concerned arose after the appellee's initial injury occurred, the appellant cannot be charged with its anticipation or prevention but only with failure to exercise reasonable care to avoid aggravation. * * *

Since the appellee was only entitled to recover for an aggravation of his injuries, the jury should have been limited and restricted in assessing the damages to the injuries that were the proximate result of the appellant's actionable negligence. * * *

The judgment is reversed with directions to sustain the appellant's motion for a new trial.

---

1. *Special Relations.* The maritime law developed the rule that a ship master was required to make reasonable efforts to rescue a seaman who fell overboard. Harris v. Pennsylvania R. Co., 50 F.2d 866 (4th Cir.1931). There are a good many cases in which this has been extended to other employers, in situations where the employee has suffered sunstroke and the like. See, for example, Carey v. Davis, 190 Iowa 720, 180 N.W. 889 (1921); Rival v. Atchison, T. & S.F.R. Co., 62 N.M. 159, 306 P.2d 648 (1957); Anderson v. Atchison, T. & S.F.R. Co., 333 U.S. 821 (1948).

2. The employer's duty is limited to situations where the employee is evidently unable to look after himself. It is also limited to the course of employment, and there is no duty to aid an employee who has stepped out on his own time for a beer. Allen v. Hixson, 111 Ga. 460, 36 S.E. 810 (1900); Matthews v. Carolina & N.W.R. Co., 175 N.C. 35, 94 S.E. 714 (1917).

3. Other special relations that have been held to impose a duty to take reasonable affirmative action to aid are:

A. Common carrier and passenger. See, for example, Middleton v. Whitridge, 213 N.Y. 499, 108 N.E. 192 (1915); Yu v. New York, N.H. & H.R. Co., 145 Conn. 451, 144 A.2d 56 (1958).

B. Innkeeper and guest, at least to the extent of aiding the guest to escape from a fire in the hotel. Dove v. Lowden, 47 F.Supp. 546 (W.D.Mo.1942).

C. Temporary legal custodian and his charge. For example, jailor and prisoner, Thomas v. Williams, 105 Ga.App. 321, 124 S.E.2d 409 (1962). The custody and control relationship may create a duty on a grade school teacher to make a reasonable effort to obtain medical aid for a pupil. See Pirkle v. Oakdale Union Grammar School Dist., 40 Cal.2d 207, 253 P.2d 1 (1953). How does this situation differ from that in Hegel v. Langsam, page 409, supra? What result when a policeman leaves a person arrested for drunkenness in a locked police car, the vehicle catches fire and the drunk is burned? See Barlow v. New Orleans, 257 La. 91, 241 So.2d 501 (1970).

4. Other courts have agreed with the principal case as to a landowner or business visitor, on premises open to the public (invitor and invitee). Connelly v. Kaufmann & Baer Co., 349 Pa. 261, 37 A.2d 125 (1944); Larkin v. Saltair Beach Co., 30 Utah 86, 83 P. 686 (1905). This was extended even to social

guests in Hutchinson v. Dickie, 162 F.2d 103 (6th Cir.1947). Cf. Depue v. Flateau, 100 Minn. 299, 111 N.W. 1 (1907), stated in the principal case.

5. In California, bar owners or employees have no duty to make an emergency call to police to protect a person threatened outside their establishment. They do have a duty, however, to allow a Good Samaritan the use of a public telephone on the premises. See Soldano v. O'Daniels, 141 Cal.App.3d 443, 190 Cal.Rptr. 310 (1983). Should it make a difference if it is a long-distance call?

6. There may be other relations. Two likely ones are those between husband and wife, and parent and child, where a duty to aid has been recognized by the criminal law, as in Rex v. Smith, 2 C. & P. 449, 172 Eng.Rep. 203 (1826). Cf. State v. Zobel, 81 S.D. 260, 134 N.W.2d 101 (1965). Assuming that intrafamily immunity has been abolished in a state, should tort law impose a duty on a parent to make a reasonable effort to protect or rescue his child? See Holodook v. Spencer, 36 N.Y.2d 35, 324 N.E.2d 338, 364 N.Y.S.2d 859 (1974).

7. *Negligent Injury by Defendant.* When the defendant by his own negligence injures another, there is general agreement that he is then under a duty to take reasonable affirmative action to aid him. Parrish v. Atlantic Coast Line R. Co., 221 N.C. 292, 20 S.E.2d 299 (1942).

8. *Innocent Injury by Defendant.* When defendant, without negligence, creates a dangerous condition in the highway, it is agreed that he is under a duty to take reasonable precautions against injury to persons using it. Thus in Hardy v. Brooks, 103 Ga.App. 124, 118 S.E.2d 492 (1961), the defendant innocently hit a cow and killed it. He was held under a duty to use reasonable care to remove it from the highway, give warning, or otherwise protect other drivers. Accord: Simonsen v. Thorin, 120 Neb. 684, 234 N.W. 628 (1931) (trolley pole knocked over into street); Montgomery v. National Convoy & Trucking Co., 186 S.C. 167, 195 S.E. 247 (1938) (truck stalled on icy road at night).

9. When the defendant, or his instrumentality, innocently injures the plaintiff, there are older cases holding that he is under no duty to do anything about it. Thus a railroad company which, without any negligence, ran over a trespasser, was held to be under no obligation to do anything at all to keep him from bleeding to death. Union Pac. R. Co. v. Cappier, 66 Kan. 649, 72 P. 281 (1903). Or even to remove the train from his body. Griswold v. Boston & Maine R. Co., 183 Mass. 434, 67 N.E. 354 (1903).

It appears unlikely that these rather appalling cases would be followed today. See Pridgen v. Boston Hous. Auth., 308 N.E.2d 467, 477 n. 7 (Mass. 1973). The Restatement (Second) of Torts has changed the rule of its § 322 to agree with the principal case. In accord are Whitesides v. Southern R. Co., 128 N.C. 229, 38 S.E. 878 (1901); and apparently Ward v. Morehead City Sea Food Co., 171 N.C. 33, 87 S.E. 958 (1916).

10. "Hit and run driver" statutes, requiring an automobile driver involved in an accident to stop and give aid, have been held in a number of states to mean that a failure to do so is negligence per se. Brumfield v. Wofford, 143 W.Va. 332, 102 S.E.2d 103 (1958); Hallman v. Cushman, 196 S.C. 402, 13 S.E.2d 498 (1941); Brooks v. E.J. Willig Truck Transp. Co., 40 Cal.2d 669, 255 P.2d 802 (1953). On these and other statutes, see Linden, Tort Liability for Criminal Nonfeasance, 44 Can.B.Rev. 25 (1966).

COFFEE v. McDONNELL–DOUGLAS CORP.

Supreme Court of California, 1972.
8 Cal.3d 551, 503 P.2d 1366, 105 Cal.Rptr. 358.

SULLIVAN, J. In this action for damages for personal injuries defendant McDonnell–Douglas Corporation appeals from a judgment entered upon a jury verdict in favor of plaintiff and from an order denying defendant's motion for a judgment notwithstanding the verdict. * * *

Plaintiff commenced the instant action against McDonnell–Douglas and its three doctor-employees (Waters, Gray, and Ruetman) alleging that defendants required plaintiff to undergo a pre-employment physical examination to determine whether or not he was physically fit to be a test pilot and that defendants performed the physical examination negligently in that they either "knew or should have known of his true condition [i.e., multiple myeloma] and negligently failed to disclose" it, or that they were so negligent in the performance of the examination that they failed to discover the presence of the disease. As a proximate result of defendants' negligence, plaintiff averred, his "disease progressed and became aggravated and spread because plaintiff was without medical treatment," thereby reducing his life expectancy, lessening his resistance to other diseases, weakening his bone structure and causing loss of wages. * * *

An employer generally owes no duty to his prospective employees to ascertain whether they are physically fit for the job they seek, but where he assumes such duty, he is liable if he performs it negligently. [Cc] The obligation assumed by an employer is derived from the general principle expressed in section 323 of the Restatement (Second) of Torts, that one who voluntarily undertakes to perform an action must do so with due care. * * *

Such a relationship was formed here when defendant undertook, although voluntarily to examine plaintiff so as to ascertain his physical fitness for duties as a pilot.

Defendant insists that the imposition of a duty "to discover" is an "undue burden." However, it has been said that an employer has failed to exercise due care when it fails "to disclose" diseased or dangerous conditions revealed in a physical examination. [Cc] Yet defendant in effect argues that if an employer fails to perform an examination with due care and thereby fails "to discover" the presence of such a condition, he should not be held liable. In other words, defendant's liability would be limited by the commission of its negligent acts. We cannot approve of such a result.

At the same time we do not say that an employer, once having required a prospective employee to submit to a physical examination in order to ascertain his fitness for the job, assumes an absolute obligation to discover any diseased conditions. In our view the proper test is this: whether the employer in such instance is liable for not discovering the disease depends upon whether or not in the light of all of the circumstances he conducted and completed the examination with due care. Included among the relevant circumstances is the purpose of the examination.

In the matter before us, the purpose of the physical examination was to determine plaintiff's physical fitness as a pilot. In order to examine prospective pilots properly, defendant decided it was essential to take a blood sample and subject it to analysis. The blood test report, indicating an inflammatory condition in plaintiff, was never seen by defendant's medical employees because of a corporate procedure allowing the report to be filed without evaluation. The question posed, already answered by the jury in the affirmative, was whether in the exercise of due care, defendant "should have known" of the results of the blood test. [C] Viewed in this context, the failure "to discover" the inflammatory condition in plaintiff was the consequence of defendant's own negligence.

The judgment is affirmed.

---

1. When does the defendant enter upon an "undertaking" by affirmative action? Defendant sees a swimmer drowning in a river; he cries, "Courage, my good fellow, I will save you!"; he starts running to a shed where there is a rope; he gets the rope; he returns to the bank; he casts the rope once and it falls short; he casts it again and the swimmer catches hold; he pulls the swimmer five feet nearer the shore; he then decides that it is all just too much trouble, and abandons the whole thing; the swimmer drowns. Suppose that there is no one else within a mile. At the end of the whole sequence, would you expect any court to hold that there is no liability? Where should the line be drawn?

2. Was there an undertaking to the plaintiff in the principal case? Sometimes an undertaking is found although there has been no affirmative effort to aid the specific victim. Thus, in Wilmington Gen. Hosp. v. Manlove, 54 Del. 15, 174 A.2d 135 (1961), a sick child was turned away from the defendant's hospital, and its condition was aggravated by the delay in obtaining medical attention. It was held that it could be found that defendant, by maintaining an emergency ward, had induced the plaintiff to forego other medical assistance, and thus had caused the delay, and so was liable. See also Stanturf v. Sipes, 447 S.W.2d 558 (Mo.1969); Annot., 35 A.L.R.3d 841 (1970); Powers, Hospital Emergency Service and the Open Door, 66 Mich.L.Rev. 1455 (1968).

3. If the defendant started to aid the plaintiff and then failed to complete the task, would his conduct have the effect of putting the plaintiff in a worse condition because third parties were deterred from rendering aid? Because they might have been deterred? Because the plaintiff was led to believe that the condition had been made safe? See Bloomberg v. Interinsurance Exchange, 162 Cal.App.3d 571, 207 Cal.Rptr. 853 (1984).

4. When can a rescuer terminate his efforts without incurring liability? The Restatement (Second) of Torts §§ 323 and 324, limits its rule to cases where the defendant leaves the plaintiff in a worse situation, as by increasing the danger, by depriving him of the chance of other aid, or by inducing him to forego it in reliance upon the undertaking. It leaves open, in Caveats to both

sections, the question whether "there may not be other situations in which one may be liable where he has entered upon performance, and cannot withdraw from his undertaking without leaving an unreasonable risk of serious harm to the other." In accord with the Restatement, see Kirshenbaum v. General Outdoor Advertising Co., 258 N.Y. 489, 180 N.E. 245 (1932); Kuchynski v. Ukryn, 89 N.H. 400, 200 A. 416 (1938). Contra: Cummings v. Henninger, 28 Ariz. 207, 236 P. 701 (1925); Bluhm v. Byram, 193 Wis. 346, 214 N.W. 364 (1927). Where does the principal case fit?

5. One of the well-known cases on this is Erie R. Co. v. Stewart, 40 F.2d 855 (6th Cir.1930). Defendant, although it was under no legal duty to do so, had maintained a watchman at a street crossing to give warning of the approach of trains. On one occasion the watchman was busy with his own affairs and failed to give warning. The driver of a truck knew of the practice of giving warning, and relied upon it in crossing the track. The truck was hit by the train, and a passenger in it was injured. Two judges allowed recovery, but only on the ground of the reliance. One, concurring, thought that a duty had been undertaken toward any vehicle crossing the track, even though the driver knew nothing about the watchman.

6. There are several cases in which a landlord, with no obligation to do so, has voluntarily attempted to make repairs on the leased premises; but, though he did not succeed in eliminating the dangerous condition, he did not make the situation worse, either by increasing the danger, by misleading the tenant into a belief of safety, or by depriving him of the opportunity of obtaining aid elsewhere. Nevertheless, the landlord has been held liable; the courts have rejected the Restatement and have said that it is a question of reasonable care under the circumstances. The best of these decisions is Bartlett v. Taylor, 351 Mo. 1060, 174 S.W.2d 844 (1943). See also Bauer v. 141–149 Cedar Lane Holding Co., 24 N.J. 139, 130 A.2d 833 (1957); Olsen v. Mading, 45 Ariz. 423, 45 P.2d 23 (1935); and the dictum of Cardozo, C.J., in Marks v. Nambil Realty Co., 245 N.Y. 256, 157 N.E. 129 (1927). Are these cases to be explained on the basis of the special relation of landlord and tenant?

7. What can the defendant do to discontinue his undertaking? If he takes charge of the victim of an accident, is he required to do more than give him first aid and call a doctor? How can a railroad discontinue a watchman whom it considers to be no longer needed? See Pennsylvania R. Co. v. Yingling, 148 Md. 169, 129 A. 36 (1925), where the court said that reasonable notice to the public was enough.

8. A recurring problem has been that of the worker's compensation insurer which, voluntarily and without any obligation, makes a safety inspection of the premises, and is negligent in doing so. Some cases, as in Nelson v. Union Wire Rope Corp., 31 Ill.2d 69, 199 N.E.2d 769 (1964), have held the insurer liable when a worker is injured by a condition that it should have discovered. The greater number of the decisions, as in Gerace v. Liberty Mut. Ins. Co., 264 F.Supp. 95 (D.D.C.1966), have held the insurer not liable, although most of them have relied on provisions of the workmen's compensation acts. See McCoid, The Third Person in the Compensation Picture, 37 Tex.L.Rev. 389 (1959); Boynton and Evans, What Price Liability for Insurance Carriers Who Undertake Voluntary Safety Inspections, 43 Notre Dame Law. 193 (1967).

9. Why should the "good Samaritan" be liable to the man he tries to help, when the priest and the Levite who pass by on the other side are not? What

kind of rule is this for the encouragement of emergency assistance and first aid?

10. *Statutes.* Doctors, who are called on much more than anyone else in such emergencies, are much disturbed about this. A survey reported in Medical Tribune, August 28, 1961, disclosed that out of 1209 doctors questioned, only about half had replied that they would stop to give aid at the scene of a medical emergency; the rest would be deterred by fear of malpractice suits. The medical profession has succeeded in obtaining the adoption, in more than forty states, of so-called "good Samaritan" statutes.

The first of these was the 1959 amendment to § 2144 of the California Business and Professions Code: "No person licensed [to practice medicine; later amended to include nurses] under this chapter, who in good faith renders emergency care at the scene of the emergency, shall be liable for any civil action for damages as a result of any acts or omissions by such person in rendering the emergency care." Good Samaritan statutes vary in many respects. For analysis and discussion of the statutes, see Notes, 64 Colum.L.Rev. 301 (1964), 38 Temp.L.Q. 418 (1965), 32 Tenn.L.Rev. 287 (1965). How helpful have the statutes proved to be? See Hessel, Good Samaritan Laws: Bad Legislation, 2 J.Leg.Med. [No. 3] 40 (1974); Weigel, Good Samaritan Laws— Who Needs Them? The Current State of Good Samaritan Protection in the United States, 21 S.Tex.L.J. 327 (1980).

11. The Alaska Good Samaritan statute (Alas.St. 09.65.090) protects a "person, who, without expecting compensation, renders emergency care" unless he engages in "reckless, wilful, or wanton misconduct." Plaintiff, a twelve-year-old girl, was attacked by a lioness. Defendant, a state trooper, came to her rescue. He killed the lioness with his first shot; however, in the melee his gun went off again, wounding his rescuee in the thigh. Should the officer be liable if he was negligent? See Lee v. State, 490 P.2d 1206 (Alaska 1971). And see Dahl v. Turner, 80 N.M. 564, 458 P.2d 816 (1969) (passing motorist). For application of a statute to a medical situation, see McKenna v. Cedars of Lebanon Hosp., 93 Cal.App.3d 282, 155 Cal.Rptr. 631 (1979).

CROWLEY v. SPIVEY

Court of Appeals of South Carolina, 1985.
285 S.C. 397, 329 S.E.2d 774.

PER CURIAM: These two wrongful death actions were brought by Timothy Crowley (Timothy), as the administrator of the estates of his two minor sons, twelve-year-old Timothy, Jr., and five-year-old Michael. The suits were brought against the children's maternal grandparents, Edward F. and Nora D. Spivey. The cases were consolidated for trial, and the jury returned verdicts for actual damages in each suit. We affirm.

The decedents were the only children of the marriage between Timothy and Joyce Lynette Crowley (Lynette), who is the Spiveys' daughter. Lynette was granted custody of the children when she and Timothy were divorced in 1975. In 1978, Timothy gained custody from Lynette, who was granted visitation rights. On the morning of April 29, 1979, while the children were visiting Lynette for a weekend at the Spiveys' home in Beaufort, Lynette shot and killed the children.

Lynette had received intermittent treatment for the mental disease paranoid schizophrenia since 1971.

The identical complaints alleged that Timothy, upon learning that Lynette had acquired a gun, advised the Spiveys that he would no longer permit visitation with the children away from his home. The Spiveys, it was alleged, then told Timothy they would supervise the care and safety of the children if the children came to visit Lynette at their home. Among the specifications of negligence charged were allegations that the Spiveys (1) unreasonably failed to discover that Lynette had access to or possession of a gun, (2) unreasonably failed to take measures to prevent Lynette from having access to a gun during the children's visitation, and (3) failed to exercise a reasonable degree of control and supervision over the visitation between Lynette and the children by allowing her to visit with the children in a locked room when the Spiveys knew or should have known that this would increase the likelihood of harm to the children.

To recover in negligence, the plaintiff must show (1) a duty of care owed by the defendant, (2) a breach of that duty by negligent act or omission, and (3) damage proximately resulting therefrom. [C] The Spiveys seek reversal of the verdict on the asserted absence of a duty of care. Alternatively, they contend that even if there was such a duty their conduct was not the proximate cause of the injury.

The duty of care in this case is grounded in the legal proposition that one who assumes to act, even though under no obligation to do so, may become subject to the duty to act with due care. [Cc] Timothy's testimony is unequivocal that he allowed visitation to resume because the Spiveys undertook to provide supervision over the children's visits with Lynette in Beaufort. The evidence also warrants the conclusion that Timothy was swayed to permit visitation because the Spiveys undertook a search for the pistol and were satisfied that Lynette no longer had it. Although the Spiveys were not obligated to so act, once their performance began, a common law duty to exercise reasonable care arose. * * *

On the Spiveys' alternative contention that their conduct was not the proximate cause of the injury, they claim that they are insulated from liability for their conduct because the intervening independent act of Lynette was not reasonably foreseeable. Stated another way, they contend there was no evidence from which the jury could conclude that they could have reasonably foreseen that Lynette would harm the children as a natural and probable consequence of their negligence. * * *

The Spiveys emphasize that Lynette had no history of violent behavior and exhibited no manifestation of ill will towards the children, whom from all indications she loved dearly. This does not conclusively show, however, that the Spiveys could not have reasonably foreseen that the children would be at risk while with Lynette when she was armed with a pistol during a period when she was deviating from a prescribed course of treatment that was necessary for her to lead a normal life.

Evidence showed the Spiveys knew Lynette had a serious mental health problem from the time she was first hospitalized in 1971. In the years that Lynette lived with the Spiveys immediately preceding the tragedy, it is inferable that they were as well acquainted as anyone with her mental disposition and the effect the failure to take her prescribed medication would have on her. Their knowledge of Lynette's condition is reflected in their testimony that as a matter of common sense Lynette should not possess a pistol. This belies the assertion that the Spiveys could not reasonably apprehend danger to others if Lynette were in possession of a pistol, a matter that is underscored by expert testimony that the danger to others is increased when a paranoid schizophrenic comes into possession of a weapon that can be used with great immediacy, such as a pistol.

Moreover, the obvious goal of Timothy's express prohibition on visitation was to protect the children. It would require no quantum leap of logic for the jury, in recognition of this fact, to infer that the Spiveys also could reasonably foresee that Lynette would pose a threat to the children if left alone with them while in possession of a pistol. Indeed, Mrs. Spivey's testimony that she and her husband searched for the pistol so that they would have "peace of mind" when the children visited could be interpreted as a recognition that potential harm to the children as a result of Lynette's having the pistol was not only foreseeable but also actually foreseen. * * *

Further, it is not necessary that the Spiveys should have foreseen the particular act which occurred, but rather only that the injury was a natural and probable consequence of their negligence. * * *

Thus the assertion that the Spiveys could not foresee the extent of the harm or the manner in which it occurred cannot shelter them from liability.

We conclude that there is sufficient evidence from which the jury could infer that the Spiveys could reasonably foresee that some harm would come to the children if they unreasonably failed to find the pistol and failed to take reasonable measures to monitor Lynette's contact with the children. Thus, the issue of proximate cause was for the jury to resolve. * * *

For these reasons, the judgment of the trial court is

Affirmed.

————

1. In the classic case of Thorne v. Deas, 4 Johns. 84 (N.Y.1809), plaintiff and defendant were co-owners of a ship, which was en route from New York to North Carolina. Plaintiff proposed that they obtain insurance, and defendant promised to do it. Ten days later, it transpired that defendant had not taken out the insurance, and plaintiff started to get the insurance but was dissuaded by defendant, who promised to get it that day. The ship was lost at sea, and

defendant had failed to effect any insurance. Chancellor Kent rendered judgment for the defendant. Contract did not lie because there was no consideration for the promise. Tort did not lie because there was no undertaking; this was nonfeasance rather than misfeasance.

2. Thorne v. Deas has been much criticized over the years. In contract law, modifications of the requirement of consideration have developed through the doctrine of promissory estoppel. See Restatement (Second) of Contracts § 90; Henderson, Promissory Estoppel and Traditional Contract Doctrine, 78 Yale L.J. 343 (1960); Hoffman v. Red Owl Stores, Inc., 26 Wis.2d 683, 133 N.W.2d 267 (1965). In torts, it has been argued forcefully that reliance on the promise placed plaintiff in a worse position, but the distinction between nonfeasance and misfeasance and the fear that adoption of the argument would cause tort law to absorb all cases of broken promises have meant that the rule of Thorne v. Deas, in its tort aspects, has continued to be applied by the great majority of the courts. This is especially true when the harm has been economic in nature. See Restatement (Second) of Torts § 323.

3. Dissatisfaction with the rule has caused courts to be acute to find an undertaking from a very minor action, apparently producing a misfeasance. See, e.g., Carr v. Maine Cent. R.R., 78 N.H. 502, 102 A. 532 (1917) (receiving papers to make application for rebate).

4. When risk of physical injury is involved, there are several decisions, besides the principal case. Consider the following:

A. In Morgan v. Yuba County, 230 Cal.App.2d 938, 41 Cal.Rptr. 508 (1964), a county sheriff's department failed to warn Mrs. Helen Morgan (as it had promised) that a dangerous prisoner was about to be released. Mrs. Morgan had played a part in the prisoner's original arrest. After the prisoner killed Mrs. Morgan, her husband brought a wrongful death claim against the county. The court held that plaintiff could state a claim if the county had induced reliance on the part of Mrs. Morgan and she had, in fact, relied on its promise. See also Williams v. United States, 450 F.Supp. 1040 (D.S.D.1978).

B. In Dudley v. Victor Lynn Lines, Inc., 48 N.J.Super. 457, 138 A.2d 53 (1958), rev'd on other grounds, 32 N.J. 479, 161 A.2d 479 (1960), a truck driver was taken ill while at work. He appeared to be suffering only from a bad cold, and apparently was quite able to look after himself. His helper called his wife, who was unable to come and take him home. She asked the assistant warehouse foreman to call a doctor; he promised to do so and did not. The illness turned out to be a heart attack and the man died. After rejecting any liability on the basis of the duty of an employer, on the ground that there was no apparent necessity for aid, the court held defendant liable in tort for breach of the promise, relied on to the man's detriment. Should a casual promise to make a phone call create liability?

C. In Rozycki v. Peley, 199 N.J.Super. 571, 489 A.2d 1272 (1984), parents of minor boys who were physically and sexually abused by defendant's husband brought suit against her, alleging that because she knew of her husband's pedophilia, she had a duty to warn either the infant plaintiffs or their parents. The court disagreed, finding that the strength of the marital relationship would be undermined were spouses required to warn others of their mate's possible dangerousness.

D. In Marsalis v. LaSalle, 94 So.2d 120 (La.App.1957), a cat bit plaintiff during a rabies scare. The cat owner promised plaintiff to keep the cat indoors while a physician determined whether plaintiff was infected with rabies. The cat escaped from the owner's yard; plaintiff sued and won medical expenses due to defendant's failure to act with reasonable care.

5. See Seavey, Reliance Upon Gratuitous or Other Conduct, 64 Harv.L. Rev. 913 (1951); Gregory, Gratuitous Undertakings and the Duty of Care, 1 DePaul L.Rev. 30 (1951); James, Scope of Duty in Negligence Cases, 47 Nw.U.L. Rev. 779 (1953).

LINDER v. BIDNER

Supreme Court of New York, Queens County, 1966.
50 Misc.2d 320, 270 N.Y.S.2d 427.

[The complaint alleged that Gary Bidner, aged 18, lived with and was subject to the control of his parents; that he had a vicious and malignant disposition, and was in the habit of mauling, assaulting and mistreating smaller children; that his parents, defendants well knew or should have known of this conduct, and did nothing to prevent or control it, but permitted him to go at large and alone, where minor children were playing; and that the said Gary Bidner assaulted and injured the plaintiff Stuart Linder. The parents moved to dismiss the complaint for failure to state a cause of action.]

J. IRWIN SHAPIRO, JUSTICE. * * * In Restatement of the Law of Torts, section 316, the statement is made that "A parent is under a duty to exercise reasonable care so to control his minor child as to prevent it from intentionally harming others or from so conducting itself as to create an unreasonable risk of bodily harm to them, if the parent (a) knows or has reason to know that he has the ability to control his child and (b) knows or should know of the necessity and opportunity for exercising such control" and this duty is not peculiar to the father alone, but "extends to the mother also in so far as her position as mother gives her an ability to control her child."

Under the allegations contained in the instant complaint, giving them every possible interpretation in support of the plaintiffs' cause of action, as one must do on a motion of this character, it is obvious that there are sufficient allegations to establish ability on the part of the parents to control their child and knowledge on their part of the necessity and opportunity for exercising such control. * * *

The allegations in the complaint, taken at their face value, show notice to the parents of the dangerous propensities of their minor son, an ability to control him in that regard and a complete default in restraining him from conduct calculated to harm others which by reason of his prior antics could reasonably have been anticipated. The parents therefore owed a duty to society to guard their son closely to see to it that he did not indulge in his vicious propensities.

In The Law of Torts (Harper and James, vol. 2, p. 1056), the authors express the same views in the following language:

"Where a parent has reason to know of a propensity for a particular type of dangerous conduct on the part of his minor child he is bound to take reasonable steps (by discipline, training or the like) to curb or guard against the propensity. The dangerous habit must be of a very specific kind, however. There is no general responsibility for the rearing of incorrigible children." [Cc]

It has uniformly been held that a parent who knows of the dangerous propensities of his child is bound to use reasonable care to control the child so as to prevent the indulgence in those propensities. [Cc]

The rule would seem to be that a parent is negligent when there has been a failure to adopt reasonable measures to prevent a *definite* type of harmful conduct on the part of the child, but that there is no liability on the part of the parents for the general incorrigibility of a child.

The motion is in all respects denied.

---

1. The duty to take affirmative action to control the conduct of a third person may arise in two different ways. Under the first, the defendant stands in a special relation to the plaintiff that requires him to exercise affirmative care to protect him against the conduct of the third person. Thus the duty of a common carrier to its passengers may require it to take steps to prevent personal attack upon them, theft of their property, or even negligent conduct which threatens to injure them. Kinsey v. Hudson & Manhattan R. Co., 130 N.J.L. 285, 32 A.2d 497 (1943).

2. A similar duty rests upon innkeepers for the protection of their guests. Modern law has extended it to occupiers of premises who hold them open to invitees, as in Peck v. Gerber, 154 Or. 126, 59 P.2d 675 (1936). The same kind of duty rests upon employers for the protection of their employees in the course of employment; and upon those who have the custody of prisoners, or children. The duty is only to exercise reasonable care. See for example Gold v. Heath, 392 S.W.2d 298 (Mo.1965).

3. In the other type of case the defendant stands in a special relation to the third person, that gives him a power of control over that person's actions. He is then required to use reasonable care to exercise that control to prevent the third person from injuring the plaintiff. Relationships include parent and child, employer and employee, automobile owner and driver, and persons who have taken charge of dangerous lunatics, criminals and persons with contagious diseases. An interesting case is Connolly v. Nicollet Hotel, 254 Minn. 373, 95 N.W.2d 657 (1959), where a convention in the defendant's hotel got out of hand and started menacing everybody and everything in the vicinity, and the management was held to be under a duty to make reasonable efforts to control it. Does a passenger in an automobile who is aware that the driver has been drinking heavily have an affirmative duty to warn other passengers who do not realize the driver's potentially impaired condition? See VanHaverbeke v. Bernhard, 654 F.Supp. 255 (S.D.Ohio 1986). Cf. Pulka v. Edelman, 40 N.Y.2d 781, 358 N.E.2d 1019, 390 N.Y.S.2d 393 (1976) (automobile garage and customers driving out over a sidewalk outside the exit).

4. Again, in all these cases, the defendant is liable only for failure to exercise the care of a reasonable person under the circumstances. In Capps v. Carpenter, 129 Kan. 462, 283 P. 655 (1930), it was held that the parent was not liable merely because the child was incorrigible, exhibited a mean disposition

and had been badly reared when the child did something that he never had done before. But in Bieker v. Owens, 234 Ark. 97, 350 S.W.2d 522 (1961), repeated attacks on other children were held to be enough. Trial court testimony on this point illustrating how the rule may work as a practical matter is set forth in Ross v. Souter, 81 N.M. 181, 464 P.2d 911, 914 (1970). In the principal case what is likely to be the result after trial?

5. There has been a temptation in the law to hold parents vicariously liable for the torts of their children. The Supreme Court of Louisiana recently took the plunge, but it based its decision on a section of the Code Napoleon that is not part of the law in common law states. See Turner v. Bucher, 308 So.2d 270 (La.1975). For an overview, see Frankel, Parental Liability for a Child's Tortious Acts, 81 Dick.L.Rev. 755 (1977).

6. Statutes in over 45 states directed at curbing juvenile delinquency place pressure upon the parent and have made him liable for damage intentionally inflicted by his child on persons or property. See Freer, Parental Liability for Torts of Children, 53 Ky.L.J. 254 (1965). The statutes have damage ceilings that may be as high as $1000. A Georgia statute with no damage ceiling was held void under the due process clauses of the state and federal constitutions. Corley v. Lewless, 227 Ga. 745, 182 S.E.2d 766 (1971).

7. In Schurk v. Christensen, 80 Wash.2d 652, 497 P.2d 937 (1972), defendants' son, while acting as a baby-sitter, sexually molested a neighbor's five-year-old daughter. The neighbors suffered severe emotional harm when they learned about this fact from their daughter and they sued defendants. What should be the major legal and factual issues in the case?

8. See generally Harper and Kime, The Duty to Control the Conduct of Another, 43 Yale L.J. 886 (1934).

TARASOFF v. REGENTS OF UNIVERSITY OF CALIFORNIA

Supreme Court of California, 1976.
17 Cal.3d 425, 551 P.2d 334, 131 Cal.Rptr. 14.

[Posenjit Poddar was an out-patient under the care of a psychologist, Dr. Lawrence Moore, at Cowell Memorial Hospital of the University of California. During the course of treatment, Dr. Moore learned from Poddar that he intended to kill Tatiana Tarasoff because she had spurned Poddar's romantic advances.

On the basis of this information, Dr. Moore had the campus police detain Poddar, apparently at the hospital. Poddar was released shortly afterward. Despite disagreement among the psychiatrists the final decision was that no further action should be taken to confine Poddar. This judgment proved to be mistaken; two months later Poddar shot and then repeatedly stabbed Tatiana. Plaintiffs, Tatiana's parents, brought a wrongful death claim against the four psychiatrists. Plaintiffs claimed that they should be liable because they failed to confine Poddar. The court rejected this claim because California Government Code Section 856 cloaked the doctors with tort immunity with regard to this type of decision. Plaintiffs also claimed that defendants should be liable for Tatiana's death because they failed to warn her or them about Poddar's threat.]

TOBRINER, JUSTICE.   *   *   * The second cause of action can be
amended to allege that Tatiana's death proximately resulted from
defendants' negligent failure to warn Tatiana or others likely to apprise
her of her danger. Plaintiffs contend that as amended, such allegations
of negligence and proximate causation, with resulting damages, establish a cause of action. Defendants, however, contend that in the
circumstances of the present case they owed no duty of care to Tatiana
or her parents and that, in the absence of such duty, they were free to
act in careless disregard of Tatiana's life and safety.   *   *   *

   Although   *   *   * under the common law, as a general rule, one
person owed no duty to control the conduct of another [cc], nor to warn
those endangered by such conduct [cc], the courts have carved out an
exception to this rule in cases in which the defendant stands in some
special relationship to either the person whose conduct needs to be
controlled or in a relationship to the foreseeable victim of that conduct
(see Rest.2d Torts, supra, §§ 315–320).   *   *   *

   Although plaintiffs' pleadings assert no special relation between
Tatiana and defendant therapists, they establish as between Poddar
and defendant therapists the special relation that arises between a
patient and his doctor or psychotherapist. Such a relationship may
support affirmative duties for the benefit of third persons. Thus, for
example, a hospital must exercise reasonable care to control the behavior of a patient which may endanger other persons. A doctor must also
warn a patient if the patient's condition or medication renders certain
conduct, such as driving a car, dangerous to others.

   Although the California decisions that recognize this duty have
involved cases in which the defendant stood in a special relationship
both to the victim and to the person whose conduct created the danger,
we do not think that the duty should logically be constricted to such
situations. Decisions of other jurisdictions hold that the single relationship of a doctor to his patient is sufficient to support the duty to
exercise reasonable care to protect others against dangers emanating
from the patient's illness. The courts hold that a doctor is liable to
persons infected by his patient if he negligently fails to diagnose a
contagious disease [c] or, having diagnosed the illness, fails to warn
members of the patient's family.   *   *   *

   Defendants contend, however, that imposition of a duty to exercise
reasonable care to protect third persons is unworkable because therapists cannot accurately predict whether or not a patient will resort to
violence. In support of this argument amicus representing the American Psychiatric Association and other professional societies cites numerous articles which indicate that therapists, in the present state of
the art, are unable reliably to predict violent acts; their forecasts,
amicus claims, tend consistently to overpredict violence, and indeed are
more often wrong than right. Since predictions of violence are often
erroneous, amicus concludes, the courts should not render rulings that

predicate the liability of therapists upon the validity of such predictions. * * *

We recognize the difficulty that a therapist encounters in attempting to forecast whether a patient presents a serious danger of violence. Obviously we do not require that the therapist, in making that determination, render a perfect performance; the therapist need only exercise "that reasonable degree of skill, knowledge, and care ordinarily possessed and exercised by members of [that professional specialty] under similar circumstances." * * *

In the instant case, however, the pleadings do not raise any question as to failure of defendant therapists to predict that Poddar presented a serious danger of violence. On the contrary, the present complaints allege that defendant therapists did in fact predict that Poddar would kill, but were negligent in failing to warn.

Amicus contends, however, that even when a therapist does in fact predict that a patient poses a serious danger of violence to others, the therapist should be absolved of any responsibility for failing to act to protect the potential victim. In our view, however, once a therapist does in fact determine, or under applicable professional standards reasonably should have determined, that a patient poses a serious danger of violence to others, he bears a duty to exercise reasonable care to protect the foreseeable victim of that danger. * * *

The risk that unnecessary warnings may be given is a reasonable price to pay for the lives of possible victims that may be saved. We would hesitate to hold that the therapist who is aware that his patient expects to attempt to assassinate the President of the United States would not be obligated to warn the authorities because the therapist cannot predict with accuracy that his patient will commit the crime.

Defendants further argue that free and open communication is essential to psychotherapy [c]; that "Unless a patient * * * is assured that * * * information [revealed by him] can and will be held in utmost confidence, he will be reluctant to make the full disclosure upon which diagnosis and treatment * * * depends." (Sen.Com. on Judiciary, comment on Evid.Code, § 1014.) The giving of a warning, defendants contend, constitutes a breach of trust which entails the revelation of confidential communications.

We recognize the public interest in supporting effective treatment of mental illness and in protecting the rights of patients to privacy [c] and the consequent public importance of safeguarding the confidential character of psychotherapeutic communication. Against this interest, however, we must weigh the public interest in safety from violent assault. The Legislature has undertaken the difficult task of balancing the countervailing concerns. In Evidence Code section 1014, it established a broad rule of privilege to protect confidential communications between patient and psychotherapist. In Evidence Code section 1024, the Legislature created a specific and limited exception to the psychotherapist-patient privilege: "There is no privilege * * * if the psychotherapist has reasonable cause to believe that the patient is in such mental or emotional condition as to be dangerous to himself or to the person or property of another and that disclosure of the communication is necessary to prevent the threatened danger." * * *

Our current crowded and computerized society compels the interdependence of its members. In this risk-infested society we can hardly tolerate the further exposure to danger that would result from a concealed knowledge of the therapist that his patient was lethal. If the exercise of reasonable care to protect the threatened victim requires the therapist to warn the endangered party or those who can reasonably be expected to notify him, we see no sufficient societal interest that would protect and justify concealment. The containment of such risks lies in the public interest. For the foregoing reasons, we find that plaintiffs' complaints can be amended to state a cause of action against defendants Moore, Powelson, Gold, and Yandell and against the Regents as their employer, for breach of a duty to exercise reasonable care to protect Tatiana. * * *

[WRIGHT, C.J., and SULLIVAN and RICHARDSON, JJ., concurred and dissented in part; and CLARK and McCOMB, JJ., dissented.]

---

1. In his dissent Justice Clark agreed with the majority that when a psychiatrist in terminating a patient increases the risk of his violence toward a particular individual, a duty to warn should arise. However, he could find neither precedent nor reason to support a duty to warn solely based on the psychiatrist-patient relationship.

2. Some courts have deemed it tortious for a psychotherapist to reveal a patient's confidential communication—at least when it was not necessary to protect the welfare of the patient or the community at large. See Shaw v. Glickman, 45 Md.App. 718, 415 A.2d 625 (1980); Horne v. Patton, 291 Ala. 701, 287 So.2d 824, 892 (1973); Berry v. Moench, 8 Utah 2d 191, 331 P.2d 814, 817 (1958). The patient then has a cause of action for emotional harm that he suffers as a result of the disclosure. Where does the principal case leave the psychotherapist? See generally Fleming and Maximov, The Patient or His Victim: The Therapist's Dilemma, 62 Calif.L.Rev. 1025 (1974); Stone, The *Tarasoff* Decision: Suing Psychotherapists to Safeguard Society, 90 Harv.L.Rev. 358 (1976); Note, 31 Stan.L.Rev. 165 (1978).

3. How dangerous should the patient be before a duty arises? Must he threaten a particular person? See Davis v. Lhim, 124 Mich.App. 291, 335 N.W.2d 481 (1983). Suppose the patient is dangerous but makes no threats against specific persons. Petersen v. State, 100 Wash.2d 421, 671 P.2d 230 (1983); see also Nova Univ., Inc. v. Wagner, 491 So.2d 1116 (Fla.1986) (private institution liable for negligently permitting dangerous juveniles to flee). Should a psychotherapist be held liable for negligent failure to accurately diagnose dangerousness? See Brady v. Hopper, 570 F.Supp. 1333 (D.Colo.1983), aff'd, 751 F.2d 329 (10th Cir.1984) (suit against John Hinckley's psychiatrist by the victims of the attempted assassination of President Reagan). On the difference of the standards of duty to warn and duty to commit, see Currie v. United States, 644 F.Supp. 1074 (M.D.N.C.1986).

4. There appears to be no duty to warn the family of a patient threatening to harm only himself. See Bellah v. Greenson, 81 Cal.App.3d 614, 146 Cal.Rptr. 535 (1978).

5. What might be the effect of this decision on other professions? Suppose a client tells his attorney about a plan to kill a witness? Should the attorney have a duty in tort law to warn the individual in potential danger? The attorney-client privilege does not extend to advice in aid of future wrongdoing. See J. Wigmore, Evidence § 2298 (McNaughton Rev.1961). But does this exception create a duty to disclose in the situation posed? Cf. McMonagle & Mallen, The Attorney's Dilemma in Defending Third Party Lawsuits: Disclosure of the Client's Confidence or Personal Liability, 14 Will.L.J. 355 (1978). Why should a professional relationship be necessary to impose the duty? Suppose a student overhears a plan to rob a grocery store. Should he have a duty to warn the owner?

6. A supervisor at a manufacturing plant was told that an employee was drunk on the job. He escorted the employee to the parking lot, asked him if he was "okay," and upon receiving assurances that he was, allowed him to drive himself home. Three miles from the plant, the employee caused an accident that killed two people. Is the company liable? Otis Eng'g Corp. v. Clark, 668 S.W.2d 307 (Tex.1983).

7. The principal case continues to fascinate law review writers. See Crocker, Judicial Expansion of the *Tarasoff* Doctrine: Doctors' Dilemma, 13 J. Psychiatry & L. 83 (1985); Dykstra, Duty to Warn of Potentially Dangerous Patients, 29 Res Gestae 461 (1986); Goodman, From Tarasoff to Hopper: The Evolution of the Therapist's Duty to Protect Third Parties, 3 Behavioral Sci. & L. 195 (1985); Laughran and Bakken, The Psychotherapist's Responsibility Toward Third Parties Under Current California Law, 12 W.St.U.L.Rev. 1 (1984); Meyers, The Legal Perils of Psychotherapeutic Practice (Part II): Coping with Hedlund and Jablonski, 12 J. Psychiatry & L. 39 (1984); Schopp and Quattrocchi, *Tarasoff,* the Doctrine of Special Relationships, and the Psychotherapist's Duty to Warn, 12 J. Psychiatry & L. 13 (1984).

3.　UNBORN CHILDREN

ENDRESZ v. FRIEDBERG
New York Court of Appeals, 1969.
24 N.Y.2d 478, 248 N.E.2d 901, 301 N.Y.S.2d 65.

FULD, CHIEF JUDGE. * * * The plaintiff, Janice Endresz, seven months pregnant, was injured in an automobile accident in the winter of 1965 and two days later was delivered of stillborn twins, a male and a female. Four actions in negligence were brought against the persons assertedly responsible for the accident. In the first two actions—one for the wrongful death of each child—the plaintiff Steve Endresz, Janice's husband, suing as administrator, seeks damages of $100,000 by reason of the distributees' "loss of anticipated * * * care, comfort and support during the minority and majority" of each infant and for "medical, hospital and funeral expenses incurred by reason of the death" of the children. * * *

Chief Justice Fuld

On motion of the defendants, the court at Special Term * * * dismissed the first two suits for wrongful death. * * *

This court has already decided that a wrongful death action may not be maintained for the death of an unborn child. [Cc] This view is held by a number of other jurisdictions and, although there is authority to the contrary, further study and thought confirm the justice and wisdom of our earlier decisions.

Section 5–4.1 of the EPTL (L.1966, ch. 952, eff. Sept. 1, 1967), * * * declares, insofar as pertinent, that "The personal representative * * * of a decedent who is survived by distributees may maintain an action to recover damages for a wrongful act, neglect or default which caused the decedent's death against a person who would have been liable to the decedent by reason of such wrongful conduct if death had not ensued." Before there may be a "decedent", there must, perforce, be birth, a person born alive, and, although the statute, enacted in 1847 (L.1847, ch. 450), is silent on the subject, it is fairly certain that the Legislature did not intend to include an "unborn" foetus within the term "decedent". Indeed, it was not until 1951, more than 100 years later, that this court—overruling a long-standing decision (Drobner v. Peters, 232 N.Y. 220, 133 N.E. 567, 20 A.L.R. 1503 [1921])—decided that "a child viable but *in utero*, if injured by tort, should, when born, be allowed to sue." (Woods v. Lancet, 303 N.Y. 349, 353, 102 N.E.2d 691, 693, 27 A.L.R.2d 1250.) If, before Woods, a child so injured had no right of action, still less was such an action intended to lie on behalf of one who, never seeing the light of day, was deprived of life while still in its mother's womb.

Our decision in the *Woods* case (303 N.Y. 349, 102 N.E.2d 691, supra) does not require us, as suggested, to reinterpret the wrongful death statute to provide compensation to the distributees of a stillborn foetus for "pecuniary injuries" resulting from its death apart from those sustained by the mother and father in their own right. The *Woods* decision, as the court recognized in Matter of Logan, 3 N.Y.2d 800, 166 N.Y.S.2d 3, 144 N.E.2d 644, supra, simply brought the common law of this State into accord with the demand of natural justice which requires recognition of the legal right of every human being to begin life unimpaired by physical or mental defects resulting from the negligence of another. The considerations of justice which mandate the recovery of damages by an infant, injured in his mother's womb and born deformed through the wrong of a third party, are absent where the foetus, deprived of life while yet unborn, is never faced with the prospect of impaired mental or physical health.

In the latter case, moreover, proof of pecuniary injury and causation is immeasurably more vague than in suits for prenatal injuries.
* * *

Beyond that, since the mother may sue for any injury which she sustained in her own person, including her suffering as a result of the stillbirth, and the father for loss of her services and consortium, an additional award to the "distributees" of the foetus would give its parents an unmerited bounty and would constitute not compensation to the injured but punishment to the wrongdoer. [Cc]

A leading law review article on the subject has clearly pointed up the differences in the two situations (Gordon, The Unborn Plaintiff, 63 Mich.L.Rev. 579, 594–595):

"The hardship of many of the decisions denying relief [in prenatal injury cases] lay in the fact that they required an infant to go through life * * * bearing the seal of another's fault. There is no such justification in the wrongful death situation. * * *

"A fundamental basis of tort law is the provision for compensation of an innocent plaintiff for the loss he has suffered. Tort law is not, as a general rule, premised upon punishing the wrongdoer. It is not submitted that the tortious destroyer of a child in utero should be able to escape completely by killing instead of merely maiming. But it is submitted that to compensate the parents any further than they are entitled by well-settled principles of law and to give them a windfall through the estate of the fetus is blatant punishment."

* * * Even if, as science and theology teach, the child begins a separate "life" from the moment of conception, it is clear that, "except in so far as is necessary to protect the child's own rights" (Matter of Roberts, 158 Misc. 698, 699, 286 N.Y.S. 476, 477), the law has never considered the unborn foetus as having a separate "juridical existence" (Drabbels v. Skelly Oil Co., 155 Neb. 17, 22, 50 N.W.2d 229) or a legal personality or identity "until it sees the light of day." (Matter of Peabody, 5 N.Y.2d 541, 547, 186 N.Y.S.2d 265, 270, 158 N.E.2d 841, 844, 845.) * * *

It is argued that it is arbitrary and illogical to draw the line at birth, with the result that the distributees of an injured foetus which survives birth by a few minutes may have a recovery while those of a stillborn foetus may not. However, such difficulties are always present where a line must be drawn. To make viability rather than birth the test would not remove the difficulty but merely relocate it and increase a hundredfold the problems of causation and damages. Thus, one commentator aptly observed that (Wenger, Developments in the Law of Prenatal Wrongful Death, 69 Dickinson L.Rev. 258, 268), "since any limitation will be arbitrary in nature, a tangible and concrete event would be the most acceptable and workable boundary. Birth, being a definite, observable and significant event, meets this requirement."

In light of all these considerations, then, we do not feel that, on balance and as a matter of public policy, a cause of action for pecuniary loss should accrue to the distributees of a foetus stillborn by reason of the negligence of another; the damages recoverable by the parents in their own right afford ample redress for the wrong done. Decidedly applicable here is the rule that "[l]iability for damages caused by wrong ceases at a point dictated by public policy or common sense." [C] * * *

The order appealed from should be affirmed, without costs.

Burke, Judge (dissenting in part). * * * The illogicalness of the majority's position was aptly demonstrated by the Supreme Court of Wisconsin, in the analogous case of Kwaterski v. State Farm Mut. Auto. Ins. Co., 34 Wis.2d 14, 20, 148 N.W.2d 107, 110, in these terms: "If no right of action is allowed, there is a wrong inflicted for which there is no remedy. Denying a right of action for negligent acts which produce a stillbirth leads to very incongruous results. For example, a doctor or midwife whose negligent acts in delivering a baby produced the baby's death would be legally immune from a lawsuit. However, if they badly injured the child they would be exposed to liability. Such a rule would produce the absurd result that an unborn child who was badly injured by the tortious acts of another, but who was born alive, could recover while an unborn child, who was more severely injured and died as the result of the tortious acts of another, could recover nothing." * * *

In summary, I am of the opinion that it is both illogical and unreasonable to distinguish between injuries wrongfully inflicted upon a viable foetus which result in death just prior to the infant's separation from the mother and those which cause either permanent injuries or death itself, but at some short interval after birth has occurred. I, therefore, dissent from that portion of the majority opinion which affirms the dismissal of the wrongful death actions by the personal representatives of these stillborn foetus.

KEATING, J., concurred.

---

1. The question of whether any duty is owed to unborn children has undergone substantial change in the law and still is not free from controversy. At one time, the answer was a simple one: no claim was allowed. See, e.g., Dietrich v. Inhabitants of Northampton, 138 Mass. 14, 52 Am.Rep. 242 (1884).

2. The reasons for denial of recovery were threefold: First, it was assumed that the fetus had no separate existence from its mother. This hypothesis was later found to be inaccurate as a matter of medical science.

Second, it was thought that the problems of proving causation in fact would be overwhelming. Medical science was of assistance here also, although highly speculative questions about causation still arise. For example, can physical trauma to a mother cause a child to be born a mongoloid? Compare Sinkler v. Kneale, 401 Pa. 267, 164 A.2d 93 (1960) (allowing plaintiff to attempt to prove a case), with Puhl v. Milwaukee Auto. Ins. Co., 8 Wis.2d 343, 99 N.W.2d 163 (1959) (finding that plaintiff had not met her burden of proof after trial). See Lintgen, The Impact of Medical Knowledge on the Law Relating to Prenatal Injuries, 110 U.Pa.L.Rev. 554 (1962).

Third, damages were thought to be too speculative. How could the jury accurately estimate a new born baby's loss of earning power? In spite of the difficulties involved, is it clear that the child has suffered a loss and would often need medical treatment in the future? Is this a sufficient reason to allow a claim?

3. Beginning in 1946 with the case of Bonbrest v. Kotz, 65 F.Supp. 138 (D.D.C.1946), an overwhelming majority of jurisdictions has held that the reasons supporting the denial of a claim were no longer persuasive and has allowed a cause of action for prenatal injuries when they were inflicted on a viable fetus who was subsequently born alive. See Annot., 40 A.L.R.3d 1222 (1971).

4. Suppose plaintiff alleges that defendant's wrongful conduct adversely affected the mother's ability to produce normal children prior to conception? Recovery has been allowed in several cases. See Bergstreser v. Mitchell, 577 F.2d 22 (8th Cir.1978) (negligent performance of caesarean—subsequent child had birth difficulties producing brain damage); Renslow v. Mennonite Hosp., 67 Ill.2d 348, 10 Ill.Dec. 484, 367 N.E.2d 1250 (1977) (wrong Rh-type blood transfusion to a 13–year–old produced injury to her child years later); Lazevnick v. Gen. Hosp., 499 F.Supp. 146 (M.D.Pa.1970) (similar); Annot., 91 A.L.R.3d 316 (1979).

5. The major controversy today focuses on the situation in the principal case. A majority of states uphold a civil claim for the wrongful death of an unborn child. See, e.g., Volk v. Baldazo, 103 Idaho 570, 651 P.2d 11 (1982); Vaillancourt v. Medical Center Hosp., Inc., 139 Vt. 138, 425 A.2d 92 (1980); cf. Kader, The Law of Tortious Prenatal Death Since Roe v. Wade, 45 Mo.L.Rev. 639 (1980). Some states also sustain criminal claims. In some jurisdictions

courts have done little more than decide that the words "death of a person" in the state wrongful death statute were only intended to include individuals who were born alive. See Kilmer v. Hicks, 22 Ariz.App. 552, 529 P.2d 706 (1974); Carroll v. Skloff, 415 Pa. 47, 202 A.2d 9 (1964). As the principal case reflects, other courts have gone beyond the matter of legislative intent (was there any?) and weighed policy considerations that support the grant or denial of a claim. Suppose the child dies during the delivery process? Duncan v. Flynn, 342 So.2d 123 (Fla.App.1977).

6. Recently a number of cases have been brought against the producer of Bendectin, a drug to prevent morning sickness. Plaintiffs alleged that the drug caused birth defects, but most of these cases resulted in no recovery. See page 277, supra. The major problem in these claims has been an inability to prove that the drug caused the children's birth defects.

7. Most wrongful death statutes allow damages only for a pecuniary loss. A few include plaintiff's "loss of society and companionship" with regard to the decedent. Should this have any bearing on the outcome? See Libbee v. Permanente Clinic, 268 Or. 258, 518 P.2d 636 (1974); White v. Yup, 85 Nev. 527, 458 P.2d 617 (1969).

8. In Roe v. Wade, 410 U.S. 113 (1973), the Supreme Court of the United States held that a fetus is not a person for the purposes of the Fourteenth Amendment to the United States Constitution and that the Due Process clause of that Amendment forbids a state from prohibiting an abortion in the first trimester of pregnancy. Does that decision have any relevancy for the problem considered in the principal case?

9. See Gordon, The Unborn Plaintiff, 63 Mich.L.Rev. 579 (1965); Muse and Spinella, Right of Infant to Recover for Prenatal Injury, 36 Va.L.Rev. 611 (1950); Murphy, Evolution of the Prenatal Duty Rule: Analysis by Inherent Determinants, 7 U.Dayton L.Rev. 351 (1982). Student notes are legion.

PROCANIK BY PROCANIK v. CILLO

Supreme Court of New Jersey, 1984.
97 N.J. 339, 478 A.2d 755.

POLLOCK, J. The primary issue on this appeal is the propriety of a grant of a partial summary judgment dismissing a "wrongful life" claim brought by an infant plaintiff through his mother and guardian *ad litem*. That judgment, which was granted on the pleadings, dismissed the claim because it failed to state a cause of action upon which relief may be granted. [C]

The infant plaintiff, Peter Procanik, alleges that the defendant doctors * * * negligently failed to diagnose that his mother, Rosemary Procanik, had contracted German measles in the first trimester of her pregnancy. As a result, Peter was born with congenital rubella syndrome. Alleging that the doctors negligently deprived his parents of the choice of terminating the pregnancy, he seeks general damages for his pain and suffering and for "his parents' impaired capacity to cope with his problems." He also seeks special damages attributable to the extraordinary expenses he will incur for medical, nursing, and other health care. The Law Division granted defendants' motion to dismiss, and the Appellate Division affirmed * * *

Justices Daniel J. O'Hern, Alan B. Handler, Robert L. Clifford,
Robert Wilentz, Sidney M. Schreiber, Stewart G. Pollock
and Marie L. Garibaldi.

We granted certification, 95 *N.J.* 176, 470 *A.*2d 404 (1983). We now
conclude that an infant plaintiff may recover as special damages the
extraordinary medical expenses attributable to his affliction, but that
he may not recover general damages for emotional distress or for an
impaired childhood. * * * Accepting as true the plaintiff's allegations, [c] the complaint discloses the following facts. * * *

On June 9, 1977, during the first trimester of her pregnancy with
Peter, Mrs. Procanik consulted the defendant doctors and informed Dr.
Cillo "that she had recently been diagnosed as having measles but did
not know if it was German measles." Dr. Cillo examined Mrs. Procanik and ordered "tests for German Measles, known as Rubella Titer
Test." The results "were 'indicative of past infection of Rubella.'"
Instead of ordering further tests, Dr. Cillo negligently interpreted the
results and told Mrs. Procanik that she "had nothing to worry about
because she had become immune to German Measles as a child." In
fact, the "past infection" disclosed by the tests was the German measles
that had prompted Mrs. Procanik to consult the defendant doctors.

Ignorant of what an accurate diagnosis would have disclosed, Mrs.
Procanik allowed her pregnancy to continue, and Peter was born on

December 26, 1977. Shortly thereafter, on January 16, 1978, he was diagnosed as suffering from congenital rubella syndrome. As a result of the doctors' negligence, Mr. and Mrs. Procanik were deprived of the choice of terminating the pregnancy, and Peter was "born with multiple birth defects," including eye lesions, heart disease, and auditory defects. The infant plaintiff states further that "he has suffered because of his parents' impaired capacity to cope with his problems," and seeks damages for his pain and suffering and for his "impaired childhood."

In April 1983, while this matter was pending in the Appellate Division, Peter moved to amend the first count to assert a claim to recover, as special damages, the expenses he will incur as an adult for medical, nursing, and related health care services. In its opinion, the Appellate Division denied without prejudice leave to amend. * * *

In this case we survey again the changing landscape of family torts. *See Schroeder v. Perkel,* 87 *N.J.* 53, 71, 432 *A.2d* 834 (1981). Originally that landscape presented a bleak prospect both to children born with birth defects and to their parents. If a doctor negligently diagnosed or treated a pregnant woman who was suffering from a condition that might cause her to give birth to a defective child, neither the parents nor the child could maintain a cause of action against the negligent doctor. *Gleitman v. Cosgrove,* 49 *N.J.* 22, 227 *A.2d* 689 (1967).

Like the present case, *Gleitman* involved a doctor who negligently treated a pregnant woman who had contracted German measles in the first trimester of her pregnancy. Reasoning from the premise that the doctor did not cause the infant plaintiff's birth defects, the *Gleitman* Court found it impossible to compare the infant's condition if the defendant doctor had not been negligent with the infant's impaired condition as a result of the negligence. Measurement of "the value of life with impairments against the nonexistence of life itself" was, the Court declared, a logical impossibility. [C] Consequently, the Court rejected the infant's claim.

The Court denied the parents' claim for emotional distress and the costs of caring for the infant, because of the impossibility of weighing the intangible benefits of parenthood against the emotional and monetary injuries sustained by them. Prevailing policy considerations, which included a reluctance to acknowledge the availability of abortions and the mother's right to choose to terminate her pregnancy, prevented the Court from awarding damages to a woman for not having an abortion. Another consideration was the Court's belief that "[i]t is basic to the human condition to seek life and hold on to it however heavily burdened." [C]

In the seventeen years that have elapsed since the *Gleitman* decision, both this Court and the United States Supreme Court have reappraised, albeit in different contexts, the rights of pregnant women and their children. The United States Supreme Court has recognized that women have a constitutional right to choose to terminate a pregnancy. *Roe v. Wade,* 410 *U.S.* 113 (1973). Recognition of that right by the high court subsequently influenced this Court in *Berman v. Allan,* 80 *N.J.* 421, 404 *A.*2d 8 [1979].

In *Berman,* the parents sought to recover for their emotional distress and for the expenses of raising a child born with Down's Syndrome. Relying on *Roe v. Wade,* the Court found that public policy now supports the right of a woman to choose to terminate a pregnancy. [C] That finding eliminated one of the supports for the *Gleitman* decision—*i.e.,* that public policy prohibited an award for depriving a woman of the right to choose whether to have an abortion. Finding that a trier of fact could place a dollar value on the parents' emotional suffering, the *Berman* Court concluded "that the monetary equivalent of this distress is an appropriate measure of the harm suffered by the parents." [C]

Nonetheless, the Court rejected the parents' claim for "medical and other expenses that will be incurred in order to properly raise, educate and supervise the child." [C] The Court reasoned that the parents wanted to retain "all the benefits inhering in the birth of the child— *i.e.,* the love and joy they will experience as parents—while saddling defendants with enormous expenses attendant upon her rearing." *Id.* Such an award would be disproportionate to the negligence of the defendants and constitute a windfall to the parents. *Id.*

The *Berman* Court also declined to recognize a cause of action in an infant born with birth defects. Writing for the Court, Justice Pashman reasoned that even a life with serious defects is more valuable than non-existence, the alternative for the infant plaintiff if his mother chose to have an abortion. [C]

More recently we advanced the parents' right to compensation by permitting recovery of the extraordinary expenses of raising a child born with cystic fibrosis, including medical, hospital, and pharmaceutical expenses. *Schroeder v. Perkel,* 87 *N.J.* at 68–69, 432 *A.*2d 834. No claim on behalf of the infant was raised in that case, [c] and we elected to defer consideration of such a claim until another day. [C] That day is now upon us, and we must reconsider the right of an infant in a "wrongful life" claim to recover general damages for diminished childhood and pain and suffering, as well as special damages for medical care and the like.

The terms "wrongful birth" and "wrongful life" are but shorthand phrases that describe the causes of action of parents and children when negligent medical treatment deprives parents of the option to terminate a pregnancy to avoid the birth of a defective child. *See Schroeder v. Perkel, supra,* 87 *N.J.* at 75–76, 432 *A.*2d 834 (Handler, J., concurring and dissenting). In the present context, "wrongful life" refers to a cause of action brought by or on behalf of a defective child who claims that but for the defendant doctor's negligent advice to or treatment of its parents, the child would not have been born. "Wrongful birth" applies to the cause of action of parents who claim that the negligent advice or treatment deprived them of the choice of avoiding conception or, as here, of terminating the pregnancy. [Cc]

Both causes of action are distinguishable from the situation where negligent injury to a fetus causes an otherwise normal child to be born in an impaired condition. [Cc] In the present case, the plaintiffs do not allege that the negligence of the defendant doctors caused the congenital rubella syndrome from which the infant plaintiff suffers. Neither do plaintiffs claim that the infant ever had a chance to be a normal child. The essence of the infant's claim is that the defendant doctors wrongfully deprived his mother of information that would have prevented his birth.

Analysis of the infant's cause of action begins with the determination whether the defendant doctors owed a duty to him. The defendant doctors do not deny they owed a duty to the infant plaintiff, and we find such a duty exists. [Cc] In evaluating the infant's cause of action, we assume, furthermore, that the defendant doctors were negligent in treating the mother. Moreover, we assume that their negligence deprived the parents of the choice of terminating the pregnancy and of preventing the birth of the infant plaintiff.

Notwithstanding recognition of the existence of a duty and its breach, policy considerations have led this Court in the past to decline to recognize any cause of action in an infant for his wrongful life. The threshold problem has been the assertion by infant plaintiffs not that they should not have been born without defects, but that they should not have been born at all. [*Gleitman*] The essence of the infant's cause of action is that its very life is wrongful. [*Berman*] Resting on the belief that life, no matter how burdened, is preferable to non-existence, the *Berman* Court stated that the infant "has not suffered any damage cognizable at law by being brought into existence." [C] Although the premise for this part of the *Berman* decision was the absence of cognizable damages, the Court continued to be troubled, as it was in *Gleitman,* by the problem of ascertaining the measure of damages. [C]

The courts of other jurisdictions have also struggled with the issues of injury and damages when faced with suits for wrongful life. Although two intermediate appellate courts in New York and California recognized an infant's claim for general damages, those decisions were rejected by the courts of last resort in both jurisdictions. * * *

Other courts have uniformly found that the problems posed by the damage issues in wrongful life claims are insurmountable and have refused to allow. the action on behalf of the infant. [Cc]

Even when this Court declined to recognize a cause of action for wrongful life in *Gleitman* and *Berman,* dissenting members urged recognition of that claim. * * *

Recently we recognized that extraordinary medical expenses incurred by parents on behalf of a birth-defective child were predictable, certain, and recoverable. [*Schroeder*] * * *

When a child requires extraordinary medical care, the financial impact is felt not just by the parents, but also by the injured child. As a practical matter, the impact may extend beyond the injured child to his brothers or sisters. Money that is spent for the health care of one child is not available for the clothes, food, or college education of another child.

Recovery of the cost of extraordinary medical expenses by either the parents or the infant, but not both, is consistent with the principle that the doctor's negligence vitally affects the entire family. * * *

Law is more than an exercise in logic, and logical analysis, although essential to a system of ordered justice, should not become a instrument of injustice. Whatever logic inheres in permitting parents to recover for the cost of extraordinary medical care incurred by a birth-defective child, but in denying the child's own right to recover those expenses, must yield to the injustice of that result. The right to recover the often crushing burden of extraordinary expenses visited by an act of medical malpractice should not depend on the "wholly fortuitous circumstance of whether the parents are available to sue." [Cc]

The present case proves the point. Here, the parents' claim is barred by the statute of limitations. Does this mean that Peter must forego medical treatment for his blindness, deafness, and retardation? We think not. His claim for the medical expenses attributable to his birth defects is reasonably certain, readily calculable, and of a kind daily determined by judges and juries. We hold that a child or his parents may recover special damages for extraordinary medical expenses incurred during infancy, and that the infant may recover those expenses during his majority. * * *

In restricting the infant's claim to one for special damages, we recognize that our colleagues, Justice Schreiber and Justice Handler, disagree with us and with each other. From the premise that "man does not know whether non-life would have been preferable to an impaired life," [c] Justice Schreiber concludes that a child does not have a cause of action for wrongful life and, therefore, that "it is unfair and unjust to charge the doctors with the infant's medical expenses." [C] Justice Handler reaches a diametrically opposite conclusion. He would allow the infant to recover not only his medical expenses, but also general damages for his pain and suffering and for his impaired childhood.

We find, however, that the infant's claim for pain and suffering and for a diminished childhood presents insurmountable problems. The philosophical problem of finding that such a defective life is worth less than no life at all has perplexed not only Justice Schreiber, but such other distinguished members of this Court as Chief Justice Weintraub, [c] Justice Proctor, [c] and Justice Pashman, [c]. We need not become preoccupied, however, with these metaphysical considerations. Our decision to allow the recovery of extraordinary medical expenses is not premised on the concept that non-life is preferable to an impaired life, but is predicated on the needs of the living. We seek only to respond to the call of the living for help in bearing the burden of their affliction.

Sound reasons exist not to recognize a claim for general damages. Our analysis begins with the unfortunate fact that the infant plaintiff never had a chance of being born as a normal, healthy child. Tragically, his only choice was a life burdened with his handicaps or no life at all. The congenital rubella syndrome that plagues him was not caused by the negligence of the defendant doctors; the only proximate result of their negligence was the child's birth.

The crux of the problem is that there is no rational way to measure non-existence or to compare non-existence with the pain and suffering of his impaired existence. Whatever theoretical appeal one might find in recognizing a claim for pain and suffering is outweighed by the essentially irrational and unpredictable nature of that claim. Although damages in a personal injury action need not be calculated with mathematical precision, they require at their base some modicum of rationality.

Underlying our conclusion is an evaluation of the capability of the judicial system, often proceeding in these cases through trial by jury, to appraise such a claim. Also at work is an appraisal of the role of tort law in compensating injured parties, involving as that role does, not only reason, but also fairness, predictability, and even deterrence of future wrongful acts. In brief, the ultimate decision is a policy choice summoning the most sensitive and careful judgment.

From that perspective it is simply too speculative to permit an infant plaintiff to recover for emotional distress attendant on birth defects when that plaintiff claims he would be better off if he had not been born. Such a claim would stir the passions of jurors about the nature and value of life, the fear of non-existence, and about abortion. That mix is more than the judicial system can digest. We believe that the interests of fairness and justice are better served through more predictably measured damages—the cost of the extraordinary medical expenses necessitated by the infant plaintiff's handicaps. Damages so measured are not subject to the same wild swings as a claim for pain and suffering and will carry a sufficient sting to deter future acts of medical malpractice.

As speculative and uncertain as is a comparison of the value of an impaired life with non-existence, even more problematic is the evaluation of a claim for diminished childhood. The essential proof in such a claim is that the doctor's negligence deprives the parents of the knowledge of the condition of the fetus. The deprivation of that information precludes the choice of terminating the pregnancy by abortion and leaves the parents unprepared for the birth of a defective child, a birth that causes them emotional harm. The argument proceeds that the parents are less able to love and care for the child, who thereby suffers an impaired childhood. [Cc]

Several considerations lead us to decline to recognize a cause of action for impaired childhood. At the outset, we note the flaw in such a claim in those instances in which the parents assert not that the information would have prepared them for the birth of the defective child, but that they would have used the information to prevent that birth. Furthermore, even its advocates recognize that a claim for "the kind of injury suffered by the child in this context may not be readily divisible from that suffered by her wronged parents." *Berman v. Allan,* *supra,* 80 *N.J.* at 445, 404 *A.*2d 8 (Handler, J., concurring and dissenting). We believe the award of the cost of the extraordinary medical care to the child or the parents, when combined with the right of the parents to assert a claim for their own emotional distress, comes closer to filling the dual objectives of a tort system: the compensation of injured parties and the deterrence of future wrongful conduct. * * *

The judgment of the Appellate Division is affirmed in part, reversed in part, and the matter is remanded to the Law Division. The infant plaintiff shall have leave to file an amended complaint asserting a claim for extraordinary medical, hospital, and other health care expenses.

[The gist of the separate partially dissenting opinions of HANDLER and SCHREIBER, JJ., is described in the majority opinion.]

———

1. *Action by the Child.* The first case involving a suit by a child for "wrongful birth" was Zepeda v. Zepeda, 41 Ill.App.2d 240, 190 N.E.2d 849 (1963). A child sued his father for wrongfully begetting him as an illegitimate child by deceiving the mother into thinking that he would marry her when he was already married. What policy issues are involved? A similar case is Williams v. State of New York, 18 N.Y.2d 481, 223 N.E.2d 343, 276 N.Y.S.2d 885 (1966), where it was alleged that the mother was an inmate in an institution for mentally deficient persons and the state had failed to provide adequate protection for her. Recovery was denied in both cases.

In accord with the principal case, see Becker v. Schwartz, 46 N.Y.2d 401, 386 N.E.2d 807, 413 N.Y.S.2d 895 (1978); Blake v. Cruz, 108 Idaho 253, 698 P.2d 315 (1984); Dorlin v. Providence Hosp., 118 Mich.App. 831, 325 N.W.2d 600 (1982); Speck v. Finegold, 497 Pa. 77, 439 A.2d 110 (1981). Contra, allowing a defective child "to recover damages for the pain and suffering to be endured during the limited life span available to such a child and any special pecuniary loss resulting from the impaired condition" is Curlender v. Bio–Science Labs, 106 Cal.App.3d 811, 165 Cal.Rptr. 477 (1980), noted in 18 Cal.W.L.Rev. 270 (1982), 25 St. Louis U.L.J. 455 (1981), 34 Okla.L.Rev. 614 (1981), 17 New Eng.L. Rev. 213 (1981). For a good article on this subject, see Collins, An Overview and Analysis: Prenatal Torts, Preconception Torts, Wrongful Life, Wrongful Death, and Wrongful Birth: Time for a New Framework, 22 J.Fam.L. 677 (1983).

California and several other states that have recognized the child's claim have compromised on the immeasurability of the value of life itself by allowing only special damages. Turpin v. Sortini, 31 Cal.3d 220, 643 P.2d 954, 182 Cal. Rptr. 337 (1982) (limiting *Curlender,* supra); Harbeson v. Parke–Davis, Inc., 98 Wash.2d 460, 656 P.2d 483 (1983).

2. *Action by the Parents.* The parents' "wrongful birth" claim generally asserts that negligent treatment or advice deprived them of the choice of terminating the pregnancy by abortion and preventing the birth of a defective child. Courts that allow recovery generally permit damages only for the extraordinary costs of rearing an impaired child.

What are some considerations in determining the amount of emotional distress damages for the wrongful birth of an impaired child? See Becker v. Schwartz, supra note 1; Speck v. Finegold, 497 Pa. 77, 439 A.2d 110 (1981); Jacobs v. Theimer, 519 S.W.2d 846 (Tex.1975).

3. Suppose the child is born healthy but is not wanted. Defendant had negligently performed an operation or a contraceptive pill or other device was ineffective. Recovery for the costs of raising the child was denied in McKernan v. Aasheim, 102 Wash.2d 411, 687 P.2d 850 (1984) (impossible to establish with reasonable certainty whether birth of a normal, healthy child "damaged" its parents). One difficulty in calculating damages for wrongful birth is whether the costs of rearing and educating a child outweigh the emotional benefits which will be conferred by that child. See Miller v. Johnson, 231 Va. 177, 343 S.E.2d 301 (1986). Recovery of these elements was held proper in Troppi v. Scarf, 31 Mich.App. 240, 187 N.W.2d 511 (1971) (druggist negligently supplied tranquilizer instead of oral contraceptive called for by prescription); cf. Jackson v. Anderson, 230 So.2d 503 (Fla.App.1970). In Coleman v. Garrison, 327 A.2d 757 (Del.Super.1974), the court refused recovery for "wrongful life" but allowed it for "wrongful pregnancy," permitting damages to the wife for pain and suffering and medical expenses. Cf. Custodio v. Bauer, 251 Cal.App.2d 303, 59 Cal.Rptr. 463 (1967). To what extent is there a contractual warranty of effectiveness? See Herrera v. Roessing, 533 P.2d 60 (Colo.App.1975) (tubal ligation); Hackworth v. Hart, 474 S.W.2d 377 (Ky.1971) (vasectomy); Whittington v. Eli Lilly & Co., 333 F.Supp. 98 (S.D.W.Va.1971) (birth-control pill).

4. An interesting situation is one where parents seek damages for unwittingly adopting a child with genetic defects. Burr v. Board of County Comm'rs, 23 Ohio St.3d 69, 491 N.E.2d 1101 (1986).

5. See, generally Kashi, The Case of the Unwanted Blessing: Wrongful Life, 31 U.Miami L.Rev. 1409 (1977); Barrett, Damages for Wrongful Birth, 21 Clev.St.L.Rev. 34 (1972); Freedman, Unplanned Pregnancies: *Damnum Absque Injuria,* 11 For the Defense 53 (1970); Goldstein & Hirsch, Wrongful Life, 28 Med.Tr.T.Q. 279 (1982); Notes, 27 Buffalo L.Rev. 537 (1978), 1978 Duke L.J. 1401 (1972); Annot., 83 A.L.R.3d 15 (1978).

4. PRIVITY OF CONTRACT

TORT AND CONTRACT

The problem of the broken promise involved in Crowley v. Spivey, supra page 418, is carried over into a host of cases in which the promise is not gratuitous, but is for consideration, so that the result is a contract, and the defendant will be liable in a contract action for breach of it. Historically, the contract action developed considerably later than the tort liability. Along with it, it remained possible to maintain the old tort action on the case in any situation where it had already been recognized. The result was a distinction, generally recognized, between "nonfeasance," where the defendant had done no more than make a promise and break it, and "misfeasance," where he had attempted performance but done the wrong thing.

Nonfeasance. In general, when there is only the promise and the breach, only the contract action will lie, and no tort action can be maintained. A good illustration is Louisville & Nashville R. Co. v. Spinks, 104 Ga. 692, 30 S.E. 968 (1898), where the defendant invited plaintiff to come to Cincinnati for employment, and promised that if it did not employ him it would furnish him with transportation back to Atlanta. He came, fell ill, and was not employed. Defendant refused to give him a ticket to Atlanta, and he was forced to walk the whole way, suffering "much from pain, weariness and blistered feet." It was held that his only remedy was an action on the contract, and no tort action would lie. See also Newton v. Brook, 134 Ala. 269, 32 So. 722 (1902), where defendants contracted to prepare a body for shipment by a certain train, and then did nothing. Again it was held that there was no tort remedy.

To this general rule there are a few recognized exceptions. One is that a common carrier, or other public utility, which has undertaken the duty of serving the public, becomes liable in tort when it fails to do so, whether or not it has made a contract. See, for example, Nevin v. Pullman Palace Car Co., 106 Ill. 222, 46 Am.Rep. 688 (1883); Zabron v. Cunard S.S. Co., 151 Iowa 345, 131 N.W. 18 (1911). Another is that a defendant who makes a contract without the intention to perform it is regarded as committing a form of misrepresentation, or fraud, for which a tort action of deceit will lie. See Burgdorfer v. Thielemann, post, page 1079. The special relation of landlord and tenant is held by some courts to give rise to a tort obligation when the landlord makes a covenant to repair the premises and does not do so. Reitmeyer v. Sprecher, 431 Pa. 284, 243 A.2d 395 (1968).

Misfeasance. When the defendant misperforms the contract, the possibility of recovery in tort is greatly augmented. In some instances this is merely the survival of the older tort action, as when a carrier remains liable in tort, as well as for breach of contract, for negligent injury to a passenger, or for loss of his baggage. In the United States this has gradually been extended to virtually any type of contract. One of the leading cases is Flint & Walling Mfg. Co. v. Beckett, 167 Ind. 491, 79 N.E. 503 (1906), where the defendant negligently installed a windmill on the plaintiff's barn, and it collapsed and wrecked the barn. In all these cases the question may arise whether the defendant has gone so far in his performance, as distinguished from mere preparation for it, as to have undertaken a tort duty.

Two good cases discussing all this are Hart v. Ludwig, 347 Mich. 559, 79 N.W.2d 895 (1956), and Kozan v. Comstock, 270 F.2d 839 (5th Cir.1959).

Election and Gravamen. In many cases it is thus possible to maintain an action in either contract or tort. When this is true, a number of questions may arise as to different rules of law applicable to the two actions. For example, a particular court may have jurisdiction over one type of action, but not the other, or certain remedies, such as summary judgment, attachment, or arrest of the defendant, may be available in one action but not the other. Different statutes of limitations may apply. There may be different rules as to the damages recoverable, especially in regard to punitive damages or for emotional harm. Some defenses, such as infancy or the statute of frauds, may be set up against one action and not the other; and so on.

In these situations the courts have proceeded along two different lines. One is to permit the plaintiff to choose the theory of his action, and dispose of the particular question accordingly. Thus in Doughty v. Maine Cent. Transp. Co., 141 Me. 124, 39 A.2d 758 (1944), an action for personal injuries received by a passenger through the negligence of the carrier would be barred by the statute of limitations if the action were in tort, but not if it were in contract. It was held that the plaintiff, having elected to treat his action as one for breach of contract, was not barred by the tort statute.

On the other hand, some courts will not give plaintiff this latitude. Rather, the court will determine the "gravamen" or "gist" of the action, which is to say the essential facts on which the plaintiff's claim rests. Thus in Webber v. Herkimer & Mohawk St. R. Co., 109 N.Y. 311, 16 N.E. 358 (1888), another case of a passenger injured by a carrier's negligence, it was held that the action was essentially founded on the negligence, and that it was governed by the tort rather than the contract statute of limitations. See also the ample discussion of the tort versus contract cause of action problem in Victorson v. Bock Laundry Mach. Co., 37 N.Y.2d 395, 335 N.E.2d 275, 373 N.Y.S.2d 39 (1975), overruling Mendel v. Pittsburgh Plate Glass Co., 25 N.Y.2d 340, 253 N.E.2d 207, 305 N.Y.S.2d 490 (1969) (personal injury—breach of implied warranty).

As these cases suggest, there is little consistency in the decisions, even in a single state, although many courts have tended to look to the policy underlying the particular rule of law or statute to be applied in order to assist themselves in making the characterization.

There is a helpful discussion of this in Prosser, The Borderland of Tort and Contract, in W. Prosser, Selected Topics on the Law of Torts, 380, at 429–450 (1954). For a review of the New York cases, see Thornton, The Elastic Concept of Tort and Contract as Applied by the Courts of New York, 14 Brooklyn L.Rev. 196 (1948).

WINTERBOTTOM v. WRIGHT
Exchequer of Pleas, 1842.
10 M. & W. 109, 152 Eng.Rep. 402.

[Defendant Wright, a manufacturer and repairer of mail coaches, contracted with the Postmaster General, Mr. Atkinson, to keep the coaches in a safe and secure condition. Defendant failed to comply with his promise and plaintiff Winterbottom, a mail coach driver, was seriously injured when a vehicle broke down due to lack of repair.]

LORD ABINGER, C.B. I am clearly of opinion that the defendant is entitled to our judgment. We ought not to permit a doubt to rest upon this subject, for our doing so might be the means of letting in upon us an infinity of actions. * * * There is no privity of contract between these parties; and if the plaintiff can sue, every passenger, or even any person passing along the road, who was injured by the upsetting of the coach, might bring a similar action. Unless we confine the operation of such contracts as this to the parties who entered into them, the most absurd and outrageous consequences, to which I can see no limit, would ensue. Where a party becomes responsible to the public, by undertaking a public duty, he is liable, though the injury may have arisen from the negligence of his servant or agent. So, in cases of public nuisances, whether the act was done by the party as a servant, or in any other capacity, you are liable to an action at the suit of any person who suffers. Those, however, are cases where the real ground of the liability is the public duty, or the commission of the public nuisance. There is also a class of cases in which the law permits a contract to be turned into a tort; but unless there has been some public duty undertaken, or public nuisance committed, they are all cases in which an action might have been maintained upon the contract. Thus, a carrier may be sued either in assumpsit or case; but there is no instance in which a party, who was not privy to the contract entered into with him, can maintain any such action. The plaintiff in this case could not have brought an action on the contract; if he could have done so, what would have been his situation, supposing the Postmaster–General had released the defendant? That would, at all events, have defeated his claim altogether. By permitting this action, we should be working this injustice, that after the defendant had done everything to the satisfaction of his employer, and after all matters between them had been adjusted, and all accounts settled on the footing of their contract, we

Lord Abinger

should subject them to be ripped open by this action of tort being brought against him.

ALDERSON, B. I am of the same opinion. The contract in this case was made with the Postmaster–General alone; and the case is just the same as if he had come to the defendant and ordered a carriage, and handed it at once over to Atkinson. If we were to hold that the plaintiff could sue in such a case, there is no point at which such actions would stop. The only safe rule is to confine the right to recover to those who enter into the contract: if we go one step beyond that, there is no reason why we should not go fifty. The only real argument in favour of the action is, that this is a case of hardship; but that might have been obviated, if the plaintiff had made himself a party to the contract. * * *

ROLFE, B. The breach of the defendant's duty stated in this declaration, is his omission to keep the carriage in a safe condition, and when we examine the mode in which that duty is alleged to have arisen, we find a statement that the defendant took upon himself, to wit, under and by virtue of the said contract, the sole and exclusive duty, charge, care, and burden of the repairs, state and condition of the said mail-coach, and, during all the time aforesaid, it had become and was the sole and exclusive duty of the defendant, to wit, under and by virtue of his said contract, to keep and maintain the said mail-coach in a fit, proper, safe, and secure state and condition. The duty, therefore, is shewn to have arisen solely from the contract; and the fallacy consists in the use of that word "duty." If a duty to the Postmaster–General be meant, that is true; but if a duty to the plaintiff be intended (and in that sense the word is evidently used), there was none. This is one of those unfortunate cases in which there certainly has been damnum, but it is damnum absque injuriâ; it is, no doubt, a hardship upon the plaintiff to be without a remedy, but by that consideration we ought not to be influenced. Hard cases, it has been frequently observed, are apt to introduce bad law.

Judgment for the defendant.

———

1. Although the principal case involved nonfeasance, it was universally interpreted as applying to any negligence of the defendant, including misfeasance; and this resulted in many decisions holding that the seller of a chattel was under no liability, in contract or in tort, to anyone other than his immediate buyer. The first major service rendered by Professor Bohlen to the law was to point out this error in his article, The Basis of Affirmative Obligations in the Law of Tort, 44 Am.L.Reg., N.S., 209, 280–285, 289–310 (1905), also in F. Bohlen, Studies in the Law of Torts, 33 (1926).

2. Judge Cardozo, in a historic opinion that eventually became the law of every state, McPherson v. Buick Motor Co., 217 N.Y. 382, 111 N.E. 105 (1916), infra page 697, abolished the privity limitation as it applied to sellers of negligently made chattels that were "reasonably certain to place life and limb in peril." This duty of reasonable care was deemed owed to all persons who were likely to use the product. It was eventually extended to bystanders who were likely to be injured by a negligently-made product.

3. The privity limitation lasted longer with regard to those who perform services. It is clear today, however, that an individual who undertakes to make a repair owes a duty to use care to those who may be foreseeably injured in case the repair is negligently made. See Lee v. Rowland, 11 N.C.App. 27, 180 S.E.2d 445 (1971) (failure properly to repair broken axle on a truck, defendant liable to those he should expect to be in the vicinity of the vehicle); Nagy v. McEachern, 28 Mich.App. 439, 184 N.W.2d 556 (1970) (failure to repair safety catch on rifle).

4. The main dispute today in failure-to-repair cases focuses on whether there was any actual undertaking by the contractor. In Wroblewski v. Otis Elevator Co., 9 A.D.2d 294, 193 N.Y.S.2d 855 (3d Dept.1959), an inspection of the elevator was enough for the court to find an undertaking and misfeasance. If the repairer had done nothing at all, the case might have been deemed one of

nonfeasance and the privity limitation might have applied. See Hanson v. Blackwell Motor Co., 143 Wash. 547, 255 P. 939 (1927) (repair shop took no steps to fix vehicle). When there is an assurance to an owner that a repair has been made even though nothing has in fact been done, many modern courts have found misfeasance and thus a breach of duty even to third parties. See Moody v. Martin Motor Co., 76 Ga.App. 456, 46 S.E.2d 197 (1948).

5. If defendant does begin performance and then fails to act, he is liable. See Waters v. Anthony, 252 Ala. 244, 40 So.2d 316 (1949); Landreth v. Phillips Petroleum, 74 F.Supp. 801 (W.D.Mo.1947).

6. On voluntary inspections by liability insurers, see Note, 18 Vand.L.Rev. 1615 (1965). Recent cases on insurance inspections include Hill v. United States F. & G. Co., 428 F.2d 112 (5th Cir.1970); and Gallichio v. Corp. Group Serv., Inc., 227 So.2d 519 (Fla.App.1969).

H.R. MOCH CO. v. RENSSELAER WATER CO.
Court of Appeals of New York, 1928.
247 N.Y. 160, 159 N.E. 896.

CARDOZO, C.J. The defendant, a waterworks company under the laws of this state, made a contract with the city of Rensselaer for the supply of water during a term of years. Water was to be furnished to the city for sewer flushing and street sprinkling; for service to schools and public buildings; and for service at fire hydrants, the latter service at the rate of $42.50 a year for each hydrant. Water was to be furnished to private takers within the city at their homes and factories and other industries at reasonable rates, not exceeding a stated schedule. While this contract was in force a building caught fire. The flames, spreading to the plaintiff's warehouse near by, destroyed it and its contents. The defendant, according to the complaint, was promptly notified of the fire, "but omitted and neglected after such notice, to supply or furnish sufficient or adequate quantity of water, with adequate pressure to stay, suppress, or extinguish the fire before it reached the warehouse of the plaintiff, although the pressure and supply which the defendant was equipped to supply and furnish, and had agreed by said contract to supply and furnish, was adequate and sufficient to prevent the spread of the fire to and the destruction of the plaintiff's warehouse and its contents." By reason of the failure of the defendant "to fulfill the provisions of the contract between it and the city of Rensselaer," the plaintiff is said to have suffered damage, for which judgment is demanded. A motion, in the nature of a demurrer, to dismiss the complaint, was denied at Special Term. The Appellate Division reversed by a divided court. * * *

We think the action is not maintainable as one for a common-law tort. * * *

If conduct has gone forward to such a stage that inaction would commonly result, not negatively merely in withholding a benefit, but positively or actively in working an injury, there exists a relation out of which arises a duty to go forward. [C] So the surgeon who operates without pay is liable, though his negligence is the omission to sterilize his instruments * * *; the engineer though his fault is in the failure to shut off steam * * *; the maker of automobiles, at the suit of some one other than the buyer, though his negligence is merely in inadequate inspection [c]. The query always is whether the putative wrongdoer has advanced to such a point as to have launched a force or instrument of harm, or has stopped where inaction is at most a refusal to become an instrument for good. * * *

The plaintiff would have us hold that the defendant, when once it entered upon the performance of its contract with the city, was brought into such a relation with every one who might potentially be benefited through the supply of water at the hydrants as to give to negligent performance, without reasonable notice of a refusal to continue, the quality of a tort. * * * We are satisfied that liability would be unduly and indeed indefinitely extended by this enlargement of the zone of duty. The dealer in coal who is to supply fuel for a shop must then answer to the customers if fuel is lacking. The manufacturer of goods, who enters upon the performance of his contract must answer, in that view, not only to the buyer, but to those who to his knowledge are looking to the buyer for their own sources of supply. Every one making a promise having the quality of a contract will be under a duty to the promisee by virtue of that promise, but under another duty, apart from contract, to an indefinite number of potential beneficiaries when performance has begun. The assumption of one relation would mean the involuntary assumption of a series of new relations, inescapably hooked together. Again we may say in the words of the Supreme Court of the United States, "The law does not spread its protection so far." Robins Dry Dock & Repair Co. v. Flint, 275 U.S. 303. * * *

We think the action is not maintainable as one for the breach of a statutory duty. * * *

The judgment should be affirmed, with costs.

———

1. What if the city's own property were destroyed by fire because of lack of sufficient water pressure? Town of Ukiah v. Ukiah Water & Improvement Co., 142 Cal. 173, 75 P. 773 (1904); Inhabitants of Milford v. Bangor Ry. & Elec. Co., 106 Me. 316, 76 A. 696 (1909).

2. What about the arguments:

A. That the defendant, by undertaking to supply water, has induced the city and the plaintiff to rely upon such protection, and to forego other protection to which they might have resorted?

B. That defendant has actually entered upon the performance of its undertaking and has performed it negligently?

C. That by entering upon performance the defendant has become a public utility, and so has entered into a relation with members of the general public that imposes a duty?

3. The principal case represents the majority rule. Some cases have allowed recovery. Harlan Water Co. v. Carter, 220 Ky. 493, 295 S.W. 426 (1927), did so on the theory that plaintiff is a third-party beneficiary of the contract with the city. In Fisher v. Greensboro Water Supply Co., 128 N.C. 375, 38 S.E. 912 (1901), and Mugge v. Tampa Water Works Co., 52 Fla. 371, 42 So. 81 (1906), the theory was one of tort for breach of a duty undertaken. In Doyle v. South Pittsburgh Water Co., 414 Pa. 199, 199 A.2d 875 (1964), the defendant was held to have entered on performance.

Both sides of the argument were presented at length in Reimann v. Monmough Consol. Water Co., 9 N.J. 134, 87 A.2d 325 (1952), which, by a vote of 4–2, adhered to the majority rule.

4. If defective water is in fact supplied under a contract with the city, the defendant may be liable to an individual for resulting injury, such as typhoid fever. Hayes v. Torrington Water Co., 88 Conn. 609, 92 A. 406 (1914).

5. There is much the same difference of opinion on the failure of a telephone company to render service under a contract with a private individual, as a result of which a third party is injured. See, for example, Mentzer v. New England Tel. & Tel. Co., 276 Mass. 478, 177 N.E. 549 (1931) (no liability); McLeod v. Pacific Tel. Co., 52 Or. 22, 94 P. 568 (1908) (liability).

6. Can the principal case be reconciled with Hall v. Consol. Edison Corp., 104 Misc.2d 565, 428 N.Y.S.2d 837 (1980), which allowed an apartment building tenant a claim for injuries when she fell in a darkened hallway after defendant cut off power without notice to the tenants?

7. The problem of the water company cases is discussed in Seavey, The Water Works Cases and Stare Decisis, 66 Harv.L.Rev. 84 (1952); Gregory, Gratuitous Undertakings and the Duty of Care, 1 De Paul L.Rev. 30, 55–67 (1951); Note, 26 Temp.L.Q. 214 (1953).

CLAGETT v. DACY

Court of Special Appeals of Maryland, 1980.
47 Md.App. 23, 420 A.2d 1285.

WILNER, JUDGE. Appellants were the high bidders at a foreclosure sale, but because the attorneys conducting the sale failed to follow the proper procedures, the sale was set aside. This occurred twice. Ultimately, the debtor discharged the loan, thus "redeeming" his land, and appellants lost the opportunity to acquire the property and make a profit on its resale. They sued the attorneys in the Circuit Court for Prince George's County to recover their loss, alleging that the attorneys in question owed them, as bidders, a duty to use care and diligence and to conduct the sale "properly and carefully." By sustaining the attorneys' demurrer without leave to amend, the court concluded that no such duty existed—at least not one from which an action for damages will arise; and, by affirming that order, we shall indicate our concurrence with the court's conclusion. * * *

Although [Prescott v. Coppage, 266 Md. 562, 296 A.2d 150 (1972)] has a most unusual factual setting, it does seem to suggest a modest relaxation of the strict privity requirement to the extent of allowing a true third party beneficiary to sue an attorney as he could sue any other defaulting or tortious party to a contract made for his benefit. This extension is not unique to Maryland. See Annot., Attorneys— Liability to Third Parties, 45 A.L.R.3d 1181.

It is, however, a limited one with a special utility. It is most often seen and applied in actions based on drafting errors in wills and other such documents or on erroneous title reports—errors that, by their very nature, will likely have a long or delayed effect and will most probably impact upon persons other than the attorney's immediate employer, [cc] although it has been applied in other contexts as well. See Donald v. Garry, 19 Cal.App.3d 769, 97 Cal.Rptr. 191 (1971) (creditor who assigned claim to collection agency for collection allowed to sue agency's attorney for negligence in prosecuting his claim).

The *Coppage* Court made clear that only those persons who qualify under the normal rules for determining third party beneficiaries will be afforded the privileged status *vis à vis* attorney defendants; i.e., creditor beneficiaries. [Cc] This would seem to limit the extension to actions based upon contract, to which the third party beneficiary theory is peculiarly applicable, and would not supply a basis for permitting third parties to sue attorneys on a pure negligence theory—violation of some general duty arising in the absence of an underlying contractual attorney-client relationship.

In Donald v. Garry, supra, the California court utilized the concept expressed in Restatement (Second) of Torts § 324A, to support a third party action, concluding that "[a]n attorney may be liable for damage caused by his negligence *to a person intended to be benefited by his performance* irrespective of any lack of privity of contract between the attorney and the party to be benefited." (Emphasis supplied.) The context of this, as noted above, was an action by the true creditor against the collection agency attorney, and the court was careful to mention that "the transaction in which the respondent's negligence occurred was intended primarily for the benefit of [the creditor]. Respondent was retained to collect an account due him."

It will, moreover, take more than general conclusory allegations to satisfy that requirement. Attorneys are not quite the free agents as some others are in the world of commerce. There are well-recognized limitations, judicially imposed and enforced, upon how they may conduct themselves, and who they may, and may not, represent in certain situations. Except in very limited circumstances, they may not represent or act for conflicting interests in a transaction; their manifest duty of loyalty to their employer/client forbids it. See, for example, Code of Professional Responsibility, Canon 5, EC5–14, 5–15, 5–16, 5–19, 5–22; DR5–105.

These limitations, predominant but not necessarily exclusive with attorneys, must, of necessity, be taken into account when dealing with actions founded upon an implied duty owed by an attorney to a person who is not his direct employer/client, or upon an employment relationship alleged to arise by implication rather than by express agreement. Thus, the duties or obligations inherent in an attorney-client relationship will not be presumed to flow to a third party and will not be presumed to arise by implication when the effect of such a presumption would be tantamount to a prohibited or improbable employment, absent the clearest exposition of facts from which such an employment may be fairly and rationally inferred.

When judged against these principles, it becomes clear that the Declaration at issue here has failed to state a cause of action. It does not sufficiently allege a proper standing on the part of appellants to sue the appellee attorneys; nor, from what *is* alleged, could it do so. Appellees were engaged to represent the mortgagee (deed of trust beneficiary), not the bidders, whose interest would likely be in conflict with that of the mortgagee. The mortgagee's economic interest, and legal obligation, is to secure the highest possible price for the property, whereas the bidders' goal is to pay as little as possible. It is evident, in that circumstance, that an attorney could not lawfully represent both the mortgagee and the bidder in the transaction; and it will not be lightly presumed or inferred that appellees did so.

Nor may the prohibited employment be inferred from an allegation that appellees' fees would ultimately be paid from the proceeds of sale. The mere fact that those fees, along with the other costs of the proceeding, may be taken from the purchase price paid by the successful bidder does not mean that the purchaser is actually paying the fees. Quite the contrary. The debtor/mortgagor ultimately pays the fees and all other costs, for he gets only the net surplus (if any) available after all such fees and costs are discharged. The bidder pays only for the property, not the cost of selling it; and he is not, therefore, the client (express or implied) of the attorney engaged to sell the property.

Judgment affirmed; appellants to pay the costs.

-----

1. One place in which the privity limitation is still significant is the area of professional relationships.

2. *Attorneys.* As the principal case reflects, the privity duty limitation has also been utilized by attorneys when they have committed an act of professional negligence. In many jurisdictions the privity limitation is still strictly applied. See Annot., 45 A.L.R.3d 1181 (1972).

3. The first major inroad on the privity rule as applied to attorneys occurred in California in Biakanja v. Irving, 49 Cal.2d 647, 320 P.2d 16 (1958), where a notary public acting as an attorney prepared a will for his "client," but negligently failed to have the will properly attested: the exception to the privity requirement was formulated along the lines of the principal case; cf. Brammer v. Taylor, ___ W.Va. ___, 338 S.E.2d 207 (1985). In Lucas v. Hamm, 56 Cal.2d 583, 364 P.2d 685, 15 Cal.Rptr. 821 (1961), cert. denied, 368 U.S. 987 (1962), the court indicated that the new rule would be applied to an actual

attorney; however, the court found that the defendant was not negligent in drafting a will provision that ran afoul of the rule against perpetuities.

Connecticut followed this lead in Licata v. Spector, 26 Conn.Supp. 378, 225 A.2d 28 (1966); but New York disagreed. See Victor v. Goldman, 74 Misc.2d 685, 344 N.Y.S.2d 672 (1973), aff'd, 43 A.D.2d 1020, 351 N.Y.S.2d 956 (1974).

4. Cases in which attorneys have been held liable to third parties generally have involved beneficiaries of wills. See Heyer v. Flaig, 70 Cal.2d 223, 449 P.2d 161, 74 Cal.Rptr. 225 (1969), where an attorney neglected to advise his client that her pending marriage would affect her intent to have all of her property flow to her daughters. But, whenever an attorney's work product is primarily for the benefit of a third party, potential liability can arise. See Donald v. Garry, 19 Cal.App.3d 769, 97 Cal.Rptr. 191 (1971) (attorney hired by collection agency liable to individual creditor). Should it matter that an attorney intentionally drafted a will in such a way that testator failed to receive what was owed her? See Kirgan v. Parks, 60 Md.App. 1, 478 A.2d 713 (1984).

5. Although California courts have formulated a "rule" almost twenty years ago, they still struggle when it must be applied in specific fact situations. For example, should an attorney be liable to an apparently intended beneficiary charitable organization when his client gave him an incorrect name of the group and this voided that provision of the will? See Ventura County Humane Society v. Holloway, 40 Cal.App.3d 897, 115 Cal.Rptr. 464 (1974). See also Roberts v. Ball, Hunt, Hart, Brown and Baerwitz, 57 Cal.App.3d 104, 128 Cal. Rptr. 901 (1976); and Goodman v. Kennedy, 18 Cal.3d 335, 556 P.2d 737, 134 Cal.Rptr. 375 (1976), both holding for the defendant. See generally, Annot., 45 A.L.R.3d 1181 (1972).

6. On an attorney's liability to a person against whom he brings a wrongful civil action, see Nelson v. Miller, 227 Kan. 271, 607 P.2d 438 (1980); see also Walter v. Doe, 93 Misc.2d 286, 402 N.Y.S.2d 723 (1978), on abuse of process. And see Thode, Groundless Case—The Lawyer's Tort Duty to His Client and to the Adverse Party, 11 St. Mary's L.J. 59 (1979).

7. Other possible areas of liability for attorneys include securities and real estate transfers. See Bradford Sec. Processing Serv., Inc. v. Plaza Bank & Trust, 653 P.2d 188 (Okl.1982), noted in 36 Okla.L.Rev. 372 (1983) (bond counsel); Page v. Frazier, 388 Mass. 55, 445 N.E.2d 148 (1983), noted in 52 U.Cin.L.Rev. 1069 (1983). See also Note, Attorney Negligence in Real Estate Title Examination and Will Drafting: Elimination of the Privity Requirement as a Bar to Recovery by Foreseeable Third Parties, 17 New Eng.L.Rev. 955 (1982); Attorney Liability to Third Parties for Corporate Opinion Letters, 64 B.U.L.Rev. 415 (1984).

8. *Physicians.* Physicians can also be protected by the privity rule. Should they be liable for malpractice to persons other than their immediate patients? For an interesting application of the privity limitation in this context, see Chatman v. Millis, 254 Ark. 451, 517 S.W.2d 504 (1975) (psychiatrist diagnosed father as a homosexual, but had only his son as a patient). Suppose a physician negligently fails to diagnose his patient's epilepsy. The patient subsequently suffers a seizure while driving and injures a third party. Should the concept of privity shield the physician from liability? See Freese v. Lemmon, 210 N.W.2d 576 (Iowa 1973). Cf. Gooden v. Tips, 651 S.W.2d 364 (Tex.

App.1983) (physician prescribed sedative without warning patient not to drive). Also relevant is the *Tarasoff* case, supra page 424.

9. *Other Professions.* For treatment of the liability of accountants in the absence of privity of contract, see chapter 21, on Misrepresentation. For treatment of the similar liability of manufacturers and other suppliers of chattels, and of architects, engineers and building contractors, see chapter 15, on Products Liability.

Chapter IX

OWNERS AND OCCUPIERS OF LAND

1. OUTSIDE THE PREMISES

TAYLOR v. OLSEN
Supreme Court of Oregon, 1978.
282 Or. 343, 578 P.2d 779.

LINDE, JUSTICE. Plaintiff sued for damages for injuries she sustained when her car, on a dark and windy January evening, struck a tree which shortly before had splintered and fallen across a * * * road. The trial court directed verdicts for * * * Marion Olsen, the adjoining landowner who was alleged to be in possession of the location. Plaintiff appeals from the judgment entered on the directed verdict for Olsen. * * *

We think * * * that, except for extreme situations, the question of the landowner's or possessor's attention to the condition of his roadside trees under a general standard of "reasonable care to prevent an unreasonable risk of harm" is to be decided as a question of fact upon the circumstances of the individual case. The extent of his responsibility either to inspect his trees or only to act on actual knowledge of potential danger cannot be defined simply by categorizing his land as "urban" or "rural." Surely it is not a matter of zoning or of city boundaries but of actual conditions. No doubt a factfinder will expect more attentiveness of the owner of an ornamental tree on a busy sidewalk [cc] than of the United States Forest Service * * *, but the great variety of intermediate patterns of land use, road use, traffic density, and preservation of natural stands of trees in urban and suburban settings prevents a simple "urban-rural" classification.

* * * [T]he onus on a homeowner of inspecting a few trees in his yard is modest, but the "practical difficulty of continuously examining each tree in the untold number of acres of forests" or in "sprawling tracts of woodland adjacent to or through which a road has been built [can be] so potentially onerous as to make property ownership an untenable burden. This would be particularly true for an absentee landowner." [C] It is less obviously true, however, for one who is engaged in logging or in actively developing the land. * * *

In this case, the road in question was a two-lane blacktop highway serving a number of communities * * *. There was testimony that it was used by an average 790 vehicles a day; in other words, a fallen tree might encounter a vehicle within an average of about two minutes, depending on the time of day. Defendant had purchased the land adjoining the road in 1973 for logging purposes, and during the five or six weeks before the accident he had logged about half the timber on his land. This included the trees adjacent to the tree on the county's right-of-way that eventually fell onto the road. Under these circumstances we conclude * * * that it would be a jury question whether defendant had taken reasonable care to inform himself of the condition of this tree, provided there was evidence that an inspection would have disclosed its hazardous condition.

The evidence is that after the tree broke and fell onto the road, the center of the tree at the point of the break proved to be decayed. However, the decay did not extend through the bark, or even to the surface below the bark except perhaps in a few places. Only by chopping or boring into the trunk of the tree would there have been a substantial chance of discovering the decay. Thus the question is not so much whether defendant had some responsibility to give his attention to the safety of this tree left behind by his logging operations as, rather, how far that responsibility extends.

There was no evidence to suggest that chopping or drilling into the trunk would have been a normal or expected way to examine a standing tree in the absence of external indications that it might not be structurally sound. * * *

It requires some evidence either that the defendant should have been on notice of possible decay in this tree, or that cutting through the bark to the trunk is a common and ordinary method of examining trees generally. In the absence of such evidence, it was not error to direct a verdict for the defendant.

Affirmed.

---

1. This chapter, like Chapter 8, considers the state of the law in an area that traditionally has involved limited duties. It specifically deals with the duty that owners of land owe to persons on and off the premises.

2. With regard to most conditions on land that arise in the state of nature, most courts have held that there is no duty upon the landholder to protect persons outside the premises. See Ponterdawe Rural District Council v. Moore–Gwynn, [1929] 1 Ch. 656 (rock falling down mountainside into village); Roberts v. Harrison, 101 Ga. 773, 28 S.E. 995 (1897) (foul swamp); Brady v. Warren, [1909] 2 Ir.Rep. 632 (rabbits).

3. This rule has been extended in a number of cases where the owner of rural land has been held not liable for the growth and spread of weeds, on the ground that they were the "natural growth of the soil," even though the cultivation was a contributing cause. Langer v. Goode, 21 N.D. 462, 131 N.W. 258 (1911) (wild mustard).

4. An exception has evolved with regard to trees, and there is agreement that the landowner is liable for negligence if he knows that the tree is defective and fails to take reasonable precautions. Turner v. Ridley, 144 A.2d 269 (Mun. App.D.C.1958); Plesko v. Allied Inv. Co., 12 Wis.2d 168, 107 N.W.2d 201 (1961).

5. The rule was clear at one time that the owner of land abutting on a rural highway is under no duty to inspect it to discover defects in trees. Chambers v. Whelen, 44 F.2d 340 (4th Cir.1930); O'Brien v. United States, 275 F.2d 696 (9th Cir.1960). The trend is toward decisions like the principal case. See Medeiros v. Honomu Sugar Co., 21 Haw. 155 (1912); Brandywine Hundred Realty Co. v. Cotillo, 55 F.2d 231 (3d Cir.1931); Hensley v. Montgomery County, 25 Md.App. 361, 334 A.2d 542 (1975).

6. In Sprecher v. Adamson Cos., 30 Cal.3d 358, 636 P.2d 1121, 178 Cal. Rptr. 783 (1981), however, the landowner's general immunity for harm outside the premises caused by natural conditions was abolished, and an uphill landowner was found to owe a legal duty of reasonable care to a downhill landowner to control a landslide condition. This decision was followed in Moeller v. Fleming, 136 Cal.App.3d 241, 186 Cal.Rptr. 24 (1982), where a landowner could be sued by a pedestrian who slipped on an irregular break in the sidewalk that was caused by tree roots from the landowner's adjacent property. Also, compare the First Restatement of Torts, § 363(2) [promulgated in 1963–64], with Restatement (Second) of Torts, § 840(2) [promulgated in 1977]; see also, id., § 840, comment c.

7. Some states recognize a "self-help" rule, under which a landowner can resort to self-help and cut-off tree branches and roots intruding onto his property from adjoining property. See, e.g., Melnick v. C.S.X. Corp., 68 Md. App. 107, 510 A.2d 592 (1986).

8. See generally Noel, Nuisances from Land in its Natural Condition, 56 Harv.L.Rev. 772 (1943); Goodhart, Liability for Things Naturally on the Land, 4 Cambridge L.J. 13 (1930); McCleary, The Possessor's Responsibilities as to Trees, 29 Mo.L.Rev. 159 (1964); May, Adjoining and Abutting Landowners: Liability for Injuries to Persons or Property, 1 Willamette L.Rev. 413 (1960); Annot., 94 A.L.R.3d 1160 (1969).

SALEVAN v. WILMINGTON PARK, INC.

Superior Court of Delaware, 1950.
45 Del. (6 Terry) 290, 72 A.2d 239.

WOLCOTT, JUDGE. The plaintiff brings suit for personal injuries received when struck in the back by a baseball while walking on East Thirtieth Street in the City of Wilmington, past the ball park of the defendant.

The defendant is the owner of land * * * on which is located the ball park in question. The business of the defendant is the maintenance and renting of the ball park and its facilities and has been carried on by the defendant for over eight years. * * *

[I]t appears that in the course of an average ball game, 16 to 18 foul balls come from inside the park into Thirtieth Street and, of them, an average of 2 or 3 foul balls come from within the park over the 10–foot fence and into the area along Thirtieth Street through which the plaintiff was passing at the time of the injury. The manager of the defendant testified that, on an average, 68 baseball games were played at Wilmington Park during the baseball season.

The plaintiff does not contend that the defendant is an insurer of persons lawfully using the highways and sidewalks adjacent to its ball park, but does contend that the defendant, as a landowner, has the duty to exercise reasonable care in the use of its land so as to prevent injury to travelers lawfully using the highways adjacent thereto. The plaintiff contends that the defendant had notice of the passage of baseballs outside of its park into East Thirtieth Street to the danger of persons using that public street, and that the failure of the defendant to take reasonable precautions to safeguard the public was negligence. * * *

It is clear that the public has a right to the free and unmolested use of the public highways, and that abutting landowners may not so use their land as to interfere with the rights of persons lawfully using the highways. * * *

The inherent nature of the game of baseball * * * is such as to require the landowner to take reasonable precautions for the protection of the traveling public. What precautions are reasonable must depend upon the facts and circumstances of the particular case. Only those precautions are required which the inherent nature of the game and its past history in the particular location make necessary for the protection of a person lawfully using the highways. * * *

While the defendant has shown that consideration was given by it to the protection of the public at the time the park was first built, the fact remains that despite the precautions taken, baseballs went out of its park into the public highway and that the defendant either knew that baseballs went out of its park or, under the circumstances, should have known. The evidence is not seriously contradicted that baseballs went out of the park into Thirtieth Street within the area through which the plaintiff was passing at the time of her injury two or three times in each game played in the defendant's park.

Under the circumstances, it seems clear to me that while the defendant took precautions to protect people passing along Thirtieth Street, those precautions were insufficient. It further seems clear that the defendant knew, or should have known, that the precautions taken initially were insufficient to protect the public engaged in its lawful right, that is, using the highways. This circumstance puts the case at bar squarely within the rule I have drawn from the reported decisions, and if this were a jury trial, would be sufficient to submit the case to the jury and would compel, in my opinion, the jury to return a verdict for the plaintiff. Accordingly, my conclusion is that judgment should be entered for the plaintiff.

Judgment being entered for the plaintiff, it remains to determine in what amount that judgment should be. Under the circumstances, I believe the sum of $2500.00 will adequately compensate the plaintiff for the injuries received as a result of the negligence of the defendant.

----

1.   Once a landowner alters a condition of his land, it becomes an "artificial" one for the purposes of tort law and the owner must exercise reasonable care for the protection of those outside of the premises. Thus Towaliga Falls Power Co. v. Sims, 6 Ga.App. 749, 65 S.E. 844 (1909) (damming a stream to form

a malarial pond); Ettl v. Land & Loan Co., 122 N.J.L. 401, 5 A.2d 689 (1939) (piling sand where the wind may blow it). This obligation will also arise with regard to a condition that may appear, on the surface, to be a natural one. See, e.g., Coates v. Chinn, 51 Cal.2d 304, 332 P.2d 289 (1958) (cultivated trees).

2. The landowner is not liable for the normal flow of surface water, which is regarded as a "natural" condition. Livezey v. Schmidt, 96 Ky. 441, 29 S.W. 25 (1895); Middlesex County v. McCue, 149 Mass. 103, 21 N.E. 230 (1889). On the same principle, it is generally held that an abutting owner is under no duty to remove snow and ice that falls naturally upon the highway. Ainey v. Rialto Amusement Co., 135 Wash. 56, 236 P. 801 (1925); Norville v. Hub Furniture Co., 59 App.D.C. 29, 32 F.2d 420 (1929).

3. Ordinances requiring the property owner to remove snow and ice from abutting sidewalks usually are construed to create a duty only to the municipality, and not to any private individual. Hanley v. Fireproof Bldg. Co., 107 Neb. 544, 186 N.W. 534 (1922); Griswold v. Camp, 149 Wis. 399, 135 N.W. 754 (1918). Usually, however, these ordinances provide that the owner must remove the snow and ice or pay the cost of removal, and are held to indicate an intent to protect the city.

4. Some courts, though, have extended an owner's responsibility for abutting sidewalks. Stewart v. 104 Wallace St., Inc., 87 N.J. 146, 432 A.2d 881 (1981) (owner liable for failing to maintain abutting sidewalks in reasonably good condition), and Cogliati v. Ecco High Frequency Corp., 92 N.J. 402, 456 A.2d 524 (1983) (current owner and predecessor in title liable for poorly maintained public sidewalks).

5. If the owner himself has altered the condition of the premises so that surface water or snow is discharged upon the highway, he may be directly held liable for negligence or nuisance. Tremblay v. Harmony Mills, 171 N.Y. 598, 64 N.E. 501 (1902); Adlington v. Viroqua, 155 Wis. 472, 144 N.W. 1130 (1914). See De Graff, Snow and Ice, 21 Cornell L.Q. 436 (1936); Note, 21 Minn.L.Rev. 703 (1937).

6. Suppose the plaintiff is injured outside the premises by something subject to the control of the owner of the premises? Compare Blake v. Dunn Farms, Inc., 274 Ind. 560, 413 N.E.2d 560 (1980) (horse runs out on highway), with Weber v. Madison, 251 N.W.2d 523 (Iowa 1977) (geese on highway). Cf. Leary v. Lawrence Sales Corp., 442 Pa. 389, 275 A.2d 32 (1971) (food dropped on shopping-center mall two feet from defendant's premises).

HAYES v. MALKAN

Court of Appeals of New York, 1970.
26 N.Y.2d 295, 258 N.E.2d 695, 310 N.Y.S.2d 281.

, JASEN, JUDGE. Plaintiff, one of three passengers in an automobile owned and operated by defendant Malkan, was injured when the vehicle struck a utility pole owned by defendant Consolidated Edison Company. The pole which Malkan's car struck was approximately seven inches from the edge of the road and was located on private property behind a two-inch granite header.[1] There is no explicit testimony as to how the car came in contact with the pole, since

---

1. When the pole was originally erected in 1929, it stood some five feet from the edge of the traveled portion of the road. However, in 1941, the State widened the traveled portion of the highway, utilizing its entire right of way.

Malkan and the plaintiff stated that they did not know precisely what occurred. The only recollection plaintiff had of the accident was that he heard a "thump" and then found himself lying by the side of the road. The other passengers did not testify.

The trial court instructed the jury that "the law imposes a duty upon the defendant [Consolidated Edison] that the pole must be so located as to avoid unreasonable and unnecessary danger to travelers upon the highway, *regardless of whether it is on private or public property.*" (Emphasis added.)

We hold this instruction to be erroneous, as a matter of law, and upon the facts of this case the complaint should be dismissed.

It is common practice in this State to locate utility poles along our highways between the edge of the traveled road and the end of the dedicated portion of the highway. When a collision with one of these poles occurs, it is frequently claimed that the proximate cause of the occurrence was the location and maintenance of the pole. In such cases, we have taken the view that placement of poles or other objects— such as fire hydrants, guardrails, culverts, trees and shrubbery—in close proximity to the pavement and within the highway right of way, raises a question of fact for jury determination as to whether the placement of that object was such as to create an unreasonable danger for travelers on the highway. [Cc]

On its face, this rule might appear to have application to this case. However, unlike the cases cited above, the pole herein was not within the public right of way, but rather was located on private property. Under such circumstances, we believe that there should be no liability against the landowner, or his licensee, for an injury to a traveler arising out of a collision with the pole. * * *

Carried to its logical conclusion, this rule would require a landowner to remove every tree, fence, post, mailbox or name sign located on his property in the vicinity of the highway, or permit them to remain, subject to possible liability. This, in our opinion, would impose an intolerable burden upon a property owner.

The rule applicable to excavations on private land adjacent to a public way is no more than an extension of the principle that one may not maintain a trap. The rule applies even to trespassers who it is known may come on the land, and, of course, a fortiori, to those who reasonably deviate from the public way. [C] There is neither practical need, nor social or economic justification, for unguarded holes. Thus, the owner ought, in any event, impose on himself minimum requirements to avoid hazard to users of the public way, whether pedestrian or motor traffic. But a utility pole is not a trap, nor is any other visible, sizeable, above-the-surface structure. * * *

Accordingly, the judgment appealed from should be reversed and the complaint dismissed.

SCILEPPI, BERGAN and BREITEL, JJ., concur with JASEN, J.; FULD, C.J., dissents and votes to affirm in a separate opinion in which BURKE and GIBSON, JJ., concur.

---

1. Most courts agree that a landholder owes a duty to a traveler who accidentally falls into excavations on land immediately adjoining the highway. Downes v. Silva, 57 R.I. 343, 190 A. 42 (1937). Also to those who inadvertently stray a short distance from the highway. Puchlopek v. Portsmouth Power Co., 82 N.H. 440, 136 A. 259 (1926) (slip); Durst v. Wareham, 132 Kan. 785, 297 P. 675 (1931).

2. The rule has even been extended, in several cases, to those who deviate intentionally from the highway for some casual purpose connected with travel. Weidman v. Consolidated Gas, E.L. & P. Co., 158 Md. 39, 148 A. 276 (1930) (stepping out to avoid crowd); Gibson v. Johnson, 69 Ohio App. 19, 42 N.E.2d 689 (1941) (stepping out to allow others to pass); Lacanfora v. Goldapel, 37 A.D.2d 721, 323 N.Y.S.2d 990 (1971) (knobless door close to sidewalk opened when child leaned on it, precipitating him to 12–foot drop).

3. In Murray v. McShane, 52 Md. 217 (1879), plaintiff, walking along the public sidewalk, sat down on defendant's doorstep to tie his shoe, and was injured when a brick fell on him out of the doorway. He was allowed to recover. In Foley v. H.F. Farnham Co., 135 Me. 29, 188 A. 708 (1936), where the plaintiff met a friend and sat down to talk to him, recovery was denied. What is the difference?

4. There is no liability as to dangers a considerable distance from the highway. Hardcastle v. South Yorkshire R. & R.D.R. Co., 4 H. & N. 67, 157 Eng.Rep. 761 (1859). In Flint v. Bowman, 42 Tex.Civ.App. 354, 93 S.W. 479 (1906), plaintiff was driving along a highway obliterated by fifteen inches of snow. He missed a right turn, and continued on across the defendant's land for nearly half a mile until he drove into an abandoned and unguarded well. Is the defendant liable to him?

5. When the land has a deceptive appearance of being a continuation of the public way, a duty may be imposed on the landholder to guard a trap or excavation even though the hazard is actually a considerable distance within private property. See Louisville & Nashville R. Co. v. Anderson, 39 F.2d 403 (5 Cir.1930); Holmes v. Drew, 151 Mass. 578, 25 N.E. 22 (1890). In such a case the entrant on the land may be deemed to be invited and not a trespasser. Is this inconsistent with the rule of Ranson v. Kitner, supra page 24.

6. In a California case, a telephone booth user, injured when the booth was struck by an automobile which had jumped the curb, sued the telephone company for dangerously locating the booth in a parking lot 15 feet from the side of a major thoroughfare and near a driveway. Bigbee v. Pacific Tel. & Tel. Co., 34 Cal.3d 49, 665 P.2d 947, 192 Cal.Rptr. 857 (1983). Contrast this situation with the facts in the principal case. Are they distinguishable? See discussion of duty owed by landowner to invitees, see infra this chapter, section 2(c). Would it make any difference if the door to the booth had jammed and he could not get out as the car approached him?

2. ON THE PREMISES

(A) TRESPASSERS

SHEEHAN v. ST. PAUL & DULUTH RY. CO.
United States Circuit Court of Appeals, Seventh Circuit, 1896.
76 Fed. 201.

[Action for damages for personal injury. While plaintiff was walking on defendant's railroad track, his foot slipped and became caught between the rail and a cattle guard. He was unable to extricate his shoe, or to get at it to untie it. Defendant's train approached, and ran over his foot. Defendant's train crew did not see him until the train was almost upon him, and it was too late to stop it. The trial court directed a verdict for defendant, on the ground that "upon the undisputed facts of the case, this injury did not occur through any wrongful action upon the part of the defendant." Plaintiff appeals.]

SEAMAN, DISTRICT JUDGE. * * * The plaintiff, at the time of his injury, was neither in the relation of passenger nor of one in a public crossing or place in which the public were licensed to travel, but, upon the undisputed facts, was a mere intruder on the tracks of the defendant,—technically, a trespasser; and this record excludes any of the elements of implied license or invitation to such use which have given rise to much discussion and diversity of views in the courts. Therefore the inquiry is here squarely presented: What is the duty which a railway company owes to a trespasser on its tracks, and how and when does the duty arise? The decisions upon this subject uniformly recognize that the trespasser cannot be treated as an outlaw; and, at the least, that, if wantonly injured in the operation of the railroad, the company is answerable in damages. Clearly, then, an obligation is placed upon the company to exercise some degree of care when the danger becomes apparent. Is it, however, bound to foresee or assume that rational beings will thus enter as trespassers in a place of danger, and to exercise in the running of its trains the constant vigilance in view of that probability which is imposed for public crossings? There are cases which would seem to hold this strict requirement [cc]; but by the great preponderance of authority, in this country, and in England, the more reasonable doctrine is pronounced, in effect, as follows: That the railroad company has the right to a free track in such places; that it is not bound to any act or service in anticipation of trespassers thereon; and that the trespasser who ventures to enter upon a track for any purpose of his own assumes all risks of the conditions which may be found there, including the operation of engines and cars. * * *

The well-established and just rule which holds the railroad company to the exercise of constant and strict care against injury through its means is applicable only to the relation on which it is founded, of an existing duty or obligation. This active or positive duty arises in favor of the public at a street crossing or other place at which it is presumable that persons or teams may be met. It is not material, so far as concerns this inquiry, whether the place is one for which a lawful right of passage exists, as it is the fact of notice to the company, arising out of its existence and the probability of its use, which imposes the positive duty to exercise care; the requirement of an extreme degree of care being superadded because of the hazards which attend the operations of the company. The case of a trespasser on the track, in a place not open to travel, is clearly distinguishable in the absence of this notice to the company. There is no constructive notice upon which to base the obligation of constant lookout for his presence there, and no actual notice up to the moment the trainmen have discovered the fact of his peril. As that peril comes wholly from his unauthorized act and temerity, the risk, and all positive duty of care for his safety, rests with the trespasser. The obligation of the company and its operatives is not, then, pre-existing, but arises at the moment of discovery, and is negative in its nature,—a duty, which is common to human conduct, to make all reasonable effort to avert injury to others from means which can be controlled. This is the issue presented here. It excludes all inquiry respecting the character of the roadbed, cattle guard, locomotive, brake appliances, or other means of operation, or of the speed or manner of running the train up to the moment of notice, because no breach of positive duty is involved. It is confined to the evidence relating to the discovery by the engineer and fireman of the plaintiff's peril, and to the efforts then made to avert the injury, and, out of that, to ascertain whether, in any view which may justly be taken, it is shown that these men, or the engineer, in disregard of the duty which then confronted them, neglected to employ with reasonable promptness the means at hand for stopping the train. * * *

The court was clearly justified in directing a verdict for the defendant, and the judgment is affirmed.

————

1. How valid are the following explanations, commonly given for the nonliability to the trespasser:

A. His presence is not reasonably to be anticipated. Suppose a railroad company, as well as everyone else, knows that people do habitually trespass on its right of way?

B. The trespasser assumes the risk. What if he does not know there is any risk or is a child too young to assume it? See Santora v. New York, N.H. & H.R. Co., 211 Mass. 464, 98 N.E. 90 (1912), where a child 27 months old got onto a railroad track and was run over.

C. He is contributorily negligent or is himself a wrongdoer not entitled to legal protection. Again, suppose that he is a child too young to be negligent? Or that under the rule of the last clear chance there would be liability to one not a trespasser even though he were negligent? Newman v. Louisville & N.R. Co., 212 Ala. 580, 103 So. 856 (1925); Dyrcz v. Missouri Pac. R. Co., 238 Mo. 33, 141 S.W. 861 (1911).

What is the explanation of the rule?

2.　The rule stated in the principal case is commonly applied to a wide variety of dangerous conditions on the land, including dangerous machinery and defective construction.

3.　The landowner's immunity toward trespassers extends to the members of his household. Sohn v. Katz, 112 N.J.L. 106, 169 A. 838 (1934). It does not extend to adjoining landowners. Fitzpatrick v. Penfield, 267 Pa. 564, 109 A. 653 (1920).

4.　The courts have not favored the immunity to trespassers, and have tended to erode it with exceptions. The first exception is that of a trespasser whose presence has been discovered. Frederick v. Philadelphia Rapid Transit Co., 337 Pa. 136, 10 A.2d 576 (1940) (plaintiff fell from subway platform onto track, train automatically stopped by "tripper", crew drove on without making adequate inspection).

A.　The earliest cases finding liability to a trespasser were those of spring guns or traps deliberately set for him. From these cases the rule developed that the defendant was not allowed to injure the trespasser negligently by an act specifically directed at him, as in Palmer v. Gordon, 173 Mass. 410, 53 N.E. 909 (1899); Magar v. Hammond, 183 N.Y. 387, 76 N.E. 474 (1906); or recklessly by conduct in conscious disregard of his danger, as in Aiken v. Holyoke St. R. Co., 184 Mass. 269, 68 N.E. 238 (1903); Trico Coffee Co. v. Clemens, 168 Miss. 748, 151 So. 175 (1933).

B.　From such decisions the rule developed that the defendant is liable for injury to a trespasser for conduct which is "wilful or wanton." Thus in Bremer v. Lake Erie & W.R. Co., 318 Ill. 11, 148 N.E. 862 (1925), the defendant was held liable when its engineer recklessly ran past a signal and injured a trespasser on the train who had not been discovered.

C.　In a number of states it is still held that there is no liability even to a discovered trespasser unless the defendant's conduct is wilful or wanton. Some of these jurisdictions have defined "wilful and wanton," as in the principal case, to include a failure to use ordinary care after discovery of the trespasser's presence. Cf. Sloniker v. Great N.R. Co., 76 Minn. 306, 79 N.W. 168 (1899).

D.　The great majority of the courts have now discarded "wilful and wanton" as a limitation, and have held that when the presence of the trespasser is discovered there is a duty to use ordinary care to avoid injuring him by active operations. This duty includes the control of operating forces, such as machinery already in motion, or a warning against it. Maldonado v. Jack M. Berry Grove Corp., 351 So.2d 967 (Fla.1977).

E.　Cases involving passive conditions on the land, as distinguished from active operations, have been infrequent. It was once held, in Buch v. Amory Mfg. Co., 69 N.H. 257, 44 A. 809 (1897), that the defendant was under no duty even to cry a warning to a trespasser whom he saw walking into a concealed danger. This apparently has now given way to the rule that he must at least warn the trespasser. Martin v. Jones, 122 Utah 597, 609, 253 P.2d 359, 261 P.2d 174 (1953); Restatement (Second) of Torts § 337.

5.　The second exception is that of frequent trespassers on a very limited area of the land. The defendant is required to anticipate the trespassers and to exercise reasonable care in his activities for their protection. In Imre v. Riegel Paper Corp., 24 N.J. 438, 132 A.2d 505 (1957), the existence of a well-defined path across the land was held to be sufficient evidence of frequent trespass.

6. The third exception is that of *tolerated intruders*. This is sometimes explained or justified on the theory that the defendant's continued toleration of the trespasses amounts to permission to use the land, so that the plaintiff becomes a licensee. In most cases, however, the mere fact that a railway company or other defendant has failed to take steps to prevent trespassing, which would be burdensome, expensive, and perhaps futile, is not in itself any indication that it consents to the entry. See Restatement (Second) of Torts § 330, comment *c;* Bohlen, The Duty of a Landowner Toward Those Entering His Premises of Their Own Right, 69 U.Pa.L.Rev. 142, 237 (1921).

7. Other exceptions include dangerous conditions obvious to an owner, Restatement (Second) of Torts § 342–343 (1965); and trapped trespassers in peril. Pridgen v. Boston Hous. Auth., 364 Mass. 696, 308 N.E.2d 467 (1974).

8. In a few jurisdictions, the courts have developed in railroad cases a special rule requiring the defendant to be on the lookout for trespassers where their presence is foreseeable and the activity carried on involves a high degree of danger to them. Pickett v. Wilmington & W.R. Co., 117 N.C. 616, 23 S.E. 264 (1895); Gulf, C. & S.F.R. Co. v. Russell, 125 Tex. 443, 82 S.W.2d 948 (1935).

9. There is a division of authority over whether a defendant using the land by permission of the owner shares the immunity of the owner toward trespassers. See, e.g., Humphrey v. Twin State Gas & Electric Co., 100 Vt. 414, 139 A. 440 (1927). Thus gratuitous licensees, invitees and holders of easements have been held liable in some cases and not in others. The Restatement (Second) of Torts §§ 383–386, has endeavored to resolve the conflict with the statement that persons on the premises who are doing work or creating artificial conditions *on behalf* of the possessor are subject to the same liability, and entitled to the same immunity, as the possessor; but that other persons on the land with his permission have no such immunity. This offers a logical approach, and serves to explain the greater number of the cases, although by no means all. See, for example, Hollett v. Dundee, Inc., 272 F.Supp. 1 (D.Del. 1967); Annot., 30 A.L.R.3d 777 (1970).

(B) LICENSEES

BARMORE v. ELMORE

Appellate Court of Illinois, Second District, 1980.
83 Ill.App.3d 1056, 38 Ill.Dec. 751, 403 N.E.2d 1355.

LINDBERG, JUSTICE. Plaintiff, Leon Barmore ("plaintiff"), appeals from an order of the Circuit Court of Winnebago County directing a verdict in favor of defendants, Thomas Elmore, Sr., and Esther Elmore ("defendants").

On August 8, 1977, at approximately 5:30 or 6:00 p.m., plaintiff came to the defendants' home. Both plaintiff and Thomas Elmore, Sr. ("Thomas, Sr.") were officers of a Masonic Lodge and plaintiff's purpose in making the visit was to discuss lodge business. During the course of plaintiff's visit, codefendant, Thomas Elmore, Jr., ("Thomas, Jr."), the defendants' 47–year old son, entered the living room with a steak knife. Thomas, Jr. said "You've been talking about me," and advanced toward plaintiff. Thomas, Sr. tried to restrain his son while plaintiff left the house. However, Thomas, Jr. was able to get away from his father, and he followed plaintiff out of the house where he stabbed the plaintiff several times in the chest area. Thomas, Sr. followed his son out of the house and, when he saw that plaintiff had been injured, he summoned help.

Based on this incident, plaintiff filed suit against [defendants.] * * * [P]laintiff's basic contention is that defendants, as landowners, were negligent in failing to protect him from a dangerous condition upon their premises—namely their son who had a history of mental illness. The extent of defendants' duty in this regard is based in part on whether the plaintiff had the status of an invitee or of a licensee at the time he visited the premises of the defendants.

* * * In order for a person to be classified as an invitee it is sufficient that he go on the land in furtherance of the owner's business. It is not necessary that the invited person gain an advantage by his entry on the land. [C] A social guest is considered a licensee and has been defined as one who enters the premises of the owner by permission, but for the licensee's own purposes. Therefore, a social guest is a person who goes on another's property for companionship, diversion, or entertainment. [C]

The duty owed by the owner of premises towards an invitee is greater than that owed towards a licensee. [C] A social guest as a licensee, generally must take the premises of his host as he finds them. However, the owner of the premises has a duty to warn the licensee of any hidden dangers which are unknown to his guest, of which he, the owner, has knowledge, and to refrain from injuring his guest willfully or wantonly. [Cc] Towards an invitee, the owner of the premises has a duty to exercise reasonable care in keeping the premises reasonably safe for use by the invitee. [C] There may be circumstances by which this duty is extended to include the responsibility to protect the invitee from criminal attacks by third parties. [C]

Plaintiff asserts that sufficient evidence was presented at trial to establish his status as an invitee at the time of the incident. Specifically, plaintiff argues that Illinois courts have recognized that the transaction of business of a fraternal organization carries with it such a status. * * *

Here, although there is evidence that Thomas, Sr. permitted lodge members to come to his home to pay their dues, the primary benefit of this service ran not to the defendant himself, but rather to the fraternal organization of which both parties were members. In sum, we conclude that plaintiff is best categorized as a licensee—social guest and thus the only duty owed to the plaintiff by the defendants was to warn him of hidden dangers unknown to the plaintiff of which the defendants had knowledge.

There is no question that defendants failed to warn plaintiff of the danger that their son might attack a house guest before the attack was underway. Thus the issue becomes whether under the facts of this case defendants had a duty to do so. Plaintiff contends that he presented sufficient evidence by which a jury could have concluded that the defendants had knowledge of previous incidents which would charge them with a duty to anticipate the criminal acts of their son toward the plaintiff. We disagree. [The Court summarizes the evidence.]

Verdicts should be directed and judgments n.o.v. entered "only in those cases in which all of the evidence, when viewed in its aspect most favorable to the opponent, so overwhelmingly favors movant that no contrary verdict based on that evidence could ever stand." [C] In our view, the evidence so overwhelmingly established that the defendants did not know or have reason to know of the possibility that Thomas, Jr. would commit a criminal act toward plaintiff that no contrary verdict could ever stand. Although they did know that their son had a history of mental problems and had been hospitalized several times, and also that approximately ten years before the present incident their son had been involved in what could be characterized as two or three violent incidents, the length of time which had passed would not give them reason to know that their son would engage in violent behavior in August, 1977. This conclusion is buttressed by the fact that plaintiff had previous contact with Thomas, Jr. without incident.

Accordingly, the judgment * * * is affirmed.

---

1. As in the case of trespassers, it was at first held that there was no duty to a licensee except to refrain from inflicting wilful or wanton injury; and there are still courts which hold this. Duff v. United States, 171 F.2d 846 (4th Cir.1949) (Maryland law); Hill v. Baltimore & Ohio R. Co., 153 F.2d 91 (7th Cir. 1946) (Illinois law). Courts often define "wilful or wanton" to include a failure to exercise ordinary care after the presence of the licensee has been discovered, or should reasonably have been expected. Atlantic Coast Line R. Co. v. Heath, 57 Ga.App. 763, 196 S.E. 125 (1938); Jackson v. Pennsylvania R. Co., 176 Md. 1, 3 A.2d 719 (1939).

2. Most of the courts now have overruled older decisions, and hold that the defendant, in conducting active operations, is under a duty of reasonable care toward licensees. This duty extends not only to licensees who are discovered, but to those whose presence might reasonably be anticipated. Babcock & Wilcox Co. v. Nolton, 58 Nev. 133, 71 P.2d 1051 (1937); Szafranski v. Radetzky, 31 Wis.2d 119, 141 N.W.2d 902 (1966) (handling gun powder).

3. If defendant landholder knows about a dangerous, latent condition on his premises that a visitor is likely to encounter, he is under a duty to warn the licensee about it. Laube v. Stevenson, 137 Conn. 469, 78 A.2d 693 (1951), involving a dangerous condition on a stairwell, is an excellent case illustrating difference in result between a defendant who knew and one who did not know about the hazard. See also Barry v. Cantrell, 150 Ga.App. 439, 258 S.E.2d 61 (1979) (hammock tied to dead tree); Rushton v. Winters, 331 Pa. 78, 200 A. 60 (1938) (defective porch railing).

The Restatement (Second) of Torts § 342 subjects the landholder to liability if he had "reason to know" about the unsafe condition. Even in this modern age when householder's liability insurance is common, this extension has not always met with approval.

4. In some jurisdictions the licensee category is broken down into two subgroups, the ordinary licensee and the "bare" licensee. The latter group includes salespersons, canvassers and social visitors who "drop in" without an express invitation. As might be expected, the duty owed to "bare" licensees is less than that owed to ordinary licensees. See Kight v. Bowman, 25 Md.App. 225, 333 A.2d 346, 350 (1975); Wilson v. Goodrich, 218 Iowa 462, 252 N.W. 142 (1934); cf. Scheibel v. Lipton, 156 Ohio St. 308, 102 N.E.2d 453 (1951). In other states, the word "bare" is simply an uncomplimentary epithet applied to all licensees.

5. *Social Guests.* Ever since Southcote v. Stanley, 1 H. & N. 247, 156 Eng. Rep. 1195 (1856), the decisions have been essentially uniform in holding that a social guest, although he is invited, and even urged to come, is not in law an invitee but is to be treated as merely a licensee. See, for example, Stevens v. Dovre, 248 Md. 15, 234 A.2d 596 (1967); Zuther v. Schild, 224 Kan. 528, 581 P.2d 385 (1978).

6. As the principal case reflects, there is general agreement that the fact that the guest renders some incidental service to his host, such as washing the dishes or repairing a broken shelf, does not change his status. And it has been held that an economic motive in inviting the defendant's employer to dinner does not make him an invitee. Cf. Hall v. Duke, 513 S.W.2d 776 (Tenn.1974).

7. Should the rule be changed? Does a social guest anticipate that the premises will be made reasonably safe for his benefit? What about the uninvited social guest, salesperson or canvasser? Does the host receive a "benefit" from a purely social guest? Is it enough to impose a duty of reasonable care? These arguments and others were explored by leading torts professors in a symposium over three decades ago. See 25 Conn.B.J. 123 (1951).

8. Should the host be liable for protecting third parties from acts of intoxicated guests? See Kelly v. Gwinnell, 96 N.J. 538, 476 A.2d 1219 (1984), supra page 324; Social Host Liability for The Negligent Acts of Intoxicated Guests, 70 Cornell L.Rev. 1058 (1985). See also Ch. 6 supra.

9. The few cases that raise the question of strict liability to licensees all have involved dangerous animals. In all of them, the strict liability has been held to extend to the licensee. See, for example, Parker v. Cushman, 195 Fed. 715 (8th Cir.1912); Marquet v. La Duke, 96 Mich. 596, 55 N.W. 1006 (1893).

10. See James, Tort Liability of Occupiers of Land: Duties Owed to Licensees and Invitees, 63 Yale L.J. 605 (1954); Marsh, The History and Comparative Law of Invitees, Licensees and Trespassers, 69 Law Q.Rev. 182, 359 (1953).

(C) Invitees

CAMPBELL v. WEATHERS
Supreme Court of Kansas, 1941.
153 Kan. 316, 111 P.2d 72.

[Defendant, as tenant of a part of a building in the city of Wichita, operated a lunch counter and cigar stand. Plaintiff entered defendant's place of business, loitered in the front part of the premises for fifteen or twenty minutes without making any purchase, and then went to the back part of the building to use the toilet. He stepped into an open trap door in a dark hallway, and was injured. In his action for negligence, the trial court sustained defendant's demurrer to the evidence and plaintiff appeals.]

WEDELL, J. * * * The first issue to be determined is the relationship between plaintiff and the lessee. Was plaintiff a trespasser, a licensee or an invitee? The answer must be found in the evidence. A part of the answer is contained in the nature of the business the lessee conducted. It is conceded lessee operated a business which was open to the public. Lessee's business was that of selling cigars and lunches to the public. It was conceded in oral argument, although the abstract does not reflect it, that the lessee also operated a bar for the sale of beer, but that beer was not being sold on Sunday, the day of the accident. Plaintiff had been a customer of the lessee for a number of years. He resided in the city of Wichita. He was a switchman for one of the railroads. He stopped at the lessee's place of business whenever he was in town. He had used the hallway and toilet on numerous occasions, whenever he was in town, and had never been advised that the toilet was not intended for public use. * * *

That the public had a general invitation to be or to become lessee's customers cannot be doubted. * * * Can we say, as a matter of law, in view of the record in this particular case, appellant had no implied invitation to use the toilet simply because he had not made an actual purchase before he was injured? * * *

The evidence of lessee's own employees was that the toilet was not regarded as a private toilet. * * * In a densely populated business district such a privilege may have constituted a distinct inducement to bring, not only old customers like appellant, but prospective customers into lessee's place of business. * * * But we need not rest our conclusion that appellant was an invitee upon the fact that according to the unqualified evidence, not only customers but everybody was permitted to use the toilet.

The writer cannot subscribe to the theory that a regular customer of long standing is not an invitee to use toilet facilities required by law to be provided by the owner of a restaurant, simply because the customer had not actually made a purchase on the particular occasion of his injury, prior to his injury. It would seem doubtful whether such a doctrine could be applied justly to regular customers of a business which the law does not specifically require to be supplied with toilet facilities, but which does so for the convenience or accommodation of its guests. Women do a great deal of shopping. They sometimes shop all day in their favorite stores and fail to make a single purchase. Shall courts say, as a matter of law, they were not invitees of the business simply because on a particular occasion they had not yet made a purchase? No business concern would contend that they were not invitees unless perchance an injury had occurred. Men frequently, during spare moments, step into a place of business, which they patronize regularly, where drinks, cigars and lunches are sold. They may not have intended definitely to presently make a purchase. They may, nevertheless, become interested, for example, in a new brand of cigars on display which they may purchase then or on some future occasion. Would the owner or operator of the business contend that they were not invitees? We do not think so. Then why should courts arbitrarily say so, as a matter of law? * * *

Manifestly this does not imply that a trespasser or a mere licensee who enters the premises on a personal errand for the advancement of his own interest or benefit is entitled to the protection due to an invitee. In the case of Kinsman v. Barton & Co., 141 Wash. 311, 251 P. 885, that court had occasion to determine what constituted an invitee, and said:

"An invitee is one who is either expressly or impliedly invited onto the premises of another in connection with the business carried on by that other. * * * If one goes into a store with a view of then, or at some other time, doing some business with the store, he is an invitee."
* * *

Of course, if it appears that a person had no intention of presently or in the future becoming a customer he could not be held to be an invitee, as there would be no basis for any thought of mutual benefit.
* * *

The order sustaining the demurrer of the lessee is reversed.

————

1. In Indermaur v. Dames, L.R. 1 C.P. 274 (1866), a journeyman gasfitter came to defendant's sugar refinery to test a patent gas regulator installed there by his employer. He fell down an open and unguarded shaft in the floor, and was injured. It was held that the defendant owed him a duty of reasonable care to make the premises safe for him, because he came "on business which concerns the occupier, and upon his invitation, express or implied."

From this case, those who enter premises "upon business which concerns the occupier" acquired the name of invitees. The early cases left it doubtful whether "business" was used in a commercial sense, to refer to a profit motive, or whether it meant to the courts only the defendant's affairs or concerns, as when we say the thing is my own business, and none of yours. Most of the early decisions did not mention any commercial motive behind the invitation, and were decided solely upon the ground that the defendant had thrown his premises open and "invited" the plaintiff to use them. See Corby v. Hill, 4 C.B., N.S., 556 (1858); Sweeney v. Old Colony & Newport R. Co., 10 Allen (Mass.) 368, 87 Am.Dec. 644 (1865); Gillis v. Pennsylvania R. Co., 59 Pa.St. 129, 87 Am.Dec. 644 (1868).

The Restatement of Torts, in § 332, discarded the term "invitees," and referred instead to "business visitors." The theory adopted was that the duty of affirmative care to make the premises safe is the price that the occupier must pay for the present or prospective economic benefit to be derived from the visitor's presence. It appears to have originated in Campbell, Law of Negligence 63–64 (2d ed. 1878) and, was espoused by the Reporter of the First Restatement in Bohlen, The Basis of Affirmative Obligations in the Law of Tort, 44 Am.L.Reg., N.S., 209, 227 (1905); Bohlen, The Duty of a Landowner

Towards Those Entering His Premises of Their Own Right, 69 U.Pa.L.Rev. 142, 340, 342 (1920).

2. Actual or potential pecuniary benefit is easily made out in the case of customers who intend to buy, or who are merely "shopping." How valid is the attempt to find it in the following situations:

A. Children accompany parents to stores or other places of business, where nothing is to be bought for the child. Anderson v. Cooper, 214 Ga. 164, 104 S.E.2d 90 (1958). Or adult friends accompany the customer. Goldsmith v. Cody, 351 Mich. 380, 88 N.W.2d 268 (1958).

B. Friends meet passengers at a railway station, or see them off. McCann v. Anchor Line, 79 F.2d 338 (2d Cir.1935). Or a potential passenger has not yet obtained a ticket on an airline. Suarez v. Trans World Airlines, Inc., 498 F.2d 612 (6th Cir.1974).

C. Tourists are invited to go through factories. Gilliland v. Bondurant, 51 S.W.2d 559 (Mo.App.1932), aff'd, 332 Mo. 881, 59 S.W.2d 679 (1933).

3. In all of the following instances the plaintiff has been held to be an invitee:

A. Those attending free public meetings. Bunnell v. Waterbury Hosp., 103 Conn. 520, 131 A. 501 (1925) (Salvation Army); Howe v. Ohmart, 7 Ind.App. 32, 33 N.E. 466 (1893) (literary society); Geiger v. Simpson M.E. Church, 174 Minn. 389, 219 N.W. 463 (1928) (social meeting at church).

B. Spectators at public amusements, entering on a free pass. Recreation Centre Corp. v. Zimmerman, 172 Md. 309, 191 A. 233 (1937); Mesa v. Spokane World Exposition, 18 Wash.App. 609, 570 P.2d 157 (1977).

C. Free use of a telephone provided for the public. Randolph v. Great Atl. & Pac. Tea Co., 2 F.Supp. 462 (W.D.Pa.1932), aff'd, 64 F.2d 247 (3d Cir.1933); Ward v. Avery, 113 Conn. 394, 155 A. 502 (1931).

D. Entering a bank to get change for a $20 bill. First Nat'l Bank of Birmingham v. Lowery, 263 Ala. 36, 81 So.2d 284 (1955).

E. Coming to get things advertised to be given away. Roper v. Commercial Fibre Co., 105 N.J.L. 10, 143 A. 741 (1928) (ashes and boxes); Edwards v. Gulf Oil Corp., 69 Ga.App. 140, 24 S.E.2d 843 (1943) (comic books at filling station).

F. Use of state or municipal land open to the public. Caldwell v. Village of Island Park, 304 N.Y. 268, 107 N.E.2d 441 (1952) (park); Lowe v. Gastonia, 211 N.C. 564, 191 S.E. 7 (1937) (golf course); Ashworth v. Clarksburg, 118 W.Va. 476, 190 S.E. 763 (1937) (swimming pool).

G. Visitors in national parks. Adams v. United States, 239 F.Supp. 503 (E.D.Okl.1965); Smith v. United States, 117 F.Supp. 525 (N.D.Cal.1953) (camper).

H. Use of paved strips adjoining the public highway. Concho Constr. Co. v. Oklahoma Natural Gas Co., 201 F.2d 673 (10th Cir.1953); Leighton v. Dean, 117 Me. 40, 102 A. 464 (1917). Or a private way given the appearance of a public thoroughfare. Southern v. Cowan Stone Co., 188 Tenn. 576, 221 S.W.2d 809 (1949); Chronopoulos v. Gil Wyner Co., 334 Mass. 593, 137 N.E.2d 667 (1956); Daisey v. Colonial Parking, Inc., 331 F.2d 777 (D.C.Cir.1963).

4. Most courts have rejected the old rule that plaintiff's status on public land depends on whether he was entering the premises for the purpose for which they were open to the public (invitee) or whether he entered the premises

for an unintended purpose (licensee). See Home Ins. Co. v. Spears, 267 Ark. 704, 590 S.W.2d 71 (1979). In other words, on public land the state, city or county owes to persons coming on the premises a duty to all persons to use reasonable care to keep the premises safe.

5. What about loafers, loiterers, and those who enter merely to get out of the rain, upon premises open for business? Dye v. Rule, 138 Kan. 808, 28 P.2d 758 (1934); Murry Chevrolet Co. v. Cotton, 169 Miss. 521, 152 So. 657 (1934). Or a man who takes a short cut through the defendant's premises? Baird v. Goldberg, 283 Ky. 558, 142 S.W.2d 120 (1940); Cook v. 177 Granite St., 95 N.H. 397, 64 A.2d 327 (1949).

6. In Guilford v. Yale Univ., 128 Conn. 449, 23 A.2d 917 (1942), plaintiff attended a class reunion on the Yale campus. Late at night, seeking to urinate, he proceeded into a dark area, fell over a low retaining wall to a level ten feet below, and was injured. It was held that he was an invitee, without regard to any question of "mutual benefit." Is this one of the purposes for which Old Eli invites its alumni to return to the hallowed elms?

7. See Prosser, Business Visitors and Invitees, 26 Minn.L.Rev. 573 (1942), reprinted in W. Prosser, Selected Topics on the Law of Torts, 243 (1953); James, Tort Liability of Occupiers of Land: Duties Owed to Licensees and Invitees, 63 Yale L.J. 605 (1954).

WHELAN v. VAN NATTA

Court of Appeals of Kentucky, 1964.
382 S.W.2d 205.

[Plaintiff came into defendant's grocery store, and purchased some cigarettes. He then asked about a box for his son. Defendant, who was busy behind the counter, replied, "Go back in the backroom. You will find some back there." Plaintiff went to the rear of the store, and opened the door of the storage room. The room was dark, and the light was not turned on. In hunting around for a box, plaintiff fell into an unseen stair well, and was injured. The defendant testified that he did not warn plaintiff of the existence of the stair well, that the light in the room had been on that morning, and that he did not know whether it was still on when the plaintiff fell.

On these facts, the court gave judgment for the defendant, and plaintiff appealed.]

MONTGOMERY, JUDGE. * * * The trial court held that appellant was a licensee at the time of his fall, to whom appellee owed no duty to provide a safe place, save and except to have abstained from doing any intentional or willful act endangering his safety or knowingly letting appellant run upon a hidden peril. [C] Appellant contends that he entered the store on business with appellee and thus had the status of an invitee and that he still occupied this status when he fell and was injured. The question is: "Did the status of appellant change from invitee to licensee after he made his purchase and went into the storage room to obtain the box?" The status of appellant determines the degree of responsibility of appellee.

Pertinent discussion of the scope of the invitation is contained in Torts, Restatement of the Law, Second, Chapter 13, Section 332, page 67 as follows:

"The possessor of land is subject to liability to another as an invitee only for harm sustained while he is on the land within the scope of his invitation. Thus an invitee ceases to be an invitee after the expiration of a reasonable time within which to accomplish the purpose for which he is invited to enter, or to remain. Whether at the expiration of that time he becomes a trespasser or a licensee will depend upon whether the possessor does or does not consent to his remaining on the land.

"Likewise, the visitor has the status of an invitee only while he is on the part of the land to which his invitation extends—or in other words, the part of the land upon which the possessor gives him reason to believe that his presence is desired for the purpose for which he has come. In determining the area included within the invitation, the purpose for which the land is held open, or the particular business purpose for which the invitation is extended is of great importance.

* * *

"If the invitee goes outside of the area of his invitation, he becomes a trespasser or a licensee, depending upon whether he goes there without the consent of the possessor, or with such consent. Thus one who goes into a shop which occupies part of the building, the rest of which is used as the possessor's residence, is a trespasser if he goes into the residential part of the premises without the shopkeeper's consent; but he is a licensee if the shopkeeper permits him to go to the bathroom, or invites him to pay a social call."

Lerman Brothers v. Lewis, 277 Ky. 334, 126 S.W.2d 461, is an example of the principle stated as applied to similar facts. There, a customer who went into a store for the purpose of doing some shopping and, with permission, proceeded to an alteration room reserved for employees in search of a particular saleswoman and who, upon entering therein, fell down a stairway, was held to be a licensee who was required to take the premises as she found them, and hence, the storekeeper was not liable for her injuries. * * *

Judgment affirmed.

———

1. A toilet is provided for the use of customers, as is usual in theatres, department stores and railway stations. The customer makes use of it, and is injured while doing so. What is his status? Knapp v. Connecticut Theatrical Corp., 122 Conn. 413, 190 A. 291 (1937); Bass v. Hunt, 151 Kan. 740, 100 P.2d 696 (1940).

2. What if the toilet is kept for the use of the occupier and his employees, and is not intended for the public, as is usual in groceries and drug stores; and the customer uses it by permission? Liveright v. Max Lifsitz Furniture Co., 117 N.J.L. 243, 187 A. 583 (1936).

3. What if the visitor is invited to go to an unusual part of the premises, such as a stock room, to make his own selection of goods? Bullock v. Safeway

Stores, 236 F.2d 29 (8th Cir.1956). Cf. Lavitch v. Smith, 224 Or. 498, 356 P.2d 531 (1960) (salesman invited into private office); Crown Cork & Seal Co. v. Kane, 213 Md. 152, 131 A.2d 470 (1957) (truck driver's helper forced to wait, going to smoking room).

4. What if the visitor is injured taking a shortcut to the parking lot? Nicoletti v. Westcor, Inc., 131 Ariz. 140, 639 P.2d 330 (1982).

WILK v. GEORGES
Supreme Court of Oregon, 1973.
267 Or. 19, 514 P.2d 877.

HOWELL, JUSTICE. Plaintiff filed this action for damages for injuries sustained when she slipped and fell on defendant's premises. A jury returned a verdict for the defendant, and plaintiff appeals.

The defendant operates a garden supply and nursery business in southeast Portland. On December 13, 1969, plaintiff and her husband went to defendant's nursery to purchase a live Christmas tree [and plaintiff slipped and fell on a plank walkway].

Defendant testified that he knew the bare planks were "slippery and dangerous" when wet, and for that reason he placed the asphalt material on them. Defendant also testified that he had placed a warning sign by the gate and one on each side of the building. The signs stated (verbatim):

"Please watch where you are going. This is a nursery where plants grow. There is four seasons: summer and winter, cold and hot, rain, icey spots. Flower petals always falling on the floor, leaves always on the floor.

"We are dealing with nature and we are hoping for the best. We are not responsible for anyone get hurt on the premises.

"Thank you."

The plaintiff and her husband testified that they did not see the signs. * * *

Plaintiff's primary assignment of error on this appeal is that the court erred in giving the following instruction:

"If a customer coming on the premises knows of a dangerous condition or if this condition is obvious, there is no duty on the part of the owner to correct or warn of the condition unless, despite the fact that the danger is known or obvious, the owner should anticipate that the dangerous condition will cause physical harm to the customer."

The plaintiff contends that the instruction was erroneous because it stated that a mere warning of a dangerous condition would satisfy the defendant's legal obligation to plaintiff. However, the defendant contends that the instruction is correct because if a prudent landowner should anticipate that an unreasonably dangerous condition will cause harm to a customer even though the danger is known or obvious, he may either (1) correct the condition, or (2) warn the customer and satisfy his duty. * * *

Under the 2 Restatement (Second) 218, Torts § 343A, comment *f*, if the possessor should anticipate that the dangerous condition will cause harm to the invitee despite the latter's knowledge, the possessor's duty of reasonable care *may* require him "to warn the invitee, *or* to take other reasonable steps to protect him * * *." (Emphasis ours.)

Dean Prosser, in the Law of Torts, discusses situations when a warning may or may not be sufficient. He points out that in the usual case there is no obligation to protect the invitee from dangers known to the invitee because it is expected that the visitor will protect himself. Under these circumstances reasonable care will require nothing more than a warning of the danger. However, where the possessor should anticipate an unreasonable risk of harm to the invitee notwithstanding his knowledge or a warning, "something more in the way of precaution may be required." Examples are situations where the invitee's attention may be distracted or conditions such as icy steps which cannot be negotiated with reasonable safety. "In all such cases the jury may find that obviousness, warning or even knowledge is not enough." Prosser, Torts (4th ed.) 394, 395, § 61. * * *

The jury should have been instructed that if they found that the condition that existed was unreasonably dangerous—a condition which cannot be encountered with reasonable safety even if the danger is known and appreciated—the owner of the premises is obligated to do more than post warning signs; he must take reasonable and feasible steps to obviate the danger. * * *

There was evidence in the instant case from which the jury could have found that the defendant as a reasonable man should have anticipated an unreasonable risk or harm to plaintiff notwithstanding the posted signs. He placed the asphalt material on most of the walkways because, as he testified, he knew that the planks were slippery and dangerous when wet. Both the bare planks and the asphalt cover were green in color, which could be misleading to one traversing a walkway looking around for a particular tree or shrub. Under these circumstances slipping and falling by a customer was easily foreseeable. * * *

Reversed and remanded.

––––––––––

1. As the principal case reflects, even though the danger is known to the plaintiff, the defendant may be found to be negligent if it is not too difficult to eliminate the danger and he should reasonably anticipate that the plaintiff might still be injured by it. See, e.g., Hechler v. McDonnell, 42 Cal.App.2d 515, 109 P.2d 426 (1941).

2. A common type of case is that in which the attention of a customer is distracted, as the defendant should reasonably expect it to be, by goods on display, and she fails to observe an entirely obvious obstacle left in the aisle, and falls over it. Is the defendant liable? Jaudon v. F.W. Woolworth Co., 303 F.2d 61 (4th Cir.1962); Yuma Furniture Co. v. Rehwinkel, 8 Ariz.App. 576, 448 P.2d 420 (1968).

3. When an obvious hazard is also a natural one such as snow, ice or rainwater, a number of jurisdictions hold that the invitor owes no duty to any invitee who slips or falls because of the hazard. See Luebeck v. Safeway Stores, Inc., 152 Mont. 88, 446 P.2d 921 (1968); Sidle v. Humphrey, 13 Ohio St.2d 45, 233 N.E.2d 589 (1968). But cf. Schoondyke v. Heil, Heil, Smart & Golee, Inc., 89 Ill.App.3d 640, 44 Ill.Dec. 802, 411 N.E.2d 1168 (1980) (company maintaining a condominium).

4. Should the duty be extended to others with business relationships to the premises? See Morrison v. MGM Grand Hotel, 570 F.Supp. 1449 (D.Nev. 1983); and Note, Innkeeper Liability for Criminal Acts of Third Parties: Should Negligence of the Franchisee Extend to the Franchisor?, 14 Mem.St. U.L.Rev. 189 (1984).

BOYD v. RACINE CURRENCY EXCHANGE, INC.

Supreme Court of Illinois, 1973.
56 Ill.2d 95, 306 N.E.2d 39.

RYAN, JUSTICE. Plaintiff's complaint was dismissed * * * for failure to state a cause of action. The appellate court reversed and remanded the cause to the circuit court. [C] We granted leave to appeal.

This is a wrongful death action against Racine Currency Exchange and Blanche Murphy to recover damages for the death of plaintiff's decedent during an attempted armed robbery. The facts surrounding that event, as alleged in the complaint and admitted by defendants' motion, are: The plaintiff's husband, John Boyd, was present in the Racine Currency Exchange on April 27, 1970, for the purpose of transacting business. While he was there, an armed robber entered and placed a pistol to his head and told Blanche Murphy, the teller, to give him the money or open the door or he would kill Boyd. Blanche Murphy was at that time located behind a bulletproof glass window and partition. She did not comply with the demand but instead fell to the floor. The robber then shot Boyd in the head and killed him. * * *

It is fundamental that there can be no recovery in tort for negligence unless the defendant has breached a duty owed to the plaintiff. [C] The plaintiff contends that a business proprietor has a duty to his invitees to honor criminal demands when failure to do so would subject the invitees to an unreasonable risk. It is claimed that this duty arises from the relationship between the landowner and a business invitee. * * *

We are aware of only two cases which have discussed issues similar to the one with which we are faced here—whether a person injured during the resistance to a crime is entitled to recover from the person who offered the resistance. In Genovay v. Fox, 50 N.J.Super. 538, 143 A.2d 229, rev'd on other grounds, 29 N.J. 436, 149 A.2d 212, a plaintiff who was shot and wounded during the robbery of a bowling alley bar claimed that the proprietor was liable because instead of complying with the criminal demand he stalled the robber and induced resistance by those patrons present. The plaintiff was shot when several patrons attempted to disarm the bandit. The court there balanced the interest of the proprietor in resisting the robbery against the interest of the patrons in not being exposed to bodily harm and held that the complaint stated a cause of action. The court stated: "The value of human life and of the interest of the individual in freedom from serious bodily injury weigh sufficiently heavily in the judicial scales to preclude a determination as a matter of law that they may be disregarded simply because the defendant's activity serves to frustrate the successful accomplishment of a felonious act and to save his property from loss." (50 N.J.Super. at 558, 143 A.2d at 239–240.) The court held that under the circumstances it was for the jury to determine whether defendant's conduct was reasonable.

In Noll v. Marian, 347 Pa. 213, 32 A.2d 18, the court held that no cause of action existed. The plaintiff was present in a bank when an armed robber entered and announced "It's a holdup. Nobody should move." The bank teller, instead of obeying this order, dropped down out of sight. The gunman then opened fire and wounded the plaintiff. The court held that even though the plaintiff might not have been injured if the teller had stood still, the teller did not act negligently in attempting to save himself and his employer's property.

In Lance v. Senior, 36 Ill.2d 516, 224 N.E.2d 231, this court noted that foreseeability alone does not result in the imposition of a duty. "The likelihood of injury, the magnitude of the burden of guarding against it and the consequences of placing the burden upon the defendant, must also be taken into account." 36 Ill.2d at 518, 224 N.E.2d at 233.

In the present case an analysis of those factors leads to the conclusion that no duty to accede to criminal demands should be imposed. The presence of guards and protective devices do not prevent armed robberies. The presence of armed guards would not have prevented the criminal in this case from either seizing the deceased and using him as a hostage or putting the gun to his head. Apparently nothing would have prevented the injury to the decedent except a complete acquiescence in the robber's demand, and whether acquiescence would have spared the decedent is, at best, speculative. We must also note that the demand of the criminal in this case was to give him the money or open the door. A compliance with this alternate demand would have, in turn, exposed the defendant Murphy to danger of bodily harm.

If a duty is imposed on the Currency Exchange to comply with such a demand the same would only inure to the benefit of the criminal without affording the desired degree of assurance that compliance with the demand will reduce the risk to the invitee. In fact, the consequence of such a holding may well be to encourage the use of hostages for such purposes, thereby generally increasing the risk to invitees upon business premises. If a duty to comply exists, the occupier of the premises would have little choice in determining whether to comply with the criminal demand and surrender the money or to refuse the demand and be held liable in a civil action for damages brought by or on behalf of the hostage. The existence of this dilemma and knowledge of it by those who are disposed to commit such crimes will only grant to them additional leverage to enforce their criminal demands. The only persons who will clearly benefit from the imposition of such a duty are the criminals. In this particular case the result may appear to be harsh and unjust, but, for the protection of future business invitees, we cannot afford to extend to the criminal another weapon in his arsenal.

For these reasons we hold that the defendants did not owe to the invitee Boyd a duty to comply with the demand of the criminal.

Accordingly, the judgment of the appellate court will be reversed, and the judgment of the circuit court of Cook County will be affirmed.

Appellate court reversed; circuit court affirmed.

GOLDENHERSH, JUSTICE (dissenting). I dissent. The majority opinion fails to take into account the principles of law clearly enunciated in Restatement (Second) of Torts, secs. 302B and 449, and on the basis of pure conjecture concludes that nothing that defendant's employee could have done would have saved the deceased from death or injury. The majority's polemic on the subject of the hazards which would be created by an application of established legal principles to this case finds little support in logic and none whatsoever in the legal authorities.

This case comes to us only on the pleadings and I agree with the appellate court that "Whether what defendants did or did not do proximately caused the injury that befell plaintiff's decedent, whether Blanche Murphy had the time so she could, under the circumstances alleged, exercise the kind of judgment expected of a person of ordinary prudence, were questions of fact which, from all the evidence, must be decided by a trier of the facts, judge or jury." I would affirm the judgment of the appellate court.

---

1. The nature and extent of a business invitor's duty to protect his invitee from third-party criminal elements has been a much litigated problem in the last decade. The general statement used by most courts to describe this duty is "reasonable care." But when it comes to interpreting what is reasonable care, courts differ. See, e.g., Preuss v. Sambo's of Arizona, Inc., 130 Ariz. 288, 635 P.2d 1210, 1211 (1981); cf. Restatement (Second) of Torts, §§ 343, 343A.

They also differ as to when the question of due care is for the court or jury. Contrast, with the principal case, Kelly v. Kroger Co., 484 F.2d 1362 (10th Cir. 1973). Robbers required the store manager to open an office safe. This caused a silent alarm in the police department, and the police arrived while the robbers were still in the store. One of them ran to the rear of the store, seized the decedent, carried her out on the street with him and shot and killed her as the police approached. It was held to be error to grant a summary judgment for defendant, since the store had previously recognized the need of not startling or alarming robbers and might therefore be found negligent in having the silent alarm attached to the safe door.

2. As suggested, they also differ regarding whether criminal attacks by third persons are "reasonably foreseeable" to their patrons. Foster v. Winston–Salem Joint Venture, 303 N.C. 636, 281 S.E.2d 36 (1981). Prior similar criminal incidents on the premises and the location and nature of the business, are factors considered in determining the foreseeability of criminal attacks on invitees. Isaacs v. Huntington Memorial Hosp., 38 Cal.3d 112, 695 P.2d 653, 211 Cal.Rptr. 356 (1985).

3. The duty to use care may apply to discovery of the dangerous criminal, cf. Townsley v. Cincinnati Gardens, Inc., 39 Ohio App.2d 5, 68 Ohio Ops.2d 72, 314 N.E.2d 409 (1974) (dictum); to becoming aware of his dangerous character, cf. Repka v. Rentalent, Inc., 477 P.2d 470 (Colo.App.1970); or to giving a warning of the danger, cf. Sinn v. Farmers' Deposit Sav. Bank, 300 Pa. 85, 150 A. 163 (1930); or to taking reasonable precaution to prevent an intoxicated patron from harming another, cf. McFarlin v. Hall, 127 Ariz. 220, 619 P.2d 729 (1980); or even to taking reasonable precautions to maintain order in a movie theater to forestall reasonably foreseeable violence to a patron in the parking lot following the movie. Silva v. Showcase Cinemas of Dedham, Inc., 736 F.2d 810 (1st Cir.1984), cert. denied, 469 U.S. 883 (1984). The duty may also extend to adjacent property, particularly entrances to the business premises if the business is aware of a dangerous condition and fails to warn invitees or take precautions. Banks v. Hyatt Corp., 722 F.2d 214 (5th Cir.1984).

4. For fact variations, see Merhi v. Becker, 164 Conn. 516, 325 A.2d 270 (1973) (violent conduct at union picnic, host failed to protect guest); F.W. Woolworth v. Kirby, 293 Ala. 248, 302 So.2d 67 (1974) (duty to control unruly crowd); Jacobsma v. Goldberg's Fashion Forum, 14 Ill.App.3d 710, 303 N.E.2d 226 (1973) (invitee attempted to apprehend felon and was injured); Jenness v. Sheraton–Cadillac Properties, Inc., 48 Mich.App. 723, 211 N.W.2d 106 (1973) (hotel guest picks up prostitute in lobby and is assaulted by her in his room).

5. See Schubowsky v. Hearn Food Store, Inc., 261 So.2d 162 (Fla.1972); Nigido v. First Nat'l Bank, 264 Md. 702, 288 A.2d 127 (1972); Annots, 72 A.L.R.3d 1269 (1976), 75 A.L.R.3d 441 (1977), and 93 A.L.R.3d 999 (1980); Degree, Nature and Extent of Business Proprietor's Duties to Protect Invitees from Criminal Assault, 30 Loy.L.Rev. 1040 (1984).

(D) PERSONS OUTSIDE THE ESTABLISHED CATEGORIES

(1) Children

Courts have been reluctant to apply to child trespassers or licensees the same limited-duty rules that would be applicable to adults. By various legal devices, most of them have imposed on landowners the duty to exercise a higher standard of care toward children. A principal reason for this is society's interest in protecting children from serious injury. See Green, Landholders' Responsibility to Children, 27 Tex.L. Rev. 1 (1948).

The Attractive Nuisance Doctrine. The first major inroad serving to raise the duty owed to child trespassers and licensees developed over a hundred years ago—it was known as the "attractive nuisance" or "turntable" doctrine. See Sioux City & Pac. R. Co. v. Stout, 84 U.S. (17

Wall.) 657 (1873); Keffe v. Milwaukee & St. Paul R. Co., 21 Minn. 207, 18 Am.Rep. 383 (1875). These cases arose when a young child entered on railroad property and was seriously injured while playing on an unlocked turntable. The courts decided that when a landholder sets before young children a temptation that he has reason to believe will lead them into danger, he must use ordinary care to protect them from harm. The courts relied on English precedents where defendants who set traps baited with strong smelling meat on their land were held liable when dogs were lured upon the land and killed in the traps.

On the basis of the turntable decisions, the doctrine acquired the misleading name "attractive nuisance." The word "nuisance" was used because of a supposed analogy to conditions dangerous to children outside the premises. The word "attractive" was applied because courts regarded it as essential that the child be lured or enticed onto the premises.

The development of the doctrine received a set-back from Justice Holmes in United Zinc & Chem. Co. v. Britt, 258 U.S. 268 (1922). In this case, two children trespassed on defendant's land and then discovered a pool of water, apparently clear but actually poisoned with sulfuric acid. The children went into the water and were harmed. Justice Holmes held that the attractive-nuisance doctrine did not apply because the children were not attracted onto the land and induced to trespass in the first instance by the thing that injured them. While at first receiving a favorable response, the *Britt* case was later rejected by a substantial majority of states.

Restatement of Torts § 339. The question of what duty should be owed to child trespassers or licensees occupied considerable time and thought in the preparation of the First Restatement of Torts. The result of these efforts was § 339, which became one of the most influential provisions of the entire Restatement. The authors abandoned the fictitious language of "attractive nuisance" and substituted the title "Artificial Conditions Highly Dangerous to Trespassing Children." As readopted, with only a few modifications, in the Restatement (Second) of Torts, it reads:

"A possessor of land is subject to liability for physical harm to children trespassing thereon caused by an artificial condition upon the land if

(a) the place where the condition exists is one upon which the possessor knows or has reason to know that children are likely to trespass, and

(b) the condition is one of which the possessor knows or has reason to know and which he realizes or should realize will involve an unreasonable risk of death or serious bodily harm to such children, and

(c) the children because of their youth do not discover the condition or realize the risk involved in intermeddling with it or in coming within the area made dangerous by it, and

Dean Francis Bohlen
Reporter for the First Restatement of Torts

(d) the utility to the possessor of maintaining the condition and the burden of eliminating the danger are slight as compared with the risk to children involved, and

(e) the possessor fails to exercise reasonable care to eliminate the danger or otherwise to protect the children."

As one can see, the Restatement rejected the *Britt* case. It is not essential that the child be attracted, lured or enticed on the premises by the thing that injures him. Nevertheless, plaintiff must show that there is a condition upon the land that would cause the possessor to know or at least have reason to know that children will appear. Thus, if children had never previously entered the premises and there was no reason to anticipate that they would, recovery may be denied. See Goll v. Muscara, 211 Pa.Super. 93, 235 A.2d 443 (1967).

Assuming that the owner knows that children are present or trespass in the area, it is not every hazardous condition that will subject him to liability. It must be one that will involve "an unreasonable risk of death or serious bodily harm to the children." Further, the plaintiff must establish that because of his youth he did not "discover the condition or realize the risk involved in meddling with it or coming within an area made dangerous by it." See Pocholec v. Giustina, 224 Or. 245, 355 P.2d 1104 (1960). Naturally, as a child gets older, proof of this becomes more difficult.

Most of the cases allowing recovery have involved children under the age of twelve. A few courts have fixed an arbitrary age limit of fourteen—a rule taken over from decisions relating to the presumed incapacity of children under that age for contributory negligence. On the other hand, a good many decisions have permitted recovery by teenagers when persons of that age might not be expected to appreciate the danger. See generally Annot., 16 A.L.R.3d 25 (1967), (245–page annotation).

Plaintiff must also show that the "utility to the possessor of maintaining the condition and burden of eliminating the danger are slight as compared with the risk for children involved." There has been little careful discussion of this aspect of Restatement of Torts § 339 in the cases. Rather, courts have relied on general language. For example, it is frequently said that "the defendant cannot be an insurer of children's safety."

Finally, the landholder is required to exercise only reasonable care to protect children from the hazard. This means, in many cases involving children who are able to read, that a clear and precise warning about the hazard will discharge the landholder's duty.

See generally Prosser, Trespassing Children, 47 Calif.L.Rev. 427 (1959); Note, Trespassing Children: A Study in Expanding Liability, 20 Vand.L.Rev. 139 (1966).

Special Limitations on the Rules Protecting Children. There are two limitations that some jurisdictions have placed on rules that create a special duty to trespassing children.

First, some courts have eliminated "common hazards" on the ground that any child of sufficient age to be allowed at large by his parents, and so to be likely to trespass, can be expected as a matter of law to appreciate the danger and avoid it, or at least make his own reasonable and intelligent choice. Hazards to which the limitation has most often been applied include drowning in water, dangers of fire, fall from a height or into an excavation, moving vehicles, ordinary visible machinery in motion, sliding or caving soil, and piles of lumber and similar materials. In some jurisdictions, the limitation has not been applied when the defendant knows or has reason to know that the children who are likely to trespass are so young that they cannot be expected to appreciate the danger. King v. Lennen, 53 Cal.2d 340, 348 P.2d 98, 1 Cal.Rptr. 665 (1959) (1½ years, swimming pool); Cockerham v. R.E. Vaughan, Inc., 82 So.2d 890 (Fla.1955) (2½ years, excavation); and the Restatement (Second) of Torts takes this position.

The common-hazard limitation has also been eliminated where there is some special and concealed danger, even though an older child is injured. Cooper v. Reading, 392 Pa. 452, 140 A.2d 792 (1958) (deep hole in muddy pool); Cicero State Bank v. Dolese & Shepard Co., 298 Ill.App. 290, 18 N.E.2d 574 (1939) (scum over pool, looking like solid ground).

The present tendency is to discard this concept as a fixed rule, and to include all these conditions with the others. The fact that the condition is one which any child likely to trespass can be expected to understand and appreciate is, however, still important, and may often defeat recovery.

A second and more enduring limitation eliminates hazards that arise in the state of nature. Courts have expressed a continuing reluctance to place a burden on the landholder to protect children from these conditions. An example is Loney v. McPhillips, 268 Or. 378, 521 P.2d 340 (1974) (windswept ocean cave particularly dangerous at high tide). See also Fitch v. Selwyn Village, 234 N.C. 632, 68 S.E.2d 255 (1951); Anneker v. Quinn–Robbins Co., 80 Idaho 1, 323 P.2d 1073 (1958). The Restatement (Second) of Torts expressed "no opinion" on whether § 339 should apply to natural conditions.

Child Licensees. While most of the cases concerning the attractive nuisance doctrine or the Restatement of Torts § 339 involve child trespassers, there are some cases that focus upon child licensees. The special rules may provide added protection for them. Thus, there may be an obligation to inform a child licensee about a risk when there would be no duty with regard to an adult. Equally important, if the child licensee is very young, a court may deem a mere warning an insufficient protection in a context when it would be sufficient if the victim were an adult. See Shannon v. Butler Homes, Inc., 102 Ariz. 312, 428 P.2d 990 (1967); Di Gildo v. Caponi, 18 Ohio St.2d 125, 47 Ohio Ops.2d 282, 247 N.E.2d 732 (1969); Restatement (Second) of Torts § 343B, Comment b; Annot., 26 A.L.R.3d 317 (1969).

(2) Persons Privileged to Enter Irrespective of Landowner's Consent

Public employees or officials do not fit very well into any of the categories that the law has established for the classification of visitors. They are not trespassers, since they are privileged to enter. This privilege is independent of any permission, consent or license of the occupier; they would be privileged to enter and could insist upon doing so even if the landholder made an active objection. They normally do not come for any of the purposes for which the premises are held open to the public, and frequently they do not enter for any benefit of the occupier, or under circumstances which would justify any expectation that the place has been prepared to receive them.

Many courts have still struggled to place public officers and employees within the category of invitees. Some public officers enter for a purpose connected with defendant's business, and are essential to it, since without them it could not legally be carried on. This is true, for example, of sanitary and safety inspectors, who are commonly held to be invitees. Swift & Co. v. Schuster, 192 F.2d 615 (10th Cir.1951); Atchley v. Berlen, 87 Ill.App.3d 61, 42 Ill.Dec. 468, 408 N.E.2d 1177 (1980); Annot., 28 A.L.R.3d 891 (1969). Economic advantage may also be made out in the case of a garbage collector, a city water-meter reader or a postman. Finnegan v. Fall River Gas Works Co., 159 Mass. 311, 34 N.E. 523 (1893); Paubel v. Hitz, 339 Mo. 274, 96 S.W.2d 369 (1936); Annot., 28 A.L.R.3d 1344 (1969). Some courts have found an economic advantage to the landholder operative in a visit from a tax collector. Wilson v. Union Iron Works Dry Dock Co., 167 Cal. 539, 140 P. 250 (1914); Anderson & Nelson Distilling Co. v. Hair, 103 Ky. 196, 44 S.W. 658 (1898).

On the other hand, both firemen and policemen have generally been held to enter under a bare license conferred by the law, and so to be no more than licensees. This means, however, that if defendant knows they are present, he must warn them of known dangers which they are unlikely to discover. James v. Cities Serv. Oil Co., 66 Ohio App. 87, 31 N.E.2d 872 (1939), aff'd, 140 Ohio St. 314, 23 Ohio Ops. 571, 43 N.E.2d 276 (1942); Rogers v. Cato Oil & Grease Co., 396 P.2d 1000 (Okl.1964).

One factor having some influence in the refusal to include firemen and policemen in the invitee category has been the fact that they are usually covered either by worker's compensation or by pension funds and thus will be compensated for their injuries. See Scheurer v. Trustees of Open Bible Church, 175 Ohio St. 163, 192 N.E.2d 38 (1963).

A practical reason for treating policemen and firemen as licensees is that they often appear at unexpected times and in unexpected places, and it might place an inordinate burden on the landholder to provide for their safety.

The general frustration with categorizing policemen and firemen into common law categories has prompted some courts to abandon the category system as applied to public officers and simply apply a general reasonable-care, negligence standard. See Mounsey v. Ellard, 297 N.E.2d 43 (Mass.1973); Armstrong v. Mailand, 284 N.W.2d 343 (Minn. 1979). Recently, Michigan refused to adopt the firemen's rule in Kreski v. Modern Wholesale Elec. Supply Co., 151 Mich.App. 376, 390 N.W.2d 244 (1986); and Oregon abolished it in Christensen v. Murphy, 296 Or. 610, 678 P.2d 1210 (1984).

If the standard of care is enlarged with regard to policemen and firemen, some interesting questions arise. For example, suppose a landholder was negligent in creating the fire that injured a fireman. Should the fireman be able to recover from the landholder for an injury of that kind? See Washington v. Atlantic Richfield Co., 66 Ill.2d 103, 5 Ill.Dec. 143, 361 N.E.2d 282 (1976). Should the so-called firemen's rule protect one who ships chemicals in containers it might have known enhanced fire risk? See Mahoney v. Carus Chem. Co., 102 N.J. 564, 510 A.2d 4 (1986). On the other hand, suppose a policeman is killed by a burglar while the officer was making a nighttime security check on defendant's property. Defendant had disconnected the power from an electric light in the area. Assuming that if the area had been properly lighted the event would not have occurred, should the defendant be liable in a wrongful death action? See Fancil v. Q.S.E. Foods, Inc., 60 Ill.2d 552, 328 N.E.2d 538 (1975).

Thus, at least five different answers have been given to the question of how public officials are to be treated. They have been: (1) classified as licensees, (2) classified as invitees, (3) held as entitled to the duty owed to licensees or invitees depending upon the highest duty which the landowner already owed to some other person at that place and time, (4) given a separate classification, with a special duty owed to it, and (5) held entitled to reasonable care under all the circumstances.

Private Persons. The same kinds of problems, with some additional complications, exist in regard to private individuals who come on the premises for self-protection or to rescue or aid someone. They may be privileged as a matter of law to enter, regardless of the landowner's consent. Should the duty owed to them be derivative, depending upon the classification of the person being rescued? What would be the effect of that person's contributory negligence? If the duty owed is an independent one owed to the rescuer in his own right, do all of the possible answers listed in the previous paragraph apply? Perhaps all of this is an appropriate introduction to the next Section.

See, in general, Bohlen, The Duty of a Landowner Towards Those Entering His Premises of their Own Right, 69 U.Pa.L.Rev. 340 (1921); Note, Landowner's Negligence Liability to Persons Entering as a Matter of Right or Under a Privilege of Private Necessity, 19 Vand.L.Rev. 407 (1966); Comment, 66 Calif.L.Rev. 585 (1978).

(E) REJECTION OR MERGING OF CATEGORIES

ROWLAND v. CHRISTIAN
Supreme Court of California, 1968.
69 Cal.2d 108, 443 P.2d 561, 70 Cal.Rptr. 97.

PETERS, JUSTICE. Plaintiff appeals from a summary judgment for defendant Nancy Christian in this personal injury action.

[The evidence was that plaintiff was a social guest in defendant's apartment; that he asked to use the bathroom; and that while there he was injured when a cracked handle of the cold water faucet on the basin broke and severed tendons and nerves on his right hand. Also that defendant had known for two weeks that the handle was cracked and had complained to the manager of the building, but that she did not say anything to the plaintiff as to its condition.]

One of the areas where this court and other courts have departed from the fundamental concept that a man is liable for injuries caused by his carelessness is with regard to the liability of a possessor of land for injuries to persons who have entered upon that land. It has been suggested that the special rules regarding liability of the possessor of land are due to historical considerations stemming from the high place which land has traditionally held in English and American thought, the dominance and prestige of the landowning class in England during the formative period of the rules governing the possessor's liability, and the heritage of feudalism. [C]

[The court reviewed the various confusing rules and exceptions that had been applied in California to licensees.]

The cases dealing with the active negligence and the trap exceptions are indicative of the subtleties and confusion which have resulted from application of the common law principles governing the liability of the possessor of land. Similar confusion and complexity exist as to the definitions of trespasser, licensee, and invitee. [C]

In refusing to adopt the rules relating to the liability of a possessor of land for the law of admiralty, the United States Supreme Court stated: "The distinctions which the common law draws between licensee and invitee were inherited from a culture deeply rooted to the land, a culture which traced many of its standards to a heritage of feudalism. In an effort to do justice in an industrialized urban society, with its complex economic and individual relationships, modern commonlaw courts have found it necessary to formulate increasingly subtle verbal

California Supreme Court
Front row: McComb, Traynor, C.J., Peters
Back row: Burke, Tobriner, Mosk, Sullivan

refinements, to create subclassifications among traditional commonlaw categories, and to delineate fine gradations in the standards of care which the landowner owes to each. Yet even within a single jurisdiction, the classifications and subclassifications bred by the common law have produced confusion and conflict. As new distinctions have been spawned, older ones have become obscured. Through this semantic morass the common law has moved, unevenly and with hesitation, towards 'imposing on owners and occupiers a single duty of reasonable care in all circumstances.' " (Footnotes omitted.) (Kermarec v. Compagnie Generale, 358 U.S. 625, 630–631.) * * *

There is another fundamental objection to the approach to the question of the possessor's liability on the basis of the common law distinctions based upon the status of the injured party as a trespasser, licensee, and invitee, the immunities from liability predicated upon where the underlying principles governing liability are based upon proper considerations. Whatever may have been the historical justifications for the common law distinctions, it is clear that those distinctions are not justified in the light of our modern society and that the complexity and confusion which has arisen is not due to difficulty in applying the original common law rules—they are all too easy to apply in their original formulation—but is due to the attempts to apply just rules in our modern society within the ancient terminology.

Without attempting to labor all of the rules relating to the possessor's liability, it is apparent that the classifications of trespasser, licensee, and invitee, the immunities from liability predicated upon those classifications, and the exceptions to those immunities, often do not reflect the major factors which should determine whether immunity should be conferred upon the possessor of land. Some of those factors, including the closeness of the connection between the injury and the defendant's conduct, the moral blame attached to the defendant's conduct, the policy of preventing future harm, and the prevalence and availability of insurance, bear little, if any, relationship to the classifications of trespasser, licensee and invitee and the existing rules conferring immunity.

Although in general there may be a relationship between the remaining factors and the classifications of trespasser, licensee, and invitee, there are many cases in which no such relationship may exist. Thus, although the foreseeability of harm to an invitee would ordinarily seem greater than the foreseeability of harm to a trespasser, in a particular case the opposite may be true. The same may be said of the issue of certainty of injury. The burden to the defendant and consequences to the community of imposing a duty to exercise care with resulting liability for breach may often be greater with respect to trespassers than with respect to invitees, but it by no means follows that this is true in every case. In many situations, the burden will be the same, i.e., the conduct necessary upon the defendant's part to meet the burden of exercising due care as to invitees will also meet his burden with respect to licensees and trespassers. The last of the major factors, the cost of insurance, will, of course, vary depending upon the rules of liability adopted, but there is no persuasive evidence that applying ordinary principles of negligence law to the land occupier's liability will materially reduce the prevalence of insurance due to increased cost or even substantially increase the cost.

Considerations such as these have led some courts in particular situations to reject the rigid common law classifications and to approach the issue of the duty of the occupier on the basis of ordinary principles of negligence. [Cc] And the common law distinctions after thorough study have been repudiated by the jurisdiction of their birth. (Occupiers' Liability Act, 1957, 5 and 6 Eliz. 2, ch. 31.)

A man's life or limb does not become less worthy of protection by the law nor a loss less worthy of compensation under the law because he has come upon the land of another without permission or with permission but without a business purpose. Reasonable people do not ordinarily vary their conduct depending upon such matters, and to focus upon the status of the injured party as a trespasser, licensee, or invitee in order to determine the question whether the landowner has a duty of care, is contrary to our modern social mores and humanitarian values. The common law rules obscure rather than illuminate the proper considerations which should govern determination of the question of duty. * * *

Once the ancient concepts as to the liability of the occupier of land are stripped away, the status of the plaintiff relegated to its proper place in determining such liability, and ordinary principles of negligence applied, the result in the instant case presents no substantial difficulties. As we have seen, when we view the matters presented on the motion for summary judgment as we must, we must assume defendant Miss Christian was aware that the faucet handle was defective and dangerous, that the defect was not obvious, and that plaintiff was about to come in contact with the defective condition, and under the undisputed facts she neither remedied the condition nor warned plaintiff of it. Where the occupier of land is aware of a concealed condition involving in the absence of precautions an unreasonable risk of harm to those coming in contact with it and is aware that a person on the premises is about to come in contact with it, the trier of fact can reasonably conclude that a failure to warn or to repair the condition constitutes negligence. Whether or not a guest has a right to expect that his host will remedy dangerous conditions on his account, he should reasonably be entitled to rely upon a warning of the dangerous condition so that he, like the host, will be in a position to take special precautions when he comes in contact with it. * * *

The judgment is reversed.

BURKE, J. I dissent. In determining the liability of the occupier or owner of land for injuries, the distinctions between trespassers, licensees and invitees have been developed and applied by the courts over a period of many years. They supply a reasonable and workable approach to the problems involved, and one which provides the degree of stability and predictability so highly prized in the law. The unfortunate alternative, it appears to me, is the route taken by the majority in their opinion in this case; that such issues are to be decided on a case by case basis under the application of the basic law of negligence, bereft of the guiding principles and precedent which the law has heretofore attached by virtue of the relationship of the parties to one another.

Liability for negligence turns upon whether a duty of care is owed, and if so, the extent thereof. Who can doubt that the corner grocery, the large department store, or the financial institution owes a greater duty of care to one whom it has invited to enter its premises as a prospective customer of its wares or services than it owes to a trespasser seeking to enter after the close of business hours and for a nonbusiness or even an antagonistic purpose? I do not think it unreasonable or unfair that a social guest (classified by the law as a licensee, as was plaintiff here) should be obliged to take the premises in the same condition as his host finds them or permits them to be. Surely a homeowner should not be obliged to hover over his guests with warnings of possible dangers to be found in the condition of the home (e.g., waxed floors, slipping rugs, toys in unexpected places, etc., etc.). Yet today's decision appears to open the door to potentially unlimited liability despite the purpose and circumstances motivating the plaintiff in entering the premises of another, and despite the caveat of the majority that the status of the parties may "have some bearing on the question of liability * * *," whatever the future may show that language to mean.

In my view, it is not a proper function of this court to overturn the learning, wisdom and experience of the past in this field. Sweeping modifications of tort liability law fall more suitably within the domain of the Legislature, before which all affected interests can be heard and which can enact statutes providing uniform standards and guidelines for the future.

I would affirm the judgment for defendant.

McComb, J., concurred.

––––––

1. Criticism of the categories as a vehicle for determining the duty a possessor of land owes to a visitor or intruder is not new. See Bohlen, The Duty of a Landholder Towards Those Entering His Premises of Their Own Right, 69 U.Pa.L.Rev. 142 (1921), also in F. Bohlen, Studies in the Law of Torts, 136, 163 (1926); Comment, The Outmoded Distinction Between Licensees and Invitees, 22 Mo.L.Rev. 186 (1957). See also Lord Denning in Dunster v. Abbott, [1953] 2 All E.R. 1572, 1574 (C.A.).

2. In 1957, as the result of a Report of the Law Reform Committee, an Occupiers' Liability Act, 5 & 6 Eliz. II, c. 31, was adopted in England. The Act declared the occupier's common duty of care to all lawful visitors (thus excluding trespassers) upon his land, and enumerated various factors to be considered in determining whether that duty had been discharged. The Eng-

lish law was subsequently supplemented by a duty to treat all trespassers with "common humanity." Keeler, Recent Developments in the Law of Occupiers and Trespassers, 46 Aust.L.J. 444 (1972); Seepersad, Duty of Care, 122 New L.J. 1004, 1006 (1972).

3. Rowland v. Christian has been followed by a number of courts. For example, Webb v. Sitka, 561 P.2d 731 (Alaska 1977); Mile High Fence Co. v. Radovich, 175 Colo. 537, 489 P.2d 308 (1971); Pickard v. Honolulu, 51 Hawaii 134, 452 P.2d 445 (1969); Richard v. Sonnier, 363 So.2d 961 (La.App.1978); Poulin v. Colby College, 402 A.2d 846 (Me.1979); Pridgen v. Boston Hous. Auth., 364 Mass. 696, 308 N.E.2d 467 (1974); Peterson v. Balach, 294 Minn. 161, 199 N.W.2d 639 (1972); Ouellette v. Blanchard, 116 N.H. 552, 364 A.2d 631 (1976); Basso v. Miller, 40 N.Y.2d 233, 386 N.Y.S.2d 564, 352 N.E.2d 868 (1976); Mariorenzi v. Di Ponte, Inc., 114 R.I. 294, 333 A.2d 127 (1975); Smith v. Arbaugh's Restaurant, Inc., 152 App.D.C. 86, 469 F.2d 97 (1972), cert. denied, 412 U.S. 939 (1973); Cates v. Beauregard Elec. Coop., Inc., 328 So.2d 367 (La. 1976), cert. denied, 429 U.S. 833 (1976).

4. A number of courts have sought middle ground by blurring the distinctions between categories of licensees and invitees, and requiring a uniform standard of care toward individuals invited onto the property. In Wood v. Camp, 284 So.2d 691 (Fla.1973), the Supreme Court of Florida included all invited persons in the category of invitees. See also Poulin v. Colby College, 402 A.2d 846 (Me.1979); Peterson v. Balach, 294 Minn. 161, 199 N.W.2d 639 (1972).

In Mounsey v. Ellard, 363 Mass. 693, 297 N.E.2d 43 (1973), the licensee-invitee categories were merged completely. See also Antoniewicz v. Reszcynski, 70 Wis.2d 836, 236 N.W.2d 1 (1975). On occasion, the change has been accomplished by the legislature. See Conn.Gen.Stat. § 5255.7(a).

5. Although about 16 states have either abolished the categories altogether or merged the categories of persons lawfully on the land, over 20 states since *Rowland* (1968) have affirmed their retention of the categories. Some have directly confronted the issue: Whaley v. Lawing, 352 So.2d 1090 (Ala.1977); Bailey v. Pennington, 406 A.2d 44 (Del.1979); Huyck v. Hecla Mining Co., 101 Idaho 299, 612 P.2d 142 (1980); Gerchberg v. Loney, 223 Kan. 446, 576 P.2d 593 (1978); Murphy v. Baltimore Gas & Elec. Co., 290 Md. 186, 428 A.2d 459 (1981) (trespassers only); Buchanan v. Prickett & Son, Inc., 203 Neb. 684, 279 N.W.2d 855 (1979); Moore v. Denune & Pipic, Inc., 26 Ohio St.2d 125, 269 N.E.2d 599 (1971); Younce v. Ferguson, 106 Wash.2d 658, 724 P.2d 991 (1986). Other courts have not directly confronted the issue, but retain the common law classifications. E.g., Nicoletti v. Westcor, Inc., 131 Ariz. 140, 639 P.2d 330 (1982); Champlin v. Walker, 249 N.W.2d 839 (Iowa 1977); Taylor v. Baker, 279 Or. 139, 566 P.2d 884 (1977); Annot., 22 A.L.R.4th 294 (1983).

6. While there is considerable agreement that the general negligence standard should be applied to all persons invited or permitted on the premises, there is less accord as to how the trespasser should be handled. Some cases deliberately apply it to a trespasser. In Mark v. Pacific Gas & Elec. Co., 7 Cal. 3d 170, 496 P.2d 1276, 101 Cal.Rptr. 908 (1972), a college student was electrocuted when he attempted to unscrew a street lamp located outside his apartment bedroom window. The Supreme Court of California reaffirmed that the negligence standard would be applied to trespassers. Many of the cases adopting *Rowland* have not involved trespass, and the Supreme Court of

Florida backed down on this issue. See Wood v. Camp, 284 So.2d 691 (Fla. 1973).

7. How far do the relative functions of judge and jury play a part in these decisions?

8. See, generally, Miner, Trespasser Beware: The Application of Occupier—Entrant Law, 51 U.Cin.L.Rev. 73 (1982); Hughes, Duties to Trespassers: A Comparative Survey and Reevaluation, 68 Yale L.J. 633 (1959); Note, Abrogation of Common–Law Entrant Classes of Trespasser, Licensee, and Invitee, 25 Vand.L.Rev. 623 (1972); Note, Invitees, Licensees and Trespassers—A Trend Towards Abolishing Classification of Entrants, 76 W.Va.L.Rev. 202 (1973).

3. LESSOR AND LESSEE

BORDERS v. ROSEBERRY
Supreme Court of Kansas, 1975.
216 Kan. 486, 532 P.2d 1366.

PRAGER, JUSTICE. * * * The sole point raised on this appeal by the plaintiff, Gary D. Borders, is that the trial court committed reversible error in concluding as a matter of law that a landlord of a single-family house is under no obligation or duty to a social guest of his tenant to repair or remedy a known condition whereby water dripped from the roof onto the front steps of a house fronting north, froze and caused the social guest to slip and fall.

Traditionally the law in this country has placed upon the lessee as the person in possession of the land the burden of maintaining the premises in a reasonably safe condition to protect persons who come upon the land. It is the tenant as possessor who, at least initially, has the burden of maintaining the premises in good repair. [Cc]

The relationship of landlord and tenant is not in itself sufficient to make the landlord liable for the tortious acts of the tenant. [Cc]

When land is leased to a tenant, the law of property regards the lease as equivalent to a sale of the premises for the term. The lessee acquires an estate in the land, and becomes for the time being the owner and occupier, subject to all of the responsibilities of one in possession, both to those who enter onto the land and to those outside of its boundaries. Professor William L. Prosser in his Law of Torts, 4th Ed. § 63, points out that in the absence of agreement to the contrary, the lessor surrenders both possession and control of the land to the lessee, retaining only a reversionary interest; and he has no right even to enter without the permission of the lessee. There is therefore, as a general rule, no liability upon the landlord, either to the tenant or to others entering the land, for defective conditions existing at the time of the lease.

The general rule of non-liability has been modified, however, by a number of exceptions which have been created as a matter of social policy. Modern case law on the subject today usually limits the liability of a landlord for injuries arising from a defective condition existing at the time of the lease to six recognized exceptions. These exceptions are as follows:

1. Undisclosed dangerous conditions known to lessor and un-known to the lessee.

This exception is stated in Restatement (Second) of Torts § 358 as follows:

"§ 358. Undisclosed Dangerous Conditions Known to Lessor

"(1) A lessor of land who conceals or fails to disclose to his lessee any condition, whether natural or artificial, which involves unreasona-ble risk of physical harm to persons on the land, is subject to liability to the lessee and others upon the land with the consent of the lessee or his sublessee for physical harm caused by the condition after the lessee has taken possession, if

"(a) the lessee does not know or have reason to know of the condition or the risk involved, and

"(b) the lessor knows or has reason to know of the condition, and realizes or should realize the risk involved, and has reason to expect that the lessee will not discover the condition or realize the risk.

"(2) If the lessee [sic] actively conceals the condition, the liability stated Subsection (1) continues until the lessee discovers it and has reasonable opportunity to take effective precautions against it. Other-wise the liability continues only until the vendee has had reasonable opportunity to discover the condition and to take such precautions."

*   *   *

It should be pointed out that this exception applies [in Kansas] only to latent conditions and not to conditions which are patent or reasona-bly discernible to the tenant. [C]

2. Conditions dangerous to persons outside of the premises.

This exception is stated in Restatement (Second) of Torts § 379 as follows:

"§ 379. Dangerous Conditions Existing When Lessor Transfers Possession

"A lessor of land who transfers its possession in a condition which he realizes or should realize will involve unreasonable risk of physical harm to others outside of the land, is subject to the same liability for physical harm subsequently caused to them by the condition as though he had remained in possession."

The theory of liability under such circumstances is that where a nuisance dangerous to persons outside the leased premises (such as the traveling public or persons on adjoining property) exists on the prem-ises at the time of the lease, the lessor should not be permitted to escape liability by leasing the premises to another.   *   *   *

3. Premises leased for admission of the public. [§ 359]

The third exception arises where land is leased for a purpose involving the admission of the public. The cases usually agree that in that situation the lessor is under an affirmative duty to exercise reasonable care to inspect and repair the premises before possession is transferred, to prevent any unreasonable risk or harm to the public who may enter. * * *

4. Parts of land retained in lessor's control which lessee is entitled to use. [§§ 360, 361]

When different parts of a building, such as an office building or an apartment house, are leased to several tenants, the approaches and common passageways normally do not pass to the tenant, but remain in the possession and control of the landlord. Hence the lessor is under an affirmative obligation to exercise reasonable care to inspect and repair those parts of the premises for the protection of the lessee, members of his family, his employees, invitees, guests, and others on the land in the right of the tenant. * * *

5. Where lessor contracts to repair. [§ 357]

At one time the law in most jurisdictions and in Kansas was that if a landlord breached his contract to keep the premises in good repair, the only remedy of the tenant was an action in contract in which damages were limited to the cost of repair or loss of rental value of the property. Neither the tenant nor members of his family nor his guests were permitted to recover for personal injuries suffered as a result of the breach of the agreement. [C] In most jurisdictions this rule has been modified and a cause of action given in tort to the injured person to enable him recovery for his personal injuries. * * *

In Steele v. Latimer, 214 Kan. 329, 521 P.2d 304, we held that the provisions of a municipal housing code prescribing minimum housing standards are deemed by implication to become a part of a lease of urban residential property, giving rise to an implied warranty on the part of the lessor that the premises are habitable and safe for human occupancy in compliance with the pertinent code provisions and will remain so for the duration of the tenancy. Such an implied warranty creates a contractual obligation on the lessor to repair the premises to keep them in compliance with the municipal housing standards as set forth in a municipal housing code.

6. Negligence by lessor in making repairs. [§ 362]

When the lessor does in fact attempt to make repairs, whether he is bound by a covenant to do so or not, and fails to exercise reasonable care, he is held liable for injuries to the tenant or others on the premises in his right, if the tenant neither knows nor should know that the repairs have been negligently made. * * * [The court found the first five exceptions not applicable in this case.]

[Exception six] comes into play only when the lessee lacks knowledge that the purported repairs have not been made or have been negligently made. Here it is undisputed that the tenant had full knowledge of the icy condition on the steps created by the absence of guttering. It seems to us that the landlord could reasonably assume that the tenant would inform his guest about the icy condition on the front steps. We have concluded that the factual circumstances do not establish liability on the landlord on the basis of negligent repairs made by him.

In his brief counsel for the plaintiff vigorously argues that the law should be changed to make the landlord liable for injuries resulting from a defective condition on the leased premises where the landlord has knowledge of that condition. He has not cited any authority in support of his position, nor does he state with particularity how the existing law pertaining to a landlord's liability should be modified. We do not believe that the facts and circumstances of this case justify a departure from the established rules of law discussed above.

The judgment of the district court is affirmed.

———

1. The principal case presents a reasonably accurate picture of the law in most states in regard to the duty in tort of a lessor toward his lessee and the lessee's guests: a general rule of "no duty," modified by a series of exceptions.

2. All courts agree that the lessor must disclose concealed dangerous conditions existing at the time of the transfer of possession, of which he has knowledge. The liability extends not only to the tenant, and the members of his family, but to his employees, his social guests and others on the premises in his right, and to a subtenant to whom he leases the premises. Most of the courts have said that it is sufficient that the lessor has information that would lead a reasonable person to conclude that the danger may exist, and that if he does he must disclose such information to the tenant. See Caesar v. Karutz, 60 N.Y. 229, 19 Am.Rep. 164 (1875) ("reasonable notice"); Cutter v. Hamlen, 147 Mass. 471, 18 N.E. 397 (1888) ("should have known"); Rhoades v. Seidel, 139 Mich. 608, 102 N.W. 1025 (1905) ("ought to have known"). The Supreme Court of California recently held that a landlord may be strictly liable for injuries resulting from latent defects in the premises existing at the time of the lease. Becker v. IRM Corp., 38 Cal.3d 454, 698 P.2d 116, 213 Cal.Rptr. 213 (1985) infra page 792.

3. Until about 1965, a majority of the courts that had considered the question held that when a landlord's covenant or contract to repair is broken, the only remedy is a contract action for the breach. An increasing number of the courts worked out a liability in tort for the lessor's failure to perform a contract to repair. The lessor thus becomes liable for resulting injuries to the tenant and also to members of his family, and to others, such as his guests, who are on the premises in the right of the tenant, and even to those outside of the land. The First Restatement of Torts, § 357, adopted the minority position, and this has been continued in the Second Restatement. It is now the majority position.

4. Several states now have statutes, such as the Tenement Act in Michaels v. Brookchester, Inc., 26 N.J. 379, 140 A.2d 199 (1958), which require the owners of certain types of dwellings to keep them in repair. The New York Multiple Dwelling Law, § 78, expressly provides for civil liability for injuries resulting from failure to repair. Even in the absence of an express provision, the statutes may be construed to result in civil liability. Compare Daniels v. Brunston, 9 N.J.Super. 294, 76 A.2d 73 (1950), aff'd, 7 N.J. 102, 80 A.2d 547

(1951), with Johnson v. Carter, 218 Iowa 587, 255 N.W. 864 (1934). See also Feuerstein and Shestack, Landlord and Tenant—The Statutory Duty to Repair, 45 Ill.L.Rev. 205 (1950). And see Restatement (Second) of Property § 17.6, providing for liability in this situation.

5. An important exception to the no-duty rule is the obligation on the landlord to use reasonable care to maintain common facilities and areas within his control. This usually includes common stairways, front steps and other passage ways. However, it may also encompass other "common facilities" under the lessor's control such as water pipes and air conditioning units. See Coleman v. Steinberg, 54 N.J. 58, 253 A.2d 167 (1969). Should the lessor owe this same duty to a social guest of a lessee? What about the argument that this would make the lessor's duty to the social guest greater than the lessee's? See Taneian v. Meghrigian, 15 N.J. 267, 104 A.2d 689 (1954). See Annot., 65 A.L.R.3d 14 (1976).

6. When premises are leased in an existing condition that is dangerous to persons on the highway, the lessor is under a duty that he cannot delegate to the tenant. See, for example, Isham v. Broderick, 89 Minn. 397, 95 N.W. 224 (1903). This is also true when the condition is a private nuisance. Wunder v. McLean, 134 Pa. 334, 19 A. 749 (1890) (cesspool); Mylander v. Beimschla, 102 Md. 689, 62 A. 1038 (1906) (downspout).

7. What if the lessor does in fact repair, and does it negligently? See Bartlett v. Taylor, 351 Mo. 1060, 174 S.W.2d 844 (1943).

8. See generally James, Tort Risks of Ownership: How Affected by Lease or Sale, 28 Conn.B.J. 127 (1954); Eldredge, Landlord's Tort Liability for Disrepair, 84 U.Pa.L.Rev. 467 (1936), reprinted in Eldredge, Modern Tort Problems, 113 (1941). There are very comprehensive treatments in Love, Landlord's Liability for Defective Premises: Caveat Lessee, Negligence, or Strict Liability, 1975 Wis.L.Rev. 19; and Browder, The Taming of a Duty—the Tort Liability of Landlords, 81 Mich.L.Rev. 99 (1982).

PAGELSDORF v. SAFECO INS. CO. OF AMERICA

Supreme Court of Wisconsin, 1979.
91 Wis.2d 734, 284 N.W.2d 55.

CALLOW, JUSTICE. We dispose of this appeal by addressing the single issue of the scope of a landlord's duty toward his tenant's invitee who is injured as a result of defective premises. Abrogating the landlord's general cloak of immunity at common law, we hold that a landlord must exercise ordinary care toward his tenant and others on the premises with permission.

The defendant Richard J. Mahnke owned a two-story, two-family duplex. There were four balcony porches: one in front and one in back of each flat. Mahnke rented the upper unit to John and Mary Katherine Blattner.   * * *

[Plaintiff Pagelsdorf was assisting Mrs. Blattner move some furniture. He leaned against the railing for the second-floor front balcony, and it collapsed with him. The railing had a dryrot condition and should have been replaced. The trial court put the case to the jury in terms of plaintiff's being a licensee of Mahnke, the landlord, and the jury found by special verdict that he had no knowledge of the defective condition of the railing. Judgment was entered on the verdict, dismissing the complaint.]

The question on which the appeal turns is whether the trial court erred in failing to instruct the jury that Mahnke owed Pagelsdorf a duty to exercise ordinary care in maintaining the premises.

Prior to December 10, 1975, the duty of an occupier of land toward visitors on the premises was determined in Wisconsin law on a sliding scale according to the status of the visitor. * * * In Antoniewicz v. Reszcynski, 70 Wis.2d 836, 854–55, 236 N.W.2d 1, 10 (1975), we abolished, prospectively, the distinction between the different duties owed by an occupier to licensees and to invitees. * * *

The classification of visitors identified the degree of duty of the possessor or occupier of the premises. [C] When the property is leased, the duty of the landlord was controlled by a different rule: That, with certain exceptions, a landlord is not liable for injuries to his tenants and their visitors resulting from defects in the premises. [C] The general rule of nonliability was based on the concept of a lease as a conveyance of property and the consequent transfer of possession and control of the premises to the tenant. [Cc]

There are exceptions to this general rule of nonliability. * * * The rule of nonliability persists despite a decided trend away from application of the general rule and toward expansion of its exceptions. [Cc]

None of the exceptions to the general rule are applicable to the facts of this case. * * *

Therefore, if we were to follow the traditional rule, Pagelsdorf was not entitled to an instruction that Mahnke owed him a duty of ordinary care. We believe, however, that the better public policy lies in the abandonment of the general rule of nonliability and the adoption of a rule that a landlord is under a duty to exercise ordinary care in the maintenance of the premises.

Such a rule was adopted by the New Hampshire court in Sargent v. Ross, 113 N.H. 388, 308 A.2d 528 (1973). The plaintiff's four-year-old child fell to her death from an outdoor stairway of a residential building owned by the defendant. In a wrongful death action against the landlord, the plaintiff claimed the stairs were too steep and the railing inadequate. The jury awarded the plaintiff damages, and the landlord appealed from a judgment entered on the verdict. After eliminating the established exceptions to the rule of nonliability, the court concluded that the rule had nothing to recommend itself in a contemporary, urban society and ought to be abandoned. Instead, general principles of negligence should apply. The court stated that the " 'quasi-sovereignty of the landowner' " had its genesis in "agrarian England of the dark ages." [C] Whatever justification the rule might once have had, there no longer seemed to be any reason to except landlords from a general duty of exercising ordinary care to prevent foreseeable harm. The court reasoned that the modern trend away from special immunities in tort law and the recognition of an implied warranty of habitability in an apartment lease transaction argued in favor of abolishing the common law rule of nonliability. Accordingly, a landlord's conduct should be appraised according to negligence principles. Questions of control, hidden defects, and common use would be relevant only as bearing on the general determination of negligence, including foreseeability and unreasonableness of the risk of harm.

In *Antoniewicz,* [c] we cited *Sargent* as one of many cases whose reasoning supported the abolition of the common law distinctions between licensees and invitees. The policies supporting our decision to abandon these distinctions concerning a land occupier's duty toward his visitors compel us, in the instant case, to abrogate the landlord's general cloak of immunity toward his tenants and their visitors. Having recognized that modern social conditions no longer support special exceptions for land occupiers, it is but a short step to hold that there is no remaining basis for a general rule of nonliability for landlords. Arguably, the landlord's relinquishment of possession, and consequently control of the premises, removes this case from the sweep of the policies embodied in *Antoniewicz.* We are not so persuaded. One of the basic principles of our tort law is that one is liable for injuries resulting from conduct foreseeably creating an unreasonable risk to others. [C] Public policy limitations on the application of this principle are shrinking. [Cc]

The modern-day apartment lease is regarded as a contract, not a conveyance. Pines v. Perssion, 14 Wis.2d 590, 111 N.W.2d 409 (1961). In *Pines* we determined that modern social conditions called for judicial recognition of a warranty of habitability implied in an apartment lease. * * *

It would be anomalous indeed to require a landlord to keep his premises in good repair as an implied condition of the lease, yet immunize him from liability for injuries resulting from his failure to do so. We conclude that there is no remaining justification for the landlord's general cloak of common law immunity and hereby abolish the general common law principle of nonliability of landlords toward persons injured as a result of their defective premises. * * *

At trial plaintiffs' counsel requested the jury be instructed that Mahnke owed Pagelsdorf, as his invitee, a duty of ordinary care. Pagelsdorf's proposed special verdict inquired whether Mahnke was "negligent in failing to keep the guardrail in question in a reasonably good state of repair." Thus Pagelsdorf preserved the assigned error for appeal. We simply reach the result he seeks by a different means. [C] * * *

Generally, a decision overruling or repudiating other cases is given retrospective operation. [C] The rule of landlords' nonliability was riddled with many exceptions; thus reliance on the rule could not have been great. [C] We find no reason to depart from the general rule of retrospective operation of the mandate herein.

In conclusion, a landlord owes his tenant or anyone on the premises with the tenant's consent a duty to exercise ordinary care. If a person lawfully on the premises is injured as a result of the landlord's negligence in maintaining the premises, he is entitled to recover from the landlord under general negligence principles. Issues of notice of the defect, its obviousness, control of the premises, and so forth are all relevant only insofar as they bear on the ultimate question: Did the landlord exercise ordinary care in the maintenance of the premises under all the circumstances?

Judgment reversed and cause remanded for proceedings consistent with this opinion.

––––––––

1. Except for early holdings in Tennessee—e.g., Wilcox v. Hines, 100 Tenn. 538, 46 S.W. 297 (1898)—Sargent v. Ross, 113 N.H. 388, 308 A.2d 528 (1973), set forth in the principal case, is the first to apply the general negligence principle to lessors. See also Brennan v. Cockrell Inv. Co., 35 Cal.App.3d 796, 111 Cal.Rptr. 122 (1973); Young v. Garwacki, 380 Mass. 162, 402 N.E.2d 1045 (1980). But cf. Francis v. Pic, 226 N.W.2d 654 (N.D.1975). The new rule has not picked up an extensive following yet. What is your opinion of the ultimate outcome? Is it Rowland v. Christian revisited, or are the problems materially different?

2. As indicated in the principal case, a number of courts in recent years have utilized an "implied warranty of habitability" to create a duty on the part of the lessor to deliver the premises in a habitable condition. See Knight v. Hallsthammar, 29 Cal.3d 46, 623 P.2d 268, 171 Cal.Rptr. 707 (1981); Lemle v. Breeden, 51 Hawaii 426, 462 P.2d 470 (1969); Marini v. Ireland, 56 N.J. 130, 265 A.2d 526 (1970); Davis & DeLaTorre, A Fresh Look at Premises Liability As Affected by the Warranty of Habitability, 59 Wash.L.Rev. 141 (1983); L'Abbate, Recovery Under the Implied Warranty of Liability, 10 Fordham Urban L.J. 285 (1982); Price, Landlord Liability—Breach of Warranty of Habitability, 16 Tr.Law.Q. 13 (1984); Annot., A.L.R. 4th 1182 (1983); Comment, Implied Warranty of Habitability: An Incipient Trend in the Law of Landlord–Tenant, 40 Fordham L.Rev. 123 (1972); Note, Implied Warranty of Habitability in Housing Leases, 21 Drake L.Rev. 300, 302–310 (1972). These decisions provided tenants only with a defense to an eviction action or a right to withhold rent until repairs were made. They did not necessarily mean that the general limitation on a landlord's duty in tort was abolished. And see Restatement (Second) of Property § 17.6.

3. At least one court has held that a theory of strict liability could be imposed on a landlord for injuries caused by latent structural defects in the premises. The court viewed apartment units as saleable goods, and characterized the lessor as one in the marketing chain who places a "product" in the stream of commerce. Becker v. IRM Corp., 38 Cal.3d 454, 698 P.2d 116, 213 Cal.Rptr. 213 (1985), infra page 792. A Washington decision of the Court of Appeals to the same effect was reversed by the Supreme Court in Hoffman v. Connall, 108 Wash.2d 69, 736 P.2d 242 (1987).

4. Efforts by lessors to immunize themselves against liability through exculpatory clauses in leases have been held to be void as against public policy, at least insofar as they seek to immunize lessors against damages caused by

negligence in maintaining common areas. Cappaert v. Junker, 413 So.2d 378 (Miss.1982).

5. What damages should be available to lessees for lessor's negligence? In Simon v. Solomon, 385 Mass. 91, 431 N.E.2d 556 (1982), the court upheld damages to the tenant for emotional distress caused by the landlord's substandard maintenance of her apartment, after evidence showed that water and sewage from an adjoining area flooded her basement apartment approximately 30 times.

KLINE v. 1500 MASSACHUSETTS AVE. APARTMENT CORP.

United States Court of Appeals, District of Columbia Circuit, 1970.
141 U.S.App.D.C. 370, 439 F.2d 477.

[Plaintiff Sarah B. Kline, a lessee of defendant, sustained serious injuries when she was criminally assaulted and robbed at approximately 10:15 P.M. while she was in the common hallway of a large (585–unit) combination office-apartment building. Although a doorman had been employed in the past, the entrances to the building were left unguarded at the time plaintiff was assaulted. This procedure was followed in spite of the fact that defendant lessor had notice of an increasing number of assaults, larcenies and robberies being perpetrated against the tenants in and from the common hallways of the building.]

WILKEY, CIRCUIT JUDGE. The appellee apartment corporation states that there is "only one issue presented for review * * * whether a duty should be placed on a landlord to take steps to protect tenants from foreseeable criminal acts committed by third parties". The District Court as a matter of law held that there is no such duty. We find that there is, and that in the circumstances here the applicable standard of care was breached. We therefore reverse and remand to the District Court for the determination of damages for the appellant.
* * *

In this jurisdiction, certain duties have been assigned to the landlord because of his *control* of common hallways, lobbies, stairwells, etc., used by all tenants in multiple dwelling units. * * *

While [prior cases have] dealt with a physical defect in the building leading to plaintiff's injury, the rationale as applied to predictable criminal acts by third parties is the same. The duty is the landlord's because by his control of the areas of common use and common danger he is the only party who has the *power* to make the necessary repairs or to provide the necessary protection.

As a general rule, a private person does not have a duty to protect another from a criminal attack by a third person. We recognize that this rule has sometimes in the past been applied in landlord-tenant law, even by this court. Among the reasons for the application of this rule to landlords are: judicial reluctance to tamper with the traditional common law concept of the landlord-tenant relationship; the notion that the act of a third person in committing an intentional tort or crime is a superseding cause of the harm to another resulting therefrom; the oftentimes difficult problem of determining foreseeability of criminal acts; the vagueness of the standard which the landlord must meet; the economic consequences of the imposition of the duty; and conflict with the public policy allocating the duty of protecting citizens from criminal acts to the government rather than the private sector.

But the rationale of this very broad general rule falters when it is applied to the conditions of modern day urban apartment living, particularly in the circumstances of this case. The rationale of the general rule exonerating a third party from any duty to protect another from a criminal attack has no applicability to the landlord-tenant relationship in multiple dwelling houses. The landlord is no insurer of his tenants' safety, but he certainly is no bystander. And where, as here, the landlord has notice of repeated criminal assaults and robberies, has notice that these crimes occurred in the portion of the premises exclusively within his control, has every reason to expect like crimes to happen again, and has the exclusive power to take preventive action, it does not seem unfair to place upon the landlord a duty to take those steps which are within his power to minimize the predictable risk to his tenants. * * *

[I]nnkeepers have been held liable for assaults which have been committed upon their guests by third parties, if they have breached a duty which is imposed by reason of the innkeeper-guest relationship. By this duty, the innkeeper is generally bound to exercise reasonable care to protect the guest from abuse or molestation from third parties, be they innkeeper's employees, fellow guests, or intruders, if the attack could, or in the exercise of reasonable care, should have been anticipated.

Liability in the innkeeper-guest relationship is based as a matter of law either upon the innkeeper's supervision, care, or control of the premises, or by reason of a contract which some courts have implied from the entrustment by the guest of his personal comfort and safety to the innkeeper. In the latter analysis, the contract is held to give the guest the right to expect a standard of treatment at the hands of the innkeeper which includes an obligation on the part of the latter to exercise reasonable care in protecting the guest.

Other relationships in which similar duties have been imposed include landowner-invitee, businessman-patron, employer-employee, school district-pupil, hospital-patient, and carrier-passenger. In all, the theory of liability is essentially the same: that since the ability of one of the parties to provide for his own protection has been limited in some way by his submission to the control of the other, a duty should be imposed upon the one possessing control (and thus the power to act) to take reasonable precautions to protect the other one from assaults by third parties which, at least, could reasonably have been anticipated. * * *

As between tenant and landlord, the landlord is the only one in the position to take the necessary acts of protection required. He is not an insurer, but he is obligated to minimize the risk to his tenants. Not only as between landlord and tenant is the landlord best equipped to guard against the predictable risk of intruders, but even as between landlord and the police power of government, the landlord is in the best position to take the necessary protective measures. * * *

We * * * hold in this case that the applicable standard of care in providing protection for the tenant is that standard which this landlord himself was employing in October 1959 when the appellant became a resident on the premises at 1500 Massachusetts Avenue. * * * [W]e hold that the same relative degree of security should have been maintained. * * *

Having said this, it would be well to state what is not said by this decision. We do not hold that the landlord is by any means an insurer of the safety of his tenants. His duty is to take those measures of protection which are within his power and capacity to take, and which can reasonably be expected to mitigate the risk of intruders assaulting and robbing tenants. The landlord is not expected to provide protection commonly owed by a municipal police department; but as illustrated in this case, he is obligated to protect those parts of his premises which are not usually subject to periodic patrol and inspection by the municipal police. We do not say that every multiple unit apartment house in the District of Columbia should have those same measures of protection which 1500 Massachusetts Avenue enjoyed in 1959, nor do we say that 1500 Massachusetts Avenue should have precisely those same measures in effect at the present time. Alternative and more up-to-date methods may be equally or even more effective. * * *

The landlord is entirely justified in passing on the cost of increased protective measures to his tenants, but the rationale of compelling the landlord to do it in the first place is that he is the only one who is in a position to take the necessary protective measures for overall protection of the premises, which he owns in whole and rents in part to individual tenants.

Reversed and remanded to the District Court for the determination of damages.

[MACKINNON, J., dissented.]

––––––––––

1. How important is the fact that the assault occurred in a common passageway? Suppose the attacker had waited outside Mrs. Kline's apartment, forced his way in and attacked her in the living room. Liability? How does this case differ from those holding a landlord liable when a tenant trips on a defective condition in a common hallway?

2. Prior to the 1970's, the courts would find no duty obligation in the instant case. See Goldberg v. Hous. Auth. of Newark, 38 N.J. 578, 186 A.2d 291 (1962); Bass v. New York, 38 A.D.2d 407, 330 N.Y.S.2d 569 (1972), aff'd, 32 N.Y.2d 894, 300 N.E.2d 154, 346 N.Y.S.2d 814 (1973) (municipally-owned dwell-

ing treated as privately owned); Daniels v. Shell Oil Co., 485 S.W.2d 948 (Tex. Civ.App.1972); Annot., 43 A.L.R.3d 331 (1972). A more recent case holding that view is Feld v. Merriam, 506 Pa. 383, 485 A.2d 742 (1984). The main arguments against imposing that duty are stated in the principal case. Also, it is said that a tenant makes a choice as to where to live and in effect "assumes the risk" of injury from criminal elements in a low security building. What about the contention that the *Kline* decision places the cost of crime on those who can least afford it—the rent-paying tenants?

3. Today there are several decisions finding the landlord liable to tenant for an attack by a third person when they were foreseeable and reasonable steps to increase security would have prevented the attack. See Graham v. M. & J. Corp., 424 A.2d 103 (D.C.App.1980); Holley v. Mt. Zion Terrace Apts., 382 So.2d 98 (Fla.1980). A few courts have extended the warranty of habitability to include security. See Trentacost v. Brussel, 82 N.J. 214, 412 A.2d 436 (1980); Secretary of HUD v. Layfield, 88 Cal.App.3d Supp. 28, 152 Cal.Rptr. 342 (1979); Brownstein v. Edison, 103 Misc.2d 316, 425 N.Y.S.2d 773 (1980).

The landlord's duty has not generally been extended to providing security for social guests of tenants. See Pippin v. Chicago Hous. Auth., 58 Ill.App.3d 1029, 16 Ill.Dec. 280, 374 N.E.2d 1055 (1978). But at least one court has extended the landlord's liability to a third person having no relationship to the landlord. Nixon v. Mr. Property Management Co., 690 S.W.2d 546 (Tex.1985). There, a minor was dragged into a vacant, dilapidated apartment and raped. The owners and managers were found liable when the Supreme Court adopted the standard of conduct imposed by a local ordinance, requiring property owners to keep doors and windows of vacant portions of structures securely closed to prevent unauthorized entry, to define the conduct of a reasonably prudent person to the general public. See, also, Nallan v. Helmsley–Spear, Inc., 50 N.Y.2d 507, 429 N.Y.S.2d 606, 407 N.E.2d 451, 457–58 (1980).

4. If a duty to protect tenants is established, an obvious problem is defining the extent of that obligation. What was defendant supposed to do in the principal case? In Johnston v. Harris, 387 Mich. 569, 198 N.W.2d 409 (1972), an elderly tenant was assaulted as he reached for the doorknob to his apartment in defendant's four-unit apartment building. The building was located in a high crime area. In Sherman v. Concourse Realty Corp., 47 A.D.2d 134, 365 N.Y.S.2d 239 (1975), the landlord of a 200–tenant multiple dwelling removed a lock cylinder from the building's security buzzer system which had been installed as a condition for a rent increase. Plaintiff-tenant was assaulted by an intruder.

5. See Henszey & Weisman, What Is the Landlord's Responsibility for Criminal Acts Committed on the Premises?, 6 Real Estate L.J. 104 (1977); Annot., 43 A.L.R.3d 331 (1969).

6. The entire topic of premises or landowners' liability is covered well in a treatise in J. Page, The Law of Premises Liability (1976).

Chapter X

DAMAGES

At one time, "damages" was treated as a separate legal subject and it was taught as a course in most American law schools. See C. McCormick, Damages (2d ed. 1935); J. Sutherland, Damages (1893). Over the past 50 years, distinct rules of damages have developed in a variety of subject matter areas; this has resulted in the topic of damages being taught usually in connection with individual areas of substantive law.

Many academicians have shied away from describing the subject of tort law damages, and most of the treatises have been written by practitioners. See, e.g., J. Stein, Damages and Recovery (1972); S. Schreiber, Damages and Personal Injury and Wrongful Death (1965). Nevertheless, the subject of damages is extraordinarily important in connection with the law of torts.

Proof of damages is an essential part of plaintiff's cause of action based on either negligence or strict liability.

The question of how much damage plaintiff suffered is often at the heart of the dispute between plaintiff and defendant. In the course of settlement negotiations, defendant's insurance company often is willing to concede the issue of liability, but it rarely will accede to plaintiff's demand for damages. Also, a good deal of trial time and effort is devoted to the topic of how much plaintiff should recover.

Some matters already considered in the chapter on duty (such as the question of whether plaintiff can recover for negligent infliction of emotional harm) can also be looked at as damage questions. In this chapter, it is assumed that a duty has been breached, that plaintiff has been injured and that the law would allow him some monetary recovery. The question here is deceptively simple: "how much"?

Throughout this casebook, you will find a variety of areas in which tort liability has been expanded in favor of the plaintiff. In general, this expansion of liability has not been accompanied by limits on damage awards. Should expansions of liability be accompanied by restrictions on damage rules? If so, which damage rules? These are questions to consider throughout this chapter.

According to Jury Verdict Research, Inc., the first million dollar product liability verdict did not occur until 1962, but there were 401 such awards in 1984. Data collected by Jury Verdict Research suggested that the average verdict in products liability cases in 1985 exceeded $1.85 million, with the average malpractice claim at $1.02 million. These figures represent the amount of verdicts only, and the amount actually paid may be less because judges sometimes reduce jury verdicts through the procedure of remittitur. See pages 513–14. While most cases are settled or reach verdicts at less than these amounts, the average verdict is high because a small number of verdicts are extremely large.

Reform of the tort system is currently a major and controversial public policy issue in the U.S. Congress and in nearly every state legislature in the country.

In 1986, the Attorney General of the United States, at the request of the President, established a Tort Policy Working Group to make recommendations regarding solutions to the crisis in availability of insurance. That Task Force identified skyrocketing damage awards as a key element in the current liability problems. See Department of Justice, Report of the Tort Policy Working Group on the Causes, Extent, and Policy Implications of the Current Crisis in Insurance Availability and Affordability, February, 1986.

The following year the Tort Policy Working Group supplemented its report and observed that data published by the Rand Corporation's Institute for Civil Justice showed substantial increases from 1960 through 1984 in average jury awards for medical malpractice and product liability cases in two locations studied—Cook County, Illinois and San Francisco, California.

In the 1986–1987 period, at least 40 state legislatures debated malpractice and tort reform, and the subject of damages has been a key element in all such legislative discussions. During that period, approximately nine states enacted limits on "caps" on damage awards.

The rules on damages contained in this chapter have sparked much of this controversy. The cases that follow are intended to illustrate the current status of damages for tort liability, as well as to challenge the student to consider the issues and implications of possible reforms.

———

There are three basic kinds of damages in tort law:

1. *Nominal Damages.* These consist of a small sum of money awarded to the plaintiff in order to vindicate his rights, make the judgment available as a matter of record in order to prevent the defendant from acquiring prescriptive rights, and carry a part of the costs of the action. The amount of the award, so long as it is trivial, is unimportant. Current practice among juries has been to award nominal damages of one dollar. Inflation has affected this also.

2. *Compensatory Damages.* These are intended to represent the closest possible financial equivalent of the loss or harm suffered by the plaintiff, and restore him to the position he occupied before the tort. Most of this chapter is concerned with these damages.

3. *Punitive Damages.* These are an additional sum, over and above the proper compensation of the plaintiff, awarded in order to punish the defendant, to make an example of him and deter others from committing similar torts.

Maximum Recovery Rule 1. **PERSONAL INJURIES**

ANDERSON v. SEARS, ROEBUCK & CO.

United States District Court, Eastern District of Louisiana, 1974.
377 F.Supp. 136.

[Plaintiff Helen Britain, a young child, was severely burned when her home was completely consumed by fire. The blaze was triggered by a heater that was held to be negligently manufactured by defendant Sears and defendant Controls Company of America. The jury awarded plaintiff $2,000,000 in damages and defendants moved for a remittitur of that verdict.]

CASSIBRY, DISTRICT JUDGE. The legal standard on which to gauge a jury verdict for remittitur purposes is the "maximum recovery rule". [Cc] This rule directs the trial judge to determine whether the verdict of the jury exceeds the maximum amount which the jury could reasonably find and if it does, the trial judge may then reduce the verdict to the highest amount that the jury could properly have awarded. Functionally, the maximum recovery rule both preserves the constitutionally protected role of the jury as finder of facts and prevents the predilections of the judge from infecting the jury's determination. Thus, the court's task is to ascertain, by scrutinizing all of the evidence as to each element of damages, what amount would be the maximum the jury could have reasonably awarded. In this case there are five cardinal elements of damages: (1) past physical and mental pain (2) future physical and mental pain (3) future medical expenses (4) loss of earning capacity and (5) permanent disability and disfigurement.

Past Physical and Mental Pain. The infant child Helen Britain, was almost burned to death in the tragic fire that swept her home. She was burned over forty per cent of her entire body; third degree burns cover eighty per cent of her scalp and second and third degree burns of the trunk and of her extremities account for the remainder. Helen Britain's immediate post-trauma treatment required hospitalization for twenty-eight days, during which time the child developed pneumonia, required numerous transfusions, suffered fever, vomiting, diarrhea, and infection, and underwent skin graft surgery, under general anesthesia, to her scalp, which was only partially successful. Keloid scarring caused webbing and ankylosis of the child's extremities and severely limited their motion. The child's fingers became adhered together; scarring bent the arm at the elbow in a burdensome, fixed position; and thick scarring on the thighs and on the side of and behind the knees impaired walking.

This child had to undergo subsequent hospitalizations for further major operations and treatment. The second major operation under general anesthesia was undertaken to graft new skin from the back and stomach to the remaining bare areas of the scalp. The third operation under general anesthesia was an attempt to relieve the deformity of her left hand caused by the webbing scars which bound down the fingers of that hand. A fourth operation under general anesthesia was performed to reduce scars which had grown back on the left hand again webbing the fingers. I cannot envisage the breadth and intensity of the pain experienced by Helen Britain throughout this ordeal.

The undisputed testimony reveals that one of the most tragic aspects of this case is that the horrible mental and emotional trauma caused to this child occurred at an age which medical experts maintain is crucial to a child's entire psyche and personality formation. Helen Britain's persistent emotional and mental disturbance is evidenced by bed wetting, nightmares, refusing to sleep alone, withdrawal, and speech impediments. Dr. Cyril Phillips, a psychiatrist, and Dr. Diamond both indicated that the child manifested to them, even at this early age, emotional illness and retarded mental growth.

The evidence reflects that an award of six hundred thousand dollars for this element of damages alone would not be unreasonable.

2) *Future Physical and Mental Pain.* There is clear evidence that the stretching, pulling, and breaking down of scars inherent in growth will continue to cause severe pain and a crippling limitation of motion in varying degrees to all of Helen Britain's upper and lower extremities. Very little can be done to improve the condition of the scalp which will never be able to breathe, sweat or grow hair. There will be risks, trauma and pain, both physical and mental, with each of the recommended twenty-seven future operations which will extend over most of the child's adult life, if she is in fact fortunate enough to be able to risk undergoing these recommended surgeries. Furthermore, Helen Britain must vigilantly guard against irritation, infection and further injury to the damaged and abnormal skin, scars and grafts because any injury, however slight, can generate cancer in these adynamic areas.

The inherent stresses and tensions of each new phase of life will severely tax this little girl's debilitated and delicate mental and emotional capacity. Throughout her future life expectancy of seventy-five years, it is reasonable to expect, that she will be deprived of a normal social life and that she will never find a husband and raise a family. On top of this, Helen Britain will always be subjected to rejection, stares and tactless inquiries from children and adults.

The court concludes that an award of seven hundred fifty thousand dollars for this element of damages alone would not be excessive.

3) *Future Medical Expenses.* A large award for future medical expenses is justified. The uncontradicted testimony was that Helen Britain would need the guidance, treatment and counselling of a team of doctors, including plastic surgeons, psychiatrists and sociologists, throughout her lifetime. Add to this the cost of the twenty-seven recommended operations and the cost of private tutoring necessitated by the child's mental and emotional needs and the jury could justifiably award a figure of two hundred and fifty thousand dollars to cover these future expenses.

4) ~~Loss of Earning Capacity~~ The evidence of Helen Britain's disabilities both physical, mental and emotional was such that this court holds that the jury could properly find that these disabilities would prevent her from earning a living for the rest of her life. Not only do the physical impairments to her extremities disable her but her emotional limitations require avoiding stress and the combined effect is the permanent incapacity to maintain serious employment.

The jury was provided with actuarial figures which accurately calculated both the deduction of interest to be earned and the addition of an inflationary buffer, on any award made for future loss of earning capacity. [Italics added.] In view of these incontrovertible projections at trial, it was within the province of the jury to award as much as $330,000.00 for the loss of earning capacity.

[margin note: large lump award will earn interest = to be deducted from total]

5) ~~Permanent Disability and Disfigurement.~~ The award for this element of damage must evaluate in monetary terms the compensation due this plaintiff for the permanent physical, mental and emotional disabilities and disfigurements proved by the evidence adduced at trial. A narration treating Miss Britain's permanent disabilities and disfigurements would be lengthy and redundant; therefore, I resort to listing.

1. The complete permanent loss of 80% of the scalp caused by the destruction of sweat glands, hair follicles and tissue—all of which effects a grotesque disfigurement and freakish appearance.

2. The permanent loss of the normal use of the legs.

3. The permanent impairment of the left fingers and hand caused by recurring webbing and resulting in limited motion.

4. The permanent impairment of the right hand caused by scars and webbing of the fingers.

5. The permanent injury to the left elbow and left arm with ankylosis and resulting in a crippling deformity.

6. The permanent destruction of 40% of the normal skin. As a result of this a large portion of the body is covered by "pigskin." Pigskin resembles the dry, cracked skin of an aged person and is highly susceptible to irritation from such ordinary things as temperature changes and washing.

7. Permanent scars over the majority of the body where skin donor sites were removed.

8. The permanent impairment of speech.

9. The loss of three years of formative and impressionable childhood. *permanence ——*

10. Permanently reduced and impaired emotional capacity.

11. The permanent impairment of normal social, recreational and educational life.

12. The permanent imprint of her mother's hand on her stomach.

Considering each of the foregoing items, the court concludes that the jury had the prerogative of awarding up to $1,100,000 for this element of damages.

By totaling the estimated maximum recovery for each element of damages, the jury's actual award is placed in proper perspective. According to my calculations the maximum jury award supported by the evidence in this case could have been $2,980,000. Obviously, the jury's $2,000,000 verdict is well within the periphery established by the maximum award test. *Can judge raise it? see n. 15, p. 513*

[Defendants] argue that the introduction of photographs of the *demonstrative* plaintiff was inflammatory. Since a part of plaintiff's claim for damages is for disfigurement and the humiliation and embarrassment resulting therefrom, I hold that these photographs were properly admitted to show the condition of the plaintiff as she appeared to others, at *Case in Oregon:* the time they were taken. [Cc] *Note = medical files entry of time of*

The defendants suggest that the presence of the child in the *admittance 1* courtroom and in the corridors of the courthouse in some way inflamed or prejudiced the jury. This allegation is unfounded; the defendants have not pointed out any wrongful conduct on the part of Helen Britain, her parents, or counsel for plaintiffs. Helen Britain was well behaved and quiet the entire time she was in the courtroom.

Accordingly I hold that there was not any bias, prejudice, or any other improper influence which motivated the jury in making its award.

The defendants' motions for a remittitur are denied.

---

1. The principal case presents a catalogue of the major elements of damages in a personal injury case. How much time and thought did plaintiff's attorney probably devote to developing proof of these items? See O'Quinn, Common Elements of Recovery in Personal Injury Cases, 18 S.Tex.L.J. 179 (1977). Although the case was based on negligence, similar items of damage can occur in actions based on intent or strict liability.

2. *Evidence of Damages.* Proof of damages is an essential part of plaintiff's cause of action, whether based on intentional conduct, negligence or strict liability. There have been extensive developments over the past few decades in techniques for presenting this proof. For example, attorneys have made growing use of what is called demonstrative evidence. This form of evidence consists of tangible items such as charts, photographs, motion pictures and models. The purpose of this evidence is to bring home to the jury the total extent of plaintiff's injury. See, e.g., Spangenberg, The Use of Demonstrative Evidence, 21 Ohio St.L.J. 178 (1960); Crocker, Demonstrative Evidence Techniques, 5 The Practical Lawyer 45 (1959); Knepper, Exhibits and Demonstrative Evidence, 30 Ins.Couns.J. 133 (1963). Much of this was set in motion by San Francisco attorney Melvin M. Belli, who empirically showed how demonstrative evidence might greatly enlarge the amount of a plaintiff's verdict. See Belli, Demonstrative Evidence and the Adequate Award, 22 Miss.L.J. 284 (1951). This development has not gone without criticism, and some observers believe that demonstrative evidence often has the effect of misleading rather

than assisting the jury. See, e.g., Milwid, The Misuse of Demonstrative Evidence, 28 Ins.Couns.J. 435 (1961).

In addition, trial lawyers have made a growing use of experts in proving damages. Experts may be used to project earnings, to detail plaintiff's medical difficulties—both physical and psychological, and in a variety of other ways. This is treated in more detail in the course of Evidence.

3. It has become customary to divide damages in a personal injury case into two separate categories.

One classification is between "general" and "special" damages; another is between "economic" and "non-economic" damages. The two classifications are not always coterminous but in personal injury cases loss of earnings and the presence of medical expenses are treated as special damages subject to objective measurement by the economic loss, while pain and suffering and emotional distress are treated as general damages without an objective economic standard to apply.

4. *Loss of Past Earnings.* If the plaintiff was employed at a fixed wage at the time of his injury, he may recover the amount of his fixed wages. On the other hand, if plaintiff was employed on some basis not susceptible to an exact computation, or if he was unemployed, he may recover for impairment of his earning capacity. Plaintiff will try to establish this by circumstantial evidence. The distinction is well discussed in Conachan v. Williams, 266 Or. 45, 511 P.2d 392 (1973). See also Oleck, Damages to Persons and Property, §§ 182, 183 (Rev. ed. 1961); Annot., 18 A.L.R.3d 88 (1968); Note, 10 Will.L.J. 278 (1974). Evidence of past profits derived from a business in which plaintiff is engaged may be admitted on the question of damages from impaired earning capacity only when the plaintiff's own efforts can be shown to have been the predominant factor in producing the profits. See Lo Schiavo v. Northern Ohio Traction & Light Co., 106 Ohio St. 61, 138 N.E. 372 (1922); see also Slagle, The Role of Profits in Personal Injury Actions, 19 Ohio St.L.J. 179 (1958).

What about persons who contribute to a family unit, but do not draw salaries or wages? Courts have come to perceive that if persons were contributing legally recognizable services during marriage, the pecuniary benefits of those services have been lost to their families on death or debilitating injury. See Johnson, Calculating the Economic Value of Lost Homemaker Services in Wrongful Death/Personal Injury Litigation, 29 Trial Law. Guide 136 (1985); Warner, Expert Testimony and the Value of a Wife and Mother, 16 Trial Law. Q. [No. 2] 19 (1984); Fuchsberg, Damages for Death of a Housespouse–Housewife, 15 Trial Law.Q. [No. 2] 41 (1983).

5. *Loss or Impairment of Future Earning Capacity.* As indicated in the principal case, even a very young plaintiff who would not be expected to engage in employment until the distant future may recover for the loss of future earnings. The jury is provided with some guidance on this issue. First, mortality tables published by insurance actuaries have been judicially noticed as accurate in every jurisdiction. See Annot., 50 A.L.R.2d 419 (1956). The jury are instructed that they are to rely on the tables only as a general guideline in determining how long plaintiff might be expected to live. They may consider how much special factors such as plaintiff's "sex, prior state of health, nature of daily employment and its perils, manner of living, personal habits, and individual characteristics" will affect the "normal" life expectancy figure provided by the mortality table. See Volz v. Dresser, 150 Pa.Super. 371, 28 A.2d 493 (1942). Moreover, it is loss of earning capacity that is being calculated and most people

do not continue to earn money for their entire lives. Thus, the jury may consider the prospects for change in plaintiff's earning capacity, taking into account not only the nature of the person's employment, but also the fact that in growing older the person may be expected to earn more, and that a point is ultimately reached at which an older person will earn less or nothing at all.

Some imaginative attorneys have utilized expert testimony of "manpower economists" who take into account a multiplicity of relevant factors and estimate the "potential impairment of future earnings." See, e.g., Hemet Dodge v. Gryder, 23 Ariz.App. 523, 534 P.2d 454 (1975); Peck and Hopkins, Economics and Impaired Earning Capacity in Personal Injury Cases, 44 Wash. L.Rev. 351 (1969). See Fisher, Use of an Economist To Prove Future Economic Losses, 18 S.Tex.L.J. 403 (1977); Annot., 23 A.L.R.3d 1189 (1969).

Loss of future earnings can be considered only when plaintiff has introduced substantial proof of permanency of his injuries. While this was not a close question in the principal case, it can be a hotly contended issue and expert testimony is usually needed. See Byrum v. Maryott, 26 Md.App. 130, 337 A.2d 142 (1975).

See generally, Hadley & Rapp, Estimating Future Lost Earnings: Some Common Problems, 21 Trial [No. 1] 28 (Feb. 1985); Zabel, A Plain English Approach to Loss of Future Earning Capacity, 24 Washburn L.J. 253 (1985).

6. *Medical Expenses.* As the principal case indicates, the plaintiff is compensated for reasonable medical expenses. There is a good deal of latitude, however, on what is reasonable. With medical expenses already incurred, the focus is on whether they were reasonable. For future medical expenses, the trier of fact must estimate what treatment will be needed in the future. Lawyers for the plaintiff and defendant may argue about the need for medical devices or surgery in the future.

[handwritten: why not order Δ to pay med ins?]

If the plaintiff has no existing physical illness or disease but sues because of the possibility of incurring an illness in the future, should the defendant be liable for the cost of medical surveillance for the possibility of developing an illness?

7. *Pain, Suffering and Mental Anguish.* It is well settled that in an action for a personal injury the plaintiff may recover damages for these general or non-economic damages. They include not only suffering prior to the trial, but also any suffering reasonably certain to result from the injury in the future. Obviously, pain, suffering and mental anguish are not capable of being reduced to any exact and accurate equivalent in money, and there can be no fixed standard of any kind by which damages for them can be measured. The best that can be done is to leave the question to the jury, subject to control by the court, to fix a reasonable amount as compensation. Culbertson v. Haynes, 127 F.Supp. 837 (D.N.D.1955); Shiers v. Cowgill, 157 Neb. 265, 59 N.W.2d 407 (1953). In American States Ins. Co. v. Audubon Country Club, 650 S.W.2d 252 (Ky.1983) it was held reversible error to accept a verdict for medical expenses but no recovery for pain and suffering.

The physical and mental complexity of human life gives rise to innumerable ways in which a life can become less happy. The topic of mental suffering can potentially be broken down into subcomponents and some courts have given plaintiffs' attorneys a good deal of leeway in this area. For example, there are holdings that allow a jury to award a recovery for the loss of sense of taste and smell, Purdy v. Swift & Co., Indus. Indem. Exch., 34 Cal.App.2d 656, 94 P.2d 389 (1939); mental suffering of a virgin of strict religious faith because her hymen

[handwritten: virginity means different things to different people]

That would be Ted.

Stop drinking so much

was ruptured by a doctor during a physical examination, Templin v. Erkekedis, 119 Ind.App. 171, 84 N.E.2d 728 (1949); acquisition of bad moral habits because of a head injury, Gorczynski v. Nugent, 335 Ill.App. 63, 80 N.E.2d 418, aff'd, 402 Ill. 147, 83 N.E.2d 495 (1948); permanent incontinence of urine, Thoren v. Myers, 151 Neb. 453, 37 N.W.2d 725 (1949); impotency and loss of desire for sexual intercourse, Sullivan v. City and County of San Francisco, 95 Cal.App.2d 745, 214 P.2d 82 (1950); shock, Crawford v. Zurich Gen. Acc. & Liab. Ins. Co., 42 So.2d 553 (La.App.1949); change of personality and change of attitude towards others, Fjellman v. Weller, 213 Minn. 457, 7 N.W.2d 521 (1942); insomnia and inability to drive a car, Napier v. Dubose, 45 Ga.App. 661, 165 S.E. 773 (1932); fear of paralysis, Dulaney Inv. Co. v. Wood, 142 S.W.2d 379 (Tex.Civ.App.1940); fear of injury to an unborn child, Domenico v. Kaherl, 160 Me. 182, 200 A.2d 844 (1964); Bee v. Liberty Mut. Ins. Co., 165 So.2d 73 (La.App.1964); and fear of developing cancer by a victim of asbestosis and damages for increased probability of suffering injury, Jackson v. Johns–Manville Sales Corp., 781 F.2d 394 (5th Cir.1986), cert. denied, ___ U.S. ___, 106 S.Ct. 3339, 92 L.Ed.2d 743 (1986); and Eagle–Picher Indus., Inc. v. Cox, 481 So.2d 517 (Fla.1985). See also Annot., 71 A.L.R.2d 338 (1959).

Who should get paid – sex further?

Regarding pain and suffering awards for fear of injury, see Birnbaum, Tort Damages for Fear and Risk of Injury, 31 Prac.Law. [No. 7] 25 (Oct.1985); Faulkner & Woods, Fear of Future Disability—An Element of Damages in a Personal Injury Action, 7 W.New.Eng.L.Rev. 865 (1985); Gale & Goyer, Recovery for Cancerphobia and Increased Risk of Cancer, 15 Cum.L.Rev. 723 (1985).

8. Scars and other disfigurements have been a fertile source of recovery for mental suffering, present and future. One of the best discussions of damages for this is in Gray v. Washington Water Power Co., 30 Wash. 665, 71 P. 206 (1903). See also Annot., 88 A.L.R.3d 117 (1969).

Should a woman recover more for facial scars than a man? Should a young unmarried woman recover more than an older woman or a married woman? Should more be awarded to those whose pleasing appearance is directly tied up with their work? For cases dealing with these problems, see Greer v. Palmer, 55 Pa.D. & C. 109 (1946); and Nikkari v. Jackson, 226 Minn. 88, 32 N.W.2d 149 (1948).

How material is the location of the scar? In Sica v. Public Serv. Co–Ordinated Transp. Co., 8 N.J.Misc. 268, 149 A. 757 (1930), the court said, "It is urged that the embarrassment of a scar on an obscure portion of the limb is not of serious import. The injury was to the calf of the leg. With the fashion industry's recurring return to short hemlines, it cannot be said that such a scar is either in an obscure place or not subject to observation and consequent embarrassment to the plaintiff." With liability insurance costs greatly increasing, is it sound public policy to limit damage awards for any of these types of harms?

9. Assuming that plaintiff is awarded damages for future pain and suffering, should that amount be capitalized at its present value? Most courts have held that since damages for pain and suffering do not have a precise market value, they are not reduced to present worth. See Texas & Pac. R. Co. v. Buckles, 232 F.2d 257 (5th Cir.), cert. denied, 351 U.S. 984 (1956); Annot., 60 A.L.R.2d 1347 (1958). A few courts have indicated that a rough attempt at reduction is better than no effort at all. See In re Millard's Estate, 251 Iowa 1282, 105 N.W.2d 95 (1960); Abbott v. Northwestern Bell Tel. Co., 197 Neb. 11, 246 N.W.2d 647 (1976). For a general discussion see O'Connell & Carpenter,

Payment for Pain and Suffering through History, 50 Ins. Couns.J. 411 (1983); Annot., 34 A.L.R. 4th 293 (1983).

10. The idea of awarding money damages for pain and suffering has been under attack in recent years. Do these damages do any good? Do they help plaintiff bear his pain? A legal-medical study concluded that damages should be allowed only for pain that has a physiological basis. See Peck, Compensation for Pain: A Reappraisal in Light of New Medical Evidence, 72 Mich.L.Rev. 1355 (1974). Professor Jeffrey O'Connell has concluded that the awarding of damages for pain and suffering is a wasteful process that is a creation of lawyers, unknown and unimportant to most of the public. See J. O'Connell and R. Simon, Payment for Pain and Suffering: Who Wants What, When and Why? (1972). See also the criticisms of Traynor, J., dissenting in Seffert v. Los Angeles Transit, 56 Cal.2d 498, 364 P.2d 337, 15 Cal.Rptr. 161 (1961); Plant, Damages for Pain and Suffering, 19 Ohio St.L.J. 200 (1958); Zelermyer, Damages for Pain and Suffering, 6 Syracuse L.Rev. 27 (1955); Morris, Liability for Pain and Suffering, 59 Col.L.Rev. 476 (1959); Jaffe, Damages for Personal Injury: The Impact of Insurance, 18 Law & Contemp.Probs. 219 (1958). When all is said and done, is the award for pain and suffering in the principal case justified? What of the argument that an award for pain and suffering is an indirect way of taking care of the plaintiff's attorney's fees, thus allowing the plaintiff the full amount of the pecuniary loss?

11. *Per-diem Argument* A disputed technique of counsel for the plaintiff in arguing to the jury has been to break physical and mental suffering down into days, hours, or even minutes, set a value on each unit, and multiply it by the total number of the units that pain and suffering has lasted and may be expected to last. Although the practice is no doubt quite old, it originated, so far as publication is concerned, with Belli, The Use of Demonstrative Evidence in Achieving "The More Adequate Award," 32–35 (1951).

There can be a certain element of duplicity in this, since it first poses an apparently reasonable and even insignificant figure, and then multiplies it by a concealed factor to attain a potentially prodigious result. Thus ten cents a minute becomes $52,560 a year, and one dollar a minute becomes ten times as much. This, together with the well-known fact that once the "threshold" of pain is crossed, the body tends to adjust to it and the suffering to diminish, has led a considerable minority of the courts to refuse to allow use of the per-diem formula technique in argument. See, for example, Botta v. Brunner, 26 N.J. 82, 138 A.2d 713 (1958); Certified T.V. & Appliance Co. v. Harrington, 201 Va. 109, 109 S.E.2d 126 (1959); Wimsatt v. Mitchell, 383 S.W.2d 154 (Mo.1964).

A majority of the courts, however, will allow the argument, assuming that juries will have intelligence enough not to be misled, and that in any case it is open to the defendant to anticipate and refute the argument. On how this last is done, see Morris, An Audio–Visual Study of Pain and Suffering in Dollars-on-a-Unit-of-Time Basis, 14 Def.L.J. 129 (1951). See permitting the argument, Weeks v. Holsclaw, 306 N.C. 655, 295 S.E.2d 596 (1982); Corkery v. Greenberg, 253 Iowa 846, 114 N.W.2d 327 (1962). And see Annot. 3 A.L.R. 4th 940 (1983) and supplements.

12. *Reduced Life Expectancy.* Traditionally, American authority has denied any damages for the shortening of the plaintiff's life expectancy itself, as distinguished from loss of prospective earnings. There have been three major factors responsible for this: (a) the belief that the common law rule against compensating for loss of life except as provided by statute must preclude

compensation for shortening life (b) the fear that duplication of damages may result; and (c) unwillingness to enter a field filled with incalculable variables. See Farrington v. Stoddard, 115 F.2d 96 (1st Cir.1940); O'Leary v. United States Lines Co., 111 F.Supp. 745 (D.Mass.1953); Rhone v. Fisher, 224 Md. 223, 167 A.2d 773 (1961); and James v. United States, 483 F.Supp. 581 (N.D.Cal.1980).

English authorities have held that the shortening of life expectancy is itself a compensable harm, constituting a distinct element of damages. See Flint v. Lovell, [1935] 1 K.B. 354 (C.A.); Yorkshire Elec. Bd. v. Naylor, [1968] A.C. 529. In Downie v. United States Lines Co., 359 F.2d 344 (3d Cir.), cert. denied, 385 U.S. 897 (1966), the court agreed with this position. There is an excellent discussion of the entire problem, including survival of actions and wrongful death in Fleming, The Lost Years: A Problem in the Computation and Distribution of Damages, 50 Calif.L.Rev. 598 (1962). See also Schultheis & Rheingold, Making Up for Lost Time: Recovering for Shortened Life Expectancy, 19 Trial [No. 2] 44 (Feb. 1983).

13. *Damage Calculation: Present Value.* In personal injury actions a plaintiff is awarded a lump sum to compensate for loss or impairment of future earning capacity. In most jurisdictions, the amount awarded is not the total arrived at by multiplying annual loss of earnings by the number of years of earnings expectancy. Rather, the jury is instructed to reduce that amount to its "present value." This smaller sum may be arrived at in two ways. One is to use present-worth tables showing the present value of a dollar paid at monthly (or other) intervals over the prospective loss period, calculated at a particular rate of interest (since this is like paying interest to the defendant for his payment in advance) and multiplied by the average monthly earnings for the period of time. The second is to use tables showing the cost of purchasing an annuity for a designated amount for the period of time. The two methods reach similar results, though they do not correspond exactly. The present-value rule applies also to such matters as future medical expenses. The discount rate should be chosen on the basis of the factors that are used to estimate the lost stream of earnings, and should represent the after-tax rate of return to the plaintiff. Jones & Laughlin Steel Corp. v. Pfeifer, 462 U.S. 523 (1983).

See generally, Restatement (Second) of Torts § 913A; Jarrell and Pulsinelli, Obtaining the Ideal Discount Rate in Wrongful Death and Injury Litigation, 32 Defense L.J. 191 (1983); Fulmer & Geraghty, The Appropriate Discount Rate to Use in Estimating Financial Loss, 32 Fed.Ins.Couns.Q. 263 (1982); McCormick, Damages, 299–314 (1935); Immel, Acturial Tables and Damage Awards, 19 Ohio St.L.J. 240 (1958); Leasure, How to Prove Reduction to Present Worth, 21 Ohio St.L.J. 205 (1960); Note, Life Expectancy and Loss of Earning Capacity, 19 Ohio St.L.J. 314 (1958); Annot., 105 A.L.R. 234 (1936). See also Lake's Monthly Installment and Interest Tables (6th Ed.1973).

14. *Future Inflation.* In recent years plaintiffs' attorneys have argued that the jury should not merely reduce lump sum awards to present value, but should also consider the countervailing effect of future inflation. They contend that an upward price movement is probable and that valuing future damages in terms of present prices does not fully compensate the victim.

Courts in about half of the states have accepted this view. Differences have arisen, however, with respect to the proper means to account for inflation, and how to mesh calculations for inflation with those for discount for present value. Three general methods have dominated the discussion: (a) the "inflation-discount method," which seeks to avoid undercompensation by increasing expected future earnings to account for inflation, and then discounting to present value by the market interest rate. Turcotte v. Ford Motor Co., 494 F.2d 173 (1st Cir.1974); (b) the "real interest method," whereby the "real" interest rate is perceived to be stable (between one percent and three percent) regardless of the level of inflation. Doca v. Marina Mercante Nicaraguense, S.A., 634 F.2d 30 (2d Cir.1980); Feldman v. Allegheny Airlines, Inc., 524 F.2d 384 (2d Cir. 1975); and (c) the "total offset method," which assumes as a matter of law that the market interest rate normally used to discount damage awards is completely offset by inflation in computing lost future income. Beaulieu v. Elliott, 434 P.2d 665 (Alaska 1967); State v. Guinn, 555 P.2d 530 (Alaska 1976); Kaczkowski v. Bolubasz, 491 Pa. 561, 421 A.2d 1027 (1980).

In Jones & Laughlin Steel Corp. v. Pfeifer, 462 U.S. 523 (1983), the Supreme Court reviewed various approaches and concluded that it should not establish one method as the exclusive federal rule for use in federal causes of action in federal courts. The Court observed that there are two stages in calculating damages (estimation of the lost stream of income and selection of an appropriate discount rate) and found that inflation should be included in both stages. It noted that two Federal Courts of Appeals allow litigants to choose the method of calculating inflation. Culver v. Slater Boat Co., 688 F.2d 280 (5th Cir.1982); and O'Shea v. Riverway Towing Co., 677 F.2d 1194 (7th Cir. 1982). Although the Court declined to establish any one method as the federal rule, it did note the attractiveness of the total offset method.

The topic is treated in: Annot., 21 A.L.R. 4th 21 (1983); Fisher & Hartnett, Admissibility of Economic Testimony on Future Inflation (1977); Winer, Adjusting Damage Awards for Future Inflation, 1982 Wis.L.Rev. 397; Note, Future Inflation and the Undercompensated Plaintiff, 4 Loy.U.Chi.L.J. 359 (1973); Note, Future Inflation, Prospective Damages, and the Circuit Courts, 63 Va.L.Rev. 105 (1977).

15. *Judicial Control of Amounts Recovered.* The principal case is not alone in approving a million-plus verdict for a plaintiff. The judicial standard by which verdicts are tested has been variously labeled. Common adjectives include "grossly excessive," "inordinate," "shocking to the judicial conscience" or "outrageous." Even the Supreme Court of the United States has gotten into the verdict-testing business. For a good example, see Grunenthal v. Long Island R. Co., 393 U.S. 156 (1968), where the court upheld an award of $305,000 to a workman who suffered a severely crushed right foot.

A verdict can be so excessive (or inadequate) in light of plaintiff's injuries as to demonstrate bias that may have affected the decision on the issue of liability, so that the trial court has authority to set it aside and order a new trial. In order to avoid the expense, inconvenience and delay of new trials in these cases, trial courts frequently, in cases of excessive verdicts, grant a motion for a new trial which is conditioned upon the refusal of the plaintiff to accept a lesser amount. This order is called a remittitur and was mentioned in the principal case above. When the verdict is inadequate the trial judge, much less frequently, may grant the motion for a new trial unless the defendant agrees to pay a larger sum set by the court. This order is called an additur or an increscitur.

It has generally been held that the remittitur does not violate the guaranty of jury trial contained in the state and Federal Constitutions. This is because the plaintiff, if he consents to accept less, has no further grounds for complaint;

and if he refuses, the court does no more than it has power to do when it orders the new trial.

On the other hand the power of additur, against the will of a plaintiff who does not consent and who insists on his new trial, has been denied to the federal courts by a 5–4 decision of the Supreme Court, Dimick v. Schiedt, 293 U.S. 474 (1935). The decisions as to the constitutionality of additur under state constitutions are in hopeless conflict. For collection of cases, see 44 Yale L.J. 318 (1934); 32 Mich.L.Rev. 538 (1934); 35 Colum.L.Rev. 202 (1934).

Is conflict in state courts hopeless, or hopeful? (laboratories for democracy) See p. 522,¶1

In Dorsey v. Barba, 38 Cal.2d 350, 240 P.2d 604 (1952), the court reviewed the entire subject at length, and held that an additur that did not increase the amount to the highest figure that could be sustained on the evidence deprived the plaintiff of his constitutional right to a jury trial, and an outright new trial must be ordered. This case was overruled, and additur placed upon the same footing as remittitur in Jehl v. Southern Pac. Co., 66 Cal.2d 821, 427 P.2d 988, 59 Cal.Rptr. 276 (1967).

See Carlin, Remittiturs and Additurs, 49 W.Va.L.Q. 1 (1942); Bender, Additur, 3 Cal.W.L.Rev. 1 (1967); Annots., 56 A.L.R.2d 213 (1958), 11 A.L.R.2d 1217 (1950).

On judicial discretion regarding additur when it applies, see Foster v. Amcon Int'l, Inc., 621 S.W.2d 142 (Tenn.1981) (although judge was justified in suggesting additur when he determined that jury verdict was inadequate, it was error to suggest an additur 30 times the amount of the jury verdict).

16. *Legislative Control of Amounts Recovered.* The number of million dollar verdicts increased from 30 in 1975 to over 400 in 1985. (Jury Verdict Research, Inc.) Can this be attributed solely to inflation?

The issue of legislative caps on damage awards has been a key element of the current efforts at "tort law reform." In 1986 and 1987, nine states enacted limits on damage awards.

The constitutionality of limitations on medical malpractice awards has been upheld in Fein v. Permanente Medical Group, 38 Cal.3d 137, 695 P.2d 665, 680, 211 Cal.Rptr. 368 (1985) ("the Legislature retains broad control over *the measure* as well as *the timing* of damages that a defendant is obligated to pay and a plaintiff is entitled to receive and * * * the Legislature may expand or limit recoverable damages so long as its action is rationally related to a legitimate state interest"); and Johnson v. St. Vincent Hosp., Inc., 273 Ind. 374, 404 N.E.2d 585 (1980).

The Supreme Court of Florida held that a statute imposing a $450,000 limit on damages for noneconomic losses was unconstitutional because it violated the state constitution's provision for open access to courts. See Smith v. Department of Insurance, 507 So.2d 1080 (Fla.1987).

Other states have invalidated damage limitations on Federal constitutional grounds. Baptist Hosp. of Southeast Texas, Inc. v. Baber, 672 S.W.2d 296 (Tex. App.1984); Carson v. Maurer, 120 N.H. 925, 424 A.2d 825 (1980); Arneson v. Olson, 270 N.W.2d 125 (N.D.1978); Simon v. St. Elizabeth Medical Center, 3 Ohio Ops.3d 164, 355 N.E.2d 903 (Com.Pl.1976); Wright v. Cent. DuPage Hosp. Ass'n, 63 Ill.2d 313, 347 N.E.2d 736 (1976); Boyd v. Bulala, 647 F.Supp. 781 (E.D.Va.1986).

HELFEND v. SOUTHERN CALIFORNIA RAPID TRANSIT DIST.

Supreme Court of California, 1970.
2 Cal.3d 1, 84, 465 P.2d 61, 84 Cal.Rptr. 173.

TOBRINER, ACTING CHIEF JUSTICE. Defendants appeal from a judgment of the Los Angeles Superior Court entered on a verdict in favor of plaintiff, Julius J. Helfend, for $16,400 in general and special damages for injuries sustained in a bus-auto collision that occurred on July 19, 1965, in the City of Los Angeles.

We have concluded that the judgment for plaintiff in this tort action against the defendant governmental entity should be affirmed. The trial court properly followed the collateral source rule in excluding evidence that a portion of plaintiff's medical bills had been paid through a medical insurance plan that requires the refund of benefits from tort recoveries. * * *

[D]efendants appealed, raising only two contentions: (1) The trial court committed prejudicial error in refusing to allow the introduction of evidence to the effect that a portion of the plaintiff's medical bills had been paid from a collateral source. (2) The trial court erred in denying defendant the opportunity to determine if plaintiff had been compensated from more than one collateral source for damages sustained in the accident. * * *

The collateral source rule as applied here embodies the venerable concept that a person who has invested years of insurance premiums to assure his medical care should receive the benefits of his thrift. The tortfeasor should not garner the benefits of his victim's providence.

The collateral source rule expresses a policy judgment in favor of encouraging citizens to purchase and maintain insurance for personal injuries and for other eventualities. Courts consider insurance a form of investment, the benefits of which become payable without respect to any other possible source of funds. If we were to permit a tortfeasor to mitigate damages with payments from plaintiff's insurance, plaintiff would be in a position inferior to that of having bought no insurance, because his payment of premiums would have earned no benefit. Defendant should not be able to avoid payment of full compensation for the injury inflicted merely because the victim has had the foresight to provide himself with insurance.

Some commentators object that the above approach to the collateral source rule provides plaintiff with a "double recovery," rewards him for the injury, and defeats the principle that damages should compensate the victim but not punish the tortfeasor. We agree with Professor Fleming's observation, however, that "double recovery is justified only in the face of some exceptional, supervening reason, as in the case of accident or life insurance, where it is felt unjust that the tortfeasor should take advantage of the thrift and prescience of the victim in having paid the premiums." (Fleming, Introduction to the Law of Torts (1967) p. 131.) * * *

Furthermore, insurance policies increasingly provide for either subrogation or refund of benefits upon a tort recovery, and such refund is indeed called for in the present case. (See Fleming, The Collateral Source Rule and Loss Allocation in Tort Law, supra, 54 Cal.L.Rev. 1478, 1479.) Hence, the plaintiff receives no double recovery; the collateral source rule simply serves as a means of by-passing the antiquated doctrine of non-assignment of tortious actions and permits a proper transfer of risk from the plaintiff's insurer to the tortfeasor by way of the victim's tort recovery. The double shift from the tortfeasor to the victim and then from the victim to his insurance carrier can normally occur with little cost in that the insurance carrier is often intimately involved in the initial litigation and quite automatically receives its part of the tort settlement or verdict.

Even in cases in which the contract or the law precludes subrogation or refund of benefits, or in situations in which the collateral source waives such subrogation or refund, the rule performs entirely necessary functions in the computation of damages. For example, the cost of medical care often provides both attorneys and juries in tort cases with an important measure for assessing the plaintiff's general damages. [C] To permit the defendant to tell the jury that the plaintiff has been recompensed by a collateral source for his medical costs might irretrievably upset the complex, delicate, and somewhat indefinable calculations which result in the normal jury verdict. [Cc]

We also note that generally the jury is not informed that plaintiff's attorney will receive a large portion of the plaintiff's recovery in contingent fees or that personal injury damages are not taxable to the plaintiff and are normally deductible by the defendant. Hence, the plaintiff rarely actually receives full compensation for his injuries as computed by the jury. The collateral source rule partially serves to compensate for the attorney's share and does not actually render a "double recovery" for the plaintiff. * * * In sum, the plaintiff's recovery for his medical expenses from both the tort-feasor and his medical insurance program will not usually give him "double recovery," but partially provides a somewhat closer approximation to full compensation for his injuries.

If we consider the collateral source rule as applied here in the context of the entire American approach to the law of torts and damages, we find that the rule presently performs a number of legitimate and even indispensable functions. Without a thorough revolution in the American approach to torts and the consequent damages, the rule at least with respect to medical insurance benefits has become so integrated within our present system that its precipitous judicial nullification would work hardship. In this case the collateral source rule lies between two systems for the compensation of accident victims: the traditional tort recovery based on fault and the increasingly prevalent coverage based on non-fault insurance. Neither system possesses such universality of coverage or completeness of compensation that we can easily dispense with the collateral source rule's approach to meshing the two systems. [C] The reforms which many academicians propose cannot easily be achieved through piecemeal common law development; the proposed changes, if desirable, would be more effectively accomplished through legislative reform. In any case, we cannot believe that the judicial repeal of the collateral source rule, as applied in the present case, would be the place to begin the needed changes. ＊ ＊ ＊ We therefore reaffirm our adherence to the collateral source rule in tort cases in which the plaintiff has been compensated by an independent collateral source—such as insurance, pension, continued wages, or disability payments—for which he had actually or constructively ＊ ＊ ＊ paid or in cases in which the collateral source would be recompensed from the tort recovery through subrogation, refund of benefits, or some other arrangement. Hence, we conclude that in a case in which a tort victim has received partial compensation from medical insurance coverage entirely independent of the tortfeasor the trial court properly followed the collateral source rule and foreclosed defendant from mitigating damages by means of the collateral payments.

[The court then held that the collateral source rule applies to governmental entities when they are defendants.]

The judgment is affirmed.

———

1. *Collateral–Source Rule.* As the principal case suggests, the collateral-benefits rule is applied when plaintiff has received accident or hospitalization insurance payments. See Annot., 77 A.L.R.3d 415 (1977). So also for other types of insurance, such as life or property insurance. See Annots., 81 A.L.R. 320 (1932) (property insurance), 95 A.L.R. 575 (1935) (personal insurance), 90 A.L.R.2d 1323 (1963) (medical expenses), 7 A.L.R.3d 1966 (employment), 12 A.L.R.3d 1245 (1967) (Federal Tort Claims Act). It also applies when he receives benefits under an employment contract, or pension funds that are deemed consideration for his services. As to pensions, see Annots., 75 A.L.R.2d 885 (1961) (injury), 81 A.L.R.2d 998 (1962) (death). As to wages, see Annot., 7 A.L.R.3d 576 (1966). The rule similarly applies to benefits obtained under social legislation, such as social security and welfare payments. See Annots., 84 A.L.R.2d 764 (1962) (social security), 68 A.L.R.2d 876 (1959) (governmental medicine).

The rule does not apply, however, to payments made by the defendant or by a joint tortfeasor or one who mistakenly thinks he is a tortfeasor, or by an insurance company or other person who makes payment in behalf of a tortfeasor. See, in general, Restatement (Second) of Torts § 920A.

2. When benefits are conferred upon the plaintiff gratuitously, as when a person is nursed without charge by the spouse, the prevailing rule is that plaintiff is entitled to recover the reasonable value of the services from the defendant, since they are a gift to him, and not to the defendant, and should not go to reduce the liability of the latter. Strand v. Grinnell Auto. Garage Co., 136 Iowa 68, 113 N.W. 488 (1907); Wells v. Minneapolis Baseball & Athletic Ass'n,

122 Minn. 327, 142 N.W. 706 (1913). The same is true when the plaintiff's employer has continued to pay his wages, as a gratuity, during the time he has been unable to work. Pryor v. Webber, 23 Ohio St.2d 104, 263 N.E.2d 235 (1970); Motts v. Michigan Cab Co., 274 Mich. 437, 264 N.W. 855 (1936). A minority rule, however, requires the deduction. See Coyne v. Campbell, 11 N.Y.2d 372, 183 N.E.2d 891, 230 N.Y.S.2d 1 (1962); Annot., 90 A.L.R.2d 1323 (1963).

3. As a corollary of the collateral-benefits rule, most courts hold that evidence of the benefits is inadmissible. In some jurisdictions, however, the fact that plaintiff received a collateral benefit for an extended period may be admissible for the limited purpose of proving that plaintiff was a malingerer. See Annot., 47 A.L.R.3d 234 (1973). Is a jury capable of making such a limited use of this evidence?

4. As the principal case states, plaintiff will not necessarily recover double when the collateral-source rule is applied. Indemnity insurance contracts may provide that the insurer is to be subrogated to the insured's tort claim. The United States government by statute has a similar right of subrogation for benefits it has paid to an injured party. See 42 U.S.C.A. § 2651 (amounts paid by the Veteran's Administration to veterans for service connected injuries excluded from the operation of the statute).

5. There has been substantial criticism of the collateral source rule, and the Attorney General's Tort Policy Working Group recommended that awards be reduced in cases in which the plaintiff can be compensated by certain collateral sources (provided by public programs or other sources, but not health or life insurance purchased by the plaintiff), in order to prevent a double recovery. Department of Justice, Report of the Tort Policy Working Group on the Causes, Extent and Policy Implications of the Current Crisis in Insurance Availability and Affordability (Feb. 1986). In 1986 and 1987, at least 14 states enacted legislation allowing admission of evidence of collateral source benefits, often either allowing court discretion or requiring reduction of awards to reflect the collateral payments. See, e.g., Florida Stat. § 768.76 (1986); New York, Ch. 220 of the Acts of 1986; Michigan, Public Act 178 of 1986.

See Schwartz, Tort Law Reform: Strict Liability and the Collateral Source Rule Do Not Mix, 39 Vand.L.Rev. 569 (1986); Lorentzen & Rankin, The Collateral Source Issue: Forging a Middle Ground, 35 Fed.Ins.Couns.Q. 3 (Fall 1984); Olson, The Not–So–Exclusive Remedy Rule, 33 Hastings L.J. 263 (1981); J. O'Connell, Ending Insult to Injury 141–147 (1975); James, Social Insurance and Tort Liability, 27 N.Y.U.L.Rev. 537 (1952); Fleming, The Collateral Source Rule and Loss Allocation in Tort Law, 54 Calif.L.Rev. 1478 (1966); Maxwell, The Collateral Source Rule in the American Law of Damages, 46 Minn.L.Rev. 669 (1962). The rule is vigorously defended in Lambert, The Case for the Collateral–Source Rule, 3 Trial Law.Q. 52 (1965). As it stands, the rule plays an important role in the rather curious calculus by which courts compute damages in personal injury cases. Other important parts of the calculus are mentioned below.

What is your view? Consider two analogies: (1) This amounts to being paid twice for the same harm. (2) This amounts to penalizing an innocent person who is richer or has more assets, because the money received from the third party on the claim against him is an asset that the plaintiff has acquired independently of the tortfeasor. Should either argument prevail? Is a compromise position better? Should the decision depend on the basis of liability imposed on the defendant, i.e., negligence or strict liability? Should it depend on the nature of the collateral source, i.e., a public source such as social security versus a private source such as a private health plan? What about subrogation rights maintained by the source itself? How does this fit into the picture?

6. *Federal Income Tax.* Plaintiff's award for personal injuries is not subject to the federal income tax. Under Section 104(a)(2) of the Internal Revenue Code of 1986, a tort victim can exclude from gross income the amount of compensatory or punitive damages he received on account of personal injuries. Punitive damages in libel and slander suits, however, are considered income. In most states, the rule regarding compensatory and punitive damage is usually the same. It seems clear that the single fact that a tort award is or is not subject to income tax should not in itself be sufficient to affect the amount of the award. A problem arises when the award, or a part of it, is to compensate for the loss of benefits that would have been subject to the tax if they had been received. The primary instance is compensation for lost wages. If no reduction is made in the award, the injured plaintiff receives more for wages than if he had not been injured. For this reason, some courts have held that the absence of income taxes must be taken into account in setting the amount of the award. Floyd v. Fruit Indus., 144 Conn. 659, 136 A.2d 918 (1957); Maus v. New York C. & St. L.R. Co., 165 Ohio St. 281, 135 N.E.2d 253 (1956). Other authorities have taken the position that "to deduct the anticipated tax saving from the recovery would nullify the tax benefit conferred by Congress"; the analogy to the collateral-source rule is obvious. Dixie Feed & Seed Co. v. Byrd, 52 Tenn.App. 619, 376 S.W.2d 745 (1964); Note, 69 Harv.L. Rev. 1495 (1956); Yorio, The Taxation of Damages: Tax and Non–Tax Policy Considerations, 62 Cornell L.Rev. 701 (1977); 16 A.L.R.4th 589 (1982) and supplements; Annot., 47 A.L.R.Fed. 735 (1980); Lost Wages Portion of Injury Settlement Is Not Taxable, 63 J.Tax'n 341 (1985); Richmond, Taxation of Personal Injury Awards: An Update, 3 Trial Advocate Q. 148 (1984); Dolin and Slessnick, Taxes and Their Effect on Compensatory Awards, 33 Fed.Ins.Couns. Q. 397 (1983); Franz, Should Income Taxes Be Excluded When Calculating Lost Earnings?, 18 Trial [No. 10] 53 (Oct.1982).

Most courts have been concerned about the speculative character of the amount of a potential deduction, at least insofar as it applies to future earnings. There is no way of telling what the tax rates will be in the future, nor what exemptions, deductions and other income the plaintiff would have, so as to determine what tax bracket he would have been in; and the whole matter is affected by possible future inflation. For these reasons, the Federal courts and most state courts have been inclined toward the position that in the case of the average taxpayer no deduction should be made, but that the other imponderables in the calculus would take care of the problem. There is a good debate on the pertinent policy issues between Judges Friendly and Lumbard in McWeeney v. New York, N.H. & H.R. R. Co., 282 F.2d 34 (2d Cir.1960), cert. denied, 364 U.S. 870 (1960). Another Federal case with good discussion is Domeracki v. Humble Oil & Ref. Co., 443 F.2d 1245 (3d Cir.), cert. denied, 404 U.S. 883 (1971). Other cases are found in Annot., 16 A.L.R.4th 589 (1983) and supplements. As indicated by the Friendly opinion, supra, different reasons may apply in the case of lost past earnings (when the amount of the tax can be accurately calculated) and the case of a taxpayer in an extremely high tax bracket, since he would receive an unduly high windfall. Should they produce a different result?

A separate problem is that of what should be said to the jury. Trial courts often find the whole matter frustrating and say nothing about it; and appellate courts usually find this within the discretion of the trial court. Other courts say that the jury should be told only that the award is not subject to income tax. The Supreme Court has ruled that in cases brought under the Federal Employers' Liability Act, evidence may be offered to show the effect of income taxes on the decedent's estimated future earnings, and may grant jury instructions that awards are tax-exempt and jurors should not consider such taxes in fixing the amount of the award. Norfolk & Western Ry. Co. v. Liepelt, 444 U.S. 490 (1980). The Court found reasonable cause for concern that tax-conscious juries would not be aware of the special statutory exception for personal injury awards contained in the Internal Revenue Code. See also Blanchfield v. Dennis, 292 Md. 319, 438 A.2d 1330 (1982). The Seventh Circuit, however, found the *Norfolk & Western* holding to be "procedural," and proceeded to apply state law to arrive at a somewhat different conclusion. In the case of In re Air Crash Disaster Near Chicago, 701 F.2d 1189 (7th Cir.1983), cert. denied, 464 U.S. 866 (1983), the court held that although an Illinois court would admit tax evidence to arrive at a measure of damages, under current Illinois practice, it was proper to refuse to instruct the jury that the damage award would not be subject to income taxes.

See Restatement, (Second) of Torts § 914A; Nordstrom, Income Taxes and Personal Injury Awards, 19 Ohio St.L.J. 212 (1958); Morris and Nordstrom, Personal Injury Recoveries and the Federal Income Tax Law, 46 A.B.A.J. 274 (1960); Phillips, Federal Income Taxation of Damages Paid or Received in Litigation, 65 A.B.A.J. 1238 (1978). On what awards are subject to income taxes, see Hartnett, Torts and Taxes, 27 N.Y.U.L.Rev. 614 (1952); Cutler, Taxation of the Proceeds of Litigation, 57 Colum.L.Rev. 470 (1957); Morrissy, Evidence and Instructions—Income Tax Issue, 1983 Tr.Law. Guide 139; Burns, A Compensation Award for Personal Injury or Wrongful Death is Tax–Exempt: Should We Tell the Jury? 14 DePaul L.Rev. 320 (1965); Inga, Damages—A Jury Should Receive Evidence and Instructions Concerning the Impact of Federal Income Taxation on an Award of Damages, 21 Santa Clara L.Rev. 873 (1981).

7. *Interest.* Because tort damages for personal injury are generally unliquidated in that plaintiff is not suing for a precise mathematical figure, courts traditionally have held that plaintiff cannot collect interest on his award until he receives a judgment. Potter v. Hartzell Propeller, Inc., 291 Minn. 513, 189 N.W.2d 499 (1971), noted in 56 Minn.L.Rev. 739 (1972). One negative result of this rule is that it may discourage early settlement by defendants. See Moore–McCormack Lines, Inc. v. Amirault, 202 F.2d 893 (1st Cir.1953), Annot., 6 A.L.R.2d 337 (1954). For this reason, legislatures in a number of states have enacted statutes that provide for interest on the amount of the award from the date of the institution of the action or from a date six months after the tort, whichever is later. See, e.g., Colo.Rev.Stat. § 41–2–1 (1963); Mich.Stat. § 27A.6013 (1962); R.I.Stat.Ann. § 9–21–10 (1969). See also N.J.S.Ct.Rule 4:42–11(b), discussed in Busik v. Levine, 63 N.J. 351, 307 A.2d 571, appeal dismissed, 414 U.S. 1106 (1973). Recently, however, a few states have begun limiting imposition of prejudgment interest on awards for some damages. See, e.g., Michigan, Public Act 178 of 1986 (future damages); Ramada Inns, Inc. v. Sharp, 101 Nev. 824, 711 P.2d 1 (1985) (punitive damages).

What is your view? Should plaintiff be paid interest on his "million dollar claim"? If so, when should interest obligations begin? Should interest cover both special and general damages? Even in the absence of statute, the jury may consider the time which has elapsed between the harm and the time of determining the amount of damages. See In re Air Crash Disaster Near Chicago, 644 F.2d 633 (7th Cir.1981) (although the relevant statute did not specify that prejudgment interest could be awarded, it could be allowed as one element of "fair and just compensation"). On interest in general, see Restatement (Second) of Torts § 913; Brown, The Availability of Prejudgment Interest in Personal Injury and Wrongful Death Cases, 16 U.S.F.L.Rev. 325 (1982); Prejudgment Interest, 26 Tr.Law.Guide 82 (1982); Williams, Pre–Judgment Interest: An Element of Damages Not To Be Overlooked, 22 Tr.Law.Guide 4 (1978); Comment, 49 U.Colo.L.Rev. 335 (1978).

8. *Expenses of Litigation.* Under the English practice, the winning party, whether plaintiff or defendant, normally recovers his expenses of litigation, including attorney's fees. C. McCormick, Damages § 60 (1935).

This is not the practice in the United States in regard to litigation in general, or tort litigation in particular, except in Alaska. Alaska Civil Rule 82. See Restatement (Second) of Torts § 914. It is sometimes suggested that in a personal-injury case, as a practical matter, the award for pain and suffering may have the effect of allowing the plaintiff to pay his attorney and still retain compensation for his pecuniary loss. Punitive damages, also, are regarded as a means of making attorney's fees available. Schlein v. Smith, 160 F.2d 22 (D.C. Cir.1947).

Chapter 21, infra, entitled "Misuse of Legal Procedure," covers the tort action for bringing a suit held to be frivolous or for using legal procedure for an improper purpose—"abuse of process." It also treats statutes and Rules of Court providing for the trial judge to impose a sanction—usually payment of attorney's fees—for conduct of this nature.

9. *The Contingent Fee.* Lawyers who represent plaintiffs in personal injury litigation are usually paid on the basis of a contingent fee contract. Under this arrangement, the lawyer agrees to render his professional services for a fee that is based on a percentage of the amount the client recovers in the case. If there is no recovery, the lawyer receives no fee. The percentage of the contingent fee varies, depending upon whether the case is settled or litigated. Also, it may vary in amount, depending on the size of recovery. While there are no reported statistics (and fee schedules among attorneys violate the antitrust laws), a common contingent fee is about 20%–25% of a settlement and 30%–40% of a final judgment. If for some reason no figure is set by attorney and client, or there is later a dispute about the amount of the figure, an attorney may bring an action against his former client for a *quantum meruit* recovery. See e.g., Nugent v. Downs, 230 So.2d 597 (La.App.1970) (fixing a fee of 30%); Annot., 57 A.L.R.3d 584 (1975). In certain situations the amount of the contingent fee may be fixed by statute. The best known example of this is the Federal Torts Claims Act, which makes it a crime for an attorney to obtain a contingent fee greater than 25% of the judgment (20% in a settlement) in a suit against the United States Government. See 28 U.S.C.A. § 2678. Jurors are not informed about the contingent fee and they are not to add that fee to their verdict. Thus, it is a basic part of the tort damage system that plaintiff, and not defendant, absorbs the costs of bringing a law suit.

As one might anticipate, the contingent fee has received harsh criticism. See M.T. Bloom, The Trouble With Lawyers (1968); Panel Discussion, Contingent Fees, 18 Fed.Ins.Couns.Q. 63 (1967); Kraut, Contingent Fee: Champerty or

Champion?, 21 Clev.St.L.Rev. 15 (1972). The contingent fee does come close to the borderline of champerty and maintenance, practices that have long been forbidden by common law. It is not champerty because the client theoretically retains control over the case and can dismiss the lawyer at any time. It does not represent maintenance because the client must pay for the out-of-pocket expenditures connected with the suit. Nevertheless, the contingent fee may result in an attorney being compensated far beyond what would be a "reasonable fee" for his efforts. Also, it may create a conflict of interest between attorney and client as to whether to accept a settlement. On the other hand, the contingent fee system has allowed poor persons to obtain good legal services when they are injured. Also, individual "fees" look less exorbitant when one considers that plaintiff attorneys also lose cases. See Brown, Some Observations on Legal Fees, 24 Sw.L.J. 565 (1970). See also Schwartz and Mitchell, An Economic Analysis of the Contingent Fee in Personal Injury Litigation, 22 Stan. L.Rev. 1125 (1970) (suggesting that the client be given a choice of fee systems: traditional contingent fee, hourly contingent fee or an hourly rate). In general see F. MacKinnon, Contingent Fees for Legal Services (1964).

The Supreme Court of New Jersey and courts in some other states, in their office as regulators of the bar, have put restrictions on the amount of the contingent fee. The New Jersey maximum fee schedule Rule 1:21–27 reads:

"* * * an attorney shall not contract for, charge, or collect a contingent fee in excess of the following limits:

"(1) 50% on the first $1000 recovered;

"(2) 40% on the next $2000 recovered;

"(3) 33⅓% on the next $47,000 recovered;

"(4) 20% on the next $50,000 recovered;

"(5) 10% on any amount recovered over $100,000; and

"(6) where the amount recovered is for the benefit of an infant or incompetent and the matter is settled without trial the foregoing limits shall apply, except that the fee on any amount recovered up to $50,000 shall not exceed 25%."

The schedule was unsuccessfully challenged on a variety of constitutional grounds by the American Trial Lawyers Association. See American Trial Lawyers Ass'n v. New Jersey Supreme Court, 66 N.J. 258, 330 A.2d 350 (1974). Is it an appropriate solution to the contingent fee dispute?

The Attorney General's Task Force made similar recommendations. How will this help cut waste and costs? Who benefits from limits on contingent fees? If we did not have them, how would poor, injured people receive justice in tort cases? European lawyers point out that there are no contingent fees in England or the European continent. Yet they claim that the poor, injured persons do receive justice. The English approach is to have the loser pay attorney's fees. Will this work? Do limits on the contingent fee help eliminate spurious claims? If not, how can society reduce or get rid of them?

10. *Periodic Payment of Damages.* When an injury is very serious, large damages are likely to be involved. The traditional common law treatment is to provide for lump-sum damages, with the money to go to the injured party for him to spend or invest as he sees fit. Practical advantages may inure to him if a settlement provides for periodic payments and he does not have the responsibility of arranging for investment to insure that the income will last during the necessary period. An additional tax advantage can also arise. Although he

does not pay income tax on the lump-sum amount, he would have to pay the tax on income from the investment. This tax may be minimized by a properly arranged periodic-payment settlement, often called a structured settlement. Benefits of a similar nature may also inure to the defendant, and sometimes also to the plaintiff's attorney. This has led to much interest in utilizing structured settlements. See Hindert, Periodic Payment of Personal Injury Damages, 31 Fed.Ins.Couns.Q. 3 (1980); Krause, Structured Settlements for Tort Victims, 66 A.B.A.J. 1527 (1980); Stone, Explaining Structured Settlements, 21 Trial 96 (Feb.1985); Winslow, Tax and Economic Considerations in Structured Settlements, 35 Fed.Ins.Couns.Q. 56 (1984); Vaughan, Tax Issues of Personal Injury and Wrongful Death Awards, 19 Tulsa L.J. 702 (1984); Staller, The Periodic Payment Settlement Act of 1982, 29 Prac.Law. [No. 3] 25 (Apr. 1983); Wells, Tax Consequences of Damages, 12 Colo.Law. 53 (1983); Leland, Periodic Payments, 3 Cal.Law. 32 (1983); Harrison, The Ethics of Structuring Settlements, 34 Drake L.Rev. 1045 (1985); Sweeney, Structured Settlements: Plaintiffs' Attorneys' Fees, 1982 Tr.Law.Guide 335.

There is also growing interest in arranging for periodic payments after a judgment has been awarded and, in 1986 and 1987, 12 states enacted legislation to permit, or in some instances require, periodic payment of damages. See, e.g., Florida, Ch. 86–160 of 1986; Michigan, Public Act 178 of 1986; New York, Ch. 682 of Acts of 1986. Constitutional challenges to statutes regarding periodic payment of punitive damages have not been successful. In American Bank & Trust Co. v. Community Hosp., 36 Cal.3d 359, 683 P.2d 670, 204 Cal.Rptr. 671 (1984), the court observed that plaintiffs have no vested property right in a particular measure of damages, and that the legislature has broad authority to modify the scope and nature of such damages.

The Uniform Laws Commissioners have prepared a Model Periodic Payment of Judgments Act, 14 Uniform Laws Ann. 2 (West, Supp.1981). The Act is discussed by the Reporter of the Act, in Henderson, Periodic Payments of Bodily Injury Awards, 66 A.B.A.J. 734 (1980). For further comment, see Corboy, Structured Injustice: Compulsory Periodic Payment of Judgments, 66 A.B.A.J. 1524 (1980); Henderson, Restoring the Tort Victim to Pre–Injury Position: A Goal on Which All Can Agree, 67 A.B.A.J. 301 (1980); Elligett, The Periodic Payment of Judgments, 46 Ins.Couns.J. 130 (1979); Grossman & Roman, The Model Periodic Payment of Judgments Act: An Economic Analysis, 18 Trial [No. 5] 62 (May 1982). See generally D. Hindert, Dehner & Hindert, Structured Settlements and Periodic Payment Judgments (1986).

ZIMMERMAN v. AUSLAND   *Duty to mitigate damages*

Supreme Court of Oregon, 1973.
266 Or. 427, 513 P.2d 1167.

[Plaintiff suffered a torn semilunar cartilage in her knee as the result of an automobile accident caused by the negligence of defendant. She obtained a jury verdict for $7,500 which included damages for *Trf = π* "permanent injury" in that she would no longer be able to engage in strenuous physical education activities. She had previously engaged in these activities in her work as a substitute teacher.

Defendant introduced a physician's expert testimony that if plaintiff had the torn cartilage "surgically excised," she "should recover completely." At the time of trial, plaintiff had not undergone the operation and she gave no indication that she would do so in the future.]

TONGUE, JUSTICE. * * * Defendant contends that the trial court erred in submitting to the jury the issue whether plaintiff sustained a permanent injury, as alleged in her complaint, and in instructing the jury on plaintiff's life expectancy, after taking judicial notice of the Standard Mortality Tables. * * *

It is * * * well established that the plaintiff in a personal injury case cannot claim damages for what would otherwise be a permanent injury if the permanency of the injury could have been avoided by submitting to treatment by a physician, including possible surgery, when a reasonable person would do so under the same circumstances. [Cc]

In this case defendant did not request an instruction on mitigation of damages, with the result that this question was not submitted to the jury. Nevertheless, if the facts are such that the court must hold, as a matter of law, that the plaintiff failed to mitigate her damages by submission to surgery when a reasonable person would have done so, the plaintiff would not be entitled to claim damages for what might otherwise be a permanent injury. It would also follow, in such an event, that defendant would be correct in contending that it was error to submit the issue of permanent injury to the jury, including consideration of the mortality tables.

In general * * * the test to be applied in determining whether a plaintiff has unreasonably failed or refused to mitigate his damages by submitting to a surgical operation is whether, under the circumstances of the particular case, an ordinarily prudent person would do so, i.e., the duty to exercise reasonable care under the circumstances. [Cc]

* * * Conversely, if under the circumstances, a reasonable person might well decline to undergo a surgical operation, a failure to do so imposes no disability against recovering full damages. [C]

The factors to be considered for this purpose ordinarily include the risk involved (i.e., the hazardous nature of the operation), the probability of success, and the expenditure of money or effort required. [C] Some courts also consider the pain involved as a factor, but no such question is presented for decision in this case. * * *

[I]t has been held that there must be evidence relating to the extent of the risk involved in a particular type of surgical operation before a jury may properly consider the contention that a plaintiff acted unreasonably in declining to submit to a surgical operation. * * *

No case has been cited to us in which it has been held that a plaintiff with a torn cartilage in the knee must submit to surgery to remove the damaged cartilage or be barred, as a matter of law, from seeking damages for an otherwise permanent injury, at least in the absence of such evidence. * * *

subj/verb agreement

We hold * * * that under the facts and circumstances of this case ⒣ the evidence supporting defendant's contention that plaintiff was required to submit to surgery upon her knee and the related contention that, for failure to do so, she is barred from claiming damages for a permanent injury to her knee, were not so clear and conclusive as to make it proper for the court to decide those questions in this case as a matter of law. This is not to say, of course, that defendant was not entitled to offer evidence of these questions and have them submitted to the jury under appropriate instructions. After examining the record in this case we also hold that testimony was offered by plaintiff from which, if believed by the jury, it could properly find that plaintiff has suffered a permanent injury, and one which interferes with her normal and usual activities, including those relating to her work as a substitute teacher. It follows that the trial court did not err in submitting that issue to the jury or in instructing it on life expectancy tables. The verdict of the jury was supported by substantial evidence and the judgment of the trial court is affirmed.

McALLISTER, J., concurs in the result.

RTL = Δ *failed to offer necessary evidence*

1. The so-called duty to mitigate damages in tort law actually is merely an inability to recover for those damages. It is often called the "avoidable consequences" rule. This rule denies recovery for any damages which could have been avoided by reasonable conduct on the part of the plaintiff after a legal wrong has been committed by defendant. It is distinguished from the defense of contributory negligence, which is unreasonable conduct on the part of plaintiff that contributes to the happening of the accident. See Restatement (Second) of Torts § 918.

2. Most decisions are in accord with the principal case in that defendant must prove that plaintiff's unreasonable conduct prevented the diminution of his injuries. See Roy v. Robin, 173 So.2d 222 (La.App.) cert. denied, 247 La. 877, 175 So.2d 110 (1965); Colton v. Benes, 176 Neb. 483, 126 N.W.2d 652 (1964). But see Barretto v. Akau, 51 Hawaii 383, 463 P.2d 917 (1969). There is division as to whether the matter must be specifically pleaded by defendant. What would be the advantage of that requirement? See Moulton v. Alamo Ambulance Serv., Inc., 414 S.W.2d 444 (Tex.1967).

3. The failure to submit to surgery that a reasonable person would undergo to mitigate injury can limit plaintiff's damages for both loss of wages and pain and suffering. See Young v. American Export Isbrandtsen Lines, Inc., 291 F.Supp. 447 (S.D.N.Y.1968) (failure to remove ruptured cartilage). The mere fact that there is some risk involved, even with a chance of fatality, may not bar the application of the avoidable consequences rule. See Bowers v. Lumbermens Mut. Casualty Co., 131 So.2d 70 (La.App.1961). See also Hayes v. United States, 367 F.2d 340 (2d Cir.1966). Is this inconsistent with the principle inherent in the law of battery that individuals should have the right to decide whether another person can violate their physical being?

4. See generally, Failure to Mitigate Damages by Showing Plaintiffs Failed to Follow Doctors' Orders, 31 Current Med. 16 (1984); Note, 45 U.Cin.L. Rev. 56 (1976); Annots., 62 A.L.R.3d 70 (1975), 62 A.L.R.3d 9 (1975), 75 A.L.R.2d 473 (1961).

2. PHYSICAL HARM TO PROPERTY

Damages for physical harm to land or chattels is closely tied in with the concept of value, or in other words, what the property is worth. If a chattel is completely destroyed, or is converted, the measure of damages is its entire value at the time and place of the tort. If it is damaged, but not destroyed or converted, the damages are measured by the difference in value before and after the injury. If there is merely deprivation of use, as in the case of dispossession for a limited time, the damages consist of the value of the use of which the plaintiff has been deprived.

Value necessarily involves the idea of some standard by which it can be determined. What we are looking for is the financial equivalent of the property, or the harm to it. In the vast majority of the cases, whether the harm is to chattels or to land, the standard set for value is the market value of the property. The theory underlying this is that the plaintiff, given this financial equivalent, can go out on the open market and replace the property by buying other property freely offered for sale. See, generally, Restatement (Second) of Torts § 911.

Market value usually is defined as what the property in question could probably have been sold for on the open market, in the ordinary course of voluntary sale by a leisurely seller to a willing buyer. C. McCormick, Damages, 165 (1935). Thus it is not the cost to the seller, or his asking price: nor is it what could be obtained on a forced sale. But since value must be looked at from the point of view of one who is complaining of being deprived of the thing valued, it is the highest price that he could have realized that we are seeking, and not the lowest price at which there could reasonably have been a sale. Also, the market value of property must be taken as a whole; and if for example, there is conversion of a stock of goods or a tract of land, it is the wholesale price of the stock of goods which is to be considered, since that is the only price at which it could have been sold in its entirety, and is the price of the land as a tract, rather than as subdivided into lots, which must be taken.

Market value ordinarily is determined on the basis of the market at the place where the wrong occurred. When there is no available market at that place, there is resort to the nearest market, with allowance made for the costs of transportation to and from it. If the goods were intended by the plaintiff for use, these costs will be added to the market price; but if they were intended for sale, they will be deducted.

Market value also is ordinarily determined as of the time of the wrong. There is, however, one exceptional group of cases in which subsequent increases in value have been taken into account. These arise where there is conversion of goods of the kind commonly dealt in on exchanges, such as stocks and bonds, and commodities such as grain. The same exception is made as to cases of breach of contract to sell such goods to the plaintiff. Even here a small minority of the courts refuse to consider subsequent increase in value, and adhere strictly to the value at the time of the wrong. Most of the American courts have made some kind of allowance for the increase. The leading cases on this are Galigher v. Jones, 129 U.S. 193 (1889) and Schultz v. Commodity Futures Trading Comm'n, 716 F.2d 136 (2d Cir.1983).

Assuming that some allowance is to be made for subsequent increase, or in other words, for successful speculation, the courts have not agreed as to just what is to be allowed. One group of cases have allowed as damages the highest value which the goods have reached during the period from the time of the wrong down to the trial of the action. This is called the "rule of the highest intermediate value." It has been criticized on the basis that it assumes that the plaintiff, if he still had the goods, would have sold them at the peak reached during that entire period; and that the longer the delay until trial the longer the time during which the plaintiff may benefit from a rise in the market. Some of the courts require, however, that the plaintiff's action must be prosecuted with reasonable diligence; and others permit recovery only of the highest intermediate value up to the commencement of the action.

Rather more than a third of the courts to consider the question follow the rule originated in New York, which, as the great commercial center, has received considerable respect in all matters concerning exchanges. The New York rule has been that the plaintiff may recover the highest market value between the time of conversion and a reasonable period within which he could have replaced the goods by purchase on the market. This is commonly known as the "highest replacement value" rule. The time for replacement does not begin at the time of the defendant's wrong, but at the time the plaintiff learns of it. The "reasonable time" for replacement is kept from being extended too far by the jury, by the view, at least in many courts, that where the facts are not in dispute, it is for the judge to say how long is a "reasonable time." See Restatement (Second) of Torts § 927.

Infrequently it will be found that chattels have no market value, simply because they are not salable. More often the market value clearly would not be adequate compensation. In these cases there may be recovery of the value to the owner, as distinguished from value to others. This is obviously true of family heirlooms and other articles that have a purely personal value, to the plaintiff and no one else. It is also true, in general, of clothing, books, pictures, furniture and household goods generally, which will obviously be worth more to the owner than their value to a second-hand store. The "personal value" so awarded is determined by consideration of whatever factors may be relevant, such as original cost of the property, the use made of it, and its condition at the time of the wrong. See, for example, Barker v. S.A. Lewis Storage & Transfer Co., 78 Conn. 198, 61 A. 363 (1905) (household goods); Blauvelt v. Cleveland, 198 App.Div. 229, 190 N.Y.S. 881 (1921) (shepherd dog); Southern Express Co. v. Owens, 146 Ala. 412, 41 So. 752

(1906) (unpublished manuscript). See also Annot., 12 A.L.R.2d 902 (1950).

All of this concerns only financial, or economic, value. Sentimental value, in the sense of the mental distress that the plaintiff feels at being deprived of the property, is not normally compensated. There are, however, occasional cases of extreme outrage, or of especial likelihood that the tort will cause mental distress, where these damages have been awarded. A recent case of this kind is Levine v. Knowles, 218 So. 2d 217 (Fla.App.1969), where the owner of a pet dog recovered for mental distress at the wrongful cremation of its body. Compare, as to invasion of the home, Watson v. Dilts, 116 Iowa 249, 89 N.W. 1068 (1902); Engle v. Simmons, 148 Ala. 92, 41 So. 1023 (1906); American Sec. Co. v. Cook, 49 Ga.App. 723, 176 S.E. 798 (1934). See also, Annot., 28 A.L.R.2d 1070 (1983).

When the property is not destroyed or converted, but only damaged, the measure becomes one of the difference in value before and after the wrong. The cost of repairing the land or chattel is admissible in evidence, on the assumption that it amounts to a restoration of the original value; but it is not conclusive, and may be challenged by either side as excessive or inadequate for the purpose. Restatement (Second) of Torts § 928. The cost of repairs may not exceed the value of the chattel prior to the injury. See Smith v. Brooks, 337 A.2d 493 (D.C. App.1975).

When there is only temporary deprivation of use, as by disposession for a limited period, the measure becomes one of the rental value of the property for that period—or in other words, the amount which the owner could have obtained in the market by renting out the property, or the cost to him of renting similar property for the specified time. See Brownstein, What's the Use? A Doctrinal and Policy Critique of the Measurement of Loss of Use Damages, 37 Rutgers L.Rev. 433 (1985).

Consequential damages may be recovered for the conversion of property, or for harm to it, when they are "proximately" caused. These might include, for example, the reasonable expense of trying to recover possession of the property, or loss of a profitable bargain resulting from deprivation of the goods, and the like. Parroski v. Goldberg, 80 Wis. 339, 50 N.W. 191 (1891); Preble v. Hanna, 117 Or. 306, 244 P. 75 (1926); Universal Credit Co. v. Wyatt, 56 S.W.2d 487 (Tex.Civ.App.1933). An interesting case in which market value, consequential damages and punitive damages all were recovered is Glass v. Brunt, 157 Kan. 27, 138 P.2d 453 (1943); see also Annot., 54 A.L.R.2d 1361 (1957).

3. PUNITIVE DAMAGES

Punitive damages, sometimes called exemplary or vindictive damages, or "smart money," consist of an additional sum, over and above the compensation of the plaintiff for the harm that he has suffered, which are awarded to him for the purpose of punishing the defendant, of admonishing him not to do it again, and of deterring others from following his example. They originated in England in the days of George III, in cases of outrageous abuses of authority by government officers, such as Huckle v. Money, 2 Wils.K.B. 205, 95 Eng.Rep. 768 (1763), and were presently taken over in the United States.

The policy of awarding punitive damages in tort cases has been a subject of much dispute. It has been condemned as undue compensation to the plaintiff beyond his just deserts, in the form of a criminal fine that should be paid to the state if to anyone and is fixed by the caprice of the jury, without any standards, and without any of the usual safeguards thrown about criminal procedure, such as proof of guilt beyond a reasonable doubt, the privilege against self-incrimination, and even the rule against double jeopardy—since, except in Indiana, the defendant may still be punished for the crime after he has been mulcted in the tort action.

Punitive damages have been defended as a salutary method of discouraging evil motives, as a partial remedy for the refusal of American civil procedure to allow compensation for the expenses of litigation including counsel fees, diverting plaintiff's desire for revenge into peaceful channels, and as an incentive to bring into court and redress a long array of petty cases of outrage and oppression, which in practice escape the notice of busy prosecuting attorneys occupied with serious crime, and which a private individual would otherwise find not worth the trouble and expense of a lawsuit.

"In forty states and in the federal courts [the allowance of punitive damages] is fully recognized. In one, Indiana, it is recognized but limited in range by the rule which forbids their allowance where the defendant's conduct is also punishable criminally. In Connecticut they are allowed but limited to the expense of litigation. New Hampshire and Michigan approximate the English view, and allow 'exemplary damages,' but regard them, not as punishment, but as extra compensation for injured feelings or sense of outrage. Four states, Louisiana, Massachusetts, Nebraska and Washington, definitely reject the doctrine altogether." C. McCormick, Damages, 278–279 (1935).

Although the above was written in 1935, it is still a reasonably accurate picture of the general state of the American law. But there have been recent changes. Some states have placed a cap or limit on the amount of punitive damages. Others have enacted legislation that would make them flow, at least in part, to the state. Large companies have been forced into bankruptcy allegedly because of punitive damages; and this has cut off the right of other people to receive compensatory damages.

GRYC v. DAYTON–HUDSON CORP.

Supreme Court of Minnesota, 1980.
297 N.W.2d 727, cert. denied, 449 U.S. 921.

TODD, JUSTICE. On December 8, 1969, Lee Ann Gryc, then 4 years of age, was clothed in pajamas made from a cotton material manufactured by defendant Riegel Textile Corporation (Riegel). The material was commercially known as "flannelette." It was not treated but did meet the <u>minimum federal standards</u> of product flammability. Lee Ann reached across the electric stove in her home to shut off a timer. Her pajamas were instantly ignited and she received severe burns over her upper body. The jury found Riegel liable for these injuries and awarded Lee Ann $750,000 in <u>compensatory damages</u> and $1,000,000 in <u>punitive damages.</u> We affirm. * * *

[Handwritten margin note: Trct =]

At trial, plaintiffs contended and presented evidence which tended to prove that the fabric used in the Gryc pajamas was defective. They claimed and their evidence tended to show that: (1) the cotton flannelette was unreasonably dangerous for use in children's sleepwear because of its highly flammable characteristics; (2) there were commercially available durable flame retardant chemicals which could have significantly increased the safety of the product; (3) there were inherently flame retardant synthetics which could have been used for children's sleepwear instead of cotton flannelette; (4) garment manufacturers, sellers, and consumers should have been warned of the flammable characteristics of the cotton flannelette; and (5) consumers should have been instructed of a simple home remedy which could have been used to flame retard the fabric after each washing. * * *

Riegel * * * contends that the trial court, in instructing the jury on the issue of punitive damages, applied an incorrect legal standard and burden of proof. Riegel argues that a "reckless disregard" standard was improperly applied and that the burden of proof on this issue should have been one of "clear and convincing evidence" rather than a "preponderance of the evidence." <u>Riegel presents these arguments for the first time on appeal.</u> These arguments were not raised at trial or in Riegel's post-trial motions.

[Handwritten margin notes: Acts to get punished; "reckless disregard"; See n. 6]

* * * [W]e hold that the <u>trial court's instructions</u> cannot now be attacked by Riegel. The <u>instructions constitute the law of the case</u> and Riegel's subsequent arguments will be reviewed on the basis of the legal standard imposed by the trial court.[6]

[Handwritten margin note: Now the "law" of subsequent cases as well]

In instructing the jury on the issue of punitive damages, the court listed several factors which the jury was to take into account in determining whether Riegel had acted in willful or reckless disregard of plaintiffs' rights:

[Handwritten margin note: list of factors]

(1) The existence and magnitude of the product danger to the public;

(2) The cost or feasibility of reducing the danger to an acceptable level;

(3) The <u>manufacturer's awareness</u> of the danger, the magnitude of the danger, and the availability of a feasible remedy;

[Handwritten margin note: = duty to be aware?]

---

6. We note that 1978 Minn.Laws c. 738, § 4, which subsequently changed the law with respect to the legal standard for punitive damages, is not applicable in this case.

4. The nature and duration of, and the reasons for, the manufacturer's failure to act appropriately to discover or reduce the danger;

5. The extent to which the manufacturer purposefully created the danger;

6. The extent to which the defendants are subject to federal safety regulation;

7. The probability that compensatory damages might be awarded against defendants in other cases; and, finally, *Consider this to what end? To leave a with money to other π's.*

8. The amount of time which has passed since the actions sought to be deterred.

We have reviewed the entire record and, after taking into consideration the above-listed factors, have concluded that there was sufficient, in fact substantial, evidence for the jury to find that Riegel acted in willful, wanton and/or malicious disregard of the rights of others in marketing its flannelette. * * *

Riegel contends that various policy considerations dictate against an award of punitive damages in this case. It argues that, in products liability cases where there is a potential for multiple plaintiffs, over-severe admonition and severe economic hardship may result if punitive damages awards are allowed. This same criticism was made by Judge Friendly in the case of Roginsky v. Richardson–Merrell, Inc., 378 F.2d 832, 838–9 (2nd Cir.1967). However, this argument has been consistently rejected by other courts and commentators who have considered this issue. * * *

Moreover, since Riegel's wealth or poverty and the degree to which it has already been punished was relevant in this case and will be relevant in future actions against it, Riegel is adequately protected against being overly punished for its misconduct.

Riegel also argues that there is no need for the deterrent of punitive damages in this case. Riegel contends that compensatory damages and loss of sales and reputation act as an adequate deterrent. Riegel also posits that since it no longer manufactures cotton flannelette and since the Flammable Fabrics Act presently has more stringent standards for children's sleepwear, no deterrent is needed. This argument ignores the fact that Riegel was shown to have acted in reckless disregard of the public for purely economic reasons in the past. A punitive damages award serves to deter Riegel from acting in a similar manner with respect to other products manufactured by it in the future. Furthermore, since the potential of compensatory damages awards and loss of sales and reputation did not serve to deter Riegel in the past, Riegel cannot now argue that these considerations act as an adequate deterrent. *Was this tried accordingly?*

Riegel also overlooks the fact that one of the functions of a punitive damages award is to punish past misconduct. This function is well served by a punitive damages award in this case.

Riegel contends that the punitive damages award of $1,000,000 was clearly excessive. This court has stated that it will not disturb a punitive damages award unless it appears that the award was actuated by passion and prejudice and is so excessive as to be deemed unreasonable. [C] We have reviewed the record in this case and find that the punitive damages award is not unreasonable in light of the evidence presented.

The evidence shows that Riegel created a substantial danger to the public by marketing its highly flammable cotton flannelette. Riegel continued to market this product even though there were economically feasible measures which could have been taken to reduce this danger to a fairly acceptable level. The evidence also showed that Riegel was aware of the danger and the means for reducing this danger. Furthermore, Riegel is a multi-million dollar corporation which reaped substantial profits through the sale of its highly flammable cotton flannelette. *You think so?* We, therefore, do not find that the punitive damages award was excessive as a matter of law. * * *

[The Court also determined that the defendant's compliance with the Flammable Fabrics Act, P.L. 90–189 § 6, 81 Stat. 568, did not preempt the jury's right to award punitive damages.]

The judgment is, therefore, affirmed. *— the state level — jury re. democracy can raise the standards; — lower them?*

———

1. A major problem involving corporate defendants and punitive damages today focuses on products. If a product is manufactured "with reckless disregard" for the safety of consumers, there may be hundreds of potential victims and the defendant may be liable for millions of dollars in punitive damages. The net result may be to deprive persons who need compensatory damages of an opportunity to recover; no matter how big the corporation, its assets are limited and the cumulative effect could result in the destruction of the company held liable. Is there any solution to this problem? It was first raised by Judge Friendly in a long dictum in Roginsky v. Richardson–Merrell, Inc., 378 F.2d 832 (2d Cir.1967).

2. In 1986, the Supreme Court of New Jersey held that punitive damages are allowable in a product liability case where the underlying claim was based on strict liability. Fischer v. Johns–Manville Corp., 103 N.J. 643, 512 A.2d 466 (1986). The defendant unsuccessfully argued that the concept of strict liability for products (see Ch. 15 infra) which theoretically focuses on the condition of the product rather than the conduct of the manufacturer, is incompatible with the concept of punitive damages, which is based on the defendant's malicious conduct. What do you think?

In Jackson v. Johns–Manville Sales Corp., 727 F.2d 506 (5th Cir.1984), cert. denied, ___ U.S. ___, 106 S.Ct. 3339, 92 L.Ed.2d 743 (1986), the court disallowed punitive damages in a mass torts case, finding that the allowance of punitive damages was incompatible with the strict liability cause of action and disrupted its viability. Deciding that strict liability seeks not merely to assure compensation for the individual plaintiff but also to achieve the broader societal objective of equitable loss distribution, it held that since the presence of a viable enterprise is essential to the maintenance of effective loss distribution under strict liability, the damages should not be allowed when an award for punitive damages would destroy the viability of the enterprise. It also noted that the basic policy objectives of punitive damages, punishment and deterrence, are satisfied by multiple exposure to compensatory damages. On rehearing, however, the court reversed itself and held that, under the applicable Mississippi law, punitive damages are available in mass tort cases in which a defendant is exposed to multiple awards of both compensatory and punitive damages. Jackson v. Johns–Manville Sales Corp., 781 F.2d 394 (5th Cir.1986), cert. denied, ___ U.S. ___, 106 S.Ct. 3339, 92 L.Ed.2d 743 (1986).

See generally Seltzer, Punitive Damages in Mass Tort Litigation: Addressing the Problems of Fairness, Efficiency, and Control, 52 Fordham L.Rev. 37 (1983); Sales, The Emergence of Punitive Damages in Product Liability Actions: A Further Assault on the Citadel, 14 St. Marys L.J. 351 (1983); Owen, Problems in Assessing Punitive Damages Against Manufacturers of Defective Products, 49 U.Chi.L.Rev. 1 (1982); Schuster, Punitive Damages Awards in Strict Products Liability Litigation: The Doctrine, the Debate, the Defenses, 42 Ohio St. L.J. 771 (1981); Ghiardi & Kircher, Punitive Damage Recovery in Products Liability Cases, 65 Marq.L.Rev. 1 (1981); Phillips, The Punitive Damage Class Action: A Solution to the Problem of Multiple Punishment, 84 U.Ill.L.Rev. 153 (1984); Annots., 11 A.L.R.4th 1261 (1982), 13 A.L.R.4th 52 (1982) and supplements.

The Uniform Product Liability Act attempted to solve this problem by providing that the judge, rather than the jury, should decide the amount of punitive damages. The jury would still decide whether they should be awarded at all. See 44 Fed.Reg. 62748. The section was based on an excellent article by Professor Owen. See Owen, Punitive Damages in Product Liability Litigation, 74 Mich.L.Rev. 1257 (1976). See also Fulton, Punitive Damages in Product Liability Cases, 15 Forum 117 (1979); Igoe, Punitive Damages in Products Liability Cases Should be Allowed, 1978 Tr. Law. Guide 24; Coccia and Morrissey, Punitive Damages in Product Liability Cases Should Not be Allowed, 1978 Tr. Law. Guide 46.

3. Punitive damages are often far in excess of any analogous criminal law fine. Is this fair to defendants? Should the defendants at least be accorded the rights given under the Constitution to criminal defendants? See Grass, The Penal Dimensions of Punitive Damages, 12 Hastings Const. L.Q. 241 (1985).

4. The decisions normally hold that punitive damages are a windfall to the plaintiff, not a right and that the jury has entire discretion to refrain from awarding them in any case. Harrison v. Ely, 120 Ill. 83, 11 N.E. 334 (1887); Petrey v. Liuzzi, 76 Ohio App. 19, 61 N.E.2d 158 (1945); Luke v. Mercantile Acceptance Corp., 111 Cal.App.2d 431, 244 P.2d 764 (1952). But see Micari v. Mann, 126 Misc.2d 422, 481 N.Y.S.2d 967 (1984), depicting a factual situation in which the court held that plaintiffs, who had been awarded only compensatory damages by a jury, were entitled to a new trial solely on the issue of punitive damages, unless the defendant stipulated to an award of $5,000 punitive damages for each plaintiff. Like an award of compensatory damages for personal injury, an award of punitive damage is not subject to federal income tax, so long as it is for personal injury. See 31 Hastings L.J. 909 (1980).

5. Punitive damages are generally permitted when defendant has committed an intentional tort such as assault, battery, false imprisonment, malicious prosecution or intentional infliction of emotional harm. Defendant's conduct need not be motivated by personal hatred; it is enough if it has the character of "outrage." Jones v. Fisher, 42 Wis.2d 209, 166 N.W.2d 175 (1969). Empirical

studies indicate that punitive damages are most frequently imposed and for greater amounts in the business torts of deceit and interference with advantageous relations, where the loss is economic in nature and the purpose to punish and deter is most appropriate. In the products liability cases with large punitive damage awards, it is often alleged that the defendant deliberately put or kept a product on the market without disclosing its known dangerous condition or even tried to conceal the danger. But, there are still times when a technically intentional tort may be committed innocently. For example, a defendant innocently buys a stolen article or falsely imprisons a person whom he reasonably believes to have stolen his property. In those cases the absence of ill will or malice will bar a claim for punitive damages. See Columbus Fin. Inc. v. Howard, 42 Ohio St.2d 178, 327 N.E.2d 654 (1975); F.B.C. Stores, Inc. v. Duncan, 214 Va. 246, 198 S.E.2d 595 (1973); Annots., 93 A.L.R.3d 1109 (1979); 94 A.L.R.3d 791 (1979).

⑥   As the principal case reflects, conduct short of intentional wrongdoing, may be sufficient to justify punitive damages. Courts use a variety of formulas to spell this out, including "wilful and wanton conduct," Smith v. Gray Concrete Pipe Co., Inc., 267 Md. 149, 297 A.2d 721 (1972); "reckless disregard" for the rights of others," Allman v. Bird, 186 Kan. 802, 353 P.2d 216 (1960); or "willful misconduct, wantonness, recklessness, or want of care indicative of indifference to consequences," In re Air Crash Disaster Near Chicago, 644 F.2d 594 (7th Cir.1981), cert. denied, 454 U.S. 878 (1981). Conduct that is merely negligent, even if it causes severe damage, is insufficient to justify punitive damages. This is usually held to be true of "grossly negligent" conduct when those terms are used as a synonym for "extreme carelessness" as opposed to "recklessness." Compare Moore v. Wilson, 180 Ark. 41, 20 S.W.2d 310 (1929), with Williamson v. McKenna, 223 Or. 366, 354 P.2d 56 (1960), superseded by statute as stated in Winn v. Gilroy, 296 Or. 718, 681 P.2d 776 (1984).

7.   In nearly every state there are statutes providing for punitive damages for torts in limited situations. A common type is the statute providing treble damages for trespass to land, destruction of trees or shrubbery, or the like.

8.   An important question upon which courts are divided concerns whether plaintiff must show actual or compensatory damages in order to recover punitive damages. In other words, should an award of nominal damages support a punitive damages award? See Shell Oil Co. v. Parker, 265 Md. 631, 291 A.2d 64 (1972), Annot., 40 A.L.R.4th 11 (1985). Should a plaintiff be required to show actual injury? A bystander who watched as a deranged man (who was having a violent reaction from his ingestion of Promaline, an 'unreasonably dangerous' drug) attack his mother and brother was allowed to state a cause of action for physical and mental suffering as well as punitive damages. The bystander suffered no physical injury, but was within the "zone of danger" of the incident. Jeannelle v. Thompson Medical Co., 613 F.Supp. 346 (E.D.Mo.1985).

9.   Conduct that is a breach of contract, but also amounts to a malicious intentional tort, can support an award of punitive damages. If plaintiff pursues a contractual remedy, however, such as return of the goods, he may be held to have "waived the tort" and also the availability of punitive damages. See Bryan Constr. Co., Inc. v. Thad Ryan Cadillac, Inc., 300 So.2d 444 (Miss. 1974).

10.   How are punitive damages calculated? The jury is told to consider "the character of defendant's act, the nature and extent of the harm to the

plaintiff and the wealth of the defendant." See Coats v. Constr. & Gen. Laborers Local # 185, 15 Cal.App.3d 908, 93 Cal.Rptr. 639 (1971). Defendant's wealth is relevant to the determination of the amount of damages that are necessary to create a punishment for defendant. The fact that the defendant's wealth is considered may justify different awards against two defendants who engaged in equally culpable conduct. See Joab, Inc. v. Thrall, 245 So.2d 291 (Fla.App.1971); Woodbury, Limiting Discovery of a Defendant's Wealth When Punitive Damages Are Alleged, 23 Duquesne L.Rev. 349 (1985); Note (1965) 20 U.Miami L.Rev. 465. Is this proper?

why?

Plaintiffs' attorneys routinely ask for punitive damages in order to be able to introduce evidence of a defendant's wealth in the case. The court then instructs the jury to ignore the evidence *unless* they find that the defendant has been reckless. The Uniform Product Liability Act § 120 prohibits this practice by requiring a separate procedure *by the court* to determine the amount of punitive damages.

A few states prohibit discovery of a defendant's wealth prior to establishment of a prima facie case. E.g., Iowa Code § 668A.1 (1986); Minn.Stat. § 549.191 (1986).

) so that at least must not be a frivolous case brought just b/c potential ∆ is rich

11. Some courts permit the defendant to show in an effort to mitigate damages that he has been criminally punished for the same wrong. See Hanover Ins. Co. v. Hayward, 464 A.2d 156 (Me.1983) (fact-finder may consider whether criminal liability has been imposed as one factor in determining whether an award of damages would serve as a meaningful deterrent). Other, chiefly older cases, refuse to allow even this mitigation. In any case, are there tactical reasons why defense counsel may decline this opportunity?

12. Some courts permit the jury to take into account plaintiff's counsel fees and other expenses of suit in determining the amount of punitive damages. Others refuse to do so, although as a practical matter it may be impossible to prevent the jury from realizing that attorneys' services are not free.

13. It is commonly said, as in Cotton v. Cooper, 209 S.W. 135 (Tex.Com. App.1919); and Hall Oil Co. v. Barquin, 33 Wyo. 92, 237 P. 255 (1925), that the amount of punitive damages must bear some reasonable proportion to the actual damages. On occasion, however, punitive awards greatly in excess of the actual damages found have been sustained. E.g., Livesey v. Stock, 208 Cal. 315, 281 P. 70 (1929) (actual damages $750, punitive $10,000); Seaman v. Dexter, 96 Conn. 334, 114 A. 75 (1921) (actual damages $318, punitive $5,000).

14. The recent campaign for legislative modification of tort law has induced some states to abolish punitive damages altogether. E.g., N.H.Rev. Stat. § 507:16 (1986). Some states enacted specific caps on punitive damage awards. E.g., Conn.Stat.Ann. § 52–240b (two times compensatory damages); Colo.Rev.Stat. § 13–21–102 (limited to amount of actual damages); Fla.Stat. § 768.73 (three times compensatory damages); Okla.Stat. § 23–9 (limited to amount of actual damages); Tex.Civ.Prac. and Rem.Code § 41.007 (four times actual damages or $200,000, whichever is greater); Va.Code § 8.01–38.1 ($350,000). Others provide that a part of the award will be paid to designated state funds. E.g., Fla.Stat. § 768.73(2)(b) (60 percent to the state Public Medical Assistance Trust Fund or the state General Revenue Fund); Iowa Code § 668.A.1 (75 percent to state civil reparations trust fund, except where action resulted from a tort specifically directed at the particular plaintiff).

15. See generally, Belli, Punitive Damages: Their History, Their Use, and Their Worth in Present Day Society, 49 UMKC L.Rev. 1 (1980). Grimshaw v.

Ford Motor Co., 119 Cal.App.3d 757, 174 Cal.Rptr. 348 (1981) involved a Ford Pinto that was struck from the rear and burst into flames, because of inadequate protection of the gas tank. The jury awarded $125,000,000 punitive damages but the trial judge reduced this to $3,500,000 and this was affirmed by the Court of Appeal. See Why the Pinto Jury Felt Ford Deserved $125 Million Penalty, Wall St.J., Feb. 14, 1978, p. 1; Launie, The Incidence and Burden of Punitive Damages, 53 Ins.Couns.J. 46 (1986); Daniels, Punitive Damages: The Real Story, 72 A.B.A.J. 60 (Aug.1986); Cowan, Zen and the Art of Exemplary Damages Assessment, 72 Ky.L.J. 897 (1984); Wheeler, The Constitutional Case for Reforming Punitive Damages Procedures, 69 Va.L.Rev. 269 (1983); Sales, Punitive Damages: A Relic that has Outlived Its Origins, 37 Vand.L.Rev. 1117 (1984); Sullivan, Defining Punitive Damages Under the Federal Tort Claims Act, 53 U.Cin.L.Rev. 251 (1984).

PRICE v. HARTFORD ACCIDENT AND INDEMNITY CO.

Supreme Court of Arizona, 1972.
108 Ariz. 485, 502 P.2d 522.

[Gary Gardner was seriously injured as a result of a drag race between Charles Price and another young man. Gardner brought a claim against Price for $100,000 compensatory and $25,000 punitive damages. Price's liability insurance company asserted that it had no duty to defend or indemnify him for the punitive-damage claim. Price's liability insurance policy issued by defendant promised to pay for "all sums" he might become liable to pay as damages "arising out of the ownership, maintenance and use" of the automobile in question. The policy had a $1,000,000 limit. In this suit, Charles Price and his mother sought a declaratory judgment that the policy included coverage for punitive damages.]

HAYS, CHIEF JUSTICE. * * * The clear, unequivocal language of the policy requires the insurance company to defend the action and pay the judgment. The only issue, therefore, is whether the public policy of the state makes the insurance contract illegal insofar as it relates to punitive damages. On this issue there is a conflict of opinion among the several states, and the matter has never been determined by this court.

The arguments favoring the view that it is against public policy to allow a defendant to insure his liability for punitive damages are well expressed in Northwestern National Casualty Co. v. McNulty, 307 F.2d 432, in which the court used the following language:

"Considering the theory of punitive damages as punitory and as a deterrent and accepting as common knowledge the fact that death and injury by automobile is a problem far from solved by traffic regulations and criminal prosecutions, it appears to us that there are especially strong public policy reasons for not allowing socially irresponsible automobile drivers to escape the element of personal punishment in punitive damages when they are guilty of reckless slaughter or maiming on the highway. * * * The delinquent driver must not be allowed to receive a windfall at the expense of the purchasers of insurance, transferring his responsibility for punitive damages to the very people—the driving public—to whom he is a menace. * * *

"If [the wrongdoer] were permitted to shift the burden to an insurance company, punitive damages would serve no useful purpose. Such damages do not compensate the plaintiff for his injury, since compensatory damages already have made the plaintiff whole. And there is no point in punishing the insurance company; it has done no wrong. In actual fact, of course, and considering the extent to which the public is insured, the burden would ultimately come to rest not on the insurance companies but on the public, since the added liability to the insurance companies would be passed along to the premium payers. Society would then be punishing itself for the wrong committed by the insured."

These arguments, at first blush, seem to have merit, but a careful analysis of them reveals several weaknesses. First, even though a driver is insured for punitive damages he cannot engage in wanton conduct with impunity. In the instant case, drag racing would subject him to criminal penalties. His insurance rates would soar. Hartford argues that the assigned risk provisions of the Arizona system would prevent them from soaring. However, the assigned risk procedure would not enable him to procure more than the minimum coverage of $15,000/30,000, and in order to replace his $1,000,000.00 limits, his premium would be tremendous. Second, Hartford has voluntarily covered its insured's liability for punitive damages, and since its premiums were based on its exposure, it may be presumed that holding it liable for what it has promised to pay would not result in additional burdens on the driving public. Third, the criminal penalties include possible loss of the driver's license and compulsory attendance at the traffic school. Fourth, punitive damages are not only designed to punish the offender but are also designed to serve as a deterrent to others. Since it is common knowledge that the vast majority of drivers do not carry million dollar liability policies, the possibility that punitive damages will exceed their policy limits will exercise a deterrent effect on them. Fifth, there is no evidence that those states which deny coverage have accomplished any appreciable effect on the slaughter on their highways. Sixth, the state of Arizona has more than one public policy. Such policy appears in many fields. One such public policy is that an insurance company which admittedly took a premium for covering *all* liability for damages, should honor its obligation. * * *

It is our holding that the premium has been paid and accepted and the protection has been tendered, and that under the circumstances public policy would be best served by requiring the insurance company to honor its obligation.

Reversed and remanded to the Superior Court for further proceedings consistent with this opinion.

[handwritten: = original to — would want Ins. Co. to pay.]

1.   As the opinion in the principal case reflects the issue before the court is a very close one.   What would be the view of Gary Gardner (the party injured by Price's alleged recklessness) on this issue?

2.   If you were house counsel for a liability insurance company that did business in Arizona, how would you advise your employer on the matter of punitive damages?   See Abbie Uriguen Oldsmobile Buick, Inc. v. United States Fire Ins. Co., 95 Idaho 501, 511 P.2d 783 (1973).

3.   Decisions in accord with the principal case include Southern Farm Bureau Casualty Ins. Co. v. Daniel, 246 Ark. 849, 440 S.W.2d 582 (1969); Dairyland County Mut. Ins. Co. v. Wallgren, 477 S.W.2d 341 (Tex.Civ.App.1972); Sinclair Oil Corp. v. Columbia Casualty Co., 682 P.2d 975 (Wyo.1984); and Anthony v. Frith, 394 So.2d 867 (Miss.1981).   Others have rejected the shift of punishment to the shoulders of the insurer, and have held it to be against public policy so to relieve the wrongdoer.   American Sur. Co. of New York v. Gold, 375 F.2d 523 (10th Cir.1966); Skyline Harvestore Systems v. Centennial Ins. Co., 331 N.W.2d 106 (Iowa 1983).   Are the arguments different when the tortious conduct is attributed to an employer due to vicarious liability for an employee?   See Dayton Hudson Corp. v. American Mut. Liab. Ins. Co., 621 P.2d 1155 (Okl.1980).

4.   See generally Pomerantz, Punitive Damages: Insurers' View, 1980 Ins. L.J. 21; Oshins, Should Punitive Damages Be Within the Coverage of Liability Insurance, 5 The Forum 78 (1969); Long, Insurance Protection Against Punitive Damages, 32 Tenn.L.Rev. 573 (1965); Formby, Insurability Against Punitive Damages: A Call for Reform, 23 S.Tex.L.J. 443 (1982); Annot., 16 A.L.R.4th 11 (1982).

5.   *Punitive Damages Against an Employer.*   Conflicting policies of a similar nature arise in connection with the question of whether punitive damages are properly awarded against an employer for the conduct of his employee.   The question is especially acute in an action against a corporation, which can act only through the conduct of its agents.   Some states take the position that a principal should be subject to punitive damages only for his own highly reprehensible conduct and so do not award them.

Others take the position that when the employee has committed conduct which subjects him to punitive damages, the employer may also be liable for them.   An especially vigorous opinion to this effect is found in Goddard v. Grand Trunk Ry., 57 Me. 202, 2 Am.Rep. 39 (1869).

A majority of the courts take a middle position and hold that the principal (whether an individual or a corporation) is liable if he authorized or ratified the act or was reckless in employing the agent, or if the agent was acting in a managerial capacity.   See Restatement (Second) of Torts § 909; Parris v. St. Johnsbury Trucking Co., 395 F.2d 543 (2d Cir.1968); Briner v. Hyslop, 337 N.W. 2d 858 (Iowa 1983).   See also Purvis v. Prattco, Inc., 595 S.W.2d 103 (Tex.1980) for a fascinating story of facts that would justify punitive damages if they are to be awarded at all.

See Owen, Problems in Assessing Punitive Damages Against Manufacturers of Defective Products, 49 U.Chi.L.Rev. 1 (1982); Sextro, Corporate Insurability of Punitive Damages Arising from Employee Acts, 11 J.Corp.L. 99 (1985); Sardell, Corporate Liability for Punitive Damages, 8 Corp.L.Rev. 184 (1985); Walden, The Publicly Held Corporation and the Insurability of Punitive Damages, 53 Fordham L.Rev. 1383 (1985).

Chapter XI

WRONGFUL DEATH AND SURVIVAL

MORAGNE v. STATES MARINE LINES, INC.

Supreme Court of the United States, 1970.
398 U.S. 375, 90 S.Ct. 1772, 26 L.Ed.2d 339.

MR. JUSTICE HARLAN delivered the opinion of the Court. We brought this case here to consider whether The Harrisburg, 119 U.S. 199, in which this Court held in 1886 that maritime law does not afford a cause of action for wrongful death, should any longer be regarded as acceptable law.

The complaint sets forth that Edward Moragne, a longshoreman, was killed while working aboard the vessel Palmetto State in navigable waters within the State of Florida. Petitioner, as his widow and representative of his estate, brought this suit in a state court against respondent States Marine Lines, Inc., the owner of the vessel, to recover damages for wrongful death and for the pain and suffering experienced by the decedent prior to his death. The claims were predicated upon both negligence and the unseaworthiness of the vessel. * * *

The Court's opinion in *The Harrisburg* acknowledged that the result reached had little justification except in primitive English legal history—a history far removed from the American law of remedies for maritime deaths. * * *

One would expect, upon an inquiry into the sources of the common-law rule, to find a clear and compelling justification for what seems a striking departure from the result dictated by elementary principles in the law of remedies. Where existing law imposes a primary duty, violations of which are compensable if they cause injury, nothing in ordinary notions of justice suggests that a violation should be nonactionable simply because it was serious enough to cause death. On the contrary, that rule has been criticized ever since its inception, and described in such terms as "barbarous." [Cc] Because the primary duty already exists, the decision whether to allow recovery for violations causing death is entirely a remedial matter. It is true that the harms to be assuaged are not identical in the two cases: in the case of mere injury, the person physically harmed is made whole for his harm, while in the case of death, those closest to him—usually spouse and children—seek to recover for their total loss of one on whom they depended. This difference, however, even when coupled with the practical difficulties of defining the class of beneficiaries who may recover for death, does not seem to account for the law's refusal to recognize a wrongful killing as an actionable tort. One expects, therefore, to find a persuasive, independent justification for this apparent legal anomaly.

Legal historians have concluded that the sole substantial basis for the rule at common law is a feature of the early English law that did not survive into this century—the felony-merger doctrine. [Cc] According to this doctrine, the common law did not allow civil recovery for an act that constituted both a tort and a felony. The tort was treated as less important than the offense against the Crown, and was merged into, or pre-empted by, the felony. [Cc] The doctrine found practical justification in the fact that the punishment for the felony was the death of the felon and the forfeiture of his property to the Crown; thus, after the crime had been punished, nothing remained of the felon or his property on which to base a civil action. Since all intentional or negligent homicide was felonious, there could be no civil suit for wrongful death.

The first explicit statement of the common-law rule against recovery for wrongful death came in the opinion of Lord Ellenborough, sitting at *nisi prius,* in Baker v. Bolton, 1 Camp. 493, 170 Eng.Rep. 1033 (1808). That opinion did not cite authority, or give supporting reasoning, or refer to the felony-merger doctrine in announcing that "[i]n a Civil court, the death of a human being could not be complained of as an injury." Ibid. Nor had the felony-merger doctrine seemingly been cited as the basis for the denial of recovery in any of the other reported wrongful-death cases since the earliest ones, in the 17th century. [Cc] However, it seems clear from those first cases that the rule of Baker v. Bolton did derive from the felony-merger doctrine, and that there was no other ground on which it might be supported even at the time of its inception. * * *

The historical justification marshaled for the rule in England never existed in this country. In limited instances American law did adopt a vestige of the felony-merger doctrine, to the effect that a civil action was delayed until after the criminal trial. However, in this country the felony punishment did not include forfeiture of property; therefore, there was nothing, even in those limited instances, to bar a subsequent civil suit. [Cc]

Nevertheless, despite some early cases in which the rule was rejected as "incapable of vindication," [cc] American courts generally adopted the English rule as the common law of this country as well. * * *

It was suggested by some courts and commentators that the prohibition of nonstatutory wrongful-death actions derived support from the ancient common-law rule that a personal cause of action in tort did not survive the death of its possessor [c], and the decision in Baker v. Bolton itself may have been influenced by this principle. [C] However, it is now universally recognized that because this principle pertains only to the victim's own personal claims, such as for pain and suffering, it has no bearing on the question whether a dependent should be permitted to recover for the injury he suffers from the victim's death. [Cc]

We need not, however, pronounce a verdict on whether *The Harrisburg,* when decided, was a correct extrapolation of the principles of decisional law then in existence. A development of major significance has intervened, making clear that the rule against recovery for wrongful death is sharply out of keeping with the policies of modern American maritime law. * * *

[L]egislatures both here and in England began to evidence unanimous disapproval of the rule against recovery for wrongful death. The first statute partially abrogating the rule was Lord Campbell's Act, 9 & 10 Vict., c. 93 (1846), which granted recovery to the families of persons killed by tortious conduct, "although the Death shall have been caused under such Circumstances as amount in Law to Felony."

In the United States, every State today has enacted a wrongful-death statute. See Smith, supra, 44 N.C.L.Rev. 402. The Congress has created actions for wrongful deaths of railroad employees, Federal Employers' Liability Act, 45 U.S.C.A. §§ 51–59; of merchant seamen, Jones Act, 46 U.S.C. § 688; and of persons on the high seas, Death on the High Seas Act, 46 U.S.C.A. §§ 761, 762. Congress has also, in the Federal Tort Claims Act, 28 U.S.C.A. § 1346(b), made the United States subject to liability in certain circumstances for negligently caused wrongful death to the same extent as a private person. [C]

These numerous and broadly applicable statutes, taken as a whole, make it clear that there is no present public policy against allowing recovery for wrongful death. The statutes evidence a wide rejection by the legislatures of whatever justifications may once have existed for a general refusal to allow such recovery. This legislative establishment of policy carries significance beyond the particular scope of each of the statutes involved. The policy thus established has become itself a part of our law, to be given its appropriate weight not only in matters of statutory construction but also in those of decisional law. See Landis, Statutes and the Sources of Law, in Harvard Legal Essays 213, 226–227 (1934).

Professor Landis has said, "much of what is ordinarily regarded as 'common law' finds its source in legislative enactment." Landis, supra, at 214. It has always been the duty of the common-law court to perceive the impact of major legislative innovations and to interweave the new legislative policies with the inherited body of common-law principles—many of them deriving from earlier legislative exertions.

[The court then concluded that it was sometimes the duty of the common law court to bend to the weight of legislative authority and noted that Congress by its failure to enact a specific remedy did not intend to forestall recovery for wrongful death in admiralty and that the doctrine of *stare decisis* does not preclude a change in law.]

Respondents argue that overruling *The Harrisburg* will necessitate a long course of decisions to spell out the elements of the new "cause of action." We believe these fears are exaggerated, because our decision does not require the fashioning of a whole new body of federal law, but merely removes a bar to access to the existing general maritime law. In most respects the law applied in personal-injury cases will answer all questions that arise in death cases. ∗ ∗ ∗

The one aspect of a claim for wrongful death that has no precise counterpart in the established law governing nonfatal injuries is the determination of the beneficiaries who are entitled to recover. General maritime law, which denied any recovery for wrongful death, found no need to specify which dependents should receive such recovery. On this question, petitioner and the United States argue that we may look for guidance to the expressions of Congress, which has spoken on this subject in the Death on the High Seas Act, the Jones Act, and the Longshoremen's and Harbor Workers' Compensation Act. Though very similar, each of these provisions differs slightly in the naming of dependent relatives who may recover and in the priority given to their claims. ∗ ∗ ∗

We do not determine this issue now, for we think its final resolution should await further sifting through the lower courts in future litigation. For present purposes we conclude only that its existence affords no sufficient reason for not coming to grips with *The Harrisburg*. If still other subsidiary issues should require resolution, such as particular questions of the measure of damages, the courts will not be without persuasive analogy for guidance. Both the Death on the High Seas Act and the numerous state wrongful-death acts have been implemented with success for decades. The experience thus built up counsels that a suit for wrongful death raises no problems unlike those that have long been grist for the judicial mill.

In sum, in contrast to the torrent of difficult litigation that has swirled about *The Harrisburg* ∗ ∗ ∗ and the problems of federal-state accommodation [it] occasioned, the recognition of a remedy for wrongful death under general maritime law can be expected to bring more placid waters. That prospect indeed makes for, and not against, the discarding of *The Harrisburg*.

We accordingly overrule *The Harrisburg*, and hold that an action does lie under general maritime law for death caused by violation of maritime duties. The judgment of the Court of Appeals is reversed, and the case is remanded to that court for further proceedings consistent with this opinion. It is so ordered.

Reversed and remanded.

----

1. American admiralty law was the last island for the common law rule that "the death of a human being could not be complained of as an injury." Baker v. Bolton, 1 Camp. 493, 170 Eng.Rep. 1033 (N.P.1808). Lord Ellenborough did not supply reasons for his rule, but later sympathizers with his result have given at least two. First, allowing a claim would lead jurors to award runaway damages and, second, it is "immoral" to place a monetary value on a human life.

2. The principal case is most unusual in making a major change away from the common law rule by the process of judicial decision. This was notable because heretofore the only way to change the common law was by statute. See Annot., 61 A.L.R.3d 906 (1975). In its subsequent decision of Sea–Land Services, Inc. v. Gaudet, 414 U.S. 573 (1974), the Supreme Court elaborated on its holding that there is a maritime common law cause of action for wrongful death. It held that the fact that the decedent had previously recovered damages for loss of wages, pain and suffering and medical expenses did not interfere with the independent common law cause of action for wrongful death resulting from the original injury, so that the later action was not precluded by res judicata. Recovery for wrongful death was held to cover damages for (1) "loss of support, * * * [including] all the financial support that the decedent would have made to his dependents had he lived," (2) "the monetary value of services the decedent provided and would have continued to provide but for his wrongful death * * * [including] the nurture, training, education, and guidance that a child would have received had not the parent been wrongfully killed * * * [plus] services the decedent performed at home or for his spouse," (3) "compensation for loss of society * * *, [embracing] a broad range of mutual benefits each family member receives from the others' continued existence, including love, affection, care, attention, companionship, comfort and protection," and (4) "damages for funeral expenses * * * in circumstances where the decedent's dependents have either paid for the funeral or are liable for its payment." The potential for double liability coming from the awards to the decedent for loss of future wages and to the defendants for loss of support was held to be controlled by the law of collateral estoppel, but it has continued to be a cause of concern to some courts. See Alfone v. Sarno, 87 N.J. 99, 432 A.2d 857 (1981) for a dicussion of duplication of damages in such cases.

3. Though it has a wrongful death statute, the state of Massachusetts has held that there is a common law action which may in some respects supplement the statutory action. In Gaudette v. Webb, 362 Mass. 60, 284 N.E.2d 222 (1972), the limitation period on the statutory action was avoided by holding that the common law action would be subject to the interpretations of the general statute of limitations allowing tolling during minority. See also the much earlier experience in Georgia in regard to a common law action for wrongful death, as described in Malone, The Genesis of Wrongful Death, 17 Stan.L.Rev. 1043, 1073–76 (1965).

4. Aside from these instances, all the states have statutes. Most of the statutes were modeled after Lord Campbell's Act, mentioned by Justice Harlan. These statutes vary in many important respects and the material considered in this Chapter is necessarily only introductory in nature. Lawyers do have the benefit of an excellent treatise on the subject that treats the statutes individually and has been kept up to date. See S. Speiser, Recovery for Wrongful Death (2d ed. 1975). The topic of wrongful death therefore differs from many others in the law of torts because it is statutory. Courts must engage in the process of statutory construction and fathoming legislative intent. This is not an easy process with regard to wrongful death statutes because there is rarely much legislative history and most statutes are over one hundred years old.

5. Representative wrongful death statutes from two states provide as follows:

South Carolina: *"Civil Action for Wrongful Act Causing Death.* Whenever the death of a person shall be caused by the wrongful act, neglect or default of another and the act, neglect or default is such as would, if death had not ensued, have entitled the party injured to maintain an action and recover damages in respect thereof, the person who would have been liable, if death had not ensued, shall be liable to an action for damages, notwithstanding the death of the person injured, although the death shall have been caused under such circumstances as make the killing in law a felony. In the event of the death of the wrongdoer, such cause of action shall survive against his personal representative." S.C.Code § 15–51–10.

"*Beneficiaries of Action for Wrongful Death; By Whom Brought.* Every such action shall be for the benefit of the wife or husband and child or children of the person whose death shall have been so caused, and, if there be no such wife, husband, child or children, then for the benefit of the parent or parents, and if there be none such, then for the benefit of the heirs at law or the distributees of the person whose death shall have been so caused. Every such action shall be brought by or in the name of the executor or administrator of such person." Id. § 15–51–20.

Ohio: "*Action for Wrongful Death.* When the death of a person is caused by wrongful act, neglect, or default which would have entitled the party injured to maintain an action and recover damages if death had not ensued, the corporation which or the person who would have been liable if death had not ensued, or the administrator or executor of the estate of such person, as such administrator or executor, shall be liable to an action for damages, notwithstanding the death of the person injured and although the death was caused under circumstances which make it aggravated murder, or manslaughter. When the action is against such administrator or executor the damages recovered shall be a valid claim against the estate of such deceased person.

"When death is caused by a wrongful act, neglect, or default in another state, or foreign country, for which a right to maintain an action and recover damages is given by a statute of such other state or foreign country, such right of action may be enforced in this state. Every such action shall be commenced within the time prescribed for the commencement of such actions by the statute of such other state or foreign country ＊ ＊ ＊" Ohio Rev.Code § 2125.01 (1985 Supp.).

"*Proceedings.* An action for wrongful death must be brought in the name of the personal representative of the deceased person, but shall be for the exclusive benefit of the surviving spouse, the children, and other next of kin of the decedent. The jury may give such damages as it thinks proportioned to the pecuniary injury resulting from such death to the persons, respectively, for whose benefit the action was brought. Except as otherwise provided by law, every such action must be commenced within two years after the death of such deceased person. Such personal representative, if he was appointed in this state, with the consent of the court making such appointment may, at any time before or after the commencement of the suit, settle with the defendant the amount to be paid." Id. § 2125.02.

"*Distribution to Beneficiaries.* The amount received by a personal representative in an action for wrongful death under sections 2125.01 and 2125.02 of the Revised Code, whether by settlement or otherwise, shall be distributed to the beneficiaries or any one or more of them, and unless the share of each is adjusted among themselves, the court making the appointment shall adjust such share in such manner as is equitable, having due regard to the pecuniary injury to each beneficiary resulting from such death and to the age and condition of such beneficiaries. In making such distribution, the court may also consider funeral expenses and other items of expense incurred by reason of the death." Id. § 2125.03.

6. *Beneficiaries.* The original Lord Campbell's Act specified that the action was for the benefit of the husband, wife, parent or child, and many American acts have limited recovery to a similar group. Interpretation problems often arise. Thus, is a step-child included? Held, no, in Steed v. Imperial Airlines, 12 Cal.3d 115, 524 P.2d 801, 115 Cal.Rptr. 329 (1974), but the statute was quickly amended. Compare Mitt v. Sec. Ins. Co., 361 So.2d 465 (1978), cert. denied, 362 So.2d 1116 (1978) (biological father of minor decedent allowed to recover but "legal" father denied recovery). See Annot., 68 A.L.R.3d 1220 (1976).

7. Another problem is whether illegitimate children come within the statute. Until the late 1960's a clear majority of American courts held that they did not. See Annot., 72 A.L.R.2d 1235 (1960). A case going against the tide was Armijo v. Wesselius, 73 Wash.2d 716, 440 P.2d 471 (1968) (illegitimate child permitted to bring a claim for the death of his natural father when the latter had both acknowledged and contributed to the support of the child). New York amended its statute specifically to create a right of action in both the illegitimate child and his father. N.Y.Est., Powers & Trusts Law § 5–4.4.

8. The Supreme Court has held that the Louisiana Wrongful Death Statute constituted a denial of equal protection of the laws when it precluded an illegitimate child from bringing a wrongful death claim on behalf of her mother. Levy v. Louisiana, 391 U.S. 68 (1968). See Annots., 78 A.L.R.3d 1230 (1977); 72 A.L.R.2d 1235 (1960) and supplements. The court also struck down a Louisiana provision that barred the claim of a mother for the wrongful death of her illegitimate child. See Glona v. American Guar. & Liab. Ins. Co., 391 U.S. 73 (1968). However, the Court upheld a Georgia statute precluding an action by the father for the wrongful death of his illegitimate child but allowing the mother's claim, finding no invidious discrimination based on sex. Parham v. Hughes, 441 U.S. 347 (1979).

9. Should parents be able to obtain recovery for the death of an unborn child? Courts have reached conflicting results. Amadio v. Levin, 509 Pa. 199, 501 A.2d 1085 (1985); Danos v. St. Pierre, 402 So.2d 633 (La.1981). But see Styles v. Y.D. Taxi Corp., Inc., 426 So.2d 1144 (Fla.App.1983). Some courts have relied on viability of the unborn child at the time of the tortious injury to determine whether a wrongful death action can be maintained. O'Grady v. Brown, 654 S.W.2d 904 (Mo.1983). See also Annot., 84 A.L.R.3d 411 (1978); Collins, An Overview and Analysis: Prenatal Torts, Preconception Torts, Wrongful Life, Wrongful Death, and Wrongful Birth: Time for a New Framework, 22 J.Fam.L. 677 (1984).

10. When the beneficiaries are specifically named, creditors of the deceased cannot share in the recovery. See State v. Cambria, 137 Conn. 604, 80 A.2d 516 (1951); Broadnax v. Broadnax, 160 N.C. 432, 76 S.E. 216 (1912). When they are not named, a special statutory provision may be necessary to exempt the award from creditors. See Kennedy v. Davis, 171 Ala. 609, 55 So. 104 (1911); Mott v. Central R. Co., 70 Ga. 680 (1883).

11. If no designated beneficiaries are living at the time of the wrongful death, the action fails. A problem of statutory interpretation occurs if the beneficiary dies after the person has been wrongfully killed, but before an action has begun or even after commencement of the action, but before judgment. How are courts to decide these things? Compare Thomas v. Eads,

400 N.E.2d 778 (Ind.App.1980), and Doyle v. Baltimore & Ohio R. Co., 81 Ohio
St. 184, 90 N.E. 165 (1909); with Gray v. Goodson, 61 Wash.2d 319, 378 P.2d 413
(1963), and McDaniel v. Bullard, 34 Ill.2d 487, 216 N.E.2d 140 (1966). See
Annot., 13 A.L.R. 4th 1060 (1982).

SELDERS v. ARMENTROUT

Supreme Court of Nebraska, 1973.
190 Neb. 275, 207 N.W.2d 686.

McCOWN, JUSTICE. * * * The sole issue on this appeal involves
the proper elements and measure of damages in a tort action in
Nebraska for the wrongful death of a minor child. The [trial] court
essentially instructed the jury that except for medical and funeral
expenses, the damages should be the monetary value of the contributions and services which the parents could reasonably have expected to
receive from the children less the reasonable cost to the parents of
supporting the children.

The defendants contend that the measure of damages is limited to
pecuniary loss and that the instructions to the jury correctly reflect the
measure and elements of damage. The plaintiffs assert that the loss of
the society, comfort, and companionship of the children are proper and
compensable elements of damage, and that evidence of amounts invested or expended for the nurture, education, and maintenance of the
children before death is proper. * * *

[A] broadening concept of the measure and elements of damages for
the wrongful death of a minor child has been in the development stage
for many years. [Cc] Following a discussion of the rigid common law
rules limiting recovery for wrongful death to the loss of pecuniary
benefits, Prosser states: "Recent years, however, have brought considerable modification of the rigid common law rules. It has been recognized that even pecuniary loss may extend beyond mere contributions
of food, shelter, money or property; and there is now a decided
tendency to find that the society, care and attention of the deceased are
'services' to the survivor with a financial value, which may be compensated. This has been true, for example, not only where a child has been
deprived of a parent, * * * but also where the parent has lost a child
* * *." Prosser, Law of Torts (4th Ed.), § 127, p. 908.

The original pecuniary loss concept and its restrictive application
arose in a day when children during minority were generally regarded
as an economic asset to parents. Children went to work on farms and
in factories at age 10 and even earlier. This was before the day of child
labor laws and long before the day of extended higher education for the
general population. A child's earnings and services could be generally
established and the financial or pecuniary loss which could be proved
became the measure of damages for the wrongful death of a child.
Virtually all other damages were disallowed as speculative or as sentimental.

The damages involved in a wrongful death case even today must of necessity deal primarily with a fictitious or speculative future life, as it might have been had the wrongful death not occurred. For that reason, virtually all evidence of future damage is necessarily speculative to a degree. The measure and elements of damage involved in a wrongful death case, however, have been excessively restrictive as applied to a minor child in contrast to an adult. Modern economic reality emphasizes the gulf between the old concepts of a child's economic value and the new facts of modern family life. To limit damages for the death of a child to the monetary value of the services which the next of kin could reasonably have expected to receive during his minority less the reasonable expense of maintaining and educating him stamps almost all modern children as worthless in the eyes of the law. In fact, if the rule was literally followed, the average child would have a negative worth. This court has already held that contributions reasonably to be expected from a minor, not only during his minority but afterwards, may be allowed on evidence justifying a reasonable expectation of pecuniary benefit. [Cc] Even with that modification, the wrongful death of a child results in no monetary loss, except in the rare case, and the assumption that the traditional measure of damages is compensatory is a pure legal fiction.

Particularly in the last decade, a growing number of courts have extended the measure of damages to include the loss of society and companionship of the minor child, even under statutes limiting recovery to pecuniary loss or pecuniary value of services less the cost of support and maintenance, or similar limitations. [Cc]

In this state, the statute has not limited damages for wrongful death to pecuniary loss but this court has imposed that restriction. For an injury to the marital relationship, the law allows recovery for the loss of the society, comfort, and companionship of a spouse. This court has allowed such a recovery for the wrongful death of a wife. [C] There is no logical reason for treating an injury to the family relationship resulting from the wrongful death of a child more restrictively. It is no more difficult for juries and courts to measure damages for the loss of the life of a child than many other abstract concepts with which they are required to deal. We hold that the measure of damages for the wrongful death of a minor child should be extended to include the loss of the society, comfort, and companionship of the child. To the extent this holding is in conflict with prior decisions of this court, they are overruled. * * *

The judgment of the trial court as to liability is affirmed, the judgment as to damages is reversed and the cause remanded for trial on the issue of damages only, consistent with our holding in this opinion.

WHITE, CHIEF JUSTICE (dissenting). * * * I submit that the majority opinion, which arbitrarily and in one stroke, after 50 years of settled law and without public hearing or consideration of the different interests and policies involved, and in violation of the 1945 legislative policy clearly announced in the statute, and unrepealed, simply throws open a death claim for a minor child to a sympathy and sentiment contest in the award of money, and is a serious mistake for us to make.

---

1. There is little doubt that the original Lord Campbell's Act and wrongful death legislation in the United States patterned after that law were intended to limit damages to "pecuniary" losses caused by the death of a loved one. This was to meet concerns of common law judges that awards made for emotional concerns connected with death would know no bounds. In approximately 40 states pecuniary loss is measured by having the trier of fact attempt to determine the monetary contribution that decedent would have made during his lifetime to the plaintiff beneficiary. As in the case of permanent injuries discussed in Chapter 10, the trier of fact is aided by mortality tables, income projections and expert testimony. Pecuniary loss may also include the market value of any services that the decedent performed for the beneficiary. At least one state limits pecuniary loss to the life expectancy of the beneficiary if it is shorter than that of the decedent. See Bowen v. Constructors Equipment Rental Co., 283 N.C. 395, 196 S.E.2d 789 (1973). Does this make good sense? See Miller, Dead Men in Torts; Lord Campbell's Act Was Not Enough, 19 Cath. U.L.Rev. 310 (1970).

2. Some states, such as Connecticut, Iowa, New Hampshire and Kentucky, compute damages on the basis of the loss to the decedent's estate. In a few states (e.g. Alabama), damages are based on the extent of the defendant's culpability. The plaintiff's pecuniary loss is immaterial.

3. As the principal case reflects, the pecuniary-loss limitation has caused problems when a child has been killed and his parents bring a wrongful death claim. In his book, Investing In Children, Thomas Espenshade estimated that it would cost a typical American family about $82,000 to raise a child in 1981. Given that the annual inflation rate has been about 25 percent since then, the figure is now over $100,000, not including college expenses. These figures did not include the loss of potential earnings of the mother (or father) who may stay at home to help raise the child. If the pecuniary-loss standard were strictly applied, defendant in a wrongful death case involving a child might counterclaim against the parents for a *quantum meruit* recovery!

4. This, of course, has not occurred. Moreover, in many states that adhere to the pecuniary-loss standard, substantial damages have been upheld on the theory that the youngster would have eventually made a corresponding monetary contribution to his parents. See Gary v. Schwartz, 72 Misc.2d 332, 339 N.Y.S.2d 39 (1972) ($98,000 to widowed mother for loss of 16–year–old son who intended to become a dentist—modified on appeal to $52,510.40), 43 A.D.2d 562, 349 N.Y.S.2d 322 (1973); Hart v. Forchelli, 445 F.2d 1018 (2d Cir.), cert. denied, 404 U.S. 940 (1971) (18–year–old son with "tentative plans to become an attorney"); Haumersen v. Ford Motor Co., 257 N.W.2d 7 (Iowa 1977) ($100,000 for loss of very intelligent seven-year-old with talent as a cartoonist). See also many similar cases collected in Annot., 49 A.L.R.3d 934 (1973) and supplements. For some helpful advice on how to obtain a maximum award in pecuniary-loss states, see Fuchsberg, Damages in Infant Death Cases, 9 Trial Law.Q. 63 (1973). On occasion courts in pecuniary-loss states attempt to adhere to the letter of the law. See Prather v. Lockwood, 19 Ill.App.3d 146, 310 N.E.2d 815 (1974) (sustaining $2000 award for death of 18–year–old). Once a court permits recovery for "loss of companionship," these "unrealistic awards based

on loss of services" will no longer be permitted. See Clark v. Icicle Irrigation Dist., 72 Wash.2d 201, 432 P.2d 541 (1967).

5. A growing number of courts have taken the route of the principal case and allowed recovery for "loss of companionship" or consortium of the child. See Bullard v. Barnes, 102 Ill.2d 505, 82 Ill.Dec. 448, 468 N.E.2d 1228 (1984); Miller v. Mayberry, 462 N.E.2d 1316 (Ind.App.1984); Wardlow v. Keokuk, 190 N.W.2d 439 (Iowa 1971); Green v. Bittner, 85 N.J. 1, 424 A.2d 210 (1980); Anderson v. Lale, 216 N.W.2d 152 (S.D.1974); Lockhart v. Besel, 71 Wash.2d 112, 426 P.2d 605 (1967). But see Siciliano v. Capitol City Shows, Inc., 124 N.H. 719, 475 A.2d 19 (1984); Annot., 69 A.L.R.3d 553 (1976), and supplements.

6. A child's right to recover for the loss of parental companionship has been a relatively recent development. See Ferriter v. Daniel O'Connell's Sons, Inc., 381 Mass. 507, 413 N.E.2d 690 (1980); Berger v. Weber, 411 Mich. 1, 303 N.W.2d 424 (1981); Gerse, Compensating the Child's Loss of Parental Love, Care, and Affection, 1983 U.Ill.L.Rev. 293.

7. Further expansion of beneficiaries who may recover for loss of companionship in wrongful death actions has been accomplished in at least one state to include decedents' brothers and sisters and all potential heirs at law. Crystal v. Hubbard, 414 Mich. 297, 324 N.W.2d 869 (1982). See also Wetering v. Eisele, 682 P.2d 1055 (Wyo.1984); Barsella, Negligent Injury to Family Relationships: A Reevaluation of the Logic of Liability, 77 Nw.U.L.Rev. 794 (1983); Annot., 31 A.L.R.3d 379 (1970), and supplements.

8. Should marriage be a prerequisite to recovery for loss of companionship? Some courts have held that an unmarried cohabitant may state a cause of action for loss of consortium in certain situations. Butcher v. Superior Court, 139 Cal.App.3d 58, 188 Cal.Rptr. 503 (1983) (relationship must be both stable and significant); and Bulloch v. United States, 487 F.Supp. 1078 (D.N.J.1980) (cohabitant may maintain suit for loss of consortium in cases where cohabitant suffered same types of injuries as legal spouses). Most courts, however, have resisted these attempts to extend the cause of action beyond the marital relationship. Taylor v. Fields, 178 Cal.App.3d 653, 224 Cal.Rptr. 186 (1986); Laws v. Griep, 332 N.W.2d 339 (Iowa 1983); Tremblay v. Carter, 390 So. 2d 816 (Fla.1980). See Saks, Loss of Spouse's Consortium: Necessity for a Valid Marriage, 17 Trial Law.Q. 42 (1985); Demidovich, Loss of Consortium: Should Marriage Be Retained as Prerequisite?, 52 U.Cin.L.Rev. (1983); Annot., 40 A.L.R.4th 553 (1985). Live-in lovers are often seen as outside the limits of the beneficiary class. Cassano v. Durham, 180 N.J.Super. 620, 436 A.2d 118 (1981). Should it make any difference if the cohabitant who sues for lack of consortium is of the same sex as the deceased cohabitant?

9. Problems with regard to the pecuniary-loss limitation of damages in wrongful death actions have also arisen with regard to nuns who have taken the vow of poverty. See Stang v. Hertz Corp., 81 N.M. 348, 467 P.2d 14 (1970), rev'd on other grounds, 83 N.M. 730, 497 P.2d 732 (1972); Goheen v. General Motors Corp., 263 Or. 145, 502 P.2d 223 (1972). They have also occurred when the victim is an elderly or retired person. See Goettelman v. Stoen, 182 N.W.2d 415 (Iowa 1970); Annots., 48 A.L.R.4th 229 (1986), 47·A.L.R.4th 100 (1986).

10. A number of state legislatures have amended their wrongful death statutes to provide for loss of companionship in all cases. See, e.g., Fla.Stat. Ann. § 768.21; Hawaii Rev.Stat. § 663-3; W.Va.Code Ann. § 55-7-6. Some jurisdictions have a built-in protection against runaway damages by placing a

ceiling on damages for loss of companionship. See Kan.Stat.Ann. § 60–1903 ($25,000); Me.Rev.Stat.Ann. tit. 18, § 2552 ($10,000 limit).

11. If damages for loss of companionship are permitted, what should defense attorneys consider during the course of their investigation of the case? Cf. Bednar v. United States Lines, Inc., 360 F.Supp. 1313, 1318 (N.D.Ohio 1973). Does allowing recovery for "loss of companionship" give plaintiff's counsel too much latitude to collect inflated damages for his client? Note how a court accepted plaintiff counsel's efforts in Anderson v. Lale, 216 N.W.2d 152, 159 (S.D.1974): "The record in this case shows that the decedent was seven years of age and a bright, affectionate, kindly child who did well in school and church activities. She was an energetic, active, obedient, helpful child and an integral part of a close-knit family." A verdict of $16,500 was upheld.

12. Some states go beyond damages for "loss of companionship" and also provide for damages based on "grief." See, e.g., Ark.Stat.Ann. § 27–909; Kan. Stat.Ann. § 60–1904. Should this be a compensable loss? More and more states are allowing these types of damages. See St. Louis Southwestern Ry. v. Pennington, 261 Ark. 650, 553 S.W.2d 436 (1977) (award for mental anguish upheld in light of evidence of unusually close family relationship); Tiner v. Tiner, 238 Ark. 222, 379 S.W.2d 425 (1964) (sustaining $25,000 award for grief— loss of 10–year–old daughter); Corman v. WEG Dial Tel., Inc., 194 Kan. 783, 402 P.2d 112 (1965) (deeming $1500 award for loss of 18–month–old son insufficient). See Speiser & Malawer, An American Tragedy: Damages for Mental Anguish of Bereaved Relatives in Wrongful Death Actions, 51 Tul.L. Rev. 1 (1976). Annots., 45 A.L.R.4th 234 (1986); 49 A.L.R.3d 934 (1973).

13. Note that courts generally do not allow recovery for purely emotional harm where the plaintiff has suffered no physical injury. See Chapter 8, Section 1, supra. How does this comport with allowing "grief" damages in wrongful death cases?

14. Almost half of the wrongful death statutes as originally enacted contained restrictions on the maximum amount that could be awarded. They represented an attempt to avoid the possibility of runaway jury verdicts. The limitations ranged from $5,000 to $20,000. Over time the limitations were raised and only a few remain. Today, the most important limitation of this type exists with regard to accidents covered by agreements derived from The Warsaw Convention. The State Department supported a $75,000 limitation in 1966, but the status of that agreement is somewhat uncertain today.

15. Suppose defendant was reckless in the manner in which he killed plaintiff's decedent. Should punitive damages be awarded to the beneficiary? See, e.g., Pease v. Beech Aircraft Corp., 38 Cal.App.3d 450, 113 Cal.Rptr. 416 (1974); S. Speiser, Recovery for Wrongful Death § 3:4 (2d ed. 1975).

16. A major controversy has arisen on whether the trier of fact should be informed that a plaintiff wife has remarried since the death of her husband. Most courts have held that this information should be withheld from the jury. See Annots., 87 A.L.R.2d 252 (1963); 88 A.L.R.3d 926 (1978). In one case, plaintiff spouse who had remarried legally changed back to her widowed name strictly for the purposes of the tort suit. Should that information be kept from the jury? See Bell Aerospace Corp. v. Anderson, 478 S.W.2d 191 (Tex.Civ.App. 1972).

17. See generally, Decof, Damages in Actions for Wrongful Death of Children, 47 Notre Dame Law. 197 (1971); Demos, Measure of Damages— Wrongful Death, 60 Ill.B.J. 518 (1972); Finkelstein, Pickrel and Glasser, The

Death of Children: A Nonparametric Statistical Analysis of Compensation for Anguish, 74 Colum.L.Rev. 884 (1974); Hare, The Rationale of Damages for the Death of a Minor or Other Dependent Person, 41 Bos.U.L.Rev. 336 (1961); Smedley, Wrongful Death—Basis of the Common Law Rules, 13 Vand.L.Rev. 605 (1960); Annot., 45 A.L.R.4th 234 (1986).

MURPHY v. MARTIN OIL CO.

Supreme Court of Illinois, 1974.
56 Ill.2d 423, 308 N.E.2d 583.

[Suit for negligently causing the death of plaintiff's husband. The husband was injured in a fire on defendant's premises, survived for nine days, and then died from the injuries. The claim was in two counts: (1) under the Wrongful Death Statute and (2) under the Survival Statute. The trial court dismissed the second count. The intermediate appellate court allowed the claim in part. Both parties appealed to the State Supreme Court.]

WARD, JUSTICE. Count I of the complaint claimed damages for wrongful death under the Illinois Wrongful Death Act. * * * The language of section 1 of the statute is:

"Whenever the death of a person shall be caused by wrongful act, neglect or default, and the act, neglect or default is such as would, if death had not ensued, have entitled the party injured to maintain an action and recover damages in respect thereof, then and in every such case the person who or company or corporation which would have been liable if death had not ensued, shall be liable to an action for damages, notwithstanding the death of the person injured, and although the death shall have been caused under such circumstances as amount in law to felony." * * *

The second count of the complaint asked for damages for the decedent's physical and mental suffering, for loss of wages for the nine-day period following his injury and for the loss of his clothing worn at the time of injury. These damages were claimed under the common law and under our survival statute, which provides that certain rights of action survive the death of the person with the right of action. (Ill. Rev.Stat.1971, ch. 3, par. 339.) The statute states:

"In addition to the actions which survive by the common law, the following also survive: actions of replevin, actions to recover damages for an injury to the person (except slander and libel), actions to recover damages for an injury to real or personal property or for the detention or conversion of personal property, actions against officers for misfeasance, malfeasance, or nonfeasance of themselves or their deputies, actions for fraud or deceit, and actions provided in Section 14 of Article VI of 'An Act relating to alcoholic liquors', approved January 31, 1934, as amended."

On this appeal we shall consider: (1) whether the plaintiff can recover for the loss of wages which her decedent would have earned during the interval between his injury and death; (2) whether the plaintiff can recover for the destruction of the decedent's personal property (clothing) at the time of the injury; (3) whether the plaintiff can recover damages for conscious pain and suffering of the decedent from the time of his injuries to the time of death.

This State in 1853 enacted the Wrongful Death Act and in 1872 enacted the so-called Survival Act (now section 339 of the Probate Act). This court first had occasion to consider the statutes in combination in 1882 in Holton v. Daly, 106 Ill. 131. The court * * * held that the Wrongful Death Act provided the exclusive remedy available when death came as a result of given tortious conduct. In considering the Survival Act the court stated that it was intended to allow for the survival of a cause of action only when the injured party died from a cause other than that which caused the injuries which created the cause of action. Thus, the court said, an action for personal injury would not survive death if death resulted from the tortious conduct which caused the injury.

This construction of the two statutes persisted for over 70 years. [Cc] Damages, therefore, under the Wrongful Death Act were limited to pecuniary losses, as from loss of support, to the surviving spouse and next of kin as a result of the death. [C] Under the survival statute damages recoverable in a personal injury action, as for conscious pain and suffering, loss of earnings, medical expenses and physical disability, could be had only if death resulted from a cause other than the one which gave rise to the personal injury action. * * *

In Prosser, Handbook of the Law of Torts (4th ed. 1971), at page 901, it is said: "[T]he modern trend is definitely toward the view that tort causes of action and liabilities are as fairly a part of the estate of either plaintiff or defendant as contract debts, and that the question is rather one of why a fortuitous event such as death should extinguish a valid action. Accordingly, survival statutes gradually are being extended; and it may be expected that ultimately all tort actions will survive to the same extent as those founded on contract." And at page 906 Prosser observes that where there have been wrongful death and survival statutes the usual holding has been that actions may be concurrently maintained under those statutes. The usual method of dealing with the two causes of action, he notes, is to allocate conscious pain and suffering, expenses and loss of earnings of the decedent up to the date of death to the survival statute, and to allocate the loss of benefits of the survivors to the action for wrongful death.

As the cited comments of Prosser indicate, the majority of jurisdictions which have considered the question allow an action for personal injuries in addition to an action under the wrongful death statute, though death is attributable to the injuries. Recovery for conscious pain and suffering is permitted in most of these jurisdictions. [Citing cases from 21 different jurisdictions.]

Too, recovery is allowed under the Federal Employers' Liability Act for a decedent's conscious pain and suffering provided it was not substantially contemporaneous with his death. [Cc]

We consider that those decisions which allow an action for fatal injuries as well as for wrongful death are to be preferred to this court's holding in Holton v. Daly that the Wrongful Death Act was the only remedy available when injury resulted in death.

The holding in *Holton* was not compelled, we judge, by the language or the nature of the statutes examined. The statutes were conceptually separable and different. The one related to an action arising upon wrongful death; the other related to a right of action for personal injury arising during the life of the injured person.

The remedy available under *Holton* will often be grievously incomplete. There may be a substantial loss of earnings, medical expenses, prolonged pain and suffering, as well as property damage sustained, before an injured person may succumb to his injuries. To say that there can be recovery only for his wrongful death is to provide an obviously inadequate justice. Too, the result in such a case is that the wrongdoer will have to answer for only a portion of the damages he caused. Incongruously, if the injury caused is so severe that death results, the wrongdoer's liability for the damages before death will be extinguished. It is obvious that in order to have a full liability and a full recovery there must be an action allowed for damages up to the time of death, as well as thereafter. Considering "It is more important that the court should be right upon later and more elaborate consideration of the cases than consistent with previous declarations" [c], we declare *Holton* and the cases which have followed it overruled. * * *

[T]he judgment of the appellate court is affirmed insofar as it held that an action may be maintained by the plaintiff for loss of property and loss of wages during the interval between injury and death, and that judgment is reversed insofar as it held that the plaintiff cannot maintain an action for her decedent's pain and suffering.

----

1. Under English common law as it was received by American courts, personal tort actions died with the person of the plaintiff or the defendant. For the historical background of this rule see W. Prosser & W. Keeton, Torts 940 (5th Ed. 1984) and materials cited.

2. In almost every jurisdiction today survival statutes have modified these rules. At the very least, these statutes provide that causes of action for injury to all tangible property survive the death of either party. The majority of statutes also allow personal injury actions to survive. Only six or seven states permit claims for intangible interests of personality (such as intentional infliction of emotional harm or defamation) to survive. A number of courts have recently considered whether a claim for punitive or exemplary damages survives the death of either the tortfeasor or the injured party. Winter v. Schneider Tank Lines, Inc., 107 Ill.App.3d 767, 63 Ill.Dec. 531, 438 N.E.2d 462 (1982); Annot., 30 A.L.R.4th 709 (1984). Obviously, these are an area in which an attorney must carefully check the statutes.

3. Two survival statutes are presented below. What are the important differences between them?

Maine: "No personal action or cause of action shall be lost by the death of either party, but the same shall survive for and against the personal representative of the deceased, except that actions or causes of action for the recovery of penalties and forfeitures of money under penal statutes and proceedings in bastardy cases shall not survive the death of the defendant. A personal representative may seek relief from a judgment in an action to which the deceased was a party to the same extent that the deceased might have done so." Me.Rev.Stat., tit. 18–A, § 3–817(a).

South Carolina: "Survival of Right of Action. Causes of action for and in respect to any and all injuries and trespasses to and upon real estate and any and all injuries to the person or to personal property shall survive both to and against the personal or real representative, as the case may be, of a deceased person and the legal representative of an insolvent person or a defunct or insolvent corporation, any law or rule to the contrary notwithstanding." S.C. Code § 10–209.

4. Generally, survival actions are brought by the executor or administrator of the estate and a recovery becomes an asset of that estate. Damages are based on loss to the estate rather than on loss to the dependants or survivors. See S. Speiser, Recovery for Wrongful Death, § 3.2 (2d ed. 1975). The recovery may be reached by creditors and it is distributed in accordance with state testacy or intestacy laws.

5. The only major argument against survival statutes is that they may result in a windfall to distant relatives who cared very little about the decedent and were not in any way dependent on him. Do you find the argument appealing? Obviously, the survival action may be vital to a relative who is not named as a beneficiary in the wrongful death statute. See, e.g., Warner v. McCaughan, 77 Wash.2d 178, 460 P.2d 272 (1969).

6. Many states have both survival and wrongful death statutes. There are then two causes of action that may be maintained separately or concurrently to successful judgment. The problem courts face in this connection is to control the damages in each action so as to avoid holding the defendant liable twice for the same elements of recovery. A good case struggling with the problem is Pezzulli v. D'Ambrosia, 344 Pa. 643, 26 A.2d 659 (1942). See Annot., 76 A.L.R.3d 125 (1977).

7. Funeral and burial expenses, and medical bills paid by the survivors after death, are normally allocated to the death action. The physical and mental pain and suffering of the decedent during his lifetime are obviously to be allocated to the survival action, as are medical expenses incurred while he is alive. His loss of potential earnings during his normal life expectancy is also considered his own damage, and is assigned to the survival action. But since it is out of these future earnings that he would have been expected to support his family, or to have made contributions to them, it is obvious that there would be a double recovery to the extent that they were allowed to recover for the loss when both actions are maintained. A frequent solution has been to allow in the survival action the potential earnings of the decedent during his life expectancy, reduced to their present value, and to deduct the probable cost of maintenance of his family, which must be recovered in the death action. See, for example, First Nat'l Bank in Greensburg v. M. & G. Convoy, Inc., 106 F.Supp. 261 (W.D.Pa.1952); and Wetzel v. McDonnell Douglas Corp., 491 F.Supp. 1288 (E.D.Pa.1980). See also Martin, Measuring Damages in Survival Actions for Tortious Death, 47 Wash.L.Rev. 609 (1972).

8. Recovery for pain and suffering is allowed only if the decedent was conscious of it. See, e.g., Schlichte v. Franklin Troy Trucks, 265 N.W.2d 725 (Iowa 1978). Thus, courtroom battles between medical experts have developed over this factual issue when the decedent lived only a short time after his injury. Compare Fialkow v. DeVoe Motors, Inc., 359 Mass. 569, 270 N.E.2d 798 (1971) (evidence of gasping, gurgling and heavy breathing insufficient to show consciousness), with Campbell v. Leach, 352 Mass. 367, 225 N.E.2d 594 (1967) (evidence that decedent cried out sufficient to support an award). See also Fuchsberg, Damages—Conscious Pain & Suffering Prior to Death, 15 Trial Law. Q. 66 (1983).

In one case, $200,000 was awarded in a survival action where the decedent had pain and suffering for 20 minutes before dying. See DeLong v. Erie County, page 630, supra.

9. In 1977 the National Conference of Commissioners on Uniform State Laws adopted a Uniform Survival and Death Act. In 1979 the title was changed to Uniform Law Commissioners' Model Survival and Death Act. The Act is set forth below. Study it to see how it meets many of the problems arising in this field. Does it contain any controversial provisions?

Model Survival and Death Act

§ 1. [Definitions]

As used in this Act:

(1) "Actionable conduct" means an act or omission that causes the death of a person for which the person could have brought and maintained a personal injury action if he had not died; the term includes an act or omission for which the law imposes strict liability or liability for breach of warranty.

(2) "Survivors of a decedent" means:

(i) the surviving spouse, ascendants and descendants of the decedent, and

(ii) individuals who were wholly or partially dependent upon the decedent for support and were members of the decedent's household or related to the decedent by blood or marriage.

(3) "Closely-related survivors" means the surviving spouse and ascendants and descendants of the decedent.

§ 2. [Survival Actions]

(a) An action or a [claim for relief] [cause of action]:

(1) does not abate by reason of the death of a person to or against whom it accrued, unless by its terms it was limited to the person's lifetime;

(2) may be maintained by or against the personal representative of a decedent; and

(3) is subject to all defenses to which it was subject during the decedent's lifetime.

(b) Damages recoverable in behalf of a decedent under this section for an injury causing his death are limited to those that accrued to him before his death, plus reasonable burial expenses paid or payable from his estate. Damages so recovered become a part of the decedent's estate and are distributable in the same manner as other assets of the estate. This section does not affect the measure of damages allowable under the law for any other damages recoverable under any other [claim for relief] [cause of action].

§ 3.   [Death Actions]

(a) With respect to any death caused by actionable conduct, the decedent's personal representative, acting in a fiduciary capacity on behalf of the survivors of the decedent, may bring and maintain a death action against any person or the estate of any person legally responsible for the damages, including an insurer providing applicable uninsured or underinsured motorist coverage. The death action is subject to all defenses that might have been asserted against the decedent had he survived.

(b) If no personal representative is appointed [within six months after decedent's death] the death action may be brought and maintained by a closely-related survivor acting in a fiduciary capacity.

(c) Any survivor having a potential conflict of interest with other survivors may be represented independently in the death action.

(d) In the death action, damages awarded to survivors of a decedent are limited to the following elements:

(1) Medical expenses incident to the injury resulting in death and reasonable burial expenses, paid or payable by the survivors, to the extent that the decedent's estate could have recovered under Section 2 had the payments been made by the decedent or his estate; [and]

(2) The [present] monetary value of support, services, and financial contributions they would have received from the decedent had death not ensued[.] [; and]

[(3) For closely-related survivors, [reasonable compensation for decedent's pain and suffering before death if not separately recoverable under Section 2, and] reasonable compensation for mental anguish and loss of companionship [not exceeding the sum of $_____].]

(e) Punitive or exemplary damages [are not recoverable] [are recoverable only if they would have been recoverable by the decedent had death not ensued].

(f) The trier of fact shall make separate awards to each of the survivors entitled to damages. Conduct of a survivor which contributed to the death is a defense to the survivor's recovery to the same extent as in other actions.

(g) The decedent's personal representative or a closely-related survivor qualifying under subsection (b) may compromise any claim arising under this section, before or after an action is brought, subject to confirmation by a judge of the court [in which the action is or could have been brought] [appointing the personal representative]. The personal representative or closely-related survivor shall apply to the court for confirmation by [petition], stating the terms of the compromise, the reasons therefor, and the names of all survivors having an interest in the distribution of the proceeds. The court, upon notice, shall hold a hearing which all survivors and their legal representatives may attend, and shall confirm or disapprove the settlement. If the settlement is confirmed and any of the survivors or their representatives disagree with the distribution prescribed by it, the judge shall order any distribution a trier of fact may make under subsection (f).

§ 4. [Joinder of Actions]

Actions under Sections 2 and 3 are separate actions but shall be joined for trial if they are based upon the same actionable conduct. Separate verdicts and awards shall be rendered in each action.

10. See Smedley, Some Order Out of Chaos in Wrongful Death Law, 37 Vand.L.Rev. 273 (1984), for an incisive analysis of the problems arising under the various types of statutes in the several states and a careful evaluation of reform proposals, including the model act just quoted.

A Note on Defenses

The interrelationship of wrongful death and survival statutes and defenses, although presented at this point, will be better appreciated by the reader after completion of Chapter 12 on Defenses. The discussion is based on W. Prosser & W. Keeton, Torts 954–60 (5th ed. 1984).

1. *Defenses Based on Conduct of the Decedent.* Since the survival type of death statute merely continues the decedent's own cause of action beyond his death and enhances it with damages for the death, any defenses that might have been set up against him if he had lived are still available to the defendant. The contrary might perhaps have been expected of the wrongful death acts, which create a separate and independent cause of action, founded upon the death itself, for the benefit of the designated survivors. The original Lord Campbell's Act, however, contained an express provision limiting the death action to those cases in which the deceased might have recovered damages if he had lived; and this provision has been carried over into most of the American acts, or has been read into them by implication when it does not expressly appear. It obviously is intended at least to prevent recovery for death when the decedent could never at any time have maintained an action, as where there was simply no tortious conduct toward him.

On the same theoretical basis, but with less manifest justification, there has been general agreement denying recovery when the defendant's conduct has been tortious toward the decedent and has caused his death, thus causing loss to the innocent survivors, but the defendant would have had a defense available against the decedent himself. This has been true of contributory negligence, assumption of risk or consent to the defendant's conduct, as well as privileges such as self-defense or defense of property. Most of the courts that have considered the question have given the same effect to the immunity of one member of a family for torts against another, although there is a strong minority view to the contrary, based upon the theory that death destroys the reason for the immunity.

It is not clear, however, that these provisions of the death acts ever were intended to prevent recovery when the deceased once had a cause of action, but it has terminated before his death. The more reasonable interpretation would seem to be that they are directed at the necessity of some original tort on the part of the defendant, under circumstances giving rise to liability in the first instance, rather than to subsequent changes in the situation affecting only the interest of the decedent. Nevertheless, a majority of the courts have held that a judgment for or against the decedent in an action for his injuries commenced during his lifetime, or the compromise and release of the action, will operate as a bar to any subsequent suit founded upon his death. This has the effect of placing in the decedent's hands the power to sell out the claim of the beneficiaries before it has come into existence. Their action is regarded as "derivative," arising out of and dependent upon the wrong done to him. The courts undoubtedly have been influenced by a fear of a double recovery. This is of course possible in point of law, not only under the survival act, but also in any jurisdiction where the decedent would be allowed to recover for the prospective earnings lost through his diminished life expectancy. Even without this, however, it is possible that a settlement made with the decedent will take into account not only his diminished earning capacity while he does live but also the decrease in his life expectancy and the earnings he would have made if he had lived out his normal term, out of which any benefits receivable by the beneficiaries would be expected to come.

Opposed to this possibility is the counter-danger of an improvident settlement by an optimistic individual, confident that he is not going to die, which takes no account of shortened life expectancy or of the interests of the survivors. Because of this, there is a substantial minority view, largely confined to jurisdictions not allowing the decedent to recover for his own curtailed life, that neither a judgment in his action nor his release of his claim will bar the action for wrongful death. The possibility of double compensation either has been ignored, on the ground that legally it could not arise, or has been met by a deduction from the award to the death beneficiaries, of the amount found to have been paid to the decedent covering the permanent destruction of his earning capacity, or the suggestion that the expectancy of the survivors be deducted from the probable earnings in the decedent's own action. No satisfactory systematic solution to the whole problem has yet been found.

On the defense of the statute of limitations, which is distinguishable only in that it does not involve the danger of double compensation, the considerable majority of the courts have held that the statute runs against the death action only from the date of death, even though at that time the decedent's own action would have been barred while he was living. Only a few courts hold that it runs from the time of the original injury and consequently that the death action may be lost before it ever has accrued. Equally inconsistent, at least in theory, is the common holding that actions may be prosecuted under both death and survival acts and that recovery or settlement under one does not bar an action under the other.

2. *Defenses Based on Conduct of the Beneficiaries.* Defenses available against the beneficiaries themselves offer a still more troublesome problem, on which the courts have not agreed. When the action is brought under a survival act, it is in theory still on behalf of the decedent, and the contributory negligence of even a sole beneficiary has been held not to prevent recovery. The same conclusion has been reached under wrongful death acts where the damages are recoverable on behalf of the decedent's estate, on the ground that the estate is distinct from the beneficiary. Under the usual death act, the recovery is for the beneficiaries, and the contributory negligence or the consent or assumption of risk of a sole beneficiary or of all beneficiaries generally is held to preclude the action, on the same principle that would bar any other plaintiff in interest. A few statutes have been construed to the contrary.

When only one of several beneficiaries is contributorily negligent, the prevailing view is that the action is not barred for those who were not negligent, but that recovery is diminished to the extent of the damages of the negligent beneficiary, who is denied all share in the proceeds. The same conclusion has been reached for assumption of risk. About all that remains of the barred action is the antique rule in a small number of states which "imputes" the negligence of one parent to the other when the action is for the death of a child. Except when it can be justified on the basis that the damages recovered will be community property, this, too, has generally been rejected as a survival of a discarded concept of marital unity. Although the death acts usually are construed to provide that only one action may be maintained for the death, it has been held that a release from one beneficiary will not prevent recovery by others and even that the statute of limitations may run against recovery on behalf of one, but not others.

3. *Comparative Negligence.* Under comparative negligence systems, there is the possibility of having the jury consider both the negligence of a beneficiary and the decedent since the negligence of either one—standing alone—will not automatically bar a claim. The process is not as complicated as it may appear: the jury simply allocates a percentage of negligence to the beneficiary and the decedent and then reduces the award to the beneficiary by that amount. In modified comparative negligence systems, recovery by that beneficiary is precluded as soon as the threshold is reached.

Chapter XII

DEFENSES

---

1. PLAINTIFF'S CONDUCT

(A) CONTRIBUTORY NEGLIGENCE

[handwritten: ⊗ Complete, affirmative defense]

BUTTERFIELD v. FORRESTER

King's Bench, 1809.
11 East 60, 103 Eng.Rep. 926.

This was an action on the case for obstructing a highway, by means of which obstruction the plaintiff, who was riding along the road, was thrown down with his horse, and injured, &c. At the trial before Bayley J. at Derby, it appeared that the defendant, for the purpose of making some repairs to his house, which was close by the road side at one end of the town, had put up a pole across this part of the road, a free passage being left by another branch or street in the same direction. That the plaintiff left a public house not far distant from the place in question at 8 o'clock in the evening in August, when they were just beginning to light candles, but while there was light enough left to discern the obstruction at 100 yards distance: and the witness, who proved this, said that if the plaintiff had not been riding very hard he might have observed and avoided it: the plaintiff however, who was riding violently, did not observe it, but rode against it, and fell with his horse and was much hurt in consequence of the accident: and there was no evidence of his being intoxicated at the time. On this evidence Bayley J. directed the jury, that if a person riding with reasonable and ordinary care could have seen and avoided the obstruction; and if they were satisfied that the plaintiff was riding along the street extremely hard, and without ordinary care, they should find a verdict for the defendant: which they accordingly did.

[handwritten left margin: Complete defense]

Vaughan Serjt. now objected to this direction, on moving for a new trial; and referred to Buller's Ni.Pri. 26(a), where the rule is laid down, that "if a man lay logs of wood across a highway; though a person may with care ride safely by, yet if by means thereof my horse stumble and fling me, I may bring an action." *[handwritten: —just not recover.]*

BAYLEY, J. The plaintiff was proved to be riding as fast as his horse could go, and this was through the streets of Derby. If he had used ordinary care he must have seen the obstruction; so that the accident appeared to happen entirely from his own fault.

LORD ELLENBOROUGH, C.J. A party is not to cast himself upon an obstruction which has been made by the fault of another, and avail

560

[handwritten: ↳ intentionally? (seems yes)]
[handwritten: → different from when is really only negligent.]

Handwritten margin notes: Did this π do this "purposely"? (intent)? π's act was volitional, but w/ what intent? to cause himself harm? This seems to be what Judes were addressing

himself of it, if he do not himself use common and ordinary caution to be in the right. In cases of persons riding upon what is considered to be the wrong side of the road, that would not authorize another purposely to ride up against them. One person being in fault will not dispense with another's using ordinary care for himself. Two things must concur to support this action, an obstruction in the road by the fault of the defendant, and no want of ordinary care to avoid it on the part of the plaintiff.

PER CURIAM. Rule refused.

Handwritten margin notes: what about proximate cause or legal cause?

Handwritten margin notes (right): π was Ⓝ = duty = breach = cause/bar/for Ⓝ would accident have happened? No = would have foreseen it (intent)

Lord Ellenborough

1. What new element has each judge added to the common law? Is the case simply one of cause-in-fact in which plaintiff was entirely to blame for the injury that befell him?

2. Consider the basic options available to the law in connection with how to treat the fact that plaintiff's negligence contributed to the happening of the accident. <u>First, the law could completely bar plaintiff's claim</u>. This approach, called contributory negligence, was taken by the court in *Butterfield*. What does it have to recommend it?

Second, the law could completely ignore plaintiff's culpable conduct. This is the approach taken under most Workers' Compensation Acts and No–Fault Automobile Accident Reparation Systems. Could this approach be justified?

Third, the law could adopt one of the first two options as a general rule and then set up other rules making exceptions for designated situations. This is what the common law later did—generally adopting option 1, but allowing exceptions to it. Note that this is still an all-or-nothing approach to the individual case; the fact that the cases may average out as a whole provides no relief for the parties to the particular case. Would it be desirable to leave to the jury the question of whether to allow the plaintiff to recover all or nothing? This may have been the practice prior to the principal case. See Cruden v. Fentham, 2 Esp. 685, 170 Eng.Rep. 496 (N.P.1799); Clay v. Wood, 5 Esp. 44, 170 Eng.Rep. 732 (N.P.1803).

Fourth, the law could arrange to compare plaintiff's fault with that of defendant and in some way apportion damages according to the measure of fault. This approach, called comparative negligence, has now been expressly adopted in 44 states, by statute or judicial decision. The six states not adopting comparative negligence are Alabama, Maryland, North Carolina, South Carolina, Tennessee and Virginia.

Which appears to be the best approach?

3. In 1854 a Pennsylvania judge reflected the feelings of many of his brethren when he called the defense of contributory negligence a "rule from time immemorial" and ventured to guess that it was "not likely to be changed for all time to come." Pennsylvania R. Co. v. Aspell, 23 Pa. 147, 149 (1854). While the judge was a poor historian (a form of comparative negligence was applied by English Admiralty Courts long before the *Butterfield* decision), he did rather well as a prognosticator. The defense has had great appeal and sticking power in the United States. It was even adopted in Louisiana—a state that could easily have utilized its code and civil law tradition to adopt a comparative negligence approach. See Malone, Comparative Negligence—Louisiana's Forgotten Heritage, 6 La.L.Rev. 125 (1945).

4. The following theories all have been advanced from time to time in explanation or justification of the defense. Which of them are valid?

A. The defense has a penal basis and plaintiff is denied recovery to punish him for his own misconduct. Is the defendant penalized for his misconduct? Suppose plaintiff has committed a criminal act? See Barker v. Kallash, 63 N.Y.2d 19, 468 N.E.2d 39, 479 N.Y.S.2d 201 (1984).

B. Plaintiff is required to come into court with "clean hands," and the court will not aid one whose own fault has participated in causing his injury.

C. The defense is a necessary deterrent to people who otherwise could expect to go ahead and be negligent, and still recover if they were injured. What about its encouraging effect upon one who is a potential defendant? Is either plaintiff or defendant really at all likely to be thinking about legal liability when he negligently drives a car?

D. Plaintiff's negligence is an intervening, superseding cause, which makes the defendant's negligence no longer "proximate." What if two negligently driven automobiles collide and injure a third person? Cordiner v. Los Angeles Traction Co., 5 Cal.App. 400, 91 P. 436 (1907); Albritton v. Hill, 190 N.C. 429, 130 S.E. 5 (1925). Does "proximate cause" differ when it is one of the drivers who is injured?

5. A good account of the history of the development of the defense of contributory negligence, with stress upon the economic factors involved and the courts' uneasy distrust of the jury, is found in Malone, The Formative Era of Contributory Negligence, 41 Ill.L.Rev. 151 (1946). See also James, Contributory Negligence, 62 Yale L.J. 691 (1953); Bohlen, Contributory Negligence, 21 Harv. L.Rev. 151 (1908); Lowndes, Contributory Negligence, 22 Geo.L.J. 674 (1934).

6. The defense of contributory negligence should be distinguished from the rule on avoidable consequences, discussed in Chapter 10, on Damages. The avoidable-consequences rule becomes material after plaintiff has been injured. He then is not permitted to recover for any injuries to himself or his property that he would have been able to avoid by taking action that a reasonable person would take. See, e.g., Ackel v. Coca Cola Bottling Co., 385 So.2d 30 (La.App. 1980) (plaintiff took no steps to preserve a damaged automobile); Dohmann v. Richard, 282 So.2d 789 (La.App.1973).

––––––

The common law rule of contributory negligence often produced results that a court or jury regarded as highly unjust. Whenever a rule of law regularly produces unjust results or lags unduly behind social and economic developments, courts usually develop ameliorating practices and a group of exceptions for avoiding its application. This tenet of judicial behavior, which might be called the Erosion Principle, has occurred in a number of important areas in the law of torts. Can you think of some illustrations?

The remainder of this Section is devoted to an exploration of the exceptions and escape devices as they have applied to the doctrine of contributory negligence. A corollary of the Erosion Principle is that eventually the avoidance techniques eradicate the original rule. For application of this corollary, see Section 2 of this chapter. In the present Section, attention will be given first to certain ameliorating practices, and then the exceptions will be considered.

ROSSMAN v. LA GREGA

New York Court of Appeals, 1971.
28 N.Y.2d 300, 270 N.E.2d 313, 321 N.Y.S.2d 588.

[Plaintiff's decedent was struck by a vehicle driven by defendant La Grega. At the time of the accident, decedent was attempting to wave traffic away from a disabled car at night on an expressway. The vehicle was situated, unlighted, in the right hand lane, and plaintiff's decedent stood to its left—the side where traffic was moving. He had been told to stand in this position by defendant Cohen, the driver of the abandoned vehicle, who had gone to telephone for assistance. The jury returned a verdict in plaintiff's favor. The intermediate appellate court reversed, regarding decedent's conduct as "so reckless * * * as to constitute contributory negligence as a matter of law." 32 App.Div. 2d 675, 300 N.Y.S.2d 648 (2d Dept.1969). Plaintiff appealed to the New York Court of Appeals.]

BERGAN, J. * * * [I]t is the majority rule in this country that in all negligence actions, including those maintained by living persons for injury or property damage, the defendant claiming contributory negligence of the plaintiff has the burden of showing it. [Cc] And it is likewise the general rule where contributory negligence is an affirmative defense the injured person "is presumed to have used due * * * care." [Cc] * * *

[T]here has been a noticeable reluctance by the court to apply strictly in death cases the doctrine of contributory negligence. The last time that the court was unanimous in holding a dead person negligent as a matter of law was almost 40 years ago in Crough v. New York Cent. R.R. Co., 260 N.Y. 227, 183 N.E. 372 (1932) and this was in a railroad crossing case, a type which fell in a special category of the law.

Indeed, the general softening of the rigidities of the doctrine of contributory negligence in New York may be seen in * * * the * * * tendency * * * to treat it almost always as a question of fact. [Cc]

The doctrine has, indeed, been long subjected to critical theoretical attack by commentators on the law of torts. Prosser has observed: "The history of the doctrine has been that of a chronic invalid who will not die." He concluded: "With the gradual change in social viewpoint, stressing the humanitarian desire to see injuries compensated, the defense of contributory negligence has gradually come to be looked upon with increasing disfavor by the courts, and its rigors have been quite extensively modified" (Prosser, Torts [3d ed.], p. 428). The theories justifying application of the doctrine were regarded by Prosser as "the antique heritage of an older day" (p. 428).

In tracing the history of the doctrine back to Butterfield v. Forrester, [supra page 560], Dean Leon Green has observed that it emerged as dictum in reviewing an otherwise properly tried and decided case to meet certain perceived or apprehended conceptions of early nineteenth century Judges in tort law (Green, Illinois Negligence Law, 39 Ill.L.Rev. 36). He characterized contributory negligence as "the harshest doctrine known to the common law of the nineteenth century."

Robert A. Leflar, in The Declining Defense of Contributory Negligence (1 Ark.L.Rev. 1), 25 years ago wrote that the doctrine "is visibly shrunken and still diminishing" and observed, as many other commen-

tators have, its inconsistency in theory and injustice in application.
* * *

One basic inconsistency that has been noted is that there is a qualitative difference, when it comes to imposing liability on such a theory as tort, between one whose negligent act does harm to others and one whose negligent act does harm to himself, and the same mechanistic standard ought not be applied undifferentially as to both. *RR: it says "I'm the one who's hurt, after all."*

It would seem to follow, then, that on any fair analysis of New York law, the question of Rossman's contributory negligence in standing where he did to wave off traffic from the danger of the standing car would be for the jury. At least we ought not extend the perimeters of this unsatisfactory doctrine wider than we need to.

If one puts himself in Rossman's situation after Cohen had a flat tire, it will be seen that his choice of action was extremely limited. He was not then a man who had a choice of sitting safely in his living room or going out in the street into traffic danger. He was in a situation of acute danger no matter what he did unless he walked well away from the car and got off the road.

If he sat in the car he would have been in danger; if he stood in back of it without a flashlight (and he had none) he would have been in danger. Had he walked 30 or 40 feet back and attempted to wave off traffic, as people are frequently seen to do along expressways, he would also have been in danger without a flashlight. <u>It did not necessarily add much to the peril by standing as Cohen told him to do, near the left door of the car and waving down traffic.</u> *Then, is Cohen liable as Δ? yes.*

It is arguable, at least, that if the car was going to be hit it would be from the rear and that standing neither in front of, nor in the rear of, the car he would be less likely to be injured. In the event, which was certainly unpredictable, the car that actually hit him swerved first to the left to avoid Cohen's car and then, out of control, to the right and at an angle into the side where decedent was standing. No one would be likely quite to anticipate this.

It is not easy to say just what would be the right thing to do to help guard against danger caused by the stalled car. It is not a situation open to dogmatic answers after the event. It is, at least, reasonably arguable; and if it is arguable it ought not be held as a matter of law that the dead man was negligent and that defendant has sustained his burden in this respect.

Defendant Tobias Cohen's negligence could readily be found from his failure to place the car on the available shoulder instead of stopping it on the driving lane; from his failure to raise the hood or trunk cover; from his failure to keep the rear lights on (as the jury could have found), and from his failure to give Rossman the flashlight he had in the glove compartment.

The order should be reversed and a new trial directed, with costs to abide the event.

---

1. The opinion in the principal case is one of the few applying the Erosion Principle to the defense of contributory negligence that states frankly the court's attitude toward the defense and admits its readiness to avoid it. Aside from the formal exceptions to the defense, there are a number of judicial devices for ameliorating its harshness. They include:

2. *Burden of Proof.* In every jurisdiction today, the burden of pleading and proving contributory negligence is on the defendant.

3. *Leaving the Question of Contributory Negligence to the Jury.* Assuming evidence of contributory negligence has been introduced, there has been a decided trend to leave the issue to the jury. This occurred, for example, when plaintiff, a competent adult, grabbed a sagging uninsulated high tension wire, Lazar v. The Cleveland Elec. Illuminating Co., 43 Ohio St.2d 131, 331 N.E.2d 424 (1975); and when plaintiff tripped over a watermelon set alongside the store aisle, Urban v. Wait's Supermarket, Inc., 294 N.W.2d 793 (S.D.1980). It has been suggested that the effect of all this is to create a *de facto* comparative negligence system in which the jury applies *sub silentio* a rule of comparative negligence and apportions damages. See Ulman, A Judge Takes the Stand, 30–34 (1933). Does this eliminate the need for comparative negligence? Is it good policy to rely on a lay jury to correct an undesirable condition of the law?

4. *Causation.* The defense of contributory negligence has also been limited by utilizing concepts related to causation.

A. *Causation in Fact.* While a few courts cling to the rule that plaintiff's negligence bars his recovery if it makes any contribution to the result, "however slight," Crane v. Neal, 389 Pa. 329, 132 A.2d 675 (1957), most courts now hold that plaintiff's negligence stands on the same footing as defendant's, and that it will bar his recovery only if it is a substantial factor in bringing about the result. See, for example, Bahm v. Pittsburgh & Lake Erie R. Co., 6 Ohio St.2d 192, 217 N.E.2d 217 (1966).

B. *Proximate Cause.* Courts have subtly confined the defense by narrowly limiting the scope of proximate cause as applied to risks that plaintiff exposed himself to by his act of negligence. Prime examples are Furukawa v. Yoshio Ogawa, 236 F.2d 272 (9th Cir.1956) (negligence as to danger of falling, but not of falling upon a hook); and Smithwick v. Hall & Upson Co., 59 Conn. 261, 21 A. 924 (1890) (negligence as to danger of slipping off an unguarded icy ledge, but not of wall collapsing on plaintiff). What should happen to these cases once a jurisdiction adopts comparative negligence? Nothing

5. *Dual Standards of Care.* Professor Fleming James has argued that the different treatment of plaintiff's contributory negligence as compared with defendant's negligence should be recognized as a formal rule. See James, Contributory Negligence, 62 Yale L.J. 691 (1953); James and Dickinson, Accident Proneness and Accident Law, 63 Harv.L.Rev. 769 (1950). The principal case is one of the few explicitly to adhere to the James approach.

Is this a good test re: even Δ's (N)? if accident may have been avoided? same/similar ⊕ to "but/for"?

DAVIES v. MANN

Exchequer, 1842.
10 M. & W. 547, 152 Eng.Rep. 588.

Trct = π   *⊛ "last clear chance"*
Exch = affd   *π's argument*

At the trial, before Erskine, J., at the last Summer Assizes for the county of Worcester, it appeared that the plaintiff, having fettered the fore feet of an ass belonging to him, turned it into a public highway, and at the time in question the ass was grazing on the off side of the road about eight yards wide, when the defendant's waggon, with a team of three horses, coming down a slight descent, at what the witness termed a smartish pace, ran against the ass, knocked it down, and the wheels passing over it, it died soon after. The ass was fettered at the time, and it was proved that the driver of the waggon was some little distance behind the horses. The learned Judge told the jury that though the act of the plaintiff, in leaving the donkey on the highway so fettered as to prevent his getting out of the way of carriages travelling along it, might be illegal, still, if the proximate cause of the injury was attributable to the want of proper conduct on the part of the driver of the waggon, the action was maintainable against the defendant; and his Lordship directed them, if they thought that the accident might have been avoided by the exercise of ordinary care on the part of the driver, to find for the plaintiff. The jury found their verdict for the plaintiff, damages 40s.

a rich man walking down the street and turned into a dumpster

more or less than violent

the wagon died

how many "proximate" causes = more than one

Godson now moved for a new trial, on the ground of misdirection.

LORD ABINGER, C.B. I am of opinion that there ought to be no rule in this case. The defendant has not denied that the ass was lawfully in the highway, and therefore we must assume it to have been lawfully there; but even were it otherwise, it would have made no difference, for as the defendant might, by proper care, have avoided injuring the animal, and did not, he is liable for the consequences of his negligence, though the animal may have been improperly there.

re: BoP on Δ
for π

PARKE, B. * * * [A]lthough the ass may have been wrongfully there, still the defendant was bound to go along the road at such a pace as would be likely to prevent mischief. Were this not so, a man might justify the driving over goods left on a public highway, or even over a man lying asleep there, or the purposely running against a carriage going on the wrong side of the road.

Do we not have so often many reason for deviation from a std = justification analogous re: π

———

1. "The groans, ineffably and mournfully sad, of Davies' dying donkey, have resounded around the earth. The last lingering gaze from the soft, mild eyes of this docile animal, like the last parting sunbeams of the softest day in spring, has appealed to and touched the hearts of men. There has girdled the globe a band of sympathy for Davies' immortal 'critter.' Its ghost, like Banquo's ghost, will not down at the behests of the people who are charged with inflicting injuries, nor can its groanings be silenced by the ranting and excoriations of carping critics. The law as enunciated in that case has come to stay." McLain, J., in Fuller v. Illinois Cent. R. Co., 100 Miss. 705, 717, 56 So. 783 (1911).

This is a man who loves this ass.

2.   Later commentators have rationalized the holding in the principal case into what has come to be known as the doctrine of ⟨last clear chance.⟩ As the title indicates, the thought is that if the defendant had the opportunity to avoid the accident after the opportunity was no longer available to the plaintiff, the defendant is the one who should bear the loss. Note that under this doctrine the whole loss is still placed on one party or the other. Does this accomplish justice between the parties?

3.   Which of the following explanations for the doctrine of last clear chance are satisfactory?

A.   The later negligence of defendant is an intervening, superseding cause, breaking the connection between plaintiff's prior negligence and his injury. See Ackerman v. James, 200 N.W.2d 818 (Iowa 1972) (collecting cases). Is this view sound? What if a third person is injured through the negligence of the two? Would the earlier negligent party be relieved of liability? Petition of Kinsman Transit Co., 338 F.2d 708 (2d Cir. 1964). — *yes*

— except in Concurrent causes

B.   The later negligence of defendant must necessarily be the greater fault: "the assumption is that he is the more culpable whose opportunity to avoid the injury was later." Kansas City S.R. Co. v. Ellzey, 275 U.S. 236 (1927). Suppose plaintiff is lying dead drunk in the street, and defendant, properly driving an automobile, sees him there and excitedly steps on the accelerator instead of the brake? Cf. Smith v. Connecticut R. & L. Co., 80 Conn. 268, 67 A. 888 (1907).

C.   The doctrine arises out of dislike of the defense of contributory negligence, and represents a retreat from its application in a group of cases where an excuse can be found. MacIntyre, The Rationale of Last Clear Chance, 53 Harv.L.Rev. 1225 (1940).

4.   What should happen to the doctrine once a jurisdiction adopts comparative negligence? See Li v. Yellow Cab Co. of California, infra page 570, and notes. *dropped*

5.   Almost all courts still following the common law rule of contributory negligence have applied the exception of last clear chance in at least one of its many forms. Application of the doctrine may depend on whether the plaintiff is (1) helpless, unable to avoid the danger, or (2) merely inattentive. The Restatement (Second) of Torts §§ 479, 480, groups the patterns around the nature of the plaintiff's conduct; the paragraphs below group them around the nature of the defendant's conduct. Is one method better than the other?

6.   *Discovered Peril (Conscious Last Clear Chance).* The simplest case arises when the defendant sees the plaintiff and becomes aware of his predicament in time to avoid the accident but negligently fails to avert it. Practically all jurisdictions continuing to use the doctrine purport to apply it in this situation, and some say they will go no further. See Woloszynowski v. New York Cent. R. Co., 254 N.Y. 206, 172 N.E. 471 (1930); Hanson v. N.H. Pre–Mix Concrete, Inc., 110 N.H. 377, 268 A.2d 841 (1970). There are difficulties in applying it. It obviously applies when the plaintiff is helpless and unable to extricate himself from the dangerous situation. Does it also apply when the plaintiff was merely inattentive? A substantial majority say yes, if the defendant is aware of this. How does one prove that the defendant was aware of the plaintiff's presence? Often the only means is by circumstantial evidence. It is still harder to ascertain when the defendant has appreciated the fact that an inattentive plaintiff is not and will not become aware of the danger in time to avert it. Two cars approach each other at a crossing—when does the driver

*[handwritten: if right of way, then not (N).
→ perhaps coming too fast.]*

who has the right of way become aware that the other driver will not stop despite the rule of the road?

7. *Discoverable Peril (Unconscious Last Clear Chance).* If the defendant did not actually become aware of the plaintiff but would have seen him by the exercise of due care, some courts have held that last clear chance is inapplicable. A majority of courts still continue to apply the doctrine, however—so long as the plaintiff has become helpless, unable to extricate himself from his predicament. The rationale is that the helpless plaintiff can no longer avert the accident, but the inattentive defendant still has a chance to avert it if he will only exercise due care. See, e.g., Williams v. Spell, 51 N.C.App. 134, 275 S.E.2d 282 (1981). If both parties are inattentive and neither discovers the peril, it cannot be said that either had the last clear chance, and there is general agreement that the exception does not apply. See, e.g., Donohue v. Rolando, 16 Utah 2d 294, 400 P.2d 12 (1965).

8. *Antecedent Negligence ("First Clear Chance").* In some situations an antecedent act of negligence on the part of the defendant may make it impossible for him to avoid the accident after he discovers the plaintiff in a position of peril. For example, defendant drives a car with defective brakes; he sees the plaintiff but cannot stop in time. The majority rule refuses to apply the last clear chance doctrine. *[handwritten: to what end? works against T.
→ still should apply b/c of continuing (N).]*

9. The whole doctrine of last clear chance has been characterized as fearfully and wonderfully complicated, and fundamentally foolish. It has been called a "transitional doctrine," a way station on the road to some other remedy, such as apportionment of damages. James, Last Clear Chance: A Transitional Doctrine, 47 Yale L.J. 704 (1938). Its effect, for many years, however, was to freeze the transition rather than to speed it.

10. *Defendant Engaged in Intentional, Wanton or Wilful or Reckless Conduct.* It is standard hornbook law that contributory negligence is not a defense to an intentional tort. See W. Prosser & W. Keeton, Torts 462 (5th ed. 1984). Thus, one cannot defend against a battery by arguing that the plaintiff was negligent in failing to duck.

The same general rule has been extended in almost every jurisdiction to situations in which defendant engaged in "wanton and willful" or reckless conduct. It is said that this conduct differs from negligence not only in degree, but also in kind and, therefore, the defense of contributory negligence is inapplicable. See, e.g., Kasanovich v. George, 348 Pa. 199, 34 A.2d 523 (1943).

As is true in the case of last clear chance, the entire amount of damages is shifted to defendant if the doctrine is applied. Should it still be applied under comparative negligence? See the section beginning on the next page.

11. *Strict Liability.* On this, see infra Chaper 15, Section 6.

12. *Defendant Violates a Statute.* Generally, contributory negligence is still held to be a defense although defendant was negligent *per se* because of violation of a statute. See Brown v. Derry, 10 Wash.App. 459, 518 P.2d 251 (1974) (motorist transported individual on outside of vehicle). Certain statutes, however, are deemed to abrogate the defense. They may be classified as follows:

A. *Statutes Explicitly Abolishing the Defense in Limited Situations.* Sometimes the legislature explicitly abolishes the contributory negligence defense in a limited situation. An example is under the F.E.L.A. when defendant

has violated a federal safety standard and that caused the injury. See 45 U.S.
C.A. § 53.

B. *Statutes "Intended" to Protect Plaintiff Against His Inability to Protect
Himself.* Statutes prohibiting child labor, the sale of firearms to minors, the
sale of liquor to intoxicated persons, and those that require safety devices to
protect factory workers, have been held to be in this category. The court must
determine that the "statute [was] enacted to protect a class of persons from
their inability to exercise self-protective care." Restatement (Second) of Torts
§ 483.

C. *Statutes Imposing Strict Liability.* Statutes creating strict liability in
tort law are often held to have impliedly abolished fault-based defenses such as
contributory negligence. See Long v. Forest–Fehlhaber, Joint Venture, 74
A.D.2d 167, 427 N.Y.S.2d 649 (1980); Evins v. St. Louis & S.F.R. Co., 104 Ark.
79, 147 S.W. 452 (1912).

D. See generally Prosser, Contributory Negligence as Defense to Violation
of Statute, 32 Minn.L.Rev. 105 (1948).

(B) COMPARATIVE NEGLIGENCE

LI v. YELLOW CAB CO. OF CALIFORNIA
Supreme Court of California, 1975.
13 Cal.3d 804, 532 P.2d 1226, 119 Cal.Rptr. 858.

[Plaintiff Nga Li, while driving a 1967 Oldsmobile, improperly
made a left-hand turn into an intersection when defendant's automobile
was approaching from the opposite direction. Defendant entered the
intersection at an unsafe speed after the traffic signal had turned
yellow. The trial court (sitting without a jury) found the defendant
negligent, but it also found that the plaintiff was contributorily negligent and entered a judgment for defendant on that basis. Plaintiff
appealed on the ground that plaintiff's contributory negligence should
not have totally barred her claim. There were numerous *amici curiae*
on both sides.]

SULLIVAN, J., delivered the opinion of the court.

In this case we address the grave and recurrent question whether
we should judicially declare no longer applicable in California courts
the doctrine of contributory negligence, which bars all recovery when
the plaintiff's negligent conduct has contributed as a legal cause in any
degree to the harm suffered by him, and hold that it must give way to a
system of comparative negligence, which assesses liability in direct
proportion to fault. * * *

It is unnecessary for us to catalogue the enormous amount of
critical comment that has been directed over the years against the "all-
or-nothing" approach of the doctrine of contributory negligence. The
essence of that criticism has been constant and clear: the doctrine is
inequitable in its operation because it fails to distribute responsibility
in proportion to fault.

California Supreme Court at the time of the *Li* decision
Front row: McComb, Wright, C.J., Peters (replaced by Clark)
Back row: Burke, Tobriner, Mosk, Sullivan

Furthermore, practical experience with the application by juries of the doctrine of contributory negligence has added its weight to analyses of its inherent shortcomings: "Every trial lawyer is well aware that juries often do in fact allow recovery in cases of contributory negligence, and that the compromise in the jury room does result in some diminution of the damages because of the plaintiff's fault. But the process is at best a haphazard and most unsatisfactory one." [Cc] * * * — so let's take it from the jury because judges will do a better job.

It is in view of these theoretical and practical considerations that to this date 25 states [6] have abrogated the "all or nothing" rule of contributory negligence and have enacted in its place general apportionment *statutes* calculated in one manner or another to assess liability in proportion to fault. In 1973 these states were joined by Florida, which effected the same result by *judicial* decision. (Hoffman v. Jones (Fla.1973) 280 So.2d 431.) We are likewise persuaded that logic, practi-

---

6. Arkansas, Colorado, Connecticut, Georgia, Hawaii, Idaho, Maine, Massachusetts, Minnesota, Mississippi, Nebraska, Nevada, New Hampshire, New Jersey, North Dakota, Oklahoma, Oregon, Rhode Island, South Dakota, Texas, Utah, Vermont, Washington, Wisconsin, Wyoming. (Schwartz, Comparative Negligence (1974), Appendix A, pp. 367–369.)

In the federal sphere, comparative negligence of the "pure" type (see infra) has been the rule since 1908 in cases arising under the Federal Employers' Liability Act (see 45 U.S.C.A. § 53) and since 1920 in cases arising under the Jones Act (see 46 U.S.C.A. § 688) and the Death on the High Seas Act (see 46 U.S.C.A. § 766.)

cal experience, and fundamental justice counsel against the retention of the doctrine rendering contributory negligence a complete bar to recovery—and that it should be replaced in this state by a system under which liability for damage will be borne by those whose negligence caused it in direct proportion to their respective fault. * * *

It is urged that any change in the law of contributory negligence must be made by the Legislature, not by this court. Although the doctrine of contributory negligence is of judicial origin—its genesis being traditionally attributed to the opinion of Lord Ellenborough in Butterfield v. Forrester (K.B.1809) 103 Eng.Rep. 926—the enactment of section 1714 of the Civil Code in 1872 codified the doctrine as it stood at that date and, the argument continues, rendered it invulnerable to attack in the courts except on constitutional grounds. Subsequent cases of this court, it is pointed out, have unanimously affirmed that— barring the appearance of some constitutional infirmity—the "all-or-nothing" rule is the law of this state and shall remain so until the Legislature directs otherwise. The fundamental constitutional doctrine of separation of powers, the argument concludes, requires judicial abstention.

[The court then presented an extensive study of the history and meaning of Civil Code Section 1714 and concluded that it was not intended to freeze the rule of contributory negligence into the law of California.]

We are thus brought to the second group of arguments which have been advanced by defendants and the amici curiae supporting their position. Generally speaking, such arguments expose considerations of a practical nature which, it is urged, counsel against the adoption of a rule of comparative negligence in this state even if such adoption is possible by judicial means.

The most serious of these considerations are those attendant upon the administration of a rule of comparative negligence in cases involving multiple parties. One such problem may arise when all responsible parties are not brought before the court: it may be difficult for the jury to evaluate relative negligence in such circumstances, and to compound this difficulty such an evaluation would not be res judicata in a subsequent suit against the absent wrongdoer. Problems of contribution and indemnity among joint tortfeasors lurk in the background. (See generally Prosser, Comparative Negligence, 41 Cal.L.Rev. 1, 33–37 (1953); Schwartz, Comparative Negligence, §§ 16.1–16.9, pp. 247–274.)

A second and related major area of concern involves the administration of the actual process of fact-finding in a comparative negligence system. The assigning of a specific percentage factor to the amount of negligence attributable to a particular party, while in theory a matter of little difficulty, can become a matter of perplexity in the face of hard facts. The temptation for the jury to resort to a quotient verdict in such circumstances can be great. (See Schwartz, supra, § 17.1, pp. 275–279.) These inherent difficulties are not, however, insurmountable.

Guidelines might be provided the jury which will assist it in keeping focussed upon the true inquiry (see, e.g., Schwartz, supra, § 17.1, pp. 278–279), and the utilization of special verdicts or jury interrogatories can be of invaluable assistance in assuring that the jury has approached its sensitive and often complex task with proper standards and appropriate reverence. (See Schwartz, supra, § 17.4, pp. 282–291; Prosser, Comparative Negligence, supra, 41 Cal.L.Rev., pp. 28–33.)

The third area of concern [is] the status of the doctrine * * * of last clear chance. Although several states which apply comparative negligence concepts retain the last clear chance doctrine (see Schwartz, supra, § 7.2, p. 134), the better reasoned position seems to be that when true comparative negligence is adopted, the need for last clear chance as a palliative of the hardships of the "all-or-nothing" rule disappears and its retention results only in a windfall to the plaintiff in direct contravention of the principle of liability in proportion to fault. (See Schwartz, supra, § 7.2, pp. 137–139; Prosser, Comparative Negligence, supra, 41 Cal.L.Rev., p. 27.) * * *

Finally there is the problem of the treatment of willful misconduct under a system of comparative negligence. In jurisdictions following the "all-or-nothing" rule, contributory negligence is no defense to an action based upon a claim of willful misconduct (see Rest.2d Torts, § 503; Prosser, Torts, supra, § 65, p. 426) [cc]. * * * As Dean Prosser has observed, "[this] is in reality a rule of comparative fault which is being applied, and the court is refusing to set up the lesser fault against the greater." (Prosser, Torts, supra, § 65, p. 426.) The thought is that the difference between willful and wanton misconduct and ordinary negligence is one of kind rather than degree in that the former involves conduct of an entirely different order, and under this conception it might well be urged that comparative negligence concepts should have no application when one of the parties has been guilty of willful and wanton misconduct. It has been persuasively argued, however, that the loss of deterrent effect that would occur upon application of comparative fault concepts to willful and wanton misconduct as well as ordinary negligence would be slight, and that a comprehensive system of comparative negligence should allow for the apportionment of damages in all cases involving misconduct which falls short of being intentional. (Schwartz, supra, § 5.3, p. 108.) The law of punitive damages remains a separate consideration. (See Schwartz, supra, § 5.4, pp. 109–111.)

The existence of the foregoing areas of difficulty and uncertainty (as well as others which we have not here mentioned—see generally Schwartz, supra, § 21.1, pp. 335–339) has not diminished our conviction that the time for a revision of the means for dealing with contributory fault in this state is long past due and that it lies within the province of this court to initiate the needed change by our decision in this case.

* * *

Forms of Comp N "Pure"

It remains to identify the precise form of comparative negligence which we now adopt for application in this state. Although there are many variants, only the two basic forms need be considered here. The first of these, the so-called "pure" form of comparative negligence, apportions liability in direct proportion to fault in all cases. This was the form adopted by the Supreme Court of Florida in Hoffman v. Jones, supra, and it applies by statute in Mississippi, Rhode Island, and Washington. Moreover, it is the form favored by most scholars and commentators. [Cc]

"Partial"

The second basic form of comparative negligence, of which there are several variants, applies apportionment based on fault *up to the point* at which the plaintiff's negligence is equal to or greater than that of the defendant—when that point is reached, plaintiff is barred from recovery. Nineteen states have adopted this form or one of its variants by statute. The principal argument advanced in its favor is moral in nature: that it is not morally right to permit one more at fault in an accident to recover from one less at fault. Other arguments assert the probability of increased insurance, administrative, and judicial costs if a "pure" rather than a "50 percent" system is adopted, but this has been seriously questioned. [Cc]

We have concluded that the "pure" form of comparative negligence is that which should be adopted in this state. In our view the "50 percent" system simply shifts the lottery aspect of the contributory negligence rule to a different ground. As Dean Prosser has noted, under such a system "[i]t is obvious that a slight difference in the proportionate fault may permit a recovery; and there has been much justified criticism of a rule under which a plaintiff who is charged with 49 percent of a total negligence recovers 51 percent of his damages, while one who is charged with 50 percent recovers nothing at all." Prosser, Comparative Negligence, supra, 41 Cal.L.Rev. 1, 25; fns. omitted. In effect "such a rule distorts the very principle it recognizes, i.e., that persons are responsible for their acts to the extent their fault contributes to an injurious result. The partial rule simply lowers, but does not eliminate, the bar of contributory negligence." [Cc]

We also consider significant the experience of the State of Wisconsin, which until recently was considered the leading exponent of the "50 percent" system. There that system led to numerous appeals on the narrow but crucial issue whether plaintiff's negligence was equal to defendant's. * * *

For all of the foregoing reasons we conclude that the "all-or-nothing" rule of contributory negligence as it presently exists in this state should be and is herewith superseded by a system of "pure" comparative negligence, the fundamental purpose of which shall be to assign responsibility and liability for damage in direct proportion to the amount of negligence of each of the parties.

[The Court held that the new rule would apply to all cases in which trial had not begun before the date its decision became final.]

The judgment is reversed.

WRIGHT, C.J., and TOBRINER and BURKE, JJ., concurred.

[MOSK, J., concurred in the judgment and in the adoption of comparative negligence, but dissented on the manner in which the majority handled the issue of retroactivity.]

CLARK, J., dissenting. * * * [T]he Legislature is the branch best able to effect transition from contributory to comparative or some other doctrine of negligence. Numerous and differing negligence systems have been urged over the years, yet there remains widespread disagreement among both the commentators and the states as to which one is best. (See Schwartz, Comparative Negligence (1974) Appendix A, pp. 367–369 and § 21.3, fn. 40, pp. 341–342, and authorities cited therein.) This court is not an investigatory body, and we lack the means of fairly appraising the merits of these competing systems. Constrained by settled rules of judicial review, we must consider only matters within the record or susceptible to judicial notice. That this court is inadequate to the task of carefully selecting the best replacement system is reflected in the majority's summary manner of eliminating from consideration all but two of the many competing proposals—including models adopted by some of our sister states.

Contrary to the majority's assertions of judicial adequacy, the courts of other states—with near unanimity—have conceded their inability to determine the best system for replacing contributory negligence, concluding instead that the legislative branch is best able to resolve the issue.

By abolishing this century old doctrine today, the majority seriously erodes our constitutional function. We are again guilty of judicial chauvinism.

MCCOMB, J., concurs.

———————

1. The basic principle underlying comparative negligence, that damages should be apportioned between the parties on the basis of their fault, can be traced to Justinian's Code in the law of ancient Rome. See Mole and Wilson, A Study of Comparative Negligence, 17 Cornell L.Q. 333, 337 (1932). The English Courts of Admiralty were influenced by international rules derived from civil law and adopted a comparative negligence system around 1700. The Supreme Court of the United States followed these English precedents in Admiralty jurisdiction.

The first significant body of comparative negligence legislation in the United States arose from a desire to salvage the fault system and make it work for the protection of injured workmen—especially railroad employees. The Second Federal Employer's Liability Act enacted in 1908 provided that an employee of an interstate railroad would not be totally barred by his own negligence in an action against his employer. 45 U.S.C.A. § 53. Rather, the jury would diminish the employee's damages in proportion to the negligence attributable to him. Congress also incorporated this principle of pure comparative negligence in the Jones Act and the Merchant Marine Act, both applicable to maritime employees, 46 U.S.C.A. § 688; and also in the Death on the High Seas Act, 46 U.S.C.A. § 766.

In the first half of the twentieth century, a number of states enacted comparative negligence statutes of limited application (collected in V. Schwartz, Comparative Negligence (2d ed. 1986), that usually protected workmen in intrastate railroad accidents. Most provinces in Canada, England (in 1945) and most Australian states have adopted a general comparative negligence system. See, e.g., G. Williams, Joint Torts and Contributory Negligence (1951). The same is true of almost every major foreign country. See Turk, Comparative Negligence on the March, 28 Chi.–Kent L.Rev. 180 & 304 (1950); Woods, Quickening March of Comparative Fault, 15 Trial [No. 11] 26 (1979).

Nevertheless, comparative negligence did not quickly achieve widespread popularity in the United States. In the mid 1960's, only six states had a general comparative negligence system: Arkansas (1955), Georgia (1904), Mississippi (1910), Nebraska (1913), South Dakota (1941) and Wisconsin (1931).

About that time attacks on the fault system began to mount again. A basic criticism was that many injured parties recover nothing because of the contributory negligence and assumption of risk defenses. See R. Keeton and O'Connell, Basic Protection for the Traffic Victim—A Blue Print for Reforming Automobile Insurance (1965). One result was a stampede toward comparative negligence. From 1965 through 1986, at least 36 states turned to such a law, bringing to a total of 44 the number of states that have adopted some form of comparative negligence.

2. Most states did so through the process of legislative enactment. Generally, courts held that the change should be left to the legislative body, though they sometimes indicated that they might have to act if the legislature did not. See McGraw v. Corrin, 303 A.2d 641 (Del.1973); Loui v. Oakley, 50 Hawaii 260, 438 P.2d 393 (1968) (hinting that it might do so in the future if the legislature failed to act—legislature acted soon after in 1968); Bourque v. Olin, 346 So.2d 1373 (La.App.1977); Haeg v. Sprague, Warner & Co., 202 Minn. 425, 281 N.W. 261 (1938) (legislature acted in 1971); Krise v. Gillund, 184 N.W.2d 405 (N.D.1971) (legislature acted in 1973); Baab v. Shockling, 61 Ohio St.2d 55, 399 N.E.2d 87 (1980) (legislature acted in 1980); Peterson v. Culp, 255 Or. 269, 465 P.2d 876 (1970) (legislature acted in 1971).

3. Prior to the principal decision, the Supreme Court of Florida had pioneered by judicially adopting the system of comparative negligence. Hoffman v. Jones, 280 So.2d 431 (Fla.1973). Florida had previously had experience with the system, both through legislative action (limited to railroad crossing accidents) and judicial construction of that legislation. Since the Li decision courts of Alaska, Michigan, West Virginia, New Mexico, Illinois, Iowa, Missouri and Kentucky have also judicially adopted a system of comparative negligence. Kaatz v. State, 540 P.2d 1037 (Alaska 1975); Placek v. Sterling Heights, 405 Mich. 638, 275 N.W.2d 511 (1978); Bradley v. Appalachian Power Co., 256 S.E.2d 79 (W.Va.1979); Alvis v. Ribar, 85 Ill.2d 1, 52 Ill.Dec. 23, 421 N.E.2d 886 (1981); Scott v. Rizzo, 96 N.M. 682, 634 P.2d 1234 (1981); Gustafsen v. Benda, 661 S.W.2d 11 (Mo.1983); Hilen v. Hays, 673 S.W.2d 713 (Ky.1984). The Illinois courts have come full circle on the issue. First, a midlevel appellate court took the plunge when the problem was referred to it by the state supreme court. Maki v. Frelk, 85 Ill.App.2d 439, 229 N.E.2d 284 (1967). This was reversed by the Supreme Court of Illinois. Maki v. Frelk, 40 Ill.2d 193, 239 N.E.2d 445

(1968). Then in 1981, the Supreme Court decided to adopt the pure form. Alvis v. Ribar, supra this note.

4. What about the argument that modern legislatures are thoroughly familiar with comparative negligence—therefore, if they do not pass a law, this amounts to an endorsement of the *status quo*? Thorough discussions of the question of whether a court should implement comparative negligence appear in the symposium on Maki v. Frelk with comments by Professors James, Kalven, R. Keeton, Leflar, Malone and Wade, 21 Vand.L.Rev. 889 (1968); Juenger, Brief for Negligence Law Section of the State Bar of Michigan in Support of Comparative Negligence as Amicus Curiae, 18 Wayne L.Rev. 3 (1972); Goldberg, Judicial Adoption of Comparative Fault in New Mexico: The Time is at Hand, 10 N.M.L.Rev. 3 (1979); Vargo, Comparative Fault: Need to Reform Indiana Tort Law, 11 Ind.L.Rev. 829 (1978). And see the argument that the Constitution requires adoption of a comparative negligence approach. C. Sowle, Comparative Negligence v. The Constitutional Guarantee of Equal Protection: A Hypothetical Judicial Decision, 1979 Duke L.J. 1083; Phillips, The Case for Judicial Adoption of Comparative Fault in South Carolina, 32 S.C.L.Rev. 295 (1980).

5. The *Li* case has been discussed in Ellerby and Gaughan, Comparative Negligence By Judicial Fiat, 42 Ins.Coun.J. 575 (1975); Fleming, Foreword: Comparative Negligence at Last—By Judicial Choice, 64 Cal.L.Rev. 239 (1976); Schwartz, Judicial Adoption of Comparative Negligence: The Supreme Court of California Takes a Historic Stand, 51 Ind.L.J. 281 (1976).

Types of Comparative Negligence Systems

A pays half of damages

1. *Modified Comparative Negligence Systems.* (A) *The Equal–Division Rule.* The simplest way to apportion damages is to divide them equally between the negligent parties. This was the original English admiralty rule, but that country abandoned it and turned to a pure system in 1911 when it conformed to the Brussels International Maritime Convention. The United States never signed that Convention and the U.S. Supreme Court clung to the equal-division rule until 1975, when it overruled an 1854 precedent and turned to pure comparative negligence. United States v. Reliable Transfer Co., 421 U.S. 397 (1975). At present, the equal-division rule is only of historic interest.

(B) *The Slight–Gross Approach.* Two states have applied comparative negligence for many years under this system. Damages are apportioned in Nebraska when plaintiff's negligence "was slight" and defendant's "was gross in comparison"; in South Dakota, when plaintiff's negligence "was slight in comparison with the negligence of the defendant."

(C) *Modified Comparative Negligence—The Two 50% Approaches.* These two approaches have the greatest number of adherents in the United States. Under the first a plaintiff who is contributorily negligent can recover diminished damages if his negligence was "not as great as" (or "not equal to") that of the defendant; otherwise the common law contributory negligence rule applies. *49/51* States adhering to this view include Arkansas, Colorado, Georgia, Idaho, Kansas, Maine, North Dakota, Oklahoma, Utah, West Virginia and Wyoming (11). The second approach permits diminished recovery if the plaintiff's negligence is "not greater than" that of the defendant. Adhering to this view are Connecticut, Delaware, Hawaii, Indiana, Iowa, Massachusetts, Minnesota, Montana, Nevada, New Hampshire, New Jersey, Ohio, Oregon, Pennsylvania, Texas, Vermont and Wisconsin (17). The difference between these two approaches is restricted to the "50-50" case. Although the distinction may not seem very important in theory, it is important as a practical matter because a 50-50 apportionment is a very comfortable one for juries. Under the "not as great as" approach, when there are only two parties who were both injured, neither one could recover anything even though both parties were fully insured, and the insurance companies could be the only winners. This is a reason why the Wisconsin legislature in 1971 shifted from a "not as great" to a "not greater than" system and started a trend.

2. *Pure Comparative Negligence.* States adopting this approach include Alaska, Arizona, California, Florida, Illinois, Kentucky, Louisiana, Michigan, Mississippi, Missouri, New Mexico, New York, Rhode Island and Washington (14). Federal statutes (FELA, Jones Act, Merchant Marine Act and Death on the High Seas Act) also follow this position, as do Puerto Rico, the Virgin Islands and the Canal Zone. England and the other common law countries all follow it. And two jurisdictions have judicially adopted a doctrine of comparative causation that amounts essentially to the same thing. See Murray v. Fairbanks Morse, Beloit Power Systems, Inc., 610 F.2d 149 (3d Cir.1979) (for the Virgin Islands); General Motors Corp. v. Hopkins, 548 S.W.2d 344 (Tex.1977) (for strict products liability, not covered by the comparative negligence Texas statute—modified by statute a decade later).

Examples of the Major Systems

1. *"Not as Great As."* Colorado:

(1) Contributory negligence shall not bar recovery in any action by any person or his legal representative to recover damages for negligence resulting in death or in injury to person or property, if such negligence was not as great as the negligence of the person against whom recovery is sought, but any damages allowed shall be diminished in proportion to the amount of negligence attributable to the person for whose injury, damage, or death recovery is made.

(2)(a) In any action to which subsection (1) of this section applies, the court, in a nonjury trial, shall make findings of fact or, in a jury trial, the jury shall return a special verdict which shall state:

(b) The amount of the damages which would have been recoverable if there had been no contributory negligence; and

(c) The degree of negligence of each party, expressed as a percentage.

(3) Upon the making of the finding of fact or the return of a special verdict, as is required by subsection (2) of this section, the court shall

reduce the amount of the verdict in proportion to the amount of negligence attributable to the person for whose injury, damage, or death recovery is made; but if the said proportion is equal to or greater than the negligence of the person against whom recovery is sought, then, in such event, the court will enter a judgment for the defendant.

(4) In a jury trial in any civil action in which contributory negligence is an issue for determination by the jury, the trial court shall instruct the jury on the effect of its finding as to the degree of negligence of each party. The attorneys for each party shall be allowed to argue the effect of the instruction on the facts which are before the jury. [Rev.Stat.Ann. § 13–22–111.]

2. *"Not Greater Than."* Wisconsin: 50/50

Contributory negligence shall not bar recovery in an action by any person or his legal representative to recover damages for negligence resulting in death or in injury to person or property, if such negligence was not greater than the negligence of the person against whom recovery is sought, but any damages allowed shall be diminished in the proportion to the amount of negligence attributable to the person recovering. [Stat.Ann. § 895.045.] =

3. *Pure System.* THE UNIFORM COMPARATIVE FAULT ACT (1979).

Section 1. [Effect of Contributory Fault]

(a) In an action based on fault seeking to recover damages for injury or death to person or harm to property, any contributory fault chargeable to the claimant diminishes proportionately the amount awarded as compensatory damages for an injury attributable to the claimant's contributory fault, but does not bar recovery. This rule applies whether or not under prior law the claimant's contributory fault constituted a defense or was disregarded under applicable legal doctrines, such as last clear chance.

(b) "Fault" includes acts or omissions that are in any measure negligent or reckless toward the person or property of the actor or others, or that subject a person to strict tort liability. The term also includes breach of warranty, unreasonable assumption of risk not constituting an enforceable express consent, misuse of a product for which the defendant otherwise would be liable, and unreasonable failure to avoid an injury or to mitigate damages. Legal requirements of causal relation apply both to fault as the basis for liability and to contributory fault.

Section 2. [Apportionment of Damages]

(a) In all actions involving fault of more than one party to the action, including third-party defendants and persons who have been released under Section 6, the court, unless otherwise agreed by all parties, shall instruct the jury to answer, special interrogatories or, if there is no jury, shall make findings, indicating:

(1) the amount of damages each claimant would be entitled to recover if contributory fault is disregarded; and

(2) the percentage of the total fault of all of the parties to each claim that is allocated to each claimant, defendant, third-party defendant, and person who has been released from liability under Section 6. For this purpose the court may determine that two or more persons are to be treated as a single party.

(b) In determining the percentages of fault, the trier of fact shall consider both the nature of the conduct of each party at fault and the extent of the causal relation between the conduct and the damages claimed.

(c) The court shall determine the award of damages to each claimant in accordance with the findings, subject to any reduction under Section 6, and enter judgment against each party liable on the basis of rules of joint-and-several liability. For purposes of contribution under Sections 4 and 5, the court also shall determine and state in the judgment each party's equitable share of the obligation to each claimant in accordance with the respective percentages of fault.

(d) Upon motion made not later than [one year] after judgment is entered, the court shall determine whether all or part of a party's equitable share of the obligation is uncollectible from that party, and shall reallocate any uncollectible amount among the other parties, including a claimant at fault, according to their respective percentages of fault. The party whose liability is reallocated is nonetheless subject to contribution and to any continuing liability to the claimant on the judgment.

Section 3. [Set-off]

A claim and counterclaim shall not be set off against each other, except by agreement of both parties. On motion, however, the court, if it finds that the obligation of either party is likely to be uncollectible, may order that both parties make payment into court for distribution. The court shall distribute the funds received and declare obligations discharged as if the payment into court by either party had been a payment to the other party and any distribution of those funds back to the party making payment had been a payment to him by the other party.

Section 4. [Right of Contribution]

(a) A right of contribution exists between or among two or more persons who are jointly and severally liable upon the same indivisible claim for the same injury, death, or harm, whether or not judgment has been recovered against all or any of them. It may be enforced either in the original action or by a separate action brought for that purpose. The basis for contribution is each person's equitable share of the obligation, including the equitable share of a claimant at fault, as determined in accordance with the provisions of Section 2.

(b) Contribution is available to a person who enters into a settlement with a claimant only (1) if the liability of the person against whom contribution is sought has been extinguished and (2) to the extent that the amount paid in settlement was reasonable.

Section 5. [Enforcement of Contribution]

(a) If the proportionate fault of the parties to a claim for contribution has been established previously by the court, as provided by Section 2, a party paying more than his equitable share of the obligation, upon motion, may recover judgment for contribution.

(b) If the proportionate fault of the parties to the claim for contribution has not been established by the court, contribution may be enforced in a separate action, whether or not a judgment has been rendered against either the person seeking contribution or the person from whom contribution is being sought.

(c) If a judgment has been rendered, the action for contribution must be commenced within [one year] after the judgment becomes final. If no judgment has been rendered, the person bringing the action for contribution either must have (1) discharged by payment the common liability within the period of the statute of limitations applicable to the claimant's right of action against him and commenced the action for contribution within [one year] after payment or (2) agreed while action was pending to discharge the common liability and, within [one year] after the agreement, have paid the liability and commenced an action for contribution.

Section 6. [Effect of Release]

A release, covenant not to sue, or similar agreement entered into by a claimant and a person liable discharges that person from all liability for contribution, but it does not discharge any other persons liable upon the same claim unless it so provides. However, the claim of the releasing person against other persons is reduced by the amount of the released person's equitable share of the obligation, determined in accordance with the provisions of Section 2.

The Uniform Act carries a prefatory note and comments on the individual sections that describe the reasons for the Act and the particular provisions in it. Specific illustrations assist in understanding the application of the provisions. These comments are well worth studying. While the Act has not been adopted as a whole in any state, portions of the Act have been a basis for portions of state legislative and judicial decisions formulating rules by the common law process.

Problems in the Implementation and Application
of Comparative Fault

Many states do little more than adopt some form of comparative fault. This leaves for the courts the task of solving the problems of administration. And, of course, if the court makes the adoption judicially, it must solve many of them piecemeal. Some of them are listed below. Observe how the Uniform Act handles each of them.

1. *Basis of Apportionment.* Should it be solely on the basis of comparative fault or with consideration given also to the relative directness with which the conduct contributed to the damages? See, taking the latter view, Cushman v. Perkins, 245 A.2d 846 (Me.1968); Lovesee v. Allied Development Corp., 45 Wis. 2d 340, 173 N.W.2d 196 (1970).

2. *Mechanics of Apportionment.* Some statutes use a special verdict or special interrogatory procedure by which the jurors inform the court as to (1) what percentage of fault was attributable to each party and (2) how much damage each claimant suffered. The court then computes the damages. Is this procedure better or is it better to let the jury return a general verdict?

3. *Set-off.* What happens if defendant files a counterclaim or set-off seeking damages? Should there be any difference between a pure system and a modified system? Will the presence of liability insurance affect the decision? Would a set-off have the effect of transferring the loss from the insurance companies to the parties? See Stuyvesant Ins. Co. v. Bournazian, 342 So.2d 471 (Fla.1976); Jess v. Herrmann, 26 Cal.3d 131, 604 P.2d 208, 161 Cal.Rptr. 87 (1979). See § 3 of the Uniform Act, supra page 580. The last sentence may be somewhat difficult to apply literally. Fortunately, it can be simplified to a formula: $D = C - O + P$ [amount $\underline{D}$istributed to a particular party equals amount $\underline{C}$laimed minus amount $\underline{O}$wed plus amount $\underline{P}$aid].

4. *Application to Persons Not Made Party to the Action.* Should their proportion of the fault be assessed and taken into consideration? Cf. Brown v. Keill, 224 Kan. 195, 580 P.2d 867 (1978), and Consolidated Freightways Corp. v. Osier, 185 Mont. 439, 605 P.2d 1076 (1979).

5. *Relationship to Contribution.* What should be done if a separate statute provides for pro rata contribution?

6. *Multiple Parties.* In a modified comparative negligence system, if there are several defendants, should plaintiff's negligence be compared with that of each defendant individually or with all of them together? The latter approach makes the problem solvable. It is provided by statute in Arkansas and Hawaii, and by decision in other states. E.g., Graci v. Damon, 376 Mass. 931, 383 N.E.2d 842 (1978); Laubach v. Morgan, 588 P.2d 1071 (Okl.1978); Bradley v. Appalachian Power Co., 163 W.Va. 332, 256 S.E.2d 879 (1979).

7. *Should Joint and Several Liability Be Abolished?* Some courts have so held. Brown v. Keill, 224 Kan. 195, 580 P.2d 867 (1978) (interpretation of statute); Bartlett v. New Mexico Welding Supply, Inc., 98 N.M. 152, 646 P.2d 579 (1982), cert. denied, 98 N.M. 336, 648 P.2d 794 (1982) (several years later, the New Mexico legislature abolished joint and several liability by statute). The current tort reform campaign has induced other states to pass statutes, but the majority position still follows the common law rule of joint and several liability. See the cases and notes at pages 355–61.

8. *Appropriate Effect of Comparative Negligence on Certain Common Law Doctrines.* (a) *Last clear chance.* The *Li* case holds that it replaces that doctrine. Most, but not all, states agree. See Danculovich v. Brown, 593 P.2d 187 (Wyo.1979); cf. Whitaker v. Burlington N., Inc., 218 Neb. 90, 352 N.W.2d 589 (1984); Notes, 6 Tex.Tech.L.Rev. 131 (1974), 28 Okla.L.Rev. 444 (1975); 6 Ga.St.B.J. 47 (1969). (b) *Res ipsa loquitur.* Should it be necessary for the plaintiff to present evidence that no negligent conduct on his part contributed to the injury? (c) *Negligence per se.* The conduct of either plaintiff or defendant may violate a statute. Should either of these affect the percentage of negligence? (d) *Imputed negligence.* (e) *Punitive damages.* (f) *Avoidable consequences.* (g) *Trial Judge's Control* of Jury (remittitur or additur).

9. *Types of Defendant's Conduct Subject to Application of Comparative Fault.* Comparative fault is, of course, applicable to negligence. What about an intentional tort? If defendant swings at plaintiff, should the damages be reduced because of plaintiff's negligent failure to duck? The answer would normally be no. What about recklessness? Wilful and wanton misconduct? Violation of a "higher degree of care" imposed on a common carrier? Strict liability for abnormally dangerous activities (Chapter 14), or for products liability based on strict liability or breach of warranty (Chapter 15)? Defendant maintains a nuisance (Chapter 16); should all nuisances be treated alike? He makes a misrepresentation that plaintiff relies upon to his detriment (Chapter 21); are intentional and negligent misrepresentations treated alike?

10. *Extent to Which Plaintiff's Condition or the Nature of His Conduct Affects the Application of Comparative Fault.* Assume plaintiff is a minor or aged, or is mentally or physically abnormal; or is an automobile guest in a state that has a different standard of care for them; he is a trespasser or licensee on defendant's land; or acted recklessly (all problems treated in earlier chapters). What if plaintiff has "assumed the risk" (next Section) or has "misused" a product manufactured by the defendant (Chapter 15).

11. *Should the Jury Be Instructed as to the Legal Consequences of Their Verdict?* For example, in a modified comparative-negligence jurisdiction, a percentage change of a single point may make a complete difference as to whether the plaintiff can recover or not. See Kaeo v. Davis, 68 Hawaii ___, 719 P.2d 387 (1986), holding that the information should be given; Brown, Federal Special Verdicts: The Doubt Eliminator, 44 F.R.D. 338 (1968); Smith, Comparative Negligence Problems With the Special Verdict: Informing the Jury of the Legal Effects of Their Verdicts, 10 Land & Water L.Rev. 199 (1975).

12. There are four treatises on comparative fault covering many of these issues. See V. Schwartz, Comparative Negligence (2d ed. 1986); H. Woods, The Negligence Case: Comparative Fault (1978); Comparative Negligence (Matthew Bender, looseleaf) (3 vols.); C.R. Heft and C.J. Heft, Comparative Negligence (1971) (based primarily on Wisconsin law). And see J. McConnell, Comparative Negligence Defense Tactics (1985); C. Gregory, Legislative Loss Distribution in Negligence Actions (1936); G. Williams, Joint Torts and Contributory Negligence (1951) (English authorities).

13. There are far too many articles on the general topic to cite more than a few. Earlier articles include: Prosser, Comparative Negligence, 51 Mich.L. Rev. 465 (1953); Mole & Wilson, A Study of Comparative Negligence, 17 Cornell L.Q. 333 & 609 (1932); Turk, Comparative Negligence on the March, 28 Chi. Kent L.Rev. 189 & 304 (1950); Eldredge, Contributory Negligence: An Outmoded Defense That Should be Abolished, 43 A.B.A.J. 52 (1957).

More recent articles include: Defense Research Institute, Practice and Procedure—Comparative Negligence Primer (1975); Fischer, Products Liability—Applicability of Comparative Negligence to Misuse and Assumption of the Risk, 43 Mo.L.Rev. 643 (1978); Fleming, Report to the Joint Committee of the California Legislature on Tort Liability on the Problems Associated with American Motorcycle Ass'n v. Superior Court, 30 Hastings L.J. 1465 (1978); George & Walkowiak, Blame and Reparation in Pure Comparative Negligence: The Multi-party Action, 8 Sw.U.L.Rev. 1 (1976); G. Schwartz, Contributory and Comparative Negligence: A Reappraisal, 87 Yale L.J. 697 (1978); R. Keeton, Legal Process in Comparative Negligence Cases, 17 Harv.J.Legis. 1 (1980); Johnson, Comparative Negligence and the Duty–Risk Analysis, 40 La.L.Rev. 319 (1980); Pearson, Apportionment of Losses under Comparative Fault, 40 La. L.Rev. 343 (1980); Schwartz, The Impact of Comparative Negligence, 23 Defense L.J. 223 (1978); Wade, Comparative Negligence—Its Development in the United States and Its Present Status in Louisiana, 40 La.L.Rev. 299 (1980); Woods, The Quickening March of Comparative Fault, 15 Trial [No. 11] 26 (1979).

A comprehensive bibliography is included in V. Schwartz, Comparative Negligence (2d ed. 1986).

(C) ASSUMPTION OF RISK

WINTERSTEIN v. WILCOM
Court of Special Appeals of Maryland, 1972.
16 Md.App. 130, 293 A.2d 821.

[Plaintiff Roland Winterstein was seriously injured when his vehicle hit a 36″ long, hundred-pound cylinder head that was lying on a drag racetrack owned by defendant. At the time plaintiff was participating in a speed contest. For this opportunity he paid defendant an entry fee.

Defendant's employees were stationed in a tower to watch "for any hazards on the track," but negligently failed to do so. Plaintiff Roland Winterstein brought a claim for his personal injuries and his wife, Barbara, brought a claim for loss of consortium. Prior to participating in the race, both plaintiffs signed releases drafted by defendant that stated in part:

"*Request and Release.* I, the undersigned, hereby request permission to enter the premises * * * and participate in auto timing and acceleration runs, tests, contests and exhibitions to be held this day. I have inspected the premises and I know the risks and dangers involved in the said activities, and that unanticipated and unexpected dangers may arise during such activities and I assume all risks of injury to my person and property that may be sustained in connection with the stated and associated activities, in and about the premises.

In consideration of the permission granted to me to enter the premises and participate in the stated activities, and in further consideration of the provisions of an insurance medical plan, I do hereby, for myself, my heirs, administrators and assigns, release, remise and discharge the owners, operators, and sponsors of the said premises, of the activities, of the vehicles, and of the equipment therein, and their respective servants, agents, officers, and officials, and all other participants in the stated activities of and from all claims, demands, actions, and causes of action of any sort, for injuries sustained by my person and/or property during my presence in said premises and participation in the stated activities due to negligence or any other fault."

Plaintiffs conceded that the risk that injured Roland fell within the terms of the release, but they contended that the release should be invalidated as a matter of "public policy." The trial court did not accept this argument and dismissed both claims. Plaintiffs appealed.]

ORTH, J. * * * In the absence of legislation to the contrary, the law, by the great weight of authority, is that there is ordinarily no public policy which prevents the parties from contracting as they see fit, as to whether the plaintiff will undertake the responsibility of looking out for himself. "It is quite possible for the parties expressly to agree in advance that the defendant is under no obligation of care for the benefit of the plaintiff, and shall not be liable for the consequences of conduct which would otherwise be negligent." Prosser, Law of Torts, 3rd Ed. (1964) § 67, p. 456. In other words, the parties may agree that there shall be no obligation to take precautions and hence no liability for negligence. * * *

There is a proviso to the general rule. The relationship of the parties must be such that their bargaining be free and open. When one party is at such an obvious disadvantage in bargaining power that the effect of the contract is to put him at the mercy of the other's negligence, the agreement is void as against public policy. The proviso is applicable on this basis between employer and employee.

It is also against public policy to permit exculpatory agreements as to transactions involving the public interest, as for example with regard to public utilities, common carriers, innkeepers and public warehousemen. Prosser feels that there has been a definite tendency to expand the exception raised by the proviso to other professional bailees who are under no public duty but deal with the public, such as garagemen, owners of parking lots, and parcel checkrooms, because the indispensable need for their services deprives the customer of all real equal bargaining power. He finds decisions divided as to other private bailees for hire, the decision likely to turn upon the extent to which it is considered that the public interest is involved. [C]

Generally, exculpatory agreements otherwise valid are not construed to cover the more extreme forms of negligence—wilful, wanton, reckless or gross. Nor do they encompass any conduct which constitutes an intentional tort. [C] And, of course, it is fundamental that if an agreement exempting a defendant from liability for his negligence is to be sustained, it must appear that its terms were known to the plaintiff, and "if he did not know of the provision in his contract and a reasonable person in his position would not have known of it, it is not binding upon him, and the agreement fails for want of mutual consent." [C] * * *

Because an exculpatory provision may not stand if it involves the public interest, see 175 A.L.R. 8 (1948), our inquiry turns to what transactions are affected with a public interest. In Tunkl v. Regents of the University of California, 60 Cal.2d 92, 383 P.2d 441, 32 Cal.Rptr. 33 (1963) the Supreme Court of California, in bank, found that in placing particular contracts within or without the category of those affected with a public interest, the courts have revealed a rough outline of that type of transaction in which exculpatory provisions will be held invalid. "Thus the attempted but invalid exemption involves a transaction which exhibits some or all of the following characteristics. It concerns a business of a type generally thought suitable for public regulation. The party seeking exculpation is engaged in performing a service of great importance to the public, which is often a matter of practical necessity for some members of the public. The party holds himself out as willing to perform this service for any member of the public who seeks it, or at least for any member coming within certain established standards. As a result of the essential nature of the service, in the economic setting of the transaction, the party invoking exculpation possesses a decisive advantage of bargaining strength against any member of the public who seeks his services. In exercising a superior bargaining power the party confronts the public with a standardized adhesion contract of exculpation, and makes no provision whereby a purchaser may pay additional reasonable fees and obtain protection against negligence. Finally, as a result of the transaction, the person or property of the purchaser is placed under the control of the seller, subject to the risk of carelessness by the seller or his agents." [C]

We note a further refinement. Although the traditional view has been that where the defendant's negligence consists of the violation of a statute, the plaintiff may still assume the risk, there is a growing tendency to the contrary where a safety statute enacted for the protection of the public is violated. The rationale is that the obligation and the right so created are public ones which it is not within the power of any private individual to waive. [Cc]

It is clear that the exculpatory provisions involved in the case before us whereby Winterstein expressly agreed in advance that Wilcom would not be liable for the consequences of conduct which would otherwise be negligent were under the general rule recognizing the validity of such provisions. There was not the slightest disadvantage in bargaining power between the parties. Winterstein was under no compulsion, economic or otherwise, to race his car. He obviously participated in the speed runs simply because he wanted to do so, perhaps to demonstrate the superiority of his car and probably with the hope of winning a prize. This put him in no bargaining disadvantage.

The business operated by Wilcom had none of the characteristics of one affected with the public interest. The legislature has not thought it suitable for public regulation for it has not sought to regulate it. Wilcom is not engaged in performing a service of great importance to the public which is a matter of practical necessity for any member of the public. Wilcom does not hold himself out as willing to perform the service for any member of the public coming within certain established standards; we see nothing to indicate that he may not arbitrarily refuse to permit any person to participate in the speed runs. Since the service is not of an essential nature Wilcom had no decisive advantage of bargaining strength against any member of the public seeking to participate. Nor was Winterstein so placed under the control of Wilcom that he was subject to the risk of carelessness by Wilcom or his agents; Winterstein was under no obligation whatsoever to race his car.

We do not believe that any safety statute of this State, enacted for the protection of the public, was involved. Our attention has not been called to, nor are we aware of, such a statute dealing with activities of the nature conducted by Wilcom.

We observe that Winterstein did not allege that the negligence he attributed to Wilcom was other than simple negligence; he characterized Wilcom's omissions and commissions as careless, not wilful, wanton, reckless or gross; he does not say that he was wronged by an intentional tort.

The short of it is that as to the releases here the effect of the exemptive clauses upon the public interest was nil. We find that each release was merely an agreement between persons relating entirely to their private affairs. In the absence of a legislative declaration, we hold that they were not void as against public policy. * * *

Judgment affirmed with costs.

————————

1. There are two basic issues involved when defendant asserts that plaintiff expressly assumed a risk. The first concerns whether the risk that injured plaintiff fell within the terms of the agreement. Suppose in the instant case plaintiff had been injured when an employee of defendant had become angry and knocked him down. Would defendant have been protected by the release? Cf. Brown v. Moore, 247 F.2d 711 (3d Cir.1957); Feigenbaum v. Brink, 66 Wash. 2d 125, 401 P.2d 642 (1965). How should a release be drafted to cover the risk?

2. The second issue is whether the contract itself violates public policy. The principal case is one of the most comprehensive in setting forth the considerations that underlie that determination. In light of those principles, how should a court rule on the validity of a document in which:

A. A patient agreed to assume all risks that had been explained to her in connection with medical diagnosis and treatment in a hospital? Meiman v. Rehabilitation Center, Inc., 444 S.W.2d 78 (Ky.1969).

Suppose the patient did not have to pay for medical services. Should that make a difference? Tunkl v. Regents of Univ. of California, 60 Cal.2d 92, 383 P.2d 441, 32 Cal.Rptr. 33 (1963) (excellent opinion by Justice Tobriner).

B.   An express assumption of risk clause is written into a contract of sale between two industrial giants.   See Delta Air Lines, Inc. v. McDonnell Douglas Corp., 503 F.2d 239 (5th Cir.1974).

C.   A passenger is given the opportunity to ride free on a common carrier, but he must relieve it of all liability to him for negligent acts committed in the course of transportation.   See Gonzales v. Baltimore & Ohio R. Co., 318 F.2d 294 (4th Cir.1963).   Suppose the passenger paid for the ticket?   See New York Cent. R. Co. v. Lockwood, 84 U.S. (17 Wall.) 357 (1873).

3.   In any case involving express assumption of risk, an attorney must research not only tort law but also appropriate regulatory laws that may affect the validity of the documents.   See, e.g., Ill.Rev.Stat., Ch. 80 § 91 (1973); N.Y. Gen.Oblig.Law § 5–321 (McKinney 1964) (declaring exculpatory clauses in rental of real property void).

4.   As indicated in a later case, comparative negligence statutes may affect implied assumption of risk, but they have no relevance on express assumption of risk.   See Gilson v. Drees Bros., 19 Wis.2d 252, 120 N.W.2d 63, 67 (1963); Lyons v. Redding Constr. Co., 83 Wash.2d 86, 515 P.2d 821, 826 (1973).

5.   See generally McClain, Contractual Limitation of Liability for Negligence, 28 Harv.L.Rev. 550 (1915); Mansfield, Informed Choice in the Law of Torts, 22 La.L.Rev. 17 (1961); Rehberg, Exculpatory Clauses in Leases, 15 Ga. B.J. 389 (1953); Annots., 49 A.L.R.3d 321 (1973) (leases), 6 A.L.R.3d 704 (1966) (medical releases).   A key issue in the 1980's is the effectiveness of releases in product liability cases.   See Annot., 93 A.L.R.3d 1296 (1979).

HILDEBRAND v. MINYARD
Arizona Court of Appeals, 1972.
16 Ariz.App. 583, 494 P.2d 1328.

[Plaintiff's decedent, George Hildebrand, was killed while he was attempting to repair a steam steering ramp on a vehicle known as a Michigan bucket loader.   The accident occurred when defendant Minyard, while driving a tractor, ran into the rear of the loader, causing it to thrust forward and crush Hildebrand.   Hildebrand had parked the loader in a passage serving as a roadway between two buildings, partially blocking the passage, but leaving room for other vehicles to pass.   When told that he ought to park elsewhere, he responded that he would be there "only a little while."

Plaintiff appeals a jury verdict for the defendant on the ground that an instruction on implied assumption of risk was unwarranted by the evidence and should not have been given.]

HOWARD, JUDGE.   *   *   *   Implied assumption of risk requires the presence of the following elements:

(1) There must be a risk of harm to plaintiff caused by defendant's conduct or by the condition of the defendant's land or chattels;

(2) Plaintiff must have actual knowledge of the particular risk and appreciate its magnitude.   [Cc]

[handwritten:) actual knowledge / 2) choice]

(3) The plaintiff must voluntarily choose to enter or remain within the area of the risk under circumstances that manifest his willingness to accept that particular risk. *[handwritten: w/in "zone of danger"?]*

As with express assumption of risk, the touchstone of implied assumption of risk is "consent." Contributory negligence arises when the plaintiff fails to exercise due care. Assumption of risk arises regardless of the due care used. It is based, fundamentally, on consent. Contributory negligence is not. [C] In the implied assumption of risk situation the consent is manifested by the plaintiff's actions after he *[handwritten: he has become knowledgeable]* has been informed of the nature and magnitude of the specific danger *[handwritten left margin: duty of Δ - to inform? No]* involved. Therefore, when the plaintiff voluntarily enters into some relationship with the defendant, with knowledge that the defendant will not protect him against the risk, he may then be regarded as tacitly or impliedly consenting to the negligence, and agreeing to take a chance. Thus he may accept employment knowing that he is expected to work with a dangerous horse; or ride in a car with knowledge that the brakes are defective and the driver incompetent; or he may enter a baseball park, sit in an unscreened seat, and thus consent that the players proceed with the game without taking any precautions to protect him from being hit by the ball. The result is that the defendant is simply relieved of the duty which would otherwise exist.

The plaintiff likewise impliedly assumes the risk when he is aware of a risk already created by the negligence of the defendant and proceeds to encounter it as where he has been supplied with a chattel which he knows to be unsafe, and proceeds to use it after he has discovered the danger. If this is voluntary choice, it may be found that he has accepted the situation, and consented to relieve the defendant of his duty. [Cc]

Putting it into its simplest terms, applying the law to the facts in this case, the question is this: "Did the deceased by his actions impliedly consent that appellee Minyard could run into the loader and that he, the deceased, was willing to take his chances and agreed to relieve Minyard from any duty of due care that Minyard may have owed to him"? Our search of the record has failed to disclose that the deceased had actual knowledge of the specific danger. Although one may *[handwritten: if risk is not]* assume the risk of the negligence of another if he is fully informed of *[handwritten: already created,]* such negligence, [c] one is not, under the doctrine of assumption of risk, *[handwritten: then ASSR must]* bound to anticipate the negligent conduct of others. [Cc] *[handwritten: be express, to anticipate neglign as in last case.]*

The failure to fully appreciate and comprehend the consequences of one's acts is not properly a matter of assumption of risk but, rather, a matter of contributory negligence. [C] *[handwritten: should have argued this]*

The standard to be applied is a subjective one, of what the particular plaintiff in fact sees, knows, understands and appreciates. [Cc] All *[handwritten: = i.e. = risk is already created]* of the evidence in this case clearly shows that the deceased thought there was room for vehicles to safely get by. In fact, several did pass through without incident prior to the accident. At most, deceased may have failed to fully appreciate the consequence of his conduct. This would constitute contributory negligence and not assumption of risk.

In speaking of implied assumption of risk, Prosser [Torts 445 (4th ed. 1971)] states:

"It is here that there is the greatest misapprehension and confusion as to assumption of risk, and its most frequent misapplication. It is not true that in any case where the plaintiff voluntarily encounters a known danger he necessarily consents to negligence of the defendant which creates it. A pedestrian who walks across the street in the middle of a block, through a stream of traffic travelling at high speed, cannot by any stretch of the imagination be found to consent that the drivers shall not use care to avoid running him down. On the contrary, he is insisting that they shall. This is contributory negligence, pure and simple; it is not assumption of risk." See also Restatement (Second) of Torts § 496(C) (1971), comment h.

While there may be situations where a person may be found to be contributorily negligent and to have assumed the risk, such as where he voluntarily consents to take an unreasonable risk, such is not the case here.

Appellant has raised other issues in her brief which will not be necessary for us to decide in view of our reversal of this case.

Reversed and remanded for new trial.

———

1. Are express and implied assumption of risk as closely related as the opinion suggests? Actual willingness may be indicated by conduct as well as by language. But assuming plaintiff knows of the risk and voluntarily encounters it, is he saying by his conduct, "Creator of this risk, I agree not to hold you responsible if I am injured"? Is implied assumption of risk virtually the same as the consent defense to intentional torts? Assumption of risk, in the sense of consent, is sometimes called *volenti*, after the Latin maxim, *Volenti non fit injuria* [To the willing, there is no injury].

2. The defense of assumption of risk originated in cases brought by injured workmen against their employers. It was easy for the courts to "imply" this as one of the provisions of the contract of employment. Along with contributory negligence and the fellow-servant rule, it was formerly one of the "unholy trinity" of defenses which barred recovery from the employer by an injured workman forced by economic necessity to work in deplorable factory conditions. Worker's compensation acts have abrogated all three defenses, and other labor legislation has almost entirely eliminated assumption of risk in this field. In most states the defense of assumption of risk has been extended to apply to all negligence cases. Few states have restricted it to the subject area of its origin. See Smith v. Blakey, 213 Kan. 91, 515 P.2d 1062 (1973).

3. In a number of states the defense of assumption of risk has been carried beyond the concept of consent and applied to any factual situation where the plaintiff consciously and voluntarily places himself in a position where he is subject to a known risk. The relationship of this type of assumption of risk to contributory negligence has given much trouble.

Sometimes the distinction is drawn by saying that the "essence of contributory negligence is carelessness; of assumption of risk, venturousness. Thus an injured person may not have acted carelessly, may have exercised the utmost care, yet may have assumed, voluntarily, a known hazard." Hunn v. Windsor Hotel Co., 119 W.Va. 215, 193 S.E. 57 (1937) (plaintiff deliberately walked down defective steps when others, not greatly more inconvenient, were also available). This blurs the distinction. No similar distinction is taken regarding defendant's conduct. And one of the types of contributory negligence is the plaintiff's "intentional and unreasonable exposure of himself to danger created by the defendant's negligence." Restatement (Second) of Torts § 466(a).

This approach gives the defendant two separate defenses for the same conduct, which is apparently what the trial court did in the principal case. Contrast the holding in the principal case with that in Ferguson v. Gardner, 533 P.2d 938 (Colo.App.1975), where under very similar facts the court held the plaintiff to have assumed the risk as a matter of law.

4. Distinguish the following. Which defense or defenses would be available to defendant in each?

A. Plaintiff voluntarily enters into a relation with defendant, which he knows to involve some not unreasonable risk. He teaches a beginner to drive an automobile. Le Fleur v. Vergilia, 280 App.Div. 1035, 117 N.Y.S.2d 244 (1952).

B. Plaintiff, entering defendant's premises in the dark, does not know that they are dangerous, and fails to exercise ordinary caution to find out.

C. Plaintiff knows that defendant's activity, or a condition created by him, involves some danger, but quite reasonably concludes that he can safely encounter it and proceeds. In an amusement park, he buys a ride on a moving belt which upsets the riders. See Judge Cardozo's terse opinion in Murphy v. Steeplechase Amusement Co., 250 N.Y. 479, 166 N.E. 173 (1929).

D. Plaintiff, fully aware of an unreasonable risk, voluntarily proceeds to encounter it. He consents to ride with a drunken driver on a dark night. Cf. Sutherland v. Davis, 286 Ky. 743, 151 S.W.2d 1021 (1941).

5. Assuming that plaintiff was contributorily negligent, why might the defense of assumption of risk have practical importance? Consider:

A. If defendant has been reckless, contributory negligence is usually avoided, see supra page 569, but assumption of risk will remain. One can assume the risk of reckless conduct. See Waltanen v. Wiitala, 361 Mich. 504, 105 N.W.2d 400 (1960); Evans v. Holsinger, 242 Iowa 990, 48 N.W.2d 250 (1951).

B. Many courts have held that assumption of risk will bar recovery in an action founded on strict liability, while plaintiff's ordinary negligence may not. See Gomes v. Byrne, 51 Cal.2d 418, 333 P.2d 754 (1959) (abnormally dangerous activity); Luque v. McLean, 8 Cal.3d 136, 501 P.2d 1163, 104 Cal.Rptr. 443 (1972) (product liability); Restatement (Second) of Torts § 402A, comment n. What problems would be created by the application of this distinction?

6. As the principal case indicates, it is essential that defendant show that plaintiff knew of the risk. Why? May one not consent to unknown risks? The best way to show this, of course, is to secure a direct admission from plaintiff or someone who heard him. See Vanderlei v. Heideman, 83 Ill.App.3d 158, 38 Ill. Dec. 525, 403 N.E.2d 756 (1980) (horseshoer testified he knew of risk of being kicked because he had been kicked several times before). But circumstantial evidence may be adequate. Cf. Wyly v. Burlington Indus., 452 F.2d 807 (5th

Cir.1971) (plaintiff contestant in "National Lap Sitting Contest" promoting wrinkle-free slacks must have been aware of risk of chair collapsing when 14 coeds sat on his lap). Suppose plaintiff is rendered incompetent by the accident. How can it be determined if he assumed the risk? See Farley v. M.M. Cattle Co., 549 S.W.2d 453 (Tex.Civ.App.1977).

7. As the principal case reflects, courts have a good deal of latitude in defining "risk." Courts that are unfavorably disposed to assumption of risk place a very narrow or specific gloss on "risk," and thereby do a great deal to undermine the practical utility of the defense. In addition to the principal case, see Gobern v. Metals & Controls, Inc., 418 F.2d 290, 296 (1st Cir.1969); Hawthorne v. Gunn, 123 Cal.App. 452, 11 P.2d 411 (1932) (young lady sitting on young man's lap in a moving car assumes certain risks, but a collision is not among them).

RUSH v. COMMERCIAL REALTY CO.

Supreme Court of New Jersey, 1929.
7 N.J.Misc. 337, 145 A. 476.

PER CURIAM. The case for the plaintiffs was that they were tenants of the defendant, which controlled the house wherein they lived and also the adjoining house, and provided a detached privy for the use of both houses; that Mrs. Rush having occasion to use this privy, went into it and fell through the floor, or through some sort of trap door therein, descended about nine feet into the accumulation at the bottom, and had to be extricated by use of a ladder. * * * The two grounds of appeal are that the trial court erred in refusing a nonsuit, and erred in refusing to direct a verdict for the defendant.

Taking the facts as the jury were entitled to find them, most favorably for the plaintiffs, the situation was that of a building under the control of the landlord for the use of tenants generally, and maintained by the landlord; a consequent duty of care in maintenance; a defective condition in the floor which the jury might say was due to negligent maintenance by the defendant; and an accident resulting therefrom. In such a situation it would seem that the argument for a nonsuit or for a direction must be restricted to the questions of contributory negligence and assumption of risk. In dealing with these, it should be observed that Mrs. Rush had no choice, when impelled by the calls of nature, but to use the facilities placed at her disposal by the landlord, to wit, a privy with a trap door in the floor, poorly maintained. We hardly think this was the assumption of a risk; she was not required to leave the premises and go elsewhere. Whether it was contributory negligence to step on a floor, which she testified was in bad order, was a question for the jury to solve according to its finding of the conditions and her knowledge of them, or what she should have known of them; it does not seem to be a court question.

We conclude that there was no error in denying motions to take the case from the jury, and the judgment will accordingly be affirmed.

1.　Apart from knowledge of the risk, plaintiff must proceed to encounter it "voluntarily." How much latitude does this concept give a court to define the scope of the defense?

2.　Defendant negligently maintains a highway, leaving a large mudhole in it. Plaintiff, knowing the condition of the highway, attempts to drive past the mudhole, and while keeping to the extreme edge of the road slides off into the ditch, and is upset and injured. Should it make any difference whether (1) plaintiff is away from home and has to get back, or (2) there is a reasonably short and convenient detour at hand, in good condition? Pomeroy v. Westfield, 154 Mass. 462, 28 N.E. 899 (1891); Campion v. Rochester, 202 Minn. 186, 277 N.W. 422 (1938).

3.　Defendant's negligent operation of a train endangers a child on the track. Plaintiff dashes on the track to save the child and is himself injured. Does he assume the risk? Bond v. Baltimore & Ohio R. Co., 82 W.Va. 557, 96 S.E. 932 (1918); Eckert v. Long Island R. Co., 43 N.Y. 502 (1871). Suppose he dashes into a burning building to save his hat?

4.　On his own property, plaintiff was bitten by a vicious boar owned by a neighbor. The jury found that plaintiff had knowledge of the vicious propensities of the boar and voluntarily exposed himself to the risk. On what basis could it be found that plaintiff did not assume the risk? See Marshall v. Ranne, 511 S.W.2d 255 (Tex.1974). Cf. Leroy Fibre Co. v. Chicago, M. & St. P.R. Co., 232 U.S. 340 (1914) (plaintiff piled straw on his own land near defendant's dangerous spark-emitting engine).

5.　Can employees be said to assume the risk of work-related activities? What might occur if they refuse to incur the risks? While there were some exceptions, as in Siragusa v. Swedish Hosp., 60 Wash.2d 310, 373 P.2d 767 (1962); and Ritter v. Beals, 225 Or. 504, 358 P.2d 1080 (1961), most courts in the past have regarded these encounters as voluntary. The case may turn on the specific facts of the job-related "encounter." Suppose a fifteen-year-old cowboy rides a particularly unruly horse and is thrown? See Farley v. M.M. Cattle Co., 549 S.W.2d 453 (Tex.Civ.App.1977).

6.　*Plaintiff's Protests.* The fact that plaintiff has protested against the defendant's conduct is of course important evidence that he does not consent to assume the risk. But having protested, he may thereafter, even though reluctantly, accept the situation, and as the courts have sometimes put it, "waive" the protest. Whether he does so is a question of fact, and usually a question for the jury. Often it will turn upon the existence of some reasonable alternative to the plaintiff's course. Compare Young v. Wheby, 126 W.Va. 741, 30 S.E.2d 6 (1944), with Ridgway v. Yenny, 223 Ind. 16, 57 N.E.2d 581 (1944).

BLACKBURN v. DORTA

Supreme Court of Florida, 1977.
348 So.2d 287.

[Several cases in the Florida District Court of Appeal had reached differing decisions on the issue of whether "the doctrine of assumption of risk is still viable as an absolute bar to recovery subsequent to adoption of the rule of comparative negligence in Hoffman v. Jones, 280 So.2d 431 (Fla.1973)." Three of them were consolidated by the state supreme court under its "conflict certiorari jurisdiction."]

SUNDBERG, JUSTICE. * * * Since our decision in Hoffman v.
Jones, supra, contributory negligence no longer serves as a complete
bar to plaintiff's recovery but is to be considered in apportioning
damages according to the principles of comparative negligence. We are
now asked to determine the effect of the *Hoffman* decision on the
common law doctrine of assumption of risk. If assumption of risk is
equivalent to contributory negligence, then *Hoffman* mandates that it
can no longer operate as a complete bar to recovery. However, if it has
a distinct purpose apart from contributory negligence, its continued
existence remains unaffected by *Hoffman*. This question was expressly
reserved in *Hoffman* as being not ripe for decision. 280 So.2d 431, 439.

At the outset, we note that assumption of risk is not a favored
defense. There is a puissant drift toward abrogating the defense. The
argument is that assumption of risk serves no purpose which is not
subsumed by either the doctrine of contributory negligence or the
common law concept of duty. It is said that this redundancy results in
confusion and, in some cases, denies recovery unjustly. * * * The
issue is most salient in states which have enacted comparative negligence legislation. Those statutes provide that the common law defense
of contributory negligence no longer necessarily acts as a complete bar
to recovery. The effect of these statutes upon the doctrine of assumption of risk has proved to be controversial. Joining the intensifying
assault upon the doctrine, a number of comparative negligence jurisdictions have abrogated assumption of risk. Those jurisdictions hold that
assumption of risk is interchangeable with contributory negligence and
should be treated equivalently. Today we are invited to join this trend
of dissatisfaction with the doctrine. For the reasons herein expressed,
we accept the invitation.

At the commencement of any analysis of the doctrine of assumption of risk, we must recognize that we deal with a potpourri of labels,
concepts, definitions, thoughts, and doctrines. The confusion of labels
does not end with the indiscriminate and interchangeable use of the
terms "contributory negligence" and "assumption of risk." In the case
law and among text writers, there have developed categories of assumption of risk. Distinctions exist between *express* and *implied;* between
primary and *secondary;* and between *reasonable* and *unreasonable* or,
as sometimes expressed, *strict* and *qualified*. It will be our task to
analyze these various labels and to trace the historical basis of the
doctrine to unravel what has been in the law an "enigma wrapped in a
mystery."

It should be pointed out that we are not here concerned with
express assumption of risk which is a contractual concept outside the
purview of this inquiry and upon which we express no opinion herein.
* * *

The breed of assumption of risk with which we deal here is that
which arises by implication or *implied* assumption of risk. Initially it
may be divided into the categories of *primary* and *secondary*. The term

primary assumption of risk is simply another means of stating that the defendant was not negligent, either because he owed no duty to the plaintiff in the first instance, or because he did not breach the duty owed. Secondary assumption of risk is an affirmative defense to an established breach of a duty owed by the defendant to the plaintiff. [C]

The concept of primary assumption of risk is the basis for the historical doctrine which arose in the master-servant relationship during the late nineteenth century. * * *

It is apparent that no useful purpose is served by retaining terminology which expresses the thought embodied in primary assumption of risk. This branch (or trunk) of the tree of assumption of risk is subsumed in the principle of negligence itself. * * * An example of this concept is presented in the operation of a passenger train. It can be said that a passenger assumes the risk of lurches and jerks which are ordinary and usual to the proper operation of the train, but that he does not assume the risk of extraordinary or unusual lurches and jerks resulting from substandard operation of the train. The same issue can be characterized in terms of the standard of care of the railroad. Thus, it can be said that the railroad owes a duty to operate its train with the degree of care of an ordinary prudent person under similar circumstances which includes some lurching and jerking while a train is in motion or commencing to move under ideal circumstances. So long as the lurching or jerking is not extraordinary due to substandard conduct of the railroad, there is no breach of duty and, hence, no negligence on the part of the railroad. The latter characterization of the issue clearly seems preferable and is consistent with the manner in which the jury is instructed under our standard jury instructions.

Having dispensed with *express* and *primary-implied* assumption of risk, we recur to *secondary-implied* assumption of risk which is the affirmative defense variety that has been such a thorn in the judicial side. The affirmative defense brand of assumption of risk can be subdivided into the type of conduct which is reasonable but nonetheless bars recovery (sometimes called *pure* or *strict* assumption of risk), and the type of conduct which is unreasonable and bars recovery (sometimes referred to as *qualified* assumption of risk). [C] Application of pure or strict assumption of risk is exemplified by the hypothetical situation in which a landlord has negligently permitted his tenant's premises to become highly flammable and a fire ensues. The tenant returns from work to find the premises a blazing inferno with his infant child trapped within. He rushes in to retrieve the child and is injured in so doing. Under the pure doctrine of assumption of risk, the tenant is barred from recovery because it can be said he voluntarily exposed himself to a known risk. Under this view of assumption of risk, the tenant is precluded from recovery notwithstanding the fact that his conduct could be said to be entirely reasonable under the circumstances. [C] There is little to commend this doctrine of implied-pure or strict assumption of risk, and our research discloses no Florida case in which it has been applied. Certainly, in light of Hoffman v. Jones, supra, there is no reason supported by law or justice in this state to give credence to such a principle of law.

There remains, then, for analysis only the principle of implied-qualified assumption of risk, and it can be demonstrated in the hypothetical recited above with the minor alteration that the tenant rushes into the blazing premises to retrieve his favorite fedora. Such conduct on the tenant's part clearly would be unreasonable. Consequently, his conduct can just as readily be characterized as contributory negligence. It is the failure to exercise the care of a reasonably prudent man under similar circumstances. It is this last category of assumption of risk which has caused persistent confusion in the law of torts because of the lack of analytic difference between it and contributory negligence. If the only significant form of assumption of risk (implied-qualified) is so readily characterized, conceptualized, and verbalized and contributory negligence, can there be any sound rationale for retaining it as a separate affirmative defense to negligent conduct which bars recovery altogether? In the absence of any historical imperative, the answer must be no. We are persuaded that there is no historical significance to the doctrine of implied-secondary assumption of risk. * * *

We find no discernible basis analytically or historically to maintain a distinction between the affirmative defense of contributory negligence and assumption of risk. The latter appears to be a viable, rational doctrine only in the sense described herein as implied-qualified assumption of risk which connotes unreasonable conduct on the part of the plaintiff. This result comports with the definition of contributory negligence appearing in Restatement (Second) of Torts § 466 (1965). Furthermore, were we not otherwise persuaded to elimination of assumption of risk as a separate affirmative defense in the context herein described, the decision of this Court in Hoffman v. Jones, supra, would dictate such a result. As stated therein:

" *   *   * A primary function of a court is to see that legal conflicts are equitably resolved. In the field of tort law, the most equitable result that can ever be reached by a court is the equation of liability with fault. Comparative negligence does this more completely than contributory negligence, and we would be shirking our duty if we did not adopt the better doctrine." 280 So.2d 431, 438.

Is liability equated with fault under a doctrine which would totally bar recovery by one who voluntarily, but reasonably, assumes a known risk while one whose conduct is unreasonable but denominated "contributory negligence" is permitted to recover a proportionate amount of his damages for injury? Certainly not. Therefore, we hold that the affirmative defense of implied assumption of risk is merged into the defense of contributory negligence and the principles of comparative negligence enunciated in Hoffman v. Jones, supra, shall apply in all cases where such defense is asserted. * * *

It is so ordered.

———

1. Assumption of risk is not favored by the courts; and it has been cordially disliked by the friends of the plaintiff, because of its long history of defeating recovery in cases of genuine hardship—particularly in those of injuries to employees before the workers' compensation acts. It has been under heavy attack from a good many legal writers. See, for example, James, Assumption of Risk, 61 Yale L.J. 141 (1952); Wade, The Place of Assumption of Risk in the Law of Negligence, 22 La.L.Rev. 5 (1961); James, Assumption of Risk: Unhappy Reincarnation, 78 Yale L.J. 185 (1968); Note, 13 Creighton L.Rev. 251 (1979) (assumption of risk and the automobile guest statute).

2. The first cases to refuse to recognize the defense at all involved the violation of statutes that were found to be enacted to protect a particular class of persons against their own consent; and it was declared that the purpose of the statute would be defeated if the defense were allowed. Child labor acts afford the obvious example. Lenahan v. Pittston Coal Mining Co., 218 Pa. 311, 67 A. 642 (1907); Terry Dairy Co. v. Nalley, 146 Ark. 448, 225 S.W. 887 (1920).

3. Apart from these special statutes, many courts have continued to hold that assumption of risk is a defense when a statute is violated, to the same extent as in cases of common law negligence. White v. Cochrane, 189 Minn. 300, 249 N.W. 328 (1933); Le Doux v. Alert Transfer & Storage Co., 145 Wash. 115, 259 P. 24 (1927).

4. Other courts have held that when any safety statute is violated, the public interest is involved to such an extent that the consent of the plaintiff to take his chances cannot be permitted to defeat the liability, unless contributory negligence is found. Casey v. Atwater, 22 Conn.Supp. 225, 167 A.2d 250 (1960); Maia v. Security Lumber & Concrete Co., 160 Cal.App.2d 16, 324 P.2d 657 (1958).

5. A growing number of courts are in accord with the holding of the principal case that implied assumption of risk does not remain an affirmative defense separate and apart from contributory negligence.

6. *Comparative Negligence.* As the principal case reflects, the advent of comparative negligence is prompting courts to implement a merger of the defenses of contributory negligence and implied assumption of risk. What are the reasons for this? The merger may occur although the comparative negligence statute is completely silent about assumption of risk. See Kopischke v. First Continental Corp., 610 P.2d 668 (Mont.1980); Gilson v. Drees Bros., 19 Wis.2d 252, 120 N.W.2d 63 (1963); Brittain v. Booth, 601 P.2d 532 (Wyo.1979). Some comparative negligence statutes have treated assumption of risk the same as contributory negligence.

7. *Reasonable Implied Assumption of Risk—Duty.* The elimination of reasonable implied assumption of risk as a defense does not necessarily mean that plaintiff will recover when "reasonably" encountering a known risk. Assuming that the risk encountered was an obvious one, the court will have to determine whether defendant violated any duty to the plaintiff and that determination may be in the negative. Thus, in Lang v. Amateur Softball Ass'n of America, 520 P.2d 659 (Okl.1974), the plaintiff was injured by a softball wildly thrown over a ten-foot fence by a pitcher warming up in the bullpen. The court held that defendant had utilized reasonable care to protect plaintiff and was under no duty to guard against this hazard. Kavafian v. Seattle Baseball Club Ass'n, 105 Wash 215, 181 P. 679 (1919); Ingersoll v. Onondaga Hockey Club, 245 App.Div. 137, 281 N.Y.S. 505 (1935) and Sunday v. Stratton

Corp., 136 Vt. 293, 390 A.2d 398 (1978) (skiing accident) illustrate the distinction between the risk that plaintiff in fact assumes and the risk that defendant may reasonably expect him to assume.

Was the court in the principal case totally accurate in its analysis? If a tenant rushed into a burning building to save his child, would that be regarded as assumption of risk by the court in the *Rush* case, supra page 592? How should courts handle the situation where a plaintiff's true assumption of risk has been reasonable, but also knowing and voluntary?

(D) FAILURE TO TAKE ADVANCE PRECAUTION AGAINST EXTENT OF INJURY

SPIER v. BARKER
New York Court of Appeals, 1974.
35 N.Y.2d 444, 323 N.E.2d 164, 363 N.Y.S.2d 916.

[Defendant negligently drove his tractor trailer into the front left portion of plaintiff's automobile. As a result of the collision, plaintiff was ejected from her vehicle, which then rolled over her, pinning her legs under the left wheel. Plaintiff did not wear an available seat belt. Defendant called as an expert witness a professor of mechanical and aerospace engineering, who gave his opinion that "if plaintiff had been wearing a seat belt, she would not have been ejected from her automobile."]

GABRIELLI, J. * * * Having permitted the defense expert to testify as to what would have probably happened to the plaintiff had she used the seat belt available to her, the trial court charged the jury as follows: "If you find that a reasonably prudent driver would have used a seat belt, and that she would not have received some or all of her injuries had she used the seat belt, then you may not award any damages for those injuries you find she would not have received had she used the seat belt. The burden of proving that some or all of her injuries would not have been received had she used the seat belt rests upon the [defendants]". Although the plaintiff's counsel took no exception to the trial court's charge, he requested the court to charge the jury "that there isn't any law in the State of New York that requires a person to wear a seat belt or to anticipate the happening of an accident." The trial court so charged.

[The jury returned a verdict for the defendant. The Appellate Division interpreted this as a finding that the plaintiff was contributorily negligent in general, and the Court of Appeals agreed. It proceeded to discuss the trial court's seat belt instruction, however, to determine whether the instruction was in error and therefore likely to have misled the jury.]

Despite the fact that the "seat belt defense", as it is commonly known, has received extensive examination in other jurisdictions as well as several legal periodicals, it is raised as a matter of first impression in this court. * * *

The cases from other jurisdictions suggest that three approaches have been advanced by defendants in support of the seat belt defense: first, it is urged that a plaintiff's nonuse of an available seat belt constitutes negligence per se which would, of course, entirely preclude the plaintiff from recovery; secondly, it is argued that, in failing to make use of an available seat belt, the plaintiff has not complied with the standard of conduct which would have been pursued by a reasonable man under similar circumstances, and, therefore, the plaintiff may be found to have been contributorily negligent; and, thirdly, it is asserted that by not fastening his seat belt the plaintiff may, under the circumstances of the particular case, be found to have acted unreasonably and in disregard of his own best interests, and, thus, should not be permitted to recover damages for those injuries which a seat belt would have obviated (see, Kircher, Seat Belt Defense—State of the Law, 53 Marq.L.Rev. 172, 173). We reject both the first and the second of these approaches and, with the modifications made herein, we accept the third.

Since section 383 of the Vehicle and Traffic Law does not require occupants of a passenger car to make use of available seat belts, we hold that a plaintiff's failure to do so does not constitute negligence per se. * * * Likewise, we do not subscribe to the holdings of those cases in which the plaintiff's failure to fasten his seat belt may be determined by the jury to constitute contributory negligence as a matter of common law. [Cc] In our view, the doctrine of contributory negligence is applicable only if the plaintiff's failure to exercise due care causes, in whole or in part, the accident, rather than when it merely exacerbates or enhances the severity of his injuries. [Cc] That being the case, holding a nonuser contributorily negligent would be improper since it would impose liability upon the plaintiff for all his injuries though use of a seat belt might have prevented none or only a portion of them. Having disapproved of these two variations of the seat belt defense, we address ourselves to the defendants' contention that nonuse of an available seat belt may be considered by the jury in assessing the plaintiff's damages where it is shown that the seat belt would have prevented at least a portion of the injuries.

As Prosser has indicated, the plaintiff's duty to mitigate his damages is equivalent to the doctrine of avoidable consequences, which precludes recovery for any damages which could have been eliminated by reasonable conduct on the part of the plaintiff (Prosser, Torts [4th ed.], § 65, pp. 422–424). Traditionally both of these concepts have been applied only to postaccident conduct, such as a plaintiff's failure to obtain medical treatment after he has sustained an injury. To do otherwise, it has been argued, would impose a preaccident obligation upon the plaintiff and would deny him the right to assume the due care of others (Kleist, Seat Belt Defense—An Exercise in Sophistry, 18 Hastings L.J. 613, 616). We concede that the opportunity to mitigate damages prior to the occurrence of an accident does not ordinarily arise, and that the chronological distinction, on which the concept of mitigation damages rests, is justified in most cases. However, in our opinion, the seat belt affords the automobile occupant an unusual and ordinarily unavailable means by which he or she may minimize his or her damages *prior* to the accident. Highway safety has become a national concern; we are told to drive defensively and to "watch out for the other driver". When an automobile occupant may readily protect himself, at least partially, from the consequences of a collision, we think that the burden of buckling an available seat belt may, under the facts of the particular case, be found by the jury to be less than the likelihood of injury when multiplied by its accompanying severity.

At this juncture, there can be no doubt whatsoever as to the efficiency of the automobile seat belt in preventing injuries. Simply stated, "[t]he seat belt, properly installed *and properly worn,* still offers the single best protection available to the automotive occupant exposed to an impact." (Snyder, Seat Belt as a Cause of Injury, 53 Marq.L.Rev. 211). Furthermore, though it has been repeatedly suggested that the seat belt itself causes injury, to date the device has never been shown to worsen an injury, but, on the contrary, has prevented more serious ones (p. 213). The studies on the subject overwhelmingly indicate that the seat belt fulfills its primary purpose of restraining the automobile occupant during and immediately after the initial impact; in so doing, it significantly reduces the likelihood of ejection and frequently prevents "the second collision" of the occupant with the interior portion of the vehicle.

Another objection frequently raised is that the jury will be unable to segregate the injuries caused by the initial impact from the injuries caused by the plaintiff's failure to fasten his seat belt. In addition to underestimating the abilities of those trained in the field of accident reconstruction, this argument fails to consider other instances in which the jury is permitted to apportion damages (i.e., as between an original tort-feasor and a physician who negligently treats the original injury). Furthermore, if the defendant is unable to show that the seat belt would have prevented some of the plaintiff's injuries, then the trial court ought not submit the issue to the jury.

In the instant case, the plaintiff was ejected from her car, which subsequently rolled over her body causing a broken leg.[5] The defense expert stated that she would have remained in the car had she used her seat belt, and that she would have sustained only minor injuries had she not been ejected. On cross-examination, plaintiff's counsel was unsuccessful in his attempts to undermine either of these opinions of the expert. In view of what has previously been stated, we hold that the trial court properly submitted this issue to the jury.

For the reasons stated, the order of the Appellate Division should be affirmed.

---

5. Full body ejection has been estimated to increase the likelihood of a fatality by nearly 500% (see Bowman, Practical Defense Problems—The Trial Lawyer's View, 53 Marq.L.Rev. 191, 196).

1. If the state had adopted comparative negligence at the time, would the case have been simple to decide? After the New York legislature adopted comparative negligence, a mid-level New York court took the approach rejected in *Spier*, holding that in certain circumstances failure to wear a seatbelt could be a cause of the accident and thereby diminish plaintiff's recovery in proportion to plaintiff's negligence on the total negligent conduct causing the accident. Curry v. Moser, 89 A.D.2d 1, 454 N.Y.S.2d 311 (1982).

2. The difficulty in characterizing the seatbelt defense under traditional tort law concepts has led some courts to reject it. Others have rejected it because of the problem connected with determining causation. Finally, some courts believe that since the ordinary person does not wear seatbelts, it is unfair to impose the burden on the reasonable person. See, e.g., Britton v. Doehring, 286 Ala. 498, 242 So.2d 666 (1970); D.W. Boutwell Butane Co. v. Smith, 244 So.2d 11 (Miss.1971); Miller v. Haynes, 454 S.W.2d 293 (Mo.App. 1970); Kopischke v. First Continental Corp., 187 Mont. 471, 610 P.2d 668 (1980).

3. A minority of the decisions are in accord with the principal case holding that evidence of plaintiff's failure to wear a seatbelt may be used to reduce the amount of damages to be awarded plaintiff. See, e.g., Tiemeyer v. McIntosh, 176 N.W.2d 819 (Iowa 1970); Insurance Co. of N. Amer. v. Pasakarnis, 451 So.2d 447 (Fla.1984); Hutchins v. Schwartz, 724 P.2d 1194 (Alaska 1986).

4. The conceptual problem underlying the seat belt cases is not new. Many tort law students of the 1930's and 1940's spent hours studying the case of Mahoney v. Beatman, 110 Conn. 184, 147 A. 762 (1929). Plaintiff drove an automobile at excessive speed and defendant negligently crossed over the median and collided with it. The proof was clear that plaintiff's speed was not responsible for the collision, but it did increase his damages. How should the court decide the case? See Green, Mahoney v. Beatman: A Study in Proximate Cause, 39 Yale L.J. 532 (1930); Gregory, Judge Maltbie's Dissent in Mahoney v. Beatman, 24 Conn.B.J. 78 (1950). Would this case be easier to handle today? Cf. East Hampton Dewitt Corp. v. State Farm Mut. Auto. Ins. Co., 490 F.2d 1234 (2d Cir.1973).

5. Suppose plaintiff motorcyclist fails to wear a helmet in violation of state criminal law. Defendant negligently crashes into him. Should the court allow defendant to show that plaintiff's injuries would have been less severe if he wore the helmet? See Rogers v. Frush, 257 Md. 233, 262 A.2d 549 (1970); Note, 41 Ohio St.L.J. 233 (1980); Annot., 40 A.L.R.3d 847 (1971). Are the issues the same as in the seat belt cases?

6. In what other situations might there be a duty imposed on plaintiff to take self-precaution against the negligence of others? Should persons have to wear gas masks in an area polluted by defendant? Should they have to wear hard hats when walking near a negligently maintained construction site? Where should the line be drawn?

7. Defendant driver removed a seatbelt warning device from his car. He then was involved in an accident in which he was not at fault. His passenger sued, claiming that he was injured because he was unaware of the law and therefore did not use the seatbelt. What considerations would be involved in that decision? Cf. Breault v. Ford Motor Co., 364 Mass. 352, 305 N.E.2d 824, 829 (1973) (dictum).

8. More states have enacted laws requiring that seatbelts be worn. Should this result in an automatic application of the seatbelt defense? What issues remain? In July, 1984, the National Highway and Traffic Safety Administration promulgated a rule mandating the installation of passive restraints in new automobiles unless states including two-thirds of the U.S. population by 1989 enacted laws requiring the mandatory use of seatbelts. 49 Fed.Reg. 28, 962. These laws must contain certain provisions regarding penalties and, among other things, reduction of damages in civil tort suits where plaintiff was not wearing a seatbelt. Many states have responded by enacting mandatory "seatbelt laws" and have addressed the question of civil liability. See, e.g., Cal.Veh.Code 27315(i) (violation not negligence per se but "negligence may be proven as a fact without regard to the violation"); Ill.Ann.Stat. 95½ 12–603.1(c) (not evidence of negligence and does not reduce recovery for damages); Iowa Code § 343.445(4) (violation can be evidence of negligence, but no more than 5% reduction); Mich.Comp.Laws 257.710e (violation may be considered evidence of negligence but shall not reduce recovery by more than 5%).

9. On the seatbelt defense, see generally Berger, The Seat Belt Defense, A.B.A. Law Notes (July 1969); Kircher, The Safety Belt Defense Current Status, 16 For the Defense 45 (1975); Kircher, Symposium, 53 Marq.L.Rev. 172 (1970); Notes, 34 Alb.L.Rev. 593 (1970), 42 St. John's L.Rev. 371 (1968), 38 Fordham L.Rev. 94 (1969); Annots., 15 A.L.R.3d 1428 (1967), 92 A.L.R.3d 9 (1979), 95 A.L.R.3d 239 (1979).

2. STATUTES OF LIMITATIONS AND REPOSE

TEETERS v. CURREY
Supreme Court of Tennessee, 1974.
518 S.W.2d 512.

HENRY, JUSTICE. This malpractice action essentially involves a determination of whether the statute of limitation begins to run from the date of the injury or from the date of the discovery of the injury.

The admitted facts are that on June 5, 1970, plaintiff gave birth to a normal child. Defendant was the attending physician. Following delivery, because of edema anemia and other medical complications, he recommended that plaintiff have a bilateral tubal ligation, the purpose of which was to avoid future pregnancies. Defendant performed this surgery on June 6, 1970, and her recovery was uneventful.

On December 6, 1972 she was hospitalized at Newell Clinic and was attended by Dr. Edgar Atkin. Dr. Atkin discovered that she was pregnant. He so advised her and referred her to other physicians for obstetrical care.

On March 9, 1973 plaintiff was delivered of a premature child and there were severe complications. Pursuant to medical advice, another bilateral tubal ligation was performed on March 11, 1973.

Plaintiff instituted suit on November 15, 1973, three years, five months and nine days after the operation, but approximately eleven months after discovering her pregnancy.

Plaintiff alleges that during the course of this latter surgery it was discovered that the earlier surgery performed by the defendant was negligently and inadequately done and was not performed in accordance with proper standards of care and good medical practice.

Specifically, she charges that defendant failed to properly or completely sever the left fallopian tube in a manner which would assure sterility and prevent future pregnancies. Further, she charges that he failed to identify the right fallopian tube in a manner which would assure sterility and prevent future pregnancies. Further, she charges that he failed to cut, sever or ligate this tube in any manner.

The defendant's answer pleads the statute of limitations and denies that he was guilty of any act of negligence. * * *

Section 28–304, T.C.A. applies to malpractice suits and provides that the action be "commenced within one (1) year after cause of action accrued."

When does the cause of action accrue?

In Bodne v. Austin, 156 Tenn. 366, 2 S.W.2d 104 (1927) the Court said: " * * * we have been referred to no authority holding that mere ignorance and failure to discover the existence of the cause of action, or the consequential damages resulting from the breach of duty or wrongful act, can prevent the running of the statute of limitations."

But this was in 1927 almost half a century ago.

In Albert v. Sherman, 167 Tenn. 133, 67 S.W.2d 140 (1934), the Court followed *Bodne*.

This was forty years ago. * * *

The time has come for us to re-examine the past holdings of our Appellate Courts in the light of contemporary standards of justice and of the holdings of the courts of last resort in other American jurisdictions. * * *

We recognize that statutes of limitations are statutes of repose designed to promote stability in the affairs of men and to avoid the uncertainties and burdens inherent in defending stale claims.

In recognition of this, traditionally our courts have held that a right of action accrues immediately upon the infliction or occurrence of injury and that mere ignorance or failure of plaintiff to discover his cause of action or the subsequent resulting damage does not toll the statute. Bodne v. Austin, supra.

That this is a harsh and an oppressive rule there can be little doubt. To counter the casualties it has produced the courts have fashioned the so-called "discovery doctrine," under which the statute does not begin to run until the negligent injury is, or should have been discovered.

This concept has been adopted by judicial interpretation in at least a majority of the American states. [C] Some of these jurisdictions limit the application of the doctrine to "foreign objects"; the majority apply it to all medical malpractice cases. * * *

As evidence of the rapidity with which the various jurisdictions have embraced this equitable doctrine, the main volume of 80 A.L.R.2d, published in *1961*, at page 388, lists *seven (7) states* as having adopted the discovery rule, viz., California, Colorado, Louisiana, Missouri, North Carolina, Pennsylvania and Texas.

The main volume of the appropriate Later Case Service, published in *1968*, lists *twelve (12) additional states,* Arizona, Delaware, Hawaii, Idaho, Iowa, Maryland, Michigan, Montana, Nebraska, New Jersey, Utah and West Virginia.

The *1974* supplement lists *nine (9) more states,* Georgia, Illinois, Kansas, Kentucky, North Dakota, Oklahoma, Oregon, Rhode Island and Washington.

This brings the total to twenty-eight (28) states.

Add Tennessee to the list.

We adopt as the rule of this jurisdiction the principle that in those classes of cases where medical malpractice is asserted to have occurred through the negligent performance of surgical procedures, the cause of action accrues and the statute of limitations commences to run when the patient discovers, or in the exercise of reasonable care and diligence for his own health and welfare, should have discovered the resulting injury. All cases contra are overruled.

In the instant case the cause of action accrued when plaintiff discovered that she was pregnant, or in the exercise of reasonable care and diligence, she should have so discovered.

We add, in meticulous fairness to the trial judge, that in ruling as he did, he properly relied upon our precedents.

We here merely recede from prior cases in order to establish a rule which we are convinced will be productive of results more nearly consonant with the demands of justice and the dictates of ethics and morality.

Reversed and remanded. Appellee will pay all costs incident to this appeal.

HARBISON, JUSTICE, concurred in a separate opinion.

----

1. Statutes of limitations in tort law may vary in length, depending upon the basis of liability, the general subject matter of the claim and the type of interest invaded. One of the first points a lawyer ascertains on undertaking a claim is what is the appropriate statute of limitations. It may be malpractice not to do so.

2. By their express language, many statutes of limitations begin to run when a cause of action "accrues." Since damage is an essential part of a cause of action based on negligence, most courts have held that the statute begins to run when there has been an actual injury to plaintiff's person or property.

When a plaintiff is exposed to toxic chemicals and is physically injured, he faces a dilemma. He would need to sue for damages on the known injury before the statute of limitations runs. However, res judicata might bar later actions for recovery if plaintiff develops cancer. See Hagerty v. L & L Marine Serv. Inc., 788 F.2d 315 (5th Cir.1986) (plaintiff's second action will not be barred by res judicata). See also Herber v. Johns–Manville Corp., 785 F.2d 79 (3d Cir.1986).

3. Suppose defendant negligently installs a lightning rod in 1980 and plaintiff's building is struck by lightning and destroyed in 1986. The appropriate statute of limitations is five years. Has plaintiff's claim been extinguished? See White v. Schnoebelen, 91 N.H. 273, 18 A.2d 185 (1941). Suppose the installation had taken place in 1940? Cf. Williams v. Polgar, 391 Mich. 6, 215 N.W.2d 149 (1974); Connelly v. Paul Ruddy's Equipment Repair & Serv. Co., 388 Mich. 146, 200 N.W.2d 70 (1972) (machine sold in 1948 caused injury in 1965).

Two states temporarily departed from the general rule and held that the statute begins to run as of the time of the sale rather than as of the time the injury is incurred. Mendel v. Pittsburgh Plate Glass Co., 25 N.Y.2d 340, 253 N.E.2d 207, 305 N.Y.S.2d 490 (1969); Jackson v. General Motors Corp., 223 Tenn. 12, 441 S.W.2d 482 (1969). But they have both subsequently overruled those decisions and adopted the general rule. Victorson v. Bock Laundry Machine Co., 37 N.Y.2d 395, 335 N.E.2d 275, 373 N.Y.S.2d 39 (1975); McCroskey v. Bryant Air Conditioning Co., 524 S.W.2d 487 (Tenn.1975). The state of New York, by statute, has now moved to the discovery rule. N.Y. Tort Reform Law § 214–c (Consol.1986). Several states have since enacted statutes that impose a bar on product liability actions brought within a specified number of . years after the date of sale. See Massey, Date-of-Sale Statutes of Limitation— A New Immunity for Product Suppliers, 1977 Ins.L.J. 535; Note, 30 Case Western L.Rev. 123 (1979). Most of these statutes simply fix a period of time after which a product seller is to be deemed no longer responsible for his product. These statutes are more properly characterized as statutes of repose. See note 13 infra, these notes. On the other hand, when New York, by statute, adopted the discovery rule, it opened up a window for *past* claims barred by the time-of-damage rule. Is this a desirable holding?

4. As the principal case reflects, the time-of-damage rule has led to difficulty in some actions for medical malpractice. The principal case, adopting a time-of-discovery rule, now represents the majority rule, although some courts have steadfastly clung to the time-of-damage approach, leaving any change for the legislature. Rod v. Farrell, 96 Wis.2d 349, 291 N.W.2d 568 (1980). Others have taken a middle position and held that the statute must begin to run when the physician-patient relationship terminates, regardless of whether the patient has discovered the injury. See Glenboski v. St. Alexis Hosp., 65 Ohio App.2d 165, 417 N.E.2d 108 (1979). While these decisions may disappoint injured plaintiffs, are they in accord with legislative intent? Some legislatures have specifically dealt with the problem and adopted a time-of-discovery rule for medical malpractice cases. See Ala.Code, tit. 7 § 25(1) (1953); Conn.Gen.Stat., § 52–584 (1969); R.S.Mo., § 516.105 (1978).

5. Some courts have limited the application of the time-of-discovery rule to situations where surgeons have left sponges, scalpels or other objects in the patient's body. They apply the time-of-damage rule to cases of negligent diagnosis or ingestion of a drug or toxic substance. What could be the reason for this distinction? See Frohs v. Greene, 253 Or. 1, 452 P.2d 564 (1969); Flanagan v. Mount Eden Gen. Hosp., 24 N.Y.2d 427, 248 N.E.2d 871, 301

N.Y.S.2d 23 (1969). What about defective products deliberately left in the patient's body, such as birth control devices and heart pacemakers? Manno v. Levi, 94 A.D.2d 556, 465 N.Y.S.2d 219 (1983).

6. The time-of-discovery rule has contributed to the rapid rise in the cost of medical malpractice insurance. Many policies used to be called an "occurrence" basis. This means that the policy covers the physician's conduct during a given year, even though a claim based on that conduct may not arise for many years. See, e.g., Ruth v. Dight, 75 Wash.2d 660, 453 P.2d 631 (1969) (23 years). Because of this fact, actuarial projections call for very high premiums. Some insurance companies have argued that the premiums could be reduced if state insurance commissioners would permit medical malpractice insurance to be issued on a "claims made" basis. These policies would cover only claims filed against the physician that year, regardless of when the act of malpractice occurred. See Special Report, DRI Medical Malpractice Conference, 16 For the Defense 59 (1975). Another approach is to place a maximum limit on the time-of-discovery rule. Ohio Rev.Code, § 2305.11(B) (1975) (four years after the act of malpractice); see also Tenn.Code Ann. § 23–3415 (Supp.1975) (modifying the rule in the principal case). See generally Anderson, The Application of Statutes of Limitations to Actions Against Physicians and Surgeons, 25 Ins.Couns.J. 237 (1958); Lillich, The Malpractice Statute of Limitations in New York and Other Jurisdictions, 47 Cornell L.Q. 339 (1962); Williams, Limitation Periods on Personal Injury Claims, 48 Notre Dame Law. 881 (1973); Witherspoon, Constitutionality of the Texas Statute Limiting Liability for Medical Malpractice, 10 Tex.Tech L.Rev. 419 (1979); Annot., 93 A.L.R.3d 218 (1979).

7. Of course, if the physician fraudulently conceals an act of malpractice, this tolls the statute of limitations. Lakeman v. La France, 102 N.H. 300, 156 A.2d 123 (1959); Ray v. Scheibert, 224 Tenn. 99, 450 S.W.2d 578 (1969). Even without active concealment, there may be a continuing duty to disclose that is breached anew each day and lasts as long as the doctor-patient relationship exists. Thatcher v. De Tar, 351 Mo. 603, 173 S.W.2d 760 (1943); Williams v. Elias, 140 Neb. 656, 1 N.W.2d 121 (1941); Glenboski v. St. Alexis Hosp., 65 Ohio App.2d 165, 19 Ohio Ops.3d 122, 417 N.E.2d 108 (1979).

8. The discovery rule itself can be narrowed or broadened depending on what the plaintiff has to discover. Should it be the harm? Its cause? The fact that plaintiff has a cause of action?

9. Problems with the time-of-damage rule have also arisen with regard to negligent acts of other professionals. When should the statute of limitations begin to run with regard to an attorney who has committed an act of malpractice? See Shideler v. Dwyer, 275 Ind. 270, 417 N.E.2d 281 (1981); Jankowski v. Taylor, Bishop and Lee, 246 Ga. 804, 273 S.E.2d 16 (1980); Biberstine v. Woodworth, 81 Mich.App. 705, 265 N.W.2d 797 (1978). See generally R. Mallen and Levit, Legal Malpractice, §§ 388–398 (2d ed. 1981); Note, 13 Val.U.L.Rev. 383 (1979). What about a tax accountant? See Chisholm v. Scott, 86 N.M. 707, 526 P.2d 1300 (1974); Annot., 26 A.L.R.3d 1438 (1969).

10. Professional negligence committed by builders, architects and engineers can present substantial problems. The latent damaging element is implanted during construction, but it may not be apparent for many, many years. How long should these professionals be subject to liability? Is it reasonable to begin the running of the statute when the construction of the building is completed and the parties' professional relationship terminated? The client then can inspect the building and determine if the structure is

sound. Compare Sosnow v. Paul, 43 A.D.2d 978, 352 N.Y.S.2d 502 (1974) (time of construction), with Malesev v. Board of County Rd. Comm'rs, 51 Mich.App. 511, 215 N.W.2d 598 (1974) (time of discovery). A number of state legislatures have enacted special statutes of limitations dealing with malpractice by builders, architects and engineers. See Knapp & Lee, Application of Special Statutes of Limitations Concerning Design and Construction, 23 St. Louis U.L.J. 351 (1979). If these classes of defendants are given special protection without any rational basis, the statute of limitations may be held to deny constitutional equal protection of the law. Kallas Millwork Corp. v. Square D Co., 66 Wis.2d 382, 225 N.W.2d 454 (1975). See Annots., 90 A.L.R.3d 507 (1979), 93 A.L.R.3d 1242 (1979).

11. *Classification of Action for the Purpose of the Statutes of Limitations.* A good deal of judicial prose has been spent in an attempt to classify actions for the purpose of the statute of limitations. Examples of problems that occur include (1) whether an action is based on "intent" or "negligence," see Lambertson v. United States, 528 F.2d 441 (2d Cir.1976); cf. Gagliardi v. Lynn, 446 Pa. 144, 285 A.2d 109 (1971) (false arrest or false imprisonment); (2) whether an action for breach of warranty is a matter of tort or contract, see, e.g., Mauran v. Mary Fletcher Hosp., 318 F.Supp. 297 (D.Vt.1970); Heavner v. Uniroyal, Inc., 118 N.J.Sup. 116, 286 A.2d 718 (1972); and cases collected in Banks and Curp, Products Liability: Use of Identity to Determine the Applicable Statute of Limitations, 3 Ohio North.L.Rev. 1 (1973); and (3) whether negligent conduct is ordinary negligence or professional malpractice. See Estate of Kohls v. Brah, 57 Wis.2d 141, 203 N.W.2d 666 (1973); Matthews v. Walker, 34 Ohio App.2d 128, 63 Ohio Ops.2d 208, 296 N.E.2d 569 (1973). Cases that have defined the terms "contract," "tort," "intent" or "malpractice" in other legal contexts are not always helpful in solving classification problems involving the statute of limitations. Why?

12. *Notice-of-Claim Statutes.* In suits against the state or municipalities, a plaintiff may be required to comply with a notice-of-claim statute in addition to a statute of limitation. The notice-of-claim statutes may be very short—as little as 60 or 90 days. Some of these statutes have been declared unconstitutional as a denial of equal protection of the laws; others remain on the books and are a trap for the unwary and ill-prepared lawyer. Compare Lunday v. Vogelmann, 213 N.W.2d 904 (Iowa 1973) (upholding 60–day statute), with Reich v. State Highway Dept., 386 Mich. 617, 194 N.W.2d 700 (1972). See generally Annot., 59 A.L.R.3d 93 (1974).

13. *Statutes of Repose.* Distinct from statutes of limitations are the closely related "statutes of repose." These statutes, which are substantive in nature, stem from a basic equity concept that a time should arrive, at some point, that a party is no longer responsible for a past act. These statutes have been enacted primarily in the area of product liability. For example, after a certain number of years from the sale or delivery of the product, claims are barred. Do you agree with their basic concept? If a product has operated without incident for 20 years, is it fair to assume that any injury occurring after that time was due to something other than an original defect in the product? What about the possibility that the product has been improperly maintained, repaired, or altered?

The Uniform Product Liability Act, Section 110(B)(1), 44 Fed.Reg. 62732, provides generally that in a claim brought after 10 years following delivery of a product, there shall be a presumption that the harm was caused after the useful sale life of the product, and no cause of action will lie. See 32 Baylor L.Rev. 137 (1980); 48 J.Air L. & Com. 449 (1981); 16 Forum 416 (1981).

The statutes create a number of problems, especially for victims of conditions with a long latency period. A few states have made special exceptions for particular products such as asbestos or diethylstilbestrol (DES). See, e.g., N.D. Cent. Code § 28–01.1–02. Some state courts have declared statutes of repose unconstitutional based on equal protection or "open courts" provisions in state constitutions. See, e.g., Lankford v. Sullivan, Long & Hagerty, 416 So.2d 996 (Ala.1982); Bolick v. American Barmag Corp., 306 N.C. 364, 293 S.E.2d 415 (1982); Hanson v. Williams County, 389 N.W.2d 319 (N.D.1986). Other courts have upheld the statutes. See, e.g., Thornton v. Mono Mfg. Co., 99 Ill.App.3d 722, 54 Ill.Dec. 657, 425 N.E.2d 522 (1981); Jones v. Five Star Eng'g, Inc., 717 S.W.2d 882 (Tenn.1986); Arsenault v. Pa–Ted Spring Co., Inc., 203 Conn. 156, 523 A.2d 1283 (1987).

3. IMMUNITIES

An immunity differs from a privilege, or justification or excuse, although the difference is largely one of degree. A privilege avoids liability for tortious conduct only under particular circumstances, and because those circumstances make it just and reasonable that the liability should not be imposed. An immunity, on the other hand, avoids liability in tort under all circumstances, within the limits of the immunity itself. It is conferred, not because of the particular facts, but because of the status or position or relation of the favored defendant. It does not deny the tort, but the resulting liability. The immunity does not mean that conduct that would amount to a tort on the part of other defendants is not still equally tortious in character, but merely that for the protection of the particular defendant, or of interests that the defendant represents, absolution from liability is granted. The "absolute privilege" to publish defamation in the course of judicial, legislative or executive proceedings (infra pages 930–35), for example, is really an immunity of those engaged in the proceedings, conferred because of the public interest in protecting them from suit.

Immunities are today very much upon the wane, as the result of years of attack from numerous legal writers, and expressed doubts on the part of many courts. On the other hand, the abolishment of immunities has produced a new and challenging question—what is to be the scope of the duty owed by defendants who were previously immune from suit.

(A) Families

FREEHE v. FREEHE
Supreme Court of Washington, 1972.
81 Wash.2d 183, 500 P.2d 771.

NEILL, ASSOCIATE JUSTICE. Plaintiff, Clifford Freehe, seeks compensation for personal injuries allegedly sustained due to defendant's negligent maintenance of a tractor and failure to warn plaintiff of the tractor's unsafe condition. The claim for relief would be just the normal action in tort for personal injury but for the fact that the defendant is the wife of the plaintiff, thus bringing into issue the doctrine of interspousal tort immunity.

The farm on which the accident took place is the separate property of defendant, doing business under the name of Hazel Knoblauch. The tractor involved in this accident, together with all other assets and income of the farm, were and remain the separate property of defendant. The business of the farm is carried on separately from any community business of the parties. Plaintiff has no interest in the farming operation. Neither was he employed by defendant.

The trial court granted defendant's motion for summary judgment solely on the basis of interspousal tort immunity. Plaintiff appeals.

*   *   *

The rule of interspousal immunity or disability is of common law origin, court made and court preserved. * * * Our cases have referred to the historical arguments supporting the common law disability. One is the "supposed unity of husband and wife." [Cc]

The "supposed unity" of husband and wife * * * is not a reference to the common nature or loving oneness achieved in a marriage of two free individuals. Rather, this traditional premise had reference to a situation, coming on from antiquity, in which a woman's marriage for most purposes rendered her a chattel of her husband.

"It has been said, whether humorously or not, that at common law husband and wife were one person, and that person was the husband. * * * [A]s to her personal and property rights, the very legal existence of the wife was regarded as suspended for the duration of the marriage, and merged into that of the husband, so that she lost the capacity to contract for herself, or to sue or be sued without joining the husband as a plaintiff or defendant. The husband acquired the right to possession and use of his wife's real and personal property, and he was entitled to all of her choses in action, provided that he 'reduced them to possession' during marriage by some act by which he appropriated them to himself, such as collecting the money or obtaining judgment in a suit in his own name. In turn he became liable for the torts of his wife, committed either before or during the marriage." (footnotes omitted) W.L. Prosser, Torts ch. 23, § 122 (4th ed. 1971) at 859–60. At old common law, with the husband entitled to the chose in action for his own torts and liable to himself for his wife's torts against him, the rule of interspousal disability made sense.

Things have changed. * * * Neither spouse is liable for the separate debts of the other. RCW 26.16.200. * * * [E]ither spouse may sue the other for invasion of separate property rights. RCW 26.16.180. [Cc] Spouses are no longer individually liable for each other's torts unless they would be jointly liable if unmarried.

Modern realities do not comport with the traditional "supposed unity" of husband and wife. In our view, this concept of legal identity is no longer a valid premise for a rule of this interspousal disability.

A second major reason given for the disability is the notion that to allow a married person to sue his or her spouse for tort damages would be to destroy the peace and tranquility of the home. On reflection, we are convinced that this is a conclusion without basis. If a state of peace and tranquility exists between the spouses, then the situation is such that either no action will be commenced or that the spouses—who are, after all, the best guardians of their own peace and tranquility—will allow the action to continue only so long as their personal harmony is not jeopardized. If peace and tranquility is nonexistent or tenuous to begin with, then the law's imposition of a technical disability seems more likely to be a bone of contention than a harmonizing factor.

* * *

A third reason advanced in support of maintaining the common law rule of disability is the suggestion that the injured spouse has an adequate remedy through the criminal and divorce laws. It has been observed that neither of these alternatives actually compensates for the damage done, or provides any remedy for nonintentional (negligent) torts. Prosser, supra, at pages 862–63. * * * To these reflections we add the observation that limiting the injured party to a divorce or criminal action against his or her tort-feasor spouse is quite inconsistent with any policy of preserving domestic tranquility. Thus, the argument based on suggested legal alternatives simply does not withstand analysis.

It has also been argued that to permit litigation between spouses over personal torts would flood the courts with a burdensome amount of trivial matrimonial disputes. * * * [T]his theoretical problem has not materialized elsewhere. Furthermore, should the courts find this possibility to be materializing, there is nothing to prevent application of established notions of "consent" or "assumption of risk" to minor annoyances associated with the ordinary frictions of wedlock. [C]

Respondent also suggests that another argument in favor of the disability rule is that to permit suits between spouses would encourage collusion and fraud where one or both of the spouses carries liability insurance. * * * In * * * Borst v. Borst, 41 Wash.2d at page 653, 251 P.2d at page 155, we stated:

"The courts may and should take cognizance of fraud and collusion when found to exist in a particular case. However, the fact that there may be greater opportunity for fraud or collusion in one class of cases than another does not warrant courts of law in closing the door to all cases of that class. Courts must depend upon the efficacy of the judicial processes to ferret out the meritorious from the fraudulent in particular cases. [C] If those processes prove inadequate, the problem becomes one for the legislature. [C] Courts will not immunize tort feasors from liability in a whole class of cases because of the possibility of fraud, but will depend upon the legislature to deal with the problem as a question of public policy."

We there cited, as an example of the ability of the legislature to cope with such a problem should it arise, the enactment of host-guest statutes (RCW 46.08.080, –.085, –.086) in automobile personal injury cases. We conclude that this possibility is not a valid premise for the common law disability rule.

Respondent also suggests that any change in the marital disability rule is a matter for the legislature * * * This argument ignores the fact that the rule is not one made or sanctioned by the legislature, but rather is one that depends for its origins and continued viability upon the common law. * * *

[The court then decided that the state's community property laws imposed no barrier to abandoning interspousal immunity.]

We are cognizant of the long standing nature of the common law rule of interspousal tort immunity. But we find more impelling the fundamental precept that, absent express statutory provision, or compelling public policy, the law should not immunize tort-feasors or deny remedy to their victims. With this in mind, we have reviewed the stated reasons for the common law rule, and have found all of them to be insufficient. Therefore, the rule of interspousal disability in personal injury cases is hereby abandoned. * * *

Reversed and remanded.

---

1. The movement toward complete abrogation of interspousal immunity began with a dissenting opinion of the first Justice Harlan in Thompson v. Thompson, 218 U.S. 611 (1910). It is now the majority rule. See generally Annot., 92 A.L.R.3d 901 (1979) and supplements for citations; Restatement (Second) of Torts § 895F.

2. Some decisions that have taken this step have placed heavy reliance on the state's married women's property act. See, e.g., Gilman v. Gilman, 78 N.H. 4, 95 A. 657 (1915); Fitzmaurice v. Fitzmaurice, 62 N.D. 191, 242 N.W. 526 (1932). These statutes, enacted in the mid–1800's, abrogated the common law disabilities of wives to sue or be sued in their own name and to buy, own or sell property. Other decisions have construed the statutes as having no intent to affect interspousal immunity. See, e.g., Emerson v. Western Seed & Irrigation Co., 116 Neb. 180, 216 N.W. 297 (1927); Oken v. Oken, 44 R.I. 291, 117 A. 357 (1922). These latter decisions may be correct in measuring legislative intent. As the principal case reflects, policies that allegedly support interspousal tort immunity are not necessarily related to legal restrictions on the rights of women.

3. *Partial Abrogation.* Many courts have partially abrogated the immunity. They refuse to apply it in one or more specific situations where they are certain that no good reason supports it. For example:

A. After divorce or marital dissolution, spouses are permitted a claim for torts that occurred prior to and in some jurisdictions during the marriage. See, e.g., Gaston v. Pittman, 224 So.2d 326 (Fla.1969) (prior); Sanchez v. Olivarez, 94 N.J.Super. 61, 226 A.2d 752 (1967) (during). Claims are also permitted when one or both spouses are dead at the time the action is brought. Asplin v. Amica Mut. Ins. Co., 121 R.I. 51, 394 A.2d 1353 (1978). How can a tort claim be allowed after a marriage is terminated if it did not exist during the relationship? Compare Ebel v. Ferguson, 478 S.W.2d 334 (Mo.1972), with the *Sanchez* case, supra this note.

B. When the tort occurred prior to the marriage and the claim is brought afterwards. See, e.g., Childress v. Childress, 569 S.W.2d 816 (Tenn.1978); Berry v. Harmon, 329 S.W.2d 784 (Mo.1959). The reason given for allowing the claim is that the spouse should not lose a property right because of entering into a marriage.

C. When the tort is an intentional one such as battery, assault or false imprisonment. See Apitz v. Dames, 205 Or. 242, 287 P.2d 585 (1955). Suppose a husband rips off his wife's clothing and, with the assistance of two friends, forces her to have intercourse with him? If a claim is allowed, how are damages to be calculated? See Lusby v. Lusby, 283 Md. 334, 390 A.2d 77 (1978).

4. The facts of the principal case are somewhat unusual as compared with most law tort suits between spouses. The overwhelming majority of these cases have involved automobile accidents, and a number of courts have expressly limited their repeal of the immunity in negligence actions to those situations. See Digby v. Digby, 120 R.I. 299, 388 A.2d 1 (1978); Richard v. Richard, 131 Vt. 98, 300 A.2d 637 (1973).

5. Suppose a wife sues her husband in tort for the injury she suffered because he prepared her food in a careless and unsanitary manner. Does she have a claim? Suppose the wife alleges that she suffered serious medical injury because her husband was negligent in his selection of a family doctor. Would she then have a claim? In Beaudette v. Frana, 285 Minn. 366, 173 N.W.2d 416 (1969), the Supreme Court of Minnesota abolished interspousal immunity, but it also observed in dictum that: "There is an intimate sharing of contact within the marriage relationship, both intentional and unintentional, that is uniquely unlike the exposure among strangers. The risks of intentional contact in marriage are such that one spouse should not recover damages from the other without substantial evidence that the injurious contact was plainly excessive or a gross abuse of normal privilege. The risks of negligent conduct are likewise so usual that it would be an unusual case in which the trial court would not instruct the jury as to the injured spouse's peculiar assumption of risk."

6. In states that have no-fault divorce and alimony, the culpability of each spouse is irrelevant to the marital dissolution proceeding. Suppose that, in a state with that type of law, one spouse has physically or emotionally abused the other during the marital relationship. Should a tort claim be permitted? See Schwartz, The Serious Marital Offender: Tort Law as a Solution, 6 Fam.L.Q. 219 (1972).

7. The history of the immunity is well described in Kahn–Freund, Inconsistencies and Injustices in the Law of Husband and Wife, 15 Mod.L.Rev. 133 (1952); and Williams, The Legal Unity of Husband and Wife, 10 Mod.L.Rev. 16 (1947). See generally McCurdy, Personal Torts Between Spouses, 4 Vill.L.Rev. 521 (1959); Herskowitz, Tort Liability Between Husband and Wife, 21 U.Miami L.Rev. 423 (1966).

ANDERSON v. STREAM

Supreme Court of Minnesota, 1980.
295 N.W.2d 595.

SCOTT, JUSTICE. These two appeals raise similar issues regarding the exceptions to the abrogation of parental immunity as adopted by this court in Silesky v. Kelman, 281 Minn. 431, 161 N.W.2d 631 (1968). In both cases, the trial courts concluded that the exceptions were applicable and thus held that the injured children had no actionable claim against their respective parent(s). We reverse.

The operative facts of these appeals have been stipulated to by the respective parties:

Anderson v. Stream v. Anderson. Edward and Ruth Anderson are the parents of Breeanna Anderson, who was born on June 16, 1975. Defendants Edna and Martin Stream live in a house next door to the Anderson home, and the two families share a common driveway. The line dividing the two properties runs generally down the center of the driveway. There is no fence between the two houses.

On Sunday morning, May 15, 1977, Breeanna, who was approximately 23 months of age, asked her parents if she could go outside and play. Breeanna was allowed to do so, but was told to "stay in the back." While Breeanna played outdoors, Mr. Anderson read the Sunday newspaper and Mrs. Anderson did housework. About 10 or 15 minutes after she began to play, Breeanna was injured when Edna Stream backed her automobile over the child's leg. * * *

Edward Anderson, as guardian for his minor daughter, and in an individual capacity, brought an action against the Streams for the damages which resulted from the child's injuries. The Streams later impleaded Mr. Anderson and his wife for contribution and indemnity. Thereafter, the Andersons moved for summary judgment against the Streams on the third-party complaint, claiming no common liability existed because they could not be held liable to their child. * * *

Nuessle v. Nuessle. On the afternoon of October 4, 1975, Michael Nuessle, who was about 3 years old at the time, accompanied his father, James Nuessle, on an errand to a drugstore located on the northwest corner of the intersection of Victoria Street and Grand Avenue in St. Paul. Defendant entered the drugstore, and after 10 to 15 seconds noticed that his son was not with him. It is unclear whether Michael actually entered the store. After looking briefly in the store for his son, defendant, through the glass door of the store, saw Michael crossing Grand Avenue. Michael was walking alongside an adult male, whom the child may have mistaken for his father. Defendant hurried outside, and without looking for traffic and in an act which defendant described as one of "panic," yelled Michael's nickname, "Micker." The child turned around, saw his father, and took a few steps to the north, recrossing the center line of Grand Avenue, while remaining in the crosswalk. Michael was then struck by the left front part of an automobile driven by a westbound driver who did not see the boy before hitting him. The child sustained serious injuries, including damage to his brain stem.

This action was commenced to recover damages against James Nuessle for Michael's injuries. Defendant subsequently moved for summary judgment on the ground that in this case the parental immunity doctrine operated to bar his son's claim. The trial court agreed, ruling that the first exception to the abolishment of parental immunity was applicable. Plaintiff now seeks review of the district court's decision. * * *

The *Silesky* decision, rendered in 1968, abrogated the long-standing doctrine of parental immunity subject to the following exceptions: "(1) where the alleged negligent act involves an exercise of *reasonable parental authority* over the child; and (2) where the alleged negligent act involves an exercise of *ordinary parental discretion* with respect to the provision of food, clothing, housing, medical and dental services, and other care." * * *

While the *Silesky* court was well-intentioned in continuing the immunity doctrine in regard to certain parental conduct, application of the exceptions has proven to be very difficult because of their precise scope is by no means clear. * * * We believe that since the problems inherent in construing the *Silesky* exceptions present a real danger of arbitrary line-drawing and in light of the fact that instructing the jury on a "reasonable parent" standard adequately protects functions which are parental in nature, the continued existence of the *Silesky* exceptions cannot be justified. * * *

Difficulty in application would not, in and of itself, cause us to cast aside the *Silesky* exceptions. The determinative consideration upon which we rest our decision is that the areas of parental authority and discretion, for which the *Silesky* exceptions were designed to provide safeguards, can be effectively protected by use of a "reasonable parent" standard, as adopted by the court in Gibson v. Gibson, 3 Cal.3d 914, 92 Cal.Rptr. 288, 479 P.2d 648 (1971). In that case, the California Supreme Court completely abolished the doctrine of parental immunity. * * *

[T]he *Gibson* opinion held that the better approach is to have the jury take into consideration the parental function when determining whether the parent acted negligently. As stated by the *Gibson* court: "The standard to be applied is the traditional one of reasonableness, but viewed in light of the parental role. Thus, we think the proper test of a parent's conduct is this: What would an ordinarily reasonable and prudent *parent* have done in similar circumstances?" 3 Cal.2d 921, 92 Cal.Rptr. 293, 479 P.2d 653 (emphasis in original). * * *

Without developing this point *in extenso*, the weight which a court or jury will ascribe to each of these and other related factors will depend on the facts peculiar to the particular case. For example, aside from the facts relating to the negligence itself, such variable matters as the age, mental and physical health, intelligence, aptitudes and needs of the child involved; the presence in the family of other children competing for parental time and attention; and the economic, social and physical environment in which the parental conduct occurs, all may be expected to play a part.

It is hard to see why such tailoring of the results of each case to its facts is not to be preferred to the erection of rigid classifications, be they catalogued as "trespasser," "licensee" or "business visitor," as "grossly" or "ordinarily" negligent or as "supervising parent." Looking to the entire picture, rather than merely the labels, is the surer path to a just result. * * *

[O]ur preference for the *Gibson* approach recognizes the practical advantages offered by utilization of a "reasonable parent" standard. It attains the *Silesky* goal of according parents some flexibility in their exercise of parental functions, but the interpretive pitfalls associated with the *Silesky* exceptions are avoided. In reaching this conclusion, we reject the contention that juries are incapable of rationally and equitably deciding whether a parent has acted negligently in exercising his parental control and discretion. Our system of justice places great faith in juries, and we see no compelling reason to distrust their effectiveness in the parent-child context. Nor do the arguments relating to family discord and collusion require a different result than that reached herein. * * *

Finally, the prevalence of liability insurance is a pertinent and important factor in subjecting parents to suit by their children. [C] After all, our paramount objective is to compensate the child for his or her injuries, and the widespread existence of homeowner's and renter's liability insurance will help effectuate this goal. To deny the injured child this source of funds on the ground that prosecution of the claim would in some way disrupt the family unit is an anomaly this court will not tolerate. * * *

In summary, by this decision we totally abolish the doctrine of parental immunity and consequently overrule *Silesky* to the extent it retained parental immunity in the form of the aforementioned exceptions. In so doing, we adopt the approach of the California Supreme Court in *Gibson,* supra, of charging the jury on a "reasonable parent" standard.

Reversed and remanded for trial.

ROGOSHESKE, JUSTICE (dissenting). I disagree with the majority's complete abrogation of parent-child tort immunity in negligence cases. I am not persuaded that the parent-child relationship, long preserved from legal interference on public policy grounds, has so declined in importance that considerations of insurance and simplified judicial administration under a jury standard warrant application of general tort principles to family interactions. In my view, the *Silesky* exceptions to abrogation of parental immunity should be retained and, on these facts, the first exception should be applied to immunize negligent parental supervision. * * *

The *Silesky* exceptions, which embrace these two special aspects of the parent-child relationship, encourage performance of parental obligations by preserving the integrity of family decisionmaking and fostering a family atmosphere of respect and trust. The exceptions implicitly acknowledge that the varied economic, educational, cultural, religious and ethnic backgrounds of parents, and the individual personalities and development paces of children result in such a multitude of permutations of parent-child relationships that no objective standard of proper child rearing is possible. While the exceptions recognize that discharge of parental functions depends on natural instinct, love and morality rather than legal sanctions, they do not assume too much by permitting parents to act negligently toward their children with impunity. * * *

SHERAN, C.J., OTIS, J. and PETERSON, J. (dissented).

---

1. Unlike the interspousal immunity doctrine which was part of the common law of England, the immunity between parent and child is a pure homegrown product. In Hewlett v. George, 68 Miss. 703, 9 So. 885 (1891), the court applied the doctrine to bar a minor daughter's false-imprisonment claim against her mother, who had wrongfully committed her to an insane asylum. Other states soon adopted the rule, applying it to actions for negligence as well as intentional torts. See, e.g., Mesite v. Kirchstein, 109 Conn. 77, 145 A. 753 (1929); Roller v. Roller, 37 Wash. 242, 79 P. 788 (1905) (15–year–old girl attempting to bring a tort claim against her father for rape). The fact that the doctrine was not announced by any of the writers of common law did not seem to trouble courts because "it was unmistakably and indelibly carved upon the tablets of Mount Sinai." Small v. Morrison, 185 N.C. 577, 585–86, 118 S.E. 12, 16 (1923).

2. *Partial Abrogation.* As in the case of interspousal immunity, courts in some states developed one or more exceptions to the general rule when they believed that the policies supporting it were inapplicable or were outweighed by the benefit of allowing a tort claim. Some of the more common exceptions include:

A. When the relation has been terminated before suit by the death of the parent or child or both. MFA Mut. Ins. Co. v. Howard Constr. Co., 608 S.W.2d 535 (Mo.App.1980). This includes action for the wrongful death of the child through the negligence of the parent. Bonner v. Williams, 370 F.2d 301 (5th Cir.1966) (Alabama law); Mosier v. Carney, 376 Mich. 532, 138 N.W.2d 343 (1965).

B. When the action is for the wrongful death of the other parent. Kaczorowski v. Kalkosinski, 321 Pa. 438, 184 A. 663 (1936); Johnson v. Ottomeier, 45 Wash.2d 419, 275 P.2d 723 (1954). See generally Annots., 62 A.L.R.3d 1299 (1975), 87 A.L.R.3d 849 (1978).

C. When the defendant is a step-parent or other person standing in loco parentis. Gillett v. Gillett, 168 Cal.App.2d 102, 335 P.2d 736 (1959); Xaphes v. Mossey, 224 F.Supp. 578 (D.Vt.1963).

D. When the child has been legally emancipated. Fitzgerald v. Valdez, 77 N.M. 769, 427 P.2d 655 (1967); Carricato v. Carricato, 384 S.W.2d 85 (Ky.1964). There is a good discussion of what constitutes emancipation in Gillikin v. Burbage, 263 N.C. 317, 139 S.E.2d 753 (1965); Small v. Rockfeld, 66 N.J. 231, 330 A.2d 335 (1974).

3. Many courts refuse to apply the immunity when the personal injury is inflicted intentionally, or is "willful" or "wanton." The usual explanation has been that that conduct is so foreign to the relation as to take the case out of it. But in Rodebaugh v. Grand Trunk W.R. Co., 4 Mich.App. 559, 145 N.W.2d 401 (1966), the court added gross negligence; and in Oldman v. Bartshe, 480 P.2d 99 (Wyo.1971), the court added wilful disregard for the well-being of a child.

4. *General Abrogation.* Abolition of the parent-child immunity lagged behind that of husband-wife, perhaps because of the absence of any statute that could be construed as so intended. The first court to announce a general abrogation of the immunity was Wisconsin, in Goller v. White, 20 Wis.2d 402, 122 N.W.2d 193 (1963). Decisions abolishing the immunity in the context of automobile negligence cases are growing each year. See generally Annot., 41 A.L.R.3d 904 (1972), for citations. Decisions with particularly well developed reasoning include Gelbman v. Gelbman, 23 N.Y.2d 434, 245 N.E.2d 192, 297 N.Y.S.2d 529 (1969); Gibson v. Gibson, 3 Cal.3d 914, 479 P.2d 648, 92 Cal.Rptr. 288 (1971); and Balts v. Balts, 273 Minn. 419, 142 N.W.2d 66 (1966). Are the policy issues the same when a child sues a parent as when a parent sues a child?

5. *Liability Insurance.* The existence or availability of liability insurance has served as an important justification for the abolishment of the parent-child immunity. Nevertheless, some courts have been steadfast in holding that the existence of insurance cannot "create liability or reduce the need for the immunity." See Maxey v. Sauls, 242 S.C. 247, 130 S.E.2d 570 (1963). A few courts have even turned the insurance argument against the plaintiff and have said that its existence is a reason to uphold the immunity because it creates an opportunity for fraud and collusion against the insurance company. The insurance company does receive some protection against this possibility from the "failure to cooperate" clause that appears in the standard liability insurance policy. But see Mutual of Enumclaw Ins. Co. v. Wiscomb, 25 Wash.App. 841, 611 P.2d 1304 (1980), where such a clause was held null and void as contrary to public policy. At least one court has abolished the immunity in negligence cases to the extent that the parent is protected by liability insurance. See Williams v. Williams, 369 A.2d 669 (Del.1976).

6. See generally Chapin, Parent–Child Tort Immunity: A Rule in Need of Change, 27 U.Miami L.Rev. 191 (1972); McCurdy, Torts Between Parent and Child, 5 Vill.L.Rev. 521 (1960); Sanford, Personal Torts Within the Family, 9 Vand.L.Rev. 823 (1956).

7. As the principal case reflects, once an immunity is abolished courts may face novel questions regarding the extent of the duty owed by a brand new class of defendants. For example, should an older sibling be held liable for negligent supervision? See Smith v. Sapienza, 52 N.Y.2d 82, 417 N.E.2d 530, 436 N.Y.S.2d 236 (1981). For a good discussion of the issues and other factual examples, as well as a result generally contra to the principal case, see Holodook v. Spencer, 36 N.Y.2d 35, 324 N.E.2d 338, 364 N.Y.S.2d 859 (1974). What result if the child alleges that he suffered emotional harm because the

parent failed to perform general parental duties? See Burnette v. Wahl, 284 Or. 705, 588 P.2d 1105 (1978). Is this a matter to be addressed by tort law?

8. The earlier Minnesota rule that the principal case overruled had originated in Goller v. White, 20 Wis.2d 402, 122 N.W.2d 193 (1963). Consider the way in which the two rules would apply in the following cases:

A. An infant (eight and one-half months) chewed an extension cord that was plugged into a live socket. Cherry v. Cherry, 295 Minn. 93, 203 N.W.2d 352 (1972).

B. A child aged two fell from a negligently constructed swing set. Cole v. Sears Roebuck & Co., 47 Wis.2d 629, 177 N.W.2d 866 (1970).

C. A child aged two caught his foot in a lawn mower. Howes v. Hansen, 56 Wis.2d 247, 201 N.W.2d 825 (1972).

D. A child aged three, left unsupervised by his mother, darted out into the street and was struck by a bus. Thoreson v. Milwaukee & Suburban Transport Co., 56 Wis.2d 231, 201 N.W.2d 745 (1972).

E. A child aged eleven fell on a loose stairway rug. Cosmopolitan Nat'l Bank of Chicago v. Heap, 128 Ill.App.2d 165, 262 N.E.2d 826 (1970).

(B) Charities

ABERNATHY v. SISTERS OF ST. MARY'S
Supreme Court of Missouri, 1969.
446 S.W.2d 599.

Henley, Chief Justice. This is an action by a patient against a hospital for $35,000 damages for personal injuries allegedly suffered as a result of negligence of defendant. Defendant moved for summary judgment, alleging that it is, and operates the hospital as, a benevolent, religious, nonprofit corporation and charitable institution and, therefore, is immune from liability for its torts. The motion was sustained, judgment was entered for defendant, and plaintiff appealed.

[Plaintiff alleged that defendant's employee negligently failed to assist him as he moved from his bed to the bathroom. Plaintiff fell and suffered multiple injuries.]

The doctrine of immunity of charitable institutions from liability for tort was adopted in this state in 1907 by a decision of the Kansas City Court of Appeals in Adams v. University Hospital, 122 Mo.App. 675, 99 S.W. 453. * * *

[T]he court said, in effect, that it is better that the individual suffer injury without compensation from the negligent charitable institution than to risk the judicially assumed probability that the public and state would be deprived of the benefits of the charity; that the interest of the latter is so supreme that the former must be sacrificed to it. * * *

There can be no doubt that at the time of its adoption the exception was a rule of expediency justifiable then, and for some time thereafter, to encourage and protect charity as vital to the growth and development of the state, but the reasons for the exception to the rule do not exist today. * * * "Today charity is big business. It often is corporate both in the identity of the donor and in the identity of the donee who administers the charity. Tax deductions sometimes make it actually profitable for doners to give to charity. Organized corporate charity takes over large areas of social activity which otherwise would have to be handled by government, or even by private business. Charity today is a large-scale operation with salaries, costs and other expenses similar to business generally. It makes sense to say that this kind of charity should pay its own way, not only as to its office expenses but as to the expense of insurance to pay for torts as well." [C] Today public liability insurance is available to charitable institutions to indemnify them against losses by way of damages for their negligence, and it is common knowledge that most charitable institutions carry such insurance and pay the premiums thereon as a part of their normal cost of operation.[12] In the states where immunity has not been accorded charity, experience has shown that the apprehension expressed here and elsewhere that the purses of donors would be closed and the funds of charity depleted if these institutions were not granted immunity was not well founded. In the quarter century since the doctrine began its decline, there has been no indication in the states which have abolished immunity that its withdrawal has discouraged donations or that the funds of these institutions have been depleted resulting in their demise.

* * *

The public is doubtless still interested in the maintenance of charitable institutions and we acknowledge society's debt to them and recognize their right to every benefit and assistance which the law can justly allow. But the day has arrived when these institutions must acknowledge the injustice of denying compensation to a person injured as a result of their negligence or the negligence of their agents or employees; when they must acknowledge that all persons, organizations and corporations stand equal before the law and must be bound or excused alike. They must recognize that " * * * immunity fosters neglect and breeds irresponsibility, while liability promotes care and caution * * *."

[The court then discussed two of the principal arguments utilized to support charitable immunity—the "implied waiver" and "trust fund" theories.]

The theory of "implied waiver," namely, that he who accepts the benefit of charity impliedly agrees he will not assert against the institution any right of recourse for wrong done him is a mere fiction. The fiction is based upon impossibility in many instances. It is impossible to say that a conscious or unconscious grievously injured accident victim carried to the emergency room of a charitable hospital, or an ill

---

12. We do not make the existence of liability insurance the criterion of liability, as some states have done; we merely emphasize its availability and widespread use as a fact and circumstance that did not exist when the doctrine was adopted. We have held that the existence of liability insurance is immaterial on the issue of liability and adhere to that decision. * * *

person received at such hospital unconscious, or a conscious ill person who enters such hospital by arrangement of others waives his rights by accepting its benefits. To say that an insane person, a minor or babe in arms waives his rights when he receives or there is administered to him the benefits of *any* charitable institution does violence to the facts; such persons have no legal capacity to will away their rights. The waiver theory obviously cannot be applied alike to all persons and this fact points up the fallacy in relying upon it to support immunity as a rule of public policy.

The "trust fund" theory as support for the doctrine of immunity rests on an illogical, and therefore weak, foundation. The essence of the theory is that the institutions' funds, given and held for charitable purposes, cannot be used to *pay* judgments resulting from tort claims. Thus, the rationale of the theory is identified solely with the right to *satisfaction* of a judgment, rather than to the fundamental question of whether an injured person has a right to maintain an action and secure a judgment. If it is reasonable to say, and it is, that the existence of liability insurance does not create liability where none exists, then it is also reasonable to say that the inability to have satisfaction of a judgment does not create or support exemption from liability where exemption does not otherwise exist. * * *

Defendant and amici curiae recognize that the court has the authority to abolish or modify the doctrine of charitable immunity, but insist the doctrine as public policy is so deeply and firmly embedded in our law that if it is to be modified or abolished the change should be made by the legislature rather than the court.

It is neither realistic nor consistent with the common law tradition to wait upon the legislature to correct an outmoded rule of case law. Nor is legislative silence as instructive or persuasive. * * *

[L]egislative indifference to remedies for private wrongs may be common enough in times when the assembly is occupied with a multitude of matters of grave public concern, but failure to enact a bill is not one of the constitutional methods by which the assembly makes law. * * *

For the reasons stated, we hold that a nongovernmental charitable institution is liable for its own negligence and for the negligence of its agents and employees acting within the scope of their employment.

Having abolished the doctrine of charitable immunity, it remains for us to determine the point of departure from precedent. We are cognizant of the fact that retrospective application of our decision could result in great hardship to those institutions which have relied on our prior decisions upholding the doctrine of charitable immunity. Therefore, feeling that justice will best be served by prospective application of the decision announced today, we hold that the new rule shall apply to this case and to all future causes of action arising after November 10, 1969, the date of the filing of this opinion.

The judgment is reversed and the cause remanded for further proceedings.

DONNELLY, J., concurs in result in separate concurring opinion filed.

––––––––––

1. Charitable immunity originated in England in 1846, in Feoffees of Heriot's Hospital v. Ross, 12 C. & F. 507, 8 Eng.Rep. 1508 (1846). It was later repudiated in Mersey Docks Trustees v. Gibbs, 11 H.L.Cas. 686 (1866). It was, however, taken up by Massachusetts in McDonald v. Massachusetts Gen. Hosp., 120 Mass. 432, 21 Am.Rep. 529 (1876), which was followed in the United States. Prior to 1942, the immunity was accepted, sometimes with various minor limitations, by all but two or three of the American courts. In that year, Judge Rutledge, in what has become a landmark opinion, abolished the immunity for the District of Columbia. See President and Directors of Georgetown College v. Hughes, 130 F.2d 810 (D.C.Cir.1942). A substantial majority of the states now follow the decision, see Annot., 25 A.L.R.2d 29 (1952) (and supp.); Rabon v. Rowan Memorial Hosp. Inc., 269 N.C. 1, 152 S.E.2d 485 (1967) (collecting cases). Are these decisions consistent in policy with federal and state tax laws that grant exemptions to qualified charitable organizations? The immunity, at least on a qualified basis, is not without its defenders. See Howard v. Bishop Byrne Council Home, Inc., 249 Md. 233, 238 A.2d 863 (1968).

2. Some jurisdictions have made one or more inroads on the immunity, but have not abolished it completely. The more common incursions include: (1) abolishing the immunity to charitable hospitals but retaining it as to religious institutions and other charities, (2) limiting the immunity to recipients of the benefits of the charity and (3) abolishing the immunity to the extent that the defendant is covered by liability insurance or to the extent that the judgment can be satisfied out of other nontrust fund assets.

3. New Jersey, by statute, has limited liability of nonprofit hospitals for negligent acts to $10,000 in damages, and charities are not liable for negligence. See 2–A N.J.S.A. § 53A–7–10 (1959). Do charities of any kind deserve special treatment under tort damage rules? What if the tort is intentional? See also Md.Ann.Code Art. 43, § 556A (1966) (limiting the liability of a charitable hospital to $100,000 if it obtains liability insurance in that amount).

4. Charitable immunity is area of tort law where state legislatures have sometimes entered. For example, several state legislatures have restored a qualified immunity after the highest court of their state had abolished it. Could a court sustain such a statute as having a "rational basis" under the Constitution? See Makar v. St. Nicholas, Etc., Church, 78 N.J.Super. 1, 187 A.2d 353 (1963); Fournier v. Miriam Hosp., 93 R.I. 299, 175 A.2d 298 (1961) (statute since repealed); cf. Neely v. St. Francis Hosp. & School of Nursing, Inc., 192 Kan. 716, 391 P.2d 155 (1964).

5. See generally Feezer, The Tort Liability of Charities, 77 U.Pa.L.Rev. 191 (1928); Fisch, Charitable Liability for Tort, 10 Vill.L.Rev. 71 (1964); Greenhill, Recent Developments in Governmental and Charitable Immunities, 22 Fed. Ins.Coun.Q. [No. 1] 123 (1970); Restatement (Second) of Torts § 895E, and Appendix.

(C) STATE AND LOCAL GOVERNMENTS

AYALA v. PHILADELPHIA BOARD OF PUBLIC EDUCATION

Supreme Court of Pennsylvania, 1973.
453 Pa. 584, 305 A.2d 877.

ROBERTS, JUSTICE. Appellants, William Ayala and William Ayala, Jr., instituted this action to recover damages for injuries suffered by William, Jr., when his arm was caught in a shredding machine in the upholstery class of the Carrol School in Philadelphia. As a result of these injuries, the 15 year old student's arm was amputated.

Appellants alleged that appellee school district, through its employees, was negligent in failing to supervise the upholstery class, in supplying the machine for use without a proper safety device, in maintaining the machine in a dangerous and defective condition, and in failing to warn the children of the dangerous condition. Appellee, the Philadelphia Board of Public Education, interposed preliminary objections asserting the defense of governmental immunity. These objections were sustained and the Superior Court affirmed in a per curiam order. [C] We granted allocatur.

We now hold that the doctrine of governmental immunity—long since devoid of any valid justification—is abolished in this Commonwealth. In so doing, we join the ever-increasing number of jurisdictions which have judicially abandoned this antiquated doctrine. [The court cited decisions from Alaska, Arizona, Arkansas, California, Colorado, the District of Columbia, Florida, Idaho, Illinois, Indiana, Kentucky, Michigan, Minnesota, Nebraska, New Jersey, Nevada, Rhode Island and Wisconsin.]

It is generally agreed that the historical roots of the governmental immunity doctrine are found in the English case of Russell v. Men of Devon, 2 T.R. 667, 100 Eng.Rep. 359 (1788). [Cc] There, the court, in extending immunity to an unincorporated county, expressed the fear that if suits against such political subdivisions were permitted, there would be "an infinity of actions." Russell v. Men of Devon, supra at 672, 100 Eng.Rep. at 362. That court was also influenced by the absence of a fund "out of which satisfaction is to be made." Id. Finally, Justice Ashurst, expressing the eighteenth century societal evaluation of the individual and local governmental interests, observed that "it is better that an individual should sustain an injury than that the public should suffer an inconvenience." Id.

While some attribute the immunity of municipal corporations and quasi-corporations to an extension of the theory that "the King can do no wrong", it has been noted that in Russell v. Men of Devon there is no mention of that phrase.　*　*　*

Additionally, it has been suggested that the doctrine of governmental immunity was a result of the English courts' difficulties with the principle of respondeat superior. * * *

"*Respondeat superior* had caused difficulties as early as the nineteenth century in England, when the question arose whether the King, who by that time could be sued in contract whenever 'right should be done,' should be held for his officers' torts. The courts denied such relief, reasoning that *respondeat superior* was based on the identity of principal and agent, because the King could not himself commit a tort, the attribution failed for want of a competent principal." Jaffe, Suits Against Governments and Officers: Damage Actions, 77 Harv.L.Rev. 209, 210 (1963) (footnote omitted).

Whatever may have been the actual basis for Russell v. Men of Devon, the doctrine it advanced was soon applied in the United States. * * *

Governmental immunity can no longer be justified on "an amorphous mass of cumbrous language about sovereignty. * * * Leflar and Kantrowitz, Tort Liability of the States, 29 N.Y.U.L.Rev. 1363, 1364 (1954). As one court has stated:

"' * * * it is almost incredible that in this modern age of comparative sociological enlightenment, and in a republic, the medieval absolutism supposed to be implicit in the maxim, "the King can do no wrong," should exempt the various branches of the government from liability for their torts, and that the entire burden of damage resulting from the wrongful acts of the government should be imposed upon the single individual who suffers the injury, rather than distributed among the entire community constituting the government, where it could be borne without hardship upon any individual, and where it justly belongs.' Barker v. City of Santa Fe, 47 N.M. 85, 136 P.2d 480, 482. * * *" Molitor v. Kaneland Community Unit Dist. No. 302 (1959) 18 Ill.2d 11, 21–22, 163 N.E.2d 89, 94. * * *

We must also reject the fear of excessive litigation as a justification for the immunity doctrine. Empirically, there is little support for the concern that the courts will be flooded with litigation if the doctrine is abandoned. * * *

Equally unpersuasive is the argument advanced in Russell v. Men of Devon * * * that immunity is required because governmental units lack funds from which claims could be paid. It is argued that funds would be diverted to the payment of claims and the performance of proper governmental functions would be obstructed. Initially, we note our disagreement with the assumption that the payment of claims is not a proper governmental function. "As many writers have pointed out, the fallacy in [the no-fund theory] is that it assumes the very point which is sought to be proved i.e., that payment of damage claims is not a proper purpose." [C]

Additionally, the empirical data does not support the fear that governmental functions would be curtailed as a result of liability for tortious conduct. * * *

The availability of public insurance removes what was the underlying reason for *Men of Devon.* [C]

[In a prior case, the court abrogated governmental immunity when a municipality engaged in a "proprietary" as compared with a "governmental" function. The court's discussion of the validity of that distinction follows.]

[T]he distinction between governmental and proprietary functions "is probably one of the most unsatisfactory known to the law, for it has caused confusion not only among the various jurisdictions but almost always within each jurisdiction." Davis, Administrative Law Treatise § 25.07 at 460 (1958). * * *

In now rejecting the immunity doctrine and the "legalistic distinctions that have only remote relationship to the fundamental considerations of municipal tort responsibility" [c], we recognize, as did Dean Prosser, that:

"Virtually all writers have agreed that no one of these reasons for denying liability is sound, and all of them can be found to have been rejected at one time or another in the decided cases. The current of criticism has been that it is better that the losses due to tortious conduct should fall upon the municipality rather than the injured individual, and that the torts of public employees are properly to be regarded, as in other cases of vicarious liability, as a cost of the administration of government, which should be distributed by taxes to the public." Prosser, supra at 1004–05 (footnotes omitted).

Imposition of tort liability will, thus, be more responsive to current concepts of justice. Claims will be treated as a cost of administration and losses will be spread among all those benefited by governmental action. [Cc]

Moreover, "where governmental immunity has had the effect of encouraging laxness and a disregard of potential harm, exposure of the government to liability for its torts will have the effect of increasing governmental care and concern for the welfare of those who might be injured by its actions." [C]

[The court then determined that it need not defer to the legislature to change "this court made rule" and that the doctrine of *stare decisis* did not bind the court to "perpetuating error." Finally, it declined to accept appellee's argument that the ruling be made totally prospective and not apply to the instant case.]

Having concluded that local governmental units—municipal corporations and quasi-corporations—are no longer immune from tort liability, the order sustaining appellee's preliminary objections is reversed and the record remanded for proceedings consistent with this opinion.

MANDERINO, J., joins in this opinion and filed a concurring opinion.
JONES, C.J., and EAGEN and O'BRIEN, JJ., dissent.

---

1. The origin of the idea of governmental immunity at common law seems
to have lain in the theory, allied with the divine right of kings, that "the King
can do no wrong," together with the feeling that it was necessarily a contradiction of his sovereignty to allow him to be sued as of right in his own courts.
The explanations for the initial acceptance of this feudal and monarchistic
doctrine in the democracy of this country are quite obscure. It was first
recognized on the purely procedural basis that the federal government could
not be sued without its consent. When justifications were finally offered, they
were consistent with this procedural rule. The explanation most commonly
quoted is that of Justice Holmes, in Kawananakoa v. Polyblank, 205 U.S. 349,
353 (1907):

"A sovereign is exempt from suit, not because of any formal conception of
obsolete theory, but on the logical and practical ground that there can be no
legal right as against the authority that makes the law on which the right
depends." With the passage of time, the idea of substantive immunity, as
distinct from the denial of the right to sue, began to appear in the federal
decisions, until in Gibbons v. United States, 75 U.S. (8 Wall.) 269 (Ct.Cl.1868), it
was held that the federal government was immune from all liability in tort.
The tort immunity of the United States has been substantially eroded by the
Federal Tort Claims Act of 1946, discussed infra pages 636–39.

2. *State Governments.* The immunity of state governments from tort
liability has the same origin as that of the United States, in feudal notions that
the King could do no wrong and that it was a denial of his sovereignty to
permit him to be sued in his own courts without his consent. The immunity
was given firmer underpinning in some state statutes and in a few state
constitutions that required legislative consent for the state to be liable in tort.
Even when consent to suit was given, some state courts held that this was not
"consent to liability" and they continued to apply the immunity.

3. The immunity was held to extend to state agencies, such as prisons,
hospitals, educational institutions, state fairs, and commissions for public
works—although a definite tendency developed to find a legislative intent in
creating the agency that it should be subject to liability.

Until around 1960, the development of the law in this area had merely
taken the form of increasing and broadening the considerable number of
exceptions.

4. *Municipal Corporations.* Municipal corporations, such as cities, school
districts, and the like have a rather curious dual character. On the one hand,
they are subdivisions of the state, acting as local governments. On the other,
they are corporate bodies, capable of much the same acts and having much the
same special interests and relations as private corporations.

The absence of any constitutional or statutory provisions requiring consent
to suit made it much easier than in the case of state immunities to develop
exceptions to the rule of non-liability. In Monell v. Department of Social Serv.
of the City of New York, 436 U.S. 658 (1978), the court decided that municipalities were persons and subject to suit for any constitutional violations, even if
committed in their governmental functions. In Owen v. Independence, 445
U.S. 622 (1980), the Court, acting under 42 U.S.C.A. § 1983 of the Civil Rights

Act, abolished any qualified immunity which municipalities or their officials could enjoy by asserting a good faith defense.

5. The principal exception was for activities that were deemed "proprietary" or "private" as contrasted with "governmental" functions. Courts imposed liability when the city or town engaged in activity that normally was carried out by the private sector of the economy. As the principal case indicates, the distinction produced a morass of confusion and inconsistency—nevertheless, a number of jurisdictions still make the attempt to apply it. See, e.g., Steelman v. New Bern, 279 N.C. 589, 184 S.E.2d 239 (1971) (public street lighting governmental rather than proprietary). Casey v. Wake County, 45 N.C.App. 522, 263 S.E.2d 360 (1980) (birth control pill dispensing is governmental).

6. When the state has authorized a municipal corporation to purchase insurance, a number of courts have held that action to be an implied waiver of the immunity to the extent of the insurance. See, e.g., Ballew v. Chattanooga, 205 Tenn. 289, 326 S.W.2d 466 (1959); Bollinger v. Schneider, 64 Ill.App.3d 758, 21 Ill.Dec. 522, 381 N.E.2d 849 (1978).

7. *Abrogation.* Beginning in 1957 with Hargrove v. Cocoa Beach, 96 So.2d 130 (Fla.1957), there have been a number of decisions abrogating the immunity of municipal corporations even for governmental functions. See the principal case, Merrill v. Manchester, 114 N.H. 722, 332 A.2d 378 (1974); Kitto v. Minot Park Dist., 224 N.W.2d 795 (N.D.1974); and Oroz v. Board of County Comm'rs of Carbon County, 575 P.2d 1155 (Wyo.1978) (except for judicial and legislative functions). Other courts have held that the matter should be left to the legislature. See O'Dell v. School Dist. of Independence, 521 S.W.2d 403 (Mo. 1975); Crowder v. Department of State Parks, 228 Ga. 436, 185 S.E.2d 908 (1971); Mayor and City Council of Baltimore v. Austin, 40 Md.App. 557, 392 A.2d 1140 (1978). Cases are collected in Annot., 60 A.L.R.2d 1198 (1958) and its supplements.

Judicial respect for governmental immunity has been greater in regard to state government. See, e.g., Krause v. State, 31 Ohio St.2d 132, 60 Ohio Ops.2d 100, 285 N.E.2d 736 (1972); Henry v. Oklahoma Turnpike Auth., 478 P.2d 898 (Okl.1970). When there has been no state constitutional barrier, some courts have abrogated the immunity. See, e.g., Stone v. Arizona Highway Comm'n, 93 Ariz. 384, 381 P.2d 107 (1963); Smith v. State, 93 Idaho 795, 473 P.2d 937 (1970) ("proprietary" functions only); Hicks v. State, 88 N.M. 588, 544 P.2d 1153 (1975); Jones v. State Highway Comm'n, 557 S.W.2d 225 (Mo.1977) (except in legislative, judicial and executive functions).

8. The rulings abolishing immunities are often prospective in nature except as applied to the parties before the court. In Holytz v. Milwaukee, 17 Wis.2d 26, 115 N.W.2d 618 (1962), the court stated that it was abolishing the immunity as a matter of substance, but it was for the legislature to determine the extent to which the state could be sued.

9. One should not lose sight of the fact that state and municipal immunities may be abrogated by legislation. Legislation regulating the matter may also be enacted after judicial abrogation. See Note, Governmental Immunity— The Doctrine of Immunity Judicially Abrogated and Legislatively Reinstated, 50 J.Urban L. 154 (1972).

Some statutes are modeled on the Federal Torts Claims Act, discussed infra page 636. Others broadly provide that the state shall be liable to the same extent as any private individual. Rather complex "codes" have been worked out in several states. See, e.g., Cal.Gov't Code §§ 810 et seq. (West 1966); N.J.

Stat.Ann. §§ 59:1–1 et seq. (Supp.1975); Utah Code Ann. §§ 63–30–1 et seq. (1968). The statute may create courts of claims and special "notice of claim" requirements (see supra page 607). This is yet another area of tort law where an attorney must research current statutory law before advising a client. See generally Cobey, New California Governmental Tort Liability Statutes, 1 Harv. J.Leg. 16 (1964); Leflar and Kantrowitz, Tort Liability of the States, 29 N.Y. U.L.Rev. 1363 (1954); Anderson, Claims Against States, 7 Vand.L.Rev. 234 (1954).

10. See generally Smith, Municipal Tort Liability, 48 Mich.L.Rev. 41 (1949); James, Tort Liability of Local Government Units and Their Officers, 22 U.Chi.L.Rev. 610 (1955); David, Tort Liability of Governmental Units, 40 Minn. L.Rev. 751 (1956); David, Tort Liability of Local Government, 6 U.C.L.A.L.Rev. 1 (1959); Hamill, The Changing Concept of Sovereign Immunity, 13 Defense L.J. 653 (1964); Schoenbrun, Sovereign Immunity, 44 Tex.L.Rev. 151 (1965); Van Alstyne, Governmental Tort Liability: A Decade of Change, 1966 U.Ill.L.F. 919; Cahn and Camper, The New Sovereign Immunity, 81 Harv.L.Rev. 919 (1968). See also Restatement (Second) of Torts §§ 895B (states), 895C (local governments); the Reporter's Note in the Appendix to these sections carries a compilation showing the position of each state on both state and local government immunity.

RISS v. NEW YORK

New York Court of Appeals, 1968.
22 N.Y.2d 579, 240 N.E.2d 860, 293 N.Y.S.2d 897.

[The description of the facts in this case is taken from the dissenting opinion of Judge Keating:

"Linda Riss, an attractive young woman, was for more than six months terrorized by a rejected suitor well known to the courts of this State, one Burton Pugach. This miscreant, masquerading as a respectable attorney, repeatedly threatened to have Linda killed or maimed if she did not yield to him: 'If I can't have you, no one else will have you, and when I get through with you, no one else will want you.' In fear for her life, she went to those charged by law with the duty of preserving and safeguarding the lives of the citizens and residents of this State. Linda's repeated and almost pathetic pleas for aid were received with little more than indifference. Whatever help she was given was not commensurate with the identifiable danger. On June 14, 1959 Linda became engaged to another man. At a party held to celebrate the event, she received a phone call warning her that it was her 'last chance.' Completely distraught, she called the police, begging for help, but was refused. The next day Pugach carried out his dire threats in the very manner he had foretold by having a hired thug throw lye in Linda's face. Linda was blinded in one eye, lost a good portion of her vision in the other, and her face was permanently scarred. After the assault the authorities concluded that there was some basis for Linda's fears, and for the next three and one-half years, she was given around-the-clock protection."]

BREITEL, J. This appeal presents, in a very sympathetic framework, the issue of the liability of a municipality for failure to provide special protection to a member of the public who was repeatedly threatened with personal harm and eventually suffered dire personal injuries for lack of such protection. * * * The issue arises upon the affirmance by a divided Appellate Division of a dismissal of the complaint, after both sides had rested but before submission to the jury. * * *

[T]his case involves the provision of a governmental service to protect the public generally from external hazards and particularly to control the activities of criminal wrongdoers. [Cc] The amount of protection that may be provided is limited by the resources of the community and by a considered legislative-executive decision as to how those resources may be deployed. For the courts to proclaim a new and general duty of protection in the law of tort, even to those who may be the particular seekers of protection based on specific hazards, could and would inevitably determine how the limited police resources of the community should be allocated and without predictable limits. This is quite different from the predictable allocation of resources and liabilities when public hospitals, rapid transit systems, or even highways are provided.

Before such extension of responsibilities should be dictated by the indirect imposition of tort liabilities, there should be a legislative determination that that should be the scope of public responsibility. * * *

When one considers the greatly increased amount of crime committed throughout the cities, but especially in certain portions of them, with a repetitive and predictable pattern, it is easy to see the consequences of fixing municipal liability upon a showing of probable need for and request for protection. To be sure these are grave problems at the present time, exciting high priority activity on the part of the national, State and local governments, to which the answers are neither simple, known, or presently within reasonable controls. To foist a presumed cure for these problems by judicial innovation of a new kind of liability in tort would be foolhardy indeed and an assumption of judicial wisdom and power not possessed by the courts.

Nor is the analysis progressed by the analogy to compensation for losses sustained. It is instructive that the Crime Victims Compensation and "Good Samaritan" statutes, compensating limited classes of victims of crime, were enacted only after the most careful study of conditions and the impact of such a scheme upon governmental operations and the public fisc (Executive Law, art. 22, § 620 et seq. [L.1966, ch. 894]; Administrative Code of City of New York, ch. 3, tit. A, § 67–3.2). And then the limitations were particular and narrow.

For all of these reasons, there is no warrant in judicial tradition or in the proper allocation of the powers of government for the courts, in the absence of legislation, to carve out an area of tort liability for police protection to members of the public. Quite distinguishable, of course, is the situation where the police authorities undertake responsibilities to particular members of the public and expose them, without adequate protection, to the risks which then materialize into actual losses (Schuster v. City of New York, 5 N.Y.2d 75).

Accordingly, the order of the Appellate Division affirming the judgment of dismissal should be affirmed.

KEATING, JUDGE (dissenting). It is not a distortion to summarize the essence of the city's case here in the following language: "Because we owe a duty to everybody, we owe it to nobody." * * * To say that there is no duty is, of course, to start with the conclusion. The question is whether or not there should be liability for the negligent failure to provide adequate police protection.

The foremost justification repeatedly urged for the existing rule is the claim that the State and the municipalities will be exposed to limitless liability. The city invokes the specter of a "crushing burden" * * *.

The fear of financial disaster is a myth. The same argument was made a generation ago in opposition to proposals that the State waive its defense of "sovereign immunity". The prophecy proved false then, and it would now. * * *

Another variation of the "crushing burden" argument is the contention that, every time a crime is committed, the city will be sued and the claim will be made that it resulted from inadequate police protection. Here, again, is an attempt to arouse the "anxiety of the courts about new theories of liability which may have a far-reaching effect" * * *.

The instant case provides an excellent illustration of the limits which the courts can draw. No one would claim that, under the facts here, the police were negligent when they did not give Linda protection after her first calls or visits to the police station in February of 1959. The preliminary investigation was sufficient. If Linda had been attacked at this point, clearly there would be no liability here. When, however, as time went on and it was established that Linda was a reputable person, that other verifiable attempts to injure her or intimidate her had taken place, that other witnesses were available to support her claim that her life was being threatened, something more was required—either by way of further investigation or protection— than the statement that was made by one detective to Linda that she would have to be hurt before the police could do anything for her. * * *

More significant, however, is the fundamental flaw in the reasoning behind the argument alleging judicial interference. It is a complete oversimplification of the problem of municipal tort liability. What it ignores is the fact that indirectly courts are reviewing administrative practices in almost every tort case against the State or a municipality, including even decisions of the Police Commissioner * * *.

DeLONG v. ERIE COUNTY

New York Supreme Court, 1982.
89 A.D.2d 376, 455 N.Y.S.2d 887.

HANCOCK, JUSTICE: * * * Before her death, Amalia DeLong, her husband, and their three young children resided at 319 Victoria Boulevard in the Village of Kenmore, a suburb of Buffalo located in Erie County. In October, 1976, the Village of Kenmore was one of the four communities outside of Buffalo fully served by the 911 emergency telephone system operated by the Central Police Services, an agency of Erie County, with the active assistance and cooperation of the Buffalo Police Department. The system was located in the 911 room in Buffalo Police Headquarters in downtown Buffalo. At 9:29:29 in the morning of October 25, 1976 Amalia DeLong dialed 911 on her telephone and was immediately connected to the 911 room. The transcript of her call is as follows:

9:29:29—Caller:		"Police?"
—Complaint Writer:		"911."
—Caller:		"Police, please come, 319 Victoria right away."
—Complaint Writer:		"What's wrong?"
—Caller:		"There's a burglar."
9:29:34—Complaint Writer:		"In there now?"
—Caller:		"I heard a burglar; I saw his face in the back; he was trying to break in the house; please come right away."
—Complaint Writer:		"Okay, right away."
9:29:43—Caller:		"Okay."

The complaint writer recorded the address on the complaint card as "219 Victoria"—not "319 Victoria". The call had lasted 14 seconds. [The evidence regarding police response time indicated that the decedent's life might have been saved if the police had not been misdirected to a nonexistent address.] As a result of the failure of proper police response, Amalia DeLong had received seven knife wounds: to the left side of the neck, the left side of the head, the second finger of the right hand, the nail of the third finger on the left hand, the thumb of the left hand, and a wound to the left shoulder. The laceration on the neck was fatal. It was deep and had severed the jugular vein and carotid artery on the left. The cuts on the fingers were described as being of a "defensive type".

The police in searching the house found evidence of a savage attack. * * *

The purpose of the 911 emergency or "hot line" system is to assist in the delivery of police services to the people in the communities served (determined by whether the telephone exchanges in the communities are such that dialing 911 will give an automatic connection with the 911 room at Buffalo police headquarters). * * *

On the morning of October 25, the complaint writer, in addition to mistakenly recording the address on the complaint card as 219 instead of 319 Victoria, failed to follow the instructions in four respects: (1) he did not ask the name of the caller; (2) he did not determine the exact location of the call; (3) he did not address the caller by name; (4) he did not repeat the address.

The operating procedures in effect on October 25, 1976 also called for follow-up action if, as with the DeLong call, the report came back to the dispatcher: "No such address." In such event, the dispatcher was required to notify the complaint writer or the 911 lieutenant (the Buffalo police lieutenant on duty in the 911 room) so that the tape recording of the call could be replayed, the Haines Directory and the street guides consulted, and other communities having street names identical or similar to the street name given by the caller immediately notified. On Amalia DeLong's call, no follow-up of any kind took place. The call was treated as a fake.

Our discussion of the questions raised concerning liability must start with Riss v. City of New York, 22 N.Y.2d 579, 293 N.Y.S.2d 897, 240 N.E.2d 860, in which the court found no legal responsibility for the tragic consequences of the city's failure to furnish police protection despite proof of Linda Riss' repeated and agonized pleas for assistance. In an opinion by then Associate Judge Breitel, the court, with one dissent, concluded: "[T]here is no warrant in judicial tradition or in the proper allocation of the powers of government for the courts, in the absence of legislation, to carve out an area of tort liability for police protection to members of the public. Quite distinguishable, of course, is the situation where the police authorities undertake responsibilities to particular members of the public and expose them, without adequate protection, to the risks which then materialize into actual losses [cc]. This fundamental rule remains the law [cc] when a relationship is created between the police and an individual which gives rise to a special duty, the municipality loses its governmental immunity and liability may result. Courts have found such a special duty to be owing "to informers [c], undercover agents [c], persons under court orders of protection [c], and school children for whom the municipality has assumed the responsibility of providing crossing guards [cc]. * * *

It is not the establishment of the emergency call system to serve the Village of Kenmore, standing alone, which creates the duty. It is the holding out of the 911 number as one to be called by someone in need of assistance, Amalia DeLong's placing of the call in reliance on that holding out, and her further reliance on the response to her plea for immediate help: "Okay, right away." This is not a mere failure to furnish police protection owed to the public generally but a case where the municipality has assumed a duty to a particular person which it must perform "in a nonnegligent manner, [although without the] voluntary assumption of that duty, none would have otherwise existed" [c]. The complaint writer's acceptance of the call, his transmittal of the complaint card to the dispatcher and the dispatcher's radio calls to the police cars were affirmative actions setting the emergency machinery in motion. This voluntary assumption of a duty to act carried with it the obligation to act with reasonable care [c].

But, defendants remind us, failing to fulfill an undertaking to provide police protection does not result in municipal liability unless it be shown that the police conduct in some way increased the risk [c]. They maintain that the evidence does not establish that the conduct had "gone forward to such a stage that inaction would commonly result, not negatively merely in withholding a benefit, but positively or actively in working an injury" [c]. In other words, defendants argue, although the hand may have been set to the task and withdrawn [c], it has resulted in no harm. We disagree.

While there could in this case be no direct evidence that Amalia DeLong relied to her ultimate detriment on the assurance of police assistance, the circumstantial evidence strongly suggests that she did so. Instead of summoning help from the Village police or from her neighbors (one of whom was a captain in the Kenmore Police Department), she waited for the response to her 911 call. Instead of taking her baby and going out the front door where she would have been safe, she remained defenseless in the house. * * *

Finally, contrary to the city's contentions, we view the evidence as supporting the jury's conclusion that the city and county were equally at fault. We find no merit in defendants' other arguments on the liability issue.

[The court found that the jury's award of $200,000 for pain and suffering was "within reasonable bounds." The period of time of decedent's fatal encounter with her assailant was between 9:30 and 9:42 a.m.]

Accordingly, the judgment insofar as it awards damages for conscious pain and suffering, should be affirmed.

Judgment affirmed with costs.

[Concurring and dissenting opinions omitted.]

————

1. In the first flush of enthusiasm in favor of general abolition of governmental immunity, little thought was given to the question of whether there might not still be situations in which the immunity should remain. Two of these arise when the government is performing a judicial or legislative function, and when the officer or employee whose conduct is in question is performing an act that lies within his discretion.

2. As the opinions in *Riss* reflect, there can be a sharp difference of opinion as to what is a discretionary function. Most would agree that "the application of the immunity here is not simply a carry-over of the concept of a governmental function as distinguished from a proprietary function." See Restatement (Second) of Torts § 895C, comment g. Where should the line be drawn? Some attempts have been made in Merrill v. Manchester, 114 N.H. 722, 332 A.2d 378, 383 (1974); Johnson v. State, 69 Cal.2d 782, 447 P.2d 352, 73 Cal.Rptr. 240 (1968). How would you classify negligent training of police? See

Carter v. Carlson, 144 U.S.App.D.C. 388, 447 F.2d 358 (1971), rev'd on other grounds sub nom. District of Columbia v. Carter, 409 U.S. 418 (1973). Compare Jones v. State, 33 N.Y.2d 275, 307 N.E.2d 236, 352 N.Y.S.2d 169 (1973) (a station house officer's decision to delay in responding to an alarm).

3. A closely related, but conceptually distinct problem focuses on the extent of the duty a government owes to its citizens. Should it be the same as that imposed on a private individual? Should it have a duty to warn citizens about the prevalence of crime in a public area? See Hayes v. State, 11 Cal.3d 469, 521 P.2d 855, 113 Cal.Rptr. 599 (1974). Suppose a failure to provide needed police protection causes plaintiff to lose his business? See Simpson's Food Fair, Inc. v. Evansville, 149 Ind.App. 387, 272 N.E.2d 871 (1971). Or a municipal housing project does not protect its tenants in a high crime area? See Bass v. New York, 38 A.D.2d 407, 330 N.Y.S.2d 569 (1972). Suppose a fire department negligently fails to save plaintiff's building from destruction. Cf. Duran v. Tucson, 20 Ariz.App. 22, 509 P.2d 1059 (1973) (fire inspection). Under the rule of the principal case, could a distinction arise between a city's failure to provide adequate police patrol versus its failure to provide good lighting in an area known to be dangerous? See Slapin v. Los Angeles Internat'l Airport, 65 Cal.App.3d 484, 135 Cal.Rptr. 296 (1976). Suppose police officers stop a drunk driver but let him go and the driver then causes a fatal accident? Irwin v. Ware, 392 Mass. 745, 467 N.E.2d 1292 (1984); and Shore v. Stonington, 187 Conn. 147, 444 A.2d 1379 (1982), noted in 15 Conn.L.Rev. 641 (1983). An interesting case arose in St. Paul, Minnesota, where the city failed to prevent vicious dogs from roaming the streets. Plaintiff was seriously injured when he was attacked by two of them. How would you decide that one? See Hansen v. St. Paul, 298 Minn. 205, 214 N.W.2d 346 (1974).

4. When a municipality through its officers has given specific assurances that it will protect an individual or group of individuals from crime or other hazards, it may be held liable for its negligent failure to do so. See Morgan v. Yuba County, 230 Cal.App.2d 938, 41 Cal.Rptr. 508 (1964); Schuster v. New York, 5 N.Y.2d 75, 154 N.E.2d 534, 180 N.Y.S.2d 265 (1958); Bloom v. New York, 78 Misc.2d 1077, 357 N.Y.S.2d 979 (1974); Grimm v. Arizona Bd. of Pardons and Paroles, 115 Ariz. 260, 564 P.2d 1227 (1977).

5. The question of whether the state should ever compensate victims of crime is susceptible to legislative as well as judicial answers. A number of jurisdictions have statutes dealing with municipal liability for riot damage. See Annot., 26 A.L.R.3d 1198 (1969); Lefkowitz, Municipal Liability for Damage Caused by Riot, 41 N.Y.S.B.J. 600 (1969). There are also broader statutes dealing with other crimes and a Uniform Crime Reparations Act has been proposed by the National Conference on Uniform State Laws. See Rothstein, How the Uniform Crime Victims Reparations Act Works, 60 A.B.A.J. 1531 (1974).

6. For those who may be interested, here is a side note on the subsequent history of the personalities in the *Riss* case. Burton Pugach, the attorney who hired the individual who partially blinded Ms. Riss, served 14 years and one month in prison for his crime. Six months after his release he proposed to Ms. Riss. She accepted and the couple were married on November 27, 1974. See N.Y. Times Nov. 28, 1974, at 1, col. 4.

7. *The Municipal Liability "Lawsuit Crisis."* In the mid–1980's, municipalities, as did other insurance customers, began to have trouble obtaining liability insurance at affordable rates. One factor was the tremendous growth

in civil rights lawsuits in the wake of *Monell* and *Owen* (see note 4, page 625). Another was the likelihood that, under the rule of joint and several liability, even when the city was only partly at fault, it would end up paying most or all of the damages (see Chapter 7). In several well-publicized cases, one large jury award emptied the treasury of a small town. Cities began cancelling fireworks displays and closing down playgrounds to minimize their exposure. As in the malpractice crisis, see page 196, the insurance companies blamed the plaintiffs' bar, and the lawyers blamed the insurance companies. The insurance industry proposed reforms such as caps on damages and contingent fees and the abolition of joint and several liability. The trial lawyers proposed greater regulation of the insurance industry. See Blodgett, Premium Hikes Stun Municipalities, 72 A.B.A.J. 48 (July 1986); Young, Tort Judgments Against Cities: The Sky's the Limit, 1983 Det.C.L.Rev. 1509; Yuhas, Recent Developments in Government Liability, 16 Urb.Law. 655 (1984). Consider the two principal cases. Many persons would be sympathetic toward the victims, but what would occur if municipalities are held liable for failure to provide adequate police or fire protection? Is it possible to formulate a rule that would be fair in these situations? Should the cost of these injuries be handled in some way other than the tort system? How?

(D) THE UNITED STATES

FITCH v. UNITED STATES

United States Court of Appeals, Sixth Circuit, 1975.
513 F.2d 1013, cert. denied, 423 U.S. 866, 96 S.Ct. 127, 46 L.Ed.2d 95 (1975).

CELEBREZZE, CIRCUIT JUDGE. This is an appeal from an award under the Federal Tort Claims Act. * * *

In November 1969, a national lottery was held to determine the order in which young men would be drafted into the Armed Forces. Clyde Fitch received number 309, which should have guaranteed that he not be drafted. An error at Local Board 69 in Inez, Kentucky resulted in transcription of his number as 132. Eligible men with this number were inducted. Clyde Fitch received his induction notice and * * * he reported for active duty on July 13, 1970. While stationed in Viet Nam, on July 9, 1971, Fitch was informed by an Army sergeant that his induction had been a mistake because of the erroneous assignment of his lottery number. Three months later he was discharged from active duty. * * *

The District Court held that the erroneous assignment of Fitch's lottery number established the United States' liability under the Federal Tort Claims Act, 28 U.S.C.A. § 2674. It assessed $11,661 in damages representing lost wages. It also held that Appellees had established "a right to punitive damages and such damages are assessed at $20,000." * * *

While we sympathize with Appellees' plight and cannot condone the negligence which caused Clyde Fitch's induction, we must reverse the award because the District Court acted beyond the authority Congress has given it.

The Federal Tort Claims Act, 28 U.S.C.A. §§ 1346(b) and 2671 et seq., is a broad waiver of the federal government's immunity from liability for the torts of its employees while acting in the scope of their employment. The Act contains various exceptions, however, and in construing the Act the courts must "carry out the legislative purpose of allowing suits against the Government for negligence with due regard for the statutory exceptions to that policy." [C]

Under 28 U.S.C.A. § 2680(h), Congress has chosen not to allow the courts to consider "any claim arising out of . . . misrepresentation." We must construe this term according to "the traditional and commonly understood legal definition of the tort." United States v. Neustadt, 366 U.S. 696, 706 (1961). It is settled that this exception includes claims arising out of negligent as well as intentional misrepresentation.

* * *

Although Appellees cast their complaint in the guise of a negligence action, this does not automatically take the case outside the misrepresentation exception. Courts must "look beyond the literal meaning of the language to ascertain the real cause of complaint." Hall v. United States, 274 F.2d 69, 71 (10th Cir.1959), quoted with approval United States v. Neustadt, 366 U.S. at 703.

In *Hall,* the plaintiff sold his cattle at a market loss after Government Inspectors mistakenly reported that his cattle were diseased. Hall argued that the inspectors' negligent testing rather than the erroneous report had caused his loss and sued the United States under the Act. The Tenth Circuit rejected this attempt to avoid the misrepresentation exception, stating:

 "Plaintiff's loss came about when the Government agents misrepresented the condition of the cattle, telling him they were diseased when, in fact, they were free from disease. * * * This stated a cause of action predicated on a misrepresentation. 274 F.2d at 71."

As in *Hall,* Appellees' complaint "arose out of" a negligent misrepresentation. It occurred when Government agents misrepresented Clyde Fitch's obligation to enter the Army, telling him that he was required to serve when, in fact, he was free from that duty. We are under the same obligation to dismiss the complaint as the Supreme Court recognized in *Neustadt:* "While we do not condone carelessness by government employees in gathering and promulgating such information, neither can we justifiably ignore the plain words Congress has used in limiting the scope of the Government's tort liability." 366 U.S. at 710–11. * * *

Finally, we observe that our action dismisses Appellees' complaint for lack of jurisdiction and does not jeopardize their opportunity to secure compensation from Congress for the injustice that befell them.

The Judgment of the District Court is reversed, with direction that an order be entered dismissing the complaint.

1. Governmental immunity has barred tort suits against the United States for the greater part of its history.

Consent to be sued began to appear in the form of private bills by Congress authorizing particular plaintiffs to sue on particular claims. Apart from the obvious possibility of political influence, this of necessity involved considerable delay and inconvenience, as well as inflicting a considerable burden upon the time of Congress. In 1855 it was largely replaced by a statute setting up a Court of Claims to hear contract cases. This was initially merely an advisory court making recommendations to Congress; but in 1863 the Court of Claims was given the power to render effective judgments. There were also a number of minor statutes permitting suit upon particular types of claims, and in a few instances some of these even authorized some relief in tort. The great majority of the tort claims against the United States remained, however, without any redress.

2. The inconvenience caused by private bills pressured Congress to provide for a general tort remedy. Between 1919 and 1946, some 18 proposals were considered. Finally, the specter of hundreds and possibly thousands of private bills flooding Congress as servicemen returned from World War II (only to be hit by postal trucks), proved too much. On August 2, 1946 the Federal Tort Claims Act was enacted. It applied to all claims accruing on and after January 1, 1945. In effect, it represented the first judicial remedy of general application available to persons who suffered tortious injury to their person or property caused by employees of the United States Government.

3. Tort claims against the Federal Government are a major source of tort litigation today. As an author of a two-volume treatise on the subject has observed:

"[L]awsuits against the United States under the Federal Tort Claims Act pending before the federal courts at one time involve[d] claims of considerably more than $300 million. New suits are filed at the rate of some 1,500 each year * * * This large volume * * * is understandable when you consider that the United States employs more than 5 million people * * * It operates more than a half a million * * * vehicles. It employs * * * more than 85,000 * * * medical personnel. * * *

"[M]otor vehicle * * * accidents comprise a little over half of the litigation under the Act * * * [T]he remainder covers virtually the entire field of torts * * *." L. Jayson, Handling Federal Tort Claims 1, 7–8 (1974).

4. The Federal Tort Claims Act is a subject for separate study. Only a few major problems under the Act will be noted here. It is of paramount importance to remember that a lawyer cannot assume that matters will be handled in "the ordinary way" under the Act. For example:

A. A person seeking recovery must present his claim to the "appropriate federal agency" before instituting suit. 28 U.S.C.A. § 2675.

B. When a claim is made, it must be filed in the United States district court in the state where the act complained of occurred. 28 U.S.C.A. § 1402.

C. The suit will be tried by a judge and not a jury. 28 U.S.C.A. § 2402.

D. The plaintiff's attorney's contingent fee is subject to express regulation and imposition of a higher fee constitutes a federal crime. 28 U.S.C.A. § 2678. (As of August, 1981, 25% of any judgment and 20% of any settlement is the maximum amount permitted.)

5. Two major sections of the Act are the jurisdiction and general liability sections. They are quoted below:

The federal district courts "shall have exclusive jurisdiction of civil actions on claims against the United States, for money damages, accruing on or after January 1, 1945, for injury or loss of property, or personal injury or death caused by the negligent or wrongful act or omission of any employee of the Government while acting within the scope of his office or employment, under circumstances where the United States, if a private person, would be liable to the claimant in accordance with the law of the place where the act or omission occurred." 28 USCA § 1346(b).

"The United States shall be liable, respecting the provisions of this title relating to tort claims, in the same manner and to the same extent as a private individual under like circumstances, but shall not be liable for interest prior to judgment or for punitive damages.

"If, however, in any case wherein death was caused, the law of the place where the act or omission complained of occurred provides, or has been construed to provide, for damages only punitive in nature, the United States shall be liable for actual or compensatory damages, measured by the pecuniary injuries resulting from such death to the persons respectively for whose benefit the action was brought, in lieu thereof." 28 U.S.C.A. § 2674.

A. What problems of statutory interpretation can you glean from each section? Why do you think Congress did not enact a complete code of federal tort law rather than rely on the "law of the place where the tort occurred"? Should the liability of the federal government vary from state to state?

B. Would the United States appear to be subject to strict liability under the Act? Suppose it engaged in an "abnormally dangerous" activity. See Chapter 15 infra, on manufacturing a "defective" product. This matter would appear to have been finally put to rest in Laird v. Nelms, 406 U.S. 797 (1972) (sonic boom), where the Supreme Court held that the Act did not authorize suit against the government based on strict or absolute liability. Nevertheless, could you make an argument the other way based on language of the Act itself? See Peck, Absolute Liability and the Federal Tort Claims Act, 9 Stan.L.Rev. 433 (1957); Jacoby, Absolute Liability Under the Federal Tort Claims Act, 24 Fed. B.J. 139 (1964).

C. Many claims have arisen on the issue of whether a government officer or employee was "acting within his office or employment" for the purpose of the Act. See Annot., 6 A.L.R.Fed. 373 (1971). Should this be decided as a matter of state or federal law? If a government employee's negligent operation of a vehicle does come under the Act, he is shielded by it and an assistant attorney general will so contend if the employee is sued in federal court. 28 U.S.C.A. § 2679(b).

6. The Act contains 13 exceptions in 28 U.S.C.A. § 2680. Most of them deal with specific activities of the government, such as the transmission of mail, the assessment or collection of customs duties, the imposition of quarantines, the fiscal operations of the Treasury, and the like, and in particular the combatant activities of military and naval forces in time of war. The Supreme Court of the United States has adhered to the proposition that it will not "extend the waiver of sovereign immunity more broadly than has been directed by Congress." United States v. Shaw, 309 U.S. 495, 502 (1940). Thus, the matter of judicial interpretation of the exceptions is of paramount importance. Three of the most important exceptions are for:

A. "Any claim based upon an act or omission of an employee of the Government, exercising due care, in the execution of a statute or regulation, whether or not such statute or regulation be valid, or based upon the exercise or performance or the failure to exercise or perform a discretionary function or duty on the part of a federal agency or an employee of the Government, whether or not the discretion involved be abused." 28 U.S.C.A. § 2680(a).

Problems regarding the interpretation of this section are not dissimilar from those that have arisen in suits against municipalities after judicial abrogation of governmental immunity. Well developed majority and dissenting opinions on the issue appear in Griffin v. United States, 500 F.2d 1059 (3d Cir. 1974), where plaintiff suffered paralysis when she ingested polio vaccine that had been approved for public consumption by the Division of Biologic Standards of the Department of Health, Education and Welfare. Both the majority and dissenting opinions relied on the same sentence from Dalehite v. United States, 346 U.S. 15, 34–36 (1953), where the Supreme Court said: "Where there is room for policy judgment and decision there is discretion." On the discretionary-function exception and its relationship to negligence, see Downs v. United States, 522 F.2d 990 (6th Cir.1975).

Subsequent Supreme Court opinions have also attempted to distinguish decisions made at the "planning" as opposed to the "operational" level. See Indian Towing Co. v. United States, 350 U.S. 61 (1955); United States v. Union Trust Co., 350 U.S. 907 (1955). See also James, The Federal Tort Claims Act and the "Discretionary Function" Exception, 10 U.Fla.L.Rev. 184 (1957); Peck, The Federal Tort Claims Act: A Proposed Construction of the Discretionary Function Exception, 31 Wash.L.Rev. 207 (1956); Symposium, 24 Fed.B.J. 133 (1964); 26 Fed.B.J. 1 (1966).

B. "Any claim arising out of assault, battery, false imprisonment, false arrest, malicious prosecution, abuse of process, libel, slander, misrepresentation, deceit, or interference with contract rights: Provided, That, with regard to acts or omissions of investigative or law enforcement officers of the United States Government, the provisions of this chapter and section 1346(b) of this title shall apply to any claim arising, on or after the date of the enactment of this proviso, out of assault, battery, false imprisonment, false arrest, abuse of process, or malicious prosecution. For the purpose of this subsection, 'investigative or law enforcement officer' means any officer of the United States who is empowered by law to execute searches, to seize evidence, or to make arrests for violations of Federal law." 28 U.S.C.A. § 2680(h).

This section contains many familiar words from tort law. Should they be construed by looking to local state or federal common law? In Moos v. United States, 118 F.Supp. 275 (D.Minn.1954), the plaintiff underwent an operation in a veteran's hospital, and the surgeon mistakenly, and negligently, operated on the wrong hip and leg. It was held that there was no liability under the Act, because under the law of Minnesota this was technically a battery. Compare Lane v. United States, 225 F.Supp. 850 (E.D.Va.1964).

In the principal case the court's construction of the word "misrepresentation" led to dismissal of plaintiff's claim. Why was not the case one of simple negligence? In Rahn v. United States, 222 F.Supp. 775 (D.C.Ga.1963), plaintiff was misled when physicians at an Air Force hospital assured her that her broken arm was properly set and progressing satisfactorily. She suffered serious permanent injury as a result. The court held that her claim was based on negligence, not misrepresentation. How is the principal case to be distinguished? This section has withstood attack on its constitutionality. See, e.g., Gardner v. United States, 446 F.2d 1195 (2d Cir.1971). But see the later case of Block v. Neal, 460 U.S. 289 (1983), involving a negligent inspection resulting in an erroneous representation, and holding that a negligence action might lie.

C. 28 U.S.C.A. § 2680(j) provides that the Federal Tort Claims Act does not apply to any "claim arising out of the combatant activities of the military or naval forces, or the Coast Guard, during time of war."

Shortly after the end of World War II, the Supreme Court held that those who served on active duty may not recover under the Federal Tort Claims Act for claims arising out of or in the course of activity incident to their service. Feres v. United States, 340 U.S. 135 (1950). Rationales for the doctrine include the need for uniformity of law, the health and welfare benefits provided to servicemen and their dependents, the absence of private liability in like circumstances, and the potential for disrupting military discipline. The doctrine has undergone close scrutiny recently in light of a variety of incidents affecting large numbers of people. See Note, The Feres Doctrine: Will It Survive the Radiation Exposure Cases?, 37 Mercer L.Rev. 839 (1986). What are the downsides of this type of immunity?

The definition of "incident to service" has been exhaustively litigated over the past 35–40 years, most of the cases involving soldiers struck by government vehicles while on varying degrees of leave. Cases are collected in 1 L. Jayson, Personal Injury: Handling Federal Tort Claims, § 155 (1986). The doctrine was extended to shield the government against contribution or indemnity claims brought by manufacturers of products who could be sued by service personnel. Stencel Aero Eng'g Corp. v. United States, 431 U.S. 666 (1977), reh'g denied, 434 U.S. 882 (1977). But the Supreme Court refused to extend this protection of the government from contribution and indemnity claims when a civilian government employee's suit was the underlying basis for the contribution claim. Lockheed Aircraft Corp. v. United States, 460 U.S. 190 (1983).

The Supreme Court in a 5–4 decision recently upheld and expanded the *Feres* Doctrine to bar tort claims by military personnel for negligence against civilian government workers. United States v. Johnson, ___ U.S. ___, 107 S.Ct. 2063, 95 L.Ed.2d 648 (1987), on remand, 828 F.2d 671 (11th Cir.1987).

7. As the principal case indicates, if a claimant is unsuccessful under the Federal Tort Claims Act, all is not necessarily lost. It is still possible to obtain relief by private bill. This is a difficult procedure requiring full cooperation of a Congressman, plus tremendous persistence by an attorney. See Note, Private Bills, 79 Harv.L.Rev. 1684 (1966).

8. See generally Wright, The Federal Tort Claims Act (1957); and there are good general discussions in Gottlieb, The Federal Tort Claims Act—A Statutory Interpretation, 35 Geo.L.J. 1 (1946); Anderson, Recovery from the United States under the Federal Tort Claims Act, 31 Minn.L.Rev. 456 (1947); Baer, Suing Uncle Sam in Tort, 26 N.C.L.Rev. 119 (1948); Gellhorn and Lauer, Federal Liability for Personal and Property Damage, 29 N.Y.U.L.Rev. 1325 (1954); Gerwig, A Decade of Litigation Under the Federal Tort Claims Act, 24 Tenn.L.Rev. 301 (1957); Gottlieb, The Tort Claims Act Revisited, 49 Geo.L.J. 539 (1961); Note, 22 Mo.L.Rev. 48 (1957). See also the symposia in 24 Fed.B.J. 133 (1964); 26 Fed.B.J. 1 (1966); and 7 Vand.L.Rev. 175 (1954).

(E) Public Officers

Public officers are subject to personal liability for tortious conduct committed in the course of their official duties. Claims against them may be predicated on the common law of torts, special statutes (a prime example being the Civil Rights Act of 1871, 42 U.S.C.A. § 1983), or a provision of the United States Constitution. See Bivens v. Six Unknown Named Agents, 403 U.S. 388 (1971), infra page 1171.

In each of these situations the public official may be shielded from liability if his conduct comes within common law official immunity—a doctrine that is separate and apart from governmental immunity. Thus, if governmental immunity is abolished, his own immunity may still protect a public official. Conversely, when the state has not consented to be sued on a matter (for example, the intentional torts exempted from coverage in the Federal Tort Claims Act), a public official may be liable if his conduct does not come within the immunity discussed in this section.

It should be noted here that sometimes when the legislature has waived governmental immunity, it has granted immunity to a public employee whose negligent conduct will now be paid for by the state. An example can be found in the Federal Tort Claims Act. 28 U.S.C.A. § 2679(b) provides that the remedy against the United States for negligent operation of motor vehicles is exclusive of any remedy against a driver employee. See Annot., 16 A.L.R.3d 1394 (1967). See also Agnew v. Porter, 23 Ohio St.2d 18, 260 N.E.2d 830 (1970) (construing state statute that protected policemen from tort claims based on their operation of motor vehicles while responding to emergency calls). If this makes sense, should it be extended to other types of torts committed by government employees?

The common law immunity for public officers would appear to be based "not so much [on a] desire to protect an erring officer as * * * [on] a recognition of the need of preserving independence of action, without deterrence or intimidation by the fear of personal liability and vexatious suits." Restatement (Second) of Torts § 895D, comment b; see the classic statement of Learned Hand, J., in Gregoire v. Biddle, 177 F.2d 579 (2d Cir.1944) (federal prosecutor).

Legislators and judges have been granted absolute immunity for acts committed within the scope of their office even if they acted in bad faith. See, e.g., Tenney v. Brandhove, 341 U.S. 367 (1951) (legislators); Pierson v. Ray, 386 U.S. 547 (1967) (judges).

Federal executive officers, even at lower levels, appeared also to benefit from the immunity. See Barr v. Matteo, 360 U.S. 564 (1959).

The President of the United States is absolutely immune for acts within the scope of his office. Nixon v. Fitzgerald, 457 U.S. 731 (1982). But presidential aides are entitled only to a qualified immunity. Harlow v. Fitzgerald, 457 U.S. 800 (1982).

State executive officers in some states also have the benefit of absolute immunity with regard to common law torts committed in the course of their official duties. In other states, the immunity is qualified; in some, it depends upon whether the harmful action was taken in good faith, and in others it depends on whether the official had a reasonable basis for taking the action.

When the immunity is qualified, it becomes similar in an operative sense to a "privilege," see supra page 608, and perhaps the major reason to preserve the label of "immunity" is to signify that it applies to negligent as well as intentional conduct.

A qualified immunity appears to be the standard developed with respect to violations of the Civil Rights Act of 1871 (42 U.S.C.A. § 1983). See Scheuer v. Rhodes, 416 U.S. 232 (1974); Wood v. Strickland, 420 U.S. 308 (1975). A state official may be deemed to have violated the act if he knew or reasonably should have known that his conduct would violate plaintiff's constitutional rights or if he took the action in bad faith. On the other hand, a prosecuting attorney is held to have absolute immunity under the Act. See Imbler v. Pachtman, 424 U.S. 409 (1976). Why should he be distinguished from officials in the executive branch of the government?

In the leading case of Butz v. Economou, 438 U.S. 478 (1978), the Supreme Court reviewed and reevaluated all of its relevant earlier cases. It held that federal executive officers are normally subject to the qualified immunity established for actions under § 1983. An absolute immunity is available, however, for an administrative officer who engages in an adjudicatory function in an administrative hearing similar to that of a judge, and also to an agency officer who performs a function similar to that of a prosecuting attorney in initiating or continuing a proceeding or arranging for the presentation of evidence in the course of an administrative adjudication. The holding in this case may prove to be quite influential on the state courts in laying down rules for state administrative officers. What about the analogy to legislators and the promulgation of administrative rules and regulations?

Official immunity is applied only with respect to acts that are "discretionary" as opposed to "ministerial" in nature. This distinction, which we have seen evolving in the area of governmental immunity, has not been an easy one to apply. Obviously, if the official was engaged in formulating policy at a high level in government, his conduct will be deemed "discretionary." Can you think of examples? How would you classify the conduct of a police chief in regard to his method of training officers? See Carter v. Carlson, 144 U.S.App.D.C. 388, 447 F.2d 358 (1971), rev'd on other grounds sub nom., District of Columbia v. Carter, 409 U.S. 418 (1973). Comment f to Section 895D of Restatement (Second) of Torts sets forth most of the factors courts have looked to when they have attempted to classify an official's conduct as "discretionary" or "ministerial."

Assuming that an official is engaged in a "discretionary" act, he will lose the cloak of the immunity if he acts "wholly" without jurisdiction. Does this seem an easy rule to apply? Two recent examples where the official went "over the line" include a judge who, without statutory authority, ordered an individual sterilized, Wade v. Bethesda Hosp., 337 F.Supp. 671 (D.C.Ohio 1971); and a city mayor who ordered his police officers to "shoot first and ask questions later." Palmer v. Hall, 380 F.Supp. 120 (D.C.Ga.1974).

While there has been little litigation on the point, the doctrine of vicarious liability would not appear to be applicable to hold public officials liable for torts committed by lower echelon employees, at least when the officials in no way personally participated in the wrongdoing. See, e.g., Carter v. Allan, 94 Idaho 190, 484 P.2d 739 (1971) (suit against mayor and city councilman for injuries caused by negligently constructed sidewalk).

See Restatement (Second) of Torts § 895D; Bermann, Integrating Governmental and Officer Tort Liability, 77 Colum.L.Rev. 1175 (1977); Black, Suits Against Government Officers and the Sovereign Immunity, 55 Harv.L.Rev. 1060 (1946); Gray, Private Wrongs of Public Servants, 47 Calif.L.Rev. 303 (1959); Jaffe, Judicial Control of Administrative Action, ch. 7 (1965); James, Tort Liability of Governmental Units and Their Officers, 22 U.Chi.L.Rev. 610 (1955); Jennings, Tort Liability of Administrative Officers, 21 Minn.L.Rev. 263 (1937); Mashaw, Civil Liability of Government Officers: Property Rights and Official Accountability, 42 L. & Cont.Prob. 8 (1978); Casto, Innovations in the Defense of Official Immunity Under § 1983, 47 Tenn.L.Rev. 47 (1979); Kattan, Knocking on Wood: Some Thoughts on the Immunities of State Officials to Civil Rights Damage Actions, 30 Vand.L.Rev. 941 (1977); Fox, The King Can Do No Wrong: A Critique of the Current Status of Sovereign and Official Immunity, 25 Wayne L.Rev. 177 (1979); K. Sowle, Qualified Immunity in § 1983 Cases: The Unresolved Issues of the Conditions for Its Use and Burden of Persuasion, 55 Tul.L.Rev. 326 (1981); Wade, Tort Law as Ombudsman, 65 Ore.L.Rev. 309 (1986). And see in general P. Schuck, Suing Government (1983).

Chapter XIII

IMPUTED NEGLIGENCE

A is negligent; B is not. "Imputed negligence" means that, by reason of some relation existing between A and B, the negligence of A is charged against B, although B has played no part in it, has done nothing to aid or encourage it, and in fact may have done all that he possibly could to prevent it. The result may be that B, in an action against C for his own injuries, is barred from recovery because of A's negligence, to the same extent as if he had been negligent himself. This is commonly called "imputed contributory negligence." Or the result may be that B, in C's action against him, becomes liable as a defendant for C's injuries, to the same extent as if he had been negligent himself. This is sometimes called "imputed negligence." More often it is called vicarious liability, or the principle is said to be that of *respondeat superior*, which may be freely translated, "look to the person higher up." The topic is covered in depth in a course in Agency. Only highlights closely related to torts are presented in this Chapter.

1. VICARIOUS LIABILITY

(A) RESPONDEAT SUPERIOR

LUNDBERG v. STATE

Court of Appeals of New York, 1969.
25 N.Y.2d 467, 255 N.E.2d 177, 306 N.Y.S.2d 947.

[Plaintiff's decedent, John Lundberg, was killed when his car was struck by an automobile negligently driven by John Sandilands, an engineering technician employed by New York State. At the time of the accident Sandilands was driving from Buffalo (his home) to a reservoir project approximately 80 miles away. The state reimbursed Sandilands for his living expenses while away from home and paid him 9 cents a mile to cover the expenses of his trip. Plaintiff brought a survival and wrongful death action against both Sandilands and the state.]

SCILEPPI, JUDGE. * * * The action against Sandilands was settled for $20,000. The one against the State went to trial and resulted in a judgment for more than $73,000. The Appellate Division, Fourth Department, unanimously affirmed and the State is appealing by permission of this court from the order of affirmance.

The sole issue presented by this appeal is whether the State of New York should be held liable, pursuant to the doctrine of *respondeat*

643

superior, for the pain and suffering and wrongful death caused by its employee's negligence. It is our opinion that Sandilands was not acting in the scope of his employment while driving from Buffalo to his work site and that, therefore, the complaint against the defendant State should have been dismissed.

Under the doctrine of *respondeat superior,* an employer will be liable for the negligence of an employee committed while the employee is acting in the scope of his employment [c]. An employee acts in the scope of his employment when he is doing something in furtherance of the duties he owes to his employer and where the employer is, or could be, exercising some control, directly or indirectly, over the employee's activities [cc]. As a general rule, an employee driving to and from work is not acting in the scope of his employment [cc]. Although such activity is work motivated, the element of control is lacking. An exception to this rule is, that an employee who uses his car in further-ance of his work is acting in the scope of his employment while driving home from his last business appointment, since such a person is working, and is under his employer's control, from the time he leaves the house in the morning until he returns at night [cc]. In the instant case, however, the employee was not driving his car in furtherance of his work at the time of the accident. He was engaged in an indepen-dent personal activity over which the State had no control. Thus, the general rule applies.   *   *   *

[I]n the instant case it is our opinion that it has been established, as a matter of law, that Sandilands was not acting in the scope of his employment. Firstly, Sandilands was not driving to satisfy an obliga-tion he owed to his employer but solely to satisfy his personal desire to visit his home in Buffalo. Moreover, the State clearly did not have the power to control Sandilands' activities after the close of work on Friday until the commencement of work on Monday. During these hours, Sandilands was free to do as he pleased. He could have chosen to remain in Salamanca or in the alternative to travel by any available means, to any place he desired, including Buffalo. In our opinion the mere fact that the State had agreed to pay Sandilands' travel expenses, in the form of a mileage allowance, did not bestow in it any right of control. To hold that by simply paying his travel expenses to his home the State opened itself to liability for any tortious act he might commit while traveling between Buffalo and the work site would be patently unfair and beyond the scope of the doctrine of *respondeat superior* (Restatement, 2d Agency, § 239; see 52 A.L.R.2d 290, 325).   *   *   *

Accordingly, the order of the Appellate Division should be reversed and the claim against the defendant dismissed.

BURKE, JUDGE (dissenting).   *   *   * Of particular relevance in this case, as distinguished from the vague and theoretical question of "right to control", is the test for liability posited by former Chief Judge Cardozo in Matter of Marks v. Gray, 251 N.Y. 90, 93–94, 167 N.E. 181, 183: "The test in brief is this: If the work of the employee creates the necessity for travel, he is in the course of his employment, though he is serving at the same time some purpose of his own" [c]. The undisputed facts in the present case clearly indicate that that test has been met. Sandilands' temporary employment at a work site 80 miles from his permanent station and home in Buffalo created the necessity for his travel between Buffalo and the work site. While so traveling, he was clearly acting in furtherance of his employment * * *. The mere fact that his traveling back and forth was motivated by his desire to see his family occasionally in no way detracts from the fact that the trips would not have been made at all had it not been for his assignment to a distant work site.

In addition, it should be recognized that the fact that the State paid Sandilands' travel expenses for these trips is significant not because it has any relation to some theoretical "right to control" but precisely because it indicates that the State recognized that Sandilands' employment necessitated such travel and acquiesced in his use of his own automobile for that travel. * * * Accordingly, the order of the Appellate Division should be affirmed.

FRUIT v. SCHREINER

Supreme Court of Alaska, 1972.
502 P.2d 133.

[Clay Fruit, a life insurance salesman, was required to attend a sales convention conducted by his employer, The Equitable Life Assurance Society. Fruit drove his own car, but was reimbursed for his expenditures. The convention included social as well as business events, and he was "encouraged to mix freely" with out-of-state insurance experts in order "to learn as much as possible about sales techniques." On the second evening of the convention, after all business-related activities and scheduled social events were long over, Fruit drove to the Waterfront Bar and Restaurant in order to look for some out-of-state colleagues. Finding none, he drove back toward the convention center. On this journey, at approximately 2:00 a.m., he skidded across a highway and struck a disabled vehicle. John Schreiner was standing in front of that vehicle and his legs were crushed in the impact. Schreiner brought a personal injury claim against both Fruit and his employer. The jury found that Fruit was negligent and awarded Schreiner $635,000.]

BOOCHEVER, JUSTICE. * * * The jury found that Fruit was an employee acting within the course and scope of his employment for Equitable at the time and place of the accident. Under the doctrine of *respondeat superior* (which simply means "let the employer answer") Equitable would thus be liable for Fruit's acts of negligence despite lack of fault on Equitable's part.

Equitable argues, however, that the evidence was insufficient to establish that Fruit was acting within the course and scope of his employment. Equitable contends that any business purpose was completed when Fruit left the Waterfront Bar and Restaurant. It cites cases holding that an employee traveling to his home or other personal destination cannot ordinarily be regarded as acting in the scope of his employment. But Fruit was not returning to his home. He was traveling to the convention headquarters where he was attending meetings as a part of his employment.

In addition, Equitable seeks to narrow the scope of *respondeat superior* to those situations where the master has exercised control over the activities of employees. Disposition of this issue requires an analysis of the doctrine of *respondeat superior,* one of the few anomalies to the general tort doctrine of no liability without fault.

The origins of the principle whereby an employer may be held vicariously liable for the injuries wrought by his employee are in dispute. Justice Holmes traces the concept to Roman law while Wigmore finds it to be of Germanic origin. The doctrine emerged in English law in the 17th Century. Initially a master was held liable for those acts which he commanded or to which he expressly assented. This was expanded to include acts by implied command or authority and eventually to acts within the scope of employment. The modern theory evolved with the growth of England's industry and commerce.

A truly imaginative variety of rationales have been advanced by courts and glossators in justification of this imposition of liability on employers. Among the suggestions are the employer's duty to hire and maintain a responsible staff of employees, to "control" the activities of his employees and thus to insist upon appropriate safety measures; the belief that the employer should pay for the inherent risks which result from hiring others to carry on his business; the observation that the employer most often has easier access to evidence of the facts surrounding the injury; and the metaphysical identification of the employer and employee as a single "persona" jointly liable for the injury which occurred in the context of the business.

Baty more cynically states: "In hard fact, the reason for the employers' liability is the damages are taken from a deep pocket." Baty, Vicarious Liability 11 (1916).

The two theories which carry the greatest weight in contemporary legal thought are respectively, the "control" theory which finds liability whenever the act of the employee was committed with the implied authority, acquiescence or subsequent ratification of the employer, and the "enterprise" theory which finds liability whenever the enterprise of the employer would have benefited by the context of the act of the employee but for the unfortunate injury.

Since we are dealing with vicarious liability, justification may not be found on theories involving the employer's personal fault such as his failure to exercise proper control over the activities of his employees or his failure to take proper precautions in firing or hiring them. Lack of care on the employer's part would subject him to direct liability without the necessity of involving *respondeat superior.* * * *

The aspect of the relationship most commonly advanced to delimit the theory is the "scope of employment" of the employee-tortfeasor. While the factual determination generally is left to the jury, many cases lying in the penumbras of "scope of employment" have produced confusing and contradictory legal results in the development of an otherwise worthy doctrine of law. To assist in delineating the areas of tortious conduct imposing liability, it is helpful to consider what we believe to be the correct philosophical basis for the doctrine.

There was a time when the artisans, shopkeepers and master craftsmen could directly oversee the activities of their apprentices and journeymen. * * * But in the present day when hundreds of persons divide labors under the same corporate roof and produce a single product for market to an unidentified consumer, the communal spirit and shared commitment of enterprises from another age is sacrificed to other efficiencies. At the same time, the impersonal nature of such complex enterprises and their mechanization make third parties considerably more vulnerable to injury incidentally arising from the pursuit of the business. Business corporations are granted a personal identification in legal fiction to limit liability of the investors, but not to insulate the corporate entity itself from liability for the unfortunate consequences of its enterprise.

"Scope of employment" as a test for application of *respondeat superior* would be insufficient if it failed to encompass the duty of every enterprise to the social community which gives it life and contributes to its prosperity. * * *

The basis of *respondeat superior* has been correctly stated as "the desire to include in the costs of operation inevitable losses to third persons incident to carrying on an enterprise, and thus distribute the burden among those benefited by the enterprise." [C]

The desirability of the result is readily discernible when an employee obviously engaged in his employer's business causes injury to a third party as a result of the employee's negligence. * * * Insurance is readily available for the employer so that the risk may be distributed among many like insureds paying premiums and the extra cost of doing business may be reflected in the price of the product.

The principle has been recognized by every state in the enactment of workmen's compensation laws whereby employees may recover compensation for injuries arising out of and in the course of their employment without reference to negligence on the part of employers. The costs to the employers are distributed to the public in the price of the product. * * *

The rule of *respondeat superior,* however, has not been extended to that length and is limited to requiring an enterprise to bear the loss incurred as a result of the employee's negligence. The acts of the employee need be so connected to his employment as to justify requiring that the employer bear that loss.

Although not usually enunciated as a basis for liability, in essence the enterprise may be regarded as a unit for tort as opposed to contract liability purposes. Employees' acts sufficiently connected with the enterprise are in effect considered as deeds of the enterprise itself. Where through negligence such acts cause injury to others it is appropriate that the enterprise bear the loss incurred.

Consistent with these considerations, it is apparent that no categorical statement can delimit the meaning of "scope of employment" once and for all times. Applicability of *respondeat superior* will depend primarily on the findings of fact in each case. In this particular case, Clay Fruit's employment contract required that he attend the sales conference. Each employee was left to his own resources for transportation, and many of the agents, including Fruit, chose to drive their own automobiles. By the admission of Equitable's agency manager, the scope of the conference included informal socializing as well as formal meetings. Social contact with the out-of-state guests was encouraged, and there is undisputed evidence that such associations were not limited to the conference headquarters * * *.

Because we find that fair-minded men in the exercise of reasonable judgment could differ as to whether Fruit's activities in returning from [the Waterfront Bar] to the convention headquarters were within the scope of his employment, we are not disposed to upset the jury's conclusion that liability for damages may be vicariously imputed to Equitable. * * *

The judgment below is affirmed.

---

1. The various rules that have imputed the negligence of one person to another in order to impose vicarious liability upon him as a defendant all have one thing in common. Each rule has involved an effort, sometimes openly declared by the court, more often unexpressed or tacitly assumed, to find a financially responsible defendant. The plaintiff is injured; his life may be utterly ruined if he is left without compensation. The person who has injured him is, or is likely to be, unable to pay that compensation. There is another who stands in such a relation to the wrongdoer that it is not unreasonable to make the responsibility his; and that other is more likely to be able to pay. So, without exonerating the wrongdoer, who remains liable to the plaintiff and will be required to indemnify the other to the extent that he is able to do so, the liability is imposed upon both.

In one sense this is strict liability, since the new person who is held liable is without any fault of his own and becomes liable only by reason of his relation to the actual wrongdoer. In another it is not. The foundation of vicarious liability is still negligence or other fault on the part of someone; and what the law does is to broaden the liability for that fault by imposing it upon an additional defendant who is himself without fault.

2. A prime example of vicarious liability is the doctrine of *respondeat superior* as discussed in the principal cases. It operates when an employee is "within the scope of his employment." There have been literally thousands of cases exploring this issue. See Prince v. Atchison, Topeka and Santa Fe Ry.

Co., 76 Ill.App.3d 898, 32 Ill.Dec. 362, 395 N.E.2d 592 (1979), aff'd, 95 Ill.App.3d 856, 51 Ill.Dec. 323, 420 N.E.2d 737 (1981), where the court used a two-pronged test to determine whether an employee who went on a "frolic" had reentered the scope of his employment. They not only focus on when employment has begun or ended, but also on whether the employee or servant is "going on a frolic of his own." (The phrase was first uttered in 1834 by Baron Parke in Joel v. Morrison, 6 C. & P. 501, 172 Eng.Rep. 1338.) In general, an employee's commuting to and from work is not considered within the scope of his employment. Robarge v. Bechtel Power Corp., 131 Ariz. 280, 640 P.2d 211 (1982). As the principal cases reflect, the resolutions to these questions may depend less on linguistics than on the rationale the court selects as a basis of *respondeat superior*. An interesting example of this is Mauk v. Wright, 367 F.Supp. 961 (M.D.Pa.1973), where the court explained how a football player on his own "free time" during training camp could still be deemed "within the scope of employment." In one case an employee became drunk at an office Christmas party, and then drove home. His negligent driving caused plaintiff's injury. Was the employee in the scope of his employment? On what does the answer depend? See Harris v. Trojan Fireworks Co., 120 Cal.App.3d 157, 174 Cal.Rptr. 452 (1981), aff'd, 155 Cal.App.3d 830, 202 Cal.Rptr. 404 (1984). In another case it was an employee's negligent handling of a cigarette that led to plaintiff's injury. Would that act come within *respondeat superior* under the *Lundberg* case? See Edgewater Motels, Inc. v. Gatzke, 277 N.W.2d 11 (Minn.1979).

3. Courts agree that the master cannot insulate himself from liability by imposing safety rules or by instructing his employees to proceed carefully—no matter how specific and detailed his orders may be. See Limpus v. London Gen. Omnibus Co., 1 H. & C. 526, 158 Eng.Rep. 993 (1862); Cosgrove v. Ogden, 49 N.Y. 255 (1872). Recently this principle was applied when a neighbor's property was damaged by fire from trash that an employee burned in violation of the employer's orders. See Poydras v. Parker, 392 So.2d 94 (La.App.1980). Also when an employee used a firearm in direct contravention of his employer's order. Frederick v. Collins, 378 S.W.2d 617 (Ky.1964).

4. *Respondeat superior* is not limited to negligent torts. An employer may be held liable for the intentional torts of his servant when they are reasonably connected with the employment and so within its "scope." Thus the master may be liable for assault and battery on the part of a servant trying to collect a debt for him, because the servant is still acting in furtherance of his master's business; and the same may be true of false imprisonment, malicious prosecution, defamation, deceit or intentional infliction of emotional distress. See Chuy v. Philadelphia Eagles Football Club, 595 F.2d 1265 (3d Cir.1979). But when the employee acts from purely personal motives, as for example out of a desire to revenge the seduction of his wife, or in a quarrel in no way connected with the master's interests, he is considered to have departed from his employment and the master is not liable. The courts have had difficulty applying this test. What should be the result: When a tenant is raped by the manager of an apartment complex? Ponticas v. K.M.S. Invs., 331 N.W.2d 907 (Minn.1983). When an employee in a bar gives a customer a "hot foot"? Sullivan v. Crowley, 307 Mass. 189, 29 N.E.2d 769 (1940). When a gas station attendant shoots a customer who refused to pay cash? Jefferson v. Rose Oil Co. of Dixie, 232 So.2d 895 (La.App.1970). When a supervisor who dislikes a subordinate employee slanderously reports that he stole company funds? Newton v. Spence, 20 Md. App. 126, 316 A.2d 837 (1974). When an employee bus driver encourages one of his passengers to assault a bicyclist? Weysham v. New Orleans Public Serv.

Inc., 385 So.2d 19 (La.App.), cert. denied, 392 So.2d 690 (La.1980). When a professional baseball pitcher intentionally "beans" a heckling spectator? Manning v. Grimsley, 643 F.2d 20 (1st Cir.1981). When an employee assaults an unarmed woman with a loaded, semi-automatic rifle? Jordan v. Medley, 228 U.S.App.D.C. 425, 711 F.2d 211 (1983). See Annots., 34 A.L.R.2d 372 (1954), 22 A.L.R.2d 1227 (1952), 172 A.L.R. 532 (1948), 38 A.L.R. 4th 225 (1983).

5.   There has been some indication of a tendency to liberalize these rules. For example, in Ira S. Bushey & Sons, Inc. v. United States, 398 F.2d 167 (2d Cir.1968), a very drunken sailor was returning from shore leave to his Coast Guard cutter, which was in the plaintiff's floating drydock. On his way along the drydock wall, the mariner decided, for no reason ever discovered, to turn three heavy wheels that controlled the water level in the drydock. As a result, the ship began to list and then fell off its blocks against the wall. This caused the drydock to partially sink. There was no indication that he had been motivated by a purpose to serve the Coast Guard. Friendly, J., threw the motive test overboard, after the drydock. He also rejected any policy questions as to who could best take out insurance or absorb the loss. Instead he went back to the much older approach and considered that when an enterprise creates risks to society the employer should be required to pay his way. It should be liable for "accidents which may be said to be characteristic of its activities." The court considered the risk here "characteristic" of the conditions of employment and not unforeseeble by the employer. Reference was made to the well-known "proclivity of seamen to find solace for solitude by copious resort to the bottle when ashore." The case is discussed in a good Note in 82 Harv.L.Rev. 1568 (1969). How would this test resolve the cases cited in note 4, supra?

6.   To be distinguished are cases in which the master is liable for his own negligence in hiring or retaining servants whom he has reason to believe will cause injury to other persons. Suppose the employer retains an employee who had previously shot a patron of employer's discotheque. Later the employee shoots another patron. Should the employer be liable? See Freeman v. Bell, 366 So.2d 197 (La.App.1978). See also Otis Eng'g Corp. v. Clark, 668 S.W.2d 307 (Tex.1983) (employer has a duty to exercise control over intoxicated employee to prevent unreasonable risk of harm to others). With so many woman entering the workforce, a growing concern is employer liability for sexual harassment. See, e.g., Machlowitz, Preventing Sexual Harassment, 73 A.B.A.J. 78 (Oct. 1, 1987). But see F & T Co. v. Woods, 92 N.M. 697, 594 P.2d 745 (1979) (employer retained an alleged rapist to deliver and repair home appliances and was sued by a rape victim).

7.   See, holding that parents were jointly and severally liable for negligently hiring an abusive babysitter, when the parents retained the babysitter despite their child's bruises and fears, Glomb v. Ginosky, 366 Pa.Super. 206, 530 A.2d 1362 (1987).

8.   In some situations, a master can seek indemnity from either a servant or an independent contractor who has assets of his own. See pages 392–403.

9.   There is a vast amount of literature about all this. See, for example, Baty, Vicarious Liability, ch. 8 (1916); Laski, The Basis of Vicarious Liability, 26 Yale L.J. 105 (1916); Smith, Frolic and Detour, 23 Colum.L.Rev. 444, 456 (1923); Seavey, Speculations as to "Respondeat Superior," Harvard Legal Essays, 433 (1934); Douglas, Vicarious Liability and the Administration of Risk,

38 Yale L.J. 584, 720 (1929); Ferson, Bases for Master's Liability and for Principal's Liability to Third Persons, 4 Vand.L.Rev. 260 (1951); Morris, Hazardous Enterprises and Risk Bearing Capacity, 61 Yale L.J. 1172 (1952); Morris, Enterprise Liability and the Actuarial Process—The Insignificance of Foresight, 70 Yale L.J. 554 (1961); Sykes, The Economics of Vicarious Liability, 93 Yale L.J. 1231 (1984); Annot., 53 A.L.R.3d 664 (1973).

(B) INDEPENDENT CONTRACTORS

MURRELL v. GOERTZ

Court of Appeals of Oklahoma, 1979.
597 P.2d 1223.

REYNOLDS, JUDGE. Mrs. C.L. Murrell, plaintiff in the trial court, appeals the order sustaining the motion for summary judgment in favor of co-defendant Oklahoma Publishing Company (appellee), in a suit for damages resulting from an alleged assault and battery by co-defendant Bruce Goertz.

On August 27, 1976, Bruce Goertz was making monthly collections for the delivery of appellant's morning newspaper, the Daily Oklahoman, which is published by appellee. Appellant questioned Goertz concerning damage to appellant's screen door caused by the newspaper carrier throwing the newspaper into it. An argument ensued culminating in appellant slapping Goertz who in turn struck appellant. As a result thereof, appellant was allegedly injured, requiring medical treatment and subsequent hospitalization. Appellant filed suit in the District Court of Oklahoma County seeking a total of $52,500 for past and future medical expenses, pain and suffering, and exemplary damages.

Appellant's petition contends that Goertz was a servant of appellee either by agreement between the co-defendants, or by appellee creating the apparent belief in appellant that Goertz was a servant by allowing Goertz to deliver the paper, advertise that product, and to collect for accounts due. Both appellee and Goertz answered denying that Goertz was appellee's servant. * * *

The line of demarcation between an independent contractor and a servant is not clearly drawn. An independent contractor is one who engaged to perform a certain service for another according to his own methods and manner, free from control and direction of his employer in all matters connected with the performance of the service except as to the result thereof. [C] The parties agree that the decisive test for determining whether a person is an employee or an independent contractor is the right to control the physical details of the work. [C] * * *

Appellant contends that the distribution of papers and the collection of money therefor is an integral part of appellee's business. Appellant cites the following factors as indicative of the high degree of control appellee possesses over the physical details of the work: ultimate control over the territorial boundaries of Goertz's route; appellee set a standard policy that paper deliveries be completed by 6 a.m.; appellee set policy that all papers were to be held by rubber bands; customers who were missed by the carrier called appellee to report it; complaints concerning the service were lodged with appellee; and new subscribers called appellee to initiate newspaper service.

Appellee submits that the affidavit of Russell Westbrook and Goertz's deposition reveal that Goertz had no contact with appellee. Westbrook stated that he was an independent newspaper distributor for appellee and that he employed Bruce Goertz as an independent carrier salesman. Westbrook further stated that Goertz was responsible only to him for the delivery of the newspapers and was in no way under the supervision, dominion, and control of appellee. By the terms of Westbrook's contract, he was an independent contractor and likewise not subject to the supervision, dominion, and control of appellee as to the manner and method of performing his job. Appellee further cites the statements of Westbrook and Goertz that Goertz was collecting money for Westbrook at the time of the incident with appellant, and that appellee received money only from Westbrook.

From a review of the record we conclude that the evidence is reasonably susceptible of but one inference. Bruce Goertz was hired as an independent carrier salesman by his friend Russell Westbrook, who was himself an independent contractor. Appellee had no input into the decision to hire Goertz and had no knowledge of his employment. Goertz had no direct contract with appellee in his business operations. While appellee established certain policies and standards to which all distributors and carriers were to adhere, such policies and standards do not rise to that level of supervision, dominion, and control over Goertz's day to day activities as to make him appellee's servant.

Affirmed.

MALONEY v. RATH

Supreme Court of California, 1968.
69 Cal.2d 442, 445 P.2d 513, 71 Cal.Rptr. 897.

[Defendant's automobile collided with a car driven by plaintiff. The accident was caused by a brake failure. The trial court found that defendant had no reason to know the brakes were defective. Three months prior to the accident, defendant had her brakes overhauled by a mechanic, Peter Evanchik. The trial court determined that Evanchik's negligent repair effort was the cause of the accident and rendered a judgment in favor of defendant. Plaintiff appealed.

The Supreme Court of California first stated that it would not hold a motorist strictly liable for damage caused by brake failure. Although the state vehicle code required that brakes be maintained "in good working order," a failure to comply could be excused by the owner's exercise of "ordinary prudence," and the court found that defendant had met that standard of care. It then discussed the question of whether defendant vehicle owner could delegate the responsibility of making a brake repair to an independent contractor.]

TRAYNOR, JUSTICE. 　*　*　* Unlike strict liability, a nondelegable duty operates, not as a substitute for liability based on negligence, but to assure that when a negligently caused harm occurs, the injured party will be compensated by the person whose activity caused the harm and who may therefore properly be held liable for the negligence of his agent, whether his agent was an employee or an independent contractor. To the extent that recognition of nondelegable duties tends to insure that there will be [a] financially responsible defendant available to compensate for the negligent harms caused by that defendant's activity, it ameliorates the need for strict liability to secure compensation. 　*　*　*

[W]e have found nondelegable duties in a wide variety of situations and have recognized that the rules set forth in the Restatement of Torts with respect to such duties are generally in accord with California law. Such duties include those imposed by a public authority as a condition of granting a franchise [cc], the duty of a condemning agent to protect a severed parcel from damage [c], the duty of a general contractor to construct a building safely [c], the duty to exercise due care when an "　*　*　* independent contractor is employed to do work which the employer should recognize as necessarily creating a condition involving an unreasonable risk of bodily harm to others unless special precautions are taken" [cc], the duty of landowners to maintain their property in a reasonably safe condition [cc], and to comply with applicable safety ordinances [cc], and the duty of employers and suppliers to comply with the safety provisions of the Labor Code [cc].

Restatement (Second) of Torts § 423 provides that "One who carries on an activity which threatens a grave risk of serious bodily harm or death unless the instrumentalities used are carefully 　*　*　* maintained, and who employs an independent contractor to 　*　*　* maintain such instrumentalities, is subject to the same liability for physical harm caused by the negligence of the contractor in 　*　*　* maintaining such instrumentalities as though the employer had himself done the work of 　*　*　* maintenance." Section 424 provides that "One who by statute or by administrative regulation is under a duty to provide specified safeguards or precautions for the safety of others is subject to liability to the others for whose protection the duty is imposed for harm caused by the failure of a contractor employed by him to provide such safeguards or precautions." Both of these sections point to a nondelegable duty in this case. The statutory provisions regulating the maintenance and equipment of automobiles constitute express legislative recognition of the fact that improperly maintained motor vehicles threaten "a grave risk of serious bodily harm or death." The responsibility for minimizing that risk or compensating for the failure to do so properly rests with the person who owns and operates the vehicle. He is the party primarily to be benefited by its use; he selects the contractor and is free to insist upon one who is financially responsible and to demand indemnity from him; the cost of his liability insurance that distributes the risk is properly attributable to his activities; and the discharge of the duty to exercise reasonable care in the maintenance of his vehicle is of the utmost importance to the public.

In the present case it is undisputed that the accident was caused by a failure of defendant's brakes that resulted from her independent contractor's negligence in overhauling or in thereafter inspecting the brakes. Since her duty to maintain her brakes in compliance with the provisions of the Vehicle Code is nondelegable, the fact that the brake failure was the result of her independent contractor's negligence is no defense.

The judgment and the order denying the motion for judgment notwithstanding the verdict on the issue of liability are reversed and the case is remanded to the trial court for a new trial on the issue of damages only.

---

1. How does the imposition of liability on the theory of a nondelegable duty differ from strict liability?

2. According to a "general rule" that developed both in English and American law, an employer of an independent contractor is not vicariously liable for his torts. The distinction between a servant and an independent contractor has been said to lie in the fact that the latter does the work on his own time, in his own way, and under no one's directions but his own, so that the employer has no control or right of control over the manner in which it is done. It is therefore to be regarded as the contractor's own enterprise, and he, rather than the employer, is the proper party to be charged with the risk. Also, no doubt, there is in the picture, although not often expressed, the fact that, taken as a class, independent contractors are in the main financially responsible parties, at least to a far greater extent than servants.

3. Conversely, it has been contended that the enterprise is still the employer's. He remains the one primarily to benefit from it; he selects the contractor and is free to choose one who is financially responsible and demand indemnity from him; and the insurance necessary to distribute the risk is properly a cost of his business rather than of the contractor. When a court places emphasis on these reasons, it may shift an employee from "independent contractor" to "servant" status. See, e.g., Konick v. Berke, Moore Co., Inc., 355 Mass. 463, 245 N.E.2d 750 (1969).

4. The "general rule" remains. But so many exceptional situations have been recognized in which vicarious liability is imposed upon the employer, that it has been observed that "the rule is now primarily important as a preamble to the catalog of its exceptions." Pacific Fire Ins. Co. v. Kenny Boiler & Mfg. Co., 201 Minn. 500, 277 N.W. 226 (1937).

5. There are four principal situations where the selection of an independent contractor will not insulate the party hiring him from liability:

A. *Negligence on the Part of the Employer.* If the employer is negligent in selecting the contractor or in giving him improper directions or equipment or in failing to stop any unnecessarily dangerous practices that come to his attention, the employer will be held liable for his own negligence, which has combined with that of the contractor. See Posner v. Paul's Trucking Serv., Inc., 380 F.2d 757 (1st Cir.1967); Annot., 78 A.L.R.3d 910 (1977).

B. *Nondelegable Duties.* There are certain responsibilities that courts will not permit an employer to delegate to an independent contractor. Maloney v. Rath contains a broad, but not totally complete, list of examples. There is no obvious criterion by which it can be determined whether a duty is "delegable" or not. In the last analysis, the cases represent *ad hoc* decisions that, as a matter of public policy, an employer cannot avoid particular responsibilities by hiring someone else to discharge them, because of the importance of the duty. See Westby v. Itasca County, 290 N.W.2d 437 (Minn.1980), where the court held the county vicariously liable for an independent contractor's failure to clear the road of mud from an exploded beaver dam. See also Misiulis v. Milbrand Maintenance Corp., 52 Mich.App. 494, 218 N.W.2d 68 (1974), where the court held that an owner of a shopping center would be vicariously liable for an independent contractor's negligent repair of a roof. See generally Peck, Negligence and Liability without Fault in Tort Law, 46 Wash.L.Rev. 225, 235 (1971).

C. *"Inherently" or "Intrinsically" Dangerous Activities.* Originally this came from Bower v. Peate, [1876] 1 Q.B.D. 321, where the foundation of plaintiff's building was undermined by an excavation. It never has been limited to activities (such as blasting) that involve an extraordinarily high degree of danger and are classified as "abnormally dangerous" for the purposes of imposing strict liability on the actor. See Chapter 14 infra. Rather, the exception is applicable when the activity involves a peculiar risk of harm that calls for more than ordinary precaution. This would be the case, for example, if the contractor were employed to transport giant logs, six feet in diameter, over the highway, in which case an obvious special danger to others arises unless the logs are properly anchored and secured. Risley v. Lenwell, 129 Cal. App.2d 608, 277 P.2d 897 (1954). Or to mark traffic lines on a busy street, where special precautions are required to keep traffic proceeding in another lane. Van Arsdale v. Hollinger, 68 Cal.2d 245, 437 P.2d 508, 66 Cal.Rptr. 20 (1968). Or to sell ice cream to small children from an ice cream vending truck on a busy street. Wilson v. Good Humor Corp., 244 U.S.App.D.C. 298, 757 F.2d 1293 (1985). See generally Annot., 34 A.L.R.4th 914 (1984).

Collateral Negligence. This exception does not apply when the independent contractor's negligence is deemed "collateral" to the risk: in other words, not recognizable in advance as particularly likely to occur or as calling for special precaution. This is sometimes referred to as the "peculiar risk" exception. Clausen v. R.W. Gibert Constr. Co., 309 N.W.2d 462 (Iowa 1981). The question of what is a collateral risk is not answered mechanically. For example, how should a court classify negligence on the part of contractor's employee in operating a wrecking crane? See Garczynski v. Darin & Armstrong Co., 420 F.2d 941 (6th Cir.1970). This general topic is well discussed in Smith, Collateral Negligence, 25 Minn.L.Rev. 399 (1941).

D. *"Illegal Activities".* An employer who contracts for performance of an illegal act is vicariously liable for any damage even if the "hiree" is an independent contractor. See King v. Loessin, 572 S.W.2d 87 (Tex.Civ.App. 1978).

6. This is a large topic, over which there has been much discussion. See Morris, The Torts of an Independent Contractor, 29 Ill.L.Rev. 339 (1935);

Harper, The Basis of the Immunity of an Independent Contractor, 10 Ind.L.J. 494 (1935); Steffen, The Independent Contractor and the Good Life, 2 U.Chi.L. Rev. 501 (1935); Ferson, Liability of Employers for Misrepresentations Made by Independent Contractors, 3 Vand.L.Rev. 1 (1949); Jacobs, Are Independent Contractors Really Independent?, 3 De Paul L.Rev. 23 (1953). For an interesting look at the doctrine, see Note, Risk Administration in the Market Place: A Reappraisal of the Independent Contractor Rule, 40 U.Chi.L.Rev. 661 (1973).

7. *A Note on Vicarious Liability of Physicians and Hospitals.* A physician who employs nurses or other paramedical personnel is vicariously liable for their torts committed in the course of employment. A physician may also be subject to liability for torts committed by hospital paramedical employees when he performs in a supervisory role over their professional activities.

The prime example of this developed in case law of the 1940's and 1950's, when a principle of agency law called "the borrowed servant rule" was applied in a number of states to place vicarious liability on the physician for the acts of nonemployee medical assistants. The "borrowed servant rule" in the area of medical malpractice developed new and fanciful terminology; the private physician performing surgery in a hospital was called the "captain of the ship" because he had a right of control over paramedical personnel. See McConnell v. Williams, 361 Pa. 355, 65 A.2d 243 (1949); Annot., 12 A.L.R.3d 1017 (1967). Vicarious liability might even be imposed on a physician for negligent acts committed by "borrowed servant" professionals such as anesthesiologists. As many physicians have pointed out, the theoretical right of control that underlies the "captain of the ship" doctrine does not equal a true power to control. If a surgeon attempted to supervise the tasks of others too stringently, he might negligently discharge his own work.

The "captain of the ship" doctrine may have been prompted by charitable immunity and a court's circuitous search to find a viable solvent defendant. With the demise of charitable immunities, the doctrine appears to have been trimmed in some states and strictly limited to the brief time surgery takes place. See Adams v. Leidholt, 579 P.2d 618 (Colo.1978). Texas further limited the doctrine to cases where the surgeon has actual control over the medical assistants in surgery. Sparger v. Worley Hosp., 547 S.W.2d 582 (Tex.1977). Nevertheless, precedents in a number of states create a potentially dangerous liability both for physicians and for other professionals. What effect does all of this have on the full and effective use of paraprofessional personnel? See generally D. Louisell & Williams, Medical Malpractice §§ 16.01–16.08 (1970); Hassard, Practice of Medicine: Delegation of Duties, 89 Calif.Med. 158 (1958); Kinkela & Kinkela, Hospital Nurses & Tort Liability, 18 Clev.–Mar.L.Rev. 53 (1969); Schwartz, The Allied Health Professions and Malpractice Liability, in New Developments in Law and Medicine, 1 (1974); Svete, Physician's Liability for Torts of Hospital Employees, 18 Clev.–Mar.L.Rev. 308 (1969); Reuter, Toward a More Realistic and Consistent Use of Respondeat Superior in the Hospital, 29 St. Louis U.L.J. 602 (1985); Note, 49 Notre Dame L.Rev. 933 (1974); Annots., 12 A.L.R.3d 1017 (1967), 29 A.L.R.3d 1065 (1970);

8. The doctrine of apparent authority has also been used by plaintiffs in medical malpractice cases to reach the "deep pocket" of hospitals when special functions, such as radiology and emergency room care, are handled by private franchises. See Mehlman v. Powell, 281 Md. 269, 378 A.2d 1121 (1977); Adamski v. Tacoma General Hosp., 20 Wash.App. 98, 579 P.2d 970 (1978); Arthur v. St. Peter's Hosp., 169 N.J.Super. 575, 405 A.2d 443 (1979). See discussion of apparent authority, infra page 663, note 9.]

(C) JOINT ENTERPRISE

The joint enterprise theory was developed by American courts to impose liability vicariously upon one person who is engaged in the same activity with another person committing the tortious act. The Restatement (Second) of Torts § 491, comment c, sets out four elements required for liability to be imposed. First, there must be either an express or implied agreement to the activity between the parties. Second, the parties must have a common purpose or goal. Third, the parties must have a common pecuniary interest in the purpose or goal; several courts require a common business purpose, limiting application of this theory to only commercial settings. Finally, there must be an equal right between the parties to control the direction of the enterprise. This does not mean power to control the other members is necessary; only the right to an equal voice is indicated. Because of these elements, each member of the joint enterprise is held to be the agent of the other; each may therefore be held liable for the acts of the other.

This theory as a means of imposing vicarious liability is on the decline, largely because of its use to impute vicarious contributory negligence. It is still most commonly applied in automobile accident cases. See Weintraub, The Joint Enterprise Doctrine in Automobile Law, 16 Cornell L.Q. 320 (1931). It has been applied occasionally in other contexts. See, e.g., Cullinan v. Tetrault, 123 Me. 302, 122 A. 770 (1923) (one party purchases liquor for a party); see Shell Oil Co. v. Prestidge, 249 F.2d 413 (9th Cir.1957) (parties are prospecting for oil). It generally does not apply to parties who take pleasure trips or other nonbusiness journeys. Fugate v. Galvin, 84 Ill.App.3d 573, 406 N.E.2d 19, 22, 40 Ill.Dec. 318 (1980) (travel arrangements to meet a mutual friend not a joint venture). In automobile cases, joint ownership without more is not enough to impose vicarious liability; there must be some business purpose involved. The person subjected to liability must also have a right to control operation of the vehicle, even when there is a common purpose for the trip and a community of business interest, such as when parties commute to and from work. See Spradley v. Houser, 247 S.C. 208, 146 S.E.2d 621 (1966).

See generally Rollison, The "Joint Enterprise" in the Law of Imputed Negligence, 6 Notre Dame L.Rev. 172 (1931); Keeton, Imputed Contributory Negligence, 13 Tex.L.Rev. 161 (1935).

(D) BAILMENTS AND OTHER BASES

LITTLES v. AVIS RENT–A–CAR SYSTEM
Supreme Court of Pennsylvania, 1969.
433 Pa. 72, 248 A.2d 837.

BELL, CHIEF JUSTICE. * * * The question to be resolved is whether the lessor of a motor vehicle is liable for damages to a passenger in a van type truck when the lessee-driver of said vehicle drove it into an overhead railroad bridge.

On August 15, 1962, Alfred Kemp rented an eight-ton truck from the Avis Rent-a-Car System. At the time of the rental, Kemp was asked whether he had had any experience in driving a truck; he replied that he had had experience in driving a pickup truck. In order to complete the transaction, Kemp produced his driver's license duly issued by the Commonwealth of Pennsylvania. Kemp was then given a receipt which, among other things, showed that the height of the truck was twelve feet.

On the same day as he rented the truck, Kemp attempted to drive the truck under a railroad bridge which was less than twelve feet high. The top of the truck hit the bridge, causing personal injury to the minor plaintiff, who was Kemp's passenger in the truck.

Plaintiffs brought suit against the Avis Rent-a-Car System, alleging that Avis was negligent in renting its truck to a person it should have known lacked the proper experience to drive such a vehicle. There are no Pennsylvania cases directly in point and the cases which plaintiffs cite from other jurisdiction do not support them.

Plaintiffs assume that because the driver hit the railroad overpass, he must have been incapable of properly driving the truck. It is quite possible, however, that the accident was not due to the inexperience or incompetency of the driver, but rather to mere lack of attention or error in judgment on his part.

Not only did defendant's agent make inquiries about Kemp's previous experience in driving trucks, but he also requested and was shown by Kemp a valid driver's license issued to him by the Commonwealth. * * *

Under the facts of this case, there is no evidence of any knowledge on the part of the lessor of lessee's inability to drive a truck or any reason for lessor to have taken any more precautions than it did before leasing the vehicle.

Order of the Superior Court ["which had dismissed plaintiff's motion to take off a compulsory nonsuit"] affirmed. * * *

ROBERTS, JUSTICE (dissenting). * * * Since the rental agent was aware of [Kemp's] experience with over-sized vehicles, I think the provisions of Restatement of Torts § 390 definitely should have applied. The section states: "One who supplies directly or through a third person a chattel for the use of another whom the supplier knows or has reason to know to be likely because of his youth, inexperience or otherwise, to use it in a manner involving unreasonable risk of physical harm to himself and others whom the supplier should expect to share in or be endangered by its use, is subject to liability for physical harm resulting to them."

Avis knew that Alfred Kemp was inexperienced in the driving of this size vehicle. He had never attempted to drive anything larger than a pick-up. Nor could the agents for Avis rely on the Pennsylvania driver's license he carried as proof of his competence despite this lack of experience. It is common knowledge that licenses are issued to any individual who is capable of driving an automobile, although such person by reason of his or her size or lack of strength would *never* be able to handle a huge tractor with its sophisticated transmission and braking systems. * * *

Since I think the nonsuit was improperly granted I dissent from the majority opinion and would remand for a determination by the jury.

SHUCK v. MEANS
Supreme Court of Minnesota, 1974.
302 Minn. 93, 226 N.W.2d 285.

KELLY, JUSTICE. * * * On March 27, 1967, an automobile owned by Hertz, leased to one George A. Codling, and driven by Means, collided with an automobile in which plaintiff Shuck was a passenger. Means was uninsured at the time of the accident and the parties later stipulated that he had been negligent. * * * [These facts present for] our consideration only the following issue: Whether a car rental agency is liable under the Minnesota Safety Responsibility Act when one of its cars is leased by one person, but operated by another in violation of the rental agreement.

The applicable owner-consent statute, Minn.St.1965, § 170.54, provides as follows: "Whenever any motor vehicle * * * shall be operated upon any public street or highway of this state, by any person other than the owner, with the consent of the owner, express or implied, the operator thereof shall in case of accident, be deemed the agent of the owner of such motor vehicle in the operation thereof."

This provision, enacted as part of the Safety Responsibility Act, was intended to make the owners of motor vehicles liable to those injured by their operation where no such liability would otherwise exist, giving such injured persons more certainty of recovery by encouraging owners to obtain appropriate liability insurance. And to that end, the statute is to be given a liberal construction. [C]

This court, in Foster v. Bock, 229 Minn. 428, 39 N.W.2d 862 (1949), was asked to decide whether a vehicle owner was liable under the owner-consent statute where a subpermittee was driving at the time of the accident, the permittee remaining in the vehicle only as a passenger. In imposing liability on the owner, the court quoted with approval the following language used in Kerns v. Lewis, 246 Mich. 423, 425, 224 N.W. 647, 648 (1929) by the Supreme Court of Michigan in construing a similar statute:

" * * * Does the essential consent mentioned in the statute relate to the *driver*, or to the vehicle, 'being driven'? The statute makes the owner liable if the 'motor vehicle is being driven with his or her express or implied consent or knowledge,' and we cannot read into it the restriction that the particular driver must be known by and his driving consented to by the owner." 229 Minn. 435, 39 N.W.2d 866.

In Granley v. Crandall, 288 Minn. 310, 180 N.W.2d 190 (1970), the restriction referred to in the above quotation was sought to be expressly imposed by the owner. The court held that notwithstanding a parent's explicit instructions to her child forbidding the operation of her automobile by anyone else, the parent is deemed to have given her consent under Minn.St. 170.54 when the car is driven by a third person with the child's permission and under its direction if the child is actually a passenger in the car.

The court [has gone] a step further in * * * holding that the presence of the permittee as a passenger in an automobile being driven by a subpermittee is not a necessary condition to liability of the owner under § 170.54.

Proving lack of consent in these situations requires a strong showing that the car was being used by the permittee without the owner's knowledge and contrary to his explicit instructions, or that the subpermittee was driving without the permission of the first permittee under conditions which approach the status of conversion or a theft. [C]

Neither of these situations is shown by the facts of the instant case, and the trial court's finding that implied consent existed is justified under the aforementioned cases unless the holdings of those cases are confined to situations involving permittees who are minor children of the owners. Such a narrow application of those cases would be inappropriate in light of the purpose of the owner-consent statute and the commercial nature of the transaction here involved.

Accordingly, the trial court was correct in concluding that Means was operating the vehicle with the implied consent of Hertz.

Affirmed.

---

1. Under the common law in the overwhelming majority of states, a bailment does not make a bailor vicariously liable for the acts of the bailee in the use of the chattel. Suppose you loan your car to a friend at law school, who gets drunk with a stranger—the stranger robs the friend and steals your car. The thief then causes an accident. Are you liable as owner of the car? See Cherokee Enterprises, Inc. v. Rogers, 451 So.2d 553 (Fla.App.1984).

2. As the *Littles* case suggests, a bailor may be liable for his own negligence in entrusting a chattel to a person whose use of it is highly likely to endanger others. See Wery v. Seff, 136 Ohio St. 307, 16 Ohio Ops. 445, 25 N.E.2d 692 (1940) (unlicensed minor driver); Snowhite v. State, 243 Md. 291, 221 A.2d 342 (1966) (owner knew driver was frequently intoxicated); Syah v. Johnson, 247 Cal.App.2d 534, 55 Cal.Rptr. 741 (1966) (epileptic). This may occur not only with automobiles, but also with other chattels. See McBerry v. Ivie, 116 Ga.App. 808, 159 S.E.2d 108 (1967) (shotgun given to a young child); Miles v. Harrison, 223 Ga. 352, 155 S.E.2d 6 (1967) (power mower); LaFaso v. LaFaso, 126 Vt. 90, 223 A.2d 814 (1966) (cigarette lighter). See generally Woods, Negligent Entrustment, 20 Ark.L.Rev. 101 (1966). Should the bailor be liable to the bailee in this context? See McDermott v. Hambright, 286 Ala. 249, 238 So.2d 876 (1970). See generally Annot., 12 A.L.R.4th 1062 (1982).

3. The common law rule on bailments has proved unsatisfactory with respect to automobiles. As a result, courts have adopted a variety of rationales to place vicarious liability on the owner of the vehicle. Among the most significant are:

A. *Presumption That Owner Controls the Vehicle.* Some courts have held in the past that the mere presence of the owner in the car establishes his right of control over the driving, so that he becomes responsible for the acts of the driver as if he were an agent. See, for example, Boker v. Luebbe, 198 Neb. 282, 252 N.W.2d 297 (1977); Reetz v. Mansfield, 119 Conn. 563, 178 A. 53 (1935).

In a number of states courts have retreated from this position even when the parties are close relatives; it is thought to be unrealistic and even may promote unnecessary back-seat driving. The effect is to make the owner merely a guest in his own car. See Rodgers v. Saxton, 305 Pa. 479, 158 A. 166 (1931); Jasper v. Freitag, 145 N.W.2d 879 (N.D.1966); Greyhound Lines Inc. v. Caster, 216 A.2d 689 (Del.1966). See also Bauer v. Johnson, 79 Ill.2d 324, 38 Ill. Dec. 149, 403 N.E.2d 237 (1980). This does not relieve the owner of a duty to object to or otherwise interfere with negligent driving once he becomes aware of it. See Sherman v. Korff, 353 Mich. 387, 91 N.W.2d 485 (1958).

Some courts take a middle position and create a rebuttable presumption that the driver is under the control of the owner. Unimpeached testimony from either of the parties may rebut the presumption. See Ross v. Burgan, 163 Ohio St. 211, 126 N.E.2d 592 (1955). See generally Annot., 37 A.L.R.4th 565 (1985).

B. *The Family Purpose Doctrine.* The "family purpose" or "family car" doctrine is a court-created legal fiction by which the owner of an automobile is held vicariously liable when the car is negligently driven by a member of the immediate household. The fiction is predicated on the assumption that the driver is implementing a "family purpose." Usually, he is only driving the automobile for his own pleasure or convenience. The car must be driven with the permission of the owner, but this may be implied from very general circumstances. The doctrine is applied in less than 20 states and has many nuances, exceptions and complications. In general, it is limited to automobiles, but the court in Stewart v. Stephens, 225 Ga. 185, 166 S.E.2d 890 (1969), extended it to a "family motorboat." Contra, Felcyn v. Gamble, 185 Minn. 357, 241 N.W. 37 (1932). See generally Annot., 8 A.L.R.3d 1191 (1966); Kidd, Vicarious Liability and the "Family Car", 121 New L.J. 529 (1971); Lattin, Vicarious Liability and the Family Automobile, 26 Mich.L.Rev. 846 (1928); Hope, The Doctrine of the Family Automobile, 8 A.B.A.J. 359 (1922); Notes, 18

S.C.L.Rev. 638 (1966), 55 Ky.L.J. 502 (1967). Who should be primarily liable as between a father or mother? What if the mother has custody of the child? See Flannigan v. Valliant, 400 So.2d 225 (La.App.1981), cert. denied, 406 So.2d 611 (1981). In Hawaii, a court held that a state "family purpose" statute did not violate the equal protection clause by discriminating against natural parents. Bryan v. Kitamura, 529 F.Supp. 394 (D.Hawaii 1982).

C. *Joint Enterprise.* The joint enterprise doctrine, discussed in the prior section, was created for the purpose of placing vicarious liability on the owner of an automobile. Although the doctrine worked in this way on occasion, see Manley v. Horton, 414 S.W.2d 254 (Mo.1967); Straffus v. Barclay, 147 Tex. 600, 219 S.W.2d 65 (1949), it more often served to impute the contributory negligence of the driver to a passenger and bar his claim against a negligent third party. See the discussion in Edlebeck v. Hooten, 20 Wis.2d 83, 121 N.W.2d 240 (1963); Clemens v. O'Brien, 85 N.J.Super. 404, 204 A.2d 895 (1964); and Jack v. Kansas City S.Ry. Co., 392 So.2d 499 (La.App.1980), cert. denied, 397 So.2d 805 (1981).

4. *Automobile Consent Statutes.* The unsatisfactory nature of common law approaches to the problem led legislatures in more than a quarter of the states to adopt statutes similar to the one construed in Shuck v. Means.

The statutes have weathered constitutional challenge and most cases that arise under them deal with problems of construction. Among the more common questions are:

A. Was the automobile being operated with the owner's "consent"? This problem is not dissimilar to making a determination about "scope of employment" in master-servant cases. Generally, violations of specific instructions as to the manner of operation will not protect the owner. But there are decisions contrary to the principal case—at least when the owner is not in the vehicle at the time of the accident. See Fischer v. McBride, 296 Mich. 671, 296 N.W. 834 (1941).

B. Will the contributory negligence of the bailee driver be imputed to the owner? Courts are divided on this issue and individual results have depended on the precise wording of the statutes and the court's view of the underlying purpose of the statute. Compare Mills v. Gabriel, 259 App.Div. 60, 18 N.Y.S.2d 78 (1940), aff'd 284 N.Y. 755, 31 N.E.2d 512 (1940), with Davis Pontiac Co. v. Sirois, 82 R.I. 32, 105 A.2d 792 (1954). Should the answer depend on whether the bailment was gratuitous? See Continental Auto Lease Corp. v. Campbell, 19 N.Y.2d 350, 227 N.E.2d 28, 280 N.Y.S.2d 123 (1967).

C. Who is an "owner" for the purpose of the statute? Should it include persons such as conditional sellers who have legal title but no power to control the vehicle? See Mason v. Automobile Fin. Co., 121 F.2d 32 (D.C.Cir.1941).

D. Suppose the owner leaves his automobile at a car wash and an attendant drives it negligently, injuring plaintiff. Should the owner be liable for that? See Allcity Ins. Co. v. Old Greenwich Delicatessen, 75 Misc.2d 898, 349 N.Y.S.2d 240 (1973). See generally Brodsky, Motor Vehicle Owners' Statutory Vicarious Liability in Rhode Island, 19 B.U.L.Rev. 448 (1939); Notes: 11 N.Y.U.Intra.L.Rev. 97 (1956), 7 Syracuse L.Rev. 312 (1956); Annot., 8 A.L.R. 4th 265 (1981).

5. The need for automobile consent statutes has been considerably lessened because of the "omnibus clause" in standard automobile liability insurance policies. This clause provides that liability insurance for the designated automobile applies to the named insured, any member of his household, and to

any person using the automobile with his permission, provided the use was within the scope of permission. How does this differ from the consent statutes? See generally R. Keeton, Insurance Law, 221–232 (1971); Gosnell, Omnibus Clauses in Automobile Insurance Policies, 1950 Ins.L.J. 237.

6. Do the policies that support an application of vicarious liability to owners of automobiles apply to any other bailors? Some attorneys have made enterprising, but unsuccessful, attempts to apply the same rule to private aircraft. See McCord v. Dixie Aviation Corp., 450 F.2d 1129 (10th Cir.1971); Rogers v. Ray Gardner Flying Serv., Inc., 435 F.2d 1389 (5th Cir.1970), cert. denied, 401 U.S. 1010 (1971) (attempting to imply the remedy from the Federal Aviation Act of 1958). A good summary of these cases is found in Broadway v. Webb, 462 F.Supp. 429 (D.C.N.C.1977).

7. There are other, occasional, instances of statutes creating vicarious liability. Some states have imposed the liability on owners of private aircraft. Another sample of statutory vicarious liability can be found in the so-called "anti-lynching" statutes, which make a municipality liable for certain torts committed by a mob. Still another example is the statutes that make parents liable (up to a fixed amount) for certain torts committed by their children. See supra page 424.

8. *Sale or Gift.* A sale or a gift of a chattel has not been utilized to impose vicarious liability. The main controversy here is whether the seller or donor should be liable for torts committed by the donee or purchaser on a negligent-entrustment theory. Suppose a parent gives an automobile to a child whom he knows to be an incompetent driver. Should the parent be liable when the child's negligent driving injures a third person? What about an automobile dealer who sells a car to the town drunk? The issue is discussed and cases are collected in Sikora v. Wade, 135 N.J.Super. 62, 342 A.2d 580 (1975).

9. *Apparent Authority.* One who expressly or impliedly represents that another party is his servant or agent may be held vicariously liable for the latter's negligent acts to the extent of that representation. This result may occur even though the negligent party is an independent contractor or even when there is no employment relationship whatsoever between the negligent actor and the party making the representation.

This theory, called apparent authority or apparent agency, may benefit an injured party who reasonably relies on the representation. See Restatement (Second) of Agency, §§ 228, 229 (1957). Lately the theory has been utilized to hold franchisors vicariously liable for the negligent conduct of their independent contractor franchisees. See Singleton v. International Dairy Queen, Inc., 332 A.2d 160 (Del.1975); Chevron Oil Co. v. Sutton, 85 N.M. 679, 515 P.2d 1283 (1973); Drexel v. Union Prescription Centers, Inc., 582 F.2d 781 (3d Cir.1978); Wood v. Holiday Inns, Inc., 508 F.2d 167 (5th Cir.1975); Annot., 81 A.L.R.3d 764 (1977). An extreme example of the application of this theory is Gizzi v. Texaco, Inc., 437 F.2d 308 (3d Cir.), cert. denied, 404 U.S. 829 (1971), where the court held Texaco's advertising and other representations to be sufficient for a jury to determine that the company had vested "apparent authority" in a dealer who sold a van on his own behalf. Texaco made no profit on the sale, but knew that the dealer engaged in the activity. Compare Weiss v. Wilkins, 313 A.2d 897 (Del.1973); Apple v. Standard Oil, Division of American Oil Co., 307 F.Supp. 107 (N.D.Cal.1969); Sanders v. Clark Oil Refining Corp., 57 Mich.App. 687, 226 N.W.2d 695 (1975). All of this has resulted in a modification in advertising techniques on the part of some franchisors. See Notes, U.Ill.L.F. 915 (1965), 41

S.Cal.L.Rev. 143 (1968), 50 N.C.L.Rev. 647 (1972), 7 Land & Water L.Rev. 263 (1972). The apparent authority theory has been the settled rule of the federal courts over the years. American Soc'y of Mechanical Eng'rs, Inc. v. Hydrolevel Corp., 456 U.S. 556 (1982).

2. IMPUTED CONTRIBUTORY NEGLIGENCE

SMALICH v. WESTFALL
Supreme Court of Pennsylvania, 1970.
440 Pa. 409, 269 A.2d 476.

EAGEN, JUSTICE. Two automobiles collided in Westmoreland County. One of the vehicles, owned by Julia Smalich, was operated by Felix Rush Westfall. Julia Smalich [was a] passenger in this automobile at the time. The other vehicle involved was operated by Stephanna Louise Blank. Julia Smalich suffered injuries in the collision which caused her death. * * *

The estate of Julia Smalich sought damages [against Westfall and Blank] in both a wrongful death action and a survival action. * * *

The trial jury found that Westfall's negligent operation of the Smalich automobile was a proximate cause of the collision. That the trial record amply supports this finding is not and cannot be questioned. After trial, the court en banc ruled that, under the facts, the contributory negligence of Westfall must be imputed to the owner of the automobile as a matter of law and this precluded recovery by the Smalich Estate against defendant Blank. * * *

[A] plaintiff ought not to be barred from recovery against a negligent defendant by the contributory negligence of a third person unless the relationship between the plaintiff and the third person is such that the plaintiff would be vicariously liable as a defendant for the negligent acts of the third person: Prosser, The Law of Torts § 73 (3d ed. 1964). See also, Restatement (Second) Torts §§ 485, 486 and 491 (1965). Placed in the context of this case, a driver's negligence will not be imputed to a passenger, unless the relationship between them is such that the passenger would be vicariously liable as a defendant for the driver's negligent acts * * *. The relationship between the passenger and the driver is therefore a very critical one, worthy of careful analysis and consideration. * * * We therefore now state unequivocally that only a master-servant relationship or a finding of joint enterprise will justify the imputation of contributory negligence.

We have serious doubt that, in the ordinary situation, the mutual understanding of the owner-passenger and the driver is that the owner-passenger reserves a right to control over the physical details of driving or that the driver consents to submit himself to the control of a "back-seat driver." It seems more reasonable that the mutual understanding is that the driver will use care and skill to accomplish a result, retaining control over the manner of operation yet subject to the duty of obedience to the wishes of the owner-passenger as to such things as destination. Such would only constitute an agency relationship and not one of master-servant, although there are undoubtedly situations where the understanding might well be such as to constitute a master-servant relationship. * * *

We do not mean, however, that the presence of the owner is entirely irrelevant, or that there is no legal significance that an owner present in his car has the power to control it. These are relevant in determining whether the owner-passenger has been actually negligent himself in failing to control the conduct of the driver. * * *

The jury rendered a verdict for the plaintiffs against defendant Blank, and therefore, must have determined that Julia Smalich had relinquished her right to control her automobile to defendant Westfall. On the facts, such a conclusion is justified under the law as we have now stated it. Judgments n.o.v. should not, therefore, have been entered in favor of defendant Blank and against the Smalich Estate. These judgments are vacated, and the record remanded with directions to enter judgments in favor of the Smalich Estate and against defendant Blank in accordance with the jury's verdict. * * *

ROBERTS, JUSTICE, concurring. I am pleased that the Court today partially repudiates the imputed contributory negligence doctrine. I am unable to join the majority's opinion, however, because I believe that in adopting a limited "both ways" test, it falls short of accomplishing the degree of reform necessary in this area. I am particularly disturbed that the majority, in continuing to apply the doctrine to the master-servant relationship, places so much weight on the physical control a master has over a servant. I therefore can only concur in the result.

The imputed contributory negligence doctrine has been criticized on two grounds. For one, it is quite obvious that the doctrine is based on the absurd fiction that the owner-passenger has the "right" to control the vehicle. In the real world, however, a passenger can in no safe way exercise operational control over the vehicle in which he rides, even if he is the owner. * * *

A second weakness in the doctrine of imputed contributory negligence arises from the fact that courts have often failed to discern the difference between using the fiction of control to impute negligence when the owner-passenger is the defendant, and using it to impute contributory negligence when the owner-passenger is the plaintiff. The assumption has been that if the driver's negligence is imputed, it is only logical to likewise impute his contributory negligence. But there is no justification for imputing contributory negligence, other than "the strong psychological appeal of all rules case in the form of balanced and logical symmetry." * * *

[T]he "both-ways test" has been strongly criticized. In 1932 it was written that "[c]ourts seem unaware that the policies involved in granting or denying the defensive plea may be different from those controlling the responsibility in damages of a master for the conduct of his servant, and that the latter are probably concerned simply with providing a financially responsible defendant." Gregory, Vicarious Responsibility and Contributory Negligence, 41 Yale L.J. 831, 833 (1932). * * *

The Supreme Court of Minnesota re-examined the whole problem of imputed contributory negligence recently in a well-reasoned opinion that deserves close study. See Weber v. Stokley–Van Camp, Inc., 274 Minn. 482, 144 N.W.2d 540 (1966). There the court repudiated the application of the doctrine to the master-servant relation in automobile negligence cases, stressing the absurdity of the control argument, and the absence of need for a solvent defendant, unlike vicarious liability cases where the master properly is held accountable for the negligence of his servant.

I look forward to the day when this Court completes its reform in this area.

––––––––

1. "Imputed negligence" has acquired a bad reputation in the law, because of a set of rules that developed in the latter part of the nineteenth century, under which entirely innocent persons, seriously injured without any fault of their own, were barred from recovery against one person who negligently injured them, because they were charged with the negligence of another who had contributed to the injury. The result was that, of the three persons involved, the entire loss fell upon the only one who was free from all negligence. Most of this is now thoroughly discredited and obsolete. See generally, Note, 26 Tenn.L.Rev. 531 (1959). For a court decision that "completed the reform" in a well-reasoned decision, see Bibergal v. McCormick, 101 Misc.2d 794, 421 N.Y.S.2d 978 (1979).

A. *Driver and Passenger.* An early English decision, Thorogood v. Bryan, 8 C.B. 115, 137 Eng.Rep. 452 (1849), "imputed" negligence of the driver of an omnibus to a passenger who was injured in a collision, so as to prevent recovery by the passenger against the other driver.

The decision has long since been overruled in England. Although some decisions in United States jurisdictions followed it for a time, those cases have also been overruled. As the principal case suggests, however, a passenger in an automobile can be charged with contributory negligence of his own. While older cases imposed a rather harsh duty on the passenger to keep a "look out," most cases today allow a passenger to rely upon a driver whom he reasonably believes to be competent. What is reasonable under the circumstances often becomes a question for the jury. See Annot., 37 A.L.R.4th 565 (1985).

B. *Husband and wife.* At common law a married woman's separate legal identity was merged with that of her husband. One result of this legal fiction was that if her spouse contributed to the happening of an accident, his negligence could be imputed to her and would bar any claim against a negligent third party. All this is ancient history. Today, the result is that, except in community property jurisdictions, the contributory negligence of one spouse is no longer imputed to bar a recovery by the other, on the basis of the marital relation alone.

C. *Parent and Child.* The common law had no similar rule of legal identity as between parent and child. The child always has been held to be entitled to the separate ownership of his own property, to the enforcement of his causes of action, and to be liable as an individual for his own torts. Consequently no statutes have been necessary to affect the situation.

On occasion a parent's negligence will be so substantial in regard to the accident that a court will treat his conduct as a superseding cause and bar the child's claim against the third party. Modern courts may be reluctant to accept this argument and will regard it as an end run attempt to restore the old rules imputing contributory negligence. See, e.g., Caroline v. Reicher, 269 Md. 125, 304 A.2d 831 (1973), noted in 34 Md.L.Rev. 155 (1975) (parent's failure to supervise child will not relieve landlord of liability for child's consumption of paint containing lead); Annot., 82 A.L.R.3d 1068 (1978).

2. As a result of all this, a general rule has developed that contributory negligence will not be imputed unless negligence could be imputed. Many courts accept the converse of this proposition: if negligence can be imputed, contributory negligence will be also. This is the so-called "both-ways test." The both-ways test has been under a slow, but steady attack. This first occurred in connection with automobile consent statutes where some courts construed the legislation as intended only to impose vicarious liability. See supra page 662, note 4. A few courts have taken the same approach in regard to the family purpose doctrine. See White v. Yup, 85 Nev. 527, 458 P.2d 617 (1969).

Although some states have clung to the both-ways test, see, e.g., Wilson v. Great N. Ry. Co., 83 S.D. 207, 157 N.W.2d 19 (1968), it has been abandoned in others, Pierson v. Edstrom, 286 Minn. 164, 174 N.W.2d 712 (1970), Kalechman v. Drew Auto Rental, Inc., 33 N.Y.2d 397, 308 N.E.2d 886, 353 N.Y.S.2d 414 (1973), and still others have indicated that they regard the test with increasing disfavor. See Adams v. Treat, 256 Or. 239, 472 P.2d 270 (1970). See generally Annots., 57 A.L.R.3d 1226 (1974); 53 A.L.R.3d 664 (1973).

3. Does the advent of comparative negligence supply a reason to retain the both-ways test? See Smedsrud v. Brown, 227 N.W.2d 572 (Minn.1975); cf. Schweidler v. Caruso, 269 Wis. 438, 69 N.W.2d 611 (1955).

4. Even courts that have indicated strong dissatisfaction with the both-ways test will apply it to impute contributory negligence of an employee onto a corporate plaintiff. What reason supports this view? See Thomas Oil, Inc. v. Onsgaard, 298 Minn. 465, 215 N.W.2d 793 (1974). Cf. Nagele–Kelly Mfg. Co. v. Hannak, 13 Mich.App. 427, 164 N.W.2d 540 (1968). Should the same result occur when the plaintiff is a partnership?

5. Where the "both ways" test is applied, the negligence of an agent (or servant) will not be imputed to a principal who is suing the agent for that very negligence. See Brown v. Poritzky, 30 N.Y.2d 289, 283 N.E.2d 751, 332 N.Y.S.2d 872 (1972) (principal victimized by two careless agents); Williams v. Knapp, 248 Md. 506, 237 A.2d 450 (1968); Dosher v. Hunt, 243 N.C. 247, 90 S.E.2d 374 (1955).

6. *Derivative Claims.* When a claim is held to be derivative in nature, the contributory negligence of an injured party will be imputed to the plaintiff. The most common example of this is a wrongful death action. See supra page 557. Other examples include claims for loss of consortium, or for negligent infliction of emotional harm based on the claimant's observation of a physical injury inflicted on a close relative. The imputation of contributory negligence is not based on principles of vicarious liability, but on the judgment of a court

or legislature that plaintiff's claim is not independent in nature but is derived from and dependent on another party's claim.

In each of these cases, an argument can be made that the plaintiff's claim is not derivative at all but an "independent injury." For example, it could be reasonably argued that a wrongful death claim is actually based on the defendant's causing an economic injury to the beneficiaries named in the statute. This line of argument has been much more popular with textwriters than with courts. See Note, 29 So.Cal.L.Rev. 344 (1956).

7. How much does the so-called "deep-pocket" theory explain the doctrines discussed in this chapter? Put another way, is the doctrinal basis of imputed negligence actually based on courts trying to find a solvent defendant? The next two chapters explore a more direct route for this result—strict and products liability.

Chapter XIV

STRICT LIABILITY

When a court imposes "strict liability" on a defendant, it is saying that he must pay damages although he neither intentionally injured plaintiff nor failed to live up to the objective standard of reasonable care that traditionally has been at the root of negligence law. Some courts and textwriters call this process "absolute liability." This description overstates the case because there are numerous defenses to an action for strict liability and sometimes, especially in the so-called "strict products liability" area (Chapter 15), fault creeps back into the system. Some other textwriters and courts group the cases in this chapter under the rubric "liability without fault." This description can be regarded as over-inclusive because there are many examples of imposition of liability without fault under the negligence and intentional tort bases of liability. Can you recall some?

As Dean Prosser observed: "Once the legal concept of 'fault' is divorced, as it has been from the personal standard of moral wrongdoing, there is a sense in which liability with or without 'fault' must beg its own conclusion. The term requires such extensive definition, that it seems better not to make use of it at all, and to refer instead to strict liability, apart from either wrongful intent or negligence." W. Prosser & W. Keeton, Torts 538 (5th ed. 1984).

Thus far we have seen that most activities are judged on the basis of negligence or objective fault. This chapter focuses on activities that have been selected by judges over the past two centuries to bear the burden of strict liability. Observe the rationales that underlie their judgments. Are they consistent? Are they sound? Should they be extended?

1. ANIMALS

Trespassing Animals. One of the first areas selected by courts for the imposition of strict liability focused on the care and maintenance of particular animals in certain situations. Somewhere around the middle of the fourteenth century, the courts began to recognize a rule making the owner of cattle liable when his animals trespassed upon the plaintiff's land. The origin of the rule is somewhat obscure. It has been attributed to a fiction that the trespass of the animals was to be attributed to the owner, because he was in some way identified with them, and responsible for what they did. According to Glanville Williams, Liability for Animals 127–34 (1939), there was no such fiction, and the early cases were those in which the owner intentionally put his cattle upon the land of the plaintiff. Liability for mere escape originated as a deliberate extension designed to remedy a gap in the law; and because it came before the full development of the action on the case, it was identified with trespass, although the invasion was an indirect one. Out of this there developed the rule that the owner of animals of a kind likely to roam and do damage is strictly liable for their trespasses.

The kinds of animals for whose trespasses their owner would be liable were limited, and they had a definite barnyard pattern. They included cattle, horses, sheep, hogs and goats, as well as such common errant fowl as turkeys, in McPherson v. James, 69 Ill.App. 337 (1896), and chickens, in Adams Bros. v. Clark, 189 Ky. 279, 224 S.W. 1046 (1920), or even pigeons, in Taylor v. Granger, 19 R.I. 410, 34 A. 153, 37 A. 13 (1896).

On the other hand, such household favorites as dogs were not included. Olson v. Pederson, 206 Minn. 415, 288 N.W. 856 (1939); McDonald v. Castle, 116 Okl. 46, 243 P. 215 (1925). The same is true of cats. Buckle v. Holmes, [1926] 2 K.B. 125; Bischoff v. Cheney, 89 Conn. 1, 92 A. 660 (1914). The reason formerly given was that dogs and cats were of no value, which is of course clearly wrong; and that their trespasses were likely to be trivial and do no serious harm. This last, of course, is unlikely to appeal to the owners of flowerbeds and poultry. A better explanation may be that of Glanville Williams, Liability for Animals 145–146 (1939), that dogs and cats are very difficult to confine or restrain, and the general custom of the community has permitted them to roam at large. In other words, the keeping of these household pets is so far sanctioned by general usage that an exception is made in their favor. Cf. Baker v. Howard County Hunt, 171 Md. 159, 188 A. 223 (1936) (trespass rule applied to pack of hunting dogs).

An early and well established exception to the rule of strict liability for trespassing cattle and the like was the case of animals straying from a highway on which they were lawfully being driven. Tillett v. Ward, L.R. 10 Q.B. 17 (1882). This obviously arose out of the necessity of getting the animals to market. It was explained as in the nature of a servitude to which owners of lands adjoining the highway were subject; and it did not apply to other lands. Thus there was strict liability when cattle strayed from the lands of A, and thence onto the land of B, removed from the highway. Wood v. Snider, 187 N.Y. 28, 79 N.E. 858 (1907).

In the United States the rule as to strict liability for animal trespass has had something of a checkered history. In the early days many of the courts, particularly in the western part of the country where cattle were customarily permitted to graze at large on open range, rejected the common law rule, as not suitable to the conditions of the country and established local custom. See for example Delaney v. Errickson, 10 Neb. 492, 6 N.W. 600 (1880); Beinhorn v. Griswold, 27 Mont. 79, 69 P. 557 (1902). These animals cases are among the leading authorities for the proposition that, under state reception statutes, the common law of England is to be followed only when it is suitable and appropriate.

As the country became more settled, these states began to enact "fencing out" statutes, which provided that if the plaintiff fenced his land properly there was strict liability when the animals broke through the fence, but otherwise there was liability only if their owner was at fault. See for example Buford v. Houtz, 133 U.S. 320 (1890); Garcia v. Sumrall, 58 Ariz. 526, 121 P.2d 640 (1942).

As the country became still more settled, the conflict between the grazing interests and developing agricultural interests—or, in other words, as the motion pictures would have it, between the range men and the "nesters" along the creek bed—resulted in many states in "fencing in" statutes, which required the owner of the animals to fence them in or otherwise restrain them, and made him strictly liable if he did not do so. See for example Ariz.Code Ann. § 50–606.

Finally, some states, particularly in the eastern part of the country, have fully returned to the common law rule. See King v. Blue Mountain Forest Ass'n, 100 N.H. 212, 123 A.2d 151 (1956).

A common type of statute today permits a county to choose the rule it wishes to apply. Thus in some states animals are permitted to run at large unless a county adopts a "fencing in" or a "fencing out" ordinance. Others permit counties to employ the fiction of designating the boundary lines of lots or tracts as lawful fences, which automatically results in a rule of strict liability. There are states in which all four variants of the rule—strict liability, fencing out, fencing in, and no liability without fault—can be found in different counties.

Dangerous Animals. Under the common law of England, the owner or possessor of a nondomesticated animal (collectively referred to by courts as "wild animals" or animals "*ferae naturae*") was subject to strict liability if the animal attacked a person. See May v. Burdett, 9 Q.B. 101 (1846) (monkey bite); Filburn v. People's Palace and Aquarium Co., Ltd., 25 Q.B.Div. 258 (C.A.1890) (attacking elephant). On the other hand the owner of a domestic animal such as a cat, dog, sheep, or horse was subject to strict liability only if the owner knew or had reason to know that the animal had vicious propensities.

This led to interesting problems of classification. Obviously lions, tigers, leopards, and bears were deemed "wild animals." What about deer? Congress & Empire Spring Co. v. Edgar, 99 U.S. 645 (1878); Briley v. Mitchell, 238 La. 551, 115 So.2d 851 (1959). A pet raccoon? Andrew v. Kilgour, 19 Man.L.Rep. 544 (1910). A hive of bees? Ammons v. Kellogg, 137 Miss. 551, 102 So. 562 (1925). Annot., 86 A.L.R.3d 829 (1978). A boar? Marshall v. Ranne, 511 S.W.2d 255 (Tex.1974). A bird able to open his own cage and startle people? See Neagle v. Morgan, 360 Mass. 864, 277 N.E.2d 482 (1971).

The customs of the community apparently enter in. In Burma an elephant is regarded as a domesticated animal, for which there is no strict liability. Maung Kayn Dun v. Ma Kyian, 2 Upper Burma Rulings, Civ. 570 (1900). Suppose a Burma elephant is brought to England to perform in a circus. Behrens v. Bertram Mills Circus, Ltd.,

[1957] 2 Q.B. 1. How about a camel, which is now domesticated virtually everywhere it is found? McQuaker v. Goddard, [1940] 1 K.B. 687.

The majority American position has followed the rule of strict liability in regard to wild animals. See Isaacs v. Powell, 267 So.2d 864 (Fla.App.1972) (chimpanzee); Franken v. Sioux Center, 272 N.W.2d 422 (Iowa 1978) (tiger); Whitefield v. Stewart, 577 P.2d 1295 (Okl.1978) (monkey).

But some courts have moved away from strict liability to a negligence standard with regard to the liability of persons who display wild animals to the public, although the standard of care is often changed to one of extreme caution. See Hansen v. Brogan, 145 Mont. 224, 400 P.2d 265 (1965) (buffalo); Vaughan v. Miller Bros. "101" Ranch Wild West Show, 109 W.Va. 170, 153 S.E. 289 (1930) (ape). The trend is more pronounced with regard to public zoos, although some of the decisions are based on the fact that the legislature authorized the activity. See, e.g., City and County of Denver v. Kennedy, 29 Colo.App. 15, 476 P.2d 762 (1970). Contra: City of Mangum v. Brownlee, 181 Okl. 515, 75 P.2d 174 (1938). What about wild animals that roam freely in animal parks where visitors drive their cars?

As for domestic animals the canard is often repeated that the common law rule is that a domestic animal such as a dog (or cat) is entitled to one bite. The cases do not bear this out. If the owner knows or has reason to know (scienter) that a domestic animal has vicious propensities, this is sufficient to classify that animal with wild ones and strict liability is imposed. See Andrews v. Smith, 324 Pa. 455, 188 A. 146 (1936); Barger v. Jimerson, 130 Colo. 459, 276 P.2d 744 (1954); Harris v. Williams, 160 Okl. 103, 15 P.2d 580 (1932). Many of the cases show interesting and imaginative efforts on the part of plaintiff's counsel to prove that the animal had such a temperament and that the owner was aware of it. See, e.g., Zarek v. Fredericks, 138 F.2d 689 (3 Cir.1943) (dog snarled at guests and was almost always accompanied by his owners); Frederickson v. Kepner, 82 Cal.App.2d 905, 187 P.2d 800 (1947); and Perkins v. Drury, 57 N.M. 269, 258 P.2d 379 (1953) (children warned to stay away from dog); Hill v. Moseley, 220 N.C. 485, 17 S.E.2d 676 (1941) (dog had bad reputation in the neighborhood). Compare the valiant but unsuccessful attempt to have German shepherds classified as "vicious by nature" in Rolen v. Maryland Casualty Co., 240 So.2d 42 (La.App.1970).

In many states the common law regarding liability for dog bites has been changed by statute. These statutes usually do away with the necessity of plaintiff's proving scienter in order to recover. The statutes may also list defenses—e.g., plaintiff committing a trespass or presence of warning sign.

Liability is also affected by statutory provisions requiring dogs to be muzzled or leashed. If a person is injured due to the failure of the owner to comply with the ordinance, the owner becomes "negligent per se" and so liable for the damages. Wistafka v. Grotowski, 205 Ill.App. 529 (1917). However, if the muzzling of the dog would not have prevented the injury, as where the dog does not bite the plaintiff but knocks him down, there is no causal connection, and the common law rule applies. Kennet v. Sossnitz, 260 App.Div. 759, 23 N.Y.S.2d 961 (1940), aff'd, 286 N.Y. 623, 36 N.E.2d 459 (1941).

In Florida, statutory immunity is created for a dog owner who displays an easily readable sign that says "BAD DOG" in a prominent place in his premises. Suppose an owner who displays such a sign says to an invitee, "Rex can be bad, but he can also be good." Rex is bad that day. See Noble v. Yorke, 490 So.2d 29 (Fla.1986). An animal receiving a lot of press attention because of its occasional viciousness is the pit bull dog. Should a landlord have a duty to tell a potential tenant that a neighbor owns a pit bull dog? See Wylie v. Gresch, 191 Cal.App.3d 412, 236 Cal.Rptr. 552 (1987) ("a vicious dog is a danger one might expect to encounter anywhere in our society").

2. ABNORMALLY DANGEROUS ACTIVITIES

RYLANDS v. FLETCHER
In the Exchequer, 3 H. & C. 774, 159 Eng.Rep. 737, 1865.
In the Exchequer Chamber, L.R. 1 Ex. 265, 1866.
In the House of Lords, L.R. 3 H.L. 330, 1868.

[Action brought in 1861 and tried at the Liverpool Summer Assizes (1862). A verdict was found for the plaintiff subject to the award of an arbitrator, who was afterwards empowered by a court order to state a special case instead of making an award. The material facts in the special case stated by the arbitrator were as follows:

The defendants were the owners of a mill. In order to supply it with water they constructed upon the nearby land of Lord Wilton, with his permission, a reservoir. The plaintiff under lease from Lord Wilton was working certain coal mines under lands close to but not adjoining the premises on which the reservoir was constructed. They worked their mine in the direction of the reservoir until they came upon certain old workings, part of which at least had been made and abandoned at a time beyond living memory. These workings consisted of horizontal passages and vertical shafts, the latter apparently filled with rubbish and marl similar to that of the solid earth surrounding them. The defendant employed a competent engineer and competent contractors to plan and construct the reservoir, and it was so planned and constructed solely by them upon a site, in the choice of which the defendants were guilty of no personal fault. In fact, the old mine workings lay beneath it and, continuing under the intermediate lands, communicated, at the point to which the plaintiff had pushed its workings in that direction, with the workings of the plaintiff. The contractors in excavating for the bed of the reservoir came upon five of the above mentioned vertical shafts; the sides or walls of these were of timber, but, because they were filled with soil of the same kind as that composing the surrounding ground, neither the contractors nor the defendants suspected that they were abandoned mine shafts. The arbitrator found that the defendants were guilty of no personal negligence or fault, but that the engineer and contractors had not in fact exercised proper care, with reference to the shafts discovered, to provide for the sufficiency of the reservoir to bear the pressure that it was designed to bear when in use.

The reservoir was completed in December, 1860, and the defendants had it partly filled. Within a few days, one of the shafts that had been met while excavating gave way and burst downward, letting the water into the abandoned workings beneath, through which it flowed, through the communications that the plaintiffs in working their mine had made between the two, into the plaintiffs' workings, flooding their mine.

The question for the opinion of the Court was whether the plaintiff was entitled to recover damages from the defendant by reason of the matters thus stated by the arbitrator.

In the Exchequer, judgment was given for the defendants by a 2-to-1 vote. Martin, B., said there was no trespass, because the damage was not "immediate," but "mediate or consequential." There was no nuisance, because the defendants were doing a lawful and reasonable act. The same rule must be applied to real property as to personal property, that there must be negligence on the part of the defendant to make him responsible. The plaintiff brought error to the Exchequer Chamber.]

BLACKBURN, J. * * * It appears from the statement in the case, that the plaintiff was damaged by his property being flooded by water which, without any fault on his part, broke out of a reservoir constructed on the defendants' land by the defendants' orders, and maintained by the defendants. * * *

The plaintiff, though free from all blame on his part, must bear the loss, unless he can establish that it was the consequence of some default for which the defendants are responsible. The question of law therefore arises, what is the obligation which the law casts on a person who, like the defendants, lawfully brings on his land something which though harmless whilst it remains there, will naturally do mischief if it escape out of his land. It is agreed on all hands that he must take care to keep in that which he has brought on the land and keeps there, in order that it may not escape and damage his neighbors; but the question arises whether the duty which the law casts upon him, under such circumstances, is an absolute duty to keep it in at his peril, or is, as the majority of the Court of Exchequer have thought, merely a duty to take all reasonable and prudent precautions, in order to keep it in, but no more. If the first be the law, the person who has brought on his land and kept there something dangerous, and failed to keep it in, is responsible for all the natural consequences of its escape. If the second

Lord Blackburn

be the limit of his duty, he would not be answerable except on proof of negligence, and consequently would not be answerable for escape arising from any latent defect which ordinary prudence and skill could not detect. *   *   *

We think that the true rule of law is that the person who for his own purposes brings on his lands and collects and keeps there any thing likely to do mischief if it escapes, must keep it in at his peril, and if he does not do so, is prima facie answerable for all the damage which is the natural consequence of its escape. He can excuse himself by showing that the escape was owing to the plaintiff's default; or perhaps that the escape was the consequence of vis major, or the act of God; but as nothing of this sort exists here, it is unnecessary to inquire what excuse would be sufficient. The general rule, as above stated, seems on principle just. The person whose grass or corn is eaten down by the escaping cattle of his neighbor, or whose mine is flooded by the water from his neighbor's reservoir, or whose cellar is invaded by the filth of his neighbor's privy, or whose habitation is made unhealthy by the fumes and noisome vapors of his neighbor's alkali works, is damnified without any fault of his own; and it seems but reasonable and just that the neighbor, who has brought something on his own property which was not naturally there, harmless to others so long as it is confined to his own property, but which he knows to be mischievous if it gets on his neighbor's, should be obliged to make good the damage which ensues if he does not succeed in confining it to his own property. But for his act in bringing it there no mischief could have accrued, and it seems but just that he should at his peril keep it there, so that no mischief may accrue, or answer for the natural and anticipated consequences. And upon authority, this we think is established to be the law, whether the things so brought be beasts, or water, or filth, or stenches.

The case that has most commonly occurred and which is most frequently to be found in the books, is as to the obligation of the owner of cattle which he has brought on his land to prevent their escaping and doing mischief. The law as to them seems to be perfectly settled from early times; the owner must keep them in at his peril, or he will be answerable for the natural consequences of their escape; that is, with regard to tame beasts, for the grass they eat and trample upon, though not for an injury to the person of others, for our ancestors have settled that it is not the general nature of horses to kick, or bulls to gore; but if the owner knows that the beast has a vicious propensity to attack man, he will be answerable for that too. * * *

Judgment for the plaintiff.

Rylands and Horrocks brought error to the House of Lords against the judgment of the Exchequer Chamber, which had reversed the judgment of the Court of Exchequer.

THE LORD CHANCELLOR (LORD CAIRNS). * * * My Lords, the principles in which this case must be determined appear to me to be extremely simple. The defendants, treating them as the owner or occupiers of the close on which the reservoir was constructed, might lawfully have used that close for any purpose for which it might in the ordinary course of the enjoyment of land be used; and if, in what I may term the natural user of that land, there had been any accumulation of water, either on the surface or underground, and if, by the operation of the laws of nature, that accumulation of water had passed off into the close occupied by the plaintiff, the plaintiff could not have complained that that result had taken place. If he had desired to guard himself against it, it would have been lain upon him to have done so, by leaving, or by interposing, some barrier between his close and the close of the defendants in order to have prevented that operation of the laws of nature.

Lord Cairns

As an illustration of that principle, I may refer to a case which was cited in the argument before your Lordships, the case of Smith v. Kendrick, in the Court of Common Pleas, 7 C.B. 515.

On the other hand, if the defendants, not stopping at the natural use of their close, had desired to use it for any purpose which I may term a non-natural use, for the purpose of introducing into the close that which in its natural condition was not in or upon it, for the purpose of introducing water either above or below ground in quantities and in a manner not the result of any work or operation on or under the land; and if in consequence of their doing so, or in consequence of any imperfection in the mode of their doing so, the water came to escape and to pass off into the close of the plaintiff, then it appears to me that that which the defendants were doing they were doing at their own peril; and, if in the course of their doing it the evil arose to which I have referred, the evil, namely, of the escape of the water and its passing away to the close of the plaintiff and injuring the plaintiff, then for the consequence of that, in my opinion, the defendants would be liable. As the case of Smith v. Kendrick is an illustration of the first principle to which I have referred, so also the second principle to which I have referred is well illustrated by another case in the same Court, the case of Baird v. Williamson, 15 C.B.N.S. 317, which was also cited in the argument at the bar. * * *

Judgment of the Court of Exchequer Chamber affirmed.

[The concurring opinion of LORD CRANWORTH is omitted.]

---

1. Why not liability simply for trespass to land? Or nuisance? The contractor who did the work was negligent in not discovering the abandoned mine shafts and blocking them up. Why was defendant not liable for the negligence of the person he employed? Would he be liable today? Was defendant negligent in having the reservoir at all? If not negligent, was he still at fault? See Keeton, Conditional Fault in the Law of Torts, 72 Harv.L.Rev. 401 (1959).

2. The reservoir in this case was located in a part of Lancashire devoted to coal mining. The American equivalent would be a reservoir in the immediate vicinity of Scranton, Pa. Has this any significance?

3. Professor Bohlen, in The Rule in Rylands v. Fletcher, 59 U.Pa.L.Rev. 298 (1911), first advanced a "materialistic" explanation of the principal case, to the effect that the judges who wrote the opinions belonged to the landed gentry, and were seeking to protect that class against the encroachments of industry. This was refuted by the painstaking biographies of the judges in Molloy, Fletcher v. Rylands: A Re-examination of Juristic Origins, 9 U.Chi.L.Rev. 266 (1942).

4. How far does the opinion of Lord Cairns limit that of Blackburn in *Rylands?* What does he mean by a "natural use" of land? Something like trees, in a state of nature? Note that he relies on Smith v. Kendrick, 7 C.B. 515, 137 Eng.Rep. 205 (1849), where defendant's normal and usual mining operations resulted in the flow of percolating water from springs into plaintiff's adjoining mine, and defendant was held not liable. A parallel case is Zampos v. United States Smelting R. & M. Co., 206 F.2d 171 (10th Cir.1953). He relies also upon Baird v. Williamson, 15 C.B. (N.S.) 376, 143 Eng.Rep. 831 (1863), where defendant pumped the water from his mine to a higher level, from which it flowed into plaintiff's mine, and was held liable.

5. Subsequent decisions in England have followed the distinction between "natural" and "nonnatural" uses of land made by Lord Cairns. In determining what is a nonnatural use, the English courts have looked not only to the character of the thing or activity in question, but also to the place and manner in which it is maintained, and its relation to its surroundings. Thus water collected in large tanks in dangerous proximity to plaintiff's land has been held to be a matter for strict liability; but water in a cistern, in household pipes, in a water closet, or in a barnyard tank supplying cattle, has not, provided there was no negligence. Fire in a fireplace, or in an authorized railway engine, is a natural use; but a traction engine shooting out sparks on the highway is not. Although the automobile is dangerous, and fatal to thousands annually, it is held to be "natural"; but a ten ton traction engine or a steam roller which crushes conduits under the street is not. See Stallybrass, Dangerous Things and the Non–Natural User of Land, 3 Cambridge L.J. 376 (1929); Fleming,

Torts, 280 (4th ed. 1971); Newark, Non–Natural Use and Rylands v. Fletcher, 24 Mod.L.Rev. 447 (1961). How would you state the English rule?

6. In Read v. J. Lyons & Co. Ltd., [1947] A.C. 156, where a government inspector was injured by an explosion in defendant's munitions plant, the court further limited Rylands v. Fletcher by holding that the rule would apply only when something "escaped" from defendant's land. The case might perhaps be justified on the ground that plaintiff had assumed the risk. Cf. E.I. Du Pont de Nemours & Co. v. Cudd, 176 F.2d 855 (10th Cir.1949), where this was held as to an employee working around a highly dangerous activity. The Read Case was, however, followed in Barrette v. Franki Compressed Pile Co., [1955] 2 Dom.L. Rep. 665, where it was held that vibration from pile driving that damaged plaintiff's building did not involve the "escape" of anything. Is the distinction sound?

7. In the United States, Rylands v. Fletcher started out with approval in Ball v. Nye, 99 Mass. 582, 97 Am.Dec. 56 (1868) (percolation of filthy water), and Cahill v. Eastman, 18 Minn. 324, 10 Am.Rep. 184 (1871) (water escaping from a tunnel). The case then was rejected in its entirety by three leading American courts in three years. Losee v. Buchanan, 51 N.Y. 476, 10 Am.Rep. 623 (1873); Marshall v. Welwood, 38 N.J.L. 339, 20 Am.Rep. 394 (1876); Brown v. Collins, 53 N.H. 442, 16 Am.Rep. 372 (1873). The first two of these involved the explosion of ordinary steam boilers, and the third a runaway horse. They were clearly cases of customary, natural uses, to which the English courts would certainly never have applied the rule. Cf. Howard v. Furness Houlder Argentine Lines, [1936] 2 All Eng.Rep. 781. In each case the attack was directed at Blackburn's broad statement in the intermediate court, and the decision in the House of Lords was given little or no attention. Rylands v. Fletcher was treated as holding that the defendant is absolutely liable whenever anything whatever escapes from his control and causes damage. In other words, the rule of the case was misstated, and as misstated was rejected, in cases in which it had no proper application in the first place.

8. These decisions gave Rylands v. Fletcher a bad name, and it was rejected in seven jurisdictions, such as Maine, New Hampshire, New York, Oklahoma, Rhode Island, Texas and possibly Wyoming. For a time a majority of the courts that considered the case by name rejected it. In recent years the American trend has been very much in favor of approval of the case, and a substantial majority now favor the case. What factors may have influenced recent courts to accept the Rylands principle? Have there been changes in society that made courts more willing to impose strict liability for hazardous activities? See Cities Service Co. v. State, 312 So.2d 799 (Fla.App.2d Dist.1975).

9. Many of the courts rejecting Rylands v. Fletcher by name have accomplished much the same result in many cases by calling the defendant's activity or condition an "absolute nuisance." See infra page 821. Also Prosser, Nuisance Without Fault, 20 Tex.L.Rev. 399 (1942).

10. Rylands v. Fletcher has been a favorite topic of legal writers. See Bohlen, The Rule in Rylands v. Fletcher, 59 U.Pa.L.Rev. 298 (1911); Thayer, Liability Without Fault, 29 Harv.L.Rev. 801 (1916); Morris, Hazardous Enterprises and Risk–Bearing Capacity, 61 Yale L.J. 1172 (1952); Stallybrass, Dangerous Things and the Non–Natural User of Land, 3 Cambridge L.J. 376 (1929); Carpenter, The Doctrine of Green v. General Petroleum Corp., 5 So.Cal.L.Rev. 263 (1932); Prosser, The Principle of Rylands v. Fletcher, in his Selected Topics on the Law of Torts 135 (1953); Baker, An Eclipse of Fault Liability, 40 Va.L.

Rev. 273 (1954); Note, The Rylands v. Fletcher Doctrine in America: Abnormally Dangerous, Ultrahazardous or Absolute Nuisance, 1978 Ariz.St.L.J. 99.

BRIDGES v. THE KENTUCKY STONE CO., INC.
Supreme Court of Indiana, 1981.
425 N.E.2d 125.

HUNTER, J. This action stems from an allegedly intentional and malicious explosion of dynamite at the home of plaintiff Charles Bridges in Johnson County, Indiana, on February 10, 1975. In the explosion, Bridges's twelve year old son was killed; a second son and Bridges both were injured in the blast * * *.

Bridges subsequently filed suit against Kentucky Stone and codefendant Webb to recover damages for the injuries sustained in the blast. Bridges's claim against William Webb rested on the allegation that he had set and ignited the explosives at Bridges's home. Kentucky Stone was named as a defendant on the basis that it had "negligently kept and stored" dynamite and other ultra-hazardous explosives at its Tyrone plant, thereby permitting Webb to obtain the explosives ultimately used at the Bridges's home in Johnson County.

The trial court held as a matter of law that the assumed negligent storage of dynamite by Kentucky Stone was not the proximate cause of the explosion and injuries to Bridges. On this basis, Kentucky Stone was granted summary judgment.

The Court of Appeals * * * reversed the summary judgment * * *.

In Yukon Equipment, Inc. v. Fireman's Fund Insurance, [585 P.2d 1206 (Alaska 1978),] thieves broke into an explosives storage magazine located in the suburbs of Anchorage and ignited 80,000 pounds of explosives, damaging homes within a two-mile radius. Notwithstanding the cause of the blast and the fact that the magazine was located on land which, by federal order, was devoted to the storage of explosives, the Alaska Supreme Court imposed absolute liability on the operators of the storage magazine. The per se rule of liability imposed stemmed from the Court's conclusion that the storage of dynamite was in and of itself an "ultra-hazardous activity."

We do not share that opinion. Rather, we are persuaded that whether the storage of dynamite in any particular circumstance is an "ultra-hazardous activity" must be determined on a case-by-case basis, as per the various factors outlined by the American Law Institute in Restatement (Second) of Torts § 520 (1977).[2] But * * * we reject the per se rule of liability adopted in Alaska. * * *

---

2. [The note quotes § 520, which is discussed in detail in the next case, and then continues:]

The storage of dynamite, we note is distinguished from the use and explosion of dynamite, the latter activity being one to which this jurisdiction accords absolute liability. Enos Coal Mining Co. v. Schuchart, (1963) 243 Ind. 692, 188 N.E.2d 406.

Here, unlike Yukon Equipment, Inc. v. Fireman's Fund Insurance, supra, the consequence of the assumed negligent storage was not contemporaneous damage to the inhabitants and property of the area surrounding the storage site. Rather, the blast occurred nearly three weeks subsequent to the theft at a location over one hundred miles from the storage site. The disappearance of the dynamite was reported to federal authorities within twenty-four hours of its discovery, as required by federal regulations 27 C.F.R. 181.127 and 181.130. The discovery and reporting occurred within twenty-four to forty-eight hours after the theft and nearly three weeks prior to the blast. In the face of these circumstances, we hold the theft of the explosive materials, the transporting of them from Tyrone to Johnson County, the preparation necessary to the discharge, and the eventual trespass and detonation at the Bridges's residence was a superseding cause of the blast precluding liability for any supposed negligence of Kentucky Stone. * * * We expressly limit our decision to the facts before us. * * * [T]he opinion of the Court of Appeals is vacated, and the judgment of the trial court is affirmed. * * * DeBRULER, J. dissents with opinion * * *.

---

1. The Restatement of Torts used the term "ultrahazardous" and applied it to an activity that "necessarily involves a risk of serious harm to the persons, land or chattels of others which cannot be eliminated by the exercise of the utmost care and * * * is not a matter of common usage." § 520. The definition is categoric. If an activity is ultrahazardous, it would be so regarded no matter where it took place. This was the approach taken by the Alaska court regarding storage of explosives in the *Yukon Equipment* case, described in the opinion in the instant case. That case carried the approach so far that it held liability on the part of the company storing the explosives, even though they were stolen by the other defendant and deliberately set off to produce the explosion. (This situation is the subject of a caveat in the Restatement.)

2. The Second Restatement, on the other hand, uses the term "abnormally dangerous" and makes the decision depend on the nature of the location where the activity takes place. Consider, for example, whether a hardware store in a small town, keeping a small amount of dynamite for the benefit of farmers clearing fields of stumps, would be subject to strict liability. Cf. Barnes v. Zettlemoyer, 25 Tex.Civ.App. 468, 62 S.W. 111 (1901). What would the Alaska court hold?

3. A majority of the courts impose strict liability for blasting if it is done in an urban area. Some, however, state that the nature of the location is important in determining whether the activity is ultrahazardous. See Liber v. Flor, 160 Colo. 7, 415 P.2d 332 (1966); Otero v. Burgess, 84 N.M. 575, 505 P.2d 1251 (1973); cf. Chavez v. Southern Pac. Transp. Co., 413 F.Supp. 1203 (D.C.Cal. 1976) (keeping 18 bomb-loaded box cars in railroad yard near town). And still others, stressing the comparative safety with which it can be carried on by the exercise of due care, hold that there is liability only for negligence. Reynolds v. W.H. Hinman Co., 145 Me. 343, 75 A.2d 802 (1956); Wadleigh v. Manchester, 100 N.H. 277, 123 A.2d 831 (1956). Sometimes strict liability is accomplished

by calling the activity a nuisance, as in Gossett v. Southern R. Co., 115 Tenn. 376, 89 S.W. 737 (1905).

LANGAN v. VALICOPTERS, INC.
Supreme Court of Washington, 1977.
88 Wash.2d 855, 567 P.2d 218.

DOLLIVER, ASSOCIATE JUSTICE. This is an appeal from a judgment against appellants for damages resulting from their crop spraying activities. * * * The Langans are organic farmers: that is, they use no nonorganic fertilizers, insecticides or herbicides to aid them in their farming but rely on natural fertilizers and natural pest control agents. They had planned to can and sell their produce to organic food buyers.

Valicopters, Inc., is a Washington corporation which engages in the aerial application of agricultural pesticides. * * * The Thalheimers, doing business as Thalheimer Farms, owned and farmed the land adjoining that of the respondents. It was their land that was being sprayed by Valicopters. * * *

On June 3, 1973, [defendant] sprayed for Colorado Beetle infestation on the Thalheimer farm with a chemical pesticide known as Thiodan. * * * Patrick Langan testified that, during one spraying pass, the helicopter began spraying while it was over his property [and] * * * that the spray settled on the entire length of their tomato, bean, garlic, cucumber and Jerusalem artichoke rows. * * *

[The Northwest Organic Food Producers' Association (NOFPA) decertified the property of the Langans after laboratory tests showed the crops had a residue higher than allowable under its by-laws.]

After a jury trial, a judgment in the amount of $5,500 was entered against appellants. They appealed to the Court of Appeals, Division Three. That court certified the case to this court and we accepted certification. * * *

The next issue is whether the trial court erred by instructing the jury that appellants would be strictly liable for damage that was proximately caused by their aerial spraying. The trial judge gave the following instruction:

"If you find that defendants' chemicals fell upon plaintiffs' crops, you are instructed that as a matter of law the defendants are liable for such damage to plaintiffs' crops, if any, as you find was proximately caused by defendants' spray application."

Liability for damage caused by crop dusting or spraying generally is imposed on the basis of either negligence or strict liability. See generally Liability for Injury Caused by Spraying or Dusting of Crops, Annot., 37 A.L.R.2d 833 (1971). The courts in most jurisdictions that have held crop dusters liable have used the theory of negligence. [Cc] However, other opinions which have ostensibly relied upon the principles of negligence have been criticized by legal writers because the reasoning is not clear or more nearly resembles strict liability * * *.

In Washington, this court has adopted the Restatement (Second) of Torts §§ 519, 520. Section 519 of the Restatement * provides:

"(1) One who carries on an abnormally dangerous activity is subject to liability for harm to the person, land or chattels of another resulting from the activity, although he has exercised the utmost care to prevent the harm.

"(2) This strict liability is limited to the kind of harm, the possibility of which makes the activity abnormally dangerous."

Section 520 lists the factors to be used when determining what constitutes an abnormally dangerous activity:

"In determining whether an activity is abnormally dangerous, the following factors are to be considered:

"(a) existence of a high degree of risk of some harm to the person, land or chattels of others;

"(b) likelihood that the harm that results from it will be great;

"(c) inability to eliminate the risk by the exercise of reasonable care;

"(d) extent to which the activity is not a matter of common usage;

"(e) inappropriateness of the activity to the place where it is carried on; and

"(f) extent to which its value to the community is outweighed by its dangerous attributes."

Whether an activity is abnormally dangerous is a question of law for the court to decide. Siegler v. Kuhlman, [81 Wash.2d 448, 502 P.2d 1181 (1972)]; Restatement (Second) of Torts § 520, comment (*l*). In making this determination, we have considered each of the factors listed in the Restatement, § 520. We note that not all of the elements listed in § 520 must weigh equally in favor of characterizing an activity as abnormally dangerous in order that we may so find it to be.

"In determining whether the danger is abnormal, the factors listed in Clauses (a) to (f) of this Section are all to be considered, and are all of importance. Any one of them is not necessarily sufficient of itself in a particular case, and ordinarily several of them will be required for strict liability. On the other hand, it is not necessary that each of them be present, especially if others weigh heavily. Because of the interplay of these various factors, it is not possible to reduce abnormally dangerous activities to any exact definition. The essential question is whether the risk created is so unusual, either because of its magnitude or because of the circumstances surrounding it, as to justify the imposition of strict liability for the harm which results from it, even though it is carried on with all reasonable care." Restatement (Second) of Torts

---

* The opinion quotes §§ 519 and 520, and their comments as they appeared in Tentative Draft No. 10 (1964). There were some minor changes in diction in the final volume, appearing in 1977. The language of the final volume is substituted here.—[Ed.]

§ 520, comment (f). [C] However, in this case, each test of the Restatement is met.

§ 520(a): *Existence of a High Degree of Risk of Some Harm to the Person, Land or Chattels of Others.* It is undisputed among the authorities cited to us that crop dusting involves an element of risk of harm. In Note, Crop Dusting: Legal Problems in a New Industry, 6 Stan.L. Rev. at 72–75, the author points out that the drift of chemicals is virtually unpredictable due to three "uncertain and uncontrollable factors: (1) the size of the dust or spray particles; (2) the air disturbances created by the [applicating aircraft]; and (3) natural atmospheric forces." The author discusses these three factors in detail and notes: "In the opinion of leading scientists who are working to alleviate the dangers of crop dusting, it is impossible to eliminate drift with present knowledge and equipment. Experience bears this out." 6 Stan.L.Rev. at 75. * * *

§ 520(b): *Likelihood That the Harm That Results from It Will Be Great.* Whether there will be great harm depends upon what adjoining property owners do with their land. For example, one property owner may grow wheat (a narrow-leafed crop) and his neighbor may grow peas (a broad-leafed crop). The wheat farmer may wish to spray his crop with the chemical herbicide (weed killer) 2,4–D, which kills only broad-leafed plants. If the 2,4–D drifts onto the pea farmer's property, his entire crop could be destroyed since peas are broad-leafed plants. Frear, Chemistry of Insecticides, Fungicides and Herbicides 316 (2d ed. 1948). The reported cases are illustrative of the many possible fact situations which indicate that neighboring property may be sensitive to and damaged by the spraying activity of an adjoining landowner. See Comment, Crop Dusting: Two Theories of Liability?, 19 Hastings L.J. 476, 479, n. 38. * * *

As the present case illustrates, it is economically damaging for an organic farmer who is a member of NOFPA to apply nonorganic materials to his crops because he would lose the association's certification. There was substantial evidence before the trial court that, once an organic farmer loses his certification, it is highly unlikely that he will be able to sell his crops on the regular commercial market due to his failure to enter into contracts with commercial produce buyers before the season begins, and, even if he could sell his crops to a commercial produce buyer, the farmer would be unable to command as high a price for his goods as he could on the organic market.

§ 520(c): *Inability to Eliminate the Risk by the Exercise of Reasonable Care.* The same elements that produce a high degree of risk of harm, namely the uncontrollability of dust or spray drift (§ 520(a) above), also cannot be eliminated by the exercise of reasonable care. [C]

§ 520(d): *Extent to Which the Activity is not a Matter of Common Usage.* The Restatement (Second) of Torts § 520(i), observes "An activity is a matter of common usage if it is customarily carried on by the great mass of mankind, or by many people in the community." Although we recognize the prevalence of crop dusting and acknowledge that it is ordinarily done in large portions of the Yakima Valley, it is carried on by only a comparatively small number of persons (approximately 287 aircraft were used in 1975) and is not a matter of common usage.

§ 520(e): *Inappropriateness of the Activity to the Place Where It Is Carried on.* Given the nature of organic farming, the use of pesticides adjacent to such an area must be considered an activity conducted in an inappropriate place.

§ 520(f): *Extent to Which Its Value to the Community Is Outweighed by Its Dangerous Attributes.* As a criterion for determining strict liability, this factor has received some criticism among legal writers. In 2 Harper & James, Law of Torts, Comment to § 14.4 (Supp. 1968), the authors suggest that § 520(f) is not a true element of strict liability: "The justification for strict liability, in other words, is that useful but dangerous activities must pay their own way." [C]

There is no doubt that pesticides are socially valuable in the control of insects, weeds and other pests. They may benefit society by increasing production. Whether strict liability or negligence principles should be applied amounts to a balancing of conflicting social interest— the risk of harm versus the utility of the activity. In balancing these interests, we must ask who should bear the loss caused by the pesticides. [C]

In the present case, the Langans were eliminated from the organic food market for 1973 through no fault of their own. If crop dusting continues on the adjoining property, the Langans may never be able to sell their crops to organic food buyers. Appellants, on the other hand, will all profit from the continued application of pesticides. Under these circumstances, there can be an equitable balancing of social interests only if appellants are made to pay for the consequences of their acts.

We realize that farmers are statutorily bound to prevent the spread of insects, pests, noxious weeds and diseases. RCW 15.08.030 and RCW 17.10.140–.150. But the fulfillment of that duty does not mean the ability of an organic farmer to produce organic crops must be destroyed without compensation.

Thus, for the reasons mentioned above, we find that the trial court did not err by instructing the jury on strict liability. * * *

There is no reversible error; the judgment of the trial court is affirmed.

---

1. Some other activities held subject to strict liability:

A. *Inflammable liquids* stored in quantity in an urban area. Zero Wholesale Gas Co. v. Stroud, 264 Ark. 27, 571 S.W.2d 74 (1978) (propane gas); Northglenn v. Chevron U.S.A., Inc., 519 F.Supp. 515 (D.Colo.1981) (service station stored large amounts of gasoline underground near a residential area and its sewer lines). Contra: Hudson v. Peavey Oil Co., 279 Or. 3, 566 P.2d 175 (1977) (filling stations common in residential areas).

B. *Pile driving,* setting up excessive vibration. Vern J. Oja & Associates v. Washington Park Towers, Inc., 89 Wash.2d 72, 569 P.2d 1141 (1977).

C. *Crop Dusting.* In addition to the principal case, see Loe v. Lenhardt, 227 Or. 242, 362 P.2d 312 (1961). Contra, requiring negligence: Lawler v. Skelton, 241 Miss. 274, 130 So.2d 565 (1961). See Notes, 9 Gonz.L.Rev. 816 (1974), 19 Hastings L.J. 476 (1968), 40 Tex.L.Rev. 527 (1962).

D. *Poisonous Gases.* Luthringer v. Moore, 31 Cal.2d 489, 190 P.2d 1 (1948) (fumigation); Langlois v. Allied Chemical Corp., 258 La. 1067, 249 So.2d 133 (1971). Contra: Fritz v. E.I. DuPont de Nemours & Co., 45 Del. 427, 75 A.2d 256 (1950).

E. *Rockets.* Defendants testing rocket fuel have been held subject to strict liability in Smith v. Lockheed Propulsion Co., 247 Cal.App.2d 774, 56 Cal. Rptr. 128 (1967); and Berg v. Reaction Motors Div., 37 N.J. 396, 181 A.2d 487 (1962).

F. *Hazardous Waste Disposal Site.* Cf. Village of Wilsonville v. SCA Services, Inc., 86 Ill.2d 1, 55 Ill.Dec. 499, 426 N.E.2d 824 (1981); Bauer, Love Canal: Common Law Approaches to a Modern Tragedy, 11 Envtl.L.Nw.U. 133 (1980); Hurley–Bruno, The Development of a Strict Liability Cause of Action for Personal Injuries Resulting from Hazardous Waste, 16 N.Eng.L.Rev. 543 (1981).

G. *Oil Wells.* Green v. General Petroleum Corp., 205 Cal. 328, 270 P. 952 (1928). Contra: Turner v. Big Lake Oil Co., 128 Tex. 155, 96 S.W.2d 221 (1936) (salt water reservoir).

H. *Water Escape.* Branch v. Western Petroleum, Inc., 657 P.2d 267 (Utah 1982); Clark–Aiken Co. v. Cromwell–Wright Co., 367 Mass. 70, 323 N.E.2d 876 (1975); Smith v. Board of County Comm'rs, 5 Mich.App. 370, 146 N.W.2d 702 (1966); Thorson v. Minot, 153 N.W.2d 764 (N.D.1967); cf. Doundoulakis v. Hempstead, 42 N.Y.2d 440, 368 N.E.2d 24, 398 N.Y.S.2d 401 (1977) (hydraulic landfill).

2. Note that these activities involve the use of property. Can the abnormally dangerous or ultrahazardous activity theory be used to establish strict liability for other activities not involving the use of land? See Perkins v. F.I.E. Corp., 762 F.2d 1250 (5th Cir.1985) (marketing of handguns—theory not applied). What about maintenance of a frequently used device that may cause injury without fault on the part of a proprietor? Cf. Brown v. Sears, Roebuck & Co., 136 Ariz. 556, 667 P.2d 750 (1983) (frayed electric cord).

3. *Aviation—Ground Damage.* In early stages of commercial aviation, airlines were held strictly liable for ground damage resulting from a crash. This view is no longer justified by the character of the planes and their accident records if the basis is an ultrahazardous or abnormally dangerous activity; and a number of courts have retreated to a negligence standard. See Wood v. United Air Lines, Inc., 32 Misc.2d 955, 223 N.Y.S.2d 692 (1961), aff'd mem., 16 A.D.2d 659, 226 N.Y.S.2d 1022 (1962), appeal dismissed, 11 N.Y.2d 1053, 230 N.Y.S.2d 207, 184 N.E.2d 180 (1962); Southern Cal. Edison Co. v. Coleman, 150 Cal.App.2d Supp. 829, 310 P.2d 504 (1957); Vrazel v. Bieri, 294 S.W.2d 148 (Tex. Civ.App.1956); In re Kinsey's Estate, 152 Neb. 95, 40 N.W.2d 526, 531 (1949). Does it make sense that as an industry becomes stronger economically or technologically it is shifted to a less stringent basis of liability? The law review

discussions do not deal directly with this point. Compare articles advocating a negligence standard—Orr, Is Aviation Ultra–Hazardous?, 21 Ins.Couns.J. 48 (1954); Symposium: Airplanes and Liability, 28 Tenn.L.Rev. 117 (1961); Whitehead, Liability of Owners and Operators of Planes, 15 Syracuse L.Rev. 1 (1963)—with those supporting strict liability—Schmidt, Piercing the Aluminum Overcast, 9 Lincoln L.Rev. 37 (1974); Vold, Strict Liability for Airplane Crashes, 5 Hastings L.J. 1 (1953); Note, 23 Stan.L.Rev. 569 (1971). After considerable wavering by the American Law Institute, a rule of strict liability was adopted in § 520A of the Second Restatement. Is there any other basis on which strict liability can be justified?

4. *"Matter of Common Usage."* Automobile accidents kill and injure more people and damage more property than any other. Why is driving an automobile not an abnormally dangerous activity subject to strict liability?

See also Beck v. Bel Air Properties, Inc., 134 Cal.App.2d 834, 286 P.2d 503 (1955) (earth moving operations incident to subdividing and grading hills and slopes with residential building sites); Rodgers v. Lovington, 91 N.M. 306, 573 P.2d 240 (1977) (burning dead leaves and grass); Insurance Co. of North America v. Sheinbein, 488 P.2d 1273 (Okl.1971) (same); cf. Zero Wholesale Gas Co. v. Stroud, 264 Ark. 27, 571 S.W.2d 74 (1978) (propane gas storage— defendant failed to raise properly the issue of common usage).

5. *"Inappropriate for the Location."* Many of the differences in the holdings of the cases cited in Note 1 supra, can be explained on the basis of the location of the activity. See also the Reporter's Note to § 520 of the Restatement, classifying the cases according to the location of the activity.

6. Professor Seavey suggested that a nuclear reactor would be a nonnatural use of land no matter where it was located. See Seavey, Torts and Atoms, 46 Calif.L.Rev. 3, 9 (1958). Compare Carolina Environmental Study Group, Inc. v. United States Atomic Energy Comm'n, 431 F.Supp. 203 (D.C.N.C. 1977), rev'd sub nom., Duke Power Co. v. Carolina Study Group, Inc., 438 U.S. 59 (1978). Accidents related to harms caused by nuclear reactors are addressed by federal legislation called the Price–Anderson Act (Atomic Energy Damages), 42 U.S.C.A. § 2210 (1957). This legislation was being reconsidered by Congress as this casebook went to press. The underlying premise of Price–Anderson is that where strict liability is to be imposed in a situation where there may be massive harm, the amount of damage paid should be *limited.* There have been Congressional debates under Price–Anderson about who should pay. Assuming innocence on the part of a defendant, should a harm be a private or public cost? What about other activities discussed in this chapter?

7. *Policy Behind the Imposition of Strict Liability.* Strict liability is "founded upon a policy of the law that imposes upon anyone who for his own purposes creates an abnormal risk of harm to his neighbors, the responsibility of relieving against that harm when it does in fact occur. The defendant's enterprise, in other words, is required to pay its way by compensating for the harm it causes because of its special, abnormal and dangerous character." Restatement (Second) of Torts § 519, comment d. The liability "is applicable to an activity that is carried on with all reasonable care, and that is of such utility that the risk involved in it cannot be regarded as so great or so unreasonable as to make it negligence merely to carry it on." Id., § 520, comment b. Observe also, that the decision of whether an activity is subject to strict liability is for the court, not the jury, to make. Id.

In other words, this liability is analogous to negligence per se, but it is not called negligence because a court makes a judgment that its value to the community is sufficiently great that the mere participation in the activity is not to be stigmatized as wrongdoing in the negligence sense. It is simply required to pay its own way, without that stigma, but it does pay with full tort damages, including pain and suffering damages when personal injury is involved. Does it make for sound social policy to make a "non-negligent" defendant pay as much as a "negligent" or "guilty" one? Should courts, as contrasted with legislatures, make judgments as to which activities should be subject to "strict liability"? What practical difference would such judgments entail?

Of course, one who carries on an abnormally dangerous activity may also be negligent in the way in which he conducts it and therefore subject to liability on both bases.

3. LIMITATIONS ON STRICT LIABILITY

FOSTER v. PRESTON MILL CO.
Supreme Court of Washington, 1954.
44 Wash.2d 440, 268 P.2d 645.

HAMLEY, JUSTICE. Blasting operations conducted by Preston Mill Company frightened mother mink owned by B.W. Foster, and caused the mink to kill their kittens. Foster brought this action against the company to recover damages. His second amended complaint, upon which the case was tried, sets forth a cause of action on the theory of absolute liability * * *.

After a trial to the court without a jury, judgment was rendered for plaintiff in the sum of $1,953.68. The theory adopted by the court was that, after defendant received notice of the effect which its blasting operations were having upon the mink, it was absolutely liable for all damages of that nature thereafter sustained. * * *

The primary question presented by appellant's assignments of error is whether, on these facts, the judgment against appellant is sustainable on the theory of absolute liability.

[The court pointed out that in Washington there is strict liability in blasting cases whether the damage is caused by trespassory or nontrespassory invasions.]

However the authorities may be divided on the point just discussed, they appear to be agreed that strict liability should be confined to consequences which lie within the extraordinary risk whose existence calls for such responsibility. [Cc] This limitation on the doctrine is indicated in the italicized portions of the rule as set forth in Restatement of Torts, § 519:

"Except as stated in §§ 521–4, one who carries on an ultrahazardous activity is liable to another whose person, land or chattels the actor should recognize as likely to be harmed by the unpreventable miscarriage of the activity for harm resulting thereto *from that which makes the activity ultrahazardous,* although the utmost care is exercised to prevent the harm." (Italics supplied.)

This restriction which has been placed upon the application of the doctrine of absolute liability is based upon considerations of policy. * * * " * * * It is one thing to say that a dangerous enterprise must pay its way within reasonable limits, and quite another to say that it must bear responsibility for every extreme of harm that it may cause. The same practical necessity for the restriction of liability within some reasonable bounds, which arises in connection with problems of 'proximate cause' in negligence cases, demands here that some limit be set. * * * This limitation has been expressed by saying that the defendant's duty to insure safety extends only to certain consequences. More commonly, it is said that the defendant's conduct is not the 'proximate cause' of the damage. But ordinarily in such cases no question of causation is involved, and the limitation is one of the policy underlying liability." Prosser on Torts, 457, § 60.

Applying this principle to the case before us, the question comes down to this: Is the risk that any unusual vibration or noise may cause wild animals, which are being raised for commercial purposes, to kill their young, one of the things which make the activity of blasting ultrahazardous?

We have found nothing in the decisional law which would support an affirmative answer to this question. The decided cases, as well as common experience, indicate that the thing which makes blasting ultrahazardous is the risk that property or persons may be damaged or injured by coming into direct contact with flying debris, or by being directly affected by vibrations of the earth or concussions of the air. * * *

The relatively moderate vibration and noise which appellant's blasting produced at a distance of two and a quarter miles was no more than a usual incident of the ordinary life of the community. See 3 Restatement of Torts 48, § 522, comment a. The trial court specifically found that the blasting did not unreasonably interfere with the enjoyment of their property by nearby landowners, except in the case of respondent's mink ranch.

It is the exceedingly nervous disposition of mink, rather than the normal risks inherent in blasting operations, which therefore must, as a matter of sound policy, bear the responsibility for the loss here sustained. We subscribe to the view expressed by Professor Harper (30 Mich.L.Rev. 1001, 1006, supra) that the policy of the law does not impose the rule of strict liability to protect against harms incident to the plaintiff's extraordinary and unusual use of land. This is perhaps but an application of the principle that the extent to which one man in the lawful conduct of his business is liable for injuries to another involves an adjustment of conflicting interests. * * *

It is our conclusion that the risk of causing harm of the kind here experienced, as a result of the relatively minor vibration, concussion, and noise from distance blasting, is not the kind of risk which makes the activity of blasting ultrahazardous. The doctrine of absolute liability is therefore inapplicable under the facts of this case, and respondent is not entitled to recover damages.

The judgment is reversed.

---

1. Suppose defendant had been found negligent in making unnecessary noise with heavy equipment, knowing of the possibility that plaintiff's mink might be frightened and kill their kittens. Should defendant be held liable? See Summit View, Inc. v. W.W. Clyde & Co., 17 Utah 2d 26, 403 P.2d 919 (1965). Suppose the defendant could postpone his blasting activity until the one-month-danger period for the mink (whelping season) was over. Under the rationale of the principal case, should that make a difference? What about liability in negligence? See MacGibbon v. Robinson, [1953] 2 D.L.R. 689; Mason v. Grandel, [1952] 1 D.L.R. 516. Should it make any difference that these cases arose in a portion of Canada where the raising of mink was an important part of the economy?

2. In accord with the principal case, upon similar facts, are Madsen v. East Jordan Irrigation Co., 101 Utah 552, 125 P.2d 794 (1942); and Gronn v. Rogers Constructors, Inc., 221 Or. 226, 350 P.2d 1086 (1960). Compare Uvalde Const. Co. v. Hill, 142 Tex. 19, 175 S.W.2d 247 (1943), where the blasting frightened a cow, which bounded against a milkmaid.

3. Without any negligence on the part of the defendant, his cow trespasses in plaintiff's garden. Plaintiff tries to drive the cow out, and the cow attacks and injures her. Strict liability? Troth v. Wills, 8 Pa.Super. 1 (1897); Nixon v. Harris, 15 Ohio St.2d 105, 238 N.E.2d 785 (1968). What about the miscegenation of the scrub bull and the pedigreed heifer? The court had some fun with this in Kopplin v. Quade, 145 Wis. 454, 130 N.W. 511 (1911). What if the cow wanders into plaintiff's barn and breaks through a rotten place in the floor; and plaintiff, entering the barn in the dark falls into the hole and is injured? Hollenbeck v. Johnson, 79 Hun 499, 29 N.Y.S. 945 (1894).

4. Defendant parades his circus elephants through the streets of a city. Plaintiff's skittish horse, seeing a large object pass at a distance of a city block, takes fright and runs away, and plaintiff is injured. Is there strict liability? Schribner v. Kelly, 32 Barb. 14 (N.Y.1862); Bostock–Ferrari Amusement Co. v. Brocksmith, 34 Ind.App. 566, 73 N.E. 281 (1875).

5. Defendant keeps a vicious dog that he knows has in the past attacked human beings. This dog, trotting peacefully down the street, accidentally runs into plaintiff and knocks him down. Strict liability? Koetting v. Conroy, 223 Wis. 550, 270 N.W. 625, 271 N.W. 369 (1937). What if the dog's owner knows that the animal has attacked other dogs and fought with them but it has never attacked a human being? Is there strict liability when it does so? Cf. Ewing v. Prince, 425 S.W.2d 732 (Ky.1968). See also Martinez v. Modenbach, 396 So.2d 471 (La.App.1981) (chasing dog away, plaintiff slips on the wet grass and falls).

6. In Behrens v. Bertram Mills Circus Ltd., [1957] 2 Q.B. 1, defendant's elephant became frightened by a dog and knocked over a tent that was inhabited by two midgets. One occupant was injured and the other was frightened. Under English precedent, elephants were deemed hazardous because they attacked man. Should it make any difference that this elephant had no desire to attack but only to avoid the fearsome canine?

GOLDEN v. AMORY

Supreme Judicial Court of Massachusetts, 1952.
329 Mass. 484, 109 N.E.2d 131.

LUMMUS, JUSTICE.   The defendants owned a hydroelectric plant in Ludlow in the Red Bridge area.   As a result of the hurricane of September 21, 1938, the Chicopee River overflowed and damaged the real estate of the several plaintiffs.   In these actions of tort the first count of the several declarations alleged that no permit or decree or approval of the county commissioners was secured by the defendants for the construction, maintenance, and operation of the Alden Street dike.   The second count alleged negligence in the maintenance of that dike.   The judge directed verdicts for the defendants on the first count, and on the second count, after verdicts for the plaintiffs, entered verdicts for the defendants under leave reserved.   To that action, as well as to the exclusion of certain evidence offered by the plaintiffs, the plaintiffs excepted.

The plaintiffs rely upon the rule stated in Fletcher v. Rylands, L.R., 1 Ex. 265, 279, and affirmed in Rylands v. Fletcher, L.R., 3 H.L. 330, 339–340, that "the person who for his own purposes brings on his lands and collects and keeps there anything likely to do mischief if it escapes, must keep it in at his peril, and, if he does not do so, is prima facie answerable for all the damage which is the natural consequence of its escape."   That rule is the law of this Commonwealth.   [Cc]   But that rule does not apply where the injury results from "vis major, the act of God * * *, which the owner had no reason to anticipate."   Gorham v. Gross, 125 Mass. 232, 238; Bratton v. Rudnick, 283 Mass. 556, 560–561, 186 N.E. 669.   In the present case the flood, as disclosed by the evidence, was plainly beyond the capacity of any one to anticipate, and was clearly an act of God.   [Citation]   For this reason the rule under discussion does not apply, and the defendants cannot be held liable for injury caused by the flood waters.

Upon the whole case, we find no error, either in the rulings of the judge or in his exclusion of evidence offered by the plaintiffs.

.   Exceptions overruled.

---

1.   In accord are Nichols v. Marsland, L.R. 2 Ex.Div. 1 (1876) (dam washed out by extraordinary rainfall); Bratton v. Rudnick, 283 Mass. 556, 186 N.E. 669 (1933) (same); Murphy v. Gillum, 73 Mo.App. 487 (1898) (seepage from dam embankment caused by unprecedented frost).   Cf. Carstairs v. Taylor, L.R. 6 Ex. 217 (1871) (rat gnawed a hole in defendant's water box).

2.   What if defendant's reservoir overflows because the owner of another reservoir upstream releases suddenly a large quantity of water?   Box v. Jubb, 4 Ex.Div. 76 (1879).   Cf. Rickards v. Lothian, [1913] A.C. 263 (malicious third person plugged up defendant's lavatory basin and turned the water on full); Kaufman v. Boston Dye House, 280 Mass. 161, 182 N.E. 297 (1932) (petroleum product ignited by third person's gasoline engine); Perry v. Kendricks Trans-

port, Ltd., [1956] 1 W.L.R. 85 (petrol in automobile tank, held to fall within Rylands v. Fletcher, exploded when boys deliberately threw lighted matches into it); Kleebauer v. Western Fuse & Explosives Co., 138 Cal. 497, 71 P. 617 (1903) (alleged murderer, pursued by police, took refuge in defendant's powder magazine and committed suicide by blowing it up). Cf. Baker v. Snell, [1908] 2 K.B. 352, 825. Defendant, the owner of a dog that he knew to be vicious, entrusted it to his servant. The servant deliberately incited it to attack the plaintiff. Two of the judges, with a third dissenting, thought there would be strict liability even if the servant were not acting within the scope of his employment.

3. See Harper, Liability Without Fault and Proximate Cause, 30 Mich.L. Rev. 1001 (1932). On the effect of an intervening act of God or of a third party, compare the provisions in Restatement (Second) of Torts §§ 504(3)(c) (livestock), 510 (wild or dangerous animals) and 522 (abnormally dangerous activities). Why the difference? Should the rule be applied any differently when the defendant has been negligent?

SANDY v. BUSHEY
Supreme Judicial Court of Maine, 1925.
124 Me. 320, 128 A. 513.

STURGIS, J. In the summer of 1923, the plaintiff turned his mare and colt out in the pasture of a neighbor. Other horses occupied the pasture during the season, including the defendant's three-year old colt. On July 14, 1923, the plaintiff went to the pasture to grain his mare, and, while so doing, was kicked by the defendant's horse and seriously injured. This action on the case is brought to recover damages for such injuries and, after verdict for the plaintiff, is before this court on a general motion.

By the common law the owners or keepers of domestic animals are not answerable for an injury done by them in a place where they have a right to be, unless the animals in fact, and to the owners' knowledge, are vicious. If, however, a person keeps a vicious or dangerous animal which he knows is accustomed to attack and injure mankind, he assumes the obligation of an insurer against injury by such animal, and no measure of care in its keeping will excuse him. His liability is founded upon the keeping of such an animal when he has knowledge of its vicious propensities, and his care or negligence is immaterial. In an action for an injury caused by such an animal, the plaintiff has only to allege and prove the keeping, the vicious propensities, and the scienter. Negligence is not the ground of liability, and need not be alleged or proved. This rule of liability of keepers of domestic animals finds its origin in the ancient common law and, except as modified by statute in case of injuries by dogs, is retained as the rule of law in this class of cases in this state. [Cc]

A careful consideration of the evidence discloses facts which fairly tend to establish that the defendant's horse had exhibited a vicious and ugly disposition at various times prior to the day on which the plaintiff was injured, and notice of the animal's vicious propensities had been brought home to the defendant. Upon these issues the jury's verdict in favor of the plaintiff was fully warranted.

The defendant, however, says that the plaintiff was guilty of contributory negligence and cannot, therefore, recover in this action. We are unable to sustain this contention under the rule of liability adopted by this court. In those jurisdictions which have departed from the ancient common-law rule and declared negligence to be the ground of liability in actions for injuries by animals, the defense of contributory negligence has been recognized, and the injured party's failure to exercise due care will defeat his action. [Cc] In this state, however, the negligence doctrine has not been accepted, and contributory negligence in the strict sense of that term cannot be held to constitute a defense to the action. Exclusion of negligence as the basis of liability forbids the inclusion of contributory negligence as a defense. Something more than slight negligence or want of due care on the part of the injured party must be shown in order to relieve the keeper of a vicious domestic animal known to be such from his liability as an insurer.

In Muller v. McKesson, 73 N.Y. 195, 29 Am.Rep. 123, which may be fairly accepted as the leading case in this country upon the question of contributory negligence as a defense to an action of this character, Church, C.J., in stating the opinion of the court, says:

"If a person with full knowledge of the evil propensities of an animal wantonly excites him, or voluntarily and unnecessarily puts himself in the say of such an animal, he would be adjudged to have brought the injury upon himself, and ought not to be entitled to recover. In such a case it cannot be said, in a legal sense, that the keeping of the animal, which is the gravamen of the offense, produced the injury. * * * But as the owner is held to a rigorous rule of liability on account of the danger to human life and limb, by harboring and keeping such animals, it follows that he ought not to be relieved from it by slight negligence or want of ordinary care. To enable an owner of such an animal to interpose this defense, acts should be proved with notice of the character of the animal, which would establish that the person injured voluntarily brought the calamity upon himself." * * *

We are convinced that the principle announced by Chief Justice Church correctly defines the degree of responsibility which must be fixed upon the injured party in order to relieve the keeper of a known vicious animal from his liability as an insurer with which he is charged in this state. The fact must be established that the injury is attributable, not to the keeping of the animal, but to the injured party's unnecessarily and voluntarily putting himself in a way to be hurt knowing the probable consequences of his act, so that he may fairly be deemed to have brought the injury upon himself.

Applying this rule to the facts in the case before us, we are of the opinion that the prima facie case against the defendant, established by the evidence, is not rebutted by the plaintiff's acts or omissions. The plaintiff led his mare away from the other horses in the pasture and started to grain her, when the defendant's horse approached in a threatening manner. The plaintiff drove him away and turned to continue feeding the mare. The colt's return was silent and swift and his attack unexpected. It cannot be said that the plaintiff voluntarily put himself in a way to be injured by the defendant's horse, knowing the probable consequences of his act. The defendant is liable, as found by the jury.

Motion overruled.

———

1. In accord is Marshall v. Ranne, 511 S.W.2d 255 (Tex.1974), where plaintiff was taunted and tormented periodically by his neighbor's wild boar. One day the boar made good on his threats and bit plaintiff.

2. The Restatement (Second) of Torts has also adopted the rule for both wild animals and abnormally dangerous activities. See §§ 515, 523, 524. Is this a logical rule? If ordinary contributory negligence is a defense when defendant is negligent, why is it not a defense when he is not even negligent?

3. Most states have adopted comparative negligence rules, reducing a plaintiff's damages by the plaintiff's percentage of negligence. If a plaintiff's negligence is no longer a complete bar to recovery, should it be a defense in strict liability cases as well as negligence cases? Is it true that conduct constituting negligence and conduct forming the basis for strict liability cannot be rationally compared?

4. Defendant keeps a bear in a cage at a circus. Plaintiff crawls under the rope in front of the cage and goes within six inches of the bars. The bear slaps at him through the bars hitting him in the face and putting out his eye. Is defendant liable? Cf. Ervin v. Woodruff, 119 App.Div. 603, 103 N.Y.S. 1051 (1907); Heidemann v. Wheaton, 72 S.D. 375, 34 N.W.2d 492 (1948). A customer at a service station put his hand in an unlocked box of snakes kept for public display at a service station. He was bitten by a rattlesnake. Is his claim barred? See Keyser v. Phillips Petroleum Co., 287 So.2d 364 (Fla.App.1973). Compare the case of a person who came within range of a bull known to be vicious. Anderson v. Anderson, 259 Minn. 412, 107 N.W.2d 647 (1961).

5. Defendant is conducting blasting operations in dangerous proximity to a highway. He stations a flagman to stop traffic when a blast is about to be set off. Plaintiff drives past the flagman, and is injured by the blast. Should it make any difference whether plaintiff does not see the flagman because he is not looking, or sees him and deliberately drives past? See Worth v. Dunn, 98 Conn. 51, 62, 118 A. 467, 471 (1922); Wells v. Knight, 32 R.I. 432, 80 A. 16 (1911).

6. *Immunity Created by Legal Sanction.* Statutory sanction for defendant's conduct has frequently been held to confer immunity from strict liability, on the ground that the defendant cannot be held liable for doing properly what the law has authorized him to do, although he will still of course be liable for any negligence. Thus the custodian of a public zoo may be held not subject to strict liability for harm done by the animals kept in it. Jackson v. Baker, 24 App.D.C. 100 (1904); Guzzi v. New York Zoological Society, 192 App.Div. 263, 182 N.Y.S. 257 (1920), aff'd, 233 N.Y. 511, 135 N.E. 897 (1922). This has been held to be true for gas or electric conduits laid in the street under legislative

authority. Gould v. Winona Gas Co., 100 Minn. 258, 111 N.W. 254 (1907). Also for common carriers required by law to ship wild animals or explosives. Actiesselskabet Ingrid v. Central R. Co. of N.J., 216 Fed. 72 (2d Cir.1914); Pope v. Edward M. Rude Carrier Corp., 138 W.Va. 218, 75 S.E.2d 584 (1953).

The rule has also been extended to a contractor doing such work as blasting for the state. Nelson v. McKenzie–Hague Co., 192 Minn. 180, 256 N.W. 96 (1934); Pumphrey v. J.A. Jones Const. Co., 250 Iowa 559, 94 N.W.2d 737 (1959). There has been a strong challenge to the proposition that a government contract alone should shield the contractor from strict liability. While such a privilege may result in lower costs to government, that saving is acquired at the expenditure of denying recovery to an innocent victim. In light of the abrogation of governmental immunity itself, modern courts may be inclined to give more consideration to the injured party and impose strict liability on the contractor who engages in an abnormally dangerous activity. There is a good discussion in Smith v. Lockheed Propulsion Co., 247 Cal.App.2d 774, 56 Cal. Rptr. 128, 139–142 (1967). See Comment, 67 Ky.L.J. 441 (1979).

7. The next chapter addresses the development of strict liability for "unreasonably dangerous" products. Is this analogous to the principle of strict liability for abnormally dangerous activities? While courts have developed a variety of tests for determining whether a product is "unreasonably dangerous," the most common test involves a balancing of the risks of the product against its utility. See Restatement (Second) of Torts § 402A (1965). Some courts apply an even more stringent strict liability test, evaluating the dangers of products that are "unreasonably dangerous per se" regardless of whether they were discoverable at the time the product was made. See Halphen v. Johns–Manville Sales Corp., 484 So.2d 110, 114 (La.1986) (asbestos); cf. Brown v. Sears, Roebuck & Co., 503 So.2d 1122 (La.App.1987), aff'd, 514 So.2d 439 (La. 1987), reh'g denied, 516 So.2d 1154 (La.1988) (initially same holding for an ordinary escalator but on petition for rehearing, holding limited to particular escalator at issue).

Chapter XV

PRODUCTS LIABILITY

"Products liability" is the name currently given to the liability of a manufacturer, seller or other supplier of chattels, to one with whom he is not in privity of contract, who suffers physical harm caused by the chattel. It may rest upon the supplier's negligence or upon a warranty, or it may be a matter of strict liability in tort.

In the 1980's, strict liability theories have become the paramount basis of liability for manufacturers of products. Moreover, the development of the strict liability basis has produced the largest case law explosion in the history of the law of torts. In the federal courts the number of cases filed have expanded from about 2,000 plus cases in 1975 to over 14,600 in 1986.

Some state courts have even extended the theories supporting the imposition of strict liability against manufacturers of products onto other classes of defendants. Thus retailers, lessors of chattels, builders and developers of real property and even sellers of services may be subject to strict liability.

This "revolution" in the common law of torts is not as radical as it may initially seem. Elements of the law of negligence, especially the "reasonableness" standard, have crept back into the strict liability basis. Courts have continued to argue that strict liability is not absolute liability, but some decisions have come close to that outer mark.

Product liability insurance premiums soared in the 1976–1978 period; for some businesses the problem reached "crisis" proportions. One result was a Federal Interagency Task Force Study of the entire product liability area. See infra page 806. The Task Force found that one of the causes of the product liability problem was uncertainties in the tort litigation system. As a result of this finding, the United States Department of Commerce developed the Uniform Product Liability Act, 44 Fed.Reg. 62714 (1979), to help bring about more stability in the system. So far it has not produced that result. The Uniform Product Liability Act is, in effect, a new attempt to restate the law of product liability, but it was developed in the public forum and based, in part, on public comment. In 1985–1986 a new insurance crisis arose. It created a stampede on the part of product manufacturers and sellers for Federal legislation on the topic of products liability. Both are referred to throughout this chapter.

The topic of products liability has sufficient material to support a separate law school course. Two major treatises, both regularly supplemented, are needed to cover the field. See R. Hursh and Bailey, American Law of Products Liability (1974); L. Frumer and Friedman,

Products Liability (Rev. ed. 1987). Also, two reporting systems have been developed to keep the attorney who specializes in this area as up to date as possible. See CCH Products Liability Reporter and BNA Products Safety and Liability Reporter. Recently, Prentice Hall entered the market with a new treatise: V. Schwartz, P. Lee, F. Souk, K. Kelly, M. Mullen, Products Liability: Cases and Trends (1986).

1. THEORIES OF RECOVERY

(A) NEGLIGENCE

MacPHERSON v. BUICK MOTOR CO.
Court of Appeals of New York, 1916.
217 N.Y. 382, 111 N.E. 1050.

Action, by Donald C. MacPherson against the Buick Motor Company. From a judgment of the Appellate Division (160 App.Div. 55, 145 N.Y.Supp. 462), affirming a judgment of the Supreme Court for plaintiff, defendant appeals.

CARDOZO, J. The defendant is a manufacturer of automobiles. It sold an automobile to a retail dealer. The retail dealer resold to the plaintiff. While the plaintiff was in the car it suddenly collapsed. He was thrown out and injured. One of the wheels was made of defective wood, and its spokes crumbled into fragments. The wheel was not made by the defendant; it was bought from another manufacturer. There is evidence, however, that its defects could have been discovered by reasonable inspection, and that inspection was omitted. There is no claim that the defendant knew of the defect and willfully concealed it. * * * The charge is one, not of fraud, but of negligence. The question to be determined is whether the defendant owed a duty of care and vigilance to any one but the immediate purchaser.

[The court discusses competing lines of precedents. One group of cases suggested that the manufacturer owed a duty of care to ultimate purchasers only when the product was "inherently dangerous." Some courts confined this classification to guns, poisons or other products whose normal function it was to injure or destroy. Other decisions suggested that a manufacturer would breach a duty of care to a foreseeable user of the product if the product was likely to cause injury if negligently made.]

We hold * * * that * * * [i]f the nature of a thing is such that it is reasonably certain to place life and limb in peril when negligently made, it is then a thing of danger. Its nature gives warning of the consequences to be expected. If to the element of danger there is added knowledge that the thing will be used by persons other than the purchaser, and used without new tests, then, irrespective of contract, the manufacturer of this thing of danger is under a duty to make it

Buick Model 10 Runabout (1909)
(The model Mr. MacPherson purchased)

carefully. That is as far as we are required to go for the decision of this case. There must be knowledge of a danger, not merely possible, but probable. It is possible to use almost anything in a way that will make it dangerous if defective. That is not enough to charge the manufacturer with a duty independent of his contract. Whether a given thing is dangerous may be sometimes a question for the court and sometimes a question for the jury. There must also be knowledge that in the usual course of events the danger will be shared by others than the buyer.

Judge Cardozo

Such knowledge may often be inferred from the nature of the transaction. But it is possible that even knowledge of the danger and of the use will not always be enough. The proximity or remoteness of the relation is a factor to be considered. We are dealing now with the liability of the manufacturer of the finished product, who puts it on the market to be used without inspection by his customers. If he is negligent, where danger is to be foreseen, a liability will follow. * * * We have put aside the notion that the duty to safeguard life and limb, when the consequences of negligence may be foreseen, grows out of contract and nothing else. We have put the source of the obligation where it ought to be. We have put its source in the law.

There is nothing anomalous in a rule which imposes upon A., who has contracted with B., a duty to C. and D. and others according as he knows or does not know that the subject-matter of the contract is intended for their use. We may find an analogy in the law which measures the liability of landlords. If A. leases to B. a tumbledown house, he is not liable, in the absence of fraud, to B.'s guests who enter it and are injured. This is because B. is then under the duty to repair it, the lessor has the right to suppose that he will fulfill that duty, and, if he omits to do so, his guests must look to him. Bohlen, Affirmative Obligations in the Law of Torts, 44 Am.Law Reg., N.S., 341. But if A. leases a building to be used by the lessee at once as a place of public entertainment, the rule is different. There injury to persons other than the lessee is to be foreseen, and foresight of the consequences involves the creation of a duty. [C]

In this view of the defendant's liability there is nothing inconsistent with the theory of liability on which the case was tried. It is true that the court told the jury that "an automobile is not an inherently dangerous vehicle." The meaning, however, is that danger is not to be expected when the vehicle is well constructed. The court left it to the jury to say whether the defendant ought to have foreseen that the car, if negligently constructed, would become "imminently dangerous." Subtle distinctions are drawn by the defendants between things inherently dangerous and things imminently dangerous, but the case does not turn upon these verbal niceties. If danger was to be expected as reasonably certain, there was a duty of vigilance, and this whether you call the danger inherent or imminent. In varying forms that thought was put before the jury. We do not say that the court would not have been justified in ruling as a matter of law that the car was a dangerous thing. If there was any error, it was none of which the defendant can complain.

We think the defendant was not absolved from a duty of inspection because it bought the wheels from a reputable manufacturer. It was not merely a dealer in automobiles. It was responsible for the finished product. It was not at liberty to put the finished product on the market without subjecting the component parts to ordinary and simple tests. [C] Under the charge of the trial judge nothing more was required of it. The obligation to inspect must vary with the nature of the thing to be inspected. The more probable the danger the greater the need of caution.   *   *   *

The judgment should be affirmed with costs.

[The dissenting opinion of WILLARD BARTLETT, C.J., is omitted.]

---

1. The early development of liability of a manufacturer or seller of chattels to third parties was strongly influenced by Winterbottom v. Wright, 10 M. & W. 109, 152 Eng.Rep. 402 (1842), supra page 444. The case was misinterpreted to state a general rule of nonliability of any contractor, including any supplier of a product, to third parties, whether in contract or in tort, and whether for nonfeasance or misfeasance. This misinterpretation was first pointed out by Professor Bohlen in a noted article in 1905. Bohlen, The Basis of Affirmative Obligations in the Law of Torts, 44 Am.L.Reg. (N.S.) 209, 280–85,

289–310 (1905). Nevertheless, most courts clung to the general rule while carving out a few exceptions for "inherently dangerous" products.

2. The manufacturer's reaction to the case is nicely illustrated in the chapter entitled "The Most Outrageous Consequences" in James Reid Parker, Attorneys at Law 95 (1942), reprinted in W. Prosser, The Judicial Humorist 14 (1952). See also D. Peck, Decision at Law, ch. 2 (1961).

3. This became a leading case, and a new point of departure. It is now accepted in all of the American jurisdictions, although one or two of them, such as Mississippi in State Stove Mfg. Co. v. Hodges, 189 So.2d 113 (Miss.1966), have jumped over negligence to the strict liability base.

4. For a time some of the courts continued to use the language of "inherent danger," although it was clear from the opinions that this meant no more than that substantial harm is to be anticipated if the chattel should be defective. This seems to have faded out almost entirely.

5. What has finally emerged has been a general rule imposing negligence liability upon all sellers of chattels—whether damage is to person or property and whether the manufacturer produced the whole product or a significant component part.

6. Since strict liability is still marked by uncertainties, the plaintiff often pleads negligence as an alternative basis of recovery, so that it is likely to appear in the decisions for a good many years to come.

7. When plaintiff can avail himself of claims in both strict liability and negligence, has he lost anything of value if the trial court erroneously dismisses his negligence claim, but lets him proceed on strict liability? See Mather v. Caterpillar Tractor Corp., 23 Ariz.App. 409, 533 P.2d 717 (1975); Jiminez v. Sears, Roebuck & Co., 4 Cal.3d 379, 482 P.2d 681, 93 Cal.Rptr. 769 (1971); Annot., 52 A.L.R.3d 92 (1973).

Most plaintiffs' lawyers still try to prove negligence. Why? An experienced practitioner has observed: "More plaintiffs would prefer to present their respective cases to a jury on a negligence, rather than on a strict liability, basis. In McLuhanesque terms negligence is 'hot' and strict liability is 'cold.' It is easier to prevail by showing that the defendant did something wrong than that there is something technically defective about the product." Rheingold, The Expanding Liability of the Product Supplier: A Primer, 2 Hofstra L.Rev. 521, 531 (1974). Can the theory affect a jury's willingness to award damages? Why?

8. A good discussion of the negligence liability is Noel, Manufacturers' Liability for Negligence, 33 Tenn.L.Rev. 444 (1966).

(B) WARRANTY

The action by the buyer of goods against his seller for breach of warranty is a freak hybrid, "born of the illicit intercourse of tort and contract," and partaking the characteristics of both. It is unique in the law. Originally the action was in tort, in an action of trespass on the case for breach of an assumed duty, and the wrong was conceived to be a form of misrepresentation, in the nature of deceit, and not at all clearly distinguished from it. Ames, History of Assumpsit, 2 Harv.L. Rev. 1, 8 (1888). In the latter part of the seventeenth century, decisions such as Cross v. Gardiner, 1 Show.K.B. 68, 89 Eng.Rep. 453 (1689), and

Medina v. Stoughton, 1 Ld.Raym. 593, 91 Eng.Rep. 1297 (1700), established the fact that the tort action would lie for a mere affirmation of fact ("express warranty") made without knowledge of its falsity or negligence. As a result warranty became a form of strict liability in tort.

In Stuart v. Wilkins, 1 Doug. 18, 99 Eng.Rep. 15 (1778), it was first held that assumpsit would lie for breach of an express warranty as a part of the contract of sale. After that decision, and over a period of more than a century, warranties gradually came to be regarded as express or implied terms of the contract of sale, and the action on the contract became the usual remedy for any breach.

Warranty has, however, never entirely lost its original tort character. There are numerous decisions holding that a tort action can be maintained for the breach, without proof of either intentional misrepresentation or negligence. See, for example, Shippen v. Bowen, 122 U.S. 575 (1887). Nor is this entirely a procedural matter. Even when the action is in form one for breach of contract its basic tort character has sometimes been recognized by the application of tort rules, such as that for survival of actions in Gosling v. Nichols, 59 Cal.App.2d 442, 139 P.2d 86 (1943). Or the statute of limitations. Rubino v. Utah Canning Co., 123 Cal.App.2d 18, 266 P.2d 163 (1954). Or the more liberal tort rule as to damages. Despatch Oven Co. v. Rauenhorst, 229 Minn. 436, 40 N.W.2d 73 (1949). And several jurisdictions allow recovery for wrongful death arising out of breach of warranty, when the action would not lie for a pure breach of contract. See for example Greco v. S.S. Kresge Co., 277 N.Y. 26, 12 N.E.2d 557 (1938); Kelley v. Volkswagenwerk Aktiengesellschaft, 110 N.H. 369, 268 A.2d 837 (1970).

The question began to be asked: if warranty is a matter of tort as well as contract and it can arise without any intent to make it a matter of contract, why should it require a contract between the parties? Why should it not arise, in tort, between parties who have not dealt at all with one another—or in other words, without privity of contract?

BAXTER v. FORD MOTOR CO.

Supreme Court of Washington, 1932.
168 Wash. 456, 12 P.2d 409.

HERMAN, J. During the month of May, 1930, plaintiff purchased a model A Ford town sedan from defendant St. John Motors, a Ford dealer, who had acquired the automobile in question by purchase from defendant Ford Motor Company. Plaintiff claims that representations were made to him by both defendants that the windshield of the automobile was made of nonshatterable glass which would not break, fly, or shatter. October 12, 1930, while plaintiff was driving the automobile through Snoqualmie pass, a pebble from a passing car struck the windshield of the car in question, causing small pieces of glass to fly into plaintiff's left eye, resulting in the loss thereof. Plaintiff brought this action for damages for the loss of his left eye and for injuries to the sight of his right eye. The case came on for trial, and, at the conclusion of plaintiff's testimony, the court took the case from the jury and entered judgment for both defendants. From that judgment, plaintiff appeals. * * *

The principal question in this case is whether the trial court erred in refusing to admit in evidence, as against respondent Ford Motor Company, the catalogues and printed matter furnished by that respondent to respondent St. John Motors to be distributed for sales assistance. Contained in such printed matter were statements which appellant maintains constituted representations or warranties with reference to the nature of the glass used in the windshield of the car purchased by appellant. A typical statement, as it appears in appellant's exhibit for identification No. 1, is here set forth:

"Triplex Shatter–Proof Glass Windshield. All of the new Ford cars have a Triplex shatter-proof glass windshield—so made that it will not fly or shatter under the hardest impact. This is an important safety factor because it eliminates the dangers of flying glass—the cause of most of the injuries in automobile accidents. In these days of crowded, heavy traffic, the use of this Triplex glass is an absolute necessity. Its extra margin of safety is something that every motorist should look for in the purchase of a car—especially where there are women and children."

Respondent Ford Motor Company contends that there can be no implied or express warranty without privity of contract, and warranties as to personal property do not attach themselves to, and run with, the article sold.

[The court here referred at length to Mazetti v. Armour & Co., 75 Wash. 622, 135 P. 663 (1913), in which a restaurant keeper was permitted to recover for damage to his business resulting when a customer was served defective canned food manufactured by the defendant.]

In the case at bar the automobile was represented by the manufacturer as having a windshield of nonshatterable glass "so made that it will not fly or shatter under the hardest impact." An ordinary person would be unable to discover by the usual and customary examination of the automobile whether glass which would not fly or shatter was used in the windshield. In that respect the purchaser was in a position similar to that of the consumer of a wrongly labeled drug, who has bought the same from a retailer, and who has relied upon the manufacturer's representation that the label correctly set forth the contents of the container. For many years it has been held that, under such circumstances, the manufacturer is liable to the consumer, even though the consumer purchased from a third person the commodity causing the damage. Thomas v. Winchester, 6 N.Y. 397, 57 Am.Dec. 455. The rule in such cases does not rest upon contractual obligations, but rather on the principle that the original act of delivering an article is wrong, when, because of the lack of those qualities which the manufacturer represented it as having, the absence of which could not be readily detected by the consumer, the article is not safe for the purposes for which the consumer would ordinarily use it.

The vital principle present in the case of Mazetti v. Armour & Co., supra, confronts us in the case at bar. In the case cited the court recognized the right of a purchaser to a remedy against the manufacturer because of damages suffered by reason of a failure of goods to comply with the manufacturer's representations as to the existence of qualities which they did not in fact possess, when the absence of such qualities was not readily discoverable, even though there was no privity of contract between the purchaser and the manufacturer.

Since the rule of caveat emptor was first formulated, vast changes have taken place in the economic structures of the English speaking peoples. Methods of doing business have undergone a great transition. Radio, billboards, and the products of the printing press have become the means of creating a large part of the demand that causes goods to depart from factories to the ultimate consumer. It would be unjust to recognize a rule that would permit manufacturers of goods to create a demand for their products by representing that they possess qualities which they, in fact, do not possess, and then, because there is no privity of contract existing between the consumer and the manufacturer, deny the consumer the right to recover if damages result from the absence of those qualities, when such absence is not readily noticeable.

"An exception to a rule will be declared by courts when the case is not an isolated instance, but general in its character, and the existing rule does not square with justice. Under such circumstances a court will, if free from the restraint of some statute, declare a rule that will meet the full intendment of the law." Mazetti v. Armour & Co., supra.

We hold that the catalogues and printed matter furnished by respondent * * * Ford Motor Company for distribution and assistance in sales were improperly excluded from evidence, because they set forth representations by the manufacturer that the windshield of the car which appellant bought contained Triplex nonshatterable glass which would not fly or shatter. The nature of nonshatterable glass is such that the falsity of the representations with reference to the glass would not be readily detected by a person of ordinary experience and reasonable prudence. Appellant, under the circumstances shown in this case, had the right to rely upon the representations made by respondent Ford Motor Company relative to qualities possessed by its products, even though there was no privity of contract between appellant and respondent Ford Motor Company. * * *

The trial court erred in taking the case from the jury and entering judgment for respondent Ford Motor Company. It was for the jury to determine under proper instructions, whether the failure of respondent Ford Motor Company to equip the windshield with glass which did not fly or shatter was the proximate cause of appellant's injury. * * *

Reversed, with directions to grant a new trial with reference to respondent Ford Motor Company; affirmed as to respondent St. John Motors.

[The second trial resulted in a verdict for plaintiff, and defendant Ford Motor Company appealed. In Baxter v. Ford Motor Co., 179 Wash. 123, 35 P.2d 1090 (1934), judgment entered on the verdict was affirmed. HOLCOMB, J., said in part:

"A new point arising out of the last trial, claimed as error, was in excluding testimony of an expert witness on behalf of appellant to the effect that there was no better windshield made than that used in respondent's car and in sustaining the objection to appellant's offer of proof on that point.

"No authorities are cited by appellant to sustain this claim, and we know of none. Indeed, it would seem that whether there was any better make of shatter-proof glass manufactured by any one at that time would be wholly immaterial, under the law as decided by us on the former appeal. Since it was the duty of appellant to know that the representations made to purchasers were true. Otherwise it should not have made them. If a person states as true material facts, susceptible of knowledge, to one who relies and acts thereon to his injury, if the representations are false, it is immaterial that he did not know they were false, or that he believed them to be true. ＊ ＊ ＊

"The court charged the jury that 'there is no proof of fraud in this case.' It has become almost axiomatic that false representations inducing a sale or contract constitute fraud in law. ＊ ＊ ＊ However, the instruction, if it was error against respondent, was cured by the verdict of the jury favorable to respondent."]

---

1. Is this an extension of a contract warranty to one who has made no contract with the defendant, or is it strict liability in tort for an innocent misrepresentation made to the plaintiff? Most of the cases have talked of "express warranty." But in Ford Motor Co. v. Lonon, 217 Tenn. 400, 398 S.W.2d 240 (1966), the court reverted to the theory of misrepresentation. It relied on the Restatement (Second) of Torts § 402B, which states the strict liability without using the word "warranty." The section reads:

"One engaged in the business of selling chattels who, by advertising, labels, or otherwise, makes to the public a misrepresentation of a material fact concerning the character or quality of a chattel sold by him is subject to liability for physical harm to a consumer of the chattel caused by justifiable reliance upon the misrepresentation, even though (a) it is not made fraudulently or negligently, and (b) the consumer has not bought the chattel from or entered into any contract relation with the seller."

See Sales, Innocent Misrepresentation Doctrine: Strict Tort Liability Under Section 402B, 16 Hous.L.Rev. 239 (1979); Green, Strict Liability Under Sections 402A and 402B: A Decade of Litigation, 54 Tex.L.Rev. 1185 (1976).

2. The principal case generally has been followed for express statements as to quality made in advertising, on labels, in brochures or other literature accompanying the product, or documents supplied to be transmitted to the ultimate purchaser. See Wade, Strict Liability of Manufacturers, 19 Sw.L.J. 5, 13 (1965). It has been extended to apply when plaintiff's property is damaged. See Randy Knitwear, Inc. v. American Cyanamid Co., 11 N.Y.2d 5, 181 N.E.2d 399, 226 N.Y.S.2d 363 (1962). How strict is this form of strict liability? Should contributory negligence or plaintiff's fault be a defense?

3. The representation must be made with the intention, or at least the expectation, that it will reach the plaintiff, or a class in which he is included; and when there is no such expectation, there is no strict liability. Cf. Barni v. Kutner, 45 Del. 550, 76 A.2d 801 (1950); Silverman v. Samuel Mallinger Co., 375 Pa. 422, 100 A.2d 715 (1953).

4. Should the plaintiff be required to rely upon the representation, either in making his purchase or in using the product? Randall v. Goodrich–Gamble Co., 238 Minn. 10, 54 N.W.2d 769 (1952); Dobbin v. Pacific Coast Coal Co., 25 Wash.2d 190, 170 P.2d 642 (1946). Most courts required this, but recently some have not. Without this requirement, what is the basis of the claim?

5. What result if a tire manufacturer advertises, "If it saves your life once, it's a bargain," and plaintiff's decedent is killed when the product "blows out"? See Collins v. Uniroyal, Inc., 64 N.J. 260, 315 A.2d 16 (1974). Suppose the manufacturer of a grinding disc states that his product is "stronger, sharper, and longer-lived than ever before available anywhere." The wheel breaks and injures plaintiff. See Jakubowski v. Minnesota Mining & Mfg., 80 N.J.Super. 184, 193 A.2d 275 (1963), rev'd on other grounds, 42 N.J. 177, 199 A.2d 826 (1964). What about a used car with a "30–day guarantee?" The car's accelerator-carburetor mechanism malfunctions within the 30–day period and plaintiff purchaser is injured. See Realmuto v. Straub Motors, Inc., 65 N.J. 336, 322 A.2d 440 (1974). Courts have stated that the promise of safety must be a specific one. However, there is a trend in recent case law to allow violation of more generalized statements to be actionable. See Payne v. Soft Sheen Prods., Inc., 486 A.2d 712 (D.C.App.1985).

6. A company manufactures a brand name painkiller called "Talwin." Extensive testing by the Food and Drug Administration and the company itself show the drug to be nonaddictive. The company advertises that "Talwin" is "free and safe from all dangers of addiction." Plaintiff, because of a rare and unforeseeable susceptibility, becomes physically dependent on the drug. Is the company liable for this result? See Crocker v. Winthrop Laboratories, 514 S.W.2d 429 (Tex.1974). Cf. Spiegel v. Saks 34th Street, 43 Misc.2d 1065, 252 N.Y.S.2d 852 (1964), aff'd mem., 26 A.D.2d 660, 272 N.Y.S.2d 972 (1966) (perfume advertised as "nonallergenic").

7. Plaintiff bought a mace gun that was advertised to "instantly stop and subdue entire groups * * *." It failed to stop an intruder who shot plaintiff. What issues does this case introduce? Cee Klages v. General Ordnance Equip. Co., 240 Pa.Super. 356, 367 A.2d 304 (1976).

HENNINGSEN v. BLOOMFIELD MOTORS, INC.
Supreme Court of New Jersey, 1960.
32 N.J. 358, 161 A.2d 69.

[Plaintiff Mrs. Henningsen was badly injured while driving a 1955 Plymouth automobile, when "something went wrong" with the steering gear, and the car turned sharply to the right into a wall. The automobile had been manufactured by defendant Chrysler Corporation, and sold by it to defendant Bloomfield Motors, a retail dealer. Mr. Henningsen purchased it from Bloomfield, and gave it to his wife for Christmas.,

When he purchased the car, Mr. Henningsen signed a contract, without reading 8½ inches of fine print on the back of it. Included in this fine print was a "warranty" clause, which provided that the manufacturer and the dealer gave no warranties, express or implied, except that they would make good at the factory any parts which became defective within 90 days after delivery of the car to the original purchaser, or before the car had been driven 4,000 miles, whichever event should first occur. In plaintiff's action against both defendants, negligence counts were dismissed by the trial court, and the cause was submitted to the jury solely on the issues of implied warranty of merchantability. Verdicts were returned for plaintiff against both defendants. Defendants appealed, and the appeal was certified directly to the Supreme Court.]

FRANCIS, J.   *   *   * In the ordinary case of sale of goods by description an implied warranty of merchantability is an integral part of the transaction. R.S. 46:30–20, N.J.S.A. If the buyer, expressly or by implication, makes known to the seller the particular purpose for which the article is required and it appears that he has relied on the seller's skill or judgment, an implied warranty arises of reasonable fitness for that purpose. R.S. 46:30–21(1), N.J.S.A. The former type of warranty simply means that the thing sold is reasonably fit for the general purpose for which it is manufactured and sold. [Cc] As Judge Cardozo remarked in Ryan v. Progressive Grocery Stores (1931) 255 N.Y. 388, 175 N.E. 105, the distinction between a warranty of fitness for a particular purpose and of merchantability in many instances is practically meaningless.   *   *   *

The uniform [sales] act codified, extended and liberalized the common law of sales. The motivation in part was to ameliorate the harsh doctrine of caveat emptor, and in some measure to impose a reciprocal obligation on the seller to beware. The transcendent value of the legislation, particularly with respect to implied warranties, rests in the fact that obligations on the part of the seller were imposed by operation of law, and did not depend for their existence upon express agreement of the parties. And of tremendous significance in a rapidly expanding commercial society was the recognition of the right to recover damages on account of personal injuries arising from a breach of warranty. [Cc]

Justice John J. Francis

The particular importance of this advance resides in the fact that under such circumstances strict liability is imposed upon the maker or seller of the product. Recovery of damages does not depend upon proof of negligence or knowledge of the defect. [Cc]

As the Sales Act and its liberal interpretation by the courts threw this protective cloak about the buyer, * * * many manufacturers took steps to avoid these ever increasing warranty obligations. Realizing that the act governed the relationship of buyer and seller, they undertook to withdraw from actual and direct contractual contact with the buyer. They ceased selling products to the consuming public through their own employees and making contracts of sale in their own names. Instead, a system of independent dealers was established; their products were sold to dealers who in turn dealt with the buying public, ostensibly solely in their own personal capacity as sellers. In the past in many instances, manufacturers were able to transfer to the dealers burdens imposed by the act and thus achieved a large measure of immunity for themselves. * * *

There is no doubt that under early common-law concepts of contractual liability only those persons who were parties to the bargain could sue for a breach of it. In more recent times a noticeable disposition has appeared in a number of jurisdictions to break through the narrow barrier of privity when dealing with sales of goods in order to give realistic recognition to a universally accepted fact. The fact is that the dealer and the ordinary buyer do not, and are not expected to, buy goods, whether they be foodstuffs or automobiles, exclusively for their own consumption or use. Makers and manufacturers know this and advertise and market their products on that assumption; witness, the "family" car, the baby foods, etc. The limitations of privity in contracts for the sale of goods developed their place in the law when marketing conditions were simple, when maker and buyer frequently met face to face on an equal bargaining plane and when many of the products were relatively uncomplicated and conducive to inspection by a buyer competent to evaluate their quality. [C] With the advent of mass marketing, the manufacturer became remote from the purchaser, sales were accomplished through intermediaries, and the demand for the product was created by advertising media. In such an economy it became obvious that the consumer was the person being cultivated. Manifestly, the connotation of "consumer" was broader than that of "buyer." He signified such a person who, in the reasonable contemplation of the parties to the sale, might be expected to use the product. Thus, where the commodities sold are such that if defectively manufactured they will be dangerous to life or limb, then society's interests can only be protected by eliminating the requirement of privity between the maker and his dealers and the reasonably expected ultimate consumer. In that way the burden of losses consequent upon use of defective articles is borne by those who are in a position to either control the danger or make an equitable distribution of the losses when they do occur. As Harper & James put it, "The interest in consumer protection calls for warranties by the maker that *do* run with the goods, to reach all who are likely to be hurt by the use of the unfit commodity for a purpose ordinarily to be expected." 2 Harper & James, Torts, 1571, 1572. * * *

Most of the cases where lack of privity has not been permitted to interfere with recovery have involved food and drugs. [Cc] In the fact, the rule as to such products has been characterized as an exception to the general doctrine. But more recently courts, sensing the inequity of such limitation, have moved into broader fields. [Cc] * * *

Under modern conditions the ordinary layman, on responding to the importuning of colorful advertising, has neither the opportunity nor the capacity to inspect or to determine the fitness of an automobile for use; he must rely on the manufacturer who has control of its construction, and to some degree on the dealer who, to the limited extent called for by the manufacturer's instructions, inspects and services it before delivery. In such a marketing milieu his remedies and those of persons who properly claim through him should not depend "upon the intricacies of the law of sales." The obligation of the manufacturer should not be based alone on privity of contract. It should rest, as was once said, upon "the demands of social justice." Mazetti v. Armour & Co., 75 Wash. 622, 135 P. 633, 635. "If privity of contract is required," then, under the circumstances of modern merchandising, "privity of contract exists in the consciousness and understanding of all right-thinking persons." Madouros v. Kansas City Coca–Cola Bottling Co., 90 S.W.2d at page 450.

Accordingly, we hold that under modern marketing conditions, when a manufacturer puts a new automobile in the stream of trade and promotes its purchase by the public, an implied warranty that it is reasonably suitable for use as such accompanies it into the hands of the ultimate purchaser. * * *

In the light of these matters, what effect should be given to the express warranty in question which seeks to limit the manufacturer's liability to replacement of defective parts, and which disclaims all other warranties, express or implied? In assessing its significance we must keep in mind the general principle that, in the absence of fraud, one who does not choose to read a contract before signing it, cannot later relieve himself of its burdens. [C] And in applying that principle, the basic tenet of freedom of competent parties to contract is a factor of importance. But in the framework of modern commercial life and business practices, such rules cannot be applied on a strict, doctrinal basis. The conflicting interests of the buyer and seller must be evaluated realistically and justly, giving due weight to the social policy evinced by the Uniform Sales Act, the progressive decisions of the courts engaged in administering it, the mass production methods of manufacture and distribution to the public, and the bargaining position, occupied by the ordinary consumer in such an economy. * * *

In a society such as ours, where the automobile is a common and necessary adjunct of daily life, and where its use is so fraught with danger to the driver, passengers and the public, the manufacturer is under a special obligation in connection with the construction, promotion and sale of his cars. Consequently, the courts must examine purchase agreements closely to see if consumer and public interests are treated fairly. * * *

[W]arranties originated in the law to safeguard the buyer and not to limit the liability of the seller or manufacturer. It seems obvious in this instance that the motive was to avoid the warranty obligations which are normally incidental to such sales. The language gave little and withdrew much. In return for the delusive remedy of replacement of defective parts at the factory, the buyer is said to have accepted the exclusion of the maker's liability for personal injuries, arising from the breach of the warranty, and to have agreed to the elimination of any other express or implied warranty. An instinctively felt sense of justice cries out against such a sharp bargain. But does the doctrine that a person is bound by his signed agreement, in the absence of fraud, stand in the way of any relief? * * *

The traditional contract is the result of free bargaining of parties who are brought together by the play of the market, and who meet each other on a footing of approximate economic equality. In such a society there is no danger that freedom of contract will be a threat to the social order as a whole. But in present-day commercial life the standardized mass contract has appeared. It is used primarily by enterprises with strong bargaining power and position. "The weaker party, in need of the goods or services, is frequently not in a position to shop around for better terms, either because the author of the standard contract has a monopoly (natural or artificial) or because all competitors use the same clauses. His contractual intention is but a subjection more or less voluntary to terms dictated by the stronger party, terms whose consequences are often understood in a vague way, if at all." Kessler, "Contracts of Adhesion—Some Thought About Freedom of Contract," 43 Colum.L.Rev. 629, 632 (1943).   *   *   *

The warranty before us is a standardized form designed for mass use. It is imposed upon the automobile consumer. He takes it or leaves it, and he must take it to buy an automobile. No bargaining is engaged in with respect to it. In fact, the dealer through whom it comes to the buyer is without authority to alter it; his function is ministerial—simply to deliver it. The form warranty is not only standard with Chrysler but, as mentioned above, it is the uniform warranty of the Automobile Manufacturers Association.   *   *   *

The gross inequality of bargaining position occupied by the consumer in the automobile industry is thus apparent. There is no competition among the car makers in the area of the express warranty. Where can the buyer go to negotiate for better protection? Such control and limitation of his remedies are inimical to the public welfare and, at the very least, call for great care by the courts to avoid injustice through application of strict common-law principles of freedom of contract. Because there is no competition among the motor vehicle manufacturers with respect to the scope of protection guaranteed to the buyer, there is no incentive on their part to stimulate good will in that field of public relations. Thus, there is lacking a factor existing in more competitive fields, one which tends to guarantee the safe construction of the article sold. Since all competitors operate in the same way, the urge to be careful is not so pressing. See "Warranties of Kind and Quality," 57 Yale L.J. 1389, 1400 (1948).   *   *   *

The task of the judiciary is to administer the spirit as well as the letter of the law. On issues such as the present one, part of that burden is to protect the ordinary man against the loss of important rights through what, in effect, is the unilateral act of the manufacturer. *   *   * In the framework of this case, illuminated as it is by the facts and the many decisions noted, we are of the opinion that Chrysler's attempted disclaimer of an implied warranty of merchantability and of the obligations arising therefrom is so inimical to the public good as to compel an adjudication of its invalidity.   *   *   *

[The court then held that the dealer, Bloomfield Motors, would not be permitted to disclaim an implied warranty of fitness with respect to personal injuries caused by the automobile in question. The problem of whether retailers should be subject to strict liability is discussed infra, at page 825.]

————

1. The first case to extend an implied warranty of the seller beyond privity of contract was Mazetti v. Armour & Co., 75 Wash. 622, 135 P. 633 (1913), which was a bad food case. It came upon the heels of a prolonged nation-wide agitation about dangerous food, and the political overturn of 1912. The decision was promptly followed in Mississippi and Kansas, and then in other states. There was a period of some twenty years over which the courts struggled to evolve various ingenious theories, most of them with an obvious element of fiction—such as agencies of the dealer to buy for the consumer or to sell for the manufacturer, or third party beneficiary contracts and the like. Finally, in Coca–Cola Bottling Works v. Lyons, 145 Miss. 876, 111 So. 305 (1927), the Mississippi court came up with the idea of an implied warranty running with the goods, by analogy to a covenant running with the land; and subsequent cases until 1963 all adopted some theory of warranty to the consumer. By 1960 nearly half of the courts had accepted the special rule as to food, and five more reached the same result under pure food statutes. The whole development is traced in Prosser, The Assault Upon the Citadel, 69 Yale L.J. 1099 (1960).

2. A gradual extension beyond food began not long after 1950, with other products for what might be called intimate bodily use, such as hair dye and clothing. Although there was an earlier case in a lower Ohio Court, which was overruled, the first decision that went the whole way was Spence v. Three Rivers Builders & Masonry Supply, Inc., 353 Mich. 120, 90 N.W.2d 873 (1958), in which the court leaped completely over food products, and applied the manufacturer's warranty to cinder building blocks when the consumer's house collapsed. Seven or eight other decisions followed, but the *Henningsen* decision became regarded as the leading case.

3. The Uniform Sales Act, discussed in the principal case, was promulgated in 1906. Its warranty provisions were intended to apply only to buyer and seller. The Uniform Sales Act has now been superseded by the Uniform Commercial Code (UCC), which has now been adopted in every state except Louisiana. While the UCC's implied-warranty provisions are similar to those in the Uniform Sales Act (UCC §§ 2–314 and 315), the Code has extended warranties to certain third parties in Section 2–318. This is one area, however, in which the Uniform Commercial Code is not uniform. State legislatures are given three alternatives to choose from:

Alternate A. A seller's warranty whether express or implied extends to any natural person who is in the family or household of his buyer or who is a guest in his home if it is reasonable to expect that such person may use, consume or be affected by the goods and who is injured in person by breach of the warranty. A seller may not exclude or limit the operation of this section.

Alternate B. A seller's warranty whether express or implied extends to any natural person who may reasonably be expected to use, consume or be affected by the goods and who is injured in person by breach of the warranty. A seller may not exclude or limit the operation of this section.

Alternate C. A seller's warranty whether express or implied extends to any person who may reasonably be expected to use, consume or be affected by the goods and who is injured by breach of the warranty. A seller may not exclude or limit the operation of this section with respect to injury to the person of an individual to whom the warranty extends. As amended 1966.

The official comment to this Section states in part: "The first alternative expressly includes as beneficiaries within its provisions the family, household and guests of the purchaser. Beyond this, the section in this form is neutral and is not intended to enlarge or restrict the developing case law on whether the seller's warranties, given to his buyer who resells, extend to other persons in the distributive chain. The second alternative is designed for states where the case law has already developed further and for those that desire to expand the class of beneficiaries. The third alternative goes further, following the trend of modern decisions as indicated by Restatement of Torts (Second) § 402A * * * in extending the rule beyond injuries to the person."

4. *Disclaimers.* The UCC, unlike the Uniform Sales Act, deals directly with the problem of disclaimers. The most important sections include 2–302, 2–316, and 2–719. Subsection (3) of the latter section is of particular interest in regard to the disclaimer problem: "Consequential damages may be limited or excluded unless the limitation or exclusion is unconscionable. Limitation of consequential damages for injury to the person in the case of consumer goods is prima facie unconscionable but limitation of damages where the loss is commercial is not."

Some states have amended their version of the UCC to prohibit the exclusion or modification of implied warranties as to consumer goods and services. See, e.g., Me.Rev.Stat.Ann., Tit. 11, § 2–316(5); Md.Ann.Code Tit. 2, § 12–316.1; Mass.Gen.Laws Ann., Ch. 106, § 2–316A. California has passed a separate Consumer Warranties Act, Cal.Civ.Code, Tit. 1.7, §§ 1790–1797.5.

5. *Notice.* Could the principal case have been decided the same way within the framework of the UCC? How? The UCC and its predecessor, the Uniform Sales Act, have a number of stumbling blocks in the way of a strict liability recovery in tort law. One of them is UCC § 2–607, which requires that a buyer must "within a reasonable time after he discovers or should have discovered the breach [of warranty] notify the seller or be barred from any remedy." The analogue Uniform Sales Act provision and the whole problem of the utility of warranty as a tort law remedy confronted Justice Traynor in the next case.

6. *Federal Acts.* The abuses discussed in the principal case have become the subject of federal regulation.

A. *The "Magnuson–Moss Warranty–Federal Trade Commission Improvement Act,"* 15 U.S.C.A. §§ 2301–12 (1975), created a comprehensive regulatory system governing the form and to some degree the content of written warranties and warranties implied by state law. The Act applies to warranties offered to "consumers" by "suppliers" of "consumer products." The Act does not require that a warranty be given; rather, it regulates the scope of warranties that are provided. While it does not affect state personal injury actions, it will affect the nature and scope of disclaimers in the sale of most consumer products that are sold with a "warranty" in the United States.

B. *The Consumer Product Safety Act.* The Consumer Product Safety Act, 15 U.S.C.A. §§ 2051 et seq. (1972), created a new federal agency, the Consumer Product Safety Commission, that has regulatory power over consumer products that are not already subject to safety regulation by other federal agencies (such as the F.D.A.). The Commission is empowered to establish and enforce uniform safety standards for consumer products and to ban products from the market if they create an "unreasonable risk" of injury to the consumer. Section 2072 of the Act provides a federal tort remedy to persons who are injured as a result of a knowing violation of a safety standard, or a rule of the Commission. See W. Kimble, Federal Consumer Product Safety Act (1975).

C. *Other Federal Regulation.* The trend toward increased federal involvement with product safety began with the National Traffic and Motor Vehicle Safety Act of 1966 which required the Secretary of Transportation to establish motor vehicle safety standards. See 15 U.S.C.A. §§ 1381 et seq.

Some of the other important federal regulatory acts relating to products include the Occupational Safety and Health Act (OSHA), 29 U.S.C.A. §§ 651 et seq. (1970), the Federal Hazardous Substances Act, 15 U.S.C.A. §§ 1261 et seq. (1960), the Poison Prevention Packaging Act, 15 U.S.C.A. §§ 1471 et seq. (1970), the Flammable Fabrics Act, 15 U.S.C.A. §§ 1191 et seq. (1972) and the Refrigerator Safety Act, 15 U.S.C.A. §§ 1211 et seq. (1956). While none of these acts creates specific civil tort remedies, violation of a specific standard issued under them may subject a defendant to liability on a negligence per se or implied tort theory. See notes 4 and 5, supra page 214; note 10, page 220.

(C) STRICT LIABILITY IN TORT

GREENMAN v. YUBA POWER PRODUCTS, INC.
Supreme Court of California, 1963.
59 Cal.2d 57, 377 P.2d 897, 27 Cal.Rptr. 697.

TRAYNOR, JUSTICE. Plaintiff brought this action for damages against the retailer and the manufacturer of a Shopsmith, a combination power tool that could be used as a saw, drill, and wood lathe. He saw a Shopsmith demonstrated by the retailer and studied a brochure prepared by the manufacturer. He decided he wanted a Shopsmith for his home workshop, and his wife bought and gave him one for Christmas in 1955. In 1957 he bought the necessary attachments to use the Shopsmith as a lathe for turning a large piece of wood he wished to make into a chalice. After he had worked on the piece of wood several times without difficulty, it suddenly flew out of the machine and struck him on the forehead, inflicting serious injuries. About ten and a half months later, he gave the retailer and the manufacturer written notice of claimed breaches of warranties and filed a complaint against them alleging such breaches and negligence.

After a trial before a jury, the court ruled that there was no evidence that the retailer was negligent or had breached any express warranty and that the manufacturer was not liable for the breach of any implied warranty. Accordingly, it submitted to the jury only the cause of action alleging breach of implied warranties against the retailer and the causes of action alleging negligence and breach of express warranties against the manufacturer. The jury returned a verdict for the retailer against plaintiff and for plaintiff against the manufacturer in the amount of $65,000. The trial court denied the manufacturer's motion for a new trial and entered judgment on the verdict. * * *

Judge Traynor

Plaintiff introduced substantial evidence that his injuries were caused by defective design and construction of the Shopsmith. His expert witnesses testified that inadequate set screws were used to hold parts of the machine together so that normal vibration caused the tailstock of the lathe to move away from the piece of wood being turned permitting it to fly out of the lathe. They also testified that there were other more positive ways of fastening the parts of the machine together, the use of which would have prevented the accident. The jury could therefore reasonably have concluded that the manufacturer negligently constructed the Shopsmith. The jury could also reasonably have concluded that statements in the manufacturer's brochure were untrue, that they constituted express warranties, and that plaintiff's injuries were caused by their breach.

The manufacturer contends, however, that plaintiff did not give it notice of breach of warranty within a reasonable time and that therefore his cause of action for breach of warranty is barred by section 1769 of the Civil Code. Since it cannot be determined whether the verdict against it was based on the negligence or warranty cause of action or both, the manufacturer concludes that the error in presenting the warranty cause of action to the jury was prejudicial.

Section 1769 of the Civil Code provides: "In the absence of express or implied agreement of the parties, acceptance of the goods by the buyer shall not discharge the seller from liability in damages or other legal remedy for breach of any promise or warranty in the contract to sell or the sale. But, if after acceptance of the goods, the buyer fails to give notice to the seller of the breach of any promise or warranty within a reasonable time after the buyer knows, or ought to know of such breach, the seller shall not be liable therefor."

Like other provisions of the uniform sales act (Civ.Code, §§ 1721–1800), section 1769 deals with the rights of the parties to a contract of sale or a sale. It does not provide that notice must be given of the breach of a warranty that arises independently of a contract of sale between the parties. Such warranties are not imposed by the sales act, but are the product of common-law decisions that have recognized them in a variety of situations. [Cc]

It is true that in many of these situations the court has invoked the sales act definitions of warranties (Civ.Code, §§ 1732, 1735) in defining the defendant's liability, but it has done so, not because the statutes so required, but because they provided appropriate standards for the court to adopt under the circumstances presented. [Cc]

The notice requirement of section 1769, however, is not an appropriate one for the court to adopt in actions by injured consumers against manufacturers with whom they have not dealt. [Cc] "As between the immediate parties to the sale, [the notice requirement] is a sound commercial rule, designed to protect the seller against unduly delayed claims for damages. As applied to personal injuries, and notice to a remote seller, it becomes a booby-trap for the unwary. The injured consumer is seldom 'steeped in the business practice which justifies the rule,' [cc] and at least until he has had legal advice it will not occur to him to give notice to one with whom he has had no dealings." [Cc] It is true that in [four prior California cases cited] the court assumed that notice of breach of warranty must be given in an action by a consumer against a manufacturer. Since in those cases, however, the court did not consider the question whether a distinction exists between a warranty based on a contract between the parties and one imposed on a manufacturer not in privity with the consumer, the decisions are not authority for rejecting the rule. [Cc] We conclude, therefore, that even if plaintiff did not give timely notice of breach of warranty to the manufacturer, his cause of action based on the representations contained in the brochure was not barred.

Moreover, to impose strict liability on the manufacturer under the circumstances of this case, it was not necessary for plaintiff to establish an express warranty as defined in section 1732 of the Civil Code. A manufacturer is strictly liable in tort when an article he places on the market, knowing that it is to be used without inspection for defects, proves to have a defect that causes injury to a human being. Recognized first in the case of unwholesome food products, such liability has now been extended to a variety of other products that create as great or greater hazards if defective. [Cc]

Although in these cases strict liability has usually been based on the theory of an express or implied warranty running from the manufacturer to the plaintiff, the abandonment of the requirement of a contract between them, the recognition that the liability is not assumed by agreement but imposed by law [cc], and the refusal to permit the manufacturer to define the scope of its own responsibility for defective products [cc], make clear that the liability is not one governed by the law of contract warranties but by the law of strict liability in tort. Accordingly, rules defining and governing warranties that were developed to meet the needs of commercial transactions cannot properly be invoked to govern the manufacturer's liability to those injured by their defective products unless those rules also serve the purposes for which such liability is imposed.

We need not recanvass the reasons for imposing strict liability on the manufacturer. * * * The purpose of such liability is to insure that the costs of injuries resulting from defective products are borne by the manufacturers that put such products on the market rather than by the injured persons who are powerless to protect themselves. Sales warranties serve this purpose fitfully at best. [C] In the present case, for example, plaintiff was able to plead and prove an express warranty only because he read and relied on the representations of the Shopsmith's ruggedness contained in the manufacturer's brochure. Implicit in the machine's presence on the market, however, was a representation that it would safely do the jobs for which it was built. Under these circumstances, it should not be controlling whether plaintiff selected the machine because of the statements in the brochure, or because of the machine's own appearance of excellence that belied the defect lurking beneath the surface, or because he merely assumed that it would safely do the jobs it was built to do. It should not be controlling whether the details of the sales from manufacturer to retailer and from retailer to plaintiff's wife were such that one or more of the implied warranties of the sales act arose. [C] "The remedies of injured consumers ought not to be made to depend upon the intricacies of the law of sales." [Cc] To establish the manufacturer's liability it was sufficient that plaintiff proved that he was injured while using the Shopsmith in a way it was intended to be used as a result of a defect in design and manufacture of which plaintiff was not aware that made the Shopsmith unsafe for its intended use. * * *

The judgment is affirmed.

---

1. The *Greenman* decision, which might be characterized as the *MacPherson* of a later day, appeared two years before the final published draft of the Restatement (Second) of Torts § 402A:

§ 402A. Special Liability of Seller of Product for Physical Harm to User or Consumer

(1) One who sells any product in a defective condition unreasonably dangerous to the user or consumer or to his property is subject to liability for physical harm thereby caused to the ultimate user or consumer, or to his property, if

(a) the seller is engaged in the business of selling such a product, and

(b) it is expected to and does reach the user or consumer without substantial change in the condition in which it is sold.

(2) The rule stated in Subsection (1) applies although

(a) the seller has exercised all possible care in the preparation and sale of his product, and

(b) the user or consumer has not bought the product from or entered into any contractual relation with the seller.

It should be noted in passing that the law was moving so fast that this Section was actually drafted three times—first as applicable only to food and drink; next, as extended also to include products for "intimate bodily use," and finally, as applicable to all products.

2. How does § 402A differ from the *Greenman* rule? Is the basic theory of each approach the same?

3. Section 402A has literally swept the country. Moreover, a number of states that formerly followed the implied warranty approach to the problem now speak of strict liability in tort. See, e.g., Heavner v. Uniroyal, Inc., 63 N.J. 130, 146–152, 305 A.2d 412 (1973) (the *Henningsen* court); Codling v. Paglia, 32 N.Y.2d 330, 298 N.E.2d 622, 345 N.Y.S.2d 461 (1973). And some courts have tried to apply both implied warranty and § 402A theories in the same action. See Hoffman v. Simplot Aviation, Inc., 539 P.2d 584 (Idaho 1975). Can there be any advantage to this approach? North Carolina has recently declined to adopt strict liability. Smith v. Fiber Controls Corp., 300 N.C. 669, 268 S.E.2d 504 (1980).

4. Whether the liability rests upon negligence, warranty or strict liability in tort, it appears clear by this time, that it applies to all types of products. Whatever limitations there may once have been as to food and drink, intimate bodily use, "inherent danger" or a high degree of danger, all have gone by the boards. The product need not even be dangerous to human beings, or injure them; and such things as animal foods that may foreseeably cause harm only to property, are within the liability. Kassab v. Central Soya, 432 Pa. 217, 246 A.2d 848 (1968); Franklin Serum Co. v. Hoover & Son, 418 S.W.2d 482 (Tex. 1967) (animal serum).

5. Also gone by the boards is a rather foolish distinction that used to plague the food cases, between the product itself and the container in which it is sold. The two are now treated as one, and if a bottled beverage explodes, it no longer makes any difference whether it is due to a defect in the bottle. Kroger Co. v. Bowman, 411 S.W.2d 339 (Ky.1967); Vallis v. Canada Dry Ginger Ale, Inc., 190 Cal.App.2d 35, 11 Cal.Rptr. 823 (1961).

6. With warranty language out of the way, a number of problems (including the notice requirement confronting the court in *Greenman*) disappear. For example, courts have held that a tort and not a contract statute of limitations applies to plaintiff's claim. See Patterson v. Her Majesty Indus., 450 F.Supp.

Committee of Advisers to the Reporter for the Restatement
(Second) of Torts (1962)

Front row: Professor Wex S. Malone,* Professor Laurence H. Eldredge,* Judge Calvert Magruder,* Dean William L. Prosser* (Reporter), Professor Fleming James, Jr.*

Back row: Professor Robert E. Keeton, Professor Allan H. McCoid,*
Francis M. Bird, Esq., Dean Samuel D. Thurman, Jr., Chief Justice
Roger J. Traynor,* Dean John W. Wade, Dean W. Page Keeton

* Deceased

425 (E.D.Pa.1978); Victorson v. Bock Laundry Mach. Co., 37 N.Y.2d 395, 335
N.E.2d 275, 373 N.Y.S.2d 39 (1975). Further, plaintiff can avail himself of both
wrongful death and survival claims. Suppose the tort law statute of limitations
has run, but the U.C.C. statute of limitations has not run? See Redfield v.
Mead, Johnson & Co., 266 Or. 273, 512 P.2d 776 (1973).

The court in Greeno v. Clark Equip. Co., 237 F.Supp. 427, 429 (N.D.Ind.
1965), stated that strict liability in tort is "hardly more than what exists under
implied warranty when stripped of the contract doctrines of privity, disclaimer,
requirements of notice of defeat, and limitation through inconsistencies with
express warranties." To the court's list might be added any limitations arising
from the UCC in terms of when the direct warranties from the seller to the
buyer arise.

7. In Cline v. Prowler Indus. of Maryland, Inc., 418 A.2d 968 (Del.1980),
the Supreme Court of Delaware declared: "In view of (1) the destructive effect
that the adoption of the strict tort liability doctrine would have on the Code
remedies available to the consumer in sales transactions; (2) the clear intent of
the General Assembly to treat consumer injuries by defective products through
the medium of sales warranty law; and (3) the lack of adequate justification for

the separate existence of a tort remedy apart from the Code in sales transactions, we conclude that the General Assembly did not intend to permit the adoption of a competing theory of liability in cases involving the sales of goods and, thus, preempted the field.

"Accordingly, we conclude that it is not within the power of this Court to adopt the doctrine of strict tort liability in sales cases due to the preeminence of the Uniform Commercial Code in the sales field of the law. If more fair and complete protective relief is to be forthcoming for consumers injured by defective products they have purchased, it must come from the General Assembly."

This argument has been presented in several law review articles, but has not been adopted by any other court. Articles discussing the issue are cited in note 11, infra.

8. Once a court has adopted strict liability in tort, should it continue to utilize implied warranty formulas in personal injury actions? See Garcia v. Texas Instruments, Inc., 610 S.W.2d 456 (Tex.1980). Contrast the approach taken under the Uniform Product Liability Act, § 103, 44 Fed.Reg. 62720.

9. Should a seller in a commercial setting be able to disclaim all tort liability to a buyer? See Delta Air Lines, Inc. v. McDonnell Douglas Corp., 503 F.2d 239 (5th Cir.1974) (nose gear of aircraft collapsed and plaintiffs sought to recover expenses made in repair); Keystone Aeronautics Corp. v. R.J. Enstrom Corp., 499 F.2d 146 (3rd Cir.1974) (helicopter purchased—crashed due to defect); Avenell v. Westinghouse Elec. Corp., 41 Ohio App.2d 150, 324 N.E.2d 583 (1974) (defective turbine broke down—specialized equipment with which both parties were familiar); Smith v. Sharpensteen Inc., 521 P.2d 394 (Okl.1974) (lease equipment arrangement—suit for cost of repairs); K–Lines, Inc. v. Roberts Motor Co., 541 P.2d 1378 (Or.1975) (truck crashed due to defect). Compare Sterner Aero AB v. Page Airmotive, Inc., 499 F.2d 709 (10th Cir.1974) (engine failed causing helicopter to crash). Suppose a machine purchased in a commercial setting fails due to a defect. The seller disclaimed all warranties under the UCC. A workman using the machine is injured as a result of the defect. Should his claim be barred? See Turner v. International Harvester Co., 133 N.J.Super. 277, 336 A.2d 62 (1975); Velez v. Craine & Clark Lumber Corp., 33 N.Y.2d 117, 305 N.E.2d 750, 350 N.Y.S.2d 617 (1973). See generally Kroll, Aviation Products Commercial Disclaimers, 1979 Ins.L.J. 615.

10. Should a seller be able to disclaim liability under Restatement (Second) of Torts § 402B (discussed Note 1, supra page 705) when he has made an express warranty that the user has relied on? See Collins v. Uniroyal, Inc., 64 N.J. 260, 315 A.2d 16 (1974). See generally Metzger, Disclaimers, Limitations of Remedy, and Third Parties, 48 U.Cin.L.Rev. 663 (1979).

11. The potential clash between the UCC and strict liability in tort has provided ample material (and some memorable titles) for articles in the law reviews. Some discussions of the subject include: Dickerson, The ABC's of Products Liability—With A Close Look at Section 402A and the Code, 36 Tenn. L.Rev. 439 (1969), and Was Prosser's Folly Also Traynor's?, 2 Hofstra L.Rev. 469 (1974); Donnelly, After the Fall of the Citadel: Exploitation of the Victory or Consideration of All Interests?, 19 Syracuse L.Rev. 1 (1967); Franklin, When Worlds Collide: Liability Theories and Disclaimers in Defective–Product Cases, 18 Stan.L.Rev. 974 (1966); Littlefield, Some Thoughts on Products Liability Law: A Reply to Professor Shanker, 18 W.Res.L.Rev. 10 (1966); McNichols, Who Says That Strict Tort Disclaimers Can Never Be Effective? The Courts

Cannot Agree, 28 Okla.L.Rev. 494 (1975); Miller, The Crossroads: The Case for the Code in Products Liability, 21 Okla.L.Rev. 411 (1968); Prosser, The Assault Upon the Citadel, 69 Yale L.J. 1099 (1960) (supplying the original rationale for § 402A), and The Fall of the Citadel, 50 Minn.L.Rev. 791 (1966); Rapson, Products Liability Under Parallel Doctrines: Contrasts Between the Uniform Commercial Code and Strict Liability in Tort, 19 Rutgers L.Rev. 692 (1965); Wade, Is § 402A of the Second Restatement of Torts Preempted by the UCC and Therefore Unconstitutional?, 42 Tenn.L.Rev. 123 (1974); Titus, Restatement (Second) of Torts § 402A and the Uniform Commercial Code, 22 Stan.L.Rev. 713 (1970); Dickerson, Products Liability: Dean Wade and the Constitutionality of Section 402A, 44 Tenn.L.Rev. 205 (1977); Wade, Tort Liability for Products Causing Physical Injury and Article 2 of the U.C.C., 48 Mo.L.Rev. 1 (1983).

12. A number of rationales have been advanced by legal writers in support of § 402A and the *Greenman* case. Which do you regard as sound?

A. The consumer finds it too difficult to prove negligence against the manufacturer.

B. Strict liability provides an effective and necessary incentive to manufacturers to make their products as safe as possible.

C. Res ipsa loquitur is in fact applied, in some cases, to impose liability upon producers who have not in fact been negligent; therefore negligence should be dispensed with.

D. Reputable manufacturers do in fact stand behind their products, replacing or repairing those which prove to be defective; and many of them issue express agreements to do so. Therefore all should be responsible when an injury results from a normal use of the product.

E. The manufacturer is in a better position to protect against harm, by insuring against liability for it, and, by adding the cost of the insurance to the price of his product, to pass the loss on to the general public.

F. Strict liability already can be accomplished by a series of actions, in which the consumer first recovers from the retailer on a warranty, and liability on warranties is then carried back through the intermediate dealers to the manufacturer. The process is time-consuming, expensive, and wasteful; there should be a short-cut.

G. By placing the product on the market, the seller represents to the public that it is fit; and he intends and expects that it will be purchased and consumed in reliance upon that representation. The middleman is no more than a conduit, a mechanical device through which the thing sold reaches the consumer.

H. The costs of accidents should be placed on the party best able to determine whether there are means to prevent that accident. When those means are less expensive than the costs of such accidents, responsibility for implementing them should be placed on the party best able to do so.

13. What about the danger of deterring manufacturers from introducing new products, or improving old ones? And what about the danger of fictitious claims? "The rats of Hamlin were as nought in comparison with that horde of mice which has sought refreshment within Coca–Cola bottles and died of a happy surfeit." Spruill, Privity of Contract as a Requisite for Recovery on

Warranty, 19 N.C.L.Rev. 551, 566 (1941). Assuming that there will be fraudulent claimants, what kind of defects in the product will they invent?

14. For discussion of legislative modifications, see infra pages 806–09.

2. UNSAFE PRODUCTS

(A) DESIGN

PHILLIPS v. KIMWOOD MACHINE CO.
Supreme Court of Oregon, 1974.
269 Or. 485, 525 P.2d 1033.

[Plaintiff was employed as a sanding machine operator by the Pope and Talbot Company. He was injured when he fed a number of thick and one thin piece of fiberboard into a sanding machine that was purchased by his employer from the defendant. The machine did not hold its grip on the thin piece of fiberboard, but suddenly expelled it. Plaintiff was injured when the fiberboard hit him in the abdomen.

At the close of all the evidence in the case, the trial court directed a verdict in defendant's favor on the ground that the sanding machine was not "unreasonably dangerous" within the meaning of Section 402A of the Restatement (Second) of Torts. Plaintiff appealed.]

HOLMAN, JUSTICE * * * Plaintiff asserts in his complaint that the machine was defective in its design and unreasonably dangerous because (1) "it * * * could not be operated in the manner and for the purpose for which it was manufactured and sold without throwing back towards the operator panels of material being sanded * * *," and (2) "* * * it did not * * * contain * * * any guards, catches, shields, barricades or similar devices to protect the operator of said machine from being struck by panels of material thrown back out of the sanding machine * * *." The two allegations assert substantially the same thing, the first one in general terms, and the second one in particular terms. In effect, they allege the machine was defective and was unreasonably dangerous because there were no safety devices to protect the person feeding the machine from the regurgitation of sheets of fiberboard.

* * * [T]here was evidence from which the jury could find that at a relatively small expense there could have been built into, or subsequently installed on, the machine a line of metal teeth which would point in the direction that the fiberboard progresses through the machine and which would press lightly against the sheet but which, in case of attempted regurgitation, would be jammed into it, thus stopping its backward motion. The evidence also showed that after the accident such teeth were installed upon the machine for that purpose by Pope and Talbot, whereupon subsequent regurgitations of thin fiberboard sheets were prevented while the efficiency of the machine was main-

tained. There was also evidence that defendant makes smaller sanders which usually are manually fed and on which there is such a safety device. * * *

In defense of its judgment based upon a directed verdict, defendant contends there was no proof of a defect in the product, and therefore strict liability should not apply. This court and other courts continue to flounder while attempting to determine how one decides whether a product is "in a defective condition unreasonably dangerous to the user." [1] It has been recognized that unreasonably dangerous defects in products come from two principal sources: (1) mismanufacture and (2) faulty design.[2] Mismanufacture is relatively simple to identify because the item in question is capable of being compared with similar articles made by the same manufacturer. However, whether the mismanufactured article is dangerously defective because of the flaw is sometimes difficult to ascertain because not every such flaw which causes injury makes the article dangerously defective.[3]

The problem with strict liability of products has been one of limitation. No one wants absolute liability where all the article has to do is to cause injury. To impose liability there has to be something about the article which makes it dangerously defective without regard to whether the manufacturer was or was not at fault for such condition. A test for unreasonable danger is therefore vital. A dangerously defective article would be one which a reasonable person would not put into the stream of commerce *if he had knowledge of its harmful character.*[4] The test, therefore, is whether the seller would be negligent if he sold the article *knowing of the risk involved.*[5] Strict liability

1. 2 Restatement (Second) of Torts § 402A, at 347 (1965).

2. Wade, On the Nature of Strict Tort Liability for Products, 44 Miss.L.J. 825, 830 (1973) (including failure to warn as a design defect).

3. The California Supreme Court recognized this problem and attempted to eliminate it by requiring only a defect that causes injury, and not an unreasonably dangerous defect. In Cronin v. J.B.E. Olson Corp., 8 Cal.3d 121, 104 Cal.Rptr. 433, 501 P.2d 1153 (1972), the court felt that requiring proof of an *unreasonably dangerous* defect would put an additional burden on plaintiff which the court deemed improper.

We, however, feel that regardless of whether the term used is "defective," as in *Cronin,* or "defective condition unreasonably dangerous," as in the Restatement, or "dangerously defective," as used here, or "not duly safe," as used by Professor Wade, the same considerations will necessarily be utilized in fixing liability on sellers; and, therefore, the supposedly different standards will come ultimately to the same

conclusion. See Wade, Strict Tort Liability of Manufacturers, 19 Sw.L.J. 5, 14–15 (1965); Wade, supra note 2.

4. See Borel v. Fibreboard Paper Products Corp., 493 F.2d 1076, 1088 (5th Cir. 1973); Welch v. Outboard Marine Corp., 481 F.2d 252, 254 (5th Cir.1973); Helene Curtis Industries, Inc. v. Pruitt, 385 F.2d 841, 850 (5th Cir.1967), cert. denied, 391 U.S. 913, 88 S.Ct. 1806, 20 L.Ed.2d 652 (1968); Olsen v. Royal Metals Corporation, 392 F.2d 116, 119 (5th Cir.1968); Dorsey v. Yoder, 331 F.Supp. 753, 759–760 (E.D.Pa. 1971), aff'd, 474 F.2d 1339 (3 Cir.1973).

See generally, P. Keeton, Manufacturer's Liability: The Meaning of "Defect" in the Manufacture and Design of Products, 20 Syracuse L.Rev. 559, 568 (1969); P. Keeton, Products Liability—Inadequacy of Information, 48 Tex.L.Rev. 398, 403–404 (1970); Wade, Strict Tort Liability of Manufacturers, 19 Sw.L.J. 5, 15–16 (1965).

5. Cf. Welch v. Outboard Marine Corp., 481 F.2d 252, 254 (5th Cir.1973). See generally Wade, supra note 2, at 834–835; P. Keeton, Products Liability—Some Observa-

imposes what amounts to constructive knowledge of the condition of the product. * * *

In the case of a product which is claimed to be dangerously defective because of misdesign, the process is not so easy as in the case of mismanufacture. All the products made to that design are the same. The question of whether the design is unreasonably dangerous can be determined only by taking into consideration the surrounding circumstances and knowledge at the time the article was sold, and determining therefrom whether a reasonably prudent manufacturer would have so designed and sold the article in question had he known of the risk involved which injured plaintiff. The issue has been raised in some courts concerning whether, in this context there is any distinction between strict liability and negligence. The evidence which proves the one will almost always, if not always, prove the other. [Nevertheless,] there is a difference between strict liability for misdesign and negligence. We [have] said:

"However, be all this as it may, it is generally recognized that the basic difference between negligence on the one hand and strict liability for a design defect on the other is that in strict liability we are talking about the condition (dangerousness) of an article which is designed in a particular way, while in negligence we are talking about the reasonableness of the manufacturer's actions in designing and selling the article as he did. The article can have a degree of dangerousness which the law of strict liability will not tolerate even though the actions of the designer were entirely reasonable in view of what he knew at the time he planned and sold the manufactured article. As Professor Wade points out, a way of determining whether the condition of the article is of the requisite degree of dangerousness to be defective (unreasonably dangerous; greater degree of danger than a consumer has a right to expect; not duly safe) is to assume that the manufacturer knew of the product's propensity to injure as it did, and then to ask whether, with such knowledge, something should have been done about the danger before it was sold. In other words, a greater burden is placed on the manufacturer than is the case in negligence because the law assumes he has knowledge of the article's dangerous propensity which he may not reasonably be expected to have, had he been charged with negligence." [Roach v. Kononen, 269 Or. 457, 465, 525 P.2d 125, 129.]

To some it may seem that absolute liability has been imposed upon the manufacturer since it might be argued that no manufacturer could reasonably put into the stream of commerce an article which he realized might result in injury to a user. This is not the case, however.

tions About Allocation of Risks, 64 Mich.L. Rev. 1329, 1335 (1966).

The Wade and Keeton formulations of the standard appear to be identical except that Keeton would impute the knowledge of dangers at time of trial to the manufacturer, while Wade would impute only the knowledge existing at the time the product was sold. Compare P. Keeton, Product Liability and the Meaning of Defect, 5 St. Mary's L.J. 30, 38 (1973), with Wade, supra note 3, at 15, and Wade, supra note 2, at 834.

The manner of injury may be so fortuitous and the chances of injury occurring so remote that it is reasonable to sell the product despite the danger. In design cases the utility of the article may be so great, and the change of design necessary to alleviate the danger in question may so impair such utility, that it is reasonable to market the product, as it is, even though the possibility of injury exists and was realized at the time of the sale. Again, the cost of the change necessary to alleviate the danger in design may be so great that the article would be priced out of the market and no one would buy it even though it was of high utility. Such an article is not dangerously defective despite its having inflicted injury.

In this case defendant contends it was Pope and Talbot's choice to purchase and use the sander without an automatic feeder, even though it was manufactured to be used with one, and, therefore, it was Pope and Talbot's business choice which resulted in plaintiff's injury and not any misdesign by defendant. However, it is recognized that a failure to warn may make a product unreasonably dangerous. * * *

It is our opinion that the evidence was sufficient for the jury to find that a reasonably prudent manufacturer, knowing that the machine would be fed manually and having the constructive knowledge of its propensity to regurgitate thin sheets when it was set for thick ones, which the courts via strict liability have imposed upon it, would have warned plaintiff's employer either to feed it automatically or to use some safety device, and that, in the absence of such a warning, the machine was dangerously defective. It is therefore unnecessary for us to decide the questions that would arise had adequate warnings been given. * * *

It is important to point out, that while the decision is made by the court whether an activity is abnormally dangerous and strict liability of the Rylands v. Fletcher type is to be applied, the determination of whether a product is dangerously defective and strict liability is to be applied has been treated as one primarily for the jury, similar to the manner in which negligence is determined. Therefore, the factors set forth by Wade [6] * * * are not the bases for instructions to the jury but are for the use of the court in determining whether a case has been made out which is submissible to the jury. If such a case has been

---

6. (1) The usefulness and desirability of the product—its utility to the user and to the public as a whole.

(2) The safety aspects of the product—the likelihood that it will cause injury, and the probable seriousness of the injury.

(3) The availability of a substitute product which would meet the same need and not be as unsafe.

(4) The manufacturer's ability to eliminate the unsafe character of the product without impairing its usefulness or making it too expensive to maintain its utility.

(5) The user's ability to avoid danger by the exercise of care in the use of the product.

(6) The user's anticipated awareness of the dangers inherent in the product and their avoidability, because of general public knowledge of the obvious condition of the product, or of the existence of suitable warnings or instructions.

(7) The feasibility, on the part of the manufacturer, of spreading the loss by setting the price of the product or carrying liability insurance. Wade, supra note 2, at 837–838.

made out, then it is submitted to the jury for its determination under instructions as to what constitutes a "dangerously defective" product, much in the same manner as negligence is submitted to the jury under the "reasonable man" rule.[7]

Defendant contends that * * * instructions were given to plaintiff's employer, Pope and Talbot, and the accident occurred because these instructions were not followed and, therefore, the sander was misused and defendant is not responsible for the accident. * * * [Nevertheless,] there is no testimony that the danger of raising the top of the sander while running material through it was ever explained to Pope and Talbot,[8] and, in the absence of such an explanation, we believe the question of whether the accident occurred because the sander was dangerously defective or because it was misused was one for the jury and should not be decided as a matter of law, as contended by defendant.

Defendant calls to our attention that one of the principal rationales behind the imposition of strict liability upon the manufacturer for injuries caused by dangerously defective products is that the manufacturer is in the position of distributing the cost of such risks among all users of the product. Defendant then argues that in the present situation Pope and Talbot would normally bear the responsibility for the injury to its employee and that because Pope and Talbot is just as capable of spreading the cost of injury by the sale of its product as is defendant, there is no logic in imposing liability without fault upon defendant for the purpose of distributing the risk. * * *

While the enterprise liability theory may be indifferent as to whether the defendant or plaintiff's employer should bear this loss, there are other theories which allow us to make a choice.

Where a defendant's product is adjudged by a jury to be dangerously defective, imposition of liability on the manufacturer will cause him to take some steps (or at least make calculations) to improve his product. Although such inducement may not be any greater under a system of strict liability than under a system of negligence recovery, it is certainly greater than if the liability was imposed on another party simply because that other party was a better risk distributor. We suspect that, in the final analysis, the imposition of liability has a

---

7. Wade, supra note 2, at 834–835. Professor Wade also suggests an appropriate jury instruction which embodies the new standard. We have taken the liberty of modifying his suggestion to a form which seems to us more appropriate for use by a jury. It is as follows:

"The law imputes to a manufacturer [supplier] knowledge of the harmful character of his product whether he actually knows of it or not. He is presumed to know of the harmful characteristics of that which he makes [supplies]. Therefore, a product is dangerously defective if it is so harmful to persons [or property] that a reasonable prudent manufacturer [supplier] with this knowledge would not have placed it on the market."

8. Where a user might not realize that a minor departure from instructions may cause serious danger, an additional duty to warn of such danger arises. Noel, Products Defective Because of Inadequate Directions or Warnings. 23 Sw.L.J. 256, 263 (1969).

beneficial effect on manufacturers of defective products both in the care they take and in the warning they give.

The case is reversed and remanded for a new trial.

———

1.　When is a product to be regarded as "defective" for the purposes of imposing strict liability?　Many courts have struggled with this broad issue and the principal case presents one of the most complete judicial discussions of the topic to date.　As the principal case reflects, courts have found that there exist functionally distinct types of defects.　These involve defects in design, construction, and inadequate warnings.

2.　The distinction between defect in design and defect in manufacture (or construction) was not well developed in early strict liability cases.　See, e.g., Greenman v. Yuba Power Prods., Inc., supra page 714; Mosier v. American Motors Co., 303 F.Supp. 44 (S.D.Tex.1967).　Today, the distinction may be quite important in terms of strict liability theory.　If a product has a material defect in construction that causes a personal injury to the user, strict liability usually will be imposed under § 402A.　The plaintiff's main problems will be in the area of factual proof—a topic developed infra, page 794.　On the other hand, when plaintiff contends that the product is defectively designed, he will confront important legal issues on which courts are divided.

3.　As indicated in the notes to Greenman v. Yuba Power Prods. Inc., supra page 714, the great majority of the states adopted the rule of § 402A of the Restatement.　Most of them utilized the language of § 402A and spoke of the requirement that the product be unreasonably dangerous.　But there were some that espoused strict liability but refused to accept the Restatement terminology.

4.　As the principal case reflects, courts have struggled with formulating a "strict liability" rule for design cases that would be distinct from traditional negligence.　For example, in Barker v. Lull Eng'g Co., 20 Cal.3d 413, 573 P.2d 443, 143 Cal.Rptr. 225 (1978), the court applied the traditional risk-utility balancing test similar to that developed by Judge Learned Hand in United States v. Carroll Towing Co., supra Chapter 4, page 145.　But in *Barker* the court placed the burden of proof on the defendant to show the product's utility and that the burden of using an alternative design outweighed the risk of danger involved in the product's design.　See also Caterpillar Tractor Co. v. Beck, 593 P.2d 871 (Alaska 1979).

5.　The Supreme Court of Oregon, in Wilson v. Piper Aircraft Corp., 282 Or. 61, 577 P.2d 1322 (1978), reh'g denied, 282 Or. 411, 579 P.2d 1287 (1978), said that a defendant cannot be found liable "unless the court is satisfied that there is evidence from which the jury could find the suggested [alternative designs] are not only technically feasible but also practicable in terms of the cost and over-all design and operation of the product."　What effect would that factor have on the principal case?

6.　Courts continue to debate whether fault standards should be preserved in design cases.　A number of courts have imputed to the defendant knowledge that it did not have when it made the product.　See Dart v. Wiebe Mfg., Inc., 147 Ariz. 242, 709 P.2d 876, 881–82 (1985) (en banc) (paper shredder).　Contrast Heritage v. Pioneer Brokerage & Sales, Inc., 604 P.2d 1059 (Alaska 1979) ("scientific knowability" refers to knowledge as of time product marketed); Freund v. Cellofilm Properties Inc., 87 N.J. 229, 432 A.2d 925 (1981) (reviewing two earlier New Jersey cases on the issue). See Powers, The Persistence of Fault in Products Liability, 61 Tex.L.Rev. 777 (1983).

7. *"Crash-proof Cars."* A strong dispute existed at one time on the issue of whether an automobile should be designed with a view to minimize the consequences of an accident. In Evans v. General Motors Corp., 359 F.2d 822 (7th Cir.1966), a new X-frame design for a car body turned out to be less safe than a conventional rectangular frame when the car was hit from the side. The court held, however, that the company was under no duty to design an accident-proof or crash-proof car, since the intended purpose of automobiles did not include its participation in a collision. Two years later another federal court in Larsen v. General Motors Corp., 391 F.2d 495 (8th Cir.1968), disagreed and held that the risk of collisions was foreseeable and the design must be prepared with this in mind. There was a long line of cases on each side. See the collection in Frericks v. General Motors Corp., 20 Md.App. 518, 317 A.2d 494 (1974); Annot., 42 A.L.R.3d 560 (1972). But the *Larsen* view soon began to prevail, and the Seventh Circuit has now changed its view and ceased to follow *Evans*. See Nanda v. Ford Motor Co., 509 F.2d 213 (7th Cir.1974). Today, the *Larsen* view has swept the field. See Hoenig & Goetz, A Rational Approach to "Crashworthy" Automobiles: The Need for Judicial Responsibility, 6 Sw.U.L. Rev. 1 (1974); Sklaw, "Second Collision" Liability: The Need for Uniformity, 4 Seton Hall L.Rev. 499 (1973); Hoenig and Werber, Automobile "Crashworthiness": An Untenable Doctrine, 20 Clev.St.L.Rev. 578 (1971); Nader and Page, Automobile Design and the Judicial Process, 55 Calif.L.Rev. 645 (1967).

8. Assuming the manufacturer owes a duty to protect the occupant of a vehicle in an accident, how far does it extend? Suppose a Volkswagen minibus has only a short space between the driver and the front of the vehicle. A more conventional design might have reduced plaintiff's injuries in a collision. Liability? See Dreisonstok v. Volkswagenwerk, A.G., 489 F.2d 1066 (4th Cir. 1974). A gearshift knob becomes brittle in sunlight; plaintiff is impaled upon the instrument the knob is supposed to protect. Liability? See Mickle v. Blackmon, 252 S.C. 202, 166 S.E.2d 173 (1969). What about an obvious hazard such as a raised, unprotected cowl on a steering wheel? Compare Burkhard v. Short, 28 Ohio App.2d 141, 57 Ohio Ops.2d 215, 275 N.E.2d 632 (1971), with Ellithorpe v. Ford Motor Co., 503 S.W.2d 516 (Tenn.1973). Suppose plaintiff is injured in a rather unforeseeable manner? Cf. Schneider v. Chrysler Motors Corp., 401 F.2d 549 (8th Cir.1968). Who should decide these things, judge or jury?

9. A four-door hardtop leaves the road and turns over and lands on its top. A corner of the roof collapses on the driver and paralyzes him. Plaintiff contends that the car should have been equipped with a roll bar or roll cage, and introduces an expert witness to testify that this was feasible technically and economically and that it was done on racing cars. But it would eliminate convertibles and perhaps hardtops, and no mass-produced automobile had ever been built this way. Can the issue go to the jury? See Turner v. General Motors Corp., 514 S.W.2d 497 (1974); Turner v. General Motors Corp., 584 S.W.2d 844 (Tex.1979).

PRENTIS v. YALE MFG. CO.
Supreme Court of Michigan, 1984.
421 Mich. 670, 365 N.W.2d 176.

BOYLE, JUSTICE. This products liability action arose out of injuries sustained in an accident involving the operation of a hand-operated forklift manufactured by defendant. The procedural events leading up to this appeal include two trials and two reversals and remands for new trials by the Court of Appeals. Plaintiffs John Prentis and his wife, Helen, brought suit alleging both negligence and breach of implied warranty, predicating defendant manufacturer's liability upon the alleged defective design of the forklift. Although the trial judge included both negligence and breach of warranty in his statement of plaintiffs' theory of the case to the jury, he refused to give plaintiffs' requested instructions on breach of implied warranty. A judgment for the defendant, upon a jury verdict of no cause of action, was reversed by the Court of Appeals, which held that the trial court's failure to charge the jury as requested was reversible error, mandating a new trial. [C]

We granted leave to appeal and limited our inquiry to the following issue: whether the trial judge's refusal to instruct the jury on breach of warranty was reversible error in this products liability action against a manufacturer for an alleged defect in the design of a product, where the jury was properly instructed on the theory of negligent design.

The facts of this case are not seriously in dispute. In April of 1970, plaintiff John Prentis, who was employed as foreman of the parts department at an automobile dealership, sustained a hip injury in an accident involving the use of a forklift manufactured by defendant Yale Manufacturing Company and sold to plaintiff's employer in 1952. The forklift was a stand-up or walking type, termed by defendant a "walkie hi-lo" model, rather than a riding or sit down variety. It was operated by lifting its handle up, much like the handle of a wagon. The forklift was estimated by plaintiff to weigh about two thousand pounds and was powered by a large battery, which had to be recharged every night. The machine was equipped with a hand controlled "dead-man" switch which normally prevented it from moving if the operator let go of the handle or controls. * * *

The accident in which Mr. Prentis was injured occurred late in the day, and he testified that he was aware at the time that the battery charge on the forklift was running low. After using the machine to assist him in placing an engine inside the cargo area of a delivery van, while the forklift was in tow behind him on a slightly inclined ramp leading from the delivery bay, Mr. Prentis attempted to start the machine by working the handle up and down. When the machine experienced a power surge, he lost his footing and fell to the ground. It appears that plaintiff's injuries were a result of the fall only, as the machine did not hit or run over him, but continued past him and stopped when it ran into a parked car. Mr. Prentis received extensive treatment for multiple fractures of his left hip. * * *

The focus of plaintiffs' proofs at both trials was an alleged defect in the design of the forklift, and the substance of the expert witness's testimony was that the design of the forklift failed to properly incorporate the operator as a "human factor" into the machine's function, specifically because it did not provide a seat or platform for the operator. * * *

During the course of trial, plaintiffs' counsel requested separate jury instructions on implied warranty and negligence theories, while counsel for defendant requested a unified jury instruction. After considerable discussion and argument and a careful review and analysis of the most recent case law under the new statute, the court instructed the jury on a unified standard of liability by using an amalgam of the common elements of proof under the implied warranty and negligence theories. * * *

Following the jury instructions on liability, the court read both parties' written theories of the case to the jury, including plaintiffs' claims under both negligence and breach of warranty. The jury panel was then given a special verdict form which first asked the following question:

"Question No. 1: Was the motorized hand truck defectively designed by Yale Manufacturing Company?

"Answer: _____ (Yes or No).

"(If your answer is no, do not answer any further questions)."

Question No. 1 was answered in the negative by the jury panel, and a judgment of no cause of action was entered by the trial court on February 28, 1980.

Plaintiff filed a timely claim of appeal in the Court of Appeals. On May 20, 1982, the Court of Appeals issued a published per curiam opinion reversing the trial court judgment and remanding for a new trial. [C] The Court of Appeals held that the trial court's failure to give the properly requested jury instruction on implied warranty was reversible error requiring a new trial. We granted defendant's application for leave to appeal on June 28, 1983. [C]

The development of the law of tort liability for physical injury caused by products is perhaps the most striking and dramatic of all the numerous stories in the portfolio of modern tort scenarios. When the societal goal of holding manufacturers accountable for the safety of their products has been threatened by the interposition of technical rules of law, it has been the rules that have gradually given way.

However, this has never meant that courts have been willing to impose absolute liability in this context and from their earliest application, theories of products liability have been viewed as tort doctrines which should not be confused with the imposition of absolute liability. * * *

Thus while courts have accepted the social policy rationale that those injured by defective products should be compensated for their injuries without being subject to the contractual intricacies of the law of sales, and have agreed that manufacturers can most effectively distribute the costs of injuries, they have never gone so far as to make sellers insurers of their products and thus absolutely liable for any and all injuries sustained from the use of those products.

Like the courts in every other state, whether a suit is based upon negligence or implied warranty, we require the plaintiff to prove that the product itself is actionable—that something is wrong with it that makes it dangerous. This idea of "something wrong" is usually expressed by the adjective "defective" and the plaintiff must, *in every case, in every jurisdiction,* show that the product was defective. [C]

As a term of art, "defective" gives little difficulty when something goes wrong in the manufacturing process and the product is not in its intended condition. In the case of a "manufacturing defect," the product may be evaluated against the manufacturer's own production standards, as manifested by that manufacturer's other like products.

However, injuries caused by the condition of a product may also be actionable if the product's design, which is the result of intentional design decisions of the manufacturer, is not sufficiently safe. Conscious design defect cases provide no such simple test. The very question whether a defect in fact exists is central to a court's inquiry. It is only in design defect cases that a court is called upon to supply the standard for defectiveness. Thus, the term "defect" in design cases is "an epithet—an expression for the legal conclusion rather than a test for reaching that conclusion." See Wade, *On product "design defects" and their actionability,* 33 Van L.R. 551, 552 (1980).

At present, questions related to "design defects" and the determination of when a product is defective, because of the nature of its design, appear to be the most agitated and controversial issues before the courts in the field of products liability. A number of appellate courts, aware that they are engaged in the conscious task of molding the law of products liability, have become concerned that they are not differentiating with sufficient clarity between various theories of recovery in design defect cases. In response, they have sought to devise significant and well-articulated distinctions. At the same time, other courts have become concerned that the differentiation is too great, and have attempted to devise means of keeping the broad scope of liability in check. The result has been several cases in which the standard for liability in the design area has been very carefully examined by courts and often vigorously debated by the judges themselves. A survey of the important recent cases in neighboring jurisdictions suggests something of the creative ferment underlying what has been described as the "rich tapestry" of the developing common law of products liability.

The approaches for determination of the meaning of "defect" in design cases fall into four general categories. The first, usually associated with Dean Wade, employs a negligence risk-utility analysis, but focuses upon whether the manufacturer would be judged negligent if it had known of the product's dangerous condition at the time it was marketed. The second, associated with Dean Keeton, compares the risk and utility of the product at the time of trial. The third focuses on consumer expectations about the product. The fourth combines the risk-utility and consumer-expectation tests. While courts have included many other individual variations in their formulations, the overwhelming consensus among courts deciding defective design cases is in the use of some form of risk-utility analysis, either as an exclusive or alternative ground of liability. Risk-utility analysis in this context always involves assessment of the decisions made by manufacturers with respect to the design of their products. * * *

The risk-utility balancing test is merely a detailed version of Judge Learned Hand's negligence calculus. See *United States v. Carroll Towing Co.*, 159 F.2d 169, 173 (2d Cir.1947). As Dean Prosser has pointed out, the liability of the manufacturer rests "upon a departure from proper standards of care, so that the tort is essentially a matter of negligence."

Although many courts have insisted that the risk-utility tests they are applying are not negligence tests because their focus is on the *product* rather than the manufacturer's *conduct*, [c] the distinction on closer examination appears to be nothing more than semantic. As a common-sense matter, the jury weighs competing factors presented in evidence and reaches a conclusion about the judgment or decision (*i.e., conduct*) of the manufacturer. The underlying negligence calculus is inescapable. As noted by Professor Birnbaum:

"When a jury decides that the risk of harm outweighs the utility of a particular design (that the product is not as safe as it *should* be) it is saying that in choosing the particular design and cost tradeoffs, the manufacturer exposed the consumer to greater risk of danger than he should have. Conceptually and analytically, this approach bespeaks negligence." Birnbaum, *Unmasking the test for design defect: From negligence [to warranty] to strict liability to negligence*, 33 Van.L.R. 593, 610 (1980) * * *

The competing factors to be weighed under a risk-utility balancing test invite the trier of fact to consider the alternatives and risks faced by the manufacturer and to determine whether in light of these the manufacturer exercised reasonable care in making the design choices it made. Instructing a jury that weighing factors concerning conduct and judgment must yield a conclusion that does not describe conduct is confusing at best.

The Model Uniform Product Liability Act (UPLA) was published in 1979 by the Department of Commerce for voluntary use by the states. The act adopts a negligence or fault system with respect to design defects. It is important to examine the rationale underlying the UPLA's adoption of negligence as the criteria for liability in design defect cases. The drafters rejected, as a reason for application of strict liability to design defect cases, the theory of risk distribution wherein the product seller distributes the costs of all product-related risks through liability insurance. They believe that a "firmer liability foundation" than strict liability is needed in a design defect case because the whole product line is at risk. Furthermore, the drafters believed that a fault system would provide greater incentives for loss prevention.

The approach of the UPLA has been approved by several commentators, whose analysis is also instructive. First, unlike manufacturing defects, design defects result from deliberate and documentable decisions on the part of manufacturers, and plaintiffs should be able to learn the facts surrounding these decisions through liberalized modern discovery rules. Access to expert witnesses and technical data are available to aid plaintiffs in proving the manufacturer's design decision was ill considered.

Second, to the extent that a primary purpose of products liability law is to encourage the design of safer products and thereby reduce the incidence of injuries, a negligence standard that would reward the careful manufacturer and penalize the careless is more likely to achieve that purpose. A greater incentive to design safer products will result from a fault system where resources devoted to careful and safe design will pay dividends in the form of fewer claims and lower insurance premiums for the manufacturer with a good design safety record. The incentive will result from the knowledge that a distinction is made between those who are careful and those who are not.

Third, a verdict for the plaintiff in a design defect case is the equivalent of a determination that an entire product line is defective. It usually will involve a significant portion of the manufacturer's assets and the public may be deprived of a product. Thus, the plaintiff should be required to pass the higher threshold of a fault test in order to threaten an entire product line. The traditional tort law of negligence better serves this purpose.

Fourth, a fault system incorporates greater intrinsic fairness in that the careful safety-oriented manufacturer will not bear the burden of paying for losses caused by the negligent product seller. It will also follow that the customers of the careful manufacturer will not through its prices pay for the negligence of the careless. As a final bonus, the careful manufacturer with fewer claims and lower insurance premiums may, through lower prices as well as safer products, attract the customers of less careful competitors.

We find the formula adopted by the UPLA on the question of defective design to have the merit of being clear and understandable. We recognize that in products liability cases against manufacturers based upon alleged defects in the design of a product, the courts of this state have attempted to avoid both the notion of fault implicit in negligence and the harshness of no-fault implicit in absolute liability. Thus, on the basis of the heritage of contract and sales law underlying concepts of implied warranty, we have in the past approved instructions that attempted to focus a jury's attention on the condition of a product rather than on the reasonableness of the manufacturer's conduct or decision. We are persuaded that in so doing in the context of cases against the manufacturers of products *based upon allegations of defective design,* we have engaged in a process that may have served to confuse, rather than enlighten, jurors, who must ultimately apply understandable guidelines if they are to justly adjudicate the rights and duties of all parties. Imposing a negligence standard for design defect litigation is only to define in a coherent fashion what our litigants in this case are in fact arguing and what our jurors are in essence analyzing. Thus we adopt, forthrightly, a pure negligence, risk-utility test in products liability actions against manufacturers of products, where liability is predicated upon defective design.

We hold that in this products liability action against a manufacturer for an alleged defect in the design of its product, where the jury was properly instructed on the theory of negligent design, the trial judge's refusal to instruct on breach of warranty was not reversible error. Such instructions could have created juror confusion and prejudicial error. Indeed, such an instruction would have been repetitive and unnecessary and could have misled the jury into believing that plaintiff could recover on the warranty count even if it found there was no "defect" in the design of the product. [C]

This opinion is limited solely to its facts. We do not suggest that implied warranty and negligence are not separate and distinct theories of recovery; [c] or that the Michigan products liability statute, M.C.L. § 600.2945; M.S.A. § 27A.2945, has merged all former products liability theories or causes of action into a single unified "products liability theory." * * *

This holding is based upon the recognition that under the common law of products liability, in an action against the manufacturer of a product based upon an alleged defect in its design, "breach of implied warranty and negligence involve identical evidence and require proof of exactly the same elements." * * *

Applying these principles to the facts of this case, although plaintiffs alleged that their injuries were proximately caused by defendant's negligence and breach of an implied warranty, their evidence and proofs at trial focused on the single claim that the defendant *defectively designed* the "walkie hi-lo" forklift, because it failed to provide a seat or platform for the operator. Thus, recovery under either theory required the jury to determine that the forklift was defectively designed by defendant. [C] The factual inquiry was: whether the design of defendant's forklift was "unreasonably dangerous" because it did not contain a seat or platform for the operator. [C]

The trial court properly recognized that the standards of liability under the theories of implied warranty and negligence were indistinguishable and that instructions on both would only confuse the jury.

Accordingly, the trial judge's instructions regarding the standard of care and theories of liability properly informed the jury of defendant's legal duties as the manufacturer of the forklift. The court set forth the necessary elements for determining whether defendant defectively designed the forklift when it stated:

"A manufacturer of a product made under a plan or design which makes it dangerous for uses for which it is manufactured is, [however,] subject to liability to others whom he should expect to use the product or to be endangered by its probable use from physical harm caused by his failure to exercise reasonable care in the adoption of a safe plan or design.

"A manufacturer has a duty to use reasonable care in designing his product and guard it against a foreseeable and unreasonable risk of injury and this may even include misuse which might reasonably be anticipated."

In essence, the jury was instructed to consider whether the manufacturer took reasonable care in light of any reasonably foreseeable use of the product which might cause harm or injury. [C]

Therefore we hold that in a products liability action against a manufacturer, based upon defective design, the jury need only be instructed on a single unified theory of negligent design.

The judgment of the Court of Appeals is reversed, and the judgment of the trial court is reinstated.

WILLIAMS, C.J., and BRICKLEY and RYAN, JJ., concur.

CAVANAGH, J., concurring in result.

LEVIN, JUSTICE (dissenting) [with opinion].

---

1. A few other courts have made similar observations about the application of a "strict liability" standard in design defect claims. See, e.g., Bilotta v. Kelley Co., 346 N.W.2d 616 (Minn.1984) ("assuming proper instruction to ensure the broadest theory of recovery, a trial court could properly submit a design-defect or failure-to-warn case to a jury on a single theory of products liability"). Do you agree or disagree with the conclusion that attempting to define a strict liability standard in cases evaluating a manufacturer's choice of design confuses jurors?

2. From the perspective of an attorney representing plaintiffs, would you choose to base your claim in a design defect case on strict liability or negligence? What would be the difference in terms of what you would try to prove under each theory?

3. What did the plaintiff allege to be the design defect in this case? How do you think the Oregon Court, which decided the *Phillips* case, supra page 722, and the *Wilson* case, supra page 727, note 5, would have decided this one? The same way?

4. Suppose the defendant in the principal case had used a part in this forklift that was made of brittle metal. Would the plaintiff be required to

prove that the defendant was negligent in failing to discover that this particular part was "defective"?

O'BRIEN v. MUSKIN CORP.
Supreme Court of New Jersey, 1983.
94 N.J. 169, 463 A.2d 298.

POLLOCK, J. Plaintiff, Gary O'Brien, seeks to recover in strict liability for personal injuries sustained because defendant, Muskin Corporation, allegedly marketed a product, an above-ground swimming pool, that was defectively designed and bore an inadequate warning. In an unreported decision, the Appellate Division reversed the judgment for defendants and remanded the matter for trial. We granted certification, [c] and now modify and affirm the judgment of the Appellate Division. * * *

O'Brien sued to recover damages for serious personal injuries sustained when he dove into a swimming pool at the home of Jean Henry, widow of Arthur Henry, now Jean Glass. Ultimately, plaintiff sued as defendants not only Muskin Corporation, the manufacturer, but also Kiddie City Inc., the distributor of the pool, charging them with placing a defectively designed pool in the stream of commerce. * * *

Muskin, a swimming pool manufacturer, made and distributed a line of above-ground pools. Typically, the pools consisted of a corrugated metal wall, which the purchaser placed into an oval frame assembled over a shallow bed of sand. This outer structure was then fitted with an embossed vinyl liner and filled with water.

In 1971, Arthur Henry bought a Muskin pool and assembled it in his backyard. The pool was a twenty-foot by twenty-four-foot model, with four-foot walls. An embossed vinyl liner fit within the outer structure and was filled with water to a depth of approximately three and one-half feet. At one point, the outer wall of the pool bore the logo of the manufacturer, and below it a decal that warned "DO NOT DIVE" in letters roughly one-half inch high.

On May 17, 1974, O'Brien, then twenty-three years old, arrived uninvited at the Henry home and dove into the pool. A fact issue exists whether O'Brien dove from the platform by the pool or from the roof of the adjacent eight-foot high garage. As his outstretched hands hit the vinyl-lined pool bottom, they slid apart, and O'Brien struck his head on the bottom of the pool, thereby sustaining his injuries.

In his complaint, O'Brien alleged that Muskin was strictly liable for his injuries because it had manufactured and marketed a defectively designed pool. In support of this contention, O'Brien cited the slippery quality of the pool liner and the lack of adequate warnings.

At trial, both parties produced experts who testified about the use of vinyl as a pool liner. One of the plaintiff's witnesses, an expert in the characteristics of vinyl, testified that wet vinyl was more than twice as slippery as rubber latex, which is used to line in-ground pools. The trial court, however, sustained an objection to the expert's opinion about alternative kinds of pool bottoms, specifically whether rubber latex was a feasible liner for above-ground pools. The expert admitted that he knew of no above-ground pool lined with a material other than vinyl, but plaintiff contended that vinyl should not be used in above-ground pools, even though no alternative material was available. A second expert testified that the slippery vinyl bottom and lack of adequate warnings rendered the pool unfit and unsafe for its foreseeable uses.

Muskin's expert testified that vinyl was not only an appropriate material to line an above-ground pool, but was the best material because it permitted the outstretched arms of the diver to glide when they hit the liner, thereby preventing the diver's head from striking the bottom of the pool. Thus, he concluded that in some situations, specifically those in which a diver executes a shallow dive, slipperiness operates as a safety feature. Another witness, Muskin's customer service manager, who was indirectly in charge of quality control, testified that the vinyl bottom could have been thicker and the embossing deeper. A fair inference could be drawn that deeper embossing would have rendered the pool bottom less slippery.

At the close of the entire case, the trial court instructed the jury on the elements of strict liability, both with respect to design defects and the failure to warn adequately. The court, however, then limited the jury's consideration to the adequacy of the warning. That is, the court took from the jury the issue whether manufacturing a pool with a vinyl liner constituted either a design or manufacturing defect.

Strict liability law, a relatively recent but rapidly growing legal phenomenon, has received uneven treatment from scholars, legislatures and courts. Underlying the various responses is a shared concern about the allocation of the risk of loss upon manufacturers, distributors and others in the stream of commerce for injuries sustained by the public from unsafe products.

One of the policy considerations supporting the imposition of strict liability is easing the burden of proof for a plaintiff injured by a defective product, a policy that is achieved by eliminating the requirement that the plaintiff prove the manufacturer's negligence. [C] Generally speaking, a plaintiff has the burden of proving that (1) the product was defective; (2) the defect existed when the product left the hands of the defendant; and (3) the defect caused injury to a reasonably foreseeable user. [C] Proof that the product was defective requires more than a mere showing that the product caused the injury. The necessity of proving a defect in the product as part of the plaintiff's *prima facie* case distinguishes strict from absolute liability, and thus prevents the manufacturer from also becoming the insurer of a product. [Cc]

Fundamental to the determination of a products liability case, including one predicated on a defective design or inadequate warning, is the duty of the manufacturer to foreseeable users. The duty includes warning foreseeable users of the risks inherent in the use of that product, [c] and not placing defective products on the market. [Cc] A manufacturer who breaches these duties is strictly liable to an injured party. That liability reflects the policy judgment that by marketing its product, a manufacturer assumes responsibility to members of the public who are injured because of defects in that product. *Restatement (Second) of Torts* § 402A comment c (1965). * * *

Critical, then, to the disposition of products liability claims is the meaning of "defect". The term is not self-defining and has no accepted meaning suitable for all strict liability cases. Implicit in the term "defect" is a comparison of the product with a standard of evaluation; something can be defective only if it fails to measure up to that standard. [C] Speaking generally, defects may be classified as design defects or manufacturing defects. In cases alleging manufacturing defects, as distinguished from design defects, defining the standard, and thus the meaning of "defect," is relatively easy. For example, the injury-causing product may be measured against the same product as manufactured according to the manufacturer's standards. If the particular product used by the plaintiff fails to conform to those standards or other units of the same kind, it is defective. An apt illustration is a mass-produced product that comes off the assembly line missing a part. The question in those cases becomes whether the product as produced by the manufacturer conformed to the product as intended. [C]

The considerations are more subtle when a plaintiff alleges that a product is defective due to any feature of its design, including the absence or inadequacy of accompanying warnings. In design defect or failure-to-warn cases, the product has been manufactured as intended and cannot be "defective" by comparison to a standard set by the manufacturer. [C] Rather, the standard to measure the product reflects a policy judgment that some products are so dangerous that they create a risk of harm outweighing their usefulness. From that perspective, the term "defect" is a conclusion rather than a test for reaching that conclusion. [C]

Although the appropriate standard might be variously defined, one definition, based on a comparison of the utility of the product with the risk of injury that it poses to the public, has gained prominence. To the extent that "risk-utility analysis," as it is known, implicates the reasonableness of the manufacturer's conduct, strict liability law continues to manifest that part of its heritage attributable to the law of negligence. [Cc] Risk-utility analysis is appropriate when the product may function satisfactorily under one set of circumstances, yet because of its design present undue risk of injury to the user in another situation.

Another standard is the consumer expectations test, which recognizes that the failure of the product to perform safely may be viewed as a violation of the reasonable expectations of the consumer. [C] In this case, however, the pool fulfilled its function as a place to swim. The alleged defect manifested itself when the pool was used for diving.

* * * [S]ome factors relevant in risk-utility analysis are:

(1) The usefulness and desirability of the product—its utility to the user and to the public as a whole.

(2) The safety aspects of the product—the likelihood that it will cause injury, and the probable seriousness of the injury.

(3) The availability of a substitute product which would meet the same need and not be as unsafe.

(4) The manufacturer's ability to eliminate the unsafe character of the product without impairing its usefulness or making it too expensive to maintain its utility.

(5) The user's ability to avoid danger by the exercise of care in the use of the product.

(6) The user's anticipated awareness of the dangers inherent in the product and their avoidability, because of general public knowledge of the obvious condition of the product, or of the existence of suitable warnings or instructions.

(7) The feasibility, on the part of the manufacturer, of spreading the loss by setting the price of the product or carrying liability insurance. [C] * * *

By implication, risk-utility analysis includes other factors such as the "state-of-the-art" at the time of the manufacture of the product. [C] The "state-of-the-art" refers to the existing level of technological expertise and scientific knowledge relevant to a particular industry at the time a product is designed. [C] Although customs of an industry may be relevant, [c] because those customs may lag behind technological development, they are not identical with the state-of-the-art. [Cc] A manufacturer may have a duty to make products pursuant to a safer design even if the custom of the industry is not to use that alternative. [C] * * *

Although state-of-the-art evidence may be dispositive on the facts of a particular case, it does not constitute an absolute defense apart from risk-utility analysis. [C] The ultimate burden of proving a defect is on the plaintiff, but the burden is on the defendant to prove that compliance with state-of-the-art, in conjunction with other relevant evidence, justifies placing a product on the market. Compliance with proof of state-of-the-art need not, as a matter of law, compel a judgment for a defendant. State-of-the-art evidence, together with other evidence relevant to risk-utility analysis, however, may support a judgment for a defendant. In brief, state-of-the-art evidence is relevant to, but not necessarily dispositive of, risk-utility analysis. That is, a product may embody the state-of-the-art and still fail to satisfy the risk-utility equation.

The assessment of the utility of a design involves the consideration of available alternatives. If no alternatives are available, recourse to a unique design is more defensible. The existence of a safer and equally efficacious design, however, diminishes the justification for using a challenged design.

The evaluation of the utility of a product also involves the relative need for that product; some products are essentials, while others are luxuries. A product that fills a critical need and can be designed in only one way should be viewed differently from a luxury item. Still other products, including some for which no alternative exists, are so dangerous and of such little use that under the risk-utility analysis, a manufacturer would bear the cost of liability of harm to others. That cost might dissuade a manufacturer from placing the product on the market, even if the product has been made as safely as possible. Indeed, plaintiff contends that above-ground pools with vinyl liners are such products and that manufacturers who market those pools should bear the cost of injuries they cause to foreseeable users.

A critical issue at trial was whether the design of the pool, calling for a vinyl bottom in a pool four feet deep, was defective. The trial court should have permitted the jury to consider whether, because of the dimensions of the pool and slipperiness of the bottom, the risks of injury so outweighed the utility of the product as to constitute a defect. In removing that issue from consideration by the jury, the trial court erred. To establish sufficient proof to compel submission of the issue to the jury for appropriate fact-finding under risk-utility analysis, it was not necessary for plaintiff to prove the existence of alternative, safer designs. Viewing the evidence in the light most favorable to plaintiff, even if there are no alternative methods of making bottoms for above-ground pools, the jury might have found that the risk posed by the pool outweighed its utility.

In a design-defect case, the plaintiff bears the burden of both going forward with the evidence and of persuasion that the product contained a defect. To establish a *prima facie* case, the plaintiff should adduce sufficient evidence on the risk-utility factors to establish a defect. With respect to above-ground swimming pools, for example, the plaintiff might seek to establish that pools are marketed primarily for recreational, not therapeutic purposes; that because of their design, including their configuration, inadequate warnings, and the use of vinyl liners, injury is likely; that, without impairing the usefulness of the pool or pricing it out of the market, warnings against diving could be made more prominent and a liner less dangerous. It may not be necessary for the plaintiff to introduce evidence on all those alternatives. Conversely, the plaintiff may wish to offer proof on other matters relevant to the risk-utility analysis. It is not a foregone conclusion that plaintiff ultimately will prevail on a risk-utility analysis, but he should have an opportunity to prove his case. ＊ ＊ ＊

We modify and affirm the judgment of the Appellate Division reversing and remanding the matter for a new trial.

CLIFFORD, J., concurring in result. SCHREIBER, J., concurring and dissenting [with opinion].

For affirmance as modified—CHIEF JUSTICE WILENTZ, and JUSTICES CLIFFORD, HANDLER, POLLOCK and O'HERN.

---

1. Recently, victims (or their heirs) of criminal shootings have sued the manufacturers of small, inexpensive handguns on the ground that, although the product worked exactly as expected, it could not be used effectively for anything but crime and was therefore "defectively marketed." They have argued that the product's risks so far outweigh its utility that the manufacturer should bear the cost of injuries it creates. So far only one court has held the manufacturer liable. Kelley v. R.G. Indus., 304 Md. 124, 497 A.2d 1143 (1985). Cf. Moore v. R.G. Indus., 789 F.2d 1326 (9th Cir.1986); Riordan v. International Armament Corp., 132 Ill.App.3d 642, 87 Ill.Dec. 765, 477 N.E.2d 1293 (1985); Rhodes v. R.G. Indus., 173 Ga.App. 51, 325 S.E.2d 465 (1984); and Patterson v. Gesellschaft, 608 F.Supp. 1206 (N.D.Tex.1985). Courts have tended to defer to legislatures in this politically sensitive area. For example, the Nevada legislature has barred lawsuits against gun manufacturers where the product has performed as intended, stating that "capability of causing serious injury or death is not a defect." Nev.Laws 1985, Ch. 480. See generally, Siegel, Liability of Manufacturers for the Negligent Design and Distribution of Handguns, 6 Hamline L.Rev. 321 (1983).

2. Courts in two states have held that manufacturers may be liable for injuries caused by dangers inherent in their products, even if the product does not contain a manufacturing or design defect or inadequate warnings. Halphen v. Johns–Manville Sales Corp., 484 So.2d 110 (La.1986) (asbestos); Johnson v. Raybestos—Manhattan, Inc., ___ Hawaii ___, 740 P.2d 548 (1987). In Louisiana, a mid-level appellate court held that ordinary escalators are "unreasonably dangerous per se" and would subject their manufacturers to liability without any showing that the escalator contained a construction or design defect or lacked adequate warnings. Brown v. Sears Roebuck & Co., 503 So.2d 1122 (La.App.1987). If an escalator manufacturer is subject to liability without a showing that escalators could be made safer by an alternative design, is this a situation where "defect" has been eliminated as a prerequisite to products liability?

3. The principal case suggested that some products are so dangerous and of such little usefulness that manufacturers who market those products should always bear the cost of injuries they cause. The Louisiana Supreme Court in Halphen, supra note 2, stated that some products are "too dangerous to be placed on the market." What would happen if courts in different states were to have conflicting views about whether a particular product was "too dangerous to be placed on the market"? Could the manufacturer avoid liability by selling his product in only those states that do not think the product should be taken off the market? Are there other ways to ban products that are unacceptably dangerous as compared to their utility to product users and society? A key issue in design liability cases is whether a defendant can avoid liability if he complied with the "state of the art" at the time he made the product. The concept of "state of the art" for products has become muddled because courts give different meaning to that term. Sometimes the term is confused with the "industry customs" defense which defeats a claim if the manufacturer was

acting in accordance with general practices used in the industry at the time the product was made. In its correct meaning, the state of the art defense requires a manufacturer to use the best scientific and medical technology that is practically and economically feasible at the time the product was made or marketed. In other words, the product is evaluated in light of knowledge and technology that were available at the time of manufacture rather than at the time of trial. A principal goal of "tort reformers" at the federal level is to incorporate state of the art into the law in all states. Would this return products liability law to negligence standards?

5. Critics of the state of the art defense argue that it allows manufacturers to be lazy and not develop safety innovations. Its supporters contend that it is unfair to impose liability where a product danger could not have been discovered and avoided, and also that the defense permits the law to distinguish between manufacturers who make safety efforts and those who do not. What do you think?

6. The state of the art defense arises primarily in cases involving claims based on design defects or inadequate product warnings. In design defect claims, there are two aspects to state of the art: (1) was the danger knowable?; and (2) was it technologically and economically feasible to make the product so that it could not only perform its intended function but also prevent the accident?

(1) As to the first question, courts are split as to whether a product should be judged at the time of manufacture or the time of trial. See Wade, On the Effect in Product Liability of Knowledge Unavailable Prior to Marketing, 58 N.Y.U.L.Rev. 734 (1983). Some courts require the claimant to prove that the danger was discoverable under existing technology. See Boatland of Houston, Inc. v. Bailey, 609 S.W.2d 743 (Tex.1980) (also requiring that alternative design be economically feasible). A few courts impute to the manufacturer knowledge available at the time of trial and ask the jury to determine whether a reasonable manufacturer would have designed the product as it was designed if he had knowledge of the danger. See, e.g., Phillips v. Kimwood Mach. Co., supra page 722; Dart v. Wiebe Mfg., Inc., 147 Ariz. 242, 709 P.2d 876 (1985) (en banc).

(2) As to the second question, most courts require the claimant to prove that an alternative safer design was feasible at the time the product was made or distributed. See, e.g., Rexrode v. American Laundry Press Co., 674 F.2d 826 (10th Cir.1982), cert. denied, 459 U.S. 862 (1982); Voss v. Black & Decker Mfg. Co., 59 N.Y.2d 102, 450 N.E.2d 204, 463 N.Y.S.2d 398 (1983); Wilson v. Piper Aircraft Corp., 282 Or. 411, 579 P.2d 1287 (1978); Nerud v. Haybuster Mfg., Inc., 215 Neb. 604, 340 N.W.2d 369 (1983). Some courts, as in the principal case, do not require proof of an alternative safer design as an element of the plaintiff's prima facie case. They make the availability of an alternative safer design a factor to be "considered" in determining whether the product was unreasonably dangerous. See, e.g., Kallio v. Ford Motor Co., 407 N.W.2d 92 (Minn.1987). At least one court has held that state of the art is irrelevant in design defect cases and has precluded the manufacturer from introducing state of the art evidence in its defense. See Elmore v. Owens–Illinois, Inc., 673 S.W.2d 434 (Mo.1984) (en banc).

For a survey of the state of the art defense throughout the states, see Klein, "Old Products": The Admissibility of State of the Art Evidence in Product Liability Cases, 9 J.Prod.Liab. 233 (1986).

7. The Uniform Product Liability Act applies a negligence standard in both design and duty-to-warn cases. See U.P.L.A. § 104, 44 Fed.Reg. 62721. What reasons support this result? Numerous federal proposals have taken the same approach; see, e.g., H.R. 7921, 96th Cong.2d Sess; S. 44, 99th Cong., 2d Sess. (1986); H.R. 1115, 100th Cong., 1st Sess. (1987).

(B) OTHER LIMITATIONS ON DESIGN

HINES v. ST. JOSEPH'S HOSPITAL
Court of Appeals of New Mexico, 1974.
86 N.M. 763, 527 P.2d 1075.

HENDLEY, JUDGE. Plaintiff, Tommie Hines, received transfusions of blood that came from defendant, Blood Services, Inc., during the course of a special fusion in July, 1970 at St. Joseph's Hospital. In September, 1970 Hines began treatment for what her doctor diagnosed as "most likely" serum hepatitis. Serum hepatitis can be transmitted by virus infected transfused blood. Hines and her husband sued St. Joseph's and Blood Services on the theories of strict liability and negligence for the damages caused by the hepatitis. The court granted defendants' motions for summary judgment on both theories. Plaintiffs appeal.

* * *

Defendants contend that their prima facie showing on strict liability [c] comes within an exception to the rule of strict liability. New Mexico has adopted the rule of strict liability stated in Restatement (Second) of Torts, § 402A (1965). [Cc] The Restatement's comments recognize an exception to the rule. It states:

"k. *Unavoidably Unsafe Products.* There are some products which, in the present state of human knowledge, are quite incapable of being made safe for their intended and ordinary use. These are especially common in the field of drugs. An outstanding example is the vaccine for the Pasteur treatment of rabies, which not uncommonly leads to very serious and damaging consequences when it is injected. Since the disease itself invariably leads to a dreadful death, both the marketing and the use of the vaccine are fully justified, notwithstanding the unavoidable high degree of risk which they involve. Such a product, properly prepared, and accompanied by proper directions and warning, is not defective, nor is it *unreasonably* dangerous. The same is true of many other drugs, vaccines, and the like, many of which for this very reason cannot legally be sold except to physicians, or under the prescription of a physician. It is also true in particular of many new or experimental drugs as to which, because of lack of time and opportunity for sufficient medical experience, there can be no assurance of safety, or perhaps even of purity of ingredients, but such experience as there is justifies the marketing and use of the drug notwithstanding a medically recognizable risk. The seller of such products, again with the qualification that they are properly prepared and marketed, and proper warning is given, where the situation calls for it, is not to be held to strict liability for unfortunate consequences attending their use, merely because he has undertaken to supply the public with an apparently useful and desirable product, attended with a known but apparently reasonable risk."

The uncontradicted evidence in this case establishes that there is a small but medically recognizable risk that transfused blood can transmit serum hepatitis. Also, at the time of Hines' transfusion, no test could adequately detect the hepatitis virus in blood. Further, no process could destroy it without damaging the blood. At the time of the transfusion in this case, therefore, blood was a product " * * * which, * * * [was] quite incapable of being made safe for [its] intended and ordinary use. * * * "

Nonetheless, blood for transfusions is not only " * * * an apparently useful and desirable product, * * * " it is at times absolutely essential to save life. The risk is outweighed by this public benefit and is thus reasonable.

Plaintiffs do not deny that the blood Hines received was "properly prepared." They contend that a "proper warning" was not given. They argue that although a written warning of the danger was attached to the blood container, Ms. Hines did not see that warning, nor was she otherwise warned.

The depositions in this case establish that blood is a prescription drug. Ordinarily the manufacturer's duty to warn of the dangers of prescription drugs is to the attending physician, not the patient. [Cc] The physician, in turn, has a duty to disclose dangers to the patient. [Cc] Blood Services placed a warning on the blood container and also "constantly distributed" an "Official Circular of Instructions for Use" to the hospital staff. Dr. Hurley, who gave the transfusion, stated he knew of the danger of hepatitis transmission in blood transfusions. Blood Services' warning was adequate.

Plaintiffs try to rebut defendants prima facie case by citing Cunningham v. MacNeal Memorial Hospital, 47 Ill.2d 443, 266 N.E.2d 897 (1970) and the reasoning therein. That case held that the exception to the Restatement's strict liability rule, quoted above, does not apply to the present type of situation since hepatitis infected blood is "impure." The exception, the court said, " * * * relates only to products which are not impure and which, even if properly prepared, inherently involve substantial risk of injury to the user. * * * " On this point *Cunningham* has been severely criticized. [Cc]

The criticism is well founded. The *Cunningham* court conveniently ignored a part of the Restatement's comment which refuted its own contention:

"It is also true in particular of many new or experimental drugs as to which, because of lack of time and opportunity for sufficient medical experience, there can be no assurance of safety, or perhaps even of *purity of ingredients,* but such experience as there is justifies the marketing and use of the drug notwithstanding a medically recognizable risk. * * *" (Emphasis added)

Although blood cannot be considered a "new or experimental" drug it is new in the sense that no adequate test had been devised to detect the hepatitis virus and even if detected, there is no process to destroy it without damage to the blood.   [C]

More importantly the *Cunningham* court, by categorically limiting the applicability of the exception to "pure" products stultified the flexible policy behind the exception. Instead of a balancing of the dangers of a particular product against its benefits, *Cunningham* would categorize a large segment of products as vulnerable to strict liability without regard to social benefits.

The granting of summary judgment as to Blood Services on strict liability was correct. It follows that under no theory would St. Joseph's be independently liable under strict liability. The granting of summary judgment as to it was also correct. * * *

---

1. The category of "unavoidably unsafe" products is an island where the state of the art principle has had great staying power because of special considerations involving drugs. Is it appropriate to confine the "unavoidably unsafe" rule to drugs?

2. One of the most difficult questions concerning products liability concerns the "unavoidably unsafe" product, which in the present state of human skill and knowledge cannot be made safe. A primary consideration is whether, in light of the known risks, it is actionable to market the product at all. This is a matter of balancing the probability and gravity of the risk of harm against the utility of the product. Cf. United States v. Carroll Towing, supra page 145. In Brown v. Superior Court (Abbott Laboratories), 182 Cal.App.3d 1125, 227 Cal. Rptr. 768, aff'd, with important opinion, 44 Cal.3d 1049, 751 P.2d 470 (1988) the court held that prescription drugs are automatically "unavoidably unsafe" if they were approved by the federal Food and Drug Administration. Do you agree? Assuming the judgment is made that it is reasonable to market the product, should the defendant be held strictly liable for an unavoidable risk? Distinguish:

A. *Common Knowledge.* The dangers of the product are generally known, so that the ordinary user may be expected to know what he is getting and understand the risk. Whiskey is such a product. It causes a wide variety of unpleasant consequences, ranging from delirium tremens and cirrhosis of the liver to drunken driving and chronic alcoholism. Butter is such a product; if one may credit current medical dogma, it may assist in bringing on heart attacks by depositing cholesterol in the arteries. A well-made automobile is such a product, as the death and accident statistics attest. Is the question one of whether the maker of the product is to be liable for the drinking, eating or driving habits of the American public?

Most courts have shied away from imposing liability. But in Collins v. Eli Lilly Co., 116 Wis.2d 166, 342 N.W.2d 37 (1984), cert. denied, 469 U.S. 826 (1984), the court indicated that comment k was not part of the law of Wisconsin. Should products such as whiskey, butter and automobiles stand on the same footing as rabies vaccine or blood? A striking example is Schemel v.

General Motors Corp., 384 F.2d 802 (7th Cir.1967), where the automobile manufacturer was held not liable for putting on the market a car that could be driven at speeds in excess of 100 miles an hour. Can this case be distinguished in principle? Should comment k be extended to products *other than* pharmaceuticals? Which products? See, e.g., Wilkinson v. Bay Shore Lumber Co., 182 Cal.App.3d 594, 227 Cal.Rptr. 327 (1986) (comment k does not apply to dry rot in lumber).

B. *Seller Knows or Should Know.* The dangers of the products are not generally known, but the seller is aware or could discover them by the exercise of reasonable care. This is a specialized application of the duty to warn, discussed in Section 2(C) of this Chapter.

With regard to prescription pharmaceuticals, a proper warning directed to the physician will be enough. See Lindsay v. Ortho Pharmaceutical Corp., 637 F.2d 87 (2d Cir.1980). However, if the manufacturer has reason to know that the drug will reach consumers without the intervention of a physician who is likely to explain the risk to the patient, it must take reasonable action to warn the consumer directly. See Reyes v. Wyeth Laboratories, 498 F.2d 1264 (5th Cir.1974); Cunningham v. Charles Pfizer & Co., Inc., 532 P.2d 1377 (Okl.1974) (mass immunization—polio vaccine). Suppose the patient is the one who decides to take the drug. See Odgers v. Ortho Pharmaceutical Corp., 609 F.Supp. 867 (E.D.Mich.1985). See Note, Mass Immunization Cases: Drug Manufacturers' Liability For Failure to Warn, 29 Vand.L.Rev. 235 (1976). Again the warning must be sufficiently explicit. See Baker v. St. Agnes Hosp., 70 A.D.2d 400, 421 N.Y.S.2d 81 (1979). Even if the printed warnings comply with F.D.A. requirements, the manufacturer may be subject to liability if its sales persons engage in high pressure promotion of the drug and "water down" the warning. See Stevens v. Parke, Davis & Co., 9 Cal.3d 51, 507 P.2d 653, 107 Cal.Rptr. 45 (1973).

C. *Unknown Danger.* The manufacturer as well as the public is unaware of the danger. The overwhelming majority of these cases have involved pharmaceuticals that have been approved for distribution by the F.D.A. When the manufacturer had no reason to know of the danger, liability has been denied. The leading case is Cochran v. Brooke, 243 Or. 89, 409 P.2d 904 (1966), where a drug utilized for the treatment of arthritis resulted in plaintiff losing her sight. See also Wolfgruber v. Upjohn Co., 72 A.D.2d 59, 423 N.Y.S.2d 95 (1979) (antibiotic-patient developed colitis); Leibowitz v. Ortho Pharmaceutical Corp., 224 Pa.Super. 418, 307 A.2d 449 (1973) (contraceptive pills—plaintiff developed a thrombophetic condition); E.R. Squibb & Sons, Inc. v. Stickney, 274 So.2d 898 (Fla.App.1973) (grafting implant material dissolved in plaintiff's body). Are the equities in these cases the same as in the transfusion decisions? Should the rule be any different if a vaccine causes the very disease it was intended to prevent? Compare Reyes v. Wyeth Laboratories, 498 F.2d 1264 (5th Cir.1974) (pure vaccine—unavoidably unsafe), with Gottsdanker v. Cutter Laboratories, 182 Cal.App.2d 602, 6 Cal.Rptr. 320 (1960) (impure vaccine—strict liability).

3. One appellate court in California held that the issue of whether a particular product is "unavoidably unsafe" should be determined by the jury by considering the product's risk and benefits. Kearl v. Lederle Laboratories, 172 Cal.App.3d 812, 218 Cal.Rptr. 453 (1985). The following year, a different California appellate court rejected that approach, stating that it "could lead to widely disparate treatment of the same drugs by different courts and different judges of the same court." Brown v. Superior Court (Abbott Laboratories), 182

Cal.App.3d 1125, 227 Cal.Rptr. 768 (1986), petition for review granted 229 Cal.Rptr. 663, 723 P.2d 1248 (1986).

4. Courts agree that the defendant will be held liable if he is negligent in testing his product and fails to find out that it is unsafe. See, e.g., Schenebeck v. Sterling Drug, Inc., 423 F.2d 919 (8th Cir.1970).

There is a good discussion of the whole problem as to drugs in Rheingold, Products Liability—The Ethical Drug Manufacturer's Liability, 18 Rutgers L.Rev. 1003 (1964); Willig, The Comment k Character: A Conceptual Barrier to Strict Liability, 29 Mercer L.Rev. 545 (1978). Annot., 94 A.L.R.3d 748 (1979). How much of a burden should be placed on a pharmaceutical company to bring the warning to the physician's attention? See Richards v. Upjohn Co., 95 N.M. 675, 625 P.2d 1192 (1980).

5. Until recently, the risk of cancer from smoking tobacco appeared to have moved from category 1C to 1A in Note 2 above. Compare Lartigue v. R.J. Reynolds Tobacco Co., 317 F.2d 19 (5th Cir.1963) (no proof that defendant was aware of danger) with Green v. American Tobacco Co., 409 F.2d 1166 (5th Cir. 1969) (unavoidably unsafe product). The dissent in the *Green* case details some of the reversals in a litigation that lasted over ten years. One case did find a breach of "implied warranty." Pritchard v. Liggett & Myers Tobacco Co., 295 F.2d 292 (3d Cir.1961). See Annot., 80 A.L.R.2d 681 (1961), and supp. Is the current "warning" on a pack of cigarettes sufficient to shield the tobacco companies from future claims? See Section 2(B) of this Chapter, infra.

6. Vendors of ordinary foods may avoid strict liability under theories quite similar to the Restatement (Second) of Torts' "unavoidably unsafe products" rationale. This occurs when plaintiffs choke on bones from meat or fish or break teeth on nut shells or pits. One group of cases has applied a "foreign-natural" test. Under this theory, there may be a recovery only if the injury-causing object is "foreign" to the food served. See, e.g., Adams v. Great Atl. and Pac. Tea Co., 251 N.C. 565, 112 S.E.2d 92 (1960); Musso v. Picadilly Cafeterias, Inc., 178 So.2d 421 (La.App.1965). A more recent line of authorities holds that the vendor of food will avoid liability only if the injury-causing object should "reasonably be expected" by a consumer in the food sold to him. Is this a better rule? Would it impose liability if a cherry pit was found in a cherry ice cream cone? See Williams v. Braum Ice Cream Stores, Inc., 534 P.2d 700 (Okl.App.1974). What about a bone in a turkey sandwich? Cf. Hochberg v. O'Donnell's Restaurant, Inc., 272 A.2d 846 (D.C.App.1971).

7. Much of the law concerning the unavoidably unsafe product was developed before a practical test to screen blood for hepatitis became available. Only one court found strict liability applicable to contaminated blood. Cunningham v. MacNeal Memorial Hosp., 47 Ill.2d 443, 266 N.E.2d 897 (1970). That decision was speedily overruled by the Illinois legislature. See Ill.Code Ann., Ch. 111½, § 5102 (1977). Other states have also enacted special blood transfusion statutes, all with the goal of avoiding a strict liability case. The statutes are collected in CCH Products Liability Reporter ¶ 1187.01 (1986).

8. The key policy issues underlying comment k are reviewed in Schwartz, Unavoidably Unsafe Products: Clarifying the Meaning and Policy Behind Comment K, 42 Wash. & Lee L.Rev. 1139 (1985).

9. *Allergic Reaction.* An allergic reaction to a drug or product may occur because of a person's unusual susceptibility to an ingredient. How does this situation differ from that in the principal case? Since the product is reasonably fit for the ordinary user, it might be said that there is no breach of implied

warranty or that the product is not defective. On the other hand, if absolute liability were imposed, the seller of the product would be liable for the consumer's adverse reaction. Courts have avoided both of these polarities. Generally, absolute liability is not imposed. See Christofferson v. Kaiser Foundation Hosp., 15 Cal.App.3d 75, 92 Cal.Rptr. 825 (1971); D'Arienzo v. Clairol, Inc., 125 N.J.Super. 224, 310 A.2d 106 (1973) (good discussion of duty to warn); Abbott Laboratories v. Gravis, 470 S.W.2d 639 (Tex.1981). See Schattman, A Cause of Action for the Allergic Consumer, 8 Hous.L.Rev. 827 (1971); Noel, The Duty to Warn Allergic Users of Products, 12 Vand.L.Rev. 331 (1959); Freedman, Allergy and Products Liability Today, 24 Ohio St.L.J. 431 (1963); Whitmore, Allergies and Other Reactions to Drugs and Cosmetics, 19 Sw.L.J. 76 (1965); Annot., 53 A.L.R.3d 298 (1973).

10. *Government Standards.* Compliance with government standards, such as the Federal Aviation Administration standards cited in Wilson v. Piper Aircraft, 282 Or. 61, 577 P.2d 1322, reh'g denied with opinion, 282 Or. 411, 579 P.2d 1287 (1978), is usually considered relevant but not conclusive on the question of reasonable care. What part, if any, should it play in a strict liability case? The Uniform Product Liability Act, § 108(A), and several state product liability statutes provide that compliance with government standards shall create a rebuttable presumption that the product was not defective. "Tort reform" advocates argue that when an agency has given expert consideration to a standard, it should not be within the province of a court or jury to ignore that standard, except in cases where the manufacturer misrepresented or withheld information from the agency. Do you agree?

11. *Government Specifications.* Suppose the government not only set standards, but set the design standards for the product? Should a manufacturer be liable for design defects in a product manufactured to government specifications? See In re Agent Orange Product Liability Litigation, 534 F.Supp. 1046 (E.D.N.Y.1982), cert. denied, 465 U.S. 1067 (1984); McKay v. Rockwell Int'l Corp., 704 F.2d 444 (9th Cir.1983), cert. denied, 464 U.S. 1043 (1984). The *Agent Orange* and *McKay* courts established a three-pronged "government specification" defense: (1) the government must be immune from liability under the *Feres* doctrine (see Ch. 12, page 639); (2) the product must conform to "reasonably precise" specifications in the government's contract; and (3) the supplier must have warned the government about the defect or danger. What are the public policy justifications for such a rule? Where does it leave injured plaintiffs? Should it be applicable to products manufactured in peacetime? See Jenkins v. Whittaker Corp., 551 F.Supp. 110 (D.Hawaii 1982), cert. denied, ___ U.S. ___, 107 S.Ct. 324, 93 L.Ed.2d 296 (1986). Suppose the product is a mixture of two commonly used agricultural toxins? See In re Agent Orange Product Liability Litigation, 597 F.Supp. 740 (E.D.N.Y.1984). What if the specification is a performance standard rather than a design? Johnston v. United States, 568 F.Supp. 351 (D.Kan.1983) (contract was for instrument dials that glow in the dark, not necessarily for radium dials). The issue of the government specifications defense has received different treatment among the federal circuit courts. At the time this book went to press, the issue was pending before the Supreme Court in Boyle v. United Technologies Corp., 792 F.2d 413 (4th Cir.1986), cert. granted, ___ U.S. ___, 107 S.Ct. 872, 93 L.Ed.2d 827 (1987).

ROYSDON v. R.J. REYNOLDS TOBACCO COMPANY

United States District Court,
Eastern District of Tennessee, 1985.
623 F.Supp. 1189.

HULL, DISTRICT JUDGE. This products liability action came to trial by jury on December 9, 1985. Plaintiffs, Mr. and Mrs. Floyd R. Roysdon, claimed that Mr. Roysdon suffers severe peripheral vascular disease as a proximate result of many years of smoking cigarettes manufactured by the defendant R.J. Reynolds Tobacco Company [R.J. Reynolds]. The Roysdons made two claims: that the defendant's cigarettes are defective and unreasonably dangerous to the health of users and that the warnings on cigarette packages and in their advertising are inadequate to fully apprise users of the medical risks involved in smoking.

Before trial, the Court dismissed that portion of the plaintiff's claim which rested on inadequate warnings. At the close of the plaintiff's proof, the Court directed a verdict for the defendant on the remaining issue, finding that the plaintiffs had failed to prove that the products at issue were "unreasonably dangerous".

This opinion will address the Court's reasoning on both issues.

In this lawsuit, it was undisputed that R.J. Reynolds had at all times pertinent fully complied with the relevant federal Cigarette Labeling and Advertising Act [the Act]. 15 U.S.C. §§ 1331–1340. The issue to be resolved was whether, in light of this compliance, plaintiff still could claim that labels were inadequate or whether the labels must be ruled adequate as a matter of law.

R.J. Reynolds took the position that Congress had preempted any claim based on the adequacy of the warning labels. It relied on very specific preemption language contained in 15 U.S.C. § 1334, which reads as follows: (a) No statement relating to smoking and health, other than the statement required by section 1331 of this title, shall be required on any cigarette package. (b) No requirement or prohibition based on smoking and health shall be imposed under State law with respect to the advertising or promotion of any cigarettes the packages of which are labeled in conformity with the provisions of this chapter.

It is obvious that this statute prohibits the Tennessee legislature from requiring R.J. Reynolds to use any statement relating to smoking and health other than the one congressionally mandated. The statute does not explicitly prohibit state common law tort actions based on labeling. However, congressional intent need not be expressly stated but may be implied from the structure and purpose of the particular statute. * * *

[I]f the courts were to impose any duty to go beyond the congressionally mandated labeling, this would thwart the stated intent of Congress to have uniformity in the warnings. For this reason, the Court found any such exposure incompatible with the intent of the legislation and dismissed any claim based on the adequacy of the warning label. The only issue remaining for trial was whether or not the defendant's products were defective and unreasonably dangerous.

This products liability action was brought pursuant to this Court's diversity jurisdiction, 28 U.S.C. § 1332(a)(1) and (c), and, accordingly, was governed by Tennessee's Products Liability Act of 1978, Tenn.Code Ann. §§ 29–28–101 *et seq.*

Through the introduction of the Surgeon General's reports and medical expert testimony, the plaintiffs made a *prima facie* case that the defendant's cigarettes are dangerous to health, and that they have been harmful to Mr. Roysdon. Of course, many dangerous products, from axes to alcohol, are in the stream of commerce and occasionally injure their users. For R.J. Reynolds, or any manufacturer, to be held liable for the harm caused by its products, the products must be found "unreasonably dangerous."

Under Tennessee law, the test of whether or not a product is unreasonably dangerous is defined as follows:

" 'Unreasonably dangerous' means that a product is dangerous to an extent beyond that which would be contemplated by the ordinary consumer who purchases it, with the ordinary knowledge common to the community as to its characteristics, or that the product because of its dangerous condition would not be put on the market by a reasonably prudent manufacturer or seller assuming that he knew of its dangerous condition." Tenn.Code Ann. § 29–28–102(8).

The Tennessee Supreme Court has stated that this is determinable from the "knowledge of the ordinary consumers of the product." *Pemberton v. American Distilled Spirits,* 664 S.W.2d 690, 692 (Tenn. 1984). Tennessee tort law has also been held to incorporate comment i to the Restatement (Second) of Torts. [Cc] Comment i used "good tobacco" (such as that at issue in this lawsuit) as an illustration of what kind of product would *not* be considered unreasonably dangerous due to the widespread common knowledge as to its characteristics.

In the *Pemberton* case, *supra,* which involved "good alcohol" rather than "good tobacco", the court took judicial notice of the widespread public understanding of the dangers inherent in alcohol. It said, "[a]lcohol has been present and used in society during all recorded history and its characteristics and qualities have been fully explored and developed and are a part of the body of common knowledge." *Id.* at 693.

In the instant action, this Court takes a similar approach. It finds that tobacco has been used for over 400 years and that its characteristics also have been fully explored. Knowledge that cigarette smoking is harmful to health is widespread and can be considered part of the common knowledge of the community. For this reason, as well as because of the language in comment i to section 402A of Restatement (Second) of Torts, this Court finds that the plaintiffs did not make a *prima facie* case that the defendant's products are "unreasonably dangerous".

Accordingly, judgment will enter on behalf of the defendant R.J. Reynolds and the plaintiffs will take nothing on their claim.

––––––––

1. Comment *i* to Restatement (Second) of Torts § 402A is commonly referred to as the "inherent characteristics" rule. It means that liability should not be imposed when harm results because of a danger or risk that is inherent in a product. Recently, the Supreme Courts of Louisiana and Hawaii have held that liability may be imposed in that situation. See Halphen v. Johns–Manville Sales Corp., 484 So.2d 110 (La.1986) (recognizing products which are "unreasonably dangerous per se" as a separate class of products); Johnson v. Raybestos–Manhattan, Inc., ––– Hawaii –––, 740 P.2d 548 (1987) (state of the art evidence not admissible in connection with strict liability action based on inherent dangerousness of a product). Both cases involved asbestos.

2. Should liability be imposed based on the inherent risks of a product? What about the examples given in comment i itself? Butter? Sugar? Whiskey? What about automobiles—don't all automobiles have the risk of causing injury if driven carelessly? Should the inherent characteristics rule apply only to certain products? Which ones? What should be the criteria for determining which products should be covered by the principle and which should not?

(C) WARNINGS

WOODILL v. PARKE DAVIS & CO.
Supreme Court of Illinois, 1980.
79 Ill.2d 26, 37 Ill.Dec. 304, 402 N.E.2d 194.

CLARK, JUSTICE: The parents of a minor child brought this action to recover damages for injuries suffered by the child during the fetal stage, the injuries having allegedly been caused by a drug, administered to the mother during delivery of the child. * * *

Ellen Woodill, the minor child's mother, entered Central Du Page Hospital as an obstetrical patient on or about November 22, 1973, at a time when the fetus was in high station. Pursuant to her physician's order for the inducement of uterine contractions, she was infused intravenously with the prescription drug, Pitocin. The product information disseminated to the medical profession by the defendant did not contraindicate the use of Pitocin for this purpose. On or about the same date, the child, delivered by the vaginal route, was born with brain damage, permanent blindness and quadriplegia. The complaint alleges that the use of Pitocin was the proximate cause of the child's injuries, and, with regard to the counts sounding in strict liability in tort, that defendant's failure to warn physicians and patients of the danger in using Pitocin while a fetus is in high station rendered the drug "not reasonably safe."

[The trial court dismissed plaintiffs' causes of action based on strict liability and breach of warranty. The appellate court affirmed that portion of the order that dismissed the strict liability causes but reversed the portion of the order that dismissed the breach of warranty cause of action.]

The issue of primary concern in this appeal is whether, in an action seeking to hold a defendant strictly liable for failure to warn of a danger attendant to the use of a product, the plaintiff must allege and prove that the defendant knew or should have known of the danger.

It is well recognized that a failure to warn of a product's dangerous propensities may serve as the basis for holding a manufacturer or seller strictly liable in tort. * * *

In support of the decision of the appellate court, the defendant argues that comment *j* of [Section 402A] requires that a manufacturer have knowledge or reason to know of the danger before it can be held liable for failure to warn. Comment *j* provides, in pertinent part:

"*Directions or warning.* In order to prevent the product from being unreasonably dangerous, the seller may be required to give directions or warning, on the container, as to its use. The seller may reasonably assume that those with common allergies, as for example to eggs or strawberries, will be aware of them, and he is not required to warn against them. Where, however, the product contains an ingredient to which a substantial number of the population are allergic, and the ingredient is one whose danger is not generally known, or if known is one which the consumer would reasonably not expect to find in the product, the seller is required to give warning against it, if he has knowledge, or by the application of reasonable, developed human skill and foresight should have knowledge, of the presence of the ingredient and the danger. Likewise in the case of poisonous drugs, or those unduly dangerous for other reasons, warning as to use may be required." (Restatement (Second) of Torts § 402A comment *j* (1965).)

Specifically, defendant points to the language in the comment which provides that the seller is required to give warning if "he has knowledge, or by the application of reasonable, developed human skill and foresight should have knowledge," of the danger. The plaintiffs argue, however, that to predicate the defendant's liability for failure to warn upon whether he knew or should have known of the danger is to revert to a negligence standard. The plaintiffs aver that the inquiry would then focus on the conduct of the manufacturer defendant rather than on the unreasonably dangerous condition of the product created by the failure to warn. There are decisions from other jurisdictions which support the plaintiffs' averment. [Cc]

On the other hand, a line of decisions, including several in our own appellate court, have stated that knowledge is an essential element in a failure-to-warn case. [Cc]

We think that the imposition of a knowledge requirement is a proper limitation to place on a manufacturer's strict liability in tort predicated upon a failure to warn of a danger inherent in a product. We do not agree with the plaintiffs that to require knowledge to be alleged and proved is to infuse negligence principles into strict liability. Indeed, liability based upon a failure to warn adequately of dangers (Restatement (Second) of Torts § 402A, comment *j* (1965)) is itself a doctrine borrowed from negligence. [C] "[T]he failure-to-warn theory in strict liability has been upheld as a distinguishable doctrine from its counter-part in negligence, based on the fact that it is the inadequacy of the warning that is looked to, rather than the conduct of the particular manufacturer, to establish strict liability."   *   *   *

We perceive that requiring a plaintiff to plead and prove that the defendant manufacturer knew or should have known of the danger that caused the injury, and that the defendant manufacturer failed to warn plaintiff of that danger, is a reasonable requirement, and one which focuses on the nature of the product and on the adequacy of the warning, rather than on the conduct of the manufacturer. The inquiry becomes whether the manufacturer, because of the "present state of human knowledge" (Restatement (Second) of Torts § 402A, comment *k* (1965)), knew or should have known of the danger presented by the use or consumption of a product. Once it is established that knowledge existed in the industry of the dangerous propensity of the manufacturer's product, then the plaintiff must establish that the defendant did not warn, in an adequate manner, of the danger. Such a rule is entirely consistent with the principles of strict liability, as first recognized and adopted as applicable to all products.   *   *   *

We believe our holding in this case is justified because of logical limit must be placed on the scope of a manufacturer's liability under a strict liability theory. To hold a manufacturer liable for failure to warn of a danger of which it would be impossible to know based on the present state of human knowledge would make the manufacturer the virtual insurer of the product, a position rejected by this court   *   *   * [c] (*Winnett v. Winnett* (1974), 57 Ill.2d 7, 11, 310 N.E.2d 1.) Strict liability is not the equivalent of absolute liability. There are restrictions imposed upon it. For example, we have previously held that where an injury is not foreseeable, that is, objectively predictable, no liability will ensue based on strict liability. [C] Also, where the plaintiff knows of the risk of injury presented by the use of a dangerously defective product but assumes the risk nonetheless, the manufacturer is absolved from liability. [Cc]

This court is acutely aware of the social desirability of encouraging the research and development of beneficial drugs. We are equally aware that risks, often grave, may accompany the introduction of these drugs into the marketplace. We simply think, however, in accordance with comments *j* and *k* of section 402A of the Restatement (Second) of Torts, that where liability is framed by the manufacturer's duty to warn adequately of dangers which may arise from the use of a drug, that liability should be based on there being some manner in which to know of the danger. Otherwise the warning itself, which is the focus of the liability, would be a meaningless exercise.

Since we are enunciating the requirement that knowledge must be alleged in a complaint for the first time in this opinion, substantial justice would seem to require that the plaintiffs be given an opportunity to amend their complaint to comply with this decision. We therefore affirm the appellate court as to count I and remand to the circuit court with directions to give the plaintiffs reasonable time to amend count I of their complaint. * * *

MORAN, JUSTICE, concurring in part and dissenting in part. * * * I dissent from that portion of the majority opinion which limits a manufacturer's liability under strict liability in tort for failure to warn of a danger inherent in its product to situations in which the manufacturer knows or has reason to know of the danger. The majority opinion sets forth the applicable section of the Restatement, Restatement (Second) of Torts § 402A (1965), but then focuses on language appearing in a comment to that section. The comment provides that a seller is required to give warning if "he has knowledge, or by application of reasonable, developed human skill and foresight should have knowledge" of the danger. (Restatement (Second) of Torts § 402A, comment *j* (1965).) In focusing upon this language, the majority ignores the rule, set forth in the body of the section, that the seller is liable even though "the seller has exercised all possible care in the preparation and sale of his product * * *." (Restatement (Second) of Torts § 402A(2)(a) (1965).) * * *

In strict liability actions, the focus is on the condition of the product and not on the conduct of the manufacturer or seller. This is the feature which primarily distinguishes strict liability from negligence. * * *

The majority's assertion that removal of the knowledge element would make the manufacturer the virtual insurer of the product is an overstatement. In my view, the manufacturer is not made an insurer when it is held answerable for injuries to someone for whom its product is intended, who uses it in the manner in which it was intended to be used, and whose injuries were proximately caused by an inherent danger in the product of which the user was unaware. The majority confesses to an awareness that risks, often grave, may accompany the introduction of beneficial drugs into the marketplace. To me, this suggests a greater need for protecting the unsuspecting and unprotected consumer, and for making recovery under strict liability available to him in fact, and not just in theory. * * *

[T]o condition plaintiff's recovery under strict liability on his pleading and proving that defendant knew or had reason to know of the danger is to inject elements of negligence into plaintiff's cause of action. Unlike negligence, the elements of a strict product liability action generally do not include knowledge or culpable fault. Consequently, inasmuch as the plaintiff is not required to plead and prove knowledge of the danger in manufacturing-defect or design-defect cases, no greater requirement should be imposed on plaintiffs in cases in which the defect is the lack of warning.

GOLDENHERSH, C.J. and WARD, J., join in this partial concurrence and partial dissent.

---

1. The principal case discussed the application of the "state of the art defense" in failure-to-warn claims based on the strict liability theory. The court made clear its belief that this was not the same as a negligence standard of liability. What is the difference?

In warnings cases, most courts still apply a negligence standard or some standard based on the manufacturer's fault. See W. Prosser & W. Keeton, Torts, § 99 at 697 (5th ed. 1984). See, e.g., Smith v. E.R. Squibb & Sons, Inc., 405 Mich. 79, 273 N.W.2d 476 (1979) ("when liability turns on the adequacy of a warning, the issue is one of reasonable care, regardless of whether the theory pled is negligence, implied warranty, or strict liability in tort").

2. The Supreme Court of New Jersey rejected the state-of-the-art defense in a case alleging failure to warn about the dangers of asbestos. Beshada v. Johns–Manville Prods. Corp., 90 N.J. 191, 447 A.2d 539 (1982). One of the court's rationales was that manufacturers and distributors of defective products are able to spread costs of injuries by incorporating the cost of liability insurance in the product's price. Two years later, however, the same court held that the *Beshada* decision was limited to asbestos cases. See Feldman v. Lederle Laboratories, 97 N.J. 429, 479 A.2d 374 (1984).

3. Is the *Beshada* court correct in its assumptions about "risk distribution"? What about the fact that many injured persons already have been paid by health or accident insurance?

4. "State of the art" was originally a scientific term rather than a legal one. One definition is the scientific and technical knowledge available to the industry at the time the product was sold. Some legal writers have used the term to refer to industry custom, industry standards, or technological feasibility. See, e.g., Neb.Rev.Stat. 25–21 ("the best technology reasonably available at the time"); Sturm, Ruger & Co. v. Day, 594 P.2d 38, 44 (Alaska 1979), cert. denied, 454 U.S. 894 (1981) (industry custom). Is there an important difference between the two definitions?

5. See, generally, Robb, A Practical Approach to Use of State of the Art Evidence in Strict Product Liability Cases, 77 Nw.U.L.Rev. 1 (1982); Spradley, Defensive Use of State of the Art Evidence in Strict Product Liability, 67 Minn. L.Rev. 343 (1982).

6. For a colorful account of the asbestos litigation from the plaintiffs' perspective, see Brodeur, Outrageous Misconduct: The Asbestos Industry on Trial (1985).

7. In general, law review writers have been critical of the *Beshada* case, but it does have some supporters. For discussion, see generally Page, Generic Product Risks: The Case Against Comment K and for Strict Tort Liability, 58 N.Y.U.L.Rev. 853, 877–82 (1982); Wade, On the Effect in Product Liability Litigation of Knowledge Unavailable Prior to Marketing, 58 N.Y.U.L.Rev. 734,

754–56 (1983); Comment, Beshada v. Johns–Manville Products Corp.: Adding Uncertainty to Injury, 35 Rutgers L.Rev. 982, 1008–15 (1983).

8. Often a case involves claims based both on defective design and inadequate warnings. Should the fact that a product contains a good warning overcome the effect of a design problem—i.e., should a warning about a design hazard preclude liability, or should the manufacturer be required to eliminate the defective design condition? See, e.g., Karns v. Emerson Elec. Co., 817 F.2d 1452 (10th Cir.1987).

9. *The Obvious Hazard.* In Posey v. Clark Equip. Co., 409 F.2d 560 (7th Cir.1969), a seller of a forklift platform that had no guard was not required to warn that large cartons might fall off it. Should a manufacturer of salami have to warn that it contains peppercorns on which a consumer might break his teeth? Hecht v. Giunta's Stop & Shop, 40 Ohio Misc. 6, 69 Ohio Ops.2d 34, 317 N.E.2d 269 (1974). Should a manufacturer of a perfume have to warn that the product is highly inflammable and should not be poured on a lit candle? See Moran v. Faberge, Inc., 273 Md. 538, 332 A.2d 11 (1975). Should a manufacturer have to indicate that a wire mesh milk container will not prevent bottles from cracking if the container is dropped on the sidewalk? Fisher v. Johnson Milk Co., 383 Mich. 158, 174 N.W.2d 752 (1970). What about the need to wear seat belts? See Marshall v. Ford Motor Co., 446 F.2d 712 (10th Cir. 1971). Should a manufacturer of pointed darts have to warn that they might injure someone's eye? See Atkins v. Arlans Dept. Store of Norman, Inc., 522 P.2d 1020 (Okl.1974). Should a manufacturer have to warn a hockey player that his helmet will not protect him from all blows to the head? Durkee v. Cooper of Canada, 99 Mich.App. 693, 298 N.W.2d 620 (1980).

Should the extent of expertise of the known user be taken into account? See Pridgett v. Jackson Iron & Metal Co., 253 So.2d 837 (Miss.1971) (metal paint drum exploded when cut by acetylene torch); Garrett v. Nissen Corp., 84 N.M. 16, 498 P.2d 1359 (1972) (experienced trampoline user landed on his head and suffered a paralyzing spinal injury).

When a hazard is open and obvious, some courts simply hold that the product is not unreasonably dangerous; they do not even reach the question of duty to warn. See, e.g., Meyer v. Gehl Co., 36 N.Y.2d 760, 329 N.E.2d 666, 368 N.Y.S.2d 834 (1975); Maas v. Dreher, 10 Ariz.App. 520, 460 P.2d 191 (1969). What about the argument that a duty to warn regarding obvious hazards reduces the impact of warnings in general? See Uniform Product Liability Act § 105(e), 44 F.R. 62726. See generally, Darling, The Patent Danger Rule: An Analysis and a Survey of Its Vitality, 29 Mercer L.Rev. 585 (1978); Phillips, Product Liability: Obviousness of Danger Revisited, 15 Ind.L.Rev. 797 (1982).

What is a manufacturer to do if one state court holds that warnings should be given about obvious hazards and another state court holds that such warnings are unnecessary?

How Much Detail is Necessary? Some recent cases have been quite severe on this issue, and terms such as "under some circumstances," and "not under prolonged operation or low fuel condition" will not be adequate. See Kritser v. Beech Aircraft Corp., 479 F.2d 1089 (5th Cir.1973) (fuel system in private aircraft—operations manual); Tucson Indus., Inc. v. Schwartz, 108 Ariz. 464, 501 P.2d 936 (1972) (cement manufacturer gave numerous warnings about its product but did not specifically state that fumes from wet cement were a hazard to the eyes). Sometimes one can discern a difference on this issue between strict liability and negligence. Under the negligence standard, the manufacturer's duty is to give a reasonable warning, not the best possible one. See Nolan v. Dillon, 261 Md. 516, 276 A.2d 36 (1971); see also Freund v. Cellofilm Properties Inc., 87 N.J. 229, 432 A.2d 925 (1981).

Directions for use, in and of themselves, may not be a sufficient warning. See McCully v. Fuller Brush Co., 68 Wash.2d 675, 415 P.2d 7 (1966). Once a detailed, clear warning is given, the manufacturer can usually assume that it will be followed. See Schmeiser v. Trus Joist Corp., 540 P.2d 998 (1975). However, in D'Arienzo v. Clairol, Inc., 125 N.J.Super. 224, 310 A.2d 106 (1973), the manufacturer of a hair coloring product gave a clear warning that a preliminary "patch test" on the skin was to be used before each application. Plaintiff used the product a number of times without adverse effect. Then she suffered a severe reaction on the occasion in question. She did not use a "patch" test. The court let the case go to the jury while noting that the issue was not "one of clarity of instructions, but of intensity sufficient to illuminate the mind of a reasonable user."

10. If a product is dangerous only to hypersensitive persons, do manufacturers have a duty to provide warnings if they know or should know of such dangers to hypersensitive persons? See Advance Chem. Co. v. Harter, 478 So. 2d 444 (Fla.App.1985).

Shifting Responsibility. In strict liability cases, as in negligence cases, it is clear that the intervening negligence of an immediate purchaser, employer or dealer in failing to discover a defect in the product will not relieve the manufacturer of § 402A liability. See Suvada v. White Motor Co., 51 Ill.App.2d 318, 201 N.E.2d 313 (1964). Should responsibility have shifted from the manufacturer to plaintiff's employer? Suppose the employer created the unsafe condition? See Kellar v. Inductotherm Corp., 498 F.Supp. 172 (D.C.Tenn. 1978), aff'd, 633 F.2d 216 (6th Cir.1978). Should it make any difference if it was the custom of the trade for the purchaser to install the safety device? See Bexiga v. Havir Mfg. Corp., 60 N.J. 402, 290 A.2d 281 (1972). What of a warning to an employer which is not passed on to the employees? Borel v. Fibreboard Paper Prod. Corp., 493 F.2d 1076 (5th Cir.1973).

Suppose the product was unreasonably unsafe and the manufacturer became aware of that fact. Should the manufacturer have any duty beyond notifying the immediate purchaser about the defect? See Ford Motor Co. v. Matthews, 291 So.2d 169 (Miss.1974); LaBelle v. McCauley Indus. Corp., 649 F.2d 46 (1st Cir.1981). Cover v. Cohen, 61 N.Y.2d 261, 461 N.E.2d 864, 473 N.Y.S.2d 378 (1984); Wash.Rev.Code § 7.72.030(c). Compare Younger v. Dow Corning Corp., 202 Kan. 674, 451 P.2d 177 (1969) (reasonable risk caused by product—manufacturer's duty discharged by warning to employer of plaintiff). What about prescription drugs? Toys? California has gone a step further; it will not permit an automobile manufacturer to shift responsibility for "service" before delivery to an automobile dealer. If the dealer does not make the proper final inspections or corrections, the manufacturer will be held liable. See Vandermark v. Ford Motor Co., 61 Cal.2d 256, 391 P.2d 168, 37 Cal.Rptr. 896, (1964). Compare Cox v. General Motors Corp., 514 S.W.2d 197 (Ky.1974) (alteration of automobile by retailer).

Suppose the machine was reasonably safe when it left the manufacturer's hands, but the purchaser altered it in a way to make it unsafe. Should the manufacturer be liable for that conduct? See Putensen v. Clay Adams, Inc., 12 Cal.App.3d 1062, 91 Cal.Rptr. 319 (1970) (plastic tubing altered by surgeon); Bond v. Transairco Co., 514 F.2d 642 (5th Cir.1975); Rios v. Niagara Mach. &

Tool Works, 59 Ill.2d 79, 319 N.E.2d 232 (1974) (safety device removed). Brown v. United States Stove Co., 98 N.J. 155, 484 A.2d 1234 (1984). When it is foreseeable that an intervening party will remove a safety device, what should the manufacturer's duty be to the ultimate consumer? See Ward v. Hobart Mfg. Co., 450 F.2d 1176 (5th Cir.1971). See generally Annot., 41 A.L.R.3d 1251 (1972). Should a manufacturer be held strictly liable for failing to improve a product already placed in the consumer's hands? See Bell Helicopter Co. v. Bradshaw, 594 S.W.2d 519 (Tex.Civ.App.1979).

11. *Learned Intermediary Rule.* In cases involving pharmaceuticals, a key issue often is whether the pharmaceutical manufacturer should provide its warnings to the prescribing physician or directly to the patient. Most courts hold that warnings and instructions should be provided to the physician, who is a "learned intermediary" and is the best person to understand the patient's needs and assess the risks and benefits of a particular course of treatment. It is assumed that the physician will decide which warnings to pass on to the patient, taking into consideration the patient's well-being. See, e.g., Salmon v. Parke, Davis & Co., 520 F.2d 1359 (4th Cir.1975); Chambers v. G.D. Searle & Co., 441 F.Supp. 377 (D.Md.1975), aff'd, 567 F.2d 269 (1977); McDaniel v. McNeil Laboratories, Inc., 196 Neb. 190, 241 N.W.2d 822 (1976).

The "learned intermediary" rule does not apply if the Food and Drug Administration has mandated that warnings be given to the patient as well as to the physician. See, e.g., 21 C.F.R. § 310.501 (1985) ("Information in lay language concerning effectiveness, contraindication, warnings, precautions, and adverse reactions shall be furnished to each patient receiving oral contraceptives"); see also McDonald v. Ortho Pharmaceutical Corp., 394 Mass. 131, 475 N.E.2d 65 (1985), cert. denied, 474 U.S. 920 (1985) (manufacturer of oral contraceptives must warn consumers because they are often actively involved in the decision to use the birth control pill, as opposed to other birth control products, and the physician usually has a relatively passive role).

A few courts have held that warnings about prescription drugs must be given directly to the consumer. See Reyes v. Wyeth Laboratories, 498 F.2d 1264 (5th Cir.1974), cert. denied, 419 U.S. 1096 (1974) (polio vaccine); Davis v. Wyeth Laboratories, Inc., 399 F.2d 121 (9th Cir.1968) (polio vaccine). Several courts have concluded that decisions requiring direct public warnings with the polio vaccine were based on the uniqueness of the nationwide program for dispensing of the vaccines. See Brooks v. Medtronic, Inc., 750 F.2d 1227 (4th Cir.1984).

12. The "learned intermediary" rule also arises in cases involving harm from products used in the workplace. There the issue is whether the employer should be responsible for warning and instructing its employees about use of the product because of the employer's control of the worksite, its knowledge of the hazards associated with products it has purchased and its ability to instruct its employees on how to protect against those hazards. See, e.g., Cook v. Branick Mfg., Inc., 736 F.2d 1442 (11th Cir.1984); Adams v. Union Carbide Corp., 737 F.2d 1453 (6th Cir.1984), cert. denied, 469 U.S. 1062 (1984). See also Welch v. Heat Research Corp., 644 F.2d 487 (5th Cir.1981) (manufacturer not required to provide warnings to independent contractor's employee who sustained injuries while fabricating a product for manufacturer in accordance with manufacturer's plans and specifications). Sometimes the product is unpackaged or in a liquid or dust form, sold to the employer in bulk containers, so it would be difficult for the manufacturer to attach its warnings directly onto the product. See, e.g., Beale v. Hardy, 769 F.2d 213 (4th Cir.1985) (silica dust).

Also, a communications expert has noted that the employer's oral communication of warnings to employees is often more effective than written information because the employer can adapt its message to particular employees of different experience, education and conceptual levels, and can answer questions, and because it is easier to demand the employee's attention with oral instruction. See Schwartz & Driver, Warnings in the Workplace: The Need for a Synthesis of Law and Communication Theory, 42 U.Cin.L.Rev. 38 (1983).

13. *Government Standards.* Manufacturers sometimes argue in court that product warnings should be considered adequate if they comply with standards under a federal law or regulation. Most courts have rejected that argument, finding that the federal law did not indicate a congressional intent to preempt common law claims. See, e.g., Bristol–Myers Co. v. Gonzales, 548 S.W.2d 416 (Tex.Civ.App.1976), aff'd, 561 S.W.2d 801 (1978); cf. Hurley v. Lederle Laboratories, 651 F.Supp. 993 (E.D.Tex.1986) (FDA mandated labeling for DPT vaccine impliedly preempts tort claims based on inadequate warnings). In the tobacco cases, however, the three Federal circuit courts that had addressed this issue at the time this casebook went to press, held that the preemption provision of the Federal Cigarette Labeling and Advertising Act precludes states and courts from imposing further requirements or prohibitions on the advertising or promotion of cigarettes. See Cipollone v. Liggett Group, Inc., 789 F.2d 181 (3d Cir.1986), cert. denied, ___ U.S. ___, 107 S.Ct. 907, 93 L.Ed.2d 857 (1987); Stephen v. American Brands, Inc., 825 F.2d 312 (11th Cir. 1987); Palmer v. Liggett Group, Inc., 825 F.2d 620 (1st Cir.1987).

14. *Post–Sale Duty to Warn.* Apart from the duty to provide warnings at the time a product is marketed, some courts have been imposing a duty on the manufacturers to provide post-sale warnings about risks that are discovered at a later time. See, e.g., Barson v. E.R. Squibb & Sons, 682 P.2d 832 (Utah 1984); Worsham v. A.H. Robins Co., 734 F.2d 676 (11th Cir.1984). However, courts generally have held manufacturers to a reasonableness standard for post-sale warnings and may consider a number of factors. See, e.g., Melancon v. Western Auto Supply Co., 628 F.2d 395 (5th Cir.1980) (obviousness of the danger); Davis v. Wyeth Laboratories, Inc., 399 F.2d 121 (9th Cir.1968) (seriousness of the potential harm); Chappuis v. Sears, Roebuck & Co., 358 So.2d 926 (La.1978), writ denied, 366 So.2d 576 (1979) (whether the danger is generally known to users); Cover v. Cohen, 61 N.Y.2d 261, 461 N.E.2d 864, 473 N.Y.S.2d 378 (1984) (burden on the manufacturer in locating those to be warned).

The question in these cases often focuses on whether the facts show that the manufacturer knew or should have known that the product presented a danger. Should a manufacturer be required to provide post-sale warnings if information about injuries is available (e.g., industry report on its product or similar products), but the manufacturer finds the evidence of potential harm "unconvincing"? See, e.g., Wooderson v. Ortho Pharmaceutical Corp., 235 Kan. 387, 681 P.2d 1038 (1984), cert. denied, 469 U.S. 965 (1984). In addition to the manufacturer's obligation to keep abreast of scientific and industry developments, should manufacturers be required to perform their own tests on their products after sale to determine if they could cause harm? See, e.g., Barson v. E.R. Squibb & Sons, 682 P.2d 832 (Utah 1984).

Very few courts have extended a manufacturer's post-sale obligations beyond a duty to take reasonable steps to provide warnings. One court imposed a duty on the manufacturer to recall or replace the product. See Bell Helicopter Co. v. Bradshaw, 594 S.W.2d 519 (Tex.Civ.App.1979). Traditionally, product recall has been a function of federal administrative agencies. See Consumer

Product Safety Act, 15 U.S.C.A. § 2064 (1982); National Traffic and Motor Vehicle Safety Act of 1966, 15 U.S.C.A. § 1414 (1982). If individual courts were to impose recall requirements, what would a manufacturer do if one court were to require a recall of a product and another court, in a different case, were to hold that the manufacturer need not recall that product?

For a general discussion of manufacturers' post-sale obligations, see Schwartz, The Post–Sale Duty to Warn: Two Unfortunate Forks in the Road to a Reasonable Doctrine, 58 N.Y.U.L.Rev. 892 (1983).

3. PROOF

FRIEDMAN v. GENERAL MOTORS CORP.
Supreme Court of Ohio, 1975.
43 Ohio St.2d 209, 72 Ohio Ops.2d 119, 331 N.E.2d 702.

[Plaintiff Morton Friedman alleged that he turned the ignition key on his 17–month-old 1966 Oldsmobile while the gearshift selector was in the "drive" position. Although he did not expect the vehicle to start, it did and the car "leaped forward, and so startled [him] that he could not regain control before the automobile ran wild * * *." Morton and three members of his family were injured in the crash.

Morton brought a claim against General Motors, the manufacturer of the vehicle. At the close of his case, the trial court granted General Motor's motion for a directed verdict on the ground that plaintiff had not proved that the vehicle was defective. The intermediate appellate court reversed the trial judge's decision and General Motors appealed to the Supreme Court of Ohio.]

PAUL W. BROWN, JUSTICE. The single issue presented by this appeal is whether the evidence introduced by the plaintiffs was of sufficient quality to overcome the defendant's motion for a directed verdict. The Court of Appeals, having thoroughly examined the entire record, concluded that reasonable minds could differ upon the evidence presented and reversed the judgment directing a verdict for the defendant. We affirm.

To sustain their allegation against General Motors, the plaintiffs were required to prove that the Oldsmobile Toronado, manufactured and sold by the defendant, was defective; that the defect existed at the time the product left the factory; and that the defect was the direct and proximate cause of the accident and injuries. [Cc]

A defect may be proven by circumstantial evidence, where a preponderance of that evidence establishes that the accident was caused by a defect and not other possibilities, although not all other possibilities need be eliminated. [Cc]

In our judgment, the evidence presented by the plaintiffs established a prima facie case of defect for which defendant General Motors would be liable.

From the testimony of [the retailer-dealer] and Morton Friedman, the jury could have found that the linkages and adjustments existing at the time of the accident were the original, factory set, adjustments, and that the defective condition, if the evidence established defect, was a defect created by the manufacturer and not by some third person after delivery.

Based upon the testimony of Morton Friedman, his wife, and his son, the jury might have concluded that the Toronado had always been started in Park, thus affording no opportunity for discovery of the alleged defect. Further, because the gear shift indicator and transmission had always operated properly, the jury might have inferred that when the gear shift indicator registered in Drive after the accident, it accurately reflected the position of the transmission.

From the testimony of eye witnesses to, and participants in, the accident, the jury might have concluded that, when Friedman started the Toronado at the Sohio station, it accelerated immediately upon ignition; that the automobile's transmission was therefore in a forward position; and that the transmission jammed, upon impact, in that same forward position.

From the testimony of [expert witnesses produced by plaintiff,] the jury could have found that, subsequent to the accident, the Toronado started with the gear shift indicator in Drive position. Based upon English's testimony, the jury might have concluded further that, upon ignition, the front wheels accelerated to a speed of 30 miles per hour in five seconds.

Finally, the record clearly established that the Toronado could not have started unless the contacts in the neutral start switch were in Neutral or Park position. Even though the transmission gears and gear shift indicator were in Drive, if the contacts in the neutral start switch were in Neutral or Park, the ignition key would start the automobile, and the front wheels would immediately rotate. In light of other facts presented, this possibility approaches probability.

Because the trial court granted the defendant's motion for a directed verdict, we must construe the evidence most strongly in favor of the plaintiffs, so as to determine if reasonable minds could differ. From the evidence heretofore summarized, we believe the jury might reasonably have concluded that the defendant was guilty of manufacturing a defective automobile, which directly and proximately caused the accident. For that reason, the judgment of the Court of Appeals is affirmed.

Judgment affirmed.

STERN, JUSTICE (dissenting). * * * In products liability cases, proof that a defect existed is often difficult and complex. Frequently the product in dispute will have been destroyed, beyond any possibility of analysis, or be so complex that a plaintiff would have a greater difficulty in determining the presence of a defect than would the manufacturer. In most cases, proof of the defect must necessarily be by circumstantial evidence and inference. No general rule can adequately apply to the wide range of such cases, each involving a different mixture of fact and inference, but fundamental to any such case is that some defect must be proved. As Prosser states, in Strict Liability to the Consumer in California, 18 Hastings L.J. 9, 52–54:

"The mere fact of an accident, as where an automobile goes into the ditch, does not make out a case that the product was defective; nor does the fact that it is found in a defective condition after the event, when it appears equally likely that it was caused by the accident itself. The addition of other facts, tending to show that the defect existed before the accident, may make out a case, and so may expert testimony. So likewise may proof that other similar products made by the defendant met with similar misfortunes, or the elimination of other causes by satisfactory evidence. In addition, there are some accidents, as where a beverage bottle explodes or even breaks while it is being handled normally, as to which there is human experience that they do not ordinarily occur without a defect. As in cases of res ipsa loquitur, the experience will give rise to the inference, and it may be sufficient to sustain the plaintiff's burden of proof."

Although plaintiff's evidence may be sufficient to permit an inference that something was wrong with the car, that alone is not sufficient to establish a defect, except perhaps in cases, analogous to res ipsa loquitur, in which ordinary human experience tells us that the event could not happen without a defect. The instant case is not such a case, for driver error, failure of some part, accidental or unwitting damage to the car, and other possibilities do provide other explanations. * * *

The particular defect that plaintiff alleges is that the indicator and the transmission gear linkages were both malaligned in a similar fashion, relative to the neutral starter switch, so that the car as manufactured could start in Drive rather than, as intended, only in Park and Neutral. There are various ways in which that particular fact could be proved, by means of several types of evidence. Keeton, Manufacturer's Liability: The Meaning of Defect in the Manufacture and Design of Products, 20 Syracuse L.Rev. 559, for example, suggests five ways by which the particular fact could be proved. [C]

(1) Plaintiff might introduce evidence by an expert based upon an examination of the product in question following the happening of the damaging event. Expert evidence would be direct evidence of an identifiable defect. * * *

(2) There may simply be evidence of a damaging event occurring in the course of or following use of a product, whether by the testimony of the user or otherwise. * * *

(3) A plaintiff may produce both evidence of a damaging event occurring in the course of or following the use of a product and expert evidence that the most likely probable cause was attributable to a defect in the product being used at the time. * * *

(4) In addition to evidence of an accident and the probable cause of such accident, evidence could be introduced to negate the existence of "probable causes" not attributable to the maker. * * *

(5) In some cases, the physical evidence of the actual condition of the product after the accident would be such that a layman could infer that it was defective. * * *

The sum of the evidence [in this case] is * * * only that something unusual happened in the car, and that a possible explanation of that happening is a defect. * * *

The same difficulty arises with regard to the issue of whether the claimed defect existed at the time the car left the hands of the defendant. * * * Here, the car was 17 months old, there was no expert testimony that the claimed defect was one which would probably have existed at the time the car was manufactured, and common experience does not permit any such inference. * * *

I agree with the trial judge that plaintiffs failed to submit sufficient evidence from which it could be inferred that a defect existed in the Friedman car at the time it left the hands of the defendant.

---

1. As the principal case reflects, problems relating to proof may be equally as important as legal theory in products liability actions. Plaintiff must be prepared to show:

A. That the product that injured him was, in fact, manufactured by defendant. Suppose an alleged manufacturer's name or trademark appeared on the product. Should that be sufficient? Compare Keegan v. Green Giant Co., 150 Me. 283, 110 A.2d 599 (1954), with Curtiss Candy Co. v. Johnson, 163 Miss. 426, 141 So. 762 (1932). See also Federal Rules of Evidence, Rule 902(7) (1975). Suppose defendant is injured by a common instrumentality that has no trademark. How does he prove it was manufactured by defendant? See Schmidt v. Archer Iron Works, Inc., 44 Ill.2d 401, 256 N.E.2d 6 (1970) (defective eye pin in a cement scoop). See generally Annot., 51 A.L.R.3d 1339 (1973). Suppose an entire industry produces allegedly defective products, but plaintiff cannot identify whose product injured him? See Sindell v. Abbott Laboratories, supra page 283; Hall v. E.I. Du Pont De Nemours & Co., Inc., 345 F.Supp. 353 (E.D.N.Y.1972) (blasting caps). In those cases, the plaintiff was able to prove that a product caused his or her injury, but was unable to prove which manufacturer made the particular product involved. In other words, the plaintiff was unable to prove that any particular manufacturer was the cause in fact of the injury. Some courts have developed a variety of theories to get the plaintiff past the requirement of proving actual causation. Other courts have refused to take this step and have applied the traditional rule that the plaintiff must prove the particular manufacturer's product caused his or her injury. Is there a middle ground? See Schwartz & Mahshigian, Failure to Identify the Defendant in Tort Law: Towards a Legislative Solution, 73 Calif.L. Rev. 941 (1985). See Chapter 5 at page 287.

B. That the product was the cause in fact of his injury. Plaintiff uses a ladder to install a television antenna on a roof top. The ladder lurches to one side and he falls to the ground. Has plaintiff shown defendant's product injured him? See Bates v. R.D. Werner Co., 419 F.2d 1118 (6th Cir.1970).

Suppose he eats a food product manufactured by defendant and becomes sick several hours later. How does he establish that it was defendant's product that caused his illness? See Geisness v. Scow Bay Packing Co., 16 Wash.2d 1, 132 P.2d 740 (1942); John Morrell & Co. v. Shultz, 208 So.2d 906 (Miss.1968). What about exposure to chemicals or pharmaceutical products? Should plaintiff's burden of proof be reduced when it is very difficult to prove a causal connection between the product and an injury? Cf. Allen v. United States, 588 F.Supp. 247 (D. Utah 1984), rev'd, 816 F.2d 1417 (10th Cir.1987) (burden of proof shifted to government that plaintiff's cancer was not caused by radiation exposure).

C. That the product was defective and he was injured as a result. The principal case and the cases in the prior section are illustrative of this problem. The crash of a plane does not make out a case until the possibility of negligent flying is eliminated. Hurley v. Beech Aircraft Corp. 355 F.2d 517 (7th Cir. 1966). Cf. Belleville Nat'l Savings Bank v. General Motors Corp., 20 Ill.App.3d 707, 313 N.E.2d 631 (1974) (automobile negligent driving). On circumstantial evidence to show that the product was defective, see Browder v. Pettigrew, 541 S.W.2d 402 (Tenn.1976).

D. That the defect existed in the product or was incipiently in it when it was sold by the particular defendant. United States Rubber Co. v. Bauer, 319 F.2d 463 (8th Cir.1963) (breaking of belt drive might have been due to other causes); Sharpe v. Danville Coca–Cola Bottling Co., 9 Ill.App.2d 175, 132 N.E.2d 442 (1956) (intermediate handling of bottle after it left the manufacturer).

2. Strictly speaking, since negligence is not in question, res ipsa loquitur has no application to a strict liability case. But the inferences that are the core of the doctrine are no less applicable to strict liability. State Farm Mut. Auto. Ins. Co. v. Anderson–Weber, Inc., 252 Iowa 1289, 110 N.W.2d 449 (1961); Kroger Co. v. Bowman, 411 S.W.2d 339 (Ky.1967).

3. In other words, the fact that the product went wrong may, in a proper case, give rise to a permissible inference that it was defective and that the defect existed when it left the hands of the defendant. See Moraca v. Ford Motor Co., 66 N.J. 454, 332 A.2d 599 (1975) (six-month-old, 11,000–mile Lincoln Continental skidded off the road—strong plaintiff case with equally strong dissent); Franks v. National Dairy Prods. Corp., 414 F.2d 682 (5th Cir.1969) (shortening exploded when user drained it from fryer into a can—a well developed case); Gherna v. Ford Motor Co., 246 Cal.App.2d 639, 55 Cal.Rptr. 94 (1966) (sudden fire in automobile engine driven 1600 miles); Bailey v. Montgomery Ward & Co., 6 Ariz.App. 213, 431 P.2d 108 (1967) (pogo stick broke after short use); MacDougall v. Ford Motor Co., 214 Pa.Super. 384, 257 A.2d 676 (1969) (malfunction of steering gear). In automobile cases, a few jurisdictions have developed a legal term for this, the "general defect" theory. See, e.g., Stewart v. Ford Motor Co., 553 F.2d 130 (D.C.Cir.1977). Should a plaintiff be permitted to have his case heard before the jury when all that he has shown is that decedent was driving a six-month old car and it suddenly turned and left the highway?

4. The most convincing evidence is a direct showing of what went wrong. This may be done by the plaintiff in an appropriate case, see Agostino v. Rockwell Mfg. Co., 345 A.2d 735 (Pa.1975) (power saw—telescopic blade guard did not function); or by an expert pinpointing the defect and giving an opinion on that basis. In the appropriate circumstances, proof of that kind will be required. For a recent example, see Green v. Safeway Stores, Inc., 541 P.2d 200 (Okl.1975) (soft drink carton collapsed—no explanation as to why). Cf. Scanlon

v. General Motors Corp., 65 N.J. 582, 326 A.2d 673 (1974) (nine-month-old Chevrolet station wagon driven 4000 miles "took off" and crashed—more proof necessary). Good advice to a client may be "save the pieces," but often the client disposes of them before he consults an attorney. If the product is destroyed in the accident, plaintiff will be left in the uncertain sphere of circumstantial proof. Obviously, clear proof of the physical facts can rebut circumstantial proof and testimony regarding an accident. See, e.g., McDonald v. Ford Motor Co., 42 Ohio St.2d 8, 326 N.E.2d 252 (1975). On authorization to test a hammer by destroying it, see Sarver v. Barrett Ace Hardware Co., 63 Ill. 2d 454, 349 N.E.2d 28 (1976).

5. *Rule on Excluding Evidence of Product Improvements To Prove Defect.* Should plaintiff be able to show that defendant redesigned or repaired his product after the accident occurred? What are the policy considerations? While many courts preclude plaintiffs from introducing this evidence, a growing number of courts will admit it if the underlying theory of liability is strict liability rather than negligence. See Herndon v. Seven Bar Flying Serv., Inc., 716 F.2d 1322 (10th Cir.1983), cert. denied, 466 U.S. 958 (1984). Cf. Werner v. Upjohn Co., 628 F.2d 848 (4th Cir.1980), cert. denied, 449 U.S. 1080 (1981); Grenada Steel Indus., Inc. v. Alabama Oxygen Co., 695 F.2d 883 (5th Cir.1983); Longenecker v. General Motors Corp., 594 F.2d 1283 (9th Cir.1979). Why would a court prohibit the introduction of evidence of product improvements in a negligence case, but permit such evidence in a strict liability case? Do you agree with these cases? Do they encourage the manufacture of safer products or do they have no effect on manufacturers' conduct? See generally Schwartz, The Exclusionary Rule on Subsequent Repairs—A Rule in Need of Repair, 7 The Forum 1 (1971); Note, 1972 Duke L.J. 837. An author of this casebook changed his mind about this issue when he drafted the Uniform Product Liability Act some nine years later. See U.P.L.A. § 107(a), 44 Fed.Reg. 62728. Should defects in design be treated differently from defects in construction with respect to admission of such evidence?

6. One of plaintiff's hurdles is tracing the defect back into the hands of the defendant. Lapse of time and long continued use will not prevent this if there is clear proof of an original defect. Pryor v. Lee C. Moore Mfg. Co., 262 F.2d 673 (10th Cir.1958) (15 years); International Derrick & Equip. Co. v. Croix, 241 F.2d 216 (5th Cir.1957) (seven years). But if the proof must be by inference, the continued use may prevent the conclusion that more probably than not the product was defective when it was sold. See Kerr v. Corning Glass Works, 284 Minn. 115, 169 N.W.2d 587 (1969) (Pyrex dish exploded seven months after purchase); Jakubowski v. Minnesota Mining & Mfg. Co., 42 N.J. 177, 199 A.2d 826 (1964); Courtois v. Chrysler Motors Co., 37 N.J. 525, 182 A.2d 545 (1962). What about design defects? Warning defects? Is it fair to impose liability on a manufacturer of a capital good that is 15 years old and had previously been used safely? What about 35 years? 50 years? In most jurisdictions, there are no strict "cut offs" on liability. See pages 607–08. But product liability "reform" proponents have sought such limitations.

7. When the defect arises after purchase, plaintiff is confronted with another facet of the problem of establishing that the product was "defective" or unreasonably unsafe. It has been said often enough that the seller does not undertake to provide a product that will not wear out. McNally v. Chrysler Motors Corp., 55 Misc.2d 128, 284 N.Y.S.2d 761 (Sup.Ct.1967) (leakage in 1963, no proof hydraulic brakes were defective when sold in 1961). On the other hand, when plaintiff's intestate was killed in 1965 by the collapse of a boom

crane that was manufactured in 1956, the Supreme Court of Oregon observed that "prolonged use of a manufactured article is but one factor, albeit an important one, in the determination of whether a defect in the product made it unsafe * * *." Tucker v. Unit Crane & Shovel Corp., 256 Or. 318, 473 P.2d 862 (1970). See also Dunham v. Vaughan & Bushnell Mfg. Co., 42 Ill.2d 339, 247 N.E.2d 401 (1969) (hammer chipped 11 months after purchase); Mickle v. Blackmon, 252 S.C. 202, 166 S.E.2d 173 (1969) (knob on the gear-shift lever of a 1949 Ford shattered in 1962). These are usually cases involving an alleged defect in design as opposed to defect in construction or manufacture. See Note, 4 Will.L.J. 394 (1967).

8. What should be the result if it appears equally likely that the defect developed in the hands of an intermediate dealer? Tiffin v. Great A. & P. Tea Co., 18 Ill.2d 48, 162 N.E.2d 406 (1959) (tinned meat opened and exposed by dealer); Sundet v. Olin Mathieson Chem. Corp., 179 Neb. 587, 139 N.W.2d 368 (1966) (reloaded cartridges, several handlers); Sharpe v. Danville Coca–Cola Bottling Co., 9 Ill.App.2d 175, 132 N.E.2d 442 (1956) (charged beverage found to be "flat" when opened).

9. Considerable leeway has been afforded the plaintiff, in cases of exploding or breaking bottles. He need not account for every moment of the bottle's existence since it left the bottler's plant, and it is enough that he introduces some evidence of careful handling in general and of the absence of unusual incidents, to permit reasonable persons to draw the conclusion that the defect existed in the hands of the defendant. On this, see Gordon v. Aztec Brewing Co., 33 Cal.2d 514, 203 P.2d 522 (1949), and Lafleur v. Coca–Cola Bottling Co. of Lake Charles, 195 So.2d 419 (La.App.1966).

Intentional tampering with a bottle is so unusual and so unlikely, that the prevailing rule is that the plaintiff need not disprove it. Miami Coca–Cola Bottling Co. v. Todd, 101 So.2d 34 (Fla.1958).

10. Some jurisdictions have assisted plaintiff by shifting the burden of tracing the defect to the shoulders of the dealer and the manufacturer. Nichols v. Nold, 174 Kan. 613, 258 P.2d 317 (1953); Loch v. Confair, 372 Pa. 212, 93 A.2d 451 (1953). Should this be applicable to any other product besides bottles?

11. See generally P. Keeton, Manufacturer's Liability: The Meaning of "Defect" in the Manufacture and Design of Products, 20 Syracuse L.Rev. 559 (1969), Products Liability—Proof of the Manufacturer's Negligence, 49 Va.L. Rev. 675 (1963) and Products Liability—Problems Pertaining to Proof of Negligence, 19 Sw.L.J. 26, 43, 76 (1965); Prosser, The Fall of the Citadel, 50 Minn.L. Rev. 791, 840–88 (1966); Spangenberg, Exploding Bottles, 24 Ohio St.L.J. 516 (1963); Bishop, Trouble in a Bottle, 16 Baylor L.Rev. 337 (1964); Phelan & Foer, Problems of Proof in Defective Design Litigation, 54 Chi.Bar.Rec. 257 (1973); Phelan & Falkof, Proving a Defect in a Commercial Products Liability Case, 24 Trial Law. Guide 10 (1980); Gallagher & Wardell, Evidence for the Plaintiff in a Products Liability Action, 19 S.Tex.L.J. 559 (1978); Annot., 51 A.L.R.3d 8 (1973).

4. PERSONS PROTECTED

WINNETT v. WINNETT
Supreme Court of Illinois, 1974.
57 Ill.2d 7, 310 N.E.2d 1.

UNDERWOOD, CHIEF JUSTICE. Four-year-old Teresa Kay Winnett was injured when she placed her hand on a moving conveyor belt or screen on a forage wagon then being operated on her grandfather's farm. An amended two-count complaint on her behalf sought recovery in count I from her grandfather predicated upon his negligence. Count II is a strict-tort-liability action against defendant Helix Corporation, manufacturer of the forage wagon. * * *

Count II of the amended complaint alleged in substance that plaintiff was visiting her grandfather by invitation at his farm home, that he was operating a forage wagon in the barnyard, and that defendant Helix Corporation had manufactured the wagon; that the forage wagon was being used for its intended purpose and the plaintiff was injured while it was being so used. Among other allegations, including the absence of rear-view mirrors and warning signs, it is charged that the conveyor belts on the wagon were exposed with no shield or guard affixed to prevent persons from coming into contact with the belts and the steel end of the wagon, and no bolts, latches or holes were present to allow for the attachment of a shield or guard. These and other conditions were alleged to render the wagon unreasonably dangerous, and it is alleged that they existed at the time the forage wagon left defendant's control and that plaintiff's injuries resulted from one or more of these conditions.

[The trial court dismissed this count of the complaint.] Whether this forage wagon was unreasonably dangerous when operated for its intended purpose by one for whose use it was intended is simply not a relevant consideration unless plaintiff is a person entitled to the protections afforded by the concepts of strict-tort-liability actions against manufacturers.

The large majority of courts which have considered the question of recovery in a strict-tort-liability action by persons other than those for whose use the product was intended have found the terms "bystander" or "innocent bystander" a convenient means of categorizing an additional group of persons for whose injuries courts have allowed recovery. [Citing cases from 15 jurisdictions.]

We also note that the Supreme Court of California has suggested that bystanders should be entitled to even greater protection than consumers or users where injury to bystanders from the defect is reasonably foreseeable, since bystanders do not have the opportunity, prior to purchase or use, to inspect products for defects as do users and consumers. Elmore v. American Motors Corp. (1969), 70 Cal.2d 578, 586, 75 Cal.Rptr. 652, 657, 451 P.2d 84, 89.

We, however, find this categorization of plaintiffs as users, consumers or innocent bystanders helpful only in a general sense. In the unusual case the application of these labels does not assist resolution of the issues. In our judgment the liability of a manufacturer properly encompasses only those individuals to whom injury from a defective product may reasonably be foreseen and only those situations where the product is being used for the purpose for which it was intended or for which it is reasonably foreseeable that it may be used. Any other approach to the problem results in making the manufacturer and those in the chain of product distribution virtual insurers of the product, a position [that has been] rejected by this court. * * *

It is apparent from the majority of cases in which recovery was allowed for injuries to persons for whose use the product was not intended that the injuries were reasonably foreseeable, and that such foreseeability was recognized by the courts as a factor in deciding the cases. Thus, it is held that injury to other vehicles, their occupants and pedestrians is the foreseeable result of defective steering mechanisms, transmissions, etc. [Cc]

Likewise, it is foreseeable that a defective shell will cause a shotgun barrel to explode and injure persons standing nearby, and recovery against the manufacturer of the shell should accordingly be allowed. * * *

Questions of foreseeability, we believe, are ordinarily for a jury to resolve, as is the question whether a product is defective or unreasonably dangerous. [C] But where the facts alleged in a complaint on their face demonstrate that the plaintiff would never be entitled to recover, that complaint is properly dismissed. [Cc] Such is the case before us. While in retrospect it can be asserted that the manufacturer of the forage wagon should have foreseen that the unfortunate event in this case might conceivably occur, we do not believe its occurrence was objectively reasonable to expect. It cannot, in our judgment, fairly be said that a manufacturer should reasonably foresee that a four-year-old child will be permitted to approach an operating farm forage wagon or that the child will be permitted to place her fingers in or on the holes in its moving screen. We believe the trial court properly dismissed plaintiff's amended complaint. * * *

Appellate court reversed; circuit court affirmed.

---

1. Most of the early cases attempting to determine the perimeters of strict liability restricted recovery to "users and consumers" of the product. See Hahn v. Ford Motor Co., 256 Iowa 27, 126 N.W.2d 350 (1964); Davidson v. Leadingham, 294 F.Supp. 155 (E.D.Ky.1968). In part, this was due to the continued influence of an implied warranty theory.

2. This uncertainty led the American Law Institute in 1965 to express "no opinion" as to whether Section 402A extended "to persons other than users and consumers." As of that year only one court had made the extension and that

case involved a rifle that exploded. See Piercefield v. Remington Arms Co., 375 Mich. 85, 133 N.W.2d 129 (1965).

3. The breakthrough came with Elmore v. American Motors Corp., 70 Cal. 2d 578, 451 P.2d 84. 75 Cal.Rptr. 652 (1969). Since that time almost every court that has specifically focused on the issue has extended strict liability recovery to the bystander. Cases are collected in Annot., 33 A.L.R.3d 415 (1970). What is the basis for holding that a manufacturer may owe a *greater* duty to a bystander than to a purchaser of a product? See White v. Jeffrey Galion, Inc., 326 F.Supp. 751 (E.D.Ill.1971).

4. Apart from pedestrians, and drivers of vehicles, which bystanders are to be protected? Is the problem simply one of foreseeability? Is it *Palsgraf* revisited? In Howes v. Hansen, 56 Wis.2d 247, 201 N.W.2d 825 (1972), a child came in contact with a power mower and suffered serious injuries. The court allowed the claim and totally rejected "foreseeability" as a criterion for deciding which bystanders may recover and said the issue was simply one of "duty." Is this approach helpful? It was utilized when a playful dog broke a defective collar, got loose and knocked a bystander plaintiff down. See Oehler v. Davis, 223 Pa.Super. 333, 298 A.2d 895 (1972). One court has held that "foreseeability" is the benchmark for determining the product seller's duty to bystanders. See Jones v. White Motor Corp., 61 Ohio App.2d 162, 401 N.E.2d 223 (1978).

5. A few of the more interesting cases include:

A. *Defects in Design That Injure Bystanders.* Plaintiff, while riding a motorcycle, collided with an automobile. She received a severe lacerating injury to the outside of her lower leg when it came in contact with an unshielded metal flipper that protruded three inches outward from the base of a right wheel cover manufactured by defendant. Liability for this injury? See Passwaters v. General Motors Corp., 454 F.2d 1270 (8th Cir.1972). Compare Nacci v. Volkswagen of Am., Inc., 325 A.2d 617 (Del.1974), where a child riding a bicycle collided with an automobile, breaking a parking light which caused the child's knee to be severed. Are the cases the same? What about the case of another young child who climbed on the rear part of a hay unloader where the driver could not see him? See Meyer v. Gehl Co., 36 N.Y.2d 760, 329 N.E.3d 666, 368 N.Y.S.2d 834 (1975). Compare the situation where a worker was killed when a driver backed up an earth moving machine that had a 48–by–20–foot blind spot in its rear view mirrors. See Pike v. Frank G. Hough Co., 2 Cal.3d 465, 467 P.2d 229, 85 Cal.Rptr. 629 (1970).

B. *Rescuers.* An oxygen mask malfunctions due to a defect and plaintiff attempts to rescue the person in peril. What are the issues when the rescuer is injured and sues the manufacturer of the mask in strict liability? See Guarino v. Mine Safety Appliance Co., 25 N.Y.2d 460, 255 N.E.2d 173, 306 N.Y.S.2d 942 (1969).

C. *Unborn Children.* On behalf of his mongoloid son, plaintiff seeks damages from defendant on the theory that its product, birth control pills, caused the birth defect; it is alleged that the untoward result occurred because the pills altered the mother's chromosome structure. See Jorgensen v. Meade Johnson Laboratories, Inc., 483 F.2d 237 (10th Cir.1973).

D. *The Public in General.* On behalf of the residents of Chicago, Illinois plaintiffs seek damages from defendants because of the injuries plaintiffs endured as the result of emissions from defendants' vehicles. See City of Chicago v. General Motors Corp., 467 F.2d 1262 (7th Cir.1972).

6. *Intervening Negligence of User.* Bystander cases present at least two distinct issues regarding intervening negligence of the user. The first is simply one of cause in fact. A truck injures a pedestrian. Did the driver fail to use reasonable care in applying the brake or was the brake assembly defective? See Bradford v. Bendix–Westinghouse Automotive Air Brake Co., 33 Colo.App. 99, 517 P.2d 406 (1973). Cf. Landry v. Adam, 282 So.2d 590 (La.App.1973) (did purchaser replace brake hose?). The second is more complicated. Should a product be deemed defective because the manufacturer failed to shield the bystander from the intervening negligent misuse of the product? See infra page 784. See also the note on shifting responsibility, supra page 757.

7. If strict liability has not been extended to bystanders, they still may be allowed to recover in negligence if in the language of the Restatement (Second) of Torts § 395 they would be "expected to be endangered by [the product's] probable use." This extension came not long after the *MacPherson* case. Would a negligence theory help plaintiff in the principal case? Cf. Jones v. Hutchinson Mfg., Inc., 502 S.W.2d 66 (Ky.1973), (five-year-old girl slipped into a corn auger).

8. See generally Noel, Defective Products: Extension of Strict Liability to Bystanders, 38 Tenn.L.Rev. 1 (1970); Notes, 8 Tulsa L.J. 216 (1972), 38 U.Chi.L. Rev. 625 (1971); 23 U.Miami L.Rev. 266 (1968).

5. INTERESTS PROTECTED

TWO RIVERS CO. v. CURTISS BREEDING SERV.
United States Court of Appeals, Fifth Circuit, 1980.
624 F.2d 1242, cert. denied, 450 U.S. 920, 101 S.Ct. 1368, 67 L.Ed.2d 348 (1981)

THORNBERRY, CIRCUIT JUDGE. This action was brought by Two Rivers Company (Two Rivers), alleging that it purchased from Hi–Pro Feeds, Inc. (Hi–Pro) semen used for artificial insemination of its cattle, and that the semen caused syndactylism in the offspring of its cattle. The semen was marketed by Curtiss Breeding Service, Division of Searle Agriculture, Inc. (Curtiss). Two Rivers' claim for damages against Curtiss and Hi–Pro is based on the doctrines of strict liability and implied warranty.

This appeal arises from a jury verdict in favor of Two Rivers. The jury apparently found that Curtiss was strictly liable for the sale of defective semen and that Curtiss breached its implied warranty of merchantability. The jury also found that Two Rivers was entitled to damages in the sum of $52,900.00. This amount represents the damage to the reputation of Two Rivers' herd of cattle as computed by the loss of the prospective market value of the cattle. The court entered judgment for plaintiff in the amount found by the jury and denied Curtiss's motion for judgment notwithstanding the verdict. We hold that, under Texas law, the district court erred in that Two Rivers is not entitled to a recovery of damages based on either strict liability or implied warranty. * * *

Curtiss markets the semen of many different breeds of cattle, including the Chianina breed. In 1972, Curtiss entered into an agreement with a Canadian firm to market in the United States the semen from a Chianina bull known as Farro AC–35. Before entering into this agreement, Curtiss conducted an examination of Farro's pedigree and of the Chianina breed.

In 1973 and 1974, Two Rivers purchased over one hundred registered one-half blood Chianina heifers with the intention of developing a purebred line of Chianina cattle by artificially breeding successive generations. To accomplish this goal, Two Rivers contracted with Mr. Tony Hall in 1974 to obtain quality semen and artificially inseminate the herd of one-half blood Chianina heifers. * * *

Hall, as an agent of Two Rivers, was given the responsibility of selecting the bull and the semen supplier. He purchased on his own account the Farro semen, which was marketed by Curtiss through Hi–Pro Feeds, Inc., that was used to breed the Two Rivers cattle. When purchasing the semen, he examined a pamphlet entitled the "1974 Curtiss Beef Breeding Guide" which contained a conspicuous disclaimer of any express or implied warranties. After consummating the purchase, Hall transported the semen to Two Rivers and inseminated the cattle. Hall charged Two Rivers a certain amount for each heifer he inseminated.

On July 24, 1974, Curtiss determined that Farro had sired offspring which might have exhibited the genetic abnormality known as syndactylism. Curtiss immediately notified its distributors and informed them that they were recalling the semen. At that time, Two Rivers had already inseminated 64 of the heifers with Farro semen. While some ranchers continued to use Farro semen, Two Rivers decided to switch to another bull. Of the 64 heifers that were artificially inseminated with Farro semen, 22 calves were born alive. Four of the Farro calves were stillborn and exhibited the genetic abnormality known as syndactylism.

Syndactylism is a genetic abnormality that can only appear when both the sire and the dam are carriers of the recessive gene. Therefore, Farro, as well as several of the heifers purchased by Two Rivers, were carriers. Syndactylism is exhibited by the fusion of nondivision of the functional digits of one or more feet of a cow. It is a hereditary genetic trait traced to the recessive gene. It is virtually impossible to detect the existence of a recessive genetic trait such as syndactylism until it is manifested by the union of two carriers of this recessive gene. * * *

The critical question presented in this case is whether Two Rivers is entitled to an award of damages pursuant to the Restatement (Second) of Torts § 402A, the implied warranties of the Uniform Commercial Code, or under both theories. To analyze this issue, it is necessary to distinguish the four types of property loss which are recognized in Texas. A different legal analysis attaches to each type of loss.

The first type of loss involves personal injury to the user (or consumer) or physical injury to the property of the user (or consumer).

It is specifically covered by the language of section 402A of the Restatement (Second) of Torts. * * * Texas courts adopted the language of section 402A in 1967 and have applied strict liability to the case of personal injuries resulting from unreasonably dangerous products, [cc] as well as to physical injuries to a consumer's property other than the product caused by a defective product. [Cc]

The second type of loss, on the complete opposite end of the spectrum, can be classified as economic loss resulting from a product with defective workmanship or materials. This category of loss was examined in Nobility Homes of Texas v. Shivers, 557 S.W.2d 77 (Tex. 1977), where an individual who purchased a mobile home sought to recover damages for economic loss suffered as the result of defects in the product. The mobile home was negligently constructed and was not fit for the purposes for which it was sold. The consumer was awarded $8,750 as the difference between the purchase price and the market value of the mobile home for his economic loss.

The court held in *Nobility Homes* that an individual may not recover for economic loss under section 402A. The court stated that an individual must instead seek damages under the implied warranties of the Uniform Commercial Code and the theory of common law negligence. Strict liability was not extended to instances of economic loss because the distinction that exists between physical damage and commercial loss had to be recognized. The Uniform Commercial Code governs the case of a mere loss of value resulting from the failure of the product to perform according to the contractual bargain and the expectations of the consumer.

A third type of loss consists of "economic loss to the purchased product itself." Mid Continent Aircraft Corp. v. Curry County Spraying Service, 572 S.W.2d 308 (Tex.1978). In *Mid Continent Aircraft,* plaintiff sought damages for physical injury to an airplane (damage to fuselage and wings) and for loss of its use value when it made a forced landing because an individual negligently failed to install a crankshaft gear bolt lock plate. Noting that the explicit language of section 402A applied only to physical harm to a person or his *other* property, the court stated that in a commercial sale, strict liability should not be extended to cover a loss resulting from damage to the product itself. * * * This is because the damage to the product is merely a loss to the purchaser of the benefit of the bargain with the seller.

The fourth type of loss is a hybrid involving physical harm to a plaintiff's *other* property as well as to the product itself. This fact pattern was presented in *Signal Oil* [& Gas Co. v. Universal Oil Products, 572 S.W.2d 320 (Tex.1978)] where a defective isomax reactor charge heater exploded. The explosion and ensuing fire at Signal Oil's Houston refinery destroyed not only the heater, but also a significant portion of the refinery (other property). It is clear that the damage to the refinery presents a strict liability cause of action under section 402A since a buyer is entitled to recover for damage to his other property. But the court went even further and held that * * * if both the product and other property are damaged, a plaintiff has a cause of action under strict liability and the U.C.C. * * *

Two Rivers asserts a cause of action based on the doctrine of strict liability against Curtiss, alleging that Curtiss sold a genetically defective product that was unreasonably dangerous. Two Rivers sought damages for the loss of the market value of the entire herd and for the value of the four calves born with syndactylism. In assessing Two Rivers' claim, the herd of calves must be divided into two groups: a group composed of those calves that received a gene for syndactyl from Farro semen (including the four syndactyl calves) and a second group composed of those calves that were not artificially inseminated with Farro semen.

Only 22 of the 98 calves born alive were the product of Farro's semen. Two Rivers claims that it is entitled to damages equal to the reduction in the market value of the 76 non-Farro calves (the second group) because of the stigma caused by having as many as 22 carriers in the herd.

After an examination of the controlling Texas case law, it is clear that Two Rivers has not stated a cause of action under strict liability with respect to the second group of calves. If anything, any damage incurred upon discovering and making publicly known a latent physical defect in the herd of one-half blood Chianina heifers purchased by Two Rivers constitutes economic loss governed by the rules of commercial law. A plaintiff in Texas is precluded from recovering for economic loss under strict liability. * * *

The crux of Two Rivers' complaint about the non-Farro calves is that everyone now knows about this potentially deleterious gene and that since it is impossible to distinguish the carrier from the noncarrier calves, the value of all the calves is reduced. This loss in market value due solely to the stigma of an accidentally discovered defective gene is, if anything, a commercial loss that is not cognizable in strict liability.

With respect to the first group of calves (artificially inseminated with Farro semen), the question is much more difficult. These calves were either born with a syndactyl gene or were possible carriers of syndactylism. The damage suffered by Two Rivers does not fit neatly into any one of the four categories discussed above. * * *

Because there are no Texas Supreme Court cases on point dealing with the situation where one product is biologically combined with another to form, by a natural process, a continuation of those products, we must decide whether the Texas Supreme Court would view this case as one that should be governed by the doctrine of strict liability or the rules of commercial law. The theoretical bases and policy rationale of contract law and strict liability have been separated and firmly established. *Mid Continent*, supra, 572 S.W.2d at 311. The Texas Supreme Court noted the distinction in *Nobility Homes* when it quoted the following language of Chief Justice Traynor:

"The law of sales has been carefully articulated to govern the economic relations between suppliers and consumers of goods. The history of the doctrine of strict liability in tort indicates that it was designed, not to undermine the warranty provisions of the sales act or of the Uniform Commercial Code but, rather, to govern the distinct problem of physical injuries. * * *

"The distinction that the law has drawn between tort recovery for physical injuries and warranty recovery for economic loss is not arbitrary and does not rest on the 'luck' of one plaintiff in having an accident causing physical injury. The distinction rests, rather, on an understanding of the nature of the responsibility a manufacturer must undertake in distributing his products. He can appropriately be held liable for physical injuries caused by the defects by requiring his goods to match a standard of safety defined in terms of conditions that create unreasonable risks of harm. He cannot be held for the level of performance of his products in the consumer's business unless he agrees that the product was designed to meet the consumer's demands." 557 S.W.2d at 77, quoting Seely v. White Motor Co., 63 Cal.2d 9, 15, 45 Cal.Rptr. 17, 23, 403 P.2d 145, 151 (1965).

This case is governed by the rules of commercial law for two reasons. First, even if the bull semen is considered to be defective, it is not unreasonably dangerous. Second, the Texas case law indicates that the policy rationale of contract law is to govern this situation. * * *

Two Rivers may not recover damages under the doctrine of strict liability because the bull semen, as a matter of law, was not unreasonably dangerous. Therefore, this case must be governed by the doctrine of commercial law. But even if the bull semen is deemed to be unreasonably dangerous, this case is still governed by the policy rationale of commercial law. * * *

Strict liability was not designed to govern every sale of a faulty product. *Mid Continent,* 572 S.W.2d at 312. Commercial law governs the case where the purchaser has lost some of the benefit of his bargain.

This is clearly demonstrated in an analogous area involving the sale of seeds that are of inferior quality and seeds that will not germinate. * * *

Essentially, Two Rivers is complaining, as a purchaser of bull semen, that the product did not fulfill its commercial expectations. * * * The presence of the recessive gene meant that the product did not fulfill Two Rivers' commercial expectations. The policy reasons behind strict liability are simply not compelling in the case of a disappointed buyer. * * *

Because this case presents a situation involving the principles of commercial law, the provisions of the Uniform Commercial Code govern the outcome. * * *

Two Rivers pleaded and the trial court found that Curtiss breached its implied warranty of merchantability to Two Rivers by distributing a product that was not fit for the purpose of artificially inseminating cattle. Without addressing the validity of this conclusion, we find that this case may be decided on the issue of disclaimer of warranty. To disclaim an implied warranty of merchantability, the disclaimer must (1) mention the word merchantability and (2) in the case of a writing, must be conspicuous.

Each sale from Curtiss to Hi–Pro included a disclaimer of all warranties, express or implied, * * *. This language appeared in large type on the back of each invoice Hi–Pro received from Curtiss when it purchased bull semen. This disclaimer was also conveyed from Curtiss, through Hi–Pro, to Tony Hall when he purchased the Farro semen. * * *

The only remaining question is whether the disclaimer that was effective against Hi–Pro and Hall could be extended to Two Rivers. While Hall purchased the semen on his own account, he did so for the benefit of Two Rivers. Hall cannot be considered a seller of bull semen. The testimony reveals that Hall merely had the semen billed to his account and that he was later reimbursed by Two Rivers in an amount equal to his cost. At least to this extent, Hall was an agent of Two Rivers. Hall also charged Two Rivers a nominal fee for the services he performed. We hold that the relationship between Hall and Two Rivers requires a finding that the disclaimer effective against Hi–Pro and Hall was also effective as to Two Rivers. * * *

In summary, in Texas the type of loss presented in this case is governed by the U.C.C. and the law of warranty. But Curtiss successfully disclaimed any and all implied warranties in this case. Therefore, the district court incorrectly allowed Two Rivers to receive damages based on the theories of strict liability and breach of an implied warranty of merchantability.

Reversed.

TATE, CIRCUIT JUDGE, dissenting. I respectfully dissent.

The majority's persuasive opinion is thoughtful and scholarly. However, like the district judge whom we reverse, my *Erie* guess is that, in the particular configuration of facts before us, the Texas courts would hold that strict liability recovery is allowable. * * *

Therefore, I would allow products liability recovery at least the damages resulting from (a) the loss of the four calves stillborn due to Farro's unreasonably dangerous semen and (b) the loss in value of the 22 calves due to their being born afflicted by the defect resulting from such semen. Accordingly, I respectfully dissent.

---

1. The leading case holding that an action in strict liability does not lie when the product did not perform as expected is Seely v. White Motor Co., 63 Cal.2d 9, 403 P.2d 145, 45 Cal.Rptr. 17 (1965) (Traynor, C.J.) (White truck

"galloped" and did not perform properly). The leading case allowing an action of strict liability is Santor v. A & M Karagheusian, 44 N.J. 52, 207 A.2d 305 (1965) (Francis, J.) (carpet wore prematurely and developed wavy lines). Chief Justice Traynor explained, however, that if there was an express warranty (including a relevant misrepresentation regarding the quality of the product), a tort action might be maintained on that basis. The difference in viewpoint has continued, with the *Seely* case followed by a majority of the courts. The principal case quotes a part of that opinion. This approach has been reaffirmed in recent cases. See Sharp Bros. Contracting Co. v. American Hoist & Derrick Co., 703 S.W.2d 901 (Mo.1986); Tri–State Ins. Co. v. Lindsay Bros., 381 N.W.2d 446 (Minn.1986). The Supreme Court has strongly endorsed the principle in admiralty cases. See East River S.S. Corp. v. Transamerica Delaval, Inc., 476 U.S. 858 (1986).

2. A few courts have created an exception to the rule. When the alleged defect creates an "unreasonable risk" of injury to persons, economic losses resulting from damages to the product itself may be compensable. See, e.g., Pennsylvania Glass Sand Corp. v. Caterpillar Tractor Co., 652 F.2d 1165 (3d Cir. 1981). Do you agree with this distinction?

3. Section 402A covers damage to property as well as persons and most courts have agreed with this extension. See, e.g., Morrow v. Caloric Appliance Co., 372 S.W.2d 41 (Mo.1963) (defective stove set fire to a house). When the property is itself destroyed by a defect most courts treat this as an economic loss not recoverable in tort. See Hawkins Constr. Co. v. Matthews Co., Inc., 190 Neb. 546, 209 N.W.2d 643 (1973) (scaffold collapsed). Other courts treat this as a "property" loss and allow recovery in strict liability. See Gherna v. Ford Motor Co., 246 Cal.App.2d 639, 55 Cal.Rptr. 94 (1966).

4. Of course, a plaintiff not in privity with the manufacturer may have a warranty claim under a state's version of UCC § 2–318. See Autrey v. Chemtrust Industries Corp., 362 F.Supp. 1085 (D.Del.1973) (applying Florida law—actual commercial loss from ineffectiveness of product); L.A. Green Seed Co. v. Williams, 246 Ark. 463, 438 S.W.2d 717 (1969); Rhodes Pharmacal Co. v. Continental Can Co., 72 Ill.App.2d 362, 219 N.E.2d 726 (1966) (implied warranty claim allowed); Morrow v. New Moon Homes, Inc., 548 P.2d 279 (Alaska 1976) (action for unsatisfactory mobile home must be in implied warranty under UCC, but court abolishes privity requirement—disclaimer therefore effective).

5. When the defective material is used in the process of manufacturing another product and that product is ruined as a result, this may be treated as damage to property and recovery will be allowed. See Spence v. Three Rivers Builders & Masonry Supply, Inc., 353 Mich. 120, 90 N.W.2d 873 (1958) (cinder blocks used in a house); Gladiola Biscuit Co. v. Southern Ice Co., 267 F.2d 138 (5th Cir.1959) (glass in ice used in dough). See Note, 66 Colum.L.Rev. 917 (1966). Suppose a burglar alarm system does not work and burglars break in and steal goods? Aronson's Men's Stores v. Potter Elec. Signal Co., 632 S.W.2d 472 (Mo.–banc, 1982).

6. When a purchaser such as a retailer suffers economic loss through a tort suit brought against him by a party injured by the product, he may shift that loss to the manufacturer by way of an indemnity claim. When the manufacturer has sold a retailer bad food and this in turn has driven his customers away, there is a well aged precedent that would allow recovery. See Mazetti v. Armour & Co., 75 Wash. 622, 135 P. 633 (1913). How is this situation to be distinguished from the principal case?

7. If there is an express warranty that is intended to reach the plaintiff, a recovery may be allowed for loss of the bargain and for intangible economic losses. See Thomas v. Olin Mathieson Chem. Corp., 255 Cal.App.2d 806, 63 Cal. Rptr. 454 (1967) (interesting case where rifle suitable for "big game hunting" failed and purchaser sued for the cost of a foreign safari); Inglis v. American Motors Corp., 3 Ohio St.2d 132, 209 N.E.2d 583 (1965). Again the end-results in these cases might be squared with the UCC, but what should be the result if the express warranty was clearly limited to replacement of the product? See Ford Motor Co. v. Olive, 234 So.2d 910 (Miss.1970) (a frequently repaired "lemon").

8. When the action is one for negligence, most cases are in accord with the principal case in denying recovery for loss of the bargain. (Wyatt v. Cadillac Motor Car Div., 145 Cal.App.2d 423, 302 P.2d 665 (1956); Trans World Airlines, Inc. v. Curtiss–Wright Corp., 1 Misc.2d 477, 148 N.Y.S.2d 284 (1955).

9. See Donnelly, After the Fall of the Citadel: Exploitation of the Victory or Consideration of All Interests? 19 Syracuse L.Rev. 1 (1967); Franklin, When Worlds Collide: Liability Theories and Disclaimers in Defective–Product Cases, 18 Stan.L.Rev. 974 (1966); Speidel, Products Liability, Economic Loss and the UCC, 40 Tenn.L.Rev. 309 (1973); Notes, 53 Neb.L.Rev. 114 (1974), 66 Colum.L. Rev. 917 (1966), 52 Va.L.Rev. 509 (1966); Annot., 16 A.L.R.3d 683 (1967).

6. PLAINTIFF'S CONDUCT

DALY v. GENERAL MOTORS CORP.
Supreme Court of California, 1978.
20 Cal.3d 725, 575 P.2d 1162, 144 Cal.Rptr. 380.

[Suit for death of the driver of an Opel automobile, thrown from his car in an accident, because of an alleged defect of the door latch. There was evidence that the driver did not use the shoulder harness system or lock the door, and that he was intoxicated. The case was submitted to the jury, which found for the defendant.]

RICHARDSON, JUSTICE. The most important of several problems which we consider is whether the principles of comparative negligence expressed by us in Li v. Yellow Cab Co. (1975) 13 Cal.2d 804, 119 Cal. Rptr. 858, 532 P.2d 1226, apply to actions founded on strict products liability. We will conclude that they do. * * *

From its inception * * * strict liability has never been, and is not now, absolute liability. As has been repeatedly expressed, under strict liability the manufacturer does not thereby become the insurer of the safety of the product's user. [Cc] On the contrary, the plaintiff's injury must have been caused by a "defect" in the product. Thus the manufacturer is not deemed responsible when injury results from an unforeseeable use of its product. [Cc] Furthermore, we have recognized that though most forms of contributory negligence do not constitute a defense to a strict products liability action, plaintiff's negligence is a complete defense when it comprises assumption of risk. [Cc] As will thus be seen, the concept of strict products liability was created and shaped judicially. In its evolution, the doctrinal encumbrances of contract and warranty, and the traditional elements of negligence, were stripped from the remedy, and a new tort emerged which extended liability for defective product design and manufacture beyond negligence but short of absolute liability.

In Li v. Yellow Cab Co., supra, 13 Cal.3d 804, 119 Cal.Rptr. 858, 532 P.2d 1126, we introduced the other doctrine with which we are concerned, comparative negligence. We examined the history of contributory negligence, the massive criticism directed at it because its presence in the slightest degree completely barred plaintiff's recovery, and the increasing defection from the doctrine. * * *

We stand now at the point of confluence of these two conceptual streams, having been greatly assisted by the thoughtful analysis of the parties and the valuable assistance of numerous amici curiae. We are by no means the first to consider the interaction of these two developing principles. As with the litigants before us, responsible and respected authorities have reached opposing conclusions stressing in various degrees the different considerations which we now examine.

Those counseling against the recognition of comparative fault principles in strict products liability cases vigorously stress, perhaps equally, not only the conceptual, but also the semantic difficulties incident to such a course. The task of merging the two concepts is said to be impossible, that "apples and oranges" cannot be compared, that "oil and water" do not mix, and that strict liability, which is not founded on negligence or fault, is inhospitable to comparative principles. The syllogism runs, contributory negligence was only a defense to negligence, comparative negligence only affects contributory negligence, therefore comparative negligence cannot be a defense to strict liability. [Cc] While fully recognizing the theoretical and semantic distinctions between the twin principles of strict products liability and traditional negligence, we think they can be blended or accommodated.

The inherent difficulty in the "apples and oranges" argument is its insistence on fixed and precise definitional treatment of legal concepts. In the evolving areas of both products liability and tort defenses, however, there has developed much conceptual overlapping and interweaving in order to attain substantial justice. The concept of strict liability itself, as we have noted, arose from dissatisfaction with the wooden formalisms of traditional tort and contract principles in order to protect the consumer of manufactured goods. Similarly, increasing social awareness of its harsh "all or nothing" consequences led us in *Li* to moderate the impact of traditional contributory negligence in order to accomplish a fairer and more balanced result. We acknowledged an intermixing of defenses of contributory negligence and assumption of risk and formally effected a type of merger. "As for assumption of risk, we have recognized in this state that this defense overlaps that of contributory negligence to some extent * * *." (*Li*, supra). * * *

We think, accordingly, the conclusion may fairly be drawn that the terms "comparative negligence," "contributory negligence" and "assumption of risk" do not, standing alone, lend themselves to the exact measurements of a micrometer-caliper, or to such precise definition as to divert us from otherwise strong and consistent countervailing policy considerations. Fixed semantic consistency at this point is less important than the attainment of a just and equitable result. The interweaving of concept and terminology in this area suggests a judicial posture that is flexible rather than doctrinaire. * * *

Given all of the foregoing, we are, in the wake of *Li*, disinclined to resolve the important issue before us by the simple expedient of matching linguistic labels which have evolved either for convenience or by custom. Rather, we consider it more useful to examine the foundational reasons underlying the creation of strict products liability in California to ascertain whether the purposes of the doctrine would be defeated or diluted by adoption of comparative principles. We imposed strict liability against the manufacturer and in favor of the user or consumer in order to relieve injured consumers "from *problems of proof* inherent in pursuing negligence * * * and warranty * * * remedies * * *." * * * As we have noted, we sought to place the burden of loss on manufacturers rather than "injured persons *who are powerless to protect themselves.*" * * *

The foregoing goals, we think, will not be frustrated by the adoption of comparative principles. Plaintiffs will continue to be relieved of proving that the manufacturer or distributor was negligent in the production, design, or dissemination of the article in question. Defendant's liability for injuries caused by a defective product remains strict. The principle of protecting the defenseless is likewise preserved, for plaintiff's recovery will be reduced *only* to the extent that his own lack of reasonable care contributed to his injury. The cost of compensating the victim of a defective product, albeit proportionately reduced, remains on defendant manufacturer, and will, through him, be "spread among society." However, we do not permit plaintiff's own conduct relative to the product to escape unexamined, and as to that share of plaintiff's damages which flows from his own fault we discern no reason of policy why it should, following *Li*, be borne by others. Such a result would directly contravene the principle announced in *Li*, that loss should be assessed equitably in proportion to fault. * * *

A second objection to the application of comparative principles in strict products liability cases is that a manufacturer's incentive to produce safe products will thereby be reduced or removed. While we fully recognize this concern we think, for several reasons, that the problem is more shadow than substance. First, of course, the manufacturer cannot avoid its continuing liability for a defective product even when the plaintiff's own conduct has contributed to his injury. The manufacturer's liability, and therefore its incentive to avoid and correct product defects remains; its exposure will be lessened only to the extent that the trier finds that the victim's conduct contributed to his injury. Second, as a practical matter a manufacturer, in a particular case, cannot assume that the user of a defective product upon whom an injury is visited will be blameworthy. * * *

In passing, we note one important and felicitous result if we apply comparative principles to strict products liability. This arises from the fact that under present law when plaintiff sues in negligence his own contributory negligence, however denominated, may diminish but cannot wholly defeat his recovery. When he sues in strict products liability, however, his "assumption of risk" *completely bars* his recovery. Under *Li,* as we have noted, "assumption of risk" is merged into comparative principles. [Cc] The consequence is that after *Li* in a negligence action, plaintiff's conduct which amounts to "negligent" assumption of risk no longer defeats plaintiff's recovery. Identical conduct, however, in a strict liability case acts as a complete bar under rules heretofore applicable. Thus, strict products liability, which was developed to free injured consumers from the constraints imposed by traditional negligence and warranty theories, places a consumer plaintiff in a worse position than would be the case were his claim founded on simple negligence. This, in turn, rewards adroit pleading and selection of theories. The application of comparative principles to strict liability obviates this bizarre anomaly by treating alike the defenses to both negligence and strict products liability actions. In each instance the defense, if established, will reduce but not bar plaintiff's claim.

A third objection to the merger of strict liability and comparative fault focuses on the claim that, as a practical matter, triers of fact, particularly jurors, cannot assess, measure, or compare plaintiff's negligence with defendant's strict liability. We are unpersuaded by the argument and are convinced that jurors are able to undertake a fair apportionment of liability. * * *

We note that the majority of our sister states which have addressed the problem, either by statute or judicial decree, have extended comparative principles to strict products liability. * * *

Of the three decisions which have declined to apply comparative negligence to strict liability, two have noted their reliance on state comparative negligence statutes which are expressly confined to "negligence" actions. [Cc] At least three jurisdictions have applied comparative negligence statutes to strict liability actions, despite language arguably limiting the statute application to negligence. [Cc] Finally, one court has judicially extended a "pure" form of comparative fault to the traditional strict liability defense of "product misuse," despite the existence of a statutory scheme of "modified" comparative negligence. (General Motors Corp. v. Hopkins (Tex.1977) 548 S.W.2d 344, 351–352.)

Moreover, we are further encouraged in our decision herein by noting that the apparent majority of scholarly commentators has urged adoption of the rule which we announce herein. * * *

We find additional significance in the provisions of the proposed Uniform Comparative Fault Act (Act). * * * Our attention has been called to the action of the Conference [of Commissioners on Uniform State Laws] in August 1977, wherein it approved adoption of the Act by a vote of 40 states to 8 (California voting favorably). The Act is the distillation of approximately five years of discussion, analysis, and contribution by a special committee and a review committee of the Conference. We quote portions of [it] * * *.

Having examined the principal objections and finding them not insurmountable, and persuaded by logic, justice, and fundamental fairness, we conclude that a system of comparative fault should be and it is hereby extended to actions founded on strict products liability. In such cases the separate defense of "assumption of risk," to the extent that it is a form of contributory negligence, is abolished. While, as we have suggested, on the particular facts before us, the term "equitable apportionment of loss" is more accurately descriptive of the process, nonetheless, the term "comparative fault" has gained such wide acceptance by courts and in the literature that we adopt its use herein. * * *

It is readily apparent that the foregoing broad expressions of principle do not establish the duties of the jury with that fixed precision which appeals to minds trained in law and logic. Nonetheless, rather than attempt to anticipate every variant and nuance of circumstance and party that may invoke comparative principles in a strict products liability context, we deem it wiser to await a case-by-case evolution in the application of the broad principles herein expressed.

By extending and tailoring the comparative principles announced in *Li,* supra, to the doctrine of strict products liability, we believe that we move closer to the goal of the equitable allocation of legal responsibility for personal injuries. We do so by relying on what Professor Schwartz aptly terms a "predicate of fairness." In making liability more commensurate with fault we undermine neither the theories nor the policies of the strict liability rule. In *Li* we took "a first step in what we deem to be a proper and just direction, * * *." [C] We are convinced that the principles herein announced constitute the next appropriate and logical step in the same direction.

The judgment is reversed.

[TOBRINER, CLARK and MANUEL, JJ., concurred; CLARK, J. filed a concurring opinion; JEFFERSON, J. (assigned), concurred in part and dissented in part and filed an opinion in which BIRD, C.J., concurred; MOSK, J., filed a dissenting opinion.]

---

1. Compare the discussion in connection with Spier v. Barker, supra [pages 601–02.] Is the situation in the principal case the same?

2. *Contributory Negligence.* The overwhelming majority of decisions have been in accord with the Restatement (Second) of Torts, holding that contributory negligence, in the sense of failure to discover a defect in the product or guard against the possibility of existence, is not a defense. See, e.g., Kassouf v. Lee Bros., 209 Cal.App.2d 568, 26 Cal.Rptr. 276 (1962) (plaintiff, without inspection, ate a chocolate bar containing worms and maggots); Bachner v. Pearson, 479 P.2d 319 (Alaska 1970) (carbon monoxide entered cabin of aircraft); Berkebile v. Brantly Helicopter Corp., 337 A.2d 893 (Pa.1975) (failure to use safety device

in crash). What is the reason for this rule? Is fault irrelevant under strict liability? Or is the rule based on the theory that a purchaser may assume the product is safe? The Restatement appeared simply to carry over the rule from the approach taken in the area of Abnormally Dangerous Activities. See supra pages 691–95.

The Uniform Product Liability Act takes a similar approach and does not require the product user or consumer to inspect a product for a defect. See U.P.L.A. § 112(A), 44 F.R. 62736.

3. *Obvious Hazard.* In some jurisdictions the Restatement approach has, as a practical matter, been narrowed by cases holding that there is no duty on a manufacturer to protect a consumer against an obvious hazard. See, e.g., Killeen v. Harmon Grain Prods., Inc., 11 Mass.App.Ct. 20, 413 N.E.2d 767 (1980) (toothpick); Blunk v. Allis–Chalmers Mfg. Co., 143 Ind.App. 631, 242 N.E.2d 122 (1968) (moving rollers on corn picker); Albert v. J. & L. Eng'g Co., 214 So.2d 212 (La.App.1968) (lack of protective guard on machine); Complaint of Diehl, 610 F.Supp. 223 (D.Idaho 1985) (aluminum sailboat mast striking power line). Can these cases be distinguished from the "unavoidably unsafe" products cases discussed at page 745? The Uniform Product Liability Act would allow for reduction of damages when the product seller proves by a preponderance of the evidence that the claimant was injured by a defective condition which would have been apparent, without inspection, to an ordinary, reasonable, prudent person. See U.P.L.A. § 112(B), 44 F.R. 62736.

4. *Assumption of Risk.* When plaintiff voluntarily confronts a known hazard, the Restatement and many courts would bar his claim. Barefield v. La Salle Coca Cola Bottling Co., 370 Mich. 1, 120 N.W.2d 786 (1963) (drinking beverage known to be full of broken glass); Ferraro v. Ford Motor Co., 423 Pa. 324, 223 A.2d 746 (1966) (driving truck with knowledge that wheels would lock on left turns and accelerator pedal tended to dislodge); Cintrone v. Hertz Truck Leasing & Rental Serv., 45 N.J. 434, 212 A.2d 769 (1965) (driving truck knowing brakes to be bad). Thus, some jurisdictions would not apply the defense when plaintiff's conduct has been "reasonable" in the context. See Young v. Aro Corp., 36 Cal.App.3d 240, 111 Cal.Rptr. 535 (1973) (worker proceeding with dangerous machinery); Moran v. Raymond Corp., 484 F.2d 1008 (7th Cir.1973) (similar); Ferraro v. Ford Motor Co., 423 Pa. 324, 223 A.2d 746 (1966) (driving with knowledge of defective wheels); Messick v. General Motors Corp., 460 F.2d 485 (5th Cir.1972) (driving with defect in front suspension system). Also, the burden of showing that plaintiff's conduct was unreasonable is placed on defendant. See Luque v. McLean, 8 Cal.3d 136, 501 P.2d 1163, 104 Cal.Rptr. 443 (1972) (plaintiff attempted to retrieve object in path of dangerous lawn mower). Finally, the impact of the defense may be lessened by a narrow construction of what is "voluntary" conduct. Henderson v. Ford Motor Co., 519 S.W.2d 87, 92 (Tex.1974) (plaintiff could not reduce speed on vehicle and crashed into pole—court observed that a "*negligent* failure to choose the best escape from the throes of peril is not a voluntary encounter"). The two concepts of "reasonableness" and "voluntary conduct" tend to overlap and merge. See Restatement (Second) of Torts § 496E.

Under the Uniform Product Liability Act, when it is clear that a claimant voluntarily and unreasonably used a product with a known defective condition, the claimant's damages are subject to reduction. In cases where the reasonableness of the claimant's knowing use of the defective product is in dispute, U.P.L.A. allows the trier of the fact to consider the claimant's conduct in the particular fact situation and to reduce damages to the extent that it is appropriate to do so. See U.P.L.A., § 112(B), 44 F.R. 62736.

5. See generally Condon, Plaintiff's Fault as a Defense to Strict Liability, 25 Food Drug Cosm.L.J. 246 (1970); Epstein, Products Liability: Defenses Based on Plaintiff's Conduct, 1968 Utah L.Rev. 267; Kissel, Defenses to Strict Liability, 60 Ill.B.J. 450 (1972); Levine, Buyer's Conduct as Affecting the Extent of Manufacturer's Liability, 52 Minn.L.Rev. 627 (1968); Horsley, Products Liability Defenses, 15 Defense L.J. 399 (1966); Noel, Defective Products: Abnormal Use, Contributory Negligence, and Assumption of Risk, 25 Vand.L.Rev. 93 (1972); R. Keeton, Assumption of Products Risks, 19 Sw.L.J. 61 (1965); Twerski, Old Wine in a New Flask—Restructuring Assumption of Risk in the Products Liability Era, 60 Iowa L.Rev. 1 (1974); Annot., 46 A.L.R.3d 240 (1972).

6. *Comparative Negligence.* On the surface many comparative negligence statutes would seem to have no bearing on strict liability cases. The statutes are usually explicitly addressed to cases based on negligence. Moreover, in the states that have judicially adopted comparative negligence, the initial decisions are carefully confined to actions based on negligence and do not disclose the relationship of the doctrine to strict liability. See Hoffman v. Jones, 280 So.2d 431 (Fla.1973); Li v. Yellow Cab Co., supra page 570; Kaatz v. State, 540 P.2d 1037 (Alaska 1975). The Arkansas statute was the first to use the word "fault" instead of "negligence," and to define fault as including the "supplying of a defective product in an unreasonably dangerous condition." See Ark.Stat.Ann., § 27–1763 (1973). The New York statute speaks of "culpable conduct." N.Y. C.P.L.R. § 1411 (Supp.1975).

Nevertheless, there is nothing in the letter of the statutes or in the judicial decisions adopting comparative negligence that would preclude the application of the doctrine to strict liability; and some courts have taken that step. Thirty jurisdictions now apply comparative fault to product liability either by statute or by judicial expansion of a comparative negligence rule. See V. Schwartz, Comparative Negligence § 12.2 (2d ed. 1986). Application of Comparative Negligence and Strict Liability: Where Are We? 47 Ins.Couns.J. 53 (1980). For cases, see Dippel v. Sciano, 37 Wis.2d 443, 155 N.W.2d 55 (1967) (reaching result by rationale of treating § 402A strict liability as "negligence per se," and so within the statute); Kennedy v. Sawyer, 228 Kan. 439, 618 P.2d 788 (1980); Cartel Capital Corp. v. Fireco of New Jersey, 81 N.J. 548, 410 A.2d 674 (1980); Sandford v. Chevrolet Div. of Gen. Motors, 292 Or. 590, 642 P.2d 624 (1982); Daly v. General Motors Corp., 20 Cal.3d 725, 575 P.2d 1162, 144 Cal.Rptr. 380 (1978); cf. Lippard v. Houdaille Indus., Inc., 715 S.W.2d 491 (Mo.1986) (en banc).

Does it make sense to reduce plaintiff's damages for plaintiff's negligence in cases where the defendant has been negligent but not in cases where the defendant is strictly liable without regard to fault?

For treatment, see Fischer, Products Liability—Applicability of Comparative Negligence, 43 Mo.L.Rev. 431 (1978); Schwartz, Strict Liability and Comparative Negligence, 42 Tenn.L.Rev. 171 (1976); Wade, Products Liability and Plaintiff's Fault—The Comparative Fault Act, 29 Mercer L.Rev. 373 (1978); Plant, Comparative Negligence and Strict Tort Liability, 40 La.L.Rev. 403 (1980).

FORD MOTOR CO. v. MATTHEWS
Supreme Court of Mississippi, 1974.
291 So.2d 169.

RODGERS, PRESIDING JUSTICE. Earnest Matthews was killed as a result of being run over by his tractor and dragged underneath a disc attachment. It was alleged that Matthews was standing beside his tractor when he started it, and the tractor was in gear at the time. The Ford tractor in question was equipped with a starter safety switch which was designed to prevent the tractor from being started in gear. It is the position of the plaintiff-administratrix that the plunger connected with the safety switch was defective and allowed the tractor to be started in gear.

[The trial court, sitting without a jury, found for the plaintiff-administratrix and entered a judgment against Ford in the amount of $74,272.65. Ford appealed.]

The appellant Ford contends that Matthews' act of standing on the ground and starting the tractor while in gear was a misuse of the product. It is argued that such misuse is an absolute limitation on Ford's liability. The basic authority for this position is Comment (h), Restatement (Second) of Torts § 402A, which reads in part: "A product is not in a defective condition when it is safe for normal handling and consumption. If the injury results from abnormal handling * * * the seller is not liable." [Restatement (Second) of Torts § 402A, at 351.] Several cases are cited by appellant to illustrate this proposition. However, in the cases cited, the court either found that there was no defect and the accident was caused by a misuse, or even if there were a defect, it played no part in the causation of the accident. Here the situation is clearly distinguishable. It is apparent that the failure of the safety switch to prevent the tractor from cranking in gear was a cause of the accident. The failure of the decedent to make sure the tractor was in neutral before starting [, if that were true] may be characterized as the omission of a customary precaution, although there is no evidence that he was warned of this danger, or that he knew of the danger. Nevertheless, this was not such a misuse of the tractor as to relieve Ford from its strict liability for the defective condition of the tractor.

Although misuse of a product that causes an injury is normally a bar to strict liability, it is said that: " * * * [T]he manufacturer is not liable for injuries resulting from abnormal or unintended use of his product, *if such use was not reasonably foreseeable. The issue is one of foreseeability and misuse may be foreseeable.*" (Emphasis added). 1 Frumer and Friedman, Products Liability § 15.01, at 351 (1973).

A recent law review writer expressed it in this manner: "In strict liability cases the same duty to foresee certain unintended uses has been recognized, and ordinarily the factual issue of the foreseeability of a particular use has been left to the jury." Noel, Defective Products:

Abnormal Use, Contributory Negligence, and Assumption of Risk, 25 Vand.L.Rev. 93, 97 (1972).

It is admitted that the tractor in question was designed to prevent its starting in gear. It is apparent that it could be foreseen by Ford that one day a tractor operator might carelessly crank the engine without first making certain that it was not in gear (as recommended in the owner's manual), especially if he were aware of the purpose of the safety switch system. In short, even if Matthews were guilty of negligence, such negligence was reasonably foreseeable by Ford and is not a bar to an action based on strict liability resulting from a defective tractor. * * *

[W]e are of the opinion that the total sum determined by the trial judge to be due was not excessive and the case should be affirmed.

Affirmed.

————

1. When plaintiff uses a product in a manner unintended by the manufacturer, courts often treat this as a matter of defense. On the other hand, could the matter be viewed more logically as an issue of duty? What is the obligation of a manufacturer to produce a product that will withstand misuse? The point is well illustrated in Swain v. Boeing Airplane Co., 337 F.2d 940 (2d Cir.1964), where the defense of contributory negligence was withdrawn because defendant could not prove which decedent was flying the plane; but it was held, nevertheless, that it could litigate the issue of abnormal use by improper flying. Cf. Galvan v. Prosser Packers, Inc., 83 Wash.2d 690, 521 P.2d 929 (1974) (treating the issue as one of "proximate cause").

2. Whether regarded as a matter of defense or a question of duty, the manufacturer is not subject to liability for an unforeseeable abnormal use of his product. Thus, when a 15–year–old boy was injured when he dove into a vinyl lined swimming pool thirty inches deep, the manufacturer was held not liable. See Colosimo v. May Dep't Store Co., 466 F.2d 1234 (3d Cir.1972).

3. There were a good many negligence cases holding that the seller is not liable when the injury is brought about by an abnormal use of the chattel. See, for example, McCready v. United Iron & Steel Co., 272 F.2d 700 (10th Cir.1959) (casements for use as window frames were used by workmen as ladders); Marker v. Universal Oil Prods. Co., 250 F.2d 603 (10th Cir.1957) (hot catalyst used in cold catalyst refining unit); Dubbs v. Zak Bros. Co., 38 Ohio App. 299, 175 N.E. 626 (1931) (shoes far too small for plaintiff's feet caused blisters).

4. Even in cases based on negligence, there are unusual uses of a product that the seller had to anticipate, and against which he was required to guard, at least to the extent of a warning. Thus standing on a chair, in Phillips v. Ogle Aluminum Furniture, Inc., 106 Cal.App.2d 650, 235 P.2d 857 (1951). Or wearing a cocktail robe in proximity to the flame of a kitchen stove, in Ringstad v. I. Magnin & Co., 39 Wash.2d 923, 239 P.2d 848 (1952). Or operating a tractor downhill at fast speed, using the engine compression as a brake, in Lovejoy v. Minneapolis–Moline Power Imp. Co., 248 Minn. 319, 79 N.W.2d 688 (1956).

5. As the principal decision reflects, one can discern in strict liability cases a clear extension of this trend and a willingness to leave the matter of "foreseeable misuse" to the jury. Perhaps the most extreme case to date is LaRue v. National Union Elec. Corp., 571 F.2d 51 (1st Cir.1978), where a

11–year–old boy sat on his mother's vacuum cleaner and rode it as if it were a toy car, and his penis slipped through openings in the casing into the fan, resulting in its amputation. The court held that the jury could find that "the vacuum cleaner presented an unreasonable risk of harm to children who might reasonably be foreseen to explore and fiddle with the device." The court noted that the "inadvertant intrusion of [the boy's] penis into the fan * * * fell within this class of dangers, even though the precise circumstances of the accident might have been improbable." See also Ritter v. Narragansett Elec. Co., 109 R.I. 176, 283 A.2d 255 (1971) (child opened oven door and stood on it— oven fell); Gardner v. Q.H.S., Inc., 448 F.2d 238 (4th Cir.1971) (plaintiff fell asleep while paraffin hair set rollers boiled on stove); Estabrook v. J.C. Penney Co., 105 Ariz. 302, 464 P.2d 325 (1970) (curious boy poked his finger between escalator and handrail guard).

6. A seller is generally entitled to expect that his clear and understandable directions and instructions for use will be followed, and when they are not the use becomes an abnormal one. This first occurred in negligence cases. See Fredendall v. Abraham & Straus, 279 N.Y. 146, 18 N.E.2d 11 (1938) (carbon tetrachloride used in enclosed space); Taylor v. Jacobson, 336 Mass. 709, 147 N.E.2d 770 (1958) (hair dye used without patch test); Landers v. Safeway Stores, 172 Or. 116, 139 P.2d 788 (1943) (bleaching solution not diluted). The same result has been obtained in strict liability cases. See McDevitt v. Standard Oil Co. of Texas, 391 F.2d 364 (5th Cir.1968) (plaintiff used tires that were the wrong size and inflated them improperly); Helene Curtis Indus. v. Pruitt, 385 F.2d 841 (5th Cir.1967) (plaintiff mixed defendant's hair color product with another brand). But warnings or instructions will not always preclude liability. If following the instructions would make it difficult to obtain the expected use of the product, the warnings will not overcome defects in the product's design or construction. For example, warnings on a fire extinguisher stating that it should not be used in a room warmer than 120 degrees. There is a trend that requires the directions to be clear, easy to understand and emphatic regarding dangers. See, e.g., D'Arienzo v. Clairol, Inc., 125 N.J.Super. 224, 310 A.2d 106 (1973) (directions about repeated preliminary testing for hair color—collecting cases). Cf. Berkebile v. Brantly Helicopter Corp., 337 A.2d 893, 902 (Pa.1975) (instructions are not "to be governed by reasonable man standard" but by "whether the seller accompanied his product with sufficient instructions and warnings so as to make his product safe").

7. Does it make any difference whether the "misuse" or "abnormal use" is that of the plaintiff or of a third party? Can both be either lack of duty or an affirmative defense?

8. The Uniform Product Liability Act would provide for a reduction or apportionment of the liability of the product seller when an injury occurs, in whole or in part, because the product user misused the product in some way that the product seller could not reasonably anticipate. Damages could be reduced or apportioned to the extent that the misuse caused the harm, and the trier of fact could determine that the harm arose solely because of product misuse. See U.P.L.A. § 112(c), 44 FR 62737. See also Helene Curtis Indus. v. Pruitt, 385 F.2d 841 (5th Cir.1967).

9. *Application of Comparative Fault.* A "comparative fault" principle may also be applied in the "foreseeable misuse" cases. Does it supply an attractive solution for those cases? See Netzel v. State Sand & Gravel Co., 51 Wis.2d 1, 186 N.W.2d 258 (1971) (plaintiff, burned in allowing defective wet cement to fall inside his shoes and remain lodged against his legs, had his

award reduced for foreseeable misuse). See generally Feinberg, Applicability of a Comparative Negligence Defense in a Product Liability Case, 42 Ins.Comp.J. 39 (1975); Schwartz, Comparative Negligence, Ch. 12 (2d ed. 1986), and Strict Liability and Comparative Negligence, 42 Tenn.L.Rev. 171 (1974); Wade, Products Liability and Plaintiff's Fault—The Uniform Comparative Fault Act, 29 Mercer L.Rev. 373 (1978).

10. *Assumption of Risk.* A number of courts have held that the plaintiff's ordinary negligence is not a defense when it consists merely of a failure to discover the defect or to guard against the possibility of its existence; but that the plaintiff's assumption of risk is a defense in strict liability cases where the plaintiff actually knew of the risk and voluntarily encountered it. Some courts in comparative negligence states treat assumption of risk as a partial, not complete, defense and use it as a basis for reducing plaintiff's damages. See generally, V. Schwartz, Comparative Negligence, §§ 12.6, 12.7 (2d ed. 1986).

7. DEFENDANTS OTHER THAN PRINCIPAL MANUFACTURERS

(A) OTHER SUPPLIERS OF CHATTELS

PETERSON v. LOU BACHRODT CHEVROLET CO.
Supreme Court of Illinois, 1975.
61 Ill.2d 17, 329 N.E.2d 785.

SCHAEFER, JUSTICE. On September 3, 1971, Maradean Peterson, age 11, and her brother, Mark Peterson, age 8, were struck by an automobile while they were walking home from school. Maradean Peterson died on the day of the accident, and Mark Peterson suffered severe injuries, including the amputation of one of his legs. The automobile involved in the accident was a used 1965 Chevrolet. James A. Peterson, administrator of the estate of Maradean Peterson, and Mark Peterson, by James A. Peterson, his father and next friend, brought this action against the driver of the used car, its owners, and the defendant involved in the appeal, Lou Bachrodt Chevrolet Company.

[The circuit court dismissed two counts of the complaint and this ruling is before the supreme court on appeal.]

One of the challenged counts sought recovery for the wrongful death of the daughter, the other for the injuries to the son. Each count alleged that the defendant, Lou Bachrodt Chevrolet Company, had sold the 1965 Chevrolet on June 11, 1971, in the ordinary course of business, and that at the time the automobile left the defendant's control it was defective and not reasonably safe for driving and operation in that:

"(a) A spring or springs in the left front wheel braking system was missing at the time of its sale;

"(b) One of the left rear brake shoes was completely worn out at the time of the sale;

"(c) A part of the cylinder braking system in the left rear wheel was missing at the time of the sale."

It was alleged that the injuries and death were a direct and proximate result of the defective conditions.

Two issues are presented on this appeal: first, whether as a matter of law, strict liability extends to the seller of a used car and, second, whether a bystander who has been struck by a defective and unreasonably dangerous car may sue under a theory of strict liability. Our disposition of the first of these issues makes it unnecessary to consider the second.

In Suvada v. White Motor Co. (1965), 32 Ill.2d 612, 210 N.E.2d 182, we held that a manufacturer is liable under a theory of strict liability if the plaintiffs "prove that their injury or damage resulted from a condition of the product, that the condition was an unreasonably dangerous one and that the condition existed at the time it left the manufacturer's control." (32 Ill.2d 612, 623, 210 N.E.2d 182, 188.) In Dunham v. Vaughan & Bushnell Mfg. Co. (1969), 42 Ill.2d 339, 247 N.E.2d 401, strict liability was imposed upon a wholesaler through whose warehouse the packaged product passed unopened. In that case we pointed out: "The strict liability of a retailer arises from his integral role in the overall producing and marketing enterprise and affords an additional incentive to safety." (42 Ill.2d 339, 344, 247 N.E.2d 401, 404.) The plaintiffs now ask that the same liability be imposed upon a defendant who is outside of the original producing and marketing chain. We decline to do so.

One of the basic grounds supporting the imposition of strict liability upon manufacturers is that losses should be borne by those "who have created the risk and reaped the profit by placing the product in the stream of commerce." (32 Ill.2d 612, 619, 210 N.E.2d 182, 186.) Imposition of liability upon wholesalers and retailers is justified on the ground that their position in the marketing process enables them to exert pressure on the manufacturer to enhance the safety of the product. [Cc] A wholesaler or retailer who neither creates nor assumes the risk is entitled to indemnity. [Cc] Therefore, although liability is imposed upon anyone who is engaged in the business of selling the product (Restatement (Second) of Torts § 402A (1965)), the loss will ordinarily be ultimately borne by the party that created the risk.

There is no allegation that the defects existed when the product left the control of the manufacturer. Nor is there any allegation that the defects were created by the used car dealer. [C] If strict liability is imposed upon the facts alleged here, the used car dealer would in effect become an insurer against defects which had come into existence after the chain of distribution was completed, and while the product was under the control of one or more consumers. See Restatement (Second) of Torts § 402A, Comment f. * * *

The judgment of the Appellate Court, Second District, is reversed.

Appellate court reversed;   circuit court affirmed.

GOLDENHERSH, JUSTICE (dissenting).   I dissent.   The rationale underlying the application of strict liability to a manufacturer is that losses should be borne by those "who have created the risk and reaped the profit by placing the product in the stream of commerce."   (Suvada v. White Motor Co., 32 Ill.2d 612, 619, 210 N.E.2d 182, 186.)   In Dunham v. Vaughan & Bushnell Mfg. Co., 42 Ill.2d 339, 247 N.E.2d 401, strict liability was made applicable to a wholesaler and retailer for the reason that "these considerations apply with equal compulsion to all elements in the distribution system."   (42 Ill.2d 339, 344, 247 N.E.2d 401, 404.)

* * *

In Galluccio v. Hertz Corp., 1 Ill.App.3d 272, 274 N.E.2d 178, appeal denied, 49 Ill.2d 575, the appellate court held strict liability applicable to the lessor of a motor vehicle.   No reason presents itself for not applying the principle to a used car dealer who places in the stream of commerce a vehicle rendered unreasonably dangerous by reason of a defect discoverable upon reasonable inspection.

I am aware of the argument made by defendant and *amici curiae* that many vehicles are sold "as is" and that the cost of repairs in some instances might exceed the value of the vehicle.   These pleadings present no such issues, and assuming, *arguendo,* that in some future case they will arise, there is precedent for weighing the cost of remedying the dangerous condition against the nature and extent of the risk which it creates.   [C]

I would affirm the judgment of the appellate court.

---

1.   The Restatement (Second) of Torts § 402A and most courts in their initial decision implementing strict products liability on tort or warranty theories have limited its reach to defendants who are "in the business of selling products."   A vital part of the development of strict liability law in the past decade has focused on: (1) which defendants fit within this definition, and (2) whether other defendants should also be included.

2.   *Retailers and Wholesaler–Distributors.*   Most courts have extended strict liability to retailers and wholesaler-distributors.   Chandler v. Anchor Serum Co., 198 Kan. 571, 426 P.2d 82 (1967); Housman v. C.A. Dawson & Co., 106 Ill.App.2d 225, 245 N.E.2d 886 (1969).   See also Keller v. Eagle Army–Navy Dep't Stores, Inc., 291 So.2d 58 (Fla.App.1974) ("dangerous instrumentalities only").   As Justice Traynor indicated in Vandermark v. Ford Motor Co., 61 Cal. 2d 256, 391 P.2d 168, 37 Cal.Rptr. 896 (1964): "In some cases the retailer may be the only member of the enterprise reasonably available to the injured plaintiff.   In other cases, the retailer himself may play a substantial part in insuring that the product is safe or may be in a position to exert pressure on the manufacturer to that end."   But see Ellis v. Rich's Inc., 233 Ga. 573, 212 S.E.2d 373 (1975); Sam Shainberg Co. v. Barlow, 258 So.2d 242 (Miss.1972) (no duty to inspect articles purchased from reputable manufacturer).   If there is privity in these cases, what about liability under the UCC?

Note that strict liability may produce substantially different results from negligence for a retailer or wholesaler.   The dealer, for example, is ordinarily not negligent in failing to open sealed containers and inspect their contents. See Frericks v. General Motors Corp., 274 Md. 288, 336 A.2d 118 (1975) (design of automobile); Kratz v. American Stores, 359 Pa. 335, 59 A.2d 138 (1948). Nor need he take the product apart. Zesch v. Abrasive Co. of Philadelphia, 353 Mo. 558, 183 S.W.2d 140 (1944). But the dealer is not absolved from the obligation to make such cursory examination as reasonably accompanies his handling of the goods. Kirk v. Stineway Drug Store Co., 38 Ill.App.2d 415, 187 N.E.2d 307 (1963). And if he knows or discovers any special reason to believe that the product may be defective, a thorough examination may be required before he sells it. Davis v. Williams, 58 Ga.App. 274, 198 S.E. 357 (1938).

3. Data show that retailers and wholesalers end up paying product liability judgments in less than five percent of cases. Nevertheless, they are brought into an overwhelming majority of product liability claims. Who benefits from all this? The Uniform Product Liability Act and proposed Federal legislation would hold retailers and wholesalers liable only for their own acts of negligence unless the manufacturer was out of business or unreachable through judicial process. Do you agree with that approach? Approximately 16 states have enacted these types of provisions limiting the liability of non-manufacturer product sellers. See, e.g., Ga.Code Ann. § 51–1–11.1 (1987); Minn.Stat. § 544.41 (1980); Mo.Rev.Stat. § 34 (1987); Ohio Rev.Code Ann. § 2305.33 (1984); Wash.Rev.Code § 7.72.040 (1981).

4. An occasional seller who does not hold himself out as having any knowledge or skill in the commercial sense will not be subject to strict liability. See Samson v. Riesing, 62 Wis.2d 698, 215 N.W.2d 662 (1974), where nine Wauwatosa Band mothers sold plaintiff defective turkey salad. They were liable only if proved negligent.

5. *Manufacturer of Component Parts.* The maker of a component part not subject to further processing or substantial change in the manufacturing process is likely to be subject to strict liability if there is a defect in that part. See Clark v. Bendix Corp., 42 A.D.2d 727, 345 N.Y.S.2d 662 (1973) (faulty power steering mechanism); Icelandic Airlines, Inc. (Loftleidir) v. Canadair, Ltd., 104 Misc.2d 239, 428 N.Y.S.2d 393 (1980) (defective hydraulic control system in airplane).

6. *Lessors and Bailors of Chattels.* Bailors for hire, including lessors, are under a duty of reasonable care, including reasonable inspection, to provide a safe chattel; and the liability for negligence extends to a foreseeable third person who is injured by reason of the defect. See, for example, Austin v. Austin, 252 N.C. 283, 113 S.E.2d 553 (1960); Scharf v. Gardner Cartage Co., 95 Ohio App. 153, 113 N.E.2d 717 (1953).

7. On the other hand, a gratuitous lender of a chattel is under no duty to inspect it for unknown defects before delivering it, but will be liable to a third party for failure to disclose any latent defects of which he has knowledge. See, for example, Hill v. Lyons Plumbing & Heating Co., 457 S.W.2d 503 (Ky.1970).

8. Strict liability was first extended to third parties not in privity in Cintrone v. Hertz Truck Leasing & Rental Serv. Co., 45 N.J. 434, 212 A.2d 769 (1965), where, in a long but good opinion, the court extended the implied warranty to the user to apply to lessors, but denied recovery to the plaintiff because of his "contributory negligence" in driving with brakes he knew to be bad. The rule that commercial lessors of chattels should be subject to strict liability has been adopted with almost uniform consistency in other states. A common situation is where a passenger or pedestrian is injured by a rented

automobile. See, e.g., Price v. Shell Oil Co., 2 Cal.3d 245, 466 P.2d 722, 85 Cal. Rptr. 178 (1970); Stewart v. Budget Rent–A–Car Corp., 52 Hawaii 71, 470 P.2d 240 (1970); Stang v. Hertz Corp., 83 N.M. 730, 497 P.2d 732 (1972).

9. *Used Products.* As the principal case reflects, some courts may decline to impose strict liability on sellers of used products. See also Ikerd v. Lapworth, 435 F.2d 197 (7th Cir.1970) (wholesaler sold used cars to retailer); Rix v. Reeves, 23 Ariz.App. 243, 532 P.2d 185 (1975) (used tire rim from salvage yard). How does this class of defendants differ from lessors of chattels or retailers?

When the defect is in a part of an automobile that the dealer specifically installed, one court has applied strict liability. See Realmuto v. Straub Motors, Inc., 65 N.J. 336, 322 A.2d 440 (1974). How does this differ from the principal case? See also Turner v. International Harvester Co., 133 N.J.Super. 277, 336 A.2d 62 (1975) (applying strict liability—truck cab collapsed on plaintiff due to defective hood latch on used truck); Cornelius v. Bay Motors, Inc., 258 Or. 564, 484 P.2d 299 (1971) ($500, seven-year-old vehicle that had been driven 50,000 miles experienced brake failure on the very morning it was purchased).

If strict liability is applied, can a seller of a used product avoid it by selling the product "as is" or "with all faults"? See Turner v. International Harvester, supra; Keystone Aeronautics Corp. v. R.J. Enstrom Corp., 499 F.2d 146 (3d Cir. 1974) (demo helicopter—commercial purchaser).

Under the Uniform Product Liability Act, a "product seller" subject to strict liability includes any party in the regular commercial distribution chain. It includes lessors and bailors of products, but excludes ordinary commercial sellers of used products. While acknowledging that the slight majority of decisions indicate that products liability law does apply to used products, the authors noted that those sellers are not held to the same standards as are sellers of new products. For this reason, resolution of the issue of potential liability of sellers of used products was left for resolution under other law of the state. See U.P.L.A. § 102(A), 44 FR 62717.

10. *Corporate Acquisitions.* An increasing business phenomenon is the acquisition of one corporation by another. How should this affect products liability? Should the acquiring corporation be subject to products liability claims in regard to items manufactured and sold before the takeover? See Ramirez v. Amsted Indus. Inc., 86 N.J. 332, 431 A.2d 811 (1981); Hausak v. Berkel, Inc., 341 A.2d 174 (Pa.1975); Domine v. Fulton Iron Works, 76 Ill.App. 3d 253, 32 Ill.Dec. 72, 395 N.E.2d 19 (1979). See generally, Phillips, Product Line Continuity and Successor Corporation Liability, 58 N.Y.U.L.Rev. 906 (1983); Schulman, Commentary: Successor Corporation Liability and the Inadequacy of the Product Line Continuity Approach, 31 Wayne L.Rev. 135 (1984); Phillips, Reply [to Schulman]: Product Line Continuity as the Basis for Successor Corporation Liability, 31 Wayne L.Rev. 149 (1984).

11. *Indemnity and Contribution.* As the principal case reflects, a relevant factor in determining which class of defendants should be subject to strict liability may be contribution or indemnity rights. There has been a good deal of litigation about these rights between retailer and manufacturer. Courts apply indemnity and contribution principles that have been utilized in negligence law. See supra pages 367–78. Suppose a retailer, by custom, inspects for defects, but fails to do so in one instance and plaintiff is injured. Who should ultimately bear this loss? Compare Ford Motor Co. v. Robert J. Poeschl, Inc., 21 Cal.App.3d 694, 98 Cal.Rptr. 702 (1972), with Goldstein v. Compudyne Corp.,

45 F.R.D. 467 (S.D.N.Y.1968). See generally, Phillips, Contribution and Indemnity in Products Liability, 42 Tenn.L.Rev. 141 (1974); Wade, Contribution and Indemnity in Products Liability Cases, 27th Ann.Miss.L.Inst. 115 (1972); Kissel, Contribution and Indemnity Among Strictly Liable Defendants, 15 For The Defense 133 (1975); Annot., 28 A.L.R.3d 943 (1969).

(B) REAL PROPERTY

BECKER v. IRM CORP.

Supreme Court of California, 1985.
38 Cal.3d 454, 698 P.2d 116, 213 Cal.Rptr. 213.

BROUSSARD, JUSTICE. In this personal injury action plaintiff's complaint asserted causes of action of strict liability and negligence against defendant landlord. Defendant moved for summary judgment urging that a landlord is not liable to a tenant for a latent defect of the rented premises absent concealment of a known danger or an expressed contractual or statutory duty to repair. The trial court granted the motion and denied a motion for reconsideration. Plaintiff appeals.

We have concluded that the trial court erred as to both causes of action.

The complaint alleged that plaintiff was injured when he slipped and fell against the frosted glass shower door in the apartment he leased from defendant. The door was made of untempered glass. It broke and severely lacerated his arm. It is undisputed that the risk of serious injury would have been substantially reduced if the shower door had been made of tempered glass rather than untempered glass.

Defendant's affidavits in support of the motion for summary judgment may be summarized as follows: Plaintiff's apartment is part of a 36–unit apartment complex built in 1962 and 1963 and acquired by defendant in 1974. Prior to the acquisition, two officers of defendant walked through most of the apartments and observed that all of the shower doors were of frosted glass and appeared to be the same. The officials, one of whom managed the property from the time of its acquisition, stated that prior to plaintiff's accident in 1978 there were no accidents involving the shower doors and that they were not advised that any of the shower doors were made of untempered glass. They first learned that some of the shower doors were of untempered glass after the accident. Their inspection of shower doors after the accident provided "no visible difference between the tempered and untempered glass in terms of visible appearance."

Defendant's maintenance man stated that after the accident he examined the glass doors, and that 31 of the doors with untempered glass were replaced by him. He also stated that in looking for the untempered glass shower doors "there was no way that a layperson could tell any difference by simply looking at the shower doors. The only way that I was able to differentiate * * * was by looking for a very small mark in the corner of each piece of glass." * * *

We follow a stream of commerce approach to strict liability in tort and extend liability to all those who are part of the "overall producing and marketing enterprise that should bear the cost of injuries from defective products." [C] The doctrine of strict liability in tort has been applied not only to manufacturers but to the various links in the commercial marketing chain including a retailer, a wholesale-retail distributor [c], personal property lessors and bailors [c], and a licensor of personalty [c]. *   *   *

We are satisfied that the rationale of the *   *   * cases, establishing the duties of a landlord and the doctrine of strict liability in tort, requires us to conclude that a landlord engaged in the business of leasing dwellings is strictly liable in tort for injuries resulting from a latent defect in the premises when the defect existed at the time the premises were let to the tenant. It is clear that landlords are part of the "overall producing and marketing enterprise" that makes housing accommodations available to renters. [Cc] A landlord, like defendant owning numerous units, is not engaged in isolated acts within the enterprise but plays a substantial role. The fact that the enterprise is one involving real estate may not immunize the landlord. *   *   *

Absent disclosure of defects, the landlord in renting the premises makes an implied representation that the premises are fit for use as a dwelling and the representation is ordinarily indispensable to the lease. [C] The tenant purchasing housing for a limited period is in no position to inspect for latent defects in the increasingly complex modern apartment buildings or to bear the expense of repair whereas the landlord is in a much better position to inspect for and repair latent defects. [C] The tenant's ability to inspect is ordinarily substantially less than that of a purchaser of the property. [C]

The tenant renting the dwelling is compelled to rely upon the implied assurance of safety made by the landlord. It is also apparent that the landlord by adjustment of price at the time he acquires the property, by rentals or by insurance is in a better position to bear the costs of injuries due to defects in the premises than the tenants.

In these circumstances, strict liability in tort for latent defects existing at the time of renting must be applied to insure that the landlord who markets the product bears the costs of injuries resulting from the defects "rather than the injured persons who are powerless to protect themselves." (*Greenman v. Yuba Power Products, Inc., supra* [page 714].)

Defendant argues that a landlord who purchases an existing building which is not new should be exempt from strict liability in tort for latent defects because, like dealers in used personalty, he assertedly is not part of the manufacturing and marketing enterprise. *   *   *

In several cases, it has been held that a seller of used machinery who does not rebuild or rehabilitate the machinery is not strictly liable in tort. [Cc] Each of these cases relied at least in part on the theory that the used machinery dealer simply by offering machinery for sale does not make any representation as to quality or durability and thus does not generate the expectation of safety involved in the sale of new goods. [Cc] When the seller of the used goods makes extensive modifications or reconditions, he is treated as a manufacturer—there is an expectation that the safety of the product has been addressed. [C]

* * *

However, a continuing business relationship is not essential to imposition of strict liability. The unavailability of the manufacturer is not a factor militating against liability of others engaged in the enterprise. The paramount policy of the strict products liability rule remains the spreading throughout society of the cost of compensating otherwise defenseless victims of manufacturing defects. [Cc] If anything, the unavailability of the manufacturer is a factor militating in favor of liability of persons engaged in the enterprise who can spread the cost of compensation. [C] Just as the unavailability of the manufacturer does not militate against liability, the absence of a continuing business relationship between builder and landlord is not a factor warranting denial of strict liability of the landlord.

Landlords are an integral part of the enterprise of producing and marketing rental housing. While used machinery is often scrapped or discarded so that resale for use may be the exception rather than the rule, landlords are essential to the rental business. They have more than a random or accidental role in the marketing enterprise. In addition, landlords have a continuing relationship to the property following the renting in contrast to the used machinery dealer who sells. As we have seen, in renting property the landlord, unlike the used machinery dealer, makes representations of habitability and safety.

The cost of protecting tenants is an appropriate cost of the enterprise. Within our marketplace economy, the cost of purchasing rental housing is obviously based on the anticipated risks and rewards of the purchase, and thus it may be expected that along with numerous other factors the price of used rental housing will depend in part on the quality of the building and reflect the anticipated costs of protecting tenants, including repairs, replacement of defects and insurance. Further, the landlord after purchase may be able to adjust rents to reflect such costs. The landlord will also often be able to seek equitable indemnity for losses.

We conclude that the absence of a continuing business relationship between builder and landlord does not preclude application of strict liability in tort for latent defects existing at the time of the lease because landlords are an integral part of the enterprise and they should bear the cost of injuries resulting from such defects rather than the injured persons who are powerless to protect themselves. (*Greenman v. Yuba Power Products, Inc., supra,* 59 Cal.2d 57, 63, 27 Cal.Rptr. 697.)

* * *

[The court also held that the defendant had a duty to inspect under negligence law even though he may not have known about the hazard.]

As to each cause of action the trial court erred in granting summary judgment in favor of defendant.

The judgment is reversed.

———

1. The law as to the negligence liability of builders and building contractors has, in general, developed along the same lines as that of the manufacturer of chattels, although it has tended to lag some twenty or thirty years behind it. The law as to the liability of lessors has lagged further still.

2. Among the misbegotten progeny of Winterbottom v. Wright were cases that construed it to mean that there could be no tort liability to any third person for the negligent performance of a contract by a builder or contractor. Included among them were a number of decisions involving mass disasters, such as Ford v. Sturgis, 56 App.D.C. 361, 14 F.2d 253 (1926), where the weight of snow on the roof of a motion picture theater collapsed the beams supporting it and the roof fell in on a theater audience. See also Galbraith v. Illinois Steel Co., 133 F. 485 (7th Cir.1904), where a huge steel water tank collapsed and fell through a building. These are now all overruled.

3. As in the case of manufacturers of chattels, the courts began their retreat from this rule by making exceptions, which gradually accumulated. In time the pressure of the analogy to chattels built up the point where the rule of the *MacPherson* case was accepted and applied to the real estate builder or contractor. Totten v. Gruzen, 52 N.J. 202, 245 A.2d 1 (1968) (all builders and contractors); Littleton v. B. & R. Constr. Co., 266 So.2d 560 (La.App.1972) (attic stairway collapsed—purchaser's spouse was injured); Jacobs v. Martz, 15 Mich. App. 186, 166 N.W.2d 303 (1968) (fireplace collapsed—purchaser of home injured); Cross v. M.C. Carlisle & Co., 368 F.2d 947 (1st Cir.1966) (negligent design).

If a financier becomes an active participant in a home construction enterprise and exercises control, he too may be subject to liability, at least with regard to the purchaser or members of his immediate family. See Connor v. Great W. Sav. & Loan Ass'n, 69 Cal.2d 850, 447 P.2d 609, 73 Cal.Rptr. 369 (1969).

4. Strict liability first entered the picture in the early 1960's when, by analogy to the sale of chattels, an implied warranty of habitability was held to run from the builder or vendor of a newly constructed home to his immediate buyer. See, e.g., Cochran v. Keeton, 287 Ala. 439, 252 So.2d 313 (1971); Carpenter v. Donohoe, 154 Colo. 78, 388 P.2d 399 (1964); Humber v. Morton, 426 S.W.2d 554 (Tex.1968). In some jurisdictions this has included not only personal injury but also damage to the purchased property. See Pollard v. Saxe & Yolles Dev. Co., 12 Cal.3d 374, 525 P.2d 88, 115 Cal.Rptr. 648 (1974); Weeks v. Slavik Builders, Inc., 384 Mich. 257, 181 N.W.2d 271 (1970). On the other hand other jurisdictions have clung to the rule of *caveat emptor* of the common law and refused to imply any warranty. See Welding Prods. of Georgia v. Kuniansky, 125 Ga.App. 537, 188 S.E.2d 278 (1972) (vendor-builder); Thomas v. Cryer, 251 Md. 725, 248 A.2d 795 (1969).

5. Courts have had difficulty applying this new warranty in specific fact situations and, as in the case of products liability, a question has arisen as to

whether there is a substantial difference between the strict liability and negligence standards. See, e.g., Shiffers v. Cunningham Shepherd Builders Co., 28 Colo.App. 29, 470 P.2d 593 (1970); Miller v. Los Angeles County Flood Control Dist., 8 Cal.3d 689, 505 P.2d 193, 106 Cal.Rptr. 1 (1973).

6. In 1965 the Supreme Court of New Jersey, in Schipper v. Levitt & Sons, Inc., 44 N.J. 70, 207 A.2d 314 (1965) extended an "implied warranty of habitability" to a third-party occupant who was scalded when he came in contact with excessively hot water drawn from the faucet in the bathroom sink. The court relied upon the fact that the defendant was involved in the "mass production and sale of homes," and indicated that the warranty meant only that the home would be "reasonably fit for the purpose for which it was sold." Berman v. Watergate West, Inc., 391 A.2d 1351 (D.C.App.1978), extended *Schipper* to cooperative apartments. To date the decision has been followed by a small number of other jurisdictions. These cases have involved a defective product or the faulty installation of a good product. See Fuqua Homes, Inc. v. Evanston Bldg. & Loan Co., 52 Ohio App.2d 399, 370 N.E.2d 780 (1977) (modular homes); Kriegler v. Eichler Homes, Inc., 269 Cal.App.2d 224, 74 Cal.Rptr. 749 (1969) (heating unit—strict liability in tort); Avner v. Longridge Estates, 272 Cal.App.2d 607, 77 Cal.Rptr. 633 (1969) (developer—improper filling and grading brought mudslide upon lot of nonpurchaser plaintiffs); State Stove Mfg. Co. v. Hodges, 189 So.2d 113 (Miss.1966) (defective hot water heater exploded).

7. *Vendors Who Are Not Builders.* A distinction is to be drawn between a vendor who sells a used house, and one who sells a house that he has himself built. The older rule of the common law was that a vendor was not liable to his vendee, or to other persons who might come upon the land, for harm resulting from a defective condition, that he did not disclose it. This has been the English rule. Bottomley v. Bannister, [1932] 1 K.B. 458. One of the leading American cases has been Smith v. Tucker, 151 Tenn. 347, 270 S.W. 66 (1925), where the vendor did not disclose his knowledge that a fireplace mantel was defective and it fell upon the tenant and injured him.

8. The Restatement of Torts § 353, stated that there was a duty upon the vendor to disclose known dangerous conditions. When this was first drawn, it was supported only by dicta in two cases and by the analogy of cases involving lessors. It has since been approved in several cases, such as Caporaletti v. A–F Corp., 137 F.Supp. 14 (D.D.C.1956), rev'd on other grounds, 240 F.2d 53 (D.C.Cir. 1957); Belote v. Memphis Dev. Co., 208 Tenn. 434, 346 S.W.2d 441 (1961); Bray v. Cross, 98 Ga.App. 612, 106 S.E.2d 315 (1958). There has also been a good deal of indirect support in cases allowing recovery for failure to disclose the known condition, in an action for deceit. In absence of fraud, the vendor will be subject to liability only until the vendee has had an opportunity to discover the condition and take appropriate precautions. See O'Connor v. Altus, 67 N.J. 106, 335 A.2d 545 (1975) (collecting cases—glass door—similar to principal case—nine years too long a time).

With regard to conditions that are disclosed, the vendor, in most states, is not subject to liability to the vendee. Compare Anderson v. Cosmopolitan Nat'l Bank of Chicago, 54 Ill.2d 504, 301 N.E.2d 296 (1973), with Farragher v. New York, 21 N.Y.2d 756, 235 N.E.2d 218, 288 N.Y.S.2d 232 (1968) (defective sprinkler—accident occurred in less time than it was possible to repair it—liability imposed).

When the hazard exposes persons outside of the premises to injury, the vendor, on a theory derived from the law of nuisance, may remain subject to liability until the vendee has had a reasonable time to correct the condition. See Narsh v. Zirbser Bros., Inc., 111 N.J.Super. 203, 268 A.2d 46 (1970) (falling tree—eleven months sufficient time for responsibility to shift).

9. When the vendor is a mass seller of homes, but takes no part in their construction or design, what tort law rules should be applied to him when a vendee or third party is injured? Cf. Bolkum v. Staab, 133 Vt. 467, 346 A.2d 210 (1975).

10. *Lessors of Real Property.* As the principal case and the cases and materials at pages 490–501 supra, indicate the lessor of real property has only recently been brought within the full negligence principle with regard to his lessee and third parties, let alone strict liability. Moreover, this development has occurred in only a few jurisdictions.

Although a number of courts have spoken of an "implied warranty of habitability" in connection with the lessor-lessee relationship, these words of art may only provide the lessee with a defense to an eviction action or with a right to withhold rent until repairs are executed. When should a lessor be subject to strict liability with respect to injuries that befall his lessee or third parties? See Love, Landlord's Liability for Defective Premises: Caveat Lessee, Negligence or Strict Liability? 1975 Wis.L.Rev. 19; Selman Products Liability at the Threshold of the Landlord–Lessor, 20 Hastings L.J. 458 (1970). Suppose the lessor rents a furnished apartment and plaintiff is injured when a defective couch collapses. Could the landlord be held strictly liable without broadly applying that theory to the lessor-lessee relationship? See Fakhoury v. Magner, 25 Cal.App.3d 58, 101 Cal.Rptr. 473 (1972). Should other jurisdictions follow the principal case? What will its effect be on the cost of apartment rentals? Is the "extra margin of protection" created by strict liability worth that cost? Can you think of cases where strict liability would result in a verdict against a landlord, but negligence principles would not?

11. *U.P.L.A. Approach.* Under the Uniform Products Liability Act, § 102(A) 44 FR 62717, the seller of real property is excluded from coverage as a "product seller," except for a builder-vendor engaged in the mass production and sale of standardized dwellings, including modular homes.

(C) SERVICES

NEWMARK v. GIMBEL'S INC.

Supreme Court of New Jersey, 1969.
54 N.J. 585, 258 A.2d 697.

[Plaintiff went to defendant's beauty parlor to have her hair washed and set. Defendant made use of a permanent wave solution called "Candle Glow," a product of Helene Curtis. As a result of the treatment, plaintiff developed acute dermatitis. Plaintiff brought suit, alleging negligence of the defendant, and breach of warranty of the product. The trial court dismissed the warranty counts, and submitted the case to the jury on the issue of negligence. The jury returned a verdict for defendant, and plaintiff appealed. The Appellate Division reversed, holding that there was a fact issue for the jury as to whether there was an implied warranty of the product applied. The Supreme Court granted the petition of defendants for certiorari.]

FRANCIS, J. * * * In dismissing the cause of action based on warranty, the trial court expressed the view that the transaction with Mrs. Newmark was not a sale within the contemplation of the Uniform Commercial Code § 2–106(1), but rather an agreement for the rendition of services. Therefore, it was not accompanied by any warranty of fitness of products used in rendering the services, and the liability of the beauty parlor was limited to the claim of negligence. Having in mind the nature of a permanent wave operation, we find that the distinction between a sale and the rendition of services is a highly artificial one. If the permanent wave solution were sold to Mrs. Newmark by defendants for consumption or application to enable her to give herself the permanent wave, unquestionably an implied warranty of fitness for that purpose would have been an integral incident of the same. Basically defendants argue that if, in addition to recommending the use of a lotion or other product and supplying it for use, they applied it, such fact (the application) would have the effect of lessening their liability to the patron by eliminating warranty and by limiting their responsibility to the issue of negligence. There is no just reason why it should. On the contrary, by taking on the administration of the product in addition to recommending and supplying it they might increase the scope of their liability, if the method of administration were improper (a result not suggested on this appeal because the jury found no negligence).

The transaction, in our judgment, is a hybrid partaking of incidents of a sale and a service. It is really partly the rendering of service, and partly the supplying of goods for a consideration. Accordingly, we agree with the Appellate Division that an implied warranty of fitness of the product used in giving the permanent wave exists with no less force than it would have in the case of a simple sale. [Cc] Obviously in permanent wave operations the product is taken into consideration in fixing the price of the service. The no-separate-charge argument puts excessive emphasis on form and downgrades the overall substance of the transaction. * * *

The oft quoted statement that in the modern commercial world the liability of a manufacturer or a retail seller of a product should not be made to depend strictly upon the intricacies of the law of sales is most pertinent here. [Cc] It was not the intention of the framers of the Uniform Commercial Code to limit the birth of implied warranties to transactions which technically meet its definition of a sale. * * * This Court has already said there is no sound reason for restricting implied warranties of fitness to conventional sales of goods. [Cc] It seems to us that the policy reasons for imposing warranty liability in the case of ordinary sales are equally applicable to a commercial transaction such as that existing in this case between a beauty parlor operator and a patron.

Although the policy reasons which generate the responsibility are essentially the same, practical administration suggests that the principle of liability be expressed in terms of strict liability in tort, thus enabling it to be applied in practice unconfined by the narrow conceptualism associated with the technical niceties of sales and implied warranties. (This seems to be the overall import of the Appellate Division statement that the "core" question is whether "warranty principles" permit a recovery in this kind of case.) One who, in the regular course of a business sells or applies a product (in the sense of the sales-service hybrid transaction involved in the present case) which is in such a dangerously defective condition as to cause harm to the consumer-patron, is liable for the harm. Consumption in this connection includes all ultimate uses for which the product is intended. * * * Obviously the ultimate use of the Helene Curtis permanent wave solution intended by both manufacturer and beauty parlor operator was its application to the hair of a patron. * * *

Defendants claim that to hold them to strict liability would be contrary to Magrine v. Krasnica (1967) 94 N.J.Super. 228, 227 A.2d 539, aff'd in Magrine v. Spector (1968) 100 N.J.Super. 223, 241 A.2d 637, aff'd 53 N.J. 259, 250 A.2d 129. We cannot agree. Magrine, a patient of the defendant-dentist, was injured when a hypodermic needle being used, concededly with due care, to administer a local anaesthetic broke off in his gum or jaw. The parties agreed that the break resulted from a latent defect in the needle. It was held that the strict liability in tort doctrine was not applicable to the professional man, such as a dentist, because the essence of the relationship with his patient was the furnishing of professional skill and services. We accepted the view that a dentist's bill for services should be considered as representing pay for that alone. The use of instruments, or the administration of medicines or the providing of medicines for the patient's home consumption cannot give the ministrations the cast of a commercial transaction. Accordingly the liability of the dentist in cases involving the ordinary relationship of doctor and patient must be tested by principles of negligence, i.e., lack of due care and not by application of the doctrine of strict liability in tort.

Defendants suggest that there is no doctrinal basis for distinguishing the services rendered by a beauty parlor operator from those rendered by a dentist or a doctor, and that consequently the liability of all three should be tested by the same principles. On the contrary there is a vast difference between the relationships. The beautician is engaged in a commercial enterprise; the dentist and doctor in a profession. The former caters publicly not to a need but to a form of aesthetic convenience or luxury, involving, the rendition of non-professional services and the application of products for which a charge is made. The dentist or doctor does not and cannot advertise for patients; the demand for his services stems from a felt necessity of the patient. In response to such a call the doctor, and to a somewhat lesser degree the dentist, exercises his best judgment in diagnosing the patient's ailment or disability, prescribing and sometimes furnishing medicines or other methods of treatment which he believes, and in some measure hopes, will relieve or cure the condition. His performance is not mechanical or routine because each patient requires individual study and formulation of an informed judgment as to the physical or mental disability or condition presented. * * *

Such men are not producers or sellers of property in any reasonably acceptable sense of the term. In a primary sense they furnish services in the form of an opinion of the patient's condition based upon their experienced analysis of the objective and subjective complaints, and in the form of recommended and, at times, personally administered medicines and treatment. * * * Thus their paramount function—the essence of their function—ought to be regarded as the furnishing of opinions and services. * * * In our judgment, the nature of the services, the utility of and the need for them involving as they do, the health and even survival of many people, are so important to the general welfare as to outweigh in the policy scale any need for the imposition on dentists and doctors of the rules of strict liability in tort. * * *

The judgment of the Appellate Division is affirmed for the reasons stated, and the cause is remanded for a new trial.

---

1. The principal case suggests the criterion for distinguishing those hybrid activities that will be subject to strict liability and those that will not is whether the activity is a professional enterprise rather than a commercial enterprise. Do you agree with the distinction made between a beautician and a dentist in this case? How would a pharmacist be treated under this criterion? See Murphy v. E.R. Squibb & Sons, Inc., 40 Cal.3d 672, 710 P.2d 247, 221 Cal. Rptr. 447 (1985).

2. A person undergoes plastic surgery in order to improve his appearance. The surgeon uses reasonable care in the course of the operation. Unfortunately, the surgical thread used by the physician proves to be defective; it dissolves too quickly and the individual's appearance is considerably worsened. Should the surgeon be subject to strict liability? Cf. Magner v. Beth Israel Hosp., 120 N.J.Super. 529, 295 A.2d 363 (1972).

3. One who renders services to another is under a duty to exercise reasonable care in doing so and is liable for any negligence to anyone who may foreseeably be expected to be injured if he fails. Thus a garage that negligently does repair work upon an automobile is liable for resulting injuries not only to the owner but to a pedestrian run down in the street by reason of the defect. Kalinowski v. Truck Equip. Co., 237 App.Div. 472, 261 N.Y.S. 657 (1933); Zierer v. Daniels, 40 N.J.Super. 130, 122 A.2d 377 (1956); Central & Southern Truck Lines v. Westfall G.M.C. Truck, Inc., 317 S.W.2d 841 (Mo.App.1958).

4. The attempt to extend strict liability to services, however, has generally failed. In Hoffman v. Simplot Aviation, Inc., 97 Idaho 32, 539 P.2d 584 (1975), plaintiff tried to impose the strict liability standard on a company that repaired a private airplane. In declining to accept plaintiff's proposal, the Supreme Court of Idaho observed: "It is sufficient to say that as contrasted with the sales of products, personal services do not involve mass production with the difficulty, if not inability, of the obtention of proof of negligence. The consumer in the personal service context usually comes into direct contact with the one offering service and is aware or can determine what work was

performed and who performed it." In Held v. 7–Eleven Food Store, 438 N.Y.S.2d 976 (1980), the court found that a concrete walkway located in front of the store which collapsed, causing injury to the plaintiff, was a service rather than a product which the defendant regularly distributed to the consuming public, and thus was not a basis for recovery under strict liability.

And in Swett v. Gribaldo, Jones & Assocs., 40 Cal.App.3d 573, 115 Cal.Rptr. 99 (1974), a California court declined to impose the strict liability rule on a soils engineer although it had applied that standard to mass builder-vendors of real estate.

Other courts have also been reluctant to impose strict liability on services. See Samuelson v. Chutich, 187 Colo. 155, 529 P.2d 631 (1974) (defendant installed a gas line); Hoover v. Montgomery Ward & Co., 270 Or. 498, 528 P.2d 76 (1974) (defendant mounted tire on vehicle); Flippo v. Mode O'Day Frock Shops of Hollywood, 248 Ark. 1, 449 S.W.2d 692 (1970) (plaintiff bit by a spider while trying on a dress); La Rossa v. Scientific Design Co., 402 F.2d 937 (3d Cir. 1968) (supervision of construction—plaintiff's decedent exposed to vanadium dust contracted cancer). What should be the result when the repairer of a product is also the manufacturer? See Young v. Aro Corp., 36 Cal.App.3d 240, 111 Cal.Rptr. 535 (1973).

Courts have also declined to impose strict liability on ordinary activities such as driving. See Hammontree v. Jenner, 20 Cal.App.3d 528, 532, 97 Cal. Rptr. 739, 742 (1971) ("it is not enough to simply say * * * that the insurance carriers should be the ones to bear the cost * * * "). One court has applied strict liability to a company that reconditioned and repaired a football helmet, on the grounds that it was not just providing a service but was an "expert in the condition of athletic equipment." Gentile v. MacGregor Mfg. Co., 201 N.J. Super. 612, 493 A.2d 647 (1985).

Are there some "products" that do not fit well within the strict liability rationales? What about a female Doberman Pinscher? See Whitmer v. Schneble, 29 Ill.App.3d 659, 331 N.E.2d 115 (1975).

5. Even when a product has been supplied in the course of the service, strict liability has often been denied. See Sergermeister v. Recreation Corp. of America, 314 So.2d 626 (Fla.App.1975) (amusement park ride); Wagner v. Coronet Hotel, 10 Ariz.App. 296, 458 P.2d 390 (1969) (bath mat in hotel room); Gilliland v. Rothermel, 83 Ill.App.3d 116, 38 Ill.Dec. 528, 403 N.E.2d 759 (1980) (service station owner loaned defective tire gauge to plaintiff). This is especially true when the defendant has been a "professional." See Carmichael v. Reitz, 17 Cal.App.3d 958, 95 Cal.Rptr. 381 (1971) (physician prescribed drug—patient suffered adverse reaction); Silverhart v. Mount Zion Hosp., 20 Cal.App.3d 1022, 98 Cal.Rptr. 187 (1971) (defective surgical needle imbedded in patient); Magrine v. Spector, 100 N.J.Super. 223, 241 A.2d 637 (1968) (dentist—hypodermic needle); Dubin v. Michael Reese Hosp. and Medical Center, 83 Ill.2d 277, 47 Ill. Dec. 345, 415 N.E.2d 350 (1980) (x-radiation).

6. On the other hand, restaurants have long been subject to strict liability when they have supplied defective food. See Friend v. Childs Dining Hall Co., 231 Mass. 65, 120 N.E. 407 (1918). And the principal case was followed in Carpenter v. Best's Apparel, Inc., 4 Wash.App. 439, 481 P.2d 924 (1971). In Worrell v. Barnes, 87 Nev. 204, 484 P.2d 573 (1971), a contractor was held strictly liable for supplying defective gas pipe fittings; and, in Hoffman v. Misericordia Hospital, 439 Pa. 501, 267 A.2d 867 (1970), the supplying of blood was held to be a "sale," not a "service" (court reserved issue as to whether

defendant might avoid strict liability on the ground that the product was "unavoidably unsafe"). Can these cases be distinguished from those in Note 5, supra? Suppose plaintiff believes she was injured by a defective contact lens and wants to bring a claim against the optician that fitted and sold them to her. Strict liability? See Barbee v. Rogers, 425 S.W.2d 342 (Tex.1968). In a number of states, court decisions holding the provision of blood or blood products to a strict liability standard resulted in the legislatures passing statutes making the distribution of blood, blood products and organs a service and not the sale of a product, in order to take it out of strict liability.

7. In Buckeye Union Fire Ins. Co. v. Detroit Edison Co., 38 Mich.App. 325, 196 N.W.2d 316 (1972), the court extended the implied warranty concept against a seller of electricity. The court said that plaintiff had to show there was a "defect" in the electricity at the time it left the plant. Cf. Pierce v. Pacific Gas & Elec., 166 Cal.App.3d 68, 212 Cal.Rptr. 283 (1985); and Smith v. Home Light & Power, 695 P.2d 788 (Colo.App.1984). In general, courts have held that electricity is not a product and not subject to strict liability, at least while it is being transmitted on utility lines. See, e.g., Public Serv. Indiana, Inc. v. Nichols, 494 N.E.2d 349 (Ind.App.1986); Smith v. Home Light & Power Co., 734 P.2d 1051 (Colo.1987); Schriner v. Pennsylvania Power & Light Co., 348 Pa.Super. 177, 501 A.2d 1128 (1985) (electricity is a "product" when it has entered the stream of commerce, i.e., after it has left the transmission lines and passed through the customer's meter).

Two other unusual cases are Schnitzer v. Nixon, 439 F.2d 940 (4th Cir.1971) (chair collapsed in hotel—implied warranty imposed); Johnson v. Sears, Roebuck & Co., 355 F.Supp. 1065 (E.D.Wis.1973) (hospitals strictly liable for administrative as opposed to medical services).

8. It has been suggested that landholders be held strictly liable for slips and falls experienced by their commercial invitees. See Ursin, Strict Liability For Defective Business Premises—One Step Beyond *Rowland* and *Greenman*, 22 UCLA L.Rev. 820 (1975). What strict liability policies support this result? What implications does it have for tort law?

9. The Uniform Product Liability Act excludes from its coverage the provider of professional services when a product is utilized or sold within the scope of such services. See U.P.L.A. § 102(A), 44 FR 62717.

10. Recall that some services may be considered "abnormally dangerous activities." See Chapter 14, supra pages 673–88. In this area, the two roads of strict liability come together. Cf. Kelley v. R.G. Indus., Inc., 304 Md. 124, 497 A.2d 1143 (1985) ("the abnormally dangerous activity doctrine does not apply to the manufacture or marketing of handguns").

11. See generally, Powers, Distinguishing Between Products and Services in Strict Liability, 62 N.C.L.Rev. 415 (1984); Dubin v. Michael Reese Hosp. & Medical Center: Seeing through the Product/Service Distinction, 48 Ins.Couns. J. 399 (1981); Application of Products Liability Principles to Professional Services, 48 Ins.Couns.J. 434 (1981); Farnsworth, Implied Warranties of Quality in Non–Sales Cases, 57 Colum.L.Rev. 653 (1957); Annots., 29 A.L.R.3d 1425 (1970); 54 A.L.R.3d 258 (1974).

(D) ENDORSERS

YUHAS v. MUDGE

Superior Court of New Jersey, 1974.
129 N.J.Super. 207, 322 A.2d 824.

HALPERN, P.J.A.D. The novel question presented on this appeal is whether a magazine publisher may be held responsible in negligence for injuries resulting from the use by a paying customer of an alleged defective product advertised in its magazine, when it does not manufacture, distribute, sell, warrant or endorse the product. The trial judge found that no actionable duty existed against the publisher and granted summary judgment in favor of respondents. We affirm.

Defendants Christie and Ecco Products, Inc., manufacturers and sellers of fireworks, placed a paid advertisement in Popular Mechanics Magazine published by respondents Popular Mechanics Corp. and Hearst Corp.[1] Defendants Floyd Mudge and Michael Lashutka saw the advertisement and purchased the fireworks directly from Christie and Ecco. Infant plaintiffs Barry Yuhas and Larry Yuhas sustained personal injuries when the fireworks were exploded by Floyd Mudge. Admittedly, respondents did not manufacture, distribute, sell, test, warrant or endorse the fireworks; nor is there any indication in the record that they have ever received any direct pecuniary benefit from any sales of the multitude of products advertised in their magazine.

This suit was instituted against William Mudge, the owner of the property where the accident occurred; Floyd Mudge the purchaser of the fireworks and the one who invited plaintiffs to see the fireworks and who exploded them; Michael Lashutka, who purchased the fireworks with Floyd Mudge; Edwin Christie and Ecco Products Inc., manufacturers and sellers of the fireworks, and respondents, printers and publishers of the advertisement.

We are concerned only with the dismissal of plaintiffs' complaint against respondents. * * *

The thesis advanced by appellants to recover from respondents is that they publish a pseudo-scientific publication which has acquired an "aura of authentativeness" in the public's mind and, therefore, they owed the reading public the duty to investigate and test inherently dangerous products advertised in their publication. They argue this is particularly true since the sale of fireworks is proscribed in New Jersey by N.J.S.A. 21:3–2. We disagree, and hold that no such legal duty rests upon respondents unless it undertakes to guarantee, warrant or endorse the product. To impose the suggested broad legal duty upon publishers of nationally circulated magazines, newspapers and other

---

1. The advertisement read:

PYROTECHNIC Caseings, stars, devices of all types. send 50¢ for samples. Ecco, Box 189, Northvale, New Jersey 07647 [sic]

UNDERWATER Fuse 81 feet $1.00. Professional green fuse, 45 feet $1.00. Christie, Box 85, Bergenfield, New Jersey 07621

publications, would not only be impractical and unrealistic, but would have a staggering adverse effect on the commercial world and our economic system. For the law to permit such exposure to those in the publishing business who in good faith accept paid advertisements for a myriad of products would open the doors "to a liability in an indeterminate amount for an indeterminate time to an indeterminate class." Ultramares Corp. v. Touche, Niven & Co., 255 N.Y. 170, 174 N.E. 441, 444 (Ct.App.1931). * * *

It is significant to note that the condemnation of the unlawful practice of unconscionable commercial advertising exempts publishers when they have "no knowledge of the intent, design or purpose of the advertiser." N.J.S.A. 56:8–2.

Affirmed.

---

1. A rule developed in negligence cases was that one who sells as his own a product manufactured by another has the responsibility of the manufacturer. Swift & Co. v. Blackwell, 84 F.2d 130 (4th Cir.1936); Penn v. Inferno Mfg. Corp., 199 So.2d 210 (La.App.1967); Sears, Roebuck & Co. v. Morris, 273 Ala. 218, 136 So.2d 883 (1961). Initially this was put on the basis of an estoppel to deny that he has made the goods himself. Today it is usually put, as in § 400 of the Restatement (Second) of Torts, on the ground that he has vouched for the product and assumed responsibility for proper care in its manufacture.

This is now being carried over to strict liability. See, for example, E.I. du Pont de Nemours and Co. v. McCain, 414 F.2d 369 (5th Cir.1969); Schwartz v. Macrose Lumber & Trim Co., 50 Misc.2d 547, 270 N.Y.S.2d 875 (Sup.Ct.1966). Cf. Gizzi v. Texaco, Inc., 437 F.2d 308 (3d Cir.1971); Chevron Oil Co. v. Sutton, 85 N.M. 679, 515 P.2d 1283 (1973).

2. Liability may also be imposed on a negligence basis when an endorser specifically certifies that a product is safe. See Hempstead v. General Fire Extinguisher Corp., 269 F.Supp. 109 (D.Del.1967). In Hanberry v. Hearst Corp., 276 Cal.App.2d 680, 81 Cal.Rptr. 519 (1969) (partially reprinted in regard to another point, infra page 1072), this was carried a bit further when defendant advertised a pair of shoes in its magazine and granted its "Good Housekeeping Seal of Approval" to the product. The seal stated, in part, "We satisfy ourselves that products advertised in Good Housekeeping are good ones and that the claims made for them in our magazine are truthful." The court held that plaintiff stated a claim for negligent misrepresentation when she fell while wearing the shoes. How does this differ from the principal case? What result should obtain if an endorsement is made by a nonprofit organization such as Consumer's Union? What about an endorsement made by a professional athlete or movie star?

3. Even the *Hanberry* court rejected strict liability. This meant, in part, that plaintiff would have to show that the shoes in question were negligently designed. She could not recover by showing that the individual shoes she purchased had a defect in construction. Why this difference? A strong dictum in Kasel v. Remington Arms Co., 24 Cal.App.3d 711, 101 Cal.Rptr. 314 (1972), suggested that strict liability be imposed on a product endorser when its conduct induced the purchase and its participatory connection was for personal profit and helped create consumer demand and reliance upon the product. Do

not advertisements in newspapers and television amount to the same thing? Is this more an area for regulation by the Federal Government than by state tort law? See Elliott, Consumer Advocates Push Print Media to Screen Advertising, Wall Street Journal 1 (6/27/75).

Most decisions are based on the law of negligent misrepresentation and appear to be in accord with the principal case. See MacKown v. Illinois Publishing & Printing Co., 289 Ill.App. 59, 6 N.E.2d 526 (1937) (dandruff formula). Cf. De Bardeleben Marine Corp. v. United States, 451 F.2d 140 (5th Cir.1971) (accuracy of map); Jaillet v. Cashman, 115 Misc. 383, 189 N.Y.S. 743 (1921), aff'd mem., 202 App.Div. 805, 194 N.Y.S. 947 (1922), aff'd mem., 235 N.Y. 511, 139 N.E. 714 (1923) (accuracy of stock market news). A recent case involving an advertisement for a hair transplant reaffirmed *Yuhas* and held that plaintiff must show recklessness on the part of the advertisers. See Suarez v. Underwood, 103 Misc.2d 445, 426 N.Y.S.2d 208 (1980).

4. See generally, Carlin, Liability of the Product Endorser—Developing a New Perspective, 15 N.Y.L.F. 835 (1969); Notes: Trademark—Strict Tort Liability in Warranty of a Franchisor—Consumer Reliance on Trade Names (1980) 71 N.Ky.L.Rev. 112; Products Liability: Imposing Strict Products Liability on the Trademark Licensor (1980) 5 U.Day.L.Rev. 409.

Legislation on the Subject of Products Liability

1. *State Legislation.* The Uniform Commercial Code has been enacted in all of the states except Louisiana. Chapter 2 of the Code, on Sales, has had an important effect, but in the great majority of states it has simply provided an additional remedy, and the common law tort remedies continue to exist.

Beginning in the 1960's, statutes directly applicable to the tort law were enacted in a number of states. For example, three of them enacted Restatement (Second) of Torts § 402A, and it became a part of the statutory law.

During the latter half of the 1970's, there occurred the experience known as the "products liability crisis." Suits had been multiplying, and based on this and judicial modification of the law in some states, liability insurance rates shot up dramatically. Manufacturers and other suppliers were led to believe that the prime cause was the substantive law of products liability. Pressures on the state legislatures became irresistible in many states, and comprehensive statutes were passed, in an emergency climate, making diverse changes in the law to decrease the size and number of recoveries against manufacturers and sellers. These statutes still remain on the books. They make changes in such legal aspects as statutes of limitation and repose, significance of state of the art, effect of alteration or misuse of the product, effect of compliance with governmental standards, elimination of strict liability against retailers, and contributory negligence and assumption of the risk. The various statutes are collected and set forth in 2 CCH Prod.Liab.Rptr., ¶¶ 90,000–92,602 (1981). There is a chart providing a convenient survey of the legislation in 17 Trial [No. 11] 92–97 (Nov. 1981).

More recently, state legislatures have shifted their approach away from product liability-specific statutes to more generic tort legislation. In 1986 and 1987, in a climate of another and even more severe "liability crisis," 41 states passed some type of tort reform legislation. Some legislation contained limits on damages, modification or elimination of joint and several liability, limitations on punitive damages, changes in the collateral source rule and regulation of attorneys' contingency fees. In some states, legislation was limited to particular categories of tort liability such as medical malpractice.

2. *Federal Action.* The crisis atmosphere also reached the Federal Government, with thousands of letters being sent to the President and Congress. In 1976, the Ford Administration established a Federal Interagency Task Force on product liability to study the problem. Chaired by Professor Victor Schwartz, the Task Force continued into the Carter Administration and issued its findings in a Final Report issued in November, 1977. See Final Report Interagency Task Force on Product Liability (National Technical Information Service—Report No. 273–220).

The Task Force found that the product liability problem related both to the liability of manufacturers for injuries caused by products and the cost and availability of product liability insurance. Product liability problems in the pharmaceutical and other high risk product lines reinforced trends against new product development. See Final Report at XXVII. Product liability costs substantially affected the cost of some products, but not all. Circumstantial evidence suggested that substantial product liability premiums were one of several factors that caused small businesses in high risk product lines to go out of business. The Task Force predicted that in the future some small businesses would be placed in default by product liability judgments.

After the Report was issued, the Carter Administration asked Professor Schwartz to set up a new Task Force at the Department of Commerce to develop remedies to address the product liability problem. The remedies that were developed focused on what the Task Force found to be the causes of the problem.

The Task Force found that one of the principal causes of the problem was overly subjective insurance rate-making practices. To address this aspect of the problem, the new Task Force designed legislation known as the "Risk Retention Act." The Risk Retention Act did two principal things. First, it facilitated the ability of businesses to form their own self-insurance cooperatives. Conflicting and overlapping state regulation had made it extremely difficult for product sellers from different states to group together in self-insurance pools. The Task Force's theory was that if product sellers had a ready means to form self-insurance groups, this would create a competitive element in the product liability insurance market that would place pressure on commercial insurers to set rates and premiums on a more accurate basis. Second, the Risk Retention Act would enable product sellers to form "purchasing groups" that could bargain collectively for lower rates on commercial liability insurance. Laws and regulations called "fictitious group prohibitions" precluded these actions in the overwhelming majority of states.

The Product Liability Risk Retention Act was enacted into law in the 97th Congress. See PL 97–45. It was the first major Federal product liability legislation enacted by the Congress of the United States. The 99th Congress enacted the Risk Retention Act Amendments of 1986 which broadened the Act to permit self-insurance of any liability risks of businesses, professionals and non-profit organizations. (H.R. 5225 and S. 2129, 99th Cong.2d Sess. (1986)). In 1986–87 several dozen risk retention groups were formed.

The Task Force found that a second major cause of the product liability problem was the uncertainty and imbalance in the tort law. The Report stated: "The instability of product liability law has increased costs apart from verdicts and settlements. It has created a climate where it may be rational for plaintiff's lawyer to bring a case, although existing rules suggest it cannot be won. It has apparently increased defense costs and investigation costs." Final Report at I–28.

To address this cause of the product liability problem, the Carter Administration asked the Task Force to draft a Uniform Product Liability Act. The Act was to help bring about more stable product liability law in the United States. It was offered as a model for state enactment. The Model Act which was published in late October of that year, has become the basis for action in a handful of states. See 44 Fed. Reg. 62714. References to pertinent provisions of the Act have been made in the Notes throughout this Chapter.

By 1981, many business and insurance organizations became convinced that the instability in the product liability problem could not be corrected by state action. This fact was also reflected in the views of some members of Congress. In June, 1982, Senator Robert Kasten, who chaired the Consumer Subcommittee of the Senate Commerce Committee, introduced S. 2531, a Federal product liability act.

The bill was reported out by the Senate Commerce Committee in the 97th Congress. Senator Kasten introduced a very similar bill, S. 44, in the 98th Congress. Again, the bill was reported out of the Senate Commerce Committee but both times Congress adjourned without Senate action on either of these bills. Senator Kasten introduced S. 100 in the 99th Congress, but that bill was defeated in the Committee. At that time, the Chairman of the Committee, Senator John C. Danforth, instructed his staff to draft a bill that would contain some of the product liability rules in the prior bills and also an alternative no-fault compensation system for injured persons. As a result of several draft bills, which were reviewed and discussed at Committee hearings, Senator Danforth substituted for the compensation system a system designed to encourage settlement of product liability claims. In June, 1986, the Committee reported out S. 2760, a bill which contains a settlement system and some uniform product liability rules. This bill was debated on the Senate Floor in September, 1986, but further action on the bill was not taken, as the Senate was pressed to move on to other matters in the waning days of the 99th Congress. Bills were reintroduced in the Senate in the 100th Congress. (S. 666, S. 687 and S. 688, 100th Cong., 1st Sess. (1987)).

The House of Representatives also has been examining proposals for Federal product liability reform legislation. In the 99th Congress, the House established a product liability task force to study and develop the proposals. The task force is made up of 27 House members. In 1987, Representative Bill Richardson of New Mexico introduced a more concise product liability bill, H.R. 1115. It restored a negligence standard for design and warning claims. During subcommittee deliberations on the bill (within the House Energy and Commerce Committee), the standard of liability was changed to strict liability, with several limitations, including defenses for state of the art, unavoidably unsafe products and products whose risks are inherent characteristics. As of March, 1988, the bill had attracted close to 100 co-sponsors in the House of Representatives, but a long and bumpy road to passage lay ahead.

A predicate for Federal action is that product liability insurance rates are set on a nationwide, not a state-by-state basis. Therefore, action by one or more individual states does little to stabilize product liability insurance rate-making practices. Moreover, it has been argued that product sellers need uniform rules in order to do business in interstate commerce. Likewise, it has been argued that it is unfair for consumer rights to vary with respect to the exact same product simply because they were injured in one state or another. Do you think that product liability law differs sufficiently from tort law to justify Federal action?

Some industries are faced with the threat of extinction because of product liability problems, so Congress has considered legislation for specific industries. One such industry is the general aviation industry for which the cost of product liability has increased from $27 million in 1977 to $210 million in 1985. Bills were introduced in the House and Senate codifying the liability standards for general aviation (small plane) manufacturers. (H.R. 2238 and S. 473, 100th Cong., 1st Sess. (1987)).

The product liability crisis faced by asbestos manufacturers became so severe that they sought Federal legislation that would set up a compensation system (as compared to a mere reform of the tort law). Representative Henry A. Waxman of California introduced a vaccine compensation bill which was passed by both the House and Senate in October, 1986 (H.R. 5546 and S. 1744, 99th Cong. 2d Sess. (1986)). President Reagan signed the bill into law on November 14, 1986, and it became effective after Congress passed separate legislation to fund the compensation program. Can product liability problems be resolved by reform of tort law or are compensation system approaches necessary? See Schwartz & Mahshigian, National Childhood Vaccine Injury Act of 1986: An Ad Hoc Remedy or a Window for the Future? 48 Ohio St.L.J. 387 (1987).

Federal statutory invasion of tort law occurs not only when Congress expressly creates a cause of action, but also when a court creates a claim by implication. This is a modern problem of negligence per se. Federal law also has been used by state courts in their own tort laws to set a standard of care.

Congress did not take the opportunity to create an entire fabric of substantive tort law when it enacted the Federal Tort Claims Act in 1946. Why do you think Congress chose to rely on state law in this instance? See Lunter, "No–Fault" and the Federal Tort Claims Act: A Conflict in Philosophies, 41 Ins.Couns.J. 609 (1974). Congress resisted the effort to reform the automobile accident reparation system at the Federal level through a Federal no-fault automobile compensation system.

Are there certain torts for which a uniform statutory approach is particularly desirable? Are they torts which, by their very nature, cannot be dealt with by one state? Are there torts that should always be regulated by the states? Do you think that the recent federal statutory developments in tort law represent a trend or an aberration?

Chapter XVI

NUISANCE

The term "nuisance" is surrounded by a great deal of legal confusion. The word itself, which is taken over from the French, means nothing more than harm, annoyance or inconvenience. The courts customarily speak of "a" nuisance as if it were a type of conduct on the part of the defendant or a condition created by him. Actually it is neither. The word has reference to a kind of interest invaded, a type of damage or harm. Nuisance is a field of liability, rather than a particular tort.

Nuisance covers two fields of liability—two distinct kinds of damage or harm. The two have little in common, and are unrelated except as each involves the basic idea of causing harm or inconvenience to someone, which is common to all torts. It is only by the accident of historical development that the same word is used to cover the two; but the use of the common term has led to the application of much the same rules to both.

Public Nuisance. The earliest cases involved purprestures, encroachments upon the royal domain or the public highway. An obstruction of the public highway is still a typical public nuisance. The remedy was gradually extended to cover other miscellaneous invasions of the public right. The remedy was exclusively a criminal one until 1536, when it was first recognized that a private individual who had suffered special damage could maintain a tort action. Y.B. 27 Hen. VIII, Mich., pl. 10 (1536).

In the United States public nuisances are now very largely covered by statute. There are many types of specific criminal provisions covering such things as black currant plants, buildings where narcotics are sold, or waters that breed mosquitoes. In addition, many states have broad criminal statutes covering "public nuisances" without attempting to define them, which are construed to include anything that would have been a public nuisance at common law.

Because of its historical development, the traditional view has been that for public nuisance to be a tort justifying private relief it must also be a crime—either a recognized crime at common law or a violation of a legislative provision. Concern for protection of the environment, however, has caused this assumption to be questioned. After considerable debate, the American Law Institute decided to go behind the statement that a public nuisance is a crime and to define it in terms that would indicate both why the interference with a public right is treated as criminal and why it should be a tort.

The Restatement (Second) of Torts § 821B now defines a public nuisance as "an unreasonable interference with a right common to the general public," and then provides that "circumstances that may sustain a holding that an interference with a public right is unreasonable include the following: (a) whether the conduct involves a substantial interference with the public health, the public safety, the public peace, the public comfort or the public convenience, or (b) whether the conduct is proscribed by a statute, ordinance or administrative regulation, or (c) whether the conduct is of a continuing nature or has produced a permanent or long-lasting effect and, to the actor's knowledge, has a substantial detrimental effect upon the public right." For discussion, see Wade, Environmental Protection, the Common Law of Nuisance and the Restatement of Torts, 8 Forum 165 (1972); and Bryson and Macbeth, Public Nuisance, the Restatement (Second) of Torts, and Environmental Law, 2 Ecology L.Q. 241 (1972).

Private Nuisance. This form of the tort action developed as an unreasonable interference with the use or enjoyment of a property interest in land. It is essentially a tort to an owner or possessor of land. It is distinguished from trespass, in that it did not require a physical entry upon the plaintiff's premises, although it might accompany a trespass.

The interference might be with the physical condition of the premises, as by blasting or vibration that damages a house; with the health of the occupant, as by unsanitary conditions adjoining; with his comfort or convenience, as by smoke, odors, noise or heat; or merely with his peace of mind, as in the case of a nearby bawdy house or funeral parlor. A threat of future injury may be treated as a present menace and interference with enjoyment, as in the case of stored explosives or a vicious dog.

Particular conduct may result in both a public and a private nuisance, or in neither. See the principal case following this introduction. See also City of Fort Smith v. Western Hide & Fur Co., 153 Ark. 99, 239 S.W. 724 (1922); Mandell v. Pivnick, 20 Conn.Sup. 99, 125 A.2d 175 (1956); and Frady v. Portland General Electric Co., 55 Or.App. 344, 637 P.2d 1345 (1981). The plaintiff may then proceed on either ground, or both, to the extent that he can make out his cause of action. Also, unless the facts show an interference with a public right, or with the use and enjoyment of land, there is simply no nuisance at all.

See generally McRae, Development of Nuisance in the Early Common Law, 1 U.Fla.L.Rev. 27 (1948); Winfield, Nuisance as Tort, 4 Camb.L.J. 189 (1931).

On the relationship of nuisance to other torts, see Friedman, Nuisance, Negligence and the Overlapping of Torts, 3 Mod.L.Rev. 305 (1940); P. Keeton, Trespass, Nuisance and Strict Liability, 59 Colum.L. Rev. 457 (1959).

PHILADELPHIA ELECTRIC COMPANY v. HERCULES, INC.

United States Court of Appeals, Third Circuit, 1985.

762 F.2d 303.

A. LEON HIGGINBOTHAM, JR., CIRCUIT JUDGE. This is an appeal from a final judgment of the district court in favor of Philadelphia Electric Company ("PECO") and against Hercules, Inc. ("Hercules") in the amount of $394,910.14, and further ordering Hercules to take all appropriate action to eliminate pollution on a property owned by PECO in Chester, Pennsylvania. The case was tried to a jury on theories of public and private nuisance. For the reasons set forth in the opinion that follows, we will reverse the judgment against Hercules on PECO's claims, and vacate the injunction. * * *

[The property in question, "the Chester site," had been owned, prior to October 1971, by the Pennsylvania Industrial Chemical Corporation ("PICCO"), where it operated a hydrocarbon resin manufacturing plant. PICCO sold the facility to "Gould" in 1971. Gould sold the site to plaintiff Philadelphia Electric Co. ("PECO") in 1974. PECO had owned an adjoining site and had full opportunity to inspect and investigate the condition of the property. Subsequently Hercules, Inc. became the successor to PICCO, expressly assuming all debts, obligations and liabilities. This action is therefore held properly brought against Hercules. The court treats the relationship between defendant Hercules and plaintiff PECO as "that of a vendor and remote vendee of land." It holds that the sale of the site was subject to the rule of caveat emptor, being between two commercial corporations with no misrepresentation or concealment and full opportunity to inspect.

In 1980 the Pennsylvania Department of Environmental Resources ("DER") discovered that resinous materials similar to those once produced by PICCO were seeping into the Delaware River and directed PECO to develop and act on a plan to eliminate the situation. In all PECO spent or lost almost $400,000.

Suit against Hercules for the damages and an injunction requiring defendant to abate any further pollution. The district court granted both. The suit is based on private nuisance, public nuisance and indemnity.]

Restatement (Second) of Torts § 821D defines a "private nuisance" as "a nontrespassory invasion of another's interest in the private use and enjoyment of land." The briefs and arguments, as well as the district court's opinion, 587 F.Supp. at 152–54, give much attention to the questions of whether the condition created by Hercules on the Chester site amounted to a nuisance, and whether Hercules remains liable for the nuisance even after vacating the land. For the purposes of our decision, we may assume that Hercules created a nuisance, and that it remains liable for this condition. See *Restatement (Second) of Torts* § 840A. The crucial and difficult question for us is *to whom* Hercules may be liable.

The parties have cited no case from Pennsylvania or any other jurisdiction, and we have found none, that permits a purchaser of real property to recover from the seller on a private nuisance theory for conditions existing on the very land transferred, and thereby to circumvent limitations on vendor liability inherent in the rule of *caveat emptor*. In a somewhat analogous circumstance, courts have not permitted *tenants* to circumvent traditional limitations on the liability of *lessors* by the expedient of casting their cause of action for defective conditions existing on premises (over which they have assumed control) as one for private nuisance. [cc] In *Harris v. Lewistown Trust Co.*, 326 Pa. 145, 191 A. 34 (1937), [c] the Supreme Court of Pennsylvania held that the doctrine that a landlord not in possession may be liable for injuries resulting from a "condition amounting to a nuisance" is confined to "the owners or occupants of near-by property, persons temporarily on such property, or persons on a neighboring highway or other places." [6] [C] Recovery on this theory was not available to tenants or their invitees: "A breach of duty owed to one class of persons cannot create a cause of action in favor of a person not within the class. A plaintiff must show that as to him there was a breach of duty." 326 Pa. at 152, 191 A. at 38. Similarly, under the doctrine of *caveat emptor* Hercules owed only a limited duty to Gould and, in turn, to PECO. PECO concedes that this duty was not violated. PECO cannot recover in private nuisance for the violation of a duty Hercules may have owed to others—namely, its neighbors.

We believe that this result is consonant with the historical role of private nuisance law as a means of efficiently resolving conflicts between *neighboring,* contemporaneous land uses. * * * Neighbors, unlike the purchasers of the land upon which a nuisance exists, have no opportunity to protect themselves through inspection and negotiation. The record shows that PECO acted as a sophisticated and responsible purchaser—inquiring into the past use of the Chester site, and inspecting it carefully. We find it inconceivable that the price it offered Gould did not reflect the possibility of environmental risks, even if the exact condition giving rise to this suit was not discovered. * * *

Where, as here, the rule of *caveat emptor* applies, allowing a vendee a cause of action for private nuisance for conditions existing on the land transferred—where there has been no fraudulent concealment—would in effect negate the market's allocations of resources and risks, and subject vendors who may have originally sold their land at appropriately discounted prices to unbargained-for liability to remote vendees. * * * Such an extension of common law doctrine is particularly hazardous in an area, such as environmental pollution, where Congress and the state legislatures are actively seeking to achieve a socially

---

6. *Cf. Restatement (Second) of Torts* § 840A and comment c thereto ("If the vendor or lessor has himself created on the land a condition that results in a nuisance, * * * *his responsibility toward those outside of his land* is such that he is not free to terminate his liability to them * * * by passing the land itself on to a third person.") (emphasis added).

acceptable definition of rights and liabilities. We conclude that PECO did not have a cause of action against Hercules sounding in private nuisance.

The doctrine of public nuisance protects interests quite different from those implicated in actions for private nuisance, and PECO's claim for public nuisance requires separate consideration. Whereas private nuisance requires an invasion of another's interest in the private use and enjoyment of land, a public nuisance is "an unreasonable interference with a right common to the general public." *Restatement (Second) of Torts* § 821B(1). An action for public nuisance may lie even though neither the plaintiff nor the defendant acts in the exercise of private property rights.[11] As William Prosser once wrote: "There are, then, two and only two kinds of nuisance, which are quite unrelated except in the vague general way that each of them causes inconvenience to someone, and in the common name, which naturally has led the courts to apply to the two some of the same substantive rules of law. A private nuisance is narrowly restricted to the invasion of interests in the use and enjoyment of land. It is only a tort, and the remedy for it lies exclusively with the individual whose rights have been disturbed. A public nuisance is a species of catch-all low-grade criminal offense, consisting of an interference with the rights of the community at large, which may include anything from the blocking of a highway to a gaming-house or indecent exposure. Although as in the case of other crimes, the normal remedy is in the hands of the state, a public nuisance may also be a private one, when it interferes with private land. The seeds of confusion were sown when courts began to hold that a tort action would lie even for a purely public nuisance if the plaintiff had suffered 'particular damage.' " Prosser, *Private Action for Public Nuisance,* 52 Va.L.Rev. 997, 999 (1966).

In analyzing the public nuisance claim, we are not concerned with the happenstance that PECO now occupies the very land PICCO occupied when it allegedly created the condition that has polluted the Delaware River waters, or that the continuing source of that pollution is located on that land. The question before us is whether PECO has *standing* to bring an individual action for damages or injunctive relief for interference with a public right.

Restatement (Second) of Torts § 821C(1) provides: "In order to recover damages in an individual action for a public nuisance, one must have suffered harm of a kind different from that suffered by other members of the public exercising the right common to the general public that was the subject of interference."

The same requirements apply to individual plaintiffs seeking injunctive relief. *Restatement (Second) of Torts* § 821C(2); Prosser, *supra,* 52 Va.L.Rev. at 1006. PECO argues that the expense it incurred in

11. Thus, commercial fishermen and clam diggers operating in public waters can recover on a public nuisance theory for harm to the waters and marine life caused by oil discharged from a tanker in transit. *See Burgess v. M/V Tamano,* 370 F.Supp. 247 (D.Me.1973).

cleaning up the offending condition constituted the harm requisite for standing to sue for public nuisance. We disagree. Though pecuniary harm certainly may be harm of a different kind from that suffered by the general public, *see Restatement (Second) of Torts* § 821C comment h,[14] we find in this case no allegation or evidence that PECO suffered this harm "exercising the right common to the general public that was the subject of interference." The public right that was interfered with was the right to "pure water". [C] PECO does not allege that it used the waters of the Delaware River itself, or that it was directly harmed in any way by the pollution of those waters. Thus, this is not a case "where an established business made commercial use of the public right with which the defendant interfered." [C] If PECO—as a riparian landowner—had suffered damage to its land or its operations as a result of the pollution of the Delaware, it would possibly have a claim for public nuisance. But the condition of the Chester site was not the *result* of the pollution, it was the *cause* of it. DER required PECO, as owner of the Chester site, to remove the sources of the pollution. PECO has been specially harmed only in the exercise of its private property rights over the Chester site. PECO has suffered no "particular damage" in the exercise of a right common to the general public, and it lacks standing to sue for public nuisance.

PECO argues that even if, as we have now held, it had no cause of action against Hercules for public or private nuisance, insofar as the judgment of the district court assessed damages against Hercules it should be affirmed on common law principles of indemnification. The short answer to PECO's contention is that under Pennsylvania law a cause of action for indemnity between jointly liable defendants and a plaintiff's cause of action for the underlying wrong are entirely distinct, [c] and as an appellate court we should be chary of upholding a judgment on the basis of a *cause of action* that was neither pleaded, proved, nor submitted to the jury by the district court. Perhaps this would be possible were there a complete identity of factual issues, but a brief review of the principles of indemnification show that such is not the case here.   *   *   *

We emphasize that our decision today should not be interpreted as standing for the general proposition that a party that contaminates land, or the successors to its assets, can escape liability by the expedient of selling the land. To the contrary, it would seem that there are many avenues by which such a party may be held accountable.[20] We hold

---

14. It may be that under Pennsylvania law harm of a *magnitude* greater than that suffered by the general public is sufficient to confer standing. *See Pennsylvania Society for the Prevention of Cruelty to Animals v. Bravo Enterprises,* 428 Pa. 350, 360, 237 A.2d 342, 348 (1968). This distinction is not, however, important in the instant case. As the discussion that follows points out, even if PECO has suffered a harm both different in kind and greater in de-

gree than that suffered by the general public, it has not suffered that harm in the exercise of a right common to the general public. *Cf. Burgess v. M/V Tamano,* 370 F.Supp. 247 (D.Me.1973) (businesses operating on beach did not have standing to sue for pollution of swimming waters, even though they lost customers as a result).

20. For example, Hercules could be liable to neighboring landowners in private

only that in this case the purchaser of that land, PECO—though we recognize that it acted as a responsible corporate citizen—had no cause of action against the vendor's successor, Hercules, for private nuisance, public nuisance, or common law indemnity. * * *

For the foregoing reasons, the injunction requiring Hercules to clean up the Chester site will be vacated, and the judgment of the district court on PECO's claims against Hercules will be reversed.

---

1. In public nuisance cases, the problem of distinguishing what is difference in "kind" and what is difference in "degree" has given courts considerable difficulty. Consider the following:

A. Defendant obstructs a public highway, forcing travelers to detour. Plaintiff, on his way to work, has to travel over the highway twice a day. Cf. Borton v. Mangus, 93 Kan. 719, 145 P. 835 (1915).

B. The same facts, except that plaintiff drives into the unguarded and unlighted obstruction, and sustains personal injury. Cf. Leahan v. Cochran, 178 Mass. 566, 60 N.E. 382 (1901); Schnitzer v. Excelsior Powder Mfg. Co., 160 S.W. 282 (Mo.App.1912).

C. The same facts, except that the obstructed highway cuts off ingress and egress to plaintiff's land. Pilgrim Plywood Co. v. Melendy, 110 Vt. 12, 1 A.2d 700 (1938). Is it enough that there is serious interference? Gates v. Bloomfield, 243 Iowa 671, 53 N.W.2d 279 (1952).

D. Noise and smoke from defendant's factory amounting to a public nuisance also interfere seriously with plaintiff's use and enjoyment of his land. Soap Corp. of America v. Reynolds, 178 F.2d 503 (5th Cir.1949); Morris v. Haledon, 24 N.J.Super. 171, 93 A.2d 781 (1952).

E. For discussion, see Reynolds, Public Nuisance: A Crime in Tort Law, 31 Okla.L.Rev. 318 (1978); Prosser, Private Action for Public Nuisance, 52 Va. L.Rev. 997 (1966); and Rothstein, Private Action for Public Nuisance: The Standing Problem, 76 W.Va.L.Rev. 453 (1974).

2. Why should it be necessary to have an injury different in kind from that of the general public? Is it because the harm suffered by the public is so trivial? Or because there would be such a flood of suits? Why not allow a class action? Or permit one member of the public to sue for an injunction that would eliminate the nuisance? The rule still persists today. But there is one solution in most states. The district attorney or other official may sue for abatement. See, e.g., State ex rel. Swann v. Pack, 527 S.W.2d 99 (Tenn.1975), cert. denied, 424 U.S. 954 (1976) (snake-handling).

3. Ferment in the field of environmental law has had as one of its major facets the utilization of private actions based on nuisance (usually public nuisance) as a means of controlling pollution of various types. This runs afoul of the difference-in-kind rule, and various writers have advocated the abolition of the rule to a greater or lesser extent. See, for example, Hanks & Hanks, An Environmental Bill of Rights: The Citizen Suit and the National Environmental Policy Act of 1969, 24 Rutgers L.Rev. 230 (1970); Jaffe, Standing to Sue in Conservation Suits, in Law and Environment 123 (1970); Jaffe, Standing Again,

nuisance, or to users of Delaware River waters in public nuisance. DER or the federal Environmental Protection Agency may be able to proceed directly against Hercules on statutory or public nuisance theories.

84 Harv.L.Rev. 633 (1971); Grad & Rockett, Environmental Litigation—Where the Action Is?, 10 Nat.Res.J. 742 (1970).

The Supreme Court holds, however, that "a mere interest in a problem, no matter how longstanding the interest and no matter how qualified the organization is in evaluating the problem, is not sufficient"; the "party seeking review must show that he is himself adversely affected." Sierra Club v. Morton, 405 U.S. 727 (1972). See also Zahn v. International Paper Co., 414 U.S. 291 (1973), holding that in a class action seeking damages for water pollution each of the members of the class must meet the federal jurisdictional amount requirement. Some states have statutes providing for suit by individual citizens or organizations to abate a public nuisance in the public interest.

4. *Use of Other Tort Remedies for Environmental Protection.* Resort has also been made to other tort actions than nuisance, with varying degrees of success. Consider the following: Trespass, Davis v. Georgia Pacific Corp., 251 Or. 239, 445 P.2d 481 (1968) (air pollution). Negligence (adds little, since nuisance will usually lie if negligence is available), Hagy v. Allied Chemical & Dye Corp., 122 Cal.App.2d 361, 265 P.2d 86 (1953) (poisonous smog). Riparian rights (also overlaps nuisance), Parker v. American Woolen Co., 195 Mass. 591, 81 N.E. 468 (1907). Strict liability for abnormally dangerous activity (also overlaps nuisance), Young v. Darter, 363 P.2d 829 (Okl.1961) (crop dusting). Products liability, City of Chicago v. General Motors Corp., 467 F.2d 1262 (7 Cir. 1972) (exhaust fumes from automobiles).

5. General treatments of potentially available tort remedies, include: Maloney, Judicial Protection of the Environment—A New Role for Common Law Remedies, 25 Vand.L.Rev. 145 (1972); Reitze, Private Remedies for Environmental Wrongs, 5 Suffolk L.Rev. 779 (1971); Warren, Nuisance Law as an Environmental Tool, 7 Wake Forest L.Rev. 211 (1970).

6. The existence of a "federal common law" of public nuisance was recognized in Illinois v. Milwaukee, 406 U.S. 91 (1972). But its scope was uncertain and, in City of Milwaukee v. States of Illinois and Michigan, 451 U.S. 304 (1981), the court held that the Federal Water Pollution Control Act Amendments of 1972, 33 U.S.C.A. §§ 1251 et seq., displaced any federal common law of nuisance. See Comments, 45 Ohio St.L.J. 791 (1984), 49 Tenn.L. Rev. 919 (1982).

MORGAN v. HIGH PENN OIL CO.
Supreme Court of North Carolina, 1953.
238 N.C. 185, 77 S.E.2d 682.

Civil action to recover temporary damages for a private nuisance, and to abate such nuisance by injunction.

[Plaintiff owned a tract of nine acres of land, on which he had his dwelling, a restaurant, and accommodations for thirty-two trailers. Defendant owned an adjoining tract on which it operated an oil refinery, at a distance of 1,000 feet from plaintiff's dwelling. Plaintiff's evidence was that for some hours on two or three different days each week the refinery emitted nauseating gases and odors in great quantities, which invaded plaintiff's land and other tracts of land within a distance of two miles, in such density as to render persons of ordinary sensitiveness uncomfortable and sick. This substantially impaired the use and enjoyment of plaintiff's land. Defendant failed to put an end to this atmospheric pollution after notice and demand from plaintiff to abate it.

Defendant's evidence was that the oil refinery was a modern plant of the type approved, known and in general use for renovating used lubricating oils; that it was not so constructed or operated as to give out noxious gases or odors in annoying quantities, and that it had not annoyed the plaintiff or other persons save on a single occasion when it suffered a brief mechanical breakdown.

The trial judge submitted to the jury the question whether the refinery was so maintained and operated as to create a nuisance. The jury returned a special verdict saying that there was a nuisance, and assessed plaintiff's damages at $2,500. The trial court entered judgment on this verdict, and enjoined defendant from continuing the nuisance. Defendant appealed.]

ERVIN, JUSTICE. * * * [The] defendant assigns as error the disallowance of its motion for a compulsory nonsuit. * * *

The High Penn Oil Company contends that the evidence is not sufficient to establish either an actionable or an abatable private nuisance. This contention rests on a twofold argument somewhat alternative in character. The High Penn Oil Company asserts primarily that private nuisances are classified as nuisances *per se* or at law, and nuisances *per accidens* or in fact; that when one carries on an oil refinery upon premises in his rightful occupation, he conducts a lawful enterprise, and for that reason does not maintain a nuisance *per se* or at law; that in such case the oil refinery can constitute a nuisance *per accidens* or in fact to the owner of neighboring land if, but only if, it is constructed or operated in a negligent manner; that there was no testimony at the trial tending to show that the oil refinery was constructed or operated in a negligent manner; and that consequently the evidence does not suffice to establish the existence of either an actionable or an abatable private nuisance. * * *

A nuisance *per se* or at law is an act, occupation or structure which is a nuisance at all times and under any circumstances, regardless of location or surroundings. [Cc] Nuisances *per accidens* or in fact are those which become nuisances by reason of their location, or by reason of the manner in which they are constructed, maintained, or operated. [Cc] The High Penn Oil Company also asserts with complete correctness that an oil refinery is a lawful enterprise and for that reason cannot be a nuisance *per se* or at law. [Cc] The High Penn Oil Company falls into error, however, when it takes the position that an oil refinery cannot become a nuisance *per accidens* or in fact unless it is constructed or operated in a negligent manner.

Negligence and nuisance are distinct fields of liability. [Cc] While the same act or omission may constitute negligence and also give rise to a private nuisance *per accidens* or in fact, and thus the two torts may coexist and be practically inseparable, a private nuisance *per accidens* or in fact may be created or maintained without negligence. [Cc] Most private nuisances *per accidens* or in fact are intentionally created or maintained, and are redressed by the courts without allegation or proof of negligence. [Cc] * * *

Much confusion exists in respect to the legal basis of liability in the law of private nuisance because of the deplorable tendency of the courts to call everything a nuisance, and let it go at that. [Cc] The confusion on this score vanishes in large part, however, when proper heed is paid to the sound proposition that private nuisance is a field of tort liability rather than a single type of tortious conduct; that the feature which gives unity to this field of tort liability is the interest invaded, namely, the interest in the use and enjoyment of land; that any substantial nontrespassory invasion of another's interest in the private use and enjoyment of land by any type of liability forming conduct is a private nuisance; that the invasion which subjects a person to liability for private nuisance may be either intentional or unintentional; that a person is subject to liability for an intentional invasion when his conduct is unreasonable under the circumstances of the particular case; and that a person is subject to liability for an unintentional invasion when his conduct is negligent, reckless or ultrahazardous. See Scope and Introduction Note to Chapter 40, American Law Institute's Restatement of the Law of Torts; [cc].

An invasion of another's interest in the use and enjoyment of land is intentional in the law of private nuisance when the person whose conduct is a question as a basis for liability acts for the purpose of causing it, or knows that it is resulting from his conduct, or knows that it is substantially certain to result from his conduct. Restatement (Second) of the Law of Torts, § 825; [cc]. A person who intentionally creates or maintains a private nuisance is liable for the resulting injury to others regardless of the degree of care or skill exercised by him to avoid such injury. [Cc] One of America's greatest jurists, the late Benjamin N. Cardozo, made this illuminating observation on this aspect of the law:

"Nuisance as a concept of the law has more meanings than one. The primary meaning does not involve the element of negligence as one of its essential factors. One acts sometimes at one's peril. In such circumstances, the duty to desist is absolute whenever conduct, if persisted in, brings damage to another. Illustrations are abundant. One who emits noxious fumes or gases day by day in the running of his factory may be liable to his neighbor though he has taken all available precautions. He is not to do such things at all, whether he is negligent or careful." McFarlane v. City of Niagara Falls, 247 N.Y. 340, 160 N.E. 391.

When the evidence is interpreted in the light most favorable to the plaintiff, it suffices to support a finding that in operating the oil refinery the High Penn Oil Company intentionally and unreasonably caused noxious gases and odors to escape onto the nine acres of the plaintiff to such a degree as to impair in a substantial manner the plaintiff's use and enjoyment of his land. This being so, the evidence is ample to establish the existence of an actionable private nuisance, entitling the plaintiff to recover temporary damages from the High Penn Oil Company. [Cc] When the evidence is taken in the light most favorable to the plaintiff, it also suffices to warrant the additional inference that the High Penn Oil Company intends to operate the oil refinery in the future in the same manner as in the past; * * * and that the issuance of an appropriate injunction is necessary to protect the plaintiff against the threatened irreparable injury. * * *

For the reasons given, the evidence is sufficient to withstand the motion of the High Penn Oil Company for a compulsory nonsuit.

[A new trial was ordered, however, because of an error in instructions to the jury.]

———

1. Relatively few nuisance cases have given much consideration to whether the tort is based upon intent, negligence or strict liability. In the usual case the defendant has continued to allow his chimney to smoke, or to spray chemicals into the air or the like, after he has been notified that it is causing damage to the plaintiff. Whatever the original conduct may have been, the continuance after this notice makes the tort an intentional one. Frequently the plaintiff is seeking an injunction, and the chief question is whether the defendant will be allowed to continue an interference that has become intentional. Cf. Vaughn v. Missouri Power & Light Co., 89 S.W.2d 699 (Mo.App. 1935); Smith v. Staso Milling Co., 18 F.2d 736 (2d Cir.1927).

2. Public nuisances frequently depend on violation of a criminal statute, and whether the violation is regarded as an intentional interference with the public right, as negligence per se or as strict liability, the result is the same. Nevertheless it is clear that either a public or a private nuisance may arise on the basis of intent, negligence or strict liability.

3. *Intentional* nuisances include such cases as the principal case, where the defendant knows that his conduct is interfering with the plaintiff's right or that it is substantially certain to do so.

4. *Negligence* is the basis of liability when the defendant has not intentionally interfered with the interest protected but has failed to exercise reasonable care to avoid the interference. Thus a city may fail to inspect and repair its highway, in which a condition dangerous to travelers has arisen. McFarlane v. Niagara Falls, 247 N.Y. 340, 160 N.E. 391 (1928); Reedy v. Pittsburgh, 363 Pa. 365, 69 A.2d 93 (1949). Or there may be failure to guard against damage to a highway from the use of heavy equipment. Denny v. Garavaglia, 333 Mich. 317, 52 N.W.2d 521 (1952). Or property may be allowed to fall into disrepair, so that a private nuisance is created. Schindler v. Standard Oil Co., 207 Mo.App. 190, 232 S.W. 735 (1921) (leaking waterpipe); Rose v. Standard Oil Co., 56 R.I. 272, 185 A. 251 (1936) (percolation of petroleum products). Or the defendant may fail to discover and abate a condition created by a third party. Lamb v. Roberts, 196 Ala. 679, 72 So. 309 (1916); City of Phoenix v. Harlan, 75 Ariz. 290, 255 P.2d 609 (1953). Also, on failure to act, see CEW Management Corp. v. First Federal Sav. & Loan Ass'n, 88 Wis.2d 631, 277 N.W.2d 766 (1979).

5. *Strict Liability.* A leading case is Heeg v. Licht, 80 N.Y. 579 (1888), holding defendant liable for damage caused by the explosion of a powder magazine that had existed for some time. Accord: Liber v. Flor, 160 Colo. 7, 415 P.2d 332 (1966) (boxes of dynamite stored). Mere storage of the explosives has been held to be sufficient for relief even though there has been no explosion. Cumberland Torpedo Co. v. Gaines, 201 Ky. 88, 255 S.W. 1046 (1923). See also Whittemore v. Baxter Laundry Co., 181 Mich. 564, 148 N.W. 437 (1914) (tank containing 20,000 gallons of gasoline kept on defendant's premises about eleven feet from plaintiff's house). What about a vicious dog? Browning v. Belue, 22 Ala.App. 437, 116 So. 509 (1928).

6. Courts frequently hold that a nuisance exists even though they would not have held that strict liability existed on the principle of Rylands v. Fletcher. Take the *Heeg* and *Liber* cases cited above. New York, at the time it decided *Heeg,* had refused to recognize Rylands v. Fletcher at all; Colorado recognized strict liability for blasting but not for storage of explosives.

On the relation between the principle of Rylands v. Fletcher and "absolute" nuisance, and the extent to which courts that purport to reject the one have in fact applied it under the name of the other, see Prosser, Nuisance Without Fault, 20 Tex.L.Rev. 399 (1942); Prosser, The Principle of Rylands v. Fletcher, in Prosser, Selected Topics on the Law of Torts 135 (1953).

7. Almost every English case imposing strict liability under the rule of Rylands v. Fletcher is duplicated by some American case under the name of nuisance. Compare Attorney–General v. Corke, [1933] Ch. 89, where the defendant harbored persons living in an unsanitary fashion who strayed onto the plaintiff's land, with the tenement full of individuals living in similar conditions in Harty v. Guerra, 269 S.W. 1064 (Tex.Civ.App.1925), and the workhouse full of criminals in District of Columbia v. Totten, 55 App.D.C. 312, 5 F.2d 374 (1925).

8. Compare Dixon v. New York Trap Rock Corp., 293 N.Y. 509, 58 N.E.2d 517 (1944), where the defendant, conducting blasting operations, shook the plaintiff's house to pieces. Plaintiff suffered mental disturbance, went into a neurotic state of anxiety, and ended with a nervous collapse. New York, at the time was one of the leading jurisdictions refusing to allow recovery for the physical consequences of mental disturbance unless there was "impact." But upon the basis that the action was one for a nuisance, recovery was allowed in *Dixon.* Open Sesame?

It has been said that nuisance is a good word with which to beg a question or to avoid a restrictive tort rule. Thus, the word has frequently been used as a talisman to avoid the effect of a rule of governmental immunity or of contributory negligence.

CARPENTER v. THE DOUBLE R CATTLE COMPANY, INC.
Supreme Court of Idaho, 1985.
108 Idaho 602, 701 P.2d 222.

BAKES, JUSTICE.   *   *   * Plaintiff appellants are homeowners who live near a cattle feedlot owned and operated by respondents. Appellants filed a complaint in March, 1978, alleging that the feedlot had been expanded in 1977 to accommodate the feeding of approximately 9,000 cattle. Appellants further alleged that "the spread and accumulation of manure, pollution of river and ground water, odor, insect infestation, increased concentration of birds, . . . dust and noise" allegedly caused by the feedlot constituted a nuisance. After a trial on the merits a jury found that the feedlot did not constitute a nuisance. The trial court then also made findings and conclusions that the feedlot did not constitute a nuisance. * * *

The case was assigned to the Court of Appeals which reversed and remanded for a new trial. The basis for this reversal was that the trial court did not give a jury instruction based upon subsection (b) of Section 826 of the Restatement (Second) of Torts. That subsection allows for a finding of a nuisance even though the gravity of harm is outweighed by the utility of the conduct if the harm is "serious" and the payment of damages is "feasible" without forcing the business to discontinue.

This Court granted defendant's petition for review. We hold that the instructions which the trial court gave were not erroneous, being consistent with our prior case law and other persuasive authority. We further hold that the trial court did not err in not giving an instruction based on subsection (b) of Section 826 of the Second Restatement, which does not represent the law in the State of Idaho. * * *

The Court of Appeals * * * adopted the new subsection (b) of Section 826 of the Second Restatement partially because of language in Koseris [v. J.R. Simplot Co., 82 Idaho 263, 352 P.2d 235 (1960)], which reads: "We are constrained to hold that the trial court erred in sustaining objections to those offers of proof [evidence of utility of conduct], since they were relevant as bearing upon the issue whether respondents, in seeking injunctive relief, were pursuing the proper remedy; nevertheless, on the theory of damages which respondents had waived, the ruling was correct." 82 Idaho at 270, 352 P.2d at 239.

The last phrase of the quote, relied on by the Court of Appeals, is clearly *dictum,* since the question of utility of conduct in a nuisance action for damages was not at issue in *Koseris.* It is very doubtful that this Court's *dictum* in *Koseris* was intended to make such a substantial change in the nuisance law. * * * The case of *McNichols v. J.R. Simplot Co.,* 74 Idaho 321, 262 P.2d 1012 (1953) should be viewed as the law in Idaho that in a nuisance action seeking damages the interests of the community, which would include the utility of the conduct, should be considered in the determination of the existence of a nuisance. The trial court's instructions in the present case were entirely consistent with *McNichols.* A plethora of other modern cases are in accord. * * *

The State of Idaho is sparsely populated and its economy depends largely upon the benefits of agriculture, lumber, mining and industrial development. To eliminate the utility of conduct and other factors listed by the trial court from the criteria to be considered in determining whether a nuisance exists, as the appellant has argued throughout this appeal, would place an unreasonable burden upon these industries.

We see no policy reasons which should compel this Court to accept appellant's argument and depart from our present law. Accordingly, the judgment of the district court is affirmed and the Court of Appeals decision is set aside.   *   *   *

BISTLINE, JUSTICE, dissenting.   *   *   * I applaud the efforts of the Court of Appeals to modernize the law of nuisance in this state. I am not in the least persuaded to join the majority with its narrow view of nuisance law as expressed in the majority opinion.

The majority today continues to adhere to ideas on the law of nuisance that should have gone out with the use of buffalo chips as fuel. We have before us today homeowners complaining of a nearby feedlot— not a small operation, but rather a feedlot which accommodates 9,000 cattle. The homeowners advanced the theory that after the expansion of the feedlot in 1977, the odor, manure, dust, insect infestation and increased concentration of birds which accompanied all of the foregoing, constituted a nuisance. If the odoriferous quagmire created by 9,000 head of cattle is *not* a nuisance, it is difficult for me to imagine what is.   *   *   *

I agree wholeheartedly that the interests of the community should be considered in determining the existence of a nuisance. However, where this primitive rule of law fails is in recognizing that in our society, while it may be desirable to have a serious nuisance continue because the utility of the operation causing the nuisance is great, at the same time, those directly impacted by the serious nuisance deserve some compensation for the invasion they suffer as a result of the continuation of the nuisance. This is exactly what the more progressive provisions of § 826(b) of the Restatement (Second) of Torts addresses. Clearly, § 826(b) recognizes that the continuation of the serious harm must remain feasible. See especially comment on clause (b), subpart f of § 826 of the Restatement. What § 826(b) adds is a method of compensating those who must suffer the invasion without putting out of business the source or cause of the invasion. This does not strike me as a particularly adventuresome or far-reaching rule of law. In fact, the fairness of it is overwhelming.   *   *   *

We should not be adopting a rule of preference which suggests that if the community interest is preferred any other interest must be disregarded. Instead, § 826(b) accommodates adverse interests by contemplating continuation of the facility which creates the nuisance while compensating those who suffer the direct impact of the nuisance—in the instant case the homeowners who live in the vicinity of the feedlot.

The majority's rule today suggests that part of the cost of industry, agriculture or development must be borne by those unfortunate few who have the fortuitous luck to live in the immediate vicinity of a nuisance producing facility. Frankly, I think this naive economic view is ridiculous in both its simplicity and its outdated view of modern economic society. The "cost" of a product includes not only the amount it takes to produce such a product but also includes the external costs:

the damage done to the environment through pollution of air or water is an example of an external cost. In the instant case, the nuisance suffered by the homeowners should be considered an external cost of operating a feedlot and producing beef for public consumption. I do not believe that a few should be required to pay this extra cost of doing business by going uncompensated for a nuisance of this sort. * * *

The majority today blithely suggests that because the State of Idaho is sparsely populated and because our economy is largely dependent on agriculture, lumber, mining and industrial development, we should forego compensating those who suffer a serious invasion. If humans are such a rare item in this state, maybe there is all the more reason to protect them from the discharge of industry. At a minimum, we should compensate those who suffer a nuisance at the hands of industry and agriculture. What the majority overlooks is that the cost of development should not be absorbed by few, but rather should be spread out and paid by all. I am not convinced that agriculture or industry will be put out of business by requiring compensation for the nuisance they generate. * * *

The decision of the Court of Appeals is an outstanding example of a judicial opinion which comes from a truly exhaustive and analytical review. See 105 Idaho 320, 669 P.2d 643 (1983). * * *

[The decision was 3 to 2.]

———

1. The decision in this case was by a vote of 3 to 2, reversing the holding of the court of appeals. As Judge Bistline said in his dissenting opinion, Judge Burnette's opinion in the intermediate court "is an outstanding example of a judicial opinion which comes from a truly exhaustive and analytical review." It is well worth reading. It appears in 105 Idaho 320, 669 P.2d 643 (1983). See also Jost v. Dairyland Power Co–Op., 45 Wis.2d 164, 172 N.W.2d 647 (1969); cf. Copart Industries, Inc. v. Consolidated Edison Co. of New York, Inc., 41 N.Y.2d 564, 362 N.E.2d 968, 394 N.Y.S.2d 169 (1977). And see Restatement (Second) of Torts §§ 826, 829A. Cf. Scott v. Jordan, 99 N.M. 567, 661 P.2d 59 (App.1983), holding, under very similar facts, that damages are not adequate and an injunction should be granted when the trial court found that the operations had resulted in the impairment of the health and comfort of the plaintiffs and their family and the enjoyment of their property.

Recent legislation in a number of states has provided that a nuisance action will not lie "against an agricultural operation that has lawfully been in operation" for a year, and providing for litigation expenses and attorney's fees for defending such an action. See, e.g., Tex.Code Ann., Agric.Code, §§ 251.001 et seq. (1982). See Hanna, "Right to Farm" Statutes—The Newest Tool in Agricultural Land Preservation, 10 Fla.St.L.Rev. 415 (1982).

2. For good discussions of when an intentional invasion is unreasonable, see Robie v. Lillis, 112 N.H. 492, 299 A.2d 155 (1972); Pendergrast v. Aiken, 293 N.C. 201, 236 S.E.2d 787 (1977) (surface water); Jacobson v. Crown Zellerbach Corp., 273 Or. 15, 539 P.2d 641 (1975) (noise and vibration from highway).

3. In order to recover damages for a nuisance, whether public or private, the plaintiff must show that he has sustained significant harm. Harndon v.

Stultz, 124 Iowa 440, 100 N.W. 329 (1904) (roots and branches extending over line); Holman v. Athens Empire Laundry Co., 149 Ga. 345, 100 S.E. 207 (1919) (occasional whiffs of smoke). See Restatement (Second) of Torts § 821F.

4. *Hypersensitivity.* It is generally held that the harm must be of a kind that would be suffered by a normal person in the community. Rogers v. Elliott, 146 Mass. 349, 15 N.E. 768 (1888) (plaintiff, in highly nervous condition from sunstroke, affected by ringing of church bell); Beckman v. Marshall, 85 So.2d 552 (Fla.1956) (noise of children playing in nursery); Venuto v. Owens–Corning Fiberglass Corp., 22 Cal.App.3d 116, 99 Cal.Rptr. 350 (1971) (allergic reactions).

5. Suppose that most people in the vicinity are hardened to the discomfort of noise, smoke, dust, vibration or odors from the defendant's factory, and do not object. Does this prevent the plaintiff from maintaining an action for a nuisance, if a normal person would be affected?

6. *Sensitive Uses of Land.* What if the defendant engages in an activity that is normally harmless to his neighbors, but the plaintiff is making an abnormally sensitive use of his land, which is adversely affected? Defendant operates a race track at night, and his flood lights, directed downward, are reflected with a light approximately equal to that of the full moon. This would be inoffensive to the ordinary landowner in the vicinity; but the plaintiff has an outdoor motion picture screen, on which his pictures are made less visible, and he loses customers. Is defendant liable on the basis of nuisance? Amphitheaters, Inc. v. Portland Meadows, 184 Or. 336, 198 P.2d 847 (1948).

Cf. Armory Park Neighborhood Ass'n v. Episcopal Community Services, 148 Ariz. 1, 712 P.2d 914 (1985), 28 Ariz.L.Rev. 121 (1986) (action to enjoin defendant from providing free meals to indigent persons because transients "frequently trespassed onto residents' yards, sometimes urinating, drinking and littering" on them); Shamhart v. Morrison Cafeteria Co., 159 Fla. 629, 32 So.2d 727 (1947), 1 Vand.L.Rev. 324 (1948) (customers queued up to enter popular cafeteria, blocking access of other customers to adjacent store).

B. Plaintiff has installed an effective solar heating system on the roof of his house. Defendant proposes to construct a house on adjoining land that will shade the heating system and impair its operation and refuses to change the location of the house sufficiently to avoid the shading. Plaintiff sues for an injunction. What problems are raised? See Prah v. Maretti, 108 Wis.2d 223, 321 N.W.2d 182 (1982); Notes, 45 Brook.L.Rev. 357 (1979), 65 Calif.L.Rev. 94 (1977), 57 Ore.L.Rev. 94 (1977).

C. In violation of a statute, defendant double parks and pins plaintiff in his parked position. Should plaintiff sue for false imprisonment, negligence per se or nuisance? See Salsbury v. United Parcel Serv., Inc., 203 Misc. 1008, 120 N.Y.S.2d 33 (1953).

WINGET v. WINN–DIXIE STORES, INC.

Supreme Court of South Carolina, 1963.
242 S.C. 152, 130 S.E.2d 363.

LEWIS, JUSTICE. Plaintiffs instituted this action for damages alleged to have been sustained from the location and operation by the defendants of a grocery supermarket in such a manner as to constitute a nuisance and for an order perpetually restraining the defendants from using the property where the supermarket was located for a retail grocery business or for any other business purpose. The trial of the case resulted in a judgment in favor of the plaintiffs for the sum of $5,000, actual damages, and a denial by the trial judge of injunctive relief. From the judgment entered in favor of the plaintiffs, the defendants have appealed. * * *

The home of the plaintiffs is located in Sumter, South Carolina, adjacent to a grocery supermarket operated by the defendant Winn–Dixie Stores, Inc., and managed at the time of the institution of this action by the defendant John Lloyd. The supermarket began operations on October 1, 1959 and this action was instituted about six weeks later. * * *

The plaintiffs have alleged, therefore, that the supermarket in the instant case was a nuisance because of both (1) its location and (2) the manner of its operation. In ruling upon the motion of the defendants for a directed verdict the lower court in effect held that there was no evidence to sustain the allegations that the supermarket was a nuisance because of its location, but submitted the issue to the jury as to whether the store was operated in such a manner as to cause injury or damage to plaintiffs. * * * The property of the plaintiffs is located on Baker Street immediately to the rear of the store lot. * * *

The business of the defendants is a lawful one and was located in an area which had been zoned by the City of Sumter for retail business and at a location which the Zoning Board determined to be suitable for a retail grocery. The record shows that every requirement of the municipal authorities was met in establishing the business in question, both in the location and the construction of the building. There is no evidence that the building was constructed in such manner as to interfere with the rights of others. Under such circumstances, it cannot be held that the location of the business in the area in question constituted a nuisance.

The fact, however, that one has been issued a license or permit to conduct a business at a particular location cannot protect the licensee who operates the business in such a manner as to constitute a nuisance. * * *

An owner of property even in the conduct of a lawful business thereon is subject to reasonable limitations. In the operation of such business he must not unreasonably interfere with the health or comfort of neighbors or with their right to the enjoyment of their property. If a lawful business is operated in an unlawful or unreasonable manner so as to produce material injury or great annoyance to others or unreasonably interferes with the lawful use and enjoyment of their property, it will constitute a nuisance. [C]

On the other hand, every annoyance or disturbance of a landowner from the use made of property by a neighbor does not constitute a nuisance. The question is not whether plaintiffs have been annoyed or disturbed by the operation of the business in question, but whether there has been an injury to their legal rights. People who live in organized communities must of necessity suffer some inconvenience and annoyance from their neighbors and must submit to annoyances consequent upon the reasonable use of property by others. * * *

In the instant case the conflict is between the rights of the plaintiffs who reside in a residential area adjacent to a district zoned for retail business and those of the defendants who operate a retail grocery supermarket in such business area. The supermarket was located in an area zoned by the City for the conduct of such business and the normal and necessary incidents to the operation thereof cannot be condemned as a nuisance.

The plaintiffs, among other things complain that (1) the store has attracted crowds of people, and many automobiles which caused noise, unhealthy fumes, blocked traffic and generally disturbed the peace and quiet of the community, and (2) trash trucks and street sweepers operated on the premises at late night hours.

In determining the respective rights of the parties in this case, it cannot be properly held that the normal traffic and noise caused by customers going to and from the supermarket would constitute a basis for declaring the operation of the business a nuisance. Of course, the purpose of the business of the defendants is to sell merchandise and in doing so to attract to their store as many customers as possible. It is a natural consequence and incident of the operation of the supermarket that there will be an increase in the number of people visiting the area.

The testimony shows that the store is operated only on week days, opening for business at 8:30 a.m. each day and never closing later than 7:30 p.m. While the record shows that the operation of the supermarket has caused an increase in the number of people and automobiles coming into the area, there is nothing to show that there was any mass entrance to or exodus from the store at unreasonable hours. On the contrary, the only reasonable inference from the record is that the traffic to and from the business was the normal traffic of patrons visiting such a grocery store over the usual business day. There is no basis for holding that the normal traffic and noise caused by customers going to and from the supermarket constituted a nuisance.

Neither do we think that the operation of trash trucks and street sweepers in connection with the removal of trash and garbage, under the facts here, can form the basis of a finding of a nuisance. * * * There is nothing to indicate that such acts were other than the usual and normal operations of the City in the gathering and removal of trash and garbage. * * *

However, with regard to other allegations of the complaint, we think that there was some evidence requiring the submission of those issues to the jury for determination. The record shows that the defendants erected fans on their building in connection with the air conditioning equipment. These fans were so directed as to blow against the trees and shrubbery on plaintiffs' property causing some damage and inconvenience. There was also some testimony that, at least, for a while after opening the supermarket, the floodlights on defendants' lot cast a bright glare over the property of plaintiffs until late at night so as to disturb the plaintiffs in the enjoyment of their home, that obnoxious odors were created from the garbage which accumulated at defendants' store, and that paper and trash from the defendants' garbage was permitted to escape onto plaintiffs' lot to an unusual extent. The record gives rise to a reasonable inference that such acts were not normal or necessary incidents of the operation of the business. We think that the foregoing testimony presented a jury issue and that the trial judge properly refused the defendants' motion for a directed verdict. * * *

The remaining issues arise under the defendants' motion for a new trial. It is contended that a new trial should be granted because of the refusal of the trial court to strike the testimony of the witness R.E. Graham relative to depreciation in value of the property of the plaintiffs. The witness Graham was asked to give his opinion as to the value of the plaintiffs' property before and after "the moving in of this Winn-Dixie Corporation." In answer to the question, he testified that the property had depreciated in value from about $12,000 to a value of $8,000 "by reason of the Winn-Dixie moving in this property." His testimony was directed solely to the question of the alleged depreciation in value of the plaintiffs' property from the location of the supermarket on the adjoining lot and not to damages that may have resulted from the manner of the operation of the business.

* * * As stated in 66 C.J.S. Nuisances § 19d, p. 771: "[A] use of property which does not create a nuisance cannot be enjoined or a lawful structure abated merely because it renders neighboring property less valuable. If there is no public or private nuisance created in the use of property, no recovery of damages can be allowed for the diminution in value of the property by reason of the lawful use of such property made by a near-by owner." * * *

The testimony was irrelevant to any issue in the case and should have been stricken upon the motion of the defendants. The failure to strike the testimony of the witness Graham was prejudicial and the lower court was in error in refusing the motion of the defendants for a new trial on this ground.

Reversed and remanded for a new trial.

---

1. In Euclid v. Ambler Realty Co., 272 U.S. 365, 388 (1926), the case in which the Supreme Court first upheld the constitutionality of zoning legislation, Justice Sutherland said: "A nuisance may be merely a right thing in the wrong place, like a pig in the parlor instead of the barnyard." It also is important where the barnyard is located. Thus, in William Aldred's Case, 9 Co.Rep. 576, 77 Eng.Rep. 816 (1610), one of the very first reported cases on private nuisance, the action was brought for maintaining a hogstye next to the plaintiff's house. Defendant "moved in arrest of judgment, that the building of the house for hogs was necessary for the sustenance of man; and one ought not to have so delicate a nose, that he cannot bear the smell of hogs * * * but it

was resolved that the action for it is * * * well maintainable." For more recent cases on the keeping of pigs, see Annot., 2 A.L.R.3d 931 (1965). For other animals, see Annots., 11 A.L.R.3d 1399 (1967) (dogs); 27 A.L.R.3d 627 (1969) (horses); 2 A.L.R.3d 965 (1965) (poultry); 58 A.L.R.3d 1126 (1974) (zoo).

2. Prior to the development of zoning programs, nuisance suits, whether brought by governmental officials or private individuals, were essentially the only way of controlling the location of certain types of activities which were undesirable to the residents in a particular area. Courts thus became virtually concerned with the extent of the undesirability of the activity. How seriously must the activity interfere with the residents? Does the decision as to a hospital depend upon the existence of health dangers (contagions), or is it sufficient to lay emphasis on such things as traffic congestion and the fear (even though irrational) of contagion? See, e.g., Everett v. Paschall, 61 Wash. 47, 111 P. 879 (1910) (tuberculosis sanitarium). There are numerous cases involving funeral parlors and their depressing mental effect on their neighbors. Two striking opinions are Williams v. Montgomery, 184 Miss. 547, 186 So. 302 (1939); and Saier v. Joy, 198 Mich. 295, 164 N.W. 507 (1917).

See Great A & P Tea Co., Inc. v. LaSalle National Bank, 77 Ill.App.3d 478, 32 Ill.Dec. 812, 395 N.E.2d 1193 (1979), in which A & P, leaseholder in a shopping center, sued the owner and lessee of the parking lot for the centers to enjoin construction of a drive-in bank facility on the ground that the facility would "deprive it of parking spaces, and disrupt the pattern of customer travel to and affect visibility of the A & P's store." The court held that a good cause of action was stated.

3. *Aesthetics.* It has been commonly held that no action lies for a dilapidated and unsightly building in an elegant residential neighborhood, whose appearance is offensive to neighboring owners. State Road Commission v. Oakes, 150 W.Va. 709, 149 S.E.2d 293 (1966); Mathewson v. Primeau, 64 Wash.2d 929, 395 P.2d 183 (1964).

But see Heston v. Ousler, 119 N.H. 58, 398 A.2d 536 (1979), where aesthetic qualities are stressed, and Puritan Holding Co. Inc. v. Holloschitz, 82 Misc.2d 905, 372 N.Y.S.2d 500 (1975), where defendant abandoned a building, which "had deteriorated, become unsightly and been taken over by derelicts." Plaintiff, owner of a recently renovated apartment building across the street, sued, claiming that its property had depreciated in value as a result. The court found the abandoned building to be a nuisance and awarded damages of $30,000. Suppose the defendant's building is later razed and the plaintiff's property values go up again? See Notes, 44 U.Cin.L.Rev. 778 (1975); 45 UMKC L.Rev. 99 (1976). On aesthetics in general, see Noel, Unaesthetic Sights as Nuisances, 25 Corn.L.Q. 1 (1939); Leighty, Aesthetics as a Legal Basis for Environmental Control, 17 Wayne L.Rev. 1347 (1971); Notes, 45 N.Y.U.L.Rev. 1075 (1970), 32 U.Cin.L.Rev. 367 (1963).

4. For collections of cases treating the question of whether certain types of activities are to be treated as nuisances in particular areas, see Annots. 50 A.L.R.2d 1324 (1956) (cemetery), A.L.R.2d 1000 (1955) (undertaking establishment), 26 A.L.R.3d 661 (1969) (gun club), 68 A.L.R.2d 1331 (1959) (golf course), 49 A.L.R.3d 652 (1973) (public swimming pool), 44 A.L.R.2d 1381 (1968) (dance hall), 32 A.L.R.3d 1127 (1970) (children's play ground), 80 A.L.R.2d 1124 (1961) (water sports), 5 A.L.R.3d 989 (1966) (saloon or tavern), 91 A.L.R.2d 572 (1963) (drive-in restaurant), 93 A.L.R.2d 1171 (1964) (drive-in theater), 24 A.L.R.2d 571 (1952) (tourist camp or motel), 58 A.L.R.3d 1134 (1974) ("pornoshop"), 41

A.L.R.3d 1273 (1972) (race track), 8 A.L.R.2d 419 (1949) (coal yard), 92 A.L.R. 974 (1963) (dairy), 18 A.L.R.2d 1033 (1951) (stockyard), 52 A.L.R.2d 1134 (public dump), 41 A.L.R.3d 1009 (1972) (incinerator), 86 A.L.R.2d 1322 (1962) (oil refinery), 50 A.L.R.3d 209 (1973) (gas storage tank), 4 A.L.R.3d 902 (1965) (electric generating plant), 56 A.L.R.2d 776 (1957) (used car lot), 84 A.L.R.2d 652 (1962) (auto wrecking ground), 40 A.L.R.2d 1177 (1955) (sewage disposal plant), 83 A.L.R.2d 936 (1962) (weeds), 58 A.L.R.3d 1134 (1974) (zoo), 100 A.L.R.3d 252 (1980) (billiard room and bowling alley), 8 A.L.R.4th 324 (1981) (funeral home), 36 A.L.R.4th 1159 (1985) (windmills), 45 A.L.R.4th 1212 (1986) (computers).

5. The question of the relationship of zoning regulations to a nuisance action has produced varying reactions from the courts. Sometimes the court treats the legislative body as preempting the topic, so that what "might have been a proper field for judicial action prior to such legislation becomes improper when the law-making branch of government has entered the field." Robinson Brick Co. v. Luthi, 115 Colo. 106, 169 P.2d 171 (1946). Other courts have held that whether an activity is conducted in an area permissible under the zoning regulations should not be controlling, since it "is the peculiar nature and location of a business, not the fact that it is a business that constitutes the private nuisance." Scallet v. Stock, 363 Mo. 721, 253 S.W.2d 143 (1952). The distinction in the principal case, between the location of an activity and the way it is carried on, makes an appropriate compromise. See also Weltshe v. Graf, 323 Mass. 498, 82 N.E.2d 795 (1948). There are holdings that violation of a zoning ordinance may make an activity a nuisance per se. Cf. Little Joseph Realty, Inc. v. Babylon, 41 N.Y.2d 738, 395 N.Y.S.2d 428, 363 N.E.2d 1163 (1977); McIvor v. Mercer–Fraser Co., 76 Cal.App.2d 247, 172 P.2d 758 (1946). See generally Beuscher and Morrison, Judicial Zoning Through Recent Nuisance Cases, 1955 Wis.L.Rev. 440; Elleckson, Alternatives to Zoning: Covenants, Nuisance Rules and Fines as Land Use Controls, 40 U.Chi.L.Rev. 681 (1973); Notes, 54 Mich.L.Rev. 266 (1955), 46 Wash.L.Rev. 47 (1970).

6. A similar problem arises in connection with the relationship of the courts, in a nuisance suit, to action taken by an administrative governmental environmental control agency. See, for example, State ex rel. Norvell v. Arizona Public Service Co., 85 N.M. 165, 510 P.2d 98 (1973), where an action was brought by the state attorney general, environmental groups and an individual to enjoin air and water pollution resulting from the operation of an electric generating plant. The court held that, under state environmental legislation, primary jurisdiction was placed in the State Board of Public Health and the Water Quality Control Commission, which were to apply state and federal standards. Discussing principles of administrative law, the court declared that it was "concerned lest the intervention of the trial court would add little to, or even hamper the solution of the overrally problem," since "nothing before us [makes] it appear that the trial court could solve the problem * * * either more quickly or better than the Agency." For collection of other cases see Annot., 60 A.L.R.3d 665 (1974). Cf. Restatement (Second) of Torts § 821B, Comment f.

ALEVIZOS v. METROPOLITAN AIRPORTS COMMISSION OF MINNEAPOLIS AND ST. PAUL

Supreme Court of Minnesota, 1974.
298 Minn. 471, 216 N.W.2d 651.

KELLY, JUSTICE. Petitioners appeal from an order of the Hennepin County District Court sustaining a demurrer to and dismissing their complaint and petition for writ of mandamus to compel respondent, Metropolitan Airports Commission of Minneapolis and St. Paul (MAC), to institute condemnation proceedings against the properties owned by petitioners and others similarly situated within their class and from the order denying their motion to have this action maintained as a class action. We reverse. * * *

Petitioners in this case have brought an action in inverse condemnation against MAC as a result of noise and pollution from the operation of airplanes directly over and near their properties. Inverse condemnation has been described as:

" * * * the popular description of a cause of action against a governmental defendant to recover the value of property which has been taken in fact by the governmental defendant, even though no formal exercise of the power of eminent domain has been attempted by the taking agency." Thornburg v. Port of Portland, 233 Or. 178, 180, note 1, 376 P.2d 100, 101 (1962).

The trial court, in its memorandum supporting the dismissal of this action, analyzed the existing case law in inverse condemnation by airplane overflight. Citing Batten v. United States, 306 F.2d 580 (10 Cir.1962), it concluded that a physical trespass is required. * * *

[The court cites and describes the Supreme Court opinions in United States v. Causby, 328 U.S. 256 (1946); and Griggs v. Allegheny County, Pa., 369 U.S. 84 (1962). Both involved overflights with planes flying low over the property involved. The opinions relied on elements of trespass (overflight) and elements of nuisance (inconvenience, frequency, interference, and rights to enjoyment and use of land). They left considerable confusion.]

The lower Federal courts which have dealt with this issue have almost unanimously allowed recovery only to those property owners located directly below the flightpath. Batten v. United States, 306 F.2d 580, 583 (10 Cir.1962); [cc]. This approach more nearly resembles the trespass theory rather than the nuisance theory. * * *

The state court decisions have largely deviated from the Federal court pattern by allowing recovery both to those property owners directly beneath the flightpath and to those near the flightpath. However, this difference in result may not be inconsistent with the Federal court decisions because the Fifth Amendment to the United States Constitution refers only to a *taking* of property, whereas many state constitutions similar to Minnesota's require compensation where private property is "taken, destroyed or damaged." Minn.Const. art. 1, § 13. * * *

A number of state courts, however, have dismissed the significance of this distinction and have allowed compensation to all parties whether in the flightpath or near it by interpreting the Causby and Griggs cases as allowing recovery based on a nuisance theory.

In the leading state decision, Thornburg v. Port of Portland, 233 Or. 178, 376 P.2d 100 (1962), the Oregon constitutional provision was similar to that of the United States Constitution. * * * The Oregon court in rejecting the majority opinion of the Batten court and following the dissent of Chief Judge Murrah, stated:

"If we accept, as we must upon established principles of the law of servitudes, the validity of the propositions that a noise can be a nuisance; that a nuisance can give rise to an easement; and that a noise coming straight down from above one's land can ripen into a taking if it is persistent enough and aggravated enough, then logically the same kind and degree of interference with the use and enjoyment of one's land can also be a taking even though the noise vector may come from some direction other than the perpendicular." 233 Or. 192, 376 P.2d 106. * * *

The court in *Thornburg* held that a compensable taking occurs whenever governmental activity substantially interferes with the useful possession of property, either by repeated trespasses or by repeated nontrespassory invasions called nuisances. Reliance on a nuisance theory would clearly give relief to any property owner living near the flightpaths who could show interference with his rights sufficient to amount to a taking. * * *

The Oregon Supreme Court * * *, when it decided a case in 1966 arising out of the same facts as the earlier decision[,] Thornburg v. Port of Portland, 244 Or. 69, 415 P.2d 750 (1966)[,] * * * held that the jury should not be asked to balance the individual property owner's rights against that of the public good derived from the airport. Rather, the court held that the jury should be instructed to determine whether the property owner's right to the use and enjoyment of his land has been infringed in such a substantial way that a loss of market value results; if so, then a taking has occurred and the jury only need determine the amount of compensation.

What, then, are the guidelines to be followed by the trial court, on remand, in reaching its initial determination? It should be pointed out initially that the Minnesota Constitution requires compensation where private property is taken, destroyed, or damaged. * * *

Property is more than the physical thing—it involves the group of rights inhering in a citizen's relation to the physical thing. Traditionally, that group of rights has included the rights to possess, use, and dispose of property. [C] Petitioners in this case do not allege that they have been dispossessed by MAC's operations. They allege that their right to use the property without undue interference has been infringed and the decrease in market value due to defendant's operations has deprived them of their right to dispose of their property for a fair price. The right to use one's property in relative freedom from irritating noise and interference can hardly be disputed in view of present-day living conditions where a great deal of governmental and private effort is spent on planning and zoning our cities in an effort to improve the quality of life. These societal efforts to protect certain land uses from irritating interferences, then, indicate that the use and enjoyment of one's property without unduly irritating noise, vibrations, and gaseous fumes have arisen to the status of a property right for which a property owner may demand compensation when it is denied to him by governmental activity.

This does not mean that every noise or interference with a property owner's use and enjoyment thereof constitutes a taking. Every landowner must continue to endure that level of inconvenience, discomfort, and loss of peace and quiet which can be reasonably anticipated by any average member of a vibrant and progressive society. But when those interferences reach the point where they cause a measurable decrease in property market value, it is reasonable to assume that, considering the permanency of the air flights, a property right has been, if not "taken or destroyed," at the very least "damaged," for which our constitution requires that compensation be paid. This will not give relief to the unusually sensitive person because the measure of recovery is decrease in market value of the property due to its decreased desirability in the general market place rather than the amount of discomfort to the individual.

We recognize that most property in a metropolitan area would have a higher value if it were completely free of any noise, smog, or other undesirable features, provided the same conveniences were available. We are sure that if the metropolitan area had no airports, freeways, buses, trucks, trains, ambulances, and many other conveniences that are sources of noise, fumes, and whatnot, that property values would be substantially reduced. Property owners cannot—and we are sure they do not expect to—have the advantages created by conveniences and yet be paid for the undesirable effects created by the same conveniences unless those effects adversely affect their property so directly and so substantially that it is manifestly unfair to require them to sustain a measurable loss in market value which the property-owning public in general does not suffer. Thus, not every inconvenience, annoyance, or loss of peace and quiet caused by air flights will give rise to a cause of action in inverse condemnation against an airport operator.

The test, then, that we prescribe will give relief to any property owner who can show a direct and substantial invasion of his property rights of such a magnitude [that] he is deprived of the practical enjoyment of the property and that such invasion results in a definite and measurable diminution of the market value of the property.

To justify an award of damages it must be proved that these invasions of property rights are not of an occasional nature, but are repeated and aggravated, and that there is a reasonable probability that they will be continued in the future. * * *

MAC finally asserts that an equitable balancing of the individual property owners' rights to compensation against the financial impact such payment would have on future aeronautical development is required as part of the mandamus action. Such a balancing, however, would be totally improper in an action which is basically one of eminent domain. The reason such a balancing is improper is that no individual seeks recovery in this action for personal injury, suffering, or inconvenience. Rather, petitioners seek compensation for a reduction in market value which amounts to a taking of property. This standard involves an inherent balancing, as was pointed out earlier in this opinion, in that the measure of recovery is based on decrease in value in the general marketplace rather than decrease in value to the individual property owner, thereby excluding recovery for the discomfort sustained by an unusually sensitive individual. This type of balancing exists when the state initiates the condemnation proceedings as well as when the injured property owner does so. But in either situation, a balancing of the individual's right to recover against that of MAC's utility to society is irrelevant. * * *

Another issue raised and argued in the briefs is: Should property owners who purchased their homes at a reduced price because of the overflight be required to set off this saving against the award of damages in this case? This question was not reached in the lower court and should be passed upon in the lower court, with respect to the damages sustained by such property owner.

Reversed and remanded for proceedings consistent with his decision.

---

1. In Nestle v. Santa Monica, 6 Cal.3d 920, 496 P.2d 480, 101 Cal.Rptr. 568 (1972), involving a similar airport situation, the plaintiffs "asserted four theories of recovery: (1) inverse condemnation, (2) nuisance, (3) negligence, and (4) zoning violations." The trial court held for the defendant on the merits on the first count and dismissed the last three counts for failure to state a cause of action. The Supreme Court affirmed the action on the first count as justified by the evidence showing no depreciation in value of the property, and reversed the trial court on the dismissal of the last three counts. See also Greater Westchester Homeowners v. Los Angeles, 26 Cal.3d 86, 603 P.2d 1329, 160 Cal. Rptr. 733 (1979).

And see Baker v. Burbank–Glendale–Pasadena Airport Authority, 39 Cal. 3d 862, 705 P.2d 866, 218 Cal.Rptr. 293 (1985), where the airport had no power of eminent domain and the court still held that an action for inverse condemnation would lie. "All that is necessary to show is that the damage resulted from an exercise of governmental power while seeking to promote the general interest in its relation to any legitimate object of government." 705 P.2d at 868. In discussing the action for nuisance, the court draws a careful distinction between a "permanent nuisance" and a "continuing nuisance." For the first, damages are "assessed once and for all." "On the other hand, if a nuisance is a use which may be discontinued at anytime, it is considered continuing in character and persons harmed by it may bring successive actions for damages until the nuisance is abated. * * * In case of doubt as to the permanency of the injury the plaintiff may elect whether to treat a particular nuisance as permanent or continuing." Id. at 870–71. In *Baker,* the plaintiffs were permitted to treat it as continuing, because the statute of limitations would otherwise have run.

2. For other cases following the *"Thornburg* line," see Henthorn v. Oklahoma City, 453 P.2d 1013 (Okl.1969); Johnson v. Greeneville, 222 Tenn. 260, 435 S.W.2d 476 (1968). State courts following the rule requiring overflight for inverse condemnation to apply have frequently granted relief on the basis of nuisance. E.g., Ferguson v. Keene, 108 N.H. 409, 238 A.2d 1 (1968); Hanover v. Morristown, 108 N.J.Super. 461, 261 A.2d 692 (1969). Courts have been very slow, however, to grant an injunction. Town of East Haven v. Eastern Airlines, Inc., 331 F.Supp. 16 (D.Conn.1971), supplemented, 333 F.Supp. 338 (1972); Antonik v. Chamberlain, 81 Ohio App. 465, 78 N.E.2d 752, 37 O.O. 305 (1947) (earlier case with frequently quoted discussion of reasonable use of property). On Federal preemption regarding noise regulation, see City of Burbank v. Lockheed Air Terminal, Inc., 411 U.S. 624 (1973); Krueger v. Mitchell, 112 Wis. 2d 28, 332 N.W.2d 733 (1983) (private airport). On zoning for airport approaches, see McShane v. Faribault, 292 N.W.2d 253 (Minn.1980).

3. There are numerous articles on the airport situation. See Eadem and Berger, A Noisy Airport Is a Damned Nuisance!, 3 Sw.U.L.Rev. 39 (1971); Baxter and Altree, Legal Aspects of Airport Noise, 15 J.L. & Econ. 1 (1972); Bell & Bell, Airport Noise; Legal Developments and Economic Alternatives, 8 Ecology L.Q. 607 (1980); Hildebrand, Noise Pollution: An Introduction to the Problem and an Outline for Future Legal Research, 70 Colum.L.Rev. 652 (1970); Spater, Noise and the Law, 63 Mich.L.Rev. 1373 (1965).

4. A problem similar to the airport situation arises when a municipal corporation discharges untreated sewage into a river, to the detriment of the downstream riparian owners. An action is held to lie for inverse condemnation or for nuisance despite the fact that the municipal government is exercising a discretionary function. See e.g., Birchwood Lakes Colony Club, Inc. v. Borough of Medford Lakes, 90 N.J. 582, 449 A.2d 472 (1982); Miotke v. Spokane, 101 Wash.2d 307, 678 P.2d 803 (1984). In Washington Market Enterprises, Inc. v. Trenton, 68 N.J. 107, 343 A.2d 408 (1975), inverse condemnation was held appropriate for suit by an adjoining property owner, when the city had started a redevelopment project and then abandoned it.

BOOMER v. ATLANTIC CEMENT CO., INC.

Court of Appeals of New York, 1970.
26 N.Y.2d 219, 257 N.E.2d 870, 309 N.Y.S.2d 312.

BERGAN, J. Defendant operates a large cement plant near Albany. These are actions for injunction and damages by neighboring land owners alleging injury to property from dirt, smoke and vibration emanating from the plant. A nuisance has been found after trial, temporary damages have been allowed; but an injunction has been denied.

Judge Bergan

The public concern with air pollution arising from many sources in industry and in transportation is currently accorded ever wider recognition accompanied by a growing sense of responsibility in State and Federal Governments to control it. Cement plants are obvious sources of air pollution in the neighborhoods where they operate.

But there is now before the court private litigation in which individual property owners have sought specific relief from a single plant operation. The threshold question raised by the division of view on this appeal is whether the court should resolve the litigation between the parties now before it as equitably as seems possible; or whether, seeking promotion of the general public welfare, it should channel private litigation into broad public objectives.

A court performs its essential function when it decides the rights of parties before it. Its decision of private controversies may sometimes greatly affect public issues. Large questions of law are often resolved by the manner in which private litigation is decided. But this is normally an incident to the court's main function to settle controversy. It is a rare exercise of judicial power to use a decision in private litigation as a purposeful mechanism to achieve direct public objectives greatly beyond the rights and interests before the court.

Effective control of air pollution is a problem presently far from solution even with the full public and financial powers of government. In large measure adequate technical procedures are yet to be developed and some that appear possible may be economically impracticable.

It seems apparent that the amelioration of air pollution will depend on technical research in great depth; on a carefully balanced consideration of the economic impact of close regulation; and of the actual effect on public health. It is likely to require massive public expenditure and to demand more than any local community can accomplish and to depend on regional and interstate controls.

A court should not try to do this on its own as a by-product of private litigation and it seems manifest that the judicial establishment is neither equipped in the limited nature of any judgment it can pronounce nor prepared to lay down and implement an effective policy for the elimination of air pollution. This is an area beyond the circumference of one private lawsuit. It is a direct responsibility for government and should not thus be undertaken as an incident to solving a dispute between property owners and a single cement plant— one of many—in the Hudson River valley.

The cement making operations of defendant have been found by the court at Special Term to have damaged the nearby properties of plaintiffs in these two actions. The total damage to plaintiffs' properties is, however, relatively small in comparison with the value of defendant's operation and with the consequences of the injunction which plaintiffs seek.

The ground for the denial of injunction, notwithstanding the finding both that there is a nuisance and that plaintiffs have been damaged substantially, is the large disparity in economic consequences of the nuisance and of the injunction. This theory cannot, however, be sustained without overruling a doctrine which has been consistently reaffirmed in several leading cases in this court and which has never been disavowed here, namely that where a nuisance has been found and where there has been any substantial damage shown by the party complaining an injunction will be granted.

The rule in New York has been that such a nuisance will be enjoined although marked disparity be shown in economic consequence between the effect of the injunction and the effect of the nuisance.

The problem of disparity in economic consequence was sharply in focus in Whalen v. Union Bag & Paper Co., 208 N.Y. 1, 101 N.E. 805. A pulp mill entailing an investment of more than a million dollars polluted a stream in which plaintiff, who owned a farm, was "a lower riparian owner." The economic loss to plaintiff from this pollution was small. This court, reversing the Appellate Division reinstated the injunction granted by the Special Term against the argument of the mill owner that in view of "the slight advantage to plaintiff and the great loss that will be inflicted on defendant" an injunction should not be granted [c]. "Such a balancing of injuries cannot be justified by the circumstances of this case," Judge Werner noted [c]. He continued: "Although the damage to the plaintiff may be slight as compared with the defendant's expense of abating the condition, that is not a good reason for refusing an injunction" [c].

Thus the unconditional injunction granted at Special Term was reinstated. The rule laid down in that case, then, is that whenever the damage resulting from a nuisance is found not "unsubstantial," viz., $100 a year, injunction would follow. This states a rule that had been followed in this court with marked consistency. * * *

Although the court at Special Term and the Appellate Division held that injunction should be denied, it was found that plaintiffs had been damaged in various specific amounts up to the time of the trial and damages to the respective plaintiffs were awarded for those amounts. The effect of this was, injunction having been denied, plaintiffs could maintain successive actions at law for damages thereafter as further damage was incurred.

The court at Special Term also found the amount of permanent damage attributable to each plaintiff, for the guidance of the parties in the event both sides stipulated to the payment and acceptance of such permanent damage as a settlement of all the controversies among the parties. The total of permanent damages to all plaintiffs thus found was $185,000. This basis of adjustment has not resulted in any stipulation by the parties.

This result at Special Term and at the Appellate Division is a departure from a rule that has become settled; but to follow the rule literally in these cases would be to close down the plant at once. This court is fully agreed to avoid that immediately drastic remedy; the difference in view is how best to avoid it. [Footnote by Court: Respondent's investment in the plant is in excess of $45,000,000. There are over 300 people employed there.]

One alternative is to grant the injunction but postpone its effect to a specified future date to give opportunity for technical advances to permit defendant to eliminate the nuisance; another is to grant the injunction conditioned on the payment of permanent damages to plaintiffs which would compensate them for the total economic loss to their property present and future caused by defendant's operations. * * * [T]he court chooses the latter alternative.

If the injunction were to be granted unless within a short period— e.g., 18 months—the nuisance be abated by improved methods, there would be no assurance that any significant technical improvement would occur.

The parties could settle this private litigation at any time if defendant paid enough money and the imminent threat of closing the plant would build up the pressure on defendant. If there were no improved techniques found, there would inevitably be applications to the court at Special Term for extensions of time to perform on showing of good faith efforts to find such techniques.

Moreover, techniques to eliminate dust and other annoying by-products of cement making are unlikely to be developed by any research the defendant can undertake within any short period, but will depend on the total resources of the cement industry nationwide and throughout the world. The problem is universal wherever cement is made.

For obvious reasons the rate of the research is beyond control of defendant. If at the end of 18 months the whole industry has not found a technical solution a court would be hard put to close down this one cement plant if due regard be given to equitable principles.

On the other hand, to grant the injunction unless defendant pays plaintiffs such permanent damages as may be fixed by the court seems to do justice between the contending parties. All of the attributions of economic loss to the properties on which plaintiffs' complaints are based will have been redressed.

The nuisance complained of by these plaintiffs may have other public or private consequences, but these particular parties are the only ones who have sought remedies and the judgment proposed will fully redress them. The limitation of relief granted is a limitation only within the four corners of these actions and does not foreclose public health or other public agencies from seeking proper relief in a proper court.

It seems reasonable to think that the risk of being required to pay permanent damages to injured property owners by cement plant owners would itself be a reasonable effective spur to research for improved techniques to minimize nuisance.

The power of the court to condition on equitable grounds the continuance of an injunction on the payment of permanent damages seems undoubted. [Cc]

The damage base here suggested is consistent with the general rule in those nuisance cases where damages are allowed. "Where a nuisance is of such a permanent and unabatable character that a single recovery can be had, including the whole damage past and future resulting therefrom, there can be but one recovery" [c].

Thus it seems fair to both sides to grant permanent damages to plaintiffs which will terminate this private litigation. The theory of damage is the "servitude on land" of plaintiffs imposed by defendant's nuisance. * * *

The judgment, by allowance of permanent damages imposing a servitude on land, which is the basis of the actions, would preclude future recovery by plaintiffs or their grantees [c].

This should be placed beyond debate by a provision of the judgment that the payment by defendant and the acceptance by plaintiffs of permanent damages found by the court shall be in compensation for a servitude on the land.

Although the Trial Term has found permanent damages as a possible basis of settlement of the litigation, on remission the court should be entirely free to re-examine this subject. It may again find the permanent damage already found; or make new findings.

The orders should be reversed, without costs, and the cases remitted to Supreme Court, Albany County to grant an injunction which shall be vacated upon payment by defendant of such amounts of permanent damage to the respective plaintiffs as shall for this purpose be determined by the court.

JASEN, J. dissenting. I agree with the majority that a reversal is required here, but I do not subscribe to the newly enunciated doctrine of assessment of permanent damages, in lieu of an injunction, where substantial property rights have been impaired by the creation of a nuisance. * * *

I see grave dangers in overruling our long-established rule of granting an injunction where a nuisance results in substantial continuing damage. In permitting the injunction to become inoperative upon the payment of permanent damages, the majority is, in effect, licensing a continuing wrong. It is the same as saying to the cement company, you may continue to do harm to your neighbors so long as you pay a fee for it. Furthermore, once such permanent damages are assessed and paid, the incentive to alleviate the wrong would be eliminated, thereby continuing air pollution of an area without abatement.

It is true that some courts have sanctioned the remedy here proposed by the majority in a number of cases, but none of the authorities relied upon by the majority are analogous to the situation before us. In those cases, the courts, in denying an injunction and awarding money damages, grounded their decision on a showing that the use to which the property was intended to be put was primarily for the public benefit. Here, on the other hand, it is clearly established that the cement company is creating a continuing air pollution nuisance primarily for its own private interest with no public benefit.

This kind of inverse condemnation [c] may not be invoked by a private person or corporation for private gain or advantage. Inverse condemnation should only be permitted when the public is primarily served in the taking or impairment of property. [Cc] The promotion of the interests of the polluting cement company has, in my opinion, no public use or benefit.

Nor is it constitutionally permissible to impose servitude on land, without consent of the owner, by payment of permanent damages where the continuing impairment of the land is for a private use. [Cc] This is made clear by the State Constitution (art. I, § 7, subd. [a]) which provides that "[p]rivate property shall not be taken for *public use* without just compensation" (emphasis added). It is, of course, significant that the section makes no mention of taking for a *private* use.

In sum, then, by constitutional mandate as well as by judicial pronouncement, the permanent impairment of private property for private purposes is not authorized in the absence of clearly demonstrated public benefit and use.

I would enjoin the defendant cement company from continuing the discharge of dust particles upon its neighbors' properties unless, within 18 months, the cement company abated this nuisance. * * *

---

1. Is the court applying inverse condemnation here in the case of a private defendant who does not possess the power of eminent domain? Does this amount to giving the power of eminent domain to the defendant and letting it force the plaintiffs to "sell out"? Are the damages to be assessed on the basis of the harm to the plaintiffs, including personal annoyance, or should they be confined to depreciation of the value of their land?

2. If an injunction is to be denied, is it wise to award permanent damages to the plaintiffs? Suppose a feasible method of controlling cement dust is later discovered. Is the defendant left with any incentive to seek to find a means of control of the dust? Suppose an injunction ordering the defendants to desist had been granted. Would this have done anything more than permit the plaintiffs to hold the defendant up and insist on a much higher price for selling out?

3. How do the two opinions in this case fit with the two opinions in Carpenter v. The Double R Cattle Co., supra page 821? Are the airport cases relevant here too? And consider again Restatement (Second) of Torts §§ 926(b), 829A (1979). What about the desirability of giving the plaintiffs the option of treating this nuisance as a permanent or continuing one, as in Baker v. Burbank–Glendale–Pasadena Airport Auth., supra page 834; cf. Restatement (Second) of Torts §§ 929, 930 (1979) (damages for harm to each for past and future invasions).

Most courts do not take a categoric position on whether an injunction should be granted in general. Instead, they engage in a process designated as "balancing the equities." A good case illustrating the process is Smith v. Staso Milling Co., 18 F.2d 736 (2d Cir.1927), where the plaintiff recovered damages for the pollution of a brook and the air with slate dust and for the jarring of his house by blasting, but an injunction to prevent the defendant from continuing was denied. In this process the courts take into consideration a number of different factors, no one of which is necessarily controlling, but any one of which may control in a particular case. Among these are the character and extent of the damage inflicted or threatened; the good faith or intentional misconduct of the defendant, or his efforts to avoid injury to the plaintiff, as in Elliott Nursery Co. v. Du Quesne Light Co., 281 Pa. 166, 126 A. 345 (1924); the financial investment of each party, and the relative economic hardship that will result to either from granting or denying the injunction; and especially the interest of the general public in the continuance of the defendant's enterprise.

4. Interesting cases illustrating the process of balancing equities and the considerations and reasoning involved are Harrison v. Indiana Auto Shredders Co., 528 F.2d 1107 (7 Cir.1975) (noise from auto shredder); Jacobson v. Crown Zellerbach Corp., 273 Or. 15, 539 P.2d 641 (1975) (vibration from logging trucks); McQuade v. Tucson Tiller Apartments, Ltd., 25 Ariz.App. 312, 543 P.2d 150 (1975) (mass rock concert); Madison v. Ducktown Sulphur, Copper & Iron Co., 113 Tenn. 331, 83 S.W. 658 (1904). In the last case a $2 million copper reduction plant that destroyed all vegetation in the area but was the total basis for existence of a town was not enjoined at the behest of landowners whose property had very little value. The plant was in the southeast corner of the state, however, and the State of Georgia, seeking original relief in the Supreme Court, obtained it. Georgia v. Tennessee Copper Co., 206 U.S. 230 (1907). For other cases, see Annot., 40 A.L.R.3d 601 (1971).

5. What should be the measure of damages? See Boomer v. Atlantic Cement Co., 72 Misc.2d 834, 340 N.Y.S.2d 97 (1972) (instant case on remand, with extensive discussion of proof and measure), aff'd sub nom. Kinley v. Atlantic Cement Co., 42 A.D.2d 496, 349 N.Y.S.2d 199 (1973).

6. In Little Joseph Realty, Inc. v. Babylon, 41 N.Y.2d 738, 363 N.E.2d 1163, 395 N.Y.S.2d 428 (1977), the court refused to apply the *Boomer* principle when an asphalt plant was located in violation of a zoning ordinance and the lower court conditioned an injunction on payment of permanent damages and abatement of the most offensive aspects. "[W]hen a continuing use flies in the face of a valid zoning restriction it must, subject to the existence of any appropriate equitable defenses, be enjoined unconditionally."

7. See generally McClintock, Discretion to Deny Injunction Against Trespass and Nuisance, 12 Minn.L.Rev. 565 (1926); Morris and Keeton, Notes on Balancing the Equities, 18 Texas L.Rev. 253 (1940); Note, Injunctive Negotiations: An Economic, Moral and Legal Analysis, 27 Stan.L.Rev. 1563 (1975); Restatement (Second) of Torts § 941.

8. *Hazardous Waste Disposal.* Village of Wilsonville v. SCA Services, Inc., 86 Ill.2d 1, 426 N.E.2d 824, 55 Ill.Dec. 499 (1981), gives a very thorough treatment to the total problem. The 130-acre disposal site was over two-thirds in the village and was located over an abandoned coal mine. There was much expert testimony regarding the method of conducting the site and the damages from the chemicals involved. The trial court granted a permanent injunction requiring that the wastes be removed. The ruling was affirmed by the appellate court and the Supreme Court. The holding was that there was both a public and a private nuisance, both existing and prospective, based on a careful balancing of the conflicting interests. Although the site served a valuable and necessary purpose and substantial sums of money had been expended on it, its maintenance could not be "justified on such grounds when we have substantial injury to individual rights, community rights, substantial damage to human beings and other living things." Other pertinent factors were that the nuisance came to the village, that a damage remedy would be inadequate, that an injunction is appropriate against prospective damage that need not be certain to take place if it would be severe, that it was feasible to remove the drums and that the approval given by the state agency was based on data collected by the defendant that had been proved at trial to be inaccurate. The injunction was held not to "deprive the defendant of its property without due process of law."

There has been much discussion of the matter. See, Baurer, Love Canal: Common Law Approaches to a Modern Tragedy, 11 Env.L.Nw.U. 133 (1980); Eckhardt, The Unfinished Business of Hazardous Waste Control, 33 Baylor L.Rev. 253 (1981); Harrington & Krupneck, Stationary Source Pollution Policy and Choices for Reform, 21 Nat.Res.J. 539 (1981); Hurley–Bruno, The Development of a Strict Liability Cause of Action for Personal Injuries Resulting from Hazardous Waste, 16 N.Eng.L.Rev. 543 (1981); Sheldon, Nuclear Waste; The Problem Remains Unburied, 32 S.C.L.Rev. 911 (1981); Zedrasser, Injuries from Hazardous Wastes, 22 Trial [No. 10] 26 (Oct.1986); Notes, Allocating the Costs of Hazardous Waste Disposal, 94 Harv.L.Rev. 584 (1981); Liability for Generators of Hazardous Waste: The Failure of Existing Mechanisms, 69 Geo.L.J. 1047 (1981); Hazardous Wastes: Preserving the Nuisance Remedy, 33 Stan.L.Rev. 675 (1981); Causation and Common Law Relief for Toxic–Substance Contamination, 14 U.Mich.J.L.Reform 53 (1980).

9. *Federal Statutes.* The Comprehensive Environmental Response, Compensation and Liability Act (CERCLA), 42 U.S.C. §§ 9601–9657 (1982) was passed in 1980. Combined with such other federal acts as the Clean Air Act, 42 U.S.C. §§ 7401–7642, the Clean Water Act, 33 U.S.C. §§ 1251–1376, the Resource Conservation and Recovery Act (RCRA), 42 U.S.C. §§ 6901–6991, and the Toxic Substance Control Act (TSCA), 15 U.S.C. §§ 2601–2629 (1982), it establishes a comprehensive and complicated system that is necessarily beyond the scope of this casebook. Specialized courses and seminars on environmental law are offered in many law schools.

On hazardous waste cleanups, see generally, F. Grad, Treatise on Environmental Law (1986); J. Stensvaag, Hazardous Waste Law and Practice (1986) (other volumes in preparation); V. Yannacone, Cohen and Davison, Environmental Rights and Remedies (1972) (with annual supplements); W. Frank and T. Atkeson, Superfund: Litigation and Cleanup (BNA, 1985); Gaba, Recovering Hazardous Waste Cleanup Costs: The Private Cause of Action Under CERCLA, 13 Ecology L.Q. 181 (1986); Freeman, Tort Law Reform: Superfund/RCRA Liability as a Major Cause of the Insurance Crisis, 21 Tort & Ins. L.J. 517 (1986).

SPUR INDUSTRIES, INC. v. DEL E. WEBB DEVELOPMENT CO.

Supreme Court of Arizona, 1972.
108 Ariz. 178, 494 P.2d 700.

CAMERON, VICE CHIEF JUSTICE. From a judgment permanently enjoining the defendant, Spur Industries, Inc., from operating a cattle feedlot near the plaintiff Del E. Webb Development Company's Sun City, Spur appeals. Webb cross-appeals. Although numerous issues are raised, we feel that it is necessary to answer only two questions. They are:

1. Where the operation of a business, such as a cattle feedlot is lawful in the first instance, but becomes a nuisance by reason of a nearby residential area, may the feedlot operation be enjoined in an action brought by the developer of the residential area?

2. Assuming that the nuisance may be enjoined, may the developer of a completely new town or urban area in a previously agricultural

area be required to indemnify the operator of the feedlot who must move or cease operation because of the presence of the residential area created by the developer?

[Farming had existed in the general area involved (about 14 to 15 miles west of urban Phoenix) prior to 1950. The property owned by Spur was well suited for cattle feeding, and Spur's predecessors began this activity. In 1959 Del Webb began to develop Sun City, some distance from Spur. The development progressed rapidly and expanded, coming into closer proximity to Spur.]

By December 1967, Del Webb's property had extended south to Olive Avenue and Spur was within 500 feet of Olive Avenue to the north. * * * Del Webb filed its original complaint alleging that in excess of 1,300 lots in the southwest portion were unfit for development for sale as residential lots because of the operation of the Spur feedlot.

Del Webb's suit complained that the Spur feeding operation was a public nuisance because of the flies and the odor which were drifting or being blown by the prevailing south to north wind over the southern portion of Sun City. At the time of the suit, Spur was feeding between 20,000 and 30,000 head of cattle, and the facts amply support the finding of the trial court that the feed pens had become a nuisance to the people who resided in the southern part of Del Webb's development. The testimony indicated that cattle in a commercial feedlot will produce 35 to 40 pounds of wet manure per day, per head, or over a million pounds of wet manure per day for 30,000 head of cattle, and that despite the admittedly good feedlot management and good housekeeping practices by Spur, the resulting odor and flies produced an annoying if not unhealthy situation as far as the senior citizens of southern Sun City were concerned. There is no doubt that some of the citizens of Sun City were unable to enjoy the outdoor living which Del Webb had advertised and that Del Webb was faced with sales resistance from prospective purchasers as well as strong and persistent complaints from the people who had purchased homes in that area. * * *

Where the injury is slight, the remedy for minor inconveniences lies in an action for damages rather than in one for an injunction. [c]. Moreover, some courts have held, in the "balancing of conveniences" cases, that damages may be the sole remedy. * * *

We have no difficulty, however, in agreeing with the conclusion of the trial court that Spur's operation was an enjoinable public nuisance as far as the people in the southern portion of Del Webb's Sun City were concerned. * * *

It is clear that as to the citizens of Sun City, the operation of Spur's feedlot was both a public and a private nuisance. They could have successfully maintained an action to abate the nuisance. Del Webb, having shown a special injury in the loss of sales, had a standing to bring suit to enjoin the nuisance. [Cc] The judgment of the trial court permanently enjoining the operation of the feedlot is affirmed. * * *

In the so-called "coming to the nuisance" cases, the courts have held that the residential landowner may not have relief if he knowingly came into a neighborhood reserved for industrial or agricultural endeavors and has been damaged thereby:

"Plaintiffs chose to live in an area uncontrolled by zoning laws or restrictive covenants and remote from urban development. In such an area plaintiffs cannot complain that legitimate agricultural pursuits are being carried on in the vicinity, nor can plaintiffs, having chosen to build in an agricultural area, complain that the agricultural pursuits carried on in the area depreciate the value of their homes. The area being *primarily agricultural,* any opinion reflecting the value of such property must take this factor into account. The standards affecting the value of residence property in an urban setting, subject to zoning controls and controlled planning techniques, cannot be the standards by which agricultural properties are judged.

"People employed in a city who build their homes in suburban areas of the county beyond the limits of a city and zoning regulations do so for a reason. Some do so to avoid the high taxation rate imposed by cities, or to avoid special assessments for street, sewer and water projects. They usually build on improved or hard surface highways, which have been built either at state or county expense and thereby avoid special assessments for these improvements. It may be that they desire to get away from the congestion of traffic, smoke, noise, foul air and the many other annoyances of city life. But with all these advantages in going beyond the area which is zoned and restricted to protect them in their homes, they must be prepared to take the disadvantages." Dill v. Excel Packing Company, 183 Kan. 513, 525, 526, 331 P.2d 539, 548, 549 (1958). * * *

Were Webb the only party injured, we would feel justified in holding that the doctrine of "coming to the nuisance" would have been a bar to the relief asked by Webb, and, on the other hand, had Spur located the feedlot near the outskirts of a city and had the city grown toward the feedlot, Spur would have to suffer the cost of abating the nuisance as to those people locating within the growth pattern of the expanding city. * * *

There was no indication in the instant case at the time Spur and its predecessors located in western Maricopa County that a new city would spring up, full-blown, alongside the feeding operation and that the developer of that city would ask the court to order Spur to move because of the new city. Spur is required to move not because of any wrongdoing on the part of Spur, but because of a proper and legitimate regard of the courts for the rights and interests of the public.

Del Webb, on the other hand, is entitled to the relief prayed for (a permanent injunction), not because Webb is blameless, but because of the damage to the people who have been encouraged to purchase homes in Sun City. It does not equitably or legally follow, however, that Webb, being entitled to the injunction, is then free of any liability to

Spur if Webb has in fact been the cause of the damage Spur has sustained. It does not seem harsh to require a developer, who has taken advantage of the lesser land values in a rural area as well as the availability of large tracts of land on which to build and develop a new town or city in the area, to indemnify those who are forced to leave as a result.

Having brought people to the nuisance to the foreseeable detriment of Spur, Webb must indemnify Spur for a reasonable amount of the cost of moving or shutting down. It should be noted that this relief to Spur is limited to a case wherein a developer has, with foreseeability, brought into a previously agricultural or industrial area the population which makes necessary the granting of an injunction against a lawful business and for which the business has no adequate relief.

It is therefore the decision of this court that the matter be remanded to the trial court for a hearing upon the damages sustained by the defendant Spur as a reasonable and direct result of the granting of the permanent injunction. Since the result of the appeal may appear novel and both sides have obtained a measure of relief, it is ordered that each side will bear its own costs.

Affirmed in part, reversed in part, and remanded for further proceedings consistent with this opinion.

---

1. The majority rule is that the plaintiff is not barred from recovery for either a public or a private nuisance by the sole fact that he "comes to the nuisance" by buying property adjoining it. See Restatement (Second) of Torts § 840D; Witham, First Come, First Served: An Economic View of Coming to the Nuisance, 9 J.Leg.Stud. 597 (1980); Notes, 41 Calif.L.Rev. 148 (1953), 17 Temple L.Q. 449 (1943).

2. The rule is not, however, an absolute one; and particularly in cases where other factors are more or less balanced, the fact that the plaintiff has come to the nuisance may be important and even decisive. An interesting case is East St. Johns Shingle Co. v. Portland, 195 Or. 505, 246 P.2d 554 (1952), where the plaintiff's shingle mill relied for its supply of logs upon rafting through a slough from the Columbia River. Defendant city discharged sewage into the river, which polluted the slough and fouled the logs, thus interfering seriously with plaintiff's business. When the plaintiff had bought its property twenty years before, the city was already polluting the slough; but with the growth of the community the condition gradually became worse. The health of the city of Portland depended in large measure upon the sewage disposal, and there was no other way to dispose of it. It was held that plaintiff was not entitled either to an injunction or to damages.

3. Defendant does not acquire a prescriptive right to continue the nuisance unless during the necessary period an action might have been maintained for it. Ireland v. Bowman & Cockrell, 130 Ky. 153, 113 S.W. 56 (1908); Hulsman v. Boiling Spring Bleaching Co., 14 N.J.Eq. 335 (1862). By the majority rule, one cannot acquire a prescriptive right to maintain a *public* nuisance, no matter how long it has continued. And this applies even to a person who is suing for damages personal to himself. Gundy v. Merrill, 250

Mich. 416, 230 N.W. 163 (1930); Smejkal v. Empire Lite–Rock, Inc., 274 Or. 571, 547 P.2d 1363 (1976).

4. The adjustment of the equities in the principal case by requiring indemnity is a new approach. It adds to the court's repertoire of remedies. How can these remedies be adjusted or combined to produce the fairest and most effective result? This topic has been the subject of some stimulating studies of the law of nuisance. See Calabresi & Melamed, Property Rules, Liability Rules and Inalienability: One View of the Cathedral, 85 Harv.L.Rev. 1089 (1972); Michelman, Pollution as a Tort: A Non–Accidental Perspective on Calabresi's Costs, 80 Yale L.J. 647 (1970); Polinski, Resolving Nuisance Disputes: The Simple Economics of Injunctive and Damage Remedies, 37 Stan.L. Rev. 1075 (1970); Rabin, Nuisance Law: Rethinking Fundamental Assumptions, 63 Va.L.Rev. 1294 (1977); Lewin, Compensated Injunction on the Evolution of Nuisance Law, 71 Iowa L.Rev. 775 (1986). For a detailed treatment of damages, see Pfennigstorf, Environment, Damages and Compensation, 1979 A.B.A.Res.J. 347.

TIMMONS v. REED

Supreme Court of Wyoming, 1977.
569 P.2d 112.

ROSE, JUSTICE. This appeal concerns the propriety of entering a summary judgment against appellant-plaintiff in his tort and nuisance action for damages arising out of a rear-end collision, which involved two trucks on a fog-covered highway near Byron, Wyoming. Defendants, James Henry Reed and NEPECO Company (hereinafter referred to as "Reed"), and defendant, Marathon Oil Company, moved for and were granted summary judgments on the grounds that there was no disputed issue of material fact, and that plaintiff was contributorily negligent as a matter of law for failure to comply with the so-called assured-clear-distance rule. We will reverse.

In his complaint, plaintiff alleged that defendants, Reed and NEPECO, were negligent; that Marathon was strictly liable for maintenance of an "abnormally dangerous activity;" and that Marathon was strictly liable for willful and intentional maintenance of a nuisance. Defendants asserted then, and now, that plaintiff's contributory negligence was a bar to his entire action for recovery. * * *

[O]n February 7, 1973, at about 7:30 a.m., plaintiff was driving an empty sugar-beet truck west on U.S. Highway 14A. It was just getting light and the temperature was about 10 degrees. Approximately two miles west of Byron, Wyoming, he encountered intermittent fog just prior to the location of an oil-treater facility maintained by Marathon. The treater facility, located immediately south of the highway, discharged 126–degree water into an enclosed conduit which ran underneath the highway to a point approximately 87 feet north of the highway. At this juncture, the heated water passes into an open ditch which conveys it to a nearby lake. Other truckdrivers, and the plaintiff, testified that on cold mornings the fog was very dense for a quarter to a half mile on either side of the water ditch, even when there was no other fog in the general area. * * *

[Plaintiff, proceeding from an earlier stop,] had reached his fourth gear (his truck had eight gears) but was in a slowing-down process because of an extremely dense fog-bank which had formed near the Marathon ditch. As the nose of his truck entered the fog, he almost immediately saw another truck, which he described to be approximately ten feet in front of him. At about the same time, the plaintiff hit his brakes but was unable to avoid colliding with the rear portion of this vehicle, which turned out to be the water-truck driven by Reed and owned by NEPECO. Plaintiff estimated his speed at the point of impact to be about twenty miles per hour or less. He testified he had been driving this stretch of road every night for about two months and was aware of the dense fog-bank near the treater facilities. Plaintiff observed no taillights on the truck, and testified further that it was his opinion that Reed was stopped on the highway when he, the plaintiff, first sighted the vehicle just inside the fog-bank.

When a driver is confronted with adverse driving conditions, such as fog, he is under the duty to exercise reasonable or ordinary care, having regard for such unusual and extraordinary circumstances. [C] In appropriate circumstances, the assured-clear-distance rule can be applied to hold a plaintiff contributorily negligent as a matter of law. [C] This is not the case, however, where a dangerous situation, which the driver of the automobile has no reason to expect, suddenly appears in front of him, and a driver is not obligated by the doctrine of ordinary care to keep a lookout for an unlighted truck in the lane of his traffic. [Cc] Where a vehicle in the same lane of traffic is unlighted, or is otherwise obscured, then, ordinarily, a following driver is not contributorily negligent as a matter of law, even though he is not able to stop within the range of his vision. [Cc]

Under the facts of record, we hold that there was a material issue of fact on the question of plaintiff's contributory negligence and the issue should not have been disposed of by summary judgment. * * *

The second question raised in this appeal is whether contributory negligence is a defense to the nuisance action against Marathon. Even if we were to find that such a defense is appropriate, our preceding discussion would indicate that, in this case, the plaintiff cannot be held contributorily negligent as a matter of law for the purposes of summary judgment. Since the case must be remanded for trial, we find it advisable to discuss the substantive issues raised by this question. Marathon admits that the defense of contributory negligence is not usually available in a nuisance action. [C] Marathon, however, would characterize plaintiff's action as essentially grounded in negligence—in which case contributory negligence is available as a defense.

Under fact situations similar to the instant appeal, the courts of other jurisdictions have spoken interchangeably about the tort concepts of negligence and nuisance. [Cc] Liability for a nuisance may be imposed on any of three bases: (1) intentional invasion of the plaintiff's interests, or (2) negligent invasion of such interests, or (3) conduct which is abnormal and out-of-place in its surroundings and so falls fairly within the principle of strict liability. Although not completely clear, plaintiff's causes of action against Marathon seem to be based on the assertion of a public nuisance from which he has received particular damages. The problem arises when plaintiff attempts to draw a dividing line between intentional and negligent conduct. Marathon may have intentionally created a public nuisance, but it may not have intended the damages which resulted to the plaintiff. [C] The distinction attempted is an important one since usually in cases based on intentional conduct, resulting in an absolute nuisance, contributory negligence is no defense—which is not the case where the claim is inherently based on negligence. [C]

The general rule applicable to the type of case now before us is stated in Restatement (Second) of Torts § 371, as follows:

"A possessor of land is subject to liability for physical harm to others outside of the land caused by an activity carried on by him thereon which he realizes or should realize will involve an *unreasonable risk* of physical harm to them under the same conditions as though the activity were carried on at a neutral place."

The defendant, therefore, is considered to have created only a risk as to injury, and with respect to the resulting damage his conduct cannot be called anything more than negligent. [C] The landowner in close proximity to a public highway must exercise reasonable care to avoid injury to the traveling public arising from unnecessarily-dangerous conditions created by him on the land, where the consequences of a failure to do so are reasonably foreseeable. [C]

A violation of this duty constitutes negligence. [Cc]

We are not prepared to hold on the basis of this record that Marathon has created an absolute nuisance—that is essentially a jury question to be resolved on the facts and circumstances disclosed at trial. We do hold, however, that the defense of contributory negligence will be available to Marathon at trial if the evidence discloses that plaintiff's nuisance action is inherently based on negligence.

The summary judgment entered against the plaintiff-appellant is reversed.

---

1. When there is an intentional private nuisance, contributory negligence is not a defense, as in the case of other intentional torts. Higginbotham v. Kearse, 111 W.Va. 264, 161 S.E. 37 (1931); Phillips Ranch, Inc. v. Banta, 273 Or. 784, 543 P.2d 1035 (1975).

2. When the nuisance arises out of negligence, most of the decisions are in accord with the principal case, that contributory negligence is a defense. See McFarlane v. Niagara Falls, 247 N.Y. 340, 160 N.E. 391 (1928) (leading case); Denny v. Garavaglia, 333 Mich. 317, 52 N.W.2d 521 (1952); Restatement (Second) of Torts § 840B.

3. The dividing line between intent and negligence has led to some difficulty in cases when the defendant has intentionally invaded the rights of the public by creating only a risk of harm to travelers on the highway, without the intent to injure the travelers. Some decisions have classified this as intentional and have held that contributory negligence is not a defense. See Delaney v. Philhern Realty Co., 280 N.Y. 461, 21 N.E.2d 507 (1939); Beckwith v. Stratford, 129 Conn. 506, 29 A.2d 775 (1942). These decisions have been criticized. See Seavey, Nuisance: Contributory Negligence and Other Mysteries, 65 Harv.L.Rev. 984 (1952); Note, Nuisance or Negligence: The Tyranny of Labels, 24 Ind.L.J. 402 (1949).

Others agree with the principal case in treating the interference as only negligence toward the plaintiff. Hartman v. Brigantine, 23 N.J. 530, 129 A.2d 876 (1957); Calder v. City and County of San Francisco, 50 Cal.App.2d 837, 123 P.2d 897 (1942).

4. When the nuisance is based on strict liability, contributory negligence of the plaintiff in failing to discover the danger is not a defense; but if he discovers the danger and deliberately proceeds to encounter it, his contributory negligence or his assumption of risk may affect his recovery. Thus if defendant is blasting in dangerous proximity to a public highway and plaintiff negligently fails to observe a warning sign, drives past it and is hurt by a blast, he may recover; but if he sees the sign, or a flagman who warns him not to proceed and he insists on doing so, he cannot recover. See Worth v. Dunn, 98 Conn. 51, 118 A. 467 (1922).

5. See generally, on the defenses of contributory negligence and assumption of risk in nuisance cases, Note, 28 Tenn.L.Rev. 561 (1961). On the effect of comparative negligence, see V. Schwartz, Comparative Negligence, ch. 11 (2d ed. 1986) (depends upon basis of action—intent, negligence or strict liability).

Self–Help to Abate a Nuisance

6. The privilege of self-help to abate a nuisance is analogous to the privilege of using reasonable force to protect the possession of land against trespass. It is open only to those to whom the condition is a nuisance. A public nuisance may be abated by a private individual only when it causes or threatens special damage to himself, apart from that to the general public. Corthell v. Holmes, 87 Me. 24, 32 A. 715 (1896); Nation v. District of Columbia, 34 U.S.App.D.C. 453 (1910).

7. It is commonly held that the privilege of abating conditions outside the actor's premises depends upon the actual existence of a nuisance, and that an honest but mistaken belief will not justify the action. Grant v. Allen, 41 Conn. 156 (1874); Humphreys Oil Co. v. Liles, 262 S.W. 1058 (Tex.Civ.App.1924), aff'd, 277 S.W. 100 (Com.App.).

8. The privilege extends to reasonable force according to the necessities of the situation, and may extend to the destruction of valuable property. Amoskeag Mfg. Co. v. Goodale, 46 N.H. 53 (dam) (1865); Maryland Tel. & Tel. Co. v. Ruth, 106 Md. 644, 68 A. 358 (telephone pole) (1907).

9. It does not extend to unnecessary damage or to damage unreasonable in extent. The actor may not burn down the adjoining house merely because it is used for prostitution. Moody v. Board of Supervisors of Niagara Cty., 46 Barb. 659 (N.Y.1866).

10. The abatement of a nuisance does not justify the infliction of personal injury or a breach of the peace. Walker v. Davis, 139 Tenn. 475, 202 S.W. 78 (1917).

11. Ordinarily, when time permits, the actor must notify the wrongdoer of the existence of the nuisance and demand removal of the condition. Hickey v. Michigan Central R. Co., 96 Mich. 498, 55 N.W. 989 (1893). This is not required when it is apparent that the wrongdoer is already aware of the nuisance and that the demand would be futile. Hickey v. Michigan Central R. Co., 96 Mich. 498, 55 N.W. 989 (1893).

Other Torts Involving Invasion of Interests in Real Property

Besides Trespass and Nuisance, there are two additional commonly recognized torts arising in behalf of a landowner or possessor of real property because of damage to his interests in the land. They are:

1. *Interference With the Support of Land.* This applies to both lateral support and subjacent support. If the withdrawal of the support is sufficient to cause a subsidence of the land in its natural condition— i.e., "naturally necessary support" is withdrawn—the liability is strict and no showing of fault on the part of the defendant is required. Damage to artificial additions to the land is also included. If the withdrawal of support would not have caused a subsidence of the land in its natural condition but does cause subsidence because of artificial additions to the land, then liability may still exist but it depends upon a finding that the actor's conduct was negligent. See Bonomi v. Backhouse, El.Bl. & El. 686, 120 Eng.Rep. 643 (1859), aff'd, 9 H.L. 503, 11 Eng.Rep. 825 (1861); Blake Constr. Co. v. United States, 585 F.2d 998 (Ct.Cl.1978); St. Louis–S.F.R.R. v. Wade, 607 F.2d 126 (5th Cir.1979); St. Joseph Light & Power Co. v. Kaw Valley Tunneling, 589 S.W.2d 260 (Mo.1979). On subsidence caused by withdrawal of ground water, see Friendswood Dev. Co. v. Smith–Southwest Industries, Inc., 576 S.W.2d 21 (Tex.1978). And see Restatement (Second) of Torts §§ 817–821 (1979).

2. *Interference with the Use of Water.* This tort covers three types of water: water in a watercourse or lake in or adjoining the land ("riparian rights"), ground water (sometime called subterranean water or underground water) and surface waters (from precipitation). On the subject of riparian rights, there are three distinct legal theories for determination of the rights involved. The first, adopted in England and used by a few American states, is the natural-flow theory—the right to have the water flow as it was wont to flow in nature, qualified only by the right of each riparian owner to make a limited use of it. The second, adopted in a majority of American states, is the reasonable-use theory—the right to be free from unreasonable uses that cause harm to the proprietor's own reasonable use. The third, adopted largely in the states of the west, is the prior-appropriation rule, that beneficial use of the water is the basis of the right to it and that priority of use is the basis of the division of it between appropriators

when there is not enough for all. The reasonable-use theory is the most flexible and adaptable one, and it has succeeded in adapting to both of the other two in terms of the factors affecting the determination of when a user is reasonable. It is now distinctly the majority rule. In a number of states, there are statutory provisions modifying the common law rules.

On the use of "ground water" (subsurface water), there are also several theories: (1) the English rule of absolute ownership, (2) the American rule of reasonable use, a rule of correlative rights, and (3) the rule that an "underground stream" is treated like a surface stream. Here too, the adaptable reasonable-use rule is growing in number of adherents, and there are statutory modification in some states. As for surface waters, there is general agreement that a landowner can use as much of them as he needs.

There is a good treatment of the whole subject in Chapter 41 of the Restatement (Second) of Torts §§ 841–864; case citations are collected in the Reporter's Notes to these sections, in the Appendix volume. And see Beuscher, Appropriation Water Law Elements in Riparian Doctrine States, 10 Buffalo L.Rev. 448 (1961); Trelease, the Concept of Reasonable Beneficial Use in the Law of Surface Streams, 12 Wyo.L.J. 1 (1957); Adams, Updating Groundwater: New Wine in Old Bottles, 39 Ohio St. L.J. 520 (1978); Davis, Wells and Stream; Relationships at Law, 37 Mo. L.Rev. 189 (1972); Maloney & Plager, Diffused Surface Water: Scourge or Bounty?, 8 Nat.Res.J. 72 (1968).

Chapter XVII

DEFAMATION

The term "tort" deriving from the Latin *tortus,* meaning twisted, is apt for the tort of defamation in two senses. The conduct involved is twisted, or crooked; and the law governing it is twisted, or wrenched sadly out of shape by its historical development. As one commentator put it, the law of defamation was "marred in the making." 1 T. Street, Foundations of Legal Liability 273 (1906). Rules and distinctions originating because of ancient controversies over jurisdiction, long since obsolete, nevertheless became frozen and crystallized.

Originally the common law courts took no jurisdiction over any defamation, leaving it to be dealt with by the local seigniorial courts. When these fell into decay, the ecclesiastical courts began to take jurisdiction over slander, regarding it as a sin and punishing it with penance. Since the cases all involved oral defamation, slander became identified with word of mouth. When the ecclesiastical courts in turn began to lose their power, there was in the sixteenth century a slow infiltration of tort actions for slander into the common law courts. The excuse for this invasion of church jurisdiction was that some "temporal" damage had been done, distinct from the mere "spiritual" offense, and that it was properly a matter for the king's courts to redress. A long conflict of jurisdiction, part of the broader contest between church and state, finally fixed this as a requirement for any slander action at common law. See Ogden v. Turner, 6 Mod.Rep. 104, 87 Eng.Rep. 862 (1703); Davies v. Gardiner, Popham 36, 79 Eng.Rep. 1155 (1593); Matthew v. Crass, Cro.Jac. 323, 79 Eng.Rep. 276 (1614). The result was that slander became actionable only in those cases where special damage of a "temporal" or pecuniary character was proved or could reasonably be assumed.

About the beginning of the seventeenth century, the Court of Star Chamber began independently to punish the crime of libel, in order to suppress the seditious publications that had multiplied with the spread of printing. In the earliest cases the libels were political, and the crime was a form of sedition. It was gradually extended to non-political libels, and still later tort damages were awarded to the person defamed, probably in order to provide a legal substitute for the duel when it was forbidden. When the Star Chamber was abolished, jurisdiction over libel in turn passed to the common law courts. Through this process, libel became identified with printed or written defamation, while slander remained oral. Instead of merging the two torts, the courts maintained their separate identity, as well as the arbitrary and illogical rules that had grown up around slander.

In the sixteenth and seventeenth centuries the judges were annoyed by the flood of rather frivolous actions let loose upon them once their jurisdiction over slander was established, and were reluctant to extend the possibilities of recovery. In addition, further development of the law of defamation was arrested when it encountered the rising tide of sentiment in favor of freedom of speech and the press, which, together with the odium attached to the memory of the Star Chamber and its political prosecutions, made any action for defamation an unpopular one, and the court somewhat reluctant in dealing with it. It is to this that we owe the general rule that defamation will not be enjoined, unless it is incident to some other tort; and more indirectly, the holding of the Supreme Court of the United States in Near v. Minnesota ex rel. Olson, 283 U.S. 697 (1931). See Pound, Equitable Relief Against Defamation and Injuries to Personality, 29 Harv.L.Rev. 640 (1916); F. Friendly, Minnesota Rag (1981).

Among the leading articles on the history of defamation are Veeder, History and Theory of the Law of Defamation, 3 Colum.L.Rev. 546 (1903), 4 Colum.L.Rev. 33 (1904); Holdsworth, Defamation in the Sixteenth and Seventeenth Centuries, 40 L.Q.Rev. 302, 397 (1924), 41 L.Q. Rev. 13 (1925); Carr, The English Law of Defamation, 18 L.Q.Rev. 255, 388 (1902); Lovell, The "Reception" of Defamation by the Common Law, 15 Vand.L.Rev. 1051 (1962). See generally L. Eldredge, Defamation (1978); R. Smolla, Defamation (1986); R. Sack, Libel, Slander and Related Problems (P.L.I.1980).

Few commentators have had a kind word to say about the general condition of the common law of defamation as it finally developed. Many calls have been made for its complete overhaul and reform. Some studies have been undertaken with this end in view. But they have failed to accomplish any really worthwhile results.

In 1964, a new reformer entered the field. The United States Supreme Court decided the case of New York Times Co. v. Sullivan, 376 U.S. 254 (1964), infra page 895, holding that the free-speech and free-press provisions of the First Amendment (acting through the Fourteenth Amendment) affected the common law of defamation.

Since that time, the decisions under the First Amendment have produced numerous changes in the law of defamation, some of them very far ranging in effect. The Supreme Court itself is still slowly feeling its way on the course to take. There have been a number of 5-to-4 decisions and even some cases decided by a plurality opinion. As a result the Court has wavered and changed its position on several matters, so that a good deal of uncertainty remains as to the extent of present and future change. For this reason, the first part of this chapter will be primarily concerned with the common law of defamation, with only incidental references to constitutional holdings. Beginning with New York Times v. Sullivan, infra page 895, the emphasis will be placed on the constitutional developments.

You have certainly observed that the law of torts involves a careful balancing of conflicting individual and social interests, with the establishment of principles, rules and standards for the purpose of enabling the court to reach the appropriate result in the particular case.   In this chapter, you will observe that the same kind of balancing of interests is followed, but that the constitutional balance may vary from the tort balance.   The social interest in freedom of expression (speech and press) regarding matters of public concern plays a very significant role, and it sometimes creates serious difficulties in maintaining orderly organization in the tort law of defamation.   It is a stimulating and sometimes frustrating process to contemplate and study.

1. NATURE OF A DEFAMATORY COMMUNICATION

BELLI v. ORLANDO DAILY NEWSPAPERS, INC.

United States Court of Appeals, Fifth Circuit, 1967.
389 F.2d 579, cert. denied 393 U.S. 825, 89 S.Ct. 88, 21 L.Ed.2d 96 (1968).

WISDOM, CIRCUIT JUDGE.   This action for damages for libel and slander is based on a false statement relating to Mr. Melvin Belli. Belli, an attorney of national prominence, is well known in the legal profession for his pioneering in the development of demonstrative evidence as a trial tactic and his success in obtaining large judgments for plaintiffs in personal injury suits.   He is well known to the general public because of his representation of Jack Ruby and others in the public eye.

In March 1964 Mr. Leon Handley, an attorney in Orlando, Florida, in a conversation with Miss Jean Yothers, a columnist for the Orlando Evening Star, repeated a story he had heard concerning Belli.   Handley told Yothers that the Florida Bar Association had invited Belli to serve as a member of one of the panels on the program of the Association at its 1955 Convention in Miami Beach.   Belli agreed, with the understanding that "since there were no funds provided in the budget for payment per se for his contribution as a lawyer to the program the Florida Bar instead would pick up the hotel tab for himself and his wife during their stay."   According to Handley, after Mr. and Mrs. Belli left Florida, the Association discovered that the Bellis "ran up a bunch of [clothing] bills" which they charged to their hotel room.   The derogatory portion of the story was admittedly false: The Bellis had not charged any purchases to their hotel account.   Unfortunately for all, Jean Yothers reported, with embellishments, this nine-year old story in her gossip column in the Orlando Evening Star for March 19, 1964.[2]

* * *

2. The article appeared in the Orlando Evening Star under the title "On the Town" by Jean Yothers and headed "Florida Bar Got the Bill".   The full text is as follows:

Jack Ruby's flamboyant attorney Melvin Belli of San Francisco makes an indelible impression whither he goeth.

The district court dismissed Belli's complaint for failure to state a claim upon which relief could be granted. The court relied on the erroneous assumption that the determination whether a statement is a libel (or slander) per se is solely for the court. We consider it a close question whether the publication is so clearly defamatory that as a matter of law the case should not be submitted to the jury. We hold, however, that the publication itself, without reference to extrinsic facts, is capable of carrying a defamatory meaning. It is for a jury to determine whether it was so understood by the "common mind". We reverse and remand. * * *

In Florida and in many states * * * a libel per se is "any publication which exposes a person to distrust, hatred, contempt, ridicule, obloquy". For example, in Briggs v. Brown, 55 Fla. 417, 46 So. 325, 330 (1908) the court states the formula for libels per se as follows:

"A civil action for libel will lie when there has been a false and unprivileged publication by letter or otherwise which exposes a person to distrust, hatred, contempt, ridicule, or obloquy * * * or which has a tendency to injure such person in his office, occupation, business, or employment. If the publication is false and not privileged, and is such that its natural and proximate consequence necessarily causes injury to a person in his personal, social, official, or business relations or life, wrong and injury are presumed and implied, and such publication is actionable per se." * * *

We find that the general law and Florida law are in agreement with Dean Prosser's conclusion: "It is for the court *in the first instance* to determine whether the words are reasonably capable of a particular interpretation, or whether they are necessarily so; it is then for the jury to say whether they were in fact understood as defamatory. If the language used is open to two meanings * * * it is for the jury to determine whether the defamatory sense was the one conveyed." (Emphasis added.) Prosser, Law of Torts § 106, at 765 (1963). * * *

Both judge and jury play a part in determining whether language constitutes libel. The Supreme Court has delineated these roles in Washington Post Co. v. Chaloner, 1919, 250 U.S. 290:

Consider the time he and Mrs. Belli were in Miami six or so years ago and Belli was a member of a panel at a program-meeting of the Florida Bar.

Here's what happened:

In making arrangements for Belli's participation it had been pointed out to him that since there were no funds provided in the budget for payment per se for his contribution as a lawyer to the program, the Florida Bar instead would pick up the hotel tab for himself and his wife during their stay.

Belli agreed.

Oops!

A local attorney remembers, with embarrassed chagrin, how the plan backfired on the Florida Bar.

After the well-dressed Mr. Belli and his well-dressed wife left town, the hotel where they had been staying received clothing bills amounting to hundreds of $s. The Bellis had shopped in Miami stores and charged clothing bills to their hotel rooms.

The Florida Bar had been taken.

It was hard to stomach but the Board of Governors of the Florida Bar picked up the Bellis' bill.

After all, that was the plan!

"A publication claimed to be defamatory must be read and construed in the sense in which the readers to whom it is addressed would ordinarily understand it.   *   *   *   When thus read, if its meaning is so unambiguous as to reasonably bear but one interpretation, it is for the judge to say whether that signification is defamatory or not. If, upon the other hand, it is capable of two meanings, one of which would be libelous and actionable and the other not, it is for the jury to say, under all the circumstances surrounding its publication, including extraneous facts admissible in evidence, which of the two meanings would be attributed to it by those to whom it is addressed or by whom it may be read."   *   *   *

The district court in this case completely excised the jury's role, a position it could take only on the assumption that the publication unambiguously carried no defamatory meaning. Since the court did not spell out its reasons, the defendants in their briefs have attempted to articulate the rationale for the holding below.

The defendants argue that the article did not "hurt" Belli as an attorney, did not imply that he was "losing his touch with demonstrative evidence", did not affect his ability to "obtain those 'more adequate awards' for seamen and railroad workers for which he is so justly famous". In effect, so the argument runs, the article was nothing more than caustic comment on the acuteness of the Florida Bar Association. Belli simply "showed the Florida lawyers that their agreement was somewhat more favorable to him tha[n] they—in their naiveté—contemplated". In its harshest sense, they say, "the article implies no more than that Mr. Belli 'put one over' on the Florida Bar", which is "not quite the same as conning a destitute widow out of her homestead". In short, Mr. Belli just got "a little more out of the agreement than the Bar Association contemplated".

The defendants make a case—just barely—for the view that the article is capable of being reasonably interpreted as non-defamatory. But since the article on its face is also capable of carrying a defamatory meaning, it is for the jury to decide whether the words were in fact so understood.

The plaintiff contends, in his brief, "No person reading the headline and the article *sub judice*   *   *   *   could conclude other than that Melvin Belli, both as a lawyer and as a private citizen is grasping, conniving, contemptible, dishonest; a cheat, swindler, trickster, deceiver, defrauder; a person to be avoided, shunned and distrusted." Without benefit of the defendants' cavalier reading of the article or the plaintiff's retort hyperbolic, we consider that the bare bones of the article are capable of carrying the meaning that Belli tricked and deceived the Florida Bar Association out of hundreds of dollars worth of clothes.   *   *   *

The author's comment seems intended to insure the common reader's understanding of what purportedly happened. The common reader is likely to understand "take", just as Miss Yothers must have understood it. A recent dictionary defines it: "To cheat, deceive"; other dictionaries agree with this definition. The man in the street is likely to understand that hotel expenses do not include "hundreds of dollars worth of clothing". But any doubts the reader might have as to what purportedly happened are likely to be resolved by the reference to Belli's "plan" to "take" the Florida Bar. We hold that a jury might reasonably conclude that the conduct imputed to Belli was incompatible with the standards of an ethical lawyer and as such violated one of the four traditional categories of libel per se. A jury might also conclude that such conduct subjected Belli to contempt and ridicule humiliating him socially and injuring him professionally.

The Court has some doubt whether the publication in question carries a non-defamatory meaning. The Court has very little doubt that it carries a defamatory meaning. The Court has concluded however that the final determination of the issue of defamation should be made by a jury.

The story is nine years old. It was not made within the context of a discussion of an important public issue. Nevertheless, the delimiting effect of the law of libel on First Amendment rights and a free press impels the Court not to excise the role of the jury. "Since one's reputation is the view which others take of him * * * [w]hether an idea injures a person's reputation depends upon the opinions of those to whom it is published." Developments in the Law: Defamation, 69 Harv.L.Rev. 875, 881–82 (1956). Thus, because it is impractical, even unreliable, to depend upon in-court testimony of recipients of the particular publication for determining whether that publication is defamatory, a logical function of the jury is to decide whether the plaintiff has been lowered in the esteem of those to whom the idea was published. As early as the seventeenth century, the court in Lord Townshend v. Dr. Hughes, 1693, 2 Mod. 150, 195, held that "words should not be construed in a rigid or in a mild sense, but according to the general and natural meaning, and agreeable to the common understanding of all men." Florida has adopted the common-mind test. Loeb v. Geronemus, Fla.1953, 66 So.2d 241. Any doubt as to the defamatory effect of a publication should be resolved by the common mind of the jury, and not by even the most carefully considered judicial pronouncement. * * *

We reverse the dismissal of the district court and remand the case for further proceedings consistent with this opinion.

---

1. The older definition of defamation was that of a communication to a third person which "tends to hold the plaintiff up to hatred, contempt or ridicule or to cause him to be shunned or avoided." This appears to have originated with Baron Parke, in Parmiter v. Coupland, 6 M. & W. 105, 108, 151 Eng.Rep. 340, 342 (1840). It is still often repeated by the courts.

2. When the question has arisen, the later cases have recognized that this definition is too narrow. Defamation is rather a communication that tends to

damage the plaintiff's "reputation," more or less in the popular sense—that is, to diminish the respect, good will, confidence or esteem in which he is held, or to excite adverse or unpleasant feelings about him.   And this is the case even though decent citizens would regard him only with pity.

3.   Which of the following are in themselves defamatory?

"He is dead."   Cf. Lemmer v. The Tribune, 50 Mont. 559, 148 P. 338 (1915). "He is under treatment for mental illness."   Cowper v. Vannier, 20 Ill.App.2d 499, 156 N.E.2d 761 (1959).   "He refuses to pay his just debts."   Thompson v. Adelberg & Berman, 181 Ky. 487, 205 S.W. 558 (1918).   "His parents were never married."   Cf. Harris v. Nashville Trust Co., 128 Tenn. 573, 162 S.W. 584 (1914).   "He is a liar."   Murphy v. Hartz, 238 Or. 226, 393 P.2d 206 (1964).   A motion picture portrays an identifiable woman as having been raped by Rasputin.   Youssoupoff v. Metro–Goldwyn–Mayer Pictures Ltd., 50 T.L.R. 581, 99 A.L.R. 864 (1934) (C.A.).   His face "resembles a hard-boiled egg," "roly-poly, like a rubber beach toy," "relentlessly small town in fashion and horizon." Raymer v. Doubleday & Co., Inc., 615 F.2d 241 (5th Cir.1980).   "Sinatra's Mouthpiece."   Rudin v. Dow Jones & Co., 510 F.Supp. 210 (D.C.N.Y.1981).

GRANT v. READER'S DIGEST ASS'N
United States Circuit Court of Appeals, Second Circuit, 1945.
151 F.2d 733.

L. HAND, CIRCUIT JUDGE.   This is an appeal from a judgment dismissing a complaint in libel for insufficiency in law upon its face. The complaint alleged that the plaintiff was a Massachusetts lawyer, living in that state; that the defendant, a New York corporation, published a periodical of general circulation, read by lawyers, judges and the general public; and that one issue of the periodical contained an article entitled "I Object To My Union in Politics," in which the following passage appeared:

"And another thing.   In my state the Political Action Committee has hired as its legislative agent one, Sidney S. Grant, who but recently was a legislative representative for the Massachusetts Communist Party."

The innuendo then alleged that this passage charged the plaintiff with having represented the Communist Party in Massachusetts as its legislative agent, which was untrue and malicious.   Two questions arise: (1) What meaning the jury might attribute to the words; (2) whether the meaning so attributed was libellous.   * * * The case therefore turns upon whether it is libellous in New York to write of a lawyer that he has acted as agent of the Communist Party, and is a believer in its aims and methods.

The interest at stake in all defamation is concededly the reputation of the person assailed; and any moral obliquity of the opinions of those in whose minds the words might lessen that reputation, would normally be relevant only in mitigation of damages.   A man may value his reputation even among those who do not embrace the prevailing moral standards; and it would seem that the jury should be allowed to appraise how far he should be indemnified for the disesteem of such persons. That is the usual rule. [Cc] The New York decisions define libel, in accordance with the usual rubric, as consisting of utterances which arouse "hatred, contempt, scorn, obloquy or shame," and the like. [Cc] However, the opinions at times seem to make it a condition that to be actionable the words must be such as would so affect "right-thinking" people. * * * The same limitation has apparently been recognized in England [c]; and it is fairly plain that there must come a point where that is true. As was said in Mawe v. Piggott, Irish Rep. 4 Comm.Law, 54, 62, among those "who were themselves criminal or sympathized with crime," it would expose one "to great odium to represent him as an informer or prosecutor or otherwise aiding in the detection of crime"; yet certainly the words would not be actionable. Be that as it may, in New York, if the exception covers more than such a case, it does not go far enough to excuse the utterance at bar. Katapodis v. Brooklyn Spectator, Inc., 287 N.Y. 17, 38 N.E.2d 112 * * * held that the imputation of extreme poverty might be actionable; although certainly "right-thinking people" ought not to shun, or despise, or otherwise condemn one because he is poor. Indeed, the only declaration of the Court of Appeals [c] leaves it still open whether it is not libellous to say that a man is insane. [Cc]

We do not believe, therefore, that we need say whether "right-thinking" people would harbor similar feelings toward a lawyer, because he had been an agent for the Communist Party, or was a sympathizer with its aims and means. It is enough if there be some, as there certainly are, who would feel so, even though they would be "wrong-thinking" people if they did. * * *

Judgment reversed; cause remanded.

––––––––

1. In accord with this decision are two excellent, and lengthy, opinions arising out of a very similar charge, in Herrmann v. Newark Morning Ledger Co., 48 N.J.Super. 420, 138 A.2d 61 (1958), second appeal, 49 N.J.Super. 551, 140 A.2d 529 (1958).

2. The leading case is Peck v. Tribune Co., 214 U.S. 185 (1909), where defendant, by mistake, published plaintiff's picture accompanying a testimonial signed by another woman, who was a nurse, in praise of the merits of Duffy's Pure Malt Whiskey. Holmes, J.: "If the advertisement obviously would hurt the plaintiff in the estimation of an important and respectable part of the community, liability is not a question of majority vote." 214 U.S. at 190.

3. What about the statement that plaintiff is obtaining a divorce? Gersten v. Newark Morning Ledger Co., 52 N.J.Super. 152, 145 A.2d 56 (1958). Or that a business man is a "price cutter"? Meyerson v. Hurlbut, 68 App.D.C. 360, 98 F.2d 232 (1938). Or that a kosher meat dealer sells bacon? Braun v. Armour & Co., 254 N.Y. 514, 173 N.E. 845 (1930).

4. There must, however, undoubtedly be an element of discredit or disgrace, even in the eyes of the particular segment of the community. Thus if a Democrat is called a Republican, it is quite probable that unpleasant feelings would be aroused against him in the minds of some other Democrats; but it can scarcely be regarded as defamatory. Cf. Steinman v. Di Roberts, 23 A.D.2d 693,

257 N.Y.S.2d 695 (1965) ("liberal"); Haas v. Evening Democrat Co., 252 Iowa 517, 107 N.W.2d 444 (1961) ("conservative").

5. A statement that plaintiff has informed the police about crime has been held not to be defamatory. Why? Mawe v. Piggott, Ir.R. 4 C.L. 54 (1869); Rose v. Borenstein, 251 N.Y. 250, 119 N.Y.S.2d 288 (1953). See the criticism of this in the Note, 58 Yale L.J. 1387 (1949). Also Riesman, Democracy and Defamation: Fair Game and Fair Comment, 42 Colum.L.Rev. 1282, 1300ff (1942).

Pleading Defamation

6. When the meaning that defames the plaintiff is clear upon the face of the words uttered, the cause of action is made out by pleading, and proving, the words themselves and their communication to a third person. Where the meaning is not clear upon the face of the words, the task of the plaintiff is more difficult. For example, take the words: "He burned down his own barn." This the plaintiff would have a perfect right to do if he chose, and on its face the statement does not defame him. Here the courts very early set up quite technical rules as to the way in which the action must be pleaded; and although these have been relaxed slightly here and there, they are in the main still rather rigidly followed. In such a case the plaintiff must plead:

A. The defamatory words, "He burned down his own barn."

B. The publication: communication of the words to a third person. "Defendant spoke these words to X."

C. Extrinsic facts, because of which the words were reasonably understood to convey a meaning defaming the plaintiff. This is called the "inducement." For example, defendant pointed at the plaintiff when he spoke, and X knew that plaintiff had insurance on the barn.

D. A formal allegation that the words were spoken of and concerning plaintiff. This is called the "colloquium." "He (meaning the plaintiff) burned down his own barn."

E. An allegation of the particular defamatory meaning conveyed by the words. This is called the "innuendo." In this case, that the words were understood by X to mean that plaintiff had burned the barn in order to defraud the insurance company, which would be the crime of arson.

F. Special damages, when they are necessary to the cause of action.

7. Both the colloquium and the innuendo must be reasonable in the light of the words spoken and the facts pleaded in the inducement. If the words, together with such facts, do not fairly support the defamatory meaning pleaded, no cause of action is made out. See also Davis v. R.K.O. Radio Pictures, 191 F.2d 901 (8th Cir.1951) (colloquium); Grice v. Holk, 268 Ala. 500, 108 So.2d 359 (1959) (innuendo).

8. On the difficulties that the pleading may give the plaintiff's attorney, see Wyse, The Complaint in Libel and Slander: A Dilemma for Plaintiff, 33 Chi.–Kent L.Rev. 313 (1955).

KILIAN v. DOUBLEDAY & CO., INC.
Supreme Court of Pennsylvania, 1951.
367 Pa. 117, 79 A.2d 657.

HORACE STERN, JUSTICE. In this action for libel the jury rendered a verdict in favor of defendant. Plaintiff appeals from the refusal of the court below to grant him a new trial.

This is the way in which the allegedly libelous article came to be written:—At the American University in Washington a course in English was conducted by Don M. Wolfe, the students being disabled veterans of World War II. The course consisted, in part, of the writing by the students of essays or stories about their personal experiences in the war; their compositions would be submitted to Dr. Wolfe, who suggested corrections and revisions. Dr. Wolfe conceived the idea of having these stories published in book form, and, after an original publication by another concern, he entered into a contract with defendant, Doubleday & Company, for that purpose. Each student in the class, 53 in all, contributed at least one article. The book was published under the title "The Purple Testament", and it was advertised in the jacket as consisting of "the native eloquence of *absolute honesty*," and as constituting "the fragments of their [the authors'] *own intimate experiences.*" Some 9000 copies were sold and distributed throughout the United States. Among the articles was one by Joseph M. O'Connell which gave rise to the present suit.

O'Connell was a soldier who had been seriously injured during the course of the Normandy invasion and was hospitalized from August to October, 1944, at a station hospital about 12 miles from Lichfield, England, where there was a large replacement depot. In the original draft of the article which he wrote he narrated incidents said to have occurred at the Lichfield camp and which, he testified at the trial, were described to him by individuals who had allegedly witnessed them. Dr. Wolfe, to whom he submitted the draft several times, stated that he "thought it was interesting, and that it was the first time he had heard about it", but twice returned it with the suggestion that O'Connell should use "more descriptive detail", that he should "make it more vivid", that it "did not have in it the sights, sounds and bits of conversation necessary to make the story readable". The result was that whereas O'Connell had originally written the article in the third person he now wrote it, in order to "make it more vivid", in the first person, purporting that the incidents he narrated occurred under his own personal observation and in his own experience.

The story, as it finally appeared in "The Purple Testament", may be condensed as follows:—I [O'Connell] and my buddy, while being transferred in an ambulance from one hospital to another in England, reached a big army camp near Lichfield. The camp was dreary and ugly; it reminded me of the rotten, filthy German prison camps I had seen in France. As we lay in the ambulance we heard a loud voice outside shouting: "Just let me catch one of you sons o'bitches loaf on this detail and you'll get twenty lashes when you get back tonight." A group of four men came to carry us into the hospital; they were all dressed in blue pants and shirts with a large letter "P" sewed on their clothes. The same loud voice I had heard a few minutes before said: "You're not supposed to talk to these _____ prisoners." A big heavy-set sergeant stepped closer to me and said, "All they are is a bunch of cowards. They are too yellow to go back to combat. They'll be glad go back when they finish with this prison." The sergeant ordered them to carry us into the hospital; as they were placing me there in my bed I noticed that one of them had all the fingers of his right hand missing and three fingers of his left. Could such things be allowed in our army? If so, it was being covered up by the brass, and the brass were making suckers of the American people. A ward attendant limping around outside the room came in and said: "I was blown out of a tank; all the muscle of my right leg was blown away. * * * I came through this way on my way [back] to combat. One day the old man (Colonel _____) ordered us out on a ten-mile hike. After about two miles I fell flat on my face. They ordered me on, but I couldn't go. So the next day they took me before the old dictator. He ordered me before a quick court martial. I got six months of hard labor. The doctor said I was unfit for hard labor, so they assigned me to this hospital. I'm still a prisoner. The other night a guard caught me stealing a piece of bread from the kitchen, and I got fifty lashes for it." * * * In the morning the old colonel himself came along to inspect the hospital. He wasn't a big guy, but he was stockily built. Behind his glasses his eyes were mean. He looked like a man who enjoys seeing another man suffer. He was surrounded by a lot of other officers. None of them looked good to me. After one scowling glance at Red [my buddy] and me, he left. As we were being carried down the hall of the ward the big sergeant was clubbing a G.I. in a corner, while some officers looked on. I only hoped that some day I would meet up with that big sergeant and the rest of the people that ran that prison. The death chair would be too good for them. But as always, Colonel _____ and the rest of the responsible officers will be protected by the big brass. Mark my word, Colonel _____ and his bullies will get off light. That is Lichfield justice.

It is not questioned that by "Colonel _____", the "old dictator", and "the old colonel", was meant Colonel Kilian, the present plaintiff, who was the commanding officer of the Lichfield camp. At the end of the article as published there was appended a footnote which Dr. Wolfe himself had added and which stated:—"On August 29, 1946, the Associated Press reported that Colonel James A. Kilian was convicted 'of permitting cruel and unusual punishment of American soldiers.' He was reprimanded by the military court and fined $500.—Editor." This insertion was obviously intended to give the impression that what was said or implied in the article in regard to Colonel Kilian was corroborated by his conviction, and further that, as the author of the article had predicted, he "got off light".

The fact in regard to plaintiff's trial before a military court in 1946 is this:—He was charged with *authorizing, aiding and abetting* the imposition of cruel, unusual and unauthorized punishments upon prisoners in confinement at the depot of which he was the Commanding Officer. The punishments referred to were itemized in the charge. A second specification was that he *knowingly permitted* the imposition of such punishments. As to the first specification—authorizing, aiding and abetting—he was acquitted; as to the second specification—knowingly permitting—he was acquitted of *knowingly* permitting and found guilty merely of *permitting;* in other words, he was convicted of neglect, but not of actual wrongdoing or of acquiescing in what occurred. Moreover, many of the alleged punishments specified in the charge as having been "permitted" were deleted by the court because they were not supported by the evidence. * * *

As affirmative defense to the action defendant pleaded justification on the ground that the publication was "a *true and accurate account of events which were observed by the author of the article in question.* " How is that defense supported by the testimony presented at the trial? As far as O'Connell being an eye-witness of any of the alleged happenings at the camp is concerned, he admitted on the witness stand that he never was at Lichfield; therefore, his article, in that respect, was wholly false. Defendant produced as witnesses three soldiers who *were* at Lichfield, who testified to punishments inflicted on them or observed by them as imposed on others, but none of the incidents they described tended to prove that a single one of the events narrated in the O'Connell article actually occurred; therefore such testimony was not properly admissible to prove the truth of the publication. While, in order to support a defense of truth, it is necessary merely to prove that it was *substantially* true, and while, therefore, if the testimony of those witnesses had shown a variance merely in the details of the events described in the article it would nevertheless have been admissible as giving support to the plea of truth, it furnished no such support by proving that other and wholly different incidents occurred although these also may have been equally blameworthy. * * * "Specific charges cannot be justified by showing the plaintiff's general bad character; and if the accusation is one of particular misconduct, such as stealing a watch from A, it is not enough to show a different offense, even though it be a more serious one, such as stealing a clock from A, or six watches from B." Prosser on Torts, p. 855, § 95. * * * None of defendant's testimony showed any instances at the camp, as alleged in O'Connell's article, of lashing, of cursing prisoners, of having a soldier whose fingers were missing act as a stretcher bearer, of ordering a badly wounded veteran on a ten-mile hike. * * * It is obvious that there was not a shred of testimony presented at the trial to prove either that the author of the article saw any of the events he narrated, or that those events or even substantially similar ones occurred, or that plaintiff was aware of any such happenings, or that he sanctioned them, or that he was a "dictator", or that in his very appearance he looked like a man who would enjoy seeing another man suffer. The court, therefore, was in error in submitting to the jury, as it did, the question whether the publication was substantially true. * * *

Judgment reversed and new trial awarded.

---

1. Under the common law the defense that the defamatory statement was true was not open to the defendant in a prosecution for criminal libel. That crime was originated to suppress sedition, and later extended to prevent breaches of the peace, and neither was likely to be minimized if the defamation were true. Hence the criminal courts took no account of any freedom to publish the truth. De Libellis Famosis, 5 Co.Rep. 125, 77 Eng.Rep. 250 (1605); Franklin's Case, 9 Hargrave St. Trials 255, 269 (1731). This explains the statement, usually attributed to Lord Mansfield, that "the greater the truth the greater the libel." In this country, the Supreme Court has held that a criminal libel statute is unconstitutional if it imposes a penalty for making a true statement about a public official. Garrison v. Louisiana, 379 U.S. 64 (1964).

2. The criminal law rule never was applied to civil actions. Johns v. Gittings, Cro.Eliz. 239, 78 Eng.Rep. 495 (1590); Hilsdon v. Saunders, Cro.Jac. 677, 79 Eng.Rep. 586 (1624). At common law there has been general agreement that an action of defamation will lie only if the statement is both defamatory and false. Statutes in a few states and judicial decisions in some others have indicated that an action may lie even for a true statement if it was not made for good motives and justifiable ends. E.g., Hutchins v. Page, 75 N.H. 215, 72 A. 689 (1909). But a statute of this nature was held unconstitutional as a violation of the First Amendment in Farnsworth v. Tribune Co., 43 Ill.2d 286, 253 N.E.2d 408 (1969). This is probably the result that the United States Supreme Court would reach if the issue were presented to it.

On the other hand, there may well be, under appropriate circumstances, a cause of action for invasion of the right of privacy. See Cox Broadcasting Co. v. Cohn, 420 U.S. 469 (1975), infra page 962, and notes following.

3. *Burden of Proof.* It has long been customary for the plaintiff to allege in his complaint that the statement is false. The common law raised a presumption of the falsity of all statements that were defamatory. As a result truth has been consistently treated as an affirmative defense, which the defendant must raise and on which he has the burden of proof. But Supreme Court decisions on the effect of the First Amendment on defamation actions had come to throw this common law position in serious doubt. There were some recent decisions that the burden of proof is now on the plaintiff. And in 1985, the Supreme Court formally held to this effect in a 5-to-4 decision. See Philadelphia Newspapers, Inc. v. Hepps, infra at page 924, where the conflicting positions can be more fully understood.

4. As the principal case indicates, the determination is whether the statement is substantially true. See, e.g., Sun Printing & Publishing Ass'n v. Schenck, 98 Fed. 925 (2d Cir.1900) (specific charge of crime not justified by proof of another and more serious crime); Crellin v. Thomas, 122 Utah 122, 247 P.2d 264 (1952) (charge that plaintiff was a "whore" not shown by evidence that she worked for a short time as a "dance hall girl" or "percentage girl"). See Restatement (Second) of Torts §§ 581A, 613, caveat.

In the principal case, O'Connell, the writer of the story, states that some of the "events" were told to him by other persons. Suppose that the story had been told to him, but it was untrue. Liability on his part?

5.   In a gubernatorial race, defendant newspaper, supporting the candidate of one party, carried a number of stories about a land transaction involving a company of which plaintiff, the other candidate, was president. The stories were essentially accurate, but the headlines and subtitles were intentionally misleading and calculated to create a false impression on the normal reader as to plaintiff's ethical conduct. Can the stories be found to be false? Sprouse v. Clay Communication, Inc., 158 W.Va. 427, 211 S.E.2d 674 (1975).

JANKLOW v. NEWSWEEK, INC.
United States Court of Appeals, Eighth Circuit, En banc, 1986.
788 F.2d 1300.

ARNOLD, CIRCUIT JUDGE.   William Janklow, the Governor of South Dakota, filed this defamation action against *Newsweek* magazine based on an article in the weekly's February 21, 1983, issue about American Indian activist Dennis Banks. The article, "Dennis Banks's Last Stand," purports to give a history of the relationship between Banks, who fled the state in the mid-1970's after his conviction on two felony counts, and Janklow, who while Attorney General prosecuted Banks and later, as Governor, sought his extradition. Janklow's claim centers on one paragraph of the article, which referred to Banks's 1974 initiation of tribal charges of assault against Janklow, in connection with an allegation (now acknowledged to be false) that the plaintiff had raped a teenaged Indian girl five years before.

The District Court granted summary judgment for the defendant magazine. The court held that *Newsweek* correctly reported the material facts of the rape allegation, that the article did not suggest the magazine believed the truth of the allegation, and that any implication that revenge motivated Janklow's prosecution of Banks was opinion and therefore nonactionable under the First Amendment.

On appeal, a divided panel of this Court upheld the first two holdings but reversed the third on the ground that "the meaning that can be drawn from the *Newsweek* article—that Janklow did not commence prosecuting Banks until after Banks attempted to bring him to justice for the alleged rape of an Indian girl—is factual." *Janklow v. Newsweek, Inc.,* 759 F.2d 644, 652 (8th Cir.1985). The panel's holding was based on four factors. The panel found that the language of the article was, on the whole, that of a factual account; that the forum—a weekly newsmagazine—was likely to be considered as offering "hard" news; that the article's implication was not "broad, unfocused or subjective" but rather a "specific factual assertion," [c]; and finally, that no cautionary language was used to signal to the reader that opinion, and not fact, was being presented. We granted defendant's petition for rehearing en banc on the question whether the article should be read as fact or opinion. We now hold it to be opinion, absolutely protected by the First Amendment, and therefore affirm the judgment dismissing the complaint with prejudice.

Opinion is absolutely protected under the First Amendment. *Gertz v. Robert Welch, Inc.*, 418 U.S. 323, 339 (1974). But it is hard to draw a bright line between "fact" and "opinion." There is a sense in which one's intention or motive in performing a certain act is properly categorized as "fact." Whether someone accused of mail fraud, say, had criminal intent is a question of "fact" to be decided by the jury in a criminal prosecution. Whether someone promising to perform a contract actually had no intention of doing so is a "fact" that, in some jurisdictions, will support a civil action for fraud. And in this sense, whether Governor Janklow prosecuted the case against Banks for revenge, or out of a genuine sense of duty, is a question of "fact." But the term "fact" need not have the same meaning in every legal context. The meaning we give to it should depend on the purposes of the law being applied. Here, that law is the First Amendment, which in the most uncompromising terms ("Congress shall make no law * * *") seeks to protect freedom of speech.

In establishing the criteria by which to judge "Dennis Banks's Last Stand," we have looked at how a variety of courts have handled the fact/opinion distinction since its importance was made clear in *Gertz*. Recently, the issue was thoroughly ventilated by the District of Columbia Circuit, *Ollman v. Evans*, 750 F.2d 970 (D.C.Cir.1984) (en banc), *cert. denied*, 471 U.S. 1127 (1985), and we choose here to adopt the four factors suggested in Judge Starr's scholarly opinion, and to expand them, for reasons we will explain, to include elements of the concurrence by Judge Bork. We emphasize, however, that these factors must be considered together, that no solitary criterion can be dispositive, and that ultimately the decision whether a statement is fact or opinion must be based on all the circumstances involved. See *Ollman*, 750 F.2d at 1060 ("important these factors not be taken mechanically") (MacKinnon, J., concurring).

The first relevant factor identified in *Ollman* was the precision and specificity of the disputed statement, 750 F.2d at 981, a concern found in many fact/opinion cases. See, *e.g.*, *Buckley v. Littell*, 539 F.2d 882 (2d Cir.1976), *cert. denied*, 429 U.S. 1062, (1977) (calling someone a "fascist" was indefinite and therefore opinion, while comparing him to a known libeller was specific and so fact). It is difficult to call a vague or imprecise statement a "fact"; in the present context, moreover, doing so would place the First Amendment at the mercy of linguistic subtleties and fourth-ranked dictionary definitions.

Tied to the concept of precision is that of verifiability. If a statement cannot plausibly be verified, it cannot be seen as "fact." *Id.* A statement regarding a potentially provable proposition can be phrased so that it is hard to establish, or it may intrinsically be unsuited to any sort of quantification. [C]

A third factor is the literary context in which the disputed statement was made. The statement must be taken as part of a whole, including tone and the use of cautionary language. [Cc] We include as well under the rubric of literary context the type of forum in which the statement was made, a factor which Judge Starr called "social context." *Ollman,* 750 F.2d at 983. This factor focuses on the category of publication, its style of writing and intended audience.

Finally, in deciding whether a statement is fact or opinion, a court must consider what we will call the "public context" in which the statement was made. It is true that the distinction between public and private figures which bears so heavily in many libel cases has no direct relevance here, see, *e.g., Ollman,* 750 F.2d at 975; *no* opinion is actionable, whether it concerns a private person or a public figure. However, when determining initially whether a statement is fact or opinion, it does a disservice to the First Amendment not to consider the public or political arena in which the statement is made and whether the statement implicates core values of the First Amendment. See *Ollman,* 750 F.2d at 1002–05 (Bork, J., concurring). In fact, as Judge MacKinnon recognized, "Judge Bork's skillful employment of 'the concept of a public, political arena' is crucial to a proper understanding of the analysis Judge Starr elucidates," *Ollman,* 750 F.2d at 1016 (MacKinnon, J., concurring).

With these factors in mind, we turn to the disputed statement in this appeal. * * *

The eight-paragraph *Newsweek* article began with an account of Dennis Banks's flight from California shortly before he could be extradited to South Dakota, described as an escape from "the clutches of his nemesis," Governor Janklow. The piece continued by recounting Banks's activities in the American Indian Movement, including his involvement in the 1973 riot at the Custer County, South Dakota, courthouse in which several police officers were hurt. The third paragraph then told readers:

"Along the way, Banks made a dangerous enemy—William Janklow. Their feud started in 1974, when Banks brought charges against Janklow in a tribal court for assault. A 15–year–old Indian girl who baby-sat for Janklow's children had claimed that he raped her in 1969. Federal officials found insufficient evidence to prosecute, but Banks persuaded the Rosebud Sioux chiefs to reopen the case under tribal law. Janklow, who was running for election as state attorney general at the time, refused to appear for the trial. But the tribal court found "probable cause" to believe the charges and barred Janklow from practicing law on the reservation. Eight months later Janklow—who had won his election despite the messy publicity—was prosecuting Banks. And his case—based on the 1973 Custer riot—was successful. Found guilty of riot and assault without intent to kill, Banks jumped bail before sentencing."

According to Janklow, the article defames him by implying that he began prosecuting Banks in revenge for the instigation of the tribal charges, when in fact Janklow, serving as special prosecutor, had initiated proceedings against Banks prior to the resurrection of the rape allegation and merely continued that prosecution as Attorney General.

Our analysis begins with the question of precision. The statement (that plaintiff "was prosecuting Banks" eight months after the tribal court's unfavorable finding) is not precise. It does not say in so many words that Janklow's motive was revenge. It does not say in so many words that the prosecution was commenced after the tribal court's decision. It certainly does not suggest that Banks had done nothing to warrant prosecution for riot and assault. It says only that the prosecution was going on eight months after the tribal court's decision, and no one can deny that that is true. The imputation of improper motive must be drawn from this sentence in the article by implication. The sentence is not nearly so precise as a direct accusation of improper motive.

Of particular concern is *why* this statement is imprecise. At bottom, we face a question of usage; had *Newsweek* changed a single word and said the plaintiff "*continued* prosecuting" Banks, the implication of revenge would be more difficult to draw, and there would not even be an arguable misstatement of underlying fact. Janklow argues that it is precisely because *Newsweek* could have written a clearer sentence that the statement is actionable. We disagree. We believe that the First Amendment cautions courts against intruding too closely into questions of editorial judgment, such as the choice of specific words. [C] Editors' grilling of reporters on word choice is a necessary aggravation. But when courts do it, there is a chilling effect on the exercise of First Amendment rights.

The second factor is verifiability. Janklow says it is "absolutely verifiable" that his prosecution of Banks was not born out of revenge, [c], because the riot prosecution began before Banks renewed the rape charge. While chronology makes it undeniable that retribution for what happened in 1974 could not motivate events in 1973, plaintiff's reading of the paragraph is not the only plausible one. It could also be seen as implying that as Attorney General, Janklow pressed the prosecution he began as special prosecutor in order to obtain revenge, personally handling the case when he prudently might have recused himself. And this implication would be difficult to prove, for unlike the rape allegation at issue in *Cianci v. New Times Publishing Co.*, 639 F.2d 54 (2d Cir.1980), the singling out of impermissible motive is a subtle and slippery enterprise, particularly when the activities of public officials are involved. [C]

As for the literary context of the statement, the panel opinion was influenced by the fact that "Dennis Banks's Last Stand" did not appear on the Op–Ed page of a newspaper, *Janklow v. Newsweek, Inc.*, 759 F.2d at 651, as did the column in *Ollman*. However, it would be a mistake rigidly to denominate some publications or pages as those dealing only with fact and others as dealing only with opinion. While the whole of the *Newsweek* article could not be classified as opinion or criticism, [c] national news magazines nevertheless are not the same as local daily newspapers. The magazines have a tradition of more colorful, even feisty language, than do dailies; they are also required to condense to a few paragraphs those issues to which local papers devote days of coverage and thousands of inches of space. [C] Here, the magazine's generally freer style of personal expression and the article's transparently pro-Banks posture would signal the reader to expect a fair amount of opinion.

Finally, we look at the public context in which this statement was made. Certainly, speech about government and its officers, about how well or badly they carry out their duties, lies at the very heart of the First Amendment. [Cc] It is vital to our form of government that press and citizens alike be free to discuss and, if they see fit, impugn the motives of public officials. Here we have criticism of the conduct of a state attorney general who now serves as governor, as well as questions about the actions of three other governors of two other states, all involving an issue of national importance, the treatment of Indian people. Few other discussions of public concern could make a greater claim for First Amendment protection.

Because the disputed statement in this case is imprecise, unverifiable, presented in a forum where spirited writing is expected, and involves criticism of the motives and intentions of a public official, we affirm the holding of the District Court that it is opinion, protected by the First Amendment. * * *

The plaintiff argues that even if the statement in *Newsweek* is to be read as opinion,[7] it is still actionable, on grounds that the magazine deliberately distorted the chronological sequence of events to suggest retribution as the motivation for the prosecution of Banks. As support, Janklow cites this Court's decision in *Lauderback v. American Broadcasting Co.*, 741 F.2d 193, 195 (8th Cir.1984), in which we held that "statements clothed as opinion which imply that they are based on undisclosed, defamatory facts are not protected" by the First Amendment.[8] Therefore, plaintiff says, a publisher also may not "disclos[e]

---

7. At oral argument before the Court en banc, plaintiff for the first time asked that we hold that close fact/opinion questions should go to the jury as trier of fact rather than be decided by the court as questions of law. We reject this suggestion. The "overwhelming weight of post-*Gertz* authority [is] that the distinction between opinion and fact is a matter of law," *Ollman*, 750 F.2d at 978.

8. A defamatory communication may consist of a statement in the form of an opinion, but a statement of this nature is actionable only if it implies the allegation of undisclosed defamatory facts as the basis for the opinion. We agree with the District of Columbia Circuit that the significant considerations raised by § 566 are "not distinct from the general evaluation of whether a statement constitutes fact or opinion," *Ollman*, 750 F.2d at 985 n. 29, and that "the tests already articulated are a sufficient aid in determining whether a statement implies the existence of undisclosed facts," *id.* at 985. As Judge Starr explains, the inquiry into precision and

'facts' which he knows to be false to support his defamatory opinion," [c] or omit facts "which would substantially alter the average reader's opinion," *Lauderback,* 741 F.2d at 198.

The situation in this case differs from that in *Lauderback,* where the television network was charged with having implied that the plaintiff either had been or was about to be indicted for insurance fraud. Nor is it similar, except superficially, to the facts of *Cianci v. New Times Publishing Co.,* 639 F.2d 54 (2d Cir.1980); there, not only was the chronology blurred in the account of a public official charged with rape, but the description of events inexorably led to a conclusion of fact—that the plaintiff had paid his alleged victim $3,000 to drop her charges when, in fact, the payment was made after the criminal charges had been dropped in order to settle a civil suit. *Id.* at 58. (" 'For the nominal sum of $3,000, Cianci managed to buy his way out of a possible felony charge.' ") No such direct suggestion of fact was made here. The implication Janklow complains of here comes from semantic ambiguity, not from false statements made by *Newsweek.* As we said above, this Court will not make editorial judgments about specific word choice in order to portray a plaintiff in the best possible light, particularly when the "sting" of the implication—that Janklow acted vengefully towards Banks—is still present when the full chronology is laid out.

Every news story (like every judicial opinion) reflects choices of what to leave out, as well as what to include. We can agree that this story would have been fairer to Janklow and more informative to the reader if the chronology of the rape charge against Janklow and the riot prosecution against Banks had been more fully explained. Certainly there can be omissions serious enough to take what is ostensibly an opinion and convert it into a fact for legal purposes. We have attempted to explain why this particular omission does not rise to that level. Courts must be slow to intrude into the area of editorial judgment, not only with respect to choices of words, but also with respect to inclusions in or omissions from news stories. Accounts of past events are always selective, and under the First Amendment the decision of what to select must almost always be left to writers and editors. It is not the business of government.

We return in conclusion to our initial point: that both in establishing the standards by which opinion is distinguished from fact, and in measuring a particular statement against those standards, we are dealing with First Amendment rights, among the most precious enjoyed by Americans. Accordingly, the judgment of the District Court is Affirmed.

BOWMAN, Circuit Judge, joined by ROSS and FAGG, Circuit Judges, dissenting. Because I do not agree that the Court's decision strikes a fair balance between the media interests represented by

verifiability covers the possibility that a statement conveys factual implications while the discussion of literary context includes an examination of how a reader might approach the statement.

Newsweek and the individual interests represented by Janklow, I respectfully dissent. * * *

I find it hard to believe that this is what Justice Powell had in mind when he penned his famous dictum in *Gertz* that "[u]nder the First Amendment there is no such thing as a false idea." *Id.* Ideas are one thing, but tawdry attacks on character and reputation are another. I do not see any reason to extend absolute protection under the First Amendment to statements that qualify as opinion rather than fact only by means of judicial semantics based on the *Ollman* factors.

For the reasons set forth in the panel opinion in this case, I believe that the meaning that a jury could draw from the Newsweek article here at issue—that Janklow prosecuted Banks because Banks had resurrected a 15–year–old Indian girl's claim that Janklow had raped her—amounts to an assertion of fact rather than an expression of opinion. * * * Clearly the [*Ollman*] factors do not yield predictability, unless the prediction is that their application almost always will result in keeping defamation actions brought by public officials and public figures from reaching a jury. * * *

What is called for, it seems to me, in cases raising the fact/opinion issue, is a thoughtful balancing of the competing interests, not the nearly total subordination of the individual's reputational interest to the media's desire for immunity from accountability to individuals harmed by defamatory material published with actual malice.

The Court's decision means that we never shall know whether Janklow would have been able to make a submissible case on the issue of actual malice. The indications, however, are that he would have made a strong showing on that issue. * * *

The Court suggests that the change of a single word in the article would have yielded a piece without even an arguable misstatement of underlying fact. * * *

But this really begs the question at hand, for all libel actions turn in one way or another on simply that—word choice. The question here is not whether courts will be making editorial judgments about these specific word choices but rather whether Newsweek will be held accountable for its editorial judgments, *i.e.*, for the words that it does choose. Moreover, considering the carefully crafted nature of the article and its blatant anti-Janklow bias, this aspect of the Court's opinion strikes me as being disingenuous.

Judge Arnold has remarked that "the article as a whole is tendentious and slanted. It is transparently pro-Banks." 759 F.2d at 657 (Arnold, J., dissenting). The District Court, in its memorandum opinion granting Newsweek's motion for summary judgment, expressed its "sense of outrage at the unfairness of the article." * * *

The issue, of course, is not whether the article is unfair. It is, and conspicuously so. The issue is not whether the implication that the article invites—that Janklow's prosecution of Banks was motivated by a desire for personal revenge—is defamatory. Clearly it is. The issue is whether this quite precise implication, readily derived from a precisely stated factual scenario, should be deemed a statement of fact or a statement of opinion. I see no good reason to distort the commonly understood meaning of a perfectly good and useful word by cloaking in the Constitutionally protected mantle of "opinion" this precise and factually based implication. To the contrary, an implication that Janklow prosecuted Banks for personal revenge is hardly the sort of idea best illuminated through public debate. It is rather a charge of serious misconduct, and as such it is ideally suited for judicial resolution. I believe that what Judge Friendly said of the charges at issue in *Cianci v. New Times Publishing Co.,* 639 F.2d 54 (2d Cir.1980), is equally applicable here.

"To call such charges merely an expression of 'opinion' would be to indulge in Humpty–Dumpty's use of language. We see not the slightest indication that the Supreme Court or this court ever intended anything of this sort and much to demonstrate the contrary." 639 F.2d at 64.

I would reverse this case and remand it to the District Court for further proceedings consistent with the panel opinion.

———

1. Under the common law, liability was imposed for both a defamatory statement of fact and a defamatory expression of opinion. The Restatement of Torts had two sections on liability for opinions, providing that a "defamatory communication may consist of a statement of opinion based upon facts known or assumed by both parties to the communication" (§ 566) and that it "may consist of a statement of opinion upon undisclosed facts" (§ 567). See, e.g., Cole v. Millspaugh, 111 Minn. 159, 126 N.W. 626 (1910) ("I would not touch him with a 10–foot pole"); Woolston v. Montana Free Press, 90 Mont. 299, 2 P.2d 1020 (1931); Triggs v. Sun Printing & Pub. Ass'n, 179 N.Y. 144, 71 N.E. 739 (1904) (strong ridicule of writings). There were, however, holdings that an action would not lie for mere words of vituperation or abuse, not intended to be taken in a literal sense, e.g., Vinson v. O'Mally, 25 Ariz. 552, 220 P. 393 (1923) ("God damn ignorant old son of a bitch"); Durr v. Smith, 90 So.2d 147 (La.App.1956) ("invective epithet which deleteriously reflected upon the validity of his parentage"); or were used only in good-natured jest or in light-hearted ridicule, e.g., Berry v. New York Ins. Co., 210 Ala. 369, 98 So. 290 (1923); Hanson v. Fueling, 160 Wis. 511, 152 N.W. 287 (1915). How about biting ridicule?

Some dispensation from the harshness of the common law rule was provided by the privilege of fair comment. But the comment or criticism had to be fair. See Restatement of Torts §§ 606–610.

2. A change came with the decision of Gertz v. Robert Welch, Inc., 418 U.S. 323 (1974), infra page 906. In his opinion, Justice Powell declared, "Under the First Amendment there is no such thing as a false idea. However pernicious an opinion may seem, we depend for its correction not on the conscience of judges and juries but on the competition of other ideas. But there is no constitutional value in false statements of fact." Infra at 908. This should be considered with Old Dominion Branch No. 496, Nat'l Ass'n of Letter Carriers v. Austin, 418 U.S. 264 (1974) (rendered on the same day as *Gertz*), holding that accusing certain employees of being "scabs" and quoting Jack

London's definition of the term as a "traitor to his god, his family and his class"—language which Justice Marshall defined as "obviously used * * * in a loose, figurative sense to demonstrate the union's strong disagreement with the views of those workers who oppose unionization, [so that] expression of such an opinion, even in the most pejorative terms, is protected under federal labor law"; and with Greenbelt Pub. Ass'n v. Bresler, 398 U.S. 6 (1970), where the term "blackmail" was used in a City Council by a member to describe a negotiating position of the plaintiff with the Council and the Court held that it could not be interpreted as a charge of actual fact.

3. On the basis of these three Supreme Court cases § 566 was amended in the Second Restatement to read: "A defamatory communication may consist of a statement in the form of an opinion, but a statement of this nature is actionable only if it implies the allegation of undisclosed defamatory facts as the basis for the opinion." For discussion of whether a "pure" opinion can constitutionally be actionable as defamatory, see Cianci v. New Times Pub. Co., 639 F.2d 54 (2d Cir.1980); Good Government Group of Seal Beach, Inc. v. Superior Court, 22 Cal.3d 672, 586 P.2d 572, 150 Cal.Rptr. 258 (1978); National Ass'n of Government Employees, Inc. v. Central Broadcasting Corp., 379 Mass. 220, 396 N.E.2d 996 (1979).

4. The case of Ollman v. Evans, 750 F.2d 970 (D.C.Cir.1984) (en banc), cert. denied, 471 U.S. 1127, 105 S.Ct. 2662, 86 L.Ed.2d 278 (1985), discussed in detail in the principal case, greatly broadens the scope of the inquiry and extends the meaning of the term "opinion" much beyond anything found in unabridged dictionaries. The principal case, like *Ollman,* involved a panel decision holding that the libel action would lie, being changed by a sharply divided court, en banc. See also Scott v. The News–Herald, 25 Ohio St.3d 243, 496 N.E.2d 699 (1986) (sports writer states "Anyone who attended the meet . . . knows in his heart that [plaintiff] lied at the hearing after . . . having given his solemn oath to tell the truth"; held expression of opinion). Compare the opinion of Judge Friendly in Cianci v. New Times Pub. Co., 639 F.2d 54 (2d Cir.1980).

NEIMAN–MARCUS v. LAIT
United States District Court, Southern District of New York, 1952.
13 F.R.D. 311.

IRVING R. KAUFMAN, DISTRICT JUDGE. * * * The defendants are authors of a book entitled "U.S.A. Confidential". The plaintiffs are the Neiman–Marcus Company, a Texas corporation operating a department store at Dallas, Texas, and three groups of its employees. They allege that the following matter libelled and defamed them: * * *

"He [Stanley Marcus, president of plaintiff Neiman–Marcus Company] may not know that some Neiman models are call girls—the top babes in town. The guy who escorts one feels in the same league with the playboys who took out Ziegfeld's glorified. Price, a hundred bucks a night.

"The salesgirls are good, too—pretty, and often much cheaper— twenty bucks on the average. They're more fun, too, not as snooty as the models. We got this confidential, from a Dallas wolf.

"Neiman–Marcus also contributes to the improvement of the local breed when it imports New York models to make a flash at style shows.

These girls are the cream of the crop. Oil millionaires toss around thousand-dollar bills for a chance to take them out.

"Neiman's was a women's specialty shop until the old biddies who patronized it decided their husbands should get class, too. So Neiman's put in a men's store. Well, you should see what happened. You wonder how all the faggots got to the wild and woolly. You thought those with talent ended up in New York and Hollywood and the plodders got government jobs in Washington. Then you learn the nucleus of the Dallas fairy colony is composed of many Neiman dress and millinery designers, imported from New York and Paris, who sent for their boy friends when the men's store expanded. Now most of the sales staff are fairies, too." ＊ ＊ ＊

[Plaintiffs sued in the following groups:]

(1) Nine individual models who constitute the entire group of models at the time of the publication ＊ ＊ ＊;

(2) Fifteen salesmen of a total of twenty-five suing on their own behalf and on behalf of the others ＊ ＊ ＊;

(3) Thirty saleswomen of a total of 382 suing on their own behalf and on behalf of the others. ＊ ＊ ＊

[T]he following propositions are rather widely accepted:

(1) Where the group or class libelled is large, none can sue even though the language used is inclusive. [Cc]

(2) Where the group or class libelled is small, and each and every member of the group or class is referred to, then any individual member can sue. [Cc]

Conflict arises when the publication complained of libels *some* or *less than all* of a designated small group. Some courts say no cause of action exists in any individual of the group. [Cc] Other courts in other states would apparently allow such an action. [Cc] ＊ ＊ ＊

[I]t is the opinion of this Court that the plaintiff salesmen, of whom it is alleged that "most ＊ ＊ ＊ are fairies" have a cause of action in New York and most likely other states ＊ ＊ ＊ Defendants' motion to dismiss as to the salesmen for failure to state a claim upon which relief can be granted is denied.

The plaintiff saleswomen are in a different category. The alleged defamatory statement in defendants' book speaks of the saleswomen generally. While it does not use the word "all" or similar terminology, yet it stands unqualified. However, the group of saleswomen is extremely large, consisting of 382 members at the time of publication. No specific individual is named in the alleged libelous statement. I am not cited to a single case which would support a cause of action by an individual member of any group of such magnitude. ＊ ＊ ＊

Giving the plaintiff saleswomen the benefit of all legitimate favorable inferences, the defendants' alleged libel cannot reasonably be said to concern more than the saleswomen as a class. There is no language referring to some ascertained or ascertainable person. Nor is the class so small that it follows that defamation of the class infects the individual of the class. This Court so holds as a matter of law since it is of the opinion that no reasonable man would take the writer seriously and conclude from the publication a reference to any individual saleswoman. [Cc]

While it is generally recognized that even where the group is large, a member of the group may have a cause of action if some particular circumstances point to the plaintiff as the person defamed, no such circumstances are alleged in the amended complaint. * * *

Accordingly, it is the opinion of this Court that as a matter of law the individual saleswomen do not state a claim for libel upon which relief can be granted and the motion to dismiss their cause of action is granted. * * *

The amended complaint is dismissed with leave to file separate complaints as to the two groups of individuals and the corporation, all in conformity with this opinion.

---

1. For which of the following statements may an individual member of the group or class maintain an action for defamation?

"All trading stamp concerns are engaged in dishonest practices." Watson v. Detroit Journal Co., 143 Mich. 430, 107 N.W. 81 (1906). "That jury was bribed." Byers v. Martin, 2 Colo. 605, 25 Am.Rep. 755 (1875). "The election board is crooked." Story v. Jones, 52 Ill.App. 112 (1893). "All men are liars." Psalms 116:11.

2. No recovery was allowed when defendant, addressing three men, said "One of you is a crook." Cohn v. Brecher, 20 Misc.2d 329, 192 N.Y.S.2d 877 (1959); and Ball v. White, 3 Mich.App. 579, 143 N.W.2d 188 (1966) (one out of five). But recovery was allowed in Farrell v. Johnson, 50 Ky. 48 (1850) (statement that a note had been altered by A or by B); Hardy v. Williamson, 86 Ga. 551, 12 S.E. 874 (1891) (eleven engineers employed by one company, "or some of them").

3. Is it a matter of degree? In Gross v. Kantor, 270 N.Y. 93, 200 N.E. 592 (1936), recovery was allowed when the statement was made of "all except one" of twelve radio critics in New York City. What if it had concerned "only one"? Cf. Blaser v. Krattiger, 99 Or. 392, 195 P. 359 (1921). Plaintiff was one of twenty Swiss sitting in a small Oregon hotel. Defendant, the landlady, came down the stairs in a state of great excitement, and said to the group, "There is a fellow stole about a thousand dollars of my jewelry, and the man is sitting right here and it is a Swiss. That son of a bitch is right in the room here." It was held that to maintain an action for slander the plaintiff must plead and prove that "he belongs to that class whose ancestry is ascribed to a canine of the female sex."

5. Group defamation has been a deliberate and sometimes potent weapon used against Jews, Catholics, Negroes, and others. As a result statutes in a few states have made group libel a crime. The Illinois Act was held constitutional in Beauharnais v. Illinois, 343 U.S. 250 (1952). See generally Riesman, Democ-

racy and Defamation: Control of Group Libel, 42 Colum.L.Rev. 727, 1085 (1942); Beth, Group Libel and Free Speech, 39 Minn.L.Rev. 167 (1954).

6. *Who Can Be Defamed?* Any living person can be defamed. Even a child ten minutes old may have a cause of action if it is called a bastard. On the other hand, it is generally agreed that there can be no actionable defamation of the dead, since there is no living person whose reputation is affected. Bello v. Random House, Inc., 422 S.W.2d 339 (Mo.1968); Gruschus v. Curtis Pub. Co., 342 F.2d 775 (10th Cir.1965). The defamation of the dead may, however, also defame the living, as where it is said that the plaintiff's deceased mother was not married to his father. Merrill v. Post Pub. Co., 197 Mass. 185, 83 N.E. 419 (1908).

7. A corporation can have no reputation in the personal sense, and cannot be defamed, for example, by being accused of unchastity. Neither can a partnership, as such. "The venereal disease was not a partnership malady. That was individual property." Bleckey, C.J., in Gilbert v. Crystal Fountain Lodge, 80 Ga. 284, 4 S.E. 905 (1887). But a corporation can maintain an action for defamation that casts an aspersion upon its honesty, credit, efficiency, or other business character. This is true even of a charitable or benevolent corporation not operated for profit, since defamation affecting its character or operations may deprive it of gifts or other sources of revenue. Boston Nutrition Society v. Stare, 342 Mass. 439, 173 N.E.2d 812 (1961); R.H. Bouligny, Inc. v. United Steelworkers of America, 270 N.C. 160, 154 S.E.2d 344 (1967). The same is true of a partnership, or an unincorporated association, such as a labor union, to the extent that the latter is recognized as a legal entity capable of bringing suit. Kirkman v. Textile Examiners & Shrinkers' Employers' Ass'n, 137 App.Div. 655, 122 N.Y.S. 460 (1910).

BINDRIM v. MITCHELL

Court of Appeal of California, Second District, 1979.
92 Cal.App.3d 61, 155 Cal.Rptr. 29, hearing denied by California Supreme Court,
1979; cert. denied 444 U.S. 984, 100 S.Ct. 490, 62 L.Ed.2d 412 (1979), reh.
denied 444 U.S. 1040, 100 S.Ct. 713, 62 L.Ed.2d 675 (1980).

[Plaintiff, Paul Bindrim, a Ph.D. and licensed psychologist, used what he designated as a "nude marathon in group therapy as a means of helping people to shed their psychological inhibitions with the removal of their clothes." Defendant Gwen Davis Mitchell, a successful novelist, registered in Bindrim's nude-therapy program, telling him that she was participating for therapeutic reasons only, and signing a contract "not to take photographs, write articles or in any manner disclose who has attended the workshop or what has transpired." Shortly thereafter, she contracted with defendant Doubleday for a novel based on the nude-therapy technique. The novel was written and published under the title of *Touching,* with a principal character, Dr. Simon Herford, using the technique.

Claiming that he was defamed by the depiction, plaintiff brought an action of libel against the two defendants. There was a jury verdict for the plaintiff in the trial court for substantial damages, and the court granted a motion for new trial conditioned on plaintiff's accepting a remittitur. Both plaintiff and the two defendants appealed.]

KINGSLEY, ASSOCIATE JUSTICE. * * * [Defendants] claim that, even if there are untrue statements, there is no showing that plaintiff was identified as the character Simon Herford, in the novel "Touching."

[They] allege that plaintiff failed to show he was identifiable as Simon Herford, relying on the fact that the character in "Touching" was described in the book as a "fat Santa Claus type with long white hair, white sideburns, a cherubic rosy face and rosy forearms" and that Bindrim was clean shaven and had short hair. Defendants rely in part on Wheeler v. Dell Publishing Co., 300 F.2d 372 (7th Cir.1962), which involved an alleged libel caused by a fictional account of an actual murder trial. The *Wheeler* court said (at p. 376):

"In our opinion, any reasonable person who read the book and was in a position to identify Hazel Wheeler with Janice Quill would more likely conclude that the author created the latter in an ugly way so that none would identify her with Hazel Wheeler. It is important to note that while the trial and locale might suggest Hazel Wheeler to those who knew the Chenoweth family, suggestion is not identification. In [Levey v. Warner Bros. Pictures, 57 F.Supp. 40 (S.D.N.Y.1944),] the court said those who had seen her act may have been reminded of her by songs and scenes, but would not reasonably identify her."

However, in *Wheeler* the court found that no one who knew the real widow could possibly identify her with the character in the novel. In the case at bar, the only differences between plaintiff and the Herford character in "Touching" were physical appearance and that Herford was a psychiatrist rather than psychologist. Otherwise, the character Simon Herford was very similar to the actual plaintiff. We cannot say, as did the court in *Wheeler,* that no one who knew plaintiff Bindrim could reasonably identify him with the fictional character. Plaintiff was identified as Herford by several witnesses and plaintiff's own tape recordings of the marathon sessions show that the novel was based substantially on plaintiff's conduct in the nude marathon.

Defendant also relies on Middlebrooks v. Curtis Publishing Co., 413 F.2d 141 (4th Cir.1969), where the marked dissimilarities between the fictional character and the plaintiff supported the court's finding against the reasonableness of identification. In *Middlebrooks,* there was a difference in age, an absence from the locale at the time of the episode, and a difference in employment of the fictional character and plaintiff; nor did the story parallel the plaintiff's life in any significant manner. In the case at bar, apart from some of those episodes allegedly constituting the libelous matter itself, and apart from the physical difference and the fact that plaintiff had a Ph.D., and not an M.D., the similarities between Herford and Bindrim are clear, and the transcripts of the actual encounter weekend show a close parallel between the narrative of plaintiff's novel and the actual real life events. Here, there were many similarities between the character, Herford, and the plaintiff Bindrim and those few differences do not bring the case under the rule of *Middlebrooks.* [C] There is overwhelming evidence that plaintiff and "Herford" were one. * * *

Defendants contend that the fact that the book was labeled as being a "novel" bars any claim that the writer or publisher could be found to have implied that the characters in the book were factual representations not of the fictional characters but of an actual nonfictional person. That contention, thus broadly stated, is unsupported by the cases. The test is whether a reasonable person, reading the book, would understand that the fictional character therein pictured was, in actual fact, the plaintiff acting as described. [C] Each case must stand on its own facts. In some cases, such as Greenbelt Pub. Assn. v. Bresler, 398 U.S. 6 (1970), an appellate court can, on examination of the entire work, find that no reasonable person would have regarded the episodes in the book as being other than the fictional imaginings of the author about how the character he had created would have acted. * * * Whether a reader, identifying plaintiff with the "Dr. Herford" of the book, would regard the passages herein complained of as mere fictional embroidering or as reporting actual language and conduct, was for the jury. Its verdict adverse to the defendants cannot be overturned by this court. * * *

Defendants raise the question of whether there is "publication" for libel where the communication is to only one person or a small group of persons rather than to the public at large. Publication for purposes of defamation is sufficient when the publication is to only one person other than the person defamed. [C] Therefore [it is] irrelevant whether all readers realized plaintiff and Herford were identical.

[The opinion also discusses whether the depiction was defamatory, the application of the "actual malice" test of New York Times v. Sullivan, infra page 895, the fact-opinion dichotomy, and damage issues.]

The judgment, as modified on the motion for a new trial, is further modified as [to damages.] * * *

Otherwise the judgment is affirmed. Neither party shall recover costs on appeal.

JEFFERSON, ASSOCIATE JUSTICE, concurring. * * * The dissent finds error in the instruction given the jury on the issue of identification. The use of the word "reasonably" in the instruction dissipates the dissent's view that only one person was required to understand the defamatory meaning. If one person "reasonably" understood the defamatory character of the language used, it describes what readers generally would "reasonably" understand. I see no basis for the dissent's view that the instruction had the result of mulcting defendants for the exercise of their first amendment right to comment on the nude marathon. The first amendment right to comment does *not* include the right to commit libel. * * *

"Of course the fictional setting does not insure immunity when a reasonable man would understand that the fictional character was a portrayal of the plaintiff. 'Reputations may not be traduced with impunity, whether under the literary forms of a work of fiction or in jest.' " [C]

FILES, PRESIDING JUSTICE (dissenting). ∗ ∗ ∗ Defendants' novel describes a fictitious therapist who is conspicuously different from plaintiff in name, physical appearance, age, personality and profession.

Indeed the fictitious Dr. Herford has none of the characteristics of plaintiff except that Dr. Herford practices nude encounter therapy. Only three witnesses, other than plaintiff himself, testified that they "recognized" plaintiff as the fictitious Dr. Herford. All three of those witnesses had participated in or observed one of plaintiff's nude marathons. The only characteristic mentioned by any of the three witnesses as identifying plaintiff was the therapy practiced. ∗ ∗ ∗

Plaintiff's brief discusses the therapeutic practices of the fictitious Dr. Herford in two categories: Those practices which are similar to plaintiff's technique are classified as identifying. Those which are unlike plaintiff's are called libelous because they are false. Plaintiff has thus resurrected the spurious logic which Professor Kalven found in the position of the plaintiff in New York Times v. Sullivan, infra page 895. Kalven wrote: "There is revealed here a new technique by which defamation might be endlessly manufactured. First, it is argued that, contrary to all appearances, a statement referred to the plaintiff; then, that it falsely ascribed to the plaintiff something that he did not do, which should be rather easy to prove about a statement that did not refer to plaintiff in the first place. ∗ ∗ ∗ " Kalven, The New York Times Case: A Note on "The Central Meaning of the First Amendment," 1964 The Supreme Court Review 191, 199.

Even if we accept the plaintiff's thesis that criticism of nude encounter therapy may be interpreted as libel of one practitioner, the evidence does not support a finding in favor of plaintiff.

Whether or not a publication to the general public is defamatory is "whether in the mind of the average reader the publication, considered as a whole, could reasonably be considered as defamatory." [C]

The majority opinion contains this juxtaposition of ideas: "Secondly, defendants' [proposed] instructions that the jury must find that a substantial segment of the public did, in fact, believe that Dr. Simon Herford was, in fact, Paul Bindrim ∗ ∗ ∗ was properly refused. For the tort of defamation, publication to one other person is sufficient."

The first sentence refers to the question whether the publication was defamatory of plaintiff. The second refers to whether the defamatory matter was published. The former is an issue in this case. The latter is not. Of course, a publication to one person may constitute actionable libel. But this has no bearing on the principle that the allegedly libelous effect of a publication to the public generally is to be tested by the impression made on the average reader. ∗ ∗ ∗

From an analytical standpoint, the chief vice of the majority opinion is that it brands a novel as libelous because it is "false," i.e., fiction; and infers "actual malice" from the fact that the author and publisher knew it was not a true representation of plaintiff. From a constitutional standpoint the vice is the chilling effect upon the publisher of any novel critical of any occupational practice, inviting litigation on the theory "when you criticize my occupation, you libel me."

I would reverse the judgment.

1. The colloquium, or reference to the plaintiff, need not be to him by name if it is reasonably understood as referring to him. Peagler v. Phoenix Newspapers, Inc., 114 Ariz. 309, 560 P.2d 1216 (1977); cf. Youssopoff v. Metro–Goldwyn–Mayer Pictures, 50 T.L.R. 581, 99 A.L.R. 864 (1934) (motion picture purportedly based on historical events; plaintiff identifiable as person raped by Rasputin). But if the words are not reasonably understood to refer to the plaintiff, there is no defamation. Arnold v. Sharpe, 296 N.C. 533, 251 S.E.2d 452 (1979); Sims v. Kiro, 20 Wash.App. 229, 580 P.2d 642 (1978).

2. Look at the latter part of the opinion in New York Times v. Sullivan, infra page 895, referring to the purported reference to Police Commissioner in the advertisement. Has it any relevance here?

3. If the novel *Touching* had contained a statement after the title page that this was a work of fiction and any similarity to existing persons was unintended, would that have made a difference?

4. For other recent cases offering variations to the problem of defamation in fiction, see Pring v. Penthouse Int'l, Inc., 695 F.2d 438 (10th Cir.1982), cert. denied, 462 U.S. 1132 (1983) (salacious story about a Miss Wyoming who performed on television at a Miss America Pageant sexual feats too fantastic to be believed; decision by the trial court for the real Miss Wyoming reversed, 2–1); Giesler v. Petrocelli, 616 F.2d 636 (2d Cir.1980) (plaintiff known to defendant, with identical name to that of the major character in a novel about a transsexual tennis player, allowed to recover); Springer v. Viking Press, 90 A.D.2d 315, 457 N.Y.S.2d 246 (1st Dept.1982), aff'd, 60 N.Y.2d 916, 458 N.E.2d 1256, 470 N.Y.S.2d 579 (1983) (plaintiff, former girl friend of author of a novel, given the same name as minor character in the book and similar physical characteristics, not allowed to recover because of insufficient basis for identifying the two).

5. There is a symposium on Defamation in Fiction, in 51 Bklyn.L.Rev. 223 (1985), including 11 articles and covering over 200 pages. See also, on the principal case, Louis, Libel in Fiction: A Chilling Decision for Authors, 6 Art & L. 3 (1983); Comment, 18 Cal.W.L.Rev. 442 (1983).

2.   LIBEL AND SLANDER

The erratic and anomalous development of the law of defamation has led to the survival until the present day of two forms of action for defamatory publication. One is libel, which originally concerned written or printed words; the other is slander, which was originally oral.

The prime significance of the distinction lies in the requirement of proof of damages. It has long been the rule as to slander that it is necessary to prove "special damages" (i.e. pecuniary loss; see Terwilliger v. Wands, infra page 884, unless the words spoken come within one of the four classes of what is called slander per se. Libel, on the other hand, did not require special damages to be actionable, though there was some disagreement on whether this applied to libel which was not defamatory on its face. The distinction has been an important one. Defamatory communications often do not produce pecuniary loss, and it is often impossible to prove when it does exist. The result is that for many types of slander no relief may be available. A natural question is, why should there be a difference? Is it solely a matter of history? Since the remarks of Sir James Mansfield, in Thorley v. Lord Kerry, 4 Taunt. 355, 128 Eng.Rep. 367 (1812), there has been no real effort to defend the distinction.

So long as the difference as to the requirement of special damages continues to be applied, however, it becomes necessary to draw the distinction between what is slander and what is libel. This is itself a question not at all free from difficulty. As it took form in the seventeenth century, the distinction was one between words that were written or printed and those that were oral. But not long afterward, libel was extended to include defamatory pictures, signs, statues, motion pictures and the like, and even conduct carrying a defamatory implication, such as hanging the plaintiff in effigy, or erecting a gallows before his door. From this it was concluded that libel is communicated by the sense of sight, while slander is conveyed by the sense of hearing. On the other hand slander was soon extended to include transitory gestures, such as the signals of a deaf-mute, or, as in Bennett v. Norban, 396 Pa. 94, 151 A.2d 476 (1959), the act of a storekeeper in publicly stopping a woman and searching her shopping bag. Furthermore, it was held to be a publication of a libel to read a defamatory writing aloud, as in Bander v. Metropolitan Life Ins. Co., 313 Mass. 337, 47 N.E.2d 595 (1943); and also to speak orally words expected to be and in fact written down, as in the case of dictation to a stenographer in Ostrowe v. Lee, 256 N.Y. 36, 175 N.E. 505 (1931), or of a statement made to a newspaper reporter in Valentine v. Gonzales, 190 App.Div. 490, 179 N.Y.S. 711 (1920). This has led some authorities to conclude that the distinction turns on embodiment of the defamation in some more or less permanent physical form. A delightful piece of spoofing as to a phonograph record and words taught to a parrot is in A.P. Herbert, Uncommon Law (7th ed. 1950) 71–76.

The advent of new methods of communication such as radio and television left the courts floundering to formulate the distinction, and led the Restatement (Second) of Torts § 568, to say that

"(1) Libel consists of the publication of defamatory matter by written or printed words, or by its embodiment in physical form, or by any other form of communication which has the potentially harmful qualities characteristic of written or printed words.

(2) Slander consists of the publication of defamatory matter by spoken words, transitory gestures, or by any form of communication other than those stated in Subsection (1).

(3) The area of dissemination, the deliberate and premeditated character of its publication, and the persistence of the defamation are factors to be considered in determining whether a publication is a libel rather than a slander."

SHOR v. BILLINGSLEY

Supreme Court, New York County, Special Term, 1956.
4 Misc.2d 857, 158 N.Y.S.2d 476.

[Action of defamation for a nationwide telecast. One person on the program "ad-libbed" the remark: "Want to know something? I wish I had as much money as he [plaintiff] owes * * * [to] everybody—oh, a lot of people." One count in the complaint was based on this remark.]

HECHT, JUSTICE. * * * That leaves for consideration the real problem in the case—whether the first cause of * * * action based upon a telecast not read from a prepared script sounds in libel or in slander.

This precise question has not been passed upon by our appellate courts, nor apparently in any other jurisdiction. Hartmann v. Winchell held that the "utterance of defamatory remarks, *read from a script* into a radio microphone and broadcast, constitute[s] publication of libel", 296 N.Y. [296,] at page 298, 73 N.E.2d [30,] at page 31, italics supplied. It expressly did not reach the question "whether broadcasting defamatory matter which has not been reduced to writing should be held to be libellous because of the potentially harmful and widespread effects of such defamation." [C] Fuld, J., concurring, held that it should "because of the likelihood of aggravated injury inherent in such broadcasting" [c].

Sorensen v. Wood, 123 Neb. 348, 353, 243 N.W. 82 (1932) [cc], likewise held libelous radio broadcasts read from a written script; Meldrum v. Australian Broadcasting Co. Ltd., [1932] Vict.L.R. 425, to the contrary, was specifically rejected in Hartmann v. Winchell, supra. * * *.

When account is taken of the vast and far-flung audience reached by radio today—often far greater in number than the readers of the largest metropolitan newspaper [c] it is evident that the broadcast of scandalous utterances is in general as potentially harmful to the defamed person's reputation as a publication by writing. That defamation by radio, in the absence of a script or transcription, lacks the measure of durability possessed by written libel, in nowise lessens its capacity for harm. Since the element of damage is, historically, the basis of the common-law action for defamation [c], and since it is as reasonable to presume damage from the nature of the medium employed when a slander is broadcast by radio as when published by writing, both logic and policy point the conclusion that defamation by radio should be actionable per se. * * *

It is true that "the delivery of the same speech over an amplifier to a vast audience in a stadium" would still be treated as a slander despite the fact that it may cause infinitely more damage than a writing seen by few, [c]. But such a speech falls so inescapably within the conventional definition of slander that in the foregoing situation "abolition of the line between libel and slander would * * * be too extreme a break with the past to be achieved without legislation." [C] But it does not follow that a court is equally powerless when dealing with the new media of radio and television. * * *

Our own courts experience no difficulty in applying the law of libel to the new instrumentality of the motion picture because "in the hands of a wrongdoer these devices have untold possibilities toward producing an effective libel". * * *

Accordingly, the motion to dismiss is denied as to the first three causes of action. * * *

----

1. This decision was affirmed without opinion by the Appellate Division, First Department, in 4 A.D.2d 1017, 169 N.Y.S.2d 416 (1957).

2. The matter is now rapidly being regulated by statute. Most of the statutes, enacted under lobbying from broadcasting companies, provide that any broadcast defamation is to be treated as slander, whether there is a script or not. See Remmers, Recent Legislative Trends in Defamation by Radio, 64 Harv.L.Rev. 727 (1951). The English Defamation Act (1952) 15 & 16 Geo. VI and Eliz. II, c. 66, provides that any broadcast is libel.

3. This has been a fertile subject of controversy in the law reviews. See, e.g., Vold, The Basis of Liability for Defamation by Radio, 19 Minn.L.Rev. 611 (1935); Donnelly, Defamation by Radio: A Reconsideration, 34 Iowa L.Rev. 12 (1948).

TERWILLIGER v. WANDS
Court of Appeals of New York, 1858.
17 N.Y. 54, 72 Am.Dec. 420.

Action for slander. The plaintiff proved by La Fayette Wands that the defendant asked him, Wands, what the plaintiff was running to Mrs. Fuller's so much for; he knew he went there for no good purpose; Mrs. Fuller was a bad woman, and plaintiff had a regular beaten path across his land to Fuller's; defendant said plaintiff went there to have intercourse with Mrs. Fuller, and that plaintiff would do all he could to keep Mrs. Fuller's husband in the penitentiary so that he could have free access there. * * *

The only damages proved were that the plaintiff was prostrated in health and unable to attend to business after hearing of the reports circulated by the defendant. A motion for a nonsuit was sustained * * *.

STRONG, J. The words spoken by the defendant not being actionable of themselves, it was necessary, in order to maintain the action, to prove that they occasioned special damages to the plaintiff. The special damages must have been the natural, immediate and legal consequence of the words. * * *

The special damages relied upon are not of such a nature as will support the action. * * * It is injuries affecting the reputation only which are the subject of the action. In the case of slanderous words actionable per se, the law, from their natural and immediate tendency to produce injury, adjudges them to be injurious, though no special loss or damage can be proved. "But with regard to words that do not apparently and upon the face of them import such defamation as will of course be injurious, it is necessary that the plaintiff should aver some particular damage to have happened." (3 Bl.Com. 124.) As to what constitutes special damages, Starkie mentions the loss of a marriage, loss of hospitable gratuitous entertainment, preventing a servant or bailiff from getting a place, the loss of customers by a tradesman; and says that in general whenever a person is prevented by the slander from receiving that which would otherwise be conferred upon him, though gratuitously, it is sufficient. * * *

It necessarily follows from the rule that the words must be disparaging to character, that the special damage to give an action must flow from disparaging it. * * * In the present case the words were defamatory, and the illness and physical prostration of the plaintiff may be assumed, so far as this part of the case is concerned, to have been actually produced by the slander, but this consequence was not, in a legal view, a natural, ordinary one, as it does not prove that the plaintiff's character was injured. The slander may not have been credited by or had the slightest influence upon any one unfavorable to the plaintiff; and it does not appear that anybody believed it or treated the plaintiff any different from what they would otherwise have done on account of it. The cause was not adapted to produce the result which is claimed to be special damages. Such an effect may and sometimes does follow from such a cause but not ordinarily; and the rule of law was framed in reference to common and usual effects and not those which are accidental and occasional. * * *

Where there is no proof that the character has suffered from the words, if sickness results it must be attributed to the apprehension of loss of character, and such fear of harm to character, with resulting sickness and bodily prostration, cannot be such special damage as the law requires for the action. The loss of character must be a substantive loss, one which has actually taken place. * * *

Judgment affirmed.

————

1. When special damages must be pleaded and proved to make out a cause of action for slander, the common law rule developed that the damages must be of a pecuniary character. This was a carry-over from the old conflict of

jurisdiction with the ecclesiastical courts, and the rule that the king's court could take jurisdiction only where there was "temporal," as distinguished from "spiritual," harm.   Hence, if no pecuniary loss is shown, it is not enough that the plaintiff has suffered acute mental distress and serious physical illness as a result of the defamation.   Allsop v. Allsop, 5 H. & N. 534, 157 Eng.Rep. 1292 (1860);   Scott v. Harrison, 215 N.C. 427, 2 S.E.2d 1 (1939).

2.   When the cause of action is once made out, either as libel or slander per se, or by proof of special damages of a pecuniary character, plaintiff may recover additional damages for his mental distress, wounded feelings and humiliation.   Pion v. Caron, 237 Mass. 107, 129 N.E. 369 (1921);   Baker v. Winslow, 184 N.C. 1, 113 S.E. 570 (1922).

3.   The original rule was that the defendant was liable only for damages due to his own publication, and was not responsible for repetition by others. Vicars v. Wilcocks, 8 East 1, 103 Eng.Rep. 244 (1806);   Hastings v. Stetson, 126 Mass. 329 (1879).   Later decisions tend to hold that the original publisher is liable for damages due to a repetition that might reasonably have been anticipated.   Elms v. Crane, 118 Me. 261, 107 A. 852 (1919);   Sawyer v. Gilmer's, Inc., 189 N.C. 7, 126 S.E. 183 (1925).

4.   The party repeating the defamation is himself liable for its publication, even though he states the source.   Haines v. Campbell, 74 Md. 158, 21 A. 702 (1891);   Times Pub. Co. v. Carlisle, 94 Fed. 762 (8th Cir.1899).   He is liable even though he states that he does not believe the imputation.   Morse v. Times–Republican Co., 124 Iowa 707, 100 N.W. 867 (1904);   Cobbs v. Chicago Defender, 308 Ill.App. 55, 31 N.E.2d 323 (1941).

Slander Per Se

Four special kinds of slander are exceptions to the general common law rule, and actionable without proof of special damages.   These are the following:

1.   *Imputations of Major Crime.*   The original basis for this exception seems to have been that the plaintiff was thus exposed to criminal prosecution.   Later the emphasis shifted to the social ostracism involved and the probability that the plaintiff must have suffered some pecuniary loss, even though he could not prove it.   Thus, the action lay without any proof of damage, even though the words made it clear that the plaintiff had been punished or pardoned, or that prosecution was barred by the statute of limitations.

In the early days of defamation most crimes were felonies.   With the extension of criminal punishment to many minor offenses, it obviously became necessary to make some distinction as to the character of the crime, since a charge of a traffic violation, for example, would not today exclude a person from society, and would do little, if any, harm to reputation.   The courts have struggled to make some kind of distinction between imputations of major and of minor crime.   The English courts decided that the crime must be one subject to corporal punishment, i.e., death or imprisonment.   American jurisdictions, added the requirement that the crime must be subject to indictment.   With the modern tendency to substitute the information for the indictment, this obviously became unsuitable.

The formula that most courts now follow is that the crime must be one involving "moral turpitude," defined as "an inherent baseness or vileness of principle in the human heart."

Today, it is not the crime, but rather the character of the act charged, that is controlling. Not every trivial assault or battery involves "moral turpitude"; but an accusation that the plaintiff beat his mother was held in Sipp v. Coleman, 179 Fed. 997 (D.N.J.1910), necessarily to do so.

2. *Loathsome Disease.* The basis of the exception for the imputation of certain diseases appears originally to have been simply the exclusion from society that would result. It began with venereal disease and leprosy, at a time when both were regarded as permanent, lingering and incurable. It was not applied to more contagious and equally repugnant disorders such as smallpox, from which one either recovered or died in a short time. James v. Rutledge, Moore 573, 4 Co. Rep. 17a, 76 Eng.Rep. 900 (1599).

The advance of medical science and a better understanding of disease tended to freeze the exception within its original limits, and today accusations of insanity, tuberculosis or other communicable diseases are not included. Furthermore, since there would not be the same social avoidance of one who had recovered, it is well settled that the imputation that the plaintiff has had even a venereal disease in the past is not sufficient to be actionable without proof of special damage. Bruce v. Soule, 69 Me. 562 (1879). The importance of this exception has been slight, and there have been almost no cases applying it in this century. Will the situation change with the advent of AIDS?

3. *Business, Trade, Profession or Office.* If the spoken words are likely to affect the plaintiff in his business, trade, profession or office, the probability of some "temporal" damage is sufficiently obvious. Any legitimate calling is included, "be it ever so base." Terry v. Hooper, 1 Lev. 115, 83 Eng.Rep. 325 (1663); cf. Fitzgerald v. Redfield, 51 Barb. 484 (N.Y.1868) (mason); Burtch v. Nickerson, 17 Johns. 217 (N.Y.1819) (blacksmith). Even uncompensated offices of confidence or trust have been included; and in Dietrich v. Hauser, 45 Misc.2d 805, 257 N.Y.S.2d 716 (1965), it was held slander per se to say of a club president that he was a cheat and a fraud.

The exception was limited to defamation of a kind incompatible with the proper conduct of the business, trade, profession or office itself. Thus it is actionable without proof of special damage to say of an attorney that he is a shyster. Nolan v. Standard Pub. Co., 67 Mont. 212, 216 P. 571 (1923). Or of a school teacher that he has been guilty of improper conduct with his pupils. Thompson v. Bridges, 209 Ky. 710, 273 S.W. 529 (1925). Or a chauffeur that he is habitually drinking. Lousiville Taxicab & Transfer Co. v. Ingle, 229 Ky. 578, 17 S.W.2d 709 (1929). Or of a bank, that it is insolvent, or of a merchant that his credit is bad. Ridgeway State Bank v. Bird, 185 Wis. 418, 202 N.W. 170 (1925). Or of the governor of a state that he is indifferent to lynching and has approved the work of a mob. Caldwell v. Crowell–Collier Pub. Co., 161 F.2d 333 (5th Cir.1947).

Thus if the defendant calls the plaintiff an illiterate, a bankrupt, a coward or a communist, it makes a difference whether the plaintiff is a professor, a merchant, an army officer or a government employee.

4. *Serious Sexual Misconduct.* The principal application of this to date has been a charge imputing unchastity to a woman. In England this was not actionable per se, until the common law rule was changed by the Slander of Women Act in 1891. Some of the American courts got around the rule, as in Kelly v. Flaherty, 16 R.I. 234, 14 A. 876 (1888), by finding that the imputation was equivalent to a charge of the crime of adultery or fornication, which involved moral turpitude. Gradually this gave way to a recognition of the essentially damaging nature of the charge, and a fourth exception is now generally recognized. Hollman v. Brady, 233 F.2d 877 (9th Cir.1956); Gnapinsky v. Goldyn, 23 N.J. 243, 128 A.2d 697 (1957).

The assumption has always been that the imputation of unchastity is not so damaging to a man, and it is still held that this is not slander per se, unless it falls into one of the other slander exceptions. Hickerson v. Masters, 190 Ky. 168, 226 S.W. 1072 (1921); Marion v. Davis, 217 Ala. 16, 114 So. 357 (1927).

Recent holdings on the constitutional requirements of equality of treatment between the sexes, while not specifically applicable to this problem, may affect the holding that an imputation of unchastity for a woman is slanderous per se while a similar imputation for a man is not. If the Constitution is held to require that they may be treated similarly, there is no indication as to which of the two applications will be changed. See Restatement (Second) of Torts § 574; Sauerhoff v. Hearst Corp., 388 F.Supp. 117 (D.Md.1974).

What about the imputation of homosexual conduct or characteristics? In Buck v. Savage, 323 S.W.2d 363 (Tex.Civ.App.1959), the statement that plaintiff was "queer on" another man was held to amount to a charge of the crime of sodomy and so to be actionable per se.

Libel Per Se and Libel Per Quod

The established rule at common law was to the effect that it is not necessary to prove special damages in order to maintain an action for libel. Some American decisions deviated from this rule, apparently through an initial mistake as to the meaning of the expression "libel per se." As applied to the requirement of proof of special damages, all libel was libel per se. But if the statement was not defamatory on its face and it was necessary to be aware of certain extrinsic (or unstated) facts in order to appreciate its defamatory implications, it was sometimes called libel per quod, meaning that the plaintiff must allege and prove those extrinsic facts in order to have a cause of action. Some

American decisions, breaking away from the established rule, apparently assumed that if the communication was not defamatory on its face and was called libel per quod, it was not libel per se and required proof of special damages. But other cases deliberately adopted the rule. Case authority was divided and a vigorous debate developed between Dean Prosser and Professor Laurence Eldredge on the status of the authorities and the arguments for the two rules. The matter was rendered largely moot, however, by the decision in Gertz v. Robert Welch, Inc., infra page 906, which held (1) that strict liability is unconstitutional and a defendant is not liable unless he was at fault and (2) that the presumed damages of the common law are unconstitutional and plaintiff can recover only "actual damages." The first holding eliminates any unfairness in the original common law rule when the defendant did not know of the extrinsic fact.

The Restatement (Second) of Torts § 569 provides that special damages are not required in any libel action. See Hinsdale v. Orange County Publications, Inc., 17 N.Y.2d 284, 217 N.E.2d 650, 270 N.Y.S.2d 592 (1966); Hinkle v. Alexander, 244 Or. 267, 417 P.2d 586 (1966). The *Gertz* holding that there can be no recovery of common law presumed damages makes the importance of defamation per se somewhat less significant.

Is it likely that some state court may now judicially abolish the distinction between slander per se and ordinary slander? Between libel and slander? This latter step was taken by the Washington Supreme Court in Grein v. La Poma, 54 Wash.2d 840, 340 P.2d 766 (1959), but the case has not yet developed a following.

3. PUBLICATION

ECONOMOPOULOS v. A.G. POLLARD CO.
Supreme Judicial Court of Massachusetts, 1914.
218 Mass. 294, 105 N.E. 896.

Action by George Economopoulos against A.G. Pollard Company. There was a verdict for defendant, and plaintiff brings exceptions.

This was an action of tort in three counts * * *; the third count charging defendant with falsely and maliciously charging plaintiff with larceny by words spoken of plaintiff, as follows: "You have stolen a handkerchief from us and have it in your pocket." There was evidence that a clerk of defendant stated in English to plaintiff, a Greek, that he had stolen a handkerchief, and that a Greek clerk stated to plaintiff in Greek that plaintiff had stolen a handkerchief. There was nothing to show that third persons heard the charge, excepting the floor walker.

LORING, J. * * * There was no evidence that anybody but the plaintiff was present when Carrier spoke to the plaintiff in English. There was no publication of this statement made in English, because on the evidence the words could not have been heard by any one but the plaintiff. [C]

Nor was there any evidence of publication of the Greek words spoken by Miralos, for although there was evidence that they were spoken in the presence of others, there was no evidence that any one understood them but the plaintiff. * * *

Exceptions overruled.

---

1. "Publication" is a word of art in defamation cases. It does not mean printing, writing or even publicity, but merely communication of the defamatory words to some one other than the person defamed. It is not enough that the words are spoken to the plaintiff himself, even in the presence of others, if no one else overhears them. Sheffill v. Van Deusen, 13 Mass. (Gray) 304, 74 Am. Dec. 632 (1859). Cf. Barnes v. Clayton House Motel, 435 S.W.2d 616 (Tex.Civ. App.1968) (letter to the plaintiff).

2. Defendant, in the presence of others who overhear him, calls plaintiff a "cocotte," which, according to the court, is a French word meaning either a prostitute or a poached egg. What else must plaintiff plead and prove in order to establish her cause of action? Rovira v. Boget, 240 N.Y. 314, 148 N.E. 534 (1925). What if the auditors are too young to know the meaning of the words? Sullivan v. Sullivan, 48 Ill.App. 435 (1892).

3. Sometimes the court presumes that some one has read and understood the defamatory words. Thus when they are published in German in a German-language newspaper circulated among subscribers who read German. Steketee v. Kimm, 48 Mich. 322, 12 N.W. 177 (1882). This presumption has also been applied to a defamatory postcard sent through the mail. Ostro v. Safir, 165 Misc. 647, 1 N.Y.S.2d 377 (1937). Other cases hold that proof of actual reading is required in such a case. McKeel v. Latham, 202 N.C. 318, 162 S.E. 747 (1932).

4. A few courts have held that there is no publication when the defamatory words are dictated to a stenographer, who is regarded as such an indispensable means of transcription in modern business as to be treated as merely equivalent to the defendant's own writing. Watson v. Wanamaker, 216 S.C. 295, 57 S.E.2d 477 (1950); Satterfield v. McLellan Stores Co., 215 N.C. 582, 2 S.E.2d 709 (1939). Most courts have held that there is a publication, although it may be privileged; and when the words are in fact taken down, there is publication of a libel. Ostrowe v. Lee, 256 N.Y. 36, 175 N.E. 505 (1931); Rickbeil v. Grafton Deaconess Hospital, 74 N.D. 525, 23 N.W.2d 247 (1946).

5. On the same basis, most courts have held that there is publication when the communication is from one officer, agent or office of a corporation to another; and when one agent of a telegraph company transmits a message to another. See Smith, Liability of a Telegraph Company for Transmitting a Defamatory Message, 20 Colum.L.Rev. 30, 369 (1920).

6. For a communication to a third party to be a publication, it must have been done intentionally or by a negligent act. See Restatement (Second) of Torts § 577. Thus there is no publication when words are spoken by defendant directly to plaintiff, with no reason to suppose that any one can overhear, and they are in fact overheard by a concealed listener. Hall v. Balkind, [1918] N.Z.L.Rep. 740. Otherwise when the words are spoken in so loud a voice that

defendant can expect that some one may overhear. McNichol v. Grandy, [1931] Can.S.C.Rep. 696.

7. If the defamation is sent by defendant to plaintiff himself in a sealed letter, which is unexpectedly opened and read by a third person, there is no publication. Barnes v. Clayton House Motel, 435 S.W.2d 616 (Tex.Civ.App. 1968). But there is liability if defendant knows that plaintiff's spouse or secretary is in the habit of reading plaintiff's mail and the words are in fact read by such a person. Rumney v. Worthley, 186 Mass. 144, 71 N.E. 316 (1904); Roberts v. English Mfg. Co., 155 Ala. 414, 46 So. 752 (1908).

8. There is a publication when a telegraph company transmits a message or a third party orally repeats a message. The postal service does not make a publication when it delivers a letter. Nor is there a publication by the telephone company when its system is used, without more for communication purposes. See Anderson v. New York Tel. Co., 35 N.Y.2d 746, 320 N.E.2d 647, 361 N.Y.S.2d 913 (1974).

9. *Publication by Plaintiff.* Ordinarily the defendant is not liable for any publication made by the plaintiff alone, since it is considered that it is plaintiff's responsibility and not the defendant's. Lyle v. Waddle, 144 Tex. 90, 188 S.W.2d 770 (1915). But suppose it is reasonable for the plaintiff to consult someone else about a defamatory communication made only to plaintiff and the defendant might expect this. The obvious case is that of the plaintiff who is blind or illiterate. Lane v. Schilling, 130 Or. 119, 279 P. 267 (1929); cf. Hedgpeth v. Coleman, 183 N.C. 309, 111 S.E. 517 (1922) (plaintiff is a child).

10. A discharged employee of the defendant, seeking other employment, is asked by all prospective employers why he left his last job. In response, he repeats, and denies, the defamatory charge. Is defendant liable? Grist v. Upjohn Co., 16 Mich.App. 452, 168 N.W.2d 389 (1969); cf. Colonial Stores v. Barrett, 73 Ga.App. 839, 38 S.E.2d 306 (1946).

11. *Failure to Remove Defamation.* In several cases defendant has been held liable for failure to remove defamation posted on his premises. See Tidmore v. Mills, 33 Ala.App. 243, 32 So.2d 769 (1947); Hellar v. Bianco, 111 Cal.App.2d 424, 244 P.2d 757 (1952). The courts have not agreed upon a theory, and have struggled with "republication," "ratification," and negligent breach of a duty to remove.

OGDEN v. ASSOCIATION OF THE UNITED STATES ARMY

United States District Court, District of Columbia, 1959.
177 F.Supp. 498.

HOLTZOFF, DISTRICT JUDGE. The question presented for decision in this case is whether from the standpoint of the statute of limitations in an action for libel every sale or delivery of a copy of a book, periodical, or newspaper containing an alleged defamatory statement, creates a separate cause of action; or whether only one cause of action arises which accrues at the time of the first publication of one or more copies of the offending material. To formulate this question in another form, should the so-called modern "single publication rule" be the law of the District of Columbia? [The book containing the alleged libel was published in November, 1955. This suit was filed on June 25, 1959.

The District of Columbia has a 1–year statute of limitations for defamation.]

The common law was originally to the effect that every sale or delivery of libelous matter was a new publication and that, therefore, a new cause of action accrued on each occasion. * * *

A leading English case on the subject is The Duke of Brunswick v. Harmer, 14 Q.B. 185, 117 Eng.Rep. 75, decided in 1849. It involved an issue of a newspaper published in 1830. A single copy was sold by the defendant seventeen years later and a suit for libel was predicated on this sale as a publication. The plea of the statute of limitations was overruled on the theory that each sale or delivery of a copy of the offending material gave rise to a new and separate cause of action. * * *

Under modern conditions the original common-law rule would give rise to an unnecessary multiplicity of suits and would practically destroy the statute of limitations as a statute of repose in actions for libel. There is no doubt, to be sure, that the number of copies of the offending publication that have been supplied to the public is a factor to be considered in determining the amount of damages to be awarded. In order to protect the plaintiff in this respect, however, it is not necessary to hold that every sale and delivery of an additional copy is a new publication and gives rise to a new cause of action.

[The court reviews decisions from many states adopting the single-publication rule and quotes the Uniform Single Publications Act, promulgated in 1952 and adopted in a number of other states.]

There are indeed a few States that expressly adhere to the original English rule in cases that were decided a great many years ago, [cc]. They are a small minority. * * *

* * * [T]he conclusion is inescapable that the modern American law of libel has adopted the so-called "single publication" rule; and, therefore, this principle must be deemed a part of the common law of the District of Columbia. In other words, it is the prevailing American doctrine that the publication of a book, periodical, or newspaper containing defamatory matter gives rise to but one cause of action for libel, which accrues at the time of the original publication, and that the statute of limitations runs from that date. It is no longer the law that every sale or delivery of a copy of the publication creates a new cause of action. * * *

The defendant's motion for summary judgment is granted.

———

1. American jurisdictions now generally agree with the principal case. Each edition of a newspaper, magazine or book is held to be one separate publication. Backus v. Look, Inc., 39 F.Supp. 662 (S.D.N.Y.1941). This is true of each broadcast or rebroadcast over radio or television, and each exhibition of a motion picture. But when a hundred different newspapers each publish in their own editions a news report supplied by Associated Press, there are a hundred publications. See Restatement (Second) of Torts § 577A.

4. BASIS OF LIABILITY

The early law apparently imposed strict liability for defamation, as in the case of most other torts. See Holdsworth, Defamation in the Sixteenth and Seventeenth Centuries, 41 L.Q.Rev. 13 (1925).

During the Seventeenth Century, at a time when the courts were not at all anxious to encourage actions for defamation, the rule developed that the plaintiff must plead and prove not only that the defendant intended to defame him, but that he was inspired by "malice," in the sense of spite, ill will, or a desire to do harm. Parson Prick's Case, cited in Cro.Jac. 91, 79 Eng.Rep. 78; Crawford v. Middleton, 1 Lev. 82, 83 Eng.Rep. 308 (1674). Apparently this was carried over from the ecclesiastical law of slander, which was concerned with the moral sin of speaking ill of one's neighbor, and from criminal libel, which required at least a criminal intent. Veeder, History and Theory of the Law of Defamation, 4 Colum.L.Rev. 33 (1904); Green, Slander and Libel, 6 Am. L.Rev. 593 (1872).

In 1825, the historic case of Bromage v. Prosser, 4 B. & C. 247, 107 Eng.Rep. 1051 (K.B.), was decided. It drew a distinction between "malice in fact and malice in law." Malice is necessary, it held, but in the ordinary defamation case, if the statement is false and defamatory and it was made intentionally, "the law implies such malice as is necessary to maintain the action." Factual malice, on the other hand, is not a necessary part of the plaintiff's case in an ordinary defamation action; but it may be important to refute a qualified privilege or to justify punitive damages. "Malice" has also come to be used, with a still different meaning, in the constitutional law cases set out in this Section.

Thus the malice implied in law became a pure fiction, and the effect of the case was that malice in fact was no longer a requisite to a prima facie case of defamation. But the courts continued to speak of malice, and the part that the term plays in an action for defamation has become one of profound confusion. With so many meanings and so much uncertainty, the term is best avoided.

Deriving from Bromage v. Prosser, decisions were rendered imposing liability for unintended and innocent defamation. The classic case was the Scottish decision of Morrison v. Ritchie & Co., 4 Sess.Cas. (Fr.) 645, 39 Scot.L.Rep. 432 (1904), where defendant newspaper published in good faith a report sent to it that plaintiff wife had given birth to twins. It was held liable when the report proved false and the plaintiffs had been married only three months.

Then came Hulton v. Jones, [1910] A.C. 20. Defendant newspaper published a report from a French correspondent from the resort of Dieppe containing a passage reading: " 'Whist! there is Artemus Jones with a woman who is not his wife, who must be you know—the other thing!' whispers a fair neighbor of mine excitedly into her bosom friend's ear. 'Really, is it not surprising how certain of our countrymen behave when they come abroad?' " The name Artemus Jones was a fictitious one, coined for the occasion, and not intended to refer to anyone. But a real Artemus Jones appeared, sued and recovered on the ground that some of his friends understood the piece to refer to him. See Smith, Jones v. Hutton: Three Conflicting Views as to Defamation, 60 U.Pa.L.Rev. 365 & 461 (1912); Holdsworth, A Chapter of Accidents in the Law of Libel, 57 L.Q.Rev. 74 (1941).

In this country, the leading case of Corrigan v. Bobbs–Merrill Co., 228 N.Y. 58, 126 N.E. 260 (1920), was similar. An author sent in a book manuscript purporting to be fictitious, and the publisher produced it without realizing that it referred in an identifiable way to a magistrate in the city of New York. "The fact that the publisher has no actual intention to defame a particular man or indeed to injure anyone does not prevent recovery of compensatory damages by one who connects himself with the publication. * * * The question is not so much who was aimed at as who was hit." There were numerous cases in accord.

Secondary Publishers. There was one important exception. A vendor or distributor of a newspaper, magazine or book is called a "secondary publisher" and is not liable if he had no knowledge of libellous matter in the publication and had no reason to be put on guard. See Vizetelly v. Mudie's Select Library, [1907] 2 Q.B. 170 (lending library); Balabanoff v. Fossani, 192 Misc. 615, 81 N.Y.S.2d 732 (1948) (newspaper vendor); McLeod v. St. Aubuyn, [1899] A.C. 549 (private lender); Grisham v. Western Union Tel. Co., 238 Mo. 480, 142 S.W. 271 (1911) (telegram innocent on its face).

A newspaper or book publishing company does not qualify as a secondary publisher, however, and was held subject to strict liability even though it innocently took the defamatory material from someone else without any reason to be put on guard. There has been sharp disagreement as to how local radio and television networks are to be classified, when they broadcast material directly from national networks or allow someone else to supply a program without opportunity for screening it. Holding that they are primary publishers: Sorenson v. Wood, 123 Neb. 348, 243 N.W. 82 (1932); Miles v. Louis Wasmer, Inc., 172 Wash. 466, 20 P.2d 847 (1933). Holding that they are secondary publishers: Kelly v. Hoffman, 137 N.J.L. 695, 61 A.2d 143 (1948); Summit Hotel Co. v. National Broadcasting Co., 336 Pa. 182, 8 A.2d 302 (1939). A number of states have statutes. See Remmers, Recent Trends in Defamation by Radio, 64 Harv.L.Rev. 727 (1951). Commentators have differed as sharply as the courts. See, e.g., Donnelly, Defamation by Radio; A Recommendation, 34 Iowa L.Rev. 212 (1948); Leflar, Radio and TV Defamation: Fault or Strict Liability?, 15 Ohio St.L.J. 252 (1954). The Restatement takes the position that a broadcasting station should be treated as an original publisher. Restatement (Second) of Torts § 581(2).

How have the Supreme Court cases in the remaining part of this Section affected all this?

NEW YORK TIMES CO. v. SULLIVAN

Supreme Court of the United States, 1964.
376 U.S. 254, 84 S.Ct. 710, 11 L.Ed.2d 686.

MR. JUSTICE BRENNAN delivered the opinion of the Court.

We are required in this case to determine for the first time the extent to which the constitutional protections for speech and press limit a State's power to award damages in a libel action brought by a public official against critics of his official conduct.

Respondent L.B. Sullivan is one of the three elected Commissioners of the City of Montgomery, Alabama. He testified that he was "Commissioner of Public Affairs and the duties are supervision of the Police Department, Fire Department, Department of Cemetery and Department of Scales." He brought this civil libel action against the four individual petitioners, who are Negroes and Alabama clergymen, and against petitioner the New York Times Company, a New York corporation which publishes the New York Times, a daily newspaper. A jury in the Circuit Court of Montgomery County awarded him damages of $500,000, the full amount claimed, against all the petitioners, and the Supreme Court of Alabama affirmed.

Respondent's complaint alleged that he had been libeled by statements in a full-page advertisement that was carried in the New York Times on March 29, 1960. Entitled "Heed Their Rising Voices," the advertisement began by stating that "As the whole world knows by now, thousands of Southern Negro students are engaged in wide-spread non-violent demonstrations in positive affirmation of the right to live in human dignity as guaranteed by the U.S. Constitution and the Bill of

Front row: Clark, Black, Warren, C.J., Douglas, Harlan
Back row: White, Brennan, Stewart, Goldberg

Rights." It went on to charge that "in their efforts to uphold these guarantees, they are being met by an unprecedented wave of terror by those who would deny and negate that document which the whole world looks upon as setting the pattern for modern freedom. * * *" Succeeding paragraphs purported to illustrate the "wave of terror" by describing certain alleged events. The text concluded with an appeal for funds for three purposes: support of the student movement, "the struggle for the right-to-vote," and the legal defense of Dr. Martin Luther King, Jr., leader of the movement, against a perjury indictment then pending in Montgomery.

The text appeared over the names of 64 persons, widely known for their activities in public affairs, religion, trade unions, and the performing arts. * * *

Of the 10 paragraphs of text in the advertisement, the third and a portion of the sixth were the basis of respondent's claim of libel. They read as follows:

Third paragraph: "In Montgomery, Alabama, after students sang 'My Country, 'Tis of Thee' on the State Capitol steps, their leaders were expelled from school, and truckloads of police armed with shotguns and tear-gas ringed the Alabama State College Campus. When the entire student body protested to state authorities by refusing to re-register, their dining hall was padlocked in an attempt to starve them into submission."

Sixth paragraph: "Again and again the Southern violators have answered Dr. King's peaceful protests with intimidation and violence. They have bombed his home almost killing his wife and child. They have assaulted his person. They have arrested him seven times—for 'speeding,' 'loitering' and similar 'offenses.' And now they have charged him with 'perjury'—a *felony* under which they could imprison him for *ten years*. * * *"

[Although plaintiff was not mentioned by name, he contended that these statements attributed misconduct to him as the Montgomery Commissioner who supervised the Police Department.]

It is uncontroverted that some of the statements contained in the two paragraphs were not accurate descriptions of events which occurred in Montgomery. Although Negro students staged a demonstration on the State Capitol steps, they sang the National Anthem and not "My Country, 'Tis of Thee." Although nine students were expelled by the State Board of Education, this was not for leading the demonstration at the Capitol, but for demanding service at a lunch counter in the Montgomery County Courthouse on another day. Not the entire student body, but most of it, had protested the expulsion, not by refusing to register, but by boycotting classes on a single day; virtually all the students did register for the ensuing semester. The campus dining hall was not padlocked on any occasion, and the only students who may have been barred from eating there were the few who had neither signed a preregistration application nor requested temporary meal tickets. Although the police were deployed near the campus in large numbers on three occasions, they did not at any time "ring" the campus, and they were not called to the campus in connection with the demonstration on the State Capitol steps, as the third paragraph implied. Dr. King had not been arrested seven times, but only four; and although he claimed to have been assaulted some years earlier in connection with his arrest for loitering outside a courtroom, one of the officers who made the arrest denied that there was such an assault.

On the premise that the charges in the sixth paragraph could be read as referring to him, respondent was allowed to prove that he had not participated in the events described. Although Dr. King's home had in fact been bombed twice when his wife and child were there, both of these occasions antedated respondent's tenure as Commissioner, and the police were not only not implicated in the bombings, but had made every effort to apprehend those who were. Three of Dr. King's four arrests took place before respondent became Commissioner. Although Dr. King had in fact been indicted (he was subsequently acquitted) on two counts of perjury, each of which carried a possible five-year sentence, respondent had nothing to do with procuring the indictment. * * *

The trial judge submitted the case to the jury under instructions that the statements in the advertisement were "libelous per se" and were not privileged, so that petitioners might be held liable if the jury found that they had published the advertisement and that the statements were made "of and concerning" respondent. * * *

Under Alabama law as applied in this case * * * once "libel per se" has been established, the defendant has no defense as to stated facts unless he can persuade the jury that they were true in all their particulars. [Cc] His privilege of "fair comment" for expressions of opinion depends on the truth of the facts upon which the comment is based. * * *

The First Amendment, said Judge Learned Hand, "presupposes that right conclusions are more likely to be gathered out of a multitude of tongues, than through any kind of authoritative selection. To many this is, and always will be, folly; but we have staked upon it our all." United States v. Associated Press, 52 F.Supp. 362, 372 (S.D.N.Y.1943). * * * Thus we consider this case against the background of a profound national commitment to the principle that debate on public issues should be uninhibited, robust and wide-open, and that it may well include vehement, caustic, and sometimes unpleasantly sharp attacks on government and public officials. [Cc] The present advertisement, as an expression of grievance and protest, on one of the major public issues of our time, would seem clearly to qualify for the constitutional protection. The question is whether it forfeits that protection by the falsity of some of its factual statements and by its alleged defamation of respondent.

Authoritative interpretations of the First Amendment guarantees have consistently refused to recognize an exception for any test of truth—whether administered by judges, juries, or administrative officials—and especially one that puts the burden of proving truth on the speaker. [C] The constitutional protection does not turn upon "the truth, popularity, or social utility of the ideas and beliefs which are offered." [C] As Madison said, "Some degree of abuse is inseparable from the proper use of everything; and in no instance is this more true than in that of the press." [C] * * *

If neither factual error nor defamatory content suffices to remove the constitutional shield from criticism of official conduct, the combination of the two elements is no less inadequate. [The Court here reviewed the history of the Sedition Act of 1798, which made it a crime to publish defamation against high officers of the United States, and reached the conclusion at this late date that the Act was unconstitutional.]

What a State may not constitutionally bring about by means of a criminal statute is likewise beyond the reach of its civil law of libel. The fear of damage awards under a rule such as that invoked by the Alabama courts here may be markedly more inhibiting than the fear of prosecution under a criminal statute. * * * Presumably a person charged with violation of [a criminal-libel] statute enjoys ordinary criminal-law safeguards such as the requirements of an indictment and of proof beyond a reasonable doubt. These safeguards are not available to the defendant in a civil action. * * *

The state rule of law is not saved by its allowance of the defense of truth. * * * A rule compelling the critic of official conduct to guarantee the truth of all his factual assertions—and to do so on pain of libel judgments virtually unlimited in amount—leads to a comparable "self-censorship." * * *

The constitutional guarantees require, we think, a federal rule that prohibits a public official from recovering damages for a defamatory falsehood relating to his official conduct unless he proves that the statement was made with "actual malice"—that is, with knowledge that it was false or with reckless disregard of whether it was false or not. An oft-cited statement of a like rule, which has been adopted by a number of state courts, is found in the Kansas case of Coleman v. MacLennan, 78 Kan. 711, 98 P. 281 (1908). The State Attorney General, a candidate for re-election and a member of the commission charged with the management and control of the state school fund sued a newspaper publisher for alleged libel in an article purporting to state facts relating to his official conduct in connection with a school-fund transaction. * * * In answer to a special question, the jury found that the plaintiff had not proved actual malice, and a general verdict was returned for the defendant. On appeal the Supreme Court of Kansas, in an opinion by Justice Burch, reasoned as follows:

"[I]t is of the utmost consequence that the people should discuss the character and qualifications of candidates for their suffrage. The importance to the state and to society of such discussions is so vast, and the advantages derived are so great that they more than counterbalance the inconvenience of private persons whose conduct may be involved, and occasional injury to the reputations of individuals must yield to the public welfare, although at times such injury may be great. The public benefit from publicity is so great and the chance of injury to private character so small that such discussion must be privileged." The court thus sustained the trial court's instruction as a correct statement of the law, saying:

"In such a case the occasion gives rise to a privilege qualified to this extent. Any one claiming to be defamed by the communication must show actual malice, or go remediless. This privilege extends to a great variety of subjects and includes matters of public concern, public men, and candidates for office." [C]

We hold today that the Constitution delimits a State's power to award damages for libel in actions brought by public officials against critics of their official conduct. Since this is such an action, the rule requiring proof of actual malice is applicable. * * *

[W]e consider that the proof presented to show actual malice lacks the convincing clarity which the constitutional standard demands, and hence that it would not constitutionally sustain the judgment for respondent under the proper rule of law. The case of the individual petitioners requires little discussion. Even assuming that they could constitutionally be found to have authorized the use of their names on the advertisement, there was no evidence whatever that they were aware of any erroneous statements or were in any way reckless in that regard. The judgment against them is thus without constitutional support.

As to the Times, we similarly conclude that the facts do not support a finding of actual malice. The statement by the Times' Secretary that, apart from the padlocking allegation, he thought the advertisement was "substantially correct," affords no constitutional warrant for the Alabama Supreme Court's conclusion that it was a "cavalier ignoring of the falsity of the advertisement, [from which] the jury could not have but been impressed with the bad faith of The Times, and its maliciousness inferable therefrom." The statement does not indicate malice at the time of the publication; even if the advertisement was not "substantially correct"—although respondent's own proofs tend to show that it was—that opinion was at least a reasonable one, and there was no evidence to impeach the witness' good faith in holding it. The Times' failure to retract upon respondent's demand, although it later retracted upon the demand of Governor Patterson, is likewise not adequate evidence of malice for constitutional purposes. Whether or not a failure to retract may ever constitute such evidence, there are two reasons why it does not here. *First,* the letter written by the Times reflected a reasonable doubt on its part as to whether the advertisement could reasonably be taken to refer to respondent at all. *Second,* it was not a final refusal, since it asked for an explanation on this point— a request that respondent chose to ignore. Nor does the retraction upon the demand of the Governor supply the necessary proof. It may be doubted that a failure to retract which is not itself evidence of malice can retroactively become such by virtue of a retraction subsequently made to another party. But in any event that did not happen here, since the explanation given by the Times' Secretary for the distinction drawn between respondent and the Governor was a reasonable one, the good faith of which was not impeached.

Finally, there is evidence that the Times published the advertisement without checking its accuracy against the news stories in the Times' own files. . . . We think the evidence against the Times supports at most a finding of negligence in failing to discover the misstatements, and is constitutionally insufficient to show the recklessness that is required for a finding of actual malice. * * *

We also think the evidence was constitutionally defective in another respect: it was incapable of supporting the jury's finding that the allegedly libelous statements were made "of and concerning" respondent.

There was no reference to respondent in the advertisement, either by name or official position. A number of the allegedly libelous statements * * * did not even concern the police. * * *

Although the statements may be taken as referring to the police, they do not on their face make even an oblique reference to respondent as an individual. * * *

This * * * has disquieting implications for criticism of governmental conduct. For good reason, "no court of last resort in this country has ever held, or even suggested, that prosecutions for libel on government have any place in the American system of jurisprudence." City of Chicago v. Tribune Co. (1923) 307 Ill. 595, 601, 139 N.E. 86, 88.

The present proposition would sidestep this obstacle by transmuting criticism of government, however impersonal it may seem on its face, into personal criticism, and hence potential libel of the officials of whom the government is composed. * * * We hold that such a proposition may not constitutionally be utilized to establish that an otherwise impersonal attack on governmental operations was a libel of an official responsible for those operations. * * *

The judgment of the Supreme Court of Alabama is reversed, and the case is remanded to that court for further proceedings not inconsistent with this opinion.

[The concurring opinions of JUSTICES BLACK and GOLDBERG are omitted. Both would categorically deny any action of defamation by a public official insofar as his public conduct is concerned. This was variously characterized as "an absolute, unconditional constitutional right to * * * say what one pleases about public affairs," "an absolute immunity for criticism of the way public officials do their public duty," and "an absolute privilege for criticism of official conduct." JUSTICE DOUGLAS joined in both opinions.]

---

1. For fuller accounts of this case and its background, see Pierce, The Anatomy of an Historic Decision: New York Times Co. v. Sullivan, 43 N.C.L. Rev. 315 (1964); Kalven, The New York Times Case: A Note on the Central Meaning of the First Amendment, 1964 S.C.Rev. 191; Lewis, New York Times v. Sullivan Reconsidered: A Return to "The Central Meaning of the First Amendment," 83 Colum.L.Rev. 603 (1983). See also Pedrick, Freedom of the Press and the Law of Libel, 49 Corn.L.Q. 581 (1964); Berney, Libel and the First Amendment—A New Constitutional Privilege, 51 Va.L.Rev. 1 (1965); Epstein, Was New York Times v. Sullivan Wrong?, 53 U.Chi.L.Rev. 783 (1986).

2. *Fair Comment.* For many years before the principal case, the courts had developed, at common law and virtually without reference to the Constitution, a privilege of criticism of public officers and their official conduct. It usually was called the privilege of "fair comment."

The existence of this qualified privilege was not disputed. There was, however, a sharp division of authority on whether it was limited to "comment" or criticism, that is, the expression of opinion, or whether it extended to false statements of fact. About three-quarters of the courts that had considered the question held that the privilege was limited to the expression of opinion, and did not include misstatements of fact. This was the position taken by the Supreme Court of Alabama in the principal case. 273 Ala. 656, 144 So.2d 25 (1962).

The leading case to this effect was Post Pub. Co. v. Hallam, 59 Fed. 530, (6th Cir.1893), an opinion of Judge (later President and Chief Justice) Taft. The reason he advanced was that if public men were to be subjected to false statements of fact, good men could not be found to take the positions. A vigorous minority, headed by Coleman v. MacLennan, 78 Kan. 711, 98 P. 281 (1908), and supported by most of the commentators, contended that the privilege extended to false statements of fact, so long as they were made in good faith. A good treatment of this is Noel, Defamation of Public Officers and Candidates, 49 Colum.L.Rev. 875 (1949). What did the principal case do to all this?

3. *Public Officials.* Rosenblatt v. Baer, 383 U.S. 75 (1966), involved comments about the supervisor of a county recreation area. The Court held that whether he was a public official was a question of federal law, not state law. The test was held to be whether "the position in government has such apparent importance that the public has an independent interest in the qualifications and performance of the person who holds it, beyond the general public interest in the qualifications and performance of all governmental employees." Cf. Tucker v. Kilgore, 388 S.W.2d 112 (Ky.1965) (patrolman); Krutech v. Schimmel, 50 Misc.2d 1052, 272 N.Y.S.2d 261 (1966) (part time accountant for public waterworks).

The *New York Times* rule is held to apply to candidates for public office. Monitor Patriot Co. v. Roy, 401 U.S. 265 (1971); Ocala Star–Banner Co. v. Damron, 401 U.S. 295 (1971).

4. *Public Figures.* The *New York Times* rule was extended to apply to "public figures" in Curtis Pub. Co. v. Butts, and Associated Press v. Walker, 388 U.S. 130 (1967). Two cases were involved: (1) suit by Coach Wally Butts of the University of Georgia (employed by a private corporation rather than the state) for a story in the Saturday Evening Post charging him with conspiring with Coach Bear Bryant to "fix" a football game, and (2) suit by Edwin A. Walker, a well-known retired army general, against the Associated Press for a story regarding his alleged part in a student disturbance at the University of Mississippi involving enrollment of its first black student. Both were held to be public figures. Recovery below was reversed in *Walker,* but affirmed in *Butts.* For an interesting book on the fact background of the *Butts* case, see J. Kirby, Fumble (1986).

The line-up of the several justices was very confusing. Justice Harlan delivered what purported to be the opinion of the Court, concurred in by Clark, Fortas and Stewart, JJ. This opinion laid down a different standard from that in *New York Times,* which would impose liability for public figures "on a showing of highly unreasonable conduct constituting an extreme departure from the standards of investigation and reporting ordinarily adhered to by responsible publishers." Applying this standard, he and the three justices concurring would reverse *Walker* and affirm *Butts.* In a separate opinion, Chief Justice Warren held that the *Times* standard of knowledge or reckless disregard should apply to public figures as well as public officials, but he concluded that applying this standard also would reverse *Walker* and affirm *Butts.* This made five justices agreeing on the affirmance-or-reversal issue. Justice Brennan, joined by Justice White, agreed with Chief Justice Warren that the *Times* standard should apply and that *Walker* should be reversed, but concluded that *Butts* should also be reversed for a new trial with more appropriate instructions. Justice Black, joined by Justice Douglas, continued to espouse the "absolute privilege" theory set forth in his separate opinion in *New York Times.* In order, however, for the Court to reach a decision, without receding from his views, he voted for the *Times* standard as set out in the Warren opinion as being nearer to his view than the Harlan opinion; he would have reversed both *Butts* and *Walker.*

The end result was that *Butts* was affirmed; and that *Walker* was reversed and remanded to the Texas court "for further proceedings not inconsistent with the opinions that have been filed herein by The Chief Justice, Mr. Justice Black and Mr. Justice Brennan." Only one of the four opinions took the position on each of the three issues that was finally adopted by a majority vote of the Court. This was the opinion of the Chief Justice, which did not have the full concurrence of any other member of the Court.

5. *Matter of Public or General Interest.* Rosenbloom v. Metromedia, Inc., 403 U.S. 29 (1971), expanded the *Times* knowing-or-reckless-disregard standard beyond public officials and public figures to apply to any matter of public or general interest. Rosenbloom had been arrested in a police drive against obscene books. Defendant, operating a radio news station, reported the arrest and used the terms "smut literature racket" and "girlie-book peddlers." Following acquittal of the criminal charges, plaintiff sued for libel. He recovered $25,000 in general damages and $725,000 in punitive damages, reduced by remittitur to $250,000. The Court of Appeals reversed, holding the *Times* standard applied, though the plaintiff was not a public figure. The Supreme Court agreed.

Once again the justices divided sharply. The plurality opinion was written by Justice Brennan, joined by Burger, C.J., and Blackmun, J. Black, J., concurred in the result but adhered to his absolute-privilege view; Douglas, J., did not participate in the case. White, J., concurred in the result on the ground that the report covered the official action of public officials. Harlan and Marshall, JJ. (joined by Stewart, J.), dissented in separate opinions deprecating the ad-hoc nature of a test depending upon whether an event was a matter of public or general interest and urged that the way for the Court to take care of the recurring cases was to limit the measure of recovery to "proven, actual damages" and to eliminate strict liability.

The plurality opinion of Justice Brennan remained the binding rule of constitutional law until it was repudiated in 1974 by Gertz v. Robert Welch, Inc., infra page 906. Does its spirit still live in Dun & Bradstreet, Inc. v. Greenmoss Builders, Inc., infra page 917?

ST. AMANT v. THOMPSON
Supreme Court of the United States, 1968.
390 U.S. 727, 88 S.Ct. 1323, 20 L.Ed.2d 262 (1968).

[Defendant St. Amant made a televised political speech, in the course of which he read questions that he had put to a union member, Albin, and Albin's answers. The answers falsely charged the plaintiff, a deputy sheriff, with criminal conduct. Plaintiff sued defendant for defamation, and was awarded damages by the trial judge. The judge then considered New York Times Co. v. Sullivan, supra page 895, decided after the trial, and denied a motion for a new trial. An intermediate appellate court reversed the judgment, finding that defendant had not acted with "actual malice" within the meaning of the New York Times rule. The Louisiana Supreme Court reversed, finding that there had been sufficient evidence that defendant had acted in "reckless disregard" of the truth. The Supreme Court granted certiorari.]

MR. JUSTICE WHITE delivered the opinion of the Court. * * *

For purposes of this case we accept the determinations of the Louisiana courts that the material published by St. Amant charged Thompson with criminal conduct, that the charge was false, and that Thompson was a public official, and so had the burden of proving that the false statements about Thompson were made with actual malice as defined in New York Times Co. v. Sullivan and later cases. We cannot, however, agree with either the Supreme Court of Louisiana or the trial court that Thompson sustained this burden.

Purporting to apply the *New York Times* malice standard, the Louisiana Supreme Court ruled that St. Amant had broadcast false information about Thompson recklessly though not knowingly. Several reasons were given for this conclusion. St. Amant had no personal knowledge of Thompson's activities; he relied solely on Albin's affidavit although the record was silent as to Albin's reputation for veracity; he failed to verify the information with those in the union office who might have known the facts; he gave no consideration as to whether or not the statements defamed Thompson and went ahead heedless of the consequences; and he mistakenly believed he had no responsibility for the broadcast because he was merely quoting Albin's words.

These considerations fall short of proving St. Amant's reckless disregard for the accuracy of his statements about Thompson. "Reckless disregard," it is true, cannot be fully encompassed in one infallible definition. Inevitably its outer limits will be marked out through case-by-case adjudication, as is true with so many legal standards for judging concrete cases, whether the standard is provided by the Constitution, statutes, or case law. Our cases, however, have furnished meaningful guidance for the further definition of a reckless publication.

In *New York Times*, the plaintiff did not satisfy his burden because the record failed to show that the publisher was aware of the likelihood that he was circulating false information. In Garrison v. State of Louisiana, 379 U.S. 64 (1964), also decided before the decision of the Louisiana Supreme Court in this case, the opinion emphasized the necessity for showing that a false publication was made with a "high degree of awareness of * * * probable falsity." Mr. Justice Harlan's opinion in Curtis Publishing Co. v. Butts, 388 U.S. 130, 153 (1967), stated that evidence of either deliberate falsification or reckless publication "despite the publisher's awareness of probable falsity" was essential to recovery by public officials in defamation actions. These cases are clear that reckless conduct is not measured by whether a reasonably prudent man would have published, or would have investigated before publishing. There must be sufficient evidence to permit the conclusion that the defendant in fact entertained serious doubts as to the truth of his publication. Publishing with such doubts shows reckless disregard for truth or falsity and demonstrates actual malice.

It may be said that such a test puts a premium on ignorance, encourages the irresponsible publisher not to inquire, and permits the issue to be determined by the defendant's testimony that he published the statement in good faith and unaware of its probable falsity. Concededly the reckless disregard standard may permit recovery in fewer situations than would a rule that publishers must satisfy the standard of the reasonable man or the prudent publisher. But *New York Times* and succeeding cases have emphasized that the stake of the people in public business and the conduct of public officials is so great that neither the defense of truth nor the standard of ordinary care would protect against self-censorship and thus adequately implement First Amendment policies. Neither lies nor false communications serve the ends of the First Amendment, and no one suggests their desirability or further proliferation. But to insure the ascertainment and publication of the truth about public affairs, it is essential that the First Amendment protect some erroneous publications as well as true ones. We adhere to this view and to the line which our cases have drawn between false communications which are protected and those which are not.

The defendant in a defamation action brought by a public official cannot, however, automatically insure a favorable verdict by testifying that he published with a belief that the statements were true. The finder of fact must determine whether the publication was indeed made in good faith. Professions of good faith will be unlikely to prove persuasive, for example, where a story is fabricated by the defendant, is the product of his imagination, or is based wholly on an unverified anonymous telephone call. Nor will they be likely to prevail when the publisher's allegations are so inherently improbable that only a reckless man would have put them in circulation. Likewise, recklessness may be found where there are obvious reasons to doubt the veracity of the informant or the accuracy of his reports. * * *

Because the state court misunderstood and misapplied the actual malice standard which must be observed in a public official's defamation action, the judgment is reversed and the case remanded for further proceedings not inconsistent with this opinion.

[JUSTICES BLACK and DOUGLAS concurred in the judgment, on the ground that there should be an absolute privilege. JUSTICE FORTAS dissented, on the ground that the defendant had a duty to check the reliability of the statement, and hence that he published it in reckless disregard of the truth.]

----

1. Almost immediately after the *New York Times* decision, the Court discarded completely the old-fashioned meaning of "malice," so far as the constitutional restriction on defamation is concerned: "The jury might well have understood these instructions to allow recovery on a showing of intent to inflict harm, rather than intent to inflict harm through falsehood. See Garrison v. Louisiana, 379 U.S. 64, 73. 'The constitutional guarantees * * * [prohibit] a public official from recovering damages for a defamatory falsehood relating to his official conduct unless he proved that the statement was made * * * with knowledge that it was false or with reckless disregard of whether it was false or not.' New York Times Co. v. Sullivan, 376 U.S. 254, 279–280 (1964)." Henry v. Collins, 380 U.S. 356, 357 (1965).

2. The test of serious doubt in *St. Amant* is admittedly subjective in nature. In Herbert v. Lando, 441 U.S. 153 (1979), a public officer, who was under the obligation of proving knowledge or reckless disregard as to falsity in his libel action based on a program of "60 Minutes," sought to depose the defendant at length with inquiries as to his state of mind and communications with other participants in the editorial process. The defendant resisted on First Amendment grounds and the Second Circuit held for him (568 F.2d 974 (2d Cir.1977)), declaring that the First Amendment grants him an absolute privilege regarding "his thoughts, opinions and conclusions with respect to the material gathered by him and about his conversations with his editorial colleagues." The Supreme Court reversed, holding that previous decisions did not authorize or presage an editorial privilege of this nature and that it did not construe the First Amendment to authorize it as a matter of constitutional law. The holding was unanimous regarding questions on state of mind, but three justices had somewhat varying views regarding forced disclosure of communications between participants in the editorial process. On remand, the Court of Appeals held, on the basis of evidence in the new trial, that summary judgment

should be granted to the defendant Herbert v. Lando, 781 F.2d 298 (2d Cir. 1986).

On state of mind, would it be better to substitute an objective test for the subjective one? This does not require a negligence test, but could be based on the language of Justice White in *St. Amant:* "publisher's allegations * * * so inherently improbable that only a reckless man would have put them in circulation."

3. A newspaper, opposing a candidate for office, carries accurate stories about his business transactions affecting the government, but deliberately prepares slanted headlines, intended to give a misleading impression to a person who did not carefully read through the story as to the candidate's ethics. Can this be found to constitute reckless disregard as to falsity? Cf. McNair v. Hearst Corp., 494 F.2d 1309 (9th Cir.1974); Sprouse v. Clay Communication, Inc., 158 W.Va. 427, 211 S.E.2d 674 (1975).

4. What is the origin of the requirement of "knowledge of falsity or reckless disregard whether it was false or not"? See Derry v. Peek, and Sovereign Pocohontas Co. v. Bond, infra, pages 1035 and 1039.

5. If "malice" is not to mean ill will, spite or a desire to do harm for its own sake, would it not be preferable to avoid using the word at all? Would "scienter" be any better?

The Court indicates that the plaintiff, if he is a public official or public figure, has the burden of proving knowledge or reckless disregard. And yet it is common to speak of a "constitutional privilege" in this regard. Is this accurate terminology, or is it more accurate to speak of a constitutional restriction on the cause of action? See Restatement (Second) of Torts § 580A, Comment e.

6. In Zerangue v. TSP Newspapers, Inc., 814 F.2d 1066 (5th Cir.1987), defendant newspaper published an inaccurate story about plaintiff officials, retracted it when the error was pointed out, then published it again some months later. It was held to be a question of fact whether the requisite malice was shown.

GERTZ v. ROBERT WELCH, INC.
Supreme Court of the United States, 1974.
418 U.S. 323, 94 S.Ct. 2997, 41 L.Ed.2d 789.

MR. JUSTICE POWELL delivered the opinion of the Court. * * *

I. In 1968 a Chicago policeman named Nuccio shot and killed a youth named Nelson. The state authorities prosecuted Nuccio for the homicide and ultimately obtained a conviction for murder in the second degree. The Nelson family retained petitioner Elmer Gertz, a reputable attorney, to represent them in civil litigation against Nuccio.

Respondent publishes American Opinion, a monthly outlet for the views of the John Birch Society. Early in the 1960's the magazine began to warn of a nationwide conspiracy to discredit local law enforcement agencies and create in their stead a national police force capable of supporting a Communist dictatorship. As part of the continuing effort to alert the public to this assumed danger, the managing editor of American Opinion commissioned an article on the murder trial of

Front row: Stewart, Douglas, Burger, C.J., Brennan, White
Back row: Powell, Marshall, Blackmun, Rehnquist

Officer Nuccio. For this purpose he engaged a regular contributor to the magazine. In March 1969 respondent published the resulting article under the title "FRAME–UP: Richard Nuccio And The War On Police." The article purports to demonstrate that the testimony against Nuccio at his criminal trial was false and that his prosecution was part of the Communist campaign against the police.

In his capacity as counsel for the Nelson family in the civil litigation, petitioner attended the coroner's inquest into the boy's death and initiated actions for damages, but he neither discussed Officer Nuccio with the press nor played any part in the criminal proceeding. Notwithstanding petitioner's remote connection with the prosecution of Nuccio, respondent's magazine portrayed him as an architect of the "frame-up." According to the article, the police file on petitioner took "a big, Irish cop to lift." The article stated that petitioner had been an official of the "Marxist League for Industrial Democracy, originally known as the Intercollegiate Socialist Society, which has advocated the violent seizure of our government." It labeled Gertz a "Leninist" and a "Communist-fronter." It also stated that Gertz had been an officer of the National Lawyers Guild, described as a Communist organization that "probably did more than any other outfit to plan the Communist attack on the Chicago police during the 1968 Democratic Convention."

These statements contained serious inaccuracies. The implication that petitioner had a criminal record was false. Petitioner had been a member and officer of the National Lawyers Guild some 15 years earlier, but there was no evidence that he or that organization had taken any part in planning the 1968 demonstrations in Chicago. There was also no basis for the charge that petitioner was a "Leninist" or a "Communist-fronter." And he had never been a member of the "Marxist League for Industrial Democracy" or the "Intercollegiate Socialist Society."

The managing editor of American Opinion made no effort to verify or substantiate the charges against petitioner. Instead, he appended an editorial introduction stating that the author had "conducted extensive research into the Richard Nuccio Case." And he included in the article a photograph of petitioner and wrote the caption that appeared under it: "Elmer Gertz of Red Guild harasses Nuccio." Respondent placed the issue of American Opinion containing the article on sale at newsstands throughout the country and distributed reprints of the article on the streets of Chicago.

Petitioner filed a diversity action for libel in the United States District Court for the Northern District of Illinois.

[The District Court denied defendant's motion to dismiss. After the evidence was in, it "ruled in effect that petitioner was neither a public official nor a public figure," and it submitted the issue of damages to the jury, which awarded $50,000. On further reflection the District Court concluded that the *New York Times* standard applied and entered judgment for defendant notwithstanding the jury verdict. This action was affirmed by the Court of Appeals for the Seventh Circuit, on the basis of Rosenbloom v. Metromedia, Inc., 403 U.S. 29 (1971), supra page 902, which had been decided in the meantime.]

II. The principal issue in this case is whether a newspaper or broadcaster that publishes defamatory falsehoods about an individual who is neither a public official nor a public figure may claim a constitutional privilege against liability for the injury inflicted by those statements. The Court considered this question on the rather different set of facts presented in Rosenbloom v. Metromedia, Inc. [c]. [The opinion describes in detail the facts and opinions in *Rosenbloom*.]

III. We begin with the common ground. Under the First Amendment there is no such thing as a false idea. However pernicious an opinion may seem, we depend for its correction not on the conscience of judges and juries but on the competition of other ideas. But there is no constitutional value in false statements of fact. Neither the intentional lie nor the careless error materially advances society's interest in "uninhibited, robust, and wide-open" debate on public issues. [C] They belong to that category of utterances which "are no essential part of any exposition of ideas, and are of such slight social value as a step to truth that any benefit that may be derived from them is clearly outweighed by the social interest in order and morality." Chaplinsky v. New Hampshire, 315 U.S. 568, 572 (1942).

Although the erroneous statement of fact is not worthy of constitutional protection, it is nevertheless inevitable in free debate. As James Madison pointed out in the Report on the Virginia Resolutions of 1798, "Some degree of abuse is inseparable from the proper use of every thing; and in no instance is this more true than in that of the press." 4 J. Elliot, Debates on the Federal Constitution of 1787, p. 571 (1876). And punishment of error runs the risk of inducing a cautious and restrictive exercise of the constitutionally guaranteed freedoms of speech and press. Our decisions recognize that a rule of strict liability that compels a publisher or broadcaster to guarantee the accuracy of his factual assertions may lead to intolerable self-censorship. Allowing the media to avoid liability only by proving the truth of all injurious statements does not accord adequate protection to First Amendment liberties. As the Court stated in New York Times Co. v. Sullivan, supra, at 279, "Allowance of the defense of truth, with the burden of proving it on the defendant, does not mean that only false speech will be deterred." The First Amendment requires that we protect some falsehood in order to protect speech that matters.

The need to avoid self-censorship by the news media is, however, not the only societal value at issue. If it were, this Court would have embraced long ago the view that publishers and broadcasters enjoy an unconditional and indefeasible immunity from liability for defamation. [Cc] Such a rule would, indeed, obviate the fear that the prospect of civil liability for injurious falsehood might dissuade a timorous press from the effective exercise of First Amendment freedoms. Yet absolute protection for the communications media requires a total sacrifice of the competing value served by the law of defamation.

The legitimate state interest underlying the law of libel is the compensation of individuals for the harm inflicted on them by defamatory falsehood. * * * The protection of private personality, like the protection of life itself, is left primarily to the individual States under the Ninth and Tenth Amendments. But this does not mean that the right is entitled to any less recognition by this Court as a basic of our constitutional system." [C]

Some tension necessarily exists between the need for a vigorous and uninhibited press and the legitimate interest in redressing wrongful injury. * * * In our continuing effort to define the proper accommodation between these competing concerns, we have been especially anxious to assure to the freedoms of speech and press that "breathing space" essential to their fruitful exercise. [C] To that end this Court has extended a measure of strategic protection to defamatory falsehood.

The New York Times standard defines the level of constitutional protection appropriate to the context of defamation of a public person. Those who, by reason of the notoriety of their achievements or the vigor and success with which they seek the public's attention, are properly classed as public figures and those who hold governmental office may recover for injury to reputation only on clear and convincing proof that the defamatory falsehood was made with knowledge of its falsity or with reckless disregard for the truth. This standard administers an extremely powerful antidote to the inducement to media self-censorship of the common-law rule of strict liability for libel and slander. And it exacts a correspondingly high price from the victims of defamatory falsehood. Plainly many deserving plaintiffs, including some intentionally subjected to injury, will be unable to surmount the barrier of the New York Times test. Despite this substantial abridgment of the state law right to compensation for wrongful hurt to one's reputation, the Court has concluded that the protection of the New York Times privilege should be available to publishers and broadcasters of defamatory falsehood concerning public officials and public figures. [C] We think that these decisions are correct, but we do not find their holdings justified solely by reference to the interest of the press and broadcast media in immunity from liability. Rather, we believe that the New York Times rule states an accommodation between this concern and the limited state interest present in the context of libel actions brought by public persons. For the reasons stated below, we conclude that the state interest in compensating injury to the reputation of private individuals requires that a different rule should obtain with respect to them.

Theoretically, of course, the balance between the needs of the press and the individual's claim to compensation for wrongful injury might be struck on a case-by-case basis. * * * But this approach would lead to unpredictable results and uncertain expectations, and it could render our duty to supervise the lower courts unmanageable. Because an ad hoc resolution of the competing interests at stake in each particular case is not feasible, we must lay down broad rules of general application. * * *

The first remedy of any victim of defamation is self-help—using available opportunities to contradict the lie or correct the error and thereby to minimize its adverse impact on reputation. Public officials and public figures usually enjoy significantly greater access to the channels of effective communication and hence have a more realistic opportunity to counteract false statements than private individuals normally enjoy. Private individuals are therefore more vulnerable to injury, and the state interest in protecting them is correspondingly greater.

More important than the likelihood that private individuals will lack effective opportunities for rebuttal, there is a compelling normative consideration underlying the distinction between public and private defamation plaintiffs. An individual who decides to seek governmental office must accept certain necessary consequences of that involvement in public affairs. He runs the risk of closer public scrutiny than might otherwise be the case. * * *

Those classed as public figures stand in a similar position. Hypothetically, it may be possible for someone to become a public figure through no purposeful action of his own, but the instances of truly involuntary public figures must be exceedingly rare. * * * Commonly, those classed as public figures have thrust themselves to the forefront of particular public controversies in order to influence the resolution of the issues involved. * * *

The communications media are entitled to act on the assumption that public officials and public figures have voluntarily exposed themselves to increased risk of injury from defamatory falsehood concerning them. No such assumption is justified with respect to a private individual. * * * He has relinquished no part of his interest in the protection of his own good name, and consequently he has a more compelling call on the courts for redress of injury inflicted by defamatory falsehood. Thus, private individuals are not only more vulnerable to injury than public officials and public figures; they are also more deserving of recovery.

For these reasons we conclude that the States should retain substantial latitude in their efforts to enforce a legal remedy for defamatory falsehood injurious to the reputation of a private individual. The extension of the New York Times test proposed by the Rosenbloom plurality would abridge this legitimate state interest to a degree that we find unacceptable. And it would occasion the additional difficulty of forcing state and federal judges to decide on an ad hoc basis which publications address issues of "general or public interest" and which do not—to determine, in the words of Mr. Justice Marshall, "what information is relevant to self-government." Rosenbloom v. Metromedia, Inc., 403 U.S., at 79. We doubt the wisdom of committing this task to the conscience of judges. Nor does the Constitution require us to draw so thin a line between the drastic alternatives of the New York Times privilege and the common law of strict liability for defamatory error. * * *

We hold that, so long as they do not impose liability without fault, the States may define for themselves the appropriate standard of liability for a publisher or broadcaster of defamatory falsehood injurious to a private individual. This approach provides a more equitable boundary between the competing concerns involved here. It recognizes the strength of the legitimate state interest in compensating private individuals for wrongful injury to reputation, yet shields the press and broadcast media from the rigors of strict liability for defamation. At least this conclusion obtains where, as here, the substance of the defamatory statement "makes substantial danger to reputation apparent." * * *

IV. Our accommodation of the competing values at stake in defamation suits by private individuals allows the States to impose liability on the publisher or broadcaster of defamatory falsehood on a less demanding showing than that required by New York Times. This conclusion is not based on a belief that the considerations which prompted the adoption of the New York Times privilege for defamation of public officials and its extension to public figures are wholly inapplicable to the context of private individuals. Rather, we endorse this approach in recognition of the strong and legitimate state interest in compensating private individuals for injury to reputation.

But this countervailing state interest extends no further than compensation for actual injury. For the reasons stated below, we hold that the States may not permit recovery of presumed or punitive damages, at least when liability is not based on a showing of knowledge of falsity or reckless disregard for the truth.

The common law of defamation is an oddity of tort law, for it allows recovery of purportedly compensatory damages without evidence of actual loss. Under the traditional rules pertaining to actions for libel, the existence of injury is presumed from the fact of publication. Juries may award substantial sums as compensation for supposed damage to reputation without any proof that such harm actually occurred. The largely uncontrolled discretion of juries to award damages where there is no loss unnecessarily compounds the potential of any system of liability for defamatory falsehood to inhibit the vigorous exercise of First Amendment freedoms. Additionally, the doctrine of presumed damages invites juries to punish unpopular opinion rather than to compensate individuals for injury sustained by the publication of a false fact. More to the point, the States have no substantial interest in securing for plaintiffs such as this petitioner gratuitous awards of money damages far in excess of any actual injury.

We would not, of course, invalidate state law simply because we doubt its wisdom, but here we are attempting to reconcile state law with a competing interest grounded in the constitutional command of the First Amendment. It is therefore appropriate to require that state remedies for defamatory falsehood reach no farther than is necessary to protect the legitimate interest involved. It is necessary to restrict defamation plaintiffs who do not prove knowledge of falsity or reckless disregard for the truth to compensation for actual injury. We need not define "actual injury," as trial courts have wide experience in framing appropriate jury instructions in tort actions. Suffice it to say that actual injury is not limited to out-of-pocket loss. Indeed, the more customary types of actual harm inflicted by defamatory falsehood include impairment of reputation and standing in the community, personal humiliation, and mental anguish and suffering. Of course, juries must be limited by appropriate instructions, and all awards must be supported by competent evidence concerning the injury, although there need be no evidence which assigns an actual dollar value to the injury.

We also find no justification for allowing awards of punitive damages against publishers and broadcasters held liable under state-defined standards of liability for defamation. In most jurisdictions jury discretion over the amounts awarded is limited only by the gentle rule that they not be excessive. Consequently, juries assess punitive damages in wholly unpredictable amounts bearing no necessary relation to the actual harm caused. And they remain free to use their discretion selectively to punish expressions of unpopular views. Like the doctrine of presumed damages, jury discretion to award punitive damages unnecessarily exacerbates the danger of media self-censorship, but, unlike the former rule, punitive damages are wholly irrelevant to the state interest that justifies a negligence standard for private defamation actions. They are not compensation for injury. Instead, they are private finds levied by civil juries to punish reprehensible conduct and to deter its future occurrence. In short, the private defamation plaintiff who establishes liability under a less demanding standard than that stated by New York Times may recover only such damages as are sufficient to compensate him for actual injury.

V. Notwithstanding our refusal to extend the New York Times privilege to defamation of private individuals, respondent contends that we should affirm the judgment below on the ground that petitioner is either a public official or a public figure. ＊ ＊ ＊

Respondent admits this but argues that petitioner's appearance at the coroner's inquest rendered him a "de facto public official." Our cases recognize no such concept. Respondent's suggestion would sweep all lawyers under the New York Times rule as officers of the court and distort the plain meaning of the "public official" category beyond all recognition. We decline to follow it.

Respondent's characterization of petitioner as a public figure raises a different question. That designation may rest on either of two alternative bases. In some instances an individual may achieve such pervasive frame or notoriety that he becomes a public figure for all purposes and in all contexts. More commonly, an individual voluntarily injects himself or is drawn into a particular public controversy and thereby becomes a public figure for a limited range of issues. In either case such persons assume special prominence in the resolution of public questions.

Petitioner has long been active in community and professional affairs. He has served as an officer of local civic groups and of various professional organizations, and he has published several books and articles on legal subjects. Although petitioner was consequently well known in some circles, he had achieved no general fame or notoriety in the community. ＊ ＊ ＊ Absent clear evidence of general fame or notoriety in the community, and pervasive involvement in the affairs of society, an individual should not be deemed a public personality for all aspects of his life. It is preferable to reduce the public-figure question to a more meaningful context by looking to the nature and extent of an individual's participation in the particular controversy giving rise to the defamation.

In this context it is plain that petitioner was not a public figure. He played a minimal role at the coroner's inquest, and his participation related solely to his representation of a private client. He took no part in the criminal prosecution of Officer Nuccio. Moreover, he never discussed either the criminal or civil litigation with the press and was never quoted as having done so. He plainly did not thrust himself into the vortex of this public issue, nor did he engage the public's attention in an attempt to influence its outcome. We are persuaded that the trial court did not err in refusing to characterize petitioner as a public figure for the purpose of this litigation.

We therefore conclude that the New York Times standard is inapplicable to this case and that the trial court erred in entering judgment for respondent. Because the jury was allowed to impose liability without fault and was permitted to presume damages without proof of injury, a new trial is necessary. We reverse and remand for further proceedings in accord with this opinion.

It is so ordered.

[This opinion was joined by STEWART, MARSHALL, BLACKMUN and REHNQUIST, JJ.; BLACKMUN, J., stating in a concurring opinion that he found some difficulties with the majority opinion, but that he joined in it to attain a "definitive ruling."

BURGER, C.J., dissented, disapproving the requirement of negligence for private defamation and urging remand for a reinstatement of the jury verdict below. DOUGLAS, J., dissented on the basis of his absolute-privilege theory and would at least retain the *Rosenbloom* rule. BRENNAN, J., dissented and would retain the *Rosenbloom* rule. WHITE, J., dissented and would retain strict liability for private defamation.]

---

1. Of the new ideas adopted in *Gertz,* the one requiring a finding of fault for private defamation had been urged in the dissenting opinion of Harlan, J., in Time, Inc. v. Hill, 385 U.S. 374 (1967) ("State should be free to hold the press to a duty of making a reasonable investigation of the underlying facts"), and the dissenting opinion of Marshall, J., in Rosenbloom v. Metromedia, Inc., 403 U.S. 29 (1971) ("only constitutional caveat should be that absolute or strict liability * * * cannot be used"). Eliminating presumed and punitive damages had been urged in *Rosenbloom* in the dissenting opinion of Marshall, J. (restrict "the award of damages to proven, actual injuries" and cut down on the "jury's wide ranging discretion * * * since the award will be based on essentially objective discernable factors"), and, to a large extent, in the dissenting opinion of Harlan, J. ("legitimate function of libel law must be understood as that of compensating individuals for actual, measurable harm caused by the conduct of others").

2. *Contracting the Coverage of the New York Times Standard.* In receding from the position taken in Rosenbloom v. Metromedia, Inc., 403 U.S. 29 (1970), that the *New York Times* standard of knowledge or reckless disregard applied to any matter of public or general interest and holding that the standard applies only to public officials and public figures, the Court was speaking only of what the Constitution requires the states to do. A state must apply the

Times standard in a suit by a public person; it is not required to do this in a suit by a private person but is entirely free to do so if it wishes. Some courts have indicated that they will continue to require knowledge or reckless disregard in all matters of public or general interest. See, e.g., Walker v. Colorado Springs Sun, Inc., 188 Colo. 86, 538 P.2d 450 (1975); AAFCO Heating & Air Conditioning Co. v. Northeast Pub. Inc., 162 Ind.App. 671, 321 N.E.2d 580 (1974); cf. Chapadeau v. Utica Observer–Dispatch Inc., 38 N.Y.2d 196, 341 N.E.2d 569, 379 N.Y.S.2d 61 (1975) (gross irresponsible manner without due consideration for the standards of information gathering and dissemination ordinarily followed by responsible parties). A majority of the courts disagree and decline to impose a requirement of knowledge or reckless disregard in an action by a private person. E.g., Stone v. Essex County Newspapers, Inc., 367 Mass. 849, 330 N.E.2d 161 (1975); Jacron Sales Co., Inc. v. Sindorf, 276 Md. 580, 350 A.2d 688 (1976); Troman v. Wood, 62 Ill.2d 292, 340 N.E.2d 292 (1975); Memphis Pub. Co. v. Nichols, 569 S.W.2d 412 (Tenn.1978); Taskett v. King Broadcasting Co., 86 Wash.2d 439, 546 P.2d 81 (1976).

3. *Scope of Fault Requirement in Action by Private Person.* *Gertz* seemed to indicate that strict liability for defamation is unconstitutional. This would require fault in regard, at least, to the falsity of the statement. There still remain some unanswered questions on the scope of the requirement, however. See, in general, Restatement (Second) of Torts § 580B, Comments d to f. And on the nature of the negligence standard, see id., Comments g and h. On the effect of the fault requirement on the whole system of conditional privileges, see id., Comment l, and the Special Note preceding § 593. And see the discussion in Jacron Sales Co. v. Sindorf, 276 Md. 580, 350 A.2d 688 (1976), infra, page 940. See Franklin & Bissel, The Plaintiff's Burden in Defamation: Awareness and Falsity, 25 Wm. & Mary L.Rev. 825 (1984).

On the standard of care, see Bloom, Proof of Fault in Media Defamation Litigation, 38 Vand.L.Rev. 247 (1985); Simon, Libel as Malpractice: News Media Ethics and the Standard of Care, 53 Ford.L.Rev. 449 (1984); Franklin, What Does Negligence Mean in Defamation Cases?, 6 Com/Ent L.J. 259 (1984); Wade, The Tort Liability of Investigative Reporters, 37 Vand.L.Rev. 301 (1984).

4. *Nonmedia Defendants.* *New York Times* and *Gertz* both involved suits against members of the news media. Were their constitutional requirements confined to suits against media defendants? Although the Supreme Court has never expressly said so, the answer for the *Times* standard seems to be clearly, "no." In *Times* itself, the suit was also against private individuals who signed the political advertisement. See also Garrison v. Louisiana, 379 U.S. 64 (1964) (press conference); Henry v. Collins, 380 U.S. 356 (1965) (letter and telephone conversation); St. Amant v. Thompson, 390 U.S. 727 (1968), supra page 903, Old Dominion Branch No. 496, Nat'l Ass'n of Letter Carriers v. Austin, 418 U.S. 264, 285 (1973) (newsletter). But cf. Hutchinson v. Proxmire, 443 U.S. 111, 133, n. 16 (1979) (Supreme Court "has never decided * * * whether the *New York Times* standard can apply to an individual defendant rather than a media defendant"). Among other courts holding that the standard applies, see Davis v. Schuchat, 510 F.2d 731 (D.C.Cir.1975); Michaud v. Livermore Falls, 381 A.2d 1110 (Me.1978).

There has been less agreement about the *Gertz* standards, the cases dividing almost evenly. But the opinions in *Greenmoss,* the next principal case, indicate that a majority of the current members of the Court would draw no distinction between media defendants and other defendants.

5. *When Is the Statement Defamatory?* Will the Supreme Court sometime decide that the question of whether a false statement is defamatory is one subject to constitutional restraint? The Supreme Court had the problem before it in 1942, when it granted certiorari on the (2–to–1) holding in Sweeney v. Schenectady Union Pub. Co., 122 F.2d 288 (2d Cir.1941), that Congressman Sweeney had a good complaint in defamation when he sued because of a charge that he had opposed the appointment of an attorney as federal judge solely because he was Jewish. After giving permission to numerous groups to file briefs amici curiae, the Court handed down a per-curiam memorandum, saying simply, "The judgment is affirmed by an equally divided court." The Court has not accepted any other cases raising the question of whether the statement is defamatory. Perhaps it has disquieting memories of its difficulties in setting a constitutional standard on when a publication is obscene.

6. *Damages.* Actual damages, as required by the Constitution under the holding in *Gertz,* are broader in scope than special damages, as required at common law for oral statements that are not slanderous per se. Special damages require pecuniary loss. Actual damages may include injury to reputation or emotional distress, without showing pecuniary loss, but the injury must be proved. It initially appeared that the purpose of this requirement was to give the trial and appellate courts greater control over the amount of damages that the jury can properly award. But the opportunity has not been utilized.

7. For discussions of *Gertz* and its implications, see Anderson, Libel and Press Self–Censorship, 53 Texas L.Rev. 422 (1975); Eaton, The American Law of Defamation Through Gertz v. Robert Welch, Inc. and Beyond: An Analytic Primer, 61 Va.L.Rev. 1349 (1975); Phillips, Defamation, Invasion of Privacy and the Constitutional Standard of Care, 16 Santa Clara L.Rev. 77 (1975); Robertson, Defamation and the First Amendment: In Praise of Gertz v. Robert Welch, Inc., 54 Texas L.Rev. 199 (1976).

Later articles include Hill, Defamation and Privacy under the First Amendment, 76 Colum.L.Rev. 1205 (1976); P. Keeton, Defamation and Freedom of the Press, 54 Texas L.Rev. 1221 (1976); Wade, The Communicative Torts and the First Amendment, 48 Miss.L.J. 671 (1977); Christie, Injury to Reputation and the Constitution: Confusion and Conflicting Approaches, 75 Mich.L.Rev. 43 (1976); Collins and Drushall, The Reaction of the State Courts to Gertz v. Robert Welch, Inc., 28 Case–W.R.L.Rev. 306 (1978); Green, Political Freedom of the Press and the Libel Problem, 56 Texas L.Rev. 391 (1978); Ingber, Defamation: A Conflict Between Reason and Decency, 65 Va.L.Rev. 785 (1979); LaRue, Living with *Gertz* : A Practical Look at Constitutional Libel Standards, 67 Va. L.Rev. 287 (1981).

More recent general treatments of the constitutional law of defamation include two important symposia: Defamation and the First Amendment: New Perspectives, 25 Wm. & Mary L.Rev. 743–968 (1984); and New Perspectives in the Law of Defamation, 74 Calif.L.Rev. 677–925 (1986). And see Smolla, Let the Author Beware: The Rejuvenation of the American Law of Libel, 132 U.Pa. L.Rev. 1 (1983); Franklin, Good Names and Bad Law: A Critique of Libel Law and a Proposal, 18 U.S.F.L.Rev. 1 (1983); McNulty, The *Gertz* Fault Standard and the Common Law of Defamation: An Argument for Predictability of Result and Certainty of Expectation, 35 Drake L.Rev. 5 (1986); Gertz, Gertz on *Gertz* : Reflections on the Landmark Libel Case, 21 Trial 66 (Oct.1985).

DUN & BRADSTREET, INC. v. GREENMOSS
BUILDERS, INC.
Supreme Court of the United States, 1985.
472 U.S. 749, 105 S.Ct. 2939, 86 L.Ed.2d 593.

[Petitioner-defendant Dun & Bradstreet supplied confidential credit rating reports to subscribers. It sent a report to five subscribers, indicating that respondent-plaintiff Greenmoss Builders had filed a voluntary petition for bankruptcy. The report was totally false, the error resulting from petitioner's use of a 17–year–old high school student to review Vermont bankruptcy proceedings. He mistakenly attributed to respondent a bankruptcy petition filed by one of respondent's former employees, and from petitioner's failure to make routine checks of accuracy. Learning of the report, respondent called petitioner's regional office, explained the error and asked for a correction. Petitioner sent out a notice which respondent regarded as inadequate, and refused to disclose the identity of the five subscribers.

Respondent sued for libel and obtained a verdict for $50,000 in compensatory or presumed damages and $300,000 in punitive damages. The trial court granted a motion for a new trial, but respondent appealed to the Vermont Supreme Court, which reversed and reinstated the verdict on the ground that the constitutional requirements of the U.S. Supreme Court did not apply when the suit was against a non-media defendant. 143 Vt. 66, 461 A.2d 414 (1983). This court granted certiorari, and affirmed the holding, "although for reasons different from those relief on by the Vermont Supreme Court."]

JUSTICE POWELL announced the judgment of the Court and delivered an opinion, in which JUSTICE REHNQUIST and JUSTICE O'CONNOR joined.

In Gertz v. Robert Welch, Inc., 418 U.S. 323, we held that the First Amendment restricted the damages that a private individual could obtain from a publisher for a libel that involved a matter of public concern. More specifically, we held that in these circumstances the First Amendment prohibited awards of presumed and punitive damages for false and defamatory statements unless the plaintiff shows "actual malice," that is, knowledge of falsity or reckless disregard for the truth. The question presented in this case is whether this rule of *Gertz* applies when the false and defamatory statements do not involve matters of public concern. * * *

In *Gertz*, we held that the fact that [an] expression concerned a public issue did not by itself entitle the libel defendant to the constitutional protections of *New York Times*. These protections, we found, were not "justified solely by reference to the interest of the press and broadcast media in immunity from liability." [C] Rather, they represented "an accommodation between [First Amendment] concern[s] and the limited state interest present in the context of libel actions brought by public persons." [C] In libel actions brought by private persons we found the competing interests different. Largely because private persons have not voluntarily exposed themselves to increased risk of injury from defamatory statements and because they generally lack effective opportunities for rebutting such statements, [c] we found that the State possessed a "strong and legitimate * * * interest in compensating private individuals for injury to reputation." [C] Balancing this stronger state interest against the same First Amendment interest at stake in *New York Times,* we held that a State could not allow recovery of presumed and punitive damages absent a showing of "actual malice." Nothing in our opinion, however, indicated that this same balance would be struck regardless of the type of speech involved. * * *

We have never considered whether the *Gertz* balance obtains when the defamatory statements involve no issue of public concern. To make this determination, we must employ the approach approved in *Gertz* and balance the State's interest in compensating private individuals for injury to their reputation against the First Amendment interest in protecting this type of expression. This state interest is identical to the one weighed in *Gertz.* There we found that it was "strong and legitimate." [C] A State should not lightly be required to abandon it. * * *

The First Amendment interest, on the other hand, is less important than the one weighed in *Gertz.* We have long recognized that not all speech is of equal First Amendment importance. It is speech on " 'matters of public concern' " that is "at the heart of the First Amendment's protection." *First National Bank of Boston v. Bellotti,* 435 U.S. 765, 776. * * *

In contrast, speech on matters of purely private concern is of less First Amendment concern. [C] As a number of state courts, including the court below, have recognized, the role of the Constitution in regulating state libel law is far more limited when the concerns that activated *New York Times* and *Gertz* are absent. * * *

While * * * speech on matters not of public concern is not totally unprotected by the First Amendment [cc], its protections are less stringent. In *Gertz,* we found that the state interest in awarding presumed and punitive damages was not "substantial" in view of their effect on speech at the core of First Amendment concern. [C] This interest, however, is "substantial" relative to the incidental effect these remedies may have on speech of significantly less constitutional interest. The rationale of the common law rules has been the experience and judgment of history that "proof of actual damage will be impossible in a great many cases where, from the character of the defamatory words and the circumstances of publication, it is all but certain that serious harm has resulted in fact." [Cc] As a result, courts for centuries have allowed juries to presume that some damage occurred from many defamatory utterances and publications. * * * [Cc] This rule furthers the state interest in providing remedies for defamation by ensuring that those remedies are effective. In light of the reduced constitutional value of speech involving no matters of public concern,

we hold that the state interest adequately supports awards of presumed and punitive damages—even absent a showing of "actual malice."
* * *

The only remaining issue is whether petitioner's credit report involved a matter of public concern. In a related context, we have held that "[w]hether * * * speech addresses a matter of public concern must be determined by [the expression's] content, form, and context * * * as revealed by the whole record." *Connick v. Myers*, 461 U.S., at 147–148. These factors indicate that petitioner's credit report concerns no public issue. It was speech solely in the individual interest of the speaker and its specific business audience. [C] This particular interest warrants no special protection when—as in this case—the speech is wholly false and clearly damaging to the victim's business reputation. [Cc] Moreover, since the credit report was made available to only five subscribers, who, under the terms of the subscription agreement, could not disseminate it further, it cannot be said that the report involves any "strong interest in the free flow of commercial information." [C] There is simply no credible argument that this type of credit reporting requires special protection to ensure that "debate on public issues [will] be uninhibited, robust, and wide-open." *New York Times Co. v. Sullivan*, 376 U.S., at 270.

In addition, the speech here, like advertising, is hardy and unlikely to be deterred by incidental state regulation. [Cc] It is solely motivated by the desire for profit, which, we have noted, is a force less likely to be deterred than others. [C] Arguably, the reporting here was also more objectively verifiable than speech deserving of greater protection. [C] In any case, the market provides a powerful incentive to a credit reporting agency to be accurate, since false credit reporting is of no use to creditors. Thus, any incremental "chilling" effect of libel suits would be of decreased significance. * * *

We conclude that permitting recovery of presumed and punitive damages in defamation cases absent a showing of "actual malice" does not violate the First Amendment when the defamatory statements do not involve matters of public concern. Accordingly, we affirm the judgment of the Vermont Supreme Court.

[CHIEF JUSTICE BURGER and JUSTICE WHITE concurred in the judgment with separate opinions. They had dissented in *Gertz* and wished it to be overruled. They also wished to reevaluate the extent of application of New York Times v. Sullivan.]

JUSTICE BRENNAN, with whom JUSTICE MARSHALL, JUSTICE BLACKMUN and JUSTICE STEVENS join, dissenting. * * *

The four who join this opinion would reverse the judgment of the Vermont Supreme Court. We believe that, although protection of the type of expression at issue is admittedly not the "central meaning of the First Amendment," [c] *Gertz* makes clear that the First Amendment nonetheless requires restraints on presumed and punitive damage awards for this expression. The lack of consensus in approach to these idiosyncratic facts should not, however, obscure the solid allegiance the principles of *New York Times v. Sullivan* continue to command in the jurisprudence of this Court. * * *

When an alleged libel involves citicism of a public official or a public figure, the need to nurture robust debate of public issues and the requirement that all state regulation of speech be narrowly tailored coalesce to require actual malice as a prerequisite to any recovery. When the alleged libel involves speech that falls outside these especially important categories, we have held that the Constitution permits states significant leeway to compensate for actual damage to reputation. The requirement of narrowly tailored regulatory measures, however, always mandates at least a showing of fault and proscribes the award of presumed and punitive damages on less than a showing of actual malice. It has remained the judgment of the Court since *Gertz* that this comprehensive two-tiered structure best accommodates the values of the constitutional free speech guarantee and the states' interest in protecting reputation. * * *

In professing allegiance to *Gertz,* the plurality opinion protests too much. As Justice White correctly observes, Justice Powell departs completely from the analytic framework and result of that case: "*Gertz* was intended to reach any false statements * * * whether or not [they] implicate[ ] a matter of public importance." [C] [11]

Even accepting the notion that a distinction can and should be drawn between matters of public concern and matters of purely private concern, however, the analyses presented by both JUSTICE POWELL and JUSTICE WHITE fail on their own terms. Both, by virtue of what they hold in this case, propose an impoverished definition of "matters of public concern" that is irreconcilable with First Amendment principles. The credit reporting at issue here surely involves a subject matter of sufficient public concern to require the comprehensive protections of *Gertz.* Were this speech appropriately characterized as a matter of only private concern, moreover, the elimination of the *Gertz* restrictions

---

11. One searches *Gertz* in vain for a single word to support the proposition that limits on presumed and punitive damages obtained only when speech involved matters of public concern. *Gertz* could not have been grounded in such a premise. Distrust of placing in the courts the power to decide what speech was of public concern was precisely the rationale *Gertz* offered for rejecting the *Rosenbloom* plurality approach. [C] It would have been incongruous for the Court to go on to circumscribe the protection against presumed and punitive damages by reference to a judicial judgment as to whether the speech at issue involved matters of public concern. At several points the Court in *Gertz* makes perfectly clear the restrictions of presumed

and punitive damages were to apply in all cases. [C]

Indeed, JUSTICE POWELL's opinion today is fairly read as embracing the approach of the *Rosenbloom* plurality to deciding when the Constitution should limit state defamation law. The limits imposed, however, are less stringent than those suggested by the *Rosenbloom* plurality. Under the approach of today's plurality, speech about matters of public or general interest receives only the *Gertz* protections against unrestrained presumed and punitive damages, not the full *New York Times v. Sullivan* protections against any recovery absent a showing of actual malice.

on presumed and punitive damages would still violate basic First Amendment requirements. * * *

The five Members of the Court voting to affirm the damage award in this case have provided almost no guidance as to what constitutes a protected "matter of public concern." JUSTICE WHITE offers nothing at all, but his opinion does indicate that the distinction turns on solely the subject matter of the expression and not on the extent or conditions of dissemination of that expression. [C] JUSTICE POWELL adumbrates a rationale that would appear to focus primarily on subject matter.[12]

The opinion relies on the fact that the speech at issue was "solely in the individual interest of the speaker and its *business* audience," [c] Analogizing explicitly to advertising, the opinion also states that credit reporting is "hardy" and "solely motivated by the desire for profit." [C] These two strains of analysis suggest that JUSTICE POWELL is excluding the subject matter of credit reports from "matters of public concern" because the speech is predominantly in the realm of matters of economic concern. * * *

Greenmoss Builders should be permitted to recover for any actual damage it can show resulted from Dun & Bradstreet's negligently false credit report, but should be required to show actual malice to receive presumed or punitive damages. Because the jury was not instructed in accordance with these principles, we would reverse and remand for further proceedings not inconsistent with this opinion.

---

1. On studying the *Gertz* case, would it have occurred to you that this case would have been decided this way? After reading *this* case, what do you think the Court will do when it reviews a case involving a private plaintiff in a matter not of public concern, when the question arises whether the *Gertz* requirement of defendant's fault is raised? What would be the effect of its decision either way?

2. The principal case does appear to settle, at least for the time being, one issue that had never been specifically decided. This is the issue of whether different standards might constitutionally be applied to media defendants and nonmedia defendants. The Vermont Supreme Court had based its decision in *Greenmoss* on the ground that the defendant was not acting as a member of the news media. Although the Supreme Court affirmed, it pointedly stated that the affirmance was not based on the reasons given by the state supreme court. Justice Brennan stated in his dissenting opinion that he counted "at least six" Justices who "agree today that, in the context of defamation law, the rights of

12. Justice Powell also appears to rely in part on the fact that communication was limited and confidential. Given that his analysis also relies on the subject matter of the credit report, it is difficult to decipher exactly what role the nature and extent of dissemination plays in JUSTICE POWELL's analysis. But because the subject matter of the expression at issue is properly understood as a matter of public concern, it may well be that this element of confidentiality is crucial to the outcome as far as JUSTICE POWELL's opinion is concerned. In other words, it may be that JUSTICE POWELL thinks this particular expression could not contribute to public welfare because the public generally does not receive it. This factor does not suffice to save the analysis. * * *

the institutional media are no greater and no less than those enjoyed by" others.

3. In Time, Inc. v. Pape, 401 U.S. 279 (1971), Time Magazine reported on a report of the U.S. Commission of Civil Rights entitled *Justice*, listing instances of police brutality which were alleged in complaints to have occurred. The allegations of one complaint, involving plaintiff, were stated as facts. Held: "In light of the totality of what was said in *Justice* we cannot agree that, when Time failed to state that the Commission in reporting the Monroe incident had technically confined itself to the allegations of a complaint, Time engaged in a 'falsification' sufficient to sustain a jury finding of 'actual malice.' * * * Time's omission of the word 'alleged' amounted to the adoption of one of a number of possible rational interpretations of a document that bristled with ambiguities. The deliberate choice of such an interpretation, though arguably reflecting a misconception, was not enough to create a jury issue of 'malice' under *New York Times*. To permit the malice issue to go to the jury because of the omission of a word like 'alleged' * * * would be to impose a much stricter standard of liability on errors of interpretation or judgment than on errors of historic fact. * * * Nothing in this opinion is to be understood as making the word 'alleged' a superfluity in published reports of information damaging to reputation."

In Time, Inc. v. Firestone, 424 U.S. 448 (1976), Time Magazine published in its "Milestones" Section this item: "Divorced, by Russell A. Firestone, Jr., 41, heir to the tire fortune, Mary Alice Sullivan Firestone, 32, his third wife; a one time Palm Beach schoolteacher; on ground of extreme cruelty and adultery; after six years marriage, one son; in West Palm Beach Florida. The 17–month intermittent trial produced enough testimony of extramarital adventures on both sides, said the judge, 'to make Dr. Freud's hair curl.' " The language in the decree was quite ambiguous but plaintiff demanded that Time retract the statement of adultery because she had been awarded alimony and under the Florida statutes she would not be entitled to alimony if found guilty of adultery. Time's refusal produced the libel action in which she was awarded $100,000 for mental distress. The Florida Supreme Court affirmed; but the Supreme Court reversed on the ground that there was never any intentional finding of fault by court or jury in the case. The Court distinguished *Pape* on the ground that it involved the *New York Times* standard while *Firestone* involved the *Gertz* standard.

4. *Repetition of Defamation.* Observe that in neither *Pape* nor *Firestone* was the court concerned with the truth or falsity of the defamatory charge or the measure of defendant's fault in ascertaining it. The defendant would apparently not have been liable even if it had actually known that the plaintiff was innocent of the charge, so long as the report of the official record was fair and accurate. It is on the issue of whether the official report was accurate and the plaintiff's fault in seeing that it was accurate that the two standards are applied.

One is not ordinarily relieved of liability for repeating a defamatory charge, even if he indicates the source and accurately repeats it—even if he also says that he does not believe it. Restatement (Second) of Torts § 578; Dixson v. Newsweek, Inc., 562 F.2d 626 (10th Cir.1977); Harris v. Minvielle, 48 La.Ann. 908, 19 So. 925 (1896) ("talebearers are as bad as talemakers"); Painter, Republication Problems in the Law of Defamation, 47 Va.L.Rev. 113 (1961); Note, Libel and The Reporting of Rumors, 92 Yale L.J. 85 (1982).

5. *The Reporter's Privilege.* At common law, there developed a special privilege, known as the "reporter's privilege" or as "record libel." It was a privilege because it did not exempt the defendant from liability unless his report was verbatim or a fair and accurate summary. *Pape* and *Firestone* now impose a constitutional requirement of fault in failing to make the report fair and accurate. But it is still a privilege, because there is no liability for repetition of a defamatory statement even though the defendant was at fault in regard to the truth or falsity of the charge itself. See Restatement (Second) of Torts § 611. There is a good discussion in Gobin v. Globe Pub. Co., 216 Kan. 223, 531 P.2d 76 (1975), decided prior to *Firestone.*

The remaining problem involves the scope of the privilege, both at common law and under the more recent constitutional doctrine, and whether they will differ or coincide.

6. *The Privilege at Common Law.* This began as a privilege to report all official proceedings in the public interest. Wason v. Walter, L.R. 4 Q.B. 573 (1868) (Parliament); Terry v. Fellows, 21 La.Ann. 375 (1869) (session of legislative committee); Hahn v. Holum, 165 Wis. 425, 162 N.W. 432 (1917) (proceeding before justice of the peace).

It has been extended also to republication of public reports filed by officials in the performance of their duties. Greenfield v. Courier–Journal & Louisville Times Co., 283 S.W.2d 839 (Ky.1955) (grand jury). Also to press releases given out by public officers as official statements in the performance of their duties. Brandon v. Gazette Pub. Co., 234 Ark. 332, 352 S.W.2d 92 (1961) (governor); Short v. News–Journal Co., 205 A.2d 6 (Del.Super.1965) (district director of Internal Revenue). It has been extended also to reporting official acts of public officers, such as an arrest and the charges made. Torski v. Mansfield Journal Co., 100 Ohio App. 538, 137 N.E.2d 679 (1956) (wrong man arrested for rape).

There have been numerous cases recognizing the privilege to report what is said at public meetings that are not official, but open to all who wish to attend. Jackson v. Record Pub. Co., 175 S.C. 211, 178 S.E. 833 (1935) (words of a candidate at a political rally); Phoenix Newspapers v. Choisser, 82 Ariz. 271, 312 P.2d 150 (1957) (same, at Chamber of Commerce "forum"); Pulverman v. A.S. Abell Co., 228 F.2d 797 (4th Cir.1956) (speech made by candidate for President); Borg v. Boas, 231 F.2d 788 (9th Cir.1956) (mass meeting held to urge calling a grand jury to investigate local law enforcement). In all of these cases, the matter reported has been one of public concern.

On the other hand, private meetings, not open to the public, have not been included. Kimball v. Post Pub. Co., 199 Mass. 248, 85 N.E. 103 (1908) (stockholders' meeting); Lewis v. Hayes, 165 Cal. 527, 132 P. 1022 (1913).

7. *Reports of Pleadings.* A few courts have held that there is a privilege to report pleadings filed in an action but not yet acted upon. Campbell v. New York Evening Post, 245 N.Y. 320, 157 N.E. 153 (1927); Langford v. Vanderbilt University, 199 Tenn. 389, 287 S.W.2d 32 (1956).

A considerable majority of the courts have held that there is an exception to the reporter's privilege in the case of pleadings filed with a court but not yet acted upon in any manner. Sanford v. Boston Herald–Traveler Corp., 318 Mass. 156, 61 N.E.2d 5 (1945); Nixon v. Dispatch Printing Co., 101 Minn. 309, 112 N.W. 258 (1907). The reason given is that the privilege to report the pleadings would afford too great an opportunity for malicious injury or even extortion by alleging almost anything in a pleading, getting it reported, and then withdrawing the suit. See Nadelmann, The Newspaper Privilege and

Extortion by Abuse of Legal Process, 54 Colum.L.Rev. 359 (1954); Barnett, The Privilege of Defamation by Private Report of Public Official Proceedings, 31 Ore.L.Rev. 185 (1952).

8. *The Privilege Under the Constitution. Pape* and *Firestone* are the only Supreme Court cases on the subject. A significant issue is raised by Edwards v. National Audubon Soc'y, Inc., 556 F.2d 113 (2d Cir.1977), cert. denied, 434 U.S. 1002 (1977), espousing a much broader privilege of "neutral reportage." The court announced as a "fundamental principle" that "when a responsible, prominent organization like the National Audubon Society makes serious charges against a public figure, the First Amendment protects the accurate and disinterested reporting of those charges, regardless of the reporter's private views regarding their validity. * * * What is newsworthy about such accusations is that they were made. We do not believe that the press may be required under the First Amendment to suppress newsworthy statements merely because it has serious doubts regarding their truth. * * * The public interest in being fully informed about controversies that often rage around sensitive issues demands that the press be afforded the freedom to report such charges without assuming responsibility for them. * * *

"Literal accuracy is not a prerequisite: if we are to enjoy the blessings of a robust and unintimidated press, we must provide immunity from defamation suits where the journalist believes, reasonably and in good faith, that his report accurately conveys the charges made."

The Second Circuit continues to espouse the principle and some other courts have relied on it. Barns v. Times Argus Ass'n, Inc., 139 Vt. 381, 430 A.2d 773 (1981). But the Third Circuit has expressly repudiated it. Dickey v. CBS, Inc., 583 F.2d 1221 (3d Cir.1978). The Supreme Court has remained silent. Cf. Franklin, Libel and Letters to the Editor: Toward an Open Forum, 57 U.Colo.L.Rev. 651 (1986).

9. On the reporter's privilege, see Bryan, Publication of Record Libel, 5 Va.L.Rev. 513 (1918); Barnett, The Privilege of Defamation by Private Report of Public Official Proceedings, 31 Ore.L.Rev. 185 (1952); K. Sowle, Defamation and the First Amendment: The Case for a Constitutional Privilege of Fair Report, 54 N.Y.U.L.Rev. 469 (1979).

PHILADELPHIA NEWSPAPERS, INC. v. HEPPS
Supreme Court of the United States, 1986.
475 U.S. 767, 106 S.Ct. 1558, 89 L.Ed.2d 783.

[Plaintiffs were Maurice S. Hepps, principal stockholder of General Programming, Inc. (GPI), a corporation engaged in franchising a chain of "Thrifty Stores" (selling beer, soft drinks and snacks), plus GPI itself and some of the franchisees. The charges were that plaintiffs "had links to organized crime and used some of those links to influence the State's governmental processes, both legislative and administrative." They were published in a series of articles by defendant, Philadelphia Newspapers, Inc., in the Philadelphia Inquirer.

Suit was in the state court, where the court followed two statutes requiring (1) a private plaintiff to prove negligence or malice by the defendant and (2) the defendant to meet the burden of proving the truth of a defamatory statement. There was also a third statute ("a

Front row: Marshall, Brennan, Rehnquist, C.J., White, Blackmun
Back row: O'Connor, Powell, Stevens, Scalia

shield law") providing that no person employed by a public medium should be required to disclose the source of information obtained. Plantiffs requested an instruction that the jury could draw a negative inference from the exercise of the shield law's privilege, and defendants requested an instruction that no reference could be drawn. The judge declined to give either instruction and the jury found for the defendants.

On appeal directly to the Pennsylvania Supreme Court, that court "held that to place the burden of drawing truth on the defendant did not unconstitutionally inhibit free debate, and remanded the case for a new trial." This court granted certiorari.]

JUSTICE O'CONNOR delivered the opinion of the Court.

This case requires us once more to "struggl[e] * * * to define the proper accommodation between the law of defamation and the freedoms of speech and press protected by the First Amendment." *Gertz v. Robert Welch, Inc.,* 418 U.S. 323, 325. In *Gertz,* the Court held that a private figure who brings a suit for defamation cannot recover without some showing that the media defendant was at fault in publishing the statements at issue. [C] Here, we hold that, at least where a newspaper publishes speech of public concern, a private-figure plaintiff cannot recover damages without also showing that the statements at issue are false.   *   *   * [The opinion describes the holdings of *New York Times, Gertz* and *Greenmoss.*]

One can discern in these decisions two forces that may reshape the common-law landscape to conform to the First Amendment. The first is whether the plaintiff is a public official or figure, or is instead a private figure. The second is whether the speech at issue is of public concern. When the speech is of public concern and the plaintiff is a public official or public figure, the Constitution clearly requires the plaintiff to surmount a much higher barrier before recovering damages from a media defendant than is raised by the common law. When the speech is of public concern but the plaintiff is a private figure, as in *Gertz,* the Constitution still supplants the standards of the common law, but the constitutional requirements are, in at least some of their range, less forbidding than when the plaintiff is a public figure and the speech is of public concern. When the speech is of exclusively private concern and the plaintiff is a private figure, as in *Dun & Bradstreet,* the constitutional requirements do not necessarily force any change in at least some of the features of the common-law landscape.

Our opinions to date have chiefly treated the necessary showings of fault rather than of falsity. Nonetheless, as one might expect given the language of the Court in *New York Times,* a public-figure plaintiff must show the falsity of the statements at issue in order to prevail on a suit for defamation.   *   *   *

Here, as in *Gertz,* the plaintiff is a private figure and the newspaper articles are of public concern. In *Gertz,* as in *New York Times,* the common-law rule was superseded by a constitutional rule. We believe that the common law's rule on falsity—that the defendant must bear the burden of proving truth—must similarly fall here to a constitutional requirement that the plaintiff bear the burden of showing falsity, as well as fault, before recovering damages.

There will always be instances when the factfinding process will be unable to resolve conclusively whether the speech is true or false; it is in those cases that the burden of proof is dispositive. Under a rule forcing the plaintiff to bear the burden of showing falsity, there will be some cases in which plaintiffs cannot meet their burden despite the fact that the speech is in fact false. The plaintiff's suit will fail despite the fact that, in some abstract sense, the suit is meritorious. Similarly, under an alternative rule placing the burden of showing truth on defendants, there would be some cases in which defendants could not bear their burden despite the fact that the speech is in fact true. Those suits would succeed despite the fact that, in some abstract sense, those suits are unmeritorious. Under either rule, then, the outcome of the suit will sometimes be at variance with the outcome that we would desire if all speech were either demonstrably true or demonstrably false.   *   *   *

In a case presenting a configuration of speech and plaintiff like the one we face here, and where the scales are in such an uncertain balance, we believe that the Constitution requires us to tip them in favor of protecting true speech. To ensure that true speech on matters of public concern is not deterred, we hold that the common-law presumption that defamatory speech is false cannot stand when a plaintiff seeks damages against a media defendant for speech of public concern.

In the context of governmental restriction of speech, it has long been established that the government cannot limit speech protected by the First Amendment without bearing the burden of showing that its restriction is justified. ＊ ＊ ＊ It is not immediately apparent from the text of the First Amendment, which by its terms applies only to governmental action, that a similar result should obtain here: a suit by a private party is obviously quite different from the government's direct enforcement of its own laws. Nonetheless, the need to encourage debate on public issues that concerned the Court in the governmental-restriction cases is of concern in a similar manner in this case involving a private suit for damages: placement by state law of the burden of proving truth upon media defendants who publish speech of public concern deters such speech because of the fear that liability will unjustifiably result. [Cc] Because such a "chilling" effect would be antithetical to the First Amendment's protection of true speech on matters of public concern, we believe that a private-figure plaintiff must bear the burden of showing that the speech at issue is false before recovering damages for defamation from a media defendant. To do otherwise could "only result in a deterrence of speech which the Constitution makes free." [C]

We recognize that requiring the plaintiff to show falsity will insulate from liability some speech that is false, but unprovably so. Nonetheless, the Court's previous decisions on the restrictions that the First Amendment places upon the common law of defamation firmly support our conclusion here with respect to the allocation of the burden of proof. In attempting to resolve related issues in the defamation context, the Court has affirmed that "[t]he First Amendment requires that we protect some falsehood in order to protect speech that matters." *Gertz,* 418 U.S., at 341. Here the speech concerns the legitimacy of the political process, and therefore clearly "matters." [C] To provide " 'breathing space,' " [c] for true speech on matters of public concern, the Court has been willing to insulate even *demonstrably* false speech from liability, and has imposed additional requirements of fault upon the plaintiff in a suit for defamation. [Cc] We therefore do not break new ground here in insulating speech that is not even demonstrably false.

We note that our decision adds only marginally to the burdens that the plaintiff must already bear as a result of our earlier decisions in the law of defamation. The plaintiff must show fault. A jury is obviously more likely to accept a plaintiff's contention that the defendant was at fault in publishing the statements at issue if convinced that the relevant statements were false. As a practical matter, then, evidence offered by plaintiffs on the publisher's fault in adequately investigating the truth of the published statements will generally encompass evidence of the falsity of the matters asserted. * * * [T]he judgment of the Pennsylvania Supreme Court is reversed, and the case is remanded for further proceedings not inconsistent with this opinion.

JUSTICE BRENNAN, with whom JUSTICE BLACKMUN joins, concurring.
* * *

JUSTICE STEVENS, with whom THE CHIEF JUSTICE, JUSTICE WHITE, and JUSTICE REHNQUIST join, dissenting. * * *

The Court, after acknowledging the need to " 'accommodat[e] * * * the law of defamation and the freedoms of speech and press protected by the First Amendment,' " [c] decides to override "the common-law presumption" retained by several states that "defamatory speech is false" because of the need "[t]o ensure that true speech on matters of public concern is not deterred." [C] I do not agree that our precedents require a private individual to bear the risk that a defamatory statement—uttered either with a mind toward assassinating his good name or with careless indifference to that possibility—cannot be proven false. By attaching no weight to the state's interest in protecting the private individual's good name, the Court has reached a pernicious result. * * *

While deliberate or inadvertent libels villify private personages, they contribute little to the marketplace of ideas. In assaying the First Amendment side of the balance, it helps to remember that the perpetrator of the libel suffers from its failure to demonstrate the truth of its accusation only if the "private-figure" plaintiff first establishes that the publisher is at "fault," either that it published its libel with "actual malice" in the *New York Times* sense * * * or that it published with that degree of careless indifference characteristic of negligence. Far from being totally in the dark about "how much of the speech affected by the allocation of the burden of proof is true and how much is false," [c] the antecedent fault determination makes irresistible the inference that a significant portion of this speech is beyond the constitutional pale. This observation is almost tautologically true with regard to libels published with "actual malice." For that standard to be met, the publisher must come close to wilfully blinding itself to the falsity of its utterance. The observation is also valid, albeit to a lesser extent, with respect to defamations uttered with "fault." Thus, while the public's interest in an uninhibited press is at its nadir when the publisher is at fault or worse, society's "equally compelling" need for judicial redress of libelous utterances is at its zenith. * * * [C]

In my opinion deliberate, malicious character assassination is not protected by the First Amendment to the United States Constitution. That Amendment does require the target of a defamatory statement to prove that his assailant was at fault, and I agree that it provides a constitutional shield for truthful statements. I simply do not understand, however, why a character assassin should be given an absolute license to defame by means of statements that can be neither verified nor disproven. The danger of deliberate defamation by reference to unprovable facts is not a merely speculative or hypothetical concern.

* * *

Even assuming that attacks on the reputation of a public figure should be presumed to be true, however, a different calculus is appropriate when a defamatory statement disparages the reputation of a private individual. In that case, the overriding concern for reliable protection of truthful statements must make room for "[t]he legitimate state interest underlying the law of libel"—"the compensation of individuals for the harm inflicted on them by defamatory falsehood." *Gertz* * * *

In my view, as long as publishers are protected by the requirement that the plaintiff has the burden of proving fault, there can be little, if any, basis for a concern that a significant amount of true speech will be deterred unless the private person victimized by a malicious libel can also carry the burden of proving falsity. The Court's decision trades on the good names of private individuals with little First Amendment coin to show for it. * * *

---

1. Who has the better of the argument? Remember, this is a decision of constitutional law, binding on both federal and state courts.

2. In Anderson v. Liberty Lobby, 477 U.S. 242 (1986), a similar question arose: In ruling on a motion for summary judgment, should the standard applied by the court vary according to whether the plaintiff is a public figure under *New York Times* or a private person under *Gertz?* Held, yes. White J.: "In sum, we conclude that the determination of whether a given factual dispute requires submission to a jury must be guided by the substantive evidentiary standards that apply to the case. This is true at both the directed verdict and summary judgment stages. Consequently, where the *New York Times* 'clear and convincing' evidence requirement applies, the trial judge's summary judgment inquiry as to whether a genuine issue exists will be whether the evidence presented is such that a jury applying that evidentiary standard could reasonably find for either the plaintiff or the defendant. Thus, where the factual dispute concerns actual malice, clearly a material issue in a *New York Times* case, the appropriate summary judgment question will be whether the evidence in the record could support a reasonable jury finding either that the plaintiff has shown actual malice by clear and convincing evidence or that the plaintiff has not." Brennan and Rehnquist, JJ., dissented, and the Chief Justice concurred with Rehnquist.

3. *Public Figures.* The scope of the concept of public figure has steadily narrowed since the decision in Curtis Pub. Co. v. Butts, 388 U.S. 130 (1967), beginning with *Gertz,* in which Justice Powell discussed it at some length, and continued through Time, Inc. v. Firestone, 424 U.S. 448 (1976) (party to sensational divorce case was held not a public figure), to Hutchinson v. Proxmire, 443 U.S. 111 (1979) (scientist research director of foundation, who received a federal research grant), and Wolston v. Reader's Digest Ass'n, Inc.,

443 U.S. 157 (1979) (nephew of two persons pleading guilty of espionage, who ignored subpoena of grand jury and was guilty of criminal contempt). It seems quite possible that if the Court were now deciding where to classify public persons, it would place them with private persons and leave the *New York Times* standard for public officers. In 1967, when Curtis Pub. Co. v. Butts was decided, this was prior to *Gertz,* and the choice was between the common law strict liability and the "actual malice" of *New York Times.*

There are three important articles on the subject of public figures in the symposium in 75 Wm. & Mary L.Rev. 905 (1984).

4. A recent Supreme Court case of importance to the constitutional law of defamation is Bose Corp. v. Consumers Union of United States, Inc., 466 U.S. 485 (1984), infra page 1092. Involving the tort of injurious falsehood (product disparagement), it holds that the issue of "constitutional malice" (knowledge or reckless disregard as to falsity) is not governed by Rule 52 of the Federal Rules of Civil Procedure, but is a determination of constitutional fact subject to independent appellate review, so that the appellate court must decide for itself whether there is "clear and convincing proof of 'actual malice.'"

5. Now that the significant Supreme Court decisions on the effect of the First Amendment on the tort law of defamation have been considered, it is well to look again at the case of Janklow v. Newsweek, Inc., supra page 866, and the fact-opinion dichotomy. Do you think Justice Powell intended to lay down a rule of constitutional law in his quotation from *Gertz,* supra, pages 906, 908? Should such a rule be pronounced? Although there are now numerous decisions on the subject, the Supreme Court has carefully abstained from granting certiorari. Why? How should the courts distinguish between fact and opinion? Can a "bright line" be drawn, or will most cases be subjected to appellate review? Will this provide for an immunity for almost every charge if the defendant takes care to word it just right?

5. PRIVILEGES

IRWIN v. ASHURST
Supreme Court of Oregon, 1938.
158 Or. 61, 74 P.2d 1127.

[Action for defamation, brought by a witness for the prosecution in a criminal trial against (1) Ashurst, the trial judge in that case (for allowing the trial to be broadcast), (2) Vandenburg, the attorney for the accused (for arguing to the jury that the plaintiff was a drug addict, a "dopefiend * * * lower than a rattlesnake," who testified to a story that her husband made up) and (3) the radio broadcasting company. The trial judge granted a nonsuit in favor of the judge, and the jury rendered verdicts in favor of the other defendants.]

BELT, JUSTICE. * * * It is well settled in England and in this country, on the ground of public policy, that a judge has absolute immunity from liability in an action for defamatory words published in the course of judicial proceedings. [Cc] The mere fact, in itself, that the defendant Ashurst permitted the installation of a microphone to report judicial proceedings affords no basis for liability. * * *

[P]laintiff contends that the absolute privilege of the court "does not extend beyond the four walls of the court room." * * *

It is difficult to see any difference in principle between radio broadcasting of court proceedings and the publication of the same in newspapers. The fundamental principles of the law of libel applicable to the publication of judicial proceedings by newspapers apply also to the broadcasting of such proceedings by radio stations. * * * In the instant case there was no comment by the radio company concerning the proceedings. All it did was to transmit to the public a true and accurate report of what was going on in the trial of the murder case. * * * Of course, if no cause of action exists against Vandenberg, it follows that the defendant broadcasting company and its manager are not liable. * * *

Under the rule in England, no action will lie against a barrister for defamatory words spoken as counsel in the course of any judicial proceeding, even though they were irrelevant to the issue and uttered maliciously. [C] Such absolute privilege with reference to counsel does not obtain in this country. A communication made by an attorney in a judicial proceeding is absolutely privileged if it is pertinent and relevant to the issues, although it may be false and malicious. [C] He cannot, however, in a judicial proceeding, utter defamatory matter wholly foreign to the issues and be protected under the shield of qualified privilege. To recover, therefore, against the defendant Vandenberg it was incumbent upon plaintiff to establish that the alleged defamatory matter spoken of and concerning her was irrelevant and impertinent to the issues in the murder case, and that it was uttered with express or actual malice. * * *

Was the argument of the defendant Vandenberg to the jury in reference to the plaintiff relevant and pertinent to the issues? * * * Defendant admits that he stated plaintiff was not truthful and that she "was lower than a rattlesnake because a rattlesnake gives warning before it strikes."

In determining whether the argument was pertinent or relevant to the issues, courts are liberal, and the privilege * * * "embraces anything that may possibly be pertinent. All doubt should be resolved in favor of its relevancy or pertinency" * * *.

It may well be that the argument of counsel in reference to plaintiff, assuming it was as alleged by plaintiff, was extremely harsh and unjust, but the vital question is whether it was foreign to the issues of the case. The credibility of the plaintiff was put in issue when she took the stand and testified as a witness. Counsel had the absolute privilege of making such deductions as he saw fit if they were relevant and pertinent to the issues, even though they were false and he was actuated by improper motives. An argument may be false and malicious and still be pertinent. * * *

The jury by its verdict in favor of the defendants must necessarily have found that what Vandenberg said was pertinent to the issues, or, assuming that it was not pertinent, that he was not actuated by express malice. * * *

The judgment of the lower court is affirmed.

---

1. *Judicial Proceedings.* The absolute privilege, or immunity, recognized in this case has been applied not only to the judge and counsel, but also to petit juries and grand juries. It makes no difference that, as in the case of a grand jury, the proceeding is not open to the public. Schultz v. Strauss, 127 Wis. 325, 106 N.W. 1066 (1906).

2. The privilege extends also to witnesses, even though they testify voluntarily, and not under subpoena. It extends to a defamatory statement in a pleading filed in the action, as in Taliaferro v. Sims, 187 F.2d 1 (5th Cir.1951), and Di Blasio v. Kolodner, 233 Md. 512, 197 A.2d 245 (1964); and also to affidavits filed in a judicial proceeding, or filed for the purpose of reopening it after judgment, as in Fleming v. Adams, 153 N.Y.S.2d 964 (Sup.Ct.1956). It makes no difference that the judicial proceeding is ex parte, and only one side of the case is heard. Beiser v. Scripps–McRae Pub. Co., 113 Ky. 383, 68 S.W. 457 (1902).

3. The privilege applies to the hearing of a sanity commission. Jarman v. Offert, 239 N.C. 468, 80 S.E.2d 248 (1954). Compare, for hearings before a grievance committee of the state bar association, Wiener v. Weintraub, 22 N.Y.2d 330, 292 N.Y.S.2d 667, 239 N.E.2d 540 (1968); Ramstead v. Morgan, 219 Or. 383, 347 P.2d 594 (1959). When the proceedings of administrative agencies are found to be judicial in character, the same privilege applies to them. Robertson v. Industrial Insurance Co., 75 So.2d 198 (Fla.1954) (revocation of insurance license).

Once the privilege is found to exist, the only limitation on it is that what is said must be found to have some reasonable bearing upon or relation to the subject of inquiry. Even the judge cannot seize upon the occasion of a judicial proceeding to voice entirely unrelated defamation. La Porta v. Leonard, 88 N.J.L. 663, 97 A. 251 (1916); Stahl v. Kincade, 135 Ind.App. 699, 192 N.E.2d 493 (1963). Of course, the privilege does not extend to what is said outside of court. Kennedy v. Cannon, 229 Md. 92, 182 A.2d 54 (1962) (attorney stating his client's contentions to the press).

But the required "relevance" or "pertinence" does not mean that what is said must come within the rules of evidence as to relevancy: and a great deal of latitude is allowed. Thus when a witness answers a question asked him and not objected to, he is privileged although both the question and the answer are entirely irrelevant to the proceeding. Greenberg v. Ackermann, 41 N.J.Super. 146, 124 A.2d 313 (1955). And if he speaks under an honest, but mistaken belief as to what is called for, as when he misunderstands the question, he is privileged. Johnson v. Dever, 201 Ark. 175, 143 S.W.2d 1112 (1940).

4. The result of the absolute privilege is that there is no civil remedy at all against the witness who gives perjured testimony in court, even though he does so in furtherance of a conspiracy to injure the plaintiff. Ginsburg v. Halpern, 383 Pa. 177, 118 A.2d 201 (1955). On the other hand, it has been held that the privilege does not protect one not himself involved in the proceeding, who procures the false testimony. Bailey v. McGill, 247 N.C. 286, 100 S.E.2d 860 (1957). See Note, 36 N.C.L.Rev. 552 (1958).

5. *Legislative Proceedings.* A similar absolute privilege is applied to members of Congress and of the state legislatures, in the performance of their legislative functions. See Cochran v. Couzens, 42 F.2d 783 (D.C.Cir.1930); and U.S. Const. Art. I, § 6, cl. 1.

6. The common law rule was that the defamation, to be privileged, must have some relation to the business of the legislature. Coffin v. Coffin, 4 Mass. 1, 3 Am.Dec. 189 (1808). Federal and state constitutional provisions have been construed, however, to extend the privilege to anything whatever said in the course of legislative proceedings themselves. Kilbourn v. Thompson, 103 U.S. 168 (1880); Cole v. Richards, 108 N.J.L. 356, 158 A. 466 (1932).

7. If the Congressman reprints his remarks in a private newsletter, and mails it out to his constituents, however, this is a republication to which the privilege does not apply. McGovern v. Martz, 182 F.Supp. 343 (D.D.C.1960); Cole v. Richards, 108 N.J.L. 356, 158 A. 466 (1932). What if he merely relates to the press what he said on the floor of Congress?

8. The privilege extends to the hearings of the legislative body, and to witnesses testifying at such hearings. Kelly v. Daro, 47 Cal.App.2d 418, 118 P.2d 37 (1941); Logan's Super Markets v. McCalla, 208 Tenn. 68, 343 S.W.2d 892 (1961). In the last case, it was held that the testimony of the witness was subject to the same rules as to pertinence to the proceeding as in the case of the judicial proceeding immunity.

9. There is disagreement on whether the legislative privilege extends to local legislative bodies, such as city councils. Cases are collected in Annot., 40 A.L.R.2d 941 (1955). The majority view grants an absolute privilege. See Noble v. Ternyik, 273 Or. 39, 539 P.2d 658 (1975).

10. A person petitioning the government for relief of grievances was held not entitled to an absolute privilege, but to the *New York Times* privilege of "actual malice," in In re IBP Confidential Business Document Litigation, 755 F.2d 1300 (8th Cir.1985).

See Veeder, Absolute Privilege in Defamation: Judicial Proceedings, 9 Colum.L.Rev. 463, 600 (1909); Veeder, Absolute Immunity in Defamation: Legislative and Executive Proceedings, 10 Colum.L.Rev. 131 (1910); Yankwich, The Immunity of Congressional Speech—Its Origin, Meaning and Scope, 99 U.Pa.L.Rev. 960 (1951). Notes, 16 U.Chi.L.Rev. 544 (1949), 18 U.Chi.L.Rev. 591 (1951).

CARR v. WATKINS

Court of Appeals of Maryland, 1962.
227 Md. 578, 177 A.2d 841.

HAMMOND, JUDGE. The appellant Carr sued Gould, an officer in the security division of the Naval Ordnance Laboratory in Silver Spring, and Watkins and Whalen officers of the Montgomery County Police Department, because they had transmitted to his employer information as to charges that had been brought against him years ago and his employer had consequently discharged him. * * * Judge Shure sustained demurrers to the declaration, holding that all the defendants were absolutely privileged as to the slander count. * * *

The validity of the counts of the declaration * * * depends in the final analysis, as we see it, on whether the defendants, in communicating or knowingly causing to be communicated to Carr's employer the charges made against him years ago, were sheltered from liability by privilege or immunity because of their status as agents of a government, performing their duties.

We find it clear that if there was immunity from liability for defamation, there was immunity from liability for the other alleged torts claimed by the declaration to have been committed. * * *

Different standards apply to the federal officer, Gould, and the Montgomery County policemen, Watkins and Whalen, in determining whether they enjoy immunity. The Supreme Court in Barr v. Matteo, 360 U.S. 564, decided that the immunity the Court had previously given executive officers of Cabinet rank in Spalding v. Vilas, 161 U.S. 483, from liability for defamation while acting as their duties required or inherently permitted, also extended to federal agents of lower standing, apparently no matter what their rank. The Court said:

"It is not the title of this office but the duties with which the particular officer sought to be made to respond in damages is entrusted—the relation of the act complained of to 'matters committed by law to his control or supervision,' Spalding v. Vilas, supra—which must provide the guide in delineating the scope of the rule which clothes the official acts of the executive officer with immunity from civil defamation suits."

The rationale of the decision was that the benefit to the public of having its governmental agents free to act as the duties of their offices required without fear of harassment or responsibility for damages at the suit of a citizen outweighed the protection of the individual against damage caused by oppressive or malicious action of a federal official. The decision, as seen above, predicated immunity on whether the act complained of was within the scope of the official's duties rather than the official's rank in the governmental hierarchy.

Since Gould is a federal employee and his defense of immunity rests upon the claim that he was acting within the scope of matters committed to his execution, supervision, or control, the federal rule is here controlling and must be applied by us as to him. The Supreme Court flatly so held in Howard v. Lyons, 360 U.S. 593, 597.

The declaration does not state or suggest that Gould was acting within the scope of his duties. On the contrary, in counts three and four it is alleged that the defendants acted outside the scope, proper authority, and duties of their offices. From the pleadings it is difficult to perceive, or indeed to conceive, how Gould's duties as an officer of the security division of the Naval Ordnance Laboratory required or permitted him appropriately to volunteer, directly or indirectly, to the employer of a former co-worker (neither of whom had any connection with the Laboratory in 1960) that the co-worker had six years before been charged with molesting a minor and with drunkenness—particularly since he had been exonerated and continued in employment until he resigned. No threat to the security of the Laboratory appears to have been involved; and no benefit to it would seem to be gained by Carr's dismissal as a guard at a shopping center.

Therefore, the question of whether Gould was or was not acting in the exercise of duties committed to him must be determined from the evidence to be adduced at the trial.

The Montgomery County police officers are in a somewhat different position. Maryland has not adopted the rule laid down in the Barr case but, on the contrary, this Court has shown reluctance to extend absolute privilege or immunity from liability for torts to government officers of a higher rank than these defendants. [Cc] It has been felt that a qualified privilege is sufficient, so that immunity is conditioned upon absence of malice (unlike the situation where there is absolute privilege) and also upon action within the scope of the actor's duties and authority. [Cc]

The matters of malice and the scope of their duties must be determined as to Watkins and Whalen from the testimony presented at the trial since a defense of qualified privilege is not available on demurrer in Maryland. * * *

Reversed.

---

1. There is general agreement that major officials of executive departments of the federal and state governments are absolutely privileged as to what they say in the discharge of their official duties. Spalding v. Vilas, 161 U.S. 483 (1896) (Postmaster General); Blair v. Walker, 64 Ill.2d 1, 349 N.E.2d 385 (1976) (governor). This has been held to include press releases to inform the public of what they are doing. Matson v. Margiotti, 371 Pa. 188, 88 A.2d 892 (1952) (state attorney general); Hackworth v. Larson, 83 S.D. 674, 165 N.W.2d 705 (1969) (state secretary of state).

2. As the principal case indicates, there is substantial disagreement on whether the absolute privilege should extend beyond executive officers to lesser administrative officials and local officers. Barr v. Matteo, 360 U.S. 564 (1959), holds that for federal officials the privilege is absolute for minor officials, as well as executive ones. There is no liability even though the communication is known to be false and was published maliciously, so long as the publication is within the "outer perimeter" of his "line of duty." See also the companion case of Howard v. Lyons, 360 U.S. 593 (1959).

3. Some state courts have adopted the federal position and extended the absolute privilege to minor or local officials. See, e.g., McNayr v. Kelly, 184 So. 2d 428, 185 So.2d 194 (Fla.1966); Sheridan v. Cresona, 14 N.Y.2d 108, 198 N.E.2d 359, 249 N.Y.S.2d 161 (1964). Many state courts, however, have not followed Barr v. Matteo, but hold that minor officials are entitled only to a qualified privilege. E.g., Ranous v. Hughes, 30 Wis.2d 453, 141 N.W.2d 251 (1966); Gardner v. Hollifield, 96 Idaho 609, 533 P.2d 730 (1975).

SINDORF v. JACRON SALES CO., INC.
Court of Special Appeals of Maryland, 1975.
27 Md.App. 53, 341 A.2d 856.

[Plaintiff Sindorf worked as salesman for Jacron Sales Co., Inc., (the parent company, of Pennsylvania). He resigned after 18 months, as a result of a dispute over his sales practices. Jacron contended that he was selling to people without adequately checking their credit ratings and apparently held up payment of his commissions until they received payment for the sales. On resigning, Sindorf kept some of his inventory, "as partial payment of the commissions due me." He soon went to work as a salesman for Tool Box Corporation of Maryland.

At the suggestion of Langton, President of Pennsylvania Jacron, a call was made to William Brose, President of Tool Box, by Bob Fridkis, Vice President of Virginia Jacron, a subsidiary of Pennsylvania Jacron, to see whether Sindorf had started working for Tool Box before leaving Jacron. Fridkis and Brose, though competitors, were friends and had had similar conversations about employees before. In a long conversation, Fridkis learned that Sindorf had not gone to work for Tool Box until after his resignation from Jacron. Fridkis told Brose that "a few cash sales and quite a bit of merchandise was not accounted for" by Sindorf, and suggested that Brose had better "watch your stock real, real carefully on trucks and things." There were other derogatory insinuations.

The trial court held that Fridkis' conversation was conditionally privileged and that no malice was shown. It granted a motion by Jacron for a directed verdict.]

ORTH, CHIEF JUDGE. * * * The first * * * question to be resolved is whether Jacron enjoyed a conditional privilege to defame Sindorf. * * *

"In an action for defamation, the plaintiff's prima facie case is made out when he has established a publication to a third person for which the defendant is responsible, the recipient's understanding of the defamatory meaning, and its actionable character. It is then open to the defendant to set up various defenses, which to some extent have moderated the rigors of the law of libel and slander." W. Prosser, Law of Torts, 776 (4th ed., 1971). One of these defenses is privilege. "It rests upon the * * * idea, that conduct which otherwise would be actionable is to escape liability because the defendant is acting in furtherance of some interest of social importance, which is entitled to protection even at the expense of uncompensated harm to the plaintiff's reputation. The interest thus favored may be one of the defendant himself, of a third person, or of the general public. If it is one of paramount importance, considerations of policy may require that the defendant's immunity for false statements be absolute, without regard to his purpose or motive, or the reasonableness of his conduct." Id. This is absolute privilege. [C] "If it has relatively less weight from a social point of view, the immunity may be qualified, and conditional upon good motives and reasonable behavior. The defendant's belief in the truth of what he says, the purpose for which he says it, and the manner of publication, all of which are immaterial when no question of privilege is involved, may determine the issue when he enters the defense of such a conditional privilege." Prosser, at 776–777. In the words of Baron Parke in Toogood v. Spyring, 1 C.M. & R. 181, 149 Eng. Rep. 1044 (1834), a publication is conditionally privileged when it is "fairly made by a person in the discharge of some public or private duty, whether legal or moral, or in the conduct of his own affairs, in matters where his interest is concerned." * * * The types of interest which are protected by a qualified privilege are classified by Prosser, at 786, as interest of the publisher, interest of others, common interest of publisher and recipient, communications made to one who may act in the public interest, and fair comment on matters of public concern. [C] "The condition attached to all such qualified privileges is that they must be exercised in a reasonable manner and for a proper purpose. The immunity is forfeited if the defendant steps outside of the scope of the privilege, or abuses the occasion. * * * [It does not] include publication to any person other than those whose hearing of it is reasonably believed to be necessary or useful for the furtherance of that interest. * * * Any reasonable and appropriate method of publication may be adopted which fits the purpose of protecting the particular interest. The dictation of a business letter to a stenographer * * * may be privileged on proper occasion. * * * [T]he fact that the communication is incidentally read or overheard by a person to whom there is no privilege to publish it will not result in liability, if the method adopted is a reasonable and appropriate one under the circumstances." Prosser, at 792–794.

The burden is upon the defendant in the first instance to establish the existence of a privileged occasion for the publication, by proof of a proper interest or duty justifying the utterance of the words. "Whether the occasion was a privileged one, is a question to be determined by the court as an issue of law, unless of course the facts are in dispute, in which case the jury will be instructed as to the proper rules to apply." Id., at 796.

The rules of law as to conditional privilege followed in Maryland generally reflect the views of the authorities above discussed. [Cc]

Thus, the law of this State is that a defamatory publication is conditionally privileged when the occasion shows that the communicating party and the recipient have a mutual interest in the subject matter, or some duty with respect thereto. [Cc] Over seventy-five years ago the Court of Appeals established that where an employer gives a character of an employee the communication is conditionally privileged under the principle that the party communicating has a duty owed, even though such duty is not a legal one, but only a moral or social duty of imperfect obligation. This is so even though the defamatory information was given voluntarily rather than upon request. Fresh v.

Cutter, 73 Md. 87, 92–94, 20 A. 774. * * * The authorities are in general agreement that where a former employer communicates with a new or prospective employer about a former employee, a conditional privilege arises from a discharge of duty owed to the new or prospective employer. * * *

The circumstances here * * * were that the defamer was the vice-president of the subsidiary of the corporation which was Sindorf's former employer, and that the communicator and recipient, even though competitors, had a close personal and business relationship. Whether based on a duty owed or a common interest, we think that a qualified privilege arose. In the absence of a dispute as to the facts, the existence *vel non* of a common interest or duty giving rise to a qualified privilege is a matter of law for the court. [Cc] There was no dispute here as to such facts. We conclude that the trial court did not err in holding as a matter of law that Fridkis, and therefore Jacron, had a conditional privilege to communicate the defamatory utterance to Brose.

The second * * * question is whether Jacron lost the privilege to defame. * * *

Because a conditional or qualified privilege is conditioned upon publication in a reasonable manner and for a proper purpose, it is defeasible. * * * The Court of Appeals said in Orrison v. Vance, 262 Md. at 295, 277 A.2d at 578: * * * "In determining an abuse of privilege all relevant circumstances are admissible, [c] including the defendant's reasonable belief in the truth of his statements, [c] the excessive nature of the language used, [c] whether the disclosures were unsolicited, id., and whether the communication was made in a proper manner and only to proper parties [c]." [7]

"Malice may be a jury question." [C] It is a jury question unless only one conclusion can be drawn from the evidence. Prosser, at 796. In other words, it is only when the evidence and all inferences fairly deducible therefrom lead to conclusions from which reasonable minds could not differ, that the issue of malice is one of law for the court and not one of fact for the jury. * * *

The motion for a directed verdict was primarily based on the theory that there was no sufficient showing by Sindorf of malice within the meaning of that word as defeating a conditional privilege. It appears that the grant of the motion was substantially bottomed on that reason. We think that the grant of the motion was wrong. We believe that the evidence, when viewed as required by the rule pertain-

---

7. "Prosser said that the qualified privilege will be lost if the defendant publishes the defamation 'in the wrong state of mind.' At 794. He thought that the statement that the privilege is defeated if the publication is 'malicious' is misleading and discounted malice in this context as a 'meaningless and quite unsatisfactory term.' At 795. He concluded, at 796: 'Probably the best statement of the rule is that the defendant is required to act as a reasonable man under the circumstances, with due regard to the strength of his belief, the grounds that he has to support it, and the importance of conveying the information.' "

ing to the grant *vel non* of a directed verdict, led to conclusions from which reasonable minds could differ. We start with the rule that the publisher's motive will be more carefully scrutinized if his statements are volunteered than if they are in response to an inquiry, in which latter instance, greater latitude is permitted. We observe that Fridkis clearly indicated that Sindorf had been fired, whereas, as far as the record shows, he resigned. It does not appear that Langton told Fridkis that Sindorf was fired, and if Fridkis did not in fact know that Sindorf was not fired, stating that he was fired could be found to be a reckless disregard of truth. * * *

We observe that the publisher will be liable if he publishes his statement to accomplish a distinct objective, which may be legitimate enough in itself but is not within the privilege. [C] We think that a reasonable person could conclude from the evidence that Fridkis's communication to Brose was an effort to pressure Sindorf into returning the material he was holding, or, perhaps, simply to ascertain, as Langton requested, the date of employment of Sindorf by Tool Box. Neither would be within the privilege. The short of it is that we cannot find, assuming the truth of all credible evidence on the issue of malice and of all inferences fairly deducible therefrom, and considering them in the light most favorable to Sindorf, that they lead to the conclusions, from which reasonable minds could not differ, that Fridkis, and through him, Jacron, did not abuse the privilege to defame by excessive publication or by use of the occasion for an improper purpose, or by lack of grounds for belief in the truth of what was said. Therefore, the question of malice was properly for the jury and the trial judge erred in granting the motion for a directed verdict. The issue of malice should have gone to the jury with appropriate instructions. We reverse the judgment and remand the case for a new trial. * * *

---

1. *Protection of Publisher's Own Interests.* A person has a qualified privilege to make defamatory statements in a reasonable effort to recover goods stolen from him; to collect money due him or prevent others from collecting it; to protest against the mismanagement of a concern in which he has a financial interest; to protect his own business against unfair competition; or to defend any other legitimate interest. See, e.g., Teichner v. Bellan, 7 A.D.2d 247, 181 N.Y.S.2d 842 (1959) (response to doctor's bill that bill was unjustified); Montgomery Ward & Co. v. Watson, 55 F.2d 184 (4th Cir.1932) (employer accuses one employee, before others, of stealing from him); Gardner v. Standard Oil Co., 179 Miss. 176, 175 So. 203 (1937) (employer warns employees that plaintiff is of bad character and they are not to deal with him).

2. Included in the privilege of protecting the defendant's own interest is the protection of his reputation against defamation on the part of others. The privilege is not limited merely to publication of the statement that the plaintiff is an unmitigated liar and the truth is not in him. The defendant may go further and attack the plaintiff's motives, to explain the defamation. Mencher v. Chesley, 193 Misc. 829, 85 N.Y.S.2d 431 (1948). On the other hand, the privilege does not extend to an irrelevant matter, as, for example, a statement

that the plaintiff beats his wife. Cf. Steinberg Mfg. Co. v. Miller, DeBrul & Peters Mfg. Co., 170 Fed. 298 (8th Cir.1909).

3. *Protection of Interests of a Third Person.* The third person is usually the recipient of the communication but need not be. The privilege exists when the publisher reasonably believes that there is information that affects a sufficiently important interest of the third party and that he publishes the information under a legal duty or in accordance with "generally accepted standards of decent conduct." Restatement (Second) of Torts § 595. Thus, there is a privilege to answer the inquiry of a prospective employer of the plaintiff concerning his character or fitness for the position. Child v. Affleck, 9 B. & C. 403, 109 Eng.Rep. 150 (1839); Zeinfeld v. Hayes Freight Lines, Inc., 41 Ill.2d 345, 243 N.E.2d 217 (1969). And a bank is privileged to answer an inquiry about the plaintiff's credit from one who has been asked to sell him goods. Melcher v. Beeler, 48 Colo. 233, 110 P. 181 (1910).

4. In determining whether the privilege should be granted, weight is given to the question of whether the information was requested by the recipient or was volunteered. Thus, volunteered statements were held not privileged in such cases as Watt v. Longsden, [1930] 1 K.B. 130, and Burton v. Mattson, 50 Utah 133, 166 P. 679 (1917), involving personal gossip. But there are occasions when it is appropriate to volunteer the information. Rose v. Tholborn, 153 Mo. App. 408, 134 S.W. 1093 (1910) (landlord informed that his tenant was undesirable).

5. *Common Interest.* The existence of a common interest between the publisher and the recipient gives rise to a privilege to speak regarding the common interest. Here there is more freedom to volunteer information. See Restatement (Second) of Torts § 596. Representative cases include Bereman v. Power Pub. Co., 93 Colo. 581, 27 P.2d 749 (1933) (labor union); Hayden v. Hasbrouk, 34 R.I. 556, 84 A. 1087 (1912) (club); Slocinski v. Radivan, 83 N.H. 501, 144 A. 787 (1929) (church members); Smith Bros. & Co. v. W.C. Agee & Co., 178 Ala. 627, 59 So. 647 (1912) (common creditors). A family relationship is given similar treatment. See Restatement (Second) of Torts § 597; Kroger Co. v. Young, 210 Va. 564, 172 S.E.2d 720 (1970); Watt v. Longsdon, [1930] 1 K.B. 130.

6. Commercial credit agencies, such as Dun & Bradstreet, are sometimes denied any privilege at all. MacIntosh v. Dunn, [1908] A.C. 390; Pacific Packing Co. v. Bradstreet Co., 25 Idaho 696, 139 P. 1007 (1914). A majority of the American courts take the view that these agencies perform a legitimate function in providing a business service to those who have a proper interest in obtaining the information. Barker v. Retail Credit Co., 8 Wis.2d 664, 100 N.W.2d 391 (1960); Retail Credit Co. v. Garraway, 240 Miss. 230, 126 So.2d 271 (1961).

JACRON SALES CO., INC. v. SINDORF
Court of Appeals of Maryland, 1976.
276 Md. 580, 350 A.2d 688.

[This is the same case as the preceding one, on appeal from the Court of Special Appeals to the Court of Appeals.]

LEVINE, JUDGE. * * * We hold * * * that the rules announced in *Gertz* apply to cases of libel and slander alike brought against non-media defendants. Consequently, the principles of *Gertz* are applicable to the instant case. We must here decide, however, the standard of liability which should govern this case, recognizing that there cannot be recovery on strict liability. While holding that "so long as they do not impose liability without fault, the States may define for themselves the appropriate standard of liability," 418 U.S. at 347, the *Gertz* Court left little doubt of its assumption that most states would adopt a negligence standard. * * *

Essential to the disposition of this case is the status of the common law conditional privileges in Maryland, especially in light of *Gertz.* As we indicated earlier, the trial judge directed a verdict for Jacron on the ground that Sindorf had failed to present sufficient evidence of "actual malice" to defeat the common law privilege protecting Jacron. In reversing, the Court of Special Appeals held that "the question of malice was properly for the jury." [C]

It has been suggested that adoption of the negligence standard of fault in defamation cases would have the practical effect of rendering obsolete the common law defense of conditional privilege. [Cc] The reasoning which underlies this position is that many jurisdictions follow the rule that one of the means by which a conditional privilege may be defeated is by proving negligence on the part of the defendant. [Cc] Indeed, the first Restatement of Torts, *supra,* at § 601 expressly adopted such a rule: "Except as stated in § 602, one who upon a conditionally privileged occasion publishes false and defamatory matter of another abuses the occasion if, although believing the defamatory matter to be true, he has no reasonable grounds for so believing."

Section 601 thus embodied the common law rule that one was held to have abused a qualified privilege if he did not believe the statement to be true or if he did not have reasonable grounds to believe in its truth. *See* Restatement (Second) of Torts § 580B, Comment 1 (Tent. Draft No. 21, 1975).

If the rule stated in § 601 of the first Restatement were the law of Maryland, we might well question the efficacy of retaining a conditional privilege defeasible by the very proof of negligence which must be presented to establish falsity and defamation in the first instance. The fault required by *Gertz* to be proved to establish liability would amount to an abuse of, and thereby defeat, a conditional privilege. In Maryland, however, we have never held that negligence is among the grounds on which the conditional privilege may be forfeited.

The Maryland cases on abuse of conditional privilege are couched in terms of "express malice" or "actual malice." [Cc] The explanation in some of the earlier cases was that malice is an element of the tort of defamation, but is generally presumed in the publication of defamatory matter unless a privilege is established, in which event the presumption is rebutted and malice must be proved. [C] Malice was variously defined in the cases as a lack of good faith, ill-will, hostility, or hatred. [C] Excessive publication and unnecessarily abusive language were held to be evidence of malice. * * *

[I]n *Stevenson v. Baltimore Club,* 250 Md. 482, 243 A.2d 533 (1968), we defined malice in part as the reckless disregard of truth:

"The privilege may be lost, however, if the plaintiff in a defamation case can show malice, which in this context means not hatred or spite but rather a *reckless disregard of truth,* the use of unnecessarily abusive language, or other circumstances which would support a conclusion that the defendant acted in an ill-tempered manner or was motivated by ill-will." 250 Md. at 486–87, 243 A.2d at 536 (emphasis added). * * *

This being a higher standard than negligence, we retain the common law conditional privilege in Maryland which, in a given case, may suffice to avoid liability even though the *Gertz* standard regarding falsity and defamation is met by the plaintiff. It should be noted, however, that in a case where a common law conditional privilege is found to exist, the negligence standard of *Gertz* is logically subsumed in the higher standard for proving malice, reckless disregard as to truth or falsity, and therefore becomes irrelevant to the trial of the case. Were the plaintiff who is confronted with a conditional privilege incapable of proving the malice necessary to overcome that hurdle, it would be of no consequence that he might have met the lesser standard of negligence.

* * *

[T]he Court of Special Appeals was correct in reversing the judgment of the circuit court and in remanding the case for a new trial.

Unless a conditional privilege is found to have existed, the plaintiff shall be required at the new trial of this case to establish the liability of the defendant through proof of negligence by the preponderance of the evidence, and may recover compensation for actual injury, as defined in *Gertz* and outlined earlier, but neither presumed nor punitive damages, unless he establishes liability under the more demanding *New York Times* standard of knowing falsity or reckless disregard for the truth. Should the court determine that a common law conditional privilege existed, the question of its forfeiture vel non shall be governed by the views expressed herein.

---

1. *Knowledge, Reckless Disregard or Negligence as to Falsity.* Courts all agree that the defendant cannot claim a qualified privilege if he knows that his defamatory statement is false or does not believe it to be true. Lawless v. Miller, 99 N.J.L. 9, 123 A. 104 (1923); Russell v. Geis, 251 Cal.App.2d 560, 59 Cal.Rptr. 569 (1967).

The majority American rule at common law is that a defendant must not only believe his statement to be true but that he must have reasonable grounds for believing it to be true. Altoona Clay Products, Inc. v. Dun & Bradstreet, Inc., 367 F.2d 625 (3d Cir.1966); Ranous v. Hughes, 30 Wis.2d 452, 141 N.W.2d 251 (1966). The English rule and that of a substantial minority of American courts, however, has been, in accordance with the principal case, that he does not lose the privilege if he acted in good faith and not in reckless disregard as to the falsity of the statement. Clark v. Molyneux; 3 Q.B.D. 237 (C.A.1877);

A.B.C. Needlecraft Co. v. Dun & Bradstreet, 245 F.2d 775 (2d Cir.1957). See Hallen, Character of Belief Necessary for the Conditional Privilege in Defamation 25 Ill.L.Rev. 865 (1931).

2. New York Times v. Sullivan, supra page 895, and its progeny have influenced a number of courts to hold that "malice" exists only if there is knowledge or reckless disregard as to the truth. See, e.g., Dun & Bradstreet, Inc. v. O'Neil, 456 S.W.2d 896 (Tex.1970); Phifer v. Foe, 443 P.2d 870 (Wyo. 1968). For a plaintiff who is already subject to this standard, a conditional privilege has no significance and is not held to exist. Wright v. Haas, 586 P.2d 1093 (Okl.1978).

In addition, the holding in Gertz v. Robert Welch, Inc., supra page 906, that the Constitution requires that the defendant be at least negligent as to falsity in other defamation cases, has meant that in order to establish a prima facie case the plaintiff must prove negligence (or lack of reasonable ground to believe the statement to be true). This would mean that according to the majority common law rule, a qualified privilege is knocked out even before it is asserted. For this reason and because of the growing use of the constitutional reckless-disregard standard, the Restatement (Second) of Torts has adopted reckless-disregard as to the test for determining whether the privilege is lost. See § 600 and the Special Note preceding § 593. This position has been adopted in numerous cases. See Luster v. Retail Credit Co., 575 F.2d 609 (8th Cir.1978); British American & Eastern Co. v. Wirth Ltd., 592 F.2d 75 (2d Cir.1979); Moore v. Smith, 89 Wash.2d 932, 578 P.2d 26 (1978). What will be the consequence if Dun & Bradstreet v. Greenmoss, supra page 917, is held to apply to the fault requirement?

3. This necessarily means that "courts will find it desirable to reassess the circumstances under which it is appropriate to grant a conditional privilege. If a proper adjustment of the conflicting interests of the parties indicates that a publisher should be held liable for failure to use due care to determine the truth of the communication before publishing it, a conditional privilege is not needed and should not be held to apply." Restatement (Second) of Torts § 593, Comment c. For application of this viewpoint to a privilege for credit-rating agencies, see § 595, Comment h; cases are collected in Annot., 40 A.L.R.3d 1049 (1971).

If a plaintiff, as a public official, is already subject to the *New York Times* standard, a conditional privilege can have no significance and is not held to exist. Wright v. Haas, 586 P.2d 1093 (Okl.1978).

PECUE v. WEST
Court of Appeals of New York, 1922.
233 N.Y. 316, 135 N.E. 515.

ANDREWS, J. During 1918 George H. West was superintendent of the law and order department of the New York Civic League. It seems to have been his duty, when he received information as to vice and immorality in a community, to convey it to the authorities and ask them to look into the matter. Charles Pecue had a saloon in Granville until September 30th, when his license expired. He then moved to a small building in the same town, which had formerly been a saloon, and used it as a restaurant and poolroom. He was a married man with children, and he and his family lived in a house next door. West had not been in Granville for three or four years and seems to have had no personal knowledge of conditions there. He was not acquainted with Pecue. Late in October he received a letter from a Mrs. Collins, so far as appears, an entire stranger to him, stating that—

"A Mr. Pecue, who kept a saloon near the railroad crossing, has been and is keeping a disorderly house."

A few days later a second letter reached him from the same Mrs. Collins. Again it contained charges against Pecue:

"The following information is received. * * * Charles Pecue, Potter avenue, who kept a saloon, is keeping girls for immoral purposes. One was taken to the hospital sick and another taken into the hospital off the street."

There was this much basis for this gossip. A servant, employed in the Pecue residence, went to the hospital at her brother's request, suffering from an attack of influenza. Otherwise it was wholly false. Nevertheless, although the second letter did not even purport to be based upon what Mrs. Collins herself knew, without making the slightest investigation, without stating that he was acting on information which he had not verified or attempted to verify, speaking as of his own personal knowledge, West wrote and sent to the district attorney of Washington county a letter containing:

"Charles Pecue, Potter avenue, formerly proprietor of a saloon, has been and is keeping girls for immoral purposes. One was taken to the hospital sick and another taken to the hospital off the street. The place is in Granville, Washington county, N.Y."

This action was brought to recover damages for libel. At the close of the trial a nonsuit was granted on the ground that the communication so made was privileged and the plaintiff had failed to show the necessary malice on the part of the defendant. This result was affirmed in the Appellate Division by a divided court. * * *

In our opinion it should not be held that the rule of absolute privilege is applicable to the circumstances before us. * * * The complaint to the district attorney is not a judicial proceeding. In receiving it he has no attributes similar to a court. It is his duty to investigate where crime is or where it may have been committed. * * * Nor do we think that any rule of public policy requires a different conclusion. It may be that the words "actual malice" have a peculiar meaning in this connection. It may be * * * that, whatever the actual ill will, there can be no recovery if the complainant had reasonable ground to believe his charge was well founded. At least, as so limited, the public interest is not likely to suffer because proper complaints are checked by fear. And it is to the general advantage that the time of public officials should not be wasted in the investigation of false charges, made maliciously and without any probable ground to believe them true.

While not a case of absolute privilege, undoubtedly a qualified privilege attaches to information as to actual or suspected crime given by the citizen to a district attorney. [C] If so, one claiming to be injured must show that the reporter was actuated by malice. If no evidence be given warranting such a conclusion, the complaint should be dismissed. [C] Malice, however, does not mean alone personal ill will. It may also mean such a wanton and reckless disregard of the rights of another as is ill will's equivalent. This means more than mere negligence or want of sound judgment. [C] It means more than hasty or mistaken action. [C]

If the defendant made the statements in good faith, believing them to be true, he will be protected, even if a man of wider reasoning powers or greater skill in sifting evidence would have hesitated. Clark v. Molyneux, 3 Q.B.Div. 237. So if he fairly and in good faith relies on hearsay, [c] which often may reasonably induce action or belief. If, however, the defendant knows the statement he makes is false, we need go no further. Again rumor may be so tenuous that the trier of fact might well decide that the statement of the defendant as to his belief in it and as to his good faith is discredited. Especially so if he reports it not as a rumor but as a statement of fact for which he vouches. "Mere reckless statements, or statements based on nothing in the way of information are not protected." [C] Nor are statements made "with knowledge that they were untrue, or without caring whether they are true or false" (Clark v. Molyneux, 3 Q.B.Div. 237); or if one states "as true what he did not know to be true, recklessly, not taking the trouble to ascertain whether it was true or not and did this by reason of his objection" to certain places of amusement. [C]

Is there any evidence from which a jury might infer such malice in the case before us? We think that there is. It is true the defendant says he had never met or heard of the plaintiff and bore him no personal ill will. Doubtless this is so. But if the jury might fairly reach the conclusion that under the circumstances his action was reckless and wanton; that he made a false charge, not caring whether it was true or false; that he was guilty of more than mere negligence or bad judgment; that he did not act in good faith, or because he in fact believed the plaintiff was guilty of the charges brought against him— then the complaint should not have been dismissed. We are not dealing with a case where a citizen transmits to a district attorney for his investigation information, suspicions, rumors, gossip, for what they are worth. Malice could not be inferred from such an act, nor would it evince bad faith or recklessness. We confine our decisions to the precise facts before us—to a false charge, made as of personal knowledge, based solely upon a statement from an unknown correspondent as to information which she had received from some unknown source. Under such circumstances, "malice," as we define the word, may be inferred.

The judgment appealed from should be reversed and a new trial granted, with costs to abide the event. * * *

HISCOCK, C.J., and HOGAN and CARDOZO, JJ., concur with ANDREWS, J. POUND, J., reads dissenting opinion, in which McLAUGHLIN and CRANE, JJ., concur.

---

1.   The privilege here is a rather narrow one, of communication to those public officers or others who may reasonably be expected to take some effective action on a matter of public, rather than purely private, importance.   Thus anyone has a qualified privilege to give information to proper authorities for the prevention or detection of crime.   Foltz v. Moore–McCormack Lines, 189 F.2d 537 (2d Cir.1951).   Or to complain about the conduct of public officers or employees to their superiors, as in the case of information given to a state health department about its employees.   Nuyen v. Slater, 372 Mich. 654, 127 N.W.2d 369 (1964).   Or to a school board about a teacher.   Fuson v. Fuson, 247 Ky. 380, 57 S.W.2d 42 (1933).

2.   At common law there were two types of privileges that were unlike the others in that they did not depend upon the measure of fault on the part of the defendant regarding falsity of the defamatory communication.   A defendant might successfully rely on the privilege even though he was aware of the fact that the statement was false.   Instead the privilege was controlled by other restrictions.   These are:

A.   The *"Reporter's Privilege."*   This privilege is to report public proceedings, public records and official acts.   The restriction is that the report must be accurate and fair.   This has been treated supra, at pages 922–23.

B.   *Privilege to Provide Means of Publication.*   When the author of the defamatory utterance is in fact privileged to publish it, those who provide him with the appropriate means of publication are likewise privileged to do so. Otherwise, of course, he would have great difficulty in making his communication.   Thus if the author is privileged to publish his statement in a newspaper, the newspaper itself can be no less privileged;   and the same is true of a stenographer taking dictation.   See Israel v. Portland News Pub. Co., 152 Or. 225, 53 P.2d 529 (1936);   Western Union Tel. Co. v. Lesesne, 182 F.2d 135 (4th Cir.1950);   Restatement (Second) of Torts § 612;   Smith, Liability of a Telegraph Company for Transmitting a Defamatory Message, 20 Colum.L.Rev. 30 (1920).

C.   *Fair Comment.*   This special type of privilege enabled the publisher to offer criticism on matters of public concern.   This included criticism of the conduct of persons who were public officials or public figures, and criticism of scientific, artistic, literary and dramatic productions and of exhibitions or entertainments presented for public approval.   According to the majority rule, the privilege applied only to an expression of opinion and not to a misstatement of fact.   The privilege might be abused and lost if the criticism did not represent the actual opinion of the critic, if it was made solely for the purpose of causing harm to the person criticized or, sometimes, if it was not one that a person of reasonable intelligence and judgment might make.   See generally the Restatement of Torts §§ 606–610 (1938).

Some courts and writers took the position that fair comment was not actually a privilege at all, but, being merely an expression of opinion and not a false statement of fact, it did not constitute defamation.   There was much to be said for this position, although it would logically have applied to all comments or expressions of opinion, not just those on matters of public concern.   As indicated earlier, it now seems to be a rule of constitutional law that there can be no recovery in defamation for a "mere" expression of opinion that does not include an implied misrepresentation of fact. See Janklow y. Newsweek, supra page 866, Restatement (Second) of Torts § 566. The result of this is that the common law "privilege" of fair comment has probably lost its significance. For this reason, no detailed treatment has been given to it.

6. REMEDIES

(1) Damages. As with most other torts the prime remedy for defamation is damages. For libel and for slander per se, it was presumed at common law that there were "general damages," and the jury were permitted to estimate the harm to plaintiff's reputation that they thought the defamation had caused, without the need of evidence to support the conclusion. This meant that there was little control by the court over the amount that the jury assessed. As a result of the holding in Gertz v. Robert Welch, Inc., supra page 906, damages were confined to "compensation for actual injury." But see Dun & Bradstreet v. Greenmoss, supra page 917.

To the extent that damages cover pecuniary, or out-of-pocket loss, an award of money damages is entirely appropriate, as it purports to make the plaintiff whole. These are the special damages that must be proved in the case of slander, if it is not actionable per se. The Supreme Court has explained, however, that "actual injury," may include "impairment of reputation and standing in the community, personal humiliation, and mental anguish and suffering," so long as there is adequate proof of these matters. This gives the court some control over the action of the jury and it remains to be seen whether the Supreme Court will take further steps to prevent the award of very large verdicts against news media in a manner that makes them a figurative sand bag. Significantly, most of the cases that the Court has entertained have involved large sums of money that can constitute a heavy burden on the news media.

There is something anomalous in attempting to convert general impairment of standing in the community, personal humiliation and mental anguish into a money award. What kind of conversion standard can there be? Would a better approach be to limit recovery to pecuniary loss but include within this concept the plaintiff's litigation expenses, including reasonable attorney's fees? This would utilize a much more objective standard and would pay the out-of-pocket costs to the plaintiff in vindicating his name. It might also have the effect of discouraging efforts to make the prosecution of the suit so expensive as to force the plaintiff to discontinue it.

Mitigation of Damages. Provocation by the plaintiff is generally regarded as admissible for the purpose of mitigating punitive damages. Palmer v. Makin, 120 Fed. 737 (8th Cir.1903). Under a minority holding, it may also be considered in mitigation of compensatory damages. Craney v. Donovan, 92 Conn. 239, 102 A. 640 (1917); Conroy v. Fall River Herald News Co., 306 Mass. 488, 28 N.E.2d 729 (1940).

Evidence that the plaintiff's reputation is bad is also admissible in mitigation. Even rumors are admissible if they are shown to be sufficiently widespread to affect his general reputation. Bleckerstaff v. Perrin, 27 Ind. 527 (1867); Stuart v. News Pub. Co., 67 N.J.L. 317, 51 A. 709 (1902). A report not so widespread as to affect the plaintiff's reputation is not admissible, however. Utah State Farm Bureau Fed. v. National Farmers Union Service Corp., 198 F.2d 20 (10th Cir.1952). And some courts have held that a person's reputation may be so bad that he is "libel-proof". See, e.g., Cardillo v. Doubleday & Co., 518 F.2d 638 (2d Cir.1975); Guccione v. Hustler Mag., Inc., 800 F.2d 298 (2d Cir. 1986); Note, The Libel–Proof Plaintiff, 98 Harv.L.Rev. 1909 (1985).

Punitive Damages. Punitive damages were freely awarded at common law, if "malice" in the literal sense of that term were shown. Gertz v. Robert Welch, Inc., supra page 906, has placed some limitations on this. It seems clear that in the absence of "malice" in the constitutional sense—i.e., knowledge or reckless disregard as to falsity—they cannot be awarded. The Court did not expressly hold whether they can be awarded then, but it seems later to have assumed that they can. Herbert v. Lando, 441 U.S. 153, 162 n. 7 (1979). See, awarding punitive damages, Davis v. Schuchat, 510 F.2d 731 (D.C.Cir.1975); Maheu v. Hughes Tool Co., 569 F.2d 459 (9th Cir.1978); Buckley v. Littell, 539 F.2d 882 (2d Cir.1976), cert. denied, 429 U.S. 1062 (1977); Newspaper Pub. Corp. v. Burke, 216 Va. 800, 224 S.E.2d 132 (1976). See generally Note, Punitive Damages and Libel Law, 98 Harv.L.Rev. 847 (1985) Committee Report, Punitive Damages in Libel Actions, 42 Record A.B.City N.Y. 20 (1987).

If they are permitted, limitations may be imposed, such as that they bear a reasonable relationship in amount to the compensatory, or that they not be awarded when the amount of compensatory damages is sufficiently large as adequately to serve the purpose of exemplary damages.

Nominal damages. Gertz v. Robert Welch held that a plaintiff cannot recover unless he proves "actual injury." If he proves that the statement is both defamatory and false, but does not prove actual injury, can he recover nominal damages? The Supreme Court has not ruled, nor does it indicate whether he can bring the initial action for the purpose of recovering only nominal damages and thus vindicating his name. It would seem, however, that the latter action ought to be allowed, and even favored. See discussion in Hearst Corp. v. Hughes, 297 Md. 112, 466 A.2d 486 (1983).

(2) Declaratory Relief. The action brought solely for nominal damages, referred to immediately above, essentially seeks declaratory relief. Its purpose is to obtain a judicial determination that the statement about the plaintiff is false, and thus to vindicate his reputation—to make him whole, as far as the law can. Declaratory-judgment proceedings, if available, may accomplish the same purpose. See Franklin, Good News and Bad Law: A Critique of Libel Law and a

Proposal, 18 U.S.F.L.Rev. 1 (1983); Note, The Defamed Reputation: Will Declaratory Judgment Bill Provide Vindication?, 13 J.Legis. 72 (1986). See also the description of the Arkansas "lie bill," found in Leflar, Legal Remedies for Defamation, 6 Ark.L.Rev. 423 (1952).

In a declaratory proceeding of this sort, should all of the requirements of an action for compensatory damage be imposed? If the plaintiff is not seeking to recover damages, but only a ruling that the statement was false, should he have to show that defendant was at fault regarding its falsity? Do privileges serve a useful purpose here? Would it be feasible to have the trial judge pose two separate questions to the jury—(1) was the statement false, and (2) was the defendant at fault regarding its falsity?

There were a number of trial innovations used in the famous Westmoreland and Sharon trials. One of special interest here was the use of "tripartite verdicts" in *Sharon*. Judge Sofaer instructed the jury to render separate special verdicts on whether the communication was defamatory, whether it was false, and whether the defendant was motivated by "actual malice." The verdicts were returned on separate days. Helpful uses of this technique should be easily apparent. For exposition, see Libel on Trial: The Westmoreland and Sharon Cases 8, 41–42 (BNA Special Report, 1986). For an interesting report of the two trials, see Adler, Annals of Law: Two Trials, The New Yorker 42 (June 6, 1986) and 34 (June 23, 1986).

(3) Self-help. "The first remedy of any victim of defamation is self-help—using available opportunities to contradict the lie or correct the error and thereby to minimize its adverse impact or reputation." Gertz v. Robert Welch, Inc., 418 U.S. 323, 344 (1974). Thus, the defamed party may make a response to the defamatory statement about him—provided he can find a suitable medium for making the response. In making response, the defamed person is given a conditional privilege. He is not liable to the original defamer unless he abuses the privilege by making irrelevant charges, or charges of his own in reckless disregard of their truth or falsity. Phifer v. Foe, 443 P.2d 870 (Wyo.1968). See also Annot., 41 A.L.R.3d 1083 (1972).

Right-of-Response Statutes. Several states have passed statutes requiring a public communications medium to give a right of response to a person who claims that he has been defamed by it. A Florida statute to this effect was held unconstitutional in Miami Herald Pub. Co. v. Tornillo, 418 U.S. 241 (1974). While the particular statute was overly broad and did not limit the requirement to cases in which there was a claim of actual defamation, the holding seems broad enough to cover a more limited statute. What about a statute requiring a newspaper to publish a news item of a defamation judgment obtained against it? See generally Danzinger, The Right of Reply in the United States and Europe, 19 N.Y.U.J.Int.L. & Pol. 171 (1986).

The person claiming to have been defamed may also go to the person publishing the defamation, explain that there has been a mistake and request a correction or a retraction. This frequently works. On the effect of refusal to retract after notice of falsity as evidence of "malice," see Morgan v. Dun & Bradstreet, Inc., 421 F.2d 1241 (5th Cir. 1970).

Retraction Statutes. There are retraction statutes in many of the states. They vary considerably in their provisions, as to the types of defamation covered, the requirement of notice, the types of plaintiffs and defendants covered, and the effect of compliance. They are collected and analyzed in 1 A. Hanson, Libel and Related Torts, ch. 15 (1969). Some may be outdated as a result of constitutional developments, as in applying only to "innocent misrepresentation," or in limiting recovery to "actual damages."

A retraction, to be effective, must be unequivocal and not partial or hesitant and hypothetical, as, for example, "We do not know whether our defamatory statement was true, but if it was not, we are sorry we published it." Cf. Monaghan v. Globe Newspaper Co., 190 Mass. 394, 77 N.E. 476 (1906); Goolsby v. Forum Printing Co., 23 N.D. 30, 135 N.W. 161 (1913). A statement that the plaintiff does not have the manners of a hog is obviously not retracted by saying he has the manners of a hog.

To the effect that the *Tornillo* case on right-of-reply statutes does not indicate the unconstitutionality of retraction statutes, see Brennan, J., concurring, in Miami Herald Pub. Co. v. Tornillo, 418 U.S. 241, 258 (1974). See generally Morris, Inadvertent Newspaper Libel and Retraction, 32 Ill.L.Rev. 36 (1937); Note, 80 Harv.L.Rev. 1730 (1967).

(4) Injunctive Relief. Ever since the decision in Near v. Minnesota, 283 U.S. 697 (1931), it has been recognized that prior restraint of a publication runs afoul of the First Amendment. (On the *Near* case, see the thorough study in F. Friendly, Minnesota Rag (1981)). Nevertheless, it remains possible that injunctive relief might become a suitable supplement to other relief when it has been formally determined in court that a statement is both defamatory and false, and the defendant persists in continuing to publish it. An injunction, carefully worded so as not to be too broad, might be both appropriate and constitutional.

See in general R. Bezanson et al., Libel Law and the Press: Myth and Reality (1987); LeBel, Reforming the Tort of Defamation: An Accommodation of the Competing Interests Within the Current Constitutional Framework, 66 Neb.L.Rev. 249 (1987); Gannett Center for Media Studies, The Cost of Libel: Economic and Policy Implications (1986).

Chapter XVIII

PRIVACY

The recognition and development of the "right of privacy" is perhaps the outstanding illustration of the influence of legal journals upon the courts. Prior to 1890, no English or American court had ever granted relief expressly based upon the invasion of this right, although there were cases that seem in retrospect to have been groping in that direction, and Judge Cooley had coined the phrase "the right to be let alone." See, e.g., DeMay v. Roberts, supra, page 101; Hardin v. Harshfield, 12 S.W. 779 (Ky.1890) (loss of marriage engagement caused by defendant's spreading a true tale of plaintiff's embarrassing combination of expelling *flatus* in a public place and her *lapsus lingua*—treated as slander).

In 1890 there appeared in 4 Harvard Law Review 193 a noted article, "The Right to Privacy," written by Samuel D. Warren and Louis D. Brandeis, which reviewed a number of older cases in which relief had been afforded on the basis of defamation, or breach of confidence or of an implied contract, in the publication of letters, portraits and the like. The article concluded that these cases were in reality founded upon a broader principle entitled to separate recognition. This principle it stated to be the right of a private individual to be let alone and protected from unauthorized publicity in his essentially private affairs.

One of the first states to consider the doctrine advanced by Warren and Brandeis was New York. After two lower courts apparently had accepted the article and recognized the right of privacy, it fell into the unfriendly hands of the Court of Appeals in Roberson v. Rochester Folding Box Co., 171 N.Y. 538, 64 N.E. 442 (1902), where the defendant had made an unauthorized use of the picture of an attractive young lady to advertise its flour. The court proceeded to reject the entire doctrine, denying the existence of any "right of privacy" at common law, and expressing a fear of a "vast amount of litigation" that would involve not only pictures, but "a comment upon one's looks, conduct, domestic relations or habits." It said that any such change in the law must be left for the legislature to make.

The immediate result of this decision was a lively public disapproval, leading to the enactment in 1903 of a statute, now New York Civil Rights Law §§ 50–51. This statute prohibits the use of the name, portrait or picture of any living person without his prior written consent for "advertising purposes" or for "purposes of trade." Similar statutes have been adopted in Virginia, Oklahoma, and Utah.

Three years later the same question was presented in Pavesich v. New England Life Ins. Co., 122 Ga. 190, 50 S.E. 68 (1905), when the defendant's insurance advertising made use of plaintiff's name and picture, together with a spurious testimonial from him. The court rejected the *Roberson* case, accepted the views of Warren and Brandeis, and recognized the existence of a distinct right of privacy. This became the leading case. For a time authority was divided; but in the 1930's the tide set in strongly in favor of recognition.

At the present time, the right of privacy is clearly recognized, in one form or another, in all but two or three states. It is limited by statute to commercial uses of the plaintiff's name or likeness in four states.

This has been a fertile field for legal writing. See, among other articles, Larremore, The Law of Privacy, 12 Colum.L.Rev. 693 (1912); Green, The Right of Privacy Today, 27 Ill.L.Rev. 237 (1932); Nizer, The Right of Privacy, 39 Mich.L.Rev. 526 (1941).

Prosser, Privacy, 48 Calif.L.Rev. 383 (1960); Kalven, Privacy in Tort Law—Were Warren and Brandeis Wrong? 31 Law & Cont.Prob. 326 (1966); Wade, Defamation and the Right of Privacy, 15 Vand.L.Rev. 1093 (1962); Bloustein, Privacy as an Aspect of Human Dignity: An Answer to Dean Prosser, 39 N.Y.U.L.Rev. 962 (1964); Shapo, Media Injuries to Personality: An Essay on Legal Regulation of Public Communication, 46 Texas L.Rev. 650 (1968); Bloustein, First Amendment and Privacy, 28 Rutgers L.Rev. 41 (1974).

Gavison, Privacy and The Limits of Law, 89 Yale L.J. 421 (1980); Zimmerman, Requiem for a Heavyweight: A Farewell to Warren and Brandeis's Privacy Tort, 68 Cornell L.Rev. 291 (1983); Emerson, Right of Privacy and Freedom of the Press, 14 Harv.C.R. & C.L.L.Rev. 329 (1979); Symposium, Toward a Resolution of the Expanding Conflict Between the Press and Privacy Interests, 64 Iowa L.Rev. 1061–1283 (1979); Symposium, Law and Economics of Privacy, 9 J.Leg.Stud. 221 (1980).

FLAKE v. GREENSBORO NEWS CO.
Supreme Court of North Carolina, 1938.
212 N.C. 780, 195 S.E. 55.

Action by Nancy Flake, by her next friend, Mrs. W.F. Flake, against the Greensboro News Company and others for damages allegedly sustained as the result of a publication of the plaintiff's photograph or likeness in connection with an advertisement which appeared in a newspaper. From an adverse judgment, the defendants appeal.

Folies de Paree was a vaudeville or stage show and advertised its performance through a system of "tie up" advertising. Under this system, some merchant and the local theatre join in the advertisement and it advertises both the product or the merchandise of the merchant and the theatre performance. Pursuant to this plan, the agent of the "Folies de Paree" solicited the defendant L. Melts, who conducted a bakery in Greensboro under the name of "Melts Bakery" and the defendant North Carolina Theatres, Inc., to join in such an advertisement and as a result a two-column advertisement was published in the Greensboro Daily News, issue of March 11, 1936. In the right portion of the advertisement there was a cut from the plaintiff's photograph showing her standing and wearing a bathing suit. To the left was the following wording, so arranged as to make four distinct statements, as follows:

"Keep that Sylph–Like Figure by eating more of Melts' Rye and Whole Wheat Bread, says Mlle. Sally Payne, exotic red haired Venus—

" 'Folies de Paree' sparkling Parisian Revue, Stage Production, National Theatre two days only, March 11 and 12.

" 'Melts' Rye and Whole Wheat Bread will give you the necessary energy, pep and vitality without adding extra weight,' says Miss Payne. Melts Bakery, 314 N. Elm St., 1829 Spring Garden St.

" 'Ask for Melts' Bread—Melts in Your Mouth.' "

In publishing this advertisement, the photograph or mat made therefrom was used without the consent of the plaintiff and was used by mistake—the defendants intending to use a cut of Sally Payne, the leading lady of Folies de Paree.

The mistake having been called to the attention of the defendant Greensboro News Company, it immediately published a full explanation of the mistake and an apology.

BARNHILL, JUSTICE. ＊ ＊ ＊ The defendants were entitled to a judgment of nonsuit on the cause of action for alleged libel.

Plaintiff's second cause of action is based upon the right of privacy, so termed. It is clear that the first issue when considered in connection with the charge of the court was submitted upon the theory of this cause of action. ＊ ＊ ＊

The question of the existence of this right is a relatively new field in legal jurisprudence. In respect to it the courts are plowing new ground and before the field is fully developed unquestionably perplexing and harassing stumps and runners will be encountered.

In determining to what extent a newspaper may publish the features of an individual under any given circumstances necessarily involves a consideration of the constitutional right of free speech and of a free press. People do not live in seclusion. When a person goes upon the street or highway or into any other public place, he exhibits his features to public inspection. Is a newspaper violating any right of the individual, or doing more than exercising the right of a free press, when it publishes a correct image of such features? Must a distinction be drawn between those in private life and those in public office or public life, and if so, when does a person cease to be a private citizen and become a public character? If a newspaper may publish the features of an individual in connection with an article that is laudatory, does it not also possess the right to publish the same in connection with an article that is critical in its nature so long as it speaks the truth? If the people are entitled to know what their Governor, or their President, or other public servant, is doing and saying, is it reasonable to hold that they are not entitled as a matter of course to ascertain and know through the newspapers his physical features and appearance? These and many other questions which may hereafter arise, in connection with this type of litigation, are not now before us for decision.

So far as we have been able to ascertain, no court has yet held that it constitutes a tort for a newspaper to publish an image of an individual when such publication is not libelous, except when such publication involves the breach of a trust, the violation of a contract, or when the photograph is used in connection with some commercial enterprise, and we are presently called upon to decide only the right of an individual to prohibit the unauthorized use of an image of her features and figure in connection with and as a part of an advertisement. * * *

The subject is * * * dealt with at length in Pavesich v. New England Life Insurance Co., 122 Ga. 190, 50 S.E. 68, 78. All former decisions are likewise fully discussed in this opinion, in which the court holds that the unauthorized publication of plaintiff's photograph in connection with an advertising enterprise gives rise to a cause of action. In the opinion Cobb, J., quoting at length and with approval from the dissenting opinion of Gray, J., in Roberson v. Rochester Folding–Box Co., 171 N.Y. 538, 64 N.E. 442, said in part: "Instantaneous photography is a modern invention, and affords the means of securing a portraiture of an individual's face and form in invitum [of] their owner. While, so far as it merely does that, although a species of aggression, I conceded it to be an irremediable and irrepressible feature of the social evolution. But if it is to be permitted that the portraiture may be put to commercial or other uses for gain, by the publication of prints therefrom, then an act of invasion of the individual's privacy results, possibly more formidable and more painful in its consequences than an actual bodily assault might be. Security of person is as necessary as the security of property, and for that complete personal security which will result in the peaceful and wholesome enjoyment of one's privileges as a member of society there should be afforded protection, not only against the scandalous portraiture and display of one's features and person, but against the display and use thereof for another's commercial purposes or gain. The proposition is to me an inconceivable one that these defendants may unauthorizedly use the likeness of this young woman upon their advertisement as a method of attracting widespread public attention to their wares, and that she must submit to the mortifying notoriety, without right to invoke the exercise of the preventive power of a court of equity. * * *

"It would be, in my opinion, an extraordinary view, which while conceding the right of a person to be protected against the unauthorized circulation of an unpublished lecture, letter, drawing, or other ideal property, yet would deny the same protection to a person whose portrait was unauthorizedly obtained and made use of for commercial purposes. * * * Whether, as incidental to that equitable relief, she should be able to recover only nominal damages, is not material, for the issuance of the injunction does not, in such a case, depend upon the amount of the damages, in dollars and cents."

We are of the opinion that the reasoning in the Pavesich Case, supra, is sound and establishes the correctness of the conclusion that the unauthorized use of one's photograph in connection with an advertisement or other commercial enterprise gives rise to a cause of action which would entitle the plaintiff, without the allegation and proof of special damages, to a judgment for nominal damages, and to injunctive relief, if and when the wrong is persisted in by the offending parties.

One of the accepted and popular methods of advertising in the present day is to procure and publish the endorsement of the article being advertised by some well-known person whose name supposedly will lend force to the advertisement. If it be conceded that the name of a person is a valuable asset in connection with an advertising enterprise, then it must likewise be conceded that his face or features are likewise of value. Neither can be used for such a purpose without the consent of the owner without giving rise to a cause of action.

We conclude therefore, that there was error in the judgment below and that the motion of the defendants for a judgment of nonsuit should have been sustained as to the plaintiff's cause of action sounding in libel, and that there should be a new trial on the cause of action alleging the unauthorized use of plaintiff's features and person in connection with said advertisement. Upon the present record, from which it appears that said photograph was used by mistake and without malice and that the defendants immediately desisted from the use thereof upon the discovery of the mistake and made due apology therefor, the plaintiff would be entitled to a judgment for nominal damages only. As the defendants have not and did not persist in the wrong complained of, the right to injunctive relief is not here involved.

New trial.

------

1. This was the first type of invasion of privacy to be recognized by the courts. Statutes in some states are limited to commercial appropriations of name or likeness. Other courts, not restricted by statute, have allowed recovery for appropriations of the plaintiff's name for non-commercial purposes. Hinish v. Meier & Frank Co., 166 Or. 482, 113 P.2d 438 (1941) (plaintiff's name signed to telegram to governor urging him to veto a bill); State ex rel. La Follette v. Hinkle, 131 Wash. 86, 229 P. 317 (1924) (use of name as candidate for office by political party); Hamilton v. Lumbermen's Mutual Cas. Co., 82 So.2d 61 (La.App.1955), (advertising in name of plaintiff for witnesses to an accident); Vanderbilt v. Mitchell, 72 N.J.Eq. 910, 67 A. 97 (1907) (providing father for child on birth certificate).

2. Most of the cases have involved advertising, or pictures accompanying an article sold; but other forms of commercial appropriation have resulted in liability. Edison v. Edison Polyform Mfg. Co., 73 N.J.Eq. 136, 67 A. 392 (1907) (use of name in title of corporation); Goodyear Tire & Rubber Co. v. Vandergriff, 52 Ga.App. 662, 184 S.E. 452 (1936) (impersonation to obtain secret

information); Binns v. Vitagraph Co. of America, 147 App.Div. 782, 132 N.Y.S. 237 (1911), aff'd, 210 N.Y. 51, 103 N.E. 1108 (1913) (motion picture based on incident in life of plaintiff, in which an actor represented him). What result if defendant sells plaintiff's name to mail advertisers? See Shibley v. Time, Inc., 45 Ohio App.2d 69, 341 N.E.2d 337 (1975).

3. It is the value of plaintiff's name that must be appropriated, rather than the name itself. Thus there is no liability for the mere use of the same name as that of the plaintiff. Swacker v. Wright, 154 Misc. 822, 277 N.Y.S. 296 (1935) (novel); Nebb v. Bell Syndicate, 41 F.Supp. 929 (S.D.N.Y.1941) (comic strip).

4. *Right of Publicity.* There has been a good deal of dispute as to whether the right here recognized is to be regarded as a right of "property." If it is not, it appears to be the same thing by another name. Thus it has been held that an exclusive licensee for the use of the name has what has been called a "right of publicity," which entitles him to enjoin its use by a third person. Haelan Laboratories v. Topps Chewing Gum, 202 F.2d 866 (2d Cir.1953). See Nimmer, The Right of Publicity, 19 L. & Cont.Prob. 202 (1954); Notes, 62 Yale L.J. 1123 (1953), 41 Geo.L.J. 583 (1953).

5. The major difference in the two theories lies in determining whether the right survives the death of the person whose image is commercially exploited. The cases are sharply divided, and the distinctions seems to lie on whether the publicity theory or the privacy theory is adopted. See Lugosi v. Universal Pictures, 25 Cal.3d 813, 603 P.2d 425, 160 Cal.Rptr. 323 (1979); Memphis Development Foundation v. Factors, Inc., 616 F.2d 956 (6th Cir.1980); Factors Etc., Inc., v. Pro Arts, Inc., 652 F.2d 278 (2d Cir.1981); Carson v. Here's Johnny Portable Toilets, Inc., 698 F.2d 831 (6th Cir.1983); cf. Martin Luther King, Jr., Center for Social Change, Inc. v. American Heritage Prod., Inc., 694 F.2d 674 (11th Cir.1983) (possessor of name need not have exploited it before death).

A recent case has combined the two theories by holding that the "law should protect both the proprietary and emotional interest." Plaintiffs had been in a serious automobile accident, disrupting their lives. Defendants provided insurance coverage and made payments to plaintiffs. They used the episode with the plaintiffs as a basis for soliciting others to purchase the coverage. Plaintiffs were allowed to recover for the benefit to defendants and their emotional distress. Candebat v. Flanagan, 487 So.2d 207 (Miss.1986).

6. *Constitutional Law.* In Zacchini v. Scripps–Howard Broadcasting Co., 433 U.S. 562 (1977), plaintiff was an entertainer commercially performing a "human cannonball act" in which he was shot from a cannon into a net 200 feet away, the performance taking some 15 seconds. Defendant broadcasting station, though requested not to do so, took a film of the act and showed it on the evening news broadcast. Plaintiff's suit for damages was held not maintainable by the Supreme Court of Ohio because of the station's privilege to report in its newscasts matters of legitimate public interest, relying on New York Times Co. v. Sullivan, supra page 895; and Time, Inc. v. Hill, 385 U.S. 374 (1967), infra page 971. The Supreme Court reversed.

Speaking for the majority, Justice White said: "The differences between [false-light privacy and appropriation privacy] are important. First, the State's interests in providing a cause of action in each instance are different. 'The interest protected' in permitting recovery for placing the plaintiff in a false light 'is clearly that of reputation, with the same overtones of mental distress as in defamation.' [C] By contrast, the State's interest in permitting a 'right of publicity' is in protecting the proprietary interest of the individual in his act in part to encourage such entertainment. As we later note, the State's interest is closely analogous to the goals of patent and copyright law, focusing on the right of the individual to reap the reward of his endeavors and having little to do with protecting feelings or reputation. Second, the two torts differ in the degree to which they intrude on dissemination of information to the public. In 'false light' cases the only way to protect the interests involved is to attempt to minimize publication of the damaging matter, while in 'right of publicity' cases the only question is who gets to do the publishing. An entertainer such as petitioner usually has no objection to the widespread publication of his act as long as he gets the commercial benefit of such publication. Indeed, in the present case petitioner did not seek to enjoin the broadcast of his act; he simply sought compensation for the broadcast in the form of damages. * * *

"Wherever the line in particular situations is to be drawn between media reports that are protected and those that are not, we are quite sure that the First and Fourteenth Amendments do not immunize the media when they broadcast a performer's entire act without his consent. The Constitution no more prevents a State from requiring respondent to compensate petitioner for broadcasting his act on television than it would privilege respondent to film and broadcast a copyrighted dramatic work without liability to the copyright owner [cc], or to film and broadcast a prize fight [c], or a baseball game [c], where the promoters or the participants had other plans for publicizing the event. There are ample reasons for reaching this conclusion."

Speaking for the dissenters, Justice Powell said: "In my view the First Amendment commands a different analytical starting point from the one selected by the Court. Rather than begin with a quantitative analysis of the performer's behavior—is this or is this not his entire act?—we should direct initial attention to the actions of the news media: what use did the station make of the film footage? When a film is used, as here, for a routine portion of a regular news program, I would hold that the First Amendment protects the station from a 'right of publicity' or 'appropriation' suit, absent a strong showing by the plaintiff that the news broadcast was a subterfuge or cover for private or commercial exploitation."

6. See, generally, Halpern, The Right of Publicity: Commercial Exploitation of the Associative Value of Personality, 39 Vand.L.Rev. 1199 (1986); Ausness, The Right of Publicity: A "Haystack in a Hurricane," 55 Temp.L.Q. 977 (1982); Gordon, Right of Property in Name, Likeness, Personality and History, 55 Nw.U.L.Rev. 553 (1961); Treece, Commercial Exploitation of Names, Likenesses and Personal Histories, 51 Tex.L.Rev. 637 (1973); Felcher & Rubin, Privacy, Publicity and the Portrayal of Real People by the Media, 88 Yale L.J. 1577 (1979); Felcher & Rubin, Descendibility of the Right of Publicity: Is There Commercial Life After Death? 89 Yale L.J. 1125 (1980); Note, An Assessment of the Commercial Exploitation Requirement As a Limit on the Right of Publicity, 96 Harv.L.Rev. 1203 (1983).

PEARSON v. DODD

United States Court of Appeals, District of Columbia Circuit, 1969.
410 F.2d 701, cert. denied 395 U.S. 947, 89 S.Ct. 2021, 23 L.Ed.2d 465 (1969).

J. SKELLY WRIGHT, CIRCUIT JUDGE. This case arises out of the exposure of the alleged misdeeds of Senator Thomas Dodd of Connecticut by newspaper columnists Drew Pearson and Jack Anderson. The District Court has granted partial summary judgment to Senator Dodd, appellee here finding liability on a theory of conversion. At the same time, the court denied partial summary judgment on the theory of invasion of privacy. Both branches of the court's judgment are before us on interlocutory appeal. We affirm the District Court's denial of summary judgment for invasion of privacy and reverse its grant of summary judgment for conversion.

The undisputed facts in the case were stated by the District Court as follows:

" * * * [O]n several occasions in June and July, 1965, two former employees of the plaintiff, at times with the assistance of two members of the plaintiff's staff, entered the plaintiff's office without authority and unbeknownst to him, removed numerous documents from his files, made copies of them, replaced the originals, and turned over the copies to the defendant Anderson, who was aware of the manner in which the copies had been obtained. The defendants Pearson and Anderson thereafter published articles containing information gleaned from these documents."

I. The District Court ruled that appellants' six newspaper columns concerning appellee, which were attached to appellee's complaint, did not establish liability for the tort of invasion of privacy. That tort, whose historical origin lies in the famous Warren and Brandeis article of 1890, is recognized in the District of Columbia. It has always been considered a defense to a claim of invasion of privacy by publication, however, that the published matter complained of is of general public interest. The columns complained of here gave appellants' version of appellee's relationship with certain lobbyists for foreign interests, and gave an interpretive biographical sketch of appellee's public career. They thus clearly bore on appellee's qualifications as a United States Senator, and as such amounted to a paradigm example of published speech not subject to suit for invasion of privacy.

Indeed, appellee has not urged with any vigor on appeal the theory that appellants' publications in themselves tortiously invaded his privacy. Rather he has argued that the District Court misapprehended his privacy claim, which went rather to the manner in which the information in the columns was obtained than to the matter contained in them.

Appellee proceeds under a branch of privacy theory which Dean Prosser has labeled "intrusion," and which has been increasingly recognized by courts and commentators in recent years. Thus it has been held that unauthorized bugging of a dwelling, tapping a telephone, snooping through windows, and overzealous shadowing amount to invasions of privacy, whether or not accompanied by trespasses to property.

Unlike other types of invasion of privacy, intrusion does not involve as one of its essential elements the publication of the information obtained. The tort is completed with the obtaining of the information by improperly intrusive means. * * *

We approve the extension of the tort of invasion of privacy to instances of intrusion, whether by physical trespass or not, into spheres from which an ordinary man in a plaintiff's position could reasonably expect that the particular defendant should be excluded. Just as the Fourth Amendment has expanded to protect citizens from government intrusions where intrusion is not reasonably expected, so should tort law protect citizens from other citizens. The protection should not turn exclusively on the question of whether the intrusion involves a technical trespass under the law of property. The common law, like the Fourth Amendment, should "protect people, not places."

The question then becomes whether appellants Pearson and Anderson improperly intruded into the protected sphere of privacy of appellee Dodd in obtaining the information on which their columns were based. In determining this question, we may assume, without deciding, that appellee's employees and former employees did commit such an improper intrusion when they removed confidential files with the intent to show them to unauthorized outsiders.[19]

Although appellee's complaint charges that appellants aided and abetted in the removal of the documents, the undisputed facts, narrowed by the District Judge with the concurrence of counsel, established only that appellants received copies of the documents knowing that they had been removed without authorization. If we were to hold appellants liable for invasion of privacy on these facts, we would establish the proposition that one who receives information from an intruder, knowing it has been obtained by improper intrusion, is guilty of a tort. In an untried and developing area of tort law, we are not prepared to go so far. A person approached by an eavesdropper with an offer to share in the information gathered through the eavesdropping would perhaps play the nobler part should he spurn the offer and shut his ears. However, it seems to us that at this point it would place too great a strain on human weakness to hold one liable in damages who merely succumbs to temptation and listens.

Of course, appellants did more than receive and peruse the copies of the documents taken from appellee's files; they published excerpts from them in the national press. But in analyzing a claimed breach of privacy, injuries from intrusion and injuries from publication should be kept clearly separate. Where there is intrusion, the intruder should generally be liable whatever the content of what he learns. An

---

19. Appellants have argued that appellee's employees and former employees committed neither conversion nor trespass nor invasion of privacy, because their actions are privileged by a public policy in favor of exposing wrongdoing. See Restatement (Second) of Agency § 395, Comment f (1958):

"An agent is privileged to reveal information confidentially acquired by him in the course of his agency in the protection of a superior interest of himself or of a third person. Thus, if the confidential information is to the effect that the principal is committing or is about to commit a crime, the agent is under no duty not to reveal it. * * *"

And compare Code of Ethics for Government Service, House Doc. No. 103, 86th Cong., 1st Sess. (1958): "Any person in government service should: * * * (IX) expose corruption wherever discovered."

eavesdropper to the marital bedroom may hear marital intimacies, or he may hear statements of fact or opinion of legitimate interest to the public; for purposes of liability that should make no difference. On the other hand, where the claim is that private information concerning plaintiff has been published, the question of whether that information is genuinely private or is of public interest should not turn on the manner in which it has been obtained. Of course, both forms of invasion may be combined in the same case.

Here we have separately considered the nature of appellants' publications concerning appellee, and have found that the matter published was of obvious public interest. The publication was not itself an invasion of privacy. Since we have also concluded that appellants' role in obtaining the information did not make them liable to appellee for intrusion, their subsequent publication, itself no invasion of privacy, cannot reach back to render that role tortious.

[The court treated the question of whether the defendants were liable for conversion of the plaintiff's files and concluded that they were not. See page 80 supra.]

Because no conversion of the physical contents of appellee's files took place, and because the information copied from the documents in those files has not been shown to be property subject to protection by suit for conversion, the District Court's ruling that appellants are guilty of conversion must be reversed.

TAMM, CIRCUIT JUDGE (concurring). Some legal scholars will see in the majority opinion—as distinguished from its actual holding—an ironic aspect. Conduct for which a law enforcement officer would be soundly castigated is, by the phraseology of the majority opinion, found tolerable; conduct which, if engaged in by government agents would lead to the suppression of evidence obtained by these means, is approved when used for the profit of the press. There is an anomaly lurking in this situation: the news media regard themselves as quasi-public institutions yet they demand immunity from the restraints which they vigorously demand be placed on government. That which is regarded as a mortal taint on information secured by any illegal conduct of government would appear from the majority opinion to be permissible as a technique or modus operandi for the journalist. Some will find this confusing, but I am not free to act on my own views under the doctrine of stare decisis which I consider binding upon me. * * *

---

1. There is a good treatment of a similar problem in Dietemann v. Time, Inc., 449 F.2d 245 (9th Cir.1971). Reporters for Life Magazine, doing a story on "Crackdown on Quackery," called on plaintiff under a ruse, were invited into his den and took secret pictures and recordings. Some of the materials were used in the story after his arrest. It was held that an action would lie for invasion of privacy, and that the publicity could be considered in assessing damages. See Lee, Privacy Intrusions While Gathering News: An Accommoda-

tion of Competing Interests, 64 Iowa L.Rev. 1243 (1979); Wade, The Tort Liability of Investigative Reporters, 37 Vand.L.Rev. 301, 319 (1984).

2. Physical intrusion upon seclusion or solitude has been recognized as a distinct form of invasion of privacy. Byfield v. Candler, 33 Ga. 275, 125 S.E. 905 (1924) (woman's stateroom on a steamboat); Welsh v. Pritchard, 125 Mont. 517, 241 P.2d 816 (1952) (landlord moving in on tenant); Sutherland v. Kroger Co., 144 W.Va. 673, 110 S.E.2d 716 (1959) (search of woman's shopping bag in store); K–Mart Corp. Store No. 7441 v. Trotti, 677 S.W.2d 632 (Tex.App.1984) (search of employee's locker).

3. As to eavesdropping, see Rhodes v. Graham, 238 Ky. 225, 37 S.W.2d 46 (1931) (wire tapping); Roach v. Harper, 143 W.Va. 869, 105 S.E.2d 564 (1958) (microphone); Hamberger v. Eastman, 106 N.H. 107, 206 A.2d 239 (1964) (landlord "bugs" tenant's bedroom). Suppose a telephone user customarily records his telephone conversations without informing the other parties? Cf. Marks v. Bell Tel. Co., 460 Pa. 73, 331 A.2d 424 (1975).

On "telephone harassment," repeated telephone calls at unreasonable hours, see Donnel v. Lara, 703 S.W.2d 257 (Tex.App.1985); cf. Ruple v. Brooks, 352 N.W.2d 652 (S.D.1984) (obscene phone calls may create liability for intentional infliction of emotional distress). And see Nader v. General Motors Corp., 25 N.Y.2d 560, 255 N.E.2d 765, 307 N.Y.S.2d 647 (1970), involving a general campaign of harassment.

4. The same principle is also applied to other forms of intrusion upon seclusion, or into private affairs. Zimmerman v. Wilson, 81 F.2d 247 (3d Cir. 1936) (unauthorized prying into private bank account); Frey v. Dixon, 141 N.J. Eq. 481, 58 A.2d 86 (1948) (invalid order requiring production of books and documents); Bednarik v. Bednarik, 18 N.J.Misc. 633, 16 A.2d 80 (1940) (illegal compulsory blood test); Vernars v. Young, 539 F.2d 966 (7th Cir.1976) (opening and reading personal mail). Cf. Galella v. Onassis, 487 F.2d 986 (2d Cir.1973) (continued surveillance and persistent harassment by taking photographs). The *Galella* case also discusses the use of injunctive relief. On this, see Note, 39 Mo.L.Rev. 647 (1974).

5. Attempting to prove that plaintiff was engaged in a homosexual liaison with her divorced husband, defendant arranged to have specimens of plaintiff's hair surreptitiously taken by a hospital orderly from his hair brush and a bandaid that had been on his arm. Actionable? Froelich v. Adair, 213 Kan. 357, 516 P.2d 993 (1973), second appeal, 219 Kan. 461, 548 P.2d 482 (1976).

6. In Souder v. Pendleton Detectives, 88 So.2d 716 (La.App.1956), relying in part upon a statute, private detectives were held liable for spying into plaintiff's windows. Cf. Alabama Electric Co-op. Inc. v. Partridge, 284 Ala. 442, 225 So.2d 848 (1969) (use of high-powered binoculars and motion picture camera). See also Note, Crimination of Peeping Toms and Other Men of Vision, 5 Ark.L.Rev. 388 (1951).

7. In Harms v. Miami Daily News, 127 So.2d 715 (Fla.1961), defendant published in its column: "If you want to hear a sexy telephone voice, call _____ and ask for Louise." Plaintiff was deluged with embarrassing telephone calls. What result? Cf. Jeppson v. United Television, Inc., 580 P.2d 1087 (Utah 1980) (dialing on television plaintiff's telephone number and name, resulting in numerous calls by viewers); House v. Peth, 165 Ohio St. 35, 133 N.E.2d 340 (1956) (creditor hounding debtor with calls); Munley v. ISC Financial Home, 584 P.2d 1336 (Okl.1978).

8.   On credit investigations and the like, see Notes, 57 Geo.L.J. 509 (1969), 17 Vand.L.Rev. 1342 (1964) (personal injury claimant); Tureen v. Equifax, Inc., 571 F.2d 411 (8th Cir.1978).

9.   There is ordinarily no liability for taking the plaintiff's photograph in a public place. Gill v. Hearst Pub. Co., 40 Cal.2d 224, 253 P.2d 441 (1953) (Farmers' Market in Los Angeles); Berg v. Minneapolis Star & Tribune Co., 79 F.Supp. 957 (D.Minn.1948) (courtroom); Nelson v. Maine Times, 373 A.2d 1221 (Me.1977) (picture of small Indian child). But in Daily Times–Democrat Co. v. Graham, 276 Ala. 380, 162 So.2d 474 (1964), where the plaintiff was photographed in a "Fun House" with her dress blown up over her head, it was held to be an invasion of privacy.

10.   This branch of the law of privacy is treated in Ezer, Intrusion on Solitude, 21 Law in Transition 63 (1961); and Note, The Emerging Tort of Intrusion, 55 Iowa L.Rev. 718 (1970).

COX BROADCASTING CORP. v. COHN

Supreme Court of the United States, 1975.
420 U.S. 469, 95 S.Ct. 1029, 43 L.Ed.2d 328.

MR. JUSTICE WHITE delivered the opinion of the Court.

The issue before us in this case is whether consistently with the First and Fourteenth Amendments a State may extend a cause of action for damages for invasion of privacy caused by the publication of the name of a deceased rape victim which was publicly revealed in connection with the prosecution of the crime. * * *

On August 1971, appellee's 17–year–old daughter was the victim of a rape and did not survive the incident. Six youths were soon indicted for murder and rape. Although there was substantial press coverage of the crime and of subsequent developments, the identity of the victim was not disclosed pending trial perhaps because of Ga.Code Ann. § 26–9901 which makes it a misdemeanor to publish or broadcast the name or identity of a rape victim. In April 1972, some eight months later, the six defendants appeared in court. Five pled guilty to rape or attempted rape, the charge of murder having been dropped. The guilty pleas were accepted by the court, and the trial of the defendant pleading not guilty was set for a later date.

In the course of the proceedings that day, appellant Wassell, a reporter covering the incident for his employer, learned the name of the victim from an examination of the indictments which were made available for his inspection in the courtroom. That the name of the victim appears in the indictments and that the indictments were public records available for inspection are not disputed. Later that day, Wassell broadcast over the facilities of station WSB–TV, a television station owned by appellant Cox Broadcasting Corporation, a news report concerning the court proceedings. The report named the victim of the crime and was repeated the following day.

In May 1972, appellee brought an action for money damages against appellants, relying on § 26–9901 and claiming that his right to privacy had been invaded by the television broadcasts giving the name of his deceased daughter. Appellants admitted the broadcasts but claimed that they were privileged under both state law and the First and Fourteenth Amendments. The trial court rejecting appellants' constitutional claims and holding that the Georgia statute gave a civil remedy to those injured by its violation, granted summary judgment to appellee as to liability, with the determination of damages to await trial by jury.

On appeal, the Georgia Supreme Court, in its initial opinion, held that the trial court had erred in construing § 26–9901 to extend a civil cause of action for invasion of privacy and thus found it unnecessary to consider the constitutionality of the statute. 231 Ga. 60, 200 S.E.2d 127 (1973). The court went on to rule, however, that the complaint stated a cause of action "for the invasion of appellee's right of privacy, or for the tort of public disclosure"—a "common law tort exist[ing] in this jurisdiction without the help of the statute that the trial judge in this case relied on." [C] Although the privacy invaded was not that of the deceased victim, the father was held to have stated a claim for invasion of his own privacy by reason of the publication of his daughter's name. The court explained, however, that liability did not follow as a matter of law and that summary judgment was improper; whether the public disclosure of the name actually invaded appellee's "zone of privacy," and if so, to what extent, were issues to be determined by the trier of fact. Also, "in formulating such an issue for determination by the fact-finder, it is reasonable to require the appellee to prove that the appellants invaded his privacy with wilful or negligent disregard for the fact that reasonable men would find the invasion highly offensive." [C] The Georgia Supreme Court did agree with the trial court, however, that the First and Fourteenth Amendments did not, as a matter of law, require judgment for appellants. The court concurred with the statement in Briscoe v. Reader's Digest Association, Inc., 4 Cal.3d 529, 541, 93 Cal.Rptr. 866, 874, 483 P.2d 34, 42 (1971), that "the rights guaranteed by the First Amendment do not require total abrogation of the right to privacy. The goals sought by each may be achieved with a minimum of intrusion upon the other."

Upon motion for rehearing the Georgia court countered the argument that the victim's name was a matter of public interest and could be published with impunity by relying on § 26–9901 as an authoritative declaration of state policy that the name of a rape victim was not a matter of public concern. This time the court felt compelled to determine the constitutionality of the statute and sustained it as a "legitimate limitation on the right of freedom of expression contained in the First Amendment." The court could discern "no public interest or general concern about the identity of the victim of such a crime as will make the right to disclose the identity of the victim rise to the level of First Amendment protection." * * *

We conclude that the Court has jurisdiction and reverse the judgment of the Georgia Supreme Court. * * *

Georgia stoutly defends both § 26–9901 and the State's common law privacy action challenged here. Her claims are not without force, for powerful arguments can be made, and have been made, that however it may be ultimately defined, there is a zone of privacy surrounding every individual, a zone within which the State may protect him from intrusion by the press, with all its attendant publicity. * * *

More compellingly, the century has experienced a strong tide running in favor of the so-called right of privacy. * * *

The version of the privacy tort now before us—termed in Georgia "the tort of public disclosure," [c]—is that in which the plaintiff claims the right to be free from unwanted publicity about his private affairs, which, although wholly true, would be offensive to a person of ordinary sensibilities. Because the gravamen of the claimed injury is the publication of information, whether true or not, the dissemination of which is embarrassing or otherwise painful to an individual, it is here that claims of privacy most directly confront the constitutional freedoms of speech and press. The face-off is apparent, and the appellants urge upon us the broad holding that the press may not be made criminally or civilly liable for publishing information that is neither false nor misleading but absolutely accurate, however damaging it may be to reputation or individual sensibilities.

It is true that in defamation actions, where the protected interest is personal reputation, the prevailing view is that truth is a defense; and the message of New York Times v. Sullivan, 376 U.S. 254 (1964); Garrison v. Louisiana, 379 U.S. 64 (1964); Curtis Publishing Co. v. Butts, 388 U.S. 130 (1967), and like cases is that the defense of truth is constitutionally required where the subject of the publication is a public official or public figure. What is more, the defamed public official or public figure must prove not only that the publication is false but that it was knowingly so or was circulated with reckless disregard for its truth or falsity. Similarly, where the interest at issue is privacy rather than reputation and the right claimed is to be free from the publication of false or misleading information about one's affairs, the target of the publication must prove knowing or reckless falsehood where the materials published, although assertedly private, are "matters of public interest." Time, Inc. v. Hill, 385 U.S., at 387–388.[19]

The Court has nevertheless carefully left open the question whether the First and Fourteenth Amendments require that truth be recog-

---

19. In another "false light" invasion of privacy case before us this Term, Cantrell v. Forest City Publishing Co., 419 U.S. 245, 250–251 (1974), we observed that we had, in that case, "no occasion to consider whether a State may constitutionally apply a more relaxed standard of liability for a publisher or broadcaster of false statements injurious to a private individual under a false-light theory of invasion of privacy, or whether the constitutional standard announced in Time, Inc. v. Hill applies to all false-light cases. Cf. Gertz v. Robert Welch, Inc., 418 U.S. 323."

nized as a defense in a defamation action brought by a private person as distinguished from a public official or public figure. Garrison held that where criticism is of a public official and his conduct of public business, "the interest in private reputation is overborne by the larger public interest, secured by the Constitution, in the dissemination of truth," [c] but recognized that "different interests may be involved where purely private libels, totally unrelated to public affairs, are concerned; therefore, nothing we say today is to be taken as intimating any views as to the impact of the constitutional guarantees in the discrete area of purely private libels." [C] In similar fashion, Time v. Hill, supra, expressly saved the question whether truthful publication of very private matters unrelated to public affairs could be constitutionally proscribed. [C]

Those precedents, as well as other considerations, counsel similar caution here. In this sphere of collision between claims of privacy and those of the free press, the interests on both sides are plainly rooted in the traditions and significant concerns of our society. Rather than address the broader question whether truthful publications may ever be subjected to civil or criminal liability consistently with the First and Fourteenth Amendments, or to put it another way, whether the State may ever define and protect an area of privacy free from unwanted publicity in the press, it is appropriate to focus on the narrower interface between press and privacy that this case presents, namely, whether the State may impose sanctions on the accurate publication of the name of a rape victim obtained from public records—more specifically, from judicial records which are maintained in connection with a public prosecution and which themselves are open to public inspection. We are convinced that the State may not do so.

In the first place, in a society in which each individual has but limited time and resources with which to observe at first hand the operations of his government, he relies necessarily upon the press to bring to him in convenient form the facts of those operations. Great responsibility is accordingly placed upon the news media to report fully and accurately the proceedings of government, and official records and documents open to the public are the basic data of governmental operations. Without the information provided by the press most of us and many of our representatives would be unable to vote intelligently or to register opinions on the administration of government generally. With respect to judicial proceedings in particular, the function of the press serves to guarantee the fairness of trials and to bring to bear the beneficial effects of public scrutiny upon the administration of justice.

Appellee has claimed in this litigation that the efforts of the press have infringed his right to privacy by broadcasting to the world the fact that his daughter was a rape victim. The commission of crime, prosecutions resulting from it, and judicial proceedings arising from the prosecutions, however, are without question events of legitimate concern to the public and consequently fall within the responsibility of the press to report the operations of government. * * *

The Restatement of Torts, § 867, embraced an action for privacy. Tentative Draft No. 13 of the Restatement (Second) of Torts, §§ 652A–652E, divides the privacy tort into four branches; and with respect to the wrong of giving unwanted publicity about private life, the commentary to § 652D states that "[t]here is no liability when the defendant merely gives further publicity to information about the plaintiff which is already public. Thus there is no liability for giving publicity to facts about the plaintiff's life which are matters of public record * * *" The same is true of the separate tort of physically or otherwise intruding upon the seclusion or private affairs of another. Section 652B, Comment c, provides that "there is no liability for examination of a public record concerning the plaintiff, or of documents which the plaintiff is required to keep and make available for public inspection." According to this draft, ascertaining and publishing the contents of public records are simply not within the reach of these kinds of privacy actions.

Thus even the prevailing law of invasion of privacy generally recognizes that the interests in privacy fade when the information involved already appears on the public record. The conclusion is compelling when viewed in terms of the First and Fourteenth Amendments and in light of the public interest in a vigorous press. * * *

By placing the information in the public domain on official court records, the State must be presumed to have concluded that the public interest was thereby being served. Public records by their very nature are of interest to those concerned with the administration of government, and a public benefit is performed by the reporting of the true contents of the records by the media. The freedom of the press to publish that information appears to us to be of critical importance to our type of government in which the citizenry is the final judge of the proper conduct of public business. In preserving that form of government the First and Fourteenth Amendments command nothing less than that the States may not impose sanctions for the publication of truthful information contained in official court records open to public inspection. * * *

Appellant Wassell based his televised report upon notes taken during the court proceedings and obtained the name of the victim from the indictments handed to him at his request during a recess in the hearing. Appellee has not contended that the name was obtained in an improper fashion or that it was not on an official court document open to public inspection. Under these circumstances, the protection of freedom of the press provided by the First and Fourteenth Amendments bars the State of Georgia from making appellants' broadcast the basis of civil liability.

Reversed.

CHIEF JUSTICE BURGER concurs in the judgment.

———

1. This is the third form of the tort of unreasonable invasion of the right of privacy. As expressed in Restatement (Second) of Torts § 652D, it applies to the giving of "publicity to a matter concerning the private life of another" which is "highly offensive to a reasonable person and is not of legitimate concern to the public."

Two important questions exist in regard to it: (1) the nature of its characteristics as they have developed at common law, and (2) the extent of the restrictions that the First Amendment to the Constitution imposes upon it.

2. *Common Law.* The cases seem to suggest that disclosure of an embarrassing private fact to only one or just a few persons does not amount to an invasion of privacy. Thus there is no invasion of privacy when defendant merely calls the plaintiff's employer and asks his help in collecting a debt from the plaintiff. Household Finance Corp. v. Bridge, 252 Md. 531, 250 A.2d 878 (1969); Timperley v. Chase Collection Service, 272 Cal.App.2d 697, 77 Cal.Rptr. 782 (1969); see Note, 36 Brooklyn L.Rev. 95 (1969). Contra: Pack v. Wise, 155 So.2d 909 (La.App.1963), writ refused, 245 La. 84, 157 So.2d 231 (1963). These cases might well be explained, however, on the basis that defendant's disclosure was privileged as a legitimate means of collecting the debt. Cf. Restatement (Second) of Torts § 652G. Suppose defendant discovers that plaintiff was an illegitimate child, and he whispers this to a few neighbors, who spread the "information?"

3. There may be other bases of liability. In Peterson v. Idaho First Nat. Bank, 83 Idaho 578, 367 P.2d 284 (1961), the private disclosure of plaintiff's finances by a bank was held not to be an invasion of privacy, but a tort action was held to lie for breach of the confidential relation. Cf. Copley v. Northwestern Mut. Life Ins. Co., 295 F.Supp. 93 (S.D.W.Va.1968) (disclosure to plaintiff's competitors of information supplied to defendant insurance company to qualify for insurance); Horne v. Patton, 291 Ala. 701, 287 So.2d 824 (1973) (doctor reveals confidential information regarding his patient to the latter's employer); Doe v. Roe, 93 Misc.2d 201, 400 N.Y.S.2d 668 (1977) (psychiatrist publishes book containing verbatim account of patient's thoughts, feelings and fantasies; plaintiff not named but identifiable); Note, Breach of Confidence: An Emerging Tort, 82 Colum.L.Rep. 1426 (1982).

In Humphers v. First Interstate Bank of Oregon, 298 Or. 706, 696 P.2d 527 (1985), plaintiff had a child out of wedlock and agreed to its being anonymously placed for adoption. The child, now grown, desired to find her natural mother and came to the doctor who delivered her seeking his help. By a subterfuge, he gave her a letter enabling her to obtain release of the sealed information. She found the plaintiff, her mother, who was married, with other children, and was very displeased with the development. She sued the doctor (actually his estate, since he had died) for invasion of privacy and disclosing confidential information. In a thorough opinion, the court held that there could be no recovery on the privacy action, but that the action for disclosure of confidential information could lie.

4. One who intentionally seeks publicity, or puts himself in the public eye, as in the case of an actor, a professional baseball player, an explorer or an inventor, is often held to become a "public figure," and to have no right to complain of a publicity that reasonably bears upon his public activity. Cohen v. Marx, 94 Cal.App.2d 704, 211 P.2d 320 (1950) (prize fighter); Koussevitzky v. Allen, Towne & Heath, 188 Misc. 479, 68 N.Y.S.2d 779 (1947), aff'd, 272 App.

Div. 759, 69 N.Y.S.2d 432 (1947) (symphony conductor); Martin v. Dorton, 210 Miss. 668, 50 So.2d 391 (1951) (sheriff).

Beyond this it frequently is held that those who unwillingly attract public attention, through association with crime or other interesting events, become reluctant public figures for a time. Thus Jones v. Herald Post Co., 230 Ky. 227, 18 S.W.2d 972 (1929) (plaintiff's husband murdered before her eyes); Berg v. Minneapolis Star & Tribune Co., 79 F.Supp. 957 (D.Minn.1948) (plaintiff engaged in divorce litigation); Stryker v. Republic Pictures Corp., 108 Cal.App.2d 191, 238 P.2d 670 (1951) (war hero); Elmhurst v. Pearson, 153 F.2d 467 (D.C.Cir. 1946) (defendant in sedition trial).

In Jacova v. Southern Radio & Television Co., 83 So.2d 34 (Fla.1955), defendant broadcast over television, by prior arrangement with the police, a gambling raid on a cigar store. Plaintiff, who had come into the store to buy a cigar, was caught in the raid and mistaken for the owner. The television broadcast showed him being questioned by two officers. He was held to have no cause of action.

In Anderson v. Fisher Broadcasting Co., 300 Or. 452, 712 P.2d 803 (1986), defendant Fisher took pictures of an automobile accident showing a recognizable plaintiff "bleeding and in pain while receiving emergency medical treatment." It did not use the tape on its news program, however, but later "used a brief excerpt showing plaintiff to illustrate promotional spots advertising a special news report about a new system for dispatching emergency medical help." Plaintiff contends that there were two violations of the right of privacy: (1) publicity given to pictures of the plaintiff that were not of legitimate public concern, and (2) appropriating the picture to its own use and commercial advantage as advertising. The court held that he could not recover on either basis, alone or the combination of the two. Judge Linde's opinion contains a penetrating analysis of the right of privacy.

5. Under the common law, there has normally been no liability for the disclosure of facts that are a matter of public record, since they are already public. Meetze v. Associated Press, 230 S.C. 330, 95 S.E.2d 606 (1956) (dates of birth and marriage); Stryker v. Republic Pictures Corp., 108 Cal.App.2d 191, 238 P.2d 670 (1951) (military service record); Bell v. Courier–Journal & Louisville Times Co., 402 S.W.2d 84 (Ky.1966) (tax delinquency); cf. Rome Sentinel Co. v. Boustedt, 43 Misc.2d 598, 252 N.Y.S.2d 10 (1964) (death certificate).

6. Defendant, an exasperated creditor, put up a placard in the show window of his garage, on the public street, stating that "Dr. W.R. Morgan owes an account here of $49.67. This account will be advertised as long as it remains unpaid." What result? Brents v. Morgan, 221 Ky. 765, 299 S.W. 967 (1927). Cf. Hamilton v. Crown Life Ins. Co., 246 Or. 1, 423 P.2d 771 (1967).

Compare Banks v. King Features Syndicate, 30 F.Supp. 352 (S.D.N.Y.1939) (newspaper publication of X-rays of woman's pelvic region); Feeney v. Young, 191 App.Div. 501, 181 N.Y.S. 481 (1920) (public exhibition of films of caesarean operation); Griffin v. Medical Society, 7 Misc.2d 549, 11 N.Y.S.2d 109 (1939) (publication in medical journal of pictures of plaintiff's deformed nose); Hawkins v. Metromedia, Inc., 288 S.C. 569, 344 S.E.2d 145 (1986) (plaintiff identified as teenage father of illegitimate child in news item).

7. On the requirement that the publicity be highly offensive to a person of ordinary sensitivities, see Bitsie v. Walston, 85 N.M. 655, 515 P.2d 659 (1973). "Traditional beliefs" of the Navajo Indians were held not to be sufficient if they were not known to defendant newspaper.

8. *Constitutional Law.* The principal case obviously establishes as rules of constitutional law many—if not all—of the common law restrictions on this form of invasion of the right of privacy. The question of whether this form of the tort invasion of the right of privacy, which involves public disclosure of true facts, can constitutionally exist at all still remains open and will not be settled until there is a clear indication by the Supreme Court. Prior to the instant case (but subsequent to Time, Inc. v. Hill), the strongest argument that the tort was not totally foreclosed by the First Amendment was found in the opinion of the California Supreme Court in Briscoe v. Reader's Digest Ass'n, Inc., 4 Cal.3d 529, 483 P.2d 34, 93 Cal.Rptr. 866 (1971). Since the principal case, there has been a careful consideration of the question, reaching the same conclusion, in Virgil v. Time, Inc., 527 F.2d 1122 (9 Cir.1975), cert. denied, 425 U.S. 998.

9. In the principal case, suppose the name, Jane Doe, had been substituted for the rape victim's true name in the indictment and in the trial itself. Could the Georgia statute then be constitutionally applied? On similar statutes in general, see Franklin, A Constitutional Problem in Privacy Protection, 16 Stan. L.Rev. 107 (1963).

In Landmark Communications, Inc. v. Virginia, 435 U.S. 829 (1978), the Virginia Judicial Inquiry and Review Commission was conducting an inquiry regarding disability or misconduct of a state judge, and the accused newspaper published an accurate story about the inquiry and identified the judge involved. This was in violation of a Virginia statute requiring that the proceedings be kept confidential, and the newspaper was prosecuted under the statute, found guilty and fined $500. The conviction was affirmed by the Supreme Court of Virginia but reversed by the Supreme Court of the United States on the ground that "the Commonwealth's interests advanced by the imposition of criminal sanctions are insufficient to justify the actual and potential encroachments of freedom of speech and of the press which follow therefrom." Id. at 838.

In Nicholson v. McClatchy Newspapers, 177 Cal.App.3d 509, 223 Cal.Rptr. 58 (1986), in accordance with statute, the Governor submitted the name of plaintiff to a committee of the State Bar for evaluation and rating as a potential appointee for judicial position. Though the statute required that the information be kept confidential, the media defendants accurately reported that the bar commission found the plaintiff not qualified. The court affirmed the lower court's sustaining of a demurrer to the complaint. Citing *Cox Publishing Company* and *Landmark*, it found the publication to be privileged and said that the allegation of a conspiracy on the part of the media defendants added nothing to the complaint. It indicated that obtaining the information by "routine reporting techniques," such as "asking persons questions, including those with confidential or restricted information," is not actionable; but obtaining the information through criminal or tortious means may be actionable.

10. The classic case for recovery for this aspect of the tort has been Melvin v. Reid, 112 Cal.App. 285, 297 P. 91 (1931). Gabrielle Darley, a prostitute, had been tried for murder and acquitted in a famous case. She subsequently married, left the state and "thereafter at all times lived an exemplary, virtuous, honorable and righteous life." Defendant produced and released a movie entitled "The Red Kimono" based on plaintiff's experiences, using her true maiden name and advertising the film as a true account. Can the holding now be justified under the *Cox* case? Suppose the defendant had publicized the married name of the plaintiff? The marriage record was probably a public record, too. Would it make any difference if the defendant

had identified the plaintiff further by disclosing her residence at the time of the movie?

11. Should lapse of time make any difference regarding either the happening of a public occurrence or the contents of a public record? Compare, in this connection, the interesting case of Sidis v. F–H Pub. Corp., 113 F.2d 806 (2 Cir.1940), involving a story in *The New Yorker* about a former child prodigy who in adulthood had sought obscurity. See also Street v. National Broadcasting Co., 645 F.2d 1227 (6th Cir.1981), involving a television historical drama of the famous Scottsboro cases of the early 1930's; plaintiff, the prosecuting witness in the prosecution for rape, was held to be still a public figure for purposes of discussion of the case and therefore unable to recover. Though the Supreme Court granted certiorari, it later dismissed the case when the parties reached a settlement. And see Montesano v. Donrey Media Group, 99 Nev. 644, 668 P.2d 1081 (1983) (newspaper picked up story of criminal conviction 20 years ago when plaintiff was only 14; no liability despite statute forbidding disclosure of conviction of minor).

12. A family supplied certain information to federal authorities to aid them in crime fighting. To prevent criminal revenge, they were given new names and identities under the federal witness protection program. Defendant discloses the information. Is this actionable? See Capra v. Thoroughbred Racing Ass'n of N.A., Inc., 787 F.2d 463 (9th Cir.1986).

CANTRELL v. FOREST CITY PUBLISHING CO.
Supreme Court of the United States, 1974.
419 U.S. 245, 95 S.Ct. 465, 42 L.Ed.2d 419.

MR. JUSTICE STEWART delivered the opinion of the Court.

Margaret Cantrell and four of her minor children brought this diversity action in a federal district court for invasion of privacy against the Forest City Publishing Company, publisher of a Cleveland newspaper, The Plain Dealer, and against Joseph Eszterhas, a reporter formerly employed by The Plain Dealer, and Richard Conway, a Plain Dealer photographer. The Cantrells alleged that an article published in The Plain Dealer Sunday Magazine unreasonably placed their family in a false light before the public through its many inaccuracies and untruths. The District Judge struck the claims relating to punitive damages as to all the plaintiffs and dismissed the actions of three of the Cantrell children in their entirety, but allowed the case to go to the jury as to Mrs. Cantrell and her oldest son, William. The jury returned a verdict against all three of the respondents for compensatory money damages in favor of these two plaintiffs.

The Court of Appeals for the Sixth Circuit reversed, holding that, in the light of the First and Fourteenth Amendments, the District Judge should have granted the respondents' motion for a directed verdict as to all the Cantrells. Cantrell v. Forest City Publishing Co., 484 F.2d 150. We granted certiorari, 418 U.S. 909.

I. In December 1967, Margaret Cantrell's husband Melvin was killed along with 43 other people when the Silver Bridge across the Ohio River at Point Pleasant, West Virginia, collapsed. The respondent Eszterhas was assigned by The Plain Dealer to cover the story of the disaster. He wrote a "news feature" story focusing on the funeral of Melvin Cantrell and the impact of his death on the Cantrell family.

Five months later, after conferring with the Sunday Magazine editor of The Plain Dealer, Eszterhas and photographer Conway returned to the Point Pleasant area to write a follow-up feature. The two men went to the Cantrell residence, where Eszterhas talked with the children and Conway took 50 pictures. Mrs. Cantrell was not at home at any time during the 60 to 90 minutes that the men were at the Cantrell residence.

Eszterhas's story appeared as the lead feature in the August 4, 1968, edition of The Plain Dealer Sunday Magazine. The article stressed the family's abject poverty; the children's old, ill-fitting clothes and the deteriorating condition of their home were detailed in both the text and accompanying photographs. As he had done in his original, prize-winning article on the Silver Bridge disaster, Eszterhas used the Cantrell family to illustrate the impact of the bridge collapse on the lives of the people in the Point Pleasant area.

It is conceded that the story contained a number of inaccuracies and false statements. Most conspicuously, although Mrs. Cantrell was not present at any time during the reporter's visit to her home, Eszterhas wrote, "Margaret Cantrell will talk neither about what happened nor about how they are doing. She wears the same mask of non-expression she wore at the funeral. She is a proud woman. She says that after it happened, the people in town offered to help them out with money and they refused to take it." Other significant misrepresentations were contained in details of Eszterhas' descriptions of the poverty in which the Cantrells were living and the dirty and dilapidated conditions of the Cantrell home.

The case went to the jury on a so-called "false light" theory of invasion of privacy. In essence, the theory of the case was that by publishing the false feature story about the Cantrells and thereby making them the objects of pity and ridicule, the respondents damaged Mrs. Cantrell and her son William by causing them to suffer outrage, mental distress, shame, and humiliation.

II. In Time, Inc. v. Hill, 385 U.S. 374, the Court considered a similar false light, invasion of privacy action. The New York Court of Appeals had interpreted New York Civil Rights Law, McKinney's Consol.Laws, c. 6, §§ 50–51 to give a "newsworthy person" a right of action when his or her name, picture or portrait was the subject of a "fictitious" report or article. Material and substantial falsification was the test for recovery. [C] Under this doctrine the New York courts awarded the plaintiff James Hill compensatory damages based on his complaint that Life Magazine had falsely reported that a new Broadway play portrayed the Hill family's experience in being held hostage by three escaped convicts. This Court, guided by its decision in New York Times Co. v. Sullivan, 376 U.S. 254, which recognized constitutional limits on a State's power to award damages for libel in actions brought by public officials, held that the constitutional protections for speech and press precluded the application of the New York statute to allow recovery for "false reports of matters of public interest in the absence of proof that the defendant published the report with knowledge of its falsity or in reckless disregard of the truth." [C] Although the jury could have reasonably concluded from the evidence in the *Hill* case that Life had engaged in knowing falsehood or had recklessly disregarded the truth in stating in the article that "the story re-enacted" the Hill family's experience, the Court concluded that the trial judge's instructions had not confined the jury to such a finding as a predicate for liability as required by the Constitution. [C]

The District Judge in the case before us, in contrast with the trial judge in Time, Inc. v. Hill, did instruct the jury that liability could be imposed only if it concluded that the false statements in the Sunday Magazine feature article on the Cantrells had been made with knowledge of their falsity or in reckless disregard of the truth. No objection was made by any of the parties to this knowing-or-reckless-falsehood instruction. Consequently, this case presents no occasion to consider whether a State may constitutionally apply a more relaxed standard of liability for a publisher or broadcaster of false statements injurious to a private individual under a false-light theory of invasion of privacy, or whether the constitutional standard announced in Time, Inc. v. Hill applies to all false-light cases. Cf. Gertz v. Welch, Inc., 418 U.S. 323. Rather, the sole question that we need decide is whether the Court of Appeals erred in setting aside the jury's verdict.

III. At the close of the petitioners' case-in-chief, the District Judge struck the demand for punitive damages. He found that Mrs. Cantrell had failed to present any evidence to support the charges that the invasion of privacy "was done maliciously within the legal definition of that term." The Court of Appeals interpreted this finding to be a determination by the District Judge that there was no evidence of knowing falsity or reckless disregard of the truth introduced at the trial. Having made such a determination, the Court of Appeals held that the District Judge should have granted the motion for a directed verdict as to all respondents. 484 F.2d, at 155.

The Court of Appeals appears to have assumed that the District Judge's finding of no malice "within the legal definition of that term" was a finding based on the definition of "actual malice" established by this Court in New York Times Co. v. Sullivan, 376 U.S. 254, 280: "with knowledge that [a defamatory statement] was false or with reckless disregard of whether it was false or not." As so defined, of course, "actual malice" is a term of art, created to provide a convenient shorthand for the standard of liability that must be established before a State may constitutionally permit public officials to recover for libel in actions brought against publishers. As such, it is quite different from the common-law standard of "malice" generally required under state tort law to support an award of punitive damages. In a false-light case, common-law malice—frequently expressed in terms of either personal ill will toward the plaintiff or reckless or wanton disregard of the plaintiff's rights—would focus on the defendant's attitude toward the plaintiff's privacy, not towards the truth or falsity of the material published. See Time, Inc. v. Hill, 385 U.S., at 396 n. 12. See generally W. Prosser, Law of Torts 9–10 (4th ed.).

Although the verbal record of the District Court proceedings is not entirely unambiguous, the conclusion is inescapable that the District Judge was referring to the common-law standard of malice rather than to the *New York Times* "actual malice" standard when he dismissed the punitive damages claims. For at the same time that he dismissed the demands for punitive damages, the District Judge refused to grant the respondents' motion for directed verdicts as to Mrs. Cantrell's and William's claims for compensatory damages. And, as his instructions to the jury made clear, the District Judge was fully aware that the Time, Inc. v. Hill meaning of the *New York Times* "actual malice" standard had to be satisfied for the Cantrells to recover actual damages. Thus, the only way to harmonize these two virtually simultaneous rulings by the District Judge is to conclude, contrary to the decision of the Court of Appeals, that in dismissing the punitive damages claims he was not determining that Mrs. Cantrell had failed to introduce any evidence of knowing falsity or reckless disregard of the truth. This conclusion is further fortified by the District Judge's subsequent denial of the respondents' motion for judgment N.O.V. and alternative motion for a new trial.

Moreover, the District Judge was clearly correct in believing that the evidence introduced at trial was sufficient to support a jury finding that the respondents Joseph Eszterhas and Forest City Publishing Company had published knowing or reckless falsehoods about the Cantrells. There was no dispute during the trial that Eszterhas, who did not testify, must have known that a number of the statements in the feature story were untrue. In particular, his article plainly implied that Mrs. Cantrell had been present during his visit to her home and that Eszterhas had observed her "wear[ing] the same mask of nonexpression she wore [at her husband's] funeral." These were "calculated falsehoods," and the jury was plainly justified in finding that Eszterhas had portrayed the Cantrells in a false light through knowing or reckless untruth.

The Court of Appeals concluded that there was no evidence that Forest City Publishing Company had knowledge of any of the inaccuracies contained in Eszterhas' article. However, there was sufficient evidence for the jury to find that Eszterhas' writing of the feature was within the scope of his employment at The Plain Dealer and that Forest City Publishing Company was therefore liable under traditional doctrines of *respondeat superior*. Although Eszterhas was not regularly assigned by The Plain Dealer to write for the Sunday Magazine, the editor of the magazine testified that as a staff writer for The Plain Dealer, Eszterhas frequently suggested stories he would like to write for the magazine. When Eszterhas suggested the follow-up article on the Silver Bridge disaster, the editor approved the idea and told Eszterhas the magazine would publish the feature if it was good. From this evidence, the jury could reasonably conclude that Forest City Publishing Company, publisher of The Plain Dealer should be held vicariously liable for the damage caused by the knowing falsehoods contained in Eszterhas' story.

For the foregoing reasons the judgment of the Court of Appeals is reversed and the case is remanded to that court with directions to enter a judgment affirming the judgment of the District Court as to the respondents Forest City Publishing Company and Joseph Eszterhas.

[JUSTICE DOUGLAS dissented, with opinion.]

———————

1. This branch of the tort of invasion of privacy can be described as placing the plaintiff in an objectionable false light in the public eye. It goes back as far as Lord Byron v. Johnston, 2 Mer. 29, 35 Eng.Rep. 851 (1816), when Byron succeeded in enjoining the circulation of a bad poem that had been attributed to his pen. See Restatement (Second) of Torts § 652E.

Representative cases include Leverton v. Curtis Pub. Co., 192 F.2d 974 (3d Cir.1951) (picture of child, hurt in automobile accident, used to illustrate article, "They Ask to be Killed"); Peay v. Curtis Pub. Co., 78 F.Supp. 305 (D.D.C.1948) (picture of honest taxi driver illustrating article on the cheating propensities of taxi drivers); Gill v. Curtis Pub. Co., 38 Cal.2d 273, 239 P.2d 630 (1952) (picture of embracing couple illustrating article on the "wrong kind of love"); Douglass v. Hustler Magazine, Inc., 769 F.2d 1128 (7th Cir.1985) (plaintiff allowed Playboy to run nude picture of her, but Hustler did it without permission; false light lies for implying that she would allow that magazine to carry the picture).

2. In Samuel v. Curtis Pub. Co., 122 F.Supp. 327 (N.D.Cal.1954), a girl stood on the edge of the Golden Gate bridge in San Francisco, about to jump. Plaintiff was photographed while trying to dissuade her. Two years later defendant published in its magazine an article on suicide, and used the picture as an illustration. This was held not to invade the plaintiff's privacy. In accord are Sarat Lahiri v. Daily Mirror, 162 Misc. 776, 295 N.Y.S. 382 (1937) (picture of Hindu illusionist illustrating article on the Indian rope trick); Oma v. Hillman Periodicals, 281 App.Div. 240, 118 N.Y.S.2d 720 (1953) (picture of boxer illustrating article on boxing); Kline v. Robert K. McBride & Co., 170 Misc. 974, 11 N.Y.S.2d 674 (1939) (picture of strike-breaker, book on strike-breaking). How are the two groups of cases to be distinguished?

3. Must there be a defamatory implication? Plaintiff signed a petition, intending it to be published, and later changed his mind and demanded that his signature be withdrawn. Defendant published the petition with his signature. This was held to be actionable. Schwartz v. Edrington, 133 La. 235, 62 So. 660 (1913). Cf. Strickler v. National Broadcasting Co., 167 F.Supp. 68 (S.D.Cal.1958) (fictitious details of conduct of plaintiff in an airplane crisis); Stryker v. Republic Pictures Corp., 108 Cal.App.2d 191, 238 P.2d 670 (1951) (fiction in motion picture film about war hero).

4. In the privacy action, what becomes of the various safeguards thrown about the freedom of the press in defamation cases, such as the necessity of a

defamatory innuendo, the requirement of proof of special damage when what is published is not actionable per se, the retraction statutes, and those requiring the filing of a bond for costs? See Prosser, Privacy, 48 Calif.L.Rev. 383, 422–23 (1960); Wade, Defamation and the Right of Privacy, 15 Vand.L.Rev. 1093 (1962). In Werner v. Times–Mirror Co., 193 Cal.App.2d 111, 14 Cal.Rptr. 208 (1961), the court recognized the problem, and applied a retraction statute even to false statements about the plaintiff that were not defamatory.

5. The privileges developed in defamation cases are generally available in privacy cases involving disclosure of private facts and creation of false light. Senogles v. Security Benefit L. Ins. Co., 217 Kan. 438, 536 P.2d 1358 (1975). See Restatement (Second) of Torts §§ 652F, 652G. During a professional football game, plaintiff, a player, consents to have his picture taken by a photographer for a national sports magazine. After the picture is published plaintiff realized that he had his fly open at the time, and he suffered both anguish and humiliation. Does he have a claim? Neff v. Time, Inc., 406 F.Supp. 858 (D.C. Pa.1976).

6. Several states have expressed doubts about false-light privacy or indicated that they do not recognize it. See e.g., Sullivan v. Pulitzer Broadcasting Co., 709 S.W.2d 475 (Mo.1986); Renwick v. News and Observer Pub. Co., 310 N.C. 312, 312 S.E.2d 405 (1984); Crump v. Beckley Newspapers, Inc., ___ W.Va. ___, 320 S.E.2d 70 (1983).

7. *Constitutional Law.* As indicated in the principal case, Time, Inc. v. Hill, 385 U.S. 534 (1967), laid down the constitutional rule that in the false-light cases, the plaintiff must prove that the defendant knew of the falsity or acted with reckless disregard of it. Gertz v. Robert Welch, Inc., supra, page 906, repudiated Rosenbloom v. Metromedia, Inc., supra, page 902, and limited the reckless-disregard formula of New York Times v. Sullivan to statements about public officials or public figures. This has given rise to speculation that the same thing will be done to Time, Inc. v. Hill and its application to the false-light cases. The principal case leaves this question undecided. See, applying the negligence standard to a false-light case, Wood v. Hustler Mag., Inc., 736 F.2d 1084 (5th Cir.1984). What effect will Dun & Bradstreet v. Greenmoss, supra page 917, have on the issue?

HUSTLER MAGAZINE v. FALWELL
Supreme Court of the United States, 1988.
___ U.S. ___, 108 S.Ct. 876, 99 L.Ed.2d 41.

CHIEF JUSTICE REHNQUIST delivered the opinion of the Court.

Petitioner Hustler Magazine, Inc., is a magazine of nationwide circulation. Respondent Jerry Falwell, a nationally known minister who has been active as a commentator on politics and public affairs, sued petitioner and its publisher, petitioner Larry Flynt, to recover damages for invasion of privacy, libel, and intentional infliction of emotional distress. The District Court directed a verdict against respondent on the privacy claim, and submitted the other two claims to a jury. The jury found for petitioners on the defamation claim [on the ground that the "ad parody could not 'reasonably be understood as describing actual facts' about plaintiff or actual events in which he participated." It also] found for respondent on the claim for intentional infliction of emotional distress and awarded damages [of $200,000, including punitive damages]. We now consider whether this award is consistent with the First and Fourteenth Amendments of the United States Constitution.

The inside front cover of the November 1983 issue of Hustler Magazine featured a "parody" of an advertisement for Campari Liqueur that contained the name and picture of respondent and was entitled "Jerry Falwell talks about his first time." This parody was modeled after actual Campari ads that included interviews with various celebrities about their "first times." Although it was apparent by the end of each interview that this meant the first time they sampled Campari, the ads clearly played on the sexual double entendre of the general subject of "first times." Copying the form and layout of these Campari ads, Hustler's editors chose respondent as the featured celebrity and drafted an alleged "interview" with him in which he states that his "first time" was during a drunken incestuous rendezvous with his mother in an outhouse. The Hustler parody portrays respondent and his mother as drunk and immoral, and suggests that respondent is a hypocrite who preaches only when he is drunk. In small print at the bottom of the page, the ad contains the disclaimer, "ad parody—not to be taken seriously." The magazine's table of contents also lists the ad as "Fiction; Ad and Personality Parody."* * *

On appeal [from the District Court,] the United States Court of Appeals for the Fourth Circuit affirmed the judgment against petitioners. *Falwell v. Flynt,* 797 F.2d 1270 (CA4 1986). The court rejected petitioners' argument that the "actual malice" standard of *New York Times Co. v. Sullivan,* 376 U.S. 254 (1964), must be met before respondent can recover for emotional distress. The court agreed that because respondent is concededly a public figure, petitioners are "entitled to the same level of first amendment protection in the claim for intentional infliction of emotional distress that they received in [respondent's] claim for libel." 797 F.2d, at 1274. But this does not mean that a literal application of the actual malice rule is appropriate in the context of an emotional distress claim. In the court's view, the *New York Times* decision emphasized the constitutional importance not of the falsity of the statement or the defendant's disregard for the truth, but of the heightened level of culpability embodied in the requirement of "knowing * * * or reckless" conduct. Here, the *New York Times* standard is satisfied by the state-law requirement, and the jury's finding, that the defendants have acted intentionally or recklessly.[3] The Court of Appeals then went on to reject the contention that because the jury found that the ad parody did not describe actual facts about respondent, the ad was an opinion that is protected by the First Amendment. As the court put it, this was "irrelevant," as the issue is

---

3. Under Virginia law, in an action for intentional infliction of emotional distress a plaintiff must show that the defendant's conduct (1) is intentional or reckless; (2) offends generally accepted standards of decency or morality; (3) is causally connected with the plaintiff's emotional distress; and (4) caused emotional distress that was severe. 797 F.2d, at 1275, n. 4 (citing Womack v. Eldridge, 215 Va. 338, 210 S.E.2d 145 (1974)).

"whether [the ad's] publication was sufficiently outrageous to constitute intentional infliction of emotional distress." [c] Petitioners then filed a petition for rehearing en banc, but this was denied by a divided court. Given the importance of the constitutional issues involved, we granted certiorari.

This case presents us with a novel question involving First Amendment limitations upon a State's authority to protect its citizens from the intentional infliction of emotional distress. We must decide whether a public figure may recover damages for emotional harm caused by the publication of an ad parody offensive to him, and doubtless gross and repugnant in the eyes of most. Respondent would have us find that a State's interest in protecting public figures from emotional distress is sufficient to deny First Amendment protection to speech that is patently offensive and is intended to inflict emotional injury, even when that speech could not reasonably have been interpreted as stating actual facts about the public figure involved. This we decline to do.

At the heart of the First Amendment is the recognition of the fundamental importance of the free flow of ideas and opinions on matters of public interest and concern. "[T]he freedom to speak one's mind is not only an aspect of individual liberty—and thus a good unto itself—but also is essential to the common quest for truth and the vitality of society as a whole." *Bose Corp. v. Consumers Union of United States, [c] Inc.,* 466 U.S. 485, 503–504 (1984). We have therefore been particularly vigilant to ensure that individual expressions of ideas remain free from governmentally imposed sanctions. The First Amendment recognizes no such thing as a "false" idea. *Gertz v. Robert Welch, Inc.,* 418 U.S. 323, 339 (1974).* * *

The sort of robust political debate encouraged by the First Amendment is bound to produce speech that is critical of those who hold public office or those public figures who are "intimately involved in the resolution of important public questions or, by reason of their fame, shape events in areas of concern to society at large." [c] Justice Frankfurter put it succinctly in *Baumgartner v. United States,* 322 U.S. 665, 673–674 (1944), when he said that "[o]ne of the prerogatives of American citizenship is the right to criticize public men and measures." Such criticism, inevitably, will not always be reasoned or moderate; public figures as well as public officials will be subject to "vehement, caustic, and sometimes unpleasantly sharp attacks," *New York Times,* supra, at 270. "[T]he candidate who vaunts his spotless record and sterling integrity cannot convincingly cry 'Foul!' when an opponent or an industrious reporter attempts to demonstrate the contrary." *Monitor Patriot Co. v. Roy,* 401 U.S. 265, 274 (1971).

Of course, this does not mean that *any* speech about a public figure is immune from sanction in the form of damages. Since *New York Times Co. v. Sullivan,* supra, we have consistently ruled that a public figure may hold a speaker liable for the damage to reputation caused by publication of a defamatory falsehood, but only if the statement was made "with knowledge that it was false or with reckless disregard of whether it was false or not." Id., at 279–280. False statements of fact are particularly valueless; they interfere with the truth-seeking function of the marketplace of ideas, and they cause damage to an individual's reputation that cannot easily be repaired by counterspeech, however persuasive or effective. See *Gertz*, 418 U.S., at 340, 344, n. 9. But even though falsehoods have little value in and of themselves, they are "nevertheless inevitable in free debate," id., at 340, and a rule that would impose strict liability on a publisher for false factual assertions would have an undoubted "chilling" effect on speech relating to public figures that does have constitutional value. "Freedoms of expression require 'breathing space.'" *Philadelphia Newspapers, Inc. v. Hepps*, 475 U.S. 767, 772 (1986) (quoting *New York Times*, 376 U.S., at 272). This breathing space is provided by a constitutional rule that allows public figures to recover for libel or defamation only when they can prove *both* that the statement was false and that the statement was made with the requisite level of culpability.

Respondent argues, however, that a different standard should apply in this case because here the State seeks to prevent not reputational damage, but the severe emotional distress suffered by the person who is the subject of an offensive publication. Cf. *Zacchini v. Scripps-Howard Broadcasting Co.*, 433 U.S. 562 (1977) (ruling that the "actual malice" standard does not apply to the tort of appropriation of a right of publicity). In respondent's view, and in the view of the Court of Appeals, so long as the utterance was intended to inflict emotional distress, was outrageous, and did in fact inflict serious emotional distress, it is of no constitutional import whether the statement was a fact or an opinion, or whether it was true or false. It is the intent to cause injury that is the gravamen of the tort, and the State's interest in preventing emotional harm simply outweighs whatever interest a speaker may have in speech of this type.

Generally speaking the law does not regard the intent to inflict emotional distress as one which should receive much solicitude, and it is quite understandable that most if not all jurisdictions have chosen to make it civilly culpable where the conduct in question is sufficiently "outrageous." But in the world of debate about public affairs, many things done with motives that are less than admirable are protected by the First Amendment. In *Garrison v. Louisiana*, 379 U.S. 64 (1964), we held that even when a speaker or writer is motivated by hatred or ill-will his expression was protected by the First Amendment: "Debate on public issues will not be uninhibited if the speaker must run the risk that it will be proved in court that he spoke out of hatred; even if he did speak out of hatred, utterances honestly believed contribute to the free interchange of ideas and the ascertainment of truth." Id., at 73.

Thus while such a bad motive may be deemed controlling for purposes of tort liability in other areas of the law, we think the First Amendment prohibits such a result in the area of public debate about public figures.

Were we to hold otherwise, there can be little doubt that political cartoonists and satirists would be subjected to damages awards without any showing that their work falsely defamed its subject. [The court discusses a number of well-known cartoon caricatures.]

Respondent contends, however, that the caricature in question here was so "outrageous" as to distinguish it from more traditional political cartoons. There is no doubt that the caricature of respondent and his mother published in Hustler is at best a distant cousin of the political cartoons described above, and a rather poor relation at that. If it were possible by laying down a principled standard to separate the one from the other, public discourse would probably suffer little or no harm. But we doubt that there is any such standard, and we are quite sure that the pejorative description "outrageous" does not supply one. "Outrageousness" in the area of political and social discourse has an inherent subjectiveness about it which would allow a jury to impose liability on the basis of the jurors' tastes or views, or perhaps on the basis of their dislike of a particular expression. An "outrageousness" standard thus runs afoul of our longstanding refusal to allow damages to be awarded because the speech in question may have an adverse emotional impact on the audience. * * * [A]s we stated in *FCC v. Pacifica Foundation*, 438 U.S. 726 (1978): "[T]he fact that society may find speech offensive is not a sufficient reason for suppressing it. Indeed, if it is the speaker's opinion that gives offense, that consequence is a reason for according it constitutional protection. For it is a central tenet of the First Amendment that the government must remain neutral in the marketplace of ideas." Id., at 745–746. See also *Street v. New York*, 394 U.S. 576, 592 (1969) ("It is firmly settled that . . . the public expression of ideas may not be prohibited merely because the ideas are themselves offensive to some of their hearers").

Admittedly, these oft-repeated First Amendment principles, like other principles, are subject to limitations. We recognized in *Pacifica Foundation*, that speech that is " 'vulgar,' 'offensive,' and 'shocking' " is "not entitled to absolute constitutional protection under all circumstances." 438 U.S., at 747. In *Chaplinsky v. New Hampshire*, 315 U.S. 568 (1942), we held that a state could lawfully punish an individual for the use of insulting " 'fighting' words—those which by their very utterance inflict injury or tend to incite an immediate breach of the peace." Id., at 571–572. These limitations are but recognition of the observation in *Dun & Bradstreet, Inc. v. Greenmoss Builders, Inc.,* 472 U.S. 749, 758 (1985), that this Court has "long recognized that not all speech is of equal First Amendment importance." But the sort of expression involved in this case does not seem to us to be governed by any exception to the general First Amendment principles stated above.

We conclude that public figures and public officials may not recover for the tort of intentional infliction of emotional distress by reason of publications such as the one here at issue without showing in addition that the publication contains a false statement of fact which was made with "actual malice," *i.e.*, with knowledge that the statement was false or with reckless disregard as to whether or not it was true. This is not merely a "blind application" of the *New York Times* standard, [c] it reflects our considered judgment that such a standard is necessary to give adequate "breathing space" to the freedoms protected by the First Amendment.

Here it is clear that respondent Falwell is a "public figure" for purposes of First Amendment law. [He cannot recover in libel and] is thus relegated to his claim for damages awarded by the jury for the intentional infliction of emotional distress by "outrageous" conduct. But for reasons heretofore stated this claim cannot, consistently with the First Amendment, form a basis for the award of damages when the conduct in question is the publication of a caricature such as the ad parody involved here. The judgment of the Court of Appeals is accordingly

Reversed.

JUSTICE WHITE, concurring in the judgment. As I see it, the decision in *New York Times v. Sullivan*, 376 U.S. 254 (1964), has little to do with this case, for here the jury found that the ad contained no assertion of fact. But I agree with the Court that the judgment below, which penalized the publication of the parody, cannot be squared with the First Amendment.

---

1. This case was decided after the copy for this edition of the casebook had been set up in proof, but it proved possible to insert the case before final page proof was entirely completed. Analytically, it might seem appropriate for Chapter 2, Section 5; but it would not have been fully understandable without a background of First-Amendment Law as laid out in the cases on defamation and privacy. Located here, it provides a good opportunity to treat the three torts together in their relationship to each other and to constitutional law.

2. Does it make sense to apply the requirement of *New York Times* "actual malice" to this situation? The Court acknowledged that it was not reasonable to apply that requirement to privacy cases involving some aspect of commercial appropriation of an element of the plaintiff's personality or career. Suppose Mr. Flynt had expressly applied to Mr. Falwell the ultra-offensive epithet implied in his parody, in a state with an actionable words statute (see supra page 57). Would it be unconstitutional to impose tort liability? Would it be necessary to show that Mr. Flynt demonstrated "actual malice"—i.e., acted with knowledge of falsity or reckless disregard regarding truth or falsity? Would the holding in Wilkinson v. Downton, supra page 53, be constitutional in the United States today?

3. Should it make any difference that this was a parody rather than frank use of the epithet? Suppose Mr. Flynt had typed the parody on a sheet of paper and sent it to Mr. Falwell with the threat that he would publish it in his magazine? What is the "idea" that is expressed? Does it involve a matter of "public interest and concern"?

Can political cartoons be distinguished from this parody? Why should it make a difference whether the plaintiff is a public figure or not? Does Justice

Powell's analysis of the reasons for drawing a distinction between public and private persons (in *Gertz* and *Greenmoss*) apply to the factual situation here?

4. In addition to the instant case, consider what actions seem appropriate in the following recent cases:

In Melvin v. Burling, 141 Ill.App.3d 786, 490 N.E.2d 1011, 95 Ill.Dec. 919 (1986), plaintiffs were harassed by dunning for payment of the cost of goods that they had not ordered. It eventually developed that defendant had ordered the goods in plaintiff's name. In Ashby v. Hustler Magazine, 802 F.2d 856 (6th Cir. 1986), plaintiff had some nude photos of herself taken by her roommate and had placed them in a jewel box in her closet. Some "friends" of her brother found them, took one and sent it in to the Hustler Magazine with fictitious name, address, and listing of "sexual fantasies." Hustler's check on the validity was somewhat perfunctory. When it appeared in a special section, acquaintances recognized her face. In Machleder v. Diaz, 804 F.2d 46 (2d Cir. 1986), a television crew confronted plaintiff on his property, with cameras rolling, raising accusatory questions about empty, hazardous drums in a weed-filled vacant adjoining area. Startled, plaintiff gave evasive responses. Subsequent explanatory statements were allegedly disregarded in the television program later broadcast. In Flynn v. Higham, 149 Cal.App.3d 677, 197 Cal.Rptr. 145 (1983), two children of the actor Errol Flynn brought action with several counts against the author of a biography of their father, contending that the book charged that he was a homosexual and a Nazi spy. Should any of the cases in this note be affected by the *Falwell* case?

For discussions (all written before these cases were decided), see Wade, Defamation and the Right of Privacy, 15 Vand.L.Rev. 1093, 1121–25 (1962); Mead, Suing Media for Emotional Distress: A Multi-Method Analysis of Tort Law Evolution, 23 Washburn L.J. 24 (1983); and Note, The Ambush Interview: A False Light Invasion of Privacy?, 34 Case W.Res.L.Rev. 72 (1983).

5. The famous case of Burton v. Crowell Publishing Co., 82 F.2d 154 (2d Cir. 1936), involved an advertisement for Camel cigarettes. Plaintiff, a gentleman steeple-chaser, was quoted as declaring that Camels "restored" him after a "crowded business day," and as endorsing the legend, "Get a lift with a Camel." In one of two photographs, he was depicted coming from a race to be weighed in, carrying his saddle in front of him. A white saddle girth hung down from the saddle in such a way as to seem on first glance to be not a part of the saddle but an indecently exposed part of his body. "So regarded, the photograph became grotesque, monstrous, and obscene and the legends, which undue violence can be made to match, reinforce the ribald interpretation. * * * [I]t is patently an optical illusion and carries its correction on its face as much as it it were a verbal utterance which expressly declared that it was false." Plaintiff had not seen the photograph before it was published. Judge Learned Hand held the advertisement to be actionable in defamation. Was he correct? Would the later Supreme Court decisions affect the holding? Consider the suitability of any other tort action.

Chapter XIX

CIVIL RIGHTS

ASHBY v. WHITE

Court of King's Bench, 1702; House of Lords, 1703.
2 Ld.Raym. 938, 92 Eng.Rep. 126; 1 Brown P.C. 62, 1 Eng.Rep. 417.

HOLT, CHIEF JUSTICE. The single question in this case is, whether, if a free burgess of a corporation, who has an undoubted right to give his vote in the election of a burgess to serve in Parliament, be refused and hindered to give it by the officer, if an action on the case will lie against such officer.

I am of opinion that judgment ought to be given in this case for the plaintiff. My brothers differ from me in opinion, and they all differ from one another in the reasons of their opinion; but notwithstanding their opinion, I think the plaintiff ought to recover, and that this action is well maintainable, and ought to lie.

But to proceed, I will do these two things: first, I will maintain that the plaintiff has a right and privilege to give his vote: secondly, in consequence thereof, that if he be hindered in the enjoyment or exercise of that right, the law gives him an action against the disturber, and that this is the proper action given by the law. * * *

If the plaintiff has a right, he must of necessity have a means to vindicate and maintain it, and a remedy if he is injured in the exercise or enjoyment of it; and indeed it is a vain thing to imagine a right without a remedy; for want of right and want of remedy are reciprocal. * * * Where a new Act of Parliament is made for the benefit of the subject, if a man be hindered from the enjoyment of it, he shall have an action against such person who so obstructed him. * * * If then when a statute gives a right, the party shall have an action for the infringement of it, is it not as forcible when a man has his right by the common law? This right of voting is a right in the plaintiff by the common law, and consequently he shall maintain an action for the obstruction of it. * * *

And I am of opinion, that this action on the case is a proper action. My brother Powell indeed thinks, that an action upon the case is not maintainable, because here is no hurt or damage to the plaintiff; but surely every injury imports a damage, though it does not cost the party one farthing, and it is impossible to prove the contrary; for a damage is not merely pecuniary, but an injury imports a damage, when a man is thereby hindered of his right. * * *. So here in the principal case, the plaintiff is obstructed of his right, and shall therefore have his action. And it is no objection to say, that it will occasion multiplicity of actions; for if men will multiply injuries, actions must be multiplied

Chief Justice Holt

too; for every man that is injured ought to have his recompence. Suppose the defendant had beat forty or fifty men, the damage done to each one is peculiar to himself, and he shall have his action. So if many persons receive a private injury by a publick nusance, every one shall have his action.   *   *   *

But in the principal case my brother says, we cannot judge of this matter, because it is a Parliamentary thing. O! By all means be very tender of that. Besides it is intricate, and there may be contrariety of opinions. But this matter can never come in question in Parliament; for it is agreed that the persons for whom the plaintiff voted were elected; so that the action is brought for being deprived of his vote; and if it were carried for the other candidates against whom he voted, his damage would be less. To allow this action will make publick officers more careful to observe the constitution of cities and boroughs, and not to be so partial as they commonly are in all elections, which is indeed a great and growing mischief, and tends to the prejudice of the peace of the nation. But they say, that this is a matter out of our jurisdiction, and we ought not to inlarge it. I agree we ought not to incroach or inlarge our jurisdiction; by so doing we usurp both on the right of the Queen and the people: but sure we may determine on a charter granted by the King, or on a matter of custom or prescription, when it comes before us without incroaching on the Parliament. And if it be a matter within our jurisdiction, we are bound by our oaths to judge of it. This is a matter of property determinable before us. Was ever such a petition heard of in Parliament, as that a man was hindred of giving his vote, and praying them to give him remedy? The Parliament undoubtedly would say, take your remedy at law. It is not like the case of determining the right of election between the candidates. * * *

Therefore my opinion is, that the plaintiff ought to have judgment. * * *

[The opinions of GOULD, POWYS and POWELL, JJ., constituting the majority in the Court of King's Bench and reversing the jury verdict for the plaintiff, are omitted.

The report of the proceeding in the House of Lords concludes: "After hearing counsel on this writ of error, a debate ensued; and the question being put, Whether this judgment should be reversed? it was resolved in the affirmative. * * * It was therefore ordered and adjudged, that the said judgment should be reversed, and that the plaintiff should recover his damages assessed by the jury; and also, the further sum of 10£. for his costs, in this behalf sustained."]

---

1. Accord: Lane v. Mitchell, 153 Iowa 139, 133 N.W. 381 (1911); Valdez v. Gonzales, 50 N.M. 281, 176 P.2d 173 (1946).

"The objection that the subject matter of the suit is political is little more than a play upon words. Of course the petition concerns political action but it alleges and seeks to recover for private damage. That private damage may be caused by such political action and may be recovered for in a suit at law hardly has been doubted for over two hundred years. * * * If the defendants' conduct was a wrong to the plaintiff the same reasons that allow a recovery for denying the plaintiff a vote at a final election allow it for denying a vote at the primary election that may determine the final result." Holmes, J., in Nixon v. Herndon, 273 U.S. 536, 540 (1927).

2. A similar action lies for depriving a person of his right to hold political office. See, e.g., Hill v. Carr, 186 Ill.App. 515 (1914), and Goetchus v. Matthewson, 61 N.Y. 420 (1875), both indicating a right to emoluments. Cf. Sutton v. Adams, 180 Ga. 48, 178 S.E. 365 (1935); Judd v. Polk, 267 Ky. 408, 102 S.W.2d 325 (1937). On both of these torts, see Restatement (Second) of Torts § 865.

3. In Morningstar v. La Fayette Hotel Co., 211 N.Y. 465, 105 N.E. 656 (1914), plaintiff was publicly refused service at the restaurant to the hotel where he resided. The reason was his refusal to pay a disputed bill of $1 for special service. Judgment had been given for the defendant. In reversing, Cardozo, J., said: "It is no concern of ours that the controversy at the root of this lawsuit may seem to be trivial. The fact supplies, indeed, the greater reason why the jury should not have been misled into the belief that justice

might therefore be denied to the suitor. To enforce one's rights when they are violated is never a legal wrong, and may often be a moral duty. It happens in many instances that the violation passes with no effort to redress it—sometimes from praiseworthy forbearance, sometimes from weakness, sometimes from mere inertia. But the law, which creates a right, can certainly not concede that an insistence upon its enforcement is evidence of a wrong." On a common law action for refusal to serve, see Restatement (Second) of Torts § 866.

4. There are also indications that interference with performance of a civil duty or responsibility may give rise to a tort cause of action. In Nees v. Hocks, 272 Or. 210, 536 P.2d 512 (1975), for example, the plaintiff was discharged from her position for failing to comply with her employer's direction that she seek to evade jury duty. She was allowed to recover damages.

5. Should these torts be confined to an intentional interference with civil rights and duties, or should they extend to a negligent interference? Should they perhaps be restricted to a purposive interference?

6. Despite the remarks of Judge Cardozo in note 3 supra, the tort action for damages sometimes proves not adequate and other remedies are needed. Thus, if a person is wrongfully prevented from voting and recovers in an action of tort, what is the measure of damages? Would it justify the plaintiff in bringing suit or the attorney in taking the case? How might this be handled?

For these reasons, in both the voting and refusal-of-service situations, statutory provisions for injunctive, criminal and administrative relief have largely replaced the common law action. On voting, there are several federal statutes, particularly the Voting Rights Act of 1965, 42 U.S.C.A. § 1971. The states also usually have legislation on the subject. On refusal to serve a customer, see particularly 42 U.S.C.A. § 2000a.

7. See Linden, Tort Law as Ombudsman, 51 Can.B.Rev. 157 (1973); Wade, Tort Law as Ombudsman, 65 Ore.L.Rev. 309 (1986).

CAREY v. PIPHUS

Supreme Court of the United States, 1978.
435 U.S. 247, 98 S.Ct. 1042, 55 L.Ed.2d 252.

[Secondary school student Jarius Piphus was discovered by the school principal engaged in activities with another student, leading him to believe that the students were "smoking marihuana." Without a hearing, he was given "the usual 20–day suspension for violation of the school rule against the use of drugs." Elementary student Silas Brisco was wearing a single small earring and refused to remove it although he was reminded of the school rule prohibiting it because it denoted membership in a street gang. Without a hearing, he was also suspended for 20 days. Both students brought action under 42 U.S.C.A. § 1983, seeking declaratory and injunctive relief and actual and punitive damages. The cases were consolidated in the federal district court, which held that both students had been suspended without procedural due process but declined to grant damages because of the lack of any evidence "which could even form the basis of a speculative inference measuring the extent of their injuries."

On appeal, the Seventh Circuit reversed and remanded. 545 F.2d 30 (1976). On the issue of damages, it held that the students "would be entitled to recover substantial 'nonpunitive' damages simply because they had been denied procedural due process," even in the absence of any other damage. The Supreme Court granted certiorari.]

MR. JUSTICE POWELL delivered the opinion of the Court. * * * Title 42 U.S.C.A. § 1983, Rev.Stat. § 1979, derived from § 1 of the Civil Rights Act of 1871, 17 Stat. 13, provides: "Every person who, under color of any statute, ordinance, regulation, custom, or usage, of any State or Territory, subjects, or causes to be subjected, any citizen of the United States or other person within the jurisdiction thereof to the deprivation of any rights, privileges, or immunities secured by the Constitution and laws, shall be liable to the party injured in an action at law, suit in equity, or other proper proceeding for redress." The legislative history of § 1983 * * * demonstrates that it was intended to "[create] a species of tort liability" in favor of persons who are deprived of "rights, privileges, or immunities secured" to them by the Constitution. Imbler v. Pachtman, 424 U.S. 409, 417 (1976).

Petitioners contend that the elements and prerequisites for recovery of damages under this "species of tort liability" should parallel those for recovery of damages under the common law of torts. In particular, they urge that the purpose of an award of damages under § 1983 should be to compensate persons for injuries that are caused by the deprivation of constitutional rights; and, further, that plaintiffs should be required to prove not only that their rights were violated, but also that injury was caused by the violation, in order to recover substantial damages. * * *

Respondents * * * contend that substantial damages should be awarded under § 1983 for the deprivation of a constitutional right *whether or not* any injury was caused by the deprivation * * * because constitutional rights are valuable in and of themselves, and because of the need to deter violations of constitutional rights. * * * Second, respondents argue that even if the purpose of a § 1983 damages award is * * * primarily to compensate persons for injuries that are caused by the deprivation of constitutional rights, every deprivation of procedural due process may be *presumed* to cause some injury. * * *

Insofar as petitioners contend that the basic purpose of a § 1983 damages award should be to compensate persons for injuries caused by the deprivation of constitutional rights, they have the better of the argument. Rights, constitutional and otherwise, do not exist in a vacuum. Their purpose is to protect persons from injuries to particular interests, and their contours are shaped by the interests they protect.

Our legal system's concept of damages reflects this view of legal rights. "The cardinal principle of damages in Anglo–American law is that of *compensation* for the injury caused to plaintiff by defendant's breach of duty." 2 F. Harper & F. James, Law of Torts § 25.1, p. 1299 (1956) (emphasis in original). The Court implicitly has recognized the applicability of this principle to actions under § 1983 by stating that damages are available under that section for actions "found * * * to have been violative of * * * constitutional rights *and to have caused compensable injury* * * *." Wood v. Strickland, 420 U.S. [308,] 319 (emphasis supplied). * * *

The Members of the Congress that enacted § 1983 did not address directly the question of damages, but the principle that damages are designed to compensate persons for injuries caused by the deprivation of rights hardly could have been foreign to the many lawyers in Congress in 1871. * * * To the extent that Congress intended that awards under § 1983 should deter the deprivation of constitutional rights, there is no evidence that it meant to establish a deterrent more formidable than that inherent in the award of compensatory damages. [Cc]

It is less difficult to conclude that damages awards under § 1983 should be governed by the principle of compensation than it is to apply this principle to concrete cases. But over the centuries the common law of torts has developed a set of rules to implement the principle that a person should be compensated fairly for injuries caused by the violation of his legal rights. These rules, defining the elements of damages and the prerequisites for their recovery, provide the appropriate starting point for the inquiry under § 1983 as well.

It is not clear, however, that common-law tort rules of damages will provide a complete solution to the damages issue in every § 1983 case. In some cases, the interests protected by a particular branch of the common law of torts may parallel closely the interests protected by a particular constitutional right. In such cases, it may be appropriate to apply the tort rules of damages directly to the § 1983 action. [C] In other cases, the interests protected by a particular constitutional right may not also be protected by an analogous branch of the common law torts. [Cc] In those cases, the task will be the more difficult one of adapting common-law rules of damages to provide fair compensation for injuries caused by the deprivation of a constitutional right. * * *

The purpose of § 1983 would be defeated if injuries caused by the deprivation of constitutional rights went uncompensated simply because the common law does not recognize an analogous cause of action. [Cc] In order to further the purpose of § 1983, the rules governing compensation for injuries caused by the deprivation of constitutional rights should be tailored to the interests protected by the particular right in question—just as the common-law rules of damages themselves were defined by the interests protected in the various branches of tort law. We agree with Mr. Justice Harlan that "the experience of judges in dealing with private [tort] claims supports the conclusion that courts of law are capable of making the types of judgment concerning causation and magnitude of injury necessary to accord meaningful compensation for invasion of [constitutional] rights." Bivens v. Six Unknown Fed. Narcotics Agents, 403 U.S. [388,] 409 (Harlan, J., concurring in judgment). With these principles in mind, we now turn to the problem of compensation in the case at hand. * * *

The Due Process Clause of the Fourteenth Amendment provides: "[N]or shall any State deprive any person of life, liberty, or property, without due process of law * * *." * * * Procedural due process rules are meant to protect persons not from the deprivation, but from the mistaken or unjustified deprivation of life, liberty, or property. Thus, in deciding what process constitutionally is due in various contexts, the Court repeatedly has emphasized that "procedural due process rules are shaped by the risk of error inherent in the truth-finding process * * *." [C] Such rules "minimize substantively unfair or mistaken deprivations of" life, liberty, or property by enabling persons to contest the basis upon which a State proposes to deprive them of protected interests. [C]

In this case, the Court of Appeals held that if petitioners can prove on remand that "[respondents] would have been suspended even if a proper hearing had been held," 545 F.2d, at 32, then respondents will not be entitled to recover damages to compensate them for injuries caused by the suspensions. The court thought that in such a case, the failure to accord procedural due process could not properly be viewed as the cause of the suspensions. [Cc] The court suggested that in such circumstances, an award of damages for injuries caused by the suspensions would constitute a windfall, rather than compensation, to respondents. [Cc] We do not understand the parties to disagree with this conclusion. Nor do we.

The parties do disagree as to the further holding of the Court of Appeals that respondents are entitled to recover substantial—although unspecified—damages to compensate them for "the injury which is 'inherent in the nature of the wrong,'" 545 F.2d, at 31, even if their suspensions were justified and even if they fail to prove that the denial of procedural due process actually caused them some real, if intangible, injury. Respondents, elaborating on this theme, submit that the holding is correct because injury fairly may be "presumed" to flow from every denial of procedural due process. Their argument is that in addition to protecting against unjustified deprivations, the Due Process Clause also guarantees the "feeling of just treatment" by the government. [C] They contend that the deprivation of protected interests without procedural due process, even where the premise for the deprivation is not erroneous, inevitably arouses strong feelings of mental and emotional distress in the individual who is denied this "feeling of just treatment." * * *

Petitioners do not deny that a purpose of procedural due process is to convey to the individual a feeling that the government has dealt with him fairly, as well as to minimize the risk of mistaken deprivations of protected interests. They go so far as to concede that, in a proper case, persons in respondents' position might well recover damages for mental and emotional distress caused by the denial of procedural due process. Petitioners' argument is the more limited one that such injury cannot be presumed to occur, and that plaintiffs at least should be put to their proof on the issue, as plaintiffs are in most tort actions.

We agree with petitioners in this respect. * * *

[We cannot] support respondents' contention that damages should be presumed to flow from every deprivation of procedural due process.

First, it is not reasonable to assume that every departure from procedural due process, no matter what the circumstances or how minor, inherently is as likely to cause distress as the publication of defamation per se is to cause injury to reputation and distress. Where the deprivation of a protected interest is substantively justified but procedures are deficient in some respect, there may well be those who suffer no distress over the procedural irregularities. Indeed, in contrast to the immediately distressing effect of defamation per se, a person may not even know that procedures *were* deficient until he enlists the aid of counsel to challenge a perceived substantive deprivation.

Moreover, where a deprivation is justified but procedures are deficient, whatever distress a person feels may be attributable to the justified deprivation rather than to deficiencies in procedure. But as the Court of Appeals held, the injury caused by a justified deprivation, including distress, is not properly compensable under § 1983.[19] This ambiguity in causation * * * provides additional need for requiring the plaintiff to convince the trier of fact that he actually suffered distress because of the denial of procedural due process itself.

Finally, we foresee no particular difficulty in producing evidence that mental and emotional distress actually was caused by the denial of procedural due process itself. Distress is a personal injury familiar to the law, customarily proved by showing the nature and circumstances of the wrong and its effect on the plaintiff. In sum, then, although mental and emotional distress caused by the denial of procedural due process itself is compensable under § 1983, we hold that neither the likelihood of such injury nor the difficulty of proving it is so great as to justify awarding compensatory damages without proof that such injury actually was caused. * * *

Even if respondents' suspensions were justified, and even if they did not suffer any other actual injury, the fact remains that they were deprived of their right to procedural due process. "It is enough to invoke the procedural safeguards of the Fourteenth Amendment that a significant property interest is at stake, whatever the ultimate outcome of a hearing * * *." Fuentes v. Shevin, 407 U.S. [67,] 87. [Cc]

Common-law courts traditionally have vindicated deprivations of certain "absolute" rights that are not shown to have caused actual injury through the award of a nominal sum of money. By making the

19. In this case, for example, respondents denied the allegations against them. They may well have been distressed that their denials were not believed. They might have been equally distressed if they had been disbelieved only after a full-dress hearing, but in that instance they would have no cause of action against petitioners.

deprivation of such rights actionable for nominal damages without proof of actual injury, the law recognizes the importance to organized society that those rights be scrupulously observed; but at the same time, it remains true to the principle that substantial damages should be awarded only to compensate actual injury or, in the case of exemplary or punitive damages, to deter or punish malicious deprivations of rights.

Because the right to procedural due process is "absolute" in the sense that it does not depend upon the merits of a claimant's substantive assertions, and because of the importance to organized society that procedural due process is observed [cc] we believe that the denial of procedural due process should be actionable for nominal damages without proof of actual injury. We therefore hold that if, upon remand, the District Court determines that respondents' suspensions were justified, respondents nevertheless will be entitled to recover nominal damages not to exceed one dollar from petitioners.

The judgment of the Court of Appeals is reversed, and the case is remanded for further proceedings consistent with this opinion.

It is so ordered.

---

1. On the legislative history of the Civil Rights Acts and the part it plays in the interpretation of liability, especially in the meaning of "color of law," see opinions in Monroe v. Pape, 365 U.S. 167 (1961); Monell v. Department of Social Services, 436 U.S. 658 (1978); Maine v. Thiboutot, 448 U.S. 1 (1980); and Chapman v. Houston Welfare Organization, 441 U.S. 600 (1979). Also Zagrans "Under Color of" What Law: A Reconstructed Model of Section 1983 Liability, 71 Va.L.Rev. 499 (1985); Eckhardt & Eckhardt, 42 U.S.C. § 1983: A Primer for the Civil Rights Lawyer, 20 Ida.L.Rev. 585 (1984); Rader, Section 1983, The Civil Rights Act on Legislation and Judicial Directions, 15 Cumb.L.Rev. 511 (1985).

2. The Supreme Court holds that certain conduct violative of an express provision of the Federal Constitution may give rise to a cause of action in tort even though the Constitution does not expressly provide for a civil action. For treatment of these "constitutional torts," see Bivens v. Six Unknown Named Agents of the Federal Bureau of Narcotics, 403 U.S. 388 (1971) infra page 1171, and notes following it. The *Bivens* doctrine imposes on federal officers about the same liability that § 1983 imposes on state officers.

3. The Attorney's Fees Award Act of 1976, 42 U.S.C.A. § 1988, provides that the court, "in its discretion," may award reasonable attorney's fees to the prevailing party in a civil rights action. See Hewitt v. Helms, ___ U.S. ___, 107 S.Ct. 2672, 96 L.Ed.2d 654 (1987); Note, 54 U.Cin.L.Rev. 987 (1986).

4. See C. Antieau, Federal Civil Rights Acts: Civil Practice (2d ed. 1980); 5 K. Davis, Administrative Law Treatise §§ 27:16–27:451 (2d ed. 1984); S. Nahmod, Civil Rights and Civil Liberties Litigation (1979).

DANIELS v. WILLIAMS

Supreme Court of the United States, 1986.
474 U.S. 327, 106 S.Ct. 662, 88 L.Ed.2d 662.

JUSTICE REHNQUIST delivered the opinion of the Court.

In *Parratt v. Taylor*, 451 U.S. 527 (1981), a state prisoner sued under 42 U.S.C. § 1983, claiming that prison officials had negligently deprived him of his property without due process of law. After deciding that § 1983 contains no independent state-of-mind requirement, we concluded that although petitioner had been "deprived" of property within the meaning of the Due Process Clause of the Fourteenth Amendment, the State's postdeprivation tort remedy provided the process that was due. Petitioner's claim in this case, which also rests on an alleged Fourteenth Amendment "deprivation" caused by the negligent conduct of a prison official, leads us to reconsider our statement in *Parratt* that "the alleged loss, even though negligently caused, amounted to a deprivation." *Id.*, at 536–537. We conclude that the Due Process Clause is simply not implicated by a *negligent* act of an official causing unintended loss of or injury to life, liberty or property.

In this § 1983 action, petitioner seeks to recover damages for back and ankle injuries allegedly sustained when he fell on a prison stairway. He claims that, while an inmate at the city jail in Richmond, Virginia, he slipped on a pillow negligently left on the stairs by respondent, a correctional deputy stationed at the jail. Respondent's negligence, the argument runs, "deprived" petitioner of his "liberty" interest in freedom from bodily injury, see *Ingraham v. Wright*, 430 U.S. 651, 673 (1977); because respondent maintains that he is entitled to the defense of sovereign immunity in a state tort suit, petitioner is without an "adequate" state remedy, cf. *Hudson v. Palmer*, 468 U.S. 517 (1984). Accordingly, the deprivation of liberty was without "due process of law."

The District Court granted respondent's motion for summary judgment. [The Court of Appeals affirmed.] * * *

In *Parratt v. Taylor*, we granted certiorari, as we had twice before, "to decide whether mere negligence will support a claim for relief under § 1983." 451 U.S., at 532. After examining the language, legislative history and prior interpretations of the statute, we concluded that § 1983, unlike its criminal counterpart, 18 U.S.C. § 242, contains no state-of-mind requirement independent of that necessary to state a violation of the underlying constitutional right. [C] We adhere to that conclusion. But in any given § 1983 suit, the plaintiff must still prove a violation of the underlying constitutional right; and depending on the right, merely negligent conduct may not be enough to state a claim.

* * *

In *Parratt*, before concluding that Nebraska's tort remedy provided all the process that was due, we said that the loss of the prisoner's hobby kit, "even though negligently caused, amounted to a deprivation [under the Due Process Clause]." 451 U.S., at 536–537. Justice Powell, concurring in the result criticized the majority for "pass[ing] over" this important question of the state of mind required to constitute a "deprivation" of property. *Id.,* at 547. He argued that negligent acts by state officials, though causing loss of property, are not actionable under the Due Process Clause. To Justice Powell, mere negligence could not "wor[k] a deprivation in the *constitutional sense.*" *Id.,* at 548. Not only does the word "deprive" in the Due Process Clause connote more than a negligent act, but we should not "open the federal courts to lawsuits where there has been no affirmative abuse of power." *Id.,* at 548–549. * * * Upon reflection, we agree and overrule *Parratt* to the extent that it states that mere lack of due care by a state official may "deprive" an individual of life, liberty or property under the Fourteenth Amendment.

The Due Process Clause of the Fourteenth Amendment provides: "[N]or shall any State deprive any person of life, liberty, or property, without due process of law." Historically, this guarantee of due process has been applied to *deliberate* decisions of government officials to deprive a person of life, liberty or property. [Cc] No decision of this Court before *Parratt* supported the view that negligent conduct by a state official, even though causing injury, constitutes a deprivation under the Due Process Clause. This history reflects the traditional and common-sense notion that the Due Process Clause, like its forebear in the Magna Carta, [c] was " 'intended to secure the individual from the arbitrary exercise of the powers of government,' " *Hurtado v. California,* 110 U.S. 516, 527. By requiring the government to follow appropriate procedures when its agents decide to "deprive any person of life, liberty, or property," the Due Process Clause promotes fairness in such decisions. And by barring certain government actions regardless of the fairness of the procedures used to implement them, [c] it serves to prevent governmental power from being "used for purposes of oppression," *Murray's Lessee v. Hoboken Land & Improvement Co.,* 18 How. (59 U.S.) 272, 277.

We think that the actions of prison custodians in leaving a pillow on the prison stairs, or mislaying an inmate's property, are quite remote from the concerns just discussed. Far from an abuse of power, lack of due care suggests no more than a failure to measure up to the conduct of a reasonable person. To hold that injury caused by such conduct is a deprivation within the meaning of the Fourteenth Amendment would trivialize the centuries-old principle of due process of law. * * *

The only tie between the facts of this case and anything governmental in nature is the fact that respondent was a sheriff's deputy at the Richmond city jail and petitioner was an inmate confined in that jail. But while the Due Process Clause of the Fourteenth Amendment obviously speaks to some facets of this relationship, see, *e.g., Wolff v. McDonnell,* 418 U.S. 539 (1974), we do not believe its protections are triggered by lack of due care by prison officials. "Medical malpractice does not become a constitutional violation merely because the victim is a prisoner," *Estelle v. Gamble,* 429 U.S. 97 (1976), and "false imprisonment does not become a violation of the Fourteenth Amendment merely because the defendant is a state official." *Baker v. McCollan,* 443 U.S. 137, 146. Where a government official's act causing injury to life, liberty or property is merely negligent, "no procedure for compensation is *constitutionally* required." *Parratt,* 451 U.S., at 548 (POWELL, J., concurring in result) (emphasis added.) [1] * * *

In support of his claim that negligent conduct can give rise to a due process "deprivation," petitioner makes several arguments, none of which we find persuasive. He states, for example, that "it is almost certain that *some* negligence claims are within § 1983," and cites as an example the failure of a State to comply with the procedural requirements of *Wolff v. McDonnell, supra,* before depriving an inmate of goodtime credit. We think the relevant action of the prison officials in that situation is their deliberate decision to deprive the inmate of good-time credit, not their hypothetically negligent failure to accord him the procedural protections of the Due Process Clause. But we need not rule out the possibility that there are other constitutional provisions that would be violated by mere lack of care in order to hold, as we do, that such conduct does not implicate the Due Process Clause of the Fourteenth Amendment. * * *

Jailers may owe a special duty of care to those in their custody under state tort law, see Restatement (Second) of Torts § 314A(4) (1965), * * * [but] we reject the contention that the Due Process Clause of the Fourteenth Amendment embraces such a tort law concept. Petitioner alleges that he was injured by the negligence of respondent, a custodial official at the city jail. Whatever other provisions of state law or general jurisprudence he may rightly invoke, the Fourteenth Amendment to the United States Constitution does not afford him a remedy.

Affirmed.

[MARSHALL and BLACKMUN, JJ., concurred in the result. JUSTICE BLACKMUN'S concurring opinion appears at the end of the succeeding case.]

DAVIDSON v. CANNON

Supreme Court of the United States, 1986.
474 U.S. 344, 106 S.Ct. 668, 88 L.Ed.2d 677.

JUSTICE REHNQUIST delivered the opinion of the Court.

Petitioner sued prison officials seeking damages under 42 U.S.C. § 1983 for injuries he suffered when they negligently failed to protect him from another inmate [of the New Jersey State Prison. He had

---

1. Accordingly, we need not decide whether, as petitioner contends, the possibility of a sovereign immunity defense in a Virginia tort suit would render that reme- dy "inadequate" under *Parratt* and *Hudson v. Palmer,* 468 U.S. 517, 104 S.Ct. 3194, 82 L.Ed.2d 393 (1984).

been threatened by the other inmate and "sent a note reporting the incident that found its way to respondent Cannon, the Assistant Superintendent of the prison, who read the note and sent it on to respondent James, a corrections sergeant." Cannon did not regard the matter as "urgent." James had other "emergency" matters to attend to and forgot about it. The assault by the other inmate took place. The Federal District Court in New Jersey held for the plaintiff, and the Third Circuit reversed.]

We granted certiorari, and set this case for oral argument with *Daniels v. Williams,* 474 U.S. 327 (1986). Finding the principles enunciated in *Daniels* controlling here, we affirm.

In *Daniels,* we held that the Due Process Clause of the Fourteenth Amendment is not implicated by the lack of due care of an official causing unintended injury to life, liberty or property. In other words, where a government official is merely negligent in causing the injury, no procedure for compensation is constitutionally required. In this case, petitioner does not challenge the District Court's finding that respondents "did not act with deliberate or callous indifference to [petitioner's] needs," [c]. Instead, he claims only that respondents "negligently failed to protect him from another inmate." [C] *Daniels* therefore controls.

Respondents' lack of due care in this case led to serious injury, but that lack of care simply does not approach the sort of abusive government conduct that the Due Process Clause was designed to prevent. [citing *Daniels.*] Far from abusing governmental power, or employing it as an instrument of oppression, respondent Cannon mistakenly believed that the situation was not particularly serious, and respondent James simply forgot about the note. The guarantee of due process has never been understood to mean that the State must guarantee due care on the part of its officials.

In an effort to limit the potentially broad sweep of his claim, petitioner emphasizes that he "does not ask this Court to read the Constitution as an absolute guarantor of his liberty from assault by a fellow prisoner, even if that assault is caused by the negligence of his jailers." Describing his claim as one of "procedural due process, pure and simple," all he asks is that New Jersey provide him a remedy. But the Fourteenth Amendment does not require a remedy when there has been no "deprivation" of a protected interest. Petitioner's claim, based on respondents' negligence, is quite different from one involving injuries caused by an unjustified attack by prison guards themselves, see *Johnson v. Glick,* 481 F.2d 1028 (CA2), or by another prisoner where officials simply stood by and permitted the attack to proceed, see *Curtis v. Everette,* 489 F.2d 516 (CA3 1973). As we held in *Daniels,* the protections of the Due Process Clause, whether procedural or substantive, are just not triggered by lack of due care by prison officials.

Accordingly, the judgment of the Court of Appeals for the Third Circuit is affirmed.

JUSTICE BLACKMUN, with whom JUSTICE MARSHALL joins, dissenting.
*   *   *

While I concur in the judgment in *Daniels,* I do not join the Court in extending that result to this case. It is one thing to hold that a commonplace slip and fall, or the loss of a $23.50 hobby kit, see *Parratt v. Taylor, supra,* does not rise to the dignified level of a constitutional violation. It is a somewhat different thing to say that negligence that permits anticipated inmate violence resulting in injury, or perhaps leads to the execution of the wrong prisoner, does not implicate the Constitution's guarantee of due process. When the State incarcerated Daniels, it left intact his own faculties for avoiding a slip and a fall. But the State prevented Davidson from defending himself, and therefore assumed some responsibility to protect him from the dangers to which he was exposed. In these circumstances, I feel that Davidson was deprived of liberty by the negligence of the prison officials. Moreover, the acts of the state officials in this case may well have risen to the level of recklessness. I therefore dissent. *   *   *

I agree that mere negligent activity *ordinarily* will not amount to an abuse of state power. Where the Court today errs, in my view, is in elevating this sensible rule of thumb to the status of inflexible constitutional dogma. The Court declares that negligent activity can *never* implicate the concerns of the Due Process Clause. I see no justification for this rigid view. In some cases, by any reasonable standard, governmental negligence is an abuse of power. This is one of those cases.
*   *   *

In the context of prisons, *   *   * once the State has taken away an inmate's means of protecting himself from attack by other inmates, a prison official's negligence in providing protection can amount to a deprivation of the inmate's liberty, at least absent extenuating circumstances. Such conduct by state officials seems to me to be the "arbitrary action" against which the Due Process Clause protects. The officials' actions in such cases thus are not remote from the purpose of the Due Process Clause and § 1983.

Even if negligence is deemed categorically insufficient to cause a deprivation under the Fourteenth Amendment, recklessness must be sufficient. Recklessness or deliberate indifference is all that a prisoner need prove to show that denial of essential medical care violated the Eighth Amendment's ban on cruel and unusual punishments. *   *   *

JUSTICE STEVENS, concurring in the judgments [in both *Daniels* and *Davidson.*] *   *   * Those aspects of a State's tort regime that defeat recovery are not constitutionally invalid, so long as there is no fundamental unfairness in their operation. Thus, defenses such as contributory negligence or statutes of limitations may defeat recovery in particular cases without raising any question about the constitutionality of a State's procedures for disposing of tort litigation. Similarly, in my judgment, the mere fact that a State elects to provide some of its agents with a sovereign immunity defense in certain cases does not justify the conclusion that its remedial system is constitutionally inadequate. There is no reason to believe that the Due Process Clause of the Fourteenth Amendment and the legislation enacted pursuant to § 5 of that Amendment should be construed to suggest that the doctrine of sovereign immunity renders a state procedure fundamentally unfair. Davidson's challenge has been only to the fact of sovereign immunity; he has not challenged the difference in treatment of a prisoner assaulted by a prisoner and a nonprisoner assaulted by a prisoner, and I express no comment on the fairness of that differentiation.

Thus, although I believe that the harms alleged by Daniels and proved by Davidson qualify as deprivations of liberty, I am not persuaded that either has raised a violation of the Due Process Clause of the Fourteenth Amendment. I therefore concur in the judgments.

———

1. In Paul v. Davis, 424 U.S. 693 (1976), the Court held that an action based on § 1983 or a "constitutional tort" will not lie for injury to reputation or invasion of privacy, since it does not involve "liability" or "property."

2. In Maine v. Theboutot, 448 U.S. 1 (1980), it held that an action under § 1983 would lie for deprival of rights a under federal statute. The action lies unless "Congress has foreclosed such enforcement of the statute in the enactment itself [or] the statute did not create enforceable rights, privileges, or immunities within the meaning of § 1983." Wright v. Roanoke Redevelopment & Housing Auth., ___ U.S. ___, ___, 107 S.Ct. 766, 770, 93 L.Ed.2d 781 (1987).

3. In Robertson v. Wegmann, 436 U.S. 584 (1978) after filing an action based on § 1983, the plaintiff died. The question was whether the federal court should "adopt as federal law a Louisiana survivorship statute, which would have required this action to abate or was free instead to create a federal common law rule allowing the action to survive." Since the Louisiana law provides for the survival of most tort actions and was not discriminatory against this action as such, it was held not to be "inconsistent" with federal law and therefore applicable. See also Goodman v. Lukens Steel Co., ___ U.S. ___, 107 S.Ct. 2617, 96 L.Ed.2d 572 (1987).

4. On the defense of immunity on the part of the defendant, see Imbler v. Pachtmen, 424 U.S. 409 (1976) (absolute immunity for certain legislative and judicial officials); Butz v. Economou, 438 U.S. 478 (1978) (good-faith immunity for executive officials performing discretionary functions); Monell v. Department of Social Services, 436 U.S. 658 (1978) (governmental immunity); Pembaur v. City of Cincinnati, 475 U.S. 469 (1986) (municipal immunity, single act); Anderson v. Creighton, ___ U.S. ___, 107 S.Ct. 3034, 3038, 97 L.Ed.2d 523 (1987). (F.B.I. officials making a warrantless search of house have "a qualified immunity, providing them immunity from civil damages immunity as long as their action could reasonably have been thought consistent with the rights they are alleged to have violated").

5. See Nahmod, Due Process, State Remedies, and Section 1983, 34 U.Kan.L.Rev. 219 (1985).

MEMPHIS COMMUNITY SCHOOL DIST. v. STACHURA
Supreme Court of the United States, 1986.
477 U.S. 299, 106 S.Ct. 2537, 91 L.Ed.2d 299.

[Respondent, a tenured teacher in the Memphis, Michigan, public schools, was suspended following parents' complaints about his teaching methods in a 7th–grade life science course that included the showing of allegedly sexually explicit pictures and films. While respondent was later reinstated, he, before being reinstated, brought suit in Federal District Court under 42 U.S.C. § 1983 against petitioner School District, Board of Education, Board Members, school administrators, and parents, alleging that his suspension deprived him of liberty and property without due process of law and violated his First Amendment right to academic freedom. He sought both compensatory and punitive damages. The District Court instructed the jury on the standard elements of compensatory and punitive damages and also charged the jury that additional compensatory damages could be awarded based on the value or importance of the constitutional rights that were violated. The jury found petitioners liable, awarding both compensatory and punitive damages. The Court of Appeals affirmed. (Facts from official syllabus.)]

JUSTICE POWELL delivered the opinion of the Court. * * *

We granted certiorari limited to the question whether the Court of Appeals erred in affirming the damages award in the light of the District Court's instructions that authorized not only compensatory and punitive damages, but also damages for the deprivation of "any constitutional right." 474 U.S. 918, 106 S.Ct. 245, 88 L.Ed.2d 254 (1985). We reverse, and remand for a new trial limited to the issue of compensatory damages. * * *

We have repeatedly noted that 42 U.S.C. § 1983[8] creates " 'a species of tort liability' in favor of persons who are deprived of 'rights, privileges, or immunities secured' to them by the Constitution." *Carey v. Piphus,* 435 U.S. 247, 253 (1978). [Cc] Accordingly, when § 1983 plaintiffs seek damages for violations of constitutional rights, the level of damages is ordinarily determined according to principles derived from the common law of torts. [Cc]

Punitive damages aside, damages in tort cases are designed to provide "*compensation* for the injury caused to plaintiff by defendant's breach of duty." 2 F. Harper & F. James, Law of Torts § 25.1, p. 1299 (1956) (emphasis in original), quoted in *Carey v. Piphus, supra.* [Cc] To that end, compensatory damages may include not only out-of-pocket loss and other monetary harms, but also such injuries as "impairment

---

8. Section 1983 reads: "Every person who, under color of any statute, ordinance, regulation, custom, or usage, of any State or Territory or the District of Columbia, subjects, or causes to be subjected, any citizen of the United States or other person within the jurisdiction thereof to the deprivation of any rights, privileges, or immunities secured by the Constitution and laws, shall be liable to the party injured in an action at law, suit in equity, or other proper proceeding for redress."

of reputation * * *, personal humiliation, and mental anguish and suffering." *Gertz v. Robert Welch, Inc.,* 418 U.S. 323, 350 (1974). See also *Carey v. Piphus, supra,* 435 U.S., at 264 (mental and emotional distress constitute compensable injury in § 1983 cases). Deterrence is also an important purpose of this system, but it operates through the mechanism of damages that are *compensatory*—damages grounded in determinations of plaintiffs' actual losses. * * * Congress adopted this common-law system of recovery when it established liability for "constitutional torts." Consequently, "the basic purpose" of § 1983 damages is "to *compensate persons for injuries* that are caused by the deprivation of constitutional rights." *Carey v. Piphus,* 435 U.S., at 254 (emphasis added). See also *id.,* at 257 ("damages awards under § 1983 should be governed by the principle of compensation").

Carey v. Piphus represents a straightforward application of these principles. * * * Where no injury was present, no "compensatory" damages could be awarded.

The instructions at issue here cannot be squared with *Carey,* or with the principles of tort damages on which *Carey* and § 1983 are grounded. The jurors in this case were told that, in determining how much was necessary to "compensate [respondent] for the deprivation" of his constitutional rights, they should place a money value on the "rights" themselves by considering such factors as the particular right's "importance * * * in our system of government," its role in American history, and its "significance * * * in the context of the activities" in which respondent was engaged. These factors focus, not on compensation for provable injury, but on the jury's subjective perception of the importance of constitutional rights as an abstract matter. *Carey* establishes that such an approach is impermissible. The constitutional right transgressed in *Carey*—the right to due process of law—is central to our system of ordered liberty. We nevertheless held that *no* compensatory damages could be awarded for violation of that right absent proof of actual injury. *Carey,* 435 U.S., at 264. *Carey* thus makes clear that the abstract value of a constitutional right may not form the basis for § 1983 damages.[11]

Respondent nevertheless argues that *Carey* does not control here, because in this case a *substantive* constitutional right—respondent's First Amendment right to academic freedom—was infringed. The

---

11. We did approve an award of nominal damages for the deprivation of due process in *Carey.* 435 U.S., at 266. Our discussion of that issue makes clear that nominal damages, and not damages based on some undefinable "value" of infringed rights, are the appropriate means of "vindicating" rights whose deprivation has not caused actual, provable injury:

"Common-law courts traditionally have vindicated deprivations of certain 'absolute' rights that are not shown to have caused actual injury through the award of

a nominal sum of money. By making the deprivation of such rights actionable for nominal damages without proof of actual injury, the law recognizes the importance to organized society that those rights be scrupulously observed; but at the same time, it remains true to the principle that substantial damages should be awarded only to compensate actual injury or, in the case of exemplary or punitive damages, to deter or punish malicious deprivations of rights." *Ibid.*

argument misperceives our analysis in *Carey*. That case does not establish a two-tiered system of constitutional rights, with substantive rights afforded greater protection than "mere" procedural safeguards. We did acknowledge in *Carey* that "the elements and prerequisites for recovery of damages" might vary depending on the interests protected by the constitutional right at issue. [C] But we emphasized that, whatever the constitutional basis for § 1983 liability, such damages must always be designed "to *compensate injuries* caused by the [constitutional] deprivation." [Cc] That conclusion simply leaves no room for noncompensatory damages measured by the jury's perception of the abstract "importance" of a constitutional right.

Nor do we find such damages necessary to vindicate the constitutional rights that § 1983 protects. See n. 11, *supra*. Section 1983 presupposes that damages that compensate for actual harm ordinarily suffice to deter constitutional violations. * * *

Moreover, damages based on the "value" of constitutional rights are an unwieldy tool for ensuring compliance with the Constitution. History and tradition do not afford any sound guidance concerning the precise value that juries should place on constitutional protections. Accordingly, were such damages available, juries would be free to award arbitrary amounts without any evidentiary basis, or to use their unbounded discretion to punish unpopular defendants. [C] Such damages would be too uncertain to be of any great value to plaintiffs, and would inject caprice into determinations of damages in § 1983 cases. We therefore hold that damages based on the abstract "value" or "importance" of constitutional rights are not a permissible element of compensatory damages in such cases. * * *

Respondent further argues that the challenged instructions authorized a form of "presumed" damages—a remedy that is both compensatory in nature and traditionally part of the range of tort law remedies. Alternatively, respondent argues that the erroneous instructions were at worst harmless error.

Neither argument has merit. Presumed damages are a *substitute* for ordinary compensatory damages, not a *supplement* for an award that fully compensates the alleged injury. When a plaintiff seeks compensation for an injury that is likely to have occurred but difficult to establish, some form of presumed damages may possibly be appropriate. [Cc]

In those circumstances, presumed damages may roughly approximate the harm that the plaintiff suffered and thereby compensate for harms that may be impossible to measure. As we earlier explained, the instructions at issue in this case did not serve this purpose, but instead called on the jury to measure damages based on a subjective evaluation of the importance of particular constitutional values. Since such damages are wholly divorced from any compensatory purpose, they cannot be justified as presumed damages.[14] Moreover, no rough substitute for compensatory damages was required in this case, since the jury was fully authorized to compensate respondent for both monetary and non-monetary harms caused by petitioners' conduct.

Nor can we find that the erroneous instructions were harmless. [Cc] When damages instructions are faulty and the verdict does not reveal the means by which the jury calculated damages, "[the] error in the charge is difficult, if not impossible, to correct without retrial, in light of the jury's general verdict." [C]

The jury was authorized to award three categories of damages: (i) compensatory damages for injury to respondent, (ii) punitive damages, and (iii) damages based on the jury's perception of the "importance" of two provisions of the Constitution. The submission of the third of these categories was error. * * *

The judgment of the Court of Appeals is reversed, and the case is remanded for further proceedings consistent with this opinion.

JUSTICE MARSHALL, with whom JUSTICE BRENNAN, JUSTICE BLACKMUN, and JUSTICE STEVENS join, concurring in the judgment.

I agree with the Court that this case must be remanded for a new trial on damages. Certain portions of the Court's opinion, however, can be read to suggest that damages in § 1983 cases are necessarily limited to "out-of-pocket loss," "other monetary harms," and "such injuries as 'impairment of reputation * * *, personal humiliation, and mental anguish and suffering.'"

I do not understand the Court so to hold, and I write separately to emphasize that the violation of a constitutional right, in proper cases, may itself constitute a compensable injury. * * *

---

14. For the same reason, *Nixon v. Herndon,* 273 U.S. 536 (1927), and similar cases do not support the challenged instructions. * * *

Nixon followed a long line of cases, going back to Lord Holt's decision in *Ashby v. White,* 2 Ld.Raym. 938, 92 Eng.Rep. 126 (1703), authorizing substantial money damages as compensation for persons deprived of their right to vote in particular elections. [Cc] Although these decisions sometimes speak of damages for the value of the right to vote, their analysis shows that they involve nothing more than an award of presumed damages for a non-monetary harm that cannot easily be quantified:

"In the eyes of the law th[e] right [to vote] is so valuable that damages are presumed from the wrongful deprivation of it without evidence of actual loss of money, property, or any other valuable thing, and the amount of the damages is a question

peculiarly appropriate for the determination of the jury, because each member of the jury has personal knowledge of the value of the right." *Ibid.* * * *

See also *Ashby v. White, supra,* at 955, 92 Eng.Rep., at 137 (Holt, C.J.) ("As in an action for slanderous words, though a man does not lose a penny by reason of the speaking [of] them, yet he shall have an action"). The "value of the right" in the context of these decisions is the money value of the particular loss that the plaintiff suffered—a loss of which "each member of the jury has personal knowledge." It is *not* the value of the right to vote as a general, abstract matter, based on its role in our history or system of government. Thus, whatever the wisdom of these decisions in the context of the changing scope of compensatory damages over the course of this century, they do not support awards of non-compensatory damages such as those authorized in this case.

Following *Carey* [*v. Piphus,* supra page 985], the courts of appeals have recognized that invasions of constitutional rights sometimes cause injuries that cannot be redressed by a wooden application of common-law damages rules. In *Hobson v. Wilson,* 237 U.S.App.D.C. 219, 275–281, 737 F.2d 1, 57–63 (1984), [c] plaintiffs claimed that defendant FBI agents had invaded their First Amendment rights to assemble for peaceable political protest, to associate with others to engage in political expression, and to speak on public issues free of unreasonable government interference. The District Court found that the defendants had succeeded in diverting plaintiffs from, and impeding them in, their protest activities. The Court of Appeals for the District of Columbia Circuit held that that injury to a First Amendment-protected interest could itself constitute compensable injury wholly apart from any "emotional distress, humiliation and personal indignity, emotional pain, embarrassment, fear, anxiety and anguish" suffered by plaintiffs. [C] The court warned, however, that that injury could be compensated with substantial damages only to the extent that it was "reasonably quantifiable"; damages should not be based on "the so-called inherent value of the rights violated."

I believe that the *Hobson* court correctly stated the law. * * * There is no reason why such an injury should not be compensable in damages. At the same time, however, the award must be proportional to the actual loss sustained.

The instructions given the jury in this case were improper because they did not require the jury to focus on the loss actually sustained by respondent. * * *

The Court therefore properly remands for a new trial on damages. I do not understand the Court, however, to hold that deprivations of constitutional rights can never themselves constitute compensable injuries. Such a rule would be inconsistent with the logic of *Carey,* and would defeat the purpose of § 1983 by denying compensation for genuine injuries caused by the deprivation of constitutional rights.

---

1. On the availability of punitive damages, see Smith v. Wade, 461 U.S. 30, 103 S.Ct. 1625, 72 L.Ed.2d 632 (1983).

2. For representative cases on police abuse, see Stringer v. Dilger, 313 F.2d 536 (10th Cir.1963); Batista v. Weir, 340 F.2d 74 (3d Cir.1965). And see Newman, Suing the Lawbreakers; Proposals to Strengthen the Section 1983 Remedy for Law Enforcers' Misconduct, 87 Yale L.J. 447 (1978); Penland & Boardmon, Section 1983—Contemporary Trends in the Police Misconduct Area, 20 Ida.L.Rev. 661 (1984). See also Briscoe v. LaHue, 460 U.S. 325 (1983) (no recovery against police officer for perjured testimony).

3. Patsy v. Board of Regents, 457 U.S. 496, 102 S.Ct. 2557, 73 L.Ed.2d 172 (1982), holds that it is not necessary to exhaust state administrative remedies before bringing suit under § 1983. The suit may be in either the Federal court or the state court. See Steinglass, The Emerging State Court § 1983 Action: A Procedural Review, 38 U.Miami L.Rev. 381 (1984).

Chapter XX

MISUSE OF LEGAL PROCEDURE

TEXAS SKAGGS, INC. v. GRAVES
Court of Civil Appeals of Texas, 1979.
582 S.W.2d 863.

[Suit for malicious prosecution. Plaintiff-appellee, Mrs. Sharon Graves, had "worked as a checker in the Skaggs store but was fired for reasons not material to this case." She continued to purchase groceries at Skaggs and had given the store two checks totaling $34.70. The checking account was in her name, but she had left a few blank checks signed by her at home, for her husband to use. The couple had separated and, unknown to her, her husband had withdrawn all of her funds. She agreed to pay "as soon as she could get the money from the Skaggs' credit union." Over two weeks later, when she received her money from the credit union, she "purchased a money order and mailed it to Skaggs to cover the 'hot' checks."

The next day, Bill Pennington, a Skaggs manager, filed an "Incident Report" with the Texarkana, Arkansas, Police Department reporting Mrs. Graves for a violation of the Arkansas Hot Check Law. Four days later, he filed an affidavit for warrant of her arrest. Over a week later, when Mrs. Graves was shopping in the Skaggs store, a manager summoned the police, who came and arrested her. She tried to explain to police sergeant Larry Arnold that she had paid the checks, but he "took her out of the store and to the police station where she was booked on a hot check charge. Arnold then telephoned Skaggs and learned that the checks had, in fact, been paid. Arnold then released Graves and returned the two checks to her (that had been attached to the Affidavit for Warrant of Arrest). "Sgt. Arnold talked to an employee of Skaggs again that afternoon and when the person he was talking to learned that Graves had been released, that person (unidentified) told Arnold that he wanted Graves prosecuted and that he did not care if she had paid the checks. The next morning, March 4th, Arnold drove to Sharon Graves' home in Texas and told her that Skaggs intended to prosecute her that afternoon. Mrs. Graves immediately hired an attorney and appeared in Court. The municipal judge dismissed the case when the prosecution could not produce the "hot checks."]

RAY, JUSTICE. * * * In Arkansas, a cause of action for malicious prosecution consists of the following elements: (1) A criminal prosecution instituted or continued by the defendant against the plaintiff; (2) Termination of the proceedings in favor of the accused; (3) Absence of probable cause for the proceeding; (4) Malice; and, (5) Damages. See

1002

Note, Malicious Prosecution—The Law in Arkansas, 22 Ark.L.Rev. 340 (1968).

In response to special issues, the jury found that Graves did not know that her bank account had insufficient funds for the payment of the two checks; that Skaggs did not have probable cause to institute the prosecution of Sharon Graves; that Skaggs acted with malice; and, that the sum of $20,000.00 would reasonably compensate Graves for her actual damages.

Institution of Criminal Proceedings. The evidence is clear and undisputed that Skaggs initiated and continued the prosecution of Sharon Graves.

Termination of the Proceedings in Favor of the Accused. The record reflects that the case against Graves was dismissed in the Municipal Court of Texarkana, Arkansas, with the notation, "dismissed on basis checks not available for presentation of case." Skaggs argues that this type of termination is indecisive and is not sufficient to establish malicious prosecution. Prosser describes types of termination that are sufficient to sustain a malicious prosecution suit:

"On the other hand, it will be enough that the proceeding is terminated in such a manner that it cannot be revived, and the prosecutor, if he proceeds further, will be put to a new one. This is true, for example, of an acquittal in court, * * * the entry of a nolle prosequi or a dismissal, abandonment of the prosecution by the prosecuting attorney or the complaining witness, * * * where any of these things have the effect of ending the particular proceeding and requiring new process or other official action to commence a new prosecution. It may be said generally, that this is true whenever the charges or the proceeding are withdrawn on the initiative of the prosecution. * * *

"On the other hand, where charges are withdrawn or the prosecution is terminated at the instigation of the accused himself, or by reason of a compromise into which he has entered voluntarily, there is no sufficient termination in favor of the accused. * * * " W. Prosser, Torts Sec. 113, pp. 857, 858 (3rd ed.1964).

Prosser is in accord with the rule established by the Restatement (Second) of Torts, §§ 658, 659 (1977). The abandonment of the proceedings because a conviction has, in the natural course of events, become impossible or improbable, is a sufficient termination in favor of the accused. [C] We are of the opinion that this case was not dismissed on technical or procedural grounds, but was an abandonment of the prosecution by the prosecuting attorney and that the inferences to be drawn from the evidence support that conclusion. We are of the further opinion that because there was a dismissal for lack of incriminating evidence, Graves could have procured a finding of "not guilty" by the municipal court had the matter been pressed for a full trial by the prosecuting attorney. Closely connected with the element of successful termination is the defense that Graves was in fact guilty of the charge. This defense was available even if Graves had been acquitted of the criminal charge. The rational basis is that the law protects only the innocent and, if guilty, the plaintiff deserved the treatment complained of. Thus, Skaggs had the option to assert the defense that Graves was in fact guilty of the charge. There was apparently some attempt to prove this defense, but the jury rejected it.

Absence of Probable Cause. Graves had the burden of proving that the criminal proceeding was initiated or continued by Skaggs without probable cause; that is, Graves had to show that Skaggs had no honest or reasonable belief in the truth of the charge however suspicious the circumstances of Graves' acts. Probable cause has been defined by the Arkansas Supreme Court in *Hitson v. Simms,* 69 Ark. 439, 441, 64 S.W. 219, 220 (1901), as follows: " * * * such a state of facts known to the prosecutor, or such information received by him from sources entitled to credit, as would induce a man of ordinary caution and prudence to believe, and did induce the prosecutor to believe, that the accused is guilty of the crime alleged, and thereby caused the prosecution * * *"

However, it is stated in 22 Ark.L.Rev. 349: "Liability is imposed on the defendant where there are sufficient facts to indicate to a reasonable man that the plaintiff was guilty but the defendant himself knew better, i.e., a subjective test. Since the test requires more than mere unfounded suspicion the courts will hold a defendant liable in cases where a reasonable man would further investigate the facts."

The facts supporting the jury's finding of lack of probable cause are that Graves was well-known by the employees of Skaggs; that the two checks were relatively small; that the checks were used to pay for groceries alone and that no cash was obtained with the checks; that Graves could have obtained large amounts of cash because she knew all of the Skaggs' employees; that she could have cashed many checks obtaining cash, but did not; that the checks were written on her regular bank account and not some fictitious bank or bank account; that once she was notified that her two checks had been returned to Skaggs, she immediately agreed to make restitution; that Graves in fact mailed her money order to Skaggs prior to the time that prosecution was instituted; that Skaggs was aware of the restitution before her arrest; that Skaggs had agreed to await restitution and to accept payment for the checks when Graves received her money from the Skaggs credit union; that Skaggs, pursuant to its agreement with Graves, had accepted restitution but issued instructions that the prosecution continue; and, that Skaggs further insisted that the prosecution continue after having been apprised of the fact that Mrs. Graves had been arrested and released by the officer after the officer had called one of Skaggs' employees and learned that restitution had been made. From the foregoing facts, and the inferences to be drawn therefrom, the jury could have reasonably concluded that Graves did not intend to defraud Skaggs and that no probable cause existed to institute or continue the prosecution proceedings. As a defense, the burden of persuasion was on Skaggs to show that the complaining witness, Bill

Pennington, believed in Graves' guilt at the time the original proceeding commenced and that this belief was supported with facts which would lead a reasonable, cautious or prudent man to the same conclusion, and which in fact did lead Pennington to this conclusion. Pennington was not called as a witness. The jury apparently believed that the testimony of Sharon Graves was more plausible than that of the employees at Skaggs and that Skaggs knew or should have known or found out from further investigation that Graves did not issue the checks knowing at the time of issuing them that she did not have sufficient funds in her bank account to cover the checks. The jury could have further believed that while a reasonable person might have concluded that Graves was guilty, Skaggs' employees knew better and should have further investigated the facts.

The "Arkansas Hot Check Law", Ark.Stat.Ann. Sec. 67–720 (Supp. 1978) provides:

"It shall be unlawful for any person to procure any article or thing of value, * * * or for any other purpose to make or draw or utter or deliver, with intent to defraud, any check, * * * upon any bank, * * * knowing at the time of such making, * * * that the maker, * * * has not sufficient funds in, or on deposit with, such bank, * * *".

Evidence of the requisite intent to defraud is supplied by Ark.Stat.Ann. Sec. 67–722 which provides that the making of a check, " * * * payment of which is refused by the drawee, shall be prima facie evidence of intent to defraud * * * ". While the statute raises the presumption of intent to defraud, such presumption may be rebutted by evidence explaining the transaction and where the evidence is sufficient to dispel any presumption of intent to defraud, the statute alone will not support a conviction under the Arkansas Hot Check Law. [Cc]. In the present case, there was no intent to defraud because there was ample evidence to support the jury finding that Graves did not know that she had insufficient funds in her bank account at the time of writing the checks with which to make payment of the two checks when they were processed for payment at her bank. And while restitution alone is not an absolute defense to the Arkansas Hot Check Law [c], the fact that Graves immediately agreed to make restitution and did in fact make restitution in some evidence that she did not intend to defraud Skaggs. Certainly, once Graves had made restitution and that fact was coupled with all the other facts known to Skaggs' employees, a conclusion that Skaggs had no probable cause to further insist upon the prosecution of Graves would be justified.

Malice. Regarding the element of malice, it is generally agreed that the lack of probable cause may give rise to an inference of malice, sufficient to carry the question to the jury. W. Prosser, Torts, Sec. 113, p. 868 (3rd ed. 1964). The courts require that malice in fact be shown in order to sustain a recovery for malicious prosecution. This is usually established by proving that the defendant had a wrongful or improper motive or was motivated by some purpose other than bringing a guilty person to justice, such as, using the prosecution as a means to recover property, to extort money, or to collect a debt. " * * * Hence, proof of malice need not be direct but may be inferred from circumstances surrounding the defendant's act. This does not mean the defendant must have acted out of hatred, ill will, spite or grudge." 22 Ark.L.Rev. 340, 353, supra. The jury could and probably did believe that Skaggs instituted the criminal proceedings without probable cause in an effort to collect the two checks. The jury finding that Skaggs acted with malice has ample support in the record. Certainly, Skaggs' insistence that the prosecution continue against Graves after she had been released by Sgt. Arnold following her arrest with the statement to the effect that Skaggs did not care if Graves had paid the checks, Skaggs wanted her prosecuted anyway, supports the inference that Skaggs continued to act maliciously.

Damages. Appellant argues that the jury verdict was so grossly excessive as to show that it was the result of passion, prejudice or other improper motives. No cases are cited to guide this Court in its determination of this issue. The general rule is as follows:

"Although the verdict is large and the trial court, in the exercise of a sound discretion, might properly have set it aside, the appellate court will not disturb the verdict, although it may seem too large, in the absence of circumstances tending to show that it was the result of passion, prejudice, or other improper motive, or that the amount fixed was not the result of a deliberate and conscientious conviction in the minds of the jury and the court, or so excessive as to shock a sense of justice in the minds of the appellate court." 17 Tex.Jur.2d Damages, Sec. 341, p. 415 (1960).

As stated in *Green v. Meadows,* 527 S.W.2d 496 (Tex.Civ.App. Houston–1st Dist. 1975, writ ref'd n.r.e.), there are no objective guidelines by which we can measure the money equivalent of mental pain.

" * * * Much discretion must be allowed the jury in fixing this amount. The trial judge refused to order a remittitur. We are unable to say that the jury's verdict is excessive to the extent that the judgment should be reversed for that reason only. * * * "

In *Green,* the jury had awarded the plaintiff $20,000.00 in a malicious prosecution suit.

The facts in the present case show that Sharon Graves has suffered substantial injury. She was arrested and paraded through the store by a uniformed policeman and the store manager in front of her friends and former fellow employees. She was taken to the police station where she was booked and suffered the humiliation of a criminal charge. She testified that because of this criminal record she was not hired by several prospective employers because of her arrest record which will follow her the rest of her life. The evidence supports the jury verdict. * * *

To recapitulate, the pleadings were adequate to support the judgment; there was sufficient evidence to establish that Skaggs had instituted and continued criminal prosecution against Sharon Graves; there was evidence that the proceeding was terminated in favor of Graves; that the evidence established an absence of probable cause for institution of the criminal proceedings against Graves; that the evidence supports the finding of malice; and, the evidence supports the jury finding of $20,000.00 in damages. * * *

---

1. There is consensus on the first four elements of the cause of action for malicious prosecution stated in the principal case. Other cases listing the requirements for liability include Hoene v. Associated Dry Goods Corp., 487 S.W.2d 479 (Mo.1972); Rose v. Whitbeck, 277 Or. 791, 562 P.2d 188 (1977). And see Restatement (Second) of Torts §§ 653 et seq.

2. *Institution of Criminal Proceedings.* This element may be met by (1) indictment or information or (2) the issuance of criminal process to bring the accused before a magistrate whose function is to determine whether he is guilty or is to be held for later determination or (3) arrest on a criminal charge. The commencement must have been either initiated or procured by the private prosecutor, or he must have played an active part in continuing the proceeding. See Wilson v. Yono, 65 Mich.App. 441, 237 N.W.2d 494 (1975); Creelman v. Svenning, 67 Wash.2d 882, 410 P.2d 606 (1966).

3. *Termination in Favor of the Accused.* This element is met by: discharge by magistrate at a preliminary hearing, Tritchler v. West Virginia Newspaper Pub. Co., 156 W.Va. 335, 193 S.E.2d 146 (1972); grand jury refusal to indict, Davis v. Quille, 248 Md. 631, 237 A.2d 745 (1968); a nolle prosequi, Bickford v. Lantay, 394 A.2d 281 (Me.1978); dismissal, Green v. Warnock, 144 Kan. 170, 58 P.2d 1059 (1936); failure to prosecute for lack of evidence, Southern Farmers Ass'n v. Whitfield, 238 Ark. 607, 383 S.W.2d 506 (1964); quashing of indictment, Davis v. McCrory Corp., 262 So.2d 207 (Fla.App.1972); or acquittal, Singer Mfg. Co. v. Bryant, 105 Va. 403, 54 S.E. 320 (1906). It is not met by an indecisive termination, Weissman v. K–Mart Corp., 396 So.2d 1164 (Fla.App.1981); Hoeg v. Strass, 567 S.W.2d 353 (Mo.App.1978); or by the impossibility of bringing the accused to trial, Halberstadt v. New York Life Ins. Co., 194 N.Y. 1, 86 N.E. 801 (1909). Perhaps the best discussion of the issue of termination is to be found in Loeb v. Teitelbaum, 77 A.D.2d 92, 432 N.Y.S.2d 487 (1980).

4. *Lack of Probable Cause.*

A. *Mistake of Fact.* The private prosecutor must have reasonable grounds for believing that the accused is guilty of the criminal charge. But if the private prosecutor does not honestly believe that the accused was guilty, there is no probable cause. Hanson v. Couch, 360 So.2d 992 (Ala.1978).

If he does so believe, he may have probable cause even though he is wrong, provided his mistake regarding the true facts is a reasonable one. This is much like the standard of the reasonable person in a negligence case, but the difference is that probable cause is for the court, rather than the jury, to decide. If there are questions of fact as to what the defendant did or did not know, the resolution of that question is for the jury under proper instructions; but whether, upon established facts, there was probable cause is not left to them. See generally Smith v. Tucker, 304 A.2d 303 (D.C.App.1973); Turner v. Chicago,

91 Ill.App.3d 931, 47 Ill.Dec. 476, 415 N.E.2d 481 (1980). If a reasonable person would investigate further to make more certain of the facts before instituting criminal proceedings and the private prosecutor fails to do so, he may be found to have acted without probable cause. Food Fair Store, Inc. v. Kincaid, 335 So. 2d 560 (Fla.App.1976); Lambert v. Sears, Roebuck & Co., 280 Or. 123, 570 P.2d 357 (1977).

In both Kroger Co. v. Standard, 283 Ark. 44, 670 S.W.2d 803 (1984), and Walmart Stores, Inc. v. Yarbrough, 284 Ark. 345, 681 S.W.2d 359 (1984), a customer was accosted after leaving the store with an article not paid for. Disbelieving the customer's explanation, the store prosecuted for shoplifting and the jury acquitted. Suit for malicious prosecution by the customer, who obtained a jury award of compensatory damages and substantial punitive damages in each. The appellate court affirmed one case and reversed the other, by a divided vote each time. What conclusions do you draw?

B. *Mistake of Law.* A layman who institutes a criminal proceeding without seeking advice of an attorney on whether the supposed facts constitute a crime may be held to have acted without probable cause if they do not; but there may be circumstances under which his conduct is reasonable. See Meadows v. Grant, 15 Ariz.App. 104, 486 P.2d 216 (1971); Ruff v. Eckerds Drugs, Inc., 265 S.C. 563, 220 S.E.2d 649 (1975). Some courts hold, however, that even a reasonable mistake of law will not support probable cause. See Thomas v. Kessler, 334 Pa. 7, 5 A.2d 187 (1939); Atkinson v. Birmingham, 44 R.I. 123, 116 A. 205 (1922).

5. *Effect of Various Occurrences on Determination of Probable Cause.*

A. Action of magistrate on preliminary hearing. Discharge is conclusive of lack of probable cause unless it was not on the merits or was based on testimony of the accused at the hearing. Hawkins v. Hawkins, 32 N.C.App. 158, 231 S.E.2d 174 (1977); Huntley v. Harberts, 264 N.W.2d 497 (S.D.1978). Contra, Hoene v. Associated Dry Goods Corp., 487 S.W.2d 479 (Mo.1972). Commitment is evidence that there was probable cause. Davis v. Quille, 248 Md. 631, 237 A.2d 745 (1968). A similar distinction is made regarding action of a grand jury.

B. Outcome of proceedings. Abandonment by the private prosecutor is evidence of lack of probable cause. See Exxon Corp. v. Kelly, 281 Md. 689, 381 A.2d 1146 (1978). Conviction is usually held to be conclusive on existence of probable cause. Early v. Harry's I.G.A., Inc., 223 Kan. 32, 573 P.2d 572 (1977); cf. J.C. Penney Co. v. Blush, 356 So.2d 590 (Miss.1978) (presumption). Acquittal does not have any effect, according to the majority rule. Meyer v. Nedry, 159 Or. 62, 78 P.2d 339 (1938). Why?

C. Advice of counsel is conclusive on the issue of probable cause, if the advice is sought in good faith and is given after a full and fair disclosure of the facts within the accuser's knowledge and information. Varner v. Hoffer, 267 Or. 175, 515 P.2d 920 (1973); Bain v. Phillips, 217 Va. 387, 228 S.E.2d 576 (1976).

6. *"Malice."* This troublesome word turns up again in malicious prosecution, and has given its name to the action. Here, it does not necessarily mean hatred, spite or ill will, but rather a purpose in initiating the prosecution other than that of bringing a criminal to justice. There is "malice" when the defendant has used the prosecution to extort money from the accused, to recover property from him, to collect a debt, or to compel performance of a contract. Dislike and ill will, which are not uncommon toward any criminal,

may not be enough for "malice," if the proper purpose is also found to exist. The courts have tended, however, to look to the primary objective of the defendant. This element is usually left to the jury, unless the facts in evidence permit only one decision. See Restatement (Second) of Torts § 668. It is generally agreed that the jury are to be instructed that lack of probable cause may be evidence of the existence of malice, but that malice is not evidence of lack of probable cause.

7. *Damages.* The plaintiff must have suffered damage from the prosecution; it is assumed by the law that some damage, such as harm to reputation, will necessarily follow. The same is true of humiliation and other mental suffering. There may, in addition, be recovery for any special damages that the plaintiff can prove, as for example those for arrest or imprisonment, discomfort or injury to health and expenses, such as attorney's fees, in defending the criminal case. This tort is clearly one appropriate for punitive damages, and it is undisputed that they can be recovered, if the jury sees fit to award them.

8. *Effect of Guilt of the Accused.* The fact that the accused was acquitted in the criminal prosecution does not necessarily mean lack of guilt. In a criminal trial, it is necessary to prove guilt beyond a reasonable doubt, and guilt or innocence of the accused may be retried in the civil action for malicious prosecution. In the civil action, a showing by the defendant that the accused (plaintiff in the civil action) was guilty is a complete defense. The defendant must raise the issue and has the burden of proof, but the measure of the burden is a preponderance of the evidence, not beyond a reasonable doubt. See MacRae v. Brant, 108 N.H. 177, 230 A.2d 753 (1967); Shoemaker v. Selnes, 220 Or. 573, 349 P.2d 473 (1960).

9. See Dobbs, Belief and Doubt in Malicious Prosecution and Libel, 21 Ariz.L.Rev. 607 (1979); Mallon, Attorney's Liability for Malicious Prosecution, 46 Ins.Coun.J. 407 (1979); Fridman, Action for Malicious Prosecution, 111 L.J. 285 (1961).

FRIEDMAN v. DOZORC

Supreme Court of Michigan, 1981.
412 Mich. 1, 312 N.W.2d 585.

LEVIN, JUSTICE. * * * Leona Serafin entered Outer Drive Hospital in May, 1970, for treatment of gynecological problems. A dilation and curettage was performed by her physician, Dr. Harold Krevsky. While in the hospital, Mrs. Serafin was referred to the present plaintiff, Dr. Friedman, for urological consultation. Dr. Friedman recommended surgical removal of a kidney stone which was too large to pass, and the operation was performed on May 20, 1970. During the surgery, the patient began to ooze blood uncontrollably. Although other physicians were consulted, Mrs. Serafin's condition continued to worsen and she died five days after the surgery. An autopsy was performed the next day; the report identified the cause of death as thrombotic thrombocytopenic purpura, a rare and uniformly fatal blood disease, the cause and cure of which are unknown.

On January 11, 1972, attorneys Dozorc and Golden, the defendants in this action, filed a malpractice action on behalf of Anthony Serafin, Jr., for himself and as administrator of the estate of Leona Serafin, against Peoples Community Hospital Authority, Outer Drive Hospital, Dr. Krevsky and Dr. Friedman, as well as another physician who was dismissed as a defendant before trial. * * * No expert testimony tending to show that any of the defendants had breached accepted professional standards in making the decision to perform the elective surgery or in the manner of its performance was presented as part of the plaintiff's case. The judge entered a directed verdict of no cause of action in favor of Dr. Friedman and the other defendants at the close of the plaintiff's proofs. The judge subsequently denied a motion for costs brought by codefendant Peoples Community Hospital Authority, pursuant to GCR 1963, 111.6. The Court of Appeals affirmed and this Court denied leave to appeal.

Dr. Friedman commenced the present action on March 17, 1976 in Oakland Circuit Court.

[The trial court granted summary judgment for the defendants. The Court of Appeals affirmed in part and reversed in part.]

This Court granted leave to appeal on both the plaintiff's application from that portion of the Court of Appeals decision affirming the dismissal of the causes of action sounding in negligence and abuse of process and on the defendants' application to cross-appeal from that portion of the decision reversing the dismissal of the cause of action for malicious prosecution. * * *

Plaintiff and amici in support urge this Court to hold that an attorney owes a present or prospective adverse party a duty of care, breach of which will give rise to a cause of action for negligence. We agree with the circuit judge and the Court of Appeals that an attorney owes no actionable duty to an adverse party.

Plaintiff and amici argue that an attorney who initiates a civil action owes a duty to his client's adversary and all other foreseeable third parties who may be affected by such an action to conduct a reasonable investigation and re-examination of the facts and law so that the attorney will have an adequate basis for a good-faith belief that the client has a tenable claim. Plaintiff contends that this duty is created by the Code of Professional Responsibility and by the Michigan General Court Rules. * * *

In a negligence action the question whether the defendant owes an actionable legal duty to the plaintiff is one of law which the court decides after assessing the competing policy considerations for and against recognizing the asserted duty. * * *

Assuming that an attorney has an obligation to his client to conduct a reasonable investigation prior to bringing an action, that obligation is not the functional equivalent of a duty of care owed to the client's adversary. We decline to so transform the attorney's obligation because we view such a duty as inconsistent with basic precepts of the adversary system. * * *

[C]reation of a duty in favor of an adversary of the attorney's client would create an unacceptable conflict of interest which would seriously hamper an attorney's effectiveness as counsel for his client. Not only would the adversary's interests interfere with the client's interests, the attorney's justifiable concern with being sued for negligence would detrimentally interfere with the attorney-client relationship. * * *

Because we are of the opinion that recognition of a cause of action for negligence in favor of a client's adversary might unduly inhibit attorneys from bringing close cases or advancing innovative theories, or taking action against defendants who can be expected to retaliate, we decline to recognize a duty of due care to the adverse party. * * *

To recover upon a theory of abuse of process, a plaintiff must plead and prove (1) an ulterior purpose and (2) an act in the use of process which is improper in the regular prosecution of the proceeding. * * *

We need not decide whether plaintiff's pleadings sufficiently allege that the defendants had an ulterior purpose in causing process to issue, since it is clear that the plaintiff has failed to allege that defendants committed some irregular act in the use of process. The only act in the use of process that plaintiff alleges is the issuance of a summons and complaint in the former malpractice action. However, a summons and complaint are properly employed when used to institute a civil action, and thus plaintiff has failed to satisfy the second element required. * * *

We note that other courts that have addressed the question whether abuse of process is a possible theory of recovery in the context of a medical malpractice countersuit have found that mere commencement of an action for malpractice is not an improper use of process. [Cc]

Plaintiff relies upon the same allegations respecting defendants' conduct and their failure to meet professional standards which assertedly constitute negligence in contending that he has pled a cause of action for malicious prosecution. He argues that the question of probable cause in a malicious prosecution action against the attorney for an opposing party turns on whether the attorney fulfilled his duty to reasonably investigate the facts and law before initiating and continuing a lawsuit. If the attorney's investigation discloses that the claim is not tenable, then it is his obligation to discontinue the action. * * *

We agree with defendants that under Michigan law special injury remains an essential element of the tort cause of action for malicious prosecution of civil proceedings. * * *

The recognition of an action for malicious prosecution developed as an adjunct to the English practice of awarding costs to the prevailing party in certain aggravated cases where the costs remedy was thought to be inadequate and the defendant had suffered damages beyond the expense and travail normally incident to defending a lawsuit. In 1698 three categories of damage which would support an action for malicious prosecution were identified: injury to one's fame (as by a scandalous allegation), injury to one's person or liberty, and injury to one's property. To this day the English courts do not recognize actions for malicious prosecution of either criminal or civil proceedings unless one of these types of injury, as narrowly defined by the cases, is present.

A substantial number of American jurisdictions today follow some form of "English rule" to the effect that "in the absence of an arrest, seizure, or special damage, the successful civil defendant has no remedy, despite the fact that his antagonist proceeded against him maliciously and without probable cause." A larger number of jurisdictions, some say a majority, follow an "American rule" permitting actions for malicious prosecution of civil proceedings without requiring the plaintiff to show special injury. * * *

The plaintiff's complaint does not allege special injury. We are satisfied that Michigan has not significantly departed from the English rule and we decline to do so today. * * *

Since this Court has not heretofore declared that an action for malicious prosecution of civil proceedings may be maintained in the absence of special injury, it remains to be decided whether we should so hold today. We are persuaded that the special injury requirement should be retained to limit the circumstances in which an action for the malicious prosecution of civil proceedings can be maintained.

Most commentators appear to favor abrogation of the special injury requirement to make the action more available and less difficult to maintain. Their counsel should, however, be evaluated skeptically. The lawyer's remedy for a grievance is a lawsuit, and a law student or tort professor may be particularly predisposed by experience and training to see the preferred remedy for a wrongful tort action as another tort action. In seeking a remedy for the excessive litigiousness of our society, we would do well to cast off the limitations of a perspective which ascribes curative power only to lawsuits.

We turn to a consideration of Dean Prosser's criticisms of the three reasons commonly advanced by courts for adhering to the English rule. First, to the assertion that the costs awarded to the prevailing party are intended as the exclusive remedy for the damages incurred by virtue of the wrongful litigation, Prosser responds that "in the United States, where the costs are set by statute at trivial amounts, and no attorney's fees are allowed, there can be no pretense at compensation even for the expenses of the litigation itself." This argument is compelling, but it does not necessarily justify an award of compensation absent the hardship of special injury or dictate that an award of compensation be assessed in a separate lawsuit. Second, to the arguments that an unrestricted tort of wrongful civil proceedings will deter honest litigants and that an innocent party must bear the costs of litigation as the price of a system which permits free access to the courts, Prosser answers that "there is no policy in favor of vexatious suits known to be groundless, which are a real and often a serious injury." But a tort action is not the only means of deterring groundless litigation, and other devices may be less intimidating to good-faith litigants. Finally, in response to the claim that recognition of the tort action will produce interminable litigation, Prosser argues that the heavy burden of proof which the plaintiff bears in such actions will safeguard bona fide litigants and prevent an endless chain of countersuits. But if few plaintiffs will recover in the subsequent action, one may wonder whether there is any point in recognizing the expanded cause of action. If the subsequent action does not succeed, both parties are left to bear the expenses of two futile lawsuits, and court time has been wasted as well.

Although this case arises upon the plaintiff doctor's assertions that the defendant attorneys wrongfully prosecuted a medical malpractice action against him, if we were to eliminate the special injury requirement that expansion of the tort of malicious prosecution would not be limited to countersuits against attorneys by aggrieved physicians. An action for malicious prosecution of civil proceedings could be brought by *any* former defendant—person, firm or corporation, private or public— in whose favor a prior civil suit terminated, against the former plaintiff or the plaintiff's attorney or both. In expanding the availability of such an action the Court would not merely provide a remedy for those required to defend groundless medical malpractice actions, but would arm all prevailing defendants with an instrument of retaliation, whether the prior action sounded in tort, contract or an altogether different area of law.

This is strong medicine—too strong for the affliction it is intended to cure. To be sure, successful defense of the former action is no assurance of recovery in a subsequent tort action, but the unrestricted availability of such an action introduces a new strategic weapon into the arsenal of defense litigators, particularly those whose clients can afford to devote extensive resources to prophylactic intimidation.

At present, a plaintiff and his attorney who know that they have less than an airtight case must, in deciding whether to continue the case or in evaluating a settlement offer, consider whether if they proceed to trial they will invest more and recover less or nothing. If the instant plaintiff's approach is adopted, all plaintiffs and their attorneys henceforth must also weigh the likelihood that if they persevere in the action and receive an unfavorable decision, they will not only take nothing but also be forced to defend an action for malicious prosecution of civil proceedings. Even if the plaintiff and his attorney had abundant cause for bringing and continuing the action and acted without malice, the expense and annoyance foreseeably involved in even a successful defense of the countersuit may induce them to abandon a problematic claim or to settle the case for less than they would otherwise accept. Some will say amen, but this would push the pendulum too far in favor of the defense, more than is necessary to rectify the evil to which this effort is directed. * * *

The cure for an excess of litigation is not more litigation. Meritorious as well as frivolous claims are likely to be deterred. There are sure to be those who would use the courts and such an expanded tort remedy as a retaliatory or punitive device without regard to the likelihood of recovery or who would seek a means of recovering the actual costs of defending the first action without regard to whether it was truly vexatious. * * *

Apart from special injury, elements of a tort action for malicious prosecution of civil proceedings are (1) prior proceedings terminated in favor of the present plaintiff, (2) absence of probable cause for those proceedings, and (3) "malice," more informatively described by the Restatement as "a purpose other than that of securing the proper adjudication of the claim in which the proceedings are based."

The following discussion addresses the chief concern of this case: the conditions under which the attorney for an unsuccessful plaintiff may be held liable. * * *

The absence of probable cause in bringing a civil action may not be established merely by showing that the action was successfully defended. To require an attorney to advance only those claims that will ultimately be successful would place an intolerable burden on the right of access to the courts.

The Court of Appeals adopted, and plaintiff endorses, the standard for determining whether an attorney had probable cause to initiate and continue a lawsuit articulated in *Tool Research & Engineering Corp. v. Henigson,* 46 Cal.App.3d 675, 683–684, 120 Cal.Rptr. 291 (1975): "The attorney is not an insurer to his client's adversary that his client will win in litigation. Rather, he has a duty 'to represent his client zealously * * * [seeking] any lawful objective through legally permissible means * * * [and presenting] for adjudication any lawful claim, issue, or defense.' (ABA, Code of Professional Responsibility, EC 7–1, DR 7–101[A][1], * * *.) So long as the attorney does not abuse that duty by prosecuting a claim which a reasonable lawyer would not regard as tenable or by unreasonably neglecting to investigate the facts and law in making his determination to proceed, his client's adversary has no right to assert malicious prosecution against the attorney if the lawyer's efforts prove unsuccessful. * * *

"The attorney's obligation is to represent his client honorably and ethically, and he may, without being guilty of malicious prosecution, vigorously pursue litigation in which he is unsure of whether his client or the client's adversary is truthful, so long as that issue is genuinely in doubt."

The *Henigson* court also said: "An attorney has probable cause to represent a client in litigation when, after a reasonable investigation and industrious search of legal authority, he has an honest belief that his client's claim is tenable in the forum in which it is to be tried."

In our view, this standard, while well-intentioned, is inconsistent with the role of the attorney in an adversary system.

Our legal system favors the representation of litigants by counsel. Yet the foregoing standard appears skewed in favor of non-representation; the lawyer risks being penalized for undertaking to present the client's claim to a court unless satisfied, after a potentially substantial investment in investigation and research, that the claim is tenable.

A lawyer may be confronted with the choice between allowing the statute of limitation to run upon a claim with which the client has only recently come forward, or promptly filing a lawsuit based on the information in hand. Such dilemmas are particularly likely to arise in connection with medical malpractice claims because a statute provides a six-month limitation period for bringing an action based on a belatedly discovered claim as an alternative to the normal two-year limitation period for malpractice actions. Time will not always permit "a reasonable investigation and industrious search of legal authority" before the lawyer must file a complaint to preserve the client's claim—and thus, perhaps, avoid an action by the client for legal malpractice.

In medical malpractice actions the facts relevant to an informed assessment of the defendant's liability may not emerge until well into the discovery process. Sometimes the relevant facts are not readily ascertainable. In the instant case, for example, defendants maintain that their efforts to acquire Mrs. Serafin's medical records were rebuffed until they commenced suit and thereupon became able to invoke established discovery procedures and the implicit power of the court to compel disclosure; it may be the practice of some doctors or hospitals to refuse to release medical records until a lawsuit has been commenced.

Moreover, the *Henigson* standard suggests rather ominously that every time a lawyer representing, say, a medical malpractice plaintiff encounters a fact adverse to the client's position or an expert opinion that there was no malpractice, he must immediately question whether to persevere in the action. An attorney's evaluation of the client's case should not be inhibited by the knowledge that perseverance may place the attorney personally at risk; the next fact or the next medical opinion may be the one that makes the case, and such developments may occur even on the eve of trial.

Indeed, a jury-submissible claim of medical malpractice may sometimes be presented even without specific testimony that the defendant physician violated the applicable standard of care. Thus, a lawyer may proceed in the good-faith belief that his proofs will establish a prima facie case of medical malpractice without expert testimony, only to find that the court disagrees. Such conduct is not the equivalent of proceeding without probable cause. * * *

This Court has said, in opinions addressed to the tort of malicious prosecution, that malice may be inferred from the facts that establish want of probable cause, although the jury is not required to draw that inference. This rule, developed in cases where damages were sought from a lay person who initiated proceedings, fails to make sufficient allowance for the lawyer's role as advocate and should not be applied in determining whether a lawyer acted for an improper purpose.

A client's total lack of belief that the action he initiates or continues can succeed is persuasive evidence of intent to harass or injure the defendant by bringing the action. But a lawyer who is unaware of such a client's improper purpose may, despite a personal lack of belief in any possible success of the action, see the client and the claim through to an appropriate conclusion without risking liability. * * *

The Restatement defines the mental element of the tort of wrongful civil proceedings as "a purpose other than that of securing the proper adjudication of the claim in which the proceedings are based." A finding of an improper purpose on the part of the unsuccessful attorney must be supported by evidence independent of the evidence establishing that the action was brought without probable cause.

We affirm that portion of the Court of Appeals decision which upheld summary judgment in favor of defendants on plaintiff's claims sounding in negligence and abuse of process. With respect to plaintiff's claim for malicious prosecution, we reverse the decision of the Court of Appeals and affirm the trial court's grant of summary judgment; we do so on the ground that an action for malicious prosecution of a civil action may not be brought absent special injury and the plaintiff failed to plead special injury.

KAVANAGH, WILLIAMS and RYAN, JJ., concur.

LEVIN, JUSTICE (concurring). Much of the discussion of the problem of unjustified litigation suffers from an undue focus upon the need to compensate the injury suffered by the defendant subjected to a groundless and malicious action. Groundless civil litigation is, however, more than an affliction visited upon a few scattered individuals; it besets the judicial system as a whole. It is, therefore, appropriate to think of it as a systemic problem and to fashion a remedy which preserves and strengthens the integrity of the civil litigation system rather than randomly providing a fortuitous amount of compensation in a handful of isolated cases.

In England, the losing party in a civil action is ordinarily required to reimburse the prevailing party for that portion of the latter's litigation costs which is determined by the judge or an officer of the court to have been "necessary." The recovery thus obtained is usually incomplete, but greater costs can be awarded if the litigation was vexatious or groundless.

The English system has been criticized because the risk of responsibility for a portion of the opponent's actual costs may deter debatable, good-faith claims.

Commentators have also been skeptical of the potential of court-administered sanctions within the original lawsuit as a remedy for groundless litigation because in this country the costs awarded to the prevailing party in a civil action are typically fixed by statute at amounts which pale beside the actual costs incurred in litigation, and American courts have generally been inclined to leave revision of costs schemes to the legislatures.

I am of the opinion, however, that this Court can appropriately devise an approach to wrongful litigation which is capable of providing both an appropriate measure of deterrence and reasonable compensation for wronged litigants without imperiling the right of free access to the courts. The remedy, quite simply, is to recognize the inadequacy of existing provisions for the taxation of costs and to adopt a new and distinct court rule authorizing the judge to whom a civil action is assigned to order payment of the prevailing party's actual expenses, including reasonable attorneys' fees and limited consequential damages, where the action was wrongfully initiated, defended or continued. Depending upon the circumstances, payment might be required of the attorney, the client or both. The factual questions implicit in such an evaluation of the losing side's conduct would be resolved by the judge after a prompt post-termination hearing at which the parties could call witnesses and they and their attorneys could testify. * * *

The sum recoverable should include all fees and administrative charges incurred because of the litigation as well as reasonable attorney's fees. The judge could award a prevailing defendant in a professional malpractice case an additional sum for loss of income-producing time and injury to professional reputation or business resulting from the wrongful action if the amount is capable of being calculated with reasonable certainty.

The rule could provide that the standard to be applied by the judge in determining whether such an award should be made is whether the losing party or his attorney had proceeded without probable cause and for an improper purpose. So defining the inquiry, in terms of the traditional elements of a cause of action for malicious prosecution of civil proceedings, allows the judge to consult existing precedent for guidance.

Having such a determination made by the judge to whom the original proceeding was assigned would have a number of advantages over assessment of these questions by judge and jury in a separate tort action:

First, a strategy for evaluating the propriety of litigation which is administered exclusively by judges is more susceptible of consistent application and careful supervision than a strategy which relies on a group of laymen chosen at random, often for one day and one trial. Confiding the question solely to the judge avoids the bifurcation of function associated with jury trial on the critical issue of probable cause in an action for malicious prosecution of civil proceedings. Limiting recovery to actual pecuniary loss, thereby eliminating recovery for emotional distress, and relying on a judge to assess damages, combined with the greater control that appellate courts exercise over a judge's findings as compared to a jury's verdict, should tend to avoid awards which might intimidate good-faith litigants.

Second, the judge would usually be familiar with the history of the case; the necessary evidence could be adduced and the relevant findings made in far more efficient fashion than if a new action and a separate trial before a different judge were required.

Third, parties who might be reluctant to initiate further litigation although they felt themselves wronged would be more likely to avail themselves of internal sanctions than of the opportunity to start a separate action which would take its place on the crowded docket and which the defendants would be likely to resist with all available means.

Groundless litigation diverts judicial resources which could otherwise be devoted to more deserving cases and represents a challenge to this Court's "general superintending control over all courts" comprising Michigan's "one court of justice." By adopting a court rule this Court would address the problem directly and in a manner compatible with its responsibility to exercise close control and supervision. * * *

WILLIAMS, J., concurs.

COLEMAN, CHIEF JUSTICE (concurring in part, dissenting in part). * * * I dissent from the portion of the majority opinion that requires proof of special injury in malicious prosecution cases. * * *

Although the majority's stated concern is to protect meritorious claims, it is nowhere contended in the opinion that the special injury requirement serves to distinguish meritorious from frivolous litigation. Nor is there a contention that special injury cases represent injury that is more egregious than in other cases. The majority's position is comprehensible only because of an unstated, although correct, premise: *most litigation does not involve special injury.*

Two noteworthy results follow from using the special injury requirement in such a way. First, in cases in which no special injury can be alleged, the non-special injury caused by the most frivolous malpractice litigation cannot be compensated. Second, assuming, as the majority does that the special injury requirement is important to protect meritorious claimants, such claimants may be deterred from raising meritorious claims in cases where the potential defendants would be able to allege special injury in a subsequent malicious prosecution case. Thus, by invoking the special injury requirement on behalf of meritorious litigants, the meritorious and frivolous claims alike are protected when no special injury can be alleged. Neither is protected when a special injury allegation might be made.

Thus, the arguments that the majority advances in favor of the special injury requirement, in reality, have no basis within the content of the special injury requirement. The same arguments could be advanced as forcefully in favor of abolishing the malicious prosecution action altogether, or even in favor of something so absurd as requiring that all malicious prosecution plaintiffs be from Kansas.

A far more reasonable approach would be to look to other elements of the malicious prosecution cause of action—such as *no probable cause* and an *improper motive*—to provide the necessary protection for bona fide litigants. * * *

In conclusion, this Court's concern should be for preserving free access to the courts *for meritorious claims.* The majority, by protecting meritorious and frivolous claims alike, has denied free access to the courts for all those who have suffered harm but no "special injury" from wrongful litigation.

I would affirm the Court of Appeals.

FITZGERALD, J., concurs.

MOODY, JUSTICE (dissenting in part). I agree with the analysis employed and the result reached by the opinion of the Court, except for [the] part which deals with a cause of action for malicious prosecution of civil proceedings. * * *

Admittedly, the special injury condition of the "English rule" limits the recovery potential for malicious prosecution of civil proceedings and thereby protects the right of free access to the courts. However, the limitation is too broad. Suits arising out of meritorious as well as vexatious actions are disallowed. The special injury requirement is not logically related to the actual damages incurred by the defendant as a result of a frivolous suit. The injury to reputation or business flowing from any defamatory matter alleged as the basis of the proceedings, and the expense of defending a lawsuit which was brought without probable cause and for an improper purpose do not depend upon a technical interference with person or property. The storekeeper whose property is attached for a few moments certainly suffers no greater injury or harm than the individual whose reputation is tarnished or who suffers a loss of business as a result of a truly vexatious lawsuit.
* * *

The strict requirements of lack of probable cause and malice, *i.e.,* improper purpose, are more appropriate guardians of free access to the courts and of promoting the honest use of the judicial process than the artificial requirement of special injury.

As an alternative to a malicious prosecution claim, an ancillary proceeding to occur immediately after judgment in the original action is suggested in a concurring opinion. Such a proposal would offer the advantages of control, availability and efficiency.

However, it may also be anticipated that this procedure could create the potential of adding an ancillary issue to every lawsuit, increase docket congestion, precipitate a conflict of interest between attorney and client, and grant too much power to the trial judge, thereby placing a premium on "judge shopping". The ease of accessibility of such a procedure may increase the likelihood of the prevailing party filing an ancillary proceeding. It could encourage, without reflection or thought, retaliatory claims. Also, since this alternative suggestion would apply to defendant and plaintiff alike, it raises an issue concerning the concept of what is an appropriate defense. * * *

---

1. The title of malicious prosecution is often expanded to cover not only criminal prosecutions but also frivolous or unwarranted civil actions. To avoid confusion the latter action is sometimes called malicious civil prosecution. The Restatement gives it the title of wrongful civil proceedings.

2. In general, the elements of the cause of action are the same for both criminal and civil prosecutions. As the principal case indicates, the major variance involves the element of damages. In the case of a civil prosecution, damages are not presumed and must be proved. The American rule is that each party to a civil action bears his own expenses of litigation, including attorney's fees. In England, attorney's fees are normally awarded to the winning party, and as a result there is no occasion for awarding them in a subsequent tort action, as part of the damages. Around a third of the American states follow the so-called "English rule"—not in awarding attorney's fees to the winner, but only in declining to allow recovery of attorney's fees as damages in the subsequent tort action. This result is distinctly anomalous: the damages that are an inevitable result of the tortious conduct and that always arise cannot be recovered, and the only recoverable damages are the abnormal special damages that are specifically proved. The Torts Restatement meets this persistant anomaly by having special provisions for certain types of injuries, such as civil proceedings involving arrest of person or deprivation of property, or repetitive actions. See §§ 677–680.

3. There are differences, too, in the two elements of lack of probable cause and "malice." The courts pride themselves in being open to the public to settle civil disputes. What is required is not a better-than-even chance that the suit will be won but a finding by the court that there was a reasonably good chance that it would. How does this concept apply when the original plaintiff was trying to persuade the court to change the law judicially?

If "malice" means bringing a civil action with an ulterior motive, how does this apply? Does it mean that the plaintiff brought the action with a subjective awareness that he had no actual chance of prevailing? Can the attorney be held liable? What is the effect of his failure to make an adequate investigation?

Is there real basis for requiring both lack of probable cause and "malice," or should either one be sufficient?

4. Is it feasible to arrange for award of appropriate litigation expenses in the original action, rather than requiring a second action in tort, with a different judge and jury? The cases have held that a countersuit, rather than a counterclaim in the same suit is required, because there must have been a termination in favor of the plaintiff at the time the tort claim is filed. A few states have provided by statute for allowing counterclaims.

5. A different solution makes use of Rules of Court. In the current Federal Rules of Civil Procedure, Rule 11 provides for a sanction against a person bringing a frivolous civil action. The sanction is imposed by the judge in the same action and may cover litigation expenses, including attorney's fees. Several states have adopted similar rules or statutes. The sanction may be imposed against the original defendant for harassing motions and other stonewalling conduct, as well as the original plaintiff. A Michigan statute, enacted

in response to the discussion in the instant case, is quoted in the Hofstra article cited below at page 464.

On this, and the questions asked above, see Wade, On Frivolous Litigation: A Study of Tort Liability and Procedural Sanctions, 14 Hofstra L.Rev. 413 (1986); Johnson and Cassady, Frivolous Lawsuits and Defensive Responses to Them—What Relief is Available? 36 Ala.L.Rev. 927 (1985); Partridge, Wilkinson and Krouse, A Complaint Based on Rumors: Countering Frivolous Litigation, 31 Loyola (N.O.) L.Rev. 221 (1985).

6. Ingenious attorneys have tried other tort actions, such as an action of negligence against the attorney for the original plaintiff in failing to determine that the suit was not warranted, and suit in negligence per se because of violation of an established ethical standard. Resort has also been made to the prima facie tort theory, to the criminal laws of champerty, maintenance and barratry, and to trespass on the case under the Statute of Westminster II; but none has been successful.

The medical profession and the news media have been particularly active in organized efforts to find effective means for preventing what they regard as unwarranted actions against them, but neither group has accomplished a breakthrough.

The principal case depicts the malpractice dispute. Other representative cases holding no cause of action on any tort basis include Berlin v. Nathan, 64 Ill.App.3d 940, 21 Ill.Dec. 682, 381 N.E.2d 1367 (1978); Wong v. Tabor, 422 N.E.2d 1279 (Ind.App.1981); and Martin v. Trevino, 578 S.W.2d 763 (Tex.Civ. App.1976). See also Tool Research and Engineering Corp. v. Heningson, 46 Cal. App.3d 675, 120 Cal.Rptr. 291 (1975) (discussion of probable cause); Nelson v. Miller, 227 Kan. 271, 607 P.2d 438 (1980) (recovery possible depending on facts); and Peerman v. Sidicane, 605 S.W.2d 242 (Tenn.App.1980) (recovery granted).

7. See generally Birnbaum, Physician's Counterattack: Liability of Lawyers for Instituting Medical-Malpractice Actions, 45 Fordham L.Rev. 1002 (1972); Lawson, The Action for Malicious Prosecution of a Civil Suit, 21 Am.L. Reg. (N.S.) 281 & 353 (1882) (good early treatment); Greenbaum, Physician Countersuits: A Cause Without Action, 12 Pac.L.J. 745 (1981); Thode, The Groundless Case—The Lawyer's Tort Duty to the Client and to the Adverse Party, 11 St. Mary's L.J. 59 (1979). There is a myriad of student Notes. Two especially good ones are Note, Liability for Proceeding With Unfounded Litigation, 33 Vand.L.Rev. 743 (1980); and Note, Groundless Litigation and the Malicious Prosecution Debate: A Historical Analysis, 88 Yale L.J. 1215 (1979).

GRAINGER v. HILL
Court of Common Pleas, 1838.
4 Bing.N.C. 212, 132 Eng.Rep. 769.

TINDAL C.J.   This is a special action on the case, in which the Plaintiff declares that he was the master and owner of a vessel which, in September 1836, he mortgaged to the Defendants for the sum of 80£, with a covenant for repayment in September 1837, and under a stipulation that, in the mean time, the Plaintiff should retain the command of the vessel, and prosecute voyages therein for his own profit: that the Defendants, in order to compel the Plaintiff through duress to give up the register of the vessel, without which he could not go to sea, before the money lent on mortgage became due, threatened to arrest him for the same unless he immediately paid the amount: that, upon the Plaintiff refusing to pay it, the Defendants, knowing he could not provide bail, arrested him under a capias, indorsed to levy 95£ 17s. 6d., and kept him imprisoned, until, by duress, he was compelled to give up the register, which the Defendants then unlawfully detained; by means whereof the Plaintiff lost four voyages from London to Caen. * * * The Defendants pleaded the general issue; after a verdict for the Plaintiff, the case comes before us * * * under an application for a nonsuit. * * *

The * * * ground urged for a nonsuit is, that there was no proof of the suit commenced by the Defendants having been terminated. But the answer to this * * * namely, the omission to allege want of reasonable and probable cause for the Defendants' proceeding, is * * * that this is an action for abusing the process of the law, by applying it to extort property from the Plaintiff, and not an action for a malicious arrest or malicious prosecution, in order to support which action the termination of the previous proceeding must be proved, and the absence of reasonable and probable cause be alleged as well as proved. * * * If the course pursued by the Defendants is such that there is no precedent of a similar transaction, the Plaintiff's remedy is by an action on the case, applicable to such new and special circumstances; and his complaint being that the process of the law has been abused, to effect an object not within the scope of the process, it is immaterial whether the suit which that process commenced has been determined or not, or whether or not it was founded on reasonable and probable cause. * * *

Judgment for Plaintiff.

---

1. A good contemporary case on abuse of process is Board of Education of Farmingdale Union Free School District v. Farmingdale Classroom Teachers Association, Inc., 38 N.Y.2d 397, 343 N.E.2d 278, 380 N.Y.S.2d 635 (1975), where, in litigation between the School District and the Teachers Association, the latter served subpoenas on all the teachers in the school system, requiring them to report to court at the same time. This harassment of the District was held to give rise to tort liability. See also Ash v. Cohn, 119 N.J.L. 54, 194 A. 174 (1937) (body execution); Ginsberg v. Ginsberg, 84 A.D.2d 573, 443 N.Y.S.2d 439 (2d Dep't 1981) (in divorce action, defendant charged with using subpoena process "for the unjustified purpose of harassing [wife] and exhausting her financial resources in order to win a collateral advantage in the legal struggle over custody of the child"); Barnett v. Reed, 51 Pa. 190 (1865) (second writ of execution issued with knowledge that the obligation had been paid).

The tort of abuse of process is not available for filing a frivolous action: Wells v. Orthwein, 670 S.W.2d 529 (Mo.App.1984); Martin v. Trevino, 578 S.W.2d 763 (Tex.Civ.App.1978).

2. See Goldoftas, Abuse of Process, 13 Clev.–Mar.L.Rev. 163 (1964); Bretz, Abuse of Process—A Misunderstood Concept, 20 Clev.St.L.Rev. 401 (1971); Notes, 28 Ark.L.Rev. 388 (1974), 10 Cumb.L.Rev. 209 (1979), 2 Valparaiso L.Rev. 129 (1967).

Chapter XXI

MISREPRESENTATION

1. INTRODUCTION

"Misrepresentation runs all through the law of torts, as a method of accomplishing various types of tortious conduct which, for reasons of historical development or as a matter of convenience, usually are grouped under categories of their own. Thus a battery may be committed by feeding the plaintiff poisoned chocolates, or by inducing his consent to a physical contact by misrepresenting its character; false imprisonment may result from a pretense of authority to make an arrest, a trespass to land from fraudulent statements inducing another to enter, or a conversion from obtaining possession of goods by false representations; and a malicious lie may give rise to a cause of action for the intentional infliction of mental suffering. A great many of the common and familiar forms of negligent conduct, resulting in invasions of tangible interests of person or property, are in their essence nothing more than misrepresentation, from a misleading signal by a driver of an automobile about to make a turn, or an assurance that a danger does not exist, to false statements concerning a chattel sold, or non-disclosure of a latent defect by one who is under a duty to give warning. In addition, misrepresentation may play an important part in the invasion of intangible interests, in such torts as defamation, malicious prosecution, or interference with contractual relations. In all such cases the particular form which the defendant's conduct has taken has become relatively unimportant, and misrepresentation has been merged to such an extent with other kinds of misconduct that neither the courts nor legal writers have found any occasion to regard it as a separate basis of liability.

"So far as misrepresentation has been treated as giving rise in and of itself to a distinct cause of action in tort, it has been identified with the common law action of deceit. * * *

"The law of misrepresentation is thus considerably broader than the action for deceit. Liability in damages for misrepresentation, in one form or another falls into the three familiar divisions with which we have dealt throughout this book—it may be based upon intent to deceive, upon negligence, or upon a policy which requires the defendant to be strictly responsible for his statements without either. For the most part, the courts have limited deceit to those cases where there is an intent to mislead, and have left negligence and strict liability to be dealt with in some other type of action. * * *" W. Prosser, Torts 683 (4th ed. 1971).

1023

Misrepresentation is thus a very complex field. The complexity results primarily from the existence of numerous alternative remedies. They include:

1. The tort action of deceit, with which this chapter is primarily concerned.

2. An action for breach of contract, when the representation is found to be an express or implied term of the contract itself. In the case of the sale of chattels, this may take the form of an action for breach of warranty, which has definite tort characteristics of its own. The contract liability is of course a strict one, and requires no intent to deceive, negligence, or other fault than the breach of the contract itself.

3. A negligence action for negligent misrepresentation. This is now recognized by nearly all courts where tangible injury to person or property results, and by most of the American jurisdictions where the only damage is financial loss.

4. A suit in equity to rescind the transaction or for other relief such as an equitable lien or a constructive trust.

5. An action at law for restitution to recover back what the plaintiff has parted with, or the unjust enrichment which the defendant has received from it.

History. The action of deceit is of very ancient origin. There was an old writ of deceit known as early as 1201, which lay only in cases of what we would now call malicious prosecution. At a later period this writ was superseded by an action on the case in the nature of deceit, which became the general common law remedy for any misrepresentation, whether fraudulent or not, which resulted in actual damage. It was used to afford a remedy for many wrongs that we should now regard as breaches of contract, such as false warranties in the sale of goods. Its use was limited almost entirely to direct transactions between the plaintiff and the defendant, and it was treated as inseparable from some contract relation. In other words, tort and contract were not at all clearly distinguished.

The bargaining ethics of that day were low. It was assumed that all sellers would lie, and if the buyer wanted protection he was expected to exact from the seller an express undertaking to be responsible, such as a warranty. "Caveat emptor"—let the buyer look out for himself. Thus in the picturesque old case of Chandelor v. Lopus, Cro.Jac. 4, 79 Eng.Rep. 3 (1603), a goldsmith sold a stone to the plaintiff, falsely stating that it was a bezar stone—a "calcareous concretion in the stomach of a goat," believed to have medicinal properties, particularly as a remedy against snake-bite. It was held that there was no liability, even though the seller knew his statement to be false, in the absence of an express undertaking to be bound.

In 1789, in Pasley v. Freeman, 3 T.R. 51, 100 Eng.Rep. 450, the action of deceit was held to lie in a case where the plaintiff had had no dealings with the defendant, but had been induced by his misrepresentation to extend credit to a third person. After that date deceit was recognized as purely a tort action, and not necessarily founded upon a contract. At about the same time, in Stuart v. Wilkins, 1 Doug. 18, 99 Eng.Rep. 15 (1778), the remedy for breach of warranty was taken over into the action of assumpsit, and it was thus established that it had a contract character. Thereafter the two lines of recovery slowly diverge, although some vestige of confusion between the two still remains, even today.

2. CONCEALMENT AND NONDISCLOSURE

SWINTON v. WHITINSVILLE SAVINGS BANK

Supreme Judicial Court of Massachusetts, 1942.
311 Mass. 677, 42 N.E.2d 808.

Action by Neil W. Swinton against Whitinsville Savings Bank to recover damages for alleged fraudulent concealment by defendant in sale of a house to plaintiff. From an order sustaining a demurrer to plaintiff's declaration, the plaintiff appeals.

QUA, JUSTICE. The declaration alleges that on or about September 12, 1938, the defendant sold the plaintiff a house in Newton to be occupied by the plaintiff and his family as a dwelling; that at the time of the sale the house "was infested with termites, an insect that is most dangerous and destructive to buildings"; that the defendant knew the house was so infested; that the plaintiff could not readily observe this condition upon inspection; that "knowing the internal destruction that these insects were creating in said house", the defendant falsely and fraudulently concealed from the plaintiff its true condition; that the plaintiff at the time of his purchase had no knowledge of the termites, exercised due care thereafter, and learned of them about August 30, 1940; and that, because of the destruction that was being done and the dangerous condition that was being created by the termites, the plaintiff was put to great expense for repairs and for the installation of termite control in order to prevent the loss and destruction of said house.

There is no allegation of any false statement or representation, or of the uttering of a half truth which may be tantamount to a falsehood. There is no intimation that the defendant by any means prevented the plaintiff from acquiring information as to the condition of the house. There is nothing to show any fiduciary relation between the parties, or that the plaintiff stood in a position of confidence toward or dependence upon the defendant. So far as appears the parties made a business deal at arm's length. The charge is concealment and nothing more; and it is concealment in the simple sense of mere failure to reveal, with nothing to show any peculiar duty to speak. The characterization of the concealment as false and fraudulent of course adds nothing in the absence of further allegations of fact. * * *

If this defendant is liable on this declaration every seller in liable who fails to disclose any nonapparent defect known to him in the subject of the sale which materially reduces its value and which the buyer fails to discover. Similarly it would seem that every buyer would be liable who fails to disclose any nonapparent virtue known to him in the subject of the purchase which materially enhances its value and of which the seller is ignorant. [C] The law has not yet, we believe, reached the point of imposing upon the frailties of human nature a standard so idealistic as this. That the particular case here stated by the plaintiff possesses a certain appeal to the moral sense is scarcely to be denied. Probably the reason is to be found in the facts that the infestation of buildings by termites has not been common in Massachusetts and constitutes a concealed risk against which buyers are off their guard. But the law cannot provide special rules for termites and can hardly attempt to determine liability according to the varying probabilities of the existence and discovery of different possible defects in the subjects of trade. The rule of nonliability for bare nondisclosure has been stated and followed by this court. * * * It is adopted in the American Law Institute's Restatement of Torts § 551. See Williston on Contracts, Rev.Ed., §§ 1497, 1498, 1499.

The order sustaining the demurrer is affirmed, and judgment is to be entered for the defendant. * * *

So ordered.

---

1. The classic statement of the effect of nondisclosure is that of Lord Cairns in Peek v. Gurney, L.R. 6 H.L. 377, 403 (1873): "Mere nondisclosure of material facts, however morally censurable, however that nondisclosure might be a ground in a proper proceeding at a proper time for setting aside an allotment or a purchase of shares, would in my opinion form no ground for an action in the nature of an action for misrepresentation. There must, in my opinion, be some active misstatement of fact, or, at all events, such a partial and fragmentary statement of fact, as that the withholding of that which is not stated makes that which is stated absolutely false." Perhaps the leading case espousing the view is Keates v. Earl of Cardogan, 10 C.B. 591, 128 Eng.Rep. 234 (1851).

2. How account for the "general rule" that an action of deceit will not lie for tacit nondisclosure, as distinguished from active misrepresentation? No tort liability for nonfeasance? Business morals developed in a day when it was taken for granted that bargaining adversaries could not trust one another, and that each would take unfair advantage if he could? Does the rule accurately portray today's business ethics? If there were a duty to disclose, what should be the test for determining when?

3. Three different rules modifying the harshness of the common law position developed quite early:

A. The courts followed a much more liberal attitude when the plaintiff sought rescission of his contract, or other equitable relief. Even mutual mistake as to a basic fact affecting the transaction is ordinarily held to be sufficient grounds for such relief; and the position of the defendant is not improved if he has knowledge of the plaintiff's mistake, failed to make disclosure, and took advantage of the situation. See, for example, Simmons v. Evans, 185 Tenn. 282, 206 S.W.2d 295 (1927).

B. Even in actions at law, the defendant was held liable for nondisclosure if the parties were in some confidential or fiduciary relation to one another, so that reliance upon good faith and full disclosure was justified. McDonough v. Williams, 77 Ark. 261, 92 S.W. 783 (1905); Brasher v. First Nat. Bank, 232 Ala. 340, 168 So. 42 (1936). "For instance, the relations of trustee and cestui que trust, principal and agent, attorney and client, physician and patient, priest and parishioner, partners, tenants in common, husband and wife, parent and child, guardian and ward, and many others of like character." Farmers State Bank of Newport v. Lamon, 132 Wash. 369, 231 P. 952 (1925). As to banker and customer, see Klein v. First Edina Nat'l Bank, 293 Minn. 418, 196 N.W.2d 619 (1972).

C. In addition, certain types of contracts, such as those of suretyship and guaranty, joint adventure, or insurance, were recognized as in themselves creating or involving something of a confidential relation, and hence as requiring the utmost good faith, and full and fair disclosure of all material facts.

4. On the precise issue of this case, existence of a duty to disclose that a building is infested with termites, the cases are sharply divided. See, in accord, Hendrick v. Lynn, 37 Del.Ch. 402, 144 A.2d 147 (1958); Fegeas v. Sherrill, 218 Md. 472, 147 A.2d 223 (1958). Contra: Williams v. Benson, 3 Mich.App. 9, 141 N.W.2d 650 (1966); Obde v. Schlemeyer, 56 Wash.2d 449, 353 P.2d 672 (1960). Other cases are collected in Annot., 22 A.L.R.3d 972 (1968).

5. In California a real estate broker is under a duty to disclose to a buyer material defects known to the broker but unknown to and unobservable by the buyer. Failure makes him guilty of "fraudulent concealment" or "negative fraud." Cooper v. Jevne, 56 Cal.App.3d 860, 128 Cal.Rptr. 724 (1976). This has recently been expanded to require the broker to "conduct a reasonably competent and diligent inspection of property he has listed for sale in order to discover defects for the benefit of the buyer." Easton v. Strassburger, 152 Cal. App.3d 90, 199 Cal.Rptr. 383 (1983) (failure to discover and disclose a potential landslide). See Note, 99 Harv.L.Rev. 1861 (1986).

LINDBERG CADILLAC CO. v. ARON
St. Louis Court of Appeals, Missouri, 1963.
371 S.W.2d 651.

WOLFE, JUDGE. This is an action in fraud in which the defendant is charged by the plaintiff with concealing defects in an automobile which he traded to plaintiff in part payment of the purchase price of a new car which the plaintiff sold to him. The trial was to the court, which found for the plaintiff in the sum of $759.00 and costs. After an unavailing motion for a new trial, the defendant appealed.

[Defendant traded in to plaintiff, an automobile dealer, a used Cadillac automobile, on the purchase of another car. He was allowed $2,290 on the trade-in. Previously, during a cold spell, the coolant in the car radiator froze, and this had resulted in two cracks on each side of the motor block. A filing station to which defendant took the car discovered the situation, and with the approval of defendant, and the expectation that the car would be traded in, filled the cracks with a "sealer," and covered them with a compound which concealed them. Plaintiff examined the car and drove it for a few minutes, but did not discover the cracks. Defendant said nothing about them. Plaintiff reconditioned the car and resold it, but the buyer complained that the car was overheating, and plaintiff returned his money. The car was finally sold to another buyer, who was told of the cracks, for $1,200.]

The first point [defendant] raises is that the appellant failed to make a prima facie showing of fraud, and that the court should have found for the defendant. The appellant asserts in support of this that he made no misrepresentation, and that his mere silence cannot be held to have been fraudulent where the matter was open to investigation by the party alleged to have been defrauded. This constitutes a complete disregard of the facts. Silence can be an act of fraud. ＊ ＊ ＊

We have in the facts before us more than a failure to speak. There is also a positive fraudulent concealment. In the case of Jones v. West Side Buick Auto Co., 231 Mo.App. 187, 93 S.W.2d 1083, ＊ ＊ ＊ we have before us facts quite similar in effect to those here under consideration. There a fraudulent seller turned back the speedometer in the car sold to 22,400 miles, when the car had in fact been driven 48,800 miles. There was no verbal or written representation by the seller, but the buyer, relying upon the mileage registered on the speedometer, purchased the car. We held that the buyer had been defrauded by the deception, stating: "＊ ＊ ＊ a representation is not confined to words or positive assertions; it may consist as well of deeds, acts, or artifices of a nature calculated to mislead another and thereby to allow the fraud-feasor to obtain an undue advantage over him." [C]

The acts of the defendant as stated above were designed to, and did, defraud the plaintiff, and there is no merit to the contention that a case in fraud was not made. ＊ ＊ ＊

We find no error present, and the judgment is affirmed.

---

1. The leading American case on active concealment is Croyle v. Moses, 90 Pa.St. 250 (1879), where defendant, selling a horse to plaintiff, hitched him up short for the purpose of concealing the fact that the horse was a cribber and a windsucker.

2. Are words necessary to a misrepresentation? In addition to Jones v. West Side Buick Auto Co., 231 Mo.App. 187, 93 S.W.2d 1083 (1936), stated in the principal case, see Chapman v. Zakzaska, 273 Wis. 74, 76 N.W.2d 537 (1956), and Kuelling v. Roderick Lean Mfg. Co., 183 N.Y. 78, 75 N.E. 1098 (1905), where defendant sold a road roller with its defects concealed with putty and paint.

3. Defendant, selling plaintiff sheets of aluminum, placed good undamaged sheets on top of bundles of sheets that were corroded or otherwise damaged. The bundles were bulky and heavy, and plaintiff did not take them apart. Is this deceit? Salzman v. Maldaver, 315 Mich. 403, 24 N.W.2d 161 (1946).

4. Suppose the defendant, in possession of the facts, denies all knowledge in response to plaintiff's inquiry, and thereby discourages him from investigating further? Smith v. Beatty, 37 N.C. 456, 40 Am.Dec. 435 (1843).

LOCK v. SCHREPPLER
Superior Court of Delaware, 1981.
426 A.2d 856.

STIFTEL, PRESIDENT JUDGE. This case is presently before me on defendant George B. Schreppler's motion for summary judgment.

The events leading to the present suit involve the plaintiffs' purchase of the house and property on Walker School Road north of Smyrna, Delaware. Plaintiffs allege that the defendant, the listing realtor in this transaction, defrauded plaintiffs by failing to reveal to plaintiffs, the buyers, his knowledge of the extensive termite damage to the beams which supported the floors in the house. Defendant denies fraudulent activity on his part in the sale of this property. * * *

[Plaintiffs inspected the interior of the house, observing a "slope in the living room floor." They] attempted to inspect the lower structure of the house using the crawl space below the house, but due to the constructed dimensions and generally filthy condition of the crawl space, [they] were unable or unwilling to go further than three feet into the space. During this limited inspection, [they] observed what appeared to be a cracked beam, which they thought might be the cause of the sloping living room floor.

[At the real estate office,] plaintiffs learned that the house was being sold in "as-is" condition, and that the house had been treated for termites. Some inquiry was made as to a termite "certificate" by plaintiffs on the third visit. When plaintiffs returned to [the real estate] office, defendant Schreppler appeared and informed plaintiffs and Mr. Taylor that there was a termite certificate, that the house had been treated for termites, and a one year guarantee against reinfestation went with the house. After further conversation, plaintiffs signed a contract for purchase of the house. * * *

Plaintiffs then took possession of the house. * * * It was several weeks after they moved in that plaintiffs, while replacing a window frame, discovered that the house had extensive termite damage. A thorough inspection of the home by an exterminator revealed that the termites had weakened the floor and ceiling supports extensively, rendering the house unfit for habitation. The extent of the damage was evidenced by the discovery that the beam supporting the rear bedroom floor was in turn being supported by an automobile jack. [They filed this suit.]

For plaintiffs to recover damages for fraudulent concealment, plaintiffs must demonstrate that defendant took some action affirmative in nature designed or intended to prevent, and which does prevent, the discovery of facts giving rise to the fraud claim, some artifice to prevent knowledge of the facts or some representation intended to exclude suspicion and prevent inquiry. * * * [C]

Comparing fraudulent concealment and fraudulent misrepresentation, the only apparent difference is the emphasis of the former on misdirection of the deceived party, as opposed to the latter concept, which seems to require a false statement of fact to be represented as true. Both require an intentional deception of the plaintiff by the defendant, which the plaintiff relies upon to his detriment. * * *

Mr. Schreppler's conversation in reference to the termite problem with the plaintiffs prior to their signing of the purchase contract created an issue as to whether the content of Mr. Schreppler's statement was such as to mislead the plaintiffs into believing there was no significant termite problem with the house. Mr. Schreppler contends that he informed the Locks that there had been a termite infestation and subsequent damage; and that the house had been treated for termites. This statement is substantiated in part by Mrs. Wojcik. * * * Even assuming that Mr. Schreppler did mention that there had been some damage, defendant does not contend that he informed the Locks of the damaged support beams. Given the conflicting accounts, there is some evidence that even if some mention was made of damage, the import of the conversation was such as to convey to the plaintiffs the impression that any damage due to the termite infestation was minor. A representation may be fraudulent even if it is true, if the defendant knows that because of facts not stated, the statement is materially misleading. [Cc] Although there is no general duty to speak, nevertheless, if a person undertakes to speak, he then has a duty to make a full and fair disclosure as to the matters about which he assumes to speak. [C] Once Mr. Schreppler undertook to inform plaintiffs of the termite problem, he had a duty to fully inform the plaintiffs so as not to mislead them with inadequate information. * * *

In summary, defendant has failed to show that his statements informing plaintiffs of the termite infestation did not misrepresent or conceal the extent of the termite problem, and to demonstrate that plaintiffs could not have justifiably relied on these statements. I conclude that defendant has not succeeded in preventing the common law action of fraud by plaintiffs. * * *

[D]efendant's motion for summary judgment as to plaintiffs' common law action for fraud is denied.

---

1. Defendant sold a rooming house to the plaintiff. He truthfully stated to plaintiff that he was then receiving rentals on rooms which totaled $297 per month. He did not mention the fact, which he knew, that the Rent Administrator of the District had not yet established war-time rent ceilings for the property, and had not approved the present rents. Plaintiff bought the house. The Rent Administrator subsequently reduced the total legal rentals payable to

$260. Will an action for deceit lie? Tucker v. Beazley, 57 A.2d 191 (Mun.App. D.C.1948).

2. Defendant sold plaintiff a tract of land, warning him that the Final Map of the Borough of Queens showed two unopened streets which, if opened, would condemn a part of the premises. He failed to mention the fact, which he knew, that the Map showed a third unopened street which, if opened, would cut the plot substantially in half. Is he liable in deceit? Junius Construction Co. v. Cohen, 257 N.Y. 393, 178 N.E. 672 (1931).

3. Defendant makes an ambiguous statement, reasonably capable of being understood in two ways, one of which is true and the other false. Plaintiff understands it in the false sense. Defendant knows that he so understands it, but says nothing further. Is defendant liable? Busch v. Wilcox, 82 Mich. 315, 46 N.W. 940 (1890); cf. Matter of Estate of Lecic, 104 Wis.2d 592, 312 N.W.2d 773 (1981).

4. Plaintiff and defendant are negotiating for the sale of defendant's brewery. In January defendant gives plaintiff accurate information as to its growth and profits for the preceding year. At the end of April plaintiff buys the brewery, relying, as defendant knows, upon the information for the previous year. After January, unknown to plaintiff, the volume of business and the profits had greatly diminished. Is defendant liable if he does not disclose the change? Loewer v. Harris, 57 Fed. 368 (2d Cir.1893).

5. In Roberts v. Ball, Hunt, Hart, Brown & Baerwitz, 57 Cal.App.3d 104, 128 Cal.Rptr. 901 (1976), a law firm prepared an opinion letter for its client stating that the client was a general partnership, but not revealing that some of the members claimed to be limited partners, not subject to full liability. Held, "the firm had a duty to reveal to plaintiff this doubt as to the status of the partnership as a general partnership, since the firm knew that the disclosure of this doubt might well be determinative of plaintiff's decision to make loans" to the client.

GRIFFITH v. BYERS CONSTR. CO. OF KANSAS, INC.

Supreme Court of Kansas, 1973.
212 Kan. 65, 510 P.2d 198.

FROMME, JUSTICE. The purchasers of new homes in Woodlawn East Addition, City of Wichita, Kansas, brought separate actions for damages because of the saline condition of the soil of their homesites. These actions were filed on alternative theories, (1) breach of an implied warranty of fitness and (2) fraud in the concealment of a material matter. The actions were brought against the developer. This appeal is from an order granting summary judgments in favor of the developer, Byers Construction Co. of Kansas, Inc. (Byers).

The petitions allege that Byers developed and advertised the addition as a choice residential area. Prior to the time of development the addition was part of an abandoned oil field which contained salt water disposal areas which Byers knew or should have known would not sustain vegetation because of the saline content of the soil. It was alleged that Byers graded and developed the whole addition for homesites in such a manner that it became impossible for a purchaser to discover the presence of these salt areas. It further appears from allegations in the petitions and testimony in depositions that each of the plaintiffs selected a homesite which was located within a salt water disposal area. After houses were constructed attempts to landscape the homesites failed. Grass, shrubs and trees were planted and died because of the saline content of the soil. * * * No inquiry was made and no assurance was given by Byers on soil fertility.

The facts of this case appear to be unique for, although many cases can be found on a vendor-builder's liability for the sale of a defective home (see 25 A.L.R.3d, p. 383), no cases are cited and we find none which discuss a developer's liability for defects arising from sterility of soil. The saline content of the soil of these homesites does not affect the structural qualities of the homes. The allegations of the petitions and deposition testimony indicate that landscaping is either impossible or highly expensive.

A real estate developer by subdividing and offering lots for sale as choice residential homesites does not by implication warrant the fertility of the soil of said lots. Liability on an implied warranty of soil fertility cannot reasonably be imposed upon the real estate developer in this case. * * *

Our next inquiry is directed to the claims based on fraud. The trial court held as a matter of law no claims for fraud could be maintained because of lack of privity between the developer and these appellants. The residential lots were sold to the builders who in turn constructed the houses and then deeded the improved lots to the appellants. * * *

The allegations of fraud appear to be viable issues for trial if nondisclosure of a known material defect in the lots constitutes actionable fraud as to the appellants.

This court has held that the purchaser may recover on the theory of fraud from a vendor-builder for nondisclosure of defects. In Jenkins v. McCormick, 184 Kan. 842, 339 P.2d 8, it is stated:

"Where a vendor has knowledge of a defect in property which is not within the fair and reasonable reach of the vendee and which he could not discover by the exercise of reasonable diligence, the silence and failure of the vendor to disclose the defect in the property constitutes actionable fraudulent concealment." * * *

This *Jenkins* rule approximates that stated in Restatement (Second) of Torts, § 551:

"(1) One who fails to disclose to another a thing that he knows may justifiably induce the other to act or refrain from acting in a business transaction is subject to the same liability to the other as though he had represented the nonexistence of the matter that he has failed to disclose, if, but only if, he is under a duty to the other to exercise reasonable care to disclose the matter in question.

"(2) One party to a business transaction is under a duty to disclose to the other before the transaction is consummated. * * *

"(e) Facts basic to the transaction, if he knows that the other is about to enter into it under a mistake as to them, and that the other, because of the relationship between them, the customs in the trade or other objective circumstances, would reasonably expect a disclosure of those facts."

A similar rule has been recognized in other states. See Bethlahmy v. Bechtel, 91 Idaho 55, 415 P.2d 698, where a drainage ditch underlay a garage and was not disclosed to the purchaser. * * * We see no reason why the rule in *Jenkins* should not be extended in the present case to a developer of residential lots.

The appellee Byers next contends, without agency, there can be no privity and without privity there can be no duty to disclose. Here, of course, appellants never dealt with the appellee, Byers. The duty to disclose the saline nature of the soil must extend to appellants if their fraud claims are to be upheld. However, the doctrine of privity provides no defense to appellee Byers if appellants were within a class of persons appellee intended to reach. * * *

Under the alleged facts of our present case, accepting the same in the light most favorable to the appellants, we must assume the appellee, Byers, had knowledge of the saline content of the soil of the lots it placed on the market. After the grading and development of the area this material defect in the lots was not within the fair and reasonable reach of the vendees, as they could not discover this latent defect by the exercise of reasonable care. The silence of the appellee, Byers, and its failure to disclose this defect in the soil condition to the purchasers could constitute actionable fraudulent concealment under the rule in Jenkins v. McCormick, supra. One who makes a fraudulent misrepresentation or concealment is subject to liability for pecuniary loss to the persons or class of persons whom he intends or has reason to expect to act or to refrain from action in reliance upon the misrepresentation or concealment.

Of course, the fraudulent concealment to be actionable has to be material to the transaction. A matter is material if it is one to which a reasonable man would attach importance in determining his choice of action in the transaction in question. (Restatement (Second) of Torts, § 538.) There is little doubt in this case a prospective purchaser of a residential building site would consider the soil condition a material factor in choosing a lot on which to build his home. It materially affected the value and acceptability of the homesite.

As to privity we do not believe it is important to categorize its existence under a particular legal theory. Suffice it to say the appellants were in that class of persons desiring building lots in a choice residential area whom appellee intended and had reason to expect would purchase and build their homes. The fact that title was first taken in the names of the builders did not change the identity of those who would be ultimately affected by any fraudulent misrepresentations or nondisclosure of material defects in the lots. The building contractors were acting on behalf of their respective purchasers as a conduit or temporary way station for the legal title which, it was understood, would pass on completion of the homes to the appellants. There is no lack of privity in this case which would prevent causes of action based on fraud, and, in this, the district court erred in entering summary judgments for the appellee, Byers. * * *

The order of the district court entering summary judgment in favor of the appellee is affirmed as to those claims based on implied warranty but reversed as to the alternative claims based on fraud, and these cases are remanded with instructions to proceed in accordance with the views expressed herein.

---

1. Defendant sold plaintiff a summer resort, located in a narrow canyon beside a state highway. Defendant did not disclose the fact, which he knew, that the resort occupied a part of the right of way of the highway. Subsequently government authorities ordered the resort moved, because of its encroachment on the highway. Since there was no room in the canyon to move it back, it had to be torn down. Is defendant liable for failure to disclose? Kallgren v. Steele, 131 Cal.App.2d 43, 279 P.2d 1027 (1955).

2. Defendant is engaged in the business of removing sand and gravel from the bed of a navigable stream and selling it. He is notified by the United States Government that such removal is affecting the channel, and ordered to stop it, under threat of legal proceedings. He decides that this is a good time to unload the business, and sells it to the plaintiff, without mentioning the notice from the Government. The Government puts a stop to the business. Is this actionable? Musgrave v. Lucas, 193 Or. 401, 238 P.2d 780 (1951).

3. There are now a good number of land-fill cases. Although some of them can be explained on the basis that the defendant's conduct amounted to an active concealment, it has come to be generally recognized that if the existence of the fill seriously affects the use to which the land is expected to be put, there is a duty to disclose. Lawson v. Citizens & Southern Nat'l Bank, 259 S.C. 477, 193 S.E.2d 124 (1971); Sorrell v. Young, 6 Wash.App. 220, 491 P.2d 1312 (1971) (rescission); Annot., (1961) 80 A.L.R.2d 1453.

4. The termite cases provide another instance of a growing tendency to permit an action for nondisclosure of basic facts going to the essence of the transaction. How is the difference in the holdings to be explained? Difference in time? Differing business standards in various parts of the country? Prevalence of termites in the area involved—which way would this work? Extent of the damages the termites had caused to the house? Custom for purchaser to inquire?

5. Currently there is much concern about radon gas seeping up from the ground into houses and harming the occupants. The presence of the gas cannot be determined except with certain specialized equipment. Some parts of the country are especially susceptible to the gas. What legal problems will arise from this and how are they likely to be handled?

6. There are now a good number of cases that more or less defy classification, where a buyer has been swindled by the sale of something seriously defective, which he would not have bought if he had been told the facts. See, for example, Kaze v. Compton, 283 S.W.2d 204 (Ky.1955) (defective drainage

under house sold); Dyke v. Zaiser, 80 Cal.App.2d 639, 182 P.2d 344 (1947) (prior police raid on amusement center, affecting its reputation and value); Herzog v. Capital Co., 27 Cal.2d 349, 164 P.2d 8 (1945) (leaky house); Morriss–Buick Co. v. Huss, 84 S.W.2d 264 (Tex.Civ.App.1935) (sale of automobile that had been wrecked and repaired); Citizens State Bank v. Gilmore, 226 Kan. 662, 603 P.2d 605 (1979) (sale of cattle known to be diseased); Caldwell v. Pop's Homes, Inc., 54 Or.App. 104, 634 P.2d 471 (1981) (sale of mobile home in park without disclosing that park had been sold and home would have to be moved); Ollerman v. O'Rourke Co., Inc., 94 Wis.2d 17, 288 N.W.2d 95 (1980) (underground well in residential lot). See also Sippy v. Cristich, infra page 1065. The Michigan Court speaks of "silent fraud." United States Fidelity and Guaranty Co. v. Black, 412 Mich. 99, 313 N.W.2d 77 (1981).

7. There is as yet little to indicate any corresponding tendency to require the buyer of property to disclose to the seller special information that he has acquired that enhances its value. The leading American case is Laidlaw v. Organ, 15 U.S. (2 Wheat.) 178 (1817), in which plaintiff took advantage of his knowledge that peace had been declared to buy a quantity of cotton from defendant, and was allowed to enforce the contract. In Hays v. Meyers, 139 Ky. 440, 107 S.W. 287 (1908), it was said that "A person may with perfect honesty and propriety use for his own advantage the superior knowledge of property he desires to purchase, that has been acquired by skill, energy, vigilance, and other legitimate means."

8. Is the test for determining when there is a duty to disclose set forth in § 551(2)(e) of the Restatement (as quoted in the principal case) sufficiently meaningful? How about the test of when "justice, equity and fair dealing" require the disclosure? This test, previously adopted in Washington from Page Keeton's article cited in the succeeding note, had been criticized. See the response, in Sorrell v. Young, 6 Wash.App. 220, 491 P.2d 1312 (1971), to the effect that when fraud is involved it is better not to be too precise. "Once let it be known what the courts consider fraudulent and those engaged in its perpetration will busy themselves in inventing some means of evasion. The courts therefore should content themselves with determining from the facts of each case whether fraud does or does not exist."

9. See generally Keeton, Fraud—Concealment and Non–Disclosure, 15 Tex.L.Rev. 1, 31–40 (1936); Goldfarb, Fraud and Nondisclosure in the Vendor–Purchaser Relation, 8 Western Res.L.Rev. 5 (1956).

3. BASIS OF LIABILITY

(A) To the Recipient

DERRY v. PEEK
House of Lords, 1889.
14 App.Cas. 337.

[This action on the case was brought by Sir Henry William Peek against William Derry, chairman, and four directors of the Plymouth, Devonport and District Tramways Company, for the fraudulent misrepresentations of the defendant; whereby the plaintiff was induced to take shares in the company.

By Section 34 of the Tramways Act, 1870, which section was incorporated in the special Act, "all carriages used on any tramway shall be moved by the power prescribed by the special Act, and where no such power is prescribed, by animal power only."

Under Section 35 of the same Act, the vehicles used on the tramways might be moved by steam or mechanical power, with the consent of the Board of Trade, for fixed periods and subject to the regulations of the Board. In February, 1883, the defendants as directors of the company issued a prospectus.

The heading, which was in large type, was as follows: "Incorporated by special Act of Parliament authorizing the use of steam or mechanical motive power." It also contained the following paragraph: "One great feature of this undertaking to which considerable importance should be attached, is, that by the special Act of Parliament obtained the company has the right to use steam or mechanical motive power, instead of horses, and it is fully expected that by means of this a considerable saving will result in the working expenses of the line as compared with other tramways worked by horses," and there were other paragraphs further setting forth the advantages to be derived from steam as compared with horse power.

Soon after the issuing of the prospectus, a copy of which the plaintiff received, he applied for and was allotted shares in the company relying, as he alleged, upon the representations of this paragraph, believing the company had an absolute right to use steam and other mechanical power.

The company proceeded to construct its tramways, but the Board of Trade refused to consent to the use of steam or mechanical power except on certain portions of the tramway, and the corporations of Devonport refused their consent to the company opening the completed part of their lines until the remainder was ready for use. In consequence the company was wound up, and immediately thereafter the plaintiff brought this action against the defendants.

At the trial the defendants all testified that they knew that consent of the Board of Trade was required for the use of steam, but that they either thought that it had been obtained, or assumed that it was assured as a matter of course once the company had been incorporated by Act of Parliament with power to use steam.

Stirling, Justice, dismissed the action, having come to the conclusion that the directors all believed that the company had the rights stated in the prospectus and that their belief was not unreasonable, nor was their conduct so reckless or careless that they ought to be held liable in an action of deceit.

On appeal the judgment of Stirling, J., was reversed on the ground that while the defendants honestly believed that the statements in the prospectus were true, the statements were made without any reasonable grounds for believing them. The defendants appealed to the House of Lords. The House of Lords unanimously reversed the decisions of the Court below and unanimously restored the opinion of Stirling, J.]

LORD HERSCHELL. * * * "This action is one which is commonly called an action of deceit, a mere common-law action." This is the description of it given by Cotton, L.J., in delivering judgment. I think it important that it should be borne in mind that such an action differs essentially from one brought to obtain rescission of a contract on the ground of misrepresentation of a material fact. The principles which govern the two actions differ widely. Where rescission is claimed it is only necessary to prove that there was misrepresentation; then, however honestly it may have been made, however free from blame the person who made it, the contract, having been obtained by misrepresentation, cannot stand. In an action of deceit, on the contrary, it is not enough to establish misrepresentation alone; it is conceded on all hands that something more must be proved to cast liability upon the

Lord Herschell

defendant, though it has been a matter of controversy what additional elements are requisite. I lay stress upon this because observations made by learned judges in actions for rescission have been cited and much relied upon at the bar by counsel for the respondent. Care must obviously be observed in applying the language used in relation to such actions to an action of deceit. * * *

I think the authorities establish the following propositions: First, in order to sustain an action of deceit there must be proof of fraud, and nothing short of that will suffice. Secondly, fraud is proved when it is shown that a false representation has been made (1) knowingly, or (2) without belief in its truth, or (3) recklessly, careless whether it be true or false. Although I have treated the second and third as distinct cases, I think the third is but an instance of the second, for one who makes a statement under such circumstances can have no real belief in the truth of what he states. To prevent a false statement being fraudulent there must, I think, always be an honest belief in its truth. And this probably covers the whole ground, for one who knowingly alleges that which is false has obviously no such honest belief. Thirdly, if fraud be proved, the motive of the person guilty of it is immaterial. It matters not that there was no intention to cheat or injure the person to whom the statement was made. * * *

In my opinion making a false statement through want of care falls far short of, and is a very different thing from, fraud, and the same may be said of a false representation honestly believed though on insufficient grounds. * * *

At the same time I desire to say distinctly that when a false statement has been made the questions whether there were reasonable grounds for believing it, and what were the means of knowledge in the possession of the person making it, are most weighty matters for consideration. The ground upon which an alleged belief was founded is a most important test of its reality. I can conceive of many cases where the fact that an alleged belief was destitute of all reasonable foundation would suffice of itself to convince the Court that it was not really entertained, and that the representation was a fraudulent one. So, too, although means of knowledge are * * * a very different thing from knowledge, if I thought that a person making a false statement had shut his eyes to the facts, or purposely abstained from inquiring into them I should hold that honest belief was absent, and that he was just as fraudulent as if he had knowingly stated that which was false. * * *

I quite admit that the statements of witnesses as to their belief are by no means to be accepted blindfolded. The probabilities must be considered. Whenever it is necessary to arrive at a conclusion as to the state of mind of another person, and to determine whether his belief under given circumstances was such as he alleges, we can only do so by applying the standard of conduct which our own experience of the ways of men has enabled us to form; by asking ourselves whether a reasonable man situated as the defendants were, with their knowledge and means of knowledge, might well believe what they state they did believe, and consider that the representations made were substantially true. * * *

I think the judgment of the Court of Appeals should be reversed. * * *

Order of the Court of Appeal reversed; order of STIRLING, J., restored.

———

1. Following this decision, the English courts concluded that deceit would not lie for a representation made negligently but in honest good faith, and that a negligence action would not lie in such a case when the damage sustained was not physical injury, but only pecuniary loss. The outstanding case was Candler v. Crane, Christmas & Co., [1951] 2 K.B. 164. There was much criticism of the rule, which left the plaintiff without a remedy.

2. It was not until 1964, in Hedley Byrne & Co. v. Heller & Partners, [1964] A.C. 465, that the House of Lords explained away its position, overruled the *Candler* case, and extended the liability for negligence to pecuniary loss in any case where some "special relation" between the parties could be found.

3. About half of the American courts to consider the question still purport to follow the principal case, at least so far as an action of deceit is concerned. See Lambert v. Smith, 235 Md. 284, 201 A.2d 491 (1964). In many of these states, however, a negligence action will lie for the pecuniary loss. See International Products Co. v. Erie R. Co., infra page 1041.

4. The unreasonableness of the defendant's belief may be strong evidence that it does not in fact exist, and that conclusion may reached as an inference of fact. For example, Kimber v. Young, 137 Fed. 744 (8th Cir.1905).

5. It is generally agreed that a bad motive, as distinguished from an intent to mislead, is not essential to the tort of deceit. The defendant is liable if he intended to deceive, notwithstanding the fact that he meant no harm, was disinterested or intended to do the plaintiff a kindness. Polhill v. Walter, 3 B. & Ald. 114, 110 Eng.Rep. 43 (1832). The presence or absence of bad motive may, however, affect the issue of punitive damages for deceit. Thompson v. Modern School of Business and Correspondence, 183 Cal. 112, 190 P. 451 (1920); Laughlin v. Hopkinson, 292 Ill. 80, 126 N.E. 591 (1920).

SOVEREIGN POCOHONTAS CO. v. BOND

United States Court of Appeals, District of Columbia, 1941.
120 F.2d 39.

EDGERTON, ASSOCIATE JUSTICE. In this action for deceit, the District Court directed a verdict for the defendants. Their alleged misstatements related to the condition of a corporation of which they were officers. There is evidence that they said it was making money, and had made about $800 in the previous quarter, and over $3,000 in the preceding year, and that they caused certain financial statements to be sent to plaintiff. Actually the corporation was losing money, and had lost about $86 in the previous quarter and $2,700 in the preceding year, and the financial statements were incorrect.

Defendant Moyer was President, and apparently defendant Bond was Secretary and Treasurer of the Corporation. Both were frequently in its office, and frequently spoke for it. It might be inferred that they were, or were among, its active managers. There is no evidence that they kept or examined its books, understood bookkeeping, prepared its financial statements, knew whether or not the statements were erroneous, or knew whether or not the corporation had made or was making money. There is evidence that the books were kept by other persons, and no evidence that those persons did not prepare the financial statements.

"The rule is settled that in an action at law where the issue is fraud the party relying upon fraud must show that the misrepresentations asserted were made either with knowledge of their untruth or in reckless disregard of the truth." [C] The evidence would, we think, justify an inference that the defendants made untrue statements of objective fact in reckless disregard of the truth. In the absence of evidence tending to show that they were themselves misled by reasonable or merely negligent reliance on what others told them, a corporation's officers may be regarded as acting recklessly when they made glaringly false statements about its current financial history and condition. An accountant testified that his interpretation of the company's books and its financial statements could not "be reconciled with good faith as to the profit and loss account."

Moreover, the evidence would support an inference that the defendants knowingly made untrue statements of subjective fact. They did not say, "We are informed and believe that the company has been making money." Had they done so, it is not likely that the plaintiff would have relied on what they said. Their alleged statements were positive and unqualified. They purported, by clear implication, to know what they were talking about. Where knowledge is possible, one who represents a mere belief as knowledge misrepresents a fact. "Where a party represents a material fact to be true to his personal knowledge, as distinguished from belief or opinion, when he does not know whether it is true or not, and it is actually untrue, he is guilty of falsehood, even if he believes it to be true, and if the statement is thus made with the intention that it shall be acted upon by another, who does so act upon it to his injury, the result is actionable fraud." Hadcock v. Osmer, 153 N.Y. 604, 608, 47 N.E. 923.

There was evidence that defendants' statements were made for the purpose of inducing plaintiff to refrain from action to collect a debt which defendants' company owed; that plaintiff did refrain, and also made a further sale to the company, in consequence; and that damage resulted, because the company's condition grew worse and plaintiff was ultimately unable to collect as much as it could have done when the representations were made. The difficulty of estimating damages is no greater than in many cases. Accordingly it was error to direct a verdict for the defendants.

Reversed.

———

1. Section 526 of the Restatement (Second) of Torts reads as follows:

"A misrepresentation is fraudulent if the maker

"(a) knows or believes that the matter is not as he represents it to be,

"(b) does not have the confidence in the accuracy of his representation that he states or implies, or

"(c) knows that he does not have the basis for his representation that he states or implies."

How does this fit with the definition of Lord Herschell in Derry v. Peek? Does it adequately include the principle of *Sovereign Pocohontas* as well?

2. Suppose the plaintiff knows that the matter represented is one upon which the defendant could not have any definite knowledge? Thus a representation that there is water under land, and it will be found when a well is drilled. Harris v. Delco Products, Inc., 305 Mass. 362, 25 N.E.2d 740 (1940).

3. Suppose the defendant makes a statement that can reasonably be understood in two ways, one true and the other false. Plaintiff understands it in the false sense, and is misled, but defendant believes that plaintiff has understood in the true one. Will an action for deceit lie? Nash v. Minnesota Title Insurance & Trust Co., 163 Mass. 574, 40 N.E. 1039 (1895).

INTERNATIONAL PRODUCTS CO. v. ERIE R.R. CO.
Court of Appeals of New York, 1927.
244 N.Y. 331, 155 N.E. 662.

[Plaintiff, an importer, was expecting a valuable consignment of goods to arrive on the steamer Plutarch, and had made arrangements with defendants to receive and store the goods until they could be reshipped. The shipment was covered by insurance until it reached the warehouse, and plaintiff desired to insure it after that time. Giving this reason for its question, it inquired of defendant where the goods would be stored. Defendant, taking time to obtain the information, replied that the goods were docked at Dock F, Weehawken. From this reply, plaintiff reasonably inferred that the goods were already received and stored, and obtained its insurance on this basis. The goods arrived later and were stored at Dock D. They were destroyed by fire, and plaintiff was unable to collect any insurance payments because of the misdescription. Plaintiff seeks to recover from defendant the sum it would have received if defendant's statement had been correct. The trial court directed a verdict for plaintiff, which was affirmed by the Appellate Division. Defendant appeals.]

ANDREWS, J. * * * Confining ourselves to the issues before us, we eliminate any theory of fraud or deceit. * * * [C] We come to the vexed question of liability for negligent language. In England the rule is fixed. "Generally speaking there is no such thing as liability for negligence in words as distinguished from act." Pollock on Torts (12th Ed.) p. 565; [c]. Dicta to the contrary may be found in earlier cases. * * * But since Derry v. Peek, L.R. 14 App.Cas. 337, although what was said was not necessary to the decision, the law is clearly to the effect "that no cause of action is maintainable for a mere statement, although untrue, and although acted upon to the damage of the person to whom the statement is made unless the statement be false to the knowledge of the person making it," [c] or, as said elsewhere, "we have to take it as settled that there is no general duty to use any care whatever in making statements in the way of business or otherwise, on which other persons are likely to act" [c]. * * *

These cases have not been without criticism. The denial, under all circumstances, of relief because of the negligently spoken or written word, is, it is said, a refusal to enforce what conscience, fair dealing, and the usages of business require. The tendency of the American courts has been towards a more liberal conclusion. The searcher of a title employed by one who delivers his abstract to another to induce action on the faith of it must exercise care. [C] So must a physician who assures a wife that she may safely treat the infected wound of her husband [c], or hired by another, examines a patient, and states the result of his diagnosis [c]. So of a telegraph company stating that a telegram was delivered when in fact it was not. [C] And the liability of such a company to the receiver for the erroneous transcription of a telegram has also sometimes been placed on this ground. [C]

In New York we are already committed to the American as distinguished from the English rule. In some cases a negligent statement may be the basis for a recovery of damages. A reference is made to the question in Carpenter v. Blake, 75 N.Y. 12. We intimated that a physician would be liable for negligent advice given to a patient after his discharge, but this suggestion was not decisive of the point we now consider. * * * Then came Glanzer v. Shepard, 233 N.Y. 236, 135 N.E. 275. A public weigher, hired by the seller to weigh goods, realizing that the buyer would rely on his certificate in paying therefor, was held liable for erroneous statements contained therein. * * *

The negligence was inferred from the issuance of a false certificate. That was the wrong for which a recovery was allowed. "Diligence was owing, not only to him who ordered, but to him also who relied."

Obviously, however, the rule we have adopted has its limits. Not every casual response, not every idle word, however damaging the result, gives rise to a cause of action. * * * Liability in such cases arises only where there is a duty, if one speaks at all, to give the correct information. And that involves many considerations. There must be knowledge, or its equivalent, that the information is desired for a serious purpose; that he to whom it is given intends to rely and act upon it; that, if false or erroneous, he will because of it be injured in person or property. Finally, the relationship of the parties, arising out of contract or otherwise, must be such that in morals and good conscience the one has the right to rely upon the other for information, and the other giving the information owes a duty to give it with care. [C] An inquiry made of a stranger is one thing; of a person with whom the inquirer has entered, or is about to enter into a contract concerning the goods which are, or are to be, its subject, is another. Even here the inquiry must be made as the basis of independent action. We do not touch the doctrine of caveat emptor. But in a proper case we hold that words negligently spoken may justify the recovery of the proximate damages caused by faith in their accuracy.

When such a relationship as we have referred to exists may not be precisely defined. All that may be stated is the general rule. In view of the complexity of modern business, each case must be decided on the peculiar facts presented. The same thing is true, however, in the usual action for personal injuries. There whether negligence exists depends upon the relations of the parties, the thing done or neglected, its natural consequences, and many other considerations. No hard and fast line may be drawn.

Here, as we view the facts, the duty to speak with care, if it spoke at all, rested on the defendant. We have [defendant] about to become the bailee of the plaintiff's goods; the inquiry made by [plaintiff] with whom [defendant] was dealing for the purpose as it knew of obtaining insurance; the realization that the information it gave was to be relied upon, and that, if false, the insurance obtained would be worthless. We have an inquiry such as might be expected in the usual course of business made of one who alone knew the truth. We have a negligent answer, untrue in fact actual reliance upon it, and resulting proximate loss. True, the answer was not given to serve the purposes of the defendant itself. This we regard as immaterial.

If there was negligence justifying a recovery, we cannot hold the plaintiff guilty of contributory negligence as a matter of law. Whether or not it should have discovered the error by an inspection of the bill of lading when it received it was a question of fact. * * *

The judgment appealed from should be affirmed, with costs.

---

1. In cases of personal injury, the courts have been quite willing to allow recovery for negligent misrepresentation. In Cunningham v. C.R. Pease House Furnishing Co., 74 N.H. 435, 69 A. 120 (1908), the defendant sold some stove blacking to the plaintiff, and negligently, but in good faith assured him that it was safe to use it on a hot stove. "The warmer the stove the better it works." Plaintiff used it on a hot stove, and was injured when it exploded. It was held that a negligence action would lie for the misrepresentation. Cf. Dalrymple v. Sinkoe, 230 N.C. 453, 53 S.E.2d 437 (1949).

2. In Weston v. Brown, 82 N.H. 157, 131 A. 141 (1925), the court carried this liability over to pecuniary loss on the purchase of a farm, saying that "it is difficult to perceive why liability should be made to depend upon the nature of the injury sustained."

3. A substantial number of the American courts have extended the negligence action from tangible injuries to pecuniary loss, and have allowed recovery in such an action. See, for example, Maxwell Ice Co. v. Brackett, Shaw & Lunt Co., 80 N.H. 236, 116 A. 34 (1921); Sult v. Scandrett, 119 Mont. 570, 178 P.2d 405 (1947). This has been approved by the Restatement (Second) of Torts § 552.

4. A few of the American courts have held that the action for deceit itself will lie for negligent misrepresentations resulting in pecuniary loss. They have either declared outright that the fault of a negligent defendant is equivalent to that of a defendant intending to deceive, or have resorted to the obvious fiction that a duty to learn the facts is the equivalent of knowledge of their existence. See, for example, Mullen v. Eastern Trust & Banking Co., 108 Me. 498, 81 A. 948 (1911); Scholfield Gear & Pulley Co. v. Scholfield, 71 Conn. 1, 40 A. 1046 (1898).

5. As to the dictum in the principal case that "not every casual response, not every idle word * * * gives rise to a cause of action," see Renn v. Provident Trust Co., 328 Pa. 481, 196 A. 8 (1938) (gratuitous supplying of copy of will, wrong will supplied by mistake); Vartan Garapedian, Inc. v. Anderson, 92 N.H. 390, 31 A.2d 371 (1943) (casual statement about credit of prospective buyer). Is an attorney or a physician, liable to one who is not his client or his patient for "curbstone advice," when it is negligently given? Fish v. Kelly, 17 C.B. (N.S.) 194, 144 Eng.Rep. 78 (1864); Buttersworth v. Swint, 53 Ga.App. 602, 186 S.E. 770 (1936).

6. There are a good many cases holding that when a truck driver comes to the crest of a hill and signals to a driver behind that it is safe to pass, he has by his affirmative conduct assumed the duty of care and so is liable if he is negligent. Thelen v. Spillman, 251 Minn. 89, 86 N.W.2d 700 (1957); Petroleum Carrier Corp. v. Carter, 233 F.2d 402 (5th Cir.1956). Can these cases be reconciled with those above?

7. What if the information, although not volunteered and given without consideration, is supplied in the course of the defendant's business or professional relations? For example, the lessor of a truck gratuitously tells the lessee, in good faith but negligently, that it is covered by insurance? Manock v. Amos D. Bridge's Sons, Inc., 86 N.H. 411, 169 A. 881 (1934). Cf. Virginia Dare Stores v. Schuman, 175 Md. 287, 1 A.2d 897 (1938) (owner to invitee).

RICHARD v. A. WALDMAN AND SONS, INC.

Supreme Court of Connecticut, 1967.
155 Conn. 343, 232 A.2d 307.

COTTER, ASSOCIATE JUSTICE. The plaintiffs, owners of a house and lot in Vernon which they purchased from the defendant corporation, instituted an action * * * for damages for alleged false representations in connection with the sale of land. * * * [Plaintiff obtained] a judgment for damages from which the defendant has appealed.
* * *

At the time of the closing, the defendant delivered to the plaintiffs a plot plan prepared by a registered engineer and land surveyor. This plan showed a sideyard of twenty feet on the southerly boundary of the lot which was in compliance with the minimum requirements for this lot according to the zoning regulations on file with the town clerk of

Vernon. A permit had previously been granted for the construction of the building, consisting of a house with an attached garage, and the survey submitted at the time the defendant made the application indicated that the structure was to be located twenty feet more or less from the southerly property line. Subsequently, a certificate of occupancy was erroneously issued based on the survey submitted by the defendant. Approximately four months after the delivery of the deed to the plaintiffs, the defendant discovered, when it set pins defining the boundaries of the premises, that the southeast corner of the foundation of the plaintiffs' house was only 1.8 feet from the southerly boundary of the lot. At this time, it was found that trespass upon adjoining property occurred in entering and leaving the plaintiffs' back door and stoop. Prior to this discovery, the parties were unaware that there was a violation of the zoning regulations as to sideyard requirements. The defendant, under a mistaken assumption, had represented by the plot plan that the structure on the lot was twenty feet from the southerly boundary. Unaware of the true fact, the plaintiffs relied on this representation.

The court concluded (1) that the defendant falsely and recklessly represented to the plaintiffs, for the purpose of inducing action, that the premises had a southerly sideyard of twenty feet and that there was no violation of the zoning regulations, and (2) that the plaintiffs were induced to rely on these representations, which were the result of a mistake on the part of the defendant but were not innocent.

The defendant claims that "[a]t most, there was an innocent misrepresentation of fact by the defendant." An innocent misrepresentation may be actionable if the declarant has the means of knowing, ought to know, or has the duty of knowing the truth. [C]

The facts, as properly found, clearly show that the plaintiffs had reasonable grounds upon which to attribute to the defendant accurate knowledge of what it represented as to the location of the structure on the lot. This was a statement of fact about which the defendant as a developer of residential real estate, had special means of knowledge, and it was a matter peculiarly relating to its business and one on which the plaintiffs were entitled to rely. [Cc] The defendant was commercially involved in and responsible for the preliminary and final plans for building and locating the structure which was then constructed on the lot by the defendant in a manner which violated the zoning ordinance. Thereafter, the defendant undertook to provide the plaintiffs with a survey and plot plan which erroneously showed a southerly sideyard of twenty feet. Actual knowledge of the falsity of the representation need not be shown under the circumstances, nor must the plaintiffs allege fraud or bad faith. They have alleged all the facts material to support their claim and demand for damages. It is immaterial whether the wrong which can be legally inferred from the facts arises in contract or in tort. The plaintiffs may seek damages resulting from the defendant's misrepresentation and at the same time retain title to the property. [C] Such a misrepresentation was "in the nature of a warranty" entitling them to a recovery under the contract "as for a breach of warranty." It would be unjust to permit the defendant under these circumstances to "retain the fruits of a bargain induced by" a material misrepresentation upon which the plaintiffs relied. * * *

There was sufficient evidence which supported the court's finding that the plaintiffs were entitled to a recovery based on the rule that the measure of damages was the difference between the actual value of the property and the value of the property had it been as represented. * * *

[In *Rich v. Rankl*, 6 Conn.Cir. 185, 269 A.2d 84 (1969), the court says: "The relief granted in the Richard case was the cost of the construction work and the moving of the house to relocate it on the plaintiffs' lot."]

The facts necessary to establish the defendant's liability were alleged in the complaint, and the conclusions of the trial court are amply supported by the facts found.

There is no error.

---

1. If the plaintiff is seeking to rescind the contract, an innocent misrepresentation that is material is basis for relief. Neither scienter nor negligence is necessary. The action is not in tort, but for restitution. See Seneca Wire & Mfg. Co. v. A.B. Leach & Co., 247 N.Y. 1, 159 N.E. 700 (1928); Ross v. Harding, 64 Wash.2d 231, 391 P.2d 526 (1964).

2. The principal case allows recovery for innocent misrepresentation in a tort action. It follows a minority position. The earliest case to carry the strict liability over to a tort action for damages for the misrepresentation was Holcomb v. Noble, 69 Mich. 396, 37 N.W. 497 (1888), where the court appears to have confused equitable relief with an action at law. But Michigan now fully and consciously follows the "doctrine of innocent misrepresentation." United States Fidelity and Guaranty Co. v. Black, 412 Mich. 99, 313 N.W.2d 77 (1981). See also Becker v. McKinnie, 106 Kan. 426, 186 P. 496 (1920); Moulton v. Norton, 184 Minn. 343, 238 N.W. 686 (1931); Pumphrey v. Quillen, 165 Ohio St. 343, 135 N.E.2d 328, 59 O.O. 460 (1956).

3. This minority position has been adopted in the Restatement (Second) of Torts. Section 552C reads as follows:

"(1) One who, in a sale, rental or exchange transaction with another, makes a misrepresentation of a material fact for the purpose of inducing the other to act or to refrain from acting in reliance upon it, is subject to liability to the other for pecuniary loss caused to him by his justifiable reliance upon the misrepresentation, even though it is not made fraudulently or negligently.

"(2) Damages recoverable under the rule stated in this Section are limited to the difference between the value of what the other has parted with and the value of what he has received in the transaction.

"*Caveat:* The Institute expresses no opinion as to whether there may not be other types of business transactions, in addition to those of sale, rental and exchange, in which strict liability may be imposed for innocent misrepresentation, under the conditions stated in this Section."

See the comprehensive discussion of the matter, disagreeing with the Restatement position, in Hill, Damages for Innocent Misrepresentation, 73 Colum.L.Rev. 679 (1973); and Hill, Breach of Contract as a Tort, 74 Colum.L. Rev. 40 (1974).

4. Is the remedy of rescission adequate to take care of the plaintiff's needs, or should he be able to keep the property and sue for damages? Is a tort action needed if an action for breach of warranty is available? Is the rule in § 552C really a development of the law of torts, or one of the law of restitution, eliminating the requirement of restoring the status quo as a condition for relief?

5. The basis of liability for misrepresentation has been a fertile subject for legal writers, and the process of development has been anticipated, followed and cheered on by a long series of articles. The initial treatment was Smith, Liability for Negligent Language, 14 Harv.L.Rev. 184 (1909), advocating liability at least for negligence. This was followed by Williston, Liability for Honest Misrepresentation, 24 Harv.L.Rev. 415 (1911), proposing strict liability. A lively discussion then broke out, most of which indicated that intent, negligence and strict liability all have their proper place: Bohlen, Misrepresentation as Deceit, Negligence or Warranty, 42 Harv.L.Rev. 733 (1929); Carpenter, Responsibility for Intentional, Negligent or Innocent Misrepresentation, 24 Ill.L.Rev. 749 (1930); Weisiger, Basis of Liability for Misrepresentation, 24 Ill.L.Rev. 866 (1930); Green, Deceit, 16 Va.L.Rev. 749 (1930); Bohlen, Should Negligent Misrepresentation Be Treated as Negligence or Fraud, 18 Va.L.Rev. 703 (1932); Green, Innocent Misrepresentation, 19 Va.L.Rev. 242 (1932).

Subsequent articles have tended to review the decisions, and bring the matter up to date. See Harper and McNeely, A Synthesis of the Law of Misrepresentation, 22 Minn.L.Rev. 939 (1939); Keeton, Actionable Misrepresentation, 1 Okla.L.Rev. 21 (1948), 2 Okla.L.Rev. 56 (1949); Keeton, Fraud: The Necessity for an Intent to Deceive, 5 UCLA L.Rev. 583 (1958). See also Keeton, Rights of Disappointed Purchasers, 32 Tex.L.Rev. 1 (1953): Green, The Duty to Give Accurate Information, 12 UCLA L.Rev. 464 (1965).

6. Statutes in some states now provide for strict liability for certain statements made in various types of commercial transactions. The Federal Securities Act of 1933, as amended in 1934, 15 U.S.C.A. §§ 77a et seq., is held to impose strict liability in many respects. Securities Law is treated as a separate course in most law schools and cannot be covered here. See generally 3 L. Loss, Securities Regulation, Chs. 9(B) and 11 (1961, and Supp.1969); Shulman, Civil Liability and the Securities Act, 43 Yale L.J. 227 (1933); Sonde, The Responsibility of Professionals under the Federal Securities Laws—Some Observations, 68 Nw.U.L.Rev. 1 (1973).

7. What changes when a misrepresentation in connection with a sale of goods causes personal injury or property damage to a person reasonably expected to rely on the statement? See Baxter v. Ford Motor Co. and notes supra pages 702–06.

(B) To Third Persons

CREDIT ALLIANCE CORPORATION v. ARTHUR ANDERSEN & CO.

Court of Appeals of New York, 1985.
65 N.Y.2d 536, 483 N.E.2d 110, 493 N.Y.S.2d 435.

JASEN, JUDGE. The critical issue common to these two appeals is whether an accountant may be held liable, absent privity of contract, to a party who relies to his detriment upon a negligently prepared financial report and, if so, within what limits does that liability extend.

[In Credit Alliance Corp. v. Andersen & Co., the defendant accountants prepared consolidated financial statements for L.B. Smith, Inc. Credit Alliance had provided financing to Smith for some time, insisting in 1978 upon audited financial statements. Smith supplied statements that had been prepared by defendant. "These statements contained an auditor's report prepared by Andersen stating that it had examined the statements in accordance with generally accepted auditing standards ('GAAS') and found them to reflect fairly the financial position of Smith in conformity with generally accepted accounting principles ('GAAP')." Plaintiff alleged that the statements were inaccurate because of failure to conduct investigations in accordance with proper auditing standards. Special Term denied defendant's motion to dismiss causes of action, based on negligence and fraud. A divided Appellate Division affirmed, 101 A.D.2d 231, 476 N.Y.S.2d 539, and certified to the Court of Appeals the question, "Was the order of the Supreme Court, as affirmed by this court, properly made?"

In European Am. Bank & Trust Co. v. Strahs & Kaye, ("S. & K."), the bank ("EAB") made substantial loans to Majestic Electro Industries. Majestic having become bankrupt, EAB sued S. & K. for seriously exaggerating Majestic's solvency assets. Special Term dismissed the complaint and Appellate Division reversed but certified a similar question to the Court of Appeals. EAB specifically alleges that S. & K. at all relevant times knew that EAB was Majestic Electro's principal lender, was familiar with the terms of the lending relationship and was fully aware that EAB was relying on the statements, and that S. & K. and Majestic were in communication during the entire course of the lending relationship.]

In the seminal case of *Ultramares Corp. v. Touche*, 255 N.Y. 170, 174 N.E. 441 [1931], this court, speaking through the opinion of Chief Judge Cardozo more than 50 years ago, disallowed a cause of action in negligence against a public accounting firm for inaccurately prepared financial statements which were relied upon by a plaintiff having no contractual privity with the accountants. This court distinguished its holding from *Glanzer v. Shepard*, 233 N.Y. 236, 135 N.E. 275 [1922], a case decided in an opinion also written by Cardozo nine years earlier. We explained that in *Glanzer*, an action in negligence against public weighers had been permitted, despite the absence of a contract between the parties, because the plaintiff's intended reliance, on the information *directly transmitted* by the weighers, created a bond so closely approaching privity that it was, in practical effect, virtually indistinguishable therefrom. This court has subsequently reaffirmed its holding in *Ultramares* which has been, and continues to be, much discussed and analyzed by the commentators and by the courts of other jurisdictions. These appeals now provide us with the opportunity to reexamine and delineate the principles enunciated in both *Ultramares* and *Glanzer*. Inasmuch as we believe that a relationship "so close as to approach that of privity" [c] remains valid as the predicate for imposing liability upon accountants to noncontractual parties for the negligent preparation of financial reports, we restate and elaborate upon our adherence to that standard today.

The doctrine of privity is said to have had its source in the classic enunciation of its rationale in *Winterbottom v. Wright,* 10 M. & W. 109, 152 Eng.Rep. 402, [supra page 444]. From *Winterbottom,* the privity doctrine developed into a general rule prevailing well into the Twentieth Century. [Cc]

By the time 90 years had passed, however, this court could note in *Ultramares* that the "assault upon the citadel of privity is proceeding in these days apace." [C] We acknowledged that inroads had been made, for example, where third-party beneficiaries or dangerous instrumentalities were involved. [C] Indeed, we referred to this court's holding in *MacPherson v. Buick Motor Co.,* 217 N.Y. 382, [supra page 697] where it was decided that the manufacturer of a defective chattel—there an automobile—may be liable in negligence for the resulting injuries sustained by a user regardless of the absence of privity—a belated rejection of the doctrine of privity as applied to the facts in *Winterbottom*. Nevertheless, regarding an accountant's liability to unknown parties with whom he had not contracted, the considerations were deemed sufficiently dissimilar to justify different treatment.

Although accountants might be held liable in fraud to nonprivy parties who were intended to rely upon the accountants' misrepresentations, we noted that "[a] different question develops when we ask whether they owed a duty to these to make [their reports] without negligence." *Ultramares Corp. v. Touche, supra.* Disputing the wisdom of extending the duty of care of accountants to anyone who might foreseeably rely upon their financial reports, Cardozo, speaking for this court, remarked: "If liability for negligence exists, a thoughtless slip or blunder, the failure to detect a theft or forgery beneath the cover of deceptive entries, may expose accountants to a liability in an indeterminate amount for an indeterminate time to an indeterminate class. The hazards of a business conducted on these terms are so extreme as to enkindle doubt whether a flaw may not exist in the implication of a duty that exposes to these consequences." [C]

In *Ultramares,* the accountants had prepared a certified balance sheet for their client to whom they provided 32 copies. The client, in turn, gave one to the plaintiff company. The latter, relying upon the misinformation contained in the balance sheet, made loans to the accountants' client who, only months later, was declared bankrupt. This court, refusing to extend the accountants' liability for negligence to their client's lender, with whom they had no contractual privity, noted that the accountants had prepared a report on behalf of their client to be exhibited generally to "banks, creditors, stockholders, purchasers or sellers, *according to the needs of the occasion*". [C] In reciting the facts, we emphasized that: "*Nothing was said as to the persons to whom these [copies] would be shown or the extent or number of the transactions in which they would be used.* In particular there was no mention of the plaintiff, a corporation doing business chiefly as a factor, which till then had never made advances to the [accountants' client], though it had sold merchandise in small amounts. The range of the transactions in which a certificate of audit might be expected to play a part was as indefinite and wide as the possibilities of the business that was mirrored in the summary." [C]

The accountants' report was primarily intended as a convenient instrumentality for the client's use in developing its business. "[O]nly incidentally or collaterally" was it expected to assist those to whom the client "might exhibit it thereafter". [C] Under such circumstances, permitting recovery by parties such as the plaintiff company would have been to impose a duty upon accountants "enforce[able] by any member of an indeterminate class of creditors, present and prospective, known and unknown." [C]

By sharp contrast, the facts underlying *Glanzer* bespoke an affirmative assumption of a duty of care to a specific party, for a specific purpose, regardless of whether there was a contractual relationship. There, a seller of beans employed the defendants who were engaged in business as public weighers. Pursuant to instructions, the weighers furnished one copy of the weight certificate to their employer, the seller, and another to the prospective buyer. In reliance upon the inaccurately certified weight, the buyer purchased beans from the seller and, thereby, suffered a loss.

Explaining the imposition upon the weighers of a "noncontractual" duty of care to the buyer, this court held: "We think the law imposes a duty toward buyer as well as seller in the situation here disclosed. The [buyer's] use of the certificates was *not an indirect or collateral consequence* of the action of the weighers. It was a consequence which, to the weighers' knowledge, was the *end and aim of the transaction.* [The seller] ordered, but [the buyer was] to use. The defendants held themselves out to the public as skilled and careful in their calling. They knew that the beans had been sold, and that on the faith of their certificate payment would be made. *They sent a copy to the [buyer] for the very purpose of inducing action.* All this they admit. In such circumstances, assumption of the task of weighing was the assumption of a duty to weigh carefully for the benefit of all whose conduct was to be governed. We do not need to state the duty in terms of contract or of privity. Growing out of a contract, it has none the less an origin not exclusively contractual. Given the contract and the relation, the duty is imposed by law." [C]

The critical distinctions between the two cases were highlighted in *Ultramares*, where we explained: "In *Glanzer v. Shepard* * * * [the certificate of weight], which was made out in duplicate, one copy to the seller and the other to the buyer, *recites that it was made by order of the former for the use of the latter* * * * Here was something more than the rendition of a service in the expectation that the one who ordered the certificate would use it thereafter in the operations of his business as occasion might require. Here was a case where *the transmission of the certificate to another was* not merely one possibility among many, but *the 'end and aim of the transaction,'* as certain and immediate and deliberately willed as if a husband were to order a gown to be delivered to his wife, or a telegraph company, contracting with the sender of a message, were to telegraph it wrongly to the damage of the person expected to receive it * * * The *intimacy of the resulting nexus* is attested by the fact that after stating the case in terms of legal duty, we went on to point out that * * * we could reach the same result by stating it in terms of contract * * * The bond was *so close' as to approach that of privity, if not completely one with it.* Not so in the case at hand [i.e., *Ultramares*]. No one would be likely to urge that there was a contractual relation, or *even one approaching it,* at the root of any duty that was owing from the [accountants] now before us to the indeterminate class of persons who, presently or in the future, might deal with the [accountants' client] in reliance on the audit. In a word, the service rendered by the defendant in *Glanzer v. Shepard* was primarily for the information of a third person, *in effect, if not in name, a party to the contract,* and only incidentally for that of the formal promisee." [C]

Several years subsequent to the decision in *Ultramares,* this court reiterated the requirement for a "contractual relationship or its equivalent" (*State St. Trust Co. v. Ernst,* 278 N.Y. 104, 111, 15 N.E.2d 416), and more recently, in *White v. Guarente,* 43 N.Y.2d 356, 401 N.Y.S.2d 474, 372 N.E.2d 315, such an equivalent was presented for our consideration. There, the accountants had contracted with a limited partnership to perform an audit and prepare the partnership's tax returns. The nature and purpose of the contract, to satisfy the requirement in the partnership agreement for an audit, made it clear that the accountants' services were obtained to benefit the members of the partnership who, like plaintiff, a limited partner, were necessarily dependent upon the audit to prepare their own tax returns. After outlining the principles articulated in *Ultramares* and *Glanzer,* this court observed that: "[T]his plaintiff seeks redress, not as a mere member of the public, but as one of a settled and particularized class among the members of which the report would be circulated *for the specific*

purpose of fulfilling the limited partnership agreed upon arrangement."
[C]

Because the accountants knew that a limited partner would have to rely upon the audit and tax returns of the partnership, and inasmuch as this was within the specific contemplation of the accounting retainer, we held that, "at least on the facts here, an accountant's liability may be so imposed." [C] The resulting relationship between the accountants and the limited partner was clearly one "approach[ing] that of privity, if not completely one with it." (*Ultramares Corp. v. Touche, supra*).

Upon examination of *Ultramares* and *Glanzer* and our recent affirmation of their holdings in *White,* certain criteria may be gleaned. Before accountants may be held liable in negligence to noncontractual parties who rely to their detriment on inaccurate financial reports, certain prerequisites must be satisfied: (1) the accountants must have been aware that the financial reports were to be used for a particular purpose or purposes; (2) in the furtherance of which a known party or parties was intended to rely; and (3) there must have been some conduct on the part of the accountants linking them to that party or parties, which evinces the accountants' understanding of that party or parties' reliance. While these criteria permit some flexibility in the application of the doctrine of privity to accountants' liability, they do not represent a departure from the principles articulated in *Ultramares, Glanzer* and *White,* but, rather, they are intended to preserve the wisdom and policy set forth therein.

We are aware that the courts throughout this country are divided as to the continued validity of the holding in *Ultramares.* Some courts continue to insist that a strict application of the privity requirement governs the law of accountants' liability except, perhaps, where special circumstances compel a different result. * * *

In all of [these] cases, the courts found the facts amenable to the imposition of accountants' liability under the principles of *Ultramares–Glanzer* or extended those principles to permit a more liberalized application. To the extent that the holdings in those cases are predicated upon certain criteria—to wit, a particular purpose for the accountants' report, a known relying party, and some conduct on the part of the accountants linking them to that party—they are consonant with the principles reaffirmed in this decision. To the extent, however, that those cases were decided upon the ground that *Ultramares* should not be followed and, instead, a rule permitting recovery by any foreseeable plaintiff should be adopted, the law in this State, as reiterated today, is clearly distinguishable. * * *

In the appeals we decide today, application of the foregoing principles presents little difficulty. In *Credit Alliance,* the facts as alleged by plaintiffs fail to demonstrate the existence of a relationship between the parties sufficiently approaching privity. Though the complaint and supporting affidavit do allege that Andersen specifically knew, should have known or was on notice that plaintiffs were being shown the reports by Smith, Andersen's client, in order to induce their reliance thereon, nevertheless, there is no adequate allegation of either a particular purpose for the reports' preparation or the prerequisite conduct on the part of the accountants. While the allegations state that Smith sought to induce plaintiffs to extend credit, no claim is made that Andersen was being employed to prepare the reports with that particular purpose in mind. Moreover, there is no allegation that Andersen had any direct dealings with plaintiffs, had specifically agreed with Smith to prepare the report for plaintiffs' use or according to plaintiffs' requirements, or had specifically agreed with Smith to provide plaintiffs with a copy or actually did so. Indeed, there is simply no allegation of any word or action on the part of Andersen directed to plaintiffs, or anything contained in Andersen's retainer agreement with Smith which provided the necessary link between them.

By sharp contrast, in *European American,* the facts as alleged by EAB clearly show that S. & K. was well aware that a primary, if not the exclusive, *end and aim* of auditing its client, Majestic Electro, was to provide EAB with the financial information it required. The prerequisites for the cause of action in negligence, as well as in gross negligence, are fully satisfied. Not only is it alleged, as in *Credit Alliance,* that the accountants knew the identity of the specific non-privy party who would be relying upon the audit reports, but additionally, the complaint and affidavit here allege both the accountants' awareness of a particular purpose for their services and certain conduct on their part creating an unmistakable relationship with the reliant plaintiff. It is unambiguously claimed that the parties remained in direct communication, both orally and in writing, and, indeed, met together throughout the course of EAB's lending relationship with Majestic Electro, for the very purpose of discussing the latter's financial condition and EAB's need for S. & K.'s evaluation. Moreover, it is alleged that S. & K. made repeated representations personally to representatives of EAB, on these occasions, concerning the value of Majestic Electro's assets. It cannot be gainsaid that the relationship thus created between the parties was the practical equivalent of privity. The parties' direct communications and personal meetings resulted in a nexus between them sufficiently approaching privity under the principles of *Ultramares, Glanzer* and *White* to permit EAB's causes of action.

Finally, disposition of the second cause of action alleged in *Credit Alliance* need not detain us long. The cause of action for fraud repeats the allegations for the negligence cause of action and merely adds a claim that Andersen recklessly disregarded facts which would have apprised it that its reports were misleading or that Andersen had actual knowledge that such was the case. This single allegation of scienter, without additional detail concerning the facts constituting the alleged fraud, is insufficient under the special pleading standards required under CPLR 3016(b), and, consequently, the cause of action should have been dismissed. [Cc].

Accordingly, in *Credit Alliance* both causes of action should be dismissed, the order of the Appellate Division reversed, with costs, and the certified question answered in the negative. In *European American,* the order of the Appellate Division should be affirmed, with costs, and the certified question answered in the affirmative.

CITIZENS STATE BANK v. TIMM, SCHMIDT & CO.
Supreme Court of Wisconsin, 1983.
113 Wis.2d 376, 335 N.W.2d 361.

[For the years 1973–76, defendant Timm, Schmidt & Co. (Timm), an accounting firm, prepared financial statements for Clintonville Fire Apparatus, Inc. (CFA), including statements of financial condition, yearly income, retained income and changes in financial condition. These were accompanied by an opinion letter to CFA stating that "the financial statements fairly presented the financial condition of CFA and that the statements were prepared in accordance with generally accepted accounting principles."

In 1975 and 1976 CFA obtained loans from Citizens State Bank amounting to $380,000, relying on Timm's statements. In 1977 Timm discovered mistakes in its statements totaling over $400,000. It notified Security, which called in all of its loans due. CFA went into receivership and was ultimately liquidated and dissolved. Still due to Citizens was $152,214. Citizens sued Timm for that amount.

Timm moved for summary judgment. All persons in the Timm firm who had worked on the CFA statements filed affidavits that they had no knowledge that CFA intended to obtain or had any loans from Citizens. There were some contradictory affidavits, especially from the CFA president, Dando, indicating that he believed that Timm knew of the dealing. The trial court granted the motion for summary judgment, and the court of appeals affirmed. The case is now before the state supreme court.]

DAY, JUSTICE * * * The question on review is whether accountants may be held liable for the negligent preparation of an audit report to a third party not in privity who relies on the report.

This is a question of first impression in this state. However, the issue has received wide consideration in both courts and law journals.

Accountants have long been held not liable for their negligence to relying third parties not in privity under an application of Judge Cardozo's decision in *Ultramares v. Touche,* 255 N.Y. 170, 174 N.E. 441 (1931). In *Ultramares,* Judge Cardozo absolved the defendant accountants from liability for overvaluing the assets of a company in an audit report to a plaintiff who had loaned money in reliance on a certified balance sheet in the report. Judge Cardozo expressed the concern that "if liability exists, a thoughtless slip or blunder * * * may expose accountants to a liability in an indeterminate amount for an indeterminate time to an indeterminate class." [C]

[At one time] *Ultramares* was relied on by every jurisdiction to consider this question to deny accountant liability to third parties. However, in recent years, *Ultramares* has received new attention and courts have started to find accountants liable to third parties.

In *Rusch Factors, Inc., v. Levin,* 284 F.Supp. 85 (D.C.RI 1968), the court, citing section 552 of the Restatement, imposed liability on an accountant to a relying third party not in privity. In *Rusch Factors,* the accountant knew the statements he prepared were to be used by his client for the purpose of obtaining credit from a third party even though they did not know of the specific relying third party. Nevertheless, the court allowed liability to be imposed. 284 F.Supp. at 93.

Similarly, in *Ryan v. Kanne,* 170 N.W.2d 395 (Iowa 1969), the Iowa Supreme Court applying Restatement section 552, determined that an accountant could be held liable to a foreseen third party who had relied upon a negligently prepared audit report. Because the relying third party was "actually known," the court did not address the extent of foreseeability that would be necessary before an accountant could be held liable to a third party not actually known. 170 N.W.2d at 403.

In this state, although the liability of accountants to third parties not in privity has not been examined, the liability of an attorney to one not in privity was recently examined in *Auric v. Continental Casualty Co.,* 111 Wis.2d 507, 331 N.W.2d 325 (1983). This court concluded that an attorney may be held liable to a will beneficiary not in privity for the attorney's negligence in supervising the execution of a will. 111 Wis.2d at 514. Part of the rationale for this decision was that the imposition of liability would make attorneys more careful in the execution of their responsibilities to their clients. [C]

That rationale is applicable here. Unless liability is imposed, third parties who rely upon the accuracy of the financial statements will not be protected. Unless an accountant can be held liable to a relying third party, this negligence will go undeterred.

There are additional policy reasons to allow the imposition of liability. If relying third parties, such as creditors, are not allowed to recover, the cost of credit to the general public will increase because creditors will either have to absorb the costs of bad loans made in reliance on faulty information or hire independent accountants to verify the information received. Accountants may spread the risk through the use of liability insurance.

We conclude that the absence of privity alone should not bar negligence actions by relying third parties against accountants.

Although the absence of privity does not bar this action, the question remains as to the extent of an accountant's liability to injured third parties. Courts which have examined this question have generally relied upon section 552 of the Restatement to restrict the class of third persons who could sue accountants for their negligent acts. Under section 552(2)(a) and (b), liability is limited to loss suffered:

"(a) By the person or one of a limited group of persons for whose benefit and guidance he [in this case the accountant] intends to supply the information or knows the recipient intends to supply it; and

"(b) Through reliance upon it in a transaction that he [the accountant] intends the information to influence or knows the recipient so intends or in a substantially similar transaction."

Under section 552, liability is not extended to all parties whom the accountant might reasonably foresee as using the information. Rather, as one commentator noted, "The Restatement's formulation of 'a limited group of persons' extends causes of action to a limited number of third parties who are expected to gain access to the financial statement information in an expected transaction." This limitation is stressed in comment h to section 552, where it is noted that:

"It is not required that the person who is to become the plaintiff be identified or known to the defendant as an individual when the information is supplied. It is enough that the maker of the representation intends it to reach and influence either a particular person or persons, known to him, or a group or class of persons, distinct from the much larger class who might reasonably be expected sooner or later to have access to the information and foreseeably to take some action in reliance upon it."

The fundamental principle of Wisconsin negligence law is that a tortfeasor is fully liable for all foreseeable consequences of his act except as those consequences are limited by policy factors. [Cc] The Restatement's statement of limiting liability to certain third parties is too restrictive a statement of policy factors for this Court to adopt.

We conclude that accountants' liability to third parties should be determined under the accepted principles of Wisconsin negligence law. According to these principles, a finding of non-liability will be made only if there is a strong public policy requiring such a finding. [Cc]

Liability will be imposed on these accountants for the foreseeable injuries resulting from their negligent acts unless, under the facts of this particular case, as a matter of policy to be decided by the court, recovery is denied on grounds of public policy. [C] This Court has set out a number of public policy reasons for not imposing liability despite a finding of negligence causing injury:

"(1) The injury is too remote from the negligence; or (2) the injury is too wholly out of proportion to the culpability of the negligent tortfeasor; or (3) in retrospect it appears too highly extraordinary that the negligence should have brought about the harm; or (4) because allowance of recovery would place too unreasonable a burden on the negligent tort-feasor; or (5) because allowance of recovery would be too likely to open the way for fraudulent claims; or (6) allowance of recovery would enter a field that has no sensible or just stopping point." *Ollerman* [v. O'Rourke Co., 94 Wis.2d 17, 48, 288 N.W.2d 95 (1980).]

Although in some cases this court has decided at the motion-to-dismiss stage that policy factors preclude the imposition of liability for negligent acts, [c] it has generally been found to be better practice to have a full factual resolution before evaluating the public policy considerations involved. *Ollerman,* [cc].

In this case we conclude that a determination of the public policy questions should be made after the facts of this case have been fully explored at trial. The question of the proper scope of these accountants' liabilities to the third party bank cannot be determined upon the information contained in the record. A full factual resolution is necessary before it can be said that public policy precludes Timm's liability for its allegedly negligent conduct.

The pleadings, affidavits and other information in the record before this court do not establish that Timm was entitled as a matter of law to summary judgment. Under the accepted principles of Wisconsin negligence law, Timm could be liable to Citizens if Timm's actions were the cause of Citizens' injuries and if the injuries were reasonably foreseeable unless public policy precluded recovery.

Timm's affidavits do not dispute that Citizen's reliance upon the financial statements led to the making of the loans and ultimately to the losses which were incurred. Each affidavit recites that Timm employees had no knowledge that the financial statements would actually be used by CFA to apply for a new bank loan or to increase existing loan indebtedness. However, the affidavit of Elmer Timm stated that "as a certified public accountant, I know that audited statements are used for many purposes and that it is common for them to be supplied to lenders and creditors, and other persons."

These affidavits and other information contained in the record do not dispose of the issue of whether it was foreseeable that a negligently prepared financial statement could cause harm to Citizens.

Therefore, Timm having failed to establish a *prima facie* case for summary judgment, we conclude the trial judge erred in granting the motion for summary judgment.

Decision of the court of appeals is reversed and cause remanded to the trial court for further proceedings not inconsistent with this opinion.

————

1. While the *Ultramares* rule, as reiterated in *Credit Alliance*, is apparently still followed by a majority of the cases, the member of defections has been growing in recent years. See, e.g., International Mortgage Co. v. John P. Butler Accountancy Corp., 177 Cal.App.3d 806, 223 Cal.Rptr. 218 (1986); H. Rosenblum, Inc. v. Adler, 93 N.J. 324, 461 A.2d 138 (1983); Sperex, Inc. v. Grant & Co., 122 N.H. 898, 451 A.2d 1308 (1982); Touche Ross & Co. v. Commercial Union Ins. Co., 514 So.2d 315 (Miss.1987). For a strong recent case

adhering to the *Ultramares* view, see Toro Co. v. Krouse, Kern & Co., Inc., 827 F.2d 155 (7th Cir.1987) (Ind. law). Cases are collected in Annot., 46 A.L.R.3d 979 (1972), and supplements.

2. As quoted in the Citizens State Bank case, the Second Restatement takes an intermediate position, confining recovery to a "limited group of persons" and to a transaction or "substantially similar transaction" intended by the defendant. A number of cases have adopted similar positions.

In Bonhiver v. Graff, 311 Minn. 111, 248 N.W.2d 291 (1976), some purchasers had taken over an insurance company and transferred all of its assets and liabilities to a newly formed company. They hired the defendant accountants to bring the insurance company's books up to date. Rumors having circulated about the company's financial condition, the state insurance commissioner arranged with the accountants to examine the books and the working papers of the company as they were being prepared. The accountants were negligent in investigating and preparing the working papers, and the insurance commissioner, misled by their apparent condition, assured plaintiff Delmont, a general agent of the insurance company, that it was financially sound. Delmont had passed this information on, and sues for loss of reputation as a result. He was allowed to recover.

3. Defendant, an attorney, is employed by A to furnish an abstract of title to A's land. Defendant knows that A intends to make use of the abstract in selling or mortgaging the land, but is not informed of any prospective purchaser or mortgagee. Defendant does the work in good faith, but negligently, so that the abstract fails to show encumbrances upon the land. Subsequently A exhibits the abstract to B, who buys the land from A, and suffers loss, in reliance upon it. Is defendant liable to B? Phoenix Title & Trust Co. v. Continental Oil Co., 34 Ariz. 219, 29 P.2d 1065 (1934); cf. Peterson v. Gales, 312 Ill. 245, 145 N.E. 833 (1926), where an inspector negligently certified the quality of second-hand steel rails. See Roady, Professional Liability of Abstractors, 12 Vand.L.Rev. 783 (1959).

4. In 1934 the defendant surveyed land for A, who owned it, and negligently provided A with an erroneous survey and description. Defendant knew that the survey reports are commonly used and relied on in transactions dealing with land, but he did not know of any contemplated transaction. In 1958, B bought the land from A, and in doing so relied on the report made in 1934. The court held that liability would not be imposed, laying emphasis on the lapse of time. Howell v. Betts, 211 Tenn. 134, 362 S.W.2d 924 (1962). But compare Tartero v. Palumbo, 224 Tenn. 262, 453 S.W.2d 780 (1970), imposing liability upon a surveyor. See also Rozny v. Marnul, 43 Ill.2d 59, 250 N.E.2d 656 (1968).

5. Compare Wice v. Schilling, 124 Cal.App.2d 735, 269 P.2d 231 (1954), where a certificate of termite clearance, with similar scienter, was given to a buyer of land, and was held to inure to the benefit of a subpurchaser, on the ground that it was intended for use by "such persons as were transacting business" with the buyer in connection with the property.

6. In M. Miller Co. v. Contra Coastal Sanitary Dist., 198 Cal.App.2d 305, 18 Cal.Rptr. 13 (1961), an engineering company was hired to prepare a soil report, knowing that it would be used by bidders for work on a sewer system. The report was negligently done and inaccurate, and the successful bidder lost money. He was allowed to recover damages although the report was not made

directly to him. But cf. Texas Tunneling Co. v. Chattanooga, 329 F.2d 402 (6th Cir.1964), rev'g, 204 F.Supp. 821 (E.D.Tenn.1962).

7. See generally Prosser, Misrepresentation and Third Persons, 19 Vand. L.Rev. 231 (1966); Keeton, The Ambit of a Fraudulent Representor's Responsibility, 17 Tex.L.Rev. 1 (1938).

There are numerous articles on accountants' liability. See. e.g., Fiflis, Current Problems of Accountants' Responsibilities to Third Parties, 28 Vand.L. Rev. 31 (1975); Gormley, Accountants' Professional Liability, 29 Bus.Law. 1205 (1974); Gormley, The Foreseen, The Foreseeable and Beyond—Accountants' Liability to Nonclients, 14 Seton Hall L.Rev. 528 (1984).

ULTRAMARES CORPORATION v. TOUCHE

Court of Appeals of New York, 1931.
255 N.Y. 170, 174 N.E. 441.

[The opinions of Judge Cardozo in Glanzer v. Shepard and Ultramares Corp. v. Touche have been well described in the opinion of Judge Jason in Credit Alliance Co., supra page 1048. The description of *Ultramares* there, however, covered only the holding regarding the accountants' liability to a third person for negligent preparation of financial statements. The *Ultramares* opinion went on to discuss liability in fraud or deceit under the American doctrine of Sovereign Pocahontas Co. v. Bond, supra page 1039. That part of the *Ultramares* opinion is set forth here.

Touche, Nivens' certificate in the case had stated: "We have examined the accounts of Fred Stern & Co. * * * and hereby certify that the annexed balance sheet is in accordance therewith and with the information and explanations given us. We further certify that * * * the said statement in our opinion presents a true and correct view of the financial condition of Fred Stern & Co. * * *."]

CARDOZO, C.J. * * * Our holding [on liability for negligence] does not emancipate accountants from the consequences of fraud. It does not relieve them if their audit has been so negligent as to justify a finding that they had no genuine belief in its adequacy, for this again is fraud. It does no more than say that, if less than this is proved, if there has been neither reckless misstatement nor insincere profession of an opinion, but only honest blunder, the ensuing liability for negligence is one that is bounded by the contract, and is to be enforced between the parties by whom the contract has been made.

The defendants certified as a fact, true to their own knowledge, that the balance sheet was in accordance with the books of account. If their statement was false, they are not to be exonerated because they believed it to be true. [Cc] We think the triers of the facts might hold it to be false.

Correspondence between the balance sheet and the books imports something more, or so the triers of the facts might say, than correspondence between the balance sheet and the general ledger, unsupported or even contradicted by every other record. The correspondence to be of any moment may not unreasonably be held to signify a correspondence between the statement and the books of original entry, the books taken as a whole. If that is what the certificate means, a jury could find that the correspondence did not exist, and that the defendants signed the certificates without knowing it to exist and even without reasonable grounds for belief in its existence. The item of $706,000, representing fictitious accounts receivable, was entered in the ledger after defendant's employee Siess had posted the December sales. He knew of the interpolation, and knew that there was need to verify the entry by reference to books other than the ledger before the books could be found to be in agreement with the balance sheet. The evidence would sustain a finding that this was never done. By concession the interpolated item had no support in the journal, or in any journal voucher, or in the debit memo book, which was a summary of the invoices, or in any thing except the invoices themselves. The defendants do not say that they ever looked at the invoices, seventeen in number, representing these accounts. They profess to be unable to recall whether they did so or not. They admit, however, that, if they had looked, they would have found omissions and irregularities so many and unusual as to have called for further investigation. When we couple the refusal to say that they did look with the admission that, if they had looked, they would or could have seen, the situation is revealed as one in which a jury might reasonably find that in truth they did not look, but certified the correspondence without testing its existence.

In this connection we are to bear in mind the principle * * * that negligence or blindness, even when not equivalent to fraud, is none the less evidence to sustain an inference of fraud. At least this is so if the negligence is gross. Not a little confusion has at times resulted from an undiscriminating quotation of statements in Kountze v. Kennedy, [47 N.Y. 124, 41 N.E. 414 (1895)] statements proper enough in their setting, but capable of misleading when extracted and considered by themselves. "Misjudgment, however gross," it was there observed, "or want of caution, however marked, is not fraud." This was said in a case where the trier of the facts had held the defendants guiltless. The judgment in this court amounted merely to a holding that a finding of fraud did not follow as an inference of law. There was no holding that the evidence would have required a reversal of the judgment if the finding as to guilt had been the other way. Even Derry v. Peek, as we have seen, asserts the probative effect of negligence as an evidentiary fact. We had no thought in Kountze v. Kennedy, of upholding a doctrine more favorable to wrongdoers, though there was a reservation suggesting the approval of a rule more rigorous. * * * No such charity of construction exonerates accountants, who by the very nature of their calling profess to speak with knowledge when certifying to an agreement between the audit and the entries.

The defendants attempt to excuse the omission of an inspection of the invoices proved to be fictitious by invoking a practice known as that of testing and sampling. A random choice of accounts is made from the total number on the books, and these, if found to be regular when inspected and investigated, are taken as a fair indication of the quality of the mass. * * * Verification by test and sample was very likely a sufficient audit as to accounts regularly entered upon the books in the usual course of business. It was plainly insufficient, however, as to accounts not entered upon the books where inspection of the invoices was necessary, not as a check upon accounts fair upon their face, but in order to ascertain whether there were any accounts at all. If the only invoices inspected were invoices unrelated to the interpolated entry, the result was to certify a correspondence between the books and the balance sheet without any effort by the auditors, as to $706,000 of accounts, to ascertain whether the certified agreement was in accordance with the truth. * * * The defendants were put on their guard by the circumstances touching the December accounts receivable to scrutinize with special care. A jury might find that, with suspicions thus awakened, they closed their eyes to the obvious, and blindly gave assent.

We conclude, to sum up the situation, that in certifying to the correspondence between balance sheet and accounts the defendants made a statement as true to their own knowledge, when they had, as a jury might find, no knowledge on the subject. If that is so, they may also be found to have acted without information leading to a sincere or genuine belief when they certified to an opinion that the balance sheet faithfully reflected the condition of the business. * * *

Upon the plaintiff's appeal as to the second cause of action, the judgment [for the defendants in the lower courts] should be reversed, and a new trial granted, with costs to abide the event.

----

1. This part of the *Ultramares* case involves liability for fraudulent, as distinguished from negligent, misrepresentation. The defendant's conduct being more reprehensible, the opinion indicates that a wider circle of liability is required. When the defendant's conduct is not only reckless but also intended to deceive, it would appear that the scope of liability would be even broader.

2. And yet many of the cases draw a circle that is narrower even than that for negligent misrepresentation. The classic case on liability in deceit to third parties is Peek v. Gurney, [1893] 6 H.L. 377, where corporate directors prepared a prospectus to induce the public to buy stock from the company, and it was held that there was no liability to a person who bought stock on the market from a stockholder. Accord: Greenville Nat'l Bank v. National Hardwood Co., 241 Mich. 524, 217 N.W. 786 (1928).

See also the following cases, denying responsibility: Defendant, seeking to induce A to buy a lot of land, knowingly made false statements about the lot to A, in the presence of B. He had no intention of inducing B to buy the lot, and no reason to believe that B would be interested. B, relying on the statements, bought the lot from another salesman. Westcliff Co. v. Wall, 153 Tex. 271, 267 S.W.2d 544 (1954). Plaintiff acted for his brother in buying some sheep from defendant. To induce plaintiff to buy for his brother, defendant deliberately and falsely stated to him that the sheep were sound. They were in fact infected with foot rot. Subsequently, after the disease had spread to the brother's entire flock, plaintiff bought all the sheep from his brother, in reliance upon the statement. Wells v. Cook, 16 Ohio St. 67, 88 Am.Dec. 436 (1865). Cf. McCane v. Wokoun, 189 Iowa 1010, 179 N.W. 332 (1920); Walker v. Choate, 228 Ky. 101, 14 S.W.2d 406 (1929).

3. How is this seeming anomaly to be explained? Apparently, it has to do with the concept of intent. Defendant intended to deceive one person but not another. Might it be appropriate to use the fiction of transferred intent here? Is it necessary?

In the first Restatement, § 533 stated that a defendant was liable to a plaintiff third party when a fraudulent misrepresentation was communicated to another "for the purpose of having him" transmit it to plaintiff "in order to influence his conduct." See Metric Inv., Inc. v. Patterson, 101 N.J.Super. 301, 244 A.2d 311 (1968). But liability was imposed when defendant supplied false information regarding his financial standing to a credit agency, and it was transmitted to the plaintiff by the agency. Dime Sav. Bank v. Fletcher, 158 Mich. 162, 122 N.W. 540 (1909); Davis v. Louisville Trust Co., 181 F. 10 (6th Cir. 1910).

The Second Restatement provides that liability extends to a third person if the maker intends or has reason to expect that the terms of the misrepresentation will be repeated or its substance communicated to him and that it will influence his conduct. Does this take care of the problem?

4. RELIANCE

WILLIAMS v. RANK & SON BUICK, INC.
Supreme Court of Wisconsin, 1969.
44 Wis.2d 239, 170 N.W.2d 807.

[Plaintiff went to defendant's used car lot on March 19 and looked at a Chrysler automobile. Plaintiff testified that he was looking for an air-conditioned car; that the salesman told him the car was air-conditioned, and that the particular car had been so described in an advertisement on which he relied. The evidence was, however, that the advertisement was first published two days after plaintiff bought the car, and defendant contended that plaintiff "seized upon an error in the ad to seek a reduction in the price previously paid for the automobile." Plaintiff was invited to take the car out for a test run, and did so, driving it for about an hour and a half. According to plaintiff, however, it was not until several days after the purchase that he discovered that the knobs marked "AIR" were for ventilation, and that the car was not air-conditioned. Plaintiff brought an action for fraud, and received a judgment for $150 damages. Defendant appeals.]

HANLEY, JUSTICE. * * * [T]here is ample evidence to warrant the trial court's finding that the oral misrepresentation of the appellant's salesman was in fact made. * * *

The question of reliance is another matter. Many previous decisions of this court have held that one cannot justifiably rely upon obviously false statements. In Jacobsen v. Whitely (1909), 138 Wis. 434, 436, 437, 120 N.W. 285, 286, the court said:

" * * * It is an unsavory defense for a man who by false statements, induces another to act to assert that if the latter had disbelieved him he would not have been injured. * * * Nevertheless courts will refuse to act for the relief of one claiming to have been misled by another's statements who blindly acts in disregard of knowledge of their falsity or with such opportunity that by the exercise of ordinary observation, not necessarily by search, he would have known. He may not close his eyes to what is obviously discoverable by him. * * * "

It is apparent that the obviousness of a statement's falsity vitiates reliance since no one can rely upon a known falsity. Were the rule otherwise a person would be free to enter into a contract with no intent to perform under the contract unless it ultimately proved profitable. On the other hand, a party who makes an inadvertent slip of the tongue or pencil would continually lose the benefit of the contract.

The question is thus whether the statement's falsity could have been detected by ordinary observation. Whether the falsity of a statement could have been discovered through ordinary care is to be determined in light of the intelligence and experience of the misled individual. Also to be considered is the relationship between the parties. [Cc] In several cases this court has held that the above factors negated the opportunity to inspect and the obviousness of the statement's falsity. [C]

In the instant case, however, no such negating factors exist. The respondent specifically testified that, being a high school graduate, he was capable of both reading and writing. It is also fair to assume that he possessed a degree of business acumen in that he and his brother operated their own business. No fiduciary relationship existed between the parties. They dealt with each other at arms' length. The appellant made no effort to interfere with the respondent's examination of the car, but, on the contrary, allowed him to take the car from the premises for a period of one and one-half hours.

Although the obviousness of a statement's falsity is a question of fact, this court has decided some such questions as a matter of law. [Cc]

In the instant case the respondent had ample opportunity to determine whether the car was air-conditioned. He had examined the car on the lot and had been allowed to remove the car from the lot unaccompanied by a salesman for a period of approximately one and one-half hours. This customers were normally not allowed to do.

No great search was required to disclose the absence of the air conditioning unit since a mere flip of a knob was all that was necessary. If air conditioning was, as stated by the respondent, the main reason he purchased the car, it is doubtful that he would not try the air conditioner. * * *

We conclude that as a matter of law the respondent under the facts and circumstances was not justified in relying upon the oral representation of the salesman. This is an action brought in fraud and not an action for a breach of warranty.

Order reversed [by a vote of 4 to 3].

WILKIE, JUSTICE (dissenting).   *   *   * I would hold that the falsity of the representation was not so obvious that it could be held as a matter of law that the respondent had no right to rely on it. It was for the finder of fact and by finding reliance the trial court, by implication, found respondent had a right to rely thereon.   *   *   *

———

1. Is the real explanation of this case that the court did not believe plaintiff's version that he requested an air-conditioned car and was told that this car was air-conditioned; that he did not discover the absence of air conditioning; and that it would be forced to leave that issue to the factfinder on his testimony?

2. In H. Hirschberg Optical Co. v. Michaelson, 1 Neb.Unof. 137, 95 N.W. 461 (1901), plaintiff, buying a pair of glasses, testified that he was told by defendant's salesman that the glass used in them had a special quality which would make them adapt themselves to his eyes. On this evidence, can the plaintiff recover for deceit? See also that foremost classic of legal humor, the sad but fascinating tale of the land of Shalam. Ellis v. Newbrough, 6 N.M. 181, 27 P. 490 (1891).

3. What if it is made clear by the evidence that plaintiff knew that the representation made to him was false? Cox v. Johnson, 227 N.C. 69, 40 S.E.2d 418 (1946). Or that he paid no attention to it, and acted for other reasons entirely? McIntyre v. Lyon, 325 Mich. 167, 37 N.W.2d 903 (1949); Tsang v. Kan, 142 Me. 83, 46 A.2d 708 (1947).

4. Suppose that A and B each make the same false statement to C, and his decision to act is substantially influenced by both. Strong v. Strong, 102 N.Y. 69, 5 N.E. 799 (1886); Shaw v. Gilbert, 111 Wis. 165, 86 N.W. 188 (1901). Does it make any difference that either statement alone would have been sufficient to induce the action? What case does this resemble?

5. Does the fact that plaintiff has made an inspection, examination or investigation of his own establish:

A. That he did not believe the representation, and so did not rely on it, but relied instead on his own investigation? See McNabb v. Thomas, 88 U.S. App.D.C. 379, 190 F.2d 608 (1951); Savings Bank Retirement System v. Clarke, 258 Md. 501, 265 A.2d 921 (1970).

In Enfield v. Colburn, 63 N.H. 218 (1884), defendant made statements to plaintiffs. Plaintiffs made an expensive investigation, and found that they were false. They sought to recover the expenses of the investigation. Recovery was denied, since "if they relied upon the representations, they did not investigate them; if they investigated them they did not rely upon them. It is a perversion of language to say they did both." Is this right?

B. That he believed the representation, and relied upon it, but sought verification before acting, and in the end relied upon both? John Hancock

Mut. Life Ins. Co. v. Cronin, 139 N.J.Eq. 392, 51 A.2d 2 (1947); Fausett & Co. v. Bullard, 217 Ark. 176, 229 S.W. 490 (1950).

6. Insured, applying for liability insurance, misrepresented his driving record. Insurance company did not obtain the record, which would cost $1. There was a finding that the company did not wish to know the truth, preferring to be in a position to rescind, if desired. Can the company now rescind after the insured has injured a third party? State Farm Mut. Auto. Ins. Co. v. Wall, 87 N.J.Super. 543, 210 A.2d 109 (1965).

7. *Materiality*. Suppose that defendant, as agent, is selling plaintiff a tract of land on behalf of a principal whom plaintiff never has seen. Defendant falsely states that his principal is left-handed. No other false statements are made. Can plaintiff recover in deceit after he buys the land? Farnsworth v. Duffer, 142 U.S. 43 (1891) (social, religious and political affiliation); Haverland v. Lane, 89 Wash. 557, 154 P. 1118 (1916) (identity of party).

8. Defendant induces plaintiff to send his daughter to a particular school by false representations that it is attended by her former classmates. Is this a material representation? Brown v. Search, 131 Wis. 109, 111 N.W. 210 (1907). What if plaintiff is induced to buy pictures by a false statement that his wife likes them? Washington Post Co. v. Sorrells, 7 Ga.App. 774, 68 S.E. 337 (1910). Or he is induced to give money to a college by a statement that it is to be named after one of his friends? Collinson v. Jefferies, 21 Tex.Civ.App. 653, 54 S.W. 28 (1899). See Restatement (Second) of Torts § 538(1)(b).

9. In Saxby v. Southern Land Co., 109 Va. 196, 63 S.E. 423 (1909), defendant, as a real estate agent, offered a farm to plaintiff, saying that it could not be purchased for less than $8,000. Actually, he had an option on it for $4,000, and the owners were anxious to sell it for that price. Is the truth material? Another part of the case is found infra at page 1065.

SIPPY v. CRISTICH

Court of Appeals of Kansas, 1980.
4 Kan.App.2d 511, 609 P.2d 204.

[Mr. and Mrs. Sippy ("the Sippys") bring this action of fraud against "the Cristiches," from whom they purchased a house, on the ground that the roof leaked. When the Sippys inspected the house, they "observed certain stains on the ceilings and floor * * * and were aware that there obviously had been leaks in the roof." They inquired of Mrs. Haggard, the agent, who told them "that the Cristiches had advised her that the roof had been repaired and was in good shape." A month after moving in, the Sippys experienced substantial damage from leakage of the roof. The trial court awarded damages of $5,278, and the vendors appeal.]

MEYER, JUDGE. * * * In response to questions by the Sippys (made to the Cristiches through Mrs. Haggard), the Sippys were assured that the roof had been repaired and was in good condition. A statement that a roof has been repaired implies that the roof has been repaired satisfactorily. This statement was not a true statement, and therefore, the first element for a fraudulent action was met.

As to the second element of fraud, while the trial court did not find that the Cristiches made known false statements, it did find that the statements of the Cristiches were recklessly made under all the circum-stances. There was substantial competent evidence to support this finding. The trial court based its finding of fraud upon the affirmative representation that the roof was in good condition or good repair.

This affirmative representation was reckless due to the fact that the roof had been in an almost constant state of repair until May 23, 1975. At the time of the sale to the Sippys in March and April of 1976, the Cristiches had not been in the house for several months, and given the history of problems and the knowledge that repairs had failed in the past, such statement was reckless.

As to the third element of fraud, appellant argues that the Sippys were not justified in relying on the statement in that Mr. Sippy had expressed concern about the roof on several occasions, had noticed water spots, and, in addition, had personally gone to the roof to inspect it. * * *

" 'A recipient of a fraudulent misrepresentation is justified in relying upon its truth without investigation, unless he knows or has reason to know of facts which make his reliance unreasonable.' * * * [T]he test is whether the recipient has 'information which would serve as a danger signal and a red light to any normal person of his intelligence and experience.' " [Citing from Restatement (Second) of Torts § 540, p. 10, and comments to § 540 at p. 12.]

Here, the fraud did not consist in the Cristiches advising the Sippys that the roof had never leaked; the fraud occurred when they claimed the roof had been repaired and was in good condition. Because of this, it is of no material significance that there were water stains upon the carpet or rug. The Sippys did, in fact, follow up on the danger signals they observed and made repeated inquiries concerning the roof and whether the leaks had been repaired. Mrs. Haggard called the Cristiches (then in Florida) and was assured by them of the roof's good repair. This was related by Mrs. Haggard to the Sippys as a statement of the Cristiches. Moreover, they were told that some of the stains were caused by watering plants.

As to the statement that the Sippys had inspected the roof, the testimony established that the defects were structural and that inspec-tion of the roof without tearing into it would not disclose its deficien-cies. Mr. Sippy is, therefore, not precluded in this action by the fact that he went to the roof to inspect it. Mr. Sippy testified the reason he did not get an independent inspection made was because he was assured that the roof was all right. Without the knowledge of the extensive and prolonged attempts to repair the roof, there was no reason to disbelieve the representation that the roof had been repaired and was now in good condition.

We conclude that the third requirement for an action in fraud has been met in that the Sippys were justified in relying on the statement of the Cristiches related to them by Mrs. Haggard. * * *

Affirmed.

---

1. *Contributory Negligence.* See, holding that contributory negligence does not bar recovery when the misrepresentation is intentional, Yorke v. Taylor, 332 Mass. 368, 124 N.E.2d 912 (1955); and Judd v. Walker, 215 Mo. 312, 114 S.W. 979 (1908) ("the laws of hospitality seem to require that strangers should be taken in in a good sense, but courts should be astute not to permit such a 'taking in' as appears here").

2. What if the defendant's representation is made without scienter or intent to deceive, but is made negligently and the action is one for negligent misrepresentation? Is contributory negligence then a defense? Maxwell Ice Co. v. Brackett, Shaw & Lunt Co., 80 N.H. 236, 116 A. 34 (1921); Gould v. Flato, 170 Misc. 378, 10 N.Y.S.2d 361 (1939). Does comparative negligence apply here?

3. The earlier decisions, such as Sherwood v. Salmon, 2 Day (Conn.) 128 (1805), adhered to the ancient idea of "caveat emptor," and laid great stress upon the plaintiff's "duty" to protect himself by proper investigation, holding that he was not entitled to rely even upon positive assertions of fact made by one with whom he was dealing at arm's length. These are now almost entirely discredited, although there is still a good deal of occasional language to the effect that the plaintiff must act reasonably, and some few cases in which the same idea is disguised under a holding that the plaintiff has no "right to rely." See Seavey, Caveat Emptor in 1960, 38 Tex.L.Rev. 439 (1960).

4. The great majority of the cases now hold that the plaintiff has no duty to make inquiry or investigation as to the truth of an apparently reliable statement made to him. This is held even though investigation could be made quickly, with little effort, by means readily at hand. Buckley v. Buckley, 230 Mich. 504, 202 N.W. 955 (1925).

5. "No rogue should enjoy his ill-gotten plunder for the simple reason that his victim is by chance a fool." Chamberlin v. Fuller, 59 Vt. 247, 9 A. 832 (1887).

6. Plaintiff, a "gullible young man," whose occupation was that of playing the piano in resorts of ill repute, inherited $40,000 from his mother. On learning this, defendant promptly offered to sell him a disreputable roadhouse, representing that it was worth $35,000. Defendant advised plaintiff not to ask questions of others, because if it got out that the place was for sale other purchasers would probably come and get the bargain away from him. Relying upon these representations, plaintiff made no inquiry, and bought the roadhouse for $35,000. It proved to be practically worthless, and had to be closed down when its license was not renewed. Plaintiff recovered from defendant. Adan v. Steinbrecher, 116 Minn. 174, 133 N.W. 477 (1911); see also Hyma v. Lee, 338 Mich. 31, 60 N.W.2d 920 (1953) ("Spanish-prisoner" fraud).

5. OPINION

SAXBY v. SOUTHERN LAND CO.
Supreme Court of Appeals of Virginia, 1909.
109 Va. 196, 63 S.E. 423.

Action to recover damages for alleged false and fraudulent representations made in regard to the sale of a certain farm known as "Winslow." A demurrer to the declaration was sustained and the suit dismissed. Plaintiff brings error.

HARRISON, J. * * * The second and third grounds of fraud alleged are that the farm contained at least 150 acres of pine timber of which about 20 acres had been burned over; whereas, there was about 120 acres in timber, of which 60 acres had been burned over.

It is well settled that a misrepresentation, the falsity of which will afford ground for an action for damages, must be of an existing fact, and not the mere expression of an opinion. The mere expression of an opinion, however strong and positive the language may be, is no fraud. Such statements are not fraudulent in law, because * * * they do not ordinarily deceive or mislead. Statements which are vague and indefinite in their nature and terms, or are merely loose, conjectural or exaggerated, go for nothing, though they may not be true, for a man is not justified in placing reliance upon them. An indefinite representation ought to put the person to whom it is made on inquiry. [C]

The declaration states that the farm in question contained 444 acres, 1 rood and 26 poles. It is manifest that the vendor was not asserting a fact in stating the number of acres in timber and the number burned over, but was merely expressing his opinion from appearances. The declaration does not charge him with saying more than that there was about 150 acres in timber and about 20 acres burned over. These expressions indicate that the defendant in error was not making statements of ascertained facts, but was merely expressing his opinion of the acreage in timber and the portion thereof which was burned over. The statements were sufficiently indefinite to have put the plaintiffs in error on their guard to make further inquiry if they regarded the matter as material.

The last two grounds of fraud alleged are that the defendant in error stated that the timber, when cut into cordwood, would readily sell at the local stations on the railroad for $4 per cord, whereas it could be sold only for a much smaller price, and that the land was specially adapted to potato culture, and would by the use of fertilizer yield 100 bushels of potatoes to the acre, whereas, by actual experiment, the land failed to produce anything like that yield by the use of fertilizers.

There is no allegation that the land had produced 100 bushels of potatoes to the acre, or that cordwood had brought $4 per cord at local stations. The production of land in the future and the price of cordwood in the future are dependent upon so many conditions that no assertion of an existing fact could be made with respect thereto.

The statements relied on as grounds of fraud cannot be regarded otherwise than as speculative expressions of opinion—mere trade talk—with respect to matters of an equally uncertain nature. * * *

We are of opinion that the demurrer to the declaration was properly sustained. The judgment complained of must, therefore, be affirmed.

---

1. Suppose that defendant had said that the farm contained "at least 444 acres" when there were only 210? Should it make any difference whether plaintiff saw the land? Is it significant that the plaintiff filed the suit two years after the transaction took place?

2. Which of the following statements, made by a seller to a buyer, are to be regarded as opinion, and which as fact?

"This land is worth $5,000." "I paid $5,000 for this land two years ago." Medbury v. Watson, 6 Metc. (Mass.) 246, 39 Am.Dec. 726 (1843). "Property exactly like this is selling for $5,000." Brody v. Foster, 134 Minn. 91, 158 N.W. 824 (1916). "I have been offered $5,000 for this land by another party." Kabatchnick v. Hanover–Elm Building Corp., 328 Mass. 341, 103 N.E.2d 692 (1952). "The lowest price at which this land can be purchased from my principal is $5,000." Hokanson v. Oatman, 165 Mich. 512, 131 N.W. 111 (1911).

3. Suppose the statement of opinion as to value is made by the buyer to the seller? The seller has had her car wrecked. She is told by the buyer that in its present condition it is worth only $200, and she sells it for that. Fossier v. Morgan, 474 S.W.2d 801 (Tex.Civ.App.1971).

4. The statement of any opinion is a statement of at least one fact—the fact that the defendant does have such an opinion. If this is false and dishonest, why should the defendant not be held liable? See Keeton, Fraud— Misrepresentation of Opinion, 21 Minn.L.Rev. 645 (1937).

5. Does a statement of opinion ever imply any other facts? In Simpson v. Western Nat'l Bank of Casper, 497 P.2d 878 (Wyo.1972), a banker, when asked about the financial condition of a customer for whose benefit the person inquiring was depositing a check, replied that he would come out all right and there was nothing wrong with his financial condition. Held, this "was an implied statement and representation that he knew of no fact incompatible with his opinion." In Wink Enterprises v. Dow, 491 S.W.2d 451 (Tex.Civ.App. 1973), an opinion was expressed to a prospective invester that a bank was "a good sound one and will continue to make money." Held, the statement "means that facts exist which lead the maker to believe the statement, or facts actually exist that the bank is in sound condition."

VULCAN METALS CO. v. SIMMONS MFG. CO.

United States Circuit Court of Appeals, Second Circuit, 1918.
248 Fed. 853.

[Two actions tried together. The Vulcan Metals Company brought action against the Simmons Manufacturing Company for deceit, by reason of misrepresentations in the sale by Simmons to Vulcan of machinery for the manufacture of vacuum cleaners, together with the patents covering their manufacture. The Simmons Company brought action against the Vulcan Company upon notes given for the purchase price, and in this action Vulcan counterclaimed for the same alleged misrepresentations.

The misrepresentations included "commendations of the cleanliness, economy and efficiency of the machine, that it was absolutely perfect in even the smallest detail; that water power, by which it worked, marked the most economical means of operating a vacuum cleaner with the greatest efficiency; that the cleaning was more thoroughly done than by beating or brushing; that, having been perfected, it was a necessity which every one could afford; that it was so simple a child of six could use it; that it worked completely and thoroughly; that it was simple, long-lived, easily operated, and effective; that it was the only sanitary portable cleaner on the market; that perfect satisfaction would result from its use; that it would last a lifetime; that it was the only practical jet machine on the market, and that perfect satisfaction would result from its use, if properly adjusted. The booklet is in general the ordinary compilation, puffing the excellence and powers of the vacuum cleaner, and asserting its superiority over all others of a similar sort." There were further representations that the vacuum cleaner never had been put on the market.

The trial court directed a verdict on each action for the Simmons Company. The Vulcan Company appeals.]

LEARNED HAND, DISTRICT JUDGE. The first question is of the misrepresentations touching the quality and powers of the patented machine. These were general commendations, or, in so far as they included any specific facts, were not disproved; e.g., that the cleaner would produce 18 inches of vacuum with 25 pounds water pressure. They raise, therefore, the question of law how far general "puffing" or "dealers' talk" can be the basis of an action for deceit.

The conceded exception in such cases has generally rested upon the distinction between "opinion" and "fact"; but that distinction has not escaped the criticism it deserves. An opinion is a fact, and it may be a very relevant fact; the expression of an opinion is the assertion of a belief, and any rule which condones the expression of a consciously false opinion condones a consciously false statement of fact. When the parties are so situated that the buyer may reasonably rely upon the expression of the seller's opinion, it is no excuse to give a false one. [C] And so it makes much difference whether the parties stand "on equality." For example, we should treat very differently the expressed opinion of a chemist, to a layman about the properties of a composition from the same opinion between chemist and chemist, when the buyer had full opportunity to examine. The reason of the rule lies, we think, in this: There are some kinds of talk which no sensible man takes seriously, and if he does he suffers from his credulity. If we were all scrupulously honest, it would not be so; but, as it is, neither party usually believes what the seller says about his own opinions, and each knows it. Such statements, like the claims of campaign managers before election, are rather designed to allay the suspicion which would attend their absence than to be understood as having any relation to objective truth. It is quite true that they induce a compliant temper in the buyer, but it is by a much more subtle process than through the acceptance of his claims for his wares.

So far as concerns statements of value, the rule is pretty well fixed against the buyer. * * * It has been applied more generally to statements of quality and serviceability. * * * But this is not always so. * * * As respects the validity of patents it also obtains. * * * Cases of warranty present the same question and have been answered in the same way. * * *

In the case at bar, since the buyer was allowed full opportunity to examine the cleaner and to test it out, we put the parties upon an equality. It seems to us that general statements as to what the cleaner would do, even though consciously false, were not of a kind to be taken literally by the buyer. As between manufacturer and customer, it may not be so; but this was the case of taking over a business, after ample chance to investigate. Such a buyer, who the seller rightly expects will undertake an independent and adequate inquiry into the actual merits of what he gets, has no right to treat as material in his determination statements like these. * * *

As respects the representation that the cleaners had never been put upon the market or offered for sale, the rule does not apply; nor can we agree that such representations could not have been material to Freeman's decision to accept the contract. The actual test of experience in their sale might well be of critical consequence in his decision to buy the business, and the jury would certainly have the right to accept his statement that his reliance upon these representations was determinative of his final decision. We believe that the facts as disclosed by the depositions of the Western witnesses were sufficient to carry to the jury the question whether those statements were false. It is quite true, as the District Judge said, that the number of sales was small, perhaps not 60 in all; but they were scattered in various parts of the Mountain and Pacific states, and the jury might conclude that they were enough to contradict the detailed statements of Simmons that the machines had been kept off the market altogether. * * *

[New trial ordered in the action of deceit.]

---

1. What about a statement that "there is no better land in Vermont"? Nichols v. Lane, 93 Vt. 87, 106 A. 592 (1919). Or that a machine is "the pride of our line," and "the best on the American market"? Prince v. Brackett, Shaw & Lunt Co., 125 Me. 31, 130 A. 509 (1925). Or that shares of stock are "hot stock," "very good," and "with unlimited possibilities"? Ryan v. Collins, 496 S.W.2d 205 (Tex.Civ.App.1973). Or that a prospect for dancing lessons had "exceptional potential to be a fine and accomplished dancer," that he was a

"natural dancer" and a "terrific dancer"? Parker v. Arthur Murray, Inc., 10 Ill.App.3d 1000, 295 N.E.2d 487 (1973). And see Letellier v. Small, 400 A.2d 371 (Me.1979), on "dealer talk."

2. In Bertram v. Reed Automobile Co., 49 S.W.2d 517 (Tex.Civ.App.1932), the seller of a second-hand automobile described it as a "dandy," a "bearcat," a "good automobile," a "good little car," and a "sweet job." The court said: "Common experience and observation causes one to marvel at the moderation of the selling agent in making his trade talk to appellant. * * * These are relative terms, they may mean anything the orator or the listener wants, and neither may be penalized if the one exaggerates or the other is disappointed. There may be something more definite in the representations that the car had been well taken care of, had good rubber on it, had been driven but 19,000 miles, had not been mistreated, that mechanics had found it in perfect condition."

3. "In Buckingham v. Thompson, 135 S.W. 652 (1911) an enterprising Texas realtor, evidently feeling that even the great state of Texas was too small a territory of operations, sent out literature to various parts of the United States concerning a particular ranch property he had listed, and described it as: richer than the valleys of Southern California; that it could not be kept from becoming a land of gold; that it was a land of fruit and flowers and happy homes; that independence was to be had there for the asking; that all eyes were on Texas, particularly Southwest Texas. * * * Due reference was made to the Garden of Eden, Monte Cristo and Aladdin's lamp. This the Texas court held to be statements 'so extraordinary that no man of ordinary sense could be supposed to take them * * * at their face.'

"When engaged in the analysis of this case we inquired of our uncle, a Texan and lawyer of note, what he thought of the decision. Barely able to control himself he gave it as his opinion that the judge who held the statements to be exaggerated ought to be hanged, and the real estate man who wrote them ought to be shot for understatement tantamount to treason. Thus we must report that (unofficially at least) the law of Texas on this point is unsettled." Obiter Dicta, 25 Ford L.Rev. 395 (1957).

4. "The rule of law is hardly to be regretted when it is considered how easily and insensibly words of hope or expectation are converted by an interested memory into statements of quality or value when the expectation has been disappointed." Holmes, J., in Deming v. Darling, 148 Mass. 504, 20 N.E. 107 (1889).

HANBERRY v. HEARST CORP.
Court of Appeal of California, 1969.
276 Cal.App.2d 680, 81 Cal.Rptr. 519.

[Plaintiff-appellant purchased from defendant Akron a pair of shoes manufactured by defendant Handal. She alleges that the shoes were defective in being "slippery and unsafe" when used on vinyl floor coverings, and that "she stepped on the vinyl floor of her kitchen, slipped, fell and sustained severe physical injuries."

She also sues defendant Hearst Corporation on the ground that it had negligently given a Good Housekeeping seal of approval to the shoes as "good ones." Hearst demurred to the causes against it, and the court granted judgment of dismissal to Hearst. Plaintiff appealed from this judgment.]

AULT, ASSOCIATE JUSTICE, PRO TEM. * * * Appellant further alleges respondent Hearst publishes a monthly magazine known as Good Housekeeping in which products, including the shoes she purchased, were advertised as meeting the "Good Housekeeping's Consumers' Guaranty Seal". With respect to this seal the magazine stated: "This is Good Housekeeping's Consumers' Guaranty" and "We satisfy ourselves that products advertised in Good Housekeeping are good ones and that the advertising claims made for them in our magazine are truthful." The seal itself contained the promise, "If the product or performance is defective, Good Housekeeping guarantees replacement or refund to consumer." * * *

In the second and eighth causes of action, appellant seeks to recover on the theory of negligent misrepresentation. * * *

The basic question presented on this appeal is whether one who endorses a product for his own economic gain, and for the purpose of encouraging and inducing the public to buy it, may be liable to a purchaser who, relying on the endorsement, buys the product and is injured because it is defective and not as represented in the endorsement. We conclude such liability may exist and a cause of action has been pleaded in the instant case. * * *

In both the second and eighth cause of action of the complaint under consideration, appellant has alleged respondent extended its certification and permitted the use of its seal in connection with the shoes, she purchased without test, inspection or examination of the shoes, or a sample thereof, or if it tested, inspected or examined, it did so in a careless and negligent manner which did not reveal their dangerous and defective condition. If either of the alternative allegations is true, respondent violated its duty of care to the appellant and the issuance of its seal and certification with respect to the shoes under that circumstance would amount to a negligent misrepresentation.

Hearst urges its representation the shoes were "good ones" was a mere statement of opinion, not a statement of a material fact, and therefore not actionable. Since the very purpose of the seal and its certification the shoes were "good ones" was to induce and encourage members of the public to buy the shoes, respondent is in poor position to argue its endorsement cannot legally be considered as the inducing factor in bringing about their sale. [C] Respondent was not the seller or manufacturer of the shoes; it held itself out as a disinterested third party which had examined the shoes, found them satisfactory, and gave its endorsement. By the very procedure and method it used, respondent represented to the public it possessed superior knowledge and special information concerning the product it endorsed. Under such circumstance, respondent may be liable for negligent representations of either fact or opinion. [C]

Respondent argues no basis for liability has been shown because, "It is a matter of common knowledge that brand new soles on brand new shoes have a tendency of being slick and slippery until the shoes have been worn sufficiently long thereafter." The argument may well have merit [c], but it is one addressed properly to the trier of fact. The case is presented to us in the pleading context. We are unwilling to hold as a matter of law that liability will not attach under any circumstance based upon a defectively designed shoe. * * *

The judgment of dismissal is * * * reversed as to the second and eighth causes of action (negligent misrepresentation).

---

1. What about the opinion of an attorney on a point of law, given to a layman with whom he is dealing? Security Savings Bank v. Kellems, 321 Mo. 1, 9 S.W.2d 967 (1928). Or the opinion of a banker, selling a note to an ordinary citizen, that the signature on the note is genuine? Wilson v. Jones, 45 S.W.2d 572 (Tex.Com.App.1932).

2. Suppose a violin expert, selling a violin, gives his opinion to a purchaser who knows nothing about such instruments, that it is a genuine Stradivarius? Powell v. Fletcher, 45 N.Y.St.Rep. 294, 18 N.Y.S. 451 (1892). What if the purchaser is another expert? Banner v. Lyon & Healy Co., 249 App.Div. 569, 293 N.Y.S. 236 (1937). Suppose a so-called "impartial expert" misleads the plaintiff into believing that he is actually impartial? Cf. Oltmer v. Zamora, 94 Ill.App.3d 651, 49 Ill.Dec. 652, 418 N.E.2d 506 (1981).

3. What if the disparity in bargaining power does not arise from any expert knowledge or special information of the defendant, but from the unusual ignorance, inexperience, illiteracy or lack of intelligence of the plaintiff? Ellis v. Gordon, 202 Wis. 134, 231 N.W. 585 (1930).

4. Why is reliance upon statements of opinion, including value, always held to be justified where there is a special relation of trust and confidence between the parties? See, for example, Jekshewitz v. Groswald, 265 Mass. 413, 164 N.E. 609 (1929) (affianced); Allen v. Frawley, 106 Wis. 638, 82 N.W. 593 (1900) (attorney and client).

5. See Keeton, Fraud—Misrepresentation of Opinion, 21 Minn.L.Rev. 645 (1937); Casey, Misrepresentations of Opinion, 28 B.U.L.Rev. 352 (1948).

6. LAW

SORENSON v. GARDNER
Supreme Court of Oregon, 1959.
215 Or. 355, 334 P.2d 471.

LUSK, JUSTICE. This is an action for deceit in which the plaintiffs recovered a judgment for $2,000 and the defendants have appealed.

The action grows out of the sale of a dwelling house. * * * The complaint alleges that the defendants falsely represented to the plaintiffs that the house was well constructed in a workmanlike manner and met all minimum code requirements, particularly with respect to electric wiring, plumbing, septic tank and sewage disposal arrangement.

* * * The plaintiff introduced evidence in support of these allegations and evidence tending to show that the representations were false.
* * *

* * * [The] general rule [is] that fraud cannot be predicated upon misrepresentations of law or misrepresentations as to matters of law. [C] Thus, misrepresentations concerning the legal effect of an instrument have been held to be not actionable. * * * [Conflicting] reasons [for this] have been repeated, sometimes in the same decision: first, that every man is presumed to know the law, and hence the plaintiff cannot be heard to say that he reasonably believed the statement made to him; and second, that no man, at least without special training, can be expected to know the law, and so the plaintiff must have understood that the defendant was giving him nothing more than an opinion." [C] The basis of the rule has been criticized by courts and textwriters.
* * *

The rule of the Restatement of Torts upon this subject is as follows:

"§ 545.   Misrepresentation of Law

"(1) If a representation as to a matter of law in a business transaction is a representation of fact the recipient is justified in relying upon it to the same extent as though it were a representation of any other fact.

"(2) If the representation as to a matter of law in a business transaction is a representation of opinion as to the legal consequences of facts known to the maker and the recipient or assumed by both to exist, the recipient is justified in relying upon it to the same extent as though it were a representation of any other opinion as stated in §§ 542, 543."

In the comment on Subsection (1) of the foregoing, it is said, "If a representation concerns the legal effect of facts not disclosed or not otherwise known to the recipient, it may justifiably be interpreted as implying that there are facts which substantiate the statement * * *. So, too, the assertion of title to a particular tract of land asserts the existence of those conveyances or relationships which are necessary to vest the title in the alleged owner. On the other hand, if all the facts believed by the maker to exist are stated to the recipient or otherwise known by him and from these facts the maker of the representation asserts that title vests in the person in question as a legal consequence, the representation is an expression of opinion and the case falls within Subsection (2)." * * *

Here we are dealing with a number of alleged misrepresentations to the effect that the house in question complied with the minimum requirements of state law. * * * There was evidence that in certain particulars the requirements of the code were not met, and evidence from which the jury could find that the defendants knew and the plaintiffs did not what the facts were in this regard. Under the rule as formulated by the Restatement, had the plaintiffs been aware of these facts and had the defendants represented to them that the facts as so known constituted a compliance with the law, then the misrepresentation in question would have been one of law and not of fact. But, the plaintiffs being ignorant of the facts, the representation in the circumstances was one of fact and the case is covered by Subsection (1) of Section 545 of the Restatement of Torts. * * * The plaintiffs are not relying on their ignorance of the law but of the facts, and the alleged representations carried with them the implication that the facts were otherwise than the evidence shows them to have been. They concerned "the legal effect of facts not disclosed or otherwise known to the recipient." * * *

Our own conclusion, which accords with the rule of the Restatement, is that such representations may, and in this case do, relate to matters of fact. Therefore, the contention of the defendants in support of the first ground of the motion for a directed verdict cannot be sustained. * * *

[Reversed, however, and new trial ordered, on the ground of error in instructions to the jury as to the measure of damages.]

---

1. Defendant, a layman, is seeking to settle a claim against plaintiff, and assures him that he is legally liable for his conduct. Plaintiff, relying upon the assurance, settles the claim. He was not in fact liable. Has he a cause of action? Williams v. Dougherty County, 101 Ga.App. 193, 113 S.E.2d 168 (1960).

2. Defendant, a layman, sold plaintiff beverages containing 18 to 25 per cent alcohol, assuring him that the local law would permit him to sell them in unbroken packages at retail. In fact, the law did not permit such sales, and plaintiff was arrested and convicted for the unlawful sale of intoxicating liquor. Defendant was held not liable. Ad. Dernehl & Sons Co. v. Detert, 186 Wis. 113, 202 N.W. 207 (1925). Cf. Gibson v. Mendenhall, 203 Okl. 558, 224 P.2d 251 (1959) (representation that plaintiff could easily obtain a license).

3. Representations as to the law of another state are treated as statements of fact, upon which the plaintiff may justifiably rely. See, for example, Hembry v. Pareco, 81 A.2d 77 (Mun.App.D.C.1951); Fireman's Ins. Co. v. Jones, 245 Ark. 179, 431 S.W.2d 728 (1968) (deception as to foreign statute of limitations).

4. What about a statement that defendant's hospital is legally accredited? Myers v. Lowery, 46 Cal.App. 682, 189 P. 793 (1920). Or that the defendant's title is good? Barnett v. Kunkle, 256 F. 644 (8th Cir.1919).

5. What about a statement of law made by an attorney to his client? By one member of a family to another? By an insurance company to its policyholder? Stark v. Equitable Life Assurance Society, 205 Minn. 138, 285 N.W. 466 (1939).

6. In cases of rescission or other equitable remedies, the courts appear to have displayed a much more liberal attitude toward mistake of law induced by the defendant's representations. See, for example, Newbern v. Gould, 162 Okl. 82, 19 P.2d 157 (1933); Hubbard & Co. v. Horne, 203 N.C. 205, 165 S.E. 347 (1932). See Restatement of Restitution, § 55 and Reporter's Note to the Section.

7. See Keeton, Fraud—Misrepresentation of Law, 15 Texas L.Rev. 409 (1937).

7. PREDICTION AND INTENTION

McELRATH v. ELECTRIC INVESTMENT CO.
Supreme Court of Minnesota, 1911.
114 Minn. 358, 131 N.W. 380.

BROWN, J.   Appeal from an order overruling a general demurrer to plaintiffs' complaint.   It appears from the complaint that the defendant was the owner of a certain summer hotel property, including the land upon which the building was situated, and certain personal property used in connection with the operation of the hotel, situated at Antlers Park, in Dakota county.   On the 15th day of April, 1909, the parties to the action entered into a contract by the terms of which defendant leased the property to plaintiffs for a term of years. * * *

The action is for damages occasioned by the alleged false and fraudulent representations made by defendant for the purpose of inducing plaintiffs to enter into the contract.   The complaint alleges: "That for the purpose of inducing said plaintiffs to enter into said contract, Exhibit A, this defendant wrongfully, falsely, and fraudulently stated and represented to these plaintiffs that the Minneapolis, St. Paul, Rochester and Dubuque Electric Traction Company would complete its electric railroad, and would run electric cars over said road from the city of Minneapolis to and beyond said Antlers Park during the summer of 1909, and about July 1st of that year; and said defendant further stated and represented to said plaintiffs that said defendant would, during said summer of 1909 and as soon as said electric railroad should run to said Antlers Park, make of said Antlers Park and surrounding ground an important summer resort for people living at said city of Minneapolis, and further stated and represented to plaintiffs that if they would enter into said contract, Exhibit A, they would make, through the assistance and efforts of said defendant, not less than fifteen hundred dollars ($1,500.00) per annum clear above all expenses of running and management. * * *

It is contended by defendant that the alleged false representations do not constitute a cause of action, for the reason that, when made, they had reference to the future intentions of the traction company, and were not representations of present existing facts, and further, that the complaint contains no allegations that the electric road was not constructed and in operation according to the representations.

We * * * hold that the complaint, in so far as it alleges the making of false representations for the purpose of inducing plaintiffs to enter into the contract, knowing the same to be false, to the effect that the electric road would be completed and in operation by July 1, 1909, states a cause of action.   While it is true as a general rule that false representations, upon which fraud may be predicated, must be of existing facts, and cannot consist of mere promises or conjectures as to future acts or events, yet, [c] if in making the representations defendant "intended to create in plaintiffs the belief that it was, as a fact, the then intention of the" traction company to complete the road at the time represented, and "the representations might be understood and were understood by plaintiffs as asserting that fact," then a charge of fraud may be based thereon, though the represented event was to occur in the future. Upon this theory, the complaint, as against a demurrer, states a cause of action. [Cc]

Upon the question of the sufficiency of the other allegations of fraud, the case comes within the general rule that promises or assurances as to future events cannot be made the basis of an action of fraud. In this respect the complaint alleges that defendant represented that it would, as soon as the electric road reached Antlers Park, "make of said Antlers Park and surrounding ground an important summer resort for people living at said City of Minneapolis." This, aside from being a mere promise to do something in the future, namely, "make an important summer resort," rests wholly in conjecture and speculation, depending for its accomplishment upon many facts, of which both parties had, presumptively, equal notice, and depending upon conditions over which neither had control. Whether an important or other summer resort may be established at a particular place depends in the main upon its location and the disposition of the public to make it a place of recreation or pleasure. * * * The naked allegation is of a promise to create a particular condition in the future, a condition surrounded with known uncertainty and beyond defendant's control, and the general rule applies. The other allegations, namely, that plaintiffs would, in the conduct of the leased property, make a specified profit during the season, also rests in conjecture and opinion, and therefore is not open to the charge of actionable fraud.

Affirmed.

––––––––

1. The following have been held not to justify reliance: A prediction that prices will remain unchanged. Coe v. Ware, 271 Mass. 570, 171 N.E. 732 (1930). That plaintiff will be able to obtain a job. Schwetters v. Des Moines Commercial College, 199 Iowa 1058, 203 N.W. 265 (1925). That building lots next to a highway will prove to be profitable. Campbell County v. Braun, 295 Ky. 96, 174 S.W.2d 1 (1943). That stock will triple in value within a year. Kennedy v. Flo–Tronics, Inc., 274 Minn. 327, 143 N.W.2d 827 (1966).

2. In Trustees of Columbia University v. Jacobsen, 53 N.J.Super. 574, 148 A.2d 63 (1959), plaintiff, a university student, claimed that the University represented to him that he would acquire "wisdom, truth, character, enlightenment, understanding, justice, liberty, honesty, courage, beauty and similar virtues and qualities; that it would develop the whole man, maturity, well-roundedness, objective thinking and the like * * *" He failed to graduate because of poor scholastic standing. What result?

3. Contrast Steinberg v. Chicago Medical Sch., 69 Ill.2d 320, 13 Ill.Dec. 699, 371 N.E.2d 634 (1977). Plaintiff applied for admission to defendant

medical school, paying the application fee, and was rejected. He alleges fraud in the catalog statements regarding selection standards to be applied, and the use of "nonacademic criteria, primarily the ability of the applicant or his family to pledge or make payment of large sums of money to the school." Held, cause of action stated and class action permitted. Recovery allowed "where the false promise or representation of future conduct is alleged to be the scheme employed to accomplish the fraud."

BURGDORFER v. THIELEMANN

Supreme Court of Oregon, 1936.
153 Or. 354, 55 P.2d 1122.

Action on the case for deceit by Charles Burgdorfer against Carl Thielemann. From a judgment in favor of plaintiff, defendant appeals.

[Plaintiff charges that defendant fraudulently induced him to exchange a $2,000 note and mortgage (plus two notes totaling $323) for two lots in the Collins View tract, by falsely promising that he would pay a $500 mortgage on the Collins View lot.]

KELLY, JUSTICE. * * * It is further alleged in plaintiff's second amended complaint:

" * * * that the defendant had no intention at the time of making the said promise, or at any time at all, of performing the promise to plaintiff hereinabove set out; * * * that the plaintiff did believe and rely on the said representations and promise of the defendant and did act thereon to his great damage; * * * "

Defendant's first assignment of error imputes error upon the part of the court in allowing plaintiff to testify as to appellant's alleged promise to pay off the mortgage on the Collins View property.

The precise objection which defendant makes is that the alleged promise could not have been performed within one year and, therefore, to be enforceable [under the statute of frauds] it must have been reduced to writing and signed by the party sought to be charged. * * *

We think that, in an action for deceit, [the] provision of the statute [of frauds] does not have the effect of rendering inadmissible testimony of an oral promise made with the fraudulent intent on the part of the promisor at the time the promise was made not to fulfill or perform the same.

One of the reasons leading to this conclusion is that the purpose of such oral testimony is not to establish an agreement, but to prove fraud. The gist of the fraud consists in the false representation of the existence of an intention which in truth and in fact has no existence. * * *

"To profess an intent to do or not to do, when the party intends the contrary, is as clear a case of misrepresentation and of fraud as could be made." Herndon v. Durham & S.R. Co., 161 N.C. 650, 656, 77 S.E. 683, 685. * * *

As stated by Bowen, L.J., in Edgington v. Fitzmaurice, Law Reports, 29 Chancery Division, 459: "There must be a misstatement of an existing fact; but the state of a man's mind is as much a fact as the state of his digestion. It is true that it is very difficult to prove what the state of a man's mind at a particular time is, but if it can be ascertained it is as much a fact as anything else. A misrepresentation as to the state of a man's mind is, therefore, a misstatement of fact."

* * *

No error was committed by allowing plaintiff to testify as to defendant's alleged promise to pay off the mortgage on the Collins View property. * * *

The judgment of the circuit court is affirmed.

----

1. All but a few courts accept the rule as to misstatements of present intention as stated. They apply it also to suits for rescission or other equitable relief. A few states reject it or do not allow an action when the intent is contained in the promise itself.

2. Suppose the proof is merely that the defendant made a contract, and after a time broke it. Is this enough for an action of deceit? Williams v. Williams, 220 N.C. 806, 18 S.E.2d 364 (1942). What if the promise is broken immediately after it is made, with no intervening change in the situation? Guy T. Bisbee Co. v. Granite Investment Co., 159 Minn. 238, 199 N.W. 14 (1924). What about a promise to pay made by one who is completely insolvent at the time? California Conserving Co. v. D'Avanzo, 62 F.2d 528 (2d Cir.1933).

3. Consider the following possible advantages of the action in deceit over a contract action for breach of the promise itself:

A. The deceit action may avoid the statute of frauds. Channel Master Corp. v. Aluminum Limited Sales, Inc., 4 N.Y.2d 403, 151 N.E.2d 833 (1958). Contra, Cassidy v. Kraft–Phenix Cheese Corp., 285 Mich. 426, 280 N.W. 814 (1938).

B. It may avoid the difficulties of the parol evidence rule, which prevents any promise not integrated into a written contract from being regarded as a part of the contract. Sabo v. Delman, 3 N.Y.2d 155, 143 N.E.2d 906 (1957). Contra: McCreight v. Davey Tree Expert Co., 191 Minn. 489, 254 N.W. 623 (1934). On this, see Sweet, Promissory Fraud and the Parol Evience Rule, 49 Cal.L.Rev. 877 (1961).

C. It may avoid the defense that the promise was without consideration. Daniel v. Daniel, 190 Ky. 210, 226 S.W. 1070 (1921). Contra: Rankin v. Burnham, 150 Wash. 615, 274 P. 98 (1929).

D. It may avoid the defense that the contract was an illegal one, if the parties are not in pari delicto. See Keeton, Fraud—Statements of Intention, 15 Texas L.Rev. 18, 213–216 (1937).

E. It may avoid the defense of the statute of limitations, since a longer period may be applicable in the deceit action, or the statute may run only from the plaintiff's discovery of the fraud. Fidelity Philadelphia Trust Co. v. Simpson, 293 Pa. 577, 143 A. 202 (1928). Contra: Brick v. Cohn-Hall-Marx, 276 N.Y. 259, 11 N.E.2d 902 (1937).

F. It may avoid a limitation of liability contained in the contract itself.

G. It may avoid a defense against the contract action, such as infancy. Wisconsin Loan & Finance Corp. v. Goodnough, 201 Wis. 101, 228 N.W. 484 (1930). Contra: Slayton v. Barry, 175 Mass. 513, 56 N.E. 574 (1900).

H. It may avoid the necessity of joining parties to a joint contract in one action. Cf. Elliott v. Hayden, 104 Mass. 180 (1870).

4. See Keeton, Fraud: Statements of Intention, 15 Tex.L.Rev. 187 (1937); Note, The Legal Effect of a Promise Made with Intent Not to Perform, 38 Colum.L.Rev. 1461 (1938).

8. DAMAGES

HINKLE v. ROCKVILLE MOTOR CO., INC.
Court of Appeals of Maryland, 1971.
262 Md. 502, 278 A.2d 42.

BARNES, JUDGE. The appellant, Donald Hinkle (Hinkle), purchased a 1969 Ford Galaxie automobile from the appellee, Rockville Motor Company, Inc. (Rockville), in January of 1970. * * * Hinkle alleged that Rockville fraudulently represented to him at the time of sale that the 1969 Galaxie was a new car when, in fact, it had over 2,000 miles on the speedometer and had been involved in an accident in the State of Tennessee. Hinkle discovered the mileage recorded on the speedometer while driving home on the day of the sale. He brought this to the attention of Rockville and an adjustment was made whereby he was compensated in the amount of $109.86, the amount of his first payment, in exchange for a release from any further claims except for those falling within his standard new car warranty. The adjustment for mileage was made on January 27, 1970. Hinkle maintains that it was not until April, 1970, that he learned the automobile had been involved in an accident in Tennessee in July of 1969. It is alleged in the declaration that the front and rear portions of the automobile had been welded together after having been severed in the accident. Hinkle alleged that Rockville had knowledge of the accident but that it "willfully concealed the true circumstances" and "willfully, maliciously and fraudulently misrepresented the quality and condition of the aforesaid Ford vehicle" and that he relied on these misrepresentations to his detriment. Damages were claimed in the amount of $100,000.

At the close of Hinkle's case, Rockville moved for a directed verdict. In granting the directed verdict, the trial court only found it necessary to consider Rockville's argument that Hinkle's failure to produce evidence in regard to the automobile's actual value at the time of sale deprived the jury of the only permissible standard by which the jury could determine the existence or amount of damages. The trial court determined this to be a correct statement of the law and directed a verdict in favor of Rockville notwithstanding the fact that Hinkle had produced expert testimony that the effects of the accident could be remedied and the car returned to new car condition by the expenditure of $800 for repairs. * * *

A majority of States will allow the plaintiffs to recover the "benefit of his bargain" if sufficiently proved. The theory is to compensate the plaintiff as though the transaction had been carried out as represented. [Cc]

Other States restrict the plaintiff to his "out of pocket" losses. The classic formula is the value of the object as represented less its actual value at the time of sale. The theory is to return the plaintiff economically to the position he was in prior to the fraudulent transaction thus allowing him recoupment of actual losses but not expected gain. This rigid limitation on the nature of recovery is often explained as being required because the action is one of tort rather than contract and that it has always been recognized that tort remedies are designed to compensate for actual harm suffered. ＊ ＊ ＊ Maryland is one of those States which has not adopted a rigid stand as far as adopting one of the above theories to the exclusion of the other. Both theories have been used and approved in Maryland. ＊ ＊ ＊

In summary, the review of the Maryland cases on this question of the proper measure of damages in fraud and deceit cases demonstrates that this Court has applied the so-called "flexibility theory" without heretofore expressly stating the factors to be considered in its application. Selman v. Shirley, 161 Or. 582, 609, 85 P.2d 384, 394, 91 P.2d 312, 124 A.L.R. 1 (1938), the first case to define expressly this flexible approach, set forth the following four rules as a guide for the proper measure of damages in these cases.

"(1) If the defrauded party is content with the recovery of only the amount that he actually lost, his damages will be measured under that rule;

"(2) if the fraudulent representation also amounted to a warranty, recovery may be had for the loss of the bargain because a fraud accompanied by a broken promise should cost the wrongdoer as much as the latter alone;

"(3) where the circumstances disclosed by the proof are so vague as to cast virtually no light upon the value of the property had it conformed to the representations, the court will award damages equal only to the loss sustained; and

"(4) where ＊ ＊ ＊ the damages under the benefit-of-the-bargain rule are proved with sufficient certainty, that rule will be employed."
＊ ＊ ＊

This position was advocated by Professor McCormick who wrote, "In the first place, it seems that in every case the defrauded plaintiff should be allowed to claim under the 'out of pocket' loss theory if he prefers. In the second place, the plaintiff should be allowed to choose the other theory, and recover the value of the bargain as represented, if the trial judge in his discretion considers that, in view of the probable moral culpability of the defendant and of the definiteness of the representations and the ascertainability of the represented value, the case is an appropriate one for such treatment." McCormick, Damages

§ 122 (1935) at p. 454. Williston on Contracts § 1392 (Rev.Ed.1937) at p. 3886 and Sutherland on Damages § 1172 (4th ed. 1916) at p. 4409 both indicate a preference for allowing the plaintiff to recover the benefit of his bargain in these cases. Sedgewick on Damages § 781 (9th ed.1912) at pp. 1629–31, while recognizing that the majority rule allows "benefit of bargain" recovery, favors a strict adherence to the "out of pocket" remedy in accordance with English common law as set forth in Peek v. Derry, 37 Ch.Div. 541 (1888). The Restatement of Torts, § 549 (1938) also sets forth the "out of pocket" rule of damages.

After the above review of cases and texts on the subject, it is concluded that the trial court erred in directing the verdict against Hinkle for failure to produce evidence upon which damages could be awarded. Hinkle's evidence in regard to the cost of necessary repairs demonstrated the existence of damages and provided an adequate measure upon which they could be predicated.

Judgment reversed and case remanded for new trial, the appellee to pay the costs.

---

1. "It is the very essence of an action of fraud or deceit that the same shall be accompanied by damage, and neither damnum absque injuria nor injuria absque damnum by themselves constitute a good cause of action." Casey v. Welch, 50 So.2d 124 (Fla.1951). In an action for rescission, it may not be necessary to show pecuniary loss and plaintiff can prevail if he did not receive what he was promised. See Hirschman v. Healey, 162 Minn. 328, 202 N.W. 734 (1925); Nance v. McClellan, 89 S.W.2d 774 (Tex.Comm.App.1936); McCleary, Damage as Requisite to Rescission for Misrepresentation, 36 Mich.L. Rev. 1 & 227 (1937).

2. Of the two "normal" measures of damages discussed here, the contract or "benefit-of-the-bargain" measure will usually result in greater damages. Thus: Price paid $5,000; Value of property purchased $3,000; Value as represented $7,000. Here the tort, or "out-of-pocket" measure results in damages of $2,000, while the "benefit-of-the-bargain" measure is $4,000.

There may, however, be cases in which the out-of-pocket measure is higher. For example, Estell v. Myers, 56 Miss. 800 (1879), where plaintiff paid $62,500 for land actually worth $27,500, and the value if the representations had been true would have been $50,000. Also Erde v. Fenster, 141 N.Y.S. 943 (1913), where plaintiff was induced to sell a claim for less than it was worth by the buyer's representation that the debtor was totally insolvent.

3. The out-of-pocket measure of damages is adopted in all deceit actions by the English courts, and by a minority of about a dozen American jurisdictions. The "benefit-of-the-bargain" rule has been adopted by about two-thirds of the American courts that have considered the question. Neither group has followed either rule with entire consistency in all cases.

4. The compromise formula, first stated in Selman v. Shirley, 161 Or. 582, 85 P.2d 384, 91 P.2d 312 (1938), has met general approval by legal writers, and has been followed in some other states. Salter v. Harris, 39 Wash.2d 826, 239 P.2d 327 (1952); Rice v. Price, 340 Mass. 502, 164 N.E.2d 891 (1960). It has been accepted, in a simplified form, by § 549 of the Restatement (Second) of Torts.

5. In addition to the "normal" measure of damages, whether it is under the tort or the contract rule, plaintiff can recover for consequential damages resulting from the misrepresentation. Thus one who buys a horse represented to him as gentle may recover for personal injuries if he is kicked by the horse. Vezina v. Souliere, 103 Vt. 190, 152 A. 798 (1931). And one who buys infected bees, represented to be healthy, may recover for damage to his other bees when the infection spreads to them. Sampson v. Penny, 151 Minn. 411, 187 N.W. 135 (1922). Plaintiff may recover for expenses to which he has been put, as when he is induced to employ an architect by misrepresentations as to his skill and compelled to incur extra expenses in completing the building as a result. Edward Barron Estate Co. v. Woodruff Co., 163 Cal. 561, 126 P. 351 (1912).

6. Questions of proximate cause can arise in misrepresentation cases, too. Plaintiff is induced to buy stock in a company by defendant's fraudulent statement. The treasurer of the company subsequently absconds with funds that he had been embezzling over a period of time and the company turns out to be insolvent. Defendant knew nothing about the treasurer's misconduct and the misrepresentation did not relate to the value of the stock. Can plaintiff recover in deceit for his loss? Fottler v. Moseley, 185 Mass. 563, 60 N.E. 788 (1904), would indicate that the answer is yes. But a majority of the courts would apparently disagree. See Boatmen's Nat'l Co. v. M.W. Elkins Co., 63 F.2d 214 (8th Cir.1933); Morrell v. Wiley, 119 Conn. 578, 178 A. 121 (1911). Plaintiff would be able to prevail if he sued in rescission. Seneca Wire & Mfg. Co. v. A.B. Leach & Co., 247 N.Y. 1, 159 N.E. 700 (1928).

7. See C. McCormick, Damages 448 et seq. (1935); Hannigan, Measure of Damages in Tort for Deceit, 18 B.U.L.Rev. 681 (1938); Note, 61 Harv.L.Rev. 113, 173–175 (1941).

8. *Statutory Provisions,* Congress has regulated in detail the preparation and selling of securities; and there are specific provisions for civil liability, plus implied remedies. See, e.g., Securities Act of 1933, 15 U.S.C.A. §§ 72a et seq.; Securities Exchange Act of 1934, 15 U.S.C.A. §§ 78a et seq.; Investment Advisor's Act of 1940, 15 U.S.C.A. §§ 80b–1 et seq.; Securities Investor Protection Act of 1970, 15 U.S.C.A. §§ 78aaa et seq. Helpful treatments are L. Loss, Fundamentals of Securities Regulation, ch. 10 (1983); D. Langevoort, Insider Trading Handbook (1987 ed.).

There are numerous state acts on this subject also, often called Blue Sky Laws. Other state laws afford protection for consumers. There are a Uniform Consumer Sales Practices Act and a Uniform Deceptive Trade Practices Act. All of these acts may impose more stringent liability than the common law of misrepresentation.

Chapter XXII

INTERFERENCE WITH
ADVANTAGEOUS RELATIONSHIPS

---

1. BUSINESS RELATIONS

(A) INJURIOUS FALSEHOOD

RATCLIFFE v. EVANS
Court of Appeal, 1892.
[1892] 2 Q.B. 524.

[Plaintiff alleged that he and his father had carried on the business of engineer and boiler maker for many years under the name Ratcliffe & Sons, that the father died but plaintiff carried on the business and that defendant, publisher of the County Herald, "falsely and maliciously" published "certain words" importing "that the plaintiff had ceased to carry on his business * * * and that the firm of Ratcliffe & Sons did not then exist."]

BOWEN, L.J. This was a case in which an action for a false and malicious publication about the trade and manufactures of the plaintiff was tried at the Chester assizes, with the result of a verdict for the plaintiff for 120*l*. Judgment having been entered for the plaintiff for that sum and costs, the defendant appealed to this Court for a new trial, or to enter a verdict for the defendant, on the ground, amongst others, that no special damage, such as was necessary to support the action, was proved at the trial. The injurious statement complained of was a publication in the *County Herald*, a Welsh newspaper. It was treated in the pleadings as a defamatory statement or libel; but this suggestion was negatived, and the verdict of the jury proceeded upon the view that the writing was a false statement purposely made about the manufactures of the plaintiff, which was intended to, and did in fact, cause him damage. The only proof at the trial of such damage consisted, however, of evidence of general loss of business without specific proof of the loss of any particular customers or orders, and the question we have to determine is, whether in such an action such general evidence of damage was admissible and sufficient. That an action will lie for written or oral falsehoods, not actionable per se nor even defamatory, where they are maliciously published, where they are calculated in the ordinary course of things to produce, and where they do produce, actual damage, is established law. Such an action is not

1085

Lord Justice Bowen

one of libel or of slander, but an action on the case for damage wilfully and intentionally done without just occasion or excuse, analogous to an action for slander of title. To support it, actual damage must be shown, for it is an action which only lies in respect of such damage as has actually occurred. It was contended before us that in such an action it is not enough to allege and prove general loss of business arising from the publication, since such general loss is general and not special damage, and special damage, as often has been said, is the gist of such an action on the case.

In an action like the present, brought for a malicious falsehood intentionally published in a newspaper about the plaintiff's business—a falsehood which is not actionable as a personal libel, and which is not defamatory in itself—is evidence to shew that a general loss of business has been the direct and natural result admissible in evidence, and, if uncontradicted, sufficient to maintain the action? In the case of a personal libel, such general loss of custom may unquestionably be alleged and proved. Every libel is of itself a wrong in regard of which the law, as we have seen, implies general damage. By the very fact that he has committed such a wrong, the defendant is prepared for the proof that some general damage may have been done. * * * "It is not special damage, [c] it is general damage resulting from the kind of injury the plaintiff has sustained." [C]

In the case before us to-day, it is a falsehood openly disseminated through the press—probably read, and possibly acted on, by persons of whom the plaintiff never heard. To refuse with reference to such a subject-matter to admit such general evidence would be to * * * involve an absolute denial of justice and of redress for the very mischief which was intended to be committed. * * *

Appeal dismissed.

----

1. This is the leading case giving sufficient scope to the "action on the case for words" to justify the use of the term "injurious falsehood"—a name suggested by Sir John Salmond in his treatise on Torts. Earlier cases had involved "slander of title" or "trade libel," which had developed as isolated torts of a limited scope. Sometimes they were joined together and the term "disparagement" was used. "Injurious falsehood" now denotes a broad general principle of liability for any false and malicious statement resulting in pecuniary loss to another. The principle is generally recognized at the present time, but the courts have been slow to adopt the name.

2. The elements necessary to the cause of action usually have been stated as follows:

(a) A false statement of a kind calculated to damage a pecuniary interest of the plaintiff.

(b) Publication to a third person.

(c) "Malice" in the publication. This element has received much the same treatment, and has caused about as much confusion, as in defamation.

(d) Resulting special damage to the plaintiff, in the form of pecuniary loss.

3. As illustrations of the broader scope of the general principle, see: Statements that the plaintiff is dead or is not in business or is going out of business. Davis v. New England Railway Pub. Co., 203 Mass. 470, 89 N.E. 565 (1909); McRoberts Protective Agency, Inc. v. Landsdell Protective Agency, Inc., 61 A.D.2d 652, 403 N.Y.S.2d 511 (1978). Or that he does not deal in certain goods. Jarrahdale Timber Co. v. Temperley, 11 T.L.R. 119 (1894). Or that another similar business is "unique," the only one in existence. Dale System v. Time, Inc., 116 F.Supp. 527 (D.C.Conn.1953). Or that plaintiff is employed by defendant, as a result of which he loses an independent sale and a commission. Balden v. Shorter, [1933] Ch. 427.

See also Gale v. Ryan, 263 App.Div. 76, 31 N.Y.S.2d 32 (1941); and Penn–Ohio Steel Corp. v. Allis–Chalmers Mfg. Co., 7 A.D.2d 441, 184 N.Y.S.2d 58 (1959) (defendant made false reports to Internal Revenue of payments made to plaintiff, as a result of which plaintiff had income-tax trouble); Al Raschid v. News Syndicate Co., 265 N.Y. 1, 191 N.E. 713 (1934) (defendant gave false information that plaintiff was not a citizen, subjecting him to deportation proceedings); Bartlett v. Federal Outfitting Co., 133 Cal.App. 747, 24 P.2d 877 (1933) (forged assignment of wages presented to an employer, in consequence of which the employee was discharged); Owens v. Mench, 81 Pa.D. & C. 314 (1952) (false report of a physician on a workman's injury necessitated suit to recover workmen's compensation); and Cooper v. Weissblatt, 154 Misc. 522, 277 N.Y.S. 709 (1935) (false statements to church authorities forced the plaintiff to defend a suit).

4. *Special Damage.* Pleading and proof of special damage are held to be essential to any cause of action for injurious falsehood. The damage must consist of pecuniary loss, and personal elements of damage such as mental distress, which are recoverable for defamation, are not sufficient to sustain this action.

5. When the damages claimed consist only of loss of prospective contracts or customers, the older and still prevailing rule is that the plaintiff must identify the particular customers who have refrained from dealing with him, and specify the transactions of which he claims to have been deprived. Wilson v. Dubois, 35 Minn. 471, 29 N.W. 68 (1886); Barquin v. Hall Oil Co., 28 Wyo. 164, 201 P. 352 (1921). It is not enough merely to show a general decline in plaintiff's business following the false publication. Ward v. Gee, 61 S.W.2d 555 (Tex.Civ.App.1933); Shaw Cleaners & Dyers v. Des Moines Dress Club, 215 Iowa 1130, 245 N.W. 231 (1932).

6. The modern tendency, deriving from the principal case, is to require the plaintiff to be specific only when it is reasonable to expect him to do so, and to allow recovery for a general decline in business if all other reasonably possible causes are excluded. Thus in Craig v. Proctor, 229 Mass. 339, 118 N.E. 647 (1918), a general allegation in the complaint was upheld, but it was said that the defendant might compel the plaintiff to furnish before trial such information as he had. Some other cases allowing recovery without identification are Erick Bowman Remedy Co. v. Jensen Salsbery Laboratories, 17 F.2d 255 (8th Cir.1926); Rochester Brewing Co. v. Certa Bottling Works, 192 Misc. 629, 80 N.Y.S.2d 925 (1948).

HORNING v. HARDY
Court of Special Appeals of Maryland, 1977.
36 Md.App. 419, 373 A.2d 1273.

["The Hardys" filed suit in trespass and ejectment against "the Hornings," claiming that they owned certain real property that the Hornings were developing. The Hornings filed a counterclaim seeking to recover damages on the two bases of slander of title and tortious interference with contract. The trial court held for the Hornings on the initial suit and for the Hardys on the counterclaim, thus allowing neither party to recover. This court agrees with the holding in the suit for trespass and ejectment, on the ground that the Hardys had failed to establish ownership through either deed descriptions or adverse possession.

On the counterclaim, the trial court regarded slander of title and interference with contract as raising the same issues and analyzed the case in terms of slander of title. The Hornings were developing land in the disputed area and had one house ready for sale. On the morning of the settlement, a phone call from the Hardys' attorney advised the parties to the settlement that the Hardys had filed suit claiming ownership on the previous day. The settlement "was immediately aborted and no sales or settlements have been consummated since that day."]

LISS, JUDGE. * * * Prosser * * * suggests that the tort we are here discussing has been incorrectly designated as "slander of title." Such nomenclature derives from the earliest cases—decided before 1600—where it applied primarily to oral aspersions on the plaintiff's ownership of land, which aspersions prevented the owner from leasing or selling the land. Prosser points out that from the beginning the tort was recognized as being only loosely allied to defamation of the person and was considered instead to be an action on the case for the special damage resulting from the defendant's interference. As the years progressed, the tort was expanded to include written aspersions on property, whether land or personalty, and the disparagement of the quality of property. The tort has, therefore, been known as "disparagement of property," "slander of goods," and "trade libel." * * *

A * * * valuable contribution to the clarification of the tort in Maryland was made by Judge Wilson K. Barnes in the case of Beane v. McMullen, 265 Md. 585, 291 A.2d 37 (1972). Quoting extensively from Prosser, Judge Barnes said:

"Injurious falsehood or disparagement, then, may consist of the publication of matter derogatory to the plaintiff's title to his property, or its quality, or to his business in general, or even to some element of his personal affairs, of a kind calculated to prevent others from dealing with him, or otherwise to interfere with his relations with others to his disadvantage. The cause of action founded upon it resembles that for defamation, but differs from it materially in the greater burden of proof resting on the plaintiff, and the necessity for special damage in all cases. The falsehood must be communicated to a third person, since the tort consists of interference with the relation with such persons. But the plaintiff must plead and prove not only the publication and its disparaging innuendo, as in defamation, but something more. There is no presumption, as in the case of personal slander, that the disparaging statement is false, and the plaintiff must establish its falsity as a part of his cause of action. Although it has been contended that there is no essential reason against liability where even the truth is published for the purpose of doing harm, the policy of the courts has been to encourage the publication of the truth, regardless of motive.

"In addition, the plaintiff must prove in all cases that the publication has played a material and substantial part in inducing others not to deal with him, and that as a result he had suffered special damage. * * *

"There is liability when the defendant acts for a spite motive, and out of a desire to do harm for its own sake; and equally so when he acts for the purpose of doing harm to the interests of the plaintiff in a manner in which he is not privileged so to interfere. There is also liability when the defendant knows that what he says is false, regardless of whether he has an ill motive or intends to affect the plaintiff at all. The deliberate liar must take the risk that his statement will prove to be economically damaging to others; and there is something like the 'scienter' found in an action of deceit. Any of these three is sufficient to constitute 'malice' and support the action. But in the absence of any of the three there is no liability, where the defendant has made his utterance in good faith, even though he may have been negligent in failing to ascertain the facts before he made it." Id. at 607–09, 291 A.2d at 49.

The law of defamation has been in a state of flux in the Supreme Court of the United States since 1964, when the decision in N.Y. Times v. Sullivan, 376 U.S. 254, supra page 895 was filed. Gertz v. Welch, 418 U.S. 323 (1974) supra page 906 held that in a purely private defamation action the States were free to adopt their own standard of liability for the defamation defendant but could not impose liability without fault.

The Court of Appeals, speaking through Judge Levine in Jacron Sales Co., Inc. v. Sindorf, 276 Md. 580, 350 A.2d 688 (1975), stated that in cases of purely private defamation it would adopt as a matter of state law the standard of negligence as set forth in Restatement (Second) of Torts, § 580B (Tentative Draft # 21, 1975), which states that liability may accrue only if the defendant a) knows that the statement is false and that it defames the other, b) the defendant acts in reckless disregard of these matters, or c) acts negligently in failing to ascertain them. The opinion further held that the quantum of proof required of the plaintiff was the usual negligence standard of the preponderance of the evidence.

In the case here being considered, there is one further complicating factor: the assertion of a qualified privilege by the appellees. Prosser * * * states the privilege to be as follows: "If [the defendant] has a present, existing economic interest to protect, such as the ownership or condition of property * * * he is privileged to prevent performance of the contract of another which threatens it; and for obvious reasons of policy he is likewise privileged to assert an honest claim, or bring or threaten a suit in good faith, to exercise the right of petition to public authorities or to settle his own case out of court."

Further justification for the recognition of the conditional privilege is stated in 1 Harper and James, The Law of Torts, § 6.2 (1956): "If, knowing that another is offering or about to offer land or other thing for sale as his own, he fails to take advantage of a readily available opportunity to inform the intending purchaser, or those likely to become purchasers, as where the sale is by auction, of his claim to the thing, he may preclude himself from afterwards asserting it against the purchaser. Therefore, he must be permitted without fear of liability to protect the enforceability of his claim by asserting it before the purchase is made."

Jacron, supra, makes it clear that the adoption of the negligence standard of fault in defamation cases does not make obsolete the defense of conditional privilege. In a case where a common law conditional privilege is asserted and found as a matter of law to exist, "the negligence standard of *Gertz* is logically subsumed in the higher standard for proving malice, reckless disregard as to truth or falsity * * *." Id. at 600, 350 A.2d at 700. If the plaintiff, faced with a conditional privilege, is unable to prove the malice necessary to overcome that defense, the proof of the lesser standard of negligence would not permit a recovery. [C] In conditional privilege cases, the privilege may be lost either by proof of "constitutional malice" in the form of reckless disregard for truth or falsity or knowing falsehood or by proof of common law malice in the form of spite or ill-will.

The question of whether a conditional privilege exists is a matter of law for the court. Whether the privilege has been abused or forfeited by malice is a question of fact for the trier of the facts. [C] The trial court found as a matter of law that the interference by Hardy with the Hornings' title was privileged. It concluded that the "original plaintiffs asserted an honest claim to the land in question which they had reason to believe was part of their property and they therefore had a present economic interest to protect." We hold this conclusion to be correct * * *.

Appellants urge strenuously that the failure of the appellees to act in good faith to verify the boundaries of the land which they claimed and in their failure to secure expert opinion as to the validity of their claim is evidence of a reckless disregard for the truth. This contention ignores, however, our holding in *Kapiloff* [v. Dunn, 27 Md.App. 514, 343 A.2d 251 (1975)], where we said:

"Although the test for reckless disregard does not avail itself of easy application, one point is clear: mere failure to investigate, in and of itself, is not sufficient evidence under the *New York Times* privilege. * * * Since failure to investigate cannot satisfy the constitutional test of reckless disregard, we cannot perceive how mere failure to seek assistance of educational experts, without more, could satisfy that standard." * * *

The trial court found as a fact that there was no abuse of the conditional privilege and we find no plain error in its conclusions. * * *

Judgments affirmed.

---

1. This was the first form of injurious falsehood. See, e.g., Gerard v. Dickenson, Cro.Eliz. 196, 76 Eng.Rep. 903 (1588), which is remarkably like the present case except that it was alleged that the defendant knew that her claim to the castle was based on forgery.

2. Any type of legally protected property interest that can be sold may be the subject of disparagement, including remainders, leases, mineral rights,

trademarks, copyrights, patents, corporate shares and literary productions. A common form of "slander of title" is the assertation, as by filing for record, of a false claim to a mortgage or other lien on the property. See, e.g., Gudger v. Manton, 21 Cal.2d 537, 134 P.2d 217 (1943), where defendant levied and recorded execution on plaintiff's property, to force him to pay a debt contracted by his wife before their marriage.

3. *Privileges.* It appears that any absolute or qualified privilege that applies to defamation under the common law applies also to injurious falsehood. Whenever the defendant is privileged to publish a false statement that is personally defamatory, he must be no less privileged to publish one that is not. See Davis v. Union State Bank, 137 Kan. 264, 20 P.2d 508 (1933) (absolute privilege for statements in pleading filed); Stewart v. Fahey, 14 Ariz.App. 149, 481 P.2d 519 (1971) (persons connected with judicial proceeding); Bearce v. Bass, 88 Me. 521, 34 A. 411 (1896) (criticism of public building as badly constructed); Mack Miller Candle Co. v. MacMillan Co., 239 App.Div. 738, 269 N.Y.S. 33 (1934) (report of judicial proceeding).

4. The defendant has a qualified privilege to protect his own interests by the assertion of a bona fide claim to any kind of property. This includes, for example, an assertion that plaintiff is infringing defendant's patent, copyright or trademark rights by the sale of his product. Oil Conservation Engineering co. v. Brooks Engineering Co., 52 F.2d 783 (6th Cir.1931); Alliance Securities Co. v. De Vilbiss, 41 F.2d 668 (6th Cir.1930). The privilege is, however, a qualified one and it is defeated if the defendant's motive is shown to be actual malice, in the sense of a desire to do harm. Sinclair Ref. Co. v. Jones Super Service Station, 188 Ark. 1075, 70 S.W.2d 562 (1934); A.B. Farquhar Co. v. National Harrow Co., 102 Fed. 714 (3d Cir.1900). It is also defeated if the defendant has acted in bad faith, as where it is found that he did not honestly believe his assertions to be true. Hopkins v. Drowne, 21 R.I. 20, 41 A. 567 (1898); Ezmirlian v. Otto, 139 Cal.App. 486, 34 P.2d 774 (1934).

As in the case of other qualified privileges, the defendant will be liable if there is excessive publication to persons whom it is not reasonably necessary to reach or if he includes statements that he knows to be untrue. Donovan v. Wilson Sporting Goods Co., 285 F.2d 714 (1st Cir.1961). See generally Restatement (Second) of Torts §§ 635, 646A.

5. Defendant oil company owned mineral rights to a large area of land, with the exception of 900 acres belonging to plaintiff, who refused to sell exploratory rights. Defendant trespassed on plaintiff's land and conducted exploratory tests that showed little likelihood of finding oil in paying quantities. The information saved defendant expenditures that would be made in drilling a dry hole, but it ruined the speculative value of the drilling rights on plaintiff's lands. Should plaintiff be able to recover for his loss? Compare Angelloz v. Humble Oil & Ref. Co., 196 La. 604, 199 So. 656 (1940), with Martel v. Hall Oil Co., 36 Wyo. 166, 253 P. 862 (1927). See Malone, Ruminations on a New Tort, 4 La.L.Rev. 309 (1942).

BOSE CORP. v. CONSUMERS UNION OF UNITED STATES, INC.

Supreme Court of the United States, 1984.
466 U.S. 485, 104 S.Ct. 1949, 80 L.Ed.2d 502.

Justice Stevens delivered the opinion of the Court.

An unusual metaphor in a critical review of an unusual loudspeaker system gave rise to product disparagement litigation that presents us with a procedural question of first impression: Does Rule 52(a) of the Federal Rules of Civil Procedure prescribe the standard to be applied by the Court of Appeals in its review of a District Court's determination that a false statement was made with the kind of "actual malice" described in *New York Times v. Sullivan,* 376 U.S. 254 (1964)?

In the May 1970 issue of its magazine, "Consumer Reports," respondent published a seven-page article evaluating the quality of numerous brands of medium priced loudspeakers. In a boxed-off section occupying most of two pages, respondent commented on "some loudspeakers of special interest," one of which was the Bose 901—an admittedly "unique and unconventional" system that had recently been placed on the market by petitioner. After describing the system and some of its virtues, and after noting that a listener "could pinpoint the location of various instruments much more easily with a standard speaker than with the *Bose* system," respondent's article made the following statements:

"Worse, individual instruments heard through the Bose system seemed to grow to gigantic proportions and tended to wander about the room. For instance, a violin appeared to be 10 feet wide and a piano stretched from wall to wall. With orchestral music, such effects seemed inconsequential. But we think they might become annoying when listening to soloists." Plaintiff's Exhibit 2, at 274.

After stating opinions concerning the overall sound quality, the article concluded: "We think the *Bose* system is so unusual that a prospective buyer must listen to it and judge it for himself. We would suggest delaying so big an investment until you were sure the system would please you after the novelty value had worn off." *Id.,* at 275.

Petitioner took exception to numerous statements made in the article, and when respondent refused to publish a retraction, petitioner commenced this product disparagement action in the United States District Court for the District of Massachusetts. [That court denied a motion for summary judgment and "ruled that the petitioner is a public figure" under Gertz v. Robert Welch, supra page 906, so that it was required to prove "by clear and convincing evidence that respondent made a false disparaging statement 'with actual malice.' "]

Based primarily on testimony by [Arnold Seligson,] the author of the article, the District Court found that instruments heard through the speakers tended to wander "along the wall," rather than "about the room" as reported by respondent. Second, it found that the statement was disparaging. Third, it concluded "on the basis of proof which it considers clear and convincing, that the plaintiff has sustained its burden of proving that the defendant published a false statement of material fact with knowledge that it was false or with reckless disregard of its truth or falsity." 508 F.Supp., at 1277. Judgment was entered for petitioner on the product disparagement claim.

The United States Court of Appeals for the First Circuit reversed. 692 F.2d 189 (1982). The court accepted the finding that the comment about wandering instruments was disparaging. It assumed, without deciding, that the statement was one of fact, rather than opinion, and that it was false, observing that "stemming at least in part from the uncertain nature of the statement as one of fact or opinion, it is difficult to determine with confidence whether it is true or false." *Id.,* at 194. After noting that petitioner did not contest the conclusion that it was a public figure, or the applicability of the *New York Times* standard, the Court of Appeals held that its review of the "actual malice" determination was not "limited" to the clearly erroneous standard of Rule 52(a); instead, it stated that it "must perform a de novo review, independently examining the record to ensure that the district court has applied properly the governing constitutional law and that the plaintiff has indeed satisfied its burden of proof." *Id.,* at 195. It added, however, that it "was in no position to consider the credibility of witnesses and must leave such questions of demeanor to the trier of fact." *Ibid.* Based on its own review of the record, the Court of Appeals concluded:

"[W]e are unable to find clear and convincing evidence that CU published the statement that individual instruments tended to wander about the room with knowledge that it was false or with reckless disregard of whether it was false or not. The evidence presented merely shows that the words in the article may not have described precisely what the two panelists heard during the listening test. CU was guilty of using imprecise language in the article—perhaps resulting from an attempt to produce a readable article for its mass audience. Certainly this does not support an inference of actual malice." *Id.,* at 197.

We granted certiorari to consider whether the Court of Appeals erred when it refused to apply the clearly erroneous standard of Rule 52(a) to the District Court's "finding" of actual malice. * * *

This is a case in which two well settled and respected rules of law point in opposite directions.

Petitioner correctly reminds us that Rule 52(a) provides: "Findings of fact shall not be set aside unless clearly erroneous, and due regard shall be given to the opportunity of the trial court to judge of the credibility of the witnesses." We have repeatedly held that the rule means what it says. [Cc] It surely does not stretch the language of the rule to characterize an inquiry into what a person knew at a given point in time as a question of "fact." In this case, since the trial judge expressly commented on Seligson's credibility, petitioner argues that the Court of Appeals plainly erred when it refused to uphold the District Court's actual malice "finding" under the clearly erroneous standard of Rule 52(a).

On the other hand, respondent correctly reminds us that in cases raising First Amendment issues we have repeatedly held that an appellate court has an obligation to "make an independent examination of the whole record" in order to make sure "that the judgment does not constitute a forbidden intrusion on the field of free expression." [Cc] Although such statements have been made most frequently in cases to which Rule 52(a) does not apply because they arose in state courts, respondent argues that the constitutional principle is equally applicable to federal litigation. We quite agree; surely it would pervert the concept of federalism for this Court to lay claim to a broader power of review over state court judgments than it exercises in reviewing the judgments of intermediate federal courts.

Our standard of review must be faithful to both Rule 52(a) and the rule of independent review applied in *New York Times v. Sullivan*. The conflict between the two rules is in some respects more apparent than real. * * *

The requirement of independent appellate review reiterated in *New York Times v. Sullivan* is a rule of federal constitutional law. It emerged from the exigency of deciding concrete cases; it is law in its purest form under our common law heritage. It reflects a deeply held conviction that judges—and particularly members of this Court—must exercise such review in order to preserve the precious liberties established and ordained by the Constitution. The question whether the evidence in the record in a defamation case is of the convincing clarity required to strip the utterance of First Amendment protection is not merely a question for the trier of fact. Judges, as expositors of the Constitution, must independently decide whether the evidence in the record is sufficient to cross the constitutional threshold that bars the entry of any judgment that is not supported by clear and convincing proof of "actual malice." * * *

The Court of Appeals was correct in its conclusions (1) that there is a significant difference between proof of actual malice and mere proof of falsity, and (2) that such additional proof is lacking in this case. * * *

Seligson's testimony does not rebut any inference of actual malice that the record otherwise supports, but it is equally clear that it does not constitute clear and convincing evidence of actual malice. Seligson displayed a capacity for rationalization. He had made a mistake and when confronted with it, he refused to admit it and steadfastly attempted to maintain that no mistake had been made—that the inaccurate was accurate. That attempt failed, but the fact that he made the attempt does not establish that he realized the inaccuracy at the time of publication.

Aside from Seligson's vain attempt to defend his statement as a precise description of the nature of the sound movement, the only evidence of actual malice on which the District Court relied was the fact that the statement was an inaccurate description of what Seligson had actually perceived. * * *

The statement in this case represents the sort of inaccuracy that is commonplace in the forum of robust debate to which the *New York Times* rule applies. *Id.,* at 292, "Realistically, * * * some error is inevitable; and the difficulties of separating fact from fiction convinced the Court in *New York Times, Butts, Gertz,* and similar cases to limit liability to instances where some degree of culpability is present in order to eliminate the risk of undue self-censorship and the suppression of truthful material." *Herbert v. Lando,* 441 U.S. 153, 171–172 (1979). "[E]rroneous statement is inevitable in free debate, and * * * must be protected if the freedoms of expression are to have the 'breathing space' that they 'need * * * to survive.'" *New York Times v. Sullivan,* 376 U.S., at 271–272. * * * [We] agree with the Court of Appeals that the difference between hearing violin sounds move around the room and hearing them wander back and forth fits easily within the breathing space that gives life to the First Amendment. We may accept all of the purely factual findings of the District Court and nevertheless hold as a matter of law that the record does not contain clear and convincing evidence that Seligson or his employer prepared the loudspeaker article with knowledge that it contained a false statement, or with reckless disregard of the truth.

It may well be that in this case, the "finding" of the District Court on the actual malice question could have been set aside under the clearly erroneous standard of review, and we share the concern of the Court of Appeals that the statements at issue tread the line between fact and opinion. Moreover, the analysis of the central legal question before us may seem out of place in a case involving a dispute about the sound quality of a loudspeaker. But though the question presented reaches us on a somewhat peculiar wavelength, we reaffirm the principle of independent appellate review that we have applied uncounted times before. We hold that the clearly erroneous standard of Rule 52(a) of the Federal Rules of Civil Procedure does not prescribe the standard of review to be applied in reviewing a determination of actual malice in a case governed by *New York Times v. Sullivan.* Appellate judges in such a case must exercise independent judgment and determine whether the record establishes actual malice with convincing clarity.

The judgment of the Court of Appeals is affirmed.

[THE CHIEF JUSTICE concurred in the judgment. WHITE, REHNQUIST and O'CONNOR, JJ., dissented.]

---

1. Perhaps the most significant aspect of this decision for the tort of injurious falsehood is the casual way in which the Court, without discussion of the matter, automatically assumed that the various constitutional restrictions on an action for defamation would also apply to an action for disparagement of a product. Both lower courts had discussed the matter at some length, and there was considerable writing on the subject. This is commercial speech and the earlier impression had been that it was not entitled to First Amendment protection. Then, when the Court held that it was entitled to the protection, in

Virginia State Board of Pharmacy v. Virginia Citizens Consumer Council, Inc., 425 U.S. 748 (1976), there were indications that the scope of the protection might be less. The instant case seems now to make clear that all of the constitutional restrictions on an action for defamation are applicable here, too. Speculation on the issue would appear to be dispelled.

2. For an early instance of an action for trade libel, see Dickes v. Fenne, March N.R. 59, 82 Eng.Rep. 411 (1639) ("Defendant having communication with some of the Customers of the Plaintiff, who was a Brewer, said, That he would give a peck of malt to his mare and she should pisse as good beare as Dickes doth Brew"; no recovery because no allegation of special damages).

3. *Intentional Infliction of Harm.* It has been said that recovery for injurious falsehood requires malice involving showing of knowledge that the statement was false, or intent to harm the plaintiff or affect his interests in an unprivileged manner. Prosser, Injurious Falsehood: The Basis of Liability, 59 Colum.L.Rev. 425 (1959). See Advance Music Corp. v. American Tobacco Co., 296 N.Y. 79, 70 N.E.2d 401 (1946) (sufficient to allege that defendants "wantonly caused damage to the plaintiff by a system of conduct [that] warrants an inference that they intend harm of that type"); Remick Music Corp. v. American Tobacco Co., 57 F.Supp. 475 (D.C.N.Y.1944) ("defendants deliberately and wilfully indulged in such unfairness"); Dale System v. General Teleradio, 105 F.Supp. 745 (1952) ("intentional publication for the sake of injuring the plaintiff"); Shapiro v. La Morta, 40 T.L.R. 201 (C.A.1923) (statement must be "not bona fide"); Balden v. Shorter, [1935] Ch. 427 (requirement of "some dishonest or otherwise improper motive"); Hahn v. Duveen, 133 Misc. 871, 234 N.Y.S. 185 (1929) (no liability "if in good faith"); cf. Demuth Development Corp. v. Merck & Co., 432 F.Supp. 990 (D.C.N.Y.1977) ("acts * * * solely malicious, * * * done 'without legal or social justification' ").

4. *Relationship of Injurious Falsehood to Defamation.* These two torts may overlap, since the same statement may both defame a person and disparage the goods he sells. See Hatchard v. Mege, 18 Q.B.D. 771 (1877). The distinction drawn by the courts is that if the statement made reflects only upon the quality of what the plaintiff has to sell, or the character of his business as such, it is merely injurious falsehood, and proof of special damage is essential to the cause of action. Evans v. Harlow, 5 Q.B. 624 (1844); National Refining Co. v. Benzo Gas Motor Fuel Co., 20 F.2d 763 (8th Cir.1927). On the other hand, if the statement imputes to the plaintiff reprehensible personal characteristics or misconduct, it is regarded as defamation. Merle v. Sociological Research Film Corp., 166 App.Div. 376, 152 N.Y.S. 829 (1915) (factory used as place of assignation); Kilpatrick v. Edge, 85 N.J.L. 7, 88 A. 839 (1913) (misconduct in a Turkish bath).

The difficulty lies in the fact that many statements do both. It might be possible to imply some accusation of personal inefficiency or incompetence, defaming the plaintiff in his business or trade, in nearly every imputation directed against a business or its product. Cf. Summit Hotel Co. v. National Broadcasting Co., 336 Pa. 182, 8 A.2d 302 (1939), where "a rotten hotel" was held to defame the management. See also Waechter v. Carnation Co., 5 Wash. App. 121, 485 P.2d 1000 (1971) (statement as to quality of milk). The courts, however, sometimes have gone to remarkable lengths in refusing to find any personal defamation. For example, Nonpareil Cork Mfg. Co. v. Keasbey & Mattison Co., 108 Fed. 721 (product a "fraud") (C.C.Pa.1901); Erick Bowman Remedy Co. v. Jensen Salsbery Laboratories, 17 F.2d 255 (8th Cir.1926) ("Barnum was right"). This is particularly true when the most that can be made out of the words is a charge of ignorance, imcompetence or negligence. Shaw Cleaners & Dyers v. Des Moines Dress Club, 215 Iowa 1130, 245 N.W. 231 (1932) (garments "only half cleaned").

Personal defamation is found when the words are found clearly to impute dishonesty or lack of integrity to the plaintiff, or say that he is deliberately perpetrating a fraud upon the public by selling a product that he knows to be defective. Tobin v. Alfred M. Best Co., 120 App.Div. 387, 105 N.Y.S. 294 (1907) ("fake" insurance policy); Rosenberg v. J.C. Penney Co., 30 Cal.App.2d 609, 86 P.2d 696 (1939) (fraud in sale).

5. See Restatement (Second) of Torts §§ 623A–652; Prosser, Injurious Falsehood: The Basis of Liability, 59 Colum.L.Rev. 925 (1959); Smith, Disparagement of Property, 13 Colum.L.Rev. 13 & 121 (1913); Wham, Disparagement of Property, 21 Ill.L.Rev. 26 (1926); Hibschman, Defamation or Disparagement, 24 Minn.L.Rev. 625 (1945); Notes, 75 Colum.L.Rev. 963 (1975), 63 Yale L.J. 1304 (1938).

TESTING SYSTEMS, INC. v. MAGNAFLUX CORP.

United States District Court, Eastern District of Pennsylvania, 1966.
251 F.Supp. 286.

[Plaintiff and defendant were competing manufacturers of equipment, devices and systems for use in testing industrial and commercial materials. The complaint alleged that defendant circulated to plaintiff's current and prospective customers a false report to the effect that the United States Government had tested plaintiff's product, and found it to be only about 40% as effective as that of the defendant. Plaintiff also claimed that at a manufacturers' convention in Philadelphia defendant's agent, in the presence of plaintiff's current and prospective customers, "did in a loud voice state that * * * [plaintiff's] * * * stuff is no good," and that "the government is throwing them out."]

LORD, DISTRICT JUDGE. This is an action for trade libel or disparagement of property. * * * The matter is now before this Court on defendant's motion to dismiss for failure to state a claim upon which relief can be granted.

For the purposes of this motion, defendant admits the truth of the allegation, but asserts that the action must nevertheless be dismissed because (1) the defendant did no more than make an unfavorable comparison of plaintiff's product with its own; and (2) even assuming that the statements were actionable, plaintiff has failed to allege his damages with the required specificity. * * *

It would serve no useful purpose to dwell at length on the issue of unfavorable comparison. Suffice it to say, as the defendant properly points out, that a statement which takes the form of an unfavorable comparison of products, or which "puffs" or exaggerates the quality of one's own product is not ordinarily actionable. [Cc] This has long been the rule in England, where the action originated, and is now well established in the vast majority of United States jurisdictions. [Cc]

However, this Court is not convinced by the defendant's arguments that his comments amounted to mere unfavorable comparison. The modern history of the doctrine of unfavorable comparison and its permissible use in the conduct of business traces its origin to the leading English case of White v. Mellin [1895] A.C. 154. There the defendant had advertised his product as being far more healthful than plaintiff's. In refusing relief the Court established the precedent that irrespective of their truth or falsity, statements by one competitor which compare his product with that of another are not actionable.

It does not follow from this, however, that every trade disparagement is protectible under the guise of unfavorable comparison merely because the perpetrator was canny enough to mention not only the product of his competitor but also his own. The decision in White v. Mellin, supra, was founded on the near impossibility of ascertaining the truth or falsity of general allegations respecting the superiority of one product over another. To decide otherwise, explained Lord Herschell, would turn the courts "into a machinery for advertising rival productions by obtaining a judicial determination [as to] which of the two was better. [C] One is expected to believe in the superiority of his wares, and he may properly declare his belief to interested parties. It has even been said that he may 'boast untruthfully of his wares.'" Phila. D. Prod. v. Quaker City I. Co., 306 Pa. 164, 172, 159 A. 3 (1932). * * *

The fine line that separates healthy competitive effort from underhanded business tactics is frequently difficult to determine. Apart from the tradesman's right of free speech, which must be vigorously safeguarded, the public has a genuine interest in learning the relative merits of particular products, however that may come about. * * *

Nonetheless, there is an outer perimeter to permissible conduct. The tradesman must be assured that his competitors will not be suffered to engage in conduct which falls below the minimum standard of fair dealing. "[I]t is no answer that they can defend themselves by also resorting to disparagement. A self-respecting business man will not voluntarily adopt, and should not be driven to adopt, a selling method which he regards as undignified, unfair, and repulsive. A competitor should not, by pursuing an unethical practice force his rival to choose between its adoption and the loss of his trade." Wolfe, Unfair Competition, 47 Yale L.J. 1304, 1334–35 (1938).

The defendant's comments in the case presently before this Court do not entitle him to the protection accorded to "unfavorable comparison." There is a readily observable difference between saying that one's product is, in general, better than another's * * * and asserting, as here, that such other's is only 40% as effective as one's own. The former, arguably, merely expresses an opinion, the truth or falsity of which is difficult or impossible of ascertainment. The latter, however, is an assertion of fact, not subject to the same frailties of proof, implying that the party making the statement is fortified with the substantive facts necessary to make it. This distinction has never been seriously questioned. See e.g. Restatement, Torts, §§ 626, 627, 628. The defendant in this case admittedly circulated to plaintiff's present and prospective customers false statements to the effect that the government had tested both products and found the defendant's to be 60% more effective than plaintiff's. This is not the sort of "comparison" that courts will protect.

Apart from this, there is at least one additional factor which withdraws the defendant's comments from the category of unfavorable comparison. Not content with making the admittedly false statements and allowing them to be evaluated independently of any extraneous influence, the defendant here gave added authenticity to its assertions, by invoking the reputation of a third party, the United States Government. It is unnecessary to speculate on the additional force the defendant's remarks must have had when coupled with the purported approval of so highly credible a source. This, of course, is to say nothing of the statements to the effect that plaintiff had been "thrown out," which by no stretch of the imagination could be termed mere comparison.

For all of the above reasons, it is the judgment of this Court that the defendant's remarks are actionable.

———

1.   How does this case compare with Vulcan Metals Co. v. Simmons Mfg. Co., supra page 1069?

2.   The competitor's "puffing" privilege permits statements of comparison, that the defendant's goods are the best in the market, that they are better than the plaintiff's, or other boasting or exaggeration, even though the defendant is fully aware that what he says is false, and the publication is made for the purpose of injuring the plaintiff by taking business away from him. One of the leading cases is White v. Mellin, [1895] A.C. 154, where the defendant sold packages of plaintiff's baby food with a wrapper affixed to them which stated that defendant's was better. This was held to be privileged. In this respect, there is an obvious difference from personal defamation, which would not be privileged under the same circumstances.

3.   Competition for business does not, however, justify intentional false statements of fact concerning the competitor's business or product, when they are not confined to comparing the product or conduct of the competitor with that of the plaintiff, and this unfair competition is not privileged. National Refining Co. v. Benzo Gas Motor Fuel Co., 20 F.2d 763 (8th Cir.1927); Hopkins Chemical Co. v. Read Drug & Chemical Co., 124 Md. 210, 92 A. 478 (1914). Sometimes the courts have leaned quite far over backwards to avoid finding an assertion to be a misstatement of fact. Thus in Nonpareil Cork Mfg. Co. v. Keasbey & Mattison Co., 108 Fed. 721 (E.D.Pa.1901), a statement that cork covering for steam pipes was a "fraud" was held to be "really but the expression of an unfavorable opinion of the goods" of its competitor. But such expressions are not uncommon among rivals in trade, and their correctness in each instance is for determination by those whose custom is sought, and not by the courts.

4.   Applying the defamation distinction between fact and opinion to product disparagement to grant an immunity for expression of opinion, see Dairy Stores, Inc. v. Sentinel Pub. Co., 104 N.J. 125, 516 A.2d 220 (1986).

(B) INTERFERENCE WITH EXISTING OR PROSPECTIVE CONTRACTUAL RELATIONS

LUMLEY v. GYE
Queen's Bench, 1853.
2 El. & Bl. 216, 118 Eng.Rep. 749.

[The declaration alleged: Plaintiff, manager of the Queens Theatre for performing operas, contracted with Johanna Wagner for her to perform in his theatre for a designated time. She agreed not to perform elsewhere during the contract term. Defendant, "knowing the premises and maliciously intruding to injure plaintiff * * *, enticed and procured Wagner to refuse to perform." Defendant demurred.]

ERLE, J. The question raised upon this demurrer is, Whether an action will lie by the proprietor of a theatre against a person who maliciously procures an entire abandonment of a contract to perform exclusively at that theatre for a certain time; whereby damage was sustained? And it seems to me that it will. The authorities are numerous and uniform, that an action will lie by a master against a person who procures that a servant should unlawfully leave his service. The principle involved in these cases comprises the present; for, there, the right of action in the master arises from the wrongful act of the defendant in procuring that the person hired should break his contract, by putting an end to the relation of employer and employed; and the present case is the same. If it is objected that this class of actions for procuring a breach of contract of hiring rests upon no principle, and ought not to be extended beyond the cases heretofore decided, and that, as those have related to contracts respecting trade, manufactures, or household service, and not to performance at a theatre, therefore they are no authority for an action in respect of a contract for such performance; the answer appears to me to be, that the class of cases referred to rests upon the principle that the procurement of the violation of the rights is a cause of action, and that, when this principle is applied to a violation of a right arising upon a contract of hiring, the nature of the service contracted for is immaterial.

It is clear that the procurement of the violation of a right is a cause of action in all instances where the violation is an actionable wrong, as in violations of a right to property, whether real or personal, or to personal security: he who procures the wrong is a joint wrongdoer, and may be sued, either alone or jointly with the agent, in the appropriate action for the wrong complained of. * * * He who maliciously procures a damage to another by violation of his right ought to be made to indemnify; and that, whether he procures an actionable wrong or a breach of contract. He who procures the non-delivery of goods according to contract may inflict an injury, the same as he who procures the abstraction of goods after delivery; and both ought on the same ground to be made responsible.   The remedy on the contract may be inadequate * * *.

The result is that there ought to be, in my opinion, judgment for the plaintiff.

[The concurring opinion of CROMPTON, J., and dissenting opinion of COLERIDGE, J., are omitted.]

———

1.   This case is generally regarded as the true beginning of the general principle that one is liable for improper interference with a contractual relationship.   Its origin goes back to very ancient times, when it was not the existence of a contract that was important, but the status, or relation recognized by the law, in which the parties stood toward one another, and with which the defendant interfered.

In 1349 a remedy was created by statute.   The Black Death had left England with a great shortage of labor, and to meet the resulting agricultural crisis the Ordinance of Labourers was enacted, by which a system of compulsory labor was introduced.   23 Edw. III, st. 1 (1350).   A penalty was provided to prevent the laborer from running away, and an action was given to the employer against anyone who received and retained him in his service.   This statutory action for enticing or harboring the servant was enforced in trespass, as was the older action for violence against the servant.   In time the two became confused and intermingled, and at last both were absorbed in the action on the case.

2.   The companion case of Lumley v. Wagner, 1 De G.M. & G. 604, 42 Eng. Rep. 687 (1852), a landmark in the law of equitable relief, affirmed injunctions preventing Miss Wagner from breaking the negative covenant in her contract with Lumley by singing for Gye and also preventing Gye from accepting her services.

3.   The principle announced in the principal case was received at first with a great deal of hesitation and disapproval.   It was reaffirmed thirty years later in Bowen v. Hall, 6 Q.B.D. 333 (1881), and then by degrees was extended—first to contracts other than those for personal services, and then to a holding that ill-will on the part of the defendant was not essential to the tort.   The present English law gives full acceptance to the proposition that intentional improper interference with any type of contract is a tort.   Jasperson v. Dominion Tobacco Co., [1923] A.C. 709.

4.   Except for the pioneering case of Aldridge v. Stuyvesant, 1 Hall 210 (N.Y.Sup.Ct.1828) (defendant wrongfully persuaded plaintiff's tenants to break their lease and leave), the American courts were reluctant to accept the principle, and rejected all liability for interference with contract except as limited to the historical basis of interference with the relation of master and servant.   These early decisions have now largely been overruled, and the American courts also give full acceptance to the principle.

5.   The primary importance of the principal case is its holding that there is liability even though the defendant does nothing unlawful except intentionally interfere with the contract.   The emphasis laid upon the existence of the contract, as something in the nature of a property interest of the plaintiff, good against the world, has been reflected in the subsequent cases.   The development of the law has extended the principle to interference with advantageous

relations of pecuniary value, even when they have not been cemented by contract. But the additional element of a definite agreement has its importance, since the person induced to break the contract is under a legal duty, for which the plaintiff has given consideration. The contract may therefore curtail the defendant's privilege to pursue his own ends at the expense of the plaintiff—as, for example, in business competition. It also fixes the limits of the plaintiff's interests, and therefore of his damages. Essentially, however, no real difference in principle is involved.

6. Defendant's tortious conduct is not confined to inducing the third person to break the contract. It may apply to other means of preventing the third person from performing. See, e.g., Phez Co. v. Salem Fruit Union, 103 Or. 514, 205 P. 970 (1922) (D refuses to carry out his contract to supply goods to T, to prevent T from supplying them to P).

7. The plaintiff must prove that the defendant knew of the contract. Imperial Ice Co. v. Rossier, 18 Cal.2d 33, 112 P.2d 631 (1931); Continental Research, Inc. v. Cruttenden, Podesta & Miller, 222 F.Supp. 190 (D.C.Minn. 1963) (circumstantial evidence of knowledge); Mid-Continent Tel. Corp. v. Home Tel. Co., 319 F.Supp. 1176 (D.C.Miss.1970) (reason to know and reasonable ignorance).

8. A third party beneficiary will be able to recover in tort for interference with the contract if he could have recovered in an action on the contract. Reynolds v. Owens, 34 Conn.Sup. 109, 380 A.2d 543 (1974).

9. If the third party has already broken the contract or decided to do so, and offers to contract with the defendant, defendant has not induced the breach. See Middleton v. Wallich's Music & Entertainment Co., 52 Ariz.App. 180, 536 P.2d 1072 (1975); Northern Wis. Coop. Tobacco Pool v. Bekkedal, 182 Wis. 571, 197 N.W. 936 (1923).

10. The first Restatement (§ 766) required that the interference be purposive. The Restatement (Second) requires that it be intentional in the sense of § 8A, but also requires that it be "improper." One of the factors in determining whether an interference is improper is the defendant's motive. (§ 767(b)).

11. In the beginning, interference with contract, like many other bases of tort liability, was much plagued with "malice." There was much dispute about the word in the older cases, some of which repeated the statement found in the first edition of Cooley on Torts 497 (1888), that "malicious motives make a bad case worse, but they cannot make that wrong which is in its essence lawful." This has now given way to a recognition that there are fields of tort liability, including this one, in which the motive or purpose of the defendant may be decisive as to his liability.

12. In South Wales Miners' Federation v. Glamorgan Coal Co., [1905] A.C. 239, it was held that "malice," in the sense of ill will, is not necessary to this tort, and that it is enough that defendant intentionally interfered with plaintiff's contract without any justification for doing so. As a result "malice" has gradually disappeared from the cases.

13. It is still true that a purely "malicious" motive, in the sense of spite or ill will and a desire to do harm for its own sake, will make the defendant liable. See for, example, Hutton v. Watters, 132 Tenn. 527, 179 S.W. 134 (1915). But so will mere officious intermeddling, for no other reason than a desire to have a finger in the pie. Sidney Blumenthal Co. v. United States, 30 F.2d 247 (2d Cir. 1929). Compare Russell v. Croteau, 98 N.H. 68, 94 A.2d 376 (1953), where no

motive or purpose appeared at all, and defendant was held liable for that reason.

14. Two classic articles on the subject of this section are Sayre, Inducing Breach of Contract, 36 Harv.L.Rev. 663 (1923); and Carpenter, Interference with Contract Relations, 41 Harv.L.Rev. 728 (1928). Two articles reaching contrasting views as to future development of the tort are Estes, Expanding Horizons in the Law of Torts—Tortious Interference, 23 Drake L.Rev. 341 (1959); and Dobbs, Tortious Interference with Contractual Relationships, 34 Ark.L.Rev. 335 (1980). And more recent important articles are Perlman, Interference with Contract and Other Economic Expectancies: A Case of Tort and Contract Doctrine, 49 U.Chi.L.Rev. 61 (1982); and Dowling, A Contract Theory for a Complex Tort: Limiting Interference with Contract Beyond The Unlawful Means Test, 48 U.Miami L.Rev. 487 (1986).

See also Green, Relational Interests, 29 Ill.L.Rev. 1041, 30 id. 1 (1935); Harper, Interference with Contract Relations, 47 Nw.L.Rev. 873 (1953); Weber, The Reasons Behind the Rules in the Law of Business Torts, 38 Neb.L.Rev. 608 (1959); Developments in the Law—Competitive Torts, 77 Harv.L.Rev. 888, 959– 69 (1964); Note, Interference with Contract Relations: A Property Limitation, 18 Stan.L.Rev. 1406 (1966); Note, Tortious Interference with Contractual Relations in the Nineteenth Century: The Transformation of Property, Contract and Tort, 93 Harv.L.Rev. 156 (1980); Note, Tortious Interference with Contract: A Reassertion of Society's Interest in Commercial Stability and Contractual Integrity, 81 Colum.L.Rev. 1491 (1987).

English treatments: J. Heydon, Economic Torts (1973); J. Fleming, Torts, 603–15 (4th ed. 1971); Stevens, Interference with Economic Relations—Some Aspects of the Turmoil in the Intentional Torts, 12 Osgoode Hall L.J. 595 (1974); Heydon, The Future of Economic Torts, 12 U.West.Aust.L.Rev. 1 (1975); Heydon, The Defence of Justification in Cases of Intentionally Caused Economic Loss, 20 U.Toronto L.J. 139 (1970).

15. Three opinions providing valuable analysis and historical treatment are Imperial Ice Co. v. Rossier, 18 Cal.2d 33, 112 P.2d 631 (1941) (apt summary by Traynor, J.); Continental Research, Inc. v. Cruttenden, Podesta & Miller, 222 F.Supp. 190 (D.C.Minn.1963) (very extensive treatment of whole subject by Larson, J.); and Top Service Body Shop, Inc. v. Allstate Ins. Co., 283 Or. 201, 582 P.2d 1365 (1978) (Linde, J.).

BACON v. ST. PAUL UNION STOCKYARDS CO.
Supreme Court of Minnesota, 1924.
161 Minn. 522, 201 N.W. 326.

[Plaintiff's complaint alleges that he was employed by the Drover Livestock Commission Co., engaged in buying, selling and dealing in livestock in the defendant's stockyards, but that the defendant "wrongfully, unlawfully, and willfully excluded plaintiff from its said stockyards, and barred and prevented him from carrying on his occupation therein, and forbade any person, firm, or corporation to employ him in or about" the stockyards. Defendant's demurrer to the complaint was sustained. Plaintiff appealed.]

PER CURIAM. * * * The wrongful interference with the contract relations of others causing a breach is a tort. We are of the opinion that the complaint states a cause of action for wrongful interference with plaintiff's employment. It appears from the complaint that the plaintiff had steady employment, and that defendant wrongfully, willfully, and unlawfully prevented him from continuing in that employment. We think such conduct is in violation of plaintiff's rights. [C] The defendant may have reasons to justify its conduct, but such reasons do not appear in the complaint. * * *

Reversed.

---

1. See Restatement (Second) of Torts § 766A. Also Harber v. Ohio Nat'l Life Ins. Co., 512 F.2d 170 (8th Cir.1975) (restricting sales of plaintiff's employee); White v. Massee, 202 Iowa 1034, 211 N.W. 839 (1927) (excluding plaintiff from place of performance); Yankee Network v. Gibbs, 295 Mass. 56, 3 N.E.2d 228 (1936) (fraudulently inducing plaintiff to break his own contract); Lichter v. Fulcher, 22 Tenn.App. 670, 125 S.W.2d 501 (1938) (depriving plaintiff of necessary labor).

2. The principle also applies to conduct making plaintiff's performance of his contract more burdensome or expensive, as by deliberate damage to a highway he is under a duty to repair. McNary v. Chamberlain, 34 Conn. 384, 91 Am.Dec. 732 (1867); Cue v. Breland, 78 Miss. 864, 29 So. 850 (1901); Piedmont Cotton Mills v. H.W. Ivey Constr. Co., 109 Ga.App. 876, 137 S.E.2d 528 (1964).

TEMPERTON v. RUSSELL
Court of Appeal, 1893.
[1893] 1 Q.B. 715.

[Members of a trade union wanted to coerce a firm of builders to comply with their demands. They requested plaintiff to stop supplying building materials to the firm. When he declined, they induced persons under contract with plaintiff to break their contracts and not to enter into further contracts with him. Plaintiff sued for his harm from both the broken contracts and the loss of prospective business.]

Lord Esher, M.R. * * * The next point is, whether the distinction taken for the defendants between the claim for inducing persons to break contracts already entered into with the plaintiff and that for inducing persons not to enter into contracts with the plaintiff can be sustained, and whether the latter claim is maintainable in law. I do not think that distinction can prevail. There was the same wrongful intent in both cases, wrongful because malicious. There was the same kind of injury to the plaintiff. It seems rather a fine distinction to say that, where a defendant maliciously induces a person not to carry out a contract already made with the plaintiff and so injures the plaintiff, it is actionable, but where he injures the plaintiff by maliciously preventing a person from entering into a contract with the plaintiff, which he would otherwise have entered into, it is not actionable. At any rate it appears to me that, on the principle acted on in the case of Gregory v. Duke of Brunswick, 6 M. & G. 953, where defendants conspire or combine together maliciously to injure the plaintiff by preventing persons from entering into contracts with him, and injury results to the plaintiff, it is actionable. ∗ ∗ ∗

It appears to me, therefore, that the combination here entered into by the defendants was wrongful both in respect of the interference with existing contracts and in respect of the prevention of contracts being entered into in the future. I cannot doubt that there was evidence from which the jury might find that people were prevented from dealing with the plaintiff by the resolution of the joint committee and the action taken by the defendants, and that the plaintiff was thereby injured, and it appears to me that the jury have so found. For these reasons I think this application must be refused. ∗ ∗ ∗

[The concurring opinions of LOPES and A.L. SMITH, L. JJ., are omitted.]

----

1. Tort liability for interference with merely prospective advantage developed at a very early date, in cases having to do with physical violence, or threats of it, to drive away customers from the plaintiff's market. Two important early cases were Garret v. Taylor, Cro.Jac. 567, 79 Eng.Rep. 485 (1621), involving threats of mayhem and vexatious suits against customers and workmen, and Tarleton v. McGawley, Peake N.P. 270, 170 Eng.Rep. 153 (1793), where the defendant fired upon African natives with whom the plaintiff was about to trade. The best early statement of the principle is found in Keeble v. Hickeringill, 11 East 574, 103 Eng.Rep. 1127 (1707), where the defendant, inspired by pure malice, fired guns to frighten ducks away from the plaintiff's pond, and so prevented him from taking them.

2. A leading American case is Tuttle v. Buck, 107 Minn. 145, 119 N.W. 946 (1909). Plaintiff's complaint alleged that the defendant, a banker and a man of wealth and influence in the community, maliciously established a barber shop, employed a barber to carry on the business, and used his personal influence to attract customers from the plaintiff's barber shop, not for the purpose of serving any legitimate purpose of his own, but for the sole purpose of maliciously injuring the plaintiff; and that as a result of this conduct the plaintiff's business was ruined. The trial court overruled a demurrer to this complaint, and the supreme court affirmed, saying:

"When a man starts an opposition place of business, not for the sake of profit to himself, but regardless of loss to himself, and for the sole purpose of driving his competitor out of business, and with the intention of himself retiring upon the accomplishment of his malevolent purpose, he is guilty of a wanton wrong and an actionable tort. In such a case he would not be exercising his legal right, or doing an act which can be judged separately from the motive which actuated him. To call such conduct competition is a perversion of terms. It is simply the application of force without legal justification, which in its moral quality may be no better than highway robbery."

3. If the defendant has a legal "right" to do what he does, how can the fact that he does it for the wrong purpose turn it into a tort? This at one time perplexed a good many courts, and it has been the subject of a good deal of discussion and exposition on the part of writers. See, for example, Ames, How Far an Act May Be a Tort Because of the Wrongful Motive of the Actor, 18 Harv.L.Rev. 411 (1905); Lewis, Should the Motive of the Defendant Affect the

Question of His Liability, 5 Colum.L.Rev. 107 (1905); Lawrence, Motive as an Element in Tort, 12 Maine L.Rev. 47 (1919); Duport, Disinterested Malevolence as an Actionable Wrong, 22 Ford.L.Rev. 185 (1953). The same problem has given trouble under the civil law. See Walton, Motive as an Element in Torts in the Common and in the Civil Law, 22 Harv.L.Rev. 501 (1909). Suppose there were two motives, one of revenge and one not entirely improper? See Beardsley v. Kilmer, 236 N.Y. 80, 140 N.E. 203 (1923).

4. Many of the cases involving interference with prospective contractual relations concern action of the defendant as a competitor for the business and prevailing over the plaintiff. As early as the Schoolmaster Case, Y.B. 11 Hen. IV, f. 47, pl. 21 (1410), it was held that the owner of an established school could not complain when a new school attracted his prospective pupils in competition. The leading modern decision is Mogul S.S. Co., Ltd. v. McGregor, Gow & Co., 23 Q.B.D. 598 (1889), affirmed in [1892] A.C. 25, where it was held that it was no tort for one group of shipowners to take business away from another by offering rebates to shippers, "smashing" rates, and concentrating ships where they would compete. See Katz v. Kapper, 71 Cal.App.2d 1, 44 P.2d 1060 (1935).

5. If it makes a difference for purposes of competition whether the plaintiff's interest is an existing contract or mere prospective advantage, how is a contract terminable at the will of either party to be classified for this purpose? The Restatement classifies it as the same as prospective advantage, thus giving a competitor the opportunity to persuade the third party to elect to terminate it. See § 768; McCluer v. Super Maid Cook–Ware Corp., 62 F.2d 426 (10th Cir.1932). How should an unenforceable contract be classified? See Guard–Life Corp. v. S. Parker Hardware Mfg. Corp., 50 N.Y.2d 183, 406 N.E.2d 445, 428 N.Y.S.2d 628 (1980), where the New York Court of Appeals divided 4 to 3, with able opinions on both sides. The majority held that it should be classified with a contract terminable at will.

6. A contract terminable at will, however, is at least a subsisting relation; and an action will lie for inducing its termination out of sheer spite, or "malice," for the purpose of injuring the plaintiff. Huskie v. Griffin, 75 N.H. 345, 74 A. 595 (1909); Ott v. Gandy, 66 Ga.App. 684, 19 S.E.2d 180 (1942). Or where the defendant is attempting to put pressure upon the plaintiff in order to coerce him into settling a claim or a lawsuit. London Guarantee & Acc. Co. v. Horn, 206 Ill. 493, 69 N.E. 526 (1903); United States F. & G. Co. v. Millonas, 206 Ala. 147, 89 So. 732 (1921).

7. Contracts that are illegal or against the public interest, as in the case of agreements intended to stifle competition in restraint of trade, are not protected against interference. Fairbanks Morse & Co. v. Texas Elec. Serv. Co., 63 F.2d 702 (5th Cir.1933).

8. Contracts to marry have received special treatment. Almost without exception, the courts have refused to hold that it is a tort to induce the parties to break them. Nelson v. Melvin, 236 Iowa 604, 19 N.W.2d 685 (1945); Brown v. Glickstein, 347 Ill.App. 486, 107 N.E.2d 267 (1952). The reason usually given is that contracts to marry are highly personal agreements, and anyone should be free to advise the parties to change their minds.

9. Inducement not to enter into a contract is normally of a third party, not the plaintiff. See Goldstein v. Kern, 82 Mich.App. 723, 267 N.W.2d 165 (1978). But preventing entry into the prospective relation may apply to either the plaintiff or a third person. See Byars v. Baptist Medical Centers, Inc., 361 So.2d 350 (Ala.1978) (hospital refused to permit nurse to be certified in nurses'

registry); Twin Falls Farm Distributing Inc. v. D & B Supply Co., 96 Idaho 351, 528 P.2d 1286 (1974) (removal of sign indicating new location of plaintiff).

STATE OF LOUISIANA ex rel. GUSTE v. M/V TESTBANK
United States Court of Appeals, Fifth Circuit (en banc), 1985.
752 F.2d 1019.

HIGGINBOTHAM, CIRCUIT JUDGE: We are asked to abandon physical damage to a proprietary interest as a prerequisite to recovery for economic loss in cases of unintentional maritime tort. We decline the invitation.

I. In the early evening of July 22, 1980, the M/V Sea Daniel, an inbound bulk carrier, and the M/V Testbank, an outbound container ship, collided at approximately mile forty-one of the Mississippi River Gulf outlet. At impact, a white haze enveloped the ships until carried away by prevailing winds, and containers aboard Testbank were damaged and lost overboard. The white haze proved to be hydrobromic acid and the contents of the containers which went overboard proved to be approximately twelve tons of pentachlorophenol, PCP, assertedly the largest such spill in United States history. The United States Coast Guard closed the outlet to navigation until August 10, 1980 and all fishing, shrimping, and related activity was temporarily suspended in the outlet and four hundred square miles of surrounding marsh and waterways. * * * [Numerous lawsuits, representing various interests,] were filed and consolidated before the same judge in the Eastern District of Louisiana. * * *

Defendants moved for summary judgment as to all claims for economic loss unaccompanied by physical damage to property. The district court granted the requested summary judgment as to all such claims except those asserted by commercial oystermen, shrimpers, crabbers and fishermen who had been making a commercial use of the embargoed waters. * * *

On appeal a panel of this court affirmed, concluding that claims for economic loss unaccompanied by physical damage to a proprietary interest were not recoverable in maritime tort. 728 F.2d 748 (5th Cir. 1984). The panel, as did the district court, pointed to the doctrine of *Robins Dry Dock & Repair Co. v. Flint,* 275 U.S. 303 (1927), and its development in this circuit. Judge Wisdom specially concurred, agreeing that the denial of these claims was required by precedent, but urging reexamination en banc. We then took the case en banc for that purpose. After extensive additional briefs and oral argument, we are unpersuaded that we ought to drop physical damage to a proprietary interest as a prerequisite to recovery for economic loss. To the contrary, our reexamination of the history and central purpose of this pragmatic restriction on the doctrine of foreseeability heightens our commitment to it. Ultimately we conclude that without this limitation foreseeability loses much of its ability to function as a rule of law.

* * *

III. The meaning of *Robins Dry Dock v. Flint*, 275 U.S. 303 (1927) (Holmes, J.) is the flag all litigants here seek to capture. We turn first to that case and to its historical setting.

Robins broke no new ground but instead applied a principle, then settled both in the United States and England, which refused recovery for negligent interference with "contractual rights." Stated more broadly, the prevailing rule denied a plaintiff recovery for economic loss if that loss resulted from physical damage to property in which he had no proprietary interest. *See, e.g., Byrd v. English*, 117 Ga. 191, 43 S.E. 419 (1903); *Cattle v. Stockton Waterworks Co.*, 10 Q.B. 453, 457 (C.A.1875). *See also* James, *Limitations on Liability for Economic Loss Caused by Negligence: A Pragmatic Appraisal*, 25 Vand.L.Rev. 43, 44–46 (1972) (discussing history of the rule); Carpenter, *Interference with Contract Relations*, 41 Harv.L.Rev. 728 (1928). Professor James explains this limitation on recovery of pure economic loss: "The explanation * * * is a pragmatic one: the physical consequences of negligence usually have been limited, but the indirect economic repercussions of negligence may be far wider, indeed virtually open-ended." James, *supra*, at 45.

Decisions such as *Stockton* illustrate the application of this pragmatic limitation on the doctrine of foreseeability. The defendant negligently caused its pipes to leak, thereby increasing the plaintiff's cost in performing its contract to dig a tunnel. The British court, writing fifty-two years before *Robins*, denied the plaintiff's claim. The court explained that if recovery were not contained, then in cases such as *Rylands v. Fletcher*, L.R. 1 Ex. 265 (1866), the defendant would be liable not only to the owner of the mine and its workers "but also to . . . every workman and person employed in the mine, who in consequence of its stoppage made less wages than he would otherwise have done." *Id.* at 457. [C]

1. In *Robins*, the time charterer of a steamship sued for profits lost when the defendant dry dock negligently damaged the vessel's propeller. The propeller had to be replaced, thus extending by two weeks the time the vessel was laid up in dry dock, and it was for the loss of use of the vessel for that period that the charterer sued. The Supreme Court denied recovery to the charterer, noting: " * * * no authority need be cited to show that, as a general rule, at least, a tort to the person or property of one man does not make the tort-feasor liable to another merely because the injured person was under a contract with that other unknown to the doer of the wrong. The law does not spread its protection so far * * * " 275 U.S. at 309. * * *

2. The principle that there could be no recovery for economic loss absent physical injury to a proprietary interest was not only well established when *Robins Dry Dock* was decided, but was remarkably resilient as well. * * * Indeed this limit on liability stood against a sea of change in the tort law. Retention of this conspicuous bright-line rule in the face of the reforms brought by the increased influence of the

school of legal realism is strong testament both to the rule's utility and to the absence of a more "conceptually pure" substitute. The push to delete the restrictions on recovery for economic loss lost its support and by the early 1940's had failed. *See* W. Prosser, *Law of Torts* § 129, at 938–940 (4th ed. 1971). In sum, it is an old sword that plaintiffs have here picked up.

3. Plaintiffs would confine *Robins* to losses suffered for inability to perform contracts between a plaintiff and others, categorizing the tort as a species of interference with contract. When seen in the historical context described above, however, it is apparent that *Robins Dry Dock* represents more than a limit on recovery for interference with contractual rights. Apart from what it represented and certainly apart from what it became, its literal holding was not so restricted. If a time charterer's relationship to its negligently injured vessel is too remote, other claimants without even the connection of a contract are even more remote. * * *

The language and the cases the *Robins* Court pointed to as "good statement[s]" of the principle make plain that the charterer failed to recover its delay claims from the dry dock because the Court believed them to be too remote. Notably, although the dry dock company did not know of the charter party when it damaged the propeller, delay losses by users of the vessel were certainly foreseeable. Thus *Robins* was a pragmatic limitation imposed by the Court upon the tort doctrine of foreseeability.

In a sense, every claim of economic injury rests in some measure on an interference with contract or prospective advantage. It was only in this sense that profits were lost in *Byrd v. English* when the electrical power to plaintiffs printing plant was cut off. The printing company's contractual right to receive power was interfered with, and in turn, its ability to print for its customers was impinged. That the printing company had a contract with the power company did not make more remote the relationship between its loss of profits and the tortious acts. To the contrary, the contract reduced this remoteness by defining an orbit of predictable injury smaller than if there were no contract between the power company and the printer. When the loss is economic rather than physical, that the loss caused a breach of contract or denied an expectancy is of no moment. If a plaintiff connected to the damaged chattels by contract cannot recover, others more remotely situated are foreclosed *a fortiori*. Indisputably, the *Robins Dry Dock* principle is not as easily contained as plaintiff would have it. * * *

4. This circuit has consistently refused to allow recovery for economic loss absent physical damage to a proprietary interest. [The court discusses in detail its own decisions and those of other circuits. It gives particular attention to Petition of Kinsman Transit Co., 388 F.2d 821 (2d Cir.1968) (Kinsman II, described in this casebook, *supra* page 315); and Union Oil Co. v. Oppen, 501 F.2d 558 (9th Cir.1974), described in this casebook page 1122.]

IV. Plaintiffs urge that the requirement of physical injury to a proprietary interest is arbitrary, unfair, and illogical, as it denies recovery for foreseeable injury caused by negligent acts. At its bottom the argument is that questions of remoteness ought to be left to the trier of fact. Ultimately the question becomes who ought to decide—judge or jury—and whether there will be a rule beyond the jacket of a given case. * * *

Those who would delete the requirement of physical damage have no rule or principle to substitute. Their approach fails to recognize limits upon the adjudicating ability of courts. We do not mean just the ability to supply a judgment; prerequisite to this adjudicatory function are preexisting rules, whether the creature of courts or legislatures. Courts can decide cases without preexisting normative guidance but the result becomes less judicial and more the product of a managerial, legislative or negotiated function.

Review of the foreseeable consequences of the collision of the [two ships in this case] demonstrates the wave upon wave of successive economic consequences and the managerial role plaintiffs would have us assume. The vessel delayed in St. Louis may be unable to fulfill its obligation to haul from Memphis, to the injury of the shipper, to the injury of the buyers, to the injury of their customers. Plaintiffs concede, as do all who attack the requirement of physical damage, that a line would need to be drawn—somewhere on the other side, each plaintiff would say in turn, of its recovery. Plaintiffs advocate not only that the lines be drawn elsewhere but also that they be drawn on an ad hoc and discrete basis. The result would be that no determinable measure of the limit of foreseeability would precede the decision on liability. We are told that when the claim is too remote, or too tenuous, recovery will be denied. Presumably then, as among all plaintiffs suffering foreseeable economic loss, recovery will turn on a judge or jury's decision. There will be no rationale for the differing results save the "judgment" of the trier of fact. Concededly, it can "decide" all the claims presented, and with comparative if not absolute ease. The point is not that such a process cannot be administered but rather that its judgments would be much less the products of a determinable rule of law. In this important sense, the resulting decisions would be judicial products only in their draw upon judicial resources.

The bright line rule of damage to a proprietary interest, as most, has the virtue of predictability with the vice of creating results in cases at its edge that are said to be "unjust" or "unfair." Plaintiffs point to seemingly perverse results, where claims the rule allows and those it disallows are juxtaposed—such as vessels striking a dock, causing minor but recoverable damage, then lurching athwart a channel causing great but unrecoverable economic loss. The answer is that when lines are drawn sufficiently sharp in their definitional edges to be reasonable and predictable, such differing results are the inevitable result—indeed, decisions are the desired product. But there is more. The line drawing sought by plaintiffs is no less arbitrary because the line drawing appears only in the outcome—as one claimant is found too remote and another is allowed to recover. The true difference is that plaintiffs' approach would mask the results. The present rule would be more candid, and in addition, by making results more predictable, serves a normative function. It operates as a rule of law and allows a court to adjudicate rather than manage.[12]

V. That the rule is identifiable and will predict outcomes in advance of the ultimate decision about recovery enables it to play additional roles. Here we agree with plaintiffs that economic analysis, even at the rudimentary level of jurists, is helpful both in the identification of such roles and the essaying of how the roles play. Thus it is suggested that placing all the consequence of its error on the maritime industry will enhance its incentive for safety. While correct, as far as such analysis goes, such *in terrorem* benefits have an optimal level. Presumably, when the cost of an unsafe condition exceeds its utility there is an incentive to change. As the costs of an accident become increasing multiples of its utility, however, there is a point at which greater accident costs lose meaning, and the incentive curve flattens. When the accident costs are added in large but unknowable amounts the value of the exercise is diminished.

With a disaster inflicting large and reverberating injuries through the economy, as here, we believe the more important economic inquiry is that of relative cost of administration, and in maritime matters administration quickly involves insurance. Those economic losses not recoverable under the present rule for lack of physical damage to a proprietary interest are the subject of first party or loss insurance. The rule change would work a shift to the more costly liability system of third party insurance. For the same reasons that courts have imposed limits on the concept of foreseeability, liability insurance might not be readily obtainable for the types of losses asserted here. As Professor James has noted, "[s]erious practical problems face insurers in handling insurance against potentially wide, open-ended liability. From an insurer's point of view it is not practical to cover, without limit, a liability that may reach catastrophic proportions, or to fix a reasonable premium on a risk that does not lend itself to actuarial measurement." James, *supra,* at 53. By contrast, first party insurance is feasible for many of the economic losses claimed here. Each businessman who might be affected by a disruption of river traffic or by a halt in fishing activities can protect against that eventuality at a relatively low cost since his own potential losses are finite and readily

---

12. Fuller, *The Forms and Limits of Adjudication,* 92 Harv.L.Rev. 353, 396 (1978). This case illustrates how our technocratic tradition masks a deep difference in attitudes toward the roles of a judiciary. The difference between the majority and dissenting opinions is far more than a choice between competing maritime rules. The majority is driven by the principle of self ordering and modesty for the judicial role; the dissent accepts a role of management which can strain the limits of adjudication.

discernible. Thus, to the extent that economic analysis informs our decision here, we think that it favors retention of the present rule.

* * *

VI.   Plaintiffs seek to avoid the *Robins* rule by characterizing their claims as damages caused by a public nuisance. They suggest that when a defendant unreasonably interferes with public rights by obstructing navigation or negligently polluting a waterway he creates a public nuisance for which recovery is available to all who have sustained "particular damages." As defined at common law such damages are those which are substantially greater than the presumed-at-law damages suffered by the general public as a result of the nuisance. *See generally Restatement (Second) of Torts* §§ 821B, 821C (1977); Prosser, *Private Action For Public Nuisance,* 52 Va.L.Rev. 997 (1966). Characterizing the problem as one of public nuisance, however, does not immediately solve the problems with plaintiffs' damage claims for pure economic losses. As Dean Prosser has explained, "courts have not always found it at all easy to determine what is sufficient 'particular damage' to support [a] private action [for a public nuisance], and some rather fine lines have been drawn in the decisions." W. Prosser, *Law of Torts* § 88 (4th ed. 1971). In drawing such lines today we are unconvinced that we should abandon the physical damage limitation as a prerequisite to recovery for economic loss.

The problem in public nuisance theory of determining when private damages are sufficiently distinct from those suffered by the general public so as to justify recovery is as difficult, if not more so, as determining which foreseeable damages are too remote to justify recovery in negligence. In each case it is a matter of degree, and in each case lines must be drawn. With economic losses such as the ones claimed here the problem is to determine who among an entire community that has been commercially affected by an accident has sustained a pecuniary loss so great as to justify distinguishing his losses from similar losses suffered by others. Given the difficulty of this task, we see no jurisprudential advantage in permitting the use of nuisance theory to skirt the *Robins* rule. * * *

VII.   In conclusion, having reexamined the history and central purpose of the doctrine of *Robins Dry Dock* as developed in this circuit, we remain committed to its teaching. Denying recovery for pure economic losses is a pragmatic limitation on the doctrine of foreseeability, a limitation we find to be both workable and useful. Nor do we find persuasive plaintiffs' arguments that their economic loses are recoverable under a public nuisance theory, as damages for violation of federal statutes, or under state law.

Accordingly, the decision of the district court granting summary judgment to defendants on all claims for economic losses unaccompanied by physical damage to property is affirmed.

GEE, CIRCUIT JUDGE, with whom CLARK, CHIEF JUDGE, joins, concurring: * * * It is my thesis that the dispute-resolution systems of courts are poorly equipped to manage disasters of such magnitude and that we should be wary of adopting rules of decision which, as would that contended for by the dissent, encourage the drawing of their broader aspects before us. * * * Such a system as ours works tolerably well in the traditional case for which it was developed, where the stakes are limited to who owns the farm or to some other finite benefit. Its deficiencies become immediately and painfully apparent, however, when the consideration of factors inherently extraneous to the dispute becomes necessary or desirable to resolving it. Of these factors, perhaps the most often encountered is that of financial reality. * * *

Extending theories of liability may not always be the more moral course, especially in such a case as this, where the extension, in the course of awarding damages to unnumbered claimants for injuries that are unavoidably speculative, may well visit destruction on enterprise after enterprise, with the consequent loss of employment and productive capacity which that entails.

[GARWOOD and WILLIAMS, JJ., concurred specially in separate opinions.]

WISDOM, CIRCUIT JUDGE, with whom ALVIN B. RUBIN, POLITZ, TATE, and JOHNSON, CIRCUIT JUDGES, join, dissenting.

Robins is the Tar Baby of tort law in this circuit. And the brier-patch is far away. This Court's application of *Robins* is out of step with contemporary tort doctrine, works substantial injustice on innocent victims, and is unsupported by the considerations that justified the Supreme Court's 1927 decision. * * *

The * * * bar for claims of economic loss unaccompanied by any physical damage conflicts with conventional tort principles of foreseeability and proximate cause. I would analyze the plaintiffs' claims under these principles, using the "particular damage" requirement of public nuisance law as an additional means of limiting claims. Although this approach requires a case-by-case analysis, it comports with the fundamental idea of fairness that innocent plaintiffs should receive compensation and negligent defendants should bear the cost of their tortious acts. Such a result is worth the additional costs of adjudicating these claims, and this rule of liability appears to be more economically efficient. Finally, this result would relieve courts of the necessity of manufacturing exceptions totally inconsistent with the expanded *Robins* rule of requiring physical injury as a prerequisite to recovery. * * *

II. THE INAPPLICABILITY OF *Robins Dry Dock* TO THIS CASE. Whatever the pragmatic justification for the original holding in *Robins,* the majority has extended the case beyond the warrant of clear necessity in requiring *a physical injury* for a recovery of economic loss in cases such as the one before the court. *Robins* prevented plaintiffs who were neither proximately nor foreseeably injured by a tortious act or product from recovering solely by claiming a contract with the injured party. The wisdom of this rule is apparent. This rule, however, has been expanded now to bar recovery by plaintiffs who would be allowed to recover if judged under conventional principles of foreseeability and proximate cause. * * *

Robins held only that if a defendant's negligence injures party *A*, and the plaintiff suffers loss of expected income or profits because it had a contract with *A*, then the plaintiff has no cause of action based on the defendant's negligence. * * *

It is a long step from *Robins* to a rule that requires *physical damage* as a prerequisite to recovery in maritime tort. The majority believes that the plaintiff's lack of any contractual connection with an injured party, taken with the *Robins* rule, forecloses liability: "If a plaintiff connected to the damaged chattels by contract cannot recover, others more remotely situated are foreclosed *a fortiori*."

This conclusion follows readily from the reasoning that if uninjured contracting parties are barred from recovery, and if contracting parties have a closer legal relationship than non-contracting parties, then a party who is not physically injured and who does not have a contractual relation to the damage is surely barred.

This argument would be sound in instances where the plaintiff suffered no loss *but for a contract* with the injured party. We would measure a plaintiff's connection to the tortfeasor by the only line connecting them, the contract, and disallow the claim under *Robins*. In the instant case, however, some of the plaintiffs suffered damages whether or not they had a contractual connection with a party physically injured by the tortfeasor. These plaintiffs do not need to rely on a contract to link them to the tort. The collision proximately caused their losses, and those losses were foreseeable. These plaintiffs are therefore freed from the *Robins* rule concerning the recovery of those who suffer economic loss because of an injury to a party with whom they have contracted.

Because *Robins* provides an overly restrictive bar on recovery, courts have over the years developed a number of exceptions. The traditional exceptions allow recovery for certain husband-wife claims, recovery for negligent interference with contract when the interference results from a tangible injury to the contractor's person or property, and recovery for persons employed on fishing boats to recover for lost income when the employment contract is disrupted by a third party's negligent injury to the ship or equipment. * * * [The opinion discusses other cases.]

One cannot deny that *Robins*'s policy of limiting the set of plaintiffs who can recover for a person's negligence and damage to physical property provides a "bright line" for demarcating the boundary between recovery and nonrecovery. Physical harm suggests a proximate relation between the act and the interference. At bottom, however, the requirement of a tangible injury is artificial because it does not comport with accepted principles of tort law. Mrs. Palsgraf, although physically injured, could not recover. Many other plaintiffs, although physically uninjured, can recover. * * *

With deference to the majority, I suggest, notwithstanding their well reasoned opinion, that the utility derived from having a "bright line" boundary does not outweigh the disutility caused by the limitation on recovery imposed by the physical-damage requirement. *Robins* and its progeny represent a wide departure from the usual tort doctrines of foreseeability and proximate cause. Those doctrines, as refined in the law of public nuisance, provide a rule of recovery that compensates innocent plaintiffs and holds the defendants liable for much of the harm proximately caused by their negligence.

III. AN ALTERNATE RULE OF RECOVERY. Rather than limiting recovery under an automatic application of a physical damage requirement, I would analyze the plaintiffs' claims under the conventional tort principles of negligence, foreseeability, and proximate causation. I would confine *Robins* to the "factual contours" of that case: A plaintiff's claim may be barred only if the claim is derived solely through contract with an injured party. The majority's primary criticism of this approach to a determination of liability is that it is potentially open ended. Yet, there are well-established tort principles to limit liability for a widely-suffered harm. Under the contemporary law of public nuisance, courts compensate "particularly" damaged plaintiffs for harms suffered from a wide-ranging tort, but deny recovery to more generally damaged parties. Those parties who are foreseeably and proximately injured by an oil spill or closure of a navigable river, for example, and who can also prove damages that are beyond the general economic dislocation that attends such disasters should recover whether or not they had contractual dealings with others who were also damaged by the tortious act. The limitation imposed by "particular" damages, together with refined notions of proximate cause and foreseeability, provides a workable scheme of liability that is in step with the rest of tort law, compensates innocent plaintiffs, and imposes the costs of harm on those who caused it.

A. Public Nuisance Law and Particular Damages. To assert a cause of action under public nuisance law, a plaintiff must assert "particular damages".[28] As Dean Prosser, Reporter for the Second Restatement of Torts, has written, although courts once required physical injury for a recovery under nuisance, this limitation was quickly abandoned: "The origin of this notion is obscure, although there is an obvious derivation from the old distinction between the actions of trespass and case. It has been expressly repudiated often enough; and the whole tenor of the cases in which particular damage has been found

---

28. The usual reason given for this requirement was that the plaintiff did not and could not represent the king, "and the vindication of royal rights was properly left to his duly constituted officers". Prosser, *Private Action for Public Nuisance,* 52 Va.L.Rev. at 1007. It seems to me, however, that the reasons were primarily practical. Courts wanted to limit access so that their time would not be consumed with complaints about public matters from a multitude of people who alleged they suffered some damage. This is especially true when damages are trivial. *See id.*

makes it quite clear that it is not now the law, if indeed it ever was."
Prosser, *Private Action for Public Nuisance,* 52 Va.L.Rev. 997, 1007–08
(1966).

Instead, to state a cause of action under public nuisance, a plaintiff
must prove "particular" damages from the alleged wrong. These
damages must be different in kind and degree from those suffered by
the general public. If other individuals suffer the same kind of damage, although in lesser degree, a private plaintiff might still recover.
Id. at 1009. "It is only when the class becomes so large and general as
to include all members of the public who come in contact with the
nuisance, that the private action will fail." *Id.*

Generally, pecuniary loss to the plaintiff results in particular
damage that sets him apart from the general public. When the
plaintiff is prevented from performing a specific contract, or is put to
additional expense in performing it, he can maintain his action because
the contract is an individual matter that is not common to the public.
Id. Also, those who have established businesses which make common
use of the public right that the nuisance infringes have been allowed
recovery. When a river is blocked, for example, a steamboat line
operating on it and a company that rafts logs or collects tolls for
passage have been permitted to maintain the action. There are also
cases in which commercial fisheries making a localized use of public
waters have been allowed to recover under nuisance law. And although plaintiffs who are delayed by a public nuisance cannot recover
money for the delay itself (e.g., the profitable opportunities that the
plaintiff had to forego), they can recover for actual additional expenses,
such as extra fuel, additional crew expenses, and greater demurrage
charges. * * *

B. *Applications of the Alternate Rule of Recovery.* Although the
requirement of "particular" damages provides a useful means of limiting claims, it must be applied within the general framework of the long-
standing requirements of proximate cause and foreseeability. It is, of
course, axiomatic in tort law that those who have been proximately and
foreseeably injured should recover. Although cause and effect can be
carried to limitless and unknowable lengths, courts have chosen to deal
with these concepts in a restrained manner that is practical and within
the scope of ordinary human understanding. These arbitrary limits
are delineated by "proximate" or "natural" causes. One must admit
that the line between recovery and nonrecovery may appear as arbitrary under a rule of proximate cause as a line created by a requirement
for physical damages. In a sense, any line that the courts draw to limit
recovery is arbitrary. But this dissent attempts to draw lines which
comport more closely with principles of intrinsic fairness than the line
based on physical damage.

1. *Requirements of Proximate Cause, Foreseeability, and "Particular" Damage.* First, the damage must be proximately caused by the
accident. Although this requirement will preclude some claims, it

provides relief for many of the claims for economic losses at issue here because of the great interdependence of the elements in the maritime industry. Hardly any claim escapes its imprimatur, and its overinclusiveness in defining the class of proper plaintiffs in this case limits its traditional utility. We therefore concentrate instead on the principles of foreseeability and "particular" damage, which are more useful here in delimiting recovery.

Foreseeability provides a mechanism for limiting claims that are proximately related to the accident. The requirement of foreseeability precludes recovery for damages resulting from gains that are allegedly lost because the accident altered the course of events upon which the expected gain was predicated. For example, the law should not compensate a shipper for purely speculative profits. Such predictions of the future are limitless in variety and incalculable in scope. Foreseeability requires that we confine the scope of claims to those arising from activities in process at the time of the accident or to claims that can be proven with certainty.

Finally, a plaintiff must assert a "particular" damage that distinguishes him from the general population. This requirement of "particular" damage basic in the law of public nuisance developed as a response to widespread losses. It was formulated to compensate those plaintiffs most seriously aggrieved by a tort while preventing open-ended liability. The distinction is useful here. In a maritime accident, a business suffers "particular" damages to the extent that the accident prevents the business from engaging in primary maritime activities, such as fishing or use of the waterways, or supplying commodities or services vital to primary maritime activities, such as those of bait and tackle shops, drydocks, marinas, and seafood wholesalers or processors. All other losses that are not peculiar to maritime activities are part of the general economic dislocation caused by the accident and are therefore not "particular".

A plaintiff must meet all three criteria for recovery. This test should provide a reasonably satisfactory equilibrium among compensation to plaintiffs, foreclosure of open-ended liability, and imposition of incentives on defendants to obtain insurance and to exercise due care.

2. Parties Entitled To Recover Under the Test. Shrimpers, crabbers, oystermen, and other commercial fishermen who routinely operated in those parts of the Mississippi River Gulf Outlet and the surrounding areas that were temporarily closed by the Coast Guard should recover. It is foreseeable that a ship carrying PCP might be in a collision and that some of the PCP containers might be lost overboard. It is also foreseeable that a PCP spill would result in the closure of fishing areas. Commercial fishermen have suffered damages that are proximately caused by this closure. Finally, they have suffered "particular" damages because, unlike members of the general public, the tort has denied them their livelihood in the maritime industry.

Ships that were trapped or delayed by the closure of the Gulf Channel Outlet are also entitled to recovery. It is foreseeable that a PCP spill would result in closure of the river to navigation. Such closure proximately caused shippers to incur additional expenses. The damage is "particular" because the operators of these ships have incurred additional pecuniary outlays in the course of their maritime activities. Ships that can alter their routes to reduce or eliminate losses should be denied recovery *pro tanto* because of their duty to mitigate damages. * * *

The land-based businesses that have claimed damages include drydocks, marinas, bait and tackle shops, seafood processors, seafood wholesalers, and restaurants. * * *

The general test of recovery for these claimants is whether their business of supplying a vital commodity or service to those engaged in the maritime industry has been interrupted by the collision, the closure, or the embargo. Marinas, for example, in the afflicted area should be allowed to recover. If all shipping and boating is suspended, then a marina or drydock in the area affected is unable to supply docking or repair services to users of the waterway. No mitigation of damages is possible. The same would be true for similarly situated boat charterers who supply marine "common carrier" services. Bait and tackle shops present a similar situation * * *

There is a point beyond which we cannot allow recovery. Seafood restaurants, for example, are not providers of a vital service to the afflicted area. Their damage is not sufficiently distinguishable from general economic dislocation to allow for recovery. They are too removed from the tortious act. A plaintiff may also be barred because it is not sufficiently involved with the afflicted area as a supplier of vital inputs peculiar to maritime activities. * * *

3. The Measure of Recovery. Generally, lost profits should be awarded to eligible claimants. Their livelihood has been compromised, and only a recovery of the value of that livelihood, however imprecise the calculation may be, can approach compensation for the losses they have suffered.

Commercial fishermen, oystermen, shrimpers, and crabbers should recover the profits that they lost during the closure of the area. * * *

Trapped shippers should recover for additional expenses of crew, fuel, demurrage, tug hire, or any other foreseeable direct expenses that these ships would not have incurred but for the accident. Loss of profit arising from maritime casualty may be awarded as long as it is proved with reasonable certainty. * * * We would * * * follow the "time-honored rule" that the "proper method of determining lost detention profits is to seek a fair average based on a number of voyages before and after."

IV. ADVANTAGES OF THE ALTERNATE RULE OF RECOVERY. The advantages of this alternate rule of recovery are that it compensates damaged plaintiffs, imposes the cost of damages upon those who have caused the harm, is consistent with economic principles of modern tort law, and frees courts from the necessity of creating a piecemeal quilt of exceptions to avoid the harsh effects of the *Robins* rule.

* * *

If tort law fails to compensate plaintiffs or to impose the cost of damages on those who caused the harm, it should be under a warrant clear of necessity. When a rule of law, once extended, leads to inequitable results and creates principles of recovery that are at odds with the great weight of tort jurisprudence, then that rule of law merits scrutiny. A strict application of the extension denies recovery to many plaintiffs who should be awarded damages. Conventional tort principles of foreseeability, proximate causation, and "particular" damages would avoid such unfairness.

It is true that application of foreseeability and proximate causation would necessitate case-by-case adjudication. But I have a more optimistic assessment of courts' ability to undertake such adjudication than the majority.[38] Certainly such an inquiry would be no different from our daily task of weighing such claims in other tort cases.

The majority opinion also states that the *Robins* rule, being free from the vagaries of factual findings in a case-by-case determination, serves an important normative function because it is more predictable and more "candid". Normative values would also be served, however, by eliminating a broad categorical rule that is insensitive to equitable and social policy concerns that would support allowing the plaintiffs' claims in many individual cases. In assessing "normative concerns", the courts' compass should be a sense of fairness and equity, both of which are better served by allowing plaintiffs to present their claims under usual tort standards. It is not clear, moreover, that a jury's finding of negligence in a case-by-case determination is "less the prod-

---

38. The majority criticizes foreseeability because it necessitates a case-by-case determination of liability. But this criticism of "foreseeability" as the criterion for judgment applies with equal force to well-established tort law for physical injury. The unquestioned concepts of foreseeability and proximate cause as established in *Palsgraf* and its progeny are open to the same condemnation that the majority makes of a rule of liability that would abandon *Robins:* "The result would be that no determinable measure of the limit of foreseeability would precede the decision on liability. We are told that where a claim is too remote, or too tenuous, recovery will be denied. Presumably then, as among all plaintiffs suffering foreseeable economic loss, recovery will turn on a judge['s] or jury's decision. * * * The

point is not that such a process cannot be administered but rather than its judgments would be much less the product of a determinable rule of law." [C]

The majority opinion favors a bright line rule, as opposed to a case-by-case determination of liability, because it enables courts to "adjudicate" rather than to "manage". A bright line rule such as the one the majority proposes, however, requires no adjudication whatsoever. Judges need merely to preside over a self-executing system of limited liability where recovery is predicated upon an easily determined physical injury. The application of such a rule, rather than a case-by-case determination, seems more "management" than adjudication.

uct of a determinable rule of law" when the finder of fact is guided in its determination by rules of law. The jury's finding of liability in this case would be no more "lawless" than a finding of proximate cause, foreseeability, and particular damages in a physical damage case.

*   *   *

The economic arguments regarding allocation of loss that purportedly favor the *Robins* rule of nonliability are not as clear to me as they appear to be to the majority. It is true that denial of recovery may effectively spread the loss over the victims. It is not certain, however, that victims are generally better insurors against the risk of loss caused by tortious acts having widespread consequences. Although the victims do possess greater knowledge of their circumstances and their potential damages, we do not know whether insurance against these types of losses is readily available to the businesses that may be affected. We do know that insurance against this kind of loss is already available for shippers. Imposition of liability upon the shippers helps ensure that the potential tortfeasor faces incentives to take the proper care. The majority's point is well taken that the incentives to avoid accidents do not increase once potential losses pass a certain measure of enormity. But in truth we have no idea what this measure is: Absent hard data, I would rather err on the side of receiving little additional benefit from imposing additional quanta of liability than err by adhering to *Robins'* inequitable rule and bar victims' recovery on the mistaken belief that a "marginal incentive curve" was flat, or nearly so. If a loss must be borne, it is no worse if a "merely" negligent defendant bears the loss than an innocent plaintiff absorb the damages.

V. Conclusion. The *Robins* approach restricts liability more severely than the policies behind limitations on liability require and imposes the cost of the accident on the victim, who is usually not in a superior position to obtain insurance to cover this loss. I would apply a rule of recovery based on conventional tort principles of proximate cause and foreseeability and limit eligibility only by the requirement that a claimant prove "particular" damages.

Alvin B. Rubin, Circuit Judge, with whom Wisdom, Politz and Tate, Circuit Judges, join, dissenting. *   *   * *Robins* should not be extended beyond its actual holding and should not be applied in cases like this, for the result is a denial of recompense to innocent persons who have suffered a real injury as a result of someone else's fault. We should not flinch from redressing injury because Congress has been indifferent to the problem.

---

1. This case follows the clear majority rule. But the disagreement in the opinions in the case is indicative of current ferment. For a strong case holding liability, see People Express Airlines, Inc. v. Consolidated Rail Corp., 100 N.J. 246, 495 A.2d 107 (1985) (tank car accident producing toxic fumes requiring evacuation of plaintiff's offices at Newark Airport, resulting in economic loss). For a good discussion of the two cases, see Robertson, Recovery in Louisiana

Tort Law for Intangible Economic Loss: Negligence Actions and the Tort of Intentional Interference with Contractual Relations, 46 La.L.Rev. 737 (1986). See also Rabin, Tort Recovery for Negligently Inflicted Loss, 37 Stan.L.Rev. 1513 (1985).

2. A different problem arises when plaintiff suffers physical harm to person or property. This is treated under the established rules of proximate cause for negligent conduct. See, e.g., Newlin v. New England Tel. & Tel. Co., 316 Mass. 234, 54 N.E.2d 929 (1944) (defendant negligently damaged electric line supplying power to heat plaintiff's mushrooms, which were lost). See also Consolidated Aluminum Corp. v. C.F. Bean Corp., 772 F.2d 1217 (5th Cir.1985), decided by the same court deciding the principal case, and holding that if there is physical damage there may be recovery for economic loss, too.

3. Representative cases denying recovery for economic loss include LaSociété Anonyme de Remorquage a Hélice v. Bennets, [1911] 1 K.B. 243 (English analog to *Robins' Dry Dock* case, discussed in principal case); Phoenix Professional Hockey Club v. Hermer, 108 Ariz. 482, 502 P.2d 164 (1972) (injury to goalie); Brink v. Wabash R. Co., 160 Mo. 87, 60 S.W. 1058 (1900) (personal injury to one whom plaintiff had contracted to support); Thompson v. Seaboard Air Line R. Co., 165 N.C. 377, 81 S.E. 315 (1914) (destruction of goods plaintiff had contracted to buy); Pure Oil Co. v. Boyle, 26 S.W.2d 161 (Tex.Com.App. 1930) (pollution of stream supplying plaintiff with water).

4. A few courts, in addition to *People Express,* have allowed recovery for economic loss resulting from negligent interference. See J'Aire v. Gregory, 24 Cal.3d 799, 157 Cal.Rptr. 407, 598 P.2d 60 (1979); Green Mountain Power Corp. v. General Elec. Corp., 496 F.Supp. 169 (D.C.Vt.1980); cf. Union Oil Co. v. Oppen, 501 F.2d 558 (9th Cir.1974) (commercial fishermen allowed to recover for fish loss due to oil spill from negligent offshore drilling).

5. See generally Schwartz, Economic Loss in American Tort Law, 23 San Diego L.Rev. 37 (1986); James, Limitations on Liability for Economic Loss Caused by Negligence: A Pragmatic Appraisal, 25 Vand.L.Rev. 43 (1972); Harvey, Economic Losses and Negligence, 50 Can.B.Rev. 580 (1972); Restatement (Second) of Torts § 766C; Notes, 16 Stan.L.Rev. 664 (1964), 88 Harv.L. Rev. 444 (1974), 60 Iowa L.Rev. 315 (1974).

ADLER, BARISH, DANIELS, LEVIN AND CRESKOFF
v. EPSTEIN

Supreme Court of Pennsylvania, 1978.
482 Pa. 416, 393 A.2d 1175.

ROBERTS, JUSTICE. Appellant, the law firm of Adler, Barish, Daniels, Levin and Creskoff, filed a Complaint in Equity in the Court of Common Pleas of Philadelphia. It sought to enjoin appellees, former associates of Adler Barish, from interfering with existing contractual relationships between Adler Barish and its clients. The court of common pleas entered a final decree granting the requested relief, but a divided Superior Court dissolved the injunction and dismissed Adler Barish's complaint. We granted allowance of appeal. We now reverse and direct reinstatement of the decree of the court of common pleas.

* * *

Appellee Alan Epstein's employment relationship with Adler Barish terminated on March 10, 1977. At his request, Epstein continued to use offices of Adler Barish until March 19. During this time, and through April 4, when Adler Barish filed its complaint, Epstein was engaged in an active campaign to procure business for his new law firm. He initiated contacts, by phone and in person, with clients of Adler Barish with open cases on which he had worked while a salaried employee. Epstein advised the Adler Barish clients that he was leaving the firm and that they could choose to be represented by him, Adler Barish, or any other firm or attorney.

Epstein's attempt to procure business on behalf of the firm did not stop with these contacts. He mailed to the clients form letters which could be used to discharge Adler Barish as counsel, name Epstein the client's new counsel and create a contingent fee agreement. Epstein also provided clients with a stamped envelope addressed to Epstein. [Similar actions were taken by other appellees.] * * *

On April 4, the court of common pleas granted Adler Barish preliminary relief, enjoining appellees' campaign to obtain the business of Adler Barish clients. One month later, on May 5, the court entered its final decree, which [enjoined defendants from communicating with Adler Barish clients who had active legal matters up until a certain date, except to announce the formation of the new firm. Those clients, however, were not prevented from voluntarily discharging Adler Barish and employing defendants or any other attorney. The Superior Court reversed, and the Supreme Court allowed an appeal.]

Adler Barish argues that appellees' conduct constitutes an intentional interference with existing contractual relationships between Adler Barish and its clients. According to Adler Barish, appellees' conduct is "deserving of censure, not encouragement." Appellees, on the other hand, contend that their conduct was "privileged," and that therefore no right of action for intentional interference lies. Moreover, they argue that their conduct is protected under the first and four-teenth amendments to the Constitution of the United States.

"[S]peech which does 'no more than propose a commercial transac-tion'" is no longer outside the protection of the first and fourteenth amendments to the Constitution of the United States. Virginia Phar-macy Board v. Virginia Consumer Council, 425 U.S. 748, 762 (1976) (striking down state statute deeming licensed pharmacists' advertising of prescription drugs "unprofessional conduct"); see Pennsylvania State Board of Pharmacy v. Pastor, 441 Pa. 186, 272 A.2d 487 (1971) (invali-dating Pennsylvania statute prohibiting advertising of "dangerous drugs" dispensible only with a physician's prescription). Accordingly, states are barred from imposing blanket prohibitions against truthful advertising of "routine" legal services. Bates v. State Bar of Arizona, 433 U.S. 350 (1977). Such a blanket prohibition "serves to inhibit the free flow of commercial information and to keep the public in igno-rance." Id., 433 U.S. at 365.

Nothing in the challenged decree prohibited appellees from engag-ing in the truthful advertising protected under *Bates*. Appellees could inform the general public, including clients of Adler Barish, of the availability of their legal services, and thus the "free flow of commer-cial information" to the public is unimpaired. Moreover, the injunction expressly permitted appellees to announce "formation of their new professional relationship in accordance with the requirements of DR 2–102 of the Code of Professional Responsibility." Appellees therefore were permitted to mail announcements to "lawyers, clients, former clients, personal friends, and relatives." Code of Professional Responsi-bility, DR 2–102(A)(2). This would include the very clients of Adler Barish whose business appellees sought. See Committee on Profession-al Ethics of the American Bar Association, Informal Decision No. 681 (August 1, 1963) (permitting departing attorney to send announcements "to those clients of the old firm for whom he had worked").

What the injunction did proscribe was appellees' "contacting and/ or communicating with those persons who up to and including April 1, 1977, had active legal matters pending with and were represented by the law firm of Adler, Barish, Daniels, Levin and Creskoff." Our task is to decide whether the conduct of appellees is constitutionally subject to sanction.

The Code of Professional Responsibility, DR 2–103(A) (as adopted, 1974), provides: "A lawyer shall not recommend employment, as a private practitioner, of himself, his partner, or associate to a non-lawyer who has not sought his advice regarding employment of a lawyer." See also Code of Professional Responsibility, DR 2–104(A). Appellees clearly violated this "proscription against self-recommenda-tion." [C] They recommended their own employment, even though clients of Adler Barish did not seek appellees' advice "regarding em-ployment of a lawyer."

Ohralik v. Ohio State Bar Association, 436 U.S. 447 (1978), makes plain that, after *Bates,* states may constitutionally impose sanctions upon attorneys engaging in conduct which violates these disciplinary rules, even though the conduct involves "commercial speech." In *Ohralik,* the state bar association suspended an attorney who "solicited" persons injured in an automobile accident by making visits to the hospital room where the persons were recovering. Mr. Justice Powell, speaking for the Court, emphasized that commercial speech does not enjoy the same constitutional protections traditionally afforded other forms of speech:

"In rejecting the notion that such speech 'is wholly outside the protection of the First Amendment,' *Virginia Pharmacy,* 425 U.S., at 761, we were careful not to hold 'that it is wholly undifferentiable from other forms' of speech. Id., at 771 n. 24. We have not discarded the 'commonsense' distinction between speech proposing a commercial transaction, which occurs in an area traditionally subject to government regulation, and other varieties of speech. Ibid. To require a parity of constitutional protection for commercial and noncommercial speech alike could invite dilution, simply by a leveling process, of the force of the Amendment's guarantee with respect to the latter kind of speech. Rather than subject the First Amendment to such a devitalization, we instead have afforded commercial speech a limited measure of protection, commensurate with its subordinate position in the scale of First Amendment values, while allowing modes of regulation that might be impermissible in the realm of noncommercial expression.

* * *

"[T]he State does not lose its power to regulate commercial activity deemed harmful to the public whenever speech is a component of that activity. Neither *Virginia Pharmacy* nor *Bates* purported to cast doubt on the permissibility of these kinds of commercial regulation." Id., 436 U.S. at 455–456. In rejecting the attorney's constitutional claim, the Court determined that the state's interests were important enough to support regulation of the attorney's conduct. * * * " [The conduct involved solicitation in person.]

Just as in *Ohralik,* appellees' conduct frustrates, rather than advances, Adler Barish clients' "informed and reliable decisionmaking." After making Adler Barish clients expressly aware that appellees' new firm was interested in procuring their active cases, Epstein provided the clients the forms that would sever one attorney-client relationship and create another. Epstein's aim was to encourage speedy, simple action by the client. All the client needed to do was to "sign on the dotted line" and mail the forms in the self-addressed, stamped envelopes. * * *

Thus, appellees were actively attempting to induce the clients to change law firms in the middle of their active cases. Appellees' concern for their line of credit and the success of their new law firm gave them an immediate, personally created financial interest in the clients' decisions. In this atmosphere, appellees' contacts posed too great a risk that clients would not have the opportunity to make a careful, informed decision. * * * [W]e must reject appellees' argument and conclude that, just as in *Ohralik,* the Constitution permits regulation of their conduct. * * *

Thus, we turn to whether the court of common pleas properly concluded that Adler Barish is entitled to relief. In Birl v. Philadelphia Electric Co., 402 Pa. 297, 167 A.2d 472 (1961), this Court adopted Restatement of Torts § 766 and its definition of the right of action for intentional interference with existing contractual relations. There, we stated:

"At least since Lumley v. Gye (1853), 2 Ell. & Bl. 216, 1 Eng.Rul. Cas. 706, the common law has recognized an action in tort for an intentional, unprivileged interference with contractual relations. It is generally recognized that one has the right to pursue his business relations or employment free from interference on the part of other persons except where such interference is justified or constitutes an exercise of an absolute right: Restatement, Torts, § 766. * * *

In its continuing effort to provide the judicial system orderly and accurate restatements of the common law, the American Law Institute has reviewed each section of the Restatement of Torts, including Section 766. Restatement (Second) of Torts § 766 (Tent.Draft No. 23, 1977), states the Institute's present view of what constitutes the elements of the cause of action before us:

"*Intentional Interference with Performance of Contract by Third Person.* One who intentionally and improperly interferes with the performance of a contract (except a contract to marry) between another and a third person by inducing or otherwise causing the third person not to perform the contract, is subject to liability to the other for the pecuniary loss resulting to the other from the third person's failure to perform the contract." * * *

An examination of this case in light of Restatement (Second) of Torts § 766, reveals that the sole dispute is whether appellees' conduct is "improper." There is no doubt that appellees intentionally sought to interfere with performance of the contractual relations between Adler Barish and its clients. While still at Adler Barish, appellees' behavior, particularly their use of expected fees from Adler Barish clients' cases, indicates appellees' desire to gain a segment of the firm's business. This pattern of conduct continued until the court of common pleas enjoined it. Indeed, appellees' intentional efforts to obtain a share of Adler Barish's business were successful. The record reveals that several clients signed the forms Epstein prepared on behalf of appellees notifying Adler Barish that the clients no longer wished the services of Adler Barish. Likewise, the record reveals that Adler Barish and its clients were parties to valid, existing contracts.

In assessing whether appellees' conduct is "improper," we bear in mind what this Court stated in Glenn v. Point Park College, 441 Pa.

[474,] 482, 272 A.2d [895,] 899, where we analyzed "privileges" in conjunction with the closely related right of action for intentional interference with prospective contract relations:

"The absence of privilege or justification in the tort under discussion is closely related to the element of intent. As stated by Harper & James, The Law of Torts, § 6.11, at 513–14: ' * * * where, as in most cases, the defendant acts at least in part for the purpose of protecting some legitimate interest which conflicts with that of the plaintiff, a line must be drawn and the interests evaluated. This process results in according or denying a privilege which, in turn, determines liability.' What is or is not privileged conduct in a given situation is not susceptible of precise definition. Harper & James refer in general to interferences which 'are sanctioned by the "rules of the game" which society has adopted', and to 'the area of socially acceptable conduct which the law regards as privileged,' id. at 510, 511, and treat the subject in detail in §§ 6.12 and 6.13."

We are guided, too, by Restatement (Second) of Torts § 767, which focuses on what factors should be considered in determining whether conduct is "improper:"

"In determining whether an actor's conduct in intentionally interfering with an existing contract or a prospective contractual relation of another is improper or not, consideration is given to the following factors:

"(a) The nature of the actor's conduct,

"(b) The actor's motive,

"(c) The interests of the other with which the actor's conduct interferes,

"(d) The interests sought to be advanced by the actor,

"[(e) The social interests in protecting the freedom of action of the actor and the contractual interests of the others,]

"[(f)] The proximity or remoteness of the actor's conduct to the interference and

"[(g)] The relations between the parties." [17]

17. Thus, new Restatement (Second) of Torts focuses upon whether conduct is "proper," rather than "privileged." Compare Restatement of Torts, § 766 (1939) ("[e]xcept as stated in Section 698 [(relating to contracts to marry)], *one who without a privilege to do so,* induces or otherwise purposely causes a third person not to ¶ (a) perform a contract with another, or ¶ (b) enter into or continue a business relation with another ¶ is liable to the other for the harm caused thereby" (emphasis added)). Comment b to Restatement (Second) of Torts, supra at § 767, explains the shift in inquiry:

"*Privilege to Interfere, or Interference not Improper.* Unlike other intentional torts such as intentional injury to person or property, or defamation, this branch of tort law has not developed a crystallized set of definite rules as to the existence or nonexistence of a privilege to act in the manner stated in §§ 766, 766A or 766B. Because of this fact, this Section is expressed in terms of whether the interference is improper or not rather than in terms of a specific privilege to act in the manner specified. The issue in each case is whether the interference is improper or not under the circumstances; whether, upon a con-

We find nothing in the "'rules of the game' which society has adopted" which sanctions appellees' conduct. Indeed, the rules which apply to those who enjoy the privilege of practicing law in this Commonwealth expressly disapprove appellees' method of obtaining clients. * * * We find such a departure from "[r]ecognized ethical codes" "significant in evaluating the nature of [appellees'] conduct." Restatement (Second) of Torts, supra at § 767 comment c.[19] All the reasons underlying our Disciplinary Rules' "proscription against [appellees'] self-recommendation," *Berlant Appeal,* 458 Pa. at 443, 328 A.2d at 474, especially the concern that appellees' contacts too easily could overreach and unduly influence Adler Barish clients with active cases, are relevant here.

Appellees' conduct adversely affected more than the informed and reliable decisionmaking of Adler Barish clients with active cases. Their conduct also had an immediate impact upon Adler Barish. Adler Barish was prepared to continue to perform services for its clients and therefore could anticipate receiving compensation for the value of its efforts. Moreover, * * * Adler Barish's fee agreements with clients were a source of anticipated revenue protected from outside interference.

It is true that, upon termination of their employment relationship with Adler Barish, appellees were free to engage in their own business venture. * * * But appellees' right to pursue their own business interests is not absolute. "[U]nless otherwise agreed, after the termination of the agency, the agent * * * has a duty to the principal not to take advantage of a still subsisting confidential relation created during the prior agency relation". Restatement (Second) of Agency, supra at § 396(d).

Appellees' contacts were possible because Adler Barish partners trusted appellees with the high responsibility of developing its clients' cases. From this position of trust and responsibility, appellees were able to gain knowledge of the details, and status, of each case to which appellees had been assigned. In the atmosphere surrounding appellees' departure, appellees' contacts unduly suggested a course of action for Adler Barish clients and unfairly prejudiced Adler Barish. No public interest is served in condoning use of confidential information which has these effects. Clients too easily may suffer in the end.[21] * * *

sideration of the relative significance of the factors involved, the conduct should be permitted without liability, despite its effect of harm to another."

[The bracketed material in the list of the factors indicates changes in the section between the Tentative Draft and the published volume. (Ed.)]

19. Restatement (Second) of Torts, supra at § 767 comment c, provides in full:

"*Business Ethics and Customs.* Recognized ethical codes for a particular area of

business activity and established customs or practices regarding approved or disapproved actions or methods may also be significant in evaluating the nature of the actor's conduct as a factor in determining whether his interference with the plaintiff's economic relations was improper or not."

21. Moreover, appellees neither occupied the same status, nor pursued the same goals, as the defendants in Watch Tower Bible & Tract Society v. Dougherty, 337 Pa.

In *Ohralik,* MR. JUSTICE POWELL emphasized:

"[T]he state bears a special responsibility for maintaining standards among members of the licensed professions. * * * 'The interest of the States in regulating lawyers is especially great since lawyers are essential to the primary governmental function of administering justice, and have historically been "officers of the courts." ' [C] While lawyers act in part as 'self-employed businessmen,' they also act 'as trusted agents of their clients, and as assistants to the court in search of a just solution to disputes.' " Ohralik v. Ohio State Bar Association, 436 U.S. at 460. Our "special responsibility" includes the obligation to assure that persons seeking professional legal assistance receive the quality advocacy and fair treatment they justifiably expect. Our responsibility also includes the duty to provide an atmosphere conducive to proper attorney-client relationships, including those situations where, as here, associates assist other members of a firm in rendering legal services. Consistent with these jurisprudential concerns, our supervisory authority over practitioners in our courts, prior decisions, the Code of Professional Responsibility, and Restatement (Second) of Torts, it must be concluded that the court of common pleas correctly determined that Adler Barish is entitled to relief.

Order of the Superior Court reversed and court of common pleas directed to reinstate its final decree. Each party pay own costs.

MANDERINO, J., filed a dissenting opinion.

---

1. *Violating ethical standards.* See Sustick v. Slatina, 48 N.J.Super. 134, 137 A.2d 54 (1957) (ultimate question is whether the conduct was "both injurious and transgressive of generally accepted standards of common morality or of law," whether it was "sanctioned by the rules of the game," and constituted "right and just dealing"); Leonard Duckworth, Inc. v. Michael L. Field & Co., 516 F.2d 952 (5th Cir.1975) ("sharp dealing or overreaching or other conduct below the behavior of fair men similarly situated"); Herron v. State Farm Mut. Ins. Co., 56 Cal.2d 202, 363 P.2d 310, 14 Cal.Rptr. 294 (1961) (rules of Nat'l Conf.Comm. on Adjusters).

2. *Other kinds of wrongful conduct.* These include physical violence, threats and intimidation: South Central Livestock Dealers, Inc. v. Security State Bank, 551 F.2d 1346 (5th Cir.1977); Williams v. Maloof, 223 Ga. 640, 157 S.E.2d 479 (1967). Misrepresentation: Gold v. Los Angeles Democratic League,

286, 11 A.2d 147 (1940). There, we concluded that defendants, leaders of their church, "cannot be mulcted in damages for protesting against the utterances of one who they believe attacks their church and misrepresents its teachings or for inducing their adherents to make similar protests." 337 Pa. at 288, 11 A.2d at 148. * * *

Appellees suggest that injunctive relief was inappropriate. "It is well settled that equity will act to prevent unjustified interference with contractual relations." Neel v. Allegheny County Memorial Park, 391 Pa. 354, 357, 137 A.2d 785, 787 (1958). Accord, Restatement (Second) of Torts, supra at § 766 comment t (approving injunctive relief "in appropriate circumstances"). Given appellees' interest in maintaining the line of credit established on the basis of Adler Barish cases, and appellees' express intent to continue their effort to gain Adler Barish clients, we believe the court of common pleas could properly conclude that equitable relief was necessary to protect all the interests at stake in this case.

49 Cal.App.3d 365, 125 Cal.Rptr. 732 (1975); Johnson v. Gustafson, 201 Minn. 629, 277 N.W. 252 (1938). Defamation: Wild v. Rarig, 302 Minn. 419, 234 N.W.2d 775 (1975); Woody v. Brush, 178 App.Div. 698, 165 N.Y.S. 867 (1917). Threats of suit: Pratt Food Co. v. Bird, 148 Mich. 631, 112 N.W. 701 (1907); Gresh v. Potter–McCune Co., 235 Pa.Super. 537, 344 A.2d 540 (1975).

LEIGH FURNITURE AND CARPET COMPANY v. ISOM
Supreme Court of Utah, 1982.
657 P.2d 293.

OAKS, JUSTICE: In 1970, Leigh Furniture and Carpet Co., a corporation, sold a furniture business in St. George to T. Richard Isom on a contract specifying a $20,000 down payment for immediate possession, with the balance of $60,000 at $500 per month plus interest for ten years.

In 1975, when the contract balance was $27,000, Leigh Furniture (hereafter "the Leigh Corporation") brought this action against Isom to repossess the business, terminate his interest under the contract, and obtain a deficiency judgment for any sums due after liquidation. Isom denied that he was in default under the agreement, alleged his tender and the Leigh Corporation's refusal to accept the sum due under the contract, and counterclaimed for $100,000 damages caused when the Corporation intentionally and maliciously forced him out of business and into bankruptcy. Isom also sought punitive damages.

The jury found for Isom in all respects, including compensatory damages of $65,000 and punitive damages of $35,000 on his counterclaim. [The trial court granted a remittitur to $13,000 on the punitive damages and entered judgment for $78,000. The Corporation appealed, and Isom cross-appealed on the issue of punitive damages.]

The issues on this appeal are exclusively concerned with Isom's recovery on the counterclaim. They are: (1) whether Utah has a cause of action for intentional interference with prospective economic relations; and, if so, (2) whether that tort was proved on the facts of this case; and (3) whether the punitive damages should have been reduced.

* * *

[The facts are stated in detail, indicating how Leigh (principal owner of the Corporation) constantly harassed Isom, interfering with his operation of the business and his relations with customers and making unreasonable and contradictory demands. These facts will become specific as the opinion discusses the application of the law. The bringing of this suit itself is one instance.]

Leigh Furniture first contends that Isom's recovery cannot be sustained as an interference with contract because the evidence showed no conduct which "intentionally and improperly interferes with the performance of a contract * * * between another and a third person by inducing or otherwise causing the third person not to perform the contract." [Cc] In this case, the only contract in evidence was the contract between Isom and the Leigh Corporation. It is settled that one party to a contract cannot be liable for the tort of interference with contract for inducing a breach by himself or the other contracting party. [Cc] Isom having failed to prove a cause of action for intentional interference with contract, we cannot sustain the verdict on that theory.

However, the right of action for interference with a specific contract is but one instance, rather than the total class, of protections against wrongful interference with advantageous economic relations. [Cc]. We therefore proceed to consider whether the jury's verdict for Isom can be sustained on the basis of the related tort of interference with prospective economic relations.　＊　＊　＊

The tort of intentional interference with prospective economic relations reaches beyond protection of an interest in an existing contract and protects a party's interest in prospective relationships of economic advantage not yet reduced to a formal contract (and perhaps not expected to be). [Cc] Although previously faced with arguments or circumstances presenting the issue [cc], we have never expressly resolved the question of whether Utah recognizes this tort. We now resolve that question, in the affirmative.

The plethora of decided cases and abundant literature on the tort of intentional interference with prospective economic relations has been helpful in our consideration. In summarizing the history of this tort, the Restatement (Second) of Torts, ch. 37, "Interference with Contract or Prospective Contractual Relation" (1979), observes that its elements are a curious blend of the principles of liability for intentional torts (in which the plaintiff proves a prima facie case of liability, subject to the defendant's proof of justification) and for negligent torts (in which the plaintiff must prove liability based on the interplay of various factors). The disagreement and confusion incident to this blend of intentional and negligent tort principles has produced two different approaches to the definition of this tort.

Influenced by the model of the intentional tort, many jurisdictions and the first Restatement of Torts define the tort of intentional interference with prospective economic relations as a prima facie tort, subject to proof of privilege as an affirmative defense. To recover, the plaintiff need only prove a prima facie case of liability, *i.e.,* that the defendant intentionally interfered with his prospective economic relations and caused him injury. As with other intentional torts, the burden of going forward then shifts to the defendant to demonstrate as an affirmative defense that under the circumstances his conduct, otherwise culpable, was justified and therefore privileged.　＊　＊　＊

The problem with the prima facie-tort approach is that basing liability on a mere showing that defendant intentionally interfered with plaintiff's prospective economic relations makes actionable all sorts of contemporary examples of otherwise legitimate persuasion, such as efforts to persuade others not to eat certain foods, use certain substances, engage in certain activities, or deal with certain entities.

The major issue in the controversy—justification for the defendant's conduct—is left to be resolved on the affirmative defense of privilege. In short, the prima facie approach to the tort of interference with prospective economic relations requires too little of the plaintiff.

Under the second approach, which is modeled after other negligent torts, the plaintiff must prove liability based on the interplay of various factors. The Restatement (Second) of Torts now defines an actionable interference with prospective economic relations as an interference that is both "intentional" and "improper." Id. at § 766B. Under this approach, the trier of fact must determine whether the defendant's interference was "improper" by balancing and counterbalancing seven factors, including the interferor's motive, the nature of his conduct and interests, and the nature of the interests with which he has interfered. Id. at § 767. In those jurisdictions which have followed the negligence model, the plaintiff bears the burden of proving that in view of all of these factors the defendant's interference was improper. This obviously imposes a very significant burden on the plaintiff and magnifies the difficulty of resolving some contested issues on the pleadings. * * * [The court describes holdings in other states, including Top Service Body Shop, Inc. v. Allstate Insurance, Co., 283 Or. 201, 582 P.2d 1365 (1978).]

We recognize a common-law cause of action for intentional interference with prospective economic relations, and adopt the Oregon definition of this tort. Under this definition, in order to recover damages, the plaintiff must prove (1) that the defendant intentionally interfered with the plaintiff's existing or potential economic relations, (2) for an improper purpose or by improper means, (3) causing injury to the plaintiff. Privilege is an affirmative defense, Searle v. Johnson, Utah, 646 P.2d 682 (1982), which does not become an issue unless "the acts charged would be tortious on the part of an unprivileged defendant."
* * *

Under the trial court's definition of "justification," the jury had to find that the Corporation's conduct was "wrongful or malicious" before they could find for Isom. Those terms are functionally equivalent to "improper means or improper purpose." Conversely, if the jury found that the Corporation "was reasonably acting to protect a legitimate economic interest of its own, arising out of or in conjunction with the May 14, 1970 agreement" (such as its right to terminate the agreement or to assert an honest claim thereunder), then the Corporation's conduct was "justified and privileged and not wrongful or malicious," and Isom was not entitled to recover. In view of this instruction, we conclude that the verdict for Isom was clearly based on the jury's finding that the Corporation was not reasonably acting to protect its legitimate economic interest under the agreement, and is tantamount to a finding that the Corporation's conduct was "wrongful or malicious." The trial court's instruction imposed an even heavier burden on the plaintiff (here, the counterclaimant, Isom) than our definition, since it required the plaintiff to negate the existence of any justification. Consequently, we proceed to consider whether the evidence was sufficient to sustain a verdict for the cause of action as we have defined it.

Reviewing the record, we conclude that there was sufficient evidence to sustain the jury's verdict against the Leigh Corporation for intentional interference with prospective economic relations that caused injury to Isom.

There was ample evidence that Isom had business relationships with various customers, suppliers, and potential business associates, and that Leigh, the former owner of the business, understood the value of those relationships. There was also substantial competent evidence that the Corporation, through Leigh, his wife, and his bookkeeper, intentionally interfered with and caused a termination of some of those relationships (actual or potential). Their frequent visits to Isom's store during business hours to confront him, question him, and make demands and inquiries regarding the manner in which he was conducting his business repeatedly interrupted sales activities, caused his customers to comment and complain, and more than once caused a customer to leave the store. Driving away an individual's existing or potential customers is the archetypical injury this cause of action was devised to remedy. [Cc].

Other actions by which the Leigh Corporation imposed heavy demands on Isom's time and financial resources to the detriment of his ability to attract and retain customers and conduct the other activities of his business included: numerous letters of complaint, Leigh's demand for an audit of Isom's books and inventory during the busy holiday season, his continued threats to cancel the contract and sell the building and business to another buyer, his refusal to pay the contracted share of the heating bills or the cost of repairing the furnace and the store's broken window, his refusal of the tendered payment of the balance due under the contract, and his suit for repossession, termination, and injunction. Leigh's refusals also prevented Isom from consummating potentially advantageous business associations with Hunter, with Talbot, and finally with Applegate, all experienced retailers able to contribute expertise and additional capital to Isom's business.

Taken in isolation, each of the foregoing interferences with Isom's business might be justified as an overly zealous attempt to protect the Corporation's interests under its contract of sale. As such, none would establish the intentional interference element of this tort, though some might give rise to a cause of action for breach of specific provisions in the contract or of the duty of good faith performance which inheres in every contractual relation. Even in small groups, these acts might be explained as merely instances of aggressive or abrasive—though not illegal or tortious—tactics, excesses that occur in contractual and commercial relationships. But in total and in cumulative effect, as a course of action extending over a period of three and one-half years and culminating in the failure of Isom's business, the Leigh Corporation's acts cross the threshold beyond what is incidental and justifiable to what is tortious. The Corporation's acts provide sufficient evidence to establish two of the elements in the definition of this tort: an intentional interference with present or prospective economic relations that caused injury to the plaintiff. ✱ ✱ ✱

The evidence was also sufficient to support the verdict under the requirement that the intentional interference with prospective economic relations (in this case, Isom's relations with his customers, suppliers, and potential business associates) must have been for an improper purpose or by the use of improper means. ✱ ✱ ✱

The alternative of improper purpose (or motive, intent, or objective) will support a cause of action for intentional interference with prospective economic relations even where the defendant's means were proper. ✱ ✱ ✱

Because it requires that the improper purpose predominate, this alternative takes the long view of the defendant's conduct, allowing objectionable short-run purposes to be eclipsed by legitimate long-range economic motivation. Otherwise, much competitive commercial activity, such as a businessman's efforts to forestall a competitor in order to further his own long-range economic interests, could become tortious. In the rough and tumble of the marketplace, competitors inevitably damage one another in the struggle for personal advantage. The law offers no remedy for those damages—even if intentional—because they are an inevitable byproduct of competition. Problems inherent in proving motivation or purpose make it prudent for commercial conduct to be regulated for the most part by the improper means alternative, which typically requires only a showing of particular conduct.

The alternative of improper purpose will be satisfied where it can be shown that the actor's predominant purpose was to injure the plaintiff. ✱ ✱ ✱

As noted earlier, there is substantial evidence that the Leigh Corporation deliberately injured Isom's economic relations. But that injury was not an end in itself. It was an intermediate step toward achieving the long-range financial goal of profitably reselling the building free of Isom's interest. Because that economic interest seems to have been controlling, we must conclude that the evidence in this case would not support a jury finding that the Corporation's predominant purpose was to injure or ruin Isom's business merely for the sake of injury alone. ✱ ✱ ✱

The alternative requirement of improper means is satisfied where the means used to interfere with a party's economic relations are contrary to law, such as violations of statutes, regulations, or recognized common-law rules. Such acts are illegal or tortious in themselves and hence are clearly "improper" means of interference, [cc] unless those means consist of constitutionally protected activity, like the exercise of First Amendment rights. [Cc] "Commonly included among improper means are violence, threats or other intimidation, deceit or misrepresentation, bribery, unfounded litigation, defamation, or disparaging falsehood." Top Service Body Shop, Inc., 582 P.2d at 1371 & n. 11. Means may also be improper or wrongful because they violate "an established standard of a trade or profession." Id. at 1371.

By forcing Isom to defend what appear to have been two groundless lawsuits, the Leigh Corporation was clearly employing an improper means of interference with Isom's business. Such use of civil litigation as a weapon to damage another's business, besides being an intolerable waste of judicial resources, may give rise to independent causes of action in tort for abuse of process and malicious prosecution. [Cc]. The jury's verdict can therefore be sustained on the ground that the Leigh Corporation intentionally interfered with Isom's economic relations by improper means.

There is also another basis for affirming that verdict on the basis of improper means.

A deliberate breach of contract, even where employed to secure economic advantage, is not, by itself, an "improper means." Because the law remedies breaches of contract with damages calculated to give the aggrieved party the benefit of the bargain, there is no need for an additional remedy in tort (unless the defendant's conduct would constitute a tort independent of the contract).

Neither a deliberate breach of contract nor an immediate purpose to inflict injury which does not predominate over a legitimate economic end will, by itself, satisfy this element of the tort. However, they may do so in combination. This is so because contract damages provide an insufficient remedy for a breach prompted by an immediate purpose to injure, and that purpose does not enjoy the same legal immunity in the context of contract relations as it does in the competitive marketplace. As a result, a breach of contract committed for the immediate purpose of injuring the other contracting party is an improper means that will satisfy this element of the cause of action for intentional interference with economic relations.

Two cases illustrate how breach of contract (or lease), when done with a purpose to injure, satisfy this element of the tort. In both cases, the defendant committed a breach not just to obtain relief from its obligation under the contract or lease (for which contract damages would have made the plaintiff whole), but to achieve a larger advantage by injuring the plaintiff in a manner not compensable merely by contract damages. In both cases, the defendant ruined the plaintiff's business by its breach, and in both cases the plaintiff was given substantial damages for the tort of interference with prospective economic relations. [The court describes in detail Buxbom v. Smith, 23 Cal.2d 535, 145 P.2d 305 (1944); and Cherberg v. Peoples National Bank of Washington, 88 Wash.2d 595, 564 P.2d 1137 (1977).]

In the case at bar, the Leigh Corporation breached its contract in various ways.

It breached its implied duty to exercise all of its rights under the contract reasonably and in good faith. [Cc] Leigh's unexplained refusal to approve Isom's prospective business partners without consideration of their merits indicates an absence of good faith and provides evidence that the Corporation's breach was intended to deprive Isom's business of additional capital and valuable expertise which (at least with regard to Talbot) Leigh himself had repeatedly urged Isom to acquire. * * * In addition, Leigh, his wife, and his bookkeeper continually interrupted sales activities with their visits, letters, threats, and demands, causing customers to comment and complain and sometimes to leave. Although the contract entitled the Corporation, as lessor and secured party, to reasonable supervision of Isom's business, the jury had sufficient evidence to conclude that this conduct constituted an unreasonable exercise of contract rights and/or was done in bad faith for the purpose of injuring Isom's business relations.

The Corporation also breached its contractual duty by refusing Isom's tender of the balance of the purchase price and by refusing to appoint an appraiser to establish a price for the sale of the entire building, thereby preventing Isom from exercising his purchase option. There is evidence of Leigh's purpose in the fact that he openly regretted his contract with Isom and frequently expressed his desire to "get Richard out" of the business and building. Furthermore, he continually contacted prospective buyers for the building, even approaching two of Isom's employees for this purpose.

All of the above provide substantial evidence from which the jury could have concluded that the Corporation breached its express and implied contractual duties for the purpose of ruining Isom's business and obtaining possession of the building in order to sell it more profitably elsewhere. By themselves, the Corporation's breaches would not satisfy the requirement of "improper means," but they could do so when coupled with the improper purpose of injuring Isom. In combination, a breach of contract and an intent to injure satisfy the improper means requirement for the cause of action for intentional interference with prospective economic relations. * * *

In defining the tort of intentional interference with prospective economic relations, we reject the two extremes of the prima facie tort and the balancing-of-factors approach. Instead, we adopt the Oregon definition, under which the plaintiff must prove that the intentional interference with existing or potential economic relations that caused injury to the plaintiff was done for an improper purpose or by improper means. The jury instructions in this case, which in effect required a finding that the Corporation's conduct was "wrongful or malicious," were sufficiently in harmony with this definition to permit the jury to return a verdict under it. There was sufficient evidence of intentional interference and causation.

To satisfy the alternative of improper purpose, the defendant's purpose to injure the plaintiff must predominate over all other purposes, including the long-range purpose of achieving some personal economic gain. Under this definition, the evidence is insufficient to justify a verdict against Leigh Corporation on the basis of improper purpose. Improper means refers primarily to actions that are contrary to law, such as violations of statutes, regulations, or recognized common-law rules. The Leigh Corporation's pursuit of two groundless lawsuits against Isom was an improper means. A deliberate breach of contract for the purpose of injuring the contracting party is also an improper means, and there is also sufficient evidence to sustain the jury's verdict on that basis. * * *

On Isom's cross-appeal, the judgment is modified to reinstate the full amount the jury awarded as punitive damages.

As modified in respect to punitive damages, the judgment on the verdict for defendant Isom is affirmed. * * *

SMITH v. FORD MOTOR CO.
Supreme Court of North Carolina, 1976.
289 N.C. 71, 221 S.E.2d 282.

[Plaintiff Smith had been brought to Winston Salem to take over as president and general manager of an unprofitable Ford dealership. A new company, Cloverdale Ford, was organized, plaintiff owning some shares and having an option to purchase all shares at the end of five years. The contract provided that the other shareholders could terminate his contract if he "proved to be unsatisfactory" in their opinion or if the Ford Motor Company found him unsatisfactory "from the standpoint of profits earned or the manner of management."

Plaintiff performed satisfactorily and made the dealership a profitable one. But he became active in "the Ford Dealer Alliance," a group of Ford dealers who had gathered together for the purpose of protecting their own interest in transactions with the defendant, the Ford Motor Company.

Plaintiff alleges that Ford was displeased when he refused to discontinue these activities, and it threatened to conclude the franchise with Cloverdale unless plaintiff's contract was terminated, with the result that plaintiff was discharged. Action against Ford for "wrongfully, maliciously and unlawfully exerting pressure" to produce plaintiff's dismissal. The lower court dismissed the action and the Court of Appeals affirmed.]

LAKE, JUSTICE. * * * The question presented to us by this appeal is: If A, knowing B is employed by C under a contract terminable at will by C, maliciously causes C to discharge B, which C would not otherwise have done, by threatening, otherwise, to terminate A's own contract with C, which contract is terminable at will by A, the sole motive for A's action being A's resentment of B's personal affiliation with an organization disapproved by A, which affiliation does not impair C's performance of its contract with A, can B maintain in the courts of this State an action against A for damages? Our conclusion is that he can. * * *

There was no breach by Cloverdale of its contract with the plaintiff, but an exercise by Cloverdale of its legal right to terminate that contract. This circumstance does not, however, defeat the plaintiff's right of action against Ford. [C] The wrong for which the courts may give redress includes also the procurement of the termination of a contract which otherwise would have continued in effect. [Cc] As Mr. Justice Hughes, later Chief Justice, said in Truax v. Raich, 239 U.S. 33 (1945), "The fact that the employment is at the will of the parties, respectively, does not make it one at the will of others." * * *

Ford contends that it did nothing to cause the termination of the plaintiff's contract with Cloverdale, except to threaten to terminate its own franchise agreement with Cloverdale if the plaintiff were not discharged, and that its contract with Cloverdale was expressly terminable at will by Ford upon the giving of proper notice. Consequently, Ford says, the complaint charges Ford with doing nothing except that which Ford had a right to do and its exercise of its own lawful right to terminate its contract with Cloverdale cannot be a tort against the plaintiff. * * *

Professor Carpenter, writing in 41 Harv.L.Rev. 728, 746 (1928), under the title "Interference With Contract Relations," says:

"The privilege [to interfere] is conditional or qualified; that is, it is lost if exercised for a wrong purpose. In general, a wrong purpose exists where the act is done other than as a reasonable and bona fide attempt to protect the interest of the defendant which is involved."

In Oakes, Organized Labor and Industrial Conflicts, § 500 (1927), it is said:

"Because one may refrain from entering into a contract with another, or may exercise a right under a contract with another, without incurring any liability to such other, irrespective of his motive in the matter, he has been said to have an absolute right to do so. This has led some courts to hold that such right is likewise absolute as to third parties. But it does not follow that because he may have an absolute right to refrain from contracting with another, or to exercise a right growing out of a contract with such other, that it is not a qualified right as to third persons injuriously affected thereby." * * *

We hold: To exert economic pressure upon an employer for the purpose of procuring the termination by him of his employment of another is a qualified privilege even though, as between the actor and the employer, the actor has an absolute right to do that which produces such pressure upon the employer. The actor is liable in damages to the employee for so procuring such termination of the employment if the actor so acted with malice and for a reason not reasonably related to the protection of a legitimate business interest of the actor. If the reason for such action be the employee's personal participation in an association not approved by the actor, the burden is upon the actor, when sued for damages for so procuring the termination of the employment relation to show that the participation by the employee in such association afforded reasonable basis for the belief that a legitimate business interest of the actor would thereby be damaged or imperiled.

The complaint of the plaintiff in this action alleges the malicious interference by the defendant with the plaintiff's employment relation without such justification. Consequently, it states a cause of action * * * and the dismissal of the action as against the Ford Motor Company was error. * * *

As to the defendant Ford Motor Company, reversed and remanded.

---

1. For other cases of exercise of economic pressure, see Johnson v. Warnaco, Inc., 426 F.Supp. 44 (D.C.Miss.1976); Jackson v. Travelers Ins. Co., 403 F.Supp. 986 (D.C.Tenn.1975); Cherburg v. People's Nat'l Bank of Washington, 88 Wash.2d 595, 564 P.2d 1137 (1977).

2. If a number of persons combine together to bring pressure by refusal to deal, it is called a boycott, thus immortalizing the name of a pariah during the troubled days in Ireland.

"Captain Boycott, an Englishman, who was agent of Lord Earne and a farmer of Lough Mask, served notices upon the lord's tenants, and they in turn, with the surrounding population, resolved to have nothing to do with him, and, as far as they could prevent it, not to allow anyone else to have. His life appeared to be in danger, and he had to claim police protection. His servants fled from him, and the awful sentence of excommunication could hardly have rendered him more helplessly alone for a time. No one would work for him, and no one would supply him with food. He and his wife were compelled to work their own fields with the shadows of armed constabulary ever at their heels; Justin MacCarthy's England Under Gladstone." Bouvier's Law Dictionary, summarizing statement in State v. Glidden, 55 Conn. 46, 8 A. 890 (1887).

3. Boycotts are "primary," where the defendant himself refuses to deal with the plaintiff, or "secondary," where he seeks to compel third persons to refuse to deal, by refusing to have dealings with them if they do.

Competition in business was held under the common law to be a sufficient justification for a primary boycott on the part of a single defendant. This has been extensively limited by statute in many jurisdictions. Discrimination in competition has been penalized by the Robinson–Patman Act, and by various acts in the states, which are beyond the scope of this book.

Secondary boycotts open up whole areas of law, particularly as to restraint of trade, antitrust acts, and labor disputes, where many complex problems have arisen, also beyond the scope of this book. They are usually dealt with in courses on unfair competition, antitrust or restraint of trade, or labor law. See Smith v. American Guild of Variety Artists, 349 F.2d 975 (8th Cir.1965); Notes, 52 Geo.L.J. 392, 406 (1964), 19 Sw.L.J. 567 (1965).

4. In Bear v. Mennonite Church, 462 Pa. 330, 341 A.2d 105 (1975), plaintiff alleged that his business collapsed after bishops of the Mennonite Church ordered all members to "shun" him. "Shunning" was a church practice that had been traditionally applied to persons who violated church rules and were excommunicated. Defendant contended that plaintiff fell within that group. Should plaintiff have a claim in tort?

5. When the defendant has no legitimate purpose and acts for a purpose that the law does not accept, he becomes liable if he interferes with a contractual relation of the plaintiff. Thus there is liability when the defendant procures the discharge of a workman to prevent him from bringing a suit, as in Johnson v. Aetna Life Ins. Co., 158 Wis. 56, 147 N.W. 32 (1914); to force him to settle it, as in London Guarantee & Accident Co. v. Horn, 206 Ill. 493, 69 N.E. 526 (1903); to force him to pay a debt, or to extort money from him, as in Warschauer v. Brooklyn Furniture Co., 159 App.Div. 81, 144 N.Y.S. 257 (1913); Hill Grocery Co. v. Carroll, 228 Ala. 376, 136 So. 789 (1931). See also Alyeska Pipeline Service Co. v. Aurora Air Service, 604 P.2d 1090 (Alaska 1979) (termination clause in contract cannot be used solely for purpose of injuring sub-contractor, without other justification).

RICHARDSON v. LA RANCHERITA LA JOLLA, INC.

California Court of Appeal, 1979.
98 Cal.App.3d 73, 159 Cal.Rptr. 285.

[Plaintiff Breg Corporation was lessee of a restaurant from La Rancherita, the lessor, under a lease providing that the lease was not subject to assignment or subletting without the written consent of the lessor. Operating at a loss, Breg negotiated a sale of the assets and assignment of the lease to Bomze, contingent upon obtaining consent of defendant. Defendant indicated that it would give consent only after a renegotiation involving increased rental and a cost-of-living escalation provision. To avoid this obstacle the Breg shareholders agreed to sell their shares to Bomze, Breg thus to continue as lessee. Defendant insisted that its consent was necessary. The sale of the stock was thus postponed for over a month but finally closed. Breg and its shareholders then sought a declaratory judgment that the consent was not necessary and recovery of damages for tortious interference with the contract between Breg's shareholders and Bomze.

The trial court gave a partial summary judgment declaring that the lessor's consent was not required, and after trial damages of $7,233.06 were awarded.]

WIENER, ASSOCIATE JUSTICE. * * * The lease provision in dispute prohibits occupancy by anyone contrary to its terms without the written consent of the lessor. Other than the issue of consent to the assignment, neither party has argued that occupancy by Breg with new shareholders violated the lease in any other respect. The lease itself did not provide that an individual was responsible for rent or liable for the performance of any other provision. The parties, at the time of their negotiations, were apparently satisfied with a corporation as lessee, making no provision to the contrary. Thus the court was asked to bar the transfer of shares of common stock in a valid corporation, permissible under corporate law, solely because of a lease provision prohibiting assignment of the lease, but containing no restraints on transfer of stock ownership. The court, under these circumstances, declined to do so, recognizing the separateness of the corporate form and properly granted plaintiffs' motion for partial summary judgment.

(See Ser–Bye Corp. v. C.P. & G. Markets, 78 Cal.App.2d [915,] 920–921, 179 P.2d 342.) * * *

An action in tort "will lie for the intentional interference by a third person with a contractual relationship either by unlawful means or by means otherwise lawful when there is a lack of sufficient justification." * * * Justification for the interference is an affirmative defense and not an element of plaintiff's cause of action. [Cc]

Defendants' arguments rest on the premise that their actions were justified. They contend their conduct was not done solely to damage plaintiffs [c], for they were motivated by the good faith belief based on their lawyers' advice that their consent to the assignment of the lease was required. Withholding their consent pending negotiations with the prospective tenant to improve their financial interest was thus proper.

The test of whether there is justification for conduct which induces a breach of contract turns on a balancing of the social and private importance of the objective advanced by the interference against the importance of the interest interfered with, considering all the circumstances including the nature of the actor's conduct and the relationship between the parties. [Cc]

In harmony with the general guidelines of the test for justification is the narrow protection afforded to a party where (1) he has a legally protected interest, (2) in good faith threatens to protect it, and (3) the threat is to protect it by appropriate means. (Rest., 2d Torts, § 773, pp. 52–53.) * * *

The financial interest which defendants sought to protect included their right to continue to receive rent and to demand compliance with the essential terms of their lease. The determinative question thus becomes whether their claim was asserted in good faith. Or, phrased differently in the context of this case, was there any reasonable basis, either factually or legally, for their counsel to believe their distinguishing of the Ser–Bye case had merit.

Ser–Bye Corp. v. C.P. & G. Markets, supra, involved a lease provision prohibiting assignment similar to the one in the case before us. In affirming a judgment on the pleadings in an unlawful detainer action in favor of the corporate lessee, the court held the sale of stock of the corporation did not constitute an assignment to void the lease. [The court found no distinguishable differences in the language of the lease clauses.]

Factual issues including elements which bear on "good faith" were properly before the trial court. [C] There was ample evidence for the court to find that defendants' concern with the assignment of the lease was only incidental to their predominant motive of terminating the existing lease to obtain a new lease upon more favorable terms to themselves. Defendants made no effort to inquire into the financial condition of the successor stockholders or their intended method of operation. They restricted their negotiations to increasing their financial return and not to preserve their interest as lessor. The record is devoid of any evidence that defendants believed their leasehold interest was threatened by the new owners. The court was justified in finding that "[t]he transaction as ultimately consummated was clearly within the parameters of the *Ser–Bye* case. * * *"

Something other than sincerity and an honest conviction by a party in his position is required before justification for his conduct on the grounds of "good faith" can be established. There must be an objective basis for the belief which requires more than reliance on counsel. It is the opinion of counsel that must be examined, recognizing that creative and conscientious lawyers should be given every opportunity to challenge outmoded precedent to permit constructive development of the law. [C] However, to merely equate reliance on an attorney's advice with "good faith" is to shield those parties from liability who seek and obtain counsel. To create such a blanket rule of immunity is unwarranted.

Judgment affirmed.

COLOGNE, ACTING P.J., concurs.

STANIFORTH, ASSOCIATE JUSTICE, dissenting. I respectfully dissent.

The trial court, in granting the challenged partial summary judgment, violated * * * elemental procedural rules governing the granting or denial of a summary judgment. * * * [It] failed to discern a multitude of factual issues that precluded granting of the summary judgment. * * *

The trial court, in granting the motion for partial summary judgment, ignored this factual dispute as to the meaning of the lease language and concluded that the decision in Ser–Bye Corp. v. C.P. & G. Markets, supra was the controlling law. *Ser–Bye* held that a sale of stock of a corporation did not constitute an assignment of the lease. The *Ser–Bye* decision is neither good law nor applicable factually to the situation at bar. * * *

A second * * * set of rules requires the case must be reversed with direction to dismiss the proceedings. Here the lessor is required to respond in damages because he had the temerity to contend—and on basis of sound legal advice which sustained him in his contention—that the attempted assignment was in violation of express terms of the lease prohibiting assignment or a change in occupancy without written consent. * * * We have not yet reached a state in this society where either a landlord or tenant may not advance a position in good faith as regards an interpretation of a document between them. There is a right and a duty upon the part of the landlord or tenant if they in good faith believe that the other party is breaching their lease to maintain that position to defend it stoutly.

The cases cited in the majority opinion involve an unjustified intermeddling with another's contractual relationships or expectancies. They authorize recovery on a tort basis from a "malicious interloper." [C] This is not a case of an officious intermeddler. Here the lessor and lessee have a valid, subsisting lease contract which clearly prohibits assignment without consent. The lessor has attempted to enforce in good faith the terms of his contract. Such a fact setting conceptually bears no relationship to the tort of interference with the prospective economic advantage. [C] In such species of interference with another's contractual relationship, the "intentional" character of the interferences, the "motive," becomes legally significant. The conceded facts here establish justification. The lessor's motives for asserting his *legal* rights are totally irrelevant. * * *

I would reverse and remand the cause with directions to dismiss proceedings.

Hearing denied [by the Supreme Court], BIRD, C.J., and TOBRINER, J., dissenting.

---

1. Of the three types of interference illustrated by the first three cases in this section, which one does this case come under?

2. On asserting a bona fide claim, see Restatement (Second) of Torts § 773, McReynolds v. Short, 115 Ariz. 166, 564 P.2d 389 (App.1977); Beane v. McMullen, 265 Md. 585, 291 A.2d 37 (1972); Allen v. Ramsey, 170 Okl. 430, 41 P.2d 658 (1935).

3. Several cases hold that there is a privilege to give disinterested advice to withdraw from a contractual relation. See Walker v. Cronin, 107 Mass. 555 (1871); Arnold v. Moffitt, 30 R.I. 310, 75 A. 502 (1910); Coakley v. Degner, 191 Wis. 170, 210 N.W. 359 (1926). But the privilege is limited to cases where the advice is requested, or otherwise called for by the circumstances, as distinguished from officious intermeddling in matters which are not the defendant's concern. Calborm v. Knudtzon, 65 Wash.2d 157, 396 P.2d 148 (1964). On whether the advice is disinterested if it also benefits other advisees, see Welch v. Bancorp. Management Advisors, Inc., 296 Or. 208, 675 P.2d 172 (1983).

4. *Burden of Proof.* Some courts place the burden on the plaintiff to show that the interference was "improper," or "malicious"—i.e., without justification. M & M Rental Tools, Inc. v. Melcham, Inc., 94 N.M. 449, 612 P.2d 241 (1980); Glenn v. Point Park College, 441 Pa. 474, 272 A.2d 895 (1971). Others place the burden on the defendant to show that the interference was justified. Lowell v. Mother's Cake & Cookie Co., 79 Cal.App.3d 13, 144 Cal.Rptr. 664 (1978). Still others suggest that it may vary, depending on the factual situation. Johnson v. Radde, 293 Minn. 409, 196 N.W.2d 478 (1972). See Restatement (Second) of Torts § 767, Comment *k*.

BRIMELOW v. CASSON
Chancery Division, 1923.
[1924] 1 Ch. 302.

[The case deals with the misfortunes of a burlesque troupe known as the Wu Tut Tut Revue, which was touring the south counties of England under the managership of one Jack Arnold. Arnold underpaid the chorus girls so badly that they were forced to eke out a living by plying another and an older trade. As the sordid tale was unfolded in court, it appeared that one of the girls had even been compelled by economic necessity to live in immorality with an abnormal and deformed dwarf, who was a member of the company. The secretary of the Actors' Association, named Lugg, took hold of the situation on behalf of the girls, and persuaded the owners of the theaters with which Arnold had contracts to cancel them unless higher wages were paid. This resulted in the troupe being stranded in the town of Maidenhead. A bill in equity was brought on behalf of the owners of the troupe against the representatives of the union to enjoin them from inducing the breaches of contract.]

RUSSELL, J. It is difficult to speak of this condition of things with restraint. A young girl, almost a child, forced by underpayment to continue in sexual association with this abnormal man is, to my mind, a terrible and revolting tragedy, but the question which I have to decide is whether the acts of the defendants make them liable to an action at the suit of the plaintiff, or whether in the circumstances of this case there exists a sufficient justification for the acts which in the absence of such justification would be actionable. * * *

Prima facie interference with a man's contractual rights and with his right to carry on his business as he wills is actionable; but it is clear on the authorities that interference with contractual rights may be justified; a fortiori the inducing of others not to contract with a person may be justified. * * *

[The unions] desire in the interest of the theatrical calling and the members thereof to stop such underpayment with its evil consequences. The only way they can do so is by inducing the proprietors of theatres not to allow persons like the plaintiff the use of their theatres, either by breaking contracts already made or by refusing to enter into contracts. They adopt this course as regards the plaintiff as the only means open to them of bringing to an end his practice of underpayment which, according to their experience, is fruitful of danger to the theatrical calling and its members. In these circumstances, have the defendants justification for their acts? That they would have the sympathy and support of decent men and women I can have no doubt. But have they in law justification for those acts? As has been pointed out, no general rule can be laid down as a general guide in such cases, but I confess that if justification does not exist here I can hardly conceive the case in which it would be present. These defendants, as it seems to me, owed a duty to their calling and to its members, and, I am tempted to add, to the public, to take all necessary peaceful steps to terminate the payment of this insufficient wage, which in the plaintiff's company had apparently been in fact productive of those results which their past experience had led them to anticipate. "The good sense" of this tribunal leads me to decide that in the circumstances of the present case justification did exist. * * *

The result is that the action is dismissed with costs.

1.　Accord, that a reasonable and disinterested motive for the protection of other individuals, or the public, will justify intentional interference with contract: Caverno v. Fellows, 300 Mass. 331, 15 N.E.2d 483 (1938) (high school supervisor, principal and superintendent reporting on conduct of teacher); Gregory v. Dealers' Equipment Co., 156 Tenn. 273, 300 S.W. 563 (1927) (agent protecting interest of his principal); Stott v. Gamble, [1916] 2 K.B. 504 (preventing improper public entertainment); Legris v. Marcotte, 129 Ill.App. 67 (1906) (mother seeking to exclude diseased person from her child's school); Porter v. King County Medical Society, 186 Wash. 410, 58 P.2d 367 (1936) (enforcing ethical rules of medical association).

2.　Instances of privilege to interfere with prospective advantage, in interest of others or the public include: NAACP v. Claiborne Hardware Co., 458 U.S. 886 (1982) (picketing and boycott activity to prevent racial discrimination); Gott v. Berea College, 156 Ky. 376, 161 S.W. 204 (1913) (for protection of its students, college ordered them not to deal with plaintiff); Julie Baking Co. v. Graymond, 152 Misc. 846, 274 N.Y.S. 250 (1934) (picketing plaintiff's bakery in protest against the high price of bread); Harris v. Thomas, 217 S.W. 1068 (Tex. Civ.App.1920) (acting to protect ethical standards of medical association).

3.　No class of law students could be expected to ignore the principal case. At the Harvard Law School in 1938, one of the students rose to the occasion by stating the case in class as follows:

"The Ballad of Brimelow v. Casson

The ladies of the chorus of the Wututtut Revue

Through economic pressure had their virtue to eschew.

'Twas economic pressure that accounts for their proclivity

To supplement their earnings with professional activity.

That poor benighted maiden didn't say this just for fun,

'If Snow White lived with seven dwarfs, well I can live with one.'

An economic royalist, Jack Arnold was his name,

Began this competition with the houses of ill fame.

'Twas some ironic destiny by which the troupe was led

That prompted them to end their tour at England's Maidenhead.

The matter was reported to our hero, labor's Lugg,

Who vowed he'd get Jack Arnold even though it meant the jug.

He gathered up the union's most persuasive breach inducers

To tell this sad and sordid tale to Arnold's pet producers.

I'm proud to say the latter said they didn't give a damn

About Jack Arnold's contract, and they closed him like a clam.

I'm prouder of the Chancellor, who didn't bat an eye,

But calmly told Jack Arnold that his action wouldn't lie.

So here's to Merrie England, let the Union Jack unfurl,

The Chancellor and Heaven will protect the working girl."

—Published in Langdell Lyrics of 1938 by Professor W. Barton Leach, of the Harvard Law School.

DUFF v. ENGELBERG
District Court of Appeal of California, 1965.
237 Cal.App.3d 505, 47 Cal.Rptr. 114.

PIERCE, PRESIDING JUSTICE. The sole question on this judgment-roll appeal by defendants Dalton Engelberg and Ann Engelberg from a plaintiff's judgment against them is, as stated in [their] brief, "whether a vendee under an executory contract to purchase real property can recover in addition to specific performance of said contract along with consequential and incidental relief damages, both compensatory and exemplary, against a third party who induced the vendor not to go forward with the sale. * * * "

Affirming the trial court's judgment we hold that he can, that the measure of damages is not the same in the cause of action against the third party tort-feasors as it is in the count for specific performance against the vendor. * * *

Plaintiffs entered into a binding contract for the purchase of a lot in Carmichael, Sacramento County, from defendants McCoy. Defendants Engelberg and Campbell, who did not want plaintiffs and their family to live in the neighborhood because plaintiffs are Negroes, maliciously caused the McCoys to refuse to perform the contract. * * * The court decreed specific performance with incidental damages against defendants McCoy. These damages consisted of interest at a higher rate that plaintiffs had to pay while they pursued their remedy of specific performance. The court also gave judgments against the Engelbergs and the Campbells for $1,000 compensatory damage and $500 punitive damages. * * *

In California Auto Court Ass'n v. Cohn, 98 Cal.App.2d 145, 219 P.2d 511 [upon similar facts] a trial court judgment for defendants on demurrer was reversed. The reviewing court stated * * *: "Each participant in the wrongful act is responsible as a joint tortfeasor for all damages ensuing from the wrong * * *." The court also stated * * *: "In the various California cases wherein damages have been awarded or injunctive relief granted for unjustifiable interference with contractual relations, it is apparent that the plaintiff is not confined to an action ex contractu against the party with whom he contracted." * * *

Professor Prosser has this to say with reference to the question under discussion: " * * * Although older cases sometimes held to the contrary, it is now agreed that the fact that there is an available action against the party who breaks the contract is no defense to the one who induces the breach, since the two are joint wrongdoers, and each is liable for the loss. Even a judgment in such action, returned unsatisfied, is no defense. Where substantial loss has occurred, one line of cases tends to adopt the contract measure of damages, limiting recovery to those damages which were within the contemplation of the parties when the original contract was made. Another, apparently somewhat more uncertain of its ground, has applied a tort measure, but has limited the damages to those which are sufficiently 'proximate' with some analogy to the rules as to negligent torts. A third, perhaps the most numerous, has treated the tort as an intentional one, and has allowed recovery for unforeseen expenses, as well as for mental suffering, damage to reputation, and punitive damages, by analogy to the cases of intentional injury to person or property. *In the light of the intent and the lack of justification necessary to the tort, this seems the most consistent result."* Prosser, Torts, 3d ed. pp. 972–973. We accept the rule last stated as being the proper one for the reasons quoted in italics.

The vice of appellants' reasoning (stated above) is that specific performance plus incidental relief does not really make the plaintiff whole. The suit for specific performance gives to plaintiff the property he was entitled to receive and the incidental expenses and other damages to which he was subjected in his efforts to pursue and recover that property. These are the expectable—Hadley v. Baxendale, [9 Ex. 341, 156 Eng.Rep. 145 (1854)]—type of damages. They are not necessarily the total damages suffered when the tort is intentional. * * *

The court awarded plaintiffs only incidental damages against defendant vendors. Plaintiffs had not charged them as members of the conspiracy. Against the conspirators committing the intentional harm, plaintiffs were entitled to recover damages for all harm resulting from their acts. [Cc]

Of course there can be no double recovery of compensatory damages. [Cc] There was no showing that a double recovery occurred here. This is a judgment-roll appeal. The findings of the court show that the award of incidental damages against defendant vendors was the difference between the rate of interest plaintiffs had to pay on moneys borrowed and the normal bank rate. There is no showing as to what the basis was for the allowance of compensatory damages in the sum of $1,000 against the defendant conspirators. The finding that plaintiffs were damaged in that sum by said defendants was a sufficient finding of ultimate fact. [C] There was no request for special findings. We cannot assume that there was an allowance of a double recovery of damages.

The allowance of punitive damages was proper. The complaint had alleged, and the court found, that the acts of the conspirators were malicious. * * *

The judgment is affirmed.

---

1. In accord, as to specific performance of the contract plus damages against the one inducing the breach, is Gentile Bros. Corp. v. Rowena Homes, Inc., 352 Mass. 584, 227 N.E.2d 338 (1967).

2. Of the three approaches to the measure of damages stated by the Prosser quotation in the principal case, the later decisions have tended definitely to swing toward the third. Thus such damages as mental suffering in an

appropriate case, damage to reputation, and unforeseen expenses, have been recovered. See Notes, 30 Colum.L.Rev. 232 (1930), 7 Santa Clara L.Rev. 140 (1966). On the scope of recovery for mental suffering, see Mooney v. Johnson Cattle Co., 291 Or. 209, 634 P.2d 1333 (1981).

3. The intentional character of the tort, and the necessary lack of justification, obviously make it an appropriate one for punitive damages, as in the principal case.

4. There are cogent reasons for believing that interference with advantageous relations is now well on the way to becoming the next burgeoning field of tort law, following medical malpractice and products liability. A prime step in its attaining this prominence is the recent case of Pennzoil Co. v. Texaco, Inc., involving an action for tortious interference with contractual relations and resulting in a completely unprecedented verdict for the plaintiff of about ten and a half billion dollars. The principal issue was whether Pennzoil's agreement to buy Getty Oil Co. had become a binding contract at the time that Texaco offered a larger sum. The jury found that it had. The verdict stood in the Texas Court of Civil Appeals, see Texaco, Inc. v. Pennzoil Co., 729 S.W.2d 768–866 (Tex.App.1987), writ ref'd n.r.e., and the Texas Supreme Court declined to review it. The defendant found it necessary to take Chapter 11 bankruptcy. The Federal Courts were involved in the side issue of the constitutionality of a Texas statute requiring a bond for the full amount of a judgment in order to be able to appeal. See Texaco, Inc. v. Pennzoil Co., 784 F.2d 1133 (2d Cir.1986), rev'd, Pennzoil Co. v. Texaco, Inc., ___ U.S. ___, 107 S.Ct. 1519, 95 L.Ed.2d 1 (1987). Numerous other legal complications arose, and the case was finally settled for the sum of three billion dollars. In early April, 1988, the settlement was completed with the payment of that sum. The appellate opinions are not suitable for use here to describe the points presented, but for succinct analyses of the central legal issues involved, see Baron & Baron, The Pennzoil-Texaco Dispute: An Independent Analysis, 38 Baylor L.Rev. 250 (1986); and Note, The 10.53 Billion Question—When Are the Parties Bound?: *Pennzoil* and the Use of Agreements in Principle in Mergers and Acquisition, 40 Vand.L.Rev. 1367 (1987). There are fascinating treatments of the whole episode in T. Petzinger, Oil & Honor: The Texaco–Penzoil Wars (1987); and S. Coll, The Taking of Getty Oil: The Full Story of the Most Spectacular and Catastrophic Takeover of All Times (1987). The cast of characters reads as if they came from the fertile imagination of a modern Dickens.

HARMON v. HARMON
Supreme Judicial Court of Maine, 1979.
404 A.2d 1020.

NICHOLS, JUSTICE. Somewhere near the frontier of the expanding field of law relating to tortious interference with an advantageous relationship we encounter the legal issue which is paramount in this appeal.

By a complaint entered November 21, 1977, in Superior Court in Cumberland County the Plaintiff, Richard Harmon, asserted that the Defendants, Harold C. Harmon and Virginia S. Harmon (who are the Plaintiff's brother and brother's wife) had by fraud and undue influence induced the Plaintiff's mother, Josephine F. Harmon, while she was 87 years old and in ill health, to transfer to the Defendants valuable property. By her 1976 will and by her more recent statements the mother had indicated her intention that the Plaintiff son should receive at least a one-half interest in this property. Thus, this transfer effectively disinherited the Plaintiff son. The mother, it appears, is still living.

Upon the Defendants' motion the Superior Court dismissed the complaint upon the grounds (a) that the complaint fails to state a claim upon which relief can be granted and (b) that the Plaintiff son lacked standing to proceed against the Defendant son and the latter's wife.

The Plaintiff son has appealed to this Court from that order of dismissal. We sustain his appeal. * * *

In Cyr v. Cote, Me., 396 A.2d 1013 (1979) we recently considered a similar question. There it was after the testator's death that certain legatees under his will commenced their action, alleging that, but for the defendants' fraud and undue influence upon the testator, they would have received the property which by such tortious conduct the Defendants obtained as an intervivos gift. In determining whether the expectancy of receiving a bequest was something which the law would protect, we had occasion to examine Perkins v. Pendleton, 90 Me. 166, 38 A. 96 (1897). There it was held that a plaintiff, employed by a company which had the right to terminate his employment at will, could bring an action against defendants who unlawfully caused the company to discharge the plaintiff. Relying upon *Perkins*, we recognized in Cyr v. Cote an action for the wrongful interference with an expected legacy or gift under a will. * * *

In *Cyr*, the interest we sought to protect was the *expectation*, and not the *certainty*, that the legatees would have received a future benefit under the will. If there had been no undue influence the testator, prior to death, could still have disinherited them or bequeathed the property to another person. Nevertheless, the wrongful conduct deprived the plaintiffs of the possibility that the testator would not have changed his mind, absent the undue influence.

Once the will has been executed an expectancy has been created in the legatee. If the legatee is injured due to some wrongful conduct on the part of a third party against the prospective testator, such act must necessarily occur within the life of the testator. The injury at this point is complete. The problem then becomes the valuation of the chance of benefit that has been lost. On this basis there may be recovery for loss of prospects falling considerably short of certainty. [C]

We find support for the precedent set by *Cyr* in a review of the historical foundations for that precedent.

The law initially proved most ready to protect commercial expectancies, such as that of entering into or continuing a business relation with another. [C] Very early cases protected a merchant whose customers were being driven away and a churchman whose donors were being harassed. [C]

Prospective or potential business relations have been protected from wrongful interference. [C]

Furthermore, it has become a settled rule in the United States that the expectancy of future contractual relations, such as the prospect of obtaining employment or employees, or the opportunity of obtaining customers, will be protected by the law from wrongful interference. [C] Tort liability for damages is the well established remedy in this situation. * * *

The law has, indeed, in the past also proved willing to protect non-commercial interests in a variety of contexts. Dean Prosser has commented:

"On this basis the earlier cases held that recovery would be denied for interference with an expected gift or a legacy under a will, even though the defendant's motives were unworthy and he had resorted to fraudulent means, because the testator might have changed his mind. There is no essential reason for refusing to protect such non-commercial expectancies, at least where there is a strong probability that they would have been realized. * * *

"The problem appears in reality to be one of satisfactory proof that the loss has been suffered, instead of the existence of a ground to tort liability." W. Prosser, Law of Torts 950–951 (4th ed. 1971) (emphasis added).

Recognition of such a cause of action was made in the Restatement (Second) of Torts § 870 (1939) which declares the imposition of liability for the intended consequences of any tortious act. Comment (b), Illustration 2, is enlightening:

"A, who is zealous in the cause of labor, is about to make a gift to B, a college, when C, for the purpose of preventing the gift, falsely represents that the president of B is opposed to collective bargaining. As a result, A refuses to make the gift, which otherwise he would have made. B is entitled to maintain an action of tort against C."

The parallel between our present factual setting and this illustration is striking indeed. * * *

Likewise, the expectancy of a beneficiary in the proceeds of an insurance policy upon the life of another is an interest which the courts are ready to protect against the wrongful interference of a third person. [Cc]

Such liability in tort is recognized notwithstanding that clearly the beneficiary's interest includes no vested right, but is a "mere" expectancy. [C] The issue is not whether the interest is vested or expectant; rather the issue is whether it is legally protected so that intentional and wrongful interference causing damage to the plaintiff gives rise to liability in tort. [C]

We conclude that where a person can prove that, but for the tortious interference of another, he would in all likelihood have received a gift or a specific profit from a transaction, he is entitled to recover for the damages thereby done to him. * * *

In the case before us, we go one step further than we did in *Cyr.* Here we recognize that one may proceed to enforce this liability, grounded in tort, before the death of the prospective testatrix occurs, even as we have seen that the victim of tortious interference with a contract of employment or with a policy of life insurance has been permitted to proceed.

There are several considerations which strongly favor according the Plaintiff brother an early day in court, notwithstanding the ambulatory nature of the mother's will and the voidable nature of a trust arrangement. These include (a) the availability of witnesses to the allegedly tortious acts while their memories are relatively fresh, (b) the present availability of relevant exhibits, and (c) especially the prospect that the court may gain the testimony of the parties' aged mother, which testimony may determine the outcome here.

While delaying the adjudication until the mother's death could solidify the Plaintiff's position as allegedly a victim of fraud or undue influence, the delay might mean that important evidence would be denied the court. [Cc]

It should be noted that the claim of the Plaintiff son is to a loss of his expectancy, not to a loss of the actual property of his mother.

Having concluded that the Plaintiff son has a justiciable interest upon which he may found this action, it is clear that he has standing to proceed with this action. Therefore, the order of dismissal was in error. * * *

Remanded for further proceedings consistent with the opinion herein.

————

1. Most of the cases dealing with interference with prospective advantage have concerned future contract relations, such as the prospect of obtaining employment or hiring employees, or the opportunity of attracting customers or purchasing property. In these cases there is a background of business experience, on the basis of which it is possible to estimate with some fair amount of success both the value of what has been lost and the likelihood that the plaintiff would have received it if the defendant had not interfered. The loss of prospective profits is a familiar element of damages in cases of breach of contract.

2. When the attempt is made to extend liability for interference beyond such commercial dealings to other "expectancies," the courts have found themselves on unfamiliar ground, and frequently have refused to allow the action. The reason usually given is that there is no sufficient degree of certainty that the plaintiff would ever have received the prospective benefits.

3. Some decisions involving interference with an expected gift or legacy under a will have denied recovery on the ground that there was not sufficient certainty that the donor would not have changed his mind. Hall v. Hall, 91 Conn. 514, 100 A. 441 (1917); Cunningham v. Edward, 52 Ohio App. 61, 3

N.E.2d 58 (1936). When reasonable certainty can be found, as when the testator has become incompetent to make a change, or the will is suppressed after his death, recovery has been allowed. Creek v. Laski, 248 Mich. 425, 227 N.W. 817 (1929); Morton v. Petit, 124 Ohio St. 241, 177 N.E. 591 (1931).

4. Other cases have granted recovery on the basis of other evidence of a high degree of probability that the testator would have made or changed a bequest. E.g., Brignati v. Medenwald, 315 Mass. 636, 53 N.E.2d 673 (1944); Bohannon v. Wachovia Bank & Trust Co., 210 N.C. 678, 188 S.E. 390 (1936). See also, allowing equitable relief in the form of a constructive trust, Latham v. Father Divine, 299 N.Y. 22, 85 N.E.2d 168 (1949); Allen v. Leybourne, 190 So.2d 825 (Fla.App.1966). See Evans, Torts to Expectancies in Decedents' Estates, 93 U.Pa.L.Rev. 187 (1944).

5. The reluctance found in will cases has been carried over to cases of other non-commercial expectancies, when there is no high degree of probability. Western Union Tel. Co. v. Crall, 39 Kan. 580, 18 P. 719 (1888) (chance of horse winning race); Cain v. Vollmer, 19 Idaho 163, 112 P. 686 (1910) (chance of winning future races); Smitha v. Gentry, 20 Ky.L.Rep. 171, 45 S.W. 515 (1898) (chance of obtaining reward); Phillips v. Pantages Theatre Co., 163 Wash. 303, 300 P. 1048 (1931) (chance of winning vaudeville contest). When the chance is attended with a high probability of success, some courts have been willing to allow recovery for the loss of value of the chance itself. Wachtel v. National Alfalfa Journal, 190 Iowa 1293, 176 N.W. 801 (1920) (prize magazine subscription contest); Chaplin v. Hicks, [1911] 2 K.B. 786 (beauty contest). See, as to damages contingent upon a chance, Note, 18 Rut.L.Rev. 875 (1964).

6. Should the plaintiff in the principal case recover the full value of the legacy, or the value of the chance that he would receive it? See Schaefer, Uncertainty and the Law of Damages, 19 Wm. & Mary L.Rev. 719 (1978).

Other "Business Torts"

There are several fields of the law in the business milieu that involve the imposition of economic injury on a person who is therefore entitled to monetary damages or an injunction against continuing the conduct. These remedies were derived essentially from the philosophy of tort law, but they have now been thoroughly merged into the legal regulation of the process of competition in business activities or the law governing the relationship of business and labor. As a result, the influence of the tort origins has decreased substantially and they have become separate fields of the law developing through statutory provisions, administrative regulations and their own independent concepts. This means that they are no longer covered in torts casebooks or treatises but have their own distinct casebooks and treatises. Only a brief reference can be made here.

1. *Copyright and Patent Infringement.* Article I, § 8, cl. 8 of the U.S. Constitution provides that Congress has the power to "promote the Progress of Science and useful Arts by securing for limited Times to Authors and Inventors the exclusive Right to their respective Writings and Discoveries." Congress has exercised this power. See 17 U.S.C.A. §§ 101 et seq. (copyright); 35 U.S.C.A. §§ 1 et seq. (patents).

There are, of course, unsettled problems. Particularly relevant is the issue of federal preemption. See, for example, the twin cases of Sears, Roebuck & Co. v. Stiffel Co., 376 U.S. 225 (1964); and Compco Corp. v. Day–Brite Lighting, Inc., 376 U.S. 234 (1964), holding that there can be no common law protection of the functional design of a product. If it is capable of being patented, compliance with the statutory procedure is necessary; if it is not, it cannot be protected by the common law. "To allow a state by use of its law of unfair competition to prevent the copying of an article which represents too slight an advance to be patented would be to permit the state to block off from the public something which federal law has said belongs to the public." The exact scope of the *Sears–Compco* holdings is yet to be worked out. And consider Copyright Act of 1976, 17 U.S.C.A. § 301, and the question of how far it preempts or supersedes common law copyright.

2. *Trade Marks and Trade Names.* A considerable body of learning has developed regarding trade marks and trade names. Much of it has been common law, but the Lanham Act (Trademark Act of 1946, 15 U.S.C.A. §§ 1051 et seq.) has extensively revised and reorganized it.

3. *Trade Secrets.* Much of this is common law, but there are state statutes and a Uniform Trade Secrets Act. Issues of federal preemption give difficulty here, too.

4. *Unfair Competition.* The three previous topics have often been combined under the generic term "unfair competition," which is also inclusive of such matters as "passing off" of one's goods as another's or misappropriation of another's ideas, news items or unpublished writings. State statutes covering unfair trade practices, false advertising and similar matters are included.

5. *Other Statutes Involving Regulation of Business.* Federal statutes include The Sherman Antitrust Act, 15 U.S.C.A. §§ 1–7 (conspiracy in restraint of trade, attempt to monopolize), Clayton Antitrust Act, 15 U.S.C.A. §§ 12–27 (restraints and monopolies); Robinson–Patman Act, 15 U.S.C.A. §§ 12 et seq. (price discrimination); Federal Trade Commission Act, 15 U.S.C.A. §§ 41–58 et seq., and regulations. There are also various state antitrust statutes.

6. *Labor Law.* Many of the early cases on tortious interference with existing or prospective economic advantage involved contests between employers and employees. Today these have all been incorporated into the law of labor relations, both federal and state, and much of it statutory or based on administrative regulations or rulings. None of these matters are presently regarded as appropriate for the course in Torts.

7. *Civil RICO.* The Racketeer Influenced and Corrupt Organizations Act, 18 U.S.C.A. §§ 1961–1968, is primarily a criminal statute. But § 1964(c) provides for a private civil action based on conducting or participating in the conduct of an enterprise "through a pattern of racketeering activity," and authorizes treble damages. As construed in Sedima, S.P.R.L. v. Imrex Co., Inc., 473 U.S. 479 (1985), it has an extensive application which may be broader than Congress intended. There are indications that Congress may amend the language. In the meantime numerous suits have been brought. See Note, Civil RICO: A Primer, 31 Loy.L.Rev. 989 (1986); CCH, RICO: Business Disputes Guide (looseleaf).

8. In the Restatement of Torts, there were chapters on The Privilege to Engage in Business (34), Confusion of Source (35), Miscellaneous Trade Practices (36), and Labor Disputes (38). All of them have been omitted from the Second Restatement as being no longer primarily based on the common law of torts. These topics are now covered in other courses than Torts in the usual law school curriculum.

9. See generally Alexander, Commercial Torts (1973); Callman, Unfair Competition, Trademarks and Monopolies (4th ed. 1981) (multi-volume); McCar-

thy, Trademarks and Unfair Competition (1973, with supps.) (2 vols.); Areeda and Turner, Antitrust Law (1978) (3 vols.).

2. FAMILY RELATIONS

NASH v. BAKER
Court of Appeals of Oklahoma, 1974.
522 P.2d 1335.

ROMANG, JUDGE. The appellants, hereinafter referred to as plaintiffs, are five minor children whose mother, Marian Nash, brings this appeal as their natural guardian and next friend. The appellee is hereinafter referred to as the defendant.

Marian Nash filed the petition in her own right and as next friend of the infant plaintiffs, alleging that after Marian Nash and James Nash had been husband and wife for about 18 years and had five children (the minor plaintiffs) of that union, the defendant, a wealthy widow, who knew or should have known of the marriage and children, lured James Nash, the husband and father, away from the plaintiffs by providing said James Nash with a finer home, sexual charms, and other inducements. The plaintiff Marian Nash sought to recover actual and punitive damages in her own right for the alienation of her husband's affections, loss of consortium, and loss of a prospective increased standard of living. In addition, as next friend of her children, she sought recovery of actual and punitive damages under the common law for alienation of their father's affections, interference with their family relationships, and "loss of the society, affection, assistance, moral support and guidance" of their father. The petition also alleged adultery by the defendant with said James Nash.

The trial court sustained the defendant's demurrer as to each of the minor plaintiffs' asserted causes of action and overruled it as to Marian Nash's suit in her own right. The latter suit was tried to a jury, resulting in a verdict for the defendant. The only questions before this court deal with whether any cause of action may be maintained on behalf of the minor children of a marriage, against a woman who entices away their father from the marital home.

The sole question remaining is whether * * * a minor child has in Oklahoma a common law right to sue a third person whose luring away of the father breaks up the parents' marriage and deprives the child of the father's society and guidance. The common law recognized no such right in the child. That the injured spouse has an action for alienation of affections, loss of consortium, or criminal conversation does not require that a cause of action be given to the child. * * * The plaintiffs cite Prosser, Law of Torts 908 (3d ed. 1964) which, although recognizing that the majority of those jurisdictions which passed on the question have denied the child an action, predicts that in the future additional jurisdictions will allow his action. On the other hand, * * * modern statutes abolishing causes of action for alienation of affections, breach of promise to marry, and related actions; the increasing failure of marriages, reportedly more than one in three ending in absolute divorce or permanent separation; and the recent liberalization of divorce in several more states, including a ground or grounds not based on "fault"; and the increase in the number of children whose parents have divorced and remarried; may well prevent the future development predicted by the late Professor Prosser. In addition, there may be a growing feeling that very often the "fault" leading to the breakup of a marriage may not be readily determinable in court, and that the "fault" which caused one spouse to be attracted to a third person was not the magnetism of such third person, but that of an emotional vacuum in the home.

Affirmed.

---

1. The law of torts has been concerned not only with the protection of interests of the personality and of property, but also with what may be called "relational" interests founded upon the relation in which plaintiff stands toward one or more third persons. W. Prosser and Keeton, Torts § 124 (5th ed. 1984); Green, Relational Interests, 29 Ill.L.Rev. 460 (1934). Much development in this area has been based on claims alleging an interference with a family relationship. See Foster, Relational Interests of the Family, 1962 U.Ill.L.F. 493. At early common law, most claims were brought by husbands for loss of economic services of a wife or child. Today there is potential for a claim to be brought by any member of the family unit and the focus is more likely to be on loss of intangible matters such as companionship or affection. The concentration here is on modern remedies.

Claims Based on Intentional Interference

2. *Alienation of Affections.*

A. *Husband and Wife.* In some states today a spouse may bring a claim against a third party for alienation of affections. The plaintiff must show that the spouse's mental attitude and conjugal kindness were converted by the defendant. Although a change in the alienated spouse's state of mind must be evidenced by external conduct, most courts hold that it is not necessary to show an act of adultery. In point of fact, the defendant need not be a romantic rival. Some cases are brought against relatives who may be privileged to act when they reasonably believe it to be in the best interest of the person "alienated." See Koehler v. Koehler, 248 Iowa 144, 79 N.W.2d 791 (1958); Bishop v. Glazener, 245 N.C. 592, 96 S.E.2d 870 (1957).

B. *Parent and Child.* If a child is abducted or defendant intentionally deprives a parent of a child's economic services, precedent supports a claim. Most courts have declined, however, to create an alienation-of-affections remedy either on behalf of a parent for loss of a child or a child for loss of a parent. See Note, 28 Okla.L.Rev. 198 (1975); Annot., 60 A.L.R.3d 931 (1974). For a recent case indicating that a claim would be allowed on behalf of a parent even though no "loss of services" was shown, see Strode v. Gleason, 9 Wash.App. 13, 510 P.2d 250 (1973), noted in (1974) 22 U.Kan.L.Rev. 684.

3. *Criminal Conversation.* This is a tort in which a married person may recover both compensatory and punitive damages by proving that the spouse

and the defendant engaged in sexual intercourse. There need be no "conversation" (a synonym for sexual intercourse) and in some jurisdictions the conduct need not violate the criminal law. How should damages be computed? When the crime of adultery has been abolished by the legislature or has been reduced to a misdemeanor with a slight fine, should this affect the tort remedy? See Jasterbowski v. Michos, 44 Ohio App.2d 201, 337 N.E.2d 627 (1975); Swartz v. Steele, 42 Ohio App.2d 1, 325 N.E.2d 910 (1974). Suppose the defendant shows that the plaintiff's spouse was the person who invited and procured the event. Should this be a defense? At early common law it was not, but these decisions were predicated on the assumption that a wife was "no more capable of giving a consent which would prejudice the husband's interests than was his horse." See 8 Holdsworth, History of England Law 430 (2d ed. 1937).

4. *Other Intentional Torts.* At common law a husband could bring an action for "enticement" or abduction of his wife. A parent could bring a claim for seduction of a minor child, an action to some extent analogous to criminal conversation. The action was not necessarily confined to claims based on an injury to female children. See White v. Nellis, 31 N.Y. 405 (1865) (alluding in dictum to "debased women who lure * * * innocent boy(s) * * * "). In general, these torts are only of historical interest today. On occasion, however, new theories of intentional interference with family relations may arise.

5. *Statutory Abolition of Actions.* Beginning in the late 1930's, legislatures in a substantial number of states have abolished tort actions based on intentional interference with family relations that carry an accusation of sexual behavior. See, e.g., Ala.Code, tit. 7, § 115; Md.Code Ann. § 5–301; N.Y. Civ.Rights Laws § 80–c. The statutes, known as "Anti–Heart Balm" laws, have generally withstood constitutional challenge. What policy reasons support them? If a state has such a statute, should a child's claim for alienation of affections be automatically barred? See Russick v. Hicks, 85 F.Supp. 281 (D.Mich.1949). The statutes are collected in H. Clark, Domestic Relations 267 (1968).

Claims Based on Negligent Interference

6. At common law a husband was legally entitled to his wife's earnings and services. Courts protected the husband's right to these "assets" against negligent interference by third parties. The action is known as one for loss of consortium. The husband may also be able to recover general damages for loss of companionship and sexual relations. Because a wife had no legal interest in her husband's personal property, she was denied a claim.

7. With the growth of legal equality between the spouses, it might be anticipated that the cause of action for loss of consortium would disappear. Instead, beginning with Hitaffer v. Argonne Co., Inc., 183 F.2d 811 (D.C.Cir. 1950), courts in many states have permitted both spouses to bring a claim for loss of consortium. See, e.g., Rodriguez v. Bethlehem Steel Corp., 12 Cal.3d 382, 525 P.2d 669, 115 Cal.Rptr. 765 (1974); Millington v. Southeastern Elevator Co., 22 N.Y.2d 498, 239 N.E.2d 897, 293 N.Y.S.2d 305 (1968). The emphasis on the damage element in the claim has shifted away from economic loss to intangibles such as loss of companionship and affection.

8. Although loss of consortium could be viewed as a wholly independent injury, most courts regard it as a derivative claim, subject to all defenses that could be asserted against the spouse who was physically injured. See Pioneer

Constr. Co. v. Bergeron, 170 Colo. 474, 462 P.2d 589 (1969); Tollett v. Mashburn, 291 F.2d 89 (8th Cir.1961).

9. Courts generally have declined to allow claims for pure loss of companionship when a child seeks a recovery of this type from a defendant who injured his parent. See Hankins v. Derby, 211 N.W.2d 581 (Iowa 1973); Russell v. Salem Transp. Co., 61 N.J. 502, 295 A.2d 862 (1972). Claims by parents solely for loss of companionship of their injured children have received similar treatment. Butler v. Chrestman, 264 So.2d 812 (Miss.1972); Ekalo v. Constructive Service Corp. of America, 46 N.J. 82, 215 A.2d 1 (1965). But see Shockley v. Prier, 66 Wis.2d 394, 225 N.W.2d 495 (1975) (medical malpractice). Is a parent's claim more deserving?

10. The material provided here is only introductory in nature. See generally Clark, Domestic Relations 261–280 (1968), and the materials cited there; and Restatement (Second) of Torts §§ 683–707A.

Chapter XXIII

SOME UNCLASSIFIED TORTS

1. TORTS "IMPLIED" FROM LEGISLATIVE PROVISIONS

BURNETTE v. WAHL
Supreme Court of Oregon, 1978.
284 Or. 705, 588 P.2d 1105.

HOLMAN, JUSTICE. Three identical cases have been consolidated for appeal. Plaintiffs are five minor children aged two to eight who, through their guardian, are bringing actions against their mothers for emotional and psychological injury caused by failure of defendant-mothers to perform their parental duties to plaintiffs. Plaintiffs appeal from orders of dismissal entered after demurrers were sustained to the complaints and plaintiffs refused to plead further.

The complaints allege that plaintiffs are in the custody of the Children's Services Division of the Department of Human Resources of the State of Oregon and are wards of Klamath County Juvenile Court.

The complaints are substantially identical, each one being in three counts. Among these counts are strewn various allegations of parental failure upon which the causes of action rest. They are:

"1. Since [date], defendant intentionally, wilfully, maliciously and with cruel disregard of the consequences failed to provide plaintiff with care, custody, parental nurturance, affection, comfort, companionship, support, regular contact and visitation.

"2. She has failed in violation of ORS 109.010[1] to maintain plaintiff, who, due to * * * age and indigency, is poor and unable to work to maintain * * * self.

"3. She has abandoned plaintiff by deserting the child with intent to abandon * * * and with intent to abdicate all responsibility for * * * care and raising, in violation of ORS 163.535.[2]

---

1. "ORS 109.010 Duty of Support. Parents are bound to maintain their children who are poor and unable to work to maintain themselves; and children are bound to maintain their parents in like circumstances."

2. "ORS 163.535 Abandonment of a Child. (1) A person commits the crime of abandonment of a child if, being a parent, lawful guardian or other person lawfully charged with the care or custody of a child under 15 years of age, he deserts the child in any place with intent to abandon it.

"(2) Abandonment of a child is a Class C felony."

1158

Oregon Supreme Court
Seated: Holman, Denecke, C.J., Tongue
Standing: Lent, Howell, Bryson, Linde

"4. She has neglected the plaintiff by negligently leaving * * * unattended in or at a place for such period of time as would have been likely to endanger the health or welfare of the plaintiff, in violation of ORS 163.545.[3]

"5. She has refused or neglected without lawful excuse to provide support for plaintiff, in violation of ORS 163.555.[4]

"6. Defendant has maliciously, intentionally, and with cruel disregard of the consequences, deserted and abandoned her child.

"7. Defendant has alienated the affections of the plaintiff in that she has intentionally, wilfully and maliciously abandoned, deserted, neglected and failed to maintain regular contact or visitation, or to provide for the plaintiff and has deprived plaintiff of the love, care, affection and comfort to which plaintiff is entitled."

3. "ORS 163.545 Child Neglect. (1) A person having custody or control of a child under 10 years of age commits the crime of child neglect if, with criminal negligence, he leaves the child unattended in or at any place for such period of time as may be likely to endanger the health or welfare of such child.

"(2) Child neglect is a Class A misdemeanor."

4. ORS 163.555 Criminal Nonsupport. (1) A person commits the crime of criminal nonsupport if, being the parent, lawful guardian or other person lawfully charged with the support of a child under 18 years of age, born in or out of wedlock, he refuses or neglects without lawful excuse to provide support for such child.

"* * *

"(3) Criminal nonsupport is a Class C felony."

It is apparent that the first allegation is general in nature and is intended to be all-encompassing. The second, third, fourth and fifth allege violation of statutory duties in which abandonment and desertion comprise the central theme. The sixth allegation is one of abandonment and desertion purportedly based on common law. The seventh allegation is an attempt to allege alienation of affections. Although these allegations of parental failure allege lack of support and physical care along with affectional neglect, from the allegations of injury in the complaint and the statements made in plaintiffs' brief, it appears that the injuries claimed are solely emotional and psychological.

Preliminary to a more detailed discussion, it should be noted that these claims of parental failure are different from those tort claims usually made upon behalf of children against parents. The adjudicated cases concern physical or emotional injuries resulting from physical acts inflicted upon children such as beatings and rapes and from automobile accidents. Plaintiffs admit they can cite no cases permitting them to recover from their parents for solely emotional or psychological damage resulting from failure to support, nurture and care for them.

The legislature, recognizing the necessity of parental nurture, support and physical care for children, has enacted a vast array of laws for the purpose of protecting or vindicating those rights. These are much more extensive and all-inclusive than are those statutes alleged to have been violated in plaintiffs' allegations of tortious conduct.[5]

ORS ch. 418 establishes extensive provisions for aid to dependent children, and it is under the provisions of this chapter and as wards of the juvenile court that plaintiffs are presently attempting to have their needs met. [The court discusses specific sections of the chapter.]

We recognize that this is not a proceeding to secure parental nurturing, support and physical care for plaintiffs, but rather an action for psychological injury claimed to have been caused by the absence of these services. However, the statutory enactments demonstrate that the legislature has put its mind to the deprivations of which plaintiff children are alleged to be victims and has attempted to remedy such situations by enacting a vast panoply of procedures, both civil and criminal, to insure that children receive proper nurturing, support and physical care. It has never undertaken to establish, however, a cause

---

5. Among these laws are ORS 108.040, providing an action against both parents for family necessities; ORS 108.110 *et seq.*, which allow a petition for the support of children to be brought against a parent by the other parent or a state agency for the support of the children; ORS ch. 110, providing both criminal and civil means for reciprocal enforcement between states of the right of support for children; ORS 411.120(4), providing for assistance to dependent children; ORS ch. 416, establish-ing the relative responsibility law (specifically see ORS 416.090, 416.100, and 416.220 for the means of enforcement); ORS ch. 418, providing for child welfare services (specifically see ORS 418.135(1) and 418.460, concerning enforcement of parental duties); ORS ch. 419, establishing juvenile courts (specifically see ORS 419.513, 419.515, and 419.517 concerning enforcement of support of children by parents).

of action for damages for any emotional injury to the child which may have been caused by a parent's refusal to provide these services. This failure of the legislature to act is significant because this is not a field of recovery which has heretofore been recognized by courts and it would therefore be natural for it to have provided such a remedy if it thought it was wise in view of the social problem it attempts to solve and the statutory provisions it has enacted for that purpose. It has had no difficulty in the past in creating new causes of action for persons aggrieved by conditions which it is attempting to rectify. Examples are the creation of causes of action, including punitive damages, in aid of enforcing ethics in the marketplace, ORS 646.638; actions for compensatory and punitive damages for unlawful discrimination by places of public accommodation, ORS 30.680, and by employers, ORS 659.030 and 659.121; and actions for double and triple damages for timber trespass, ORS 105.810 and 105.815.

The establishment by courts of a civil cause of action based on a criminal or regulatory statute is not premised upon legislative intent to create such an action. It is obvious that had the legislature intended a civil action it would have provided for one, as legislatures many times do. Therefore, the underlying assumption is that it was not intended that the statute create any civil obligation or afford civil protection against the injuries which it was designed to prevent. When neither the statute nor the common law authorizes an action and the statute does not expressly deny it, the court should recognize that it is being asked to bring into existence a new type of tort liability on the basis of its own appraisal of the policy considerations involved. If a court decides to create a cause of action for the act or omission which violates the statute, the interest which is invaded derives its protection solely from the court although the legislative action in branding the act or omission as culpable is taken into consideration by the court in deciding whether a common law action should be established. If a civil cause of action based upon a statute is established by a court, it is because the court, not the legislature, believes it is necessary and desirable to further vindicate the right or to further enforce the duty created by statute.

Because it is plain to the legislature that it could have created the civil liability and it has not, courts must look carefully not only at the particular statute establishing the right or duty but at all statutes which might bear either directly or indirectly on the legislative purpose. If there is any chance that invasion into the field by the court's establishment of a civil cause of action might interfere with the total legislative scheme, courts should err on the side of non-intrusion because it is always possible for the legislature to establish such a civil cause of action if it desires. Courts have no omnipotence in the field of planning, particularly social planning of the kind involved here. Courts should exercise restraint in fields in which the legislature has attempted fairly comprehensive social regulation.

There is no doubt but that the statutory provisions previously cited show a strong state policy of requiring the kind of parental nurturing, support and physical care of children which the defendants here are alleged to have denied their children. As previously indicated, it does not follow as a matter of course that it would be wise or judicious to vindicate that policy by a tort action for damages by children against their mothers. The state also has other policies within its statutory plan of which such a cause of action might well be destructive, particularly the policy of reuniting abandoned children with their parents, if possible. * * *

It is recognized by the statutory scheme that in some instances the reestablishment of a biological family is impossible and it therefore provides for a proceeding to terminate parental rights in order that a new family unit for the child may be formed. * * *

It is significant that plaintiffs' complaints do not allege that proceedings for the termination of the defendants' parental rights have taken place. In such circumstances, it would be exceedingly unwise for this court to step in and to initiate a new and heretofore unrecognized cause of action in a field of social planning to which the legislature has devoted a great deal of time and effort in evolving what appears to be an all-encompassing plan. Those persons designated by statute for aiding the plaintiffs in these cases have not yet taken the step for which the plan provides when there is no longer any hope of reestablishing these children in a family unit with their mothers. Tort actions such as the present ones might well be destructive of any plans the social agencies and the juvenile court might have for these children. It is inappropriate for this court to insert a new cause of action into the picture.

An exhaustive search of the legal literature finds only one article dealing with a right of action by children for emotional damage caused by ineffectual parents: The Rights of Children: A Trust Model, 46 Fordham L.Rev. 669 (1978). It suggests an analogy to the broad equitable principles of trust law as a model for defining the rights and duties existing among the child, his parents and the state. Even such a radical departure from present views does not advocate an action for money damages such as the present one. * * *

This state has provided appropriate remedies, as suggested by the article. The article further says, at 739, "The possibility of a monetary recovery for lack of nurturing should be limited to adult plaintiffs." While our position does not purport to be one of approval or disapproval of the positions asserted by the authors, the article demonstrates that even those who advocate radical changes in our method of thinking concerning the rights of children do not endorse actions such as those asserted here. Plaintiffs are unable to point to any literature in the field of child care or family planning which advocates an action for money damages to vindicate a right of the kind asserted here.

In addition, there is a limitation to the extent to which use may be made of tort actions for the purpose of accomplishing social aims. If there is ever a field in which juries and general trial courts are ill equipped to do social engineering, it is in the realm of the emotional relationship between mother and child. It is best we leave such matters to other fields of endeavor. There are certain kinds of relationships which are not proper fodder for tort litigation, and we believe this to be one of them. There are probably as many children who have been damaged in some manner by their parents' failure to meet completely their physical, emotional and psychological needs as there are people. A tort action for damages by emotionally deprived persons against their parents is, in our opinion, not going to solve the social problem in the same manner in which the legislature is attempting to solve it.

In addition to the contention that defendants should be liable for civil damages because of their violation of criminal and regulatory statutes, plaintiffs also contend that defendants are responsible because of the infliction of severe emotional distress by intentional acts. Plaintiffs allege that defendants intentionally deserted and abandoned them; however, they do not contend that defendants deserted them for the purpose of inflicting emotional harm upon them. We recognize that this tort usually also encompasses the infliction of emotional harm under circumstances from which a reasonable person would conclude that harm was almost certain to result. We believe this latter rationale is inapplicable as between parents and children. If it were otherwise, the children of divorced parents would almost always have an action for emotional damage against their parents. Divorce has become a way of life with almost certain emotional trauma of a greater or lesser degree to the children from the legal dissolution of the family and the resultant absence of at least one of the parents and sometimes both.

In addition, plaintiffs contend that the common law tort of alienation of affections is applicable. They argue that because such a cause of action is intended to compensate one spouse for the intentional alienation of the other spouse's affections by a third party, and that because in one case, Daily v. Parker, 152 F.2d 174 (7th Cir.1945), this cause of action has been extended to the children, it should exist against the parent himself. The statement of the argument is its refutation. Also, the tort of alienation of affections has recently been abolished by the legislature, Oregon Laws 1975, ch. 562, § 1.

Plaintiffs generally contend that without respect to previously recognized theories of recovery, we should recognize a new tort of parental desertion. For all the reasons previously given in declining to use recognized theories of recovery, we also decline this invitation.

The judgment of the trial court is affirmed.

TONGUE, JUSTICE, concurring. * * * The doctrine of intrafamily tort immunity has been previously abandoned by this court with respect to intentional torts resulting in physical injuries. In my opinion, however, it does not follow that the doctrine should also be abandoned with respect to intrafamily torts resulting in "mental and emotional injuries" for reasons stated by the majority, although not in the context of intrafamily tort immunity.

LENT, JUSTICE, concurring in part; dissenting in part. I agree with the majority that the asserted cause of action for alienation of affections must fall. I further agree with the majority that from a technical, pleading standpoint plaintiff * * * has failed to state a cause of action for "outrageous conduct" for failure to state that defendant intended to cause the severe emotional distress described in the complaint.

In dissenting, I have joined in the dissent of Linde, J. but desire to add some additional reasons for finding that a civil cause of action for damages should obtain. * * *

At present there are over one-third of a million children in the United States who are dependent upon the community for their parental care. In Oregon during fiscal year 1976–77 the number of dependent children was over 6,000. The future is bleak for the vast majority of these children, at least those in the position of the plaintiffs, whose parents have abandoned them permanently. Only approximately five percent of such children are ever adopted and placed in a permanent parental situation.

The costs—in dollars and cents—of taking care of these children is staggering. In 1972, the total cost at all levels of government was 712.5 million dollars. The present cost may be estimated at approximately 800 million dollars. In Oregon the Children's Services Division budget for the 1977–1979 biennium to provide "family services" for dependent children is over 43 million dollars.

It is estimated that the total direct cost to the community of foster care in 1972 for a child from the age of one to eighteen was $122,500. This is about five times the cost of raising a child in a low-budget family situation. In Oregon the cost of foster care is approximately $200 per month per child. Other types of dependent child care cost as much as $978.57 per child per month.

However, the dollars-and-cents picture is not complete, since it measures only the direct, monetary loss to the community. Indirect costs are those which result from the *effects* of prolonged foster care— delinquency, economic dependency, crimes and corrections. Possibly the greatest costs are those which cannot be measured by dollars and cents at all—the loss in human potential. This latter cost to the community can best be stated in the words of those who have done the pioneering research on this subject.

All researchers report the psychological phenomenon known as "separation trauma," the trauma produced by the initial separation from the mother regardless of the circumstances of the case. A second element noted by researchers is the development of ambiguous relationships by the dependent child, with a concomitant loss of self-identity.

A third general phenomenon found by the researchers stems from the instability of the foster care system itself, where multiple placements are the norm.   This instability in relationships fosters personality disturbance.   *   *   *

While indirect monetary costs to society are more difficult to document and quantify, they are just as real.   Maas reports that forty to fifty percent of the foster children involved in his study exhibited symptoms of maladjustment.   Eisenberg reports that the referral rate for psychiatric services for foster children is thirty per one thousand population, about ten times that of the general population.   Meier reports a higher than normal incidence of marital breakdown and illegitimate births among former foster children.   Finally, McCord reports that "a significantly higher proportion of those who had been placed in foster homes had criminal records in adulthood" when compared to a control group of potentially delinquent boys living at home.   *   *   *

The sum of the cost to the community—direct and indirect, monetary and intangible—cannot be computed with complete accuracy; however, Maas and Engler summarized their findings as follows:

"Adequate care of children is not inexpensive.   It is just as costly to mend a child emotionally crippled by disorganized family life as it is to cure the crippled leg of a child stricken with polio.   For children in need of parents the community will pay the price sooner or later.   The high incidence of mental disorders, criminality, or at best economic dependency among adults who as children had lived in the limbo of foster care, is clear evidence of this."   *   *   *

[The opinion is quite detailed and specific, citing authority for data offered and quoting from and discussing social studies in the field, including H. Maas and Engler, Children in Need of Parents (1959); J. Goldstein, Freud and Solnit, Beyond the Best Interests of the Child (1973); Fanshel and Shinn, Dollars and Sense in the Foster Care of Children (Child Welfare League, 1972); Eisenburg, The Sins of the Fathers: Urban Decay and Social Pathology, 32 Am.J. Orthopsychiatry 14 (1962); Maas, Highlights of the Foster Care Project; Introduction, 38 Child Welfare 5 (1959); McCord, McCord and Thurber, the Effects of Foster–Home Placement in the Prevention of Adult Anti–Social Behavior, 34 Soc.Sci.Rev. 415 (1960); Mnookin, Foster Care—In Whose Best Interest?, 43 Harv.Ed.Rev. 599 (1973); Meier, Current Circumstances of Former Foster Children, 44 Child Welfare 192 (1965).]

In view of the costs, both tangible and intangible to society of caring for these dependent children who have well been termed the "orphans of the living" and the character of defendant's conduct as admitted by the demurrer, I believe defendant should shoulder so much of the financial burden as her resources permit.   Further, I would hold that the emotional harm which the demurrer admits plaintiff has suffered is such as the community should conclude is monetarily compensable. As stated in Justice Linde's dissent plaintiff has alleged a cause of action.

LINDE, JUSTICE, dissenting. * * * The simple issue before us is whether a young child who allegedly has suffered severe mental and emotional injuries as a result of being deserted and abandoned by a parent acting "maliciously, intentionally, and with cruel disregard of the consequences"—conduct which the legislature has declared to be a crime—may upon proper proof hold the parent responsible in damages for these severe mental and emotional injuries. Contrary to the majority opinion, I believe that these allegations, which plead a violation of ORS 163.535, state a claim on which a child so injured may go to trial.[1]

In reaching this conclusion, I differ with the majority's treatment of its two crucial premises: (1) the source of civil liability for violation of criminal laws, and (2) the significance to be accorded to Oregon's child protection laws.

Liability for Damages from Prohibited Conduct. It should be noted at the outset that awarding civil damages for violations of prohibitory laws is not an uncommon or radical theory of recovery. The question when the victim of criminal or otherwise prohibited conduct may recover damages from the wrongdoer is increasingly important in many areas of law. In a number of recent cases the issue has occupied the United States Supreme Court and the federal courts, whose greater attention to statutory premises of liability probably reflects the fact that these courts are not empowered to formulate common law torts unrelated to the Constitution or laws of the United States. [C] Thus the Supreme Court has also referred to potential civil liability under state law as one factor in determining whether such liability arises implicitly from an act of Congress. [C] Apart from these differences, however, federal and state courts face the same question when prohibitory legislation implies a civil liability toward those for whose protection the legislation is enacted and when it does not. The answer depends first on whether a legislative policy to allow or to deny a civil remedy can be discerned in the text or the legislative history of the statute. If neither can be discerned, then it depends on whether the plaintiff belongs to the class for whose special protection the statute was enacted and whether the civil remedy would contribute to or perhaps detract from achieving the object of the legislation. [C]

This court has had a number of recent occasions to undertake this analysis. In Davis v. Billy's Con–Teena, Inc., Or., 587 P.2d 75 (1978), we based potential liability for damages caused by unlawfully selling alcohol to minors on a stated legislative purpose to protect the safety

---

1. ORS 163.535:

(1) A person commits the crime of abandonment of a child if, being a parent, lawful guardian or other person lawfully charged with the care or custody of a child under 15 years of age, he deserts the child in any place with intent to abandon it.

(2) Abandonment of a child is a Class C felony.

Since the complaint alleges at least one cause of action, the validity of the other theories of recovery contained in the complaint need not be considered in overruling the demurrer. * * *

and health of other persons beyond the minors themselves. In Farris v. United States Fidelity, Or., 587 P.2d 1015 (1978), on the other hand, we found that the statutory penalties provided for violations of the insurance code precluded inferring a damage claim for emotional suffering or punitive damages for the violation in question. O'Toole v. Franklin, 279 Or. 513, 569 P.2d 561 (1977), recognized that a knowing violation of a provision of the Oregon State Bar act could give rise to a damage action by a member of the class for whose protection it was enacted. And only this week we found in a prohibition against discharging an employee for claiming workers' compensation a public policy that supported a civil claim for damages by a worker so discharged. Brown v. Transcon Lines, Or., 588 P.2d 1087 (1978). The American Law Institute's Restatement (Second) of Torts, Tentative Draft No. 23, 1977, lists a number of other illustrations in its discussion of proscriptive or prescriptive statutes as sources of civil liability.[2] Sometimes a common law court will assimilate the statutory duty into an existing principle of liability, as for instance the negligence action in Davis v. Billy's Con-Teena, supra, but that is not always so. See Restatement (Second) of Torts, Tentative Draft No. 23, 1977, § 874A, Comment f.[3]

Of course, the question of civil recovery for breach of a statutory duty can be an issue only when the legislation itself is silent on the point. If the legislature either provides for a civil remedy or clearly indicates that it means other provisions for enforcement to be complete and exclusive, there is nothing for a court to decide. It would help to clarify not only private rights but also the particular public policy if the legislative assembly as a routine step in the drafting of penal legislation faced the question of its civil consequences, or alternatively, if it were

2. Restatement (Second) of Torts § 874A (Tentative Draft No. 23, 1977):

"3. A statute makes it a crime to have sexual intercourse with a previously chaste female under the age of 17, even though she factually consents. The court may hold that the tort action of battery will lie, regardless of the consent.

"4. A federal act makes it a crime to intercept and divulge a telephone conversation. The court may 'assimilate' this conduct to the torts of defamation and invasion of the right of privacy and grant damages. * * *

"6. A statute makes it a crime to utter insulting and abusive language to another publicly. The court may hold that a civil action will lie, amounting to the intentional infliction of emotional distress. * * *

"8. A statute makes it a crime to seduce a woman under promises of marriage. The court may hold that this conduct gives rise to a tort action for damages. * * *

"14. A statute imposes a criminal penalty upon an employer who, upon request of a former employee, fails to supply a 'service letter' providing details of his service. The court may supply a civil action for damages for violation.

3. As early as 1934, and until 1965, the original Restatement (Second) of Torts, § 286, stated:

"The violation of a legislative enactment by doing a prohibited act, or by failing to do a required act, makes the actor liable for an invasion of an interest of another if:

"(a) the intent of the enactment is exclusively or in part to protect an interest of the other as an individual; and

"(b) the interest invaded is one which the enactment is intended to protect; and,

"(c) where the enactment is intended to protect an interest from a particular hazard, the invasion of the interests results from that hazard; and,

"(d) the violation is a legal cause of the invasion, and the other has not so conducted himself as to disable himself from maintaining an action.

to enact a general formula for determining these consequences when a statute is otherwise silent.

Unfortunately legislatures do neither, but nothing can be inferred from that fact, given the existing practice of recognizing such consequences when the nature of the protective statute appears to imply them. The majority overstates the case when it equates legislative silence with an "underlying assumption * * * that it was not intended that the statute create any civil obligation or afford civil protection against the injuries which it was designed to prevent." Nor does it follow, when a court finds that the duty created or defined by the statute does imply a civil cause of action, that the court is engaged in pronouncing common law. The difference between a new common law theory of recovery in tort or otherwise and a civil claim based on a statute is obvious: The latter claim stands and falls with the statute from which it is implied, and it will disappear as soon as the amendment or repeal of the statute indicates a reconsideration of the previous public policy. Thus, while a court is often left at large to divine the implications of a statutory policy, it is equally an overstatement to say that the court simply makes its own judgment whether to "create a cause of action" deriving "solely" from the court's own appraisal whether additional protection for the claimed interest is "necessary and desirable." [4]

The relevance of criminal or regulatory laws to civil liability is more complex than merely being an element "taken into consideration by the court in deciding whether a common law action should be established," as the majority puts it. Such laws express distinct kinds of policies. First, the most familiar criminal laws are redefinitions of common-law crimes against private persons or property. They have equally familiar civil analogues in common-law torts. Only "victimless crimes" and crimes deemed to endanger the public as a collectivity, such as bribery, counterfeiting, or tax evasion, are likely to lack a corresponding civil liability. Violations of game laws or environmental protection laws may be other examples. Second, regulatory laws specify standards of socially responsible conduct for the protection of persons endangered by the conduct. While the tort standard may go further, we have recognized the force of the criminal or regulatory standard in negligence cases even when it was set by agencies or local governments that presumably could not themselves create civil liability whether or

---

4. Long ago, Chief Justice Harlan F. Stone deplored the reluctance of "modern courts [to] resort to standards of conduct set up by legislation" as sources of liability or other consequences beyond those provided by the legislation. "The statute was looked upon as in the law but not of it, a formal rule to be obeyed, it is true, since it is the command of the sovereign, but to be obeyed grudgingly, by construing it narrowly and treating it as though it did not exist for any purpose other than that embraced within the strict construction of its words. It is difficult to appraise the consequences of the perpetuation of incongruities and injustices in the law by this habit of narrow construction of statutes and by the failure to recognize that, as recognitions of social policy, they are as significant and rightly as much a part of the law, as the rules declared by judges." Stone, The Common Law in the United States, 50 Harv.L.Rev. 4 (1936).

not they had such an intent. [Cc] Third, governmental sanctions, penal or otherwise, may be enacted to add governmental enforcement to the recognized obligations of a relationship existing apart from the legislation. In such a situation the "underlying assumption," to use the majority's phrase, is hardly that the penal sanction makes the civil obligation unnecessary. Rather, the statute shows that the obligation is considered of such importance that it deserves enforcement by public prosecution.

The Child Protection Laws. It can hardly be questioned that a statute like 163.535, which makes it a crime intentionally to desert and abandon a child, is of the third kind. It and the related sections did not enact a novel prohibition against parental neglect for the convenience of the general public or the protection of taxpayers. They enacted a legislative definition and public enforcement of certain minimal obligations of an existing relationship. Jurisprudentially it might be said that parents have a duty not to abandon and desert their young children because ORS 163.535 makes it a crime to do so, but a legislator would surely think ORS 163.535 should make it a crime to abandon and desert a child because the parent's existing duty—the duty to the child, not to the state—deserved governmental reenforcement. It is the parent's duty thus recognized under Oregon law that plaintiffs invoke in these cases.

The majority does not really deny that ORS 163.535 constitutes such a legislative recognition and reenforcement of the parent's private obligation to the child, not of some socially convenient behavior. Rather, the majority would deny a remedy for the intentional breach of this obligation on the ground that other public policies militate against such a remedy. Upon examination, the majority's statutory citations refer to the single policy of maintaining and preserving the position of the child within a functioning family as long as this is possible. Without in any way questioning that this is indeed the state's public policy, I do not agree that it supports the conclusion that the legislature meant to deny the child a remedy for injuries from a parent's unlawful acts.

First, it must be kept in mind what conduct violates ORS 163.535. The statute makes it a felony to desert one's child with intent to abandon it. Of course, we have no evidence of the actual facts in these cases, but the allegations are that defendants did desert and abandon their children "maliciously, intentionally, and with cruel disregard of the consequences." If that is true, the parents have in fact ended the family unit, so that solicitude about not impairing it by litigation may sacrifice the children's legal rights to a pious hope. Contrary to the majority, I do not believe it is this court's own judgment of the possible effects of litigation on family relations that matters (a question on which counsel was unable to enlighten us and that, if taken seriously, is hardly within judicial notice) but rather what view of these effects may be attributed to the legislature. More important for interpreting the legislative policy, however, the statute means that a district attorney or grand jury on the alleged facts could prosecute the parents for a felony.

It is incongruous to hold that the legislature provided for a felony prosecution of parents who egregiously violate a duty toward their children, but that it meant to exclude civil actions on behalf of the maliciously abandoned children for fear of impairing the family unit. To hold that the plaintiffs cannot invoke this duty, one must assume a legislative policy that a deserted and abandoned child (or a guardian on its behalf) should ask a district attorney to seek the criminal punishment of the parent for this desertion, but that the child should have no claim that would be of any benefit to itself. That seems to unlikely a policy to attribute to the legislature without some showing that it was intended.

Moreover, the majority's premise proves too much. For purposes of the issue of law before us on these demurrers, it can be assumed that the plaintiffs have suffered actual, demonstrable injuries of a kind for which the law provides money damages against defendants other than parents, that defendants have assets from which these real injuries of the plaintiffs could be compensated, and that defendants caused these injuries by intentionally breaching a specific duty toward plaintiffs that is recognized in Oregon law. Perhaps the explanation for the majority's unwillingness to follow these assumptions to their conclusion is that the injuries alleged are psychological and emotional rather than physical. But if a civil remedy is denied on the majority's premise that it is precluded by a state policy of preserving family unity, that premise would apply equally to bar recovery of damages by a child crippled by physical abuse.[5] And despite the majority's reference to statutory proceedings for the termination of parental rights, it is at least questionable that a termination proceeding would create rights to a financial recovery to compensate for such very real and costly harm caused before the termination proceeding.

Although the majority does not say so, its premise is the equivalent of the doctrine of intrafamily tort immunity which Oregon has abandoned at least with respect to intentional torts, though attributed here to a supposed legislative policy subordinating legal claims of children against their parents to reliance on "protective social services." I perceive no such prescribed reliance on social services when parents who have deliberately mistreated their children in a manner made criminal by statute have the assets to be responsible for the harm caused thereby. In my view, plaintiffs have alleged at least one triable

---

5. Defendant presented a "parade of horribles" such as actions for psychological or emotional injury from receiving fewer Christmas gifts than a sibling and the like. I note this only to point out that the argument misses the point. The nature of the *breach of duty* in this case is fixed by ORS 163.535 and would not give rise to an expandable common law precedent. As far as the present issue is concerned, the case would be the same if a child had been deliberately abandoned in an unheated mountain cabin and lost a limb to frostbite or suffered other permanent injuries from lack of food or pneumonia.

Nothing is said here about claims based on other statutes invoked by plaintiffs that deal with general but unintentional neglect or nonsupport of children. The provision of alternative social services relied on by the majority may militate against implying a civil remedy for these less final and culpable violations of parental duty.

cause of action arising from an alleged intentional violation of duties recognized in ORS 163.535. Therefore, the demurrers should have been overruled.

LENT, J., joins in this dissent.

---

1. The three opinions in this case present three different views of the approach to be adopted by a court in deciding the effect that a criminal or administrative statute should have on the existing common law of torts. Identify and evaluate them. See Restatement (Second) of Torts § 874A. And see the interesting further discussion by the members of the same court in Bob Godfrey Pontiac, Inc. v. Roloff, 291 Or. 318, 630 P.2d 840 (1981) (violation of statute setting forth ethical duties of attorneys).

2. For some typical examples, see Bishop v. Liston, 112 Neb. 559, 199 N.W. 825 (1924) (criminal age-of-consent statute held to affect tort action); Herman Saks & Sons, Inc. v. Ivey, 26 Ala.App. 240, 157 So. 265 (1934) (criminal statute on insulting and abusive language to another in public, tort action applied); Creek v. Laski, 248 Mich. 425, 227 N.W. 817 (1929) (criminal statute on malicious destruction of a will, tort action); Laczko v. Jules Meyers, Inc., 276 Cal.App.2d 293, 80 Cal.Rptr. 798 (1969) (criminal statute against altering mileage on car odometer); Brinkman v. Urban Realty Co., 10 N.J. 113, 89 A.2d 394 (1952) (criminal statute against rental overcharge); Heuer v. John R. Thompson Co., 251 S.W.2d 980 (Mo.App.1952) (statute imposes criminal penalty for failure to supply a "service letter" to former employee); Hatcher v. Range, 98 Tex. 85, 81 S.W. 289 (1914) (crime to impute unchastity to a woman—creates slander per se).

3. Observe that the court may assimilate the cause of action to the nearest related tort and modify that tort under its common law authority or may create a new tort action. On factors influencing the determination of whether the court should supply a tort remedy, see Restatement (Second) of Torts § 874A, comment h. And see comment i on the scope of the legislative purpose.

4. See Foy, Some Reflections on Legislation, Adjudication, and Implied Private Actions in the State and Federal Courts, 71 Cornell L.Rev. 501 (1986); Forell, The Interrelationship of Statutes and Tort Actions, 66 Ore.L.Rev. 201 (1987); Gamm & Eisberg, The Implied Rights Doctrine, 4 UMKC L.Rev. 292 (1972); Note, The Use of Criminal Statutes in the Creation of New Torts, 48 Colum.L.Rev. 456 (1948); Comment, Implied Causes of Action in the State Courts, 30 Stan.L.Rev. 1243 (1978); Comment, Private Remedies Under the Consumer Fraud Acts: The Judicial Approaches of Statutory Interpretation and Implication, 67 Nw.L.Rev. 413 (1972).

BIVENS v. SIX UNKNOWN NAMED AGENTS OF FEDERAL BUREAU OF NARCOTICS

Supreme Court of the United States, 1971.
403 U.S. 388, 91 S.Ct. 1999, 29 L.Ed.2d 619.

MR. JUSTICE BRENNAN delivered the opinion of the Court. The Fourth Amendment provides that: "The right of the people to be secure in their persons, houses, papers, and effects, against unreasonable searches and seizures, shall not be violated. * * * "

In Bell v. Hood, 327 U.S. 678 (1946), we reserved the question whether violation of that command by a federal agent acting under color of his authority gives rise to a cause of action for damages consequent upon his unconstitutional conduct. Today we hold that it does. * * *

Petitioner's complaint alleged that * * * respondents, agents of the Federal Bureau of Narcotics acting under claim of federal authority, entered his apartment and arrested him for alleged narcotics violations. The agents manacled petitioner in front of his wife and children, and threatened to arrest the entire family. They searched the apartment from stem to stern. * * *

[H]is complaint [also] asserted that the arrest and search were effected without a warrant, and that unreasonable force was employed in making the arrest, [and, by implication,] that the arrest was made without probable cause. Petitioner claimed to have suffered great humiliation, embarrassment, and mental suffering as a result of the agents' unlawful conduct, and sought $15,000 damages from each of them. The District Court, on respondents' motion, dismissed the complaint on the ground, *inter alia,* that it failed to state a cause of action.[2] 276 F.Supp. 12 (EDNY 1967). The Court of Appeals * * * affirmed on that basis. 409 F.2d 718 (CA2 1969). We granted certiorari. 399 U.S. 905 (1970). We reverse. * * *

Respondents do not argue that petitioner should be entirely without remedy for an unconstitutional invasion of his rights by federal agents. In respondents' view, however, the rights that petitioner asserts—primarily rights of privacy—are creations of state and not of federal law. Accordingly, they argue, petitioner may obtain money damages to redress invasion of these rights only by an action in tort, under state law, in the state courts. In this scheme the Fourth Amendment would serve merely to limit the extent to which the agents could defend the state law tort suit by asserting that their actions were a valid exercise of federal power: if the agents were shown to have violated the Fourth Amendment, such a defense would be lost to them and they would stand before the state law merely as private individuals. * * *

We think that respondents' thesis rests upon an unduly restrictive view of the Fourth Amendment's protection against unreasonable searches and seizures by federal agents, a view that has consistently been rejected by this Court. Respondents seek to treat the relationship between a citizen and a federal agent unconstitutionally exercising his authority as no different from the relationship between two private citizens. In so doing, they ignore the fact that power, once granted, does not disappear like a magic gift when it is wrongfully used. An

2. The agents were not named in petitioner's complaint, and the District Court ordered that the complaint be served upon "those federal agents who it is indicated by the records of the United States Attorney participated in the November 25, 1965, arrest of the [petitioner]." * * * Five agents were ultimately served.

agent acting—albeit unconstitutionally—in the name of the United States possesses a far greater capacity for harm than an individual trespasser exercising no authority other than his own. [Cc] Accordingly, as our cases make clear, the Fourth Amendment operates as a limitation upon the exercise of federal power regardless of whether the State in whose jurisdiction that power is exercised would prohibit or penalize the identical act if engaged in by a private citizen. It guarantees to citizens of the United States the absolute right to be free from unreasonable searches and seizures carried out by virtue of federal authority. And "where federally protected rights have been invaded, it has been the rule from the beginning that courts will be alert to adjust their remedies so as to grant the necessary relief." Bell v. Hood, 327 U.S., at 684. * * *

Our cases have long since rejected the notion that the Fourth Amendment proscribes only such conduct as would, if engaged in by private persons, be condemned by state law. * * *

The interests protected by state laws regulating trespass and the invasion of privacy, and those protected by the Fourth Amendment's guarantee against unreasonable searches and seizures, may be inconsistent or even hostile. Thus, we may bar the door against an unwelcome private intruder, or call the police if he persists in seeking entrance. The availability of such alternative means for the protection of privacy may lead the State to restrict imposition of liability for any consequent trespass. A private citizen, asserting no authority other than his own, will not normally be liable in trespass if he demands, and is granted, admission to another's house. [Cc] But one who demands admission under a claim of federal authority stands in a far different position. [Cc] The mere invocation of federal power by a federal law enforcement official will normally render futile any attempt to resist an unlawful entry or arrest by resort to the local police; and a claim of authority to enter is likely to unlock the door as well. * * *

That damages may be obtained for injuries consequent upon a violation of the Fourth Amendment by federal officials should hardly seem a surprising proposition. Historically, damages have been regarded as the ordinary remedy for an invasion of personal interests in liberty. [Cc] Of course, the Fourth Amendment does not in so many words provide for its enforcement by an award of money damages for the consequences of its violation. But "it is * * * well settled that where legal rights have been invaded, and a federal statute provides for a general right to sue for such invasion, federal courts may use any available remedy to make good the wrong done." Bell v. Hood, 327 U.S., at 684 (footnote omitted). The present case involves no special factors counselling hesitation in the absence of affirmative action by Congress. * * * Finally, we cannot accept respondents' formulation of the question as whether the availability of money damages is necessary to enforce the Fourth Amendment. For we have here no explicit congressional declaration that persons injured by a federal officer's violation of the Fourth Amendment may not recover money damages from the agents, but must instead be remitted to another remedy, equally effective in the view of Congress. The question is merely whether petitioner, if he can demonstrate an injury consequent upon the violation by federal agents of his Fourth Amendment rights, is entitled to redress his injury through a particular remedial mechanism normally available in the federal courts. [Cc] "The very essence of civil liberty certainly consists in the right of every individual to claim the protection of the laws, whenever he receives an injury." Marbury v. Madison, 1 Cranch 137, 163 (1803). Having concluded that petitioner's complaint states a cause of action under the Fourth Amendment * * * we hold that petitioner is entitled to recover money damages for any injuries he has suffered as a result of the agents' violation of the Amendment. *. * *

Judgment reversed and case remanded.

MR. JUSTICE HARLAN, concurring in the judgment. * * * I am of the opinion that federal courts do have the power to award damages for violation of "constitutionally protected interests" and I agree with the Court that a traditional judicial remedy such as damages is appropriate to the vindication of the personal interests protected by the Fourth Amendment. * * *

[T]he interest which Bivens claims—to be free from official conduct in contravention of the Fourth Amendment—is a federally protected interest. [C] Therefore, the question of judicial power to grant Bivens damages is not a problem of the "source" of the "right"; instead, the question is whether the power to authorize damages as a judicial remedy for the vindication of a federal constitutional right is placed by the Constitution itself exclusively in Congress' hands. * * *

[I]n suits for damages based on violations of federal statutes lacking any express authorization of a damage remedy, this Court has authorized such relief where, in its view, damages are necessary to effectuate the congressional policy underpinning the substantive provisions of the statute. J.I. Case Co. v. Borak, 377 U.S. 426 (1964).[4] [Cc] * * *

Initially, I note that it would be at least anomalous to conclude that the federal judiciary—while competent to choose among the range of traditional judicial remedies to implement statutory and common-law policies, and even to generate substantive rules governing primary behavior in furtherance of broadly formulated policies articulated by

---

4. The Borak case is an especially clear example of the exercise of federal judicial power to accord damages as an appropriate remedy in the absence of any express statutory authorization of a federal cause of action. There we "implied"—from what can only be characterized as an "exclusively procedural provision" affording access to a federal forum [citation] a private cause of action for damages for violation of § 14(a) of the Securities Exchange Act of 1934, 48 Stat. 895, 15 U.S.C.A. § 78n(a). * * *

The exercise of judicial power involved in Borak simply cannot be justified in terms of statutory construction [c]: nor did the Borak Court purport to do so. [C] The notion of "implying" a remedy, therefore, as applied to cases like Borak, can only refer to a process whereby the federal judiciary exercises a choice among traditionally available judicial remedies according to reasons related to the substantive social policy embodied in an act of positive law. [C]

statute or Constitution [cc] is powerless to accord a damages remedy to vindicate social policies which, by virtue of their inclusion in the Constitution, are aimed predominantly at restraining the Government as an instrument of the popular will. * * *

If explicit congressional authorization is an absolute prerequisite to the power of a federal court to accord compensatory relief regardless of the necessity or appropriateness of damages as a remedy simply because of the status of a legal interest as constitutionally protected, then it seems to me that explicit congressional authorization is similarly prerequisite to the exercise of equitable remedial discretion in favor of constitutionally protected interests. Conversely, if a general grant of jurisdiction to the federal courts by Congress is thought adequate to empower a federal court to grant equitable relief for all areas of subject-matter jurisdiction enumerated therein, see 28 U.S.C.A. § 1331(a), then it seems to me that the same statute is sufficient to empower a federal court to grant a traditional remedy at law. * * *

Although conceding that the standard of determining whether a damage remedy should be utilized to effectuate statutory policies is one of "necessity" or "appropriateness," [cc] the Government contends that questions concerning congressional discretion to modify judicial remedies relating to constitutionally protected interests warrant a more stringent constraint on the exercise of judicial power with respect to this class of legally protected interests. [C]

These arguments for a more stringent test to govern the grant of damages in constitutional cases seem to be adequately answered by the point that the judiciary has a particular responsibility to assure the vindication of constitutional interests such as those embraced by the Fourth Amendment. To be sure, "it must be remembered that legislatures are ultimate guardians of the liberties and welfare of the people in quite as great a degree as the courts." [C] But it must also be recognized that the Bill of Rights is particularly intended to vindicate the interests of the individual in the face of the popular will as expressed in legislative majorities * * *.

The question then, is, as I see it, whether compensatory relief is "necessary" or "appropriate" to the vindication of the interest asserted. [Cc] In resolving that question, it seems to me that the range of policy considerations we may take into account is at least as broad as the range a legislature would consider with respect to an express statutory authorization of a traditional remedy. In this regard I agree with the Court that the appropriateness of according Bivens compensatory relief does not turn simply on the deterrent effect liability will have on federal official conduct. Damages as a traditional form of compensation for invasion of a legally protected interest may be entirely appropriate even if no substantial deterrent effects on future official lawlessness might be thought to result. Bivens, after all, has invoked judicial processes claiming entitlement to compensation for injuries resulting from allegedly lawless official behavior, if those injuries are properly compensable in money damages. I do not think a court of law—vested with the power to accord a remedy—should deny him his relief simply because he cannot show that future lawless conduct will thereby be deterred.

And I think it is clear that Bivens advances a claim of the sort that, if proved, would be properly compensable in damages. The personal interests protected by the Fourth Amendment are those we attempt to capture by the notion of "privacy"; while the Court today properly points out that the type of harm which officials can inflict when they invade protected zones of an individual's life are different from the types of harm private citizens inflict on one another, the experience of judges in dealing with private trespass and false imprisonment claims supports the conclusion that courts of law are capable of making the types of judgment concerning causation and magnitude of injury necessary to accord meaningful compensation for invasion of Fourth Amendment rights. * * *

It seems to me entirely proper that these injuries be compensable according to uniform rules of federal law, especially in light of the very large element of federal law which must in any event control the scope of official defenses to liability. [C] Certainly, there is very little to be gained from the standpoint of federalism by preserving different rules of liability for federal officers dependent on the State where the injury occurs. [C]

Putting aside the desirability of leaving the problem of federal official liability to the vagaries of common-law actions, it is apparent that some form of damages is the only possible remedy for someone in Bivens' alleged position. * * *

However desirable a direct remedy against the Government might be as a substitute for individual official liability, the sovereign still remains immune to suit. * * *

The only substantial policy consideration advanced against recognition of a federal cause of action for violation of Fourth Amendment rights by federal officials is the incremental expenditure of judicial resources that will be necessitated by this class of litigation. There is, however, something ultimately self-defeating about this argument. For if, as the Government contends, damages will rarely be realized by plaintiffs in these cases because of jury hostility, the limited resources of the official concerned, etc., then I am not ready to assume that there will be a significant increase in the expenditure of judicial resources on these claims. Few responsible lawyers and plaintiffs are likely to choose the course of litigation if the statistical chances of success are truly de minimis. And I simply cannot agree with my Brother Black that the possibility of "frivolous" claims—if defined simply as claims with no legal merit—warrants closing the courthouse doors to people in Bivens' situation. There are other ways, short of that, of coping with frivolous lawsuits.

On the other hand, if—as I believe is the case with respect, at least, to the most flagrant abuses of official power—damages to some degree will be available when the option of litigation is chosen, then the question appears to be how Fourth Amendment interests rank on a scale of social values compared with, for example, the interests of stockholders defrauded by misleading proxies. See J.I. Case Co. v. Borak, supra. Judicial resources, I am well aware, are increasingly scarce these days. Nonetheless, when we automatically close the courthouse door solely on this basis, we implicitly express a value judgment on the comparative importance of classes of legally protected interests. And current limitations upon the effective functioning of the courts arising from budgetary inadequacies should not be permitted to stand in the way of the recognition of otherwise sound constitutional principles. * * *

For these reasons, I concur in the judgment of the Court.

MR. CHIEF JUSTICE BURGER, dissenting. I dissent from today's holding which judicially creates a damage remedy not provided for by the Constitution and not enacted by Congress. We would more surely preserve the important values of the doctrine of separation of powers— and perhaps get a better result—by recommending a solution to the Congress as the branch of government in which the Constitution has vested the legislative power. Legislation is the business of the Congress, and it has the facilities and competence for that task—as we do not. * * * [The opinion suggests that the problem of a substitute for the "exclusionary rule" might be considered with the problem in this case and legislation recommended to Congress.]

MR. JUSTICE BLACK, dissenting. * * * Congress could create a federal cause of action for damages for an unreasonable search in violation of the Fourth Amendment. Although Congress has created such a federal cause of action against state officials acting under color of state law, it has never created such a cause of action against federal officials. If it wanted to do so, Congress could, of course, create a remedy against federal officials who violate the Fourth Amendment in the performance of their duties. But the point of this case and the fatal weakness in the Court's judgment is that neither Congress nor the State of New York has enacted legislation creating such a right of action. For us to do so is, in my judgment, an exercise of power that the Constitution does not give us.

Even if we had the legislative power to create a remedy, there are many reasons why we should decline to create a cause of action where none has existed since the formation of our Government. The courts of the United States as well as those of the States are choked with lawsuits. The number of cases on the docket of this Court have reached an unprecedented volume in recent years. A majority of these cases are brought by citizens with substantial complaints—persons who are physically or economically injured by torts or frauds or governmental infringement of their rights; persons who have been unjustly deprived of their liberty or their property; and persons who have not yet received the equal opportunity in education, employment, and pursuit of happiness that was the dream of our forefathers. Unfortunately, there have also been a growing number of frivolous lawsuits, particularly actions for damages against law enforcement officers whose conduct has been judicially sanctioned by state trial and appellate courts and in many instances even by this Court. My fellow Justices on this Court and our brethren throughout the federal judiciary know only too well the time-consuming task of conscientiously poring over hundreds of thousands of pages of factual allegations of misconduct by police, judicial, and corrections officials. Of course, there are instances of legitimate grievances, but legislators might well desire to devote judicial resources to other problems of a more serious nature. * * *

But that is not my task. The task of evaluating the pros and cons of creating judicial remedies for particular wrongs is a matter for Congress and the legislatures of the States. * * *

Should the time come when Congress desires such lawsuits, it has before it a model of valid legislation, 42 U.S.C.A. § 1983, to create a damage remedy against federal officers. * * *

---

1. In this, the first Supreme Court case implying a cause of action from a constitutional provision, the Court laid considerable reliance upon earlier cases involving actions "implied" from federal statutes, particularly J.I. Case Co. v. Borak, 377 U.S. 426 (1964) (Securities Exchange Act). Observe that *Bivens* established essentially the same cause of action against federal officers as that existing against state officers under 42 U.S.C.A. § 1983. See Carey v. Piphus, supra page 985.

2. Since *Bivens* there have been other Supreme Court cases giving rise to a cause of action deriving from a constitutional provision. See, e.g., Davis v. Passman, 442 U.S. 228 (1979) (5th Amendment—due process and sex discrimination); Carlson v. Green, 446 U.S. 14 (1980) (8th Amendment—cruel and inhuman punishment).

3. See Hill, Constitutional Remedies, 69 Colum.L.Rev. 1109 (1969); Dellinger, Of Rights and Remedies: The Constitution as a Sword, 85 Harv.L.Rev. 1532 (1972); Love, Damages: A Remedy for Violation of Constitutional Rights, 67 Calif.L.Rev. 1242 (1978); Whitman, Government Responsibility for Constitutional Torts, 85 Mich.L.Rev. 225 (1986); Note, Damage Awards for Constitutional Torts, 93 Harv.L.Rev. 966 (1980).

TRANSAMERICA MORTG. ADVISORS, INC. (TAMA)
v. LEWIS
Supreme Court of the United States, 1979.
444 U.S. 11, 100 S.Ct. 242, 62 L.Ed.2d 146.

MR. JUSTICE STEWART delivered the opinion of the Court. The Investment Advisers Act of 1940, 15 U.S.C.A. §§ 80b–1 et seq. was enacted to deal with abuses that Congress had found to exist in the investment advisers industry. The question in this case is whether that Act creates a private cause of action for damages or other relief in favor of persons aggrieved by those who allegedly have violated it.

The respondent, a shareholder of petitioner Mortgage Trust of America (Trust), brought this suit in a Federal District Court as a derivative action on behalf of the Trust and as a class action on behalf of the Trust's shareholders. Named as defendants were the Trust, several individual trustees, the Trust's investment adviser, Transamerica Mortgage Advisors, Inc. (TAMA), and two corporations affiliated with TAMA. * * *

The respondent's complaint alleged that the petitioners in the course of advising or managing the Trust had been guilty of various frauds and breaches of fiduciary duty. The complaint set out three causes of action, each said to arise under the Investment Advisers Act of 1940. The first alleged that the advisory contract between TAMA and the Trust was unlawful because TAMA and Transamerica were not registered under the Act and because the contract had provided for grossly excessive compensation. The second alleged that the petitioners breached their fiduciary duty to the Trust by causing it to purchase securities of inferior quality from Land Capital. The third alleged that the petitioners had misappropriated profitable investment opportunities for the benefit of other companies affiliated with Transamerica. The complaint sought injunctive relief to restrain further performance of the advisory contract, rescission of the contract, restitution of fees and other considerations paid by the Trust, an accounting of illegal profits, and an award of damages.

The trial court ruled that the Investment Advisers Act confers no private right of action, and accordingly dismissed the complaint. The Court of Appeals reversed, Lewis v. Transamerica Corp., 575 F.2d 237, holding that "implication of a private right of action for injunctive relief and damages under the Advisers Act in favor of appropriate plaintiffs is necessary to achieve the goals of Congress in enacting the legislation." Id., at 239. We granted certiorari to consider the important federal question presented. 439 U.S. 952.

The Investment Advisers Act nowhere expressly provides for a private cause of action. * * * The argument is made, however, that the clients of investment advisers were the intended beneficiaries of the Act and that courts should therefore imply a private cause of action in their favor. [Cc]

The question whether a statute creates a cause of action, either expressly or by implication, is basically a matter of statutory construction. [Cc] While some opinions of the Court have placed considerable emphasis upon the desirability of implying private rights of action in order to provide remedies thought to effectuate the purposes of a given statute, e.g., J.I. Case Co. v. Borak, [377 U.S. 426 (1964),] what must ultimately be determined is whether Congress intended to create the private remedy asserted, as our recent decisions have made clear. [Cc]

We accept this as the appropriate inquiry to be made in resolving the issues presented by the case before us.

Accordingly, we begin with the language of the statute itself. [Cc] It is asserted that the creation of a private right of action can fairly be inferred from the language of two sections of the Act. The first is § 206, which broadly proscribes fraudulent practices by investment advisers, making it unlawful for any investment adviser "to employ any device, scheme, or artifice to defraud * * * [or] to engage in any transaction, practice, or course of business which operates as a fraud or deceit upon any client or prospective client," or to engage in specified transactions with clients without making required disclosures.[6] The second is § 215, which provides that contracts whose formation or performance would violate the Act "shall be void * * * as regards the rights of" the violator and knowing successors in interest.[7]

It is apparent that the two sections were intended to benefit the clients of investment advisers, and, in the case of § 215, the parties to advisory contracts as well. As we have previously recognized, § 206 establishes "federal fiduciary standards" to govern the conduct of investment advisers. [Cc] Indeed, the Act's legislative history leaves no doubt that Congress intended to impose enforceable fiduciary obligations. [Cc]

---

6. Section 206, 54 Stat. 852, as amended, as set forth in 15 U.S.C.A. § 80b–6, reads as follows:

"§ 80b–6. Prohibited Transactions by Investment Advisers

"It shall be unlawful for any investment adviser, by use of the mails or any means or instrumentality of interstate commerce, directly or indirectly—

"(1) to employ any device, scheme, or artifice to defraud any client or prospective client;

"(2) to engage in any transaction, practice, or course of business which operates as a fraud or deceit upon any client or prospective client;

"(3) acting as principal for his own account, knowingly to sell any security to or purchase any security from a client, or acting as broker for a person other than such client, knowingly to effect any sale or purchase of any security for the account of such client, without disclosing to such client in writing before the completion of such transaction the capacity in which he is acting and obtaining the consent of the client to such transaction. The prohibitions of this paragraph shall not apply to any transaction with a customer of a broker or dealer if such broker or dealer is not acting as an investment adviser in relation to such transaction;

"(4) to engage in any act, practice, or course of business which is fraudulent, deceptive, or manipulative. The Commission shall, for the purposes of this paragraph (4) by rules and regulations define, and prescribe means reasonably designed to prevent, such acts, practices, and courses of business as are fraudulent, deceptive, or manipulative." * * *

7. Section 215, 54 Stat. 856, as set forth in 15 U.S.C.A. § 80b–15 reads in part as follows:

"§ 80b–15. Validity of Contracts
* * *

"(b) Every contract made in violation of any provision of this subchapter and every contract heretofore or hereafter made, the performance of which involves the violation of, or the continuance of any relationship or practice in violation of any provision of this subchapter, or any rule, regulation, or order thereunder, shall be void (1) as regards the rights of any person who, in violation of any such provision, rule, regulation, or order, shall have made or engaged in the performance of any such contract, and (2) as regards the rights of any person who, not being a party to such contract, shall have acquired any right thereunder with actual knowledge of the facts by reason of which the making or performance of such contract was in violation of any such provision."

But whether Congress intended additionally that these provisions would be enforced through private litigation is a different question.

On this question the legislative history of the Act is entirely silent—a state of affairs not surprising when it is remembered that the Act concededly does not explicitly provide any private remedies whatever. [C] But while the absence of anything in the legislative history that indicates an intention to confer any private right of action is hardly helpful to the respondent, it does not automatically undermine his position. This Court has held that the failure of Congress expressly to consider a private remedy is not inevitably inconsistent with an intent on its part to make such a remedy available. [C] Such an intent may appear implicitly in the language or structure of the statute, or in the circumstances of its enactment.

In the case of § 215, we conclude that the statutory language itself fairly implies a right to specific and limited relief in a federal court. By declaring certain contracts void, § 215 by its terms necessarily contemplates that the issue of voidness under its criteria may be litigated somewhere. At the very least Congress must have assumed that § 215 could be raised defensively in private litigation to preclude the enforcement of an investment advisers contract. But the legal consequences of voidness are typically not so limited. A person with the power to avoid a contract ordinarily may resort to a court to have the contract rescinded and to obtain restitution of consideration paid. [Cc] And this Court has previously recognized that a comparable provision, § 29(b) of the Securities Exchange Act of 1934, 15 U.S.C.A. § 78cc(b) confers a "right to rescind" a contract void under the criteria of the statute. Mills v. Electric Auto–Lite Co., 396 U.S. 375, 388. Moreover, the federal courts in general have viewed such language as implying an equitable cause of action for rescission or similar relief. [Cc]

For these reasons we conclude that when Congress declared in § 215 that certain contracts are void, it intended that the customary legal incidents of voidness would follow, including the availability of a suit for rescission or for an injunction against continued operation of the contract, and for restitution. Accordingly, we hold that the Court of Appeals was correct in ruling that the respondent may maintain an action on behalf of the Trust seeking to void the investment advisers contract.

We view quite differently, however, the respondent's claims for damages and other monetary relief under § 206. Unlike § 215, § 206 simply proscribes certain conduct, and does not in terms create or alter any civil liabilities. If monetary liability to a private plaintiff is to be found, it must be read into the Act. Yet it is an elemental canon of statutory construction that where a statute expressly provides a particular remedy or remedies, a court must be chary of reading others into it. "When a statute limits a thing to be done in a particular mode, it includes the negative of any other mode." [Cc] Congress expressly provided both judicial and administrative means for enforcing compliance with § 206. First, under § 217, 15 U.S.C.A. § 80b–17, willful violations of the Act are criminal offenses, punishable by fine or imprisonment, or both. Second, § 209 authorizes the Commission to bring civil actions in federal courts to enjoin compliance with the Act, including, of course, § 206. Third, the Commission is authorized by § 203 to impose various administrative sanctions on persons who violate the Act, including § 206. In view of these express provisions for enforcing the duties imposed by § 206, it is highly improbable that "Congress absentmindedly forgot to mention an intended private action." Cannon v. University of Chicago, 441 U.S., at 742 (Powell, J., dissenting).

Even settled rules of statutory construction could yield, of course, to persuasive evidence of a contrary legislative intent. [Cc] But what evidence of intent exists in this case, circumstantial though it be, weighs against the implication of a private right of action for a monetary award in a case such as this. Under each of the securities laws that preceded the Act here in question, and under the Investment Company Act of 1940 which was enacted as companion legislation, Congress expressly authorized private suits for damages in prescribed circumstances. For example, Congress provided an express damages remedy for misrepresentations contained in an underwriter's registration statement in § 11(a) of the Securities Act of 1933, and for certain materially misleading statements in § 18(a) of the Securities Exchange Act of 1934. "Obviously, then, when Congress wished to provide a private damages remedy, it knew how to do so and did so expressly." [Cc] The fact that it enacted no analogous provisions in the legislation here at issue strongly suggests that Congress was simply unwilling to impose any potential monetary liability to a private suitor. [C]

The omission of any such potential remedy from the Act's substantive provisions was paralleled in the jurisdictional section, § 214. Early drafts of the bill had simply incorporated by reference a provision of the Public Utility Holding Company Act of 1935, which gave the federal courts jurisdiction "of all suits in equity and actions at law brought to enforce any liability or duty created by" the statute (emphasis added). [Cc] After hearings on the bill in the Senate, representatives of the investment advisers industry and the staff of the Commission met to discuss the bill, and certain changes were made. The language that was enacted as § 214 first appeared in this compromise version of the bill. [C] That version, and the version finally enacted into law [c] both omitted any references to "actions at law" or to "liability." The unexplained deletion of a single phrase from a jurisdictional provision is, of course, not determinative of whether a private remedy exists. But it is one more piece of evidence that Congress did not intend to authorize a cause of action for anything beyond limited equitable relief.

Relying on the factors identified in Cort v. Ash, 422 U.S. 66, the respondent and the Commission, as amicus curiae, argue that our inquiry in this case cannot stop with the intent of Congress, but must consider the utility of a private remedy, and the fact that it may be one not traditionally relegated to state law. We rejected the same contentions last term in Touche Ross & Co. v. Redington [442 U.S. 560], where it was argued that these factors standing alone justified the implication of a private right of action under § 17(a) of the Securities Exchange Act of 1934. We said in that case:

"It is true that in Cort v. Ash, the Court set forth four factors * that it considered 'relevant' in determining whether a private remedy is implicit in a statute not expressly providing one. But the Court did not decide that each of these factors is entitled to equal weight. The central inquiry remains whether Congress intended to create, either expressly or by implication, a private cause of action. Indeed, the first three factors discussed in Cort—the language and focus of the statute, its legislative history, and its purpose, [c] are ones traditionally relied upon in determining legislative intent." [C]

The statute in Touche Ross by its terms neither granted private rights to the members of any identifiable class, nor proscribed any conduct as unlawful. [C] In those circumstances it was evident to the Court that no private remedy was available. Section 206 of the Act here involved concededly was intended to protect the victims of the fraudulent practices it prohibited. But the mere fact that the statute was designed to protect advisers' clients does not require the implication of a private cause of action for damages on their behalf. [Cc] The dispositive question remains whether Congress intended to create any such remedy. Having answered that question in the negative, our inquiry is at an end.

For the reasons stated in this opinion, we hold that there exists a limited private remedy under the Investment Advisers Act of 1940 to void an investment advisers contract, but that the Act confers no other private causes of action, legal or equitable.[14] Accordingly, the judgment of the Court of Appeals is affirmed in part and reversed in part, and the case is remanded to that court for further proceedings consistent with this opinion.

MR. JUSTICE POWELL, concurring. I join the Court's opinion, which I view as compatible with my dissent in Cannon v. University of Chicago, 441 U.S. 677, 730.†

---

* These four factors are quoted in note 3, of the dissenting opinion, infra page 1184. [Ed.]

14. Where rescission is awarded, the rescinding party may of course have restitution of the consideration given under the contract, less any value conferred by the other party. See 5 A. Corbin, Contracts § 1114 (1964). Restitution would not, however, include compensation for any diminution in the value of the rescinding party's investment alleged to have resulted from the adviser's action or inaction. Such relief could provide by indirection the equiv-

alent of a private damages remedy that we have concluded Congress did not confer.

† Justice Powell's dissenting opinion in *Cannon* said in part: "The time has come to reappraise our standards for the judicial implication of private causes of action. * * * In recent history the Court has tended to stray from the Art. III and separation-of-powers principle of limited jurisdiction. * * * The 'four factor' analysis of [Cort v. Ash, 422 U.S. 66] is an open invitation to federal courts to legislate causes of action not authorized by Congress. It is an analysis not faithful to

MR. JUSTICE WHITE, with whom MR. JUSTICE BRENNAN, MR. JUSTICE MARSHALL, and MR. JUSTICE STEVENS join, dissenting.

The Court today holds that private rights of action under the Investment Advisers Act of 1940 (Act) are limited to actions for rescission of investment advisers contracts. In reaching this decision, the Court departs from established principles governing the implication of private rights of action by confusing the inquiry into the existence of a right of action with the question of available relief. By holding that damages are unavailable to victims of violations of the Act, the Court rejects the conclusion of every United States Court of Appeals that has considered the question. [Cc] The Court's decision cannot be reconciled with our decisions recognizing implied private actions for damages under securities laws with substantially the same language as the Act. By resurrecting distinctions between legal and equitable relief, the Court reaches a result that, as all parties to this litigation agree, can only be considered anomalous.

I. This Court has long recognized that private rights of action do not require express statutory authorization. [Cc] The preferred approach for determining whether a private right of action should be implied from a federal statute was outlined in Cort v. Ash, 422 U.S. 66, 78 (1975). See Cannon v. University of Chicago, 441 U.S. 677 (1979). Four factors were thought relevant,[3] and although subsequent decisions have indicated that the implication of a private right of action "is limited solely to determining whether Congress intended to create the private right of action," [c] these four factors are "the criteria through which this intent could be discerned." [C] Proper application of the factors outlined in Cort clearly indicates that § 206 of the Act, creates a private right of action.

II. In determining whether respondent can assert a private right of action under the Act, "the threshold question under Cort is whether the statute was enacted for the benefit of a special class of which the plaintiff is a member." [C] The instant action was brought by respondent as both a derivative action on behalf of Mortgage Trust of America and a class action on behalf of Mortgage Trust's shareholders. Respondent alleged that Mortgage Trust had retained Transamerica Mortgage Advisors, Inc. (TAMA), as its investment adviser and that violations of

constitutional principles and should be rejected. Absent the most compelling evidence of affirmative congressional intent, a federal court should not infer a private cause of action." 441 U.S. at 730, 731. [Ed.]

3. "First, is the plaintiff 'one of the class for whose especial benefit the statute was enacted,' Texas & Pacific R. Co. v. Rigsby, 241 U.S. 33, 39 (1916) (emphasis supplied)—that is, does the statute create a federal right in favor of the plaintiff? Second, is there any indication of legislative intent, explicit or implicit, either to create such a remedy or to deny one? See, e.g., National Railroad Passenger Corp. v. National Assn. of Railroad Passengers, 414 U.S. 453, 458, 460 (1974) (Amtrak). Third, is it consistent with the underlying purposes of the legislative scheme to imply such a remedy for the plaintiff? See, e.g., Amtrak, supra [cc]. And finally, is the cause of action one traditionally relegated to state law, in an area basically the concern of the States, so that it would be inappropriate to infer a cause of action based solely on federal law? [Cc]" Cort v. Ash, 422 U.S. 66, 78 (1975).

the Act by TAMA had injured the client corporation. Thus the question under Cort is whether the Act was enacted for the special benefit of clients of investment advisers.

The Court concedes that the language and legislative history of § 206 leave no doubt that it was "intended to benefit the clients of investment advisers," as we have previously recognized. [Cc] Because respondent's claims were brought on behalf of a member of the class the Act was designed to benefit, i.e., the clients of investment advisers, the first prong of the *Cort* test is satisfied in this case.

III. The second inquiry under the *Cort* approach is whether there is evidence of an express or implicit legislative intent to negate the claimed private rights of action. As the Court noted in *Cannon:* "[T]he legislative history of a statute that does not expressly create or deny a private remedy will typically be equally silent or ambiguous on the question. Therefore, in situations such as the present one 'in which it is clear that federal law has granted a class of persons certain rights, it is not necessary to show an intention to *create* a private cause of action, although an explicit purpose to *deny* such cause of action would be controlling.' *Cort,* 422 U.S. at 82 (emphasis in original)." 441 U.S., at 694.

I find no such intent to foreclose private actions. Indeed, the statutory language evinces an intent to create such actions. In § 215(b) of the Act Congress provided that contracts made in violation of any provision of the Act "shall be void." As the Court recognizes, such a provision clearly contemplates the existence of private rights under the Act. Similar provisions in the Investment Company Act of 1940, the Securities Exchange Act of 1934, and the Public Utility Holding Company Act have been recognized as reflecting an intent to create private rights of action to redress violations of substantive provisions of those Acts. [Cc]

The Court's conclusion that § 215, but not § 206, creates an implied private right of action ignores the relationship of § 215 to the substantive provisions of the Act contained in § 206. Like the jurisdictional provisions of a statute, § 215 "creates no cause of action of its own force and effect; it imposes no liabilities." [C] Section 215 merely specifies one consequence of a violation of the substantive prohibitions of § 206. The practical necessity of a private action to enforce this particular consequence of a § 206 violation suggests that Congress contemplated the use of private actions to redress violations of § 206. It also indicates that Congress did not intend the powers given to the SEC to be the exclusive means for enforcement of the Act.

The Court's holding that private litigants are restricted to actions for contract rescission confuses the question whether a cause of action exists with the question of the nature of relief available in such an action. Last Term in Davis v. Passman, 442 U.S. at 239, we recognized that "the question of whether a litigant has a 'cause of action' is analytically distinct and prior to the question of what relief, if any, a litigant may be entitled to receive." Once it is recognized that a statute creates an implied right of action, courts have wide discretion in fashioning available relief. Sullivan v. Little Hunting Park, Inc., 396 U.S. 229, 239. ("The existence of a statutory right implies the existence of all necessary and appropriate remedies"). As the Court stated in Bell v. Hood, 327 U.S. 678, 684 (1946), "where legal rights have been invaded, and a federal statute provides for a general right to sue for such invasion, federal courts may use any available remedy to make good the wrong done." Thus, in the absence of any contrary indication by Congress, courts may provide private litigants exercising implied rights of action whatever relief is consistent with the congressional purpose. [Cc] The very decisions cited by the Court to support implication of an equitable right of action from contract voidance provisions of a statute, indicate that the relief available in such an action need not be restricted to equitable relief. * * *

The fundamental problem with the Court's focus on § 214 is that it attmepts to discern congressional intent to deny a private cause of action from a jurisdictional, rather than a substantive, provision of the Act. Because § 214 is only a jurisdictional provision, "[i]t creates no cause of action of its own force and effect; it imposes no liabilities." [C] Since the source of implied rights of action must be found "in the substantive provisions of [the Act] which they seek to enforce, not in the jurisdictional provision," § 214's failure to refer to "actions at law" does not indicate that private actions for damages are unavailable under the Investment Advisers Act. The subject-matter jurisdiction of the federal courts over respondent's action is unquestioned, regardless of how § 214 is interpreted, because jurisdiction is provided by the "arising under" clause of 28 U.S.C.A. § 1331. [Cc] Where federal courts have jurisdiction over actions to redress violations of federal statutory rights, relief cannot be denied simply because Congress did not expressly provide for independent jurisdiction under the statute creating the federal rights.

IV. The third portion of the *Cort* standard requires consideration of the compatibility of a private right of action with the legislative scheme. While a private remedy will not be implied to the frustration of the legislative purpose, "when that remedy is necessary or at least helpful to the accomplishment of the statutory purpose, the Court is decidedly receptive to its implication under the statute." * * *

Implication of a private right of action for damages unquestionably would be not only consistent with the legislative goal of preventing fraudulent practices by investment advisers, but also essential to its achievement. While the Act empowers the SEC to take action to seek equitable relief to prevent offending investment advisers from engaging in future violations, in the absence of a private right of action for damages, victimized clients have little hope of obtaining redress for their injuries. Like the statute in *Cannon,* the Act does not assure that the members of the class it benefits are able "to activate and participate in the administrative process contemplated by the statute." [C]

Moreover, the SEC candidly admits that, given the tremendous growth of the investment advisory industry, the magnitude of the enforcement problem exceeds the Commission's limited examination and enforcement capabilities. The Commission maintains that private litigation therefore is a necessary supplement to SEC enforcement activity. Under the circumstances of this case, this position seems unassailable. [Cc]

V. The final consideration under the *Cort* analysis is whether the subject matter of the cause of action has been so traditionally relegated to state law as to make it inappropriate to infer a federal cause of action. Regulation of the activities of investment advisers has not been a traditional state concern. * * *

Although some practices proscribed by the Act undoubtedly would have been actionable in common-law actions for fraud, "Congress intended the Investment Advisers Act to establish federal fiduciary standards for investment advisers." [Cc] While state law may be applied to parties subject to the Act, "as long as private causes of action are available in federal courts for violation of the federal statutes, [the] enforcement problem is obviated." [C]

VI. Each of the *Cort* factors points toward implication of a private cause of action in favor of clients defrauded by investment advisers in violation of the Act. The Act was enacted for the special benefit of clients of investment advisers, and there is no indication of any legislative intent to deny such a cause of action, which would be consistent with the legislative scheme governing an area not traditionally relegated to state law. Under these circumstances an implied private right of action for damages should be recognized.

---

1. Early Supreme Court cases giving rise to a tort cause of action because of a statute are Texas & P.R. Co. v. Rigsby, 241 U.S. 33 (1916) (Safety Appliance Act); J.I. Case Co. v. Borak, 377 U.S. 426 (1964) (Securities Exchange Act); Allen v. State Board of Elections, 393 U.S. 544 (1969) (Voting Rights Act). As a result of these cases and *Bivens,* supra page 1171, there were numerous cases in the federal courts making use of the principle.

2. But the tide changed with Cort v. Ash, 422 U.S. 66 (1975) (statute prohibiting political contributions from corporations). A sharply divided court has declined to find a cause of action available in Securities Investor Protection Corp. v. Barbour, 421 U.S. 412 (1975) (Investor Protection Act); Piper v. Chris-Craft Indus., Inc., 430 U.S. 1 (1977) (statute on tender offers); Chrysler Corp. v. Brown, 441 U.S. 281 (1979) (Freedom of Information Act); Touche, Ross & Co. v. Redington, 442 U.S. 560 (1979) (Securities Exchange Act); California v. Sierra Club, 451 U.S. 287 (1981); and Middlesex County Sewerage Auth. v. National Sea Cleaners Ass'n, 453 U.S. 1 (1981) (Federal Water Pollution Control Act). But see Cannon v. University of Chicago, 441 U.S. 677 (1979) (prohibition of sex discrimination); Merrill Lynch v. Curran, 456 U.S. 353 (1982) (Commodities Exchange Act; perhaps starting a reverse trend).

3. The result therefore is that, at present, different positions are taken regarding constitutional and statutory provisions, with dissenting opinions in

most cases. One basis for explaining this is that the Constitution is not self-executing and requires court action, while the Congress can always provide for an action if it defines it. Other factors: (1) There is no federal common law of torts that the courts have the authority to modify; as a result, the Court must "imply" a cause of action from the legislation. But compare the remarks of Justice Harlan, supra page 1174, n. 4. This is the reason why the Supreme Court lays such heavy emphasis on "implying" a cause of action. (2) Some justices are vitally concerned over implications of the principle of separation of powers. (3) Some justices are concerned from a practical standpoint with the "flood of cases" likely to develop, and want to insist that the Congress provide for a cause of action if it wants it.

4. See McMahon & Rodos, Judicial Implication of Private Causes of Action: Reappraisal and Retrenchment, 80 Dick.L.Rev. 167 (1976); Pillai, Negative Implication: The Demise of Private Rights of Action in the Federal Courts, 47 U.Cin.L.Rev. 1 (1978); Frankel, Implied Rights of Action, 67 Va.L. Rev. 553 (1981); Note, Implied Private Action under Federal Statutes—The Emergence of a Conservative Doctrine, 18 Wm. & M.L.Rev. 419 (1976); Note, A New Direction for Implied Causes of Action, 48 Ford.L.Rev. 505 (1980).

2. PRIMA FACIE TORT

PORTER v. CRAWFORD & CO.
Missouri Court of Appeals, Western District, 1980.
611 S.W.2d 265.

DIXON, JUDGE. * * * The principal issue to be resolved is whether or not the law of Missouri will permit a recovery in tort for a lawful act performed maliciously and with the intent of causing harm to a plaintiff. * * *

Plaintiff had sustained damage in an automobile collision involving a motorist insured by defendant Carriers Insurance. Crawford & Company, acting as the agent and adjuster for Carriers, settled the plaintiff's claim and delivered a draft in exchange for a full release of the plaintiff's claim against the other motorist. The plaintiff deposited the draft in the National Bank in North Kansas City, third party defendant here, and upon the basis of that deposit, wrote checks on plaintiff's account. Carriers had, unbeknownst to the plaintiff, stopped payment on the draft; and, as a consequence, the plaintiff's checks were returned to the payees as being drawn against insufficient funds, and the bank subsequently assessed service charges in connection with those insufficient funds checks.

[In two counts directed respectively at Carriers and at Crawford, the plaintiff alleged (1) that Carriers "without having given any notice to plaintiff and for no cause or reason attributable to plaintiff, and without just cause or reason, stopped payment, * * * [that] said acts were done and committed by defendant in careless and reckless disregard of the rights of plaintiff and with intent to injury [sic] plaintiff, * * * that the acts and omissions * * * were wilful, wanton, and malicious," and that this produced embarrassment, humiliation and reputation damages; and (2) that Crawford failed to notify plaintiff, "with the intent to cause actual injury and damage, wilfully and knowingly failed to notify plaintiff of the act of Carriers in stopping payment," with the same damages. The trial court sustained motions to dismiss both counts.]

To facilitate the discussion, a statement of the elements of [the prima-facie] theory of tort liability will be stated in summary form as gleaned from the sources to be later discussed. The elements so summarized are:

1. Intentional lawful act by the defendant.

2. An intent to cause injury to the plaintiff.

3. Injury to the plaintiff.

4. An absence of any justification or an insufficient justification for the defendant's act. * * *

[Defendants concede] that the petition pleads the essential elements of that doctrine. The question is thus squarely presented as to whether or not Missouri will undertake to recognize a recovery upon the basis of an intentional tort under the principles of the case law in other jurisdictions developing what has been styled, "the prima facie tort doctrine."

Prima facie tort doctrine is a result of a controversy that has been waged for generations among the legal scholars with respect to the fundamental concept of tort liability. * * *

In the early development of tort law, it was assumed that the only tort liability which could be recognized was tort liability arising within the framework of one of the specific trespass writs. Maitland, The Forms of Action at Common Law, pp. 4–5 (1941). [C] Scholarly research has indicated that this was a misconception and that the early common law recognized the flexibility of trespass on the case to deal with other forms of tort action not specifically included in the traditional trespass writs. [C]

There is no need to detail the long and convoluted history of the dispute over the nature and function of the tort law. It is clear that modern scholarship considers that there exists a residue of tort liability which has not been explicated in specific forms of tort action and which is available for the courts to develop as common law tort actions as the needs of society require such development. [C] The emerging products liability recovery theories and the relatively recent development of theories in the recovery of damages for intentional infliction of emotional distress are demonstrative of the willingness of the courts to draw upon traditional concepts of tort liability and impose liability in new forms and under new factual situations. * * *

The origin of the prima facie tort doctrine in the United States is found in Aikens v. Wisconsin, 195 U.S. 194 (1904). In that case, Justice Holmes conceptualized the tort in the following language: "Prima facie, the intentional infliction of temporal damages is a cause of action which as a matter of substantive law, whatever may be the form of the pleading, requires a justification if the defendant is to escape." Other language in that case gave rise to the notion of "disinterested malevolence" as characterizing the motivation for conduct justifying the imposition of tort liability. By that phrase, Justice Holmes looked to the ordinarily lawful conduct and indicated that if conduct otherwise lawful was not done to achieve a beneficial end for the actor but was done solely with a malevolent intent to injure the plaintiff, the conduct became actionable.

The case law development clearly has tempered the requirement that an act be totally malevolent before it became actionable. This is based in part upon criticism that disinterested malevolence and justification represent a contradiction. The argument is that a wholly malevolent act can never be justified and that a purpose other than malevolent desire to injure the plaintiff is, in itself, a justification for the act. [Cc]

Thus, the modern authority seems to agree that what is involved in the two concepts of malevolence and justification is that the plaintiff's cause of action must include proof of an actual intent to injure and if another purpose appears in the actor's conduct which amounts to a justification, then the wrongful act and the justification will be weighed to determine whether the justification in terms of societal value outweighs the wrongful motive of the defendant in attempting injury to the plaintiff.

Justice Holmes' opinion in *Aikens,* supra, is often cited as the seminal case in the field of intentional tort in the performance of a lawful act. *Aikens,* however, but reflects the earlier opinions of Justice Holmes when he was sitting as a member of the Massachusetts court. Justice Holmes developed the doctrine in a very early line of Massachusetts cases. Moran v. Dunphy, 177 Mass. 485, 59 N.E. 125 (1901); Plant v. Woods, 176 Mass. 492, 504, 57 N.E. 1011, 1015 (1900) (dissenting opinion); Vegelahn v. Guntner, 167 Mass. 92, 104, 44 N.E. 1077, 1079 (1896) (dissenting opinion). Holmes, in Privilege, Malice, and Intent, 8 Harv.L.Rev. 1 (1894), provides the theoretical underpinning for the Massachusetts decisions and ultimately for *Aikens,* supra. Even those early Massachusetts cases had a sound basis in the English authority for the development of the doctrine. The most frequently cited English case is Mogul Steamship Co. v. McGregor Gow & Co., 23 Q.B.D. 598 (1889), affirmed, [1892] A.C. 25; but it, too, rests upon earlier cases developing the doctrine from a theoretical basis to applications in the case law. The English cases, no doubt, were strongly influenced by the Statute of Westminster, the Second: "let a writ be made by those learned in the law so that for the future it shall not befall that the court fail in doing justice to complaints." 13 Edw. I, c. 24 (1285) (Plucknett trans.).

The general sense of the great English statute referred to exists in our own organic law in Mo. Const. Art. I, § 14, "certain remedy for every injury to person, property or character." A case resting the theory of recovery in tort for alienation of affections resulting in loss of support by plaintiff children upon the broad ground of a similar provision of the Illinois Constitution, Art. 2, § 19, is Daily v. Parker, 152 F.2d 174 (7 Cir.1945). The theory of liability does not rest alone upon the theoretical basis and ancient authority thus far discussed.

* * *

Despite the early development of the Massachusetts law, the leading modern authorities arise in New York. Other states have, in part, adopted similar theories but in no state other than New York has the doctrine been developed with such care.

Many of the nominative tort theories, such as trespass, now rigidly defined, were evolved on a case-by-case basis. The development process tends to produce some confusion and uncertainty as to the courts' struggle with new and different fact settings and as the circumstances and ingenuity of counsel raise new issues for resolution. The history of the development of the prima facie tort doctrine is a classic example of that developmental process. The early adoption of the prima facie tort theory in New York and the willingness of the New York courts to recognize and confront the issues presents an unusual opportunity to vicariously assess the whole ambit of issues involved in the development and application of the theory.

The early cases in New York adopted the doctrine along the lines of *Aikens* and the Massachusetts cases. [Cc] Apparently fearful of expansion of tort liability beyond reasonable bounds, the New York courts devised limitations upon the doctrine. [C] Those limitations, upon further analysis and consideration, have been largely eliminated, or at least made less restrictive than the early statements of them would suppose. An early limitation—that the doctrine would not support a cause of action if the facts would also support a nominative tort—has been largely dispelled by the analysis which suggests that under modern pleading, alternative and even contradictory theories may be pleaded. Board of Education, etc. v. Farmingdale Classroom Tchrs., 38 N.Y.2d 397, 343 N.E.2d 278, 380 N.Y.S.2d 635 (1975).

New York case law at one point also restricted the doctrine to cases where malice was the sole motivation for the acts complained of by the plaintiff. Reinforce, Inc. v. Birney, 308 N.Y. 164, 124 N.E.2d 104 (1954), but in *Farmingdale Classroom Tchrs.*, supra, the New York Court of Appeals found the pleading sufficient and left to the proof in the case the balancing of the defendant's motivation in performing the act causing the injury (the evidence of bad motive) against the claim of justification of the act. The notion of the need to prove maliciousness as a sole motivation is subject to the same criticism as Justice Holmes' "disinterested malevolence not otherwise justified;"—an act wholly malicious cannot be justified.

The Restatement (Second) of Torts (1977) has resolved the issue on the basis of a balancing of interests. The plaintiff must allege and prove bad motive on the part of the defendant. The defendant may plead and prove any justification. The court first must weigh and consider the balance of social values to determine if the defendant's acts are tortious. This balancing reflects the traditional role of the court in the direction of a verdict. Ultimately, the jury must balance the bad motivation of the defendant against the claimed justification for the act. Restatement (Second) of Torts § 870, Comment e, pp. 281–283, Comment k, p. 286 (1977). That position is consistent with the general principle underlying the statement of the doctrine. "Tort law involves a balancing of the conflicting interests of the litigants in the light of the social and economic interests of society in general." Restatement (Second) of Torts § 870, Comment c, p. 280 (1977).

A great many cases in New York have turned on the issue of the necessity for pleading "special damages." [C]

The general rule is that "general damages" are those that flow as a natural and necessary result of the act complained of and that "special damages" are damages which actually result from the act by reason of the special circumstances of the case and not as a necessary result of the act. Special damages may be pecuniary, but not inevitably so.

*   *   *

The Restatement (Second) of Torts has resolved the issue in § 870 by resorting to the definitions of "harm," "injury," and "damages," concepts established for all forms of recovery in tort. "Harm" is defined in Restatement (Second) § 7, p. 12 as "the existence of loss or detriment in fact of any kind." The word "injury" is defined by the same section as "the invasion of any legally protected interest of another." Comment A to § 7 Restatement (Second) of Torts makes it clear that "injury" may occur without "harm" and "harm" may occur with injury. "Harm" as so defined gives rise to a cause of action only when it results *from* the invasion of a legally protected interest, i.e., "injury." Section 870 thus focuses upon "injury" as necessary before any cause of action arises under the prima facie tort doctrine. The earlier drafts of the Restatement contained language suggesting harm. The debate preceding the adoption of the present language of § 870, Restatement (Second) of Torts, makes it clear that the omission of harm and the inclusion of injury was intended to restrict the section's application to the invasion of a legally protected interest. 53 ALI Proceedings 64 (1976).

Upon the basis of this analysis, the rule as to pleading special or general damages can take its proper place. An "injury" as an invasion of a legally protected right may cause either general or special damages. If the former, no special pleading is required. If the latter, the pleading must set forth the factual matters that give reasonable notice of the nature and extent of the claim.

What has been said thus far should suffice to show that the notion of a tort action based on common law precepts is accurately described in Restatement (Second) of Torts § 870 (1977). It should also appear from the analysis that the stricture upon the doctrine of the New York case law requiring pleading and proof of pecuniary loss in not analytically sound.

The only remaining question is a policy question concerning the propriety of the adoption of such a theory of tort liability in Missouri.

There seems to be no sound reason based upon either precedent or policy why Missouri should not adopt the New York view. None of the principles relied upon in the evolution of the doctrine are foreign to our law. The concept is consistent with the mandate of our organic law that there should be a remedy for every injury. Mo.Const.Art. I, § 14. Missouri has not been reluctant to adopt new forms of action in tort based on Restatement principles. In Annbar Associates v. American Express Co., 565 S.W.2d 701 (Mo.App.1978), the tort of injurious falsehood, a cause of action based upon § 623A Restatement (Second) of Torts, was recognized. Corcoran v. Southwestern Bell Tel. Co., 572 S.W.2d 212 (Mo.App.1978), in analyzing a claim for invasion of privacy, relied upon Restatement (Second) of Torts § 652A. Our products liability cases have relied heavily on Restatement (Second) of Torts § 402A. [Cc] Nor does such a tort require a name; *Annbar Associates,* supra.

The doctrine has been well developed in several states and Restatement (Second) of Torts § 870 has refined the principles of the case law into a workable guide for application of the doctrine. It must be concluded that, like New York and Massachusetts, as well as other states which have found support for the doctrine in common law principles, Missouri should adopt the Restatement view imposing such liability.

Applying this analysis to the instant case, the plaintiff's petition states a cause of action against the defendants Carrier and Crawford. As noted above, the defendants do not attack the pleading as deficient in stating a cause of action under the prima facie tort doctrine except for the assertion that there is no pleading of special pecuniary damages. The pleadings in the instant case, by asserting the pecuniary loss by reason of bank charges for returned checks, would satisfy the narrowest view of any of the case law discussing the issue of special damages. The pleading here need not rest on that narrow ground. * * *

The concern implicit or expressed, that the creation of a new theory of tort liability pursuant to the guidelines of Restatement (Second) of Torts § 870, will result in a flood of litigation, is unfounded. The burden of proof upon the plaintiff to show an intent to injure, not merely an intentional act, as well as the preservation of the right of the defendant to plead and prove a justification for the act, make it unlikely that the theory will be subject to abuse.

The defendant in the instant case may, of course, plead and prove any facts establishing a justification for the act of stopping payment on the draft. All that is determined here is that if the plaintiff proves what has been alleged, a submissible case is made. The proof of a justification by the defendants may either result in a directed verdict for the defendants or a jury verdict in their favor dependent upon issues of the nature of the proof and the credibility of the evidence, which cannot now be anticipated. * * *

The ruling of the trial court dismissing plaintiff's petition against Carriers and Crawford is reversed; * * * and the cause is remanded to the trial court with directions to reinstate plaintiff's petition against Carriers and Crawford.

ON MOTION FOR REHEARING

PER CURIAM. Both Crawford & Company and Carriers Insurance Company have filed motions for rehearing and for transfer. Both continue to argue that there is no violation of a legal duty and thus there can be no cause of action because the defendants had a statutory right to stop payment on the check. Thus, the defendants continue to refuse to recognize the principle that the duty violated in any intentional tort is the duty to avoid intentionally causing harm to another without justification.

It is not the exercise of the lawful right to stop payment which creates the tort. The opinion shows that the *pleadings* in this case plead that the act was done with *intent to injure* and *without justification.* * * *

The motions for rehearing are overruled, and the motions to transfer are denied.

———

1. *Prima Facie Tort.* The origin of the prima facie tort theory is a statement made by Bowen, L.J., in Mogul S.S. Co., Ltd. v. McGregor, Gow & Co., 23 Q.B.D. 598, 613 (1889), aff'd [1892] A.C. 25: "Now, intentionally to do that which is calculated in the ordinary course of events to damage, and which does, in fact, damage another in that other person's property or trade, is actionable if done without just cause or excuse. Such intentional action when done without just cause or excuse is what the law calls a malicious wrong [citations]. The acts of the defendants which are complained of here were intentional and were also calculated, no doubt, to do the plaintiffs' damage in their trade. But in order to see whether they were wrongful we have still to discuss the question whether they were without just cause or excuse." The acts (using rebates to attract business from competitors) were held not to be wrongful.

Compare the remarks of Lord Herschell, referring to the quotation above: "It will be noted that the learned judge here makes no distinction between acts which interfere with property and those which interfere with trade. For the purpose then in hand the statement of the law may be accurate enough, but if it means that a man is bound in law to justify or excuse every wilful act which may damage another in his property or trade, then I say, with all respect, the proposition is far too wide; everything depends on the nature of the act and whether it is wrongful or not." Allen v. Flood, [1898] A.C. 1, 139–40.

2. The quotation from Justice Holmes' opinion in Aikens v. Wisconsin, found in the principal case, is generally regarded as the origin in this country. The other Holmes opinions, cited in the principal case, are also often referred

to. See also Holmes, The Common Law, Lect. 4 (1881); Ames, How Far An Act May Be a Tort Because of the Wrongful Motive of the Actor, 18 Harv.L.Rev. 411 (1905).

3. *Restatement of Torts.* Restatement (Second) of Torts § 870 provides: "One who intentionally causes injury to another is subject to liability to the other for that injury, if his conduct is generally culpable and not justifiable under the circumstances. This liability may be imposed although the actor's conduct does not come within a traditional category of tort liability."

The comments spell out in detail the considerations to be balanced by a court in determining whether to declare the existence of a new cause of action or to extend the parameters of an existing cause.

4. Will an action for prima facie tort lie if a more traditional tort would also lie? The New York courts seemed to indicate that it would not until 1975, when the Court of Appeals held that it would, although duplication of damages would not be permitted. Board of Education of Farmingdale Union Free Sch. Dist. v. Farmingdale Classroom Teachers Ass'n, 38 N.Y.2d 397, 343 N.E.2d 278, 380 N.Y.S.2d 635 (1975). Missouri holds that it will not be permitted. Bandag of Springfield, Inc. v. Bandag, Inc., 662 S.W.2d 546 (Mo.App.1983).

5. See Halpern, Intentional Torts and the Restatement, 7 Buffalo L.Rev. 7 (1951). Also, Albertsworth, Recognition of New Interests in the Law of Torts, 10 Calif.L.Rev. 461 (1922); Epstein, Intentional Harms, 4 J.Leg.Stud. 391 (1975); Smith, Torts Without Particular Names, 69 U.Pa.L.Rev. 91 (1921).

MORRISON v. NATIONAL BROADCASTING CO., INC.

New York Supreme Court, Appellate Division, First Department, 1965.
24 A.D.2d 284, 266 N.Y.S.2d 406.

BREITEL, JUSTICE PRESIDING. This appeal involves a unique combination of operative facts. While the combination is unique and its novelty is the source of the difficulties in analysis, each of the facts is of a kind found in one or more of the recognized classifications in the law of torts.

Two questions are raised. The first is whether plaintiff's complaint states a cause of action, and the second is, if a claim is stated, whether it is barred by an applicable statute of limitations. * * *

The gist of the claim is that defendants, associated in various ways in television, acting in concert, falsely represented to plaintiff, a young university academic, that they were conducting an authentic and honest contest on television, a "quiz" show, when in fact it was rigged. They made these misrepresentations in order to induce his participation as a contestant. As a result of his innocent participation and the public scandals thereafter occurring, plaintiff sustained harm to his good reputation and in particular was deprived of scholastic fellowships for which he had applied. For purposes of this appeal the description of the promotion and sponsorship of the program must be assumed to be true. As for the harm to plaintiff's reputation and prospects, and his innocent participation in the contest, for the present this too must be assumed to be true. The claim then charges defendants with corrupt purposes, lying to plaintiff to induce his innocent participation in a corrupt enterprise, as a result of which, on public exposure of the enterprise, plaintiff sustained harm to his reputation and academic prospects. In referring to corrupt purposes or enterprises it is not intended to suggest essential illegality but to import necessarily a violation of strong and prevalent moral standards with respect to competitive contests for material awards. The point is that everything that is not illegal is not therefore legitimate or sanctioned conduct.

Notably, each of the ultimate elements of the claim is a recognized element in the law of remedies for one sustaining harms. Nevertheless, defendants contend that there is a failure to state a claim or cause of action because the separate elements do not all fall into any one classic category of tort but are found only in a combination of such categories. If this be right, then once again our jurisprudence would suffer a hardening of its categories making neither for sense nor justice and mark a return to a specious procedural formalism. [C]

In the first place, misplaced speculation about the applicability of "prima facie tort" doctrine to this case should be eliminated. That open-ended, non-category, class or sub-class of tort covers "disinterested malevolence," that is, the intentional malicious injury to another by otherwise lawful means without economic or social justification, but solely to harm the other [c]. The elements in this case are distinguishable and stronger. The means used were not lawful or privileged, in the sense of affirmatively sanctioned conduct, but were intentional falsehood without benevolent purpose uttered to induce action by another to his detriment. The ultimate purpose and the scheme were corrupt, in the sense that no socially useful purpose but only gain by deceit was intended, although perhaps not "illegal." Defendants were engaged in operating a dishonest contest. Innocent contestants were being cheated of the chances for rewards they thought they had. The public was being deceived as to the kind of spectacle it was viewing. Defendants lied to plaintiff to induce his innocent participation. They were engaged in the pursuit of economic gain for themselves. Hence, this is no instance of otherwise lawfully privileged means being made actionable, because without economic or social justification, and because of the exclusive purpose to injure plaintiff, which are the identifying qualities of so-called "prima facie" tort.

Secondly, the claim is not for defamation, as defendants correctly argue, because defendants did not publish in any form anything derogatory to or concerning plaintiff. Instead, they put him in an unduly hazardous position where his reputation might be injured, not because this was their purpose, but because they did not care what happened to him in the pursuit of their purposes for selfish gain. Yet the harm sustained is exactly like that from defamation, albeit induced neither by slander nor libel. Thus, the causative acts are different from those in defamation, but the effect, that is, harm to reputation, is the same.

Thirdly, the acts of defendants are not in deceit although they fit precisely all but one of the several elements of deceit. They fall short with respect to the nature of the harm sustained by plaintiff. There is knowing misrepresentation of fact, for the purpose of inducing plaintiff to act, upon which he relies. But the resulting harm is not the obtaining of plaintiff's property, or even his services; instead, it is the putting him into a hazardous false position, that is, of a cheater or corrupt contestant, to which he would not have consented if he had known the truth. While the harm to plaintiff was never intended, for defendants were gambling that there would be no exposure, the risk of harm to plaintiff's reputation was known or should have been known and therefore completely foreseeable to defendants [c]. In this last respect there is a touch of an element in the law of negligence. But the claim is not for negligence, because while the harm may not have been intended, the act and effect of putting plaintiff into the false position of appearing to be a cheater was. It is not necessary that the intent in tort law be hostile [cc].

In short, and in repetition, every element in plaintiff's claim descriptive of defendants' acts, his reliance, and the harm sustained, are identifiable in the most ancient of the tort categories and in the law of negligence. What is more important, the elements of defendants' conduct and the harm to plaintiff fall neatly within general principles of law, even if not within any of the numbered forms of a form book. The intentional use of wrongful means and the intentional exposure of another to the known, unreasonable risk of harm, which results in such harm, provides classic basis for remedy. The harm must, of course, have been intended, foreseeable, or the "natural consequence" of the wrong. Even in intentional tort there is no liability for "remote" harms [cc]. What troubled the lawyers in another day was not the intentional infliction of harm by wrongful means or for wrongful purpose, but harms inflicted without intention or by otherwise lawfully privileged conduct.

The root of the present trouble is that every kind of wrongful conduct, like lying, is not actionable *per se.* The analysis should not stop short, however, but must continue by examination of the purpose for which one lies, the harm produced by the lie, and whether the harm was foreseeable or the natural consequence of the wrong. The problem may also be looked at conversely. If there be no remedy, then the law would be saying in effect that one is free to lie to another as distinguished from lying about another (which is defamation), for one's private gain, so long as the consequence of the lie is not to take the victim's property (which is deceit), but rather to expose him and his reputation to likely injury.

In passing it should be observed that criminal statutes which must be explicitly directed to conduct forbidden are not involved. Rather this case explores the common law reach in providing a remedy for foreseeable harms resulting from intentional conduct.

In the late nineteenth and early twentieth centuries a great controversy raged over whether there was a law of tort based on general principles or only a law of torts based on specific remedies which could not be rationally correlated but only historically explained. Pollock in England was the chief exponent for the view of a general theory of tort and Salmond was the chief exponent for the contrary view (see Pollock on Torts [15th ed.], pp. 16–17 and Salmond on Torts [12th ed.], pp. 17–19, 20–31; see, also, Advance Music Corp. v. American Tobacco Co., 296 N.Y. 79, 83–84, 70 N.E.2d 401–403). It is significant that the later editors of Salmond retreat from his hard position that "every plaintiff must bring his case under one of the recognized heads of tort." (Salmond, op. cit., supra, at pp. 17–19.) And there is no doubt that the generality of Pollock's position must be a bit restrained, if history is not to be ignored (Prosser, op. cit., supra, p. 4).

But there is no need to join in the overseas controversy. The Court of Appeals in the *Advance Music* case, supra, resolved the dispute for this State. After discussing the Pollock–Salmond controversy, Chief Judge Loughran had this to say (296 N.Y. at p. 84, 70 N.E.2d at p. 403):

"This difference over the general principles of liability in tort was composed for us in Opera on Tour, Inc., v. Weber, 285 N.Y. 348, 34 N.E.2d 349, 136 A.L.R. 267. We there adopted from Aikens v. State of Wisconsin, [195 U.S. 194, esp. at 204, per Holmes, J.,] the declaration that '*prima facie,* the intentional infliction of temporal damage is a cause of action, which * * * requires a justification if the defendant is to escape.'"

Then, dropping the commas around the words "prima facie," a new name was created in this State for not such a new tort, the Chief Judge saying: "The above second cause of action alleges such a prima facie tort and, therefore, is sufficient in law on its face."

It is not important to the present analysis that the so-called "prima facie" tort was thus rationalized. It is important that the Court aligned itself with the Holmes–Pollock view that tort concepts of liability did not depend solely upon procedural categories, important as they were, and that intentional harm, without excuse or justification, was actionable, *simpliciter.* The extension of these principles is well beyond what has been since dubbed the "prima facie" tort. Indeed, the subclassification of "prima facie" tort has perhaps caused more trouble in understanding than what it was supposed to clarify. * * * What should be clear enough is that "prima facie" tort does not embrace all intentional tort outside the classic categories of intentional torts.

Even before the *Advance Music* case, this Court had no trouble in recognizing as actionable an intentional wrong that did not classify into any of the formal categories. In Gale v. Ryan, 263 App.Div. 76, 31 N.Y.S.2d 732 the complaint charged defendants, for their own tax evasion purposes, and without hostile intention toward plaintiff, with having given false information to the revenue authorities concerning plaintiff's earnings. As a result, plaintiff allegedly was investigated and sustained damage because of these false statements. The Court, recognizing that the claim did not come within any of the classic tort categories, analogized it to various causes of action for injurious false-hood and sustained the complaint. It quoted from Ratcliffe v. Evans, ([1892] 2 Q.B. 524, 527–528, [supra page 1149]). * * * [I]n Penn–Ohio Steel Corp. v. Allis–Chalmers Mfg., 7 A.D.2d 441, at pp. 443–444, 184 N.Y.S.2d 58, at pp. 60, 61, the Court, per M.M. Frank, J., said:

"The parties to the litigation agree that the complaint does not charge a conventional tort, such as malicious prosecution or defamation. * * * It seems inadvisable to lump all malicious and intentional harms into a grab bag labelled 'prima facie tort', especially since it is impossible to tabulate the infinite varieties of misconduct that give rise to actionable wrongs. It is generally accepted that 'There is no necessity whatever that a tort must have a name. New and nameless torts are being recognized constantly'. (Prosser, Torts, 2d Ed., p. 3.) What is important is that there must be the infliction of intentional harm, resulting in damage, without legal excuses or justification. [Cc] The utterance or furnishing of false and misleading information may be actionable if done maliciously or with the intention to harm another, or so recklessly and without regard to its consequences, that a reasonably prudent person should anticipate that damage to another will naturally follow. * * *"

Mr. Justice Frank well summarized the grounds for liability to be found in the instant pleading, and demonstrated the inapplicability of a parochial adherence to ancient forms of action and the futility of manipulating labels rather than concepts in the law of torts.

There has been some discussion whether plaintiff's reputation could have been harmed, turning on whether it was reasonable, and therefore credible, for the public to generalize that the corruption exposed applied to all rather than only to some of the contestants in the rigged contest. That is a question of fact. The pleading alleges that it happened. The proof of the pleading may well be another matter. Then it will be time enough to speak of what plaintiff has shown. At this stage he succeeds merely by alleging, so long as he alleges enough.

Sufficient has already been said to suggest the answer to the limitations problem. Only if plaintiff were suing in defamation would the one-year statute for libel or slander apply (Civ.Prac.Act, § 51, subd. 3). The acts charged here are neither libel nor slander; only the harm which resulted was the same as that in the law of defamation. Consequently, the applicable statute of limitation is the six-year statute covering personal injuries other than those covered elsewhere in the limitation statutes under the Civil Practice Act. * * *

It has been assumed by most in the discussion of this case that plaintiff has the burden of alleging special damages. If he does, the allegations are somewhat deficient but only in a very technical sense; and if so, these could and should be easily cured by allowing him to amend. But plaintiff's claim should not depend upon the allegation and proof of special damages. The reason is that the harm to reputation alleged here is exactly of the kind for which in the law of defamation recovery is allowed in the way of general damages. In short, on plaintiff's allegations he was in effect exposed to the charge of being a cheat, that is, a corrupt conniver in a scheme to divert rewards in a contest from those entitled to them to those who cheated. Put another way: defendants never said of plaintiff that he was a cheater, they only caused him to appear to be one. It hardly requires additional proof that this is destructive of plaintiff's standing or prospects as a university teacher of the young. * * *

[W]here the conduct is purposively corrupt by conventional standards, intentional as to consequences, or utilizes vicious means (again by conventional standards), the law will allow general recovery for foreseeable harm to established protected interests, such as reputation in trade or occupation, reputation for chastity or honesty, consortium, and, at one time, the love and affection of another. * * *

In conclusion, it should be observed that the classical categories of tort were merely classifications, and incomplete ones at that. Omitted were all the law of negligence, the intentional tort committed by lawful means but solely out of malevolence (the "prima facie" tort), and innumerable other remediable wrongs wrought in the later common law years from the formless mold of "action on the case," out of which even the action on assumpsit had to arise because the "contract" categories had hardened into debt, covenant, and the like. This history should create no problems for a modern court but, instead, provides modes of solution, especially so where the claim rests on elements each of which, considered separately, has been recognized as an operative fact in the law of torts. Nor should a slavish formalism apply to the rule of damages any more than to the statement of a substantive claim. In either case, a rule should stand or fall because of its reason or lack of it. * * *

Orders * * * modified, on the law, to the extent of denying defendants' motions to dismiss the first cause of action.

[EAGER, JUSTICE dissented only to the holding that special damages are not required.]

STEUER, JUSTICE (dissenting). * * * Concededly [the facts here] do not fall within any of the accepted categories. Neither libel nor slander can be claimed because no statement derogatory or otherwise concerning plaintiff is charged. Even though plaintiff was deceived by the implied representation that the program was honestly and fairly conducted, that deceit did not cause him any damage. What is alleged to have injured him is the unwarranted assumption by the public that, because plaintiff was a participant in a show which deliberately fooled the public, he was one of those who was misleading them.

It is undeniable that the action of the defendants in palming off this program as a bona fide contest and exaggerating the abilities of the favored contestants was a hoax on the public. But aside from inducing them to listen to the program it is difficult to see how any member of the public was injured or how anyone was defrauded. Naturally some persons would be resentful and form unfavorable opinions of the perpetrators of the hoax, including those who took part in the supposed contest. But it is quite another matter to assume that the public would form the same opinion of a person who appeared as a legitimate contestant. * * *

Plaintiff's claim is based on the contention that the public did not distinguish among contestants and wrongfully assumed that all were parties to the deception. If this contention is invalid, plaintiff has not shown that he suffered. If it is valid, he has not shown that any act or word of the defendants is responsible for the public's false assumption. So what plaintiff apparently relies on is that the public is prone to accept guilt by association. It is submitted that neither these defendants nor anyone else should be held responsible for this human failing.

The majority rests its decision on the finding that this is an action on the case of a hitherto unspecified character. Undoubtedly at times new inventions as well as new customs give rise to injuries in a manner not before experienced. And the absence of precise precedent is no bar to recovery. * * *

While an action on the case is designed to cover situations where a wrong has been committed and no existing remedy is provided for it (see Case, Action on, 14 C.J.S., p. 3) yet it is not entirely amorphous. There are some rules. It does not apply where conventional actions exist or where force, the usual damaging agent, is present (see C.J.S., op. cit., § 3). An action on the case may accrue from an injury to reputation, but only if the false utterance is made maliciously with intent to harm the plaintiff [cc]. No such element is here present. * * *

---

1. This decision was reversed by the Court of Appeals, 19 N.Y.2d 453, 227 N.E.2d 572, 280 N.Y.S. 641 (1967), on the ground that the 1–year statute of limitations for defamation applied, since the "harm assertedly sustained by the plaintiff—injury to his reputation—is precisely the same as that caused by defamation." But a short time later the Court of Appeals expressly declared that it "adopted [the] approach" of (then) Chief Judge Breitel in this opinion. Board of Education of Farmingdale Union Free School Dist. v. Farmingdale Classroom Teachers Ass'n., Inc., 38 N.Y.2d 397, 406n, 343 N.E.2d 278, 284n, 380 N.Y.S.2d 635, 645n (1975).

2. Leading New York cases on prima facie tort include: Beardsley v. Kilmer, 236 N.Y. 80, 140 N.E. 203 (1923); Al Raschid v. News Syndicate, 265 N.Y. 1, 191 N.E. 713 (1934); Opera on Tour, Inc. v. Weber, 285 N.Y. 348, 34 N.E.2d 349 (1941); Advance Music Corp. v. American Tobacco Co., 296 N.Y. 79, 70 N.E.2d 401 (1946); Fieger v. Glen Oaks Village, 309 N.Y. 527, 132 N.E.2d 492 (1956); Board of Education v. Farmingdale Classroom Teachers Ass'n, 38 N.Y.2d 397, 343 N.E.2d 278, 380 N.Y.S.2d 635 (1975).

3. Many of these cases would be decided the same way in other states, but with the utilization of a different concept, such as injurious falsehood, abuse of process, interference with contractual relations, invasion of privacy and others.

4. See Brown, The Rise and Threatened Demise of the Prima Facie Tort Principle, 54 Nw.U.L.Rev. 563 (1959); Forkosch, An Analysis of the Prima Facie Tort "Cause of Action", 42 Cornell L.Q. 465 (1957); Hale, Prima Facie Torts, Combination and Non–Feasance, 46 Colum.L.Rev. 196 (1946); Note, The Prima Facie Tort Doctrine, 52 Colum.L.Rev. 503 (1952); Note, The Prima Facie Doctrine in New York—Another Writ?, 42 St. John's L.Rev. 530 (1968).

3. OTHER TORTS

MARGOLIN v. MORTON F. PLANT HOSP. ASS'N, INC.
District Court of Appeal of Florida, Second District, 1977.
342 So.2d 1090.

GRIMES, JUDGE. This is an appeal from the dismissal of a complaint which alleged that the plaintiff/doctor was prevented from conducting surgery at Morton Plant Hospital in Clearwater by being improperly deprived of the necessary anesthesia services. * * *

The essential allegations of Count I may be summarized in the following manner. The plaintiff is a licensed physician engaged in the practice of ear, nose, throat and cosmetic surgery in Pinellas County. He is a member in good standing of the medical staff of Morton Plant Hospital. The defendant, Roger White, is the Executive Director and Administrator of the hospital, and the defendant, Dr. Straub, is president of the hospital's medical staff. The other defendants, characterized as the group, are licensed physicians who practice anesthesiology as members of the hospital staff. The defendants comprising the group are the only anesthesiologists on the Morton Plant Hospital staff and are alleged to be exercising absolute control over the availability and rendering of general anesthesia services to all surgeons and their patients at the hospital.

The plaintiff alleges that the admission of his patients into the surgical facilities of Morton Plant Hospital, and the obtaining of general anesthesia services are essential to his practice as a surgeon in Clearwater. He says that since 1973 until the happening of the events alleged in the complaint, all of his patients who required general anesthesia were treated at Morton Plant Hospital. * * * He further alleges that for the past several years he has performed surgery on hundreds of patients at the hospital during which members of the group have routinely and regularly rendered general anesthesia services. Yet, he contends that subsequent to March 28, 1975, the members of the group have wantonly and maliciously combined and conspired with each other and with the defendants, White and Straub, to boycott the plaintiff and his patients by denying them the availability of anesthesia services and thereby the use of the hospital's surgical facilities. The plaintiff alleges that by virtue of their unique position as the only anesthesiologists on the hospital staff and their concerted refusal to provide him with general anesthesia services, the members of the group have interfered with the contractual rights between him and his patients.

[He specifically alleges also that some of the defendants "acting in concert and in behalf of themselves and the other defendants" informed plaintiff that the group's] "refusal to render general anesthesia services to plaintiff and his patients and the restrictions against plaintiff's use of the surgical facilities of MPH would continue until such time as a lawsuit filed on March 28, 1975, by plaintiff's wife, Dr. Ann Margolin, in Federal Court in Tampa, Florida, against all defendants but Straub was dismissed, and general anesthesia services from the Group would be available to plaintiff and his patients only after said action by Dr. Ann Margolin was dismissed." [Also that defendants] "combined and conspired to block and prevent the appointment of at least two additional M.D. anesthesiologists to the staff of MPH [Morton Plant Hospital], thereby preserving the absolute control of the Group over the rendering of anesthesia services at MPH and continuing the effectiveness of the boycott directed against plaintiff and his patients by preventing other anesthesiologists not controlled by the Group from becoming qualified to render services to plaintiff and his patients at MPH." The purpose is said to be to bring about the plaintiff's financial ruin by driving him out of his established practice of medicine in Clearwater. * * *

The plaintiff concludes that as a result of the conspiracy he has been denied the opportunity to practice any surgery at Morton Plant Hospital. As a consequence, he seeks compensatory and punitive damages for lost surgical patients, the decrease in the number of referral patients, the denial of the right to practice a vital portion of his profession, and the damage to his professional reputation and ability to earn a living.

In support of his claim to a cause of action, the plaintiff relies heavily upon Snipes v. West Flagler Kennel Club, Inc., 105 So.2d 164 (Fla.1958). The complaint in that case alleged that five racetrack corporations and others connected with them had wrongfully conspired to refuse to permit him to race his greyhounds at their tracks. The complaint further alleged that the defendants, through their force of numbers and economic stature, had intimidated other dog tracks in the state and made them unwilling partners in the boycott and conspiracy being directed toward the plaintiff. The plaintiff contended that the conspiracy was being carried on not to gain any financial benefit but rather to precipitate his financial ruin by driving him out of the greyhound business. The court first stated the general rule in Florida was that an act which did not constitute a cause of action against one person could not be made the basis of a civil action for conspiracy. However, the court went on to point out that an exception to this rule existed in which by reason of the force of numbers or other exceptional circumstances the conduct of the defendants acting in concert could be such as to give rise to an independent wrong. The court quoted with approval from a Massachusetts case in which it was said that in order to prove an independent tort for conspiracy upon this basis, it must be shown that there was some " 'peculiar power of coercion of the plaintiff possessed by the defendants in combination which any individual standing in like relation to the plaintiff would not have had.' " The court held that the allegations of the complaint fell within the exception and were thereby sufficient to state a cause of action for civil conspiracy.

Though the facts are quite different, the rationale of Snipes is applicable to the instant case. Certainly, any one of the group could decline to render services to the plaintiff for whatever reason he might have. Yet, when all of them declined to do so, the effect is to preclude the plaintiff from conducting surgery at Morton Plant Hospital. While the plaintiff is admittedly free to seek to perform his surgery at some other hospital, the loss of his opportunity to perform surgery at Morton Plant when he is a fully accredited member of that hospital's staff is a substantial deprivation of his rights. When a surgeon loses his right to operate at a major hospital in his community where all of his general surgical procedures have previously been conducted, he is bound to suffer a substantial impairment of his economic well-being.

The defendants point out that there are other hospitals in the Tampa Bay area, but we would be naive to think that this is a practical alternative to using a major hospital in the plaintiff's locale. The gravamen of the exception in Snipes is the effectiveness of the boycott and not its geographical scope. There, the effectiveness arose from the defendant's absolute control over five dog tracks where Snipes conducted his racing business. Here, the effectiveness of the boycott arises from the group's absolute control over anesthesia services at an institution where the plaintiff practiced all of his general surgery before the commencement of the boycott. The power of coercion over the plaintiff with respect to his use of Morton Plant Hospital is evident from the allegations that the members of the group are the only anesthesiologists on the staff and that the defendants have conspired to block the appointment of additional anesthesiologists who might be willing to work with the plaintiff.

The case of Cowan v. Gibson, 392 S.W.2d 307 (Mo.1965), warrants consideration because of its analysis of the effect upon a doctor when he cannot practice in a particular hospital. There, the Missouri Supreme Court upheld a complaint by a doctor alleging that other doctors comprising the staff of a private hospital had wrongfully conspired to prevent him from acquiring membership on the medical staff so as to force his patients to seek the services of the defendants in their individual practice in order to obtain proper medical treatment. While the motivation of the defendants was different than that alleged in the instant case, the Missouri court pointed out the defendants' unjustified refusal to admit the doctor to the staff constituted an inference with the plaintiff's contractual rights with his patients. * * *

Apropos to our discussion is Section 765 of the Restatement of Torts (1939) which reads as follows:

"§ 765. Concerted Refusal to Deal

"(1) Persons who cause harm to another by a concerted refusal in their business to enter into or to continue business relations with him are liable to him for that harm, even though they would not be liable for similar conduct without concert, if their concerted refusal is not justified under the circumstances.

"(2) In the issue of justification under the rule stated in Subsection (1), the following are important factors:

"(a) the objects sought to be accomplished and the interests sought to be advanced by the actors' conduct;

"(b) the extent of the hardship caused to the person against whom the actors' conduct is directed and his opportunities for mitigating the hardship;

"(c) the appropriateness of the actors' conduct as a means of advancing their interests and the availability of less harmful means to that end;

"(d) the relations between the actors and the person against whom the conduct is directed and their relative economic power;

"(e) the effects of the actors' conduct and of its objects on the social interest in business enterprise and competition."

While the terminology in *Snipes* and that of the Restatement is different, we think this difference is little more than semantics. The *Snipes* exception of coercion falls within the scope of Section 765(2)(d). In essence, even though a person has the privilege of selecting those with whom he wishes to conduct business, when several persons who occupy a coercive position with respect to another act in concert to decline to do business with him, their refusal may under certain circumstances constitute an independent tort.

We hasten to point out that we simply hold that Count I states a cause of action. As recognized in Section 765(2)(a) of the Restatement, there may be a number of legitimate reasons why the group has declined to render services to the plaintiff, but these are matters of defense which do not appear on the face of the complaint.

The order dismissing Count I is reversed. * * *

------

1. Conspiracy is a crime at common law and under modern criminal statutes. As a basis for civil liability in tort, the concept is far less clear, and there are comparatively few cases that discuss it helpfully.

2. Many of the references to conspiracy in tort cases amount to no more than a pejorative way of saying that the parties acted in concert. And, under the law of joint tortfeasors, those who act in concert are liable jointly for what each of them did. See supra pages 352–54. The real significance of conspiracy, therefore, lies in the case in which the actor would not be liable if he had done the act alone. See generally Note, Civil Conspiracy: A Substantial Tort, 50 B.U.L.Rev. 921 (1979).

3. In Olivet v. Frischling, 104 Cal.App.3d 851, 164 Cal.Rptr. 87 (1980), it was held that in the case of a conspiracy to induce a breach of contract, a party to the contract might be held liable if he participated, even though he could not individually be liable for the tort of interfering with his own contract. See Note, Civil Conspiracy and Interference with Contract Relations, 8 Loyola L.A.L.Rev. 302 (1975).

4. Agnew v. Parks, 172 Cal.App.2d 746, 343 P.2d 118 (1959), is an interesting case involving a "conspiracy to obstruct orderly prosecution of a civil action"—the so-called "conspiracy of silence" in medical malpractice cases. The court held that there would be no liability for pressure to prevent a doctor from testifying against another by threatening to expel him from the medical association and to arrange for his malpractice insurance to be cancelled, especially when the statute of limitations had run; but that an action would lie for fraudulently inducing the judge to appoint one of the association members as an objective doctor who did not know the defendant in the malpractice suit, and recovery could be had of the fee paid him and punitive damages.

5. Compare Gregory v. Duke of Brunswick, 1 Car. & P. 25, 174 Eng.Rep. 696 (N.P.1843), aff'd, 6 Man. & G. 953, 134 Eng.Rep. 1178 (C.P.1844). Plaintiff alleged that in a performance he was to play the part of Hamlet and that the defendants had conspired to "hoot, hiss, groan and yell at and against the plaintiff during the performance" and had engaged 200 persons to attend and participate. He was hooted off the stage. Does he have a cause of action if he can prove the conspiracy?

NEIBUHR v. GAGE

Supreme Court of Minnesota, 1906.
99 Minn. 149, 108 N.W. 884.

ELLIOTT, J. This action was brought to recover damages which the plaintiff claims he suffered by reason of being required while under duress to transfer to the defendant certain shares of stock in a corporation. In the court below he recovered a verdict for $8,478. The trial court denied the defendant's motion for judgment notwithstanding the verdict, but granted a new trial. Both parties appealed. * * *

[Plaintiff possessed 91 shares of stock in Gage, Hayden & Co., having a face value of $9,100. Defendant Gage accused him of the felony of grand larceny and threatened to have him convicted unless he transferred the shares to Gage. Plaintiff alleged that he was innocent and that Gage led him to believe that Gage "would produce false testimony against him, in order to establish and justify [the] false accusation." Under threat of immediate arrest and imprisonment and without opportunity for consultation, plaintiff transferred the shares.]

The defendant contends * * * that if the contract resulted from duress it was voidable, and the sole remedy of the injured party was either to rescind and to restore the benefits, and then bring his action for what he had parted with, or bring his action in equity for a rescission and for such relief as he was entitled to upon rescission. * * *

In form this is an action at law to recover damages for an injury caused by the wrongful act of the defendant Gage. It was so regarded by the trial court, and the plaintiff's evidence was offered and received upon this theory. The pleadings do not raise the question of ratification or laches. The defendant stands squarely upon the proposition that there was no duress and that the plaintiff admitted that he was an embezzler, and for the purpose of paying an acknowledged debt to Gage, Hayden & Co. freely and voluntarily transferred the stock to Gage.

* * *

The remedies which are available to one who has been induced to part with his property or execute a contract by ordinary fraud are well understood. He may keep what he has received under the contract and bring an action to recover the damages which he has sustained by reason of the fraud, or he may rescind the contract by his own act, and sue at law for what he parted with by reason of the fraud, or he may sue in equity for a rescission of the contract by the court and recover what he parted with upon such conditions as the court may deem equitable. * * * If he seeks equitable relief, he must proceed promptly and comply with all the conditions which equity imposes. If he elects to rescind by his own act and sue at law for what he parted with by reason of the fraud, he must do all that he reasonably can to place the defendant in statu quo. [C]

The plaintiff abandoned his stock to the defendant. He asks no equitable relief. He ratifies and affirms the contract, but not the fraud by which it was obtained. The equitable doctrine of laches has no application in an action at law to recover damages. * * * In an action for damages where no rescission is sought a return of the consideration received under the contract is unnecessary.

But is a party who has been injured by duress entitled to the same remedies as one who has been injured by deception? We are unable to see why there should be any distinction made between these two classes of cases. Fraud is ordinarily accomplished by deceit, but it is also accomplished by many other practices. As commonly understood, fraud is a wrong accomplished by deception but * * * duress is a species of fraud in which compulsion in some form takes the place of deception in accomplishing the injury. [C]

We find no principle * * * which limits the remedy by reason of some inherent quality found in the definition of the word "deceit." The practice in either case is equally bad, and there is no reason why the remedy should not be as comprehensive and complete in one as in the other. The wrongdoer accomplishes the same wrong in each case, and does it with the same bad intent. The cases are at least analogous and on principle the remedies should be the same. It is not necessary that the law should show any special and extraordinary consideration for the wrongdoer. All he is entitled to is a fair opportunity to make good the damages resulting from his wrong without unnecessary injury to himself. It is not for him to determine the choice of remedies for the injured party. If the remedy of an action at law for damages is available to a person who has been injured by deceit, it should not lie in the mouth of the wrongdoer to say that the remedy is more restricted when the wrong is the result of the more gross and brutal acts which are known as "duress." * * * A party who has been injured by duress is entitled to the same remedies which are available in cases of deceit. * * *

The entire record has been carefully read, and we are satisfied that there is evidence to sustain the verdict. * * *

The order granting a new trial is reversed, with directions to the trial court to enter a judgment in favor of the plaintiff upon the verdict.

---

1. The crime of extortion, including blackmail, is well formulated in criminal law. Should tort law provide a suitable civil counterpart? The law of restitution is available to allow the victim to recover any unjust enrichment obtained from the victim of duress, and to invalidate any consent that would otherwise be a defense to a regular court action such as assault or false imprisonment. Is the newly developed tort of intentional infliction of mental distress adequate for the purpose or is an independent tort action for duress desirable? There is comparatively little authority.

2. See, in accord with the principal case, Housing Authority of the City of Dallas v. Hubbell, 325 S.W.2d 880 (Tex.Civ.App.1959) (economic pressure). And compare Silsbee v. Webber, 171 Mass. 378, 50 N.E. 555 (1898), where defendant, employer of plaintiff's son, whom he charged with embezzlement of funds, threatened to go to the father to raise the matter. As both parties knew, the father was an invalid in a delicate physical condition, who might die from the interview. To prevent this, plaintiff transferred to defendant some property of her own. Should plaintiff be allowed to recover for her own emotional distress? Should it make any difference whether the son had actually embezzled funds and, if so, whether the property transferred exceeded the value? Plaintiff was not personally liable for any embezzlement. See Note, Duress as a Tort, 39 Harv.L.Rev. 108 (1925). And see State Nat'l Bank of El Paso v. Farah Mfg. Co., 678 S.W.2d 661 (Tex.App.1984) (lenders' liability).

SILLIMAN v. DOBNER
Supreme Court of Minnesota, 1925.
165 Minn. 87, 205 N.W. 696.

[Plaintiff Silliman gave a note for $10,000 to the National Rendering Company to be used with funds similarly raised to build a rendering plant under an oral agreement that it would be payable when a sufficient number of similar notes were obtained. He alleges that there was a conspiracy between the officers and certain other persons to defraud him, and the court finds that the evidence justifies this conclusion. The note was negotiated to appellant (Dobner). He subsequently sold it to a bona fide purchaser, who was able to collect on it. Suit was brought against participants in the scheme, and Dobner was included as a defendant. Jury verdict for plaintiff against all defendants. Dobner is the only defendant to appeal the denial of a motion for a new trial.]

WILSON, C.J.　*　*　* The record does not permit a holding that there was a conditional delivery.　*　*　*

The [parol evidence rule] does not prevent the proof of oral contemporaneous statements for the purpose of showing fraud. The record would support a finding by the jury that these notes were fraudulently procured, and that they were negotiated to appellant by the payee in breach of faith and under such circumstances as amounted to fraud. Notice of an executory agreement between the maker and the payee of a note that the payee should do certain things does not affect a purchaser who has no notice or knowledge that the payee has broken his contract. But the basis of liability, if any, in this case, is fraud and not breach of contract.　*　*　*

The record will justify the jury in finding that at a certain stage of the transaction appellant came upon the scene and helped to carry it through, and participated in the fruits of the enterprise to, at least, the extent of $1,500, and that he did this with knowledge of the fraud, or, at least, under circumstances charging him with knowledge thereof. We believe there was sufficient evidence to justify the court in submitting the question of conspiracy to the jury.

The court in its charge to the jury said this:

"But if you find that there was no conspiracy, or that there is no evidence to establish a conspiracy, if you find from the evidence that the defendant Dobner was the means after he had notice of the defect in the title of the note, that he was the means of conveying the notes into the hands of an innocent holder, then he would be liable, and your verdict should be against him, notwithstanding you find there was no conspiracy."

The foregoing is an erroneous statement of the law because it permits the imposition of liability, even though appellant acted honestly and without fraud. Dishonesty and the fraudulent purpose of the conspiracy of impressing a liability upon plaintiffs in causing them to pay these notes without getting anything for their money to the benefit of the wrongdoer is the gist of this action. [C] Plaintiffs were entitled to a charge covering their right to a verdict against appellant, even if they did not find the existence of a conspiracy. Such liability, however, would be predicated upon the theory that he fraudulently acquired and transferred the notes, with knowledge of the breach of faith, for the purpose of imposing upon the plaintiffs a liability, incident to a bona fide holder in due course, to which they would have no defense. If he so acted, he would be liable, regardless of the existence of a conspiracy. [C] Such conduct would amount to a wrong and being followed by damages would constitute a cause of action in tort.

The term "fraud" in such case is used synonymously with malice, which is the basis for liability in a wrongful interference with another's business or contract rights.　*　*　*

A new trial is granted.

1. Compare St. Charles Mercantile Co. v. Armour & Co., 156 S.C. 397, 153 S.E. 470 (1930), where it was alleged that defendant as the payee to a post-dated check from the plaintiff, changed the date and presented it for payment, thus damaging the plaintiff's credit. See also Porter v. Crawford & Co., supra page 1188.

2. Cases involving intentionally false statements: Al Raschid v. News Syndicate Co., 265 N.Y. 1, 191 N.E. 713 (1938) (plaintiff subjected to deportation proceedings because of false information that he was not a citizen); Gale v. Ryan, 263 App.Div. 76, 31 N.Y.S.2d 732 (1946) (false report to IRS of payments made to plaintiff as an employee, creating income tax difficulties). These cases were treated under the New York concept of prima facie tort and may also be explained on the basis of the tort of injurious falsehood.

3. In Seidel v. Greenburg, 108 N.J.Super. 248, 260 A.2d 863 (1963), defendants, the officers and principal stockholders of a corporation, arranged to burn the lumber yard of the corporation. Plaintiff, a key employee who was innocent, was prosecuted for arson. He was given recovery. What basis?

GRUENBERG v. AETNA INSURANCE CO.

Supreme Court of California, 1973.
9 Cal.3d 566, 510 P.2d 1032, 108 Cal.Rptr. 480.

SULLIVAN, JUSTICE. Plaintiff appeals from a judgment of dismissal entered upon an order sustaining, with leave to amend, defendants' general demurrers to plaintiff's complaint, plaintiff having thereafter declined to amend.

Plaintiff's complaint, containing only one count, alleged in substance the following: On and after April 7, 1969, plaintiff was the owner of a cocktail lounge and restaurant business in Los Angeles known as the Brass Rail. The business premises were insured against fire loss in the aggregate sum of $35,000 by the three defendant insurers, Aetna Insurance Company (Aetna), Yosemite Insurance Company (Yosemite), and American Home Assurance Company (American).

In the early hours of the morning of November 9, 1969, a fire occurred at the Brass Rail. Plaintiff was notified and immediately went to the scene. While there, he became involved in an argument with a member of the arson detail of the Los Angeles Fire Department and was placed under arrest.

On November 10, 1969, defendant insurers, upon being informed of the fire, engaged the services of defendant P.E. Brown and Company (Brown). Carl Busching, a claims adjuster employed by Brown, went to the Brass Rail to investigate the fire and inspect the premises. While he was there, he stated to an arson investigator of the Los Angeles Fire Department that plaintiff had excessive coverage under his fire insurance policies. Eventually the premises were locked and nothing was removed until November 14, 1969, when Busching authorized the removal of the rubble and debris.

About November 13, 1969, plaintiff was charged in a felony complaint with the crimes of arson (Pen.Code, § 448a) and defrauding an insurer (Pen.Code, § 548). A preliminary hearing was set for January 12, 1970.

Defendant insurance companies also retained defendant law firm Cummins, White, Briedenbach & Alphson (Cummins) to represent them in the matter of plaintiff's claim of fire loss. On November 25, 1969, defendant Donald Ricketts, an attorney-employee of Cummins, demanded in writing that plaintiff appear at the offices of said firm on December 12, 1969, to submit to an examination under oath and to produce certain documents. On November 26, 1969, plaintiff's attorney responded by letter to Ricketts explaining that he had advised plaintiff not to make any statements concerning the fire loss while criminal charges were pending. The letter also requested that the insurers waive the requirement of an examination until the criminal charges lodged against plaintiff were concluded. Ricketts refused the request and warned that failure to appear for the examination would void coverage under the policies. On December 16, 1969, Ricketts, on behalf of the Cummins law firm, advised plaintiff's attorney in writing that defendant insurers were denying liability under the policies because of plaintiff's failure to submit to an examination under oath and to produce documents.

On January 12, 1970, a preliminary hearing was held on the complaint charging plaintiff with arson and defrauding an insurer. Busching appeared as a witness for the prosecution and restated his belief that plaintiff had excessive fire insurance coverage for his business. The charges were dismissed by the magistrate for lack of probable cause.

On January 26, 1970, plaintiff's attorney advised defendant insurers that plaintiff was now prepared to submit himself for an examination. However, the insurers reaffirmed their position that they were denying liability because of plaintiff's failure to appear.

According to the allegations of the complaint, all defendants other than the insurance company defendants were the agents and employees of the three defendant companies and were acting within the scope of such agency and employment when the acts attributed to them were committed. It was further alleged that "the defendants and each of them joined together and acted in concert to falsely imply that the plaintiff had a motive to deliberately set fire to and burn down his place of business [and that] [t]he purpose of the defendants in creating such false implication was to establish a grounds [sic] upon which the defendant Insurers could avoid paying the amounts due to plaintiff under the policies of insurance issued by the defendant Insurers." To carry out their purpose, defendants "conducted themselves in the following manner": (a) defendant Busching stated to an arson investigator that plaintiff had acquired excessive fire insurance coverage; (b) defendant insurers demanded that plaintiff submit to an examination under oath and to produce certain documents "in order to enable them to secure further evidence to support the false implication that plaintiff was guilty of arson"; and (c) defendant Busching, appearing as a witness for the People at the preliminary hearing on the felony complaint, reaffirmed his statement made to the arson investigator.

As a "direct and proximate result of the outrageous conduct and bad faith of the defendants," plaintiff suffered "severe economic damage," "severe emotional upset and distress," loss of earnings and various special damages. Plaintiff sought both compensatory and punitive damages.

Defendants filed general demurrers to the complaint which were sustained with leave to amend. Plaintiff elected to stand on his complaint and an order of dismissal was entered. This appeal followed.

* * *

Plaintiff contends that he has stated sufficient facts to constitute a cause of action in tort against defendants for breach of an implied duty of good faith and fair dealing. The duty of an insurer to deal fairly and in good faith with its insured is governed by our decisions in Crisci v. Security Ins. Co. (1967) 66 Cal.2d 425, 58 Cal.Rptr. 13, 426 P.2d 173, and Comunale v. Traders & General Ins. Co. (1958) 50 Cal.2d 654, 328 P.2d 198. We explained that this duty, the breach of which sounds in both contract and tort, is imposed because "[t]here is an implied covenant of good faith and fair dealing in every contract [including insurance policies] that neither party will do anything which will injure the right of the other to receive the benefits of the agreement." [C] Therefore, "an insurer * * * who refuses to accept a reasonable settlement within the policy limits in violation of its duty to consider in good faith the interest of the insured in settlement, is liable for the entire judgment against the insured even if it exceeds the policy limits." [C]

* * *

In those two cases, we considered the duty of the insurer to act in good faith and fairly in handling the claims of third persons against the insured, described as a "duty to accept reasonable settlements"; in the case before us we consider the duty of an insurer to act in good faith and fairly in handling the claim of an insured, namely a duty not to withhold unreasonably payments due under a policy. These are merely two different aspects of the same duty. That responsibility is not the requirement mandated by the terms of the policy itself—to defend, settle, or pay. It is the obligation, deemed to be imposed by the law, under which the insurer must act fairly and in good faith in discharging its contractual responsibilities. Where in so doing, it fails to deal *fairly and in good faith* with its insured by refusing, without proper cause, to compensate its insured for a loss covered by the policy, such conduct may give rise to a cause of action in tort for breach of an implied covenant of good faith and fair dealing.

[The court quotes from and discusses Richardson v. Employers Liab. Assur. Corp., 25 Cal.App.2d 232, 239, 102 Cal.Rptr. 547, 552 (1972); and Fletcher and Western National Life Ins. Co., 10 Cal.App.3d 376, 89 Cal.Rptr. 78 (1970).]

It is manifest that a common legal principle underlies all of the foregoing decisions; namely, that in every insurance contract there is an implied covenant of good faith and fair dealing. The duty to so act is imminent in the contract whether the company is attending to the claims of third persons against the insured or the claims of the insured itself. Accordingly, when the insurer unreasonably and in bad faith withholds payment of the claim of its insured, it is subject to liability in tort.

In the case at bench plaintiff has alleged in essence that defendants wilfully and maliciously entered into a scheme to deprive him of the benefits of the fire policies. * * * We conclude therefore that while the complaint is far from a model pleading, it does allege in substance a breach on the part of defendant insurance companies of their duty of good faith and fair dealing which they owed plaintiff. * * *

While it might be argued that defendants would be excused from their contractual duties * * * if plaintiff breached his obligations under the policies, we do not think that plaintiff's alleged breach excuses defendants from their duty, implied by law, of good faith and fair dealing. In other words, the insurer's duty is unconditional and independent of the performance of plaintiff's contractual obligations. * * *

In summary, we conclude that plaintiff has stated facts sufficient to constitute a cause of action in tort against defendant insurance companies for breach of their implied duty of good faith and fair dealing; that plaintiff's failure to appear at the office of the insurers' counsel in order to submit to an examination under oath and to produce certain documents, as appearing from the allegations of the complaint, is not fatal to the statement of such cause of action; and that plaintiff has stated facts sufficient for the recovery of damages for mental distress whether or not these facts constitute "extreme" or "outrageous" conduct. On the other hand, since the remaining defendants were not subject to the implied duty arising from the contractual relationship, we conclude that the complaint does not state sufficient facts to constitute a cause of action against them and that the judgment of dismissal in their favor was proper.

As to defendants Aetna Insurance Company, Yosemite Insurance Company and American Home Assurance Company, the judgment is reversed and the cause is remanded to the trial court with directions to overrule the demurrers and to allow said defendants a reasonable time within which to answer. As to the remaining defendants, the judgment is affirmed. * * *

[ROTH, JUSTICE PRO TEM., dissented, with opinion.]

---

1. A growing number of states and cases have been recognizing this "new tort" of bad faith in the performance of an insurance policy. Fact patterns have usually fallen into two categories: (1) Turning down a claim without even investigating its validity. United Services Auto. Ass'n v. Werley, 526 P.2d 28

(Alaska 1974); Egan v. Mutual of Omaha Ins. Co., 63 Cal.App.3d 659, 133 Cal. Rptr. 899 (1976); Anderson v. Continental Ins. Co., 85 Wis.2d 675, 271 N.W.2d 368 (1978). (2) Declining to pay in order to bring economic pressure on the insured in his straitened condition. Neal v. Farmers Ins. Exchange, 21 Cal.3d 910, 582 P.2d 980, 148 Cal.Rptr. 389 (1978); Egan v. Mutual of Omaha Ins. Co., 63 Cal.App.3d 659, 133 Cal.Rptr. 899 (1976); United States Fidelity & Guar. Co. v. Peterson, 91 Nev. 617, 540 P.2d 1070 (1975).

2. *Bases for the Action.* The principal case suggests breach of an "implied covenant of good faith and fair dealing." The implied-covenant concept is, of course, a means of expanding contract responsibility. But the court says that the action sounds in both contract and tort. Another basis is violation of a fiduciary obligation. This is a tort action though it has traditionally sounded in equity. See Restatement (Second) of Torts § 874; Rowen v. LeMars Mut. Ins. Co. of Iowa, 282 N.W.2d 639 (Iowa 1979); Doe v. Roe, 93 Misc.2d 201, 400 N.Y.S.2d 668 (1977). It requires the step, however, of holding that there is a fiduciary relation between the insurer and the insured. Perhaps something akin to the "tort" of duress or abuse of economic pressure may be utilized. See Neibuhr v. Gage, supra page 1206. Might this be treated as a reciprocal counterpart to the tort of wrongful civil proceedings (supra Chapter 20)— frivolous or unwarranted defenses? The suggestion has been made that the tort is justified by the quasi-public nature of insurance companies and the need to control them for the benefit of the public. Christian v. American Home Assurance Co., 577 P.2d 899 (Okl.1978). Some states impose a statutory penalty on an insurance company for failure to make prompt payment. E.g., Tenn.Code § 56–7–105 (1980). Compare the statement in D'Ambrosio v. Pennsylvania Nat'l Mut. Cas. Ins. Co., 262 Pa.Super. 331, 396 A.2d 780 (1979): "The insurer's promise to the insured to 'simplify his life,' to put him 'in good hands,' to back him with 'a piece of the rock' or to be 'on his side' hardly suggests that the insurer will abandon the insured in his time of need."

3. An insurance company was found to have breached the "implied covenant of good faith and fair dealing" in the manner in which it terminated disability payments to plaintiff, its policyholder. Held, the action is in tort and plaintiff can recover the future policy benefits that he would have received if the contract had been honored by the insurer, plus compensation for emotional distress (amounting to a total of $44,550). Punitive damages of $1,000,000 were held not excessive, since they amounted to only .00002% of the insurer's gross assets. Pistorious v. Prudential Ins. Co. of America, 123 Cal.App.3d 541, 176 Cal.Rptr. 660 (1981).

4. In L'Orange v. Medical Protective Co., 394 F.2d 57 (6th Cir.1968), plaintiff alleged that the defendant cancelled his malpractice insurance when he testified against another dentist in an action for medical malpractice. Held, the complaint states a good cause for action for breach of contract. The cancellation is against public policy, especially in view of the state's statutory policy against intimidating a witness. It is not clear whether the plaintiff can merely recover damages for breach of contract or can obtain a declaration that the policy is still in effect. Is there any basis on which an action of tort might be maintained? On the other hand, would a better solution be to insist that actions of this general nature be in contract rather than tort, and to modify the contract law to allow broader consequential damages and perhaps punitive damages when the defendant acts intentionally and in bad faith?

5. Whether the tort or contract basis is adopted, should the general concept be extended beyond insurance policies to contracts in general?

6. See Schwartz, Statutory Strict Liability for an Insurer's Failure to Settle: A Balanced Plan for an Unresolved Problem, 1975 Duke L.J. 901; Gage, Recovery of Unlimited Insurance Proceeds Based Upon Bad Faith and Unfair Dealings, 5 San Fernando L.Rev. 367 (1977); Shernoff & Blickenstaff, Investigating for Bad Faith: The Role of Plaintiff's Attorney, 14 Forum 132 (1978).

PALMATEER v. INTERNATIONAL HARVESTER CO.
Supreme Court of Illinois, 1981.
85 Ill.2d 124, 52 Ill.Dec. 13, 421 N.E.2d 876.

SIMON, JUSTICE: The plaintiff, Ray Palmateer, complains of his discharge by International Harvester Company (IH). He had worked for IH for 16 years, rising from a unionized job at an hourly rate to a managerial position on a fixed salary. Following his discharge, Palmateer filed a * * * complaint against IH, alleging * * * that he had suffered a retaliatory discharge. According to the complaint, Palmateer was fired both for supplying information to local law-enforcement authorities that an IH employee might be involved in a violation of the Criminal Code of 1961 [c] and for agreeing to assist in the investigation and trial of the employee if requested. The circuit court * * * ruled the complaint failed to state a cause of action and dismissed it; the appellate court affirmed in a divided opinion. [C] We granted Palmateer leave to appeal to determine the contours of the tort of retaliatory discharge approved in Kelsay v. Motorola, Inc. (1978), 74 Ill.2d 172, 23 Ill.Dec. 559, 384 N.E.2d 353.

In *Kelsay* the plaintiff was discharged in retaliation for filing a worker's compensation claim. The court noted that public policy strongly favored the exercise of worker's compensation rights; if employees could be fired for filing compensation claims, that public policy would be frustrated. Despite a dissent urging that the creation of a new tort should be left to the legislature, the court said, "We are convinced that to uphold and implement this public policy a cause of action should exist for retaliatory discharge." [C] The court then considered the claim for damages, and decided that punitive damages would be allowed in retaliatory discharge cases, but only in the future. The creation of the new tort, at a time when decisions in other jurisdictions conflicted on whether such a firing would be actionable, was sufficiently unexpected that Motorola was not required to pay punitive damages to Kelsay. This court directed, however, that in subsequent cases punitive damages would be available. [C]

With *Kelsay,* Illinois joined the growing number of States recognizing the tort of retaliatory discharge. The tort is an exception to the general rule that an "at-will" employment is terminable at any time for any or no cause. [C] This general rule is a harsh outgrowth of the notion of reciprocal rights and obligations in employment relationships—that if the employee can end his employment at any time under any condition, then the employer should have the same right. [C] As one 19th century court put it: "May I not refuse to trade with any one? May I not forbid my family to trade with any one? May I not dismiss my domestic servant for dealing, or even visiting, where I forbid? And if my domestic, why not my farm-hand, or my mechanic, or teamster? * * * All may dismiss their employes at will, be they many or few, for good cause, for no cause or even for cause morally wrong, without being thereby guilty of legal wrong." Payne v. Western & Atlantic R.R. Co. (1884), 81 Tenn. (13 Lea) 507, 518–20.

Recent analysis has pointed out the shortcomings of the mutuality theory. With the rise of large corporations conducting specialized operations and employing relatively immobile workers who often have no other place to market their skills, recognition that the employer and employee do not stand on equal footing is realistic. [C] In addition, unchecked employer power, like unchecked employee power, has been seen to present a distinct threat to the public policy carefully considered and adopted by society as a whole. As a result, it is now recognized that a proper balance must be maintained among the employer's interest in operating a business efficiently and profitably, the employee's interest in earning a livelihood, and society's interest in seeing its public policies carried out.

By recognizing the tort of retaliatory discharge, *Kelsay* acknowledged the common law principle that parties to a contract may not incorporate in it rights and obligations which are clearly injurious to the public. [C] This principle is expressed forcefully in cases which insist that an employer is in contempt for discharging an employee who exercises the civic right and duty of serving on a jury. [Cc] But the Achilles heel of the principle lies in the definition of public policy. When a discharge contravenes public policy in any way the employer has committed a legal wrong. However, the employer retains the right to fire workers at will in cases "where no clear mandate of public policy is involved." [C] But what constitutes clearly mandated public policy?

There is no precise definition of the term. In general, it can be said that public policy concerns what is right and just and what affects the citizens of the State collectively. It is to be found in the State's constitution and statutes and, when they are silent, in its judicial decisions. [C] Although there is no precise line of demarcation dividing matters that are the subject of public policies from matters purely personal, a survey of cases in other States involving retaliatory discharges shows that a matter must strike at the heart of a citizen's social rights, duties, and responsibilities before the tort will be allowed. Thus, actions for retaliatory discharge have been allowed where the employee was fired for refusing to violate a statute. Examples are: Petermann v. International Brotherhood of Teamsters Local 396 (1959), 174 Cal.App.2d 184, 344 P.2d 25 (for refusing to commit perjury); Tameny v. Atlantic Richfield Co. (1980), 27 Cal.3d 167, 610 P.2d 1330, 164 Cal.Rptr. 839 (for refusing to engage in price-fixing); Harless v. First National Bank (W.Va.1978), 246 S.E.2d 270 (for refusing to violate a consumer credit code); O'Sullivan v. Mallon (1978), 160 N.J.Super. 416, 390 A.2d 149 (for refusing to practice medicine without a license). It has also been allowed where the employee was fired for refusing to evade jury duty (Nees v. Hocks (1975), 272 Or. 210, 536 P.2d 512; Reuther v. Fowler & Williams, Inc. (1978), 255 Pa.Super. 28, 386 A.2d 119), for engaging in statutorily protected union activities (Glenn v. Clearman's Golden Cock Inn, Inc. (1961), 192 Cal.App.2d 793, 13 Cal. Rptr. 769), and for filing a claim under a worker's compensation statute (Sventko v. Kroger Co. (1976), 69 Mich.App. 644, 245 N.W.2d 151; Frampton v. Central Indiana Gas Co. (1973), 260 Ind. 249, 297 N.E.2d 425).

The action has not been allowed where the worker was discharged in a dispute over a company's internal management system (Keneally v. Orgain (1980), Mont., 606 P.2d 127), where the worker took too much sick leave (Jones v. Keogh (1979), 137 Vt. 562, 409 A.2d 581), where the worker tried to examine the company's books in his capacity as a shareholder (Campbell v. Ford Industries, Inc. (1976), 274 Or. 243, 546 P.2d 141), where the worker impugned the company's integrity (Abrisz v. Pulley Freight Lines, Inc. (Iowa 1978), 270 N.W.2d 454), where the worker refused to be examined by a psychological-stress evaluator (Larsen v. Motor Supply Co. (1977), 117 Ariz. 507, 573 P.2d 907), where the worker was attending night school (Scroghan v. Kraftco Corp. (Ky. App.1977), 551 S.W.2d 811), or where the worker improperly used the employer's Christmas fund (Jackson v. Minidoka Irrigation District (1977), 98 Idaho 330, 563 P.2d 54).

The cause of action is allowed where the public policy is clear, but is denied where it is equally clear that only private interests are at stake. Where the nature of the interest at stake is muddled, the courts have given conflicting answers as to whether the protection of the tort action is available. Compare the inconsistent results where the discharge was for opposition to sexual discrimination or harassment (McCluney v. Jos. Schlitz Brewing Co. (E.D.Wis.1980), 489 F.Supp. 24, and Monge v. Beebe Rubber Co. (1974), 114 N.H. 130, 316 A.2d 549), for refusal to falsify official reports (Hinrichs v. Tranquilaire Hospital (Ala. 1977), 352 So.2d 1130, and Trombetta v. Detroit, Toledo & Ironton R.R. Co. (1978), 81 Mich.App. 489, 265 N.W.2d 385), and over internal company disputes regarding product safety (Geary v. United States Steel Corp. (1974), 456 Pa. 171, 319 A.2d 174, and Pierce v. Ortho Pharmaceutical Corp. (1979), 166 N.J.Super. 335, 399 A.2d 1023).

It is clear that Palmateer has here alleged that he was fired in violation of an established public policy. * * * There is no public policy more basic, nothing more implicit in the concept of ordered liberty, [c] than the enforcement of a State's criminal code. [Cc] There is no public policy more important or more fundamental than the one favoring the effective protection of the lives and property of citizens. [Cc]

No specific constitutional or statutory provision requires a citizen to take an active part in the ferreting out and prosecution of crime, but public policy nevertheless favors citizen crime-fighters. * * * Public policy favors Palmateer's conduct in volunteering information to the law-enforcement agency. Once the possibility of crime was reported, Palmateer was under a statutory duty to further assist officials when requested to do so. [C] Public policy thus also favors Palmateer's agreement to assist in the investigation and prosecution of the suspected crime.

The foundation of the tort of retaliatory discharge lies in the protection of public policy, and there is a clear public policy favoring investigation and prosecution of criminal offenses. Palmateer has stated a cause of action for retaliatory discharge.

IH contends that even if there is a public policy discouraging violations of the Criminal Code, that public policy has too wide a sweep. IH points out that the crime here might be nothing more than the theft of a $2 screwdriver. It feels that in the exercise of its sound business judgment it ought to be able to properly fire a managerial employee who recklessly and precipitously resorts to the criminal justice system to handle such a personnel problem. But this response misses the point. The magnitude of the crime is not the issue here. It was the General Assembly, the People's representatives, who decided that the theft of a $2 screwdriver was a problem that should be resolved by resort to the criminal justice system. IH's business judgment, no matter how sound, cannot override that decision. * * *

Appellate court affirmed in part and reversed in part * * * cause remanded, with directions.

UNDERWOOD, JUSTICE, dissenting: For the reasons stated in my dissent in Kelsay v. Motorola, Inc. (1978), 74 Ill.2d 172, 190, 23 Ill.Dec. 559, 384 N.E.2d 353, I believe the court there erred. The thoughts expressed in that dissent regarding judicial self-restraint are equally applicable here. In addition, I share Mr. Justice Ryan's criticism of the court's action in this case.

RYAN, JUSTICE, also dissenting: Although I authored the opinion in Kelsay v. Motorola, Inc. (1978), 74 Ill.2d 172, 23 Ill.Dec. 559, 384 N.E.2d 353, I cannot agree to extend the cause of action for retaliatory discharge approved in that case into the nebulous area of judicially created public policy, as has been done by the opinion in this case. I fear that the result of this opinion will indeed fulfill the prophesy of Mr. Justice Underwood's dissent in *Kelsay*. "Henceforth, no matter how indolent, insubordinate or obnoxious an employee may be, * * * [the] employer may thereafter discharge him only at the risk of being compelled to defend a suit for retaliatory discharge and unlimited punitive damages * * *" Kelsay v. Motorola, Inc. (1978), 74 Ill.2d 172, 192, 23 Ill.Dec. 559, 384 N.E.2d 353. * * *

By departing from the general rule that an at-will employment is terminable at the discretion of the employer, the courts are attempting to give recognition to the desire and expectation of an employee in continued employment. In doing so, however, the courts should not concentrate solely on promoting the employee's expectations. The courts must recognize that the allowance of a tort action for retaliatory discharge is a departure from, and an exception to, the general rule. The legitimate interest of the employer in guiding the policies and destiny of his operation cannot be ignored. The new tort for retaliatory discharge is in its infancy. In nurturing and shaping this remedy, courts must balance the interests of employee and employer with the hope of fashioning a remedy that will accommodate the legitimate expectations of both. In the process of emerging from the harshness of the former rule, we must guard against swinging the pendulum to the opposite extreme.　*　*　*

In order to establish the necessary balance between employer and employee interests, I would hold that the employee may maintain an action for retaliatory discharge only when the discharge has been violative of some *strong* public policy that has been *clearly* articulated. Usually, that clear articulation would be found in legislative enactment. I do not think that an employer should be compelled to defend a tort action and possibly, be forced to pay a disgruntled discharged employee compensatory, and possibly substantial, punitive damages because of a violation of some vague concept of public policy that has never been articulated by anyone except four members of this court.

I therefore respectfully dissent.

THOMAS J. MORAN, J., joins in this dissent.

---

1. The sampling of retaliatory-discharge cases given in the opinion of the instant case is appropriately representative. For later decisions with good discussion, see Adler v. American Standard Corp., 291 Md. 31, 432 A.2d 464 (1981); Sides v. Duke University, 74 N.C.App. 331, 328 S.E.2d 818 (1985) (nurse anesthetist gives truthful, rather than perjured, testimony; doctors inducing her discharge also liable for inducing breach of contract); Wagenseller v. Scottsdale Mem. Hosp., 147 Ariz. 370, 710 P.2d 1025 (1985), 1986 Ariz.St.L.J. 161 (1986) (discusses, at length, various legal doctrines bearing on the problem of wrongful discharge).

2. Some courts speak of the implied covenant of good faith and fair dealing and use it to give rise to a cause of action for breach of contract. A leading case is Monge v. Beebe Rubber Co., 114 N.H. 130, 316 A.2d 549 (1974) (sexual harassment). Two recent cases from Massachusetts have carried the approach further than the torts cases have. In Fortune v. National Cash Register Co., 373 Mass. 96, 364 N.E.2d 1251 (1977), the court held that to discharge an at-will employee in order to avoid paying him his bonus credit and earned commissions amounted to bad faith and he could recover for breach of contract. In McKinney v. National Dairy Council, 491 F.Supp. 1108 (D.C.Mass. 1980), the court held that the same principle might apply to a discharge given because plaintiff was reaching retirement age. At present many courts follow the principal case in treating the action as based on tort.

3. See Love, Retaliatory Discharge for Filing a Worker's Compensation Claim: The Development of a Modern Tort Action, 37 Hastings L.J. 551 (1986); Lopatka, The Emerging Law of Wrongful Discharge, 40 Bus.Law. 1 (1984); Mauk, Wrongful Discharge: The Erosion of 100 Years of Employer Privilege, 21 Ida.L.Rev. 201 (1985); Linzer, The Decline of Assent: At–Will Employment as a Case Study of the Breakdown of Private Law Theory, 20 Ga.L.Rev. 323 (1986);

Blades, Employment at Will v. Individual Freedom: On Limiting the Abusive Exercise of Employer Power, 67 Colum.L.Rev. 1404 (1976); Peck, Unjust Discharge from Employment: A Necessary Change in the Law, 40 Ohio St.L.J. 1 (1979).

SEAMAN'S DIRECT BUYING SERVICE, INC. v. STANDARD OIL COMPANY OF CALIFORNIA

Supreme Court of California, In Bank, 1984.
36 Cal.3d 752, 686 P.2d 1158, 206 Cal.Rptr. 354.

[The city of Eureka, planning extensive redevelopment in its harbor area, condemned the area in which the plaintiff, Seaman's, was located. Seaman's was engaged in general activities for the benefit of incoming vessels, including "a small marine fueling station." It negotiated with the city for becoming a part of the redevelopment by substantially enlarging its business. The negotiations were conditioned on Seaman's providing evidence of financial responsibility to the city and the federal Economic Development Agency (EDA).

Seaman's entered into negotiations with Standard Oil of California for a commitment to supply gasoline, the two companies "reaching an agreement on all major points." A writing was prepared and signed by both Seaman's and Standard. Based on this, the city signed a 40–year lease for the area desired by Seaman's.

Before Seaman's expanded facility was completed, action by OPEC nations produced a serious oil shortage throughout the world, creating a seller's market. Standard notified Seaman's that it was sorry that it would be unable to supply the oil promised in their agreement because of federal regulations limiting the allocation of petroleum products to existing customers. Seaman's finally succeeded in obtaining an exception from the federal agency, allowing Standard to supply the gasoline to Seaman's as a new customer.

Once this had been done, Standard changed its position and contended that no binding agreement had ever been reached. The federal agency indicated that it would direct Standard to fulfill supply obligations to Seaman's upon receiving copy of a court decree that a valid contract existed between the parties. Seaman's asked Standard to stipulate the existence of a contract, but the Standard representative refused, laughed and left, saying "See you in court."

Seaman's brought suit charging "breach of contract, fraud, breach of the implied covenant of good faith and fair dealing and interference with Seaman's contractual relationship with the city." The jury returned a verdict for the plaintiff on all counts except fraud. Total damages amounted to $3,970,500 compensation and $22,077,620 punitive. The trial judge required a remittitur to $7,000,000 on the punitive damages. Both parties appealed.

The court holds that the writing satisfies the statute of frauds. It also holds that the tort of intentional interference with an existing contract requires intent and that it was error to instruct that a person "is deemed to have acted intentionally if it knew that disruption or interference with an advantageous relationship was substantially certain to result from its conduct." For this, it quotes the first Restatement that the "essential thing is the purpose to cause the result." This eliminated the damages for intentional interference with contract.]

BY THE COURT: The principal issue * * * is whether, and under what circumstances, a breach of the implied covenant of good faith and fair dealing in a commercial contract may give rise to an action in tort. Standard contends that a tort action for breach of the implied covenant has always been, and should continue to be, limited to cases where the underlying contract is one of insurance. Seaman's, pointing to several recent cases decided by this court and the Courts of Appeal, challenges this contention. A brief review of the development of the tort is in order.

It is well settled that, in California, the law implies in *every* contract a covenant of good faith and fair dealing. [Cc] Broadly stated, that covenant requires that neither party do anything which will deprive the other of the benefits of the agreement. [C]

California courts have recognized the existence of this covenant, and enforced it, in cases involving a wide variety of contracts. * * *

While the proposition that the law implies a covenant of good faith and fair dealing in all contracts is well established, the proposition advanced by Seaman's—that breach of the covenant always gives rise to an action in tort—is not so clear. In holding that a tort action is available for breach of the covenant in an insurance contract, we have emphasized the "special relationship" between insurer and insured, characterized by elements of public interest, adhesion, and fiduciary responsibility. [C] No doubt there are other relationships with similar characteristics and deserving of similar legal treatment.

When we move from such special relationships to consideration of the tort remedy in the context of the ordinary commercial contract, we move into largely uncharted and potentially dangerous waters. Here, parties of roughly equal bargaining power are free to shape the contours of their agreement and to include provisions for attorney fees and liquidated damages in the event of breach. They may not be permitted to disclaim the covenant of good faith but they are free, within reasonable limits at least, to agree upon the standards by which application of the covenant is to be measured. In such contracts, it may be difficult to distinguish between breach of the covenant and breach of contract, and there is the risk that interjecting tort remedies will intrude upon the expectations of the parties. This is not to say that tort remedies have no place in such a commercial context, but that it is wise to proceed with caution in determining their scope and application.

For the purposes of this case it is unnecessary to decide the broad question which Seaman's poses. Indeed, it is not even necessary to predicate liability on a breach of the implied covenant. It is sufficient to recognize that a party to a contract may incur tort remedies when, in addition to breaching the contract, it seeks to shield itself from liability by denying, in bad faith and without probable cause, that the contract exists.

It has been held that a party to a contract may be subject to tort liability, including punitive damages, if he coerces the other party to pay more than is due under the contract terms through the threat of a lawsuit, made " 'without probable cause and with no belief in the existence of the cause of action.' " [C] There is little difference, in principle, between a contracting party obtaining excess payment in such manner, and a contracting party seeking to avoid all liability on a meritorious contract claim by adopting a "stonewall" position ("see you in court") without probable cause and with no belief in the existence of a defense. Such conduct goes beyond the mere breach of contract. It offends accepted notions of business ethics. [C] Acceptance of tort remedies in such a situation is not likely to intrude upon the bargaining relationship or upset reasonable expectations of the contracting parties.

Turning to the facts of this case, the jury was instructed that "where a binding contract [has] been agreed upon, the law implies a covenant that neither party will deny the existence of a contract, since doing so violates the legal prohibition against doing anything to prevent realization of the promises of the performance of the contract." * * *

Since Standard's denial of the existence of a binding contract would not have been tortious if made in good faith, the trial court erred in failing to so instruct the jury. It is then necessary to decide whether this error requires that the judgment be reversed. * * *

In this case, there is a considerable degree of conflict in the evidence on the issue of whether Standard denied the existence of a contract in bad faith. [The opinion treats this in detail.] Here, it seems probable that the jury may have imposed liability on Standard as a result of the trial court's failure to instruct as to the bad faith requirement. Accordingly, the judgment in favor of Seaman's for breach of the duty of good faith and fair dealing must be reversed. * * *

The judgment in favor of Seaman's for breach of contract is affirmed. The judgment for intentional interference with contractual relations and for breach of the duty of good faith and fair dealing is reversed with directions to conduct further proceedings consistent with this opinion.

BIRD, CHIEF JUSTICE, concurring and dissenting. * * * [T]he assumption that parties may breach at will, risking only contract damages, is one of the cornerstones of contract law. * * * In most commercial contracts, recognition of this economic reality leads the parties to accept the possibility of breach, particularly since their right to recover contract damages provides adequate protection.

For example, one party to a contract may decide to breach if it concludes that the market will bring a higher price for its product than that set forth in the contract. In commercial contracts, the risk of such a breach is widely recognized and generally accepted. * * *

When the breaching party acts in bad faith to shield itself entirely from liability for contract damages, however, the duty of good faith and fair dealing is violated. * * *

This type of conduct violates the non-breaching party's justified expectation that it will be able to recover damages for its losses in the event of a breach. That expectation must be protected. Otherwise, the acceptance of the possibility of breach by the contracting parties and by society as a whole may be seriously undermined.

There is no danger that permitting tort recovery for bad faith denial of the existence of a valid commercial contract will make every breach of contract a tort. * * *

[T]ort "[l]iability is imposed *not* for a bad faith breach of the contract, but for failure to meet the duty . . . included within the implied covenant of good faith and fair dealing." [C] There are many situations in which a defendant's actions may sound both in tort and contract. The fact that overlapping remedies may exist in some situations does not make every breach of contract a tort. * * *

[Here the] duty of good faith and fair dealing was violated because a party attempted to avoid all liability for a contract breach by denying, in bad faith, the very existence of the contract. Such conduct violates the nearly universal expectation that the injured party will be compensated for losses caused by the breaching party's failure to perform. This tort remedy was recognized by this court in its earlier decisions involving the implied covenant of good faith and fair dealing. Those decisions should be the basis for the holding here. * * *

A breach of contract may also constitute a tortious breach of the covenant of good faith and fair dealing in a situation where the possibility that the contract will be breached is not accepted or reasonably expected by the parties. * * *

On this record, there is ample evidence to support the conclusion that the parties' reasonable expectations did not include the possibility of breach. Standard was repeatedly informed that Seaman's needed a "binding commitment." Throughout the negotiations, there was an emphasis on the need for such a commitment and for a stable relationship between Seaman's and its supplier. Standard knew that Seaman's lease, and, to some extent, the entire marina development depended on these factors. Under these circumstances, it would be reasonable to conclude that the parties' justified expectations did not include the possibility of breach.

Under this cause of action, no independent showing of bad faith should be required. Where the possibility of breach was not reasonably expected at the inception of the contract, the voluntary breach of an acknowledged contract is in itself a violation of the duty to deal fairly and in good faith. * * *

Standard's denial of the existence of the contract to the federal agency and the subsequent refusal to stipulate were anticipatory breaches of the contract. [C] Neither the breach nor the underlying resistance to an assertion of contract liability is a tort if undertaken in good faith. [C] In this case, * * * Standard did not deny that a contract existed until it had been ordered by the federal government to supply fuel to Seaman's. Moreover, Standard did not make its denials forthrightly as a defense to an action for breach of contract. It used them as a trump card in its final attempt to avoid all liability for nonperformance. The timing and the intended effect of both denials tend strongly to establish that they were made in bad faith.

I would affirm the judgment for Seaman's for breach of contract and breach of the duty of good faith and fair dealing.

---

1. Consider the implications of this case on the future development of contract and tort and their relationship. How likely is it to produce a following? For two extensive critiques of the case, see Comments, 71 Iowa L.Rev. 893 (1986); and 69 Minn.L.Rev. 1161 (1985). See also Nicholson v. United Pacific Ins. Co., __ Mont. __, 710 P.2d 1342 (1985), involving lease of office space, to be remodeled, in which lessee sought to rescind the lease after the remodeling was almost completed, because of a decision not to locate in Montana. The opinion cites other Montana cases in which liability was imposed for breach of the covenant of good faith and fair dealing. And see K.M.C. Co. v. Irving Trust Co., 757 F.2d 752 (6th Cir.1985) (bank's refusal to honor request to draw funds on line of credit); Commercial Cotton Co. v. United Calif. Bank, 163 Cal.App.3d 511, 209 Cal.Rptr. 551 (1985).

2. See Summers, Good Faith in the General Contract Law and the Sale Provisions of the UCC, 54 Va.L.Rev. 195 (1968); Burton, Breach of Contract and the Common Law Duty to Perform in Good Faith, 94 Harv.L.Rev. 369 (1980); Burton, More on Good Faith Performance of a Contract: A Reply to Professor Summers, 69 Iowa L.Rev. 497 (1984); Sullivan, Punitive Damages in the Law of Contract: The Reality and the Illusion of a Legal Change, 61 Minn.L.Rev. 207 (1977); Note, The Expanding Availability of Punitive Damages in Contract Actions, 8 Ind.L.Rev. 668 (1975).

3. See Diamond, The Tort of Bad Faith Breach of Contract: When, If at All, Should It Be Extended Beyond Insurance Transactions?, 64 Marq.L.Rev. 426 (1981); Louderback & Jurika, Standards for Limiting the Tort of Bad Faith Breach of Contract, 16 U.S.F.L.Rev. 187 (1982); Ryan, The Bad Faith Blast, 28 For the Defense 20 (Mar. 1986).

4. Smith Furniture Co. is a small furniture manufacturer in a small town. Jones Furniture Company is a wholesaler. It orders furniture from Smith, increases the orders and reaches the point where it is taking 90% of Smith's production. After this happens it delays paying for a period of six months and then sends a letter to Smith asserting that the products delivered during that period were found to be inferior and that it cannot conscientiously pay more than half the agreed price. Smith, which is in debt because of borrowing

money during the six-months period to pay wages and supplies, comes to you to ask what to do. Can you offer any helpful advice?

5. Was the court correct in its holding that an action would not lie for an intentional interference with an existing contract (see the last paragraph in the bracketed statement of facts)? Compare Restatement (Second) of Torts §§ 8A, 13 (1965); Jung & Levine, Whence Knowledge Intent? Whither Knowledge Intent?, 20 U.C. Davis L.Rev. 551 (1987).

Chapter XXIV

COMPENSATION SYSTEMS AS SUBSTITUTES FOR TORT LAW

1. EMPLOYMENT INJURIES

If this casebook were being prepared at the beginning of this century, it would have differed in many respects from its present form. But the greatest difference undoubtedly would be that it would include a long, and most important, chapter on employee injuries arising through industrial accidents. The formative period of the law of negligence coincided with the existence of the Industrial Revolution and was substantially affected by it. Out of the numerous cases arose an elaborate doctrinal system. Thus, among others, the employer had the general duties of using due care to provide a safe place to work and to supply safe tools and appliances. There were exceptions and counter-exceptions—e.g., the simple-tool doctrine as an exception to the second duty above, and the inexperienced-employee doctrine as an exception to it. See generally Labatt, Master and Servant (1913), vols. 3 and 4.

But the most significant aspect of the doctrinal development was the existence of a group of three defenses—assumption of risk, contributory negligence and the fellow-servant rule. This "unholy trinity," added to the requirement of proving negligence on the part of the employer, meant that the injured workman was successful in obtaining reparations for less than a quarter of the accidents. When he did recover, it was likely to be after a long, drawn-out litigation placing severe financial burdens upon him. And finally, the comparatively rare recoveries did not create a pressing incentive on the employer to spend money to avoid accidents. All of this produced mounting and explosive dissatisfaction.

In 1894, Germany, under Kaiser Wilhelm II, was the first major country to pass a system of compensation for work-related injuries. England, France and other European powers soon followed suit as their industries became machine dependent.

In the United States, the initial response to the mounting pressure was to pass statutes changing the most detrimental common law rules. Congress acted early, passing the first Employers' Liability Act in 1906.

This legislation attempted to create a federal tort rule protecting railroad employees. The Supreme Court held the Act to be unconstitutional. Employers' Liability Cases, 207 U.S. 463 (1908). Congress tried again in 1908 and enacted the second Federal Employers' Liability Act, which made federal (rather than state) law determinative when injury or death occurs to a railroad employee "while he is employed" in interstate commerce by the carrier. See 45 U.S.C.A. §§ 51 et seq. (1908). This time the Court upheld the statute. Second Employers' Liability Cases, 223 U.S. 1 (1912). Much judicial construction has evolved under this Act. A brief review can be found in the variety of opinions in Kelley v. Southern Pac. Co., 419 U.S. 318 (1974). This Act remains a tort law statute, requiring proof of employer negligence for recovery. Injured railroad employees are covered by this Act, and not by state or federal workers' compensation systems that now cover most other employment injuries. See Schwartz and Mahshigian, The Federal Employers' Liability Act, A Bane for Workers, A Bust for Railroads, A Boon for Lawyers, 23 San Diego L.Rev. 1 (1986).

Congress also substituted national standards for state tort law in 1927, when it enacted the Longshoremen's and Harbor Workers' Compensation Act. See 33 U.S.C.A. §§ 901 et seq. (as amended 1972). This act provided a workers' compensation system for those workers and also prescribed tort rules regarding their claims against shipowners. See Pascal, The Longshoremen's and Harbor Workers' Act Amendments of 1972, 10 Forum 1263 (1975) (describing legislative changes in both jurisdictional scope and substantive tort rules).

In the states, the culmination of the reaction began with the enactment in 1910 of a workers' compensation act in the State of New York, and the rapid spread of the acts throughout the rest of the states. In 1911 Wisconsin became the first state to pass a constitutional system of workers' compensation law.

The rallying theme for the movement was that the enterprise should bear the loss rather than permit it to lie on the unfortunate employee who fortuitously incurred the injury: "The cost of the product should bear the blood of the workman." The employer was liable to the injured employee regardless of fault, so long as the injury occurred in the course of employment. Early workers' compensation laws only protected employees from work-related injuries, but not occupational diseases. Today these are also included under the workers' compensation scheme. For further historical background, see J. Weinstein, The Corporate Ideal in the Liberal State, 1900–1918, ch. 2 (1968).

Workers' compensation has developed into a complex and highly specialized field of law. Each year there are literally hundreds of case law interpretations of a variety of statutes. Typical questions include whether an injury fell within the scope of employment, see, e.g., Nemchick v. Thatcher Glass Mfg. Co., 203 N.J.Super. 137, 495 A.2d 1372 (App.Div.1985) (employee's injury while driving home from work after completion of an assigned off-premises task occurred in "course of employment"); or whether the injury suffered was caused by conditions of employment. See, e.g., State Accident Ins. Fund v. Noffsinger, 80 Or. App. 640, 723 P.2d 358 (1986) (psychic injury as a result of verbal harassment and horseplay at workplace); Graver Tank & Mfg. Co. v.

Industrial Comm'n, 97 Ariz. 256, 399 P.2d 664 (1965) (suicide). Generally courts consider whether the injury may reasonably be regarded as an incident of employment rather than whether the injury was specifically foreseeable. See, e.g., Burns v. Merritt Eng'g Co., 302 N.Y. 131, 135, 96 N.E.2d 739, 741 (1951).

With the advancement of knowledge regarding harmful effects of substances often found in the working environment, many recent cases have challenged definitional limitations on coverage as well as notice and filing requirements that may limit recovery for occupational disease claims involving diseases not readily discoverable or easily associated with employment. See Solomons, Workers' Compensation for Occupational Disease Victims: Federal Standards and Threshold Problems, 41 Albany L.Rev. 195 (1977).

Perhaps the best summary of how these laws function has been provided by the author of the leading treatise in the field:

"The right to [workers'] compensation benefits depends on one simple test: Was there a work-connected injury? Negligence, and, for the most part, fault, are not in issue and cannot affect the result. Let the employer's conduct be flawless in its perfection, and let the employee's be abysmal in its clumsiness, rashness and ineptitude: if the accident arises out of and in the course of the employment, the employee receives his award. Reverse the positions, with a careless and stupid employer and a wholly innocent employee: the same award issues.

"Thus, the test is not the relation of an individual's personal quality (fault) to an event, but the relationship of an event to an employment. The essence of applying the test is not a matter of assessing blame, but of marking out boundaries.

"The typical [workers'] compensation act has these features: (a) the basic operating principle is that an employee is automatically entitled to certain benefits whenever he suffers a 'personal injury by accident arising out of and in the course of employment'; (b) negligence and fault are largely immaterial, both in the sense that the employee's contributory negligence does not lessen his rights and in the sense that the employer's complete freedom from fault does not lessen his liability; (c) coverage is limited to persons having the status of employee, as distinguished from independent contractor; (d) benefits to the employee include cash-wage benefits, usually around one-half to two-thirds of his average weekly wage, and hospital and medical expenses; in death cases benefits for dependents are provided; arbitrary maximum and minimum limits are ordinarily imposed; (e) the employee and his dependents, in exchange for these modest but assured benefits, give up their common-law right to sue the employer for damages for any injury covered by the act; (f) the right to sue third persons whose negligence caused the injury remains, however, with the proceeds usually being applied first to reimbursement of the employer for the compensation outlay, the balance (or most of it) going to the employee; (g) administration is typically in the hands of administrative commissions; and, as far as possible, rules of procedure, evidence, and conflict of laws are relaxed to facilitate the achievement of the beneficent purposes of the legislation; and (h) the employer is required to secure his liability through private insurance, state-fund insurance in some states, or 'self-insurance'; thus the burden of compensation liability does not remain upon the employer but passes to the consumer, since compensation premiums, as part of the cost of production, will be reflected in the price of the product." 1 A. Larson, The Law of Workmen's Compensation, 1–2, 5 (1985). (Copyright Matthew Bender and Company, Inc. Reprinted by permission.)

Workers' compensation has not been an ideal solution to the work-related accident problem. In some states compensation rates have been kept abnormally low and in many jurisdictions the system has been plagued with delay and excessive litigation. See Report of National Commission on State Workmen's Compensation Laws (1972); Schroeder and Shapiro, Responses to Occupational Disease: The Role of Markets, Regulation, and Information, 72 Geo.L.J. 1231 (1984).

Although legislation has been introduced at the federal level to ameliorate these problems, it has not shown much chance for enactment. A number of states have improved their workers' compensation laws in key areas. See U.S. Chamber of Commerce, Analysis of Workers' Compensation Laws (1985).

The modest benefits provided by the workers' compensation system are particularly conspicuous in light of the recent developments of expanded liability for tortious conduct; restriction or abolishment of the defenses of contributory negligence, assumption of the risk and the fellow servant rule; plus the award of damages for pain and suffering and for mental distress. A few courts have responded to this growing imbalance between what an employee recovers under workers' compensation and what he could have recovered in a tort action by construing statutes to limit employer immunity by finding ways to circumvent the worker compensation immunity shield.

BLANKENSHIP v. CINCINNATI MILACRON CHEMICALS, INC.

Supreme Court of Ohio, 1982.
69 Ohio St.2d 608, 433 N.E.2d 572, cert. denied, 459 U.S. 857, 103 S.Ct. 127, 74 L.Ed.2d 110 (1982).

[Eight current or former employees of Cincinnati Milacron Chemicals, Inc. (Milacron) brought an action against Milacron, alleging that exposure to fumes of certain chemicals within the scope of their employment rendered them sick, poisoned, and permanently disabled. The employees alleged that Milacron knew that such conditions existed, failed to correct the conditions, failed to warn the employees of the damages and conditions that existed, and failed to report the conditions to various state and Federal agencies to which they were required to report by law. The employees further alleged that Milacron failed to warn the employees that certain occupational diseases were being contracted and failed to provide medical examinations as required by law, and that Milacron's omissions were intentional, malicious, and in willful and wanton disregard of the duty to protect the health of employees.

The trial court dismissed on the ground that the action was barred by relevant sections of the Ohio Constitution and the Ohio Workers' Compensation Act, which afforded an employer and his employees total immunity from civil suit. Employees appealed the trial court's holding and the Court of Appeals affirmed. The cause is now before this court pursuant to the allowance of a motion to certify the record.]

BROWN, J. * * * The sole issue raised in this appeal is whether the trial court properly granted appellees' motion to dismiss appellants' complaint on the grounds that an employee is barred by Section 35, Article II of the Ohio Constitution, and R.C. 4123.74 and 4123.741 from prosecuting an action at law for an intentional tort. * * *

The primary focus of the dispute between the parties centers upon the question of whether the Workers' Compensation Act (R.C. 4123.35 et seq.) is intended to cover an intentional tort committed by employers against their employees. Section 35, Article II of the Ohio Constitution, serves as a basis for legislative enactments in the area of workers' compensation by providing, in pertinent part:

"For the purpose of providing compensation to workmen and their dependents, for death, injuries or occupational disease, occasioned in the course of such workmen's employment, laws may be passed establishing a state fund to be created by compulsory contribution thereto by employers, and administered by the state, determining the terms and conditions upon which payment shall be made therefrom. Such compensation shall be in lieu of all other rights to compensation, or damages, for such death, injuries, or occupational disease, and any employer who pays the premium or compensation provided by law, passed in accordance herewith, shall not be liable to respond in damages at common law or by statute for such death, injuries or occupational disease. * * *"

The constitutional mandate has been implemented by R.C. 4123.74 which provides: "Employers who comply with section 4123.35 of the Revised Code shall not be liable to respond in damages at common law or by statute for any injury, or occupational disease, or bodily condition, received or contracted by any employee in the course of or arising out of his employment * * * whether or not such injury, occupational disease [or] bodily condition * * * is compensable under sections 4123.01 to 4123.94, inclusive, of the Revised Code." * * *

[W]here an employee asserts in his complaint a claim for damages based on an intentional tort, " * * * the substance of the claim is not an injury * * * received or contracted by any employee in the course of or arising out of his employment within the meaning of R.C. 4123.74 * * *." Id. No reasonable individual would equate intentional and unintentional conduct in terms of the degree of risk which faces an employee nor would such individual contemplate the risk of an intentional tort as a natural risk of employment. Since an employer's intentional conduct does not arise out of employment, R.C. 4123.74 does not bestow upon employers immunity from civil liability for their intentional torts and an employee may resort to a civil suit for damages. [C]

This holding not only comports with constitutional and statutory requirements, but it is also consistent with the legislative goals which underlie the Workers' Compensation Act.

The workers' compensation system is based on the premise that an employer is protected from a suit for negligence in exchange for compliance with the Workers' Compensation Act. The Act operates as a balance of mutual compromise between the interests of the employer and the employee whereby employees relinquish their common law remedy and accept lower benefit levels coupled with the greater assurance of recovery and employers give up their common law defenses and are protected from unlimited liability. But the protection afforded by the Act has always been for negligent acts and not for intentional tortious conduct. Indeed, workers' compensation acts were designed to improve the plight of the injured worker, and to hold that intentional torts are covered under the Act would be tantamount to encouraging such conduct, and this clearly cannot be reconciled with the motivating spirit and purpose of the Act.

It must also be remembered that the compensation scheme was specifically designed to provide less than full compensation for injured employees. Damages such as pain and suffering and loss of services on the part of a spouse are unavailable remedies to the injured employee. Punitive damages cannot be obtained. Yet, these damages are available to individuals who have been injured by intentional tortious conduct of third parties, and there is no legitimate reason why an employer should be able to escape from such damages simply because he committed an intentional tort against his employee.

In addition, one of the avowed purposes of the Act is to promote a safe and injury-free work environment. [C] Affording an employer immunity for his intentional behavior certainly would not promote such an environment, for an employer could commit intentional acts with impunity with the knowledge that, at the very most, his workers' compensation premiums may rise slightly. * * * [The court holds that the question of whether Milacron's conduct and omissions amounted to an intentional tort should have been determined by the trier of fact, and that the trial court improperly dismissed the action. Judgment of the Court of Appeals is reversed and case remanded for further proceedings].

[CELEBREZZE, C.J., and SWEENEY and CLIFFORD F. BROWN, JJ., concur. LOCHER, J., concurs in part and dissents in part. HOLMES and KRUPANSKY, JJ., dissent. The dissenting opinion of Holmes argues that tort actions should be permitted against employers only in cases of actual intent to injure the employees. Krupansky's dissent argues that there should be no judicial creation of an intentional misconduct exception to the employers' tort immunity because there is no express exception in the Ohio Workers' Compensation Act].

---

1. Several years after this decision, Ohio enacted a statute to deal with intentional tort claims against employers. Ohio Rev.Code § 4121.80 (1986). If an employee proves that the employer committed an intentional tort, as defined in this statute, an industrial commission determines the amount of damages to award taking into consideration workers' compensation benefits payable and the financial loss to the employee. Those damages may be no less than 50 percent of, and no more than three times, total workers' compensation receivable by the employee, and in no event may they be more than $1 million. The damages are paid from an intentional tort fund comprised of annual payments by all public and private employers. Do you think this is a fair way to compensate "intentionally" injured employees without totally removing employers' tort immunity in those circumstances?

2. The Supreme Court of West Virginia created a similar exception for employers' "willful, wanton, or reckless misconduct" in Mandolidis v. Elkins Indus., Inc., 161 W.Va. 695, 246 S.E.2d 907 (1978). Later, the West Virginia legislature modified the *Mandolidis* rule by specifying the type of *intentional* conduct that will give rise to the exception to employers' tort immunity. It also established a special "Employer's Excess Liability Fund" under which employers may voluntarily insure against this type of liability.

3. There have been numerous other attempts to make an end-run around workers' compensation. The exception recognized in the principal case concerns an intentional tort committed by the employer such as deliberately exposing an employee to hazardous or toxic substances. See also Noonan v. Spring Creek Forest Prods., Inc., ___ Mont. ___, 700 P.2d 623 (1985); Note, Intentional Torts Under Workers' Compensation Statutes: A Blessing or a Burden? 12 Hofstra L.Rev. 181 (1983). Another exception is the dual capacity theory, whereby the employer is treated as a third-party tortfeasor as, for example, where an employer also manufactures or designs a product that injures the employee. See, e.g., Mercer v. Uniroyal, Inc., 49 Ohio App.2d 279, 361 N.E.2d 492, 3 Ohio Ops.3d 333 (1976); Annot., 9 A.L.R. 4th 873 (1983). Other exceptions include: suits against successor corporations, Billy v. Consolidated Mach. Tool Corp., 51 N.Y.2d 152, 412 N.E.2d 934, 432 N.Y.S.2d 879 (1980); third party actions for indemnity or contribution against the employer, Lambertson v. Cincinnati Corp., 312 Minn. 114, 257 N.W.2d 679 (1977); Tarpley and Jagmin, Workers' Compensation: Third Party Actions Against Employers Under Comparative Causation, 47 J.Air L. & Com. 187 (1982); and actions for damages of a type not covered by the workers' compensation statute, Foley v. Polaroid Corp., 381 Mass. 545, 413 N.E.2d 711 (1980) (injury to reputation resulting from libel).

4. Is the result in the principal case likely to occur so long as no-fault compensation systems are set as islands within the tort litigation system? Ohio

is among states with more limited recovery in worker compensation. Would the result have been different if worker compensation awards had been more adequate? See U.S. Chamber of Commerce, Analysis of Workers' Compensation Laws (1981) for recent changes in state statutes; Ashford & Johnson, Negligence vs. No–Fault Liability: An Analysis of the Workers' Compensation Example, 12 Seton Hall L.Rev. 725 (1982).

5. The subject of Workers' Compensation has found a separate place in the curriculum of most law schools, and this brief introduction is therefore all that appears warranted in this casebook.

2. AUTOMOBILE ACCIDENT INJURIES

Motor vehicle reparation plans, or no-fault automobile insurance as they are commonly called, are of much later origin than the worker's compensation statutes, and they have been unable to obtain the widespread adoption of the worker's compensation statutes. The impetus for automobile no-fault plans may be traced to a book written in 1965 by Professors Robert E. Keeton and Jeffrey O'Connell, titled Basic Protection for the Accident Victim—A Blueprint for Reforming Automobile Insurance. The plan was accompanied by a model no-fault statute. Through the 1970s and early 1980s, 24 states and the District of Columbia passed automobile no-fault statutes of various types. In more recent years no new no-fault statute has been passed, and Nevada repealed its statute as of January 1, 1980. See American Insurance Association, Summary of Selected State Laws and Regulations Relating to Automobile Insurance 2–17 (1983). These statutes vary in several ways, but all of them rely on "first-party" insurance by which an insured recovers from the insured's own insurer for economic losses, up to a fixed level.

MONTGOMERY v. DANIELS
New York Court of Appeals, 1975.
38 N.Y.2d 41, 340 N.E.2d 444, 378 N.Y.S.2d 1.

JONES, J. We hold that the New York no-fault automobile accident compensation law is not unconstitutional.

This case comes to us on direct appeal * * * from a judgment at Special Term which, on cross motions for summary judgment, declared Insurance Law Article 18 in violation of the due process and equal protection clauses of the Federal and State Constitutions and a denial of the right to trial by jury guaranteed by our State Constitution.

The New York No–Fault Act. * * * Under the title, "Comprehensive Automobile Insurance Reparations Act", Article 18 of the Insurance Law (as added by L.1973, c. 13, in full effect Feb. 1, 1974) provides a plan for compensating victims of automobile accidents without regard to fault. In essence, it is a two-pronged, partial modification of the pre-existing system of reparation for personal injuries suffered in automobile accidents under which system liability was grounded in negligence under classic principles of tort law. One prong deals with compensation; the other with limitation of tort actions.

The first prong lays down the requirement that every owner of a motor vehicle provide himself, members of his household, operators, occupants and pedestrians with compensation for "basic economic loss" resulting from injuries occasioned by the use or operation of that vehicle in this State, regardless of fault (§ 672[1]). "Motor vehicle" is defined to exclude motorcycles from the Act's coverage (§ 671[6]). "Basic economic loss," subject to a maximum of $50,000 per person, is defined to include:

"(a) Treatment Expense—All 'reasonable and necessary expenses' for medical, hospital, surgical, nursing, dental, ambulance, x-ray, prescription drug and prosthetic services, as well as for psychiatric care, other professional health services, and any nonmedical remedial care rendered in accordance with a religious method of healing recognized by the laws of this State, all without limitation as to time, provided that, within one year after the date of the accident causing injury, it is ascertainable that further expenses may be incurred as a result of the injury (§ 671[1][a]);

"(b) Lost Earnings—Loss of earnings and expenses incurred in obtaining substitute services up to $1,000 per month for not more than three years from the date of the accident (§ 671[1][b]); and

"(c) Other Expenses—All other reasonable and necessary expenses incurred, up to $25 per day for not more than one year from the date of the accident (§ 671[1][c])."

Compensation for basic economic loss is payable as "first party benefits" after reducing the gross amount of such loss by deducting (a) 20% of "lost earnings" (§ 671[2][a]), (b) all amounts recoverable under state or federal laws providing social security disability benefits or workmen's compensation benefits (§ 671[2][b]), and (c) amounts deductible under the applicable insurance policy (§ 671[2][c]). "First party benefits" become due and payable "as the loss is incurred" and "are overdue if not paid within thirty days after the claimant supplies proof of the fact and amount of loss sustained" (§ 675[1]). Any dispute with the insurer as to benefits may be resolved expeditiously by submission to binding arbitration at the option of the claimant (§ 675[2]).

The right to first party benefits accrues to the injured person regardless of fault or negligence on the part of the covered person, except that the insurer may exclude from coverage a person who intentionally causes his own injury, is injured as a result of operating a motor vehicle while in an intoxicated condition or while his ability to operate such vehicle is impaired by the use of a drug, or is injured while committing an act which would constitute a felony, seeking to avoid lawful apprehension or arrest, participating in a race or speed test, or operating or occupying a vehicle he knows to be stolen (§ 672[2]).

The second prong of the Act imposes two limitations on tort recovery for personal injuries, applicable, however, only to actions between "covered persons" (as defined in § 671[10]): (1) there can be no duplicate tort compensation for "basic economic loss" (§ 673[1]); and (2) damages for noneconomic loss (i.e., pain and suffering) are not recoverable in tort unless the plaintiff can establish that he has suffered a "serious injury" (Id). Serious injury is defined in § 671(4) as a personal injury:

"(a) which results in death; dismemberment; significant disfigurement; a compound or comminuted fracture; or permanent loss of use of a body organ, member, function, or system; or

"(b) if the reasonable and customary charges for medical, hospital, surgical, nursing, dental, ambulance, x-ray, prescription drug and prosthetic services necessarily performed as a result of the injury would exceed five hundred dollars."

Thus, an injured party may bring a third-party tort action and may recover therein for economic loss over $50,000, for treatment expenses not ascertainable within one year of injury, for lost earnings which exceed $1,000 per month or continue beyond three years, and for other reasonable and necessary expenses which exceed $25 per day or continue after one year. Damages for pain and suffering may likewise still be recovered in a tort action if there was a "serious injury." Finally, Article 18 erects no bar whatever to tort actions seeking recovery for personal injury against noncovered persons or for property damage against covered or noncovered persons.

[The court reviews (1) the long process of study and investigation that preceded the enactment of Article 18, and (2) the arguments for and against the adoption of a no-fault automobile compensation system. It then gives consideration to plaintiff's argument that he was deprived of due process when the legislature partially abolished his right to sue for damages caused by another's negligent conduct.]

[T]his aspect of plaintiffs' challenge is to be viewed as presenting two inquiries: in enacting Article 18 was the Legislature acting in pursuit of permissible state objectives and, if so, were the means adopted in Article 18 reasonably related to the accomplishment of those objectives? We conclude that each inquiry must be answered in the affirmative. * * *

The Legislature was acting to correct what it viewed as * * * basic infirmities or defects in that fault system and was acting on the basis of findings which certainly supported its perception of the problems * * *. Plaintiffs' claim that "examination of these 'evils' of the tort system shows that in fact no such problems exist" must be rejected. "Where the question of what the facts establish is a fairly-debatable one, we accept and carry into effect the opinion of the legislature." [Cc] This judicial approach takes on added substance where the Legislature has engaged in extensive and thorough investigation as in this instance. [C]

Likewise, we reject plaintiff's argument that there is no reasonable basis between reform as undertaken in Article 18 and the objective of remedying the defects perceived by the Legislature to inhere in the fault-based tort system for compensating automobile accident personal injury claimants. On the contrary we conclude that, by eliminating recovery for pain and suffering in relatively minor cases and by simultaneously guaranteeing prompt and full compensation for economic losses up to $50,000 without the necessity of recourse to the courts, the Legislature acted reasonably to eliminate much of the wasted expenditures of premium dollars on expenses extraneous to treatment of injury (e.g., legal and investigative costs involved in determining fault and in establishing the value of the alleged pain and suffering). Such action may further be viewed as reasonably related to guaranteeing full and fair recovery to all victims by reducing pressure on a seriously injured person to compromise down his claims in order to obtain funds for treatment while at the same time eliminating pressure on insurers to compromise up claims by persons suffering minor injuries in order to avoid the expense of investigating and defending against such minor claims. Finally, it cannot be said that by partially obviating recourse to the courts the statute was unreasonable in relation to its purpose to reduce the long delays in the payment of claims experienced under judicial procedures and to lessen the burden on our State Courts and judicial resources. * * * We hold only that Article 18 is reasonably related to the promotion of the public welfare and thus represents a legitimate exercise of our State's police power.

Plaintiffs posit another due process claim on the argument that Article 18 unconstitutionally abrogates their common law right to sue in tort without providing an adequate substitute remedy. * * *

For the purposes of disposing of this appeal we conclude, however, that it is unnecessary to decide when, if ever, due process requires that a legislature in abrogating causes of action under the common law must provide an adequate substitute remedy. * * * [W]e would conclude here that the issue is not present because under any analysis the law now challenged provides more than an adequate substitute for the cause of action it abrogates. * * *

Finally under the due process heading, we find no merit in plaintiffs' additional claim that the term "significant disfigurement," as used in § 671(4)(a) to define a "serious injury," is unconstitutionally vague. * * * The challenged phrase is no less vague than that found in our State's Workmen's Compensation Law § 15(3)(t)(1) which provides that the "Board may award proper and equitable compensation for serious facial and head disfigurement"—a provision which has been interpreted and applied without constitutional difficulty.

[The court considers plaintiff's claims that Article 18 violates plaintiff's Fourteenth Amendment right to "equal protection" of the law.]

We here apply the traditional equal protection test as expressed in Dandridge v. Williams, 397 U.S. 471, 485:

"In the area of economics and social welfare, a State does not violate the Equal Protection Clause merely because the classifications made by its laws are imperfect. If the classification has some 'reasonable basis,' it does not offend the Constitution simply because the classification 'is not made with mathematical nicety or because in practice it results in some inequality.'"

Plaintiffs first contend that the operation of § 673 creates an arbitrary and capricious classification as between covered and noncovered persons. Subdivision 1 of that section bars a suit in tort in actions between covered persons unless the injured party sustains a serious injury or incurs expenses in excess of basic economic loss. Under subdivision 2 of that section, however, no such bar attaches where a noncovered person is a party to the suit. Noncovered persons under Article 18 include: (1) an owner, operator or passenger on a motorcycle (§ 671[6][b]); (2) the owner, operator or occupant of an uninsured motor vehicle (§§ 671[9] and [10]); and (3) the owner or operator of an out-of-state motor vehicle whose insurance policy does not include no-fault coverage for New York operation (§ 676). Plaintiffs claim that there can be no rational basis for a scheme which determines whether a right to recover in tort exists by reference to the identity of the motorist involved. Such a claim does not withstand analysis.

There was a rational basis for the exclusion of motorcycles from the definition of motor vehicle. The Legislature had before it evidence that the premium cost to motorcyclists, should they have been required to purchase first-party coverage under the no-fault plan, would have been prohibitively high. * * *

Similarly it was not unreasonable for the Legislature to have excluded persons operating uninsured vehicles from coverage under Article 18. Such persons operate their vehicles in violation of the law of our State (Vehicle and Traffic Law, Arts. 6 and 8) and further make no contribution to the automobile injury compensation system designed to spread the risk of loss among all who drive.

Finally with respect to this contention, we find no infirmity in the exclusion from coverage of an out-of-state motor vehicle whose insurance policy does not include no-fault coverage for operation in our State. Certainly the Legislature cannot be faulted for not extending the requirement of coverage to those over whom the Legislature had no power to act. * * *

Still urging their claim of denial of equal protection plaintiffs next challenge the legislative definition of "serious injury" (§ 671[4]) by which it is determined whether or not a party shall or shall not have a right to sue for pain and suffering (§ 673), as creating an arbitrary and capricious classification. * * *

We find the classifications created by the Legislature to be reasonably related to the end of establishing a rational line of distinction and of eliminating the evils which that body perceived to exist. True it may be that certain injuries not listed might well have been included within the class of serious injuries or that the threshold amount might more wisely have been set at $400 or $600. But such decisions are not of determinative concern to this Court. "[E]very line drawn by a legislature leaves out some that might well have been included. That exercise of discretion, however, is a legislative, not a judicial, function." [Cc]

Plaintiffs' attack on the $500 threshold amount on the grounds that particular charges for medical services vary from one locality to another and in operation might discriminate against the poor is not persuasive.[20] Section 671(4)(b) provides that the threshold requirement is met when it is determined that "reasonable and customary" charges would exceed $500. We note the difference in diction employed by the Legislature in different provisions of Article 18. The standard for proof of a claimant's basic economic loss is "all *reasonable and necessary* expenses incurred", i.e., an individualized standard related to the expenses in fact incurred by the particular plaintiff (§ 671[1][a]). The standard for determination of the threshold amount, by contrast, is "the *reasonable and customary* charges for ∗   ∗   ∗ services necessarily performed" (§ 671[4][b]), a general standard in the application of which payments actually made by the particular claimant will not be determinative.   ∗   ∗   ∗ Dispute as to what is "reasonable and customary" is a question of fact not dissimilar to many issues of damages which can be and are effectively determined by a jury or judge without a jury. [Cc]

Finally plaintiffs argue that Article 18 in limiting their right to recover in tort, infringes on their right to trial by jury, protected by Article 1, § 2 of our State Constitution.

Article 18 does not replace the jury as trier of fact with some other trier of fact. Rather it modifies the substantive law and redefines the rights of those personally injured in automobile accidents. The constitution guarantees the right to trial by jury if the plaintiff has a claim to assert. If, as here, the Legislature otherwise properly abrogates the claim in part, to that extent there remains nothing to which the right to trial by jury may attach.   ∗   ∗   ∗

Finally we conclude that there is no merit to plaintiffs' contention that even if it be assumed that total abolition of a common law cause of action would not violate Article 1, Section 2 because nothing would be left for a jury to try, a different result should follow when as here there

---

20. We note in passing that there were findings before the Legislature that the tort system worked particularly to the disadvantage of people who were poor and uneducated. The United States Department of Transportation found that where family income was $10,000 or more accident victims recovered 61% of their economic loss, but where it was below $5,000 they recovered only 38% of their economic loss. (U.S. Dept. of Transportation, Economic Consequences of Automobile Accident Injuries, 54 [1970].) Likewise it was shown that seriously injured victims with post-graduate education recovered 73% of their economic loss while those with only five to eight years of formal education recovered only 27% of their economic loss. (Id., at 52.)

has been only a partial abrogation of a common law cause of action. Again, *pro tanto,* there is nothing left for a jury to try.

The judgment of Supreme Court should be reversed, summary judgment granted to defendants, and the case remitted to Supreme Court for a declaration consistent with the views expressed in this opinion.

FUCHSBERG, J. (concurring). If I were acting in the capacity of legislator, I would vote against Article 18, for I believe that the concept that the individual is the basic and ultimate unit in society must be supported by recognition of the value of one's physical, mental and emotional integrity, including freedom from pain and suffering and the ability to live an uncrippled life.

The automobile, a modern bane and boon, daily threatens that integrity for millions of people. And Article 18, while not in any way alleviating that threat, strips a class which includes most automobile accident victims of the right to be fairly compensated for injuries and pain and suffering, no matter how genuine and how clearly the result of negligence by others. In so doing, I believe it does not operate in the public interest, and I cannot view with equanimity the emasculation of common law principles whose long-developing emphasis on personal and human rights promised full and fair compensation for all such individuals.

But I do not sit here as a legislator or even in the capacity of citizen alone. As a judge, my role and my obligation is a different one. It requires me to respect and uphold a reasonable exercise of the legislative power to deal with the public health, safety, morals and welfare of my fellow citizens of this state, regardless of whether that exercise is, in my judgment, wise or unwise. Laws are passed, amended and repealed all the time, and whether they are the best of even desirable means to accomplish their intended purposes is not subject to judicial review. It is not our business to choose from among "the earnest conflict of serious opinion".

[The opinion reviews the arguments that suggest a no-fault system is unnecessary.]

Much of what has been noted derives from the fact that Article 18 is not in fact a true "no-fault" law. A true no-fault law, based on the conclusion that the automobile is a sufficiently dangerous instrumentality, while it would impose the concept of strict liability for injuries resulting from automobile accidents and thus eliminate the need to determine fault, would provide for full and fair compensation for *all* damages, including general damages for injuries as well as special damages for monetary losses. Seven other states, in enacting their own forms of hybrid no-fault legislation, have come closer to the ideal of full recovery by providing for compulsory, first-party benefit insurance, as does New York's Article 18, while at the same time permitting non-duplicative recovery by suit against tortfeasors at common law. [Citing statutes from Arkansas, Delaware, Maryland, Oregon, South Dakota, Texas and Virginia.] * * *

Whatever movement there may have been toward more flexibility in this area, it has not reached the economic issues involved here today. I am, therefore, constrained to agree that, under a test which requires the court not only to search the record for reasons but also to ask itself whether it can "conceive" of any, Article 18 is constitutional. * * *

---

1.   As the concurring judge makes clear the New York statutory no-fault system is a very different proposition from a common law process of imposing liability without fault on persons who cause accidents.   This is true with respect to most no-fault plans that have been enacted.   See notes 3 and 4, infra. As a practicing attorney, Judge Fuchsberg was a vigorous opponent of no-fault legislation.

2.   *"No–Lawsuit" Automobile No-fault Plans.*   Under the original Keeton–O'Connell Plan, unless damages for pain and suffering exceeded $5,000, or other personal damages exceeded $10,000, the no-fault insurance coverage replaced any tort action for non-fatal damages.   Fourteen states and Puerto Rico now apply variations of this approach to automobile no-fault, and in these jurisdictions the right to recover economic damages by a tort action has also been eliminated to the extent the claimant would be entitled to recover from no-fault insurance.   See ABA Special Committee on Automobile Insurance Legislation, Automobile Accident Reparation Systems: A Comparative Study of the National Experience (scheduled for publication by ABA).   Common features of these no-fault plans include:

A.   Persons protected within the system include the motorist, passenger in the motorist's vehicle and pedestrians struck by the vehicle.   In some states, however, only persons who operate, register, maintain or use a motor vehicle are covered.   See, e.g., Whiteman v. Lowe, 702 S.W.2d 436 (Ky.1986) (nine-year-old bicyclist struck by a car not covered by no-fault plan).   Is a motorcycle, dirt bike or ATV (all terrain vehicle) a "motor vehicle" under no-fault statutes? See Pistorius v. Travelers Ins. Co., 348 Pa.Super. 527, 502 A.2d 670 (1985).

B.   The no-fault basic protection is a package that includes medical payments and loss of earnings (or a percentage thereof) but excludes damages for pain and suffering up to certain limits.   It may also include loss of services and death benefits.   All of the automobile no-fault insurance plans, with the exception of Michigan's statute, apply only to bodily injury claims and not to property damage claims.   U.S. Dep't of Transp., Compensating Auto Accident Victims: A Follow–Up Report on No–Fault Auto Insurance Experiences 18 (DOT–P–30–84–20) (1985).   Benefits vary widely among different plans.   For example, in Georgia and Connecticut aggregate limits are set at $5,000; New York has an aggregate limit of $50,000.   See F. Harper, F. James and O. Gray, The Law of Torts § 13.8 (1986).

C.   Persons protected by the no-fault system are barred from bringing a claim, at least to the extent of that protection, against a negligent motorist who injures them.

D.   Persons within the system are given an immunity in tort to the extent of an individual's no-fault benefits.

E.   The fault system returns when damages reach a certain level or a certain kind of injury occurs. In the case of serious injury, a claimant may sue in tort for damages that are above a defined threshold. For example, in some jurisdictions tort actions for general damages (pain, suffering, disfigurement) are barred unless medical expenses exceed $5,000. In other plans, however, medical thresholds are quite low ($400) and do not effectively deter litigation of general damages claims. In addition to medical-economic thresholds, some plans establish narrative or descriptive criteria, e.g., descriptions of the seriousness of the injury as "bone fracture," or "fracture to weight bearing bones," or "serious injury." See R. Keeton, Teaching Compensation Systems, 26 J. Legal Ed. 433, 438–39 (1975). Finally, some states employ a pure economic or out-of-pocket loss criterion for permitting re-entry into the tort system. See Maroney, No–Fault Automobile Insurance: A Success or Failure after Eleven Years, 51 Ins.Couns.J. 75 (1984). Is it logical to exclude large claims from the no-fault system? See Blum & Kalven, Ceilings, Costs and Compulsion in Auto Compensation Legislation, 1973 Utah L.Rev. 341, 350.

F.   Persons protected may be able to collect only actual economic loss, and the collateral source rule, to some extent, may not apply. The purpose of this restriction was to avoid "wasteful overlapping" of protection. See R. Keeton & J. O'Connell, Basic Protection for the Accident Victim—A Blueprint for Reforming Automobile Insurance 400–10 (1965).

G.   The protection is compulsory: every registered motorist must obtain a minimum level of no-fault protection. Is this efficient or wise? See O'Connell & Joost, Giving Motorists A Choice Between Fault and No–Fault Insurance, 72 Va.L.Rev. 61 (1986); Epstein, Automobile No–Fault Plans: A Second Look at First Principles, 13 Creighton L.Rev. 769 (1980).

3.   *"Add–On" Automobile No–Fault Plans.* In nine states and the District of Columbia, the tort law remains unchanged and the insured retains the right to bring a claim against a negligent tortfeasor. Insurers, however, are required to offer no-fault coverage. The average amount of no-fault benefits available per victim in an add-on state is significantly less than the amount of no-fault benefits available under a no-lawsuit no-fault plan. In add-on no-fault states, insurance companies have subrogation rights to receive reimbursement from any tort recovery made by the insured to the extent of no-fault benefits that were paid to the insured. In some add-on states (e.g., South Carolina), the insured must purchase no-fault protection; in other states (e.g., Pennsylvania), coverage is optional.

4.   *Constitutionality.* The personal injury portion of automobile no-fault laws have survived attacks under the due process and equal protection clauses of the Federal Constitution in all state courts of last resort. The reasoning of the principal case is typical. Most of the decisions have looked to the analogy of workers' compensation laws in order to meet the due process claim. Under those laws in most states a worker can elect to retain his common law rights, and so the analogy is not entirely congruent. (Most workers have declined to make this election).

The equal protection arguments against the no-fault thresholds have given the courts more difficulty, but the thresholds have been sustained. The first major case was Pinnick v. Cleary, 360 Mass. 1, 271 N.E.2d 592 (1971). See also Manzanares v. Bell, 214 Kan. 589, 522 P.2d 1291 (1974) ($500 medical threshold); Lasky v. State Farm Ins. Co., 296 So.2d 9 (Fla.1974) ($500 medical threshold); Fann v. McGuffey, 534 S.W.2d 770 (Ky.1975) ($500 medical threshold); Singer v. Sheppard, 464 Pa. 387, 346 A.2d 897 (1975) ($750 medical threshold). In Gentile v. Altermatt, 169 Conn. 267, 363 A.2d 1 (1975) ($500 medical threshold), the Supreme Court dismissed the appeal, 423 U.S. 1041 (1976). Two state courts of final jurisdiction have rendered opinions that sustain the basic premises of two-party no-fault systems as set forth in note 5, supra. See Opinion of the Justices, 113 N.H. 205, 304 A.2d 881 (1973) ($1000 medical threshold); In re Requests of the Governor and Senate, Etc., 389 Mich. 411, 208 N.W.2d 469 (1973) ("serious impairment of bodily function" and "permanent serious disfigurement" thresholds); and see Shavers v. Kelly, 402 Mich. 554, 267 N.W.2d 72 (1978).

The strongest judicial opinion attacking no-fault on federal constitutional grounds is the opinion of the trial court in the principal case. See Montgomery v. Daniels, 81 Misc.2d 373, 367 N.Y.S.2d 419 (1975). See also Gaines v. Mohawk Motor, Inc., 43 U.S.L.W. 2074 (Mich.Cir.Ct. Aug. 1, 1974) (plan restricting injured parties' remedies if tortfeasor is insured, but not if tortfeasor is uninsured, violates equal protection).

The Supreme Court of Illinois struck down that state's no-fault law under a section of the state's constitution that prohibited a "special law" when a general law could be made applicable. The court found this provision breached because the Illinois no-fault law barred recovery for pain and suffering to all persons in the state, not merely those subject to no-fault protection. Should this approach create federal constitutional problems also?

The Supreme Court of Florida held a no-fault provision regarding damage to the insured vehicle violative of due process when it simply shifted the cost of that risk from the tortfeasor to the injured party. See Kluger v. White, 281 So. 2d 1 (Fla.1973). Most no-fault plans do not cover property damage and there is debate as to whether they should.

The Michigan Supreme Court has upheld the state's statute against numerous equal-protection objections. See O'Donnell v. State Farm Mut. Auto. Ins. Co., 404 Mich. 524, 273 N.W.2d 829 (1979).

In regard to constitutionality of no-fault statutes, see generally R. Keeton & J. O'Connell, Basic Protection for the Traffic Victim—A Blue Print for Reforming Automobile Insurance, 483–514 (1965); Hart, The Constitutionality of the New York State Comprehensive Automobile Insurance Reparations Act, 43 Ford.L.Rev. 400 (1974); Notes, 1969 U.Ill.L.F. 266, 4 Mem.St.U.L.Rev. 635 (1974), 49 Tul.L.Rev. 691 (1975), 21 Cath.U.L.Rev. 421 (1972), 20 U.Kan.L.Rev. 324 (1972), 55 Marq.L.Rev. 198 (1972), 6 Suffolk U.L.Rev. 123 (1971), 40 U.Cin.L. Rev. 849 (1971); Annot. 42 A.L.R.3d 229 (1972).

5. *Deterrence and Costs.* Does the adoption of a no-fault compensation plan for automobile accidents result in increased accident rates? See Landes, Insurance Liability and Accidents: A Theoretical and Empirical Investigation of the Effects of No–Fault Accidents, 25 J.L. & Econ. 49 (1982). Cf. O'Connell & Levmore, A Reply to Landes: A Faulty Study of No–Fault's Effect on Fault? 48 Mo.L.Rev. 649 (1983). Are some no-fault laws "out-of-balance," in that they cause higher insurance premiums because total no-fault benefits exceed the reduction of tort liability payments? See O'Connell & Joost, Giving Motorists a Choice Between Fault and No–Fault Insurance, 72 Va.L.Rev. 61 (1986).

3. OTHER NO–FAULT COMPENSATION SYSTEMS

The tort system compensates personal injuries and other losses by a system of fault assessment and liability insurance. Even in cases involving strict products liability or abnormally dangerous activities, there is a measure of moral, economic, or legal fault: the product is defective or unreasonably dangerous; the activity involves abnormal risks that outweigh its value to the community. See, e.g., Powers, The Persistence of Fault in Products Liability, 61 Tex.L.Rev. 777 (1983); J. O'Connell, Ending Insult to Injury: No–Fault Insurance for Products and Services 57 (1975). Litigating fault and using the court system to compensate victims involves substantial transaction costs and expenses of administration. Critics charge that, for reasons of both efficiency and fairness, a no-fault compensation system should replace the traditional tort system's method of compensating accident victims. See, e.g., J. O'Connell, Ending Insult to Injury: No–Fault Insurance for Products and Services (1975); P. Atiyah, Accidents, Compensation and the Law (3d ed. 1980); 1 (U.K.) Royal Commission on Civil Liability and Compensation for Personal Injury (the "Pearson Commission") 209–12 (Cmnd. 7054–I) (1978).

1. In 1972 New Zealand adopted the first comprehensive administrative system that replaced tort claims with a new no-fault remedy for virtually all accidental injuries. The plan, administered by the government, is a social insurance system that pays limited benefits to all persons who suffer "personal injury by accident." The plan is financed through car-owner, employer, and general tax levies. See G. Palmer, Compensation for Incapacity: A Study of Law and Social Change in New Zealand and Australia (1979); Willy, The Accident Compensation Act and Recovery for Losses Arising From Personal Injury and Death by Accident, 6 N.Z.U.L.Rev. 250 (1975). The New Zealand plan does not replace the tort system in cases involving property damage, nonworkplace disease, economic losses, business torts or medical malpractice. See Henderson, The New Zealand Accident Compensation Reform, 48 U.Chi.L.Rev. 781 (1981); Franklin, Personal Injury Accidents in New Zealand and the United States, Some Striking Similarities, 21 Stan.L.Rev. 653 (1975); Phillips, In Defense of the Tort System, 27 Ariz. L.Rev. 603, 605 (1986). Under a social insurance compensation plan as in effect in New Zealand, is there a trade-off in lowered accident deterrence and diminished incentives for safety? See T. Ison, Accident Compensation 165 (1980); Love, Punishment and Deterrence: A Comparative Study of Tort Liability for Punitive Damages Under No–Fault Compensation Legislation, 16 U.C.Davis L.Rev. 232 (1983). Is such a plan feasible in the United States? How much would it cost?

2. In the United States, no-fault approaches to injury compensation have been applied or proposed in a number of contexts other than workers' compensation and automobile accidents:

A. *Federal Compensation Plans.* In 1969, Congress passed the Black Lung Act, 30 U.S.C.A. §§ 901 et seq., to compensate coal miners and their dependents for the disabling respiratory disease known as "black lung." Whether viewed as a compensation system to miners, a subsidy to the mining industry, or as a type of welfare benefit, the federal black lung program represents an innovative solution to compensation in a case in which traditional tort and workers' compensation remedies proved inadequate because of the progressive nature of the disease and the effect of statutes of limitations and workers' compensation statutes that, at that time, failed to cover occupational diseases. See Ramsey & Habermann, The Federal Black Lung Program—The View From the Top, 87 W.Va.L.Rev. 575 (1985); Millus, A Haunting Nightmare, Best's Review 38 (July 1986) (an overview of the applicability of workers' compensation to occupational disease).

Similarly, compensation bills have been introduced in Congress to deal with the problems of asbestos-related diseases, see, e.g., Asbestos Workers' Recovery Act, S. 1265, 99th Cong., 1st Sess. (June 3, 1985), Comment, Relief for Asbestos Victims: A Legislative Analysis, 20 Harv. J. Legis. 179 (1983); and injuries by veterans from exposure to nuclear radiation and the herbicide "Agent Orange," see, e.g., Veterans' Dioxin and Radiation Exposure Compensation Standards Act, 38 U.S.C.A. § 354 (Supp.1986); Comment, Agent Orange as a Problem of Law and Social Policy, 77 Nw.U.L.Rev. 48 (1982).

As discussed in Chapter 15, another example of a federal no-fault proposal involves compensation for victims of adverse reactions or other harmful medical effects from vaccines. Because of the number of lawsuits and occasional multi-million dollar awards against vaccine manufacturers, particularly manufacturers of polio vaccine and DPT (diphtheria, pertussis and tetanus shots), various bills were introduced in Congress to secure the adequacy of the supply of vaccines, to reduce costs, and to ensure compensation for all victims. The first no-fault compensation program was introduced in 1984 as an alternative to litigation (S. 827). In 1986 Congress again considered a no-fault statute, the National Vaccine Injury Compensation Program, as an amendment to S. 1744, the State Comprehensive Mental Health Services Plan Act of 1986, 99th Cong., 2d Sess. (1986). This bill was passed by both the House and Senate, and signed into law by President Reagan on November 14, 1986. It establishes automatic recovery from a federal fund for particular listed side-effects of vaccines. If a claimant elects to reject this compensation and bring a law suit against the vaccine manufacturer, the manufacturer is afforded certain defenses provided in the Act. The vaccine fund will be financed by an excise tax on the price of vaccines, but only after Congress passes an additional statute authorizing this tax. Congress had begun to take action on this matter when this casebook went to press.

Other examples of federal programs to compensate victims are the National Swine Flu Immunization Program, 42 U.S.C.A. § 247(b) (note) (1982), see Appel, Liability in Mass Immunization Programs, 1980 B.Y.

U.L.Rev. 69; and The Superfund Act, 42 U.S.C.A. § 9601, that provides for payment for the cost of cleaning up toxic waste disposal sites. See Freeman, Toxic Torts, Hazardous Waste and the Superfund, 2 J.Prod. Liab. 149 (Sept. 1983). On a broader scale, social security represents a comprehensive social insurance or welfare solution for the problems of unemployment, hospital and medical expenses, disability, retirement and survivor's benefits.

B. *Medical Malpractice.* Along the lines of automobile no-fault, Professor O'Connell and others have proposed a no-fault approach to medical malpractice claims. Introduced in 1984, the Moore–Gephardt Alternative Liability Act, H.R. 5400, 98th Cong., 2d Sess., 130 Cong.Rec. 2553 (1984), would have created a partial no-fault compensation system that would abolish the right to recover non-economic losses for patients in federally funded health care programs and would serve as a model for state programs. See Moore & O'Connell, Foreclosing Medical Malpractice Claims by Prompt Tender of Economic Loss, 44 La.L.Rev. 1267 (1984); Smith, Battling a Receding Tort Frontier: Constitutional Attacks on Medical Malpractice Laws, 38 Okla.L.Rev. 195, 198 (1985). Similar bills were introduced in 1986 in the Senate (S.1960) and House (H.R. 3084).

C. *Products Liability.* In an effort to reduce insurance and transaction costs and to ensure basic protection for injured victims, commentators have proposed both private and statutory no-fault compensation systems for product injuries. See J. O'Connell, Ending Insult to Injury: No–Fault Insurance for Products Liability and Services (1975); O'Connell, Offers That Can't be Refused: Foreclosure of Personal Injury Claims by Defendant's Prompt Tender of Claimant's Net Economic Losses, 77 Nw.L.Rev. 589 (1983); Freedman, No–Fault and Products Liability: An Answer to a Maiden's Prayer, 627 Ins.L.J. 199 (1975). For victims, these plans would provide a relative certainty of payment for economic or out-of-pocket losses; however, claimants would lose (in whole or in part) the opportunity to recover non-economic losses for pain, suffering, psychic harm, and punitive damages. For product makers, total liability for injuries caused by product defects would be reduced, although, arguably, with at least some loss of deterrence or incentive for accident safety. See Ford, The Fault with No–Fault, 61 A.B.A.J. 1071 (1975).

In the 99th Congress, two bills were introduced that would have given injured parties the option of bringing no-fault products liability claims to recover solely for economic loss (i.e., lost wages, medical expenses, rehabilitation costs), and which would have superseded some aspects of state law for parties who sought tort remedies. Senator Dodd introduced the "Product Manufacturers' Responsibility Act of 1985," 131 Cong.Rec.S. 3183 (March 19, 1985). Senator Gorton introduced the "Product Liability and Compensation Act," 131 Cong.Rec.S. 6090 (May 14, 1985). Subsequently, elements of these bills were combined in S. 1999, introduced by Senator Danforth on December 20, 1985. On August 14, 1986, Senator Danforth introduced S. 2760 to replace the no-fault claim system embodied in S. 1999 with an expedited settlement procedure that provides economic incentives for both plaintiffs and defendants to settle lawsuits. Either party could offer to settle for the amount of economic losses plus, in certain cases involving serious injury, a specified amount for pain and suffering. If the defendant offered to settle and the plaintiff refused the offer, there would be a limit on the amount of pain and suffering damages the plaintiff could recover at trial. If the plaintiff offered to settle and the defendant refused and the damages awarded at trial were greater than the settlement offer, the defendant would have to pay the plaintiff's attorney's fees. See Report of the Senate Committee on Commerce, Science and Transportation, "Product Liability Reform Act, S.2760," August 15, 1986. Do you think these economic incentives would encourage parties to settle a lawsuit? Is settlement of a lawsuit for the plaintiff's economic losses, plus a limited amount for pain and suffering, a goal which a product liability statute should encourage?

D. *Elective No–Fault Insurance Contracts.* To cover athletic injuries, particularly those sustained in high school football, many school districts purchase insurance contracts that oblige insurance companies to make prompt offers to pay an injured athlete's medical expenses and other economic losses set forth in the policy. But the world of politics did not treat these approaches favorably, and they were opposed by both consumer and business groups.

If the claimant accepts the payment, a release is obtained and no tort suit may be brought. If the payment is not accepted, the victim may proceed with a tort suit. See "Whatever Happened to No–Fault?," Nat'l L.J., Nov. 18, 1985, p. 1, col. 3; O'Connell, Elective No–Fault Liability by Contract—With or Without An Enabling Statute, 1975 U.Ill.L.Forum 59–72 (1975).

E. Additional proposals for substituting compensation plans for the tort system have been prepared and forcefully presented. See, for example, T. Isom, The Forensic Lottery (1967); Franklin, Replacing the Negligence Lottery: Compensation and Selective Reimbursement, 53 Va.L.Rev. 774 (1967); Pierce, The Limits of Tort Law and Government Regulation, 33 Vand.L.Rev. 1281 (1980); Sugarman, Doing Away With Tort Law, 73 Calif.L.Rev. 558 (1985).

4. THE FUTURE

The fifth edition of this casebook was published 17 years ago, in 1971. The first automobile no-fault statute had just been passed by the Massachusetts legislature. No cases had been decided on the statute but the concept was being ardently pushed by its proponents and just as strongly opposed by its detractors. The subject could not then be treated in the traditional casebook fashion, but that edition contained a chapter entitled "Automobile Accidents—Tort Law or Reparation System?" The text described the alleged deficiencies in the existing systems, the steps that had been taken in some states to alleviate them, and the various proposals for extensive reform; and it identified the "policy issues" involved in the decisions to be made. It concluded with a reference to the future and presented this challenge:

"It takes more than a crystal ball to predict what the state of the law will be 20 to 40 years from now. But that is the time when you will be in your prime as a lawyer. Whatever develops, it will be a legal matter and as an attorney you are likely to be deeply involved in it. Speculate now, with the wisdom and background you presently have, both as to what will be the state of the law 30 years from now and as to what [you think] it should be. Why not do it in writing so as to make your thoughts more lucid and concrete? And then you can check yourself as the years roll by to see both how good a legal prognosticator you are and whether your viewpoints on desirable solutions have changed." Prosser and Wade, Cases and Materials on Torts 650 (5th ed. 1971).

The options are greater now than they were then. The pressure for adoption of a reparation system is not as intense at present, but it is steady. We would like to repeat this challenge to you now. You will find the experience a stimulating one. What do you predict as the ultimate outcome, and what do you wish that outcome to be?

ABBREVIATIONS USEFUL FOR NOTE-TAKING IN TORT CLASSES *

π	plaintiff	Tp	trespass	kw/RD	knowledge or reckless disregard
△	defendant	pvg	privilege		
θ	third party	Tfz	tortfeasor		
c.l.	common law	JTz	joint tortfeasor	Ab Dg Ak	abnormally dangerous activity
c/a	cause of action	lz	license		
DV/△	directed verdict for defendant	lzc	licensee		
		n̄vt	invitee	ulhz	ultrahazardous
JV/π	jury verdict for plaintiff	tpr	trespasser	inj	injunction
		nf k¢	informed consent	b.f.p.	bona fide purchaser
S/J	summary judgment			br/wt	breach of warranty
R&R	reversed & remanded	ktb	contribution	mp w̄t	implied warranty
		ndt	indemnity	xp wt	express warranty
Dem	demurrer	L̄r	lessor	dft	defect
$	suppose	Lee	lessee	dsn	design
Q	question	CN	contributory negligence	WD	wrongful death
O	owner			Svv	survival
axn	action	CpN	comparative negligence	m-	mal-, mis-
R2T	Restatement, Second, of Torts	LCC	last clear chance	m-fz	misfeasance
stat	statute	rsb	reasonable	m-pr	malpractice
L	liable, liability	RPP	reasonable prudent person	m-rep	misrepresentation
nj	injury			n-	non-
B̄x	Blackacre	A/R	assumption of risk	n-fz	nonfeasance
JD	John Doe Jane Doe	cz	cause	[	not, un-
ntt	intent	px cz	proximate cause	[4cb	unforeseeable
d̄mg	damages	cz/f	cause in fact	cov [sue	covenant not to sue
dfs	defense	dp iv cz	dependent intervening cause	jdr	joinder
b/p	burden of proof			kct	concert
s/l	statute of limitations	ndp cz	independent cause	mut	immunity
		s̄s cz	superseding cause	ndp kr	independent contractor
s/f	statute of frauds	RIL	res ipsa loquitur		
K	contract	4cb	foreseeable	mp	implied
T	tort	dfm	defamation	mpt	imputed
IT	intentional tort	Dct	deceit	kvn	conversion
N	negligence	lbl	libel	jfc	justification
SL	strict liability	sld	slander	std	standard
Az	assault			vln	violation
Bt	battery			pun	punitive
A&B	assault & battery			nom	nominal
FI	false imprisonment			nzc	nuisance
IIED	intentional infliction of emotional distress			stfn	satisfaction
				rls	release
				pvt	privity
				r̄em	remedy
Sb/L	subject to liability			p.f.	prima facie

* There are only a few abbreviations that are generally conventional, like those for plaintiff, defendant and contract. Students should adopt their own system of abbreviations. These have helped some students in the past and may help you. The system should be enlarged and may vary from class to class.

INDEX *

References are to Pages

* The Editors express appreciation to Mr.
Gordon Copland for substantial assistance
in preparing this Index.

†

The Heard Museum

"A Few Balm of Gilead Trees"
- Env. Racism - "different borders"
- Env. Sta's = Tribe as State (Territorial)
- land/people connection as text + context = treaty

A sense of place
The Process

- Got Joel's paper re: Envir. Racism/ Talk w/ Melanie

- Cathedral Mountains, Temple Trees
    ... need no monuments